PRICE GUIDE 2005

antiques

MILLER'S 2005

PRICE GUIDE 2005

antiques

ELIZABETH NORFOLK *GENERAL EDITOR*

2005
VOLUME XXV

MILLER'S ANTIQUES PRICE GUIDE 2005

Created and designed by
Miller's
The Cellars, High Street
Tenterden, Kent, TN30 6BN
Tel: 01580 766411
Fax: 01580 766100

General Editor: Elizabeth Norfolk
Managing Editor: Valerie Lewis
Production Co-ordinator: Kari Reeves
Editorial Co-ordinator: Deborah Wanstall
Editorial Assistants: Melissa Hall, Joanna Hill
Production Assistants: June Barling, Caroline Bugeja, Ethne Tragett
Advertising Executive: Jill Jackson
Advertising Assistants: Emma Gillingham, Carol Woodcock
Advertising Co-ordinator & Administrator: Melinda Williams
Designer: Philip Hannath
Advertisement Designer: Simon Cook
Indexer: Hilary Bird
Production: Sarah Rogers
Jacket Design: Victoria Bevan
Additional Photographers: Robin Saker, Emma Gillingham, David Mereweather, Dennis O'Reilly

First published in Great Britain in 2004
by Miller's, a division of Mitchell Beazley,
imprints of Octopus Publishing Group Ltd,
2–4 Heron Quays, London E14 4JP

A CIP catalogue record for this book is
available from the British Library

ISBN 1 84000 976 4

Colour origination: 1.13, Whitstable, Kent
Lab 35, Milton Keynes, Bucks
Printed and bound: Rotolito Lombarda, Italy

Front cover illustrations:
A Coalport bowl, c1820, 7in (18cm) diam. **£130–145 / €190–210 / $220–240 ⊞ DAN**
A pollarded oak work table, c1830, 29½in (75cm) high. **£2,650–2,950 / €3,800–4,200 / $4,500–5,000 ⊞ RGC**
A brass lantern clock, with eight-day platform movement, French, c1920, 10in (25.5cm) high.
£390–435 / €560–630 / $660–730 ⊞ PTh

Half title illustration:
A Charlotte Rhead Burleigh Ware pottery wall plaque, tube-lined with a maiden in profile, with a stylized floral border, c1930, 10in (25.5cm) diam.
£3,400–4,100 / €4,900–5,900 / $5,800–6,900 AH

Contents illustration:
A Tiffany glass and metal Bellflower lamp, impressed marks, c1925, 21¾in (55.5cm) high.
£15,500–17,200 / €22,300–24,800 / $26,000–28,900 ⊞ LUA

CHURCH HILL ANTIQUES CENTRE

ANTIQUES AND INTERIORS

Susan Miller and Simon Ramm
6 Station Street
Lewes
East Sussex
BN7 2DA

Tel: +44 (0)1273 474842
Fax: +44 (0)1273 846797
Email: churchhilllewes@aol.com
Website: www.church-hill-antiques.com

Opening Hours:
Mon–Sat 9.30am–5.00pm

Pugh's Antiques

Pugh's Farm, Monkton
Nr. Honiton, Devon EX14 9QH
3 miles north of Honiton on A30

Tel: 01404 42860 Fax: 01404 47792
Email: sales@pughsantiques.com
Internet: www.pughsantiques.com

There are six barns of furniture (6,000 sq. feet) Edwardian to Victorian. Furniture imported fortnightly from France = Louis XV - country - French - armoires - dressers, etc. Exciting range of root furniture. New range of Queen size beds (as on website)

Speciality antique beds

OPEN MONDAY-SATURDAY

home
antique
new
eclectic
illuminating
upstairs
downstairs
decorative
garden

Blender Antiques Limited
Cotefield Farm
Oxford Road (A4260)
Bodicote, Banbury
Oxon OX15 4AQ

Tel: 01295 254754
Mobile: 07969 922 531
www.blenderantiques.co.uk

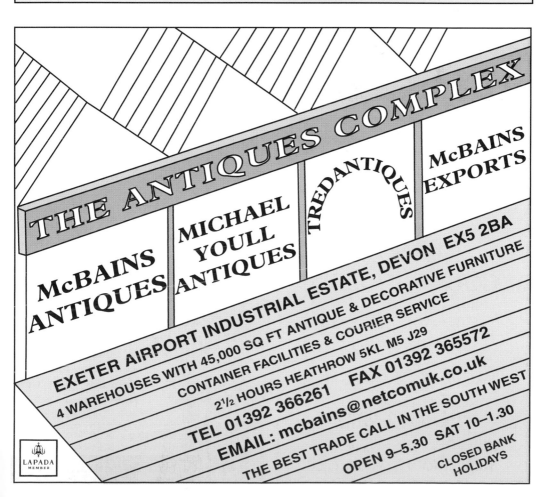

Jubilee Hall Antiques
the really different centre
Spoil yourself! Discover a really different type of antiques centre. Twenty five experienced dealers in furniture and furnishing objects and art, who are dedicated to quality, integrity, and value for money.
WWW.JUBILEEHALL.CO.UK
Tel: 01367 253777
HOW TO FIND US
We are easy to find on the A361 in Lechlade. We can be reached via either the M4 or the A40. Or you could even sail leisurely up The River Thames!
OPENING TIMES
Mon-Sat 10 to 5
Sundays 11 to 5
Open every Bank Holiday except Christmas
To Cheltenham
A40
Stow on the wold
Chipping Norton
Burford
To Gloucester
The
Witney
A361
Cirencester
Fairford
Jubilee Hall Antiques
To Oxford
Lechlade
Free and easy parking
Tetbury
Cotswolds
A417
To Bristol
Swindon
J15
M4
J17
To London
To Bath
To Marlbro'
To Salisbury
Oak Street
LECHLADE
on Thames
Gloucestershire
England. GL7 3AY

<table>
<tr><th>Dates</th><th>British Monarch</th><th>British Period</th><th>French Period</th></tr>
<tr><td>1558–1603</td><td>Elizabeth I</td><td>Elizabethan</td><td rowspan="2">Renaissance</td></tr>
<tr><td>1603–1625</td><td>James I</td><td>Jacobean</td></tr>
<tr><td>1625–1649</td><td>Charles I</td><td>Carolean</td><td>Louis XIII
(1610–1643)</td></tr>
<tr><td>1649–1660</td><td>Commonwealth</td><td>Cromwellian</td><td rowspan="6">Louis XIV
(1643–1715)</td></tr>
<tr><td>1660–1685</td><td>Charles II</td><td>Restoration</td></tr>
<tr><td>1685–1689</td><td>James II</td><td>Restoration</td></tr>
<tr><td>1689–1694</td><td>William & Mary</td><td>William & Mary</td></tr>
<tr><td>1694–1702</td><td>William III</td><td>William III</td></tr>
<tr><td>1702–1714</td><td>Anne</td><td>Queen Anne</td></tr>
<tr><td>1714–1727</td><td>George I</td><td>Early Georgian</td><td>Régence
(1715–1723)</td></tr>
<tr><td>1727–1760</td><td>George II</td><td>Early Georgian</td><td>Louis XV
(1723–1774)</td></tr>
<tr><td>1760–1811</td><td>George III</td><td>Late Georgian</td><td>Louis XVI
(1774–1793)

Directoire
(1793–1799)

Empire
(1799–1815)</td></tr>
<tr><td>1812–1820</td><td>George III</td><td>Regency</td><td rowspan="2">Restauration
Charles X
(1815–1830)</td></tr>
<tr><td>1820–1830</td><td>George IV</td><td>Regency</td></tr>
<tr><td>1830–1837</td><td>William IV</td><td>William IV</td><td rowspan="3">Louis Philippe
(1830–1848)

2nd Empire
Napoleon III
(1848–1870)

3rd Republic
(1871–1940)</td></tr>
<tr><td>1837–1901</td><td>Victoria</td><td>Victorian</td></tr>
<tr><td>1901–1910</td><td>Edward VII</td><td>Edwardian</td></tr>
</table>

German Period	U.S. Period	Style	Woods
Renaissance	Early Colonial	Gothic	Oak Period (to c1670)
		Baroque (c1620–1700)	
Renaissance/ Baroque (c1650–1700)			Walnut period (c1670–1735)
	William & Mary		
	Dutch Colonial	Rococo (c1695–1760)	
Baroque (c1700–1730)	Queen Anne		Early mahogany period (c1735–1770)
Rococo (c1730–1760)	Chippendale (from 1750)		
Neo–classicism (c1760–1800)	Early Federal (1790–1810)	Neo–classical (c1755–1805)	Late mahogany period (c1770–1810)
Empire (c1800–1815)	American Directoire (1798–1804) American Empire (1804–1815)	Empire (c1799–1815)	
Biedermeier (c1815–1848)	Late Federal (1810–1830)	Regency (c1812–1830)	
Revivale (c1830–1880)		Eclectic (c1830–1880)	
Jugendstil (c1880–1920)	Victorian	Arts & Crafts (c1880–1900)	
	Art Nouveau (c1900–1920)	Art Nouveau (c1900–1920)	

contents

Acknowledgments

The publishers would like to acknowledge the great assistance given by our consultants. We would also like to extend our thanks to all auction houses and their press offices, as well as dealers and collectors, who have assisted us in the production of this book.

FURNITURE:	Elaine Binning, Dreweatt Neate, Donnington Priory, Newbury, Berkshire RG13 2JE
MINIATURE FURNITURE:	Robert Timms, S. &. S Timms, 2–4 High Street, Shefford, Bedfordshire SG17 5DG
OAK & COUNTRY FURNITURE:	Robert Young, 68 Battersea Bridge Road, London SW11 3AG
POTTERY:	John Axford, Woolley & Wallis, 51–61 Castle Street, Salisbury, Wiltshire SP1 3SU
MASON'S IRONSTONE:	Janice Paull, PO Box 100, Kenilworth, Warwickshire CV8 1JX
PORCELAIN:	Phil Howell, Sotheby's Olympia, Hammersmith Road, London W14 8UX
ASIAN CERAMICS & WORKS OF ART:	Peter Wain, Anglesey
GLASS:	Andy McConnell decanterman@freezone.co.uk
SILVER & SILVER PLATE:	Hugh Gregory, Thomson, Roddick & Medcalf, Coleridge House, Shaddongate, Carlisle, Cumbria CA2 5TU
CLOCKS:	Richard Price, Middlesex
BAROMETERS:	Derek & Tina Rayment, Orchard House, Barton, Nr Farndon, Cheshire SY14 7HT
DECORATIVE ARTS:	John Masters & Chrissie Painell, The Design Gallery 1850–1950, 5 The Green, Westerham, Kent TN16 1AS
Extra information on Doulton Lambeth ware provided by:	Richard Marks, Caniche Decorative Arts, PO Box 350, Watford
RUGS & CARPETS:	Jonathan Wadsworth, Wadsworth's, Marehill, Pulborough, West Sussex RH20 2DY
TEXTILES:	Joanna Proops, Antique Textiles & Lighting, 34 Belvedere, Bath, Somerset BA1 5HR
JEWELLERY:	Charlotte Sayers, Stand 313, Gray's Antiques Market, 58 Davies Street, London W1K 5LP
PEWTER:	David Moulson dmoulson@hotmail.com
ANTIQUITIES:	Peter A. Clayton FSA, Seaby Minerva, 14 Old Bond Street, London W1S 4PP
TRIBAL ART:	Fiona McKinnon, Elms Lester, 1–3–5 Flitcroft Street, Soho, London WC2H 8DH
SCIENTIFIC INSTRUMENTS & MARINE:	Jon Baddeley, Bonhams, 10 Salem Road, Bayswater, London W2 4DL
FOCUS ON SCOTLAND:	Gordon McFarlan, Bonhams, 176 St Vincent Street, Glasgow G2 5SG

How to use this book

In order to find a particular item, consult the contents list on page 19 to find the main heading – for example, Furniture. Having located your area of interest, you will find that larger sections have been sub-divided. If you are looking for a particular factory, designer or craftsman, consult the index which starts on page 804.

BONHEURS DU JOUR • BOOKCASES 31

FURNITURE

Bonheurs du Jour

A Sheraton-style satinwood bonheur du jour, c1790, 19¼in (49cm) wide.
£5,200–5,800
€7,550–8,400
$8,800–9,800 ⊞ GGD

Miller's Compares

I. A Louis XV-style kingwood and parquetry bonheur du jour, with gilt-metal mounts and Sèvres-style porcelain plaques, with three drawers, c1880, 31½in (80cm) wide.
£3,350–4,000
€4,800–5,700
$5,600–6,700 ⚒ S(O)

II. A Louis XV-style walnut and kingwood crossbanded serpentine bonheur du jour, with gilt-metal mounts and leather inset slide, c1870, 37¾in (96cm) wide.
£1,800–2,150
€2,600–3,100
$3,000–3,600 ⚒ S(O)

The parquetry panels, porcelain mounts and additional detail to the frieze of Item I mark it out as being a superior example of cabinet-making. The parquetry would have taken much longer to execute than the standard veneers of Item II.

A satinwood and marquetry inlaid bonheur du jour, by Edwards & Roberts, London, c1880, 45in (114.5cm) high.
£27,000–30,000
€39,000–43,000
$45,000–50,000 ⊞ GEO
The value of this item is due to the reputation of the manufacturer and the quality of the wood that was used.

An inlaid rosewood bonheur du jour, the crossbanded top with fitted box and leather inset above a single drawer, late 19thC, 30in (76cm) wide.
£590–710 / €850–1,000
$1,000–1,200 ⚒ PF

Bonheurs du jour

Bonheur du jour is a French term for a lady's desk of small proportions, generally with a superstructure of drawers and fittings above a writing surface. Bonheurs du jour command high prices as they are small and often highly ornamented with marquetry, fine quality timbers, ormolu or porcelain mounts.

An Edwardian mahogany and marquetry inlaid bonheur du jour, the two cupboard doors enclosing fitted stationery compartments, 27½in (70cm) wide.
£440–530 / €630–760
$740–890 ⚒ B(Kn)

Bookcases

A mahogany bookcase, the upper section with two glazed doors enclosing shelves, the base with shelves and cupboard doors, c1810, 45in (114cm) wide.
£3,850–4,600
€5,500–6,600
$6,400–7,700 ⚒ S(O)

A walnut bookcase, the two glazed doors enclosing shelves, damaged, Italian, early 19thC, 58in (147cm) high.
£230–270 / €330–390
$390–460 ⚒ BR

A Gothic-style flame mahogany bookcase, early 19thC, 57in (145cm) wide.
£14,000–15,500
€20,200–23,300
$23,500–26,000 ⊞ GDB

A Victorian mahogany bookcase, with moulded cornice and glazed doors, 54in (137cm) wide.
£530–640 / €760–920
$890–1,050 ⚒ B(Kn)

Further reading

Miller's Late Georgian to Edwardian Furniture Buyer's Guide, Miller's Publications, 2003

Page tab
identifies the main heading under which larger sections have been sub-divided, therefore, allowing easy access to the various sections.

Miller's Compares
explains why two items which look similar have realized very different prices.

Information box
covers relevant collecting information on factories, makers, care and restoration, fakes and alterations.

Price guide
this is based on actual prices realized. Remember that Miller's is a price guide not a price list and prices are affected by many variables such as location, condition, desirability and so on. Don't forget that if you are selling it is quite likely you will be offered less than the price range. Price ranges for items sold at auction tend to include the buyer's premium and VAT if applicable. The exchange rate used in this edition is 1.44 for € and 1.68 for $.

Source code
refers to the Key to Illustrations on page 794 that lists the details of where the item was photographed. The ⚒ icon indicates the item was sold at auction. The ⊞ icon indicates the item originated from a dealer.

Caption
provides a brief description of the item including the maker's name, medium, year it was made and in some cases condition.

Further reading
directs the reader towards additional sources of information.

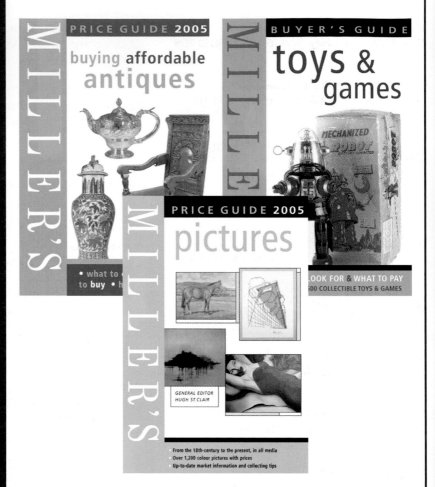

2004 BACA *Winners...*

CATEGORY 1
General Antiques Dealer

UK: NORTH OF M62
Heathcote Antiques
Cross Hills, Nr Keighley, West Yorkshire BD20 7DS

M62 SOUTH, TO M4 / M25
Christopher Clarke Antiques
Stow-on-the-Wold, Gloucestershire GL54 1JS

LONDON (INSIDE M25)
sponsored by CHRISTIE'S
David Brower
113 Kensington Church Street,
London W8 7LN

SOUTH AND SOUTH-WEST OF ENGLAND
Spencer Swaffer
30 High Street, Arundel, West Sussex BN18 9AB

CATEGORY 2
Specialist Antiques Dealers

FURNITURE
Butchoff Interiors
154 Kensington Church Street, London W8 4BN

COLLECTABLES
H. Blairman & Sons Ltd
119 Mount Street, London W1K 3NL

SILVER & PLATE
Koopman Rare Art
London Silver Vaults, Chancery House,
Chancery Lane, London WC2A 1QX

ART NOUVEAU & ART DECO
Editions Graphique
3 Clifford Street, London W15 2LF

OIL PAINTINGS
Messum's Fine Art
8 Cork Street, London W1S 3LJ

CLOCKS, WATCHES & SCIENTIFIC INSTRUMENTS
Trevor Philip & Son Ltd
75a Jermyn Street, London SW1Y 6NP

JEWELLERY
Tadema Gallery
10 Charlton Place, London N1 8AJ

CERAMICS
Brian Haughton Antiques
3b Burlington Gardens, London W1S 3EP

CATEGORY 3
Auction Houses

UK: NORTH OF M62
Lyon & Turnbull Auctioneers
33 Broughton Place, Edinburgh,
Scotland EH1 3RR

M62 SOUTH, TO M4 / M25
Bosley's Military Auctioneers
Marlow, Buckinghamshire SL7 1AH

INSIDE M25
Bonhams
101 New Bond Street, London W1S 1SR

SOUTH AND SOUTH-WEST OF ENGLAND
Dreweatt Neate
Donnington Priory, Newbury,
Berkshire RG14 2JE

CATEGORY 4
Associated Awards

AUCTIONEER OF THE YEAR
Richard Allen
Halls Fine Art Auctions, Welsh Bridge,
Shrewsbury SY3 8LA

MILLER'S CLUB BEST TOWN/VILLAGE
sponsored by

Petworth, West Sussex

BEST ANTIQUES CENTRE VOTED FOR BY THE READERS OF BBC HOMES & ANTIQUES
sponsored by BBC HOMES & ANTIQUES MAGAZINE
The Swan Antiques Centre, Tetsworth OX9 7AB

IN-HOUSE EXHIBITION
Art Deco Postmodernism
A Legacy of British Art Deco Glass,
10–20th September 2003, Richard Dennis
Gallery, London W8 (40pp illustrated catalogue
by Jeanette Hayhurst & Nigel Benson)

MILLER'S LIFE-TIME ACHIEVEMENT
sponsored by MILLER'S
Roger Warner
Burford, Oxfordshire

Introduction

Today many of us are obsessed with 'the look without the price' concept, fuelled by the many television make-over shows that demonstrate how a home can be furnished without great financial outlay and by careful shopping. However, the perennial popularity of *Miller's Antiques Price Guide* demonstrates that this is only a very small part of the story. We all have a choice, and the many thousands of us who purchase this book are showing that we are curious for individual design and style, whether it is 17th-century oak and country furniture or fine examples of early 20th-century craftmanship or Art Deco design.

For me it has been fascinating reading the introductions to the various sections in this guide. Robert Young, writing about Oak and Country Furniture, believes that there are three reasons that vernacular furniture has out-performed all other areas of the antiques market. I would like to suggest a fourth reason, 'stability'. My company exhibits often in America and since the events of 9/11 I have noticed a slow change in tastes. The minimal look is disappearing fast and I am finding that increasingly people want reminders of the old days, things with character and, as Robert Young says, 'nostalgia for old values'. As I look through glossy magazines I see more and more homes being treated with chintz and country house clutter; in other words, back to the good old days and a more lived-in, comfortable feeling.

Over the last ten years the market has been flooded with modern mass-produced disposable items but it can be seen from even a quick glance at *Miller's Antiques Price Guide* that quality pieces will always sell. Andy McConnell, in his introduction to Glass, reminds us that one of the reasons for the shortage of good pieces is that collections are remaining with their owners for far longer because of increasing longevity. That, of course, goes for all collections, resulting in fewer of the more unusual and top quality items being available so, when they are released, prices for these tend to rocket.

Writing about the furniture market, Elaine Binning says 'the key shift has been a drop in the market for mid-range furniture while selective furniture at the top end has been increasing in value' and, if we compare prices of plain brown furniture over the same period, the market has dramatically weakened and prices have fallen considerably. Of course, the upside of this is that, for those of us who still prefer well made antique pieces, there are thousands of bargains to be found. Anyone furnishing a house will find that prices for standard antique furniture compete favourably with newly made furniture. Added to this is the beauty of patination, individuality and the durability of these pieces. There is also an enormous advantage to the environment, since recycling protects the world's forests. The antiques business is truly a green industry.

Dining room furniture is very reasonably priced today compared with a few years ago because people do not have the time in their busy lives to entertain on the scale they used to. It is an effort getting the dining room ready for a dinner party whereas eating in the kitchen is a much more relaxed affair, so the demand for formal furniture is not as strong. However, at these competitive prices it might be worth considering buying an extending dining table which, according to how many of the leaves are inserted, can be used as a round, oval, hall or occasional table or even two console tables. The accompanying chairs can also be used around the house in various rooms, and the advantage of this is that when one does want to entertain formally the furniture required is already in the house. However, for kitchen entertaining, English or French farmhouse tables and chairs are ideal. Prices for these are increasing steadily – I can see this trend accelerating.

I believe that during the coming year we are going to see strong movement in the Asian market. The Chinese economy is getting stronger and for the last few years we have experienced more Chinese from the mainland paying ever higher prices to repatriate their heritage. Furthermore, after 10 years of the Japanese market being in recession, there are signs that it is beginning to improve and I expect that in the future we will see more Japanese chasing fine pieces.

As Peter Wain expresses in his introduction to Japanese ceramics, the best pieces will still find a ready market. That has been the case for all disciplines during the past few years and will remain so in the future. As we say in our industry: 'one never regrets paying too much for something, one only regrets one's bargains.'

Edward Reily Collins

Furniture

The past year has seen a variety of changes to the buying and selling patterns in the antique furniture market. The key shift has been a drop in the market for mid-range furniture both internationally and nationwide, while selective furniture at the top end of the market has been increasing in value.

It is difficult to generalize about the most important factors affecting the value of a piece of furniture, but age, fashion, quality, size, condition, design and freshness to market all feature in the equation. Many of the old ideas of what to buy and sell and what are traditionally sound investments are changing.

For example, age is still significant but has arguably less relevance to value than in recent years. This is illustrated by examples of quality furniture of classical design from the late 19th and early 20th centuries commanding high sums despite their relative lack of age.

Sometimes, rather perversely, in order to be successful an antique needs to fall in line with current styling as relayed through television programmes and interior design magazines. This interpretation of fashion has seen much of the ornately carved high Victorian furniture drop in value while those pieces from any period with a sleek design, compatible with contemporary interiors, have risen.

Alongside this fickle world of fashion, functionality is important. The market remains as strong as ever for key furniture such as bedside cabinets, dining tables and usable long sets of chairs. Buyers and sellers alike tend not to want to clutter up their houses with 'white elephant' antique furniture that serves no purpose. Minimalism is in: furniture has to earn its way in a home by being useful. For example, canterburies were originally used to store sheet music but are now used to hold newspapers and magazines.

The trend of the last few years continues for bureaux, as demand is low and their prices as a result have dropped. Computers, requiring desk space and wires are blamed for their demise, particularly for the ubiquitous George III mahogany examples. Curiously, this trend does not appear to have spread to bureau cabinets and bureau bookcases.

Buyers continue to be thrilled by the unusual. Intriguing and novel designs such as the bear chair (see page 54); metamorphic furniture (see page 52) and miniature furniture (see page 85) are increasing in value. As a general rule of thumb, prices are enhanced by good provenance, freshness to market, top-quality materials and makers' stamps, and many such pieces are highlighted with footnotes in the following pages. **Elaine Binning**

Beds & Cradles

An Empire mahogany bed, with brass and patinated-bronze mounts, French, 1799–1815, 47¾in (121cm) wide.
£4,800–5,700 / €6,900–8,200
$8,000–9,600 ⚒ S(O)

A walnut *lit en bateau*, with gilt-metal mounts, French, 19thC, 80¼in (204cm) wide.
£420–500 / €600–710
$700–840 ⚒ B(Kn)

A William IV mahogany four-poster bed, with dentil-moulded canopy, 82¼in (209cm) wide.
£820–900 / €1,150–1,400
$1,400–1,650 ⚒ B(Kn)
A major expense with four-poster beds is the cost of the mattress and hangings.

Lits en bateau

Lits en bateau, extremely popular in France in the 19th century, are so-called because they are somewhat similar in form to a small boat. They have two straight, often rolled-over, ends of equal height joined by a steeply curved traverse and they were sometimes overhung with a canopy. As they were intended to be placed in an alcove, only one of the four sides bore any elaborate form of decoration. This type of bed is particularly associated with the Biedermeier period (1815–48).

► **A Louis Philippe figured mahogany *lit en bateau*,** 1830–48, 79in (113cm) wide.
£165–200 / €240–290
$280–340 ⚒ B(Kn)
Mahogany furniture from this period typically has well-figured cuts of veneers, including flame mahogany as in this example. This bed appears to be an inexpensive piece as it is not a standard size in modern terms and single beds tend to sell better in pairs.

A Victorian mahogany half-tester bed, the bowfronted tester with a moulded cornice and turned curtain rail with dropped finials, the shaped and bowed footboard with applied rococo mouldings, 48in (122cm) wide.
£1,300–1,500
€1,850–2,250
$2,200–2,600 TEN

A Victorian mahogany half-tester bed, the tester with ball angle pendants on square posts, the arched panelled footboard with spiral-turned posts with gadrooned finials, 58in (147.5cm) wide.
£850–1,000
€1,200–1,450
$1,400–1,650 PF

◄ **A Victorian mahogany bed,** with spiral-carved end supports, 59in (150cm) wide.
£760–910
€1,100–1,300
$1,300–1,550
B(Kn)

Metal-framed beds

Tubular brass was used for beds from the 1820s and became particularly fashionable from the 1880s following the Industrial Revolution. Cast-iron beds were also made in increasing numbers as manufacturing techniques were improved during the 19th century. They would have been infinitely cheaper than timber-veneered examples and in large country houses would have been typically used in servants' quarters rather than main bedrooms.

A cast-iron bed, with black finish, c1875, 54in (137cm) wide.
£810–900 / €1,150–1,300
$1,350–1,500 SeH

A mahogany rocking cradle, the turned uprights joined by a stretcher, on platforms with flattened bun feet, 19thC, 39¼in (100cm) long.
£260–310 / €370–450
$430–520 PFK

A cast-iron bed, c1875, 60in (152.5cm) wide.
£1,900–2,100
€2,700–3,000
$3,200–3,550 SeH

A cast-iron half-tester bed, c1880, 60in (152.5cm) wide.
£1,800–2,000
€2,600–2,850
$3,000–3,350 SeH

► **A pair of cast-iron beds,** c1880, 36in (91.5cm) wide.
£1,600–1,800
€2,300–2,600
$2,700–3,000
SeH

► **A cast-iron bed,** c1875, 60in (152.5cm) wide.
£1,150–1,300
€1,650–1,850
$1,950–2,200
SeH

A cast-iron bed, c1880, 54in (137cm) wide.
£810–900 / €1,150–1,300
$1,350–1,500 SeH

A cast-iron bed, c1880, 36in (91.5cm) wide.
£810–900 / €1,150–1,300
$1,350–1,500 SeH

◄ **A Louis XVI-style plum pudding mahogany and satinwood-banded bed,** French, c1880, 63in (160cm) wide.
£2,150–2,600 / €3,100–3,750
$3,600–4,350 S(O)
The term plum pudding refers to the spotted figuring of this mahogany.

A Renaissance-style rosewood bed, the carved head and footboards with ebonized decoration, with carved wood side rails, French, c1890, 54in (137cm) wide.
£1,700–1,900 / €2,450–2,700
$2,850–3,200 SWA

A carved mahogany bed, late 19thC, 57½in (146cm) wide.
£370–440 / €530–630
$620–740 B(Kn)

A brass and iron bed, c1895, 54in (137cm) wide.
£720–800 / €1,050–1,150
$1,200–1,350 ⊞ SeH

A flame mahogany bed, with acorn finials, c1895, 36in (91.5cm) wide.
£1,600–1,800 / €2,300–2,600
$2,700–3,000 ⊞ SeH

A Louis XV-style rosewood bed, with carved pediment, French, c1895, 54in (137cm) wide.
£1,100–1,200 / €1,550–1,700
$1,800–2,000 ⊞ SeH

A Louis XVI-style mahogany bed, with ormolu decoration, French, c1895, 60in (152.5cm) wide.
£1,600–1,800 / €2,300–2,600
$2,700–3,000 ⊞ SeH

A walnut bed, with gilt-metal mounts, French, late 19thC, 58in (147cm) wide.
£130–155 / €190–230
$220–260 B(Kn)

A pair of painted beds, Italian, late 19thC, 81in (221cm) long.
£760–910 / €1,100–1,300
$1,300–1,550 B(Kn)

A mahogany four-poster bed, the acanthus-carved and reeded posts with pineapple finials, American, late 19thC, 52in (132cm) wide.
£2,200–2,650 / €3,150–3,800
$3,700–4,450 NOA

A polychrome and giltwood bed, with moulded headboard and engraving depicting the Madonna and Child, on acanthus-carved and stepped block feet, Italian, late 19thC, 70in (178cm) wide.
£2,300–2,750 / €3,300–3,950
$3,850–4,600 S(Am)

A cherrywood bed, with burr-elm panels and inlays, French, c1900, 54in (137cm) wide.
£1,100–1,200 / €1,600–1,750
$1,850–2,050 ⊞ SWA

A Louis XV-style walnut bed, French, c1900, 60in (152.5cm) wide.
£810–900 / €1,150–1,300
$1,350–1,500 ⊞ PUGH

A Louis XVI-style walnut and marquetry bed, French, c1900, 60in (152.5cm) wide.
£810–900 / €1,150–1,300
$1,350–1,500 ⊞ PUGH

A pair of brass beds, c1910, 42in (106.5cm) wide.
£1,800–2,000 / €2,600–2,900
$3,000–3,350 ⊞ SeH

Items in the Furniture section have been arranged in date order within each sub-section.

An Empire-style bed, with figured walnut panels and ormolu mounts, French, c1910, 60in (152.5cm) wide.
£1,350–1,500 / €1,950–2,150
$2,250–2,500 ⊞ SWA

◄ **A satinwood bed,** with quarter-veneered panels and rosewood-crossbanded head and footboards, c1910, 60in (152.5cm) wide.
£990–1,100
€1,400–1,600
$1,650–1,850 ⊞ SWA

A Louis XV-style beechwood and cane bed, with side rails, central support and double-caned footboard, French, c1910, 46½in (118cm) wide.
£480–580 / €690–830
$810–970 ⚒ S(O)

An Empire-style bed, with gilded kingwood mounts and rosewood crossbanding, French, c1910, 60in (152.5cm) wide.
£2,150–2,400
€3,100–3,450
$3,600–4,050 ⊞ SWA

► **A painted bed,** probably beech, c1920, 72in (183cm) wide.
£1,100–1,200
€1,600–1,750
$1,850–2,050
⊞ PUGH

Benches

◄ **A mahogany bench,** with end scrolls and turned legs, c1840, 36¼in (92cm) wide.
£880–1,050
€1,250–1,500
$1,500–1,750
⚒ SWO

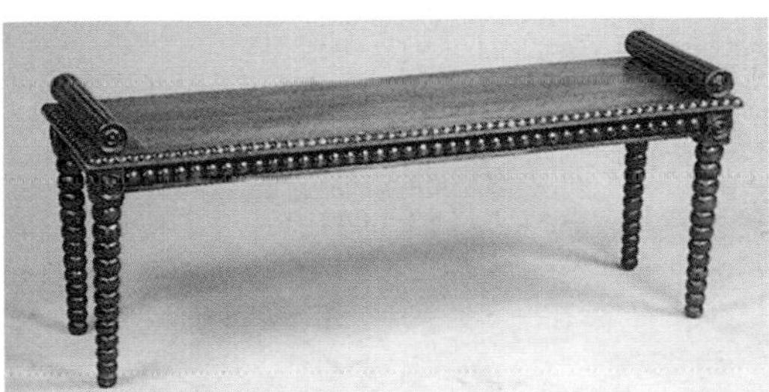

A turned oak hall bench, c1850, 48½in (123cm) wide.
£560–670 / €800–960
$940–1,100 ⚒ B(Kn)

► **A Victorian mahogany hall bench,** on ring-turned baluster legs, 36in (91.5cm) wide.
£870–1,050
€1,250–1,500
$1,450–1,750
⚒ WW

Bonheurs du Jour

A Sheraton-style satinwood bonheur du jour, c1790, 19¼in (49cm) wide.
£5,200–5,800
€7,550–8,400
$8,800–9,800 ⊞ GGD

An inlaid rosewood bonheur du jour, the crossbanded top with fitted box and leather inset above a single drawer, late 19thC, 30in (76cm) wide.
£590–710 / €850–1,000
$1,000–1,200 ⚒ PF

Miller's Compares

I. A Louis XV-style kingwood and parquetry bonheur du jour, with gilt-metal mounts and Sèvres-style porcelain plaques, with three drawers, c1880, 3½in (80cm) wide.
£3,350–4,000
€4,800–5,700
$5,600–6,700 ⚒ S(O)

II. A Louis XV-style walnut and kingwood crossbanded serpentine bonheur du jour, with gilt-metal mounts and leather inset slide, c1870, 37¾in (96cm) wide.
£1,800–2,150
€2,600–3,100
$3,000–3,600 ⚒ S(O)

The parquetry panels, porcelain mounts and additional detail to the frieze of Item I mark it out as being a superior example of cabinet-making. The parquetry would have taken much longer to execute than the standard veneers of Item II.

Bonheurs du jour

Bonheur du jour is a French term for a lady's desk of small proportions, generally with a superstructure of drawers and fittings above a writing surface. Bonheurs du jour command high prices as they are small and often highly ornamented with marquetry, fine quality timbers, ormolu or porcelain mounts.

A satinwood and marquetry inlaid bonheur du jour, by Edwards & Roberts, London, c1880, 45in (114.5cm) high.
£27,000–30,000
€39,000–43,000
$45,000–50,000 ⊞ GEO
The value of this item is due to the reputation of the manufacturer and the quality of the wood that was used.

An Edwardian mahogany and marquetry inlaid bonheur du jour, the two cupboard doors enclosing fitted stationery compartments, 27½in (70cm) wide.
£440–530 / €630–760
$740–890 ⚒ B(Kn)

Bookcases

A mahogany bookcase, the upper section with two glazed doors enclosing shelves, the base with shelves and cupboard doors, c1810, 45in (114cm) wide.
£3,850–4,600
€5,500–6,600
$6,400–7,700 ⚒ S(O)

A walnut bookcase, the two glazed doors enclosing shelves, damaged, Italian, early 19thC, 58in (147cm) high.
£230–270 / €330–390
$390–460 ⚒ BR

A Gothic-style flame mahogany bookcase, early 19thC, 57in (145cm) wide.
£14,000–15,500
€20,200–23,300
$23,500–26,000 ⊞ GDB

A Regency mahogany and brass-inlaid bookcase, the pediment over two glazed doors enclosing a refitted interior, the base with brass-inlaid top edge and crossbanded doors enclosing shelves, on carved paw feet, 45¾in (116cm) wide.
£5,400–6,500
€7,800–9,300
$9,100–10,900 ⚒ TEN

A George IV mahogany bookcase, with moulded cornice above two astragal-glazed doors and two panelled doors, on a platform base, 61¾in (157cm) wide.
£5,000–6,000
€7,200–8,600
$8,400–10,100 JAd

A pair of Victorian mahogany-veneered bookcases, each with a glazed ash door enclosing shelves, over a concave moulded drawer and two doors enclosing shelves, 38in (96.5cm) wide.
£3,650–4,400
€5,200–6,300
$6,200–7,400 WW

A mahogany bookcase, the two glazed doors enclosing shelves, the base with panelled doors enclosing shelves, c1850, 42in (106.5cm) wide.
£760–910 / €1,100–1,300
$1,300–1,500 PF

A Pugin-style Gothic oak bookcase, c1860, 84in (213.5cm) wide.
£4,900–5,500
€7,000–7,800
$8,200–9,200 GEO

Gothic revival style

During the 19th century, there was a resurgence of interest in the medieval period, due in some part to the popularity of the novels of Walter Scott. The high point of this fervour was the staging of the Eglington Tournament in Ayrshire in 1839 by the Earl of Eglington. This was an extravaganza of feasting, jousting and archery in rather belated honour of Queen Victoria's coronation in 1837, the celebrations for which the Earl felt should have been more redolent of the Age of Chivalry.

Such was the enthusiasm for all things medieval that after the Palace of Westminster burned down in 1834 it was decided to rebuild it in the Gothic rather than Classical taste and the furniture designs of the time followed the fashion. Initially the effect was produced by applying architectural detail to existing forms – later A. W. N. Pugin was to invent his own style based on Gothic forms. Bookcases particularly lent themselves to the Gothic revival style which, being a rather masculine style, was considered appropriate for the Victorian library. Pieces were generally made of oak and were either of a plain, functional appearance with decorative architectural details grafted on, or of a more authentic interpretation with exposed joints.

An oak library bookcase, the two glazed doors enclosing shelves over two frieze drawers with foliate-carved handles and two pairs of linen-fold panelled doors enclosing shelves, 1880s, 75in (190.5cm) wide.
£1,200–1,450
€1,750–2,100
$2,000–2,400 TRM

A Victorian mahogany bookcase, with moulded cornice and glazed doors, 54in (137cm) wide.
£530–640 / €760–920
$890–1,050 B(Kn)

A walnut bookcase, late 19thC, 54in (137cm) wide.
£1,450–1,600
€2,100–2,300
$2,450–2,700 SWA

A Victorian mahogany bookcase, the arched glazed doors enclosing three shelves, the base with two panelled doors enclosing two banks of 15 glass-topped specimen drawers, 41¼in (105cm) wide.
£1,300–1,550
€1,850–2,250
$2,200–2,600 DD

A mahogany and satinwood-crossbanded bookcase, with astragal-glazed doors, c1890, 37in (94cm) wide.
£3,350–3,700
€4,800–5,300
$5,600–6,200 GBr

A pair of rosewood, boxwood-strung and mother-of-pearl-inlaid bookcases, the upper section with bevelled glass doors and brass glazing bars enclosing a stained bird's-eye maple interior, the lower section with one panelled door, on a plinth base, Austrian, c1905, 86in (218.5cm) wide.
£760–910 / €1,100–1,300
$1,300–1,550 DN

Bureau Bookcases

A walnut bureau bookcase, the double domed and moulded cornice with giltwood urns, c1700, 84in (213.5cm) wide.
£15,300–17,000
€22,000–24,500
$25,700–28,600 ⊞ GEO

A George I walnut bureau bookcase, the associated top with moulded cornice over two glazed doors enclosing three shelves, the base with a fully fitted interior over two short and two long drawers, restored, 42½in (108cm) wide.
£5,200–6,200
€7,500–9,000
$8,700–10,500 HAM

A George III mahogany bureau bookcase, with glazed doors and adjustable shelves, the fall-front enclosing drawers and pigeonholes above two short and three long graduated drawers, 47in (119.5cm) wide.
£1,900–2,300
€2,750–3,300
$3,200–3,800 HYD

A George III figured mahogany bureau bookcase, with mirror doors and fitted interior, 87in (221cm) high.
£11,200–12,500
€16,200–18,000
$18,900–21,000 ⊞ GGD

Miller's Compares

I. A satinwood bureau bookcase, with painted floral decoration, astragal-glazed doors and three drawers, c1890, 31¼in (79.5cm) wide.
£8,400–10,100
€12,100–14,500
$14,100–17,000 S(O)

II. A mahogany and inlaid bureau bookcase, with astragal-glazed doors and two drawers, c1910, 30¾in (78cm) wide.
£720–860
€1,050–1,250
$1,200–1,450 S(O)

Despite being the same size and of a similar date, Item I sold for ten times more because of its superior craftsmanship. Item I is veneered in satinwood – a more desirable wood than the mahogany of Item II and the architectural pediment, outswept feet and extra drawer of Item I also enhance its value. The dentil cornice, oval veneer to the bureau fall and the painted decoration of Item I are further indications of a quality piece.

A mahogany cylinder bureau bookcase, the glazed doors enclosing adjustable shelves, the fall-front enclosing a pull-out leather-inset writing top, burr-maple-veneered drawers and pigeonholes above two panelled doors, c1840, 45in (114.5cm) wide.
£2,600–3,100
€3,750–4,450
$4,350–5,200 NSal

▶ **A Victorian mahogany cylinder bureau bookcase,** the roll top with turned handles enclosing a pull-out writing surface, drawers and pigeonholes, 50in (127cm) wide.
£2,000–2,400
€2,900–3,450
$3,350–4,000 DN

A rococo revival rosewood bureau bookcase, with two glazed doors over a cyma-shaped fold-out writing surface with a segmented interior, the lower half with panelled doors and ogee-moulded frame, American, 19thC, 54in (137cm) wide.
£2,200–2,650
€3,150–3,800
$3,700–4,450 NOA

Low Bookcases

◀ **A Victorian oak inverted breakfront bookcase,** with a beaded frieze and four glazed doors enclosing adjustable shelves, 98¾in (251cm) wide.
£880–1,050 / €1,250–1,500
$1,450–1,700 ⚒ CGC

A Victorian burr-oak low bookcase, by Johnstone, Jeanes & Co, with glazed doors, stamped maker's mark, 41in (104cm) wide.
£640–770 / €920–1,100
$1,100–1,300 ⚒ SWO

Johnstone, Jupe & Co, of New Bond St, London, made the first Jupe patent expanding dining tables from 1835 to 1840. The firm became Johnstone & Jeanes after 1842, and exhibited at the 1851 Great Exhibition.

► **A Regency-style mahogany breakfront bookcase,** late 19thC, 74¾in (190cm) wide.
£820–980 / €1,200–1,400
$1,400–1,650 ⚒ B(Kn)

Open Bookcases

A late George III mahogany open bookcase, stand possibly later, 77½in (197cm) wide.
£1,450–1,750
€2,100–2,500
$2,450–2,950 ⚒ B(Kn)

A Regency mahogany open bookcase, with ebony stringing, graduated shelves and two brass grille doors, slight damage, 35¾in (91cm) wide.
£3,750–4,500
€5,400–6,500
$6,300–7,500 ⚒ Bea

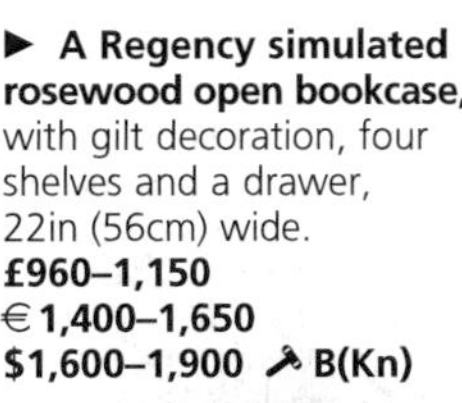

► **A Regency simulated rosewood open bookcase,** with gilt decoration, four shelves and a drawer, 22in (56cm) wide.
£960–1,150
€1,400–1,650
$1,600–1,900 ⚒ B(Kn)

A simulated rosewood open bookcase, with adjustable shelves, formerly with a rail to the top, c1815, 20in (51cm) wide.
£1,800–2,150
€2,600–3,100
$3,000–3,600 ⚒ S(O)

A Regency mahogany open bookcase, 48¾in (124cm) wide.
£1,140–1,350
€1,650–1,950
$1,900–2,250 ⚒ S(O)

A Regency painted, ebonized and gilt bookcase, the frieze drawer, panelled door and uprights painted with foliage, anthemia and guilloche, 24½in (62cm) wide.
£1,450–1,750
€2,100–2,500
$2,450–2,950 ⚒ Bea

A Regency mahogany open bookcase, with two drawers and brass carrying handles, 48in (122cm) wide.
£3,800–4,550
€5,400–6,500
$6,400–7,600 ⚒ B

► **A George IV rosewood breakfront open bookcase,** with a marble top above a frieze drawer and adjustable shelves, 78in (198cm) wide.
£2,350–2,800 / €3,400–4,050
$3,950–4,700 ⚒ LFA

A mahogany open book-case, with adjustable shelves, c1840, 34¾in (88.5cm) wide.
£640–770 / €920–1,100
$1,100–1,300 PFK

A Victorian mahogany open bookcase, the top with a pierced brass gallery, with adjustable shelves, 48¾in (124cm) wide.
£1,000–1,200 / €1,450–1,700
$1,700–2,000 PFK

A Victorian figured walnut breakfront open bookcase, the adjustable shelves flanked by fretwork doors enclosing further adjustable shelves, 75¼in (191cm) wide.
£2,100–2,500 / €3,000–3,600
$3,500–4,200 CGC

► **An Edwardian mahogany, harewood, satinwood, crossbanded and marquetry bookcase,** by Edwards & Roberts, the superstructure with sunburst pediment and urn finials, above two shelves and a central panel with foliate inlay, the top and sides with similar decoration, inscribed maker's label, 41in (104cm) wide.
£4,500–5,400 / €6,500–7,800
$7,600–9,100 B(Ed)
Edwards & Roberts was founded in London in 1845 and by the late 19th century the company was one of the leading English cabinet-makers. They produced furniture of modern design as well as reproductions of earlier French and English styles and their name is associated with high-quality workmanship and materials.

An Edwardian mahogany and satinwood-banded open bookcase, 33in (84cm) wide.
£500–600 / €720–860
$840–1,000 B(Kn)

Revolving Bookcases

◄ **An oak revolving bookcase,** c1870, 24in (61cm) wide.
£800–980 / €1,250–1,400
$1,500–1,650 MTay

An Edwardian inlaid mahogany revolving bookcase, 19¾in (50cm) high.
£280–330 / €400–480
$470–550 L&E

A walnut revolving bookcase, 19thC, 19¼in (49cm) wide.
£1,000–1,200 / €1,450–1,700
$1,700–2,000 S(P)

◄ **An Edwardian mahogany revolving bookcase,** the top with satinwood crossbanding, boxwood stringing and central medallion, 18¼in (46.5cm) wide.
£900–1,050 / €1,300–1,500
$1,500–1,750 DD

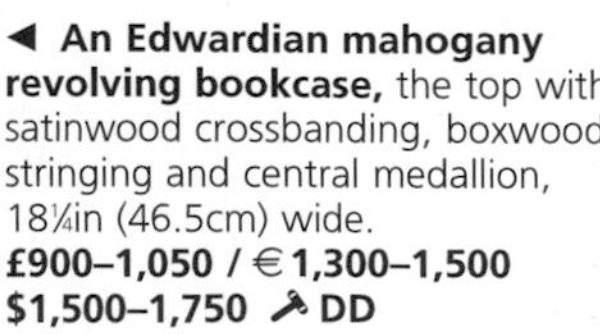

► **An Edwardian mahogany revolving bookcase,** 19¼in (49cm) wide.
£1,000–1,200 / €1,450–1,700
$1,700–2,000 B(Kn)

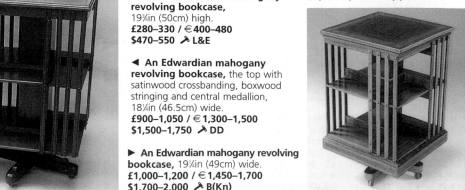

An Edwardian mahogany revolving bookcase, 19¼in (49cm) high.
£350–420 / €500–600
$590–710 L&E

An Edwardian mahogany and satinwood-crossbanded revolving bookcase, the top with a marquetry cartouche, 18½in (47cm) wide.
£640–770 / €920–1,100
$1,100–1,300 TRM

An Edwardian mahogany revolving bookcase, 18½in (47cm) wide.
£350–420 / €500–600
$590–710 WilP

Secretaire Bookcases

A George III satinwood secretaire bookcase, 34in (86.5cm) wide.
£13,200–14,700
€19,100–21,200
$22,200–24,800 GGD

A mahogany secretaire bookcase, the two astragal-glazed doors enclosing shelves, the lower section with three drawers and secretaire drawer fitted with baize-lined writing surface, bowfronted drawers with pigeonholes, c1790, 44in (112cm) wide.
£7,900–8,750
€11,400–12,600
$13,300–14,700 JC

A George III mahogany secretaire bookcase, the scrolled, carved and fret-pierced pediment over a dentilled cornice and blind-fretted frieze, the two astragal-glazed doors enclosing adjustable shelves over a fitted secretaire drawer and three long drawers, 45¼in (115cm) wide.
£9,600–11,600
€13,900–16,700
$16,200–19,500 TEN

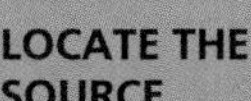

LOCATE THE SOURCE

The source of each illustration in Miller's can be found by checking the code letters below each caption with the Key to Illustrations, pages 794–800.

► **A George III satinwood and kingwood secretaire bookcase,** 29¼in (74.5cm) wide.
£5,000–6,000
€7,200–8,650
$8,400–10,100 S(O)

A George III Chippendale-style mahogany secretaire bookcase, the two astragal-glazed doors enclosing shelves, the lower section with two dummy drawers opening to a writing surface with an arrangement of secretaire drawers and pigeonholes, above three long graduated drawers, 43in (109cm) wide.
£5,400–6,500
€7,800–9,300
$9,100–10,900 HYD

A George III mahogany secretaire bookcase, the two astragal-glazed doors enclosing shelves, the base with a pull-out secretaire fitted with four short drawers, the panelled doors enclosing two shelves, 39in (99cm) wide.
£1,400–1,700
€2,000–2,450
$2,350–2,850 TMA

A mahogany breakfront secretaire bookcase, with four glazed doors, the secretaire enclosing a leather-inset writing surface and fitted interior, over a bank of graduated drawers flanked by cupboard doors with pull-out work surface above, c1800, 89in (226cm) wide.
£3,900–4,700
€5,600–6,700
$6,600–7,900 NOA

A mahogany bowfronted secretaire bookcase, the astragal-glazed doors enclosing adjustable shelves, the secretaire drawer fitted with dummy front with bird's-eye maple-veneered drawers, pigeonholes and central panelled door, over three boxwood-strung graduated drawers, c1820, 48in (122cm) wide.
£2,000–2,400
€2,900–3,450
$3,350–4,050 AG

This bookcase is probably associated. The upper section is a very good match to the base, having figured veneer and boxwood stringing that is very similar to the drawer fronts.

► **A mahogany and crossbanded secretaire bookcase,** c1835, 35½in (90cm) wide.
£2,750–3,300
€4,000–4,800
$4,600–5,500 S(O)

A Victorian walnut secretaire bookcase, the two glazed doors over a fitted and panelled secretaire drawer and two panelled doors with carved decoration, 44in (112cm) wide.
£1,350–1,600
€1,950–2,300
$2,250–2,700 SWO

A mahogany secretaire bookcase, with astragal-glazed doors, the crossbanded secretaire above three long drawers, c1815, 46½in (118cm) wide.
£1,750–2,100
€2,500–3,000
$2,950–3,550 B(Kn)

A Victorian mahogany secretaire bookcase, with four glazed doors, the base with a secretaire drawer flanked by two short drawers, above four panelled doors, 64½in (164cm) wide.
£2,450–2,950
€3,500–4,250
$4,100–4,950 DN

A Regency mahogany, satinwood and ebony-strung secretaire bookcase, the two glazed doors enclosing adjustable shelves, the base with fall-front drawer enclosing a fitted interior, 48¾in (124cm) wide.
£3,750–4,500
€5,400–6,500
$6,300–7,500 DN

A mahogany secretaire bookcase, attributed to William Cradock of Leyburn, with glazed doors and moulded drawers, above a fitted secretaire drawer and two panelled doors, 19thC, 41¼in (105cm) wide.
£1,500–1,800
€2,150–2,600
$2,500–3,000 TEN

A mahogany secretaire bookcase, with glazed doors, the secretaire drawer with leather surface, eight drawers and pigeonholes, above three drawers, c1820, 87in (221cm) wide.
£5,800–6,500
€8,400–9,400
$9,800–10,900 YOX

A mahogany secretaire bookcase, the later top with astragal-glazed doors enclosing adjustable shelves, the base with a secretaire drawer fitted with drawers and compartments, above three graduated drawers, 19thC, 42½in (108cm) wide.
£610–730 / €880–1,050
$1,000–1,200 DD

◄ **An Edwardian inlaid mahogany secretaire bookcase,** the glazed doors enclosing adjustable shelves, the secretaire drawer with fitted interior above two doors, 46in (117cm) wide.
£880–1,050
€1,250–1,500
$1,450–1,750 PF

Boxes-on-Stands

A walnut domed casket, restored, on a later stand, Flemish, 18thC, 33in (84cm) wide.
£470–560 / €680–810
$790–940 B(Kn)

For further information on
Boxes see page 150

A George III mahogany reading/writing box-on-stand, with a hinged panel on a ratchet support above a drawer, the stand fitted with a side drawer, on casters, restored, 31¾in (80.5cm) high.
£2,500–3,000
€3,600–4,300
$4,200–5,000 S(NY)

An Edwardian mahogany work box, decorated with inlay, 33in (84cm) high.
£360–400 / €520–580
$600–670 WAA

A satinwood drinks casket, by Maple & Co, inlaid with marquetry and rosewood crossbanding, the mechanically divided hinged top enclosing a removable glass tray, with maker's label, c1910, 24in (61cm) wide.
£3,800–4,600
€5,500–6,600
$6,400–7,700 S(O)

Buckets

A brass-bound mahogany plate bucket, late 18thC, 14½in (37cm) high.
£2,650–3,200
€3,800–4,600
$4,450–5,400 S

A George III brass-bound mahogany bucket, with brass carrying handles, restored, 15¾in (40cm) high.
£570–680 / €820–980
$960–1,150 Bea

A brass-bound mahogany bucket, with a brass liner, c1770, 13¾in (35cm) high.
£840–1,000
€1,200–1,450
$1,400–1,650 S(O)

A brass-bound mahogany plate bucket, c1780, 15in (38cm) high.
£1,800–2,000
€2,600–2,900
$3,000–3,350 JeA

Buffets

A Regency mahogany buffet, the shelves above a brushing slide, the platform base with a mirror back, scrolled supports and an inlaid lyre, 62¼in (158cm) wide.
£880–1,050 / €1,250–1,500
$1,500–1,800 SWO

A Victorian mahogany Jersey buffet, the pierced top rail and upper tier on reeded column supports, with a cupboard below, 42¼in (107.5cm) wide.
£240–280 / €340–400
$400–470 B&L

A Victorian mahogany three-tier buffet, 48in (122cm) wide.
£1,550–1,750 / €2,200–2,500
$2,600–2,900 WAA

LOCATE THE SOURCE
The source of each illustration in Miller's can be found by checking the code letters below each caption with the Key to Illustrations, pages 794–800.

Bureaux

A George I walnut bureau, with crossbanding and featherbanding, the later baize-lined fall-front enclosing four pigeonholes, two secret drawers, seven small drawers and a chequerbanded sliding well, above a frieze drawer and three graduated drawers, 36¼in (92cm) wide.
£2,850–3,400 / €4,100–4,900 $4,800–5,700 ⚒ B

A George III mahogany bureau, the fall-front enclosing a fitted interior above two short and three long drawers, with later brass handles, 33in (84cm) wide.
£820–980 / €1,200–1,400 $1,400–1,650 ⚒ DN

A walnut bureau, the top and fall-front with matching quarter veneers and herringbone banding, above three long graduated drawers, interior and bracket feet later, 19thC, 33½in (85cm) wide.
£1,050–1,250 / €1,500–1,800 $1,750–2,100 ⚒ AMB

A George I walnut bureau, inlaid with feather stringing, 38½in (98cm) wide.
£1,100–1,300 / €1,550–1,850 $1,850–2,200 ⚒ L

A George III mahogany bureau, the fall-front enclosing a fitted interior, above a central drawer flanked by two short over three long drawers, 48in (122cm) wide.
£610–730 / €880–1,050 $1,000–1,200 ⚒ CHTR
It is unusual to have the fall resting on drawers rather than lopers.

An inlaid walnut bureau, the banded fall-front enclosing a central cupboard flanked by drawers and pigeonholes, the lower section with a serpentine front and three long drawers, Italian, late 18thC, 41½in (105.5cm) wide.
£2,450–2,950 / €3,550–4,250 $4,100–4,900 ⚒ NOA

► **A mahogany cylinder bureau,** the cylinder enclosing a leather writing surface and three drawers, south German or Austrian, c1820, 45¼in (115cm) wide.
£1,250–1,500 / €1,800–2,150 $2,100–2,500 ⚒ S(Am)

A George II plum pudding mahogany bureau, the fall-front enclosing a fitted interior over four long drawers between fluted quarter-columns, 41¾in (106cm) wide.
£5,500–6,600 / €7,900–9,500 $9,200–11,100 ⚒ TEN

A George III flame mahogany bureau, the fall-front enclosing a fitted interior with 12 short drawers and five pigeonholes above four long graduated drawers, restored, 42¼in (107.5cm) wide.
£850–1,000 / €1,200–1,400 $1,400–1,650 ⚒ BR

A mahogany tambour-top bureau, the interior fitted with 11 drawers above a slide, c1780, 36¾in (93.5cm) wide.
£2,650–3,200 / €3,800–4,500 $4,500–5,400 ⚒ S(O)

A Louis XVI-style lady's rosewood bureau, the two-tiered gallery above a figured fall-front enclosing an inset feltwork surface and fitted interior, with a crossbanded drawer, on foliate-carved legs, restored, American, 1850–75, 30½in (77.5cm) wide.
£1,650–2,000
€2,400–2,900
$2,800–3,350 NOA

◄ **A walnut, fruitwood and ivory *alla certosina* parquetry *bureau de dame,*** with all-over geometrical and stylized-flower inlay, the top with a one-drawer box superstructure above a frieze drawer, Italian, c1870, 33½in (85cm) wide.
£900–1,100 / €1,300–1,550
$1,500–1,850 S(Am)

***Alla certosina* is the term used for this type of decorative geometrical inlay in ivory or bone, seen quite often in Italian 19th-century furniture. The style originates from north Africa and was originally in common use for decoration in the 16th century.**

► **An ebonized bureau,** with marquetry decoration and ivory and ebony banding, Dutch, c1880, 29in (73.5cm) wide.
£2,150–2,400
€3,100–3,450
$3,600–4,000
⊞ HiA

A walnut *bureau de dame,* early 20thC, 39in (99cm) wide.
£290–350 / €420–500
$500–600 B(Kn)

Cabinets

A walnut cabinet, the two panelled doors enclosing shelves and drawers, restored, Dutch, 1650–1700, 80¼in (204cm) wide.
£2,300–2,750
€3,300–4,000
$3,850–4,600 S(Am)

A Regency mahogany hanging cabinet, with four internal drawers, 19in (48.5cm) wide.
£1,500–1,650
€2,200–2,400
$2,500–2,750 ⊞ GGD

A Regency mahogany collector's cabinet, with ebony stringing, the wire mesh doors enclosing 12 graduated long drawers, on reeded bun feet, 36½in (92.5cm) wide.
£960–1,150 / €1,400–1,650
$1,600–1,900 Bea

A Victorian rosewood medal cabinet, the top with an inscribed presentation plaque, the glazed doors enclosing drawers numbered 1–53, damaged, three drawers missing, 30in (76cm) wide.
£2,800–3,350
€4,000–4,800
$4,700–5,600 L&E

Bedside Cabinets

A George III mahogany bowfronted bedside cabinet, the tray top with pierced handles, above a cupboard and a converted drawer, 22¼in (56.5cm) wide.
£810–970 / €1,200–1,400
$1,400–1,650 HYD

A George III mahogany bedside cabinet, 23in (58.5cm) wide.
£1,150–1,300
€1,650–1,850
$1,950–2,200 ⊞ APO

A George III mahogany tray-top bedside cabinet, with outline stringing, the cupboard door above a sliding commode drawer, 21¼in (54cm) wide.
£800–960 / €1,150–1,350
$1,350–1,600 B(W)

A George III inlaid mahogany bedside cabinet, the tray top with gallery, above two doors inlaid with star motifs, the inlaid dummy drawer pulls out to reveal a commode, the sides with pierced carrying handles, 19in (48.5cm) wide.
£410–490 / €590–700
$690–820 PF

A bedside cabinet, the two doors inlaid with flame mahogany panels, c1790, 31in (78.5cm) high.
£1,650–1,850
€2,400–2,650
$2,750–3,100 ⊞ GEO

A mahogany bedside cabinet, the galleried top above a cockbeaded door, with cut-out carrying handles, c1820, 13½in (34.5cm) wide.
£1,100–1,250
€1,600–1,800
$1,850–2,100 ⊞ JC

► **A mahogany bedside cabinet,** the three-quarter gallery over a panelled door, 19thC, 17in (43cm) wide.
£360–400 / €520–580
$600–670 ⊞ WAA

A pair of mahogany bedside cabinets, altered, c1860, 29in (73.5cm) high.
£1,300–1,450
€1,900–2,100
$2,200–2,450 ⊞ GEO

A George III mahogany tray-top bedside cabinet, the galleried top with pierced decoration, above two panelled doors, with a fitted drawer below, 21¾in (55.5cm) wide.
£940–1,100
€1,350–1,600
$1,550–1,850 ⚒ B(B)

A pair of mahogany bedside cabinets, each with a three-quarter gallery, on rope-twist tapering legs, probably Cork, Irish, early 19thC, 17in (43cm) wide.
£2,100–2,500
€3,000–3,600
$3,500–4,200 ⚒ HOK

A Victorian mahogany commode, with a pull-out leather-inset step, top 17½ x 18½in (44.5 x 47cm).
£270–300 / €390–430
$450–500 ⊞ WAA

A mahogany bedside cabinet, the top with a three-quarter gallery above a cockbeaded door with a brass knob, c1800, 14in (35.5cm) wide.
£850–950 / €1,200–1,350
$1,400–1,600 ⊞ JC

A William IV mahogany bedside cabinet, the three-quarter galleried top over two cedar-lined drawers with wooden handles, 16½in (42cm) wide.
£470–560 / €680–810
$790–940 ⚒ WW

A mahogany bedside cabinet, the panelled door above a drawer, with pierced brass plate side handles and pot stretcher, top later, 19thC, 15¼in (38.5cm) wide.
£120–145 / €175–210
$200–240 ⚒ WW

► **A pair of mahogany bedside cabinets,** c1860, 29in (73.5cm) high.
£1,450–1,600
€2,100–2,300
$2,450–2,700 ⊞ GEO

A George III mahogany bedside cabinet, the rising top above two doors, the base with two long drawers, 24½in (62cm) wide.
£330–400 / €480–580
$560–670 ⚒ L

A mahogany bedside cabinet, the three-quarter galleried top over a bowfronted door, 19thC, 15in (38cm) wide.
£1,450–1,650
€2,100–2,400
$2,400–2,800 ⊞ GGD

A Victorian mahogany bedside cabinet, with a later ring handle, 14in (35.5cm) wide.
£190–230 / €280–330
$320–380 ⚒ WW

A pair of Victorian mahogany bedside cabinets, the three-quarter galleries over panelled doors each enclosing a shelf, 15in (38cm) wide.
£950–1,150
€1,350–1,600
$1,600–1,900 ⚒ WW

A pair of walnut bedside cabinets, c1870, 30in (76cm) high.
£1,400–1,550
€2,000–2,250
$2,350–2,600 ⊞ MTay

A fruitwood bedside cabinet, c1890, 28in (71cm) high.
£380–420 / €550–610
$630–700 ⊞ WAA

A pair of Louis XV-style kingwood and parquetry night commodes, with marble tops, the fronts with two real and one dummy drawer, single drawers to each side, French, early 20thC, 22in (56cm) wide.
£2,300–2,750
€3,300–3,950
$3,850–4,600 ⚒ S(O)

Bureau Cabinets

► A George II mahogany bureau cabinet, with two fielded panelled doors enclosing shelves, the fall-front enclosing nine pigeonholes and drawers above two short and three long graduated drawers, the top and base with brass carrying handles, 48in (122cm) wide.
£2,650–3,200
€3,850–4,600
$4,500–5,400 ⚒ B

◄ A George I walnut bureau cabinet, the two feather-strung and inlaid panelled doors enclosing shelves and drawers, the bureau with a fall-front enclosing a fitted interior and a well, 40½in (103cm) wide.
£9,400–11,300 / €13,500–16,300
$15,800–19,000 ⚒ L

A Queen Anne-style walnut bureau cabinet, the sloping fall enclosing a fitted interior, c1920, 32¾in (83cm) wide.
£2,650–3,200
€3,800–4,500
$4,500–5,400 ⚒ S(O)

Cabinets-on-Chests

◄ A walnut cabinet-on-chest, the inlaid doors with engraved escutcheon plates, enclosing a central cupboard flanked by 12 oak-lined drawers, all with herringbone inlay and brass handles, on bun feet, the whole with three secret drawers, c1710, 44in (112cm) wide.
£25,000–30,000
€36,000–43,000
$42,000–50,000 ⊞ JC
This is a very fine piece, retaining its original metalwork and of a very pleasing colour and patination.

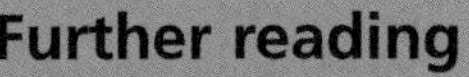

Further reading

Miller's Late Georgian to Edwardian Furniture Buyer's Guide, Miller's Publications, 2003

A George I walnut and inlaid cabinet-on-chest, with a cushion-moulded cornice drawer, the doors enclosing 12 drawers flanking a central cupboard with three further drawers, altered, 40½in (103cm) wide.
£6,000–7,200
€8,600–10,300
$10,100–12,100 ⚒ S(O)

A mahogany and boxwood-strung cabinet-on-chest, the breakfront upper section with a satinwood-banded frieze and door enclosing shelves, c1810, 48in (122cm) wide.
£840–1,000
€1,200–1,400
$1,400–1,650 ⚒ S(O)

Corner Cabinets

A George II japanned corner cabinet, 23½in (59.5cm) wide.
£750–900 / €1,100–1,300
$1,250–1,500 L

A George III mahogany bowfronted corner cabinet, the moulded cornice above two doors enclosing shelves, 28¼in (72cm) wide.
£940–1,150
€1,350–1,600
$1,600–1,900 CGC

A fruitwood and mahogany corner cabinet, with two glazed doors enclosing a velvet-lined interior with shaped shelves, early 19thC, 32¾in (83cm) wide.
£150–180 / €220–260
$250–300 DN

► **A mahogany bowfronted corner cabinet,** 19thC, 50¾in (129cm) high.
£300–360 / €430–510
$500–600 SWO

A lacquered bowfronted corner cabinet, with a three-tier stepped pediment, the door with chinoiserie decoration, c1750, 48in (122cm) high.
£2,000–2,250
€2,900–3,250
$3,350–3,800 Man

A late George III mahogany and marquetry bowfronted corner cabinet, with two panelled doors enclosing shelves and drawers, on a later stand, 32¼in (82cm) wide.
£850–1,000
€1,200–1,450
$1,450–1,700 DN

A japanned corner cabinet, with gilt chinoiserie decoration and a part-glazed panelled door, 18thC, 30¾in (78cm) wide.
£960–1,150
€1,400–1,650
$1,600–1,900 B(B)

A mahogany corner cabinet, the glazed doors over two panelled doors, c1790, 45in (114.5cm) wide.
£3,150–3,500
€4,550–5,000
$5,300–5,900 Che

A mahogany double corner cabinet, the moulded cornice above two glazed doors enclosing shaped shelves, the base with two panelled doors, with canted corners, Welsh, c1850, 41in (104cm) wide.
£760–910 / €1,100–1,300
$1,300–1,500 PF

A George III crossbanded mahogany bowfronted corner cabinet, the moulded cornice above two doors enclosing shelves, over a spice drawer flanked by dummy drawers, 48in (122cm) wide.
£330–400 / €470–560
$560–670 L&E

A George III corner cabinet, the glazed door enclosing shaped shelves, 36½in (92.5cm) wide.
£1,000–1,200
€1,450–1,700
$1,700–2,000 B(Kn)

An Edwardian bowfronted mahogany corner cabinet, 51in (129.5cm) high.
£450–500 / €650–720
$760–840 SV

Display Cabinets

A polychrome decorated vitrine, painted with sprigs of flowers, the internal back panel with a landscape scene, restored, French, 1723–74, 41in (104cm) high.
£450–540 / €650–780
$760–910 B(Kn)

An ebonized, inlaid and penwork display cabinet-on-stand, with glass shelves, four finials missing, c1880, 42½in (108cm) wide.
£3,350–4,000
€4,800–5,700
$5,600–6,700 S(O)

An inlaid and gilt-trimmed kingwood display cabinet, French, c1880, 24in (61cm) wide.
£3,800–4,250
€5,500–6,100
$6,400–7,100 RAN

► **A Gothic revival walnut display cabinet/bookcase,** with a drawer below, French, c1880, 45in (114.5cm) wide.
£2,700–3,000
€3,900–4,300
$4,550–5,000 SWA

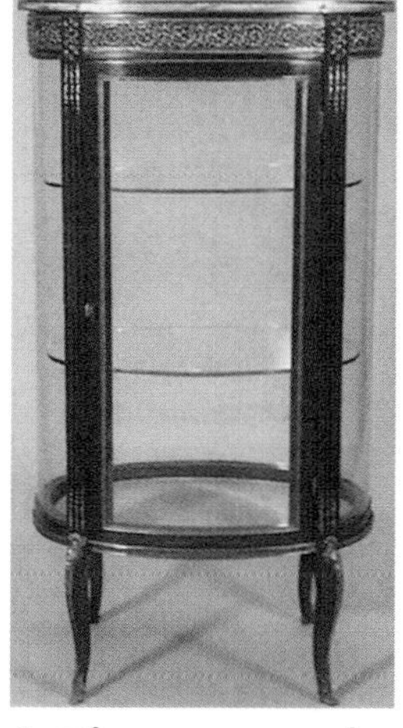

A mahogany-veneered oval vitrine, with gilt-brass mounts, the bevelled glass top above a bowed door with fluted stiles enclosing glass shelves, French, late 19thC, 24½in (62cm) wide.
£2,600–3,100
€3,750–4,450
$4,350–5,200 WW

◄ **A mahogany display cabinet,** the mirror-backed arched pediment moulded with scrolls, the glazed door enclosing shelves, late 19thC, 24in (61cm) wide.
£400–480 / €580–690
$670–800 GAK

► **A Victorian mahogany and marquetry-inlaid display cabinet,** the glazed display section with a mirrored back flanked by open shelves and carved and reeded pillars, the base with a drawer, on turned and lobed front legs, 45¾in (116cm) wide.
£1,500–1,800
€2,200–2,600
$2,500–3,000 HYD

A Victorian walnut vitrine, with a gilt-brass balustrade gallery, the door flanked by Corinthian columns, 36¼in (92cm) wide.
£2,350–2,800
€3,400–4,000
$4,000–4,700 B(Kn)

A Louis XVI-style kingwood and marquetry-inlaid display cabinet, French, c1890, 35in (89cm) wide.
£960–1,150
€1,400–1,650
$1,600–1,900 S(O)

An Edwardian mahogany display cabinet, with satinwood banding and inlay, the swan-neck pediment over a caddy top and two astragal-glazed doors, with undertier, 42in (106.5cm) wide.
£1,000–1,200
€1,450–1,750
$1,700–2,000 G(B)

An Edwardian inlaid satinwood display cabinet, the top crossbanded in ebony and rosewood, above a painted frieze of ribbons and floral garlands, with two bevelled glass panelled doors, 42in (106.5cm) wide.
£1,700–2,000
€2,450–2,950
$2,900–3,450 JAd

An Edwardian mahogany and satinwood-banded display cabinet, the astragal-glazed and foliate-carved doors enclosing adjustable shelves, 58¾in (149cm) high.
£610–730 / €880–1,050
$1,000–1,200 WW

An Edwardian French-style mahogany display cabinet, inlaid with floral sprays and musical trophies, the gilt-metal beaded glazed and panelled doors enclosing three shelves, 37in (94cm) wide.
£1,300–1,550
€1,850–2,200
$2,200–2,600 JM

A George III neo-classical/ Adam-style mahogany display cabinet, the top with a reeded frieze above two glazed and panelled doors with carved flowerheads and bellflower swags, enclosing three shelves, three panes cracked, early 20thC, 41in (104cm) wide.
£330–400 / €470–560
$560–670 PFK

An Edwardian mahogany display cabinet, with a glass shelf, 36in (91.5cm) high.
£900–1,000
€1,300–1,450
$1,500–1,700 MTay

An Edwardian satinwood and tulipwood-crossbanded display cabinet, 48in (122cm) wide.
£2,100–2,500
€3,000–3,600
$3,500–4,200 B(Kn)

French style

Throughout the 18th and 19th centuries, furniture in Britain and the United States was profoundly influenced by French styles, and in particular the designs of the Louis XV and XVI periods. The sinuous forms of display cabinets produced at this time took advantage of developments of glass-making techniques that facilitated curving and sweeping panes. French examples were constructed typically of kingwood or tulipwood, while English pieces were usually of mahogany or walnut. Both types would be applied with ornate gilt-metal mounts and often marquetry panels as well.

An Edwardian mahogany and satinwood-strung display cabinet, the moulded top outlined with chequerbanding, with two shelves, 14¼in (36cm) wide.
£290–350 / €420–500
$490–590 DD

► **A brass-framed display cabinet on an oak stand,** with two doors and a double shelf, early 20thC, 69¼in (176cm) wide.
£640–770 / €920–1,100
$1,100–1,300 SWO

An Edwardian mahogany serpentine display cabinet, with stringing and floral marquetry, the two brass-trimmed doors enclosing shelves, shaped apron, label for Christopher Pratt, Bradford, 42in (106.5cm) wide.
£1,600–1,900
€2,300–2,750
$2,700–3,200 AH

Music Cabinets

A Victorian mahogany music cabinet, the hinged moulded satinwood-crossbanded top above a glazed door inlaid with musical trophies, enclosing three shelves, the whole outlined with satinwood banding, 19in (48.5cm) wide.
£590–710 / €850–1,000
$1,000–1,200 ⚒ DD

A Victorian figured walnut music cabinet, with a three-quarter gilt-metal gallery above a glazed door, enclosing four tooled leather shelves, with canted corners, 21in (53.5cm) wide.
£430–510 / €610–730
$720–860 ⚒ TMA

A simulated rosewood music cabinet, the arched top over a shelf with a mirror below, supported by a short gallery, the frieze drawer over a mirrored door with an urn motif, late 19thC, 22in (56cm) wide.
£430–510 / €610–730
$720–860 ⚒ GAK

An Edwardian mahogany and satinwood-banded music cabinet, the mirror-backed top over a glazed door, 23½in (59.5cm) wide.
£175–210 / €250–300
$300–350 ⚒ BR

For further information on
Music see pages 612–621

Secretaire Cabinets

A quarter-veneered kingwood *secrétaire à abattant,* with a marble top, frieze drawer and fall-front enclosing six drawers and open shelves, cupboards below, on cabriole feet with ormolu rococo sabots, French, 1723–74, 39in (99cm) wide.
£1,550–1,850
€2,200–2,650
$2,600–3,100 ⚒ B(Kn)

A figured mahogany secretaire cabinet, the two panelled doors above a fitted cockbeaded drawer, over two further cockbeaded drawers, c1760, 80in (203cm) high.
£6,300–7,000
€9,100–10,100
$10,600–11,800 ⊞ YOX

◄ A Biedermeier mahogany *secrétaire à abattant,* with gilt-metal mounts, the frieze drawer with brass handles, above a panelled fall-front enclosing a pedimented central cupboard with satinwood banding flanked by drawers and pigeonholes, with two drawers below, Continental, early 19thC, 39in (99cm) wide.
£1,750–2,100
€2,500–3,000
$2,950–3,500 ⚒ AH

A Sheraton-style mahogany gentleman's secretaire cabinet, the top converted to a cocktail cabinet, the two doors with inlaid stringing and flame-veneered panels with rosewood crossbanding, the base with a fall-front secretaire drawer, over three long graduated drawers with inlaid stringing and brass handles, late 18thC, 50in (127cm) wide.
£1,600–1,900
€2,300–2,750
$2,700–3,200 ⚒ NSal

► An elm and mahogany *secrétaire à abattant,* with gilt-metal mounts, the fall enclosing seven drawers and pigeonholes, French, early 19thC, 28in (71cm) wide.
£1,750–2,100
€2,500–3,000
$2,950–3,500 ⚒ S(O)

A walnut and marquetry *secrétaire à abattant,* the arched cornice with inlaid decoration, above a cushion drawer and a fall-front enclosing a central door and secret sliding panel flanked by pigeonholes and drawers, over two long and two short drawers, on bracket feet, two small drawers missing, Dutch, 18thC and later, 50in (127cm) wide.
£2,700–3,250
€3,900–4,600
$4,600–5,500 ⚒ Gam

A mahogany secretaire cabinet, with gilt-brass mounts and a marble top, the fall-front enclosing pigeonholes, a door modelled as two drawer fronts and six short drawers, Italian, early 19thC, 35in (89cm) wide.
£1,900–2,300
€2,750–3,300
$3,200–3,850 ⚒ NOA

A Louis XV-style ebony and amboyna secretaire cabinet, the top with two doors enclosing shelves, above a fitted drawer, c1860, 50¾in (129cm) high.
£2,900–3,500
€4,200–5,000
$4,900–5,900 ⚒ S(O)

A figural marquetry secretaire cabinet, the fitted interior with secret compartments and three drawers, Italian, 19thC, 36in (91.5cm) wide.
£3,200–3,850
€4,600–5,500
$5,400–6,500 ⚒ HOLL

A walnut and parquetry escritoire, the marble top above a drawer, the fall-front enclosing a fitted interior and two drawers with brass handles, Continental, 19thC, 35½in (90cm) wide.
£920–1,100
€1,300–1,550
$1,500–1,800 ⚒ DN

A Gothic-style rosewood secretaire cabinet, with a fitted interior, German, c1840, 42in (106.5cm) wide.
£5,200–5,800
€7,500–8,400
$8,700–9,700 ⊞ RAN

► **A Louis XV-style quarter-veneered kingwood *secrétaire à abattant,*** with a marble top and serpentine front, a frieze drawer above the fall-front and three drawers, with floral marquetry inlay on crossbanded panels and ormolu mounts and escutcheons, French, 19thC, 55in (139.5cm) wide.
£960–1,150 / €1,400–1,650
$1,600–1,900 ⚒ JM

A mahogany and marquetry secretaire cabinet, the fall-front enclosing pigeonholes above a recess and six drawers flanking a cupboard, the base with two panelled doors enclosing a shelf, Dutch, c1840, 45in (114.5cm) wide.
£2,400–2,900
€3,500–4,200
$4,000–4,800 ⚒ S(O)

A flame mahogany *secrétaire à abattant,* the marble top above a frieze drawer and a fall-front enclosing a leather writing surface and a shelf over drawers, the base with two cupboard doors, on ebonized paw feet, French, c1850, 38¾in (98.5cm) wide.
£2,200–2,650
€3,200–3,800
$3,700–4,450 ⚒ NOA

A rococo revival figured walnut secretaire, the case edged with beaded moulding, the fall-front fitted with a mirror enclosing a writing surface with leather inset, drawers and pigeonholes, American, 1850–75, 26in (66cm) wide.
£1,150–1,400
€1,700–2,000
$2,000–2,350 ⚒ NOA

◄ **A French-style burr-walnut and ebony writing cabinet,** the upper section with a recessed mirrored compartment flanked by cabinets, the frieze with a writing drawer, with gilt-brass and gilt-metal mounts and Sèvres-style porcelain plaques, on fluted and blocked columns with a platform base, late 19thC, 48¾in (124cm) wide.
£2,800–3,350
€4,000–4,800
$4,700–5,600 ⚒ HOK

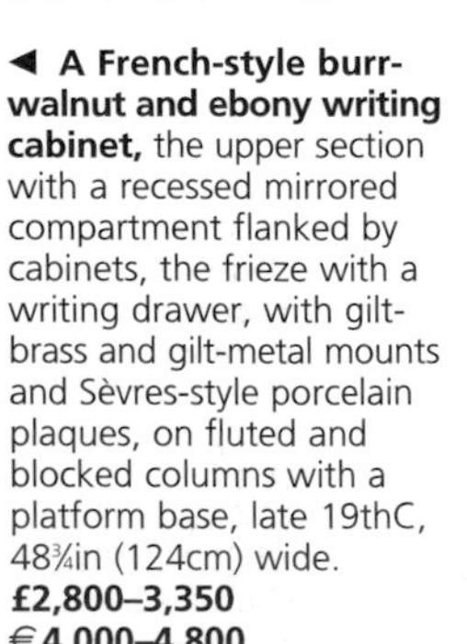

A walnut secretaire/gentleman's dressing table/folding bed, by C. R. Jeanselme, the fall-front enclosing an extending bed, French, c1890, 32¾in (83cm) wide.
£1,650–2,000
€2,400–2,900
$2,800–3,400 ⚒ S(O)
The Jeanselme family were important cabinet-makers from the 1820s, flourishing under various names until 1871.

Side Cabinets

A mahogany side cabinet, cross-banded in tulipwood and boxwood, c1790, 40in (101.5cm) wide.
£7,600–8,500 / €11,000–12,300 $12,800–14,300 ⊞ CAT

A rosewood side cabinet, the two doors with silk pleating and brass grilles flanked by spiral columns, on gilt-brass claw feet, early 19thC, 48in (122cm) wide.
£2,100–2,500 / €3,000–3,600 $3,500–4,200 ⚒ HOK

An Empire rosewood chiffonier, with gilt-metal bands and mounts, the mirrored back with a shelf and turned columns, the base with a drawer over two panelled doors flanked by columns, gallery and some veneer missing, French, early 19thC, 42in (106.5cm) wide.
£680–820 / €1,000–1,200 $1,150–1,400 ⚒ DN

A Regency figured rosewood chiffonier, the marble top above two doors with pleated silk panels, 49in (124.5cm) wide.
£2,100–2,500 / €3,000–3,600 $3,500–4,200 ⚒ HOLL

◄ **A mahogany pier cabinet,** the marble top over a frieze drawer and two panelled doors, early 19thC, 35½in (90cm) wide.
£1,100–1,300 / €1,600–1,900 $1,850–2,200 ⚒ AH

A walnut and floral marquetry serpentine side cabinet, Dutch, c1820, 36in (91.5cm) high.
£4,750–5,300 €6,800–7,600 $8,000–8,900 ⊞ GEO

A Regency mahogany chiffonier, with a galleried shelf and panelled back, above a drawer over a cupboard base with two panelled doors, 33in (84cm) wide.
£760–910 / €1,100–1,300 $1,250–1,500 ⚒ TMA

◄ **A walnut demi-lune side cabinet,** with a drawer over two tambour compartments, Dutch, 19thC, 35¾in (91cm) wide.
£1,250–1,500 €1,800–2,150 $2,100–2,500 ⚒ S(O)

A William IV mahogany chiffonier, the convex frieze drawer over two doors, on reeded bun feet, back missing, 36in (91.5cm) wide.
£420–500 / €600–720
$700–840 G(L)

A Victorian walnut credenza, 66in (167.5cm) wide.
£3,400–3,750 / €4,900–5,400
$5,700–6,300 MTay

A rococo revival side cabinet, attributed to J. H. Belter, New York, with a pierced and carved crest over a triple-arched mirror plate flanked by mirror-backed shelves, the marble top above the conforming base with a mirrored cupboard door flanked by shelves, American, c1850, 59in (150cm) wide.
£31,500–37,800 / €45,300–54,400
$53,000–63,500 NOA

The designs of John Henry Belter (1804–63) are typically sumptuously carved and of heavy proportions. Intended to grace the houses of America's nouveau riche, pieces were rarely exported and therefore seldom found outside the United States.

An ebonized and boulle-work side cabinet, 19thC, 59½in (151cm) wide.
£1,000–1,200 / €1,450–1,700
$1,700–2,000 L

A rosewood chiffonier, with a mirrored back and doors and a marble top, c1850, 49in (124.5cm) wide.
£860–950 / €1,200–1,350
$1,450–1,600 HiA

A Victorian Louis XVI-style ebonized and boulle bowfront side cabinet, decorated with applied brass egg-and-dart moulding and foliate banding, the brass-inlaid cupboard door flanked by glazed panels, 47¼in (120cm) wide.
£2,000–2,400 / €2,900–3,450
$3,350–4,000 JAd

A walnut side cabinet/vitrine, the frieze with inlaid foliate scroll-work, above an arch-glazed door enclosing a shelf, flanked by foliate scroll-inlaid pilasters with ormolu mounts, 19thC, 30½in (77.5cm) wide.
£560–670 / €810–960
$940–1,100 PFK

A mahogany chiffonier, c1850, 38in (96.5cm) wide.
£430–480 / €620–690
$720–810 MTay

Papier-mâché

Papier-mâché, a hard wood-like material made from pulped paper, and similar to Oriental lacquer, was first made in Europe in the 17th century. British makers such as Henry Clay in the late 18th century and Jennens & Bettridge in the 19th century patented various techniques of manufacture and stamped their wares. Papier-mâché pieces were painted or japanned and decorated in polychrome and gilt, often with flowers, exotic birds and scrolls, sometimes incorporating mother-of-pearl inlay. While many examples of trays, boxes, caddies and chairs exist, larger pieces are less commonly seen.

◀ **A papier-mâché chiffonier,** painted with birds of paradise and sprigs of flowers, the top with scrolled supports above a frieze and two panelled doors, c1870, 34¼in (87cm) wide.
£1,750–2,100 / €2,500–3,000
$2,950–3,500 B(Kn)

A Victorian burr-walnut, ebony and marquetry-inlaid chiffonier, in the style of Gillows, the central column with a classical monopodium flanked by glazed cupboards, 48in (122cm) wide.
£1,750–2,100 / €2,500–3,000 $2,950–3,500 HYD

An Edwardian inlaid mahogany side cabinet, the inlaid foliate scroll frieze above two satinwood-crossbanded and boxwood-strung doors, 42in (106.5cm) wide.
£2,600–3,100 / €3,750–4,450 $4,350–5,200 SWO

A bleached sycamore side cabinet, with gilt-metal mounts and inset porcelain plaques, the door enclosing shelves, c1880, 64¼in (163cm) wide.
£3,600–4,300 / €5,200–6,200 $6,000–7,200 S(O)

Sycamore can sometimes resemble satinwood but, rather than being an exotically grown and imported timber, it is native to England. When used in veneer form, as on this cabinet, the figuring often has a rippled or striped appearance. Sycamore was also used in the solid, to make rustic items such as turned bowls. Sycamore veneers were stained green for use in decorative marquetry and the timber is referred to as harewood.

▶ **A marquetry-inlaid rosewood side cabinet,** the mirrored top above a bowfronted base with three cupboards and shelves with spindle galleries, late 19thC, 54in (137cm) wide.
£580–700 / €830–1,000 $1,000–1,200 PF

A Sheraton revival rosewood-banded satinwood side cabinet, with painted decoration and four doors, c1885, 60in (152.5cm) wide.
£10,350–11,500 / €14,900–16,600 $17,400–19,300 ⊞ Che

Cabinets-on-Stands

A tortoiseshell, ormolu and ebonized cabinet-on-stand, the pediment top with a pierced gallery applied with a double eagle and two recumbent lions, above eight short drawers and a door applied with a relief of Hercules enclosing five further drawers, on a later stand, Spanish, 17thC, 48¾in (124cm) wide.
£7,400–8,900
€10,600–12,800
$12,500–15,000 ⚒ S(Am)

A japanned cabinet-on-stand, the two doors enclosing an arrangement of 11 drawers, the sides of the stand centred by a carved shell and pierced foliate decoration, stand resilvered, late 17thC, 44in (112cm) wide.
£15,600–18,700
€22,450–26,900
$26,200–31,400 ⚒ S

Items in the Furniture section have been arranged in date order within each sub-section.

A George III japanned cabinet-on-stand, the doors decorated with figures, buildings and birds, with gilt-metal hinges and escutcheon, on a later Oriental-style stand, 38½in (98cm) wide.
£1,550–1,850
€2,250–2,650
$2,600–3,100 ⚒ WW

A Louis XVI-style walnut and parquetry cabinet-on-stand, the broken pediment above glazed doors flanked by Corinthian columns and cupboard doors, the interior veneered with bird's-eye maple, over a frieze drawer and two spring-release drawers, c1890, 45¼in (115cm) wide.
£4,250–5,100
€6,100–7,350
$7,150–8,550 ⚒ B(Kn)

◄ A burr-walnut cabinet-on-stand, c1920, 30in (76cm) wide.
£790–880 / €1,150–1,250
$1,300–1,500 ⊞ MTay

Table Cabinets

A walnut and stained burr-elm table cabinet, with cherrywood-crossbanded drawers, one later, on later bun feet, German, 18thC, 41in (104cm) wide.
£530–640 / €760–920
$890–1,050 ⚒ B(Kn)

A Victorian inlaid walnut table cabinet, 11in (28cm) wide.
£190–230 / €280–330
$320–380 ⚒ AMB

A chinoiserie-style japanned table cabinet, heightened in gilt, the hinged top enclosing a red-painted interior, the two doors enclosing six drawers and a stepped recess, early 19thC, 18in (45.5cm) high.
£1,900–2,250 / €2,750–3,250
$3,200–3,750 ⚒ TEN

An Edwardian mahogany table cabinet, the two doors with inner panels decorated in black lacquer and gilt, with a leather-lined drawer above a base drawer, 24in (61cm) wide.
£720–860 / €1,050–1,250
$1,200–1,400 ⚒ TMA

A collector's walnut table cabinet, the panelled doors enclosing three drawers, 19thC, 13in (33cm) high.
£210–250 / €300–360
$350–420 ⚒ CGC

A thuya wood table cabinet, the carved panel doors with diamond stringing, enclosing 50 drawers, two secret drawers and a velvet-lined recess, together with a receipt from Spink & Sons dated 1936, early 20thC, 20in (51cm) wide.
£1,750–2,100 / €2,500–3,000
$2,900–3,500 ⚒ B(L)

Canterburies

A mahogany canterbury, c1800, 19in (48.5cm) wide.
£1,700–1,900 / €2,450–2,750
$2,850–3,200 ⊞ GEO

Originally designed to hold sheet music, canterburies remain popular today for use as magazine racks. Those with a handle on one of the divisions often suffer damage as the handles are rarely strong enough to lift the canterbury full of heavy papers.

A Victorian walnut canterbury, with shaped and pierced divisions and a drawer, on turned legs with casters, 19¾in (50cm) wide.
£420–500 / €600–720
$700–840 ⚒ L

A boxwood-strung walnut canterbury, with a gilt-metal gallery, pierced fretwork uprights above a frieze drawer, 19thC, 24in (61cm) wide.
£940–1,100 / €1,450–1,650
$1,600–1,850 ⚒ GAK

A Regency rosewood canterbury, 22in (56cm) wide.
£2,900–3,250 / €4,200–4,700
$4,850–5,400 ⊞ GGD

A rosewood canterbury, on turned legs with casters, c1830, 21in (53.5cm) wide.
£2,100–2,350 / €3,000–3,400
$3,500–3,950 ⊞ GEO

► **A rosewood canterbury,** with a single drawer, on turned baluster legs with ceramic casters, late 19thC, 21in (53.5cm) wide.
£370–440 / €530–630
$620–740 ⚒ EH

A Victorian walnut canterbury, the divisions carved with scrolls and foliage above a drawer, 21in (53.5cm) wide.
£610–730 / €880–1,050
$1,000–1,200 ⚒ E

► **An Edwardian mahogany and brass revolving canterbury,** on a brass tripod, stamped 'S. H. & S.', 17in (43cm) wide.
£300–360 / €430–520
$500–600 ⚒ G(L)

A Regency mahogany canterbury, with double baluster and block supports and a drawer, on shaped tapering legs with brass caps and casters, repaired, 19½in (49.5cm) wide.
£680–820 / €1,000–1,200
$1,150–1,350 ⚒ MCA

A rosewood canterbury, with spindled sides and divisions above a single drawer, trade label for James Shoolbred & Co, c1850, 22in (56cm) wide.
£680–820 / €1,000–1,200
$1,150–1,350 ⚒ NOA

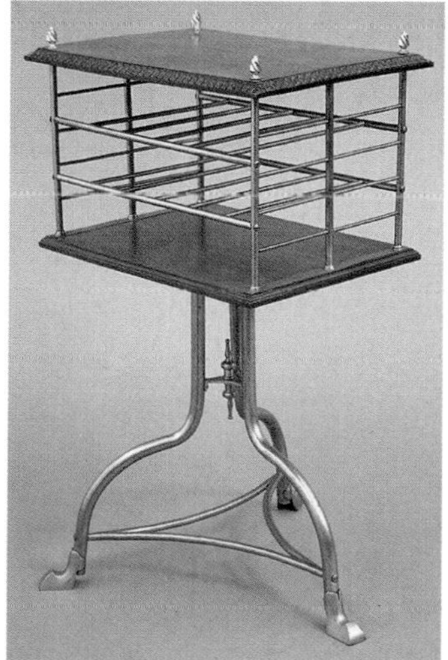

Open Armchairs

A walnut open armchair, with padded back and seat and acanthus-carved scrolling arm rests, Dutch, 17thC.
£1,050–1,250
€1,500–1,800
$1,750–2,100 S(Am)

A pair of mahogany 'drunkard's' chairs, with applied yew wood roundels, c1790.
£4,000–4,500
€5,800–6,500
$6,700–7,500 GDB
The extensions to the base and the width of the chair make it very difficult to tip over.

A pair of Regency ebonized open armchairs, with gilt highlights.
£3,600–4,000
€5,200–5,750
$6,000–6,700 GGD

► **A mahogany open armchair,** c1820.
£580–650 / €850–950
$1,000–1,100 DY

A Hepplewhite-style mahogany-framed open armchair, with upholstered back and seat, on cabriole legs, 18thC.
£1,300–1,550
€1,900–2,250
$2,200–2,600 BWL

A pair of mahogany *faux* bamboo cockpen chairs, c1800.
£1,950–2,150
€2,800–3,100
$3,300–3,650 BMi
It is often thought that these chairs get their name from their use by gentlemen while watching cock fights, but in fact the Laird of Cockpen had chairs of similar design in his pew at Cockpen church, near Dalhousie Castle, Dalkeith, Scotland.

A painted and parcel-gilt open armchair, Italian, c1750.
£1,100–1,300
€1,600–1,850
$1,850–2,200 S(O)

A Regency mahogany open armchair.
£1,100–1,250
€1,600–1,800
$1,900–2,100 WAA

A mahogany and inlaid open armchair, c1820.
£1,650–1,850
€2,400–2,650
$2,800–3,100 GEO

A George III mahogany open armchair, with spindle back and stuff-over seat, north country.
£500–600 / €700–860
$840–1,000 BR

A mahogany metamorphic library step chair, after Morgan & Sanders, c1815.
£13,100–14,500
€18,800–20,900
$22,000–24,300 REI
Metamorphic furniture invariably commands a premium.

A karelian birch open armchair, probably Russian, c1830.
£750–900 / €1,100–1,300
$1,250–1,500 S(P)

A William IV mahogany-framed open armchair, with brass casters, repaired.
£430–520 / €630–750
$730–870 BR

◄ **A William IV mahogany-framed open armchair.**
£220–260 / €310–370
$370–440 WilP

A mahogany open armchair, with a pierced splat and drop-in seat, on square chamfered legs, 19thC.
£210–250 / €300–360
$350–420 WW

A carved walnut Savonarola, with embossed leather seat and back, Spanish, 19thC.
£350–420 / €500–600
$590–700 B(Kn)

A mahogany open armchair, with needlework seat, 19thC.
£135–150 / €200–220
$220–250 HiA

An 18thC-style mahogany open armchair, possibly by Butler, with claw-and-ball feet, Irish, 19thC.
£2,750–3,300
€3,950–4,750
$4,600–5,500 B

A carved thorn wood open armchair, with an inscribed plaque and red leather button-upholstered seat, c1840.
£3,150–3,500
€4,450–5,000
$5,300–5,900 GEO
The plaque on this chair reads: 'This chair was constructed from the wood of a thorn tree, felled in 1814, which stood behind the hall of the Royal College of Physicians. The site is now occupied by the Commercial Bank of Scotland, who took possession of their building in George Street on 5 April 1847'.

A Victorian rosewood open armchair, the buttoned back with a floral-carved surmount, the arms with scroll terminals, with a carved shell apron, on cabriole front legs and brass casters.
£590–710 / €850–1,000
$1,000–1,200 PFK

A mahogany-framed open armchair, with carved scrollwork, c1840.
£520–620 / €750–900
$870–1,000 SWO

A walnut folding open armchair, by George Hunzinger, with *faux* bamboo folding X-frame, incised stamp, American, 1850–75.
£610–730 / €880–1,050
$1,000–1,200 NOA
George Hunzinger (1835–98) was born in Germany, and having already trained as a cabinet-maker, emigrated to New York at the age of 20. He was an enthusiastic inventor and in his lifetime was awarded 21 patents for the design of various items of furniture.

A Victorian walnut open arm desk chair, the scrolled back relief-carved with a cartouche with a coronet and initials, flanked by gadrooned moulded vase-turned pillars, on turned legs with casters.
£165–200 / €240–290
$280–330 PF

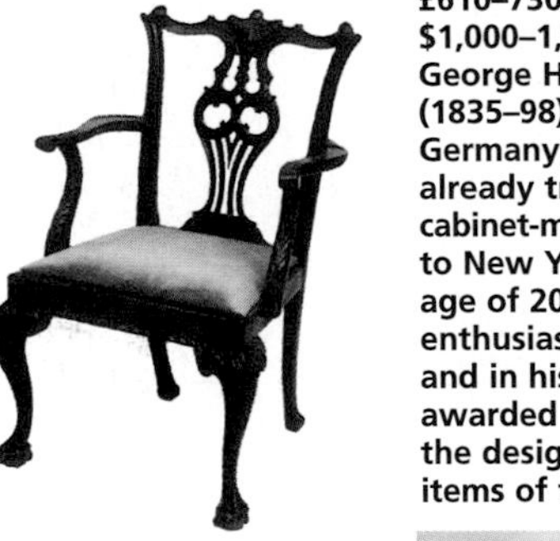

A mid-18thC-style mahogany elbow open armchair, by James Shoolbred & Co, with a carved pierced splat, drop-in seat and a brass trade label, on cabriole legs with claw-and-ball feet, late 19thC.
£350–420 / €500–600
$590–700 NSal

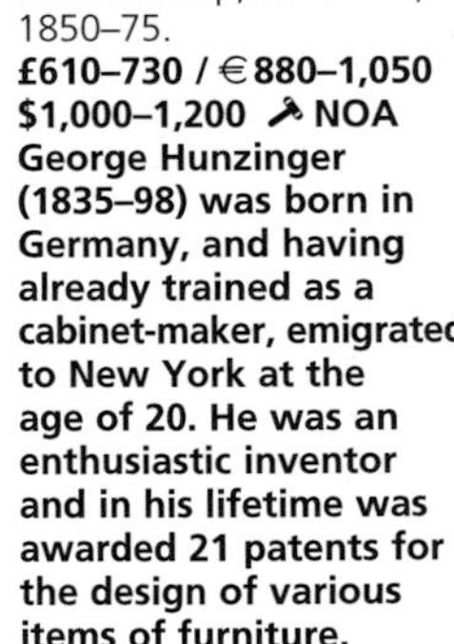

A Victorian mahogany and leather club armchair, in the manner of Howard & Sons, the arms fitted with brass light sockets, on turned bun feet with brass casters.
£1,400–1,650
€2,000–2,450
$2,350–2,800 EH
Howard & Sons were throne makers and manufacturers of high quality deep-seated armchairs. The casters are usually stamped.

A simulated rosewood reclining open armchair, with an adjustable ladder back and swept arms, on turned front legs with brass toe caps and casters, c1840.
£175–200 / €250–300
$300–350 HYD

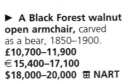

► **A Black Forest walnut open armchair,** carved as a bear, 1850–1900.
£10,700–11,900
€15,400–17,100
$18,000–20,000 NART

◀ **A pair of Louis XV-style walnut upholstered *fauteuils*,** with gilt-metal mounts, Scandinavian, c1870.
£780–940
€1,100–1,300
$1,300–1,550 S(O)

A set of 12 open elbow chairs, including a chairman's chair, with reeded backs and scrolling arms on turned supports, with stuff-over seats, on turned tapering front legs, late 19thC.
£1,200–1,450
€1,700–2,000
$2,000–2,400 AH

An inlaid mahogany tub-shaped armchair, c1900.
£200–230 / €290–330
$340–380 MTay

An Edwardian mahogany tub-shaped chair, with openwork back and tapestry seat, on square tapering legs.
£350–420 / €500–600
$590–700 G(L)

A pair of mahogany tub open armchairs, with nailed upholstery, late 19thC.
£1,100–1,300
€1,600–1,900
$1,850–2,200 L

A pair of mahogany X-frame open armchairs, with carved and pierced backs, damaged, late 19thC.
£560–670 / €810–960
$940–1,150 SWO

A pair of George II-style upholstered oak open armchairs, early 20thC.
£1,150–1,300
€1,650–1,850
$1,900–2,100 MHA

A parcel-gilt rosewood open armchair, by Gustav Herter, American, c1870.
£3,050–3,650
€4,400–5,300
$5,100–6,100 S(NY)

Gustav Herter emigrated from Germany to New York with his half-brother Christian in the mid-19th century. Gustav's designs were fairly conventional and tended towards the revivalist style, while Christian produced more adventurous pieces.

An inlaid mahogany open armchair, with a shield-shaped back, late 19thC.
£130–160 / €200–230
$220–260 LF

A pair of Gustavian-style birch open armchairs, Swedish, 1910–20.
£2,600–2,900
€3,800–4,200
$4,350–4,800 CAV

A pair of Sheraton revival satinwood open armchairs, with painted decoration, c1885.
£4,000–4,500
€5,800–6,500
$6,700–7,500 Che

A Sheraton revival satin-wood open armchair, with an interlaced splat back, the arms inlaid with ebonized boxwood and satinwood stringing, on square tapering front legs, late 19thC.
£330–400 / €490–580
$560–670 GAK

A walnut swivelling desk chair, with leather squab seat, on square tapering legs, American, early 20thC.
£230–270 / €330–390
$390–460 GAK

LOCATE THE SOURCE

The source of each illustration in Miller's can be found by checking the code letters below each caption with the Key to Illustrations, pages 794–800.

Upholstered Armchairs

A William & Mary ebonized beechwood wing armchair, with carved stretcher and S-scroll front legs.
£1,900–2,300
€2,750–3,300
$3,200–3,850 HYD

A George I walnut wing chair, with 18thC petit point upholstery and carved cabriole legs, restored and repaired.
£3,300–3,950
€4,750–5,700
$5,500–6,600 HAM

A George III mahogany wing armchair, with padded wings and arms and a sprung seat, on casters.
£610–730 / €880–1,050
$1,000–1,200 PF

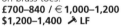

An early George III mahogany wing armchair, upholstery worn.
£2,450–2,950
€3,550–4,250
$4,100–4,900 CGC
This chair sold for over four times its low estimate despite its distressed condition, which shows that it is fresh to the market. Although its poor state of repair might seem off-putting, the shape of the back is stunning and all it needs is reupholstering, waxing and probably frame tightening.

A mahogany campaign armchair, attributed to Ross & Co, with buttoned back and sprung seat, late 19thC.
£1,750–1,950
€2,500–2,800
$2,950–3,300 ChC

A club armchair, on turned mahogany legs and casters, recovered in hide, c1870.
£1,900–2,100
€2,750–3,050
$3,200–3,550 RGa

◄ **A Victorian mahogany spoon-back armchair,** with upholstered buttoned back, carved serpentine front rail and tapering legs on brass toes.
£700–840 / €1,000–1,200
$1,200–1,400 LF

A Victorian mahogany spoon-back armchair, with buttoned back and padded seat, on brass casters.
£800–960 / €1,150–1,400
$1,350–1,600 BR

A pair of carved giltwood armchairs, Italian, late 19thC.
£1,250–1,400
€1,800–2,000
$2,100–2,350 HiA

A shell-shaped occasional chair, on turned walnut legs with casters, late 19thC.
£220–260 / €310–370
$370–440 NSal

A pair of shell-shaped armchairs, early 20thC.
£590–710 / €850–1,000
$1,000–1,200 DN

Bergères

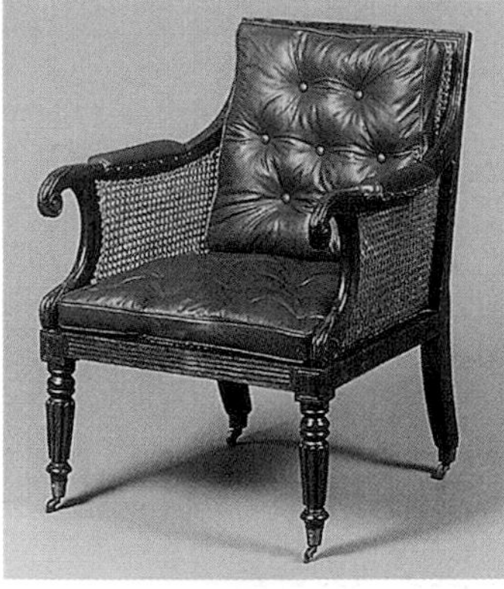

A mahogany bergère, with buttoned leather cushions, on turned legs, c1825.
£3,800–4,550 / €5,500–6,500
$6,400–7,600 S(O)

A pair of Biedermeier-style birchwood bergères, Swedish, c1910.
£4,500–5,000 / €6,500–7,200
$7,500–8,400 ⊞ CAV

◄ **A Louis XV-style giltwood bergère,** French, late 19thC.
£860–1,000 / €1,250–1,450
$1,450–1,750 NOA

Children's Chairs

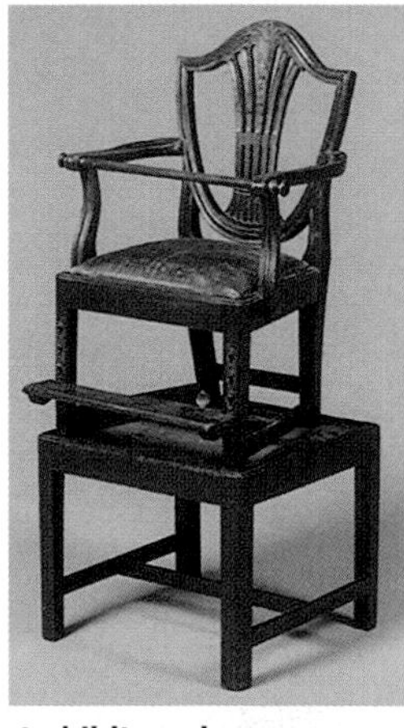

A child's mahogany high chair, c1790, 35¾in (91cm) high.
£3,450–4,150
€4,950–6,000
$5,800–7,000 S(O)

A child's mahogany armchair, c1820.
£700–780 / €1,000–1,100
$1,150–1,300 ⊞ WAA

A George IV child's mahogany bergère high chair, base missing, footrest and bar replaced.
£260–310 / €380–450
$440–520 G(L)

A child's mahogany high chair, 19thC, 32¼in (82cm) high.
£270–320 / €390–460
$450–540 B(Kn)

Further reading

Miller's Buying Affordable Antiques Price Guide, Miller's Publications, 2003

► **A Victorian child's bentwood rocking chair,** with a caned seat and back.
£560–670
€810–960
$940–1,000
B&L

A Victorian child's mahogany high chair, with arched top rail above scrolling arms, the base with baluster-turned legs.
£400–480 / €570–680
$670–810 CGC

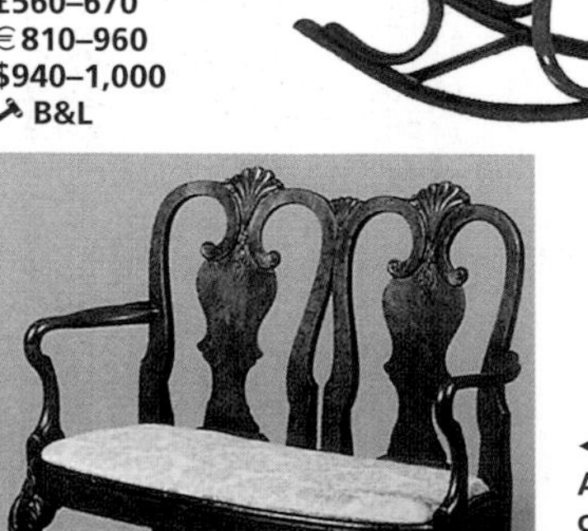

◄ **A Queen Anne-style child's walnut double-back chair,** c1880.
£3,000–3,600
€4,300–5,200
$5,000–6,000
S(O)

A Queen Anne-style child's walnut chair, late 19thC.
£2,650–2,950
€3,800–4,250
$4,450–4,950 ⊞ GGD

Corner Chairs

A George II mahogany corner chair, the cresting rail over a silhouette baluster splat, the cabriole front leg with a claw-and-ball foot.
£1,650–2,000 / €2,400–2,850
$2,750–3,350 ⚒ HYD

A George III mahogany corner chair, with pierced splats and drop-in seat, on turned legs.
£700–840 / €1,000–1,200
$1,200–1,400 ⚒ SWO

▶ A George III mahogany corner chair, with solid splats.
£940–1,100 / €1,350–1,600
$1,600–1,850 ⚒ DN

An early George III mahogany corner chair.
£700–840 / €1,000–1,200
$1,200–1,400 ⚒ L

LOCATE THE SOURCE

The source of each illustration in Miller's can be found by checking the code letters below each caption with the Key to Illustrations, pages 794–800.

Dining Chairs

A George II mahogany dining chair, with a vase splat back and drop-in seat, on cabriole legs.
£190–230 / €270–320
$320–380 PFK

A walnut dining chair, with a pierced splat back and upholstered drop-in seat, on cabriole front legs, Dutch, 18thC.
£610–730 / €880–1,050
$1,000–1,200 GAK

A set of six mahogany dining chairs, with waisted slatted backs, the arched top rail on shaped stiles above tapestry drop-in seats, late 18thC.
£1,700–2,050
€2,450–2,950
$2,850–3,450 AH

A set of three George III mahogany dining chairs, the arched foliate-carved backs with pierced splats, drop-in seats, on square tapering legs.
£440–530 / €640–760
$740–890 B(B)

► **A set of eight mahogany dining chairs,** with pierced swag splats, c1770.
£6,700–7,500
€9,700–10,800
$11,300–12,600
YOX

A mahogany ladder-back chair, c1775.
£300–330 / €430–480
$500–550 WAA

A set of six Chippendale-style mahogany dining chairs, c1770.
£10,800–12,000
€15,500–17,300
$18,100–20,100 GDB

Regency style (1790–1830)

- Named after George, Prince of Wales, who was Prince Regent from 1811 to 1820 during the illness of his father, George III
- Style inspired by classical art and architecture
- Painted, carved or stencilled decoration was particularly popular
- Early Regency designs are ornate but relatively light and elegant with flowing lines incorporating scrolls, and with sabre legs
- By the George IV (High Regency) period (1820–30), designs had become heavier with an emphasis on carving
- Typical motifs in the early period were acanthus, guilloche and palmettes, while those of the High Regency period reflected the Prince's taste for the exotic, such as dolphins, sphinxes, crocodiles and Orientals
- Key creative figures were Thomas Hope and George Smith

A set of 10 Regency dining chairs, including two carvers, the carved cresting rails above reeded central splats, inlaid panels and calico-covered seats.
£4,700–5,600
€6,700–8,100
$7,900–9,500 G(L)

A Hepplewhite-style mahogany dining chair, with pierced back and swag carving, c1790.
£430–480 / €620–690
$720–810 WAA

A set of eight mahogany dining chairs, including two carvers, c1810.
£19,800–22,000 / €28,500–32,000
$33,000–37,000 JC
These chairs are an excellent rich colour, in fine condition and with original patination.

A set of six Regency mahogany dining chairs, including two carvers, with reeded brass line-inlaid top rails and crossbars, on ring-turned front legs.
£1,250–1,500
€1,800–2,150
$2,100–2,500 Bea

◀ A set of four Regency mahogany dining chairs, with tablet backs and sabre legs.
£260–310
€380–450
$440–520
SWO

A set of six Regency mahogany dining chairs, the bar backs with veneered tablets, above drop-in seats, on turned tapering front legs.
£1,700–2,000
€2,400–2,900
$2,700–3,200 Mit

◀ A set of six mahogany dining chairs, c1820.
£2,200–2,500
€3,200–3,600
$3,700–4,200 DY

A set of ten Regency mahogany dining chairs, the cresting rails with carved acanthus scrolls and brass inlay, the central horizontal splats with chrysanthemum and scroll motif, above drop-in seats.
£7,100–8,500
€10,200–12,200
$11,900–14,300 M

A set of six Regency beechwood dining chairs, painted to simulate rosewood and gilt-decorated, with stylized palmettes above horse-hair upholstered drop-in seats, some restoration.
£2,300–2,750
€3,300–3,950
$3,850–4,600 DN

► A set of five Regency mahogany dining chairs, including one carver, with carved top rails above drop-in seats, on sabre legs.
£940–1,100
€1,350–1,600
$1,550–1,850 AH

Styles of chair backs

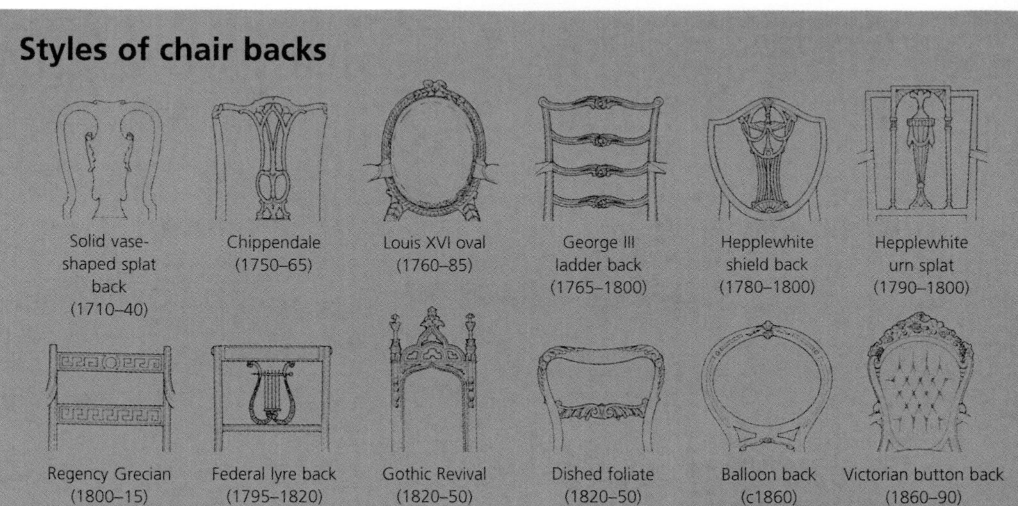

A set of six George IV mahogany dining chairs, the horizontal rails with central roundels flanked by bellflowers, above padded seats, on turned tapering front legs.
£1,500–1,800
€2,150–2,600
$2,500–3,000 ⚒ **PF**

A William IV rosewood dining chair, in the style of Gillows.
£120–145 / €170–200
$200–240 ⚒ **B(Kn)**

Items in the Furniture section have been arranged in date order within each sub-section.

A set of eight George IV mahogany dining chairs, with scroll-carved crest rails and veneered panels, above drop-in seats.
£3,900–4,700
€5,600–6,700
$6,600–7,900 ⚒ **DN**

A set of five mahogany dining chairs, the curved top rails above scroll and tablet bar backs, with stuff-over leather-upholstered seats, 1830s.
£350–420 / €500–600
$590–710 ⚒ **AH**

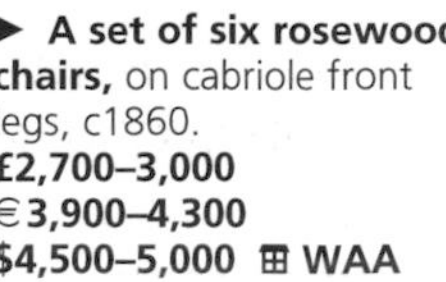

► **A set of six rosewood chairs,** on cabriole front legs, c1860.
£2,700–3,000
€3,900–4,300
$4,500–5,000 ⊞ **WAA**

► **A set of four William IV mahogany bar-back dining chairs,** on turned tapering front legs.
£280–330
€400–480
$470–550
⚒ **SWO**

A set of eight mahogany dining chairs, including two carvers, the top rails with inlaid stringing, above drop-in seats, restored, 19thC.
£1,200–1,400
€1,700–2,000
$2,000–2,350 ⚒ **WW**

A set of six mahogany dining chairs, including two carvers, with leather-upholstered stuff-over seats, c1850.
£760–910 / €1,100–1,300
$1,300–1,550 ⚒ **CGC**

A pair of walnut dining chairs, c1870.
£180–200 / €260–290
$300–330 ⊞ **GBr**

A set of six Victorian rosewood dining chairs, with stuff-over seats, some damage and repairs.
£470–560 / €670–800
$790–940 SWO

A set of six Sheraton-style mahogany dining chairs, with trellis backs, 19thC.
£760–850 / €1,100–1,250
$1,300–1,450 ⊞ HiA

A set of six Hepplewhite-style mahogany dining chairs, 19thC.
£2,550–2,850
€3,700–4,100
$4,300–4,800 ⊞ RAN

► **A set of 14 Victorian oak dining chairs,** including two carvers.
£2,250–2,700
€3,250–3,900
$3,800–4,500
B(Kn)

► **A set of six Victorian rosewood balloon-back dining chairs,** with double scrolled splats above tapestry seats, on cabriole front legs.
£430–520
€620–750
$720–870
TRM

A set of eight Hepplewhite-style mahogany dining chairs, with wheatsheaf splats and leather-upholstered seats, 19thC.
£3,150–3,500
€4,550–5,000
$5,300–5,900 ⊞ NoC

A set of six Victorian mahogany dining chairs, stamped 'Holland & Sons', three damaged.
£1,650–2,000
€2,400–2,900
$2,800–3,350 MAR

A set of eight Victorian carved mahogany balloon-back dining chairs, with serpentine front seats, on turned and fluted legs.
£1,650–2,000 / €2,400–2,850
$2,800–3,350 WilP

Hall Chairs

A mahogany hall chair, with painted panel, c1790.
£570–630 / €820–910
$960–1,100 ⊞ GEO

A set of three mahogany hall chairs, c1810.
£1,100–1,250
€1,600–1,800
$1,850–2,100 ⊞ GEO

A pair of George III mahogany hall chairs, the shield backs with painted crests, restored.
£940–1,100
€1,350–1,600
$1,600–1,850 ⚒ B(Kn)

A Regency mahogany hall chair, with a shell and C-scroll back, on sabre legs.
£260–310 / €370–450
$440–520 ⚒ EH

Items in the Furniture section have been arranged in date order within each sub-section.

A pair of WIlliam IV mahogany hall chairs, with pierced and carved backs, on turned tapering front legs.
£260–310 / €370–450
$440–520 ⚒ WW

A pair of Gothic-style oak hall chairs, 1830–40.
£4,000–4,500
€5,800–6,500
$6,700–7,500 ⊞ GDB

A pair of mahogany hall chairs, c1860.
£540–600 / €780–860
$910–1,000 ⊞ DY

A pair of oak hall chairs, c1870.
£530–590 / €760–850
$890–990 ⊞ GBr

Library Chairs

A William IV mahogany library armchair, with pull-out footrest.
£1,050–1,250
€1,500–1,800
$1,750–2,100 ⚒ MAR

An early Victorian oak library chair, the reverse carved with a stag crest.
£3,750–4,500
€5,400–6,500
$6,300–7,500 ⚒ LFA

A mahogany library chair, upholstered in leather, with Buckingham Palace inventory mark, 1866.
£3,350–3,700
€4,800–5,300
$5,600–6,200 ⊞ SAW

A mahogany library chair, the padded arm supports with carved animal head terminals, upholstered in leather, French, 19thC.
£880–1,000
€1,250–1,450
$1,500–1,700 ⚒ HYD

Salon Chairs

A Hepplewhite-style mahogany salon chair, with silk upholstery, late 18thC.
£2,150–2,400
€3,100–3,450
$3,600–4,000 ⊞ GGD

A pair of birch Klismos salon chairs, Swedish, c1790–1800.
£3,000–3,400
€4,300–4,900
$5,000–5,700 ⊞ CAV
This style was based on chairs featured on ancient Greek vases and illustrated in *House-hold Furniture & Interior Decoration* pubished in 1807 by Thomas Hope.

◄ A Victorian walnut salon chair, with pierced arms, on cabriole legs and knurled feet.
£220–260 / €320–370
$370–440 ⚒ L&E

► A pair of gilt-gesso salon chairs, French, 19thC.
£280–340
€400–480
$470–550 ⚒ L&E

A pair of Edwardian inlaid mahogany salon chairs, with upholstered seats, on square tapering front legs.
£175–210 / €250–300
$300–350 ⚒ PFK

Further reading

Miller's Buying Affordable Antiques Price Guide,
Miller's Publications, 2003

Side Chairs

A pair of walnut side chairs, with fret-carved crests, c1690.
£2,500–2,800
€3,600–4,000
$4,200–4,700 ⊞ NAW

A Queen Anne walnut side chair, the moulded top rail and vase-shaped splat above a drop-in needlework seat, on cabriole front legs and pad feet.
£1,050–1,250
€1,500–1,800
$1,750–2,100 ⚒ B
This side chair was once owned by Rev Lord Augustus FitzClarence who was the illegitimate son of William IV.

A George III mahogany ribbon-back side chair, on square legs joined by stretchers.
£1,200–1,400
€1,750–2,100
$2,000–2,400 ⚒ AH

A mahogany campaign side chair, with a caned seat, late 18thC.
£400–450 / €570–650
$670–750 ⊞ ChC
This type of chair is often referred to as a Naval chair, since Admiral Lord Nelson had a similar set of chairs on HMS *Victory*

Items in the Furniture section have been arranged in date order within each sub-section.

► **A pair of carved rosewood side chairs,** c1860.
£4,250–4,700
€6,100–6,800
$7,150–7,900 ⊞ GGD

◄ **A set of six early Victorian rosewood balloon-back side chairs,** with pierced tied scroll horizontal splats, on cabriole front legs.
£910–1,100
€1,350–1,600
$1,550–1,850 ⚒ NSal

A Louis XVI-style carved giltwood side chair, the beaded crest above a lyre back, French, late 19thC.
£290–340 / €410–490
$480–570 ⚒ NOA

A set of four Edwardian side chairs.
£340–380 / €490–550
$570–640 ⊞ AMG

Miscellaneous Chairs

◄ **A walnut chair,** with carved and moulded decoration surrounding a caned back and seat, seat recaned and feet restored, French, 1723–74.
£580–700 / €840–1,000
$970–1,150 ⚒ S(P)
This chair was from the collection of Lady Mendl (also known as Elsie de Wolfe), who had a villa at Versailles. She has been described as 'the most successful interior designer of the 20th century'.

A silverwood grotto rocking chair, decorated with sea creatures, Italian, c1900.
£2,500–3,000
€3,600–4,300
$4,200–5,000 ⚒ S(O)

A Victorian walnut prie dieu, with carved and twist-turned decoration and contemporary woolwork upholstery.
£350–420 / €500–600
$590–700 ⚒ SWO

Chaises Longues

A laminated rosewood *méridienne*, attributed to J. H. Belter, the back-crest with fruit and floral carving, on cabriole legs, American, c1850, 36½in (92.5cm) high.
£2,350–2,800 / €3,400–4,000
$4,000–4,700 ⚒ NOA

French in origin, *méridienne* is the Regency name for a couch with one scrolled end higher than the other, usually on paw feet and casters.

► **A Victorian rosewood chaise longue,** with a scrolled back and later turned feet, 82¾in (210cm) long.
£400–480 / €580–690
$670–800 ⚒ B&L

► **A Victorian walnut chaise longue,** 73½in (186.5cm) long.
£380–460 / €550–660
$640–770 ⚒ B(Kn)

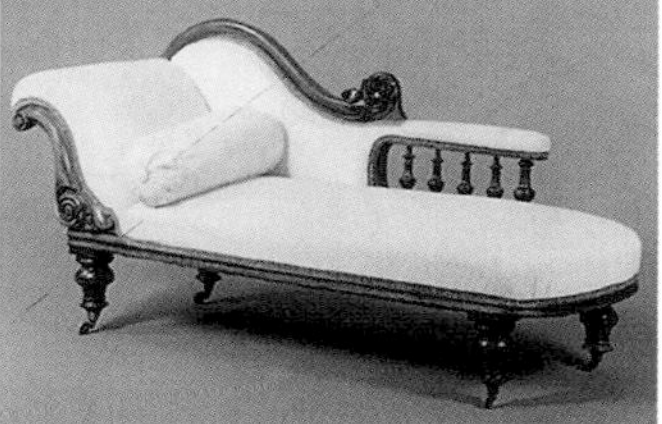

A mahogany chaise longue, with a bolster cushion, c1860, 72in (183cm) long.
£700–840 / €1,000–1,200
$1,200–1,400 ⚒ S(O)

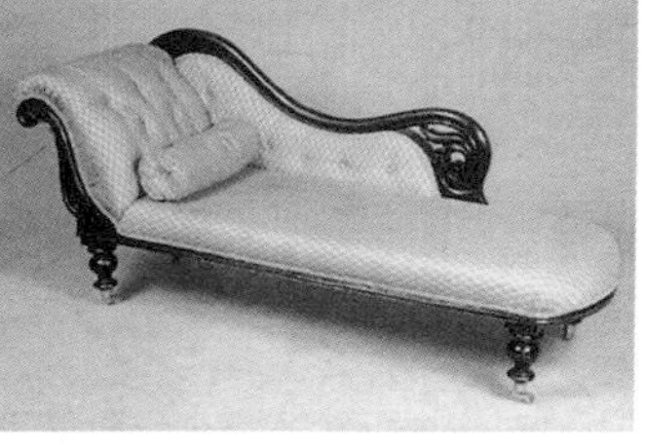

A giltwood *duchesse brisée*, carved with scrolls, flowers and acanthus, the two chairs with caned backs and sides, the stool of serpentine form, all with carved cabriole legs, canework damaged, French, late 19thC, 101in (256.5cm) high.
£1,050–1,250 / €1,500–1,800
$1,750–2,100 ⚒ DN

Chests & Coffers

A walnut *cassone*, the hinged lid enclosing a compartment and shelf, the front carved with a double-headed eagle within a circle and sunbeams, the corners carved with acanthus pilasters, slight damage, north Italian or Tyrolean, 16th/17thC, 71¼in (181cm) wide.
£1,800–2,150 / €2,600–3,100
$3,000–3,600 ⚒ S(Am)

A mahogany mule chest, by T. Willson, with a hinged top over a panelled front, the stand with a drawer, maker's stamp, 19thC, 48in (122cm) wide.
£280–340 / €400–480
$470–560 ⚒ SWO

Thomas Willson's firm of cabinet-makers and retailers was established in London in 1818, dealing in new and second-hand items. The firm was run by Thomas's wife Mary from 1830 to 1837, and then by their son Matthew from 1838 to 1854.

► **A mahogany blanket chest-on-stand,** with brass carrying handles, c1770, 48in (122cm) wide.
£1,900–2,300
€2,750–3,300
$3,200–3,850 ⚒ S(O)

◄ **A George III mahogany mule chest,** the rising top above four real and four dummy drawers with reeded corners, 63¾in (162cm) wide.
£1,150–1,350
€1,700–1,950
$2,000–2,300 ⚒ B(Kn)

A brass-bound camphorwood and hardwood studwork chest, with an internal box, three drawers to the base, carrying handles, 19thC, 50¼in (127.5cm) wide.
£1,000–1,200 / €1,450–1,700
$1,700–2,000 ⚒ SWO

Chests-on-Chests

A George II walnut chest-on-chest, with a moulded cavetto cornice over two short and three long graduated drawers, above two short and three long drawers, on paw-and-ball feet carved with scrolling acanthus leaves, 45in (114.5cm) wide.
£19,000–22,800
€27,000–32,000
$32,000–38,000 HYD

This fine chest, executed in well-figured walnut, boasts the rare feature of carved feet, seldom seen on English case furniture of this period.

A mahogany and inlaid chest-on-chest, Channel Islands, early 19thC, 44in (112cm) wide.
£2,200–2,600
€3,150–3,750
$3,700–4,350 S(O)

► **A Regency mahogany chest-on-chest,** with two short and three long drawers, over three long graduated drawers, with a shaped apron, on outswept bracket feet, 31in (78.5cm) wide.
£3,200–3,850
€4,600–5,600
$5,400–6,500 B

A mahogany secretaire chest-on-chest, the dentil cornice and blind fret frieze above an arrangement of drawers, with fluted canted corners, c1780, 44in (112cm) wide.
£2,600–3,100
€3,750–4,500
$4,350–5,200 B(Kn)

A George III mahogany chest-on-chest, cross-banded and with stringing, the two short and three long drawers flanked by inlaid quarter columns, the base with three long drawers, on bracket feet, 46¼in (117.5cm) wide.
£2,100–2,500
€3,000–3,600
$3,500–4,200 AH

A mahogany chest-on-chest, c1780, 42in (106.5cm) wide.
£2,900–3,250
€4,200–4,700
$4,900–5,500 ⊞ GGD

A mahogany chest-on-chest, the dentil cornice above graduated oak-lined drawers, c1800, 36in (91.5cm) wide.
£4,400–4,900
€6,300–7,000
$7,400–8,200 ⊞ YOX

A mahogany chest-on-chest, the cornice above two short and three long drawers, over three long drawers, c1850, 44in (112cm) wide.
£1,100–1,300
€1,600–1,900
$1,850–2,200 DN

A mahogany-veneered chest-on-chest, with satinwood and rosewood decoration, c1790, 40in (101.5cm) wide.
£10,800–12,000
€15,500–17,300
$18,000–20,000 ⊞ GDB

A George III mahogany chest-on-chest, the dentil and blind fret cornice over two short and three long graduated drawers, above a brushing slide and three further long drawers, with deal sides, some veneer replaced, 43in (109cm) wide.
£1,300–1,550
€1,850–2,200
$2,200–2,600 EH

A mahogany chest-on-chest, c1900, 46in (117cm) wide.
£2,300–2,750
€3,350–4,000
$3,850–4,600 S(O)

Chests of Drawers & Commodes

An oyster-veneered walnut chest of drawers, c1700, 35in (89cm) high.
£8,900–9,900 / €12,800–14,200
$15,000–16,600 ⊞ ANAn

Oyster veneering

This technique was introduced in the late 17th century and was fashionable until the mid-18th century. The name derives from the appearance of the wood grain which resembles an oyster shell. It is achieved by slicing the veneer transversely across the end grain of small branches. The most frequently used woods were walnut, kingwood, laburnum and olivewood.

A Queen Anne japanned chest, with three short and three long drawers, 40in (101.5cm) wide.
£5,400–6,500
€7,800–9,400
$9,100–10,900 L

A Queen Anne figured walnut chest of drawers, the quarter-veneered crossbanded top over three short and three long herringbone-banded drawers with brass drop handles, on bun feet, damaged, 40¼in (102cm) wide.
£360–430 / €520–630
$600–720 Bri

An early George III mahogany chest of drawers, with brass handles and ogee bracket feet, 43in (109cm) wide.
£1,150–1,350 / €1,650–1,950
$1,900–2,250 DN

A mahogany, elm and oak commode, Dutch, 1750–1800, 40¼in (102cm) wide.
£840–1,000
€1,200–1,400
$1,400–1,650 S(O)

► **A walnut and boxwood-strung serpentine commode,** Maltese, c1760, 55½in (141cm) wide.
£4,800–5,750
€6,900–8,300
$8,000–9,600
S(O)

A Louis XV/XVI Transitional amaranth and parquetry commode, by Louis Noël Malle, the marble top above two long inlaid drawers, flanked by rounded angles with simulated flutes and gilt-bronze capitals, on cabriole legs with sabots, maker's stamp, French, 50½in (128.5cm) wide.
£4,650–5,600 / €6,650–8,000
$7,900–9,400 B

Louis Noël Malle was received Master in 1765 and worked during the reigns of Louis XV and XVI. He was a talented cabinet-maker, using rare and exotic woods, mother-of-pearl, bone and ivory, and is renowned for the quality of his marquetry work.

A mahogany chest of drawers, the three short cockbeaded walnut-lined drawers above three long drawers, 1780, 41¼in (105cm) wide.
£2,400–2,650 / €3,450–3,800
$4,000–4,400 ⊞ JC

A Baroque-style walnut chest of drawers, the drawer fronts with parquetry inlay, Swedish, c1790, 34in (86.5cm) high.
£5,800–6,500 / €8,400–9,400
$9,800–10,900 ⊞ GEO

A mahogany chest of drawers, with two short drawers above three long drawers, c1785, 43in (109cm) wide.
£1,650–1,850 / €2,350–2,650
$2,750–3,000 ⊞ WAA

A mahogany chest of drawers, with later handles, c1790, 39in (99cm) wide.
£850–950 / €1,200–1,350
$1,450–1,600 ⊞ GGD

A Hepplewhite-style figured mahogany serpentine chest of drawers, with four graduated cockbeaded long drawers, c1785, 42½in (108cm) wide.
£7,900–8,800 / €11,300–12,600
$13,300–14,700 ⊞ RGa

A George III mahogany serpentine commode, the two long drawers flanked by serpentine sides, on moulded legs, 44½in (113cm) wide.
£6,500–7,800 / €9,400–11,300
$11,000–13,200 ⚒ B

Drawer linings

Although it is not always stated in the various descriptions for these chests of drawers, one point that can be an indicator of the quality of a piece is the type of timber used for drawer linings. It is important to use other factors in combination when assessing any piece of furniture, such as proportions, condition etc. Oak or cedar drawer linings generally suggest a higher quality piece when compared to pine drawer linings.

◄ **A George III mahogany chest of drawers,** with four long drawers, 32in (81.5cm) wide.
£1,600–1,900 / €2,300–2,750
$2,700–3,200 ⚒ JAd

A George III mahogany chest of drawers, with two short over three long drawers, 43½in (110.5cm) wide.
£1,150–1,300 / €1,650–1,850
$2,000–2,200 ⊞ SWA

◄ **A George III mahogany chest of drawers,** with a crossbanded top, 40in (101.5cm) wide.
£350–420 / €500–600
$600–700 ⚒ L

A George III mahogany bowfronted chest of drawers, the top drawer with a fitted writing slide, 40in (101.5cm) wide.
£3,400–3,800 / €4,900–5,400
$5,700–6,400 ⊞ GGD

A George III mahogany-veneered chest of drawers, with two short and three long graduated drawers, handles and escutcheons replaced, 32½in (82.5cm) wide.
£1,200–1,450 / €1,700–2,000
$2,000–2,400 ⚒ NSal

A pair of walnut commodes, the marble tops above three banded drawers, on cabriole legs with acanthus carving and claw-and-ball feet, Continental, late 18thC, 20in (51cm) wide.
£3,750–4,500 / €5,400–6,500
$6,300–7,500 NOA

A George III mahogany chest of drawers, on shaped bracket feet, 43¼in (110cm) wide.
£1,000–1,200
€1,450–1,700
$1,700–2,000 Bea

A mahogany chest of drawers, with two short drawers over four long drawers, late 18thC, 43in (109cm) wide.
£900–1,000 / €1,300–1,450
$1,500–1,700 HiA

A rosewood, purplewood, tulipwood and calamander marquetry serpentine commode, the marble top above three long drawers inlaid with panoramic views of houses, flanked by canted angles inlaid with harewood flutes, the sides inlaid with tasselled drapes and classical urns, on shaped bracket feet, top later, restored, Russian, c1800, 46¾in (119cm) wide.
£10,600–12,700 / €15,200–18,300
$17,800–21,400 B(Kn)

A walnut and fruitwood-banded serpentine commode, the upper drawer with later compartments, south German, c1800, 49¾in (126.5cm) wide.
£840–1,000 / €1,200–1,400
$1,450–1,700 S(O)

A mahogany chest of drawers, with a brushing slide over four graduated drawers, c1800, 34in (86.5cm) wide.
£2,700–3,000 / €3,900–4,300
$4,550–5,000 YOX

An Empire mahogany commode, with a fossil marble top and gilt-bronze handles, French, 1799–1815, 39in (99cm) wide.
£610–730 / €880–1,050
$1,000–1,200 B(Kn)

Miller's Compares

I. A mahogany and rosewood-crossbanded bowfronted chest of drawers, Channel Islands, early 19thC, 41in (104cm) wide.
£1,900–2,300 / €2,750–3,300
$3,200–3,850 S(O)

II. A mahogany chest of drawers, c1810, 37½in (95.5cm) wide.
£720–860 / €1,050–1,250
$1,200–1,400 S(O)

Furniture from the Channel Islands is, of course, much scarcer than that from the mainland, and Item I has the added advantage of being an example of top-quality cabinet-making. The top is crossbanded and the drawer fronts inlaid with stringing and shells to the corners. The keyholes are ivory-inlaid rather than the more usual brass surrounds of Item II, and the brass ring handles are more desirable than the plain mahogany knobs of Item II. The bowed shape and scalloped apron of Item I is also very pleasing, demonstrating additional craftsmanship and time involved in the construction of this piece, while Item II is of a much plainer design and more straightforward to make, although with attractive figuring to the drawer fronts.

◀ **A mahogany chest of drawers,** with two short and three long graduated cockbeaded drawers, one brass handle missing, early 19thC, 36in (91.5cm) wide.
£370–440 / €530–630
$620–740 PF

A bowfronted chest of drawers, with two short over three long drawers, c1810, 40in (101.5cm) wide.
£1,350–1,500 / €1,950–2,150
$2,250–2,500 ⊞ CGA

A mahogany-veneered chest of drawers, with an applied reeded edge over four long drawers, early 19thC, 36½in (92.5cm) wide.
£420–500 / €600–720
$700–840 ⚒ WW

A mahogany and brass-mounted bowfronted commode, the reeded top above three long figured drawers flanked by fluted stiles with rounded capitals, Russian, early 19thC, 36¼in (92cm) wide.
£4,300–5,100 / €6,200–7,400
$7,200–8,600 ⚒ B

A Regency mahogany chest of drawers, with five small drawers over three long graduated drawers, on reeded feet, 49½in (125.5cm) wide.
£440–530 / €640–760
$740–890 ⚒ WilP

A late Georgian mahogany chest of drawers, 31in (78.5cm) wide.
£1,250–1,400 / €1,800–2,000
$2,100–2,350 ⊞ APO

A mahogany-veneered bowfronted chest of drawers, with two short and two long drawers, early 19thC, 35in (89cm) wide.
£940–1,100 / €1,350–1,600
$1,550–1,850 ⚒ WW

A mahogany bowfronted chest, the reeded frieze over two short and three long drawers, early 19thC, 43¾in (111cm) wide.
£590–710 / €850–1,000
$1,000–1,200 ⚒ DN

A mahogany chest of drawers, with four long drawers, handles replaced, Welsh, 19thC, 43¼in (110cm) wide.
£700–840 / €1,000–1,200
$1,200–1,400 ⚒ SWO

A mahogany bowfronted chest of drawers, the brushing slide over three graduated cockbeaded drawers, early 19thC, 41¼in (105cm) wide.
£1,100–1,300 / €1,600–1,900
$1,850–2,200 ⚒ DD

A mahogany bowfronted chest of drawers, with two short drawers over three long drawers, early 19thC, 42in (106.5cm) wide.
£520–570 / €740–820
$870–960 ⊞ MTay

A Regency mahogany bowfronted chest of drawers, the three drawers flanked by reeded pilasters, on turned feet, 39¾in (101cm) wide.
£1,450–1,750 / €2,100–2,500
$2,450–2,950 ⚒ HOLL

A fruitwood commode, with canted corners and three long drawers, on tapering legs with brass caps, Continental, 1825–50, 36in (91.5cm) high.
£1,000–1,200 / €1,450–1,700
$1,700–2,000 ⚒ NOA

A mahogany-veneered chest of drawers, the moulded cornice above six drawers flanked by capped columns, on bracketed block feet, handles replaced, Dutch, 19thC, 42in (106.5cm) wide.
£800–960 / €1,200–1,400
$1,350–1,600 WW

A figured mahogany chest of drawers, by Heal & Son, the stage top with a raised back over two short and three long drawers with recessed brass handles, 19thC, 48in (122cm) wide.
£820–980 / €1,200–1,400
$1,400–1,650 GH
The recessed brass handles to this piece are strongly influenced by campaign furniture.

A mahogany bowfronted chest of drawers, with two short and three long graduated cockbeaded drawers, c1850, 44in (112cm) high.
£880–1,050 / €1,250–1,500
$1,500–1,750 PF

A Biedermeier satin-birch chest of drawers, c1850, 41in (104cm) wide.
£1,000–1,200
€1,450–1,700
$1,700–2,000 S(O)

A mahogany architect's chest of drawers, with five drawers, c1860, 49in (124.5cm) wide.
£2,200–2,450
€3,150–3,500
$3,700–4,100 MHA

A Victorian mahogany bowfronted chest of drawers, with two short and four long drawers, 42¼in (107.5cm) wide.
£610–730 / €880–1,050
$1,000–1,200 SWO

A Victorian collector's mahogany specimen chest, with ten graduated drawers, on compressed bun feet, 19¼in (49cm) wide.
£590–700 / €850–1,000
$1,000–1,200 PFK

A mahogany and marquetry dressing chest, the rising top above three drawers, on claw feet, Dutch, 19thC, 35in (89cm) wide.
£2,000–2,200
€2,900–3,200
$3,350–3,700 HiA

A Louis XV-style figured walnut chest, the marble top over five drawers, 19thC, 30in (76cm) wide.
£1,450–1,750
€2,100–2,500
$2,450–2,950 S(O)

A satinwood and crossbanded bowfronted commode, the quarter-veneered top above two drawers, French, 19thC, 29in (73.5cm) wide.
£700–840 / €1,000–1,200
$1,200–1,400 TRM

► **A kingwood commode,** with a marble top and floral marquetry panels, French, c1880, 35in (89cm) wide.
£3,000–3,350
€4,400–4,900
$5,100–5,700
RAN

◄ **A mahogany specimen chest,** the two sets of seven long graduated drawers with central locking bar, late 19thC, 48in (122cm) wide.
£590–710
€850–1,000
$1,000–1,200
LAY

A figured walnut and gilt-metal-mounted chest, with four drawers, German, late 19thC, 24½in (62cm) wide.
£1,650–2,000
€2,450–2,900
$2,750–3,300 TEN

A walnut chest of drawers, by Maple & Co, with chamfered corners and seven drawers, late 19thC, 26¾in (68cm) wide.
£1,050–1,250
€1,500–1,800
$1,750–2,100 DN

Military Chests

◄ **A teak military secretaire chest,** with brass-bound edges, the fall-front with a writing surface and drawers, the front with brass stringing and fleur-de-lys-inlaid corners, the base with two short and two long drawers, distressed, side handles missing, c1850, 19in (48.5cm) wide.
£2,000–2,400 / €3,000–3,500
$3,350–4,000 ⚒ DN

A camphorwood secretaire campaign chest, c1850, 41in (104cm) wide.
£3,150–3,500 / €4,500–5,000
$5,200–5,700 ⊞ GBr

A Victorian mahogany military chest, the two sections with brass corners and handles and two short and three long drawers, 39in (99cm) wide.
£1,050–1,250 / €1,500–1,800
$1,750–2,100 ⚒ NSal

A teak campaign chest, the two sections with brass corners and two short drawers above three long drawers, on removable turned legs, 19thC, 38in (96.5cm) wide.
£800–960 / €1,200–1,400
$1,350–1,600 ⚒ G(B)

A satinwood military secretaire chest, c1860, 42in (106.5cm) high.
£2,500–2,800 / €3,600–4,000
$4,200–4,700 ⊞ GEO

Secretaire Chests

◄ **A George III mahogany and crossbanded secretaire chest,** with a fitted interior, 32¼in (82cm) wide.
£960–1,150 / €1,400–1,650
$1,600–1,900 ⚒ B(Kn)

A late George III mahogany secretaire chest, the fall-front above two flame-veneered doors enclosing a sliding tray, 49in (124.5cm) wide.
£1,450–1,750 / €2,100–2,500
$2,450–2,950 ⚒ DN

A George III mahogany secretaire chest, with three long crossbanded and boxwood-strung drawers, 50in (127cm) wide.
£760–910 / €1,100–1,300
$1,300–1,500 ⚒ TRM

◄ **A Regency mahogany secretaire chest,** the fall-front secretaire with twin dummy fronts enclosing a fitted interior, above two long drawers, with later bookcase top, damaged, 43¼in (110cm) wide.
£590–710 / €850–1,000
$1,000–1,200 ⚒ BR

A mahogany secretaire chest, Irish, c1860, 44in (112cm) wide.
£950–1,050 / €1,350–1,500
$1,600–1,800 ⊞ HON

Chests-on-Stands

◄ A gilt and painted **vargueño,** with secret drawers and compartments, on a later wood and metal stand, Spanish, 17thC, 25in (63.5cm) high.
£8,000–9,000
€11,500–13,000
$13,400–15,100 ⊞ ANAn

An oyster-veneered olivewood chest-on-stand, with holly banding and stringing, the ovolo-moulded top over two short and three long drawers, the stand with one long drawer, feet missing, damaged, late 17thC, 41¾in (106cm) wide.
£7,000–8,400 / €10,100–12,100
$11,800–14,100 ⚒ TEN

This is a good example of how a piece of furniture has evolved over the years. The chest is now lacking its feet and the handles were replaced in Victorian times. It is in a shabby state, but is an honest piece and the condition shows that it is fresh to the market. This is very appealing to prospective buyers and although the purchaser will, in all probability, immediately have it restored, the advantage of buying it in this condition is that the restoration can be carried out to personal requirements.

A William and Mary oyster-veneered olivewood chest-on-stand, the hinged top enclosing a fitted interior above a drawer, on stained ash spiral-turned legs, interior refitted, c1700.
£4,200–5,000 / €6,000–7,200
$7,100–8,400 ⚒ S(O)

A walnut and marquetry chest-on-stand, inlaid with mother-of-pearl, Dutch, c1700, 32in (81.5cm) wide.
£6,100–7,300 / €8,800–10,500
$10,200–12,300 ⚒ LFA

A walnut chest-on-stand, the interior refitted as a cocktail cabinet, early 18thC, 37¼in (94.5cm) wide.
£2,000–2,400
€2,950–3,500
$3,400–4,000 ⚒ B(Kn)

An oyster-veneered walnut chest-on-stand, with parquetry inlay and crossbanding, two short and three long graduated drawers, the base with a moulded top above a drawer, on later bracket feet, early 18thC, 31in (78.5cm) wide.
£13,500–16,200
€19,500–23,400
$22,700–27,000 ⚒ CGC

A walnut-veneered chest-on-stand, the moulded cornice above three short and three long featherbanded drawers, over three further drawers, later brass handles, early 18thC, 42in (106.5cm) wide.
£1,050–1,250
€1,500–1,800
$1,750–2,100 ⚒ WW

A George I walnut chest-on-stand, the drawers with feather crossbanding, 38½in (98cm) wide.
£1,200–1,450
€1,700–2,000
$2,000–2,400 ⚒ L

◄ **A George I burr-elm-veneered chest-on-stand,** the sectioned, stepped and moulded cavetto cornice above three drawers, over three long graduated drawers, all inlaid with boxwood and holly stringing, the stand with a central drawer flanked by two further drawers, on cabriole legs and club feet, 40½in (103cm) wide.
£108,000–120,000 / €155,000–173,000
$181,000–201,000 ⊞ JC

The quality and condition of this chest-on-stand is exceptional. It can be considered an extremely rare piece of English furniture of a period where very few pieces have survived in original and untouched condition. After research, the vendors are of the opinion that this chest-on-stand can be attributed to John Coxed and Thomas Woster, who produced many fine bureaux, cabinets and chests, dating from the period 1700 to 1730, at the White Swan, St Paul's Churchyard, London.

A George II walnut chest-on-stand, some replacements, 40¼in (102cm) wide.
£2,800–3,300
€4,000–4,700
$4,600–5,500 ⚒ S(O)

Wellington Chests

A Regency mahogany Wellington chest, the 11 drawers with lion-mask handles, 18in (45.5cm) wide.
£1,050–1,250
€1,500–1,800
$1,750–2,100 B(Kn)

It is unusual to have a door on such pieces. Generally, Wellington chests just have a locking pilaster or pilasters.

► **A Victorian oak Wellington chest,** the 10 drawers flanked by pilasters, 16in (40.5cm) wide.
£780–940 / €1,100–1,300
$1,300–1,600 BR

◄ **A Victorian oak Wellington chest,** with seven drawers, 21¼in (54cm) wide.
£590–700 / €850–1,000
$1,000–1,200 SWO

A Victorian walnut secretaire Wellington chest, 30in (76cm) wide.
£3,750–4,500
€5,400–6,500
$6,300–7,500 B(Kn)

► **A Victorian walnut Wellington chest,** with seven graduated drawers and carved mounts, 19¼in (49cm) wide.
£470–560 / €680–810
$790–940 WilP

A Victorian figured walnut Wellington chest, with carved scroll mounts, six drawers and twin locking pilasters, 16in (40.5cm) high.
£870–1,050
€1,250–1,500
$1,500–1,750 JM

Clothes & Linen Presses

A George III mahogany linen press, the panelled doors enclosing slides, above two short and two long drawers, 52in (132cm) wide.
£2,100–2,500
€3,000–3,600
$3,500–4,200 SWO

The value of clothes and linen presses can be affected by the presence or lack of sliding trays in the upper section.

► **A Regency mahogany linen press,** stamped 'Gillows of Lancaster', 50in (127cm) wide.
£4,500–5,000
€6,500–7,200
$7,500–8,400 APO

A George III figured mahogany linen press, with two panelled doors, 52in (132cm) wide.
£1,900–2,300
€2,750–3,300
$3,200–3,900 CDC

A George III figured mahogany and satinwood-crossbanded linen press, decorated with floral marquetry, the two panelled doors enclosing sliding trays, 48in (122cm) wide.
£1,800–2,150
€2,600–3,100
$3,000–3,600 JM

► **A mahogany and boxwood-strung clothes press,** the doors with flame mahogany veneers and crossbanding enclosing four sliding trays, early 19thc, 52in (132cm) wide.
£2,450–2,900
€3,500–4,200
$4,100–4,900 DN

A George III mahogany linen press, with flame mahogany panelled doors over two long and two short drawers, feet replaced, 49in (124.5cm) wide.
£5,200–5,800
€7,500–8,300
$8,700–9,700 GGD

A mahogany linen press, with ebony stringing, c1815, 48in (122cm) wide.
£3,500–3,900
€5,000–5,600
$5,900–6,600 ⊞ Che

A mahogany linen press, the two doors with papier-mâché inset panels depicting figures, enclosing sliding trays, c1820, 47¼in (120cm) wide.
£3,800–4,550
€5,500–6,600
$6,400–7,600 ⚒ S(O)

A William IV mahogany and crossbanded linen press, the pediment with brass urn and moulded brass roundels above two doors enclosing sliding trays, 48in (122cm) wide.
£3,750–4,500
€5,400–6,500
$6,300–7,500 ⚒ AG

A mahogany and inlaid clothes press, the two panelled doors enclosing a later hanging rail, early 19thC, 56in (142cm) wide.
£1,500–1,800
€2,150–2,600
$2,500–3,000 ⚒ WW

A George IV mahogany linen press, 49in (124cm) wide.
£1,050–1,250
€1,500–1,800
$1,750–2,100 ⚒ L

A mahogany linen press, c1840, 50in (127cm) wide.
£2,100–2,350
€3,000–3,400
$3,500–4,000 ⊞ MTay

LOCATE THE SOURCE

The source of each illustration in Miller's can be found by checking the code letters below each caption with the Key to Illustrations, pages 794–800.

A Regency figured mahogany linen press, the two doors enclosing four sliding trays, the drawers with later handles, 49½in (125.5cm) wide.
£1,250–1,500
€1,800–2,150
$2,100–2,500 ⚒ Bri

A mahogany linen press, the fretwork cornice above two doors with rosewood-crossbanded and ebony and boxwood-strung panels enclosing hanging space, 19thC, 48¾in (124cm) wide.
£1,750–2,100
€2,500–3,000
$2,900–3,500 ⚒ PFK

A Victorian plum pudding mahogany-veneered clothes press, the two panelled doors enclosing hanging space, with later bracket feet and back, stamped 'Heal & Son, London', 51½in (131cm) wide.
£560–670 / €800–960
$940–1,100 ⚒ WW

A crossbanded mahogany linen press, c1820, 48in (122cm) wide.
£2,700–3,000
€3,900–4,300
$4,500–5,000 ⊞ GBr

A mahogany linen press, with arched pediment, the doors with oval panels, c1830, 50in (127cm) wide.
£6,200–6,900
€8,900–9,900
$10,400–11,500 ⊞ RAN

A mahogany linen press, the two panelled doors enclosing a later hanging rail, above three drawers with replaced handles, late 19thC, 48in (122cm) wide.
£2,000–2,400
€2,900–3,450
$3,350–4,000 ⚒ WW

Columns & Pedestals

A pair of *brêche violette* marble pedestals, with gilt-metal mounts, French, 19thC, 51¾in (130cm) high.
£6,300–7,600
€9,200–11,000
$10,700–12,800 B(B)

A late Victorian *verde antico* marble pedestal, with revolving top and carved decoration, 42in (106.5cm) high.
£650–780 / €940–1,100
$1,100–1,300 NOA

A marble pedestal column, with brass mounts, late 19thC, 44in (112cm) high.
£360–430 / €520–620
$600–720 S(O)

A pair of mahogany fluted columns, with brass mounts, late 19thC, 41¼in (105cm) high.
£5,000–6,000
€7,200–8,600
$8,400–10,100 S(P)

A *verde antico* marble pedestal, with revolving top, c1900, 38in (96.5cm) high.
£580–700 / €840–1,000
$970–1,150 NOA

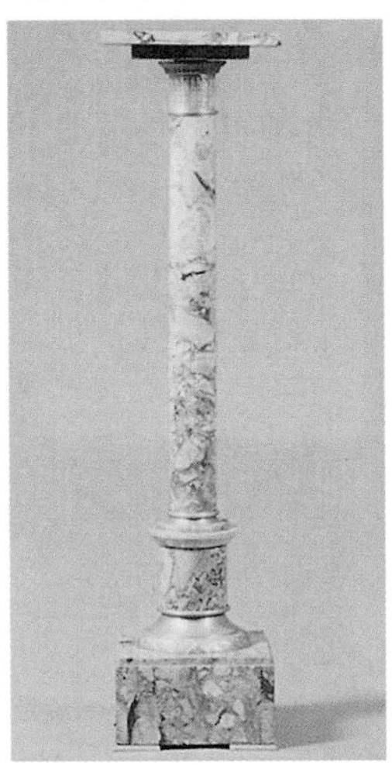

A marble and gilt-bronze pedestal column, c1900, 41¼in (105cm) high.
£1,000–1,200
€1,450–1,700
$1,700–2,000 S(O)

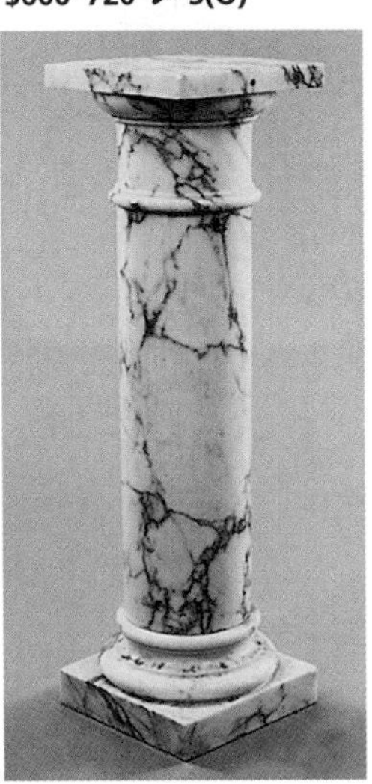

A marble pedestal, with revolving top, Continental, c1900, 48¼in (122.5cm) high.
£510–610 / €730–880
$860–1,000 NOA

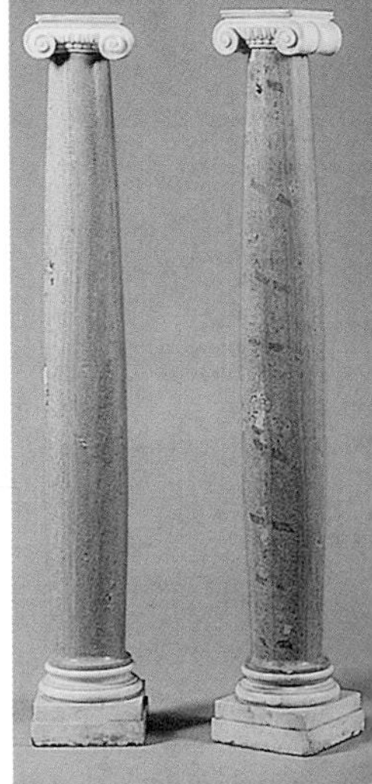

A pair of marble columns, early 20thC, 48½in (123cm) high.
£2,750–3,300
€4,000–4,750
$4,600–5,500 S(O)

Conversation Seats

A Victorian button-backed conversation seat, on mahogany legs with brass casters.
£410–500 / €590–720
$700–840 B(Kn)

A walnut and upholstered conversation seat, c1870, 52½in (133.5cm) wide.
£1,800–2,150 / €2,600–3,100
$3,000–3,600 S(O)

A pair of Victorian conversation seats, with hinged reversible backs and walnut and parcel-gilt scroll feet on horn casters, 47¼in (120cm) wide.
£910–1,100 / €1,350–1,600
$1,550–1,850 DN

FURNITURE

Davenports

A calamander davenport, by Miles & Edwards, the sliding upper section with a leather writing surface and brass gallery above four drawers, stamped, 1825–50, 19in (48.5cm) wide.
£1,550–1,850
€2,250–2,650
$2,600–3,100 Bea

Miles & Edwards, cabinet-makers and upholsterers, flourished from 1822 to 1844. Their clients included the Empress of Russia, the British Ambassador in Paris and the Turkish Ambassador in London. The firm was taken over by Charles Hindley & Sons in 1844.

A George IV fiddle-back mahogany davenport, c1830, 36in (91.5cm) high.
£2,400–2,650
€3,450–3,800
$4,000–4,450 GEO

A burr-walnut davenport, c1880, 27in (86.5cm) wide.
£3,500–3,900
€5,000–5,600
$5,900–6,600 WAA

A burr-walnut davenport, c1860, 21in (53.5cm) wide.
£3,150–3,500
€4,500–5,000
$5,300–5,900 GGD

A Victorian burr-walnut piano-top davenport, the fall-front enclosing a tooled-leather adjustable writing surface, 21½in (54.5cm) wide.
£2,300–2,750
€3,300–4,000
$3,850–4,600 Bri

An olivewood and inlaid davenport, the hinged storage compart-ment above a fall-front, with a panel door to one side enclosing drawers, Jerusalem, c1875, 25¼in (64cm) wide.
£5,250–6,300
€7,550–9,100
$8,800–10,600 S(O)

A late Victorian ebonized davenport, the fitted interior enclosing a rear stationery compartment, with four real and four dummy drawers, 22in (56cm) wide.
£420–500 / €600–720
$700–840 WilP

Daybeds

A Victorian daybed, on mahogany turned legs and brass casters, 78¼in (199cm) long.
£3,500–4,200 / €5,000–6,000
$5,900–7,000 DN

◄ A Louis XVI-style polychrome and cane daybed, early 20thC, 80in (203cm) long.
£550–650
€790–940
$920–1,100
NOA

A beechwood daybed, the uprights moulded with scrolls and foliage, French, late 19thC, 75in (190.5cm) long.
£500–600 / €720 860
$840–1,000 GAK

A Louis XVI-style beechwood daybed, with reeded moulded frame and padded headboard and footboard, late 19thC, 78in (198cm) long.
£950–1,150 / €1,400–1,650
$1,600–1,900 NOA

Desks

A walnut crossbanded and strung kneehole desk, c1720, 31in (78.5cm) wide.
£4,000–4,450 / €5,700–6,400
$6,700–7,500 ⊞ GGD

A George III mahogany kneehole desk, 52½in (133cm) wide.
£960–1,150 / €1,400–1,650
$1,600–1,900 ⚒ S(O)

A burr-maple desk, inlaid with rosewood and brass, French, 1830–48, 52¼in (133cm) wide.
£3,300–3,950 / €4,800–5,700
$5,500–6,600 ⚒ S(P)

A Victorian mahogany partner's desk, the leather inset top above three drawers, 60in (152.5cm) wide.
£2,700–3,000 / €3,900–4,300
$4,500–5,000 ⊞ WAA

A George II walnut and featherbanded kneehole desk, 31¼in (82cm) wide.
£7,000–8,400 / €10,100–12,100
$11,800–14,100 ⚒ TEN

A walnut pedestal desk, French, 18thC, 43in (109cm) wide.
£680–820 / €980–1,150
$1,150–1,400 ⚒ B(Kn)

A Victorian mahogany partner's desk, the crossbanded and leather-inset top above 11 drawers, with three opposing drawers and two cupboard doors with false drawer fronts, 59¾in (152cm) wide.
£3,400–4,100 / €4,900–5,900
$5,700–6,900 ⚒ DN

A Victorian walnut-veneered desk, with later gilt tooled-leather insets, later handles but originals present, 47¼in (120cm) wide.
£940–1,100 / €1,350–1,600
$1,550–1,850 ⚒ WW

◄ **A Victorian mahogany partner's desk,** the *faux* leather-inset top above nine drawers with opposing doors, damaged, 71in (180cm) wide.
£2,000–2,400 / €2,900–3,450
$3,350–4,000 ⚒ Bri

A George III mahogany partner's desk, with leather top, 57in (145cm) wide.
£7,650–8,500 / €11,000–12,200
$12,800–14,300 ⊞ APO

A partner's fiddle-back mahogany desk, with cedar-lined drawers, stamped 'M. Willson', c1825, 59¾in (152cm) wide.
£1,050–1,250 / €1,500–1,800
$1,750–2,100 ⚒ S(O)
Furniture which was stamped M. Willson was either made or retailed through Mary and Thomas Willson's furniture broking and cabinet-making business.

A Victorian walnut partner's desk by Johnstone & Jeanes, the leather-inset top above a frieze drawer flanked by two drawers over panelled and carved cupboard doors enclosing shelves, stamped, 57¾in (147cm) wide.
£4,700–5,600 / €6,750–8,000
$7,900–9,400 ⚒ B(NW)

For further information on
Johnstone & Jeanes see page 33

A Victorian rosewood and kingwood pedestal desk, with pull-out writing slope and brass edges, 42¼in (107.5cm) wide.
£1,300–1,550 / €1,900–2,200
$2,200–2,600 ⚒ B(Kn)

A Victorian mahogany pedestal desk, the leather-inset top above 11 drawers, the reverse with dummy drawers above domed panels, 48½in (123cm) wide.
£1,150–1,250 / €1,500–1,800
$1,750–2,100 NSal

A mahogany pedestal writing desk, the top with hinged writing surface and drawers, a dummy frieze drawer below, repaired, 19thC, 53¼in (135cm) wide.
£530–630 / €760–910
$890–1,000 SWO

A Biedermeier-style rosewood desk, the roll-top enclosing a fitted interior of drawers and pigeonholes above a recessed sliding writing surface, 19thC, 46½in (118cm) high.
£820–980 / €1,200–1,400
$1,400–1,650 GAK

An oak double-sided library desk, the pedestal drawers with opposing panelled doors carved with musical trophies, Franco/Flemish, c1880, 59in (150cm) wide.
£1,150–1,250 / €1,500–1,800
$1,750–2,100 S(O)

► A walnut and marquetry-inlaid cylinder desk, with marble top and ormolu mounts, French, c1880, 26in (66cm) wide.
£3,150–3,500 / €4,500–5,000
$5,300–5,900 ⊞ GEO

A Victorian mahogany pedestal desk, crossbanded with stringing, the top with shell marquetry above a frieze drawer with hinged writing slope, the kneehole cupboard flanked by eight drawers, 48in (122cm) wide.
£1,100–1,300 / €1,600–1,900
$1,850–2,200 AH

An oak desk, by Gillows of Lancaster, late 19thC, 66in (167.5cm) wide.
£5,400–6,000 / €7,800–8,600
$9,100–10,100 ⊞ APO

► An inlaid mahogany writing desk, c1890, 48in (122cm) wide.
£2,400–2,650
€3,450–3,800
$4,000–4,450
⊞ MTay

◄ A Georgian-style mahogany partner's desk, c1900, 72in (183cm) wide.
£4,000–4,500
€5,800–6,500
$6,700–7,600
⊞ GEO

A crossbanded walnut kneehole writing desk, stamped 'FF Jost', German, c1900, 43in (109cm) wide.
£1,150–1,350 / €1,650–1,950
$1,850–2,200 ⚒ S(O)

An Edwardian lady's carved walnut desk, with lap drawer and two further drawers, 35¾in (91cm) wide.
£350–420 / €500–600
$590–700 ⚒ WilP

A George III-style mahogany desk, c1920, 59in (150cm) wide.
£5,600–6,200 / €8,100–8,900
$9,500–10,500 ⊞ GEO

An Edwardian mahogany, boxwood and ebony line-inlaid kidney-shaped desk, the leather-inset top above nine drawers, 49in (124.5cm) wide.
£1,750–2,100 / €2,500–3,000
$2,900–3,500 ⚒ E

An Edwardian walnut pedestal desk, with three-quarter brass gallery above a tambour front enclosing a fitted interior with leather-inset writing slide, above six drawers, 36in (91.5cm) wide.
£820–980 / €1,200–1,400
$1,400–1,650 ⚒ PF

An Edwardian inlaid mahogany writing desk, the mirrored back with two stationery compartments, above a leather writing surface and two drawers, 35¾in (91cm) wide.
£330–400 / €470–570
$550–670 ⚒ CHTR

A George III-style inverted breakfront desk, alterations, early 20thC, 59¾in (152cm) wide.
£540–650 / €780–940
$910–1,100 ⚒ B(Kn)

► **A Queen Anne-style walnut partner's desk,** the reverse with cupboards, c1930, 67¾in (172cm) wide.
£2,850–3,400 / €4,100–4,900
$4,800–5,700 ⚒ S(O)

Dumb Waiters

A pair of William IV walnut telescopic dumb waiters, 39½in (100cm) high.
£2,300–2,750 / €3,300–4,000
$3,850–4,600 ⚒ JAd

A mahogany dumb waiter, the three rise-and-fall tiers above carved supports, c1850, 47in (119.5cm) wide.
£820–980 / €1,200–1,400
$1,400–1,650 ⚒ Mit

A walnut dumb waiter, with three tiers, c1880, 35in (89cm) high.
£900–1,000 / €1,300–1,450
$1,500–1,700 ⊞ MTay

Etagères

An ebonized marquetry and inlaid three-tier étagère, the top tier with brass gallery, French, c1860, 31in (78.5cm) high.
£450–500 / €650–720
$760–840 ⊞ AMG

A walnut and ebonized three-tier étagère, each tier set with a musical trophy, French, 19thC, 16½in (42cm) wide.
£330–390 / €470–560
$550–650 ⚒ L

A pair of mahogany and mahogany-stained walnut three-tier étagères, on tapering legs, late 19thC, 30in (76cm) high.
£1,300–1,550
€1,900–2,250
$2,200–2,600 ⚒ S(P)

An ebonized three-tier étagère, inlaid with gilt-metal banding, French, late 19thC, 33½in (85cm) high.
£280–330 / €400–480
$470–550 ⚒ B(Kn)

LOCATE THE SOURCE
The source of each illustration in Miller's can be found by checking the code letters below each caption with the Key to Illustrations, pages 794–800.

Frames

A parcel-gilt and painted frame, Spanish, 17thC, 29 x 22in (73.5 x 56cm).
£4,250–5,100
€6,100–7,300
$7,100–8,500 ⚒ B(Kn)

A gilded frame, with flowerhead corners, Italian, 18thC, 11¼ x 8¾in (28.5 x 22.5cm).
£1,650–2,000
€2,400–2,900
$2,800–3,350 ⚒ B(Kn)

► **A gilt frame,** late 19thC, 70½ x 58¾in (179 x 149cm).
£360–430 / €510–620
$600–720 ⚒ SWO

A giltwood frame, French, c1720, aperture 31 x 25in (78.5 x 63.5cm).
£1,050–1,250
€1,500–1,800
$1,750–2,100 ⚒ DuM

A giltwood or gilt gesso frame, French, 1830–60, aperture 14¼ x 11¼in (36 x 28.5cm).
£700–840 / €1,000–1,200
$1,200–1,400 ⚒ DuM

A Florentine-style gilded frame, trade label for Thomas Beatty, 18thC, aperture 38½ x 33in (98 x 84.5cm).
£820–980 / €1,200–1,400
$1,400–1,650 ⚒ L

A giltwood frame, Italian, Florence, 19thC, 20½ x 15½in (52 x 39.5cm).
£370–440 / €530–630
$620–740 ⚒ DN

► **A Renaissance-style giltwood frame,** Italian, 1880–1910, aperture 11½ x 8in (29 x 20.5cm).
£360–430 / €520–620
$600–720 ⚒ DuM

A Régence-style giltwood frame, French, 18thC, aperture 24½ x 20in (62 x 51cm).
£630–750 / €910–1,100
$1,000–1,200 ⚒ DuM

A pair of chinoiserie japanned wood frames, 19thC, aperture 10¼ x 5½in (26 x 14cm).
£500–600 / €720–860
$840–1,000 ⚒ SWO

Jardinières

A mahogany jardinière, with brass swing handle and metal liner, c1810, 13½in (34.5cm) high.
£660–790 / €950–1,150 $1,100–1,300 S(O)

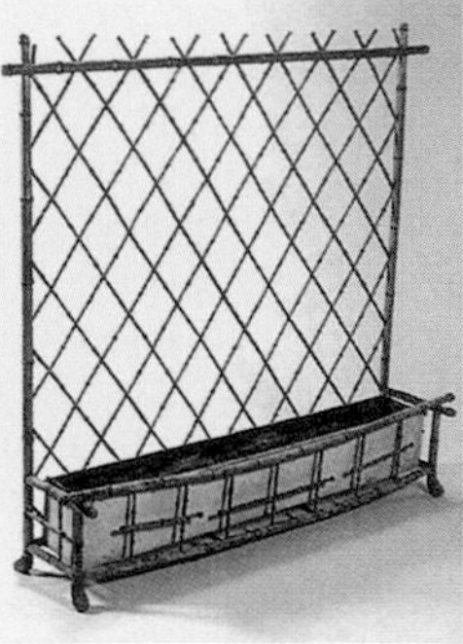

A giltwood jardinière, turned to simulate bamboo trellis, with a metal liner and feet, French, 19thC, 47¼in (120cm) high.
£490–590 / €710–850 $820–990 DN

Insurance values

Always insure your valuable antiques for the cost of replacing them with similar items, regardless of the original price paid. Both dealers and auctioneers can provide a valuation service for a fee.

► A mahogany jardinière, with gilt-metal mounts, French, c1815, 35in (89cm) high.
£1,650–2,000 €2,350–2,900 $2,800–3,350 S(O)

An Edwardian mahogany and satinwood-banded jardinière, with later base and insert, 22¾in (58cm) high.
£105–125 / €150–180 $175–210 B(Kn)

An Edwardian mahogany jardinière, with brass liner, distressed, 33in (84cm) high.
£260–310 / €370–440 $430–520 WW

Lowboys

A crossbanded walnut lowboy, with three drawers, alterations, early 18thC, 29½in (75cm) wide.
£1,300–1,550 / €1,850–2,200 $2,200–2,600 B(Kn)

A George I crossbanded walnut lowboy, the top with moulded border above three drawers and an arched apron, 29in (73.5cm) wide.
£760–910 / €1,100–1,300 $1,250–1,500 HYD

A crossbanded walnut lowboy, the quarter-veneered boxwood-strung top above three boxwood-strung drawers, c1725, 32in (81.5cm) wide.
£7,000–7,800 / €10,100–11,200 $11,800–13,100 RGa

A walnut lowboy, with veneered frieze and later brasses, c1740, 29¼in (74.5cm) wide.
£4,350–4,850 / €6,300–7,000 $7,300–8,100 RGa

A George II crossbanded mahogany lowboy, with pierced fret apron, 34in (86.5cm) wide.
£1,300–1,550 / €1,850–2,200 $2,200–2,600 B

A George IV mahogany lowboy, with three drawers, 30in (76cm) wide.
£1,000–1,200 / €1,400–1,700 $1,650–2,000 G(L)

Miniature Furniture

Many pieces of miniature furniture started life as travelling salesmen's samples. They would have been made of exactly the same materials, be of the same construction and in exact proportion to their full-size counterparts. These pieces were obviously a lot easier for a salesman to carry around the country and enabled him to show potential customers his workshop's current stock. The bureaux, chest-on-chest and extending dining table shown on these pages were no doubt made for this purpose.

A far smaller amount of miniature furniture was actually made by apprentices. This was a very good way of testing a young trainee's ability and workmanship without wasting what were sometimes extremely valuable materials if things were to go wrong. The miniature chest of drawers with bone handles (see page 86) is a good example of this.

Some pieces would have been individual commissions, although this was not as common with miniature pieces as it was with the slightly larger and more practical children's furniture. They would generally have been used for display purposes or as a useful storage article, such as the velvet-covered miniature couch (see page 87).

As you can see from the pictures on the following pages, more chests of drawers of various shapes and sizes were made than any other type of miniature furniture. This is reflected in the market, as small plain miniature chests make fairly modest prices when compared to, say, a miniature bureau of similar date and quality, due to the fact that the latter is harder to find.

Miniature furniture of superb quality and great rarity continue to rise steadily in price and will continue to do so, as these pieces become less readily available and therefore more desirable. The middle to lower end of the market has held up reasonably well, with prices generally rising slightly. However, the more standard and readily available pieces are liable to fluctuate in value from year to year and place to place, although in time they may become scarcer which will cause prices to increase.

These delightful little objects are proving to be a sound investment and are likely to continue so, even in periods where their larger counterparts are struggling. **Robert Timms**

A walnut-veneered miniature bureau, inlaid with stringing, base missing, 18thC, 10in (25.5cm) wide.
£4,700–5,600 / €6,800–8,100
$7,900–9,400 ⚒ WW

A George II oak miniature bureau, the fall-front enclosing a fitted interior, above four drawers, with retailer's label for Bellamy, 9in (23cm) wide.
£1,400–1,700 / €2,000–2,400
$2,350–2,850 ⚒ HYD

A Queen Anne-style walnut miniature bureau, c1920, 9in (23cm) high.
£760–850 / €1,100–1,200
$1,250–1,450 ⊞ TIM

A mahogany miniature corner cabinet, c1920, 23in (58.5cm) high.
£1,500–1,650
€2,150–2,350
$2,500–2,750 ⊞ TIM

Items in the Miniature Furniture section have been arranged in alphabetical order.

◄ **A figured walnut-veneered miniature chest-on-chest,** the two short and three long drawers over three graduated long drawers, with later silvered gilt-brass bun drop handles, c1740, 15¾in (40cm) high.
£2,450–2,950
€3,500–4,250
$4,100–5,000 ⚒ TEN

► **A beech miniature Windsor armchair,** c1860, 11in (28cm) high.
£300–330 / €430–480
$500–550 ⊞ TIM

A George III mahogany miniature chest of drawers, the top with a central satinwood panel, 9in (23cm) wide.
£420–500 / €600–720
$700–840 HYD

A mahogany miniature chest of drawers, with boxwood stringing and bone handles, c1785, 10in (25.5cm) wide.
£1,150–1,300 / €1,650–1,850
$1,950–2,200 WAA

A George III mahogany miniature bowfronted chest of drawers, with a crossbanded top, 15½in (39cm) wide.
£610–730 / €880–1,000
$1,000–1,200 L

A mahogany miniature chest of drawers, c1820, 11in (28cm) wide.
£590–650 / €850–940
$990–1,100 F&F

A mahogany miniature chest of drawers, with boxwood stringing and bone handles, on bracket feet, early 19thC, 15in (38cm) wide.
£820–980 / €1,200–1,400
$1,400–1,650 TEN

A pine miniature chest of drawers, with painted decoration, c1820, 14in (35.5cm) wide.
£1,100–1,250 / €1,600–1,800
$1,850–2,100 TIM

A mahogany miniature chest of drawers, c1825, 8½in (21.5cm) wide.
£300–330 / €430–480
$500–550 F&F

A rosewood and parquetry-inlaid miniature chest of drawers, c1830, 17in (43cm) wide.
£2,500–2,750 / €3,600–4,000
$4,200–4,600 TIM

A pine miniature chest of drawers, with painted decoration, c1830, 11in (28cm) wide.
£1,000–1,150 / €1,450–1,650
$1,700–1,900 TIM

A mahogany miniature chest of drawers, with bone handles, minor damage, 19thC, 8¾in (22cm) wide.
£330–400 / €470–570
$550–670 L&E

A mahogany miniature chest of drawers, 19thC, 19¾in (50cm) wide.
£260–310 / €370–440
$440–520 B(Kn)

A mahogany miniature chest of drawers, c1860, 17in (43cm) wide.
£800–880 / €1,150–1,300
$1,300–1,450 GGD

A Victorian rosewood-veneered miniature Wellington chest, the six drawers with side locking pilaster, minor damage, 15¾in (40cm) high.
£230–270 / €330–390
$380–450 ⚒ WW

A pine miniature dresser base, c1880, 19in (48.5cm) wide.
£390–430 / €560–620
$650–720 ⊞ SAW

A mahogany miniature tripod table, c1825, 9½in (24cm) diam.
£540–600 / €780–860
$910–1,000 ⊞ F&F

A walnut miniature chiffonier, with mirrored back and doors, c1860, 24in (61cm) wide.
£2,400–2,650 / €3,450–3,800
$4,000–4,450 ⊞ TIM

A Victorian mahogany miniature sideboard, with one long drawer over Gothic arched cupboard doors, the interior with three sliding shelves, 12¾in (32.5cm) wide.
£530–640 / €760–920
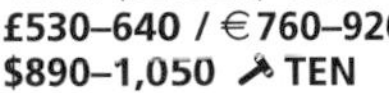
$890–1,050 ⚒ TEN

► A mahogany miniature dining table, with a loose leaf extension, on turned legs, c1840, 13in (33cm) wide.
£3,800–4,200
€5,500–6,100
$6,400–7,100
⊞ TIM

◄ A walnut miniature three-tiered whatnot, stamped 'Evan Llewellyn, London', c1860, 8in (20.5cm) wide.
£1,300–1,450 / €1,900–2,100
$2,200–2,400 ⊞ TIM

A velvet-covered wooden miniature couch, the base forming a box, c1860, 8¼in (21cm) long.
£70–80 / €100–115
$115–130 ⊞ F&F

An oak miniature side table, with a single drawer, c1820, 12½in (32cm) wide.
£790–880 / €1,100–1,250
$1,300–1,450 ⊞ TIM

◄ A walnut-veneered miniature centre table, with a turned column and triform base, c1840, 10½in (26.5cm) wide.
£1,400–1,600 / €2,000–2,300
$2,350–2,700 ⊞ RGa

A mahogany and marquetry-inlaid miniature tilt-top loo table, c1860, 8in (20.5cm) diam.
£1,800–2,000 / €2,600–2,900
$3,000–3,350 ⊞ TIM

Cheval Mirrors

A mahogany cheval mirror, the spiral-turned uprights with urn finials, probably Irish, early 19thC, 67¼in (171cm) high.
£3,600–4,300
€5,200–6,200
$6,000–7,200 B

A Regency mahogany cheval mirror, on a bobbin-turned part-ebonized frame, 25¼in (64cm) wide.
£1,250–1,500
€1,800–2,150
$2,100–2,500 SWO

A mahogany cheval mirror, c1835, 60in (152.5cm) high.
£760–850 / €1,050–1,200
$1,250–1,400 GEO

A Victorian mahogany cheval mirror, 29½in (75cm) wide.
£940–1,100
€1,350–1,600
$1,600–1,900 CGC

A mahogany cheval mirror, c1860, 62in (157.5cm) high.
£1,050–1,150
€1,500–1,650
$1,750–1,950 GEO

A mahogany cheval mirror, c1900, 36½in (92.5cm) wide.
£1,350–1,600
€1,950–2,300
$2,250–2,700 NOA

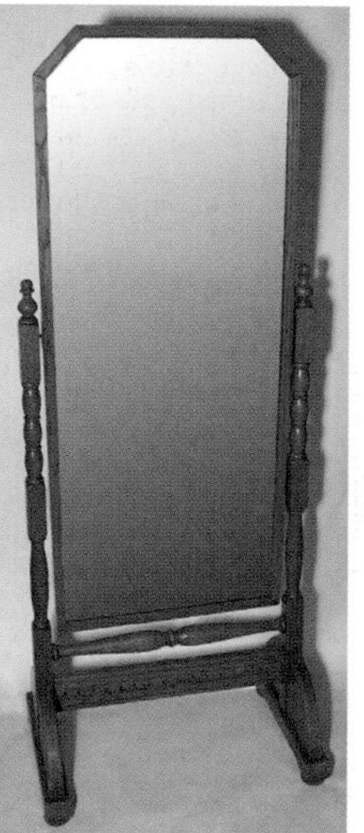

A blonde oak cheval mirror, c1910, 67in (170cm) high.
£430–480 / €620–690
$720–800 GEO

◄ **A mahogany cheval mirror,** c1870, 65in (165cm) high.
£1,150–1,300 / €1,650–1,850
$2,000–2,200 GEO

Dressing Table Mirrors

◄ **A walnut dressing table mirror,** c1750, 29in (73.5cm) high.
£800–900 / €1,150–1,300
$1,350–1,500 GEO

► **An early George III mahogany dressing table mirror,** 16in (40.5cm) wide.
£165–200 / €240–280
$280–330 L

A George III mahogany dressing table mirror, 17in (43cm) wide.
£300–360 / €430–510
$500–600 L

Miller's Compares

I. A walnut dressing table mirror, with oak-lined drawers, c1710, 23in (58.5cm) high.
£2,550–2,850
€3,700–4,100
$4,300–4,800 ⊞ FHA

II. A mahogany dressing table mirror, with oak-lined drawers, c1785, 23in (58.5cm) high.
£700–850
€1,100–1,250
$1,250–1,400 ⊞ FHA

Item I is a fine example of a Queen Anne dressing table mirror, the mirror plate and attractive patination both being original. Item II, although also in good condition, is a George III example in the Queen Anne style. It is made of mahogany rather than the more desirable walnut and the mirror plate is a late 19th-century replacement.

Items in the Furniture section have been arranged in date order within each sub-section.

A mahogany dressing table mirror, stamped 'Rumney & Love', Liverpool, 19thC, 41¼in (105cm) high.
£540–650 / €780–930
$920–1,100 ⚒ HOK

Condition

The condition is absolutely vital when assessing the value of an antique. Damaged pieces on the whole appreciate much less than perfect examples. However a rare desirable piece may command a high price even when damaged.

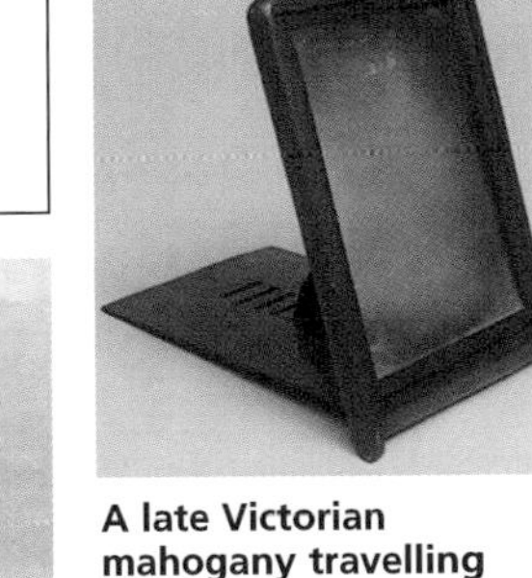

A late Victorian mahogany travelling mirror, with an easel support, 19in (48.5cm) high.
£90–110 / €140–160
$150–180 ⚒ NSal

An Edwardian tortoiseshell-veneered dressing table mirror, decorated with ivory stringing, 13in (33cm) wide.
£700–840 / €1,000–1,200
$1,200–1,400 ⚒ NSal

A George III mahogany dressing table mirror, with boxwood stringing, the bowfronted base with one long and two short drawers, 30½in (77.5cm) wide.
£270–320 / €390–460
$450–540 ⚒ PFK

A Victorian Queen Anne-style walnut dressing table mirror, the bureau-style base with a serpentine drawer, 13in (33cm) wide.
£500–600 / €720–860
$840–1,000 ⚒ G(L)

A mahogany dressing table mirror, decorated with crossbanding and cut brass inlay, the base with two drawers, c1820, 21in (53.5cm) wide.
£780–870 / €1,100–1,250
$1,300–1,450 ⊞ JC

A flame mahogany dressing table mirror, c1850, 26in (66cm) high.
£400–450 / €580–650
$670–760 ⊞ AMG

Miller's Compares

I. A George III mahogany-veneered and inlaid dressing table mirror, the tulipwood-banded double concave base with two drawers, one foot replaced, 18in (45.5cm) wide.
£640–770
€920–1,100
$1,100–1,300 ⚒ WW

II. A George III mahogany-veneered dressing table mirror, with boxwood stringing and brass urn finials, the serpentine base with tulipwood banding and three drawers, some losses, 17in (43cm) wide.
£380–460 / €550–660
$640–770 ⚒ WW

Item I has an unusual double concave-shaped base whereas the serpentine shape of Item II or a flat front is more common in these pieces. The marquetry shell and ivory mounts on Item I are also desirable features and its lighter colour is preferable to the much darker colour of Item II. The drawers of Item I are also attractively figured.

Wall Mirrors

A George I cross-grained walnut wall mirror, 26½in (67.5cm) wide.
£1,300–1,550
€1,850–2,200
$2,200–2,600 HOLL

A walnut wall mirror, bevelled plate later, early 18thC, 36½in (92.5cm) high.
£410–490 / €590–700
$690–820 PFK

A George II giltwood wall mirror, in the style of William Kent, the egg-and-dart inner frame surmounted by a stylized scallop shell, surrounded by bullrushes and acanthus leaves, 33in (84cm) wide.
£9,150–11,000
€13,200–15,800
$15,400–18,500 HYD

A George II walnut fret frame wall mirror, the crest pierced with a shell, the inner moulding gilded, with a bevelled plate, some repairs, 25¼in (64cm) wide.
£770–920 / €1,100–1,300
$1,300–1,550 DN

A mahogany and parcel-gilt wall mirror, restored, c1740, 52in (132cm) high.
£8,600–9,600
€12,400–13,800
$14,500–16,100 JeA

A carved giltwood wall mirror, Continental, c1750, 27in (68.5cm) high.
£3,400–3,800
€4,900–5,500
$5,700–6,400 GGD

A carved wood and gilt wall mirror, surmounted by a *ho-o* bird and foliate decoration, c1765, 26in (66cm) wide.
£8,800–9,800
€12,700–14,100
$14,800–16,450 RGC

A Sheraton-style mahogany pier mirror, with an inlaid frieze and side columns, c1785, 15in (38cm) wide.
£1,000–1,200
€1,600–1,800
$1,800–2,000 WAA

An Adam-style giltwood wall mirror, with carved rosette and reel decoration, c1790, 20in (51cm) wide.
£1,300–1,550 / €1,850–2,200
$2,200–2,600 B(Kn)

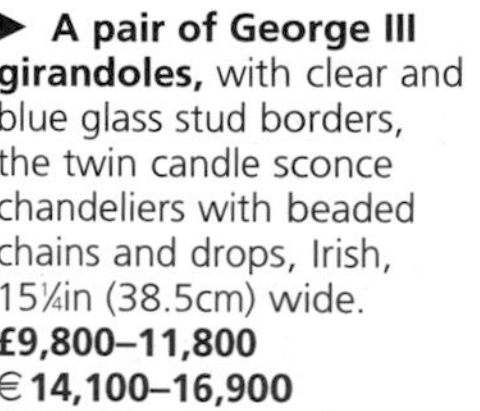

► **A pair of George III girandoles,** with clear and blue glass stud borders, the twin candle sconce chandeliers with beaded chains and drops, Irish, 15¼in (38.5cm) wide.
£9,800–11,800
€14,100–16,900
$16,500–19,800 JAd

A George III giltwood wall mirror, surmounted by a shell and C-scrolls, 38½in (98cm) high.
£1,900–2,300
€2,750–3,300
$3,200–3,850 B(B)

A carved giltwood and gesso wall mirror, the moulded frame applied with flowering foliate vines surmounted by a scrolling urn, c1800, 19¾in (50cm) wide.
£1,000–1,200
€1,450–1,700
$1,700–2,000 CGC

A giltwood gesso and ebonized overmantel mirror, the leaf and baton frame with lion-head masks, the scrolling foliate frieze with a central shell, early 19thC, 51½in (131cm) wide.
£1,000–1,200 / €1,450–1,700
$1,700–2,000 ⚒ WW

A Regency gilt wall mirror, the cornice with applied gilt balls over a griffin and foliate scroll frieze, the central mirror flanked by two further mirrors, 53¼in (135.5cm) wide.
£700–840 / €1,000–1,200
$1,200–1,400 ⚒ CHTR

A gilt convex wall mirror, with candle sconces, c1810, 18in (45.5cm) wide.
£2,700–3,000
€3,900–4,300
$4,500–5,000 ⊞ GDB

A Regency giltwood convex wall mirror, 21¼in (54cm) diam.
£640–770 / €920–1,100
$1,100–1,300 ⚒ SWO

LOCATE THE SOURCE

The source of each illustration in Miller's can be found by checking the code letters below each caption with the Key to Illustrations, pages 794–800.

◄ **A Regency giltwood and gesso convex girandole,** the crest with a foliate scroll motif flanked by mythical birds, the plate with a ropetwist and leaf border, the foliate-carved base with two candle arms with lustre drops, 27½in (70cm) wide.
£3,000–3,600
€4,300–5,150
$5,000–6,000 ⚒ DN

A Regency gilt convex wall mirror, with a ball-decorated frame and ebonized slip, plate 17½in (44.5cm) diam.
£850–1,000
€1,200–1,400
$1,450–1,700 HOLL

A mahogany pier mirror, with inlaid panels and fluted side columns, c1840, 22in (56cm) wide.
£500–550 / €720–790
$840–920 WAA

A Victorian giltwood and gesso convex girandole, with a carved seahorse surmount, flanked by two sconces, converted to electricity, 22in (56cm) wide.
£980–1,200
€1,450–1,700
$1,700–2,000 JAd

A gilt convex wall mirror, c1820, 26in (66cm) diam.
£500–550 / €720–790
$840–920 GGD

A carved giltwood wall mirror, Irish, c1850, 60in (152.5cm) wide.
£2,400–2,650
€3,500–3,850
$4,000–4,400 HON

A Biedermeier satin birch pier mirror, with a later plate, c1840, 38½in (98cm) wide.
£540–650 / €780–930
$920–1,100 S(O)

► **An etched glass wall mirror,** Italian, 19thC, 29½in (75cm) wide.
£960–1,150 / €1,400–1,650
$1,600–1,950 S(O)

A mahogany and chequer-strung overmantel mirror, the inverted breakfront cornice above a marquetry panel, the bevelled plate with faceted pilasters, early 19thC, 17¾in (45cm) wide.
£610–730 / €880–1,050
$1,000–1,200 DN

A Victorian giltwood overmantel mirror, the scrolling foliate crest with central anthemion and garlands, 66¼in (168.5cm) wide.
£1,750–2,100
€2,500–3,000
$2,950–3,500 EH

A giltwood and composition pier glass or overmantel mirror, the anthemia-decorated frieze flanked by cinquefoils, Buchan & Sons trade label, c1825, 74in (188cm) wide.
£4,800–5,700
€6,900–8,200
$8,000–9,500 S

Henry Buchan was born in 1794 and in 1814 at the age of 20 he established a decorating business at 9 Keppel Row, Portsmouth. In 1823 he moved to 46 High Street, Southampton, where he sold frames and, according to his advertisement, supplied artists with 'every material for drawing and painting', while he continued his successful business as a house decorator for Hampshire and the surrounding counties. In 1827 he expanded the partnership to 159 High Street and is recorded there as a carver and gilder. From 1836 to 1839, the partnership of Buchan & Slodden are recorded trading from the same premises. Towards the end of his life Henry Buchan retired in favour of his only son Henry Joseph Buchan. After the death of his father in 1865, H. J. Buchan continued to trade from the same premises and is recorded in *Cox's Southampton Directory* of 1880.

Antique mirrors

- 18th-century glass is usually thin and the bevelling soft and shallow
- 19th-century glass is thicker, the bevelling is cut at an acute angle and the cutting is more regular
- original glass is naturally more desirable: if it is cloudy it may be possible to have it resilvered, but replacing the glass should generally be avoided. Some mirrored glass is sprayed to give it the appearance of age
- composition frames are vulnerable to damage but are less expensive than giltwood or silvered carved wood frames

A mahogany and satinwood-inlaid overmantel mirror, the crossbanded and over-hung friezes flanked by half-column supports, c1890, 56½in (143.5cm) wide.
£300–360 / €440–520
$500–600 WL

A giltwood and gesso overmantel mirror, the frieze decorated with a rural scene, the three bevelled plates flanked by Corinthian columns, 19thC, 55in (139.5cm) wide.
£1,000–1,200 / €1,450–1,700
$1,700–2,000 AH

A gilt gesso and ebonized overmantel mirror, the moulded cornice with ball decoration, the scrolled acanthus frieze flanked by caryatid figures, above a triple bevelled-edged plate, 19thC, 58¾in (149cm) wide.
£770–920 / €1,100–1,300
$1,300–1,550 TRM

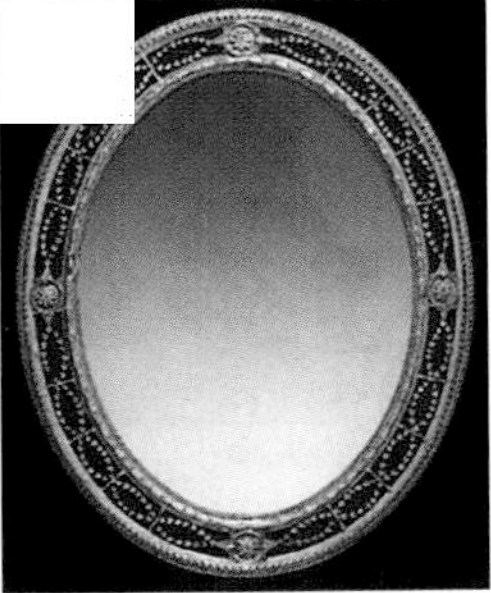

An Adam-style gilt composition wall mirror, regilt, 19thC, 40¼in (102cm) wide.
£530–630 / €760–910
$890–1,050 B(Kn)

A giltwood wall mirror, 19thC, 22in (56cm) diam.
£290–350 / €420–500
$490–590 NSal

◄ A Renaissance revival burr-wood pier mirror, with gilt-incised and ebony decoration, American, 1850–75, 37in (94cm) wide.
£750–900 / €1,100–1,300
$1,250–1,500 NOA

A giltwood pier mirror, with leaf capitals to the cluster columns, fabric panel later, 19thC, 23in (58.5cm) wide.
£175–210 / €250–300
$300–350 WW

A Victorian giltwood mirror, with four bracket shelves, c1890, 23¾in (60.5cm) wide.
£590–710 / €850–1,000
$1,000–1,200 B(Kn)

A Louis XV-style painted wall mirror, French, late 19thC, 40½in (103cm) wide.
£840–1,000
€1,200–1,440
$1,450–1,700 S(O)

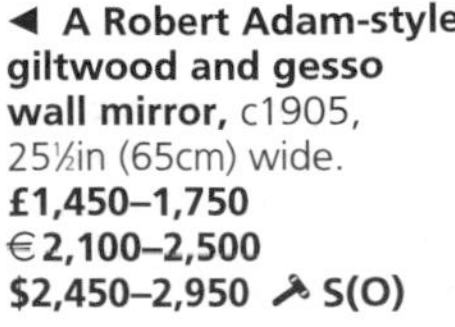

◄ A Robert Adam-style giltwood and gesso wall mirror, c1905, 25½in (65cm) wide.
£1,450–1,750
€2,100–2,500
$2,450–2,950 S(O)

Ottomans

A Biedermeier-style walnut ottoman, 19thC, 31in (78.5cm) wide.
£450–540 / €650–780
$760–910 SWO

A Victorian ottoman, on bun feet with casters, 27½in (70cm) wide.
£400–480 / €580–690
$680–810 B(B)

A Victorian ottoman, with rosewood mouldings, on ceramic casters, 21½in (54.5cm) wide.
£175–210 / €250–300
$300–350 WW

Screens

A painted vellum three-fold screen, decorated with musical trophies, swags and ribbon-ties, some damage, 19thC, 49¼in (125cm) wide.
£330–400 / €490–580
$560–670 DN

A Louis XV-style painted gilt composition three-fold screen, with 13 panels, regilded, late 19thC, 81in (205.5cm) wide.
£1,100–1,300
€1,600–1,900
$1,850–2,200 B(Kn)

An Adam-style satinwood three-fold screen, each section with a glazed panel over a fabric panel, c1900, 49½in (125.5cm) wide.
£480–580 / €690–830
$810–970 NOA

A mahogany three-fold screen, each section with a glazed top and carved floral swags above floral-embroidered panels, with beaded and carved surrounds, ribbon surmount damaged, early 20thC, 67¼in (171cm) wide.
£290–350 / €420–500
$490–590 PFK

Fire Screens

A pair of George III painted pole screens, with vase-turned uprights, 59in (150cm) high.
£1,300–1,550 / €1,900–2,250
$2,200–2,600 TEN

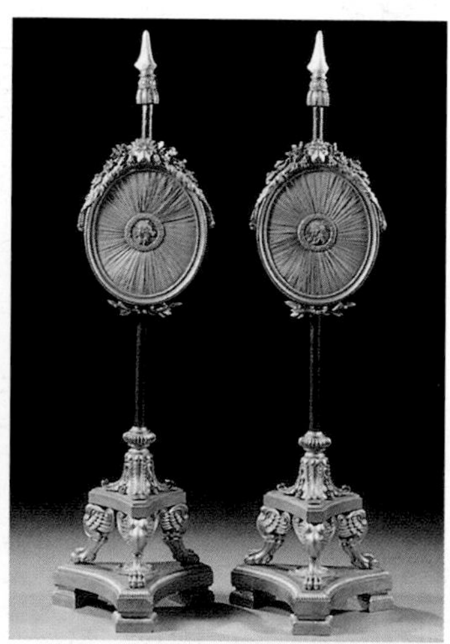

A pair of Regency giltwood and gilt-brass-mounted pole screens, the pleated silk panels replaced, regilded, 66in (167.5cm) high.
£7,800–9,300 / €11,200–13,400
$13,100–15,600 S

A rosewood pole screen, the embroidered panel with foliate moulding, on a baluster-turned column and platform base, early 19thC, 54½in (138.5cm) high.
£150–180 / €220–260
$250–300 L&E

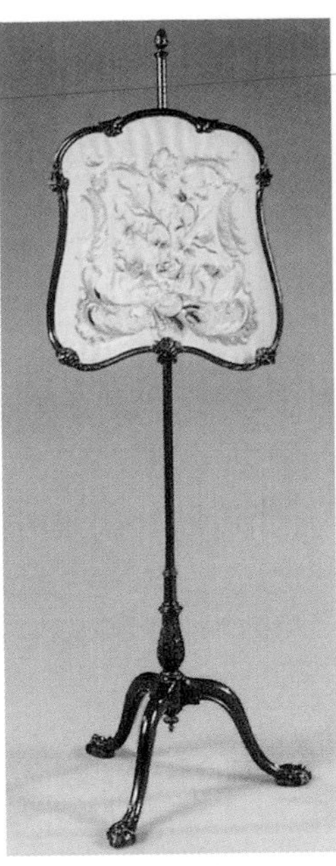

A mahogany pole screen, with silk needlework panel, the pole with a leaf-carved baluster base on a cabriole tripod with claw feet, 19thC, 54¼in (138cm) high.
£450–540 / €650–780
$760–910 TEN

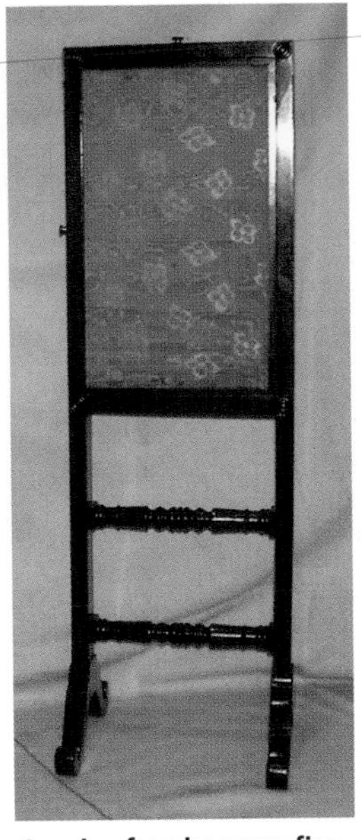

A pair of mahogany fire screens, with silk panels, c1830, 37in (94cm) high.
£1,750–1,950
€2,500–2,800
$2,950–3,300 FHA

A pair of mahogany pole screens, the panels framing two watercolours, c1850, 47in (119.5cm) high.
£1,350–1,500
€1,950–2,150
$2,250–2,500 GEO

A rosewood fire screen, the acanthus-carved pediment above a needlework panel, on carved outswept legs with acanthus-leaf scrolled decoration joined by a turned stretcher, c1850, 24in (61cm) wide.
£410–490 / €590–700
$690–820 B(W)

► **A Louis Philippe mahogany fire screen,** the tapestry panel with a foliate surmount, on splayed legs with acanthus carving and paw feet, French, c1850, 42½in (108cm) high.
£620–740 / €890–1,050
$1,000–1,200 NOA

◄ **A Victorian walnut fire screen,** with a tapestry panel, the frame with spiral-turned supports, on bun feet, 38¼in (97cm) wide.
£880–1,050
€1,250–1,500
$1,500–1,800 B(B)

A gilt-bronze fire screen, French, c1890, 21¾in (55.5cm) wide.
£840–1,000
€1,200–1,400
$1,450–1,700 S(O)

Settees & Sofas

◄ **An Empire sofa,** with gilt-brass mounts, French, 1799–1815, 67in (170cm) wide.
£610–730
€880–1,050
$1,000–1,200
SWO

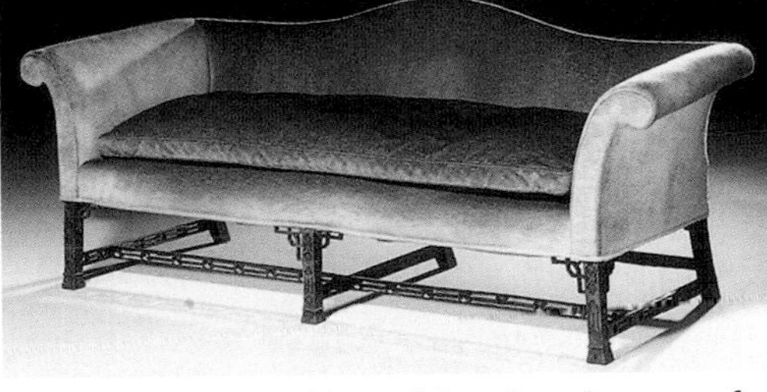

A George III Chinese Chippendale-style mahogany sofa, on fret-carved front legs joined by a pierced H-stretcher, 86½in (219.5cm) wide.
£5,900–7,100 / €8,500–10,200
$9,900–11,900 B

There was a fascination with the Far East throughout the 17th and 18th centuries in Europe. Reflecting this, Chippendale incorporated many Chinese features into his furniture, such as lacquer work, pagodas and fretwork. Chippendale was commissioned to design and make furniture for great English country houses such as Nostell Priory and Harewood House in Yorkshire, where whole rooms were decorated in the Chinese taste.

◄ **A George III mahogany settee,** with moulded shell-carved seat rails, on cabriole legs, 70½in (179cm) wide.
£730–880 / €1,050–1,250
$1,200–1,400 B(L)

A Regency carved mahogany settee, the low arm carved with a cornucopia and the high arm with an acanthus scroll, on outswept legs with lion-paw feet, 84¼in (214cm) wide.
£1,650–2,000 / €2,450–2,900
$2,800–3,350 Bri

A Regency simulated rosewood canapé, inlaid with cut-brass panels and rosette motifs, with a shaped back and scrolled terminals, on reeded turned tapering legs with brass toes and casters, 77in (195.5cm) wide.
£590–710 / €850–1,000
$1,000–1,200 AH

A mahogany ladder-back settee, formed as three chair backs, with scrolled arms, on grooved legs joined by stretchers, Irish, 18thC, 61in (155cm) wide.
£1,450–1,750 / €2,100–2,500
$2,450–2,950 HOK

► **A fruitwood canapé,** French, late 18thC, 32¼in (82cm) wide.
£960–1,150
€1,400–1,650
$1,600–1,900
S(O)

A mahogany sofa, German, c1830, 82¾in (210cm) wide.
£3,850–4,600 / €5,500–6,600
$6,500–7,700 S(O)

An ebonized and gilt sofa, with a fluted top rail and turned arm supports, on curved front legs with brass casters, early 19thC, 59½in (151cm) wide.
£820–980 / €1,200–1,400
$1,400–1,650 L&E

A Federal mahogany sofa, with a rolled crest and carved scrolled horns, on cornucopia wings with carved hairy paw feet, American, early 19thC, 80in (203cm) wide.
£1,050–1,250 / €1,500–1,800
$1,750–2,100 COBB

A William IV mahogany sofa, with carved scroll ends, 83in (211cm) wide.
£6,100–6,750 / €8,800–9,700
$10,200–11,300 GGD

A mahogany settee, with scroll ends, c1850, 81in (205.5cm) wide.
£2,900–3,250 / €4,200–4,700
$4,900–5,500 MTay

A mahogany-veneered settee, with a carved apron, on scroll feet, Continental, 19thC, 77in (195.5cm) wide.
£540–650 / €780–930
$920–1,100 WW

A rosewood-veneered settee, attributed to J. and J. W. Meeks, New York, the back with foliate-carved crest, carved serpentine seat rail, on cabriole legs, American, c1850, 66in (167.5cm) wide.
£2,600–3,100 / €3,700–4,400
$4,350–5,200 ⚒ NOA
J. and J. W. Meeks of New York (1797–1868) produced fine furniture in the rococo style during the 1850s and 1860s.

A Victorian mahogany sofa, the back with a C-scroll and berry-moulded mount, joined to splayed sides by C-scroll mounts, with similarly decorated uprights terminating in a serpentine apron, on hoof feet, 74in (188cm) wide.
£1,000–1,200 / €1,450–1,700
$1,700–2,000 ⚒ GAK

◄ A Victorian beech-framed sofa, on casters, 57in (145cm) wide.
£160–190
€230–270
$270–320
⚒ B(Kn)

A pair of 18thC-style mahogany-framed sofas, the frames carved with acanthus and pendant flowers, the moulded seat rail on six acanthus-carved cabriole legs, on claw-and-ball feet, 1920s, 77in (195.5cm) wide.
£4,250–5,100 / €6,100–7,300
$7,100–8,500 ⚒ M

A Victorian carved walnut double chairback settee, on cabriole legs, 70in (178cm) wide.
£1,300–1,550 / €1,850–2,200
$2,200–2,600 ⚒ SWO

► A Victorian Chesterfield sofa, with giltwood feet, 85¾in (218cm) wide.
£840–1,000
€1,200–1,450
$1,400–1,700
⚒ S(O)

A major development in the evolution of the sofa was the use of the coil spring, which was patented in 1828. These springs were supported by a layer of hessian webbing and covered with more webbing, which was in turn covered with horsehair stuffing and padding and finally the upholstery fabric. This resulted in bulkier and squatter designs that were far less elegant in appearance, but infinitely more comfortable.
The button-upholstered Chesterfield, the first fully-upholstered sofa, originated in mid-Victorian times, which was possibly the golden age of upholstery. Stuffing had been growing steadily thicker from the 1840s, and buttons were introduced to prevent the thread that held the stuffing in place from pulling the covering material.

A walnut settee, c1870, 78in (198cm) wide.
£2,500–2,800 / €3,600–4,000
$4,200–4,700 ⊞ MIay

◄ A mahogany-framed settee, with a boxwood-strung back rail, the back with an inlaid splat, on boxwood-strung tapering legs, early 20thC, 43in (109cm) wide.
£250–300
€360–430
$420–500 ⚒ PFK

Shelves

A George III painted and parcel-gilt satinwood hanging shelf, decorated with roses, 25½in (65cm) wide.
£2,500–3,000 / €3,600–4,300
$4,200–5,000 ⚒ S(NY)

A mahogany three-tier wall shelf, early 19thC, 29¾in (75.5cm) wide.
£660–790 / €950–1,100
$1,100–1,300 ⚒ L

A mahogany three-tier hanging shelf, c1820, 15in (38cm) wide.
£340–380 / €490–550
$570–640 ⊞ F&F

A pair of mahogany bowfronted hanging shelves, c1820, 30¼in (77cm) wide.
£1,200–1,400 / €1,700–2,000
$2,000–2,350 ⚒ S(O)

A carved and pierced rosewood hanging bookshelf, the four shelves on turned barley-twist supports, c1830, 24¼in (61.5cm) wide.
£1,300–1,450 / €1,850–2,100
$2,200–2,450 ⊞ JC

An ebonized wall shelf, the three graduated shelves with X-frame supports, the base with two drawers, restored, 19thC, 36in (91.5cm) wide.
£350–420 / €500–600
$590–710 ⚒ WW

Sideboards

A George III inlaid mahogany bowfronted sideboard, the two drawers flanked by a cellaret drawer and cupboard, 60¾in (154cm) wide.
£2,300–2,750 / €3,300–3,900
$3,850–4,600 ⚒ WilP

A George III mahogany bowfronted sideboard, with tambour door, restored, 52in (132cm) wide.
£820–980 / €1,200–1,400
$1,400–1,650 ⚒ B(Kn)

A George III mahogany break-front sideboard, the top inlaid with boxwood and ebony stringing with a crossbanded edge, the frieze drawer flanked by deep drawers, one lead-lined, 71½in (181.5cm) wide.
£3,000–3,600 / €4,300–5,200
$5,000–6,000 ⚒ L

A George III mahogany sideboard, altered, 54in (137cm) wide.
£1,900–2,250 / €2,700–3,250
$3,200–3,800 ⚒ S(O)

A mahogany serpentine sideboard, c1790, 68in (172.5cm) wide.
£8,700–9,700 / €12,600–14,000
$14,700–16,400 ⊞ Che

A George III mahogany and satinwood-banded sideboard, 74½in (189cm) wide.
£2,700–3,250 / €3,900–4,700
$4,500–5,400 ⚒ B(Kn)

A George III mahogany serpentine sideboard, crossbanded with stringing, the drawer flanked by a cellaret drawer and two further drawers, with oubliette compartment, 61in (155cm) wide.
£3,300–3,950 / €4,700–5,700 $5,500–6,600 AH

A George III mahogany, kingwood-banded and line-inlaid bowfronted sideboard, the frieze drawer flanked by two deep drawers, restored, 54in (137cm) wide.
£3,400–4,100 / €4,900–5,900 $5,700–6,800 BR

A mahogany bowfronted sideboard, the top with kingwood crossbanding and boxwood stringing, above an oak-lined drawer flanked by a lead-lined cellaret drawer and a divided drawer with removable oak-lined tray, c1790, 38in (96.5cm) wide.
£5,100–5,700 / €7,300–8,200 $8,600–9,600 JC

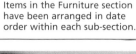

Items in the Furniture section have been arranged in date order within each sub-section.

An inlaid mahogany bowfronted breakfront sideboard, the top with a three-quarter gallery and ebony and boxwood chevron, the frieze drawer flanked by deep drawers, one with cellaret, on tapering legs with harewood inlay, c1800, 79½in (202cm) wide.
£2,650–3,150 / €3,800–4,500 $4,450–5,300 HOK

A George III mahogany bowfronted pedestal sideboard, the two central drawers flanked by rotating cupboards above a further cupboard and drawers, with lion-mask handles, 54¼in (138cm) wide.
£2,000–2,400 / €2,900–3,450 $3,350–4,000 WilP

A George III mahogany serpentine sideboard, with fitted interior including cellaret drawer, 60¼in (153cm) wide.
£1,900–2,300 / €2,750–3,300 $3,200–3,850 B(Kn)

A mahogany serpentine sideboard, c1790, 45¼in (115cm) wide.
£6,000–6,600 / €8,600–9,500 $10,100–11,100 RGa

A late George III mahogany serpentine sideboard, inlaid with boxwood lines, the top with turned brass rail, 73¼in (186cm) wide.
£4,750–5,700 / €6,800–8,200 $8,000–9,600 B

► **A brass-inlaid mahogany sideboard,** the top enclosing a two-tier folding plate rack with drawers, with two central dummy drawers, early 19thC, 50¼in (128cm) wide.
£1,300–1,550 / €1,850–2,200 $2,200–2,600 SWO

A George III mahogany-veneered demi-lune sideboard, with inlaid stringing, the central frieze drawer flanked by a pair of drawers and cupboard doors, 64in (162.5cm) wide.
£3,750–4,500 / €5,400–6,500 $6,300–7,500 WW

A George III mahogany sideboard, on acanthus leaf-carved legs, 72½in (184cm) wide.
£1,600–1,900 / €2,300–2,700 $2,700–3,200 B(Kn)

A mahogany bowfronted sideboard, the crossbanded top above a frieze drawer flanked by a deep cellaret drawer and a cupboard, c1790, 62in (157.5cm) wide.
£10,800–12,000 / €15,500–17,300 $18,100–20,100 YOX

A mahogany bowfronted sideboard, with a recessed drawer flanked by four drawers, early 19thC, 57¼in (145cm) wide.
£1,200–1,450 / €1,700–2,100 $2,000–2,400 DN

Styles of handles

Solid backplate (1600–50)	Split tail (1680–1715)	Solid backplate (1710–40)	Chippendale Rococo (1755–65)	Chinoiserie (1755–80)	American Rococo (1760–80)
Plain drop (c1760)	Ring (1770–1800)	American Federal (1790–1810)	Regency lion-mask (1790–1820)	Turned rounded pull (1810–30)	Plain knob (1840–1900)

A brass-mounted mahogany cylinder sideboard, the fitted interior over three drawers, Irish, Cork, early 19thC, 71in (180cm) wide.
£3,400–4,100 / €4,900–5,900
$5,700–6,900 ⚒ HOK

A Regency mahogany sideboard, the central short drawer above a concave drawer flanked by a cellaret drawer and a cupboard, 42in (106.5cm) wide.
£1,400–1,700 / €2,000–2,400
$2,350–2,800 ⚒ G(B)

A mahogany bowfronted sideboard, inlaid with boxwood stringing, the central drawer flanked by two cellaret cupboards, 19thC, 72in (183cm) wide.
£2,300–2,750 / €3,300–4,000
$3,850–4,600 ⚒ HOLL

► A mahogany and inlaid sideboard, the two drawers flanked by a cupboard and a deep drawer, Dutch, 19thC, 56¾in (144cm) wide.
£1,400–1,700 / €2,000–2,400
$2,350–2,800 ⚒ S(O)

A Regency mahogany inverted breakfront sideboard, the central drawer flanked by cupboards, on ring-turned tapering legs, 78in (198cm) wide.
£1,400–1,700 / €2,000–2,400
$2,350–2,850 ⚒ GAK

A Regency mahogany breakfront sideboard, with beaded and coin mouldings, the top with a brass rail above a drawer, a cellaret drawer and a cupboard, 75¼in (191cm) wide.
£1,500–1,800 / €1,150–2,600
$2,500–3,000 ⚒ B(Kn)

A George IV mahogany breakfront sideboard, the ebony-strung top with fitted sliding compartments, over three frieze drawers and deep side drawers, 85¾in (218cm) wide.
£4,000–4,800 / €5,800–6,900
$6,700–8,000 ⚒ JAd

A Regency crossbanded mahogany bowfronted sideboard, in the manner of Robert Gillow, the two doors simulating four drawers, some alterations, 54in (137cm) wide.
£1,250–1,500 / €1,800–2,150
$2,100–2,500 ⚒ Bea

A Regency mahogany sideboard, the three-quarter gallery above dummy frieze drawers and pedestal cupboards with panelled doors, 36in (91.5cm) high.
£1,400–1,700 / €2,000–2,400
$2,350–2,800 ⚒ HYD

A Regency mahogany-veneered bowfronted breakfront sideboard, with two drawers and a cupboard, 48in (122cm) wide.
£2,350–2,800 / €3,400–4,000
$4,000–4,700 ⚒ LAY

A mahogany sideboard, the three-quarter gallery above a central drawer and two cupboards, with leaf-carved scrolled brackets, c1850, 85in (216cm) wide.
£800–960 / €1,150–1,400
$1,350–1,600 DN

A figured walnut sideboard, attributed to William McCracken, the upper section with pierced crest above two shelves supported by scroll-carved brackets, the lower section with a marble top over three drawers and three panelled cupboard doors with ribbon-moulding, American, c1850, 54½in (138.5cm) wide.
£1,600–1,900 / €2,300–2,750
$2,750–3,300 NOA

A mahogany sideboard, c1865, 45in (114.5cm) wide.
£1,350–1,500 / €1,950–2,150
$2,250–2,500 MTay

Insurance values

Always insure your valuable antiques for the cost of replacing them with similar items, regardless of the original price paid. Both dealers and auctioneers can provide a valuation service for a fee.

A mahogany inverted breakfront sideboard, with three frieze drawers and a zinc-lined cellaret drawer, c1850, 78in (198cm) wide.
£1,250–1,500 / €1,800–2,150
$2,100–2,500 B(Kn)

A mahogany pedestal sideboard, the three frieze drawers above tapering pilaster doors, c1850, 84in (213.5cm) wide.
£370–440 / €530–630
$620–740 SWO

A Victorian rosewood breakfront sideboard, the central door flanked by panelled doors with gilded, painted and mother-of-pearl-inlaid floral decoration, with four gilt spiral-turned columns, 76¼in (193.5cm) wide.
£2,800–3,350 / €4,000–4,800
$4,700–5,600 JAd

A mahogany sideboard, c1870, 60in (152.5cm) wide.
£1,100–1,250 / €1,600–1,800
$1,850–2,100 MTay

A Hepplewhite-style mahogany and line-inlaid serpentine sideboard, with three drawers and four cupboard doors, c1850, 72¼in (183.5cm) wide.
£1,400–1,650 / €2,000–2,400
$2,400–2,900 COBB

A mahogany bowfronted pedestal sideboard, the top with scroll-carved crest above three frieze drawers and two cupboard doors, one enclosing two cellarets, c1850, 74in (188cm) wide.
£530–630 / €760–910
$890–1,000 PF

A Victorian mahogany sideboard, the scroll-carved back above three cushion-moulded frieze drawers and four panelled doors enclosing shelves, slides and a cellaret drawer, 59¾in (152cm) wide.
£1,200–1,450 / €1,750–2,100
$2,000–2,400 CGC

A Victorian mahogany pedestal sideboard, the panelled back above three drawers and two cupboard doors with carved decoration, 73¾in (187cm) wide.
£680–810 / €980–1,150
$1,150–1,350 SWO

◄ **A Victorian oak sideboard,** the mirrored back over four panelled doors enclosing cupboards and fitted drawers, 72in (183cm) wide.
£350–420 / €500–600
$590–710 TRM

A mahogany sideboard, with four doors, c1870, 78in (198cm) wide.
£2,000–2,250 / €2,900–3,200
$3,350–3,800 ⊞ MTay

A pollarded oak mirrored-back sideboard, the inverted breakfront above one drawer and two panelled cupboard doors, c1890, 77½in (197cm) wide.
£1,150–1,400 / €1,700–2,000
$1,950–2,350 ⚒ WL

A mahogany bowfronted sideboard, with boxwood and ebonized stringing, the central drawer flanked by cupboards, late 19thC, 48in (122cm) wide.
£700–840 / €1,000–1,200
$1,200–1,400 ⚒ GAK

A flame mahogany-veneered breakfront sideboard, the back with a carved shell motif, over two short drawers flanked by panelled cupboard doors, one enclosing a cellaret drawer, early 20thC, 71½in (182cm) wide.
£520–620 / €750–890
$870–1,000 ⚒ FHF

◄ **A crossbanded mahogany bowfronted sideboard,** by Redman & Hales, the central drawer flanked by cupboards, 1920s, 58in (147cm) wide.
£400–480 / €570–690
$670–800 ⚒ SWO

A Victorian mahogany pedestal sideboard, decorated with Chippendale and Adam-style motifs, the three frieze drawers flanked by two arched panelled cupboard doors enclosing shelves, on claw-and-ball feet, 83½in (212cm) wide.
£1,200–1,450 / €1,750–2,100
$2,000–2,400 ⚒ B(Kn)

A George III-style mahogany bowfronted sideboard, the central drawer above an arched recess flanked by cupboard doors, early 20thC, 48¼in (122.5cm) wide.
£840–1,000 / €1,200–1,400
$1,400–1,650 ⚒ BR

A Georgian-style mahogany sideboard, c1930, 72in (183cm) wide.
£1,300–1,450 / €1,850–2,100
$2,200–2,450 ⊞ MTay

Folio Stands

A mahogany folio stand, with adjustable reading slope and two candle slides, losses, c1800, 18¾in (47.5cm) wide.
£3,000–3,600
€4,300–5,200
$5,000–6,000 ⚒ S(O)

A Regency rosewood and brass-strung folio stand, with a frieze drawer, eight folio divisions and a long drawer, on lion-paw front feet, 30in (76cm) wide.
£4,450–5,300
€6,400–7,600
$7,500–8,900 ⚒ HYD

A Victorian walnut folio stand, the hinged adjustable sides on simulated bamboo mouldings and supports, 32¼in (82cm) wide.
£960–1,150
€1,400–1,650
$1,600–1,900 ⚒ Bea

A Victorian rosewood folio stand, with a moulded gallery, 17¾in (45cm) wide.
£430–510 / €620–730
$720–850 ⚒ S(O)

Hat & Stick Stands

◄ **A mahogany hat, coat and stick stand,** c1800, 60in (152.5cm) high.
£1,100–1,250
€1,600–1,800
$1,850–2,100 ⊞ GEO

Hat and stick stands come in a variety of forms, with Victorian examples as rectangular pieces of furniture to go against a wall, often incorporating a mirror. Other examples can be found made of bentwood and even as Bavarian full-size carved wood bears.

► **A mahogany hat and coat stand,** early 19thC, 69in (175.5cm) high.
£1,650–1,850
€2,400–2,650
$2,800–3,100 ⊞ GEO

A Regency mahogany and brass hat and coat stand, 68¼in (173cm) wide.
£2,900–3,500
€4,200–5,000
$4,900–5,900 ⚒ Bea

Kettle & Urn Stands

A George III mahogany kettle stand, with a slide, 26in (66cm) high.
£2,700–3,000
€3,900–4,300
$4,500–5,000 ⊞ GGD

A George III kettle stand, the top with a pierced lattice gallery on a carved baluster stem and cabriole legs, 24in (61cm) high.
£4,800–5,800
€6,900–8,300
$8,100–9,700 ⚒ S

A figured mahogany and boxwood-inlaid kettle stand, c1785, 27in (68.5cm) high.
£2,000–2,200
€2,900–3,200
$3,350–3,700 ⊞ WAA

A crossbanded and inlaid mahogany tea urn stand, c1790, 25in (63.5cm) high.
£2,600–2,900
€3,750–4,200
$4,350–4,900 ⊞ JeA

Auction or dealer?

All the pictures in our price guides originate from auction houses ⚒ and dealers ⊞. When buying at auction, prices can be lower than those of a dealer, but a buyer's premium and VAT will be added to the hammer price. Equally, when selling at auction, commission, tax and photography charges must be taken into account. Dealers will often restore pieces before putting them back on the market. Both dealers and auctioneers can provide professional advice, so it is worth researching both sources before buying or selling your antiques.

► **An Edwardian satinwood-veneered urn stand,** with polychrome decoration, 12¼in (31cm) wide.
£230–270
€330–390
$390–450
⚒ WW

Music Stands

A George III mahogany music stand, the double-sided adjustable top with hinged music rests, on a fluted and turned column, 51¼in (130cm) high.
£1,250–1,500
€1,800–2,150
$2,100–2,500 SWO

A rosewood duet stand, the music rests decorated with lyres, on a turned baluster stem, c1850, 17in (43cm) wide.
£960–1,150
€1,400–1,650
$1,600–1,900 G(L)

An oak and copper folding music/book stand, early 20thC, 9½in (24cm) high.
£30–35 / €45–50
$50–55 ⊞ ChC
This stand folds down to a bar less than 1in (2.5cm) thick and just over 7in (18cm) long when not in use. It could be used as either a book lectern or a music stand.

◄ **A walnut duet stand,** the lyre-decorated music rests with a candle holder above, the adjustable brass stem on carved supports, c1850, 61in (155cm) high.
£2,600–2,900
€3,700–4,200
$4,350–4,900 ⊞ YOX

Miscellaneous Stands

A pair of Victorian mahogany candle stands, 36in (91.5cm) high.
£1,100–1,250
€1,600–1,800
$1,850–2,100 ⊞ GEO

Items in the Miscellaneous Stands section have been arranged in alphabetical order.

◄ **A Victorian mahogany luggage stand,** with a slatted top, on vase-turned tapering legs, 30in (76cm) wide.
£330–390
€470–560
$550–650
WW

An Edwardian mahogany plant stand, on cabriole legs, 38in (96.5cm) high.
£340–380 / €490–550
$570–640 ⊞ WAA

A Regency mahogany and rosewood-banded adjustable reading stand, inlaid with stringing, the ratcheted top on a reeded frame and scroll legs, 21in (53.5cm) wide.
£1,900–2,300
€2,750–3,300
$3,200–3,850 WW

A mahogany shaving stand, the adjustable mirror above a shelf and two drawers, on a square tapering column with reeded supports, 19thC, 16in (40.5cm) wide.
£520–620 / €750–900
$870–1,000 TRM

A mahogany whip and boot stand, with turned supports, early 19thC, 37in (94cm) high.
£320–380 / €460–550
$530–640 Bea

Steps

A set of George IV mahogany library steps, with turned uprights, 32in (81cm) high.
£1,300–1,550 / €1,900–2,200
$2,200–2,600 B

A set of George III-style mahogany library steps, early 20thC, 24in (61cm) high.
£570–630 / €820–910
$960–1,100 GEO

A set of Regency-style mahogany folding library steps, c1900, 88in (223.5cm) high.
£1,600–1,900 / €2,300–2,700
$2,700–3,200 NOA

Stools

A Régence stained beech stool, carved with shells and acanthus leaves, restored, 1715–23, French, 15¾in (40cm) wide.
£1,300–1,550 / €1,900–2,200
$2,200–2,600 S(P)

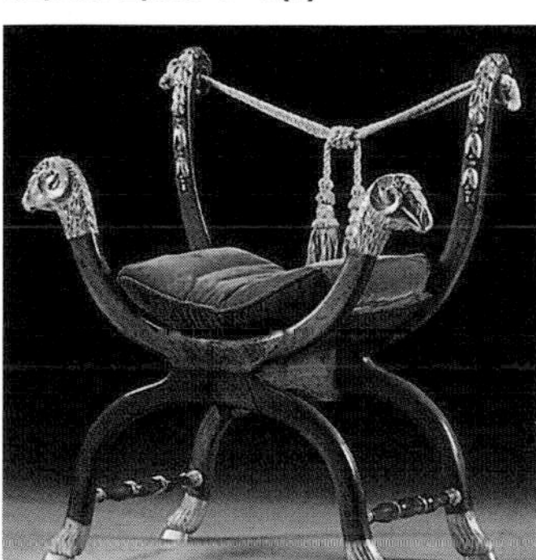

A carved walnut and parcel-gilt X-frame stool, Italian, early 19thC.
£4,000–4,800 / €5,800–6,900
$6,700–8,000 S(P)

► **A rosewood and leather-upholstered stool,** c1830, 18in (45.5cm) wide.
£1,650–1,850 / €2,350–2,650
$2,750–3,100 GGD

A walnut dressing table stool, c1760, 16in (40.5cm) wide.
£450–500 / €650–720
$750–840 F&F

A simulated rosewood foot-stool, worm damage, early 19thC, 15in (38cm) wide.
£110–130 / €160–190
$180–210 WW

A George III mahogany dressing table stool, with stuff-over seat and cabriole legs with carved knees, 18½in (47cm) wide.
£1,500–1,800 / €2,150–2,600
$2,500–3,000 HOLL

A rosewood footstool, c1830, 15in (38cm) wide.
£450–500 / €650–720
$750–840 GEO

For further information on
Stools see pages 177–178

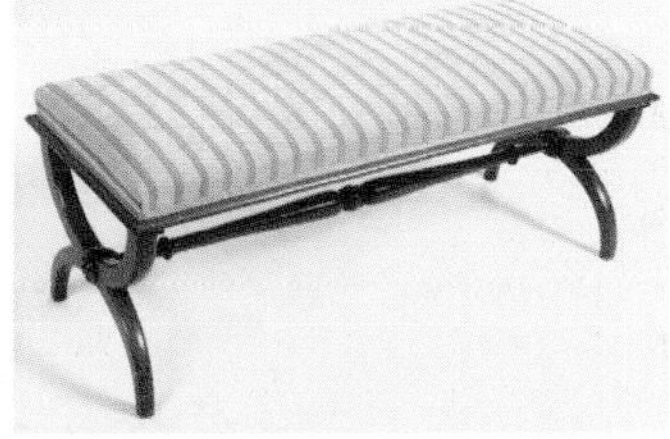

A mahogany stool, the stretcher with bull's-eye turnings at the ends, c1835, 42in (106.5cm) wide.
£1,400–1,550 / €2,000–2,200
$2,350–2,600 MTay

An early Victorian mahogany X-frame stool, with later tapestry seat, repaired, 21¾in (55.5cm) wide.
£210–250 / €300–360
$350–420 WW

A giltwood footstool, with original woolwork top, c1850, 11in (28cm) diam.
£145–160 / €210–230
$240–270 GGD

A pair of parcel-gilt walnut footstools, with woolwork tops, the frames punched with quatrefoils, on splayed scroll feet, c1850, 17in (43cm) square.
£1,700–2,000 / €2,450–2,900
$2,850–3,350 Bea

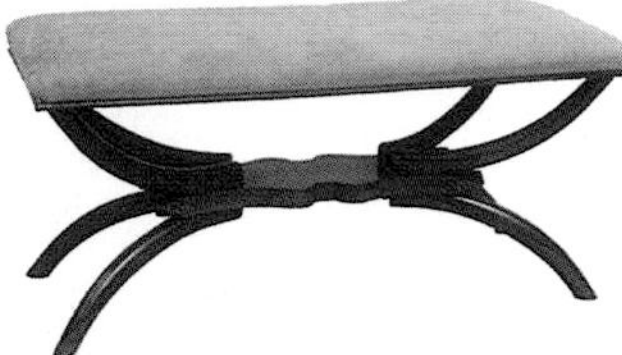

A rosewood stool, with a shaped central platform stretcher and down-swept legs, c1850, 35in (89cm) wide.
£640–770 / €920–1,100
$1,100–1,300 NSal

A rosewood stool, with cabriole legs, c1850, 21in (53.5cm) wide.
£1,350–1,500 / €1,950–2,150
$2,250–2,500 WAA

A walnut stool, stamped 'Gillow & Co', c1850, 17in (43cm) wide.
£450–540 / €650–780
$750–900 S(O)

A Victorian walnut fender stool, on cabriole legs, 48in (122cm) wide.
£150–180 / €220–260
$250–300 PFK

A giltwood footstool, c1860, 12in (30.5cm) wide.
£250–280 / €360–400
$420–470 WAA

A Victorian walnut stool, with a Berlin woolwork stuff-over seat, on a scroll-moulded X-frame with ring-turned stretcher, 23¼in (59cm) wide.
£270–320 / €390–460
$450–540 DD

A Victorian carved rosewood stool, the X-frame supports joined by a turned stretcher, 16½in (42cm) wide.
£410–490 / €590–700
$690–820 WW

A carved mahogany footstool, c1870, 14in (35.5cm) wide.
£380–420 / €550–600
$640–710 GEO

A mahogany footstool, the scroll feet with gilt-brass mounts, needlework later, 19thC, 15in (38cm) wide.
£120–140 / €170–200
$200–230 WW

A Louis XV-style carved giltwood and gesso stool, French, c1870, 33in (84cm) wide.
£3,000–3,600 / €4,300–5,200
$5,000–6,000 S(O)

A Victorian rosewood stool, the X-frame with spindle stretchers and scroll feet, 24in (61cm) high.
£610–730 / €880–1,000
$1,000–1,200 GAK

A George II-style mahogany stool, c1870, 22½in (57cm) wide.
£600–720 / €850–1,000
$1,000–1,200 S(O)

A walnut X-frame stool, with carved lion-head terminals and lion-paw feet, c1880, 27in (68.5cm) wide.
£1,100–1,250
€1,600–1,800
$1,850–2,100 WAA

A Queen Anne-style walnut stool, on cabriole legs, c1880, 21in (53.5cm) high.
£760–850 / €1,100–1,250
$1,250–1,400 GEO

A pair of mahogany footstools, c1880, 16in (40.5cm) wide.
£800–900 / €1,150–1,300
$1,350–1,500 WAA

► **A rosewood stool,** carved with foliage and C-scrolls, the frieze with knurled toes on bun feet, losses, late 19thC, 39¾in (101cm) wide.
£2,350–2,800
€3,400–4,000
$4,000–4,700 WW

Music Stools

A rosewood revolving music stool, c1830.
£880–980 / €1,250–1,400
$1,500–1,650 SAW

A mahogany music stool, on ring-turned front legs, c1837, 34¼in (87cm) high.
£175–210 / €250–300
$290–350 PFK

A rosewood and leather harpist's adjustable music stool, c1860.
£900–1,000
€1,300–1,450
$1,500–1,700 GGD

A Victorian carved rosewood adjustable piano stool, on a gadrooned baluster column with claw feet.
£200–240 / €290–340
$340–400 SWO

◄ **A Victorian rosewood adjustable music stool,** on cabriole legs.
£420–500 / €600–720
$700–840 B(Kn)

► **A Victorian mahogany piano stool,** 19in (48cm) high.
£140–170 / €200–240
$240–280 B(Kn)

A mahogany and inlaid adjustable piano stool, on cabriole legs, c1910, 14in (35.5cm) diam.
£390–430 / €560–620
$650–720 AMG

Bedroom Suites

A mahogany three-piece bedroom suite, comprising a bed, a chest of drawers and a dressing bureau, with gilt-bronze mounts, American, late 19thC, dressing bureau 85in (216cm) high.
£8,500–10,200 / €12,200–14,700
$14,300–17,100 ⚒ S(NY)

A walnut four-piece bedroom suite, comprising a half-tester bed, armoire, dressing bureau and marble mirror back washstand, bed shortened in height, American, 1875–1900, bed 92½in (235cm) high.
£2,600–3,100 / €3,700–4,450
$4,350–5,200 ⚒ NOA

A Renaissance-style burr-elm and walnut six-piece bedroom suite, comprising a cheval mirror, a chest of drawers, an armoire, a pair of bedside cupboards and a bed, with carved decoration and burr-wood panels, c1900, bed 74in (188cm) wide.
£2,850–3,400 / €4,100–4,900
$4,800–5,700 ⚒ NOA

Salon Suites

A walnut and button-upholstered salon suite, comprising a single chair, an armchair and a chaise longue, c1860.
£1,000–1,200 / €1,400–1,700
$1,700–2,000 ⚒ S(O)

A mahogany salon suite, comprising a chaise longue, a gentleman's armchair and a lady's armchair, c1870.
£700–840 / €1,000–1,200
$1,200–1,400 ⚒ WL

A Victorian carved walnut parlour suite, comprising a couch, an armchair and a nursing chair, couch 73¾in (187cm) wide.
£2,250–2,700 / €3,250–3,900
$3,800–4,500 ⚒ DD

A mahogany seven-piece drawing room suite, comprising a settee, two armchairs and four side chairs, with foliate-carved pierced top rails, late 19thC.
£760–910 / €1,100–1,300
$1,250–1,500 ⚒ PF

◀ An Edwardian mahogany seven-piece salon suite, with floral-carved pierced backs.
£190–230 / €270–330
$320–380 ⚒ AMB

▶ A giltwood and gesso three-piece salon suite, with Aubusson tapestry, French, early 20thC, settee 64½in (164cm) wide.
£1,800–2,150 / €2,600–3,100
$3,000–3,600 ⚒ S(O)

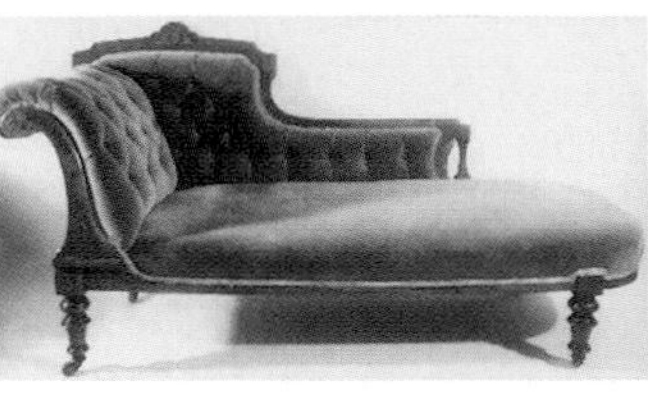

A Victorian walnut and inlaid part salon suite, comprising a chaise longue, an open armchair and three standard chairs.
£370–440 / €530–630
$620–740 ⚒ L&E

An Edwardian walnut bergère suite, comprising a settee and two armchairs, each with a boys and crown top rail.
£880–1,000 / €1,250–1,400
$1,500–1,700 ⚒ B&L

Boys and crown is a term for a type of carving found particularly on the cresting rails of chairs, depicting a crown supported by two flying, naked boys.

Architects' Tables

A George II mahogany architect's table, the ratchet top with candle-stands, the drawer with baize-lined slide and compartments, c1750, 35¾in (91cm) wide.
£2,150–2,600 / €3,100–3,700
$3,600–4,350 ⚒ S(O)

A Georgian mahogany architect's table, with an adjustable top, 35¾in (91cm) wide.
£2,450–2,900 / €3,500–4,200
$4,100–4,900 ⚒ TRM

A mahogany architect's table, with a rachet-action top and a fitted drawer, c1790, 35¾in (91cm) wide.
£1,800–2,150 / €2,600–3,100
$3,000–3,600 ⚒ S(O)

Items in the Furniture section have been arranged in date order within each sub-section.

Card Tables

A George I mahogany card table, with a triple-action top and a frieze drawer, 34in (86.5cm) wide.
£1,750–2,100 / €2,500–3,000
$2,900–3,500 ⚒ B(Kn)

A Louis XV-style mahogany card table, the serpentine-shaped hinged top enclosing a fitted interior of compartments above a frieze drawer and one side drawer, Dutch, 18thC, 28¾in (73cm) wide.
£1,450–1,750 / €2,100–2,500
$2,450–2,900 ⚒ S(Am)

LOCATE THE SOURCE
The source of each illustration in Miller's can be found by checking the code letters below each caption with the Key to Illustrations, pages 794–800.

A walnut card table, the fold-over top above a frieze drawer, some restoration, early 18thC, 34in (86.5cm) wide.
£1,000–1,200 / €1,450–1,700
$1,700–2,000 ⚒ TMA

A mahogany card table, the baize-lined playing surface with counter well and candle recesses, Irish, c1740, 38¼in (97cm) wide.
£4,650–5,600 / €6,700–8,000
$7,800–9,400 ⚒ S(NY)

A crocuswood card table, the quarter-veneered fold-over top enclosing a baize-lined playing surface with counter wells and candlestands, some restoration, c1735, 34in (86.5cm) wide.
£9,600–11,500 / €13,800–16,500
$16,100–19,300 ⚒ S
The streaked crocuswood veneer of this piece is indigenous to the West Indies and rare on a table of this type and date. It is characterized by its dark heartwood and prominent white sapwood.

A satinwood and rosewood-crossbanded card table, the baize-lined fold-over top with harewood stringing and banding, the front with inlaid panels of acorns and oak leaves, c1770, 36in (91.5cm) wide.
£5,600–6,300 / €8,100–9,100
$9,500–10,600 ⊞ YOX

◄ **A George III mahogany card table,** with inlaid oak leaf paterae, 36in (91.5cm) wide.
£3,400–3,800 / €4,900–5,400
$5,700–6,400 ⊞ GGD

A Hepplewhite-style mahogany card table, with a fold-over top, stamped 'H. Tibats', French, c1775, 34in (86.5cm) wide.
£10,000–11,000 / €14,400–15,800
$16,800–18,500 ⊞ RGa

The earliest tables designed specifically for playing cards date from the end of the 17th century. Gambling in general and card playing in particular became extremely popular in the 18th century and tables were produced in great numbers to cater for this craze. Most commonly made of mahogany or walnut, they had fold-over tops with a baize surface, and sometimes dished surfaces or slides for candles, and wells for counters at the corners. From c1720, the best quality tables incorporated a popular concertina action to ensure greater symmetry and stability. Designs became ever more ingenious and some examples incorporated separate leaves for backgammon, chess, writing and cards.

By 1770, the mania for gambling was causing such concern that George III and Queen Charlotte forbade it at the royal palaces, but this had little effect. It was not until Parliament intervened that the situation improved, with the result that card and games tables became less fashionable during the Regency period.

A walnut card table, with a baize-lined hinged top, German, c1785, 34in (86.5cm) wide.
£1,000–1,200 / €1,450–1,700
$1,700–2,000 ⚒ S(Am)

A rosewood card table, the hinged baize-lined top enclosing a mahogany-framed interior, with gilt-brass beading, c1810, 36in (91.5cm) wide.
£2,900–3,200 / €4,150–4,600
$4,850–5,400 ⊞ JC

A mahogany and brass-bound card table, with a triple-action top, north European, early 19thC, 43in (109cm) wide.
£1,300–1,550 / €1,850–2,200
$2,200–2,600 ⚒ S(O)

A Regency rosewood and brass-inlaid card table, with gilt-metal mounts and a swivel top, 36in (91.5cm) wide.
£1,400–1,700 / €2,000–2,400
$2,350–2,850 ⚒ AH

A Regency mahogany and calamander-crossbanded card table, 35in (89cm) wide.
£1,500–1,800 / €2,150–2,600
$2,500–3,000 ⚒ G(L)

A mahogany-veneered, satinwood- and rosewood-banded card table, veneer cracked, early 19thC, 35½in (90cm) wide.
£400–480 / €570–690
$670–800 ⚒ WW

A Regency rosewood and crossbanded card table, with inlaid brass stringing, 35in (89cm) wide.
£910–1,100 / €1,300–1,550
$1,550–1,850 ⚒ L

◄ A rosewood card table, attributed to George Oakley, early 19thC, 36in (91.5cm) wide.
£4,000–4,500 / €5,800–6,500
$6,700–7,500 ⊞ JeA

► A mahogany card table, c1820, 35¾in (91cm) wide.
£840–1,000 / €1,200–1,400
$1,400–1,650 ⚒ S(O)

A George IV mahogany card table, minor damage, 36in (91.5cm) wide.
£530–630 / €760–900
$890–1,000 ⚒ WW

A George IV mahogany card table, the baize-lined fold-over top above a flame-figured frieze, minor damage and restoration, 35¾in (91cm) wide.
£470–560 / €680–810
$790–940 ⚒ BR

Further reading

Miller's Buying Affordable Antiques Buyer's Guide, Miller's Publications, 2003

A rosewood card table, with a fold-over top, c1840, 36in (91.5cm) wide.
£1,700–1,900 / €2,450–2,700
$2,850–3,250 ⊞ WAA

A William IV mahogany card table, Irish, 36in (91.5cm) wide.
£950–1,050 / €1,350–1,500
$1,600–1,800 ⊞ HON

A rosewood card table, the baize-lined fold-over top above a carved frieze, c1850, 36in (91.5cm) wide.
£700–840 / €1,000–1,200
$1,200–1,400 ⚒ DN

► A rosewood card table, with a baize-lined fold-over top, c1850, 36in (91.5cm) wide.
£680–810 / €980–1,150
$1,150–1,350 ⚒ PF

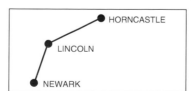

A mahogany and marquetry card table, the top with bird and floral decoration enclosing card-decorated candlestands, the frieze with a single short drawer and a square drawer to one side, Dutch, 19thC, 29½in (75cm) wide.
£2,600–3,100 / €3,700–4,450
$4,350–5,200 ⚒ AMB
This table is inlaid with 'playing cards', which is common with Dutch pieces to achieve a trompe l'oeil effect.

A pollarded oak card table, with a fold-over top, c1860, 36in (91.5cm) wide.
£2,100–2,350 / €3,000–3,400
$3,500–4,000 ⊞ GEO

A Victorian figured walnut loo table, 40½in (103cm) wide.
£1,400–1,650 / €2,000–2,400
$2,350–2,750 ⚒ B(Kn)

An Edwardian inlaid rosewood card table, the baize-lined fold-over top above a drawer, 20in (51cm) wide.
£340–410 / €490–590
$570–690 ⚒ PF

A Victorian walnut loo table, the quarter-veneered top with a gadrooned edge, 58¼in (148cm) diam.
£960–1,150 / €1,400–1,650
$1,600–1,900 ⚒ SWO

A Victorian walnut card table, the fold-over top with brass banding, c1870, 29in (73.5cm) high.
£2,100–2,350 / €3,000–3,400
$3,500–4,000 ⊞ GEO

An Edwardian satinwood and mahogany-crossbanded card table, with a baize-lined fold-over top, maker's mark 'C.V.S.', 21in (53.5cm) wide.
£490–590 / €710–850
$820–990 ⚒ TRM

A Victorian rosewood card table, 36¼in (92cm) wide.
£440–530 / €630–760
$740–890 ⚒ CHTR

A fruitwood card table, the glazed top inset with portrait miniatures, mounted with a plaque inscribed 'F. W. Papke', late 19thC, 28¾in (73cm) wide.
£330–390 / €470–560
$550–660 ⚒ B(Kn)

A pair of George III-style satinwood card tables, decorated with vignettes of lovers, vases of flowers and floral trellis, c1910, 33in (84cm) wide.
£5,300–5,900 / €7,600–8,500
$8,900–9,900 ⊞ RAN

Centre Tables

A rosewood-veneered and crossbanded centre table, the top with ormolu moulding, on a *faux* rosewood column and carved feet, c1815, 47¼in (120cm) diam.
£10,800–12,000 / €15,500–17,300
$18,100–20,100 ⊞ HA

A Regency rosewood and brass-inlaid centre table, on a square column and platform base, brass paw feet later, some restoration, 51¼in (130cm) diam.
£2,800–3,350 / €4,000–4,800
$4,700–5,600 ⚒ SWO

A figured mahogany-veneered centre table, on a turned and lobed pedestal, c1820, 52in (132cm) diam.
£5,600–6,200 / €8,100–9,000
$9,400–10,400 ⊞ RGa

A Regency rosewood centre table, the central column with carved lamb's tongue detail, on a triform base with roundel feet and casters, 51¼in (130cm) diam.
£420–500 / €600–720
$700–840 WilP

A William IV mahogany centre table, the snap-action top with a recessed crossbanded frieze, on a quatre-form base and lion-paw feet, 53in (134.5cm) wide.
£1,250–1,500 / €1,800–2,150
$2,100–2,500 Mit

A Regency brass-inlaid and mounted mahogany centre table, the satinwood and ebony-banded top inlaid with cut-brass star motifs, each end standard applied with flowerheads above a caduceus, on splayed scroll feet with brass casters, some losses and alterations, 49¼in (125cm) wide.
£29,000–34,000 / €42,000–50,000
$49,000–57,000 Bea

Given a cautious estimate because it is lacking its frieze drawer, this table attracted a great deal of interest from the trade. It is a very stylish piece with the meandering trellis band around the top and the caduceus applied to the sides. It is in the manner of George Oakley, who produced high quality Grecian-style furniture.

► **A burr-poplar and mahogany tilt-top centre table,** on a hexagonal column and trefoil plinth base, probably Baltic, c1830, 55in (140cm) wide.
£5,300–6,300 / €7,600–9,100
$8,900–10,600 S(Am)

A George IV mahogany centre table, the top inset with figured rosewood crossbanding, the base with acanthus capped and reeded details, with cast lotus casters, 48in (122cm) diam.
£2,100–2,500 / €3,000–3,600
$3,500–4,200 HOLL

A rosewood centre table, on a tripod scroll base, mid-19thC, 49¼in (125cm) diam.
£900–1,100 / €1,300–1,550 $1,500–1,800 ⚒ HOK

A rococo revival rosewood centre table, the inset marble top above a floral and foliate-carved frieze, on scrolled acanthus-carved legs, American, c1850, 43½in (103cm) wide.
£740–890 / €1,100–1,300 $1,250–1,500 ⚒ NOA

A Louis Philippe mahogany centre table, the marble top above a plain frieze, on a baluster-turned and fluted column, French, 19thC, 38in (96.5cm) wide.
£1,500–1,800 / €2,150–2,600 $2,500–3,000 ⚒ HYD

A Victorian walnut centre table, on a turned and carved central column, 54in (137cm) wide.
£1,850–2,100 / €2,650–3,000 $3,100–3,500 ⊞ MTay

► **A carved mahogany centre table,** on C-scrolled legs with caryatid flower and leaf-carved capitals, on acanthus leaf scrolled feet and casters, Dutch, c1890, 61¾in (157cm) wide.
£800–960 / €1,150–1,350 $1,350–1,600 ⚒ BR

Breakfast tables

- Early examples are small, as breakfast and supper were generally eaten in the bedroom or small parlour from the 16th to the 18th century
- 18th-century examples are usually of mahogany with hinged flaps, a frieze drawer and a storage shelf below for china, cutlery or condiments
- By the 1770s the undershelf is increasingly uncommon and the type begins to take on the form of a Pembroke table. Lighter varieties of mahogany, satinwood and other exotic timbers are used, embellished with marquetry or painted decoration
- In the late 18th and early 19th centuries it was very fashionable to have tables with a central column and splayed legs. These tables are generally large enough to seat about eight people, as eating breakfast was becoming a more sociable affair. They often have round, oval or rectangular tilting or snap tops, enabling them to be tipped into a vertical position and casters on their feet for added flexibility of use. Mahogany or rosewood are commonly used but some of the finest examples are made of calamander
- In the mid-19th century the shape of the top became more varied, and octagonal, quatrefoil and lobed examples were all commonly seen. Typical woods are mahogany, oak and highly figured timbers such as walnut, enhanced with marquetry, brass inlay or carved decoration

A rosewood tilt-top centre table, on carved legs, c1850, 56in (142cm) wide.
£2,900–3,200 / €4,150–4,600 $4,850–5,400 ⊞ MTay

A burr-walnut centre table, c1860, 29in (73.5cm) high.
£2,700–3,000 / €3,900–4,300 $4,500–5,000 ⊞ GEO

A walnut-veneered centre table, the top veneered, c1860, 47in (119.5cm) wide.
£1,550–1,750 / €2,200–2,500 $2,600–2,900 ⊞ JSt

A mahogany centre table, by Gillows, with a fretwork frieze and gadrooned rim, on tapering Gothic-style legs, Gillows label, c1890, 39in (99cm) wide.
£1,250–1,500 / €1,800–2,150 $2,100–2,500 ⚒ SWO

A carved walnut centre table, the top with a gadrooned frieze above a pillar-arcaded stretcher, carved with panels of classical mythological scenes, Italian, c1890, 54in (137cm) wide.
£880–1,050 / €1,250–1,500 $1,450–1,750 ⚒ HOLL

Console & Pier Tables

A Sheraton-period satinwood demi-lune console table, with inlaid fan decoration and kingwood crossbanding, late 18thC, 42in (106.5cm) wide.
£17,100–19,000 / €24,600–27,400
$28,800–32,000 ⊞ GGD

A mahogany console table, with a marble top, French, c1800, 37¾in (96cm) wide.
£2,400–2,900 / €3,450–4,150
$4,000–4,800 ⚒ S(O)

A pair of Louis Philippe marble console tables, French, 19thC, 30¾in (78cm) wide.
£3,100–3,750 / €4,500–5,400
$5,200–6,300 ⚒ S(Am)

A pair of Adam-style mahogany demi-lune console tables, the friezes with central carved tablets, late 19thC, 61in (155cm) wide.
£1,650–1,950 / €2,350–2,800
$2,750–3,300 ⚒ CDC

A mahogany and chequer-banded demi-lune console table, the top with a marquetry shell above two frieze drawers, Dutch, late 18thC, 31¼in (79.5cm) wide.
£530–630 / €760–900
$890–1,000 ⚒ DN

A rosewood and giltwood console table, c1825, 39in (99cm) wide.
£6,400–7,200 / €9,200–10,300
$10,800–12,100 ⊞ RGa

A giltwood and gesso console table, the top painted to simulate marble, the frieze with stiff-leaf and scrolling acanthus, 19thC, 78in (198cm) wide.
£1,600–1,900 / €2,300–2,750
$2,700–3,200 ⚒ DN

A polished steel console table, the marble top above a frieze drawer, French, c1860, 45in (114.5cm) wide.
£3,000–3,300 / €4,300–4,750
$5,000–5,500 ⊞ PICA

► **A satinwood and inlaid demi-lune console table,** c1905, 52½in (133.5cm) wide.
£3,100–3,700 / €4,450–5,300
$5,200–6,200 ⚒ S(O)

A mahogany demi-lune console table, with two drawers, c1790, 29in (73.5cm) wide.
£1,100–1,250 / €1,600–1,800
$1,850–2,100 ⊞ GEO

A mahogany pier table, with a marble top, American, c1835, 41in (104cm) wide.
£1,500–1,800 / €2,150–2,600
$2,500–3,000 ⚒ NOA

A Louis XVI-style giltwood demi-lune console table, the marble top above a pierced scrolling frieze, mid-19thC, 23in (58.5cm) wide.
£1,300–1,550 / €1,850–2,200
$2,150–2,600 ⚒ NOA

Dining Tables

◀ **A George II mahogany drop-leaf dining table,** altered, 104¾in (266cm) extended.
£5,000–6,000
€7,200–8,600
$8,400–10,100
⚒ S(O)

A George III plum pudding mahogany extending dining table, with two extra leaves, the recessed legs possibly adapted, 101½in (258cm) extended.
£940–1,100 / €1,350–1,600
$1,600–1,850 ⚒ DN

A George III figured mahogany extending dining table, with three extra leaves, 137¾in (350cm) extended.
£2,900–3,500 / €4,150–5,000
$4,850–5,900 ⚒ RTo

A George III mahogany drop-leaf dining table, possibly Irish, 94in (239cm) extended.
£2,600–3,100 / €3,700–4,450
$4,350–5,200 ⚒ HOLL

A George III mahogany extending dining table, with two extra leaves, 88in (223.5cm) wide.
£940–1,100 / €1,350–1,600
$1,600–1,850 ⚒ PF

A late Georgian figured mahogany metamorphic extending dining table, with a concertina action and four extra leaves, 117in (297cm) extended.
£5,200–6,200 / €7,500–8,900
$8,700–10,400 ⚒ M

A mahogany drop-leaf dining table, early 19thC, 117½in (298.5cm) extended.
£4,450–5,300 / €6,400–7,600
$7,400–8,900 ⚒ WW

◀ **A Regency mahogany extending dining table,** with two extra leaves, on tapering reeded legs, leaves damaged, 97¾in (248cm) extended.
£6,600–7,900
€9,500–11,450
$11,100–13,300
⚒ Bri

A Regency mahogany twin pedestal extending dining table, with two extra leaves, 121¼in (308cm) extended.
£2,750–3,300 / €4,000–4,750
$4,600–5,500 ⚒ S(O)

▶ **A Regency mahogany and ebony-inlaid triple pedestal dining table,** one different pedestal, 91¼in (232cm) wide.
£15,500–18,600 / €22,300–26,800
$26,000–31,000 ⚒ B

Extending tables

Value can be affected by the length to which the table can be extended, which can be as much as 192in (487.5cm), as well as the patination and figuring of the table tops and the originality of the loose leaves. Ensure that the table is firm and steady when fully extended and that the superstructure can withstand the weight when fully laid. Finally, check the height of the frieze under the table top – make sure you can sit at it and get your knees under it.

A Regency mahogany extending dining table, with a concertina action and three extra leaves, 99¾in (253cm) wide.
£2,900–3,500 / €4,150–5,000
$4,900–5,900 ⚒ Bea

► A George IV mahogany and kingwood-crossbanded extending dining table, in the manner of Gillows, with a concertina action and two extra leaves, 102½in (260cm) wide.
£3,200–3,800
€4,600–5,500
$5,400–6,400 ⚒ S(O)

A George IV mahogany drop-leaf dining table, 106¾in (271cm) wide.
£7,100–8,500 / €10,200–12,200
$11,900–14,300 ⚒ B

A mahogany extending dining table, with seven associated extra leaves, one mahogany and six oak, 19thC, 56¼in (143cm) wide.
£4,150–5,000 / €6,000–7,200
$7,000–8,400 ⚒ S(P)

A mahogany extending dining table, with two extra leaves, c1850, 108¼in (275cm) wide.
£2,100–2,500 / €3,000–3,600
$3,500–4,200 ⚒ B(Kn)

A mahogany extending dining table, with three extra leaves and swivel ends, 19thC, 109in (277cm) extended.
£2,450–2,900 / €3,500–4,150
$4,100–4,850 ⚒ WW

A mahogany extending dining table, with concertina action and two extra leaves, one leaf later, c1825, 95in (241cm) extended.
£5,000–6,000 / €7,200–8,600
$8,400–10,100 ⚒ S(O)

A George IV mahogany extending dining table, with telescopic action and two extra leaves, 74½in (189cm) extended.
£1,200–1,450 / €1,750–2,100
$2,000–2,400 ⚒ S(O)

A mahogany extending dining table, with two extra leaves, minor damage, c1850, 91in (231cm) wide.
£2,000–2,400 / €2,900–3,450
$3,350–4,000 ⚒ EH

◄ An oak extending dining table, with five extra leaves, c1860, 186¼in (473cm) extended.
£2,400–2,900 / €3,450–4,150
$4,000–4,800 ⚒ S(O)

A mahogany extending dining table, by Johnstone & Jeanes, with two extra sets of eight leaves, one set larger than the other, stamped, c1845, smaller leaves 59¼in (150.5cm) wide, medium leaves 72¼in (183.5cm) wide, larger leaves 83½in (211cm) wide.
£160,000–192,000
€230,000–276,000
$269,000–322,000 ⚒ G(B)

This dining table was discovered in an East Sussex farmhouse by one of the valuers from the auction house. It is a rare patent circular expanding example which, with the addition of two sets of extra leaves, offers the three diameter options of 60in (152.5cm), 72in (183cm) and 84in (213.5cm).

Such tables are always sought after. With numerous telephone bidders and much activity in the room the bidding rose steadily from £30,000 / €43,200 / $50,400 to its final figure, eventually selling to a leading member of the London trade.

◄ **A walnut extending dining table,** with four extra leaves, American, c1865, 93in (236cm) extended.
£680–810
€980–1,150
$1,150–1,350
NOA

A Victorian mahogany extending dining table, with telescopic action and three extra leaves, 105¼in (267.5cm) extended.
£1,500–1,800 / €2,150–2,600
$2,500–3,000 WW

A Victorian mahogany extending dining table, with six extra leaves contained in a grained-pine cabinet with a panelled door, 187½in (476cm) wide.
£7,500–9,000 / €10,800–13,000
$12,600–15,100 Bea

A Victorian oak extending dining table, with five extra leaves, 176¼in (447cm) wide.
£3,200–3,800 / €4,600–5,500
$5,400–6,400 B(Kn)

A Victorian mahogany extending dining table, with telescopic action and three extra leaves, 106¼in (270cm) wide.
£1,500–1,800 / €2,150–2,600
$2,500–3,000 Bri

A Victorian mahogany extending dining table, with two extra leaves and a winding handle, 81½in (207cm) wide.
£720–860 / €1,000–1,200
$1,200–1,450 B(Kn)

A Victorian mahogany extending dining table, with telescopic action and two extra leaves, 106in (269cm) extended.
£940–1,100 / €1,350–1,600
$1,550–1,850 WW

A Victorian mahogany extending dining table, with two extra leaves, 168in (426.5cm) extended.
£3,300–3,950 / €4,750–5,700
$5,500–6,600 MAR

Auction or dealer?

All the pictures in our price guides originate from auction houses and dealers. When buying at auction, prices can be lower than those of a dealer, but a buyer's premium and VAT will be added to the hammer price. Equally, when selling at auction, commission, tax and photography charges must be taken into account. Dealers will often restore pieces before putting them back on the market. Both dealers and auctioneers can provide professional advice, so it is worth researching both sources before buying or selling your antiques.

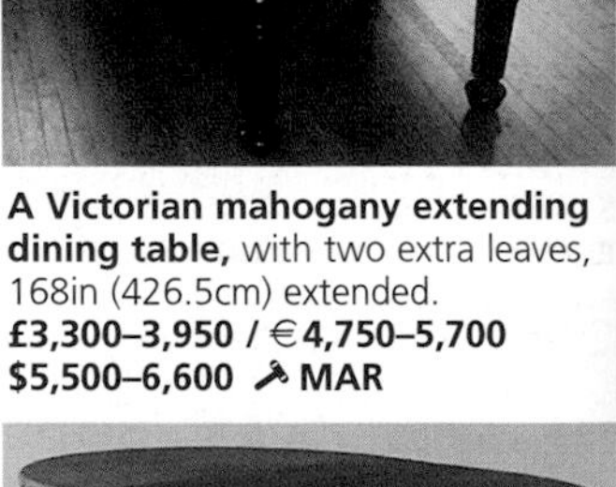

An oak extending dining table, in the style of Gillows, with three extra leaves and a winding handle, c1880, 129½in (329cm) extended.
£1,550–1,850 / €2,200–2,650
$2,600–3,100 S(O)

A Victorian mahogany wind-out extending dining table, with four extra leaves, 116¼in (295cm) extended.
£2,600–3,100 / €3,700–4,450
$4,350–5,200 Bri

A Victorian mahogany extending dining table, with one extra leaf and a winding mechanism, handle missing, 47¾in (121.5cm) extended.
£1,000–1,200 / €1,450–1,700
$1,700–2,000 WW

► **A Victorian mahogany extending dining table,** with two extra leaves, 94½in (240cm) wide.
£1,350–1,600 / €1,900–2,300
$2,250–2,700 B(Kn)

An oak extending dining table, with three extra leaves and two winding handles, stamped '57', c1890, 117¾in (299cm) extended.
£1,000–1,200 / €1,450–1,700
$1,700–2,000 S(O)

A walnut extending dining table, with two extra leaves and winding handle, stamped 'J. Lamb, Manchester 31683', late 19thC, 68½in (174cm) extended.
£410–490 / €590–700
$690–820 PFK

A late Victorian mahogany extending dining table, with a telescopic action and three extra leaves, with embossed plaque inscribed 'Joseph Fittle, Patentee, Birmingham', 118¼in (300cm) extended.
£1,400–1,650 / €2,000–2,350
$2,350–2,750 WW

A mahogany dining table, on a split pedestal, with four extra leaves, American, late 19thC, 54in (137cm) wide.
£1,900–2,300 / €2,750–3,300
$3,200–3,850 NOA

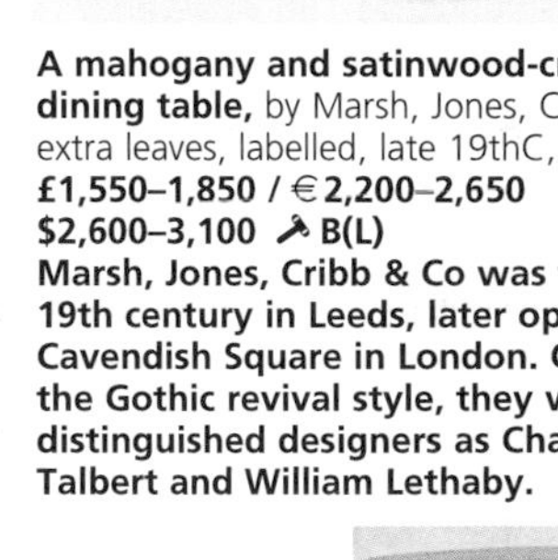

A mahogany and satinwood-crossbanded extending dining table, by Marsh, Jones, Cribb & Co, with three extra leaves, labelled, late 19thC, 115¼in (293cm) wide.
£1,550–1,850 / €2,200–2,650
$2,600–3,100 B(L)
Marsh, Jones, Cribb & Co was founded in the mid-19th century in Leeds, later opening a premises in Cavendish Square in London. Great proponents of the Gothic revival style, they worked with such distinguished designers as Charles Bevan, Bruce Talbert and William Lethaby.

► **An oak wind-out extending dining table,** with one extra leaf, c1900, 48in (122cm) wide.
£850–950
€1,200–1,350
$1,450–1,600
MIN

◄ **A walnut dining table,** early 20thC, 84in (213.5cm) wide.
£2,600–3,100
€3,750–4,450
$4,350–5,200
DN

A George III-style mahogany wind-out extending dining table, with three extra leaves, early 20thC, 94in (239cm) wide.
£1,400–1,650 / €2,000–2,350
$2,350–2,750 PF

A mahogany extending dining table, with six extra leaves, early 20thC, 89in (226cm) extended.
£1,800–2,150 / €2,600–3,100
$3,000–3,600 S(O)

A walnut extending dining table, with two extra leaves, a winding handle and three felt protection mats, 1930s, 117in (297cm) extended.
£1,000–1,200 / €1,450–1,700
$1,700–2,000 S(O)

Display Tables

A Victorian mahogany display table, with a slanted top, on turned legs, 49¼in (125cm) wide.
£330–400 / €490–580
$560–670 SWO

A Regency-style painted satinwood display table, c1890, 29in (73.5cm) high.
£2,700–3,000 / €3,900–4,300
$4,550–5,000 GEO

A Louis XV-style giltwood display table, on cabriole legs, late 19thC, 24¾in (63cm) wide.
£1,050–1,250 / €1,500–1,800
$1,750–2,100 B(Kn)

A kingwood-crossbanded yew wood display table, the legs with simulated ebonized stringing, early 20thC, 22¾in (57.5cm) wide.
£120–140 / €170–200
$200–240 PFK

An Edwardian inlaid mahogany display table, 20¾in (53cm) wide.
£380–460 / €550–660
$640–770 AMB

An Edwardian painted satinwood display table, decorated with foliate swags and bellflowers, 17¾in (45cm) wide.
£1,050–1,250 / €1,500–1,800
$1,750–2,100 JAd

Dressing Tables

A Louis XV gilt-bronze-mounted rosewood-veneered *coiffeuse*, by L. Boudin et Jme, the top with three flaps, the central flap with a mirror, French, 31in (78.5cm) wide.
£4,600–5,500 / €6,600–7,900
$7,700–9,250 S(P)
Léonard Boudin was received Master in 1761. He initially carried out commissions for the cabinet-maker Pierre III Migeon but as he became known for his elaborate and innovative marquetry he began to attract important clients of his own.

► **A George II padoukwood gentleman's dressing table,** the swing mirror above two flaps enclosing a space for wash bowls, 17in (43cm) wide.
£4,800–5,700
€6,900–8,300
$8,000–9,600
S(O)

A George III mahogany dressing stand, the top enclosing a basin and soap dishes, with a rising mirror, above a cupboard and two drawers, on square legs, the stretcher with a pierced stand, 18in (45.5cm) wide.
£3,850–4,600
€5,500–6,600
$6,500–7,700 S

A satinwood and mahogany crossbanded gentleman's dressing table, c1790, 28in (71cm) wide.
£2,300–2,750 / €3,300–3,900
$3,850–4,600 S(O)

A Regency mahogany and crossbanded bowfronted dressing table, 32in (81.5cm) wide.
£1,300–1,550 / €1,900–2,250
$2,200–2,600 B(Kn)

A walnut marquetry dressing table, with two drawers, Dutch, c1820, 66in (167.5cm) high.
£4,500–5,000 / €6,500–7,200
$7,600–8,400 GEO

► **A rosewood, tortoiseshell and brass boullework-inlaid *poudreuse,*** inlaid with brass stringing, the dished lidded top enclosing a mirrored and fitted interior, above a drawer and workbasket, on spiral-turned legs, French, c1860, 20½in (52cm) wide.
£850–1,000 / €1,200–1,400
$1,400–1,650 B(Kn)

A Georgian mahogany dressing table/washstand, the folding top enclosing a rising mirror, pigeonholes and drawer compartments, above a pull-out wash bowl and further drawers, one formed as a bidet, on tapering legs, 16in (40.5cm) wide.
£700–840 / €1,000–1,200
$1,150–1,350 GAK

A Regency travelling dressing table, c1820, 40½in (103cm) wide.
£4,000–4,500 / €5,800–6,500
$6,700–7,600 RGa
The front and back legs of this piece unscrew.

A maple dressing table, with five drawers, on cabriole legs, Continental, 19thC, 40in (103cm) wide.
£680–820 / €1,000–1,200
$1,150–1,350 BWL

An Empire mahogany and gilt-metal-mounted *coiffeuse,* with a moulded marble top, French, 1799–1815, 34¾in (88.5cm) wide.
£1,100–1,300 / €1,600–1,900
$1,850–2,200 S(O)

A mahogany dressing table/desk, the top with a three-quarter gallery, above four drawers flanking an arch, on spiral-turned legs, part of gallery missing, mid-19thC, 44in (112cm) wide.
£280–330 / €400–480
$470–550 PF

A rosewood dressing table, attributed to William and James McCracken, the plate flanked by narrow cupboards with Gothic panel doors, the base with four drawers and a scalloped apron, on cabochon and shell-carved feet, American, mid-19thC, 47in (119.5cm) wide.
£1,250–1,500 / €1,800–2,150
$2,100–2,500 NOA

A mahogany breakfront dressing table, with three frieze drawers, 19thC, 34in (86.5cm) wide.
£420–500 / €600–720
$700–840 B(Kn)

An Edwardian mahogany and marquetry-inlaid dressing table, 48in (122cm) wide.
£770–920 / €1,100–1,300
$1,300–1,550 B(Kn)

A Louis XV-style kingwood and rosewood marquetry *poudreuse*, with a bird's-eye maple fitted interior, c1870, 22¾in (58cm) wide.
£590–710 / €850–1,000
$1,000–1,200 B(Kn)

An Edwardian satinwood dressing table, mirror missing, 48in (122cm) wide.
£290–350 / €420–500
$490–590 B(Kn)

◄ **A George II-style walnut dressing table,** the hinged quarter-veneered panelled top enclosing a satinwood-veneered fitted interior, containing shagreen, ivory and silver-mounted accessories, marked 'CB & S London 1929', the kneehole flanked by two drawers, on cabriole legs and pad feet, c1929, 30¾in (78cm) wide.
£4,700–5,600 / €6,800–8,100
$7,900–9,500 B(Kn)

A Louis XV-style kingwood and marquetry *poudreuse*, c1890, 29in (73.5cm) high.
£1,150–1,300 / €1,650–1,850
$2,000–2,200 ⊞ Che

An Empire-style satinwood dressing table, with a swing mirror and marble top, c1910, 38in (96.5cm) wide, with a matching chair.
£760–850 / €1,050–1,200
$1,250–1,400 ⊞ SWA

Drop-leaf Tables

A mahogany drop-leaf table, with a concealed lateral drawer, on leather-clad casters, c1740, 43¾in (111cm) wide.
£1,800–2,150 / €2,600–3,100
$3,000–3,600 S(O)

A mahogany drop-leaf table, on cabriole legs with pointed pad feet, c1750, 42in (106.5cm) wide.
£3,000–3,350 / €4,300–4,800
$5,100–5,700 ⊞ RGa

► **A George II mahogany drop-leaf table,** 45¾in (116cm) diam.
£1,000–1,200 / €1,450–1,700
$1,700–2,000 SWO

A mahogany drop-leaf table, on cabriole legs with pointed pad feet, mid-18thC, 48in (122cm) diam.
£920–1,100 / €1,350–1,600
$1,550–1,850 PF

A George II mahogany drop-leaf table, on pad feet, 47in (119.5cm) diam.
£890–1,050 / €1,250–1,500
$1,500–1,750 HYD

A mahogany drop-leaf table, with claw feet, Irish, mid-18thC, 45in (114.5cm) diam.
£3,100–3,700 / €4,500–5,300
$5,200–6,200 HOK

A mahogany drop-leaf table, c1770, 54½in (138.5cm) wide.
£1,150–1,400 / €1,700–2,000
$2,000– 2,350 L

Items in the Furniture section have been arranged in date order within each sub-section.

A mahogany drop-leaf table, on tapering legs with pad feet, late 18thC, 37¼in (94.5cm) extended.
£480–580 / €690–830
$810–970 NOA

A mahogany drop-leaf spider table, c1770, 31in (78.5cm) wide.
£2,700–3,000 / €3,900–4,300
$4,500–5,000 JeA

A George III mahogany drop-leaf table, on square legs, 64¼in (163cm) wide.
£1,300–1,550 / €1,900–2,250
$2,200–2,600 JAd

► **A mahogany drop-leaf table,** on ring-turned tapering legs, some damage, early 19thC, 69½in (176.5cm) wide.
£300–360 / €440–520
$500–600 WW

Drum Tables

An olivewood drum table, the segmented veneered top centred with a parquetry Maltese cross, above four frieze drawers, on a panelled triform stem, on three later bun feet, some later veneering, Maltese, early 19thC, 22¾in (58cm) diam.
£2,100–2,500 / €3,000–3,600
$3,500–4,200 WW

Maltese furniture attracts a small group of specialist buyers and sale prices often seem high to the British eye, when comparing the quality with similar British furniture. Pieces are generally veneered in olive-wood and decorative marquetry often includes a Maltese cross.

A mahogany drum table, the leather inset top with a moulded edge, above a frieze with four real and four dummy drawers, on a turned column with three outswept reeded legs on brass casters, c1810, 35in (89cm) diam.
£11,200–12,500 / €16,000–18,000
$18,900–21,000 RGa

A George IV satinwood drum table, the top inlaid with ebony star and foliate motifs within ebony stringing and calamander crossbanding, the frieze with eight alternate angular pivoting and straight drawers, one lock stamped 'Bramah', c1825, 47¼in (120cm) diam.
£19,200–23,000 / €27,700–33,000
$32,000–38,000 S

The use of Bramah locks often reflects the high quality of a piece of furniture. Originally a cabinet-maker, Joseph Bramah (1748–1814) patented a lock in 1784 which, due to its complex design, remained unpicked for more than 50 years. As such it was a popular choice for pieces of furniture such as this, that could be used to hold valuable papers.

◄ **A fruitwood drum table,** the frieze with two drawers, Italian, early 19thC, 65¾in (167cm) diam.
£3,100–3,700 / €4,500–5,300
$5,200–6,200 S(O)

Games Tables

A mahogany and satinwood-crossbanded games table, with later marquetry inlay, c1790, 18in (45.5cm) wide.
£1,800–2,150 / €2,600–3,100
$3,000–3,550 ⚒ S(O)

A late Regency rosewood games table, the sliding top reversing with inlaid chess board, the interior inlaid with a backgammon board, on foliate carved legs and scroll bar feet, damaged, 32½in (82.5cm) wide.
£2,100–2,500 / €3,000–3,600
$3,500–4,200 ⚒ L&E

A rosewood games/work table, the fold-over top enclosing bird's-eye maple marquetry-veneered chequerboards for chess/draughts, backgammon and cribbage, above a single frieze drawer and pull-out basket, on turned feet with wooden casters, silk missing, c1850, 20in (51cm) wide.
£590–710 / €850–1,000
$1,000–1,200 ⚒ BR

► **A marquetry games table,** the folding top with a chequerboard insert, the corners inlaid with suits of cards, a frieze drawer below, on cabriole legs with gilt-metal mounts, Continental, late 19thC, 28in (71cm) wide.
£500–600 / €720–860
$840–1,000 ⚒ GAK

A Regency yew wood and satinwood games table, 28in (71cm) wide.
£2,100–2,500 / €3,000–3,600
$3,500–4,200 ⚒ S(O)

A mahogany fold-over games table, the hinged swivel-action top enclosing a maple and rosewood chequerboard inlay, above a single frieze drawer on tapering legs with scroll feet and brass casters, c1830, 21½in (54.5cm) wide.
£750–900 / €1,100–1,300
$1,250–1,500 ⚒ WL

A Victorian walnut games table, the swivel drop-leaf top inlaid with a chequer and backgammon board above a frieze drawer, the spiral-incised turned stem on carved cabriole legs, 29in (73.5cm) wide.
£290–340 / €420–490
$490–570 ⚒ WW

A Regency amboyna and rosewood games table, fitted for backgammon and with a reversible chessboard top, flanked by bowed ends with a pierced brass gallery, on gilt-mounted lyre end supports, 31in (78.5cm) wide.
£2,700–3,250 / €3,900–4,600
$4,600–5,500 ⚒ G(B)

A William IV rosewood-veneered and marble-inset games table, on a quatreform base with turned feet and brass casters, 24in (61cm) wide.
£740–890 / €1,100–1,300
$1,250–1,500 ⚒ WW

A Victorian papier-mâché and ebonized games table, the piecrust top painted and shell-inlaid with floral decoration and a chessboard, on a fluted baluster stem and claw feet, 25in (63.5cm) diam.
£570–680 / €820–980
$960–1,150 ⚒ G(L)

Library Tables

A Regency rosewood and gilt library table, with two frieze drawers and four dummy drawers, restored, 57in (145cm) wide.
£2,100–2,500 / €3,000–3,600
$3,500–4,200 B(Kn)

A George IV rosewood library table, with two cedar-lined frieze drawers opposing dummy drawers, flanked by leaf brackets, on double-end supports and bases carved with stiff leaves, the reeded bun feet with recessed casters, 60¼in (153cm) wide.
£3,200–3,850 / €4,650–5,600
$5,400–6,500 DN

A George IV amboyna and parcel-gilt library table, in the style of George Smith, the leather-inset top above two frieze drawers, the panelled trestle ends joined by a lotus-carved stretcher, on lotus-corbelled bar bases with foliate feet and casters, 60¼in (153cm) wide.
£5,500–6,600 / €7,900–9,500
$9,200–11,100 B

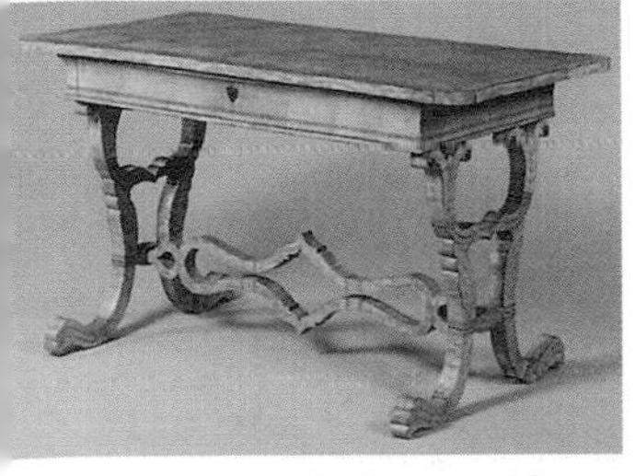

A Biedermeier ash library table, inlaid with ebony stringing, with a drawer, Continental, c1840, 53¼in (135.5cm) wide.
£4,200–5,000 / €6,000–7,200
$7,100–8,500 S(O)

A Regency mahogany library table, with two real and two dummy drawers, on lyre-shaped ends carved with honeysuckle, on raised scroll feet with brass casters, 63¾in (162cm) wide.
£2,900–3,500 / €4,200–5,000
$5,000–6,000 G(L)

A goncalo alves library table, with two drawers and dummy drawers to the reverse, c1825, 60¼in (153cm) wide.
£4,800–5,700 / €6,900–8,200
$8,100–9,600 S(O)

Goncalo alves (*Astronium fraxinifolium*) is a South American timber similar in appearance to rosewood.

A William IV rosewood library table, the leather-inset top with a crossbanded edge, above two frieze drawers, flanked by foliate scrolled carvings, with turned stylized tulip-carved ends, on foliate-carved feet with casters, 45in (114.5cm) wide.
£1,000–1,200 / €1,450–1,700
$1,700–2,000 Mit

A rosewood library table, the carved frieze with two drawers, on tapering end supports with scrolled feet, c1850, 48in (122cm) wide.
£650–780 / €940–1,000
$1,100–1,300 G(L)

A rosewood library table, with two drawers, c1820, 28in (71cm) high.
£3,350–3,750 / €4,850–5,400
$5,600–6,300 GEO

A rosewood library table, with two drawers, Irish, 1820–40, 52in (132cm) wide.
£2,800–3,100 / €4,000–4,400
$4,700–5,200 HON

A William IV rosewood library table, with two frieze drawers, on pierced lyre end supports and lion-paw feet, 44in (112cm) wide.
£820–980 / €1,200–1,400
$1,350–1,600 HYD

An oak library table, in the style of J. G. Crace, the top inset with tooled leather, over two frieze drawers, the stretcher with tusked tenons, on rosette-carved trestle bases with casters, c1850, 54¼in (138cm) wide.
£2,900–3,500 / €4,200–5,000
$4,900–5,900 TEN

J. G. Crace was one of the leading decorating companies in the 18th and 19th centuries, undertaking commissions for the Royal Pavilion in Brighton for the Prince Regent and the Gothic Victorian mansion of Tyntesfield, near Bristol, among others. Several pieces of their furniture were displayed with the pre-Raphaelite paintings in the collection of Andrew Lloyd Webber at the Royal Academy in 2003.

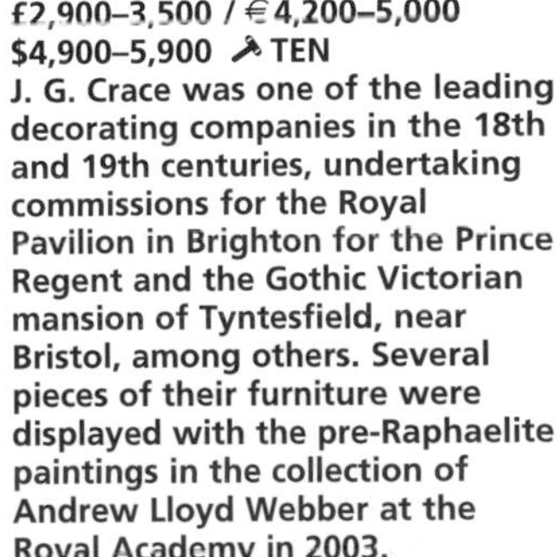

Nests of Tables

A Regency burr-walnut nest of three tables, c1820, 28in (71cm) high.
£1,950–2,150 / €2,800–3,100
$3,250–3,600 ⊞ GEO

A set of mahogany quartetto tables, with amboyna veneer, harewood crossbanding and line-inlaid tops, c1890, largest 20in (51cm) wide.
£3,150–3,500 / €4,500–5,000
$5,200–5,900 ⊞ YOX

A set of Georgian-style mahogany quartetto tables, c1890, 27in (68.5cm) high.
£1,700–1,900 / €2,450–2,750
$2,850–3,200 ⊞ GEO

A set of painted papier-mâché and turned wood quartetto tables, decorated with landscapes, late 19thC, largest 21½in (54.5cm) wide.
£600–720 / €860–1,000
$1,000–1,200 ⚒ S(O)

A set of Edwardian mahogany and satinwood-strung quartetto tables, largest 22in (56cm) wide.
£350–420 / €500–600
$590–700 ⚒ B(Kn)

A set of Edwardian mahogany quartetto tables, with beaded tops, largest 22in (56cm) wide.
£470–560 / €680–810
$790–940 ⚒ WilP

Occasional Tables

A Sheraton-style rosewood-veneered occasional table, with brass stringing, the top cross-banded in harewood, the cedar-lined frieze drawer with turned wood knobs and brass lock, the sides with candle slides, the tapering legs with satinwood banding, late 18thC, 20in (51cm) wide.
£2,000–2,400
€2,950–3,500
$3,350–4,000 ⚒ NSal

► **A George III mahogany occasional table,** 21in (53.5cm) wide.
£300–360 / €440–520
$500–600 ⚒ L

A satinwood, ebonized hardwood and mahogany occasional table, with a serpentine edge and single drawer, on tapering legs with original casters, c1790, 28in (71cm) wide.
£4,400–4,900
€6,300–7,000
$7,400–8,200 ⊞ HA

A mahogany occasional table, the lifting top over one real and one dummy drawer, with brass casters, c1805, 29in (73.5cm) wide.
£2,150–2,400
€3,100–3,450
$3,600–4,000 ⊞ HA

◄ **A Regency mahogany occasional table,** with a scalloped gadrooned edge, the beaded platform base with three brass paw feet, retailer's label for Druce & Co, 21¼in (54cm) diam.
£3,000–3,600
€4,350–5,200
$5,000–6,000 ⚒ TEN

A teak campaign occasional table, the top with a reeded edge, the turned column on four legs, c1820, 22¼in (56.5cm) wide.
£1,000–1,100
€1,450–1,600
$1,700–1,900 ⊞ ChC

This teak table breaks down into three pieces with the top, stem and base unscrewing. The turned column is fitted with a brass collar at either end to strengthen it and teak was used to withstand climate change. Although simple in construction, this piece still follows the fashion of the day.

A pair of mahogany occasional tables, with flame mahogany tops, c1845, 10in (25.5cm) wide.
£8,500–9,500
€12,200–13,700
$14,300–16,000 ⊞ CAT

A walnut and ebony occasional table, with marquetry inlay, c1880, 22in (56cm) diam.
£700–780 / €1,000–1,100
$1,200–1,350 ⊞ MTay

A rosewood occasional table, c1830, 24in (61cm) wide.
£1,650–1,850
€2,350–2,650
$2,750–3,100 ⊞ WAA

An early Victorian burr-maple occasional table, on a tapering carved column and conforming platform base, 37½in (95.5cm) wide.
£2,800–3,350
€4,000–4,800
$4,700–5,600 ⚒ G(B)

A Victorian lacquered papier-mâché tilt-top occasional table, with mother-of-pearl inlay, on a double baluster column and base, 26in (66cm) diam.
£280–340 / €400–480
$470–560 ⚒ MCA

A French Empire-style mahogany and brass-banded occasional table, c1890, 30in (76cm) high.
£1,350–1,500
€1,950–2,150
$2,250–2,500 ⊞ GEO

A rosewood occasional table, with a marble top, the bobbin-turned pillar on a quatrefoil base, with lobed feet, c1830, 15in (38cm) diam.
£1,350–1,500
€1,950–2,150
$2,250–2,500 ⊞ YOX

A rosewood occasional table, with a single drawer, on turned and reeded legs with brass caps and casters, mid-19thC, 19in (48.5cm) wide.
£1,050–1,250
€1,500–1,800
$1,750–2,100 ⚒ SWO

► **An Edwardian mahogany occasional table,** the top hand-painted with garlands of roses, musical instruments and with line inlays, 24in (61cm) diam.
£770–850 / €1,100–1,250
$1,300–1,450 ⊞ AMG

A mahogany-veneered and brass-mounted occasional table, the marble top with a brass gallery, on four tapering legs united by a stretcher with a central urn finial, on brass paw feet, Continental, 19thC, 33in (84cm) diam.
£2,400–2,900
€3,500–4,200
$4,000–4,800 ⚒ COBB

A walnut and Sorrento marquetry occasional table, the top decorated with a marquetry panel of a musician and serving girl, on a turned column with downswept legs, stencilled initials 'C.V', Italian, mid-19thC, 23½in (60cm) square.
£1,100–1,300
€1,600–1,900
$1,850–2,200 ⚒ B(Kn)

Marquetry

Marquetry is a veneer composed of numerous woods applied as an embellishment to a plain surface. Designs typically incorporate flowers, arabesques and birds. It was first employed during the Italian Renaissance and quickly adopted in Germany and the Low Countries but the technique did not reach France until the early 17th century and Britain until after the Restoration in 1660. It became fashionable again in the 1840s and was the speciality of Italian cabinet-makers in Sorrento, who produced elaborately inlaid occasional tables decorated with rustic scenes.

FURNITURE

Pembroke Tables

A mahogany and satinwood-banded Pembroke table, with a frieze drawer, on tapering legs, Irish, c1800, 29½in (75cm) wide.
£3,000–3,600 / €4,350–5,200
$5,000–6,000 ⚒ HOK

A George III mahogany Pembroke table, with a frieze drawer, on tapering legs and casters, 44in (112cm) wide.
£1,450–1,750 / €2,100–2,500
$2,450–2,950 ⚒ B

A Regency mahogany Pembroke table, by Gillow, with a frieze drawer, on tapering legs with brass-capped casters, stamped 'Gillow', retailer's mark, 36in (91.5cm) wide.
£2,350–2,800 / €3,400–4,000
$3,900–4,650 ⚒ Mit

A George IV mahogany Pembroke table, the rosewood-crossbanded and strung top above a frieze drawer and dummy drawer, on a turned column and four ebony-strung outswept legs with brass terminals and casters, top warped, 37¾in (96cm) wide.
£880–1,050 / €1,250–1,500
$1,500–1,800 ⚒ DN

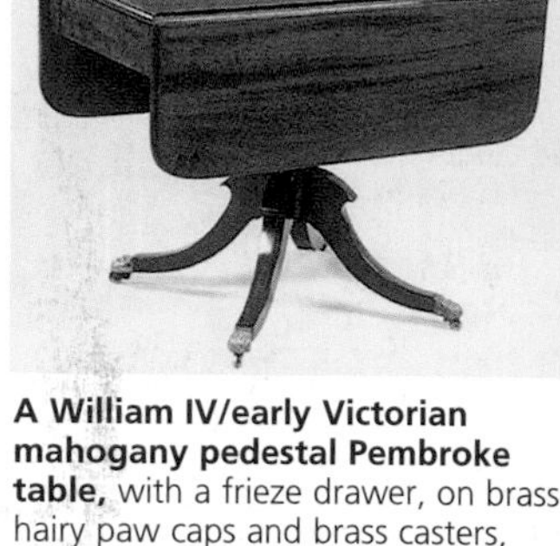

A William IV/early Victorian mahogany pedestal Pembroke table, with a frieze drawer, on brass hairy paw caps and brass casters, 44¼in (112.5cm) extended.
£410–490 / €590–700
$690–820 ⚒ PFK

A Regency mahogany Pembroke table, the top with line inlay, above a frieze drawer fitted with three compartments, on tapering legs with brass caps and leather casters, 37in (94cm) wide.
£1,300–1,550 / €1,900–2,250
$2,200–2,600 ⚒ CGC

► **A mahogany Pembroke table,** with one real and one dummy crossbanded drawer, on turned and reeded legs with brass casters, American, Phyfe School, New York, 19thC, 34in (86.5cm) wide.
£820–980 / €1,200–1,400
$1,400–1,650 ⚒ COBB

Reading Tables

A Regency mahogany reading table, the top with ratchet support, 35¾in (91cm) wide.
£760–910 / €1,100–1,300
$1,250–1,500 ⚒ SWO

An oak reading table, with a ratcheted top, c1860, 39in (99cm) wide.
£960–1,150 / €1,400–1,650
$1,600–1,900 ⚒ S(O)

A Victorian mahogany adjustable reading table, with a ratcheted book rack and telescopic stem, 29in (73.5cm) wide.
£410–490 / €590–700
$690–820 ⚒ G(L)

Serving Tables

A George III mahogany serpentine serving table, with two frieze drawers, on moulded chamfered legs, alterations, 56in (142cm) wide.
£880–1,050 / €1,250–1,500
$1,500–1,750 ⚒ B(Kn)

A mahogany bowfronted serving table, with satinwood-banded legs, c1800, 52¾in (134cm) wide.
£580–700 / €830–1,000
$1,000–1,200 ⚒ S(O)

A George III mahogany serving table, decorated with three paterae, with two drawers, on chamfered and moulded legs, 48in (122cm) wide.
£1,900–2,300 / €2,750–3,300
$3,200–3,850 ⚒ PFK

Items in the Furniture section have been arranged in date order within each sub-section.

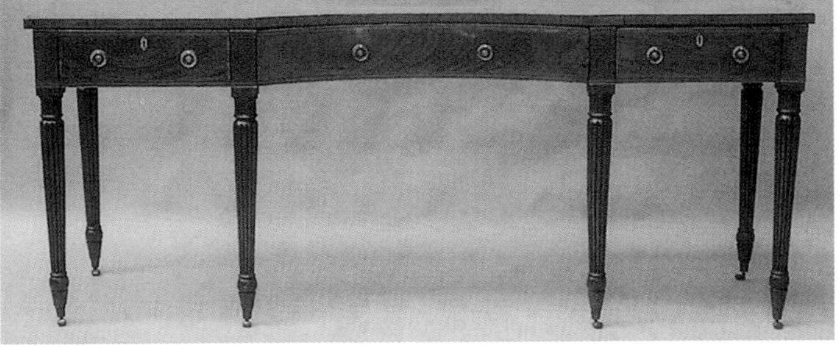

A mahogany inverted bow breakfront serving table, the top with ebonized banding above a dummy drawer flanked by two drawers outlined with satinwood and ebonized banding, on tapering supports with brass sockets and barrel casters, alterations, 19thC, 78¾in (200cm) wide.
£3,000–3,600 / €4,350–5,200
$5,000–6,000 ⚒ DD

A mahogany serving table, with inlaid stringing, two frieze drawers, one divided, with inlaid fruitwood panels, on tapering legs and spade feet, late 19thC, 48in (122cm) wide.
£610–730 / €880–1,050
$1,000–1,200 ⚒ WW

Side Tables

A William III walnut side table, with a fruitwood-inlaid frieze drawer, on bobbin-turned legs and an undulating stretcher, on bun feet, 34¼in (87cm) wide.
£4,300–5,100 / €6,200–7,400
$7,200–8,600 B

An olivewood and boxwood-strung side table, Maltese, c1770, 41in (104cm) wide.
£5,400–6,500 / €7,800–9,350
$9,100–10,900 S(O)

A George III mahogany bowfront side table, with a drawer, on tapering legs, 35in (89cm) wide.
£570–680 / €820–980
$960–1,150 L

A mahogany side table, with a frieze drawer and shaped apron, on turned tapering legs and pad feet, mid-18thC, 28½in (72.5cm) wide.
£590–710 / €850–1,000
$1,000–1,200 WW

A George III Adam-style mahogany and pine side table, the bowfront top with boxwood stringing and crossbanding, above a fluted frieze, with a central ram's, on tapering stop-fluted legs with paterae tops and spade feet, 72in (183cm) wide.
£16,500–19,800 / €23,700–28,500
$27,700–33,000 HYD

Period Adam-style tables of these proportions and design were made in the late 18th century for some of the grandest houses. Period examples fetch many times more than those of similar style made in the late 19th century.

A mahogany and satinwood-banded side table, the top inlaid with a conch shell motif, above a frieze drawer, on tapering legs and brass ball feet, some losses, Dutch, late 18thC, 38¼in (97cm) wide.
£1,050–1,250 / €1,500–1,800
$1,750–2,100 B

◄ **An ebonized and parcel-gilt side table,** the top with an Oriental-style painted frieze, on a stiff-leaf and fluted baluster column with outswept legs with turned finials and feet, paintwork worn, early 19thC, 41in (104cm) wide.
£2,000–2,400 / €2,950–3,500
$3,400–4,000 DN

A Chippendale-style mahogany side table, c1770, 60in (152.5cm) wide.
£9,000–10,000 / €13,000–14,400
$15,100–16,800 GDB

A George III mahogany side table, the moulded edge above a frieze drawer, on chamfered legs, 30in (76cm) wide.
£700–840 / €1,000–1,200
$1,200–1,400 WW

A George III mahogany serpentine-front side table, 28in (71cm) wide.
£1,050–1,250 / €1,500–1,800
$1,750–2,100 B(Kn)

A burr-walnut side table, French, c1815, 19in (48.5cm) wide.
£840–1,000 / €1,200–1,400
$1,450–1,700 S(O)

A George III-style mahogany side table, with pad feet, c1860, 29in (73.5cm) high.
£2,250–2,500 / €3,250–3,600
$3,750–4,200 ⊞ GEO

A mahogany side table, with a moulded top, on turned barley-twist legs, c1890, 31¼in (79.5cm) wide.
£500–600 / €720–860
$840–1,000 ⚒ SWO

► An Edwardian Sheraton revival marquetry-inlaid satinwood side table, in the style of Edwards & Roberts, on tapered legs with an X-stretcher, some damage, 19¾in (50cm) wide.
£760–910 / €1,100–1,300
$1,300–1,550 ⚒ EH

A Victorian satinwood side table, with two drawers, on turned legs, 36in (91.5cm) wide.
£630–700 / €910–1,000
$1,050–1,200 ⊞ WAA

An oak side table, with two frieze drawers, the stretcher centred with a carved medallion, on moulded square feet, Italian, c1900, 60in (152.5cm) wide.
£1,000–1,200 / €1,450–1,700
$1,700–2,000 ⚒ NOA

A Victorian burr-elm side table, the three frieze drawers with ebonized banding, with shaped trestles, stamped 'Lamb, Manchester', 50in (127cm) wide.
£3,350–4,000 / €4,800–5,700
$5,600–6,700 ⚒ S

James Lamb (1816–1903), founded a cabinet-making workshop in Manchester which flourished during the boom years of the Industrial Revolution. The firm exhibited at the 1862 London Universal Exhibition, and in Paris in 1867 and 1878, winning several awards. Principally associated with the Aesthetic Movement, Lamb worked in association with several key designers of the period including Alfred Waterhouse and Charles Bevan. An obituary in *The Journal of Decorative Art and British Decorator* for September 1903 states 'His name was a synonym for the best in everything he did from 1850 to 1885, and he towered over everybody in Lancashire and Yorkshire as a maker of high-class furniture, and to middle-aged and older men connected with the furniture and decorating business, his name for fifty years stood as a benchmark for all that was best in both spheres of industrial art.'

Silver Tables

A George II mahogany silver table, with a moulded gallery and valanced fretwork frieze over cabriole legs with faceted pad feet, 28¾in (73cm) wide.
£10,800–13,000 / €15,500–18,600
$18,100–21,800 ⚒ S

A mahogany silver table, with a rounded shaped frieze, on cabriole legs and pad feet, top cracked, mid-18thC, 29½in (75cm) wide.
£3,750–4,500 / €5,400–6,500
$6,300–7,500 ⚒ WW

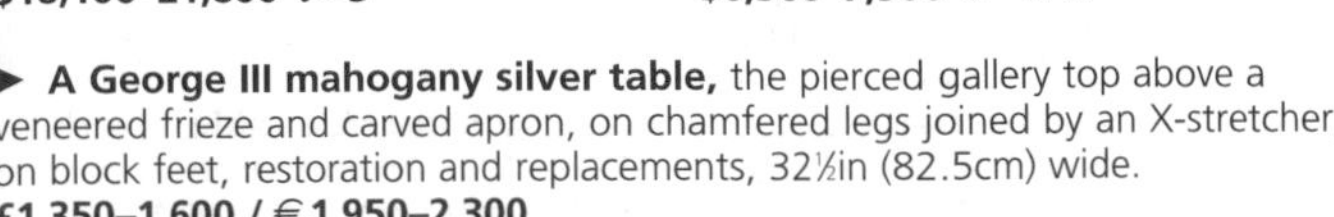

► A George III mahogany silver table, the pierced gallery top above a veneered frieze and carved apron, on chamfered legs joined by an X-stretcher, on block feet, restoration and replacements, 32½in (82.5cm) wide.
£1,350–1,600 / €1,950–2,300
$2,250–2,700 ⚒ WW

A Georgian mahogany silver table, Irish, 32in (81cm) wide.
£13,200–15,800 / €19,000 22,500
$22,000–26,500 ⚒ S

Sofa Tables

A Regency mahogany sofa table, the plum figured top crossbanded in rosewood, over two banded frieze drawers, on splayed legs with brass caps and casters, 58in (147.5cm) wide.
£2,350–2,800 / €3,350–4,000 $3,900–4,600 ⚒ B(Pr)

A Regency rosewood sofa table, with satinwood crossbanding and tulipwood banding, 37½in (95.5cm) wide.
£3,300–3,950 / €4,750–5,700 $5,500–6,600 ⚒ B(Kn)

This example shows a high arched stretcher which gives a pleasing effect rather than a pedestal base or a low stretcher cutting across. Combined with quality, age and condition, this type of arched support can positively effect the value.

A Regency rosewood sofa table, with brass stringing, two frieze drawers and two dummy drawers, 37¾in (96cm) wide.
£1,750–2,100 / €2,500–3,000 $2,950–3,500 ⚒ B(Kn)

A George IV mahogany sofa table, c1825, 35in (89cm) wide.
£2,650–3,200 / €3,800–4,550 $4,500–5,400 ⚒ S(O)

A Regency partridgewood sofa table, with satinwood banding and tulipwood crossbanding, inlaid with boxwood and ebonized lines, with two frieze drawers and two dummy drawers, on lyre end supports with brass roundels, the downswept legs with brass paw caps and casters, 62¼in (158cm) wide.
£5,900–7,100 / €8,500–10,000 $10,000–12,000 ⚒ B

A Regency mahogany sofa table, the rosewood-banded top above two frieze drawers and two dummy drawers, the obelisk stem and quatreform base with moulded reeded-edge splayed legs with brass sabots and casters, slight repairs, handles later, 36in (91.5cm) wide.
£940–1,100 / €1,350–1,600 $1,600–1,900 ⚒ NSal

A Regency rosewood and brass-inlaid sofa table, the crossbanded and brass-strung top above two cedar-lined frieze drawers and two dummy drawers, on lyre end supports with brass paw caps and casters, stamped 'T. Sharples, Liverpool', 41in (104cm) wide.
£8,700–10,400 / €12,500–15,000 $14,600–17,500 ⚒ SWO

The partnership of Sharples & Rainford is first recorded trading in 1804 in Liverpool. By 1809, Thomas Sharples was trading alone and is listed in Liverpool directories until 1834.

A Regency rosewood sofa table, the satinwood-crossbanded top above two frieze drawers inlaid with satinwood stringing, on a turned column, the hipped sabre legs with brass caps and casters, 59in (150cm) extended.
£1,600–1,900 / €2,300–2,750 $2,700–3,200 ⚒ HYD

A rosewood sofa table, with two cedar-lined frieze drawers and two dummy drawers, c1810, 61in (155cm) extended.
£5,350–6,400 / €7,700–9,200 $9,000–10,750 ⚒ S(NY)

A mahogany and rosewood-banded sofa table, with banded frieze drawers, the turned pedestal on a platform base with sabre legs, lotus cast-brass caps and casters, c1820, 60in (152.5cm) wide.
£4,750–5,300 / €6,800–7,600 $7,900–8,900 ⊞ YOX

A George IV rosewood sofa table, with satinwood crossbanding within brass lines, the trestle legs with Gothic piercing flanked by turned pilasters, 37in (94cm) wide.
£3,400–4,100 / €4,900–5,900 $5,700–6,800 ⚒ L

Sutherland Tables

A mahogany Sutherland table, on turned legs and pad feet, 19thC, 32in (81.5cm) wide.
£590–710 / €850–1,000
$1,000–1,200 SWO

A Victorian walnut Sutherland table, on downswept legs, 22¾in (58cm) wide.
£375–450 / €540–650
$640–760 AMB

A rosewood Sutherland table, with a moulded-edge top, on turned legs with brass cup casters, repolished, c1850, 42in (106.5cm) wide.
£1,300–1,450 / €1,850–2,100
$2,200–2,450 JC

◄ **A mahogany Sutherland table,** with pierced supports and curved feet, late 19thC, 39½in (100.5cm) wide.
£250–300 / €360–430
$420–500 B(Kn)

► **A Sheraton-style mahogany double Sutherland table,** c1910, 28in (71cm) wide.
£760–850 / €1,050–1,200
$1,250–1,400 GEO

Tea Tables

A mahogany tea/card table, Irish, c1770, 31½in (80cm) wide.
£1,700–2,050 / €2,450–2,900
$2,850–3,400 ⚒ S(O)

A George III mahogany and chequer-banded fold-over tea table, 36¼in (92cm) wide.
£360–430 / €520–620
$600–720 ⚒ B(Kn)

A George III mahogany tea/card table, line-inlaid and with rosewood crossbanding, with a fold-over top, on later fluted legs, 38in (96.5cm) wide.
£1,950–2,350 / €2,850–3,400
$3,250–3,900 ⚒ HOLL

A mahogany fold-over tea table, on a U-shaped stretcher, the down-swept legs with brass caps and casters, early 19thC, 36in (91.5cm) wide.
£590–710 / €850–1,000
$1,000–1,200 ⚒ B(NW)

A George III mahogany serpentine tea table, 35¾in (91cm) wide.
£2,050–2,450 / €3,000–3,550
$3,500–4,150 ⚒ S(O)

A Regency mahogany folding tea table, the top with swivel action, the platform base with brass lion-paw feet and casters, 36in (91.5cm) wide.
£880–1,050 / €1,250–1,500
$1,500–1,850 ⚒ AH

◄ **A mahogany tea table,** early 19thC, 36¼in (92cm) wide.
£350–420 / €500–600
$590–700 ⚒ B(Kn)

► **A William IV mahogany tea table,** the top inlaid with brass stringing, on a spiral reeded and turned column, with a platform base on scrolled reeded supports with brass caps and casters, 36in (91.5cm) wide.
£1,250–1,500 / €1,800–2,150
$2,100–2,500 ⚒ TRM

Tripod Tables

A mahogany tripod table, on a birdcage support, c1730, 28in (71cm) diam.
£3,600–4,000
€5,200–5,800
$6,000–6,700 ⊞ SEA

A walnut tripod table, the tilting dish-top with a scratch stock moulded edge, on a ring-turned barrel column with three legs, c1770, 28in (71cm) wide.
£2,550–2,850
€3,700–4,100
$4,300–4,800 ⊞ JC

A George III mahogany tripod table, the tilt-top on a birdcage support and turned column, with cabriole legs and pad feet, 28in (71cm) diam.
£450–540 / €650–780
$760–910 ⚒ PF

An early George III mahogany tripod table, on a spiral carved and knopped shaft with cabriole legs and pointed pad feet, 18¼in (46.5cm) wide.
£4,800–5,700
€6,900–8,300
$8,000–9,600 ⚒ B

A mahogany two-tier tripod table, on original casters, c1810, 34in (86.5cm) high.
£3,850–4,300
€5,500–6,200
$6,500–7,200 ⊞ JeA

A rosewood tripod table, the tilt-top with satinwood banding and brass edging, the column with brass inlay, c1820, 29in (73.5cm) high.
£2,500–2,800
€3,600–4,000
$4,250–4,700 ⊞ FHA

◄ A walnut parquetry tripod table, Italian, 19thC, 62in (157.5cm) diam.
£350–420 / €500–600
$590–710 ⚒ EH

► A mahogany tripod table, with a tilt-top, on a turned and reeded column, with casters, 1840–45, 22in (56cm) diam.
£2,000–2,200
€2,900–3,200
$3,350–3,700 ⊞ GGD

A mahogany and inlaid tripod table, on a turned column with fret-carved legs, 19thC, 19in (48.5cm) wide.
£360–400 / €520–580
$600–660 ⊞ WAA

A mahogany wine table, c1825, 22in (56cm) wide.
£530–590 / €760–850
$890–990 ⊞ GBr

A mahogany and brass revolving tripod table, stamped 'Hall', c1900, 18in (45.5cm) wide.
£700–780 / €1,000–1,100
$1,150–1,300 ⊞ GEO

Two-tier Tables

A mahogany and marquetry two-tier table, with a folding top, Dutch, c1820, 30in (76cm) high.
£2,000–2,200
€2,900–3,200
$3,350–3,700 ⊞ GEO

A walnut two-tier table, on turned legs, c1880, 17in (43.5cm) diam.
£240–270 / €350–390
$400–450 ⊞ GBr

A pair of satinwood two-tier tables, banded and strung with harewood, with pierced gilt-brass edges, carved and engraved leaf knees and paw feet, c1880, 13in (33cm) diam.
£2,450–2,700
€3,500–3,900
$4,100–4,550 ⊞ YOX

A walnut and gilt-metal-mounted two-tier table, with a marble top, French, c1880, 15¾in (40cm) wide.
£900–1,100
€1,350–1,600
$1,500–1,800 ⚒ S(O)

A mahogany two-tier table, c1890, 15in (38cm) diam.
£500–550 / €720–800
$840–920 ⊞ MTay

An Edwardian satinwood two-tier table, with inlay and crossbanding, 24½in (62cm) wide.
£610–730 / €880–1,050
$1,000–1,200 ⚒ SWO

► **An Edwardian satinwood-veneered two-tier table,** inlaid with leaf and ribbon decoration, on tapering legs and spade feet, 35¾in (91cm) wide.
£680–820 / €1,000–1,200
$1,200–1,400 ⚒ SWO

Items in the Furniture section have been arranged in date order within each sub-section.

A Louis XV-style kingwood, tulipwood and amboyna two-tier table, with a marble top and ebony stringing, the front slide enclosing two drawers, on gilt-metal sabots, French, early 20thC, 16¼in (41.5cm) diam.
£1,700–2,000
€2,500–2,900
$2,850–3,400 ⚒ S(O)

Work Tables

A George III burr-yew drum work table, includes other woods, adapted, 17¼in (44cm) wide.
£350–420 / €500–600
$590–700 ⚒ B(Kn)

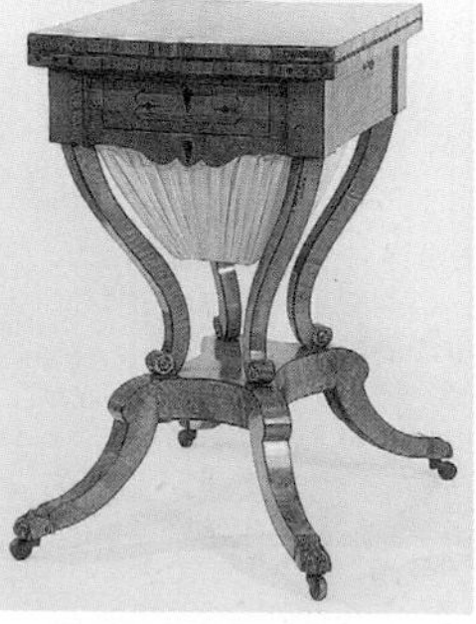

A George III bird's-eye maple work table, cross-banded with stringing and gilt-metal mounts, with brass lion-paw toes and casters, 16¼in (41.5cm) wide.
£1,900–2,300
€2,750–3,300
$3,200–3,850 ⚒ AH

A satinwood and rosewood-banded work table, with ebony and boxwood stringing, the two short and two long drawers with ivory knobs, on tapering legs with original casters, c1780, 24in (61cm) wide.
£2,500–2,800
€3,600–4,000
$4,200–4,700 ⊞ YOX

A satinwood work table, the papier-mâché top decorated in the style of Angelica Kauffmann, restored, c1790, 20in (51cm) wide.
£4,300–4,750
€6,200–6,900
$7,200–8,000 ⊞ NAW

A George III rosewood-veneered work table, with inlaid stringing, the ratcheted inlaid leather top with a rest, above a leather-lined slide and dummy drawer, with divided writing drawer, the pleated work bag with an ivory escutcheon, the back with a lift-up screen, on tapering legs with brass casters, 23in (58.5cm) wide.
£3,400–4,100
€4,900–5,900
$5,800–6,900 WW

A Regency rosewood and brass-inlaid work table, the hinged top with a gadrooned edge, enclosing a shallow well, over a fitted drawer to one side with a workbag under, on scrolled X-supports, the carved and hipped sabre feet with brass caps and casters, 15¾in (40cm) wide.
£5,600–6,700
€8,100–9,600
$9,400–11,200 TEN

A rosewood work table, the swivel top enclosing a writing table with leather inset, on scrolled feet with casters, c1830, 27in (68.5cm) high.
£1,350–1,500
€1,950–2,150
$2,100–2,500 ⊞ AMG

A George III plum pudding mahogany pedestal work table, the top drawer with a hinged writing surface and pen slide, on a column with reeded inverted sabre legs, 20in (51cm) wide.
£1,350–1,600
€1,950–2,300
$2,250–2,700 HOLL

A Regency tortoiseshell-veneered work table, the hinged top enclosing a velvet-covered tapering well, 12½in (32cm) wide.
£400–480 / €580–690
$670–800 HYD

A rosewood work table, c1830, 29in (73.5cm) high.
£2,400–2,650
€3,500–3,800
$4,050–4,450 ⊞ GEO

A rosewood and boxwood-strung work table, the hinged top enclosing a recess above a compartmented drawer, on splayed legs with convex stretchers, early 19thC, 19in (48.5cm) wide.
£1,300–1,550
€1,900–2,250
$2,200–2,600 DN

A Regency mahogany work table, the hinged top with a leather inset, over a frieze drawer and work basket, 28¼in (72cm) wide.
£940–1,100
€1,350–1,600
$1,600–1,900 SWO

A pollarded oak work table, the figured top with a gadrooned edge, enclosing a fitted interior, on an acanthus carved and reeded column, over a platform base with paw feet and concealed casters, c1830, 20in (51cm) wide.
£2,700–2,950
€3,900–4,200
$4,500–5,000 ⊞ RGC

A rosewood work table, with a twin-flap top, fitted real and opposing dummy drawers, on a platform base with C-scroll feet, c1820, 18in (45.5cm) wide.
£2,900–3,200
€4,200–4,600
$4,900–5,400 ⊞ GGD

A Regency mahogany work table, the top above two frieze drawers and two dummy drawers, on scrolled supports and a platform base, above four scrolled legs with brass casters, top replaced, formerly with drop flaps, 24in (61cm) wide.
£330–400 / €490–580
$560–670 BR

A mahogany work table, the hinged top revealing a compartmented interior with a storage well, the front with applied foliate carving, the column with a base on scrolled feet, c1835, 15in (38cm) wide.
£340–410 / €490–590
$580–690 NOA

◄ **A japanned chinoiserie-decorated work table,** the top revealing a fitted interior with ivory sewing accessories, above a sliding basket, on lyre end supports and lion-paw feet, 19thC, 24½in (62cm) wide.
£590–710 / €850–1,000
$1,000–1,200 B(Kn)

A mahogany work/writing table, French, 19thC, 22in (56cm) wide.
£3,600–4,000
€5,200–5,800
$6,000–6,700 ⊞ GGD

An Empire-style burr-oak work table, the hinged top above a frieze drawer, on turned column supports with engraved brass capitals, 19thC, 21in (53.5cm) wide.
£1,200–1,450
€1,750–2,100
$2,000–2,400 ⚒ BWL

A mahogany work table, c1840, 34in (86.5cm) wide.
£1,250–1,400
€1,800–2,000
$2,100–2,350 ⊞ MTay

A rosewood work table, the top with brass stringing above a frieze drawer and silk bag, on sledge supports with brass paw casters, c1850, 23½in (59.5cm) wide.
£3,150–3,500
€4,500–5,000
$5,300–5,900 ⊞ Man

A satinwood work table, the top enclosing a silk-covered interior, the frieze with applied bosses, the angles with stylized floral motifs, above a sliding work bag, the end supports united by a padded footrest on scrolled feet with casters, c1850, 21in (53.5cm) wide.
£260–310 / €380–450
$440–520 ⚒ PF

For further information on antique furniture see the full range of Miller's books at **www.millers.uk.com**

A Victorian painted satinwood work table, 15in (38cm) wide.
£1,000–1,100
€1,450–1,600
$1,700–1,900 ⊞ AMG

A Victorian walnut work table, the quarter-veneered top above a frieze drawer and slide-out work bag, on turned carved baluster supports with downswept legs, 23¾in (60.5cm) wide.
£570–680 / €820–980
$960–1,150 ⚒ AMB

A Victorian papier-mâché and mother-of-pearl work table, the gilt-decorated lid enclosing a fitted interior with ivory sewing accessories, above a vine-decorated fretwork apron, the baluster support on a platform base with scroll feet and brass casters, 20½in (52cm) wide.
£2,700–3,250
€3,900–4,650
$4,600–5,500 ⚒ Bri

A Victorian inlaid walnut work/writing table, the interior fitted with a leather inset, above a workbox drawer and well, on turned supports, 16½in (42cm) wide.
£1,650–2,000
€2,450–2,900
$2,800–3,350 ⚒ JAd

A Victorian rosewood-veneered work table, the top above a fitted and part-lidded interior, on a tapering stem with a triform base on flat feet, 16¾in (42.5cm) diam.
£330–400 / €490–580
$560–670 ⚒ WW

A Victorian walnut and marquetry work table, with a fitted interior, on carved toes, 30in (76cm) high.
£1,350–1,500
€1,950–2,150
$2,250–2,500 ⊞ GEO

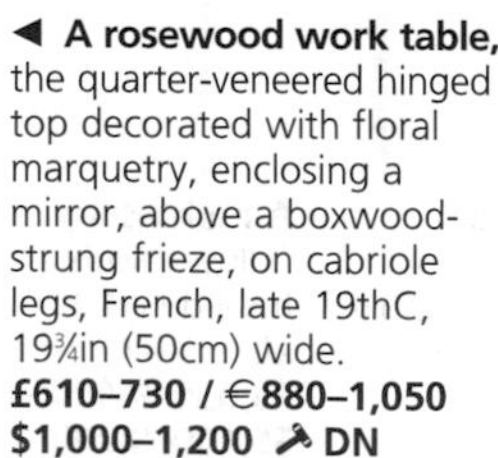

◀ **A rosewood work table,** the quarter-veneered hinged top decorated with floral marquetry, enclosing a mirror, above a boxwood-strung frieze, on cabriole legs, French, late 19thC, 19¾in (50cm) wide.
£610–730 / €880–1,050
$1,000–1,200 ⚒ DN

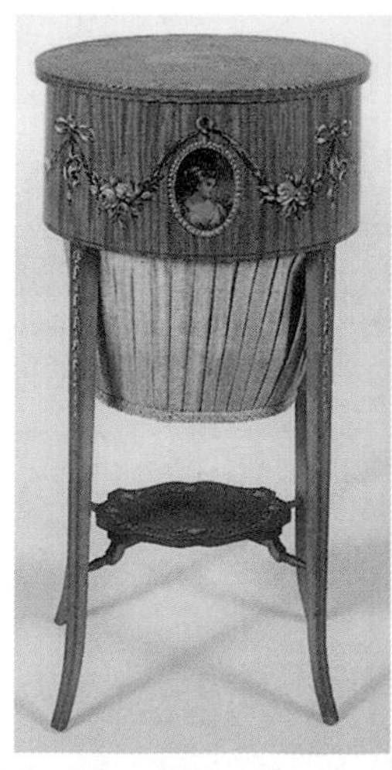

An Edwardian painted satinwood work table, the top painted with a central cartouche, enclosing a fitted interior and silk workbag, on tapering legs, 15¼in (38.5cm) diam.
£1,450–1,750
€2,100–2,500
$2,450–2,950 ⚒ LJ

Writing Tables

A George III mahogany and cross-banded writing table, the panelled top with hinged flaps, the sliding central panel enclosing a ratcheted writing surface and lidded compartment with fitted interior, above dummy drawers, 38½in (98cm) extended.
£3,000–3,600 / €4,350–5,200
$5,000–6,000 ⚒ B

A Regency rosewood writing table, the top with ratchet action, above three frieze drawers, 37½in (95.5cm) wide.
£3,400–4,100 / €4,900–5,900
$5,800–6,900 ⚒ B(O)

A pale mahogany writing table, with a fitted writing drawer above two drawers, the opposing side with dummy drawers, c1810, 39½in (100.5cm) wide.
£3,350–4,000 / €4,800–5,700
$5,600–6,700 ⚒ S(O)

A satinwood and tulipwood-banded writing table, the leather inset over a frieze drawer, on cabriole legs, 19thC, 44½in (113cm) wide.
£1,350–1,600 / €1,950–2,300
$2,250–2,700 ⚒ TEN

A mahogany kidney-shaped writing table, with a leather top, early 19thC, 36in (91.5cm) wide.
£3,500–3,900 / €5,000–5,600
$5,900–6,600 ⊞ JeA

A Regency mahogany writing table, with concave front, the cleated reeded-edge top above a frieze drawer, flanked by two further drawers, with trade label for Norman Adams, crack to top, handles replaced, 41¾in (106cm) wide.
£1,750–2,100 / €2,500–3,000
$2,950–3,500 ⚒ WW

A mahogany kidney-shaped writing table, on brass casters, c1820, 42in (106.5cm) wide.
£2,800–3,100 / €4,000–4,450
$4,700–5,200 ⊞ SAW

A mahogany writing table, by Gillows, with an integral inkwell, on turned legs and brass casters, 19thC, 28in (71cm) wide.
£3,050–3,400 / €4,400–4,900
$5,100–5,700 ⊞ APO

A mahogany and rosewood-crossbanded writing table, the leather-inset top above a gadrooned frieze with two drawers, early 19thC, 30¾in (78cm) wide.
£1,600–1,900 / €2,300–2,750
$2,700–3,200 ⚒ B

A Regency mahogany writing table, with leather-inset top above two frieze drawers, 42½in (108cm) wide.
£1,200–1,450 / €1,750–2,100
$2,000–2,400 ⚒ CGC

A rosewood writing table, with two frieze drawers, c1835, 35¾in (91cm) wide.
£1,200–1,450 / €1,750–2,100
$2,000–2,400 ⚒ S(O)

A gilt-bronze-mounted mahogany writing table, with a frieze drawer, the legs joined by an X-stretcher, French, 19thC, 19¼in (49cm) wide.
£3,150–3,800 / €4,600–5,500
$5,300–6,400 ⚒ S(P)

A mahogany writing table, the top with an applied moulding and leather inset, above a frieze drawer, on tapering legs with brass casters, c1850, 23in (58.5cm) wide.
£590–710 / €850–1,000
$1,000–1,200 WW

A burr-walnut kidney-shaped writing table, with a leather top, c1860, 29in (73.5cm) high.
£4,500–5,000 / €6,500–7,200
$7,600–8,400 GEO

A Victorian oak writing table, with three frieze drawers to each side, 49½in (125.5cm) wide.
£660–790 / €1,000–1,150
$1,100–1,300 L

A Victorian mahogany two-tier writing table, the top with a rear shelved gallery, above two frieze drawers, 50¾in (129cm) wide.
£350–420 / €500–600
$590–700 WilP

A Louis XV-style walnut writing table, with gilt-metal mounts and porcelain plaques, the serpentine frieze with one drawer, c1850, 48in (122cm) wide.
£2,900–3,500 / €4,150–5,000
$4,900–5,900 S(O)

A Victorian carved oak and marquetry writing table, c1860, 48in (122cm) wide.
£3,000–3,600 / €4,400–5,200
$5,000–6,000 S(O)

A Victorian oak writing table, the top with a leather inset, above a frieze with six opposing drawers, on reeded legs with ceramic casters, 28in (71cm) wide.
£920–1,100 / €1,350–1,600
$1,550–1,850 BR

A Victorian mahogany partner's writing table, the top with a *faux* leather inset over a central arch flanked by two drawers, opposing three drawers to the frieze, the ends with dummy drawers, damaged, 69¾in (177cm) wide.
£1,250–1,500 / €1,800–2,150
$2,100–2,500 Bri

◄ **A kingwood, marquetry and ormolu *bureau plat*,** French, c1880, 50in (127cm) wide.
£6,200–6,900 / €8,900–9,900
$10,400–11,600 Che

► **A marquetry *bureau plat*,** c1890, 54in (137cm) wide.
£8,500–9,500 / €12,300–13,700
$14,300–16,000 SAW

A Régence-style kingwood and gilt-bronze-mounted *bureau plat*, the moulded top with a leather inset, above three frieze drawers opposed by three dummy drawers, on cabriole legs, on gilt-bronze claw sabots, French, c1850, 70in (178cm) wide.
£5,900–7,100 / €8,500–10,200
$9,900–11,900 S(Am)

A walnut and ebony-inlaid writing table, with a leather top and brass trim, French, c1860, 54in (137cm) wide.
£4,700–5,200 / €6,750–7,500
$7,900–8,700 MTay

A Victorian oak writing table, the top with a leather inset, moulded foliate border and adjustable writing slope, above two frieze drawers, 42in (106.5cm) wide.
£320–350 / €450–500
$540–600 FHF

A Louis XV-style kingwood and marquetry serpentine *bureau plat*, French, c1880, 46in (117cm) wide.
£3,000–3,350 / €4,300–4,800
$5,000–5,600 Che

Teapoys

► **A Regency mahogany teapoy,** inlaid with ebony, the top on splayed legs with brass paw caps and casters, damage and losses to interior, 16in (40.5cm) wide.
£1,700–2,050
€2,450–2,900
$2,950–3,500 Bea

A Regency rosewood and brass-inlaid teapoy, the top enclosing four lidded caddies and two original glass mixing bowls, on a lyre-shaped support, 16¼in (41.5cm) wide.
£3,400–4,100
€4,900–5,900
$5,800–6,900 SWO

A rosewood teapoy, c1850, 17¾in (45cm) wide.
£600–720 / €860–1,000
$1,000–1,200 S(O)

A Regency rosewood teapoy, with brass inlay, the top enclosing four caddies and two recesses for bowls, on a lyre-shaped support, mixing bowls missing, 16½in (42cm) wide.
£1,100–1,300
€1,600–1,900
$1,850–2,200 DN

► **A Louis XV-style burr-walnut teapoy,** by Gillows of Lancaster, the interior with two canisters and a removable tray, c1860, 22½in (57cm) wide.
£2,050–2,450
€2,950–3,500
$3,500–4,150 S(O)

A rosewood teapoy, the hinged cover enclosing a vacant interior, the column on short scroll feet, c1835, 15½in (39.5cm) wide.
£420–500 / €600–720
$700–840 WL

Torchères

A George III mahogany torchère, the reeded stem with stiff-leaf carving, on downswept carved cabriole legs with claw-and-ball feet, 63in (160cm) high.
£375–450 / €540–650
$640–760 Mit

A mahogany torchère, with an inset onyx top, French, c1890, 30in (76cm) high.
£430–480 / €620–690
$720–800 AMG

A Louis XIV-style carved giltwood torchère, c1890, 69¼in (176cm) high.
£1,800–2,150
€2,600–3,100
$3,000–3,600 S(O)

A Sheraton revival satin-wood torchère, late 19thC, 51in (129.5cm) high.
£1,250–1,400
€1,800–2,000
$2,100–2,300 APO

Towel Rails

A mahogany double-gate towel rail, with a lacquered brass fastener, on a platform base with scroll feet, early 19thC, 37in (94cm) wide.
£400–480 / €580–690
$670–800 WW

A mahogany towel rail, c1850, 27½in (70cm) wide.
£2,050–2,450 / €2,950–3,500
$3,450–4,100 S(O)

A turned mahogany folding towel rail, 19thC, 23¾in (60.5cm) wide.
£260–310 / €380–450
$440–520 SWO

Trays

► **A mahogany butler's tray,** with pierced handles, on a later stand, c1820, 24½in (62cm) wide.
£3,000–3,350 / €4,350–4,800
$5,000–5,600 RGa

A George III mahogany butler's tray, on an associated stand, 24½in (62cm) wide.
£420–500 / €600–720
$700–840 S(O)

A papier-mâché tray, on a later *faux* bamboo stand, c1860, 20in (51cm) high.
£1,050–1,150 / €1,500–1,650
$1,750–1,950 GEO

◄ **A painted papier-mâché tray,** on a stand, c1880, 25in (63.5cm) wide.
£880–980 / €1,250–1,400
$1,500–1,650 JSt

Wall Brackets

A carved giltwood wall bracket, the top with egg-and-dart and guilloche mouldings above a plumed foliate support, c1770, 18¾in (47.5cm) wide.
£9,600–11,500
€13,800–16,500
$16,100–19,300 S

A pair of painted wood wall brackets, some losses, c1770, 6¾in (17cm) wide.
£2,150–2,600
€3,100–3,700
$3,600–4,300 S(NY)

A bronzed plaster wall bracket, by Lawrence Gahagan, with maker's name and date 1804 in Latin, Irish, 11¾in (30cm) wide.
£820–980 / €1,200–1,400
$1,400–1,650 S(O)

A pair of carved giltwood wall brackets, with cruciform-style backplates, Italian, c1900 and later, 15in (38cm) wide.
£650–780 / €920–1,100
$1,100–1,300 NOA

Wardrobes

A polychrome-decorated wardrobe, redecorated, Italian, late 18thC, 63in (160cm) wide.
£3,000–3,600 / €4,300–5,200
$5,000–6,000 ⚒ B(Kn)

A brass and wrought-iron-mounted lacquered armoire, decorated with chinoiserie bamboo motifs, French, c1800, 65¼in (165.5cm) wide.
£7,500–9,000 / €10,800–13,000
$12,600–15,100 ⚒ NOA

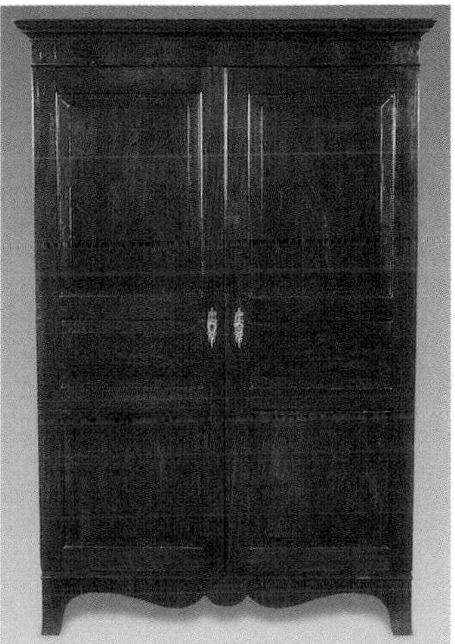

A mahogany wardrobe, the panelled doors enclosing a brass hanging rail above removable shelves, Jersey, c1830, 54in (137cm) wide.
£4,000–4,500 / €5,800–6,500
$6,800–7,500 ⊞ JC

A Sheraton-style mahogany wardrobe, with cedar-lined trays and drawers, original gilded brasswork and exotic timber inlaid decoration, c1800, 96in (244cm) wide.
£15,300–17,000 / €22,000–24,500
$25,700–28,600 ⊞ GDB

A mahogany breakfront wardrobe, the central doors and drawers flanked by full length cupboards, early 19thC, 100in (254cm) wide.
£1,550–1,850 / €2,250–2,650
$2,600–3,100 ⚒ S(O)

A William IV mahogany breakfront wardrobe, the seven drawers flanked by two doors, 85in (216cm) wide.
£620–740 / €890–1,000
$1,000–1,200 ⚒ DN

A mahogany wardrobe, the egg-and-dart carved cornice above fielded panel doors, Channel Islands, c1800, 57½in (146cm) wide.
£1,200–1,450 / €1,750–2,100
$2,000–2,400 ⚒ B(Kn)

A Regency mahogany wardrobe, the panelled doors enclosing slides and hanging space above drawers, 79½in (202cm) wide.
£1,300–1,550 / €1,900–2,250
$2,200–2,600 ⚒ CGC

A mahogany breakfront wardrobe, the panelled doors now enclosing hanging space, c1835, 88½in (225cm) wide.
£2,000–2,400 / €2,900–3,450
$3,350–4,000 ⚒ S(O)

◄ **A mahogany breakfront wardrobe,** the two central panelled doors enclosing a fitted tray and two drawers, flanked by doors enclosing hanging space, Dutch, 19thC, 84½in (214.5cm) wide.
£1,700–2,050 / €2,450–2,900
$2,950–3,500 ⚒ BR

A Victorian mahogany wardrobe, the two doors flanked by fluted columns and enclosing a partially fitted interior, above two drawers, 60in (152.5cm) wide.
£1,350–1,500 / €1,950–2,150
$2,250–2,500 ⊞ SWA

Wardrobes are a natural development from clothes and linen presses, the term first coming into use in the second half of the 18th century when it was popularized by George Hepplewhite. They were intended to hang clothing rather than storing it folded as in the earlier presses but did not entirely supersede these as storage furniture until the late 19th century. Hanging was often from pegs, as rails came in later with the use of coat hangers in the early 20th century.

A mahogany wardrobe, the panelled doors enclosing drawers and hanging rails, c1875, 54in (137cm) wide.
£650–780 / €930–1,100
$1,100–1,300 ⚒ NOA

A mahogany wardrobe, the recessed cupboard doors above five drawers flanked by cupboards, c1850, 84in (213.5cm) wide.
£1,300–1,550 / €1,900–2,250
$2,200–2,600 ⚒ NOA

A Victorian mahogany wardrobe, with a fitted interior, 81in (206cm) wide.
£410–490 / €590–700
$690–820 ⚒ B(Kn)

An Edwardian mahogany, marquetry-inlaid and kingwood-banded wardrobe, 85¾in (218cm) wide.
£780–930 / €1,100–1,300
$1,300–1,550 ⚒ BR

► **An Empire-style satinwood quarter-veneered armoire,** c1910, 74in (188cm) wide.
£1,600–1,800 / €2,300–2,600
$2,700–3,000 ⊞ SWA

A Victorian rosewood wardrobe, the panelled doors with carved decoration, 48in (122cm) wide.
£450–540 / €650–780
$760–910 ⚒ EH

A Victorian walnut-veneered breakfront wardrobe, the panelled doors enclosing hanging space and drawers, stamped 'Johnstone & Jeanes', 107½in (273cm) wide.
£1,100–1,300 / €1,600–1,900
$1,850–2,200 ⚒ WW

An Edwardian mahogany and satinwood-crossbanded compactum wardrobe, 65in (165cm) wide.
£820–980 / €1,200–1,400
$1,400–1,650 ⚒ B(Kn)

LOCATE THE SOURCE

The source of each illustration in Miller's can be found by checking the code letters below each caption with the Key to Illustrations, pages 794–800.

Washstands

A George III mahogany washstand, the hinged splash-back above a cupboard and a small drawer flanked by dummy drawers, 27in (68.5cm) wide.
£880–1,000
€1,250–1,450
$1,500–1,700 AH

A mahogany washstand, with a later top, c1775, 30in (76cm) high.
£520–580 / €750–840
$870–970 WAA

A George III mahogany washstand, 13½in (34cm) wide.
£120–145 / €170–200
$200–240 L

A George III mahogany washstand, 12½in (32cm) wide.
£360–430 / €520–620
$600–720 S(O)

A mahogany corner washstand, by Gillows of Lancaster, with boxwood stringing, stamped, 1780–1810, 23in (58.5cm) wide.
£1,300–1,450
€1,900–2,100
$2,200–2,450 WAA

► **A pair of George III mahogany bowfronted corner washstands,** c1800, 42¼in (107cm) high.
£840–1,000
€1,200–1,450
$1,400–1,650
S(O)

A George III mahogany washstand, the hinged top enclosing a mirror, above a dummy drawer, a cupboard and a real drawer, 16in (40.5cm) wide.
£100–120 / €145–170
$170–200 TRM

◄ **A mahogany washstand,** the top with cross-banding and box-wood stringing, above three frieze drawers, early 19thC, 43in (109cm) wide.
£1,200–1,450
€1,750–2,100
$2,000–2,400
DN

A George III mahogany washstand, the top enclosing a mirror and spaces for wash bowls above a dummy drawer front, 37½in (95cm) wide.
£230–270 / €330–390
$390–450 PFK

A mahogany corner washstand, the central frieze drawer flanked by two dummy drawers, top later, early 19thC, 26in (66cm) wide.
£370–440 / €530–630
$620–740 WW

A mahogany washstand, inset with a pottery bowl, early 19thC, 22½in (57cm) diam.
£400–480 / €580–690
$670–810 SWO

A marble washstand, the mirrored back above dummy drawers, c1850, 40¼in (102cm) wide.
£780–930 / €1,100–1,300
$1,300–1,550 S(O)

Further reading

Miller's Antiques Encyclopedia, Miller's Publications, 2003

Whatnots

A George III mahogany whatnot, with a bookcase, 46in (117cm) high.
£4,000–4,500
€5,800–6,500
$6,700–7,500 ⊞ GGD

A rosewood three-tier whatnot, with a drawer, on casters, 19thC, 39in (99cm) high.
£2,150–2,400
€3,100–3,450
$3,600–4,000 ⊞ WAA

A burr-walnut and brass-mounted three-tier whatnot, c1870, 37in (94cm) high.
£2,100–2,350
€3,000–3,400
$3,500–3,900 ⊞ GEO

A Regency mahogany whatnot, the top drawer above three tiers and a further drawer, losses, 20in (51cm) wide.
£960–1,150
€1,400–1,650
$1,600–1,900 ⚒ WW

A Victorian rosewood three-tier whatnot, each tier with a drawer, with spiral supports, c1840, 44¾in (114cm) high.
£1,100–1,300
€1,600–1,900
$1,850–2,200 ⚒ B(Kn)

A mahogany four-tier whatnot, with a cabinet, c1830, 64½in (164cm) high.
£2,400–2,900
€3,450–4,150
$4,000–4,800 ⚒ S(O)

A burr-walnut four-tier corner whatnot, c1860, 57in (145cm) high.
£1,000–1,150
€1,450–1,650
$1,700–1,950 ⊞ MTay

◄ **A Victorian walnut three-tier serpentine whatnot,** with a pierced fret gallery, baluster-turned supports and a base drawer, 45½in (115.5cm) high.
£700–840 / €1,000–1,200
$1,200–1,400 ⚒ AH

► **An ebonized three-tier whatnot,** c1900, 39¾in (101cm) high.
£700–840 / €1,000–1,200
$1,200–1,400 ⚒ S(O)

A pair of mahogany whatnots, c1830, 58in (147.5cm) high.
£8,300–9,200
€12,000–13,200
$14,000–15,500 ⊞ GEO

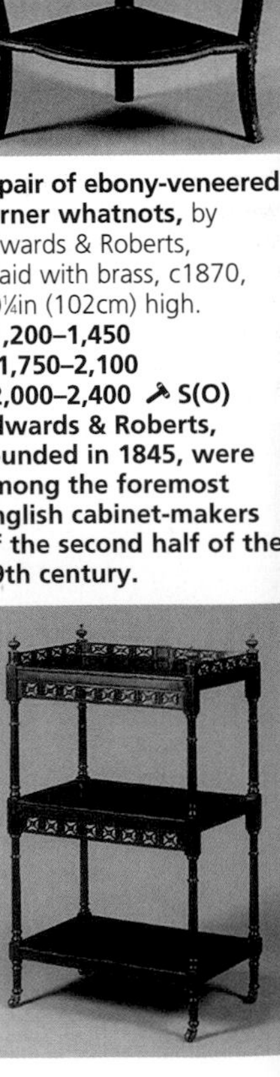

A pair of ebony-veneered corner whatnots, by Edwards & Roberts, inlaid with brass, c1870, 40¼in (102cm) high.
£1,200–1,450
€1,750–2,100
$2,000–2,400 ⚒ S(O)
Edwards & Roberts, founded in 1845, were among the foremost English cabinet-makers of the second half of the 19th century.

Window Seats

A carved giltwood window seat, with traces of painted decoration beneath later gilding, c1775.
£9,000–10,800 / €13,000–15,500
$15,100–18,100 S
Window seats similar to this example were supplied by Thomas Chippendale to Edwin Lascelles for Harewood House.

A painted birch window seat, Swedish, c1800, 43in (109cm) wide.
£2,600–2,900 / €3,700–4,200
$4,350–4,850 ⊞ CAV

A Louis XVI-style gilt and gesso window seat, c1830.
£2,450–2,750 / €3,500–4,000
$4,100–4,600 ⊞ GGD

► **A mahogany window seat,** c1830, 45in (114.5cm) wide.
£2,800–3,150 / €4,000–4,500
$4,700–5,300 ⊞ GEO

Further reading

Miller's Late Georgian to Edwardian Furniture Buyer's Guide, Miller's Publications, 2003

Wine Coolers

A brass-bound mahogany wine cooler, the lead-lined interior with seven compartments, c1780, 17in (43cm) wide.
£4,000–4,500
€5,800–6,500
$6,700–7,500 ⊞ JC

A brass-bound mahogany wine cooler, with a lead lining, c1780, 27in (68.5cm) high.
£3,900–4,400
€5,600–6,300
$6,500–7,400 ⊞ JeA

A George III satin-wood cellaret, with later decoration, 15½in (39.5cm) wide.
£2,000–2,400
€2,900–3,450
$3,350–4,000 B(Ed)

A George III brass-bound mahogany cellaret-on-stand, damaged, 19¼in (49cm) wide.
£840–1,000
€1,200–1,450
$1,400–1,650 S(O)

A George III brass-bound mahogany wine cooler, stamped 'Gillows, London and Lancaster', 21in (53.5cm) wide.
£6,100–7,300
€8,800–10,500
$10,200–12,200 TEN

A George III mahogany wine cooler, 16½in (42cm) diam.
£1,050–1,250
€1,500–1,800
$1,750–2,100 B(Kn)

A George III Chippendale-style mahogany wine cooler, with blind fret frieze, reeded sides and lead-lined interior, on a later plinth base and brass bun feet, 23¾in (60.5cm) wide.
£5,000–6,000
€7,200–8,600
$8,400–10,100 B

A George III brass-bound mahogany cellaret, with lead-lined interior, 23¼in (59cm) wide.
£960–1,150
€1,400–1,650
$1,600–1,900 S(O)

A pair of George III mahogany wine coolers, restored, 24in (61cm) wide.
£3,250–3,900 / €4,700–5,600
$5,400–6,500 S(O)

A George III mahogany wine cooler, with zinc liner, handles later, 26¾in (68cm) wide.
£1,050–1,250
€1,500–1,800
$1,750–2,100 B(Kn)

A mahogany wine cooler, in the manner of Gillows, with lead liner, on gadrooned feet with casters, c1830, 36½in (92.5cm) wide.
£6,400–7,700 / €9,300–11,100
$10,800–13,000 M

A Regency mahogany sarcophagus-shaped cellaret, 35in (89cm) wide.
£2,900–3,250 / €4,150–4,650
$4,850–5,400 GEO

A Regency oak wine cooler, on lion-paw feet, 29in (73.5cm) wide.
£6,000–6,700 / €8,600–9,700
$10,000–11,200 GGD

A Regency mahogany wine cooler, with lead liner, partitions missing, 28¼in (72cm) wide.
£2,250–2,700 / €3,250–3,900
$3,750–4,500 B(Kn)

A mahogany wine cooler, with a lead-lined divided interior, stamped for Wilkinson of London, c1830, 39¾in (101cm) wide.
£6,000–7,200 / €8,600–10,300
$10,000–12,000 S

The firm of Wilkinson was established c1790 by William Wilkinson, working in partnership with a relation, Thomas Wilkinson. By 1808, William had established a business of his own at 14 Ludgate Hill, London, and by 1825 had brought his two sons into the business, who continued to trade under the family name after their father's death in 1833. From this location Wilkinson built up a flourishing trade, winning significant commissions from such distinguished clients as the Goldsmiths Company. A versatile designer and craftsman, Wilkinson worked in a variety of styles, producing furniture in the Egyptian, rococo and Grecian styles.

A Regency mahogany sarcophagus-shaped wine cooler, with zinc liner, on claw feet, 27in (68.5cm) wide.
£7,200–8,000 / €10,400–11,500
$12,100–13,400 GGD

A Regency mahogany and crossbanded cellaret, on later lion-paw feet, 22in (56cm) wide.
£440–530 / €630–760
$740–890 B(Kn)

A mahogany cellaret, on stylized claw feet, c1830, 22in (56cm) high.
£4,700–5,200 / €6,700–7,500
$7,900–8,800 GEO

A William IV mahogany wine cooler, with brass handles, on bun feet with casters, 28in (71cm) wide.
£1,900–2,250 / €2,700–3,250
$3,200–3,800 CGC

◄ **A George II-style mahogany wine cooler,** with ring-turned legs and pad feet, c1880, 23in (58.5cm) diam.
£1,800–2,000 / €2,600–2,900
$3,000–3,350 GEO

► **A George III-style brass-bound mahogany wine cooler,** with brass handles, c1890, 17in (43cm) high.
£2,100–2,350 / €3,000–3,350
$3,500–3,900 GEO

Oak & Country Furniture

Today's market in oak and country furniture offers genuine opportunities to buyers at all levels. Middle- to lower-range pieces, largely suitable for country house furnishing, are still very affordable and compare favourably with contemporary alternatives. The higher end of the market and fine collector's pieces on the other hand are becoming increasingly rare and sought after – which has produced a strong rising market and a good opportunity for investment.

It has been widely reported that the growth in both interest and value of vernacular furniture has out-performed all other areas of the antique furniture market. There seems to be three main reasons for this. Firstly, 30 years ago when records of comparative values started to be collated, country furniture was the poor relation in the field. Fine walnut and mahogany were the market leaders and were in popular and growing demand. Oak and country pieces were therefore often overlooked, under appreciated and commensurately low in value, creating enormous scope for growth.

Secondly, as the world keeps changing, values and tastes gradually shift. It seems that nostalgia for old values and the 'back to nature' ethos have influenced the modern lifestyle. Organic food, small independent producers and artisans, folk music, 'peasant'-inspired clothing have all apparently benefited from this changed mood and interest.

Finally the individual, sometimes eccentric, nature of ancient country pieces ooze the kind of eclectic character that contemporary artists, designers and decorators have come to cherish. Oak and country furniture with its bold structural forms and solid timbers represents something solid and unpretentious. There is no veneer on its character and it is understood and appreciated for its honest lines and sometimes quirky details. Scars and bruises are borne proudly as evidence of age and years of service.

It is a combination of originality, colour, surface and character, the visible patination of age and wear, rich and crusty or naturally washed out and faded surfaces, sculptural forms and aesthetic lines, that go to make up 'the look'. Original painted decoration is enhanced by signs of wear, cracking, pitting, blooming, losses and crackelure. All of these are appreciated and searched for by an increasingly discerning collectors' market. Look for unusual scale, untouched condition, charm and personality. These characteristics are irresistible to the dedicated and enthusiastic collector. **Robert Young**

Beds & Cradles

An oak tester bed, the headboard with strapwork carving and panels, with later oak parts, 17thC, 63½in (161cm) wide.
£4,250–5,100 / €6,100–7,300
$7,100–8,500 ⚒ B(NW)

An oak tester bed, the headboard with guilloche carving above punchwork-decorated panels, 17thC, 74¾in (190cm) wide.
£2,100–2,500 / €3,000–3,600
$3,500–4,200 ⚒ B(NW)

An oak boarded cradle, with a pierced flowerhead motif, north European, c1700, 36¾in (93cm) long.
£95–110 / €135–160
$160–185 ⚒ S(O)

The children's furniture illustrated in this guide no longer complies with EC safety regulations and must not be used for its original purpose.

An oak cradle, on rockers, 18thC, 35in (89cm) long.
£470–560 / €670–800
$790–940 ⚒ HYD

► **A walnut rocking cradle,** the sides with scroll shaping, American, early 19thC, 40½in (103cm) wide.
£270–320
€390–460
$460–540
⚒ NOA

Benches

An oak boarded bench, with an ogee arched apron, losses, 16thC, 93in (236cm) long.
£2,750–3,300 / €4,000–4,750
$4,600–5,500 S(O)
Oak boarded benches or stools of the 16th century are seldom found.

An oak bench, repaired, Welsh, c1720, 70½in (179cm) long.
£1,900–2,300 / €2,700–3,300
$3,400–3,850 S(O)

► **A beech bench,** c1920, 63in (160cm) long.
£280–310 / €400–450
$470–520 DFA

A Charles II oak and elm joined bench, formerly with a central stretcher, 76in (193cm) long.
£670–800 / €960–1,150
$1,150–1,350 S(O)

An ash bench, 19thC, 86¾in (220cm) long.
£240–290 / €340–410
$400–480 SWO

Boxes

An oak desk box, with sloping lid and fitted interior, 1650–1700, 27in (68.5cm) wide.
£1,100–1,200 / €1,550–1,700
$1,800–2,000 KEY

An oak Bible box, with later iron handles, 18thC, 23½in (59.5cm) wide.
£310–350 / €440–500
$520–590 CHAC

An oak Bible box, the hinged lid above foliate strapwork, late 17thC, 26in (66cm) wide.
£240–290 / €340–410
$400–480 PF

◄ **An oak wall hanging candle box,** Welsh, c1760, 18¾in (47.5cm) high.
£340–380
€490–550
$570–640
F&F

An oak Bible box, the sloping lid with knotwork motifs and replacement hinges and lockplate, late 17thC, 30¼in (77cm) wide.
£210–250 / €300–360
$350–420 PFK

An oak Bible box, initialled, on later wrought-iron supports, 18thC, 21¾in (55.5cm) wide.
£220–260 / €310–370
$370–440 SWO

Buffets, Side Cabinets & Bookcases

A carved oak buffet, Flemish, early 16thC, 33½in (85cm) wide.
£3,000–3,600 / €4,300–5,200
$5,000–6,000 ⚒ S

An oak side cabinet, the later top above two doors enclosing a shelf, the left side with a frieze initialled 'IH', c1680, 60¼in (153cm) wide.
£600–720 / €860–1,000
$1,000–1,200 ⚒ S(O)

An oak country buffet, with two drawers above two doors, French, c1780, 53in (134.5cm) wide.
£1,600–1,800 / €2,300–2,600
$2,700–3,000 ⊞ DAC

► **A carved oak side cabinet,** the two frieze drawers above two cupboard doors, Flemish, 19thC, 58¾in (149cm) wide.
£330–390 / €470–560
$550–650 ⚒ B(Kn)

Further reading

Miller's Pine & Country Furniture Buyer's Guide, Miller's Publications, 2001

► **A walnut buffet,** 1800–25, 57in (145cm) wide.
£3,400–4,100
€4,900–5,900
$5,700–6,800
⚒ NOA

A Victorian oak library bookcase, the upper section with a moulded and carved cornice above four shelves, the lower section with a pair of panelled doors, 38¾in (98.5cm) wide.
£1,000–1,200
€1,450–1,700
$1,700–2,000 ⚒ HYD

A Gothic carved oak *buffet à deux corps*, French, 19thC, 51in (129.5cm) wide.
£2,150–2,400
€3,100–3,450
$3,600–4,000 ⊞ APO

► **A Louis XV-style fruitwood *buffet à deux corps*,** the glazed door flanked by two panelled cupboard doors, the lower section with three drawers above three cupboard doors, French, c1900, 62½in (159cm) wide.
£1,650–2,000
€2,450–2,900
$2,750–3,350 ⚒ NOA

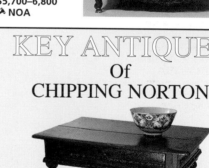

Paul Hopwell Antiques

Early English Oak

Dressers, tables and chairs always in stock

A fine Queen Anne oak three-drawer dresser base with shaped cockbeaded apron. On baluster-turned legs. English c1710

A Charles II oak-joined press cupboard. Decorated with tulips, strap and chip carving. English c1680

A small 17th century oak side table with single carved drawer. Gloucestershire c1700

Bureaux

An oak bureau-on-stand, the hinged sloping fall-front enclosing a fitted interior of pigeonholes and small drawers around a central well, above a frieze drawer, late 17thC, 28in (71cm) wide.
£1,000–1,200 / €1,450–1,700
$1,650–2,000 ⚒ B(NW)

An oak bureau, the fitted interior with a well, c1720, 33in (84cm) wide.
£1,650–2,000 / €2,400–2,900
$2,750–3,350 ⚒ S(O)

An early Georgian oak bureau, the fall-front enclosing a fitted interior with drawers and pigeon-holes, above two short and three long drawers, with later handles, 34in (86.5cm) wide.
£1,000–1,200 / €1,450–1,700
$1,650–2,000 ⚒ AH

Fall-front bureaux have been out of fashion for the last few years and prices have remained comparatively low. It is thought that flat-top desks and tables have been in higher demand because of their compatibility with home computers. With the widespread use of lap-tops and keen pricing of bureaux they could now be a very prudent investment. Look for an example 36in (91.5cm) wide or less, with a comprehensively fitted interior of pigeonholes, drawers and cupboards. A 'well' (a sliding compartment concealed within an interior to house writing paper and envelopes) is also desirable. With any piece of case furniture, original handles, escutcheons, locks and similar details are always value points, as are overall good condition, original feet, drawer linings, colour, original surface and patination.

An oak bureau, with a fitted interior, above four drawers, 18thC, 31in (78.5cm) wide.
£1,300–1,550 / €1,850–2,200
$2,200–2,600 ⚒ BWL

A George III oak bureau, the fall-front inlaid with a star motif and enclosing a fitted interior, above five drawers, 34in (86cm) wide.
£470–560 / €670–810
$790–940 ⚒ CHTR

A George III oak bureau, the fall-front enclosing a fitted interior, above four drawers, 36in (91.5cm) wide.
£510–610 / €730–870
$860–1,000 ⚒ NOA

An oak bureau, the fall-front enclosing a fitted interior, Dutch, 18thC, 41½in (105cm) wide.
£670–800 / €960–1,150
$1,100–1,300 ⚒ L&E

► **A George III oak bureau,** the fall-front enclosing a fitted interior, with later brass handles and escutcheons, on bracket feet, 37¾in (96cm) wide.
£470–560 / €670–800
$790–940 ⚒ DN

A George III oak bureau, the fall-front enclosing a fitted interior, above three drawers, 38in (96.5cm) wide.
£820–980 / €1,200–1,400
$1,400–1,650 ⚒ HYD

Bureau Cabinets

An oak bureau cabinet, the double dome bookcase with panelled doors enclosing pigeonholes and two drawers and two candle slides below, the lower section with a fall-front enclosing a stepped interior with a sliding well and three secret drawers, above two short and two long drawers, with later brass handles and bun feet, early 18thC, 38½in (98cm) wide.
£2,800–3,350
€4,000–4,800
$4,700–5,600 DMC

A George II oak bureau cabinet, the two panelled doors above a fall-front and four short and one long drawer, on bracket feet, 32¾in (83cm) wide.
£1,250–1,500
€1,800–2,150
$2,100–2,500 DN

► An elm bureau cabinet, c1780, 75in (190.5cm) high.
£3,750–4,200
€5,400–6,000
$6,300–7,000 ANAn

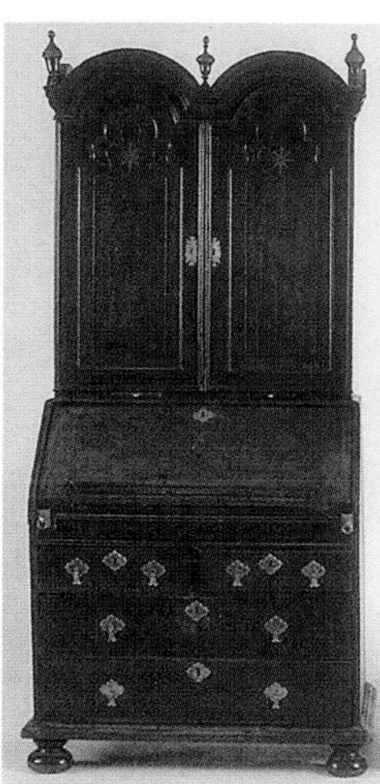

An oak bureau cabinet, the shaped doors with later inlay enclosing shelves, the lower section with a fall-front enclosing a stepped interior with drawers and pigeonholes around a well, above two short and two long drawers, with later brass handles and bun feet, 18thC, 36¼in (92cm) wide.
£3,400–4,100
€4,900–5,900
$5,700–6,900 B(NW)

► An oak and mahogany-crossbanded bureau cabinet, the panelled doors enclosing three adjustable shelves above a fall-front with a fitted interior, brushing slide, two short and three long graduated drawers, c1780, 45¾in (116cm) wide.
£3,800–4,500
€5,400–6,500
$6,400–7,600 S(O)

An oak bureau cabinet, the two arched doors with crossbanding and fruitwood line inlay, enclosing a part fitted interior, the cross-banded fall-front enclosing a fitted interior, above one long and three short drawers, mid-18thC, 31½in (80cm) wide.
£2,250–2,700
€3,200–3,900
$3,800–4,550 B(NW)

OAK & COUNTRY FURNITURE

Candle Stands

◄ An oak candle stand, c1700, 39in (99cm) high.
£2,000–2,400
€2,900–3,450
$3,350–4,000 S(O)

► An oak candle stand, with a rounded draft excluder, on a ring-turned shaft and tripartite down-swept legs, mid-18thC, 36½in (92.5cm) high.
£6,600–7,900
€9,500–11,400
$11,100–13,300 B(NW)
This piece is desirable because the candle shield is particularly tall and the stand has excellent proportions, scale and colour. These factors, combined with rarity, lead to a high value.

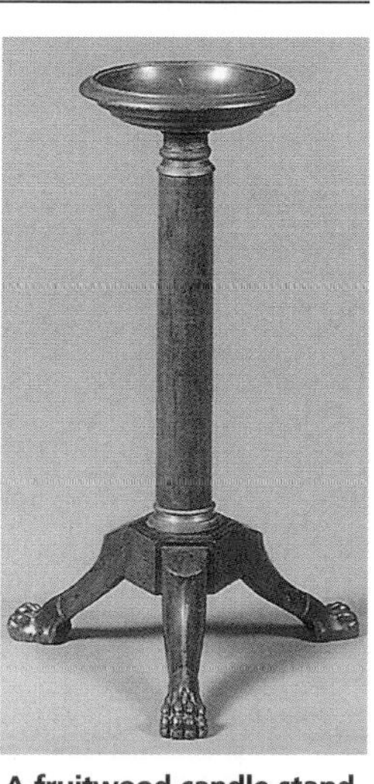

A fruitwood candle stand, with gilt-metal mounts, French, early 19thC, 28in (71cm) high.
£720–860 / €1,000–1,200
$1,200–1,450 S(O)

Chairs

A walnut friar's chair, with reeded finials, downscrolling arms, leather seat and back, Spanish, c1600.
£3,100–3,700
€4,450–5,300
$5,200–6,200 ⚒ S

A pair of oak side chairs, one depicting Charles II at his coronation and the other the allegorical figure of Autumn, both carved with the family initials 'HHM' in the triangular formation associated with a marriage, Lancashire, c1660.
£12,100–13,500
€17,500–19,400
$20,400–22,700 ⊞ KEY

It is very probable that these two chairs have come from a larger set with the other seasons being portrayed and the portrait of the king being added to celebrate the restoration of the monarchy. The carved back panels with the caryatids flanking the central figures in an arcaded surround are of a style popular in the earlier 17th century and would perhaps suggest the chairs were made for an old, established family with traditional royalist values.

An oak open armchair, 17thC.
£1,150–1,300
€1,650–1,850
$1,900–2,200 ⊞ APO

An oak armchair, the scrolled top rail above an inlaid panelled back and scrolled downswept arms, Yorkshire, late 17thC.
£1,400–1,650
€2,000–2,350
$2,350–2,750 ⚒ AH

An oak lambing armchair, the shaped crest above a fielded panel and shaped side panels, above a drawer, on four stile supports, probably Yorkshire, c1760.
£4,700–5,600
€6,800–8,100
$7,900–9,500 ⚒ Bri

This chair is desirable because of the bold wings, well shaped crest rail, broad arms and original drawer.

An oak armchair, Yorkshire, 1620–30.
£3,150–3,500
€4,500–5,000
$5,300–5,900 ⊞ KEY

An oak chair, with a panelled back, Lancashire, c1690.
£1,350–1,500
€1,900–2,150
$2,250–2,500 ⊞ SEA

An oak corner chair, on splayed peg legs, Welsh, 18thC.
£940–1,100
€1,350–1,600
$1,550–1,850 ⚒ CGC

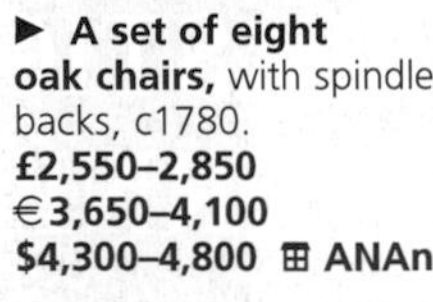

► **A set of eight oak chairs,** with spindle backs, c1780.
£2,550–2,850
€3,650–4,100
$4,300–4,800 ⊞ ANAn

An oak rocking chair, the panelled back carved with 'Ruth 1689', 17thC.
£300–360 / €430–520
$500–600 ⚒ G(L)

An oak wing armchair, painted, with leather upholstery, c1700.
£6,750–7,500
€9,700–10,800
$11,300–12,600 ⊞ RYA

An ash and sycamore Windsor comb-back armchair, with traces of original paint, 1760–80.
£3,800–4,200
€5,500–6,000
$6,400–7,000 ⊞ RYA

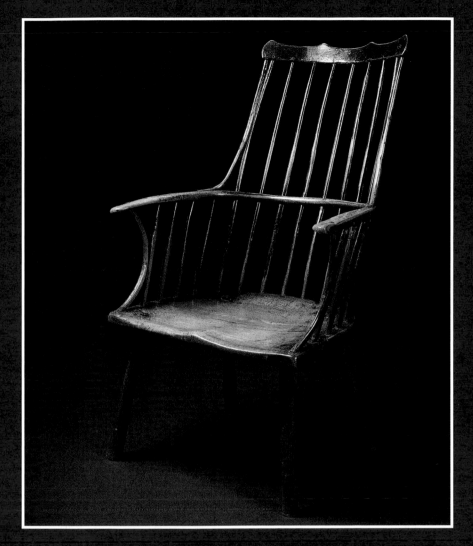

A pair of yew wood Windsor chairs, with pierced splats, turned supports and crinoline stretchers, c1800.
£2,900–3,500
€4,150–5,000
$4,850–5,900 E

Windsor chairs

Windsor chairs are currently enjoying enormous popularity. It is individual qualities that the market values. With primitive comb-back chairs, look for a quirky piece. A shaped saddle or tractor seat, well shaped and defined cresting rail and generous height and width are all value points. With traditional double bow Windsors, yew wood remains the choice timber. Maker's name, branded initials and provenance all add interest and value, as do crinoline stretchers, interestingly shaped splats and original full length legs. It is important to inspect these chairs very carefully for originality and authenticity as restorers have historically rebuilt chairs out of old elements. Genuine untouched colour and patination and original paint surface where applicable is of the upmost importance.

An ash and pine wing-back armchair, the solid back and seat on square tapering legs, early 19thC.
£2,700–3,200
€3,900–4,600
$4,500–5,400 DN
The design of this attractive, country-made chair is extremely rare.

A fruitwood, beech and elm Windsor chair, from the High Wycombe area, c1820.
£1,100–1,200
€1,550–1,700
$1,800–2,000 SEA

An elm Windsor chair, with a spindle back, on turned supports, 19thC.
£100–120 / €145–170
$170–200 WilP

◄ **An elm and ash smoker's bow,** c1850.
£400–450 / €580–650
$670–750 MIN

A japanned rocking chair, the curved crest rail above turned splats and overscrolled arms, stencilled with Oriental scenes, foliage and fruit, possibly American, 19thC.
£1,900–2,300
€2,750–3,300
$3,200–3,850 S

An elm and beech smoker's bow, c1870.
£430–480 / €620–690
$720–810 COF

► **An ash and elm elbow chair,** with a shell motif and a rush seat, Lancashire, c1870.
£300–330 / €430–480
$500–550 WiB

Miller's Compares

I. An ash and elm comb-back Windsor chair, the narrow top rail above a spindle back, bowed arms and block seat, on splayed peg legs, 19thC.
£4,000–4,800
€5,800–6,900
$6,700–8,000 CGC

II. An ash and elm comb-back Windsor chair, the bowed top rail above a spindle back, bowed arms and block seat, on splayed peg legs, 19thC.
£420–500 / €600–720
$700–840 CGC

These two chairs are very similar in appearance but all the interest in the saleroom focused on Item I, because of its small sculptural comb and the inward curving sticks to the upper part, which is known as a 'lobster pot' back. This lends great character to the chair and is aesthetically more pleasing than the square upright line of Item II. Item I also retains much of its original green paint and has a desirable saddle-shaped seat. In contrast, the less attractive seat of Item II has a split through it which greatly reduces its value and desirability, resulting in it failing to reach its reserve in the auction room and selling after the sale for a tenth of the price of Item I.

Miller's Compares

I. A set of eight ash dining chairs, including two open armchairs, with ladder backs and rush seats, Lancashire, 19thC.
£1,700–2,000
€2,450–2,900
$2,850–3,350 WW

II. A set of four ash side chairs, with ladder backs, solid seats and turned supports, worm damage, 19thC.
£410–490 / €590–700
$690–820 WW

One might think that a set of eight chairs would sell for approximately double the price of a similar set of four chairs, but in fact the differential between these two sets is more than quadruple. This is in part due to the fact that Item I has the advantage of including a pair of open armchairs but, more importantly, a set of eight chairs is far less common, and more desirable, than a set of four. Item I also has attractive patination and vastly superior crest rails to those of Item II although the rush seats are in need of repair.

A pair of oak stick-back chairs, c1875.
£340–380 / €490–550
$570–640 Byl

A pair of oak chairs, with spindle backs, c1890.
£430–480 / €620–690
$720–810 AMG

A set of four ash and elm bow-back Windsor chairs, c1880.
£810–900 / €1,150–1,300
$1,350–1,500 PICA
This set of chairs could be American in origin. Round seated models with broad arms are commonly seen in Connecticut and New England.

A beech smoker's bow, c1910.
£150–165 / €210–240
$250–280 PaA

OAK & COUNTRY FURNITURE

Children's Chairs

A child's chestnut boarded commode chair, 17thC.
£780–930 / €1,150–1,300
$1,300–1,550 S(O)

A late Victorian child's ash and elm chair.
£220–250 / €320–360
$370–420 SDA

A George II child's elm, oak and walnut rocking chair, on cabriole legs and rockers, some repairs.
£1,100–1,300
€1,600–1,900
$1,850–2,250 TEN
It is unusual to find a country child's chair of such quality. This is a rare and quirky interpretation of a George II period open armchair with well detailed and carved arms and legs. The condition is poor (there are iron brace repairs to the top rail) but in spite of this a high price was achieved. This is a rare collectable piece.

A child's beech Windsor armchair, with a painted top rail, on turned supports, 19thC.
£140–170 / €200–240
$240–290 PF

The children's furniture illustrated in this guide no longer complies with EC safety regulations and must not be used for its original purpose.

▶ **A child's beech side chair,** late 19thC.
£110–120 / €160–170
$180–200 F&F

A Victorian child's elm Windsor rocking chair, with oak rockers.
£400–450 / €570–650
$670–750 MFB

Chests & Coffers

An oak clamp front ark, with a carved lid, c1535, 31½in (80cm) wide.
£3,100–3,700 / €4,450–5,300
$5,200–6,200 S(O)
The ark is a development of the clamp-fronted chest of the Middle Ages and would have been used in the kitchen to store grains, flour, meal and bread. The lids were not originally attached, so they could be inverted to serve as kneading troughs or even as hand barrows with the insertion of carrying poles.

An oak blanket box, the hinged top with four panels, the frieze carved with scrolled strapwork, 17thC, 62½in (159cm) wide.
£560–670 / €800–960
$940–1,100 DD

An oak coffer, with bog oak and poplar inlay, Leeds, c1680, 48in (122cm) wide.
£1,800–2,000 / €2,600–2,900
$3,000–3,350 KEY
The front of this piece has distinctive lozenge carving surrounded by deeply carved pennants with scrolling terminals. Dog-tooth inlay of bog oak and poplar outlines the panels on the stiles and rails. The carving and inlay are common to a group of furniture from this area with other examples in St John's Church, Leeds and at Bolling Hall, Leeds.

A boarded oak chest, with a carved front panel, with later strap hinges, altered and restored, c1600, 50½in (128cm) wide.
£1,000–1,200 / €1,450–1,700
$1,700–2,000 BR
A genuine unrestored example of an early Gothic coffer of this type would sell for £8,000–12,000 / €11,500–17,300 / $13,400–20,200.

A boarded oak chest, 17thC, 33¾in (85.5cm) wide.
£150–180 / €220–260
$250–300 BR

◄ A carved and panelled oak coffer, 17thC, 39in (99cm) wide.
£910–1,100 / €1,300–1,550
$1,550–1,850 TMA

An oak coffer, the twin-panelled top and front with a central carved muntin, 17thC, 38½in (98cm) wide.
£440–520 / €630–750
$740–870 L

A carved oak coffer, c1680, 29½in (75cm) wide.
£1,200–1,350 / €1,700–1,900
$2,000–2,250 F&F

► A William and Mary oak, elm and fruitwood mule chest, the hinged top above pierced corbels, three panels with two short drawers and one long drawer, 43¼in (110cm) wide.
£1,300–1,550 / €1,850–2,200
$2,200–2,600 HYD

An oak and inlaid 'nonsuch' chest, with some later inlay and mouldings to the front, restorations, c1615, 46½in (118cm) wide.
£2,750–3,300 / €4,000–4,700
$4,600–5,500 S(O)
'Nonsuch' chests were elaborately inlaid and made in Germany or the Low Countries, or by German or Flemish craftsmen working in England in the late 16th and 17th centuries. They are distinctive for their patterned architectural inlays on a background of intricate mosaic wood. 'Nonsuch' chests are so named because they depict elements of the famous Nonsuch Palace built by Henry VIII and lost to fire. It was reportedly a fabulous palace with no expense spared on the decoration which used imported exotic woods, including pine which at the time was not indigenous to southern England.

An oak coffer, the hinged top above a panelled and carved front, with a later iron clasp, 17thC, 37in (94cm) wide.
£440–520 / €630–750
$740–870 NSal

An oak coffer, the moulded top above three panels, with a candle box, raised on stile supports, initialled, c1680, 52in (132cm) wide.
£970–1,150 / €1,400–1,650
$1,600–1,900 F&C

An inlaid oak coffer, the two-piece plank top above a parquetry-inlaid frieze and four panels with relief-carved lozenges, late 17thC, 60in (152.5cm) wide.
£610–730 / €880–1,000
$1,000–1,200 ⚒ PF

An oak mule chest, with a panelled and hinged top above a front and sides with two drawers, early 18thC, 63¾in (162cm) wide.
£440–520 / €630–750
$740–870 ⚒ DN

A George I oak mule chest, with four Gothic arched panels converted to cupboard doors, above three drawers, early 18thC, 56in (142cm) wide.
£940–1,100 / €1,350–1,600
$1,600–1,850 ⚒ HYD

An oak mule chest, the hinged plank top above a front with raised fielded panels and two drawers, 18thC, 51in (129.5cm) wide.
£460–550 / €660–790
$770–920 ⚒ JM

An oak and mahogany-banded mule chest, the hinged top enclosing a candle box, above six drawers, late 18thC, 74in (188cm) wide.
£1,100–1,300 / €1,600–1,850
$1,850–2,200 ⚒ E

A Louis XIV oak coffer, the panelled sides with geometric and scroll carving, restorations, French, 67½in (171.5cm) wide.
£1,000–1,200 / €1,450–1,700
$1,700–2,000 ⚒ NOA

An oak blanket chest, the hinged top enclosing a candle box, the front with four panels, early 18thC, 61in (155cm) wide.
£230–270 / €330–390
$380–450 ⚒ WL

An oak blanket chest, the interior fitted with a tray and a drawer, above two drawers, on a platform base, 18thC, 50in (127cm) wide.
£420–500 / €600–720
$700–840 ⚒ CUN

A George III oak mule chest, the top with three panels enclosing a candle box, the panelled front with initials, date and two drawers, three bale handles missing, 55½in (141cm) wide.
£230–270 / €330–390
$380–450 ⚒ PFK

An oak *coffor bach*, the loose top above a plain front with a single drawer, Welsh, late 18thC, 24in (61cm) wide.
£470–560 / €670–800
$790–940 ⚒ PF

An oak coffer, the front with three geometric moulded panels, losses, c1700, 44½in (113cm) wide.
£470–560 / €670–800
$790–940 ⚒ SWO

An oak mule chest, the top with three panels, above a hand-carved frieze, three panels and two short drawers, early 18thC, 48in (122cm) wide.
£230–270 / €330–390
$380–450 ⚒ SWO

An oak coffer, the hinged and panelled top above an arcaded frieze with lozenge inlaid panels, 18thC, 49½in (125.5cm) wide.
£1,000–1,200 / €1,450–1,700
$1,700–2,000 ⚒ DMC

A George III yew wood mule chest, with two short drawers, 35½in (90cm) wide.
£750–900 / €1,100–1,300
$1,250–1,500 ⚒ L

An oak linen chest, the hinged top above six dummy drawers and three real drawers, Lancashire, c1800, 61in (155cm) wide.
£640–760 / €920–1,100
$1,100–1,300 ⚒ B(Kn)

Chests of Drawers

An oak chest of drawers, with simulated wild grain walnut and geometrically-moulded decoration, later handles, 1670–90, 40in (101.5cm) wide.
£6,700–7,500 / €9,700–10,800 $11,300–12,600 ⊞ RYA
This is one of a few surviving examples of early provincial case and joined frame furniture paint-decorated to simulate figured walnut on an oak or pine carcass.

An oak chest of drawers, with applied geometric mouldings, 17thC, 30in (76cm) high.
£2,550–2,850 / €3,700–4,100 $4,300–4,800 ⊞ ANAn

An oak chest of drawers, the four long drawers with geometric mouldings, on stile feet, c1680, 38½in (98cm) wide.
£2,900–3,500 / €4,200–5,000 $5,000–5,900 ⚒ WW

Miller's Compares

I. An oak chest of drawers, in two sections, the drawer fronts inlaid with fruitwood, 17thC, 40½in (103cm) wide.
£2,000–2,400 / €2,900–3,450 $3,350–4,000 ⚒ L

II. An oak chest of drawers, with four long drawers, 17thC, 36¾in (93.4cm) wide.
£590–700 / €850–1,000 $1,000–1,200 ⚒ L

These two chests of drawers are of the same period and style and both have four long drawers. Item I, however, benefits from being constructed in two parts, having a broad dentilled cornice, a cushion or coffered moulded front with interesting geometric shapes, narrow and broad drawer configuration and a rich overall colour and patination. Despite being larger than Item II, these details make it more desirable.

Moulded front chests of drawers

Prices for these vary enormously and, apart from overall originality, colour and patination, there are a few other general points to look for. The earlier examples tend to split into two parts beneath the second of four drawers. The drawers of these chests are usually side-hung, meaning that the side drawer linings have a deep groove cut into them that houses a bearer fixed inside the carcass, which acts as a support for each drawer. A complex variety of geometric and cushioned mouldings always adds interest, particularly when there is a marked difference in the depth of each drawer. Unlike later Georgian chests which have a graduated column of drawers, the better early chests tend to have a drawer configuration. Small and low-waisted chests always tend to fetch high prices but three-drawer chests remain generally less popular than those with four long or two short and three long drawers.

An oak chest of drawers, in two parts, on bun feet, c1680, 41¾in (106cm) wide.
£1,200–1,450 / €1,700–2,000 $2,000–2,400 ⚒ S(O)

◄ An oak and walnut chest of drawers, the two parts with carved decoration, the four long drawers with geometric moulding, on bun feet, c1680, 47in (119.5cm) wide.
£2,350–2,800 / €3,350–4,000 $3,900–4,700 ⚒ B(NW)

An oak chest of drawers, with two short and three long drawers, c1680, 35in (89cm) wide.
£3,200–3,600 / €4,600–5,100 $5,350–6,000 ⊞ TRI

Further reading

Miller's Late Georgian to Edwardian Furniture Buyer's Guide, Miller's Publications, 2003

An oak chest of drawers, on later bracket feet, c1690, 36¾in (93.5cm) wide.
£1,800–2,150 / €2,600–3,100
$3,000–3,600 S(O)

An oak chest of drawers, with two short over three long drawers and panelled sides, on turned bun feet, handles later, marked 'W. D.', early 18thC, 41½in (105.5cm) wide.
£530–630 / €760–910
$890–1,100 WW

The chest of drawers evolved in Britain during the 17th century, although the coffer was still the principal item of storage furniture at that time. The concept of the drawer became widespread from the mid-16th century, due to the popularity of the Spanish *vargueño*, a chest which incorporated numerous small drawers in its design. In general, British furniture did not contain drawers until the end of the 16th century, when they were added to coffers and cabinets. They were called 'tills' or 'drawing boxes', which gave rise to the word 'drawer'. The chest of drawers in the form that we know it dates from the end of the 17th century.

An oak chest of drawers, the two short and three long drawers with geometric mouldings, with panelled sides and stile feet, handles later, late 17thC, 47in (119.5cm) wide.
£590–700 / €850–1,000
$1,000–1,200 AH

A Queen Anne oak chest of drawers, the two short and three long drawers with geometric moulding, on later bun feet, 36in (91.5cm) wide.
£3,600–4,300 / €5,200–6,200
$6,000–7,200 S

A George III oak chest of drawers, with two short over three long drawers, on bracket feet, with later handles and escutcheons, 37½in (95.5cm) wide.
£560–670 / €800–960
$940–1,100 DN

◀ **A George III oak chest of drawers,** with two short over three long graduated drawers, on bracket feet, 22¼in (56cm) wide.
£590–700 / €850–1,000
$990–1,200 AMB

▶ **A George III oak chest of drawers,** with two short over three long drawers, on bracket feet, 31in (78.5cm) high.
£2,000–2,200 / €2,900–3,200
$3,350–3,700 ANAn

An oak and elm chest of drawers, with two short and three long drawers, on bun feet, early 18thC, 38½in (98cm) wide.
£440–530 / €630–760
$740–890 G(B)

A cherrywood and walnut *bombé* chest of drawers, with three long drawers, French, c1750, 48in (122cm) wide.
£14,400–16,000 / €20,700–23,000
$24,200–27,000 RYA
This is a fine example of early French provincial rococo furniture. It is raised on rare carved *pieds de biche* and has a delicately shaped apron.

A George III oak chest of drawers, with two short and three long drawers, on bracket feet, 35in (89cm) wide.
£700–840 / €1,000–1,200
$1,200–1,400 L

A Louis XVI fruitwood chest of drawers, distressed, French, 38¼in (97cm) wide.
£700–840 / €1,000–1,200
$1,200–1,400 ⚒ B(Kn)

A George III oak chest of drawers, with mahogany crossbanding, the brushing slide over two short and two long drawers, on bracket feet, 34½in (87.5cm) wide.
£880–1,050 / €1,250–1,500
$1,450–1,750 ⚒ AH

◄ An oak chest of drawers, the shaped frieze over three short and three long drawers, on bracket feet, East Anglian, early 19thC, 31½in (80cm) wide.
£1,050–1,250 / €1,500–1,800
$1,750–2,100 ⚒ SWO

► A Regency oak chest of drawers, the four drawers over a serpentine apron, on tapering legs, 36¾in (93.5cm) wide.
£350–420 / €500–600
$590–700 ⚒ EH

An oak chest of drawers, with mahogany crossbanding and two short over three long drawers, early 19thC, 40¾in (103.5cm) wide.
£590–700 / €850–1,000
$1,000–1,200 ⚒ SWO

OAK & COUNTRY FURNITURE

Chests-on-Stands

An oak chest-on-stand, with four long drawers and a double scroll-shaped apron, on stile feet, 17thC, 38in (96.5cm) wide.
£640–770 / €920–1,100
$1,150–1,300 ⚒ TRM

► An oak chest-on-stand, the moulded dentil cornice over two short and three long walnut-crossbanded graduated drawers, the stand with two deep and one short drawer, on cabriole legs, early 18thC, 40½in (103cm) wide.
£3,000–3,600 / €4,300–5,200
$5,000–6,000 ⚒ B(NW)

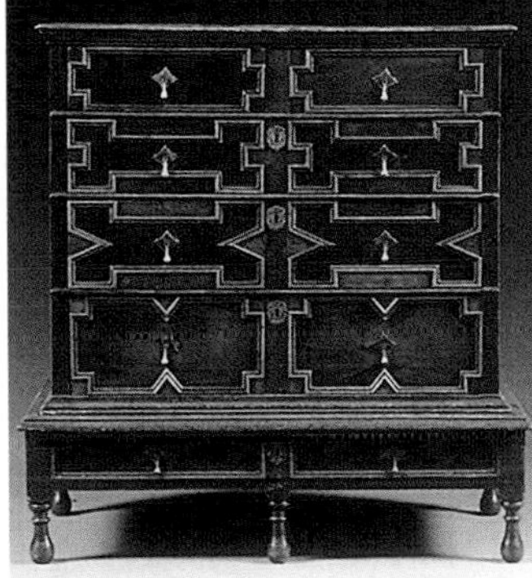

An oak chest-on-stand, with panelled sides and back and geometrically moulded drawers, c1700, 42½in (107.5cm) wide.
£1,400–1,650 / €2,000–2,350
$2,350–2,750 ⚒ S(O)

◄ An elm chest-on-stand, with fitted secretaire, northern England, c1760, 44in (112cm) wide.
£18,000–22,000 / €26,000–31,700
$30,200–37,000 ⊞ RYA

A George III oak chest-on-stand, the two short over three long drawers above a pierced scrollwork apron, on square legs, 40in (101.5cm) wide.
£2,700–3,250 / €3,900–4,700
$4,550–5,400 ⚒ PF

Clothes & Linen Presses

An oak and marquetry-inlaid clothes press, the stepped inverted cornice above two panelled doors with inlaid spandrels, over two dummy drawers and two short frieze drawers, on block feet, c1700, 63in (160cm) wide.
£5,200–6,200 / €7,500–8,900
$8,700–10,400 ⚒ WL

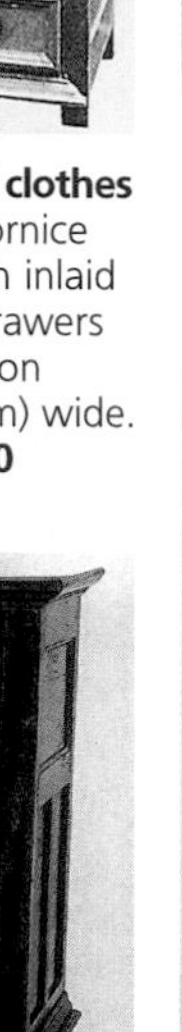

A George III oak clothes press, the fielded panelled doors above an arrangement of four small drawers, 54in (137cm) wide.
£940–1,100 / €1,350–1,600
$1,550–1,850 ⚒ HYD

► **An oak clothes press,** the shaped and moulded panelled doors flanked by reeded pilasters, over five dummy drawers and a long drawer, 18thC, 51½in (131cm) high.
£1,200–1,450 / €1,700–2,000
$2,000–2,400 ⚒ SWO

A George II oak clothes press, in two parts, associated, Welsh, 51½in (131cm) wide.
£1,800–2,150 / €2,600–3,100
$3,000–3,600 ⚒ S(O)

A George III oak clothes press, the two ogee panelled doors enclosing hanging space, flanking similar central panel, over six small drawers, handles and feet later, 72in (183cm) wide.
£3,500–4,200 / €5,000–6,000
$5,900–7,000 ⚒ AH

◄ **An oak clothes press,** the two fielded panelled doors enclosing a shelf, over five short drawers, on bracket feet, Welsh, early 19thC, 54in (137cm) wide.
£1,050–1,250 / €1,500–1,800
$1,750–2,100 ⚒ PF

An oak clothes press, the raised and fielded panelled doors above four crossbanded and cockbeaded drawers, with panelled sides, c1750, 56¼in (143cm) wide.
£1,950–2,350 / €2,800–3,350
$3,250–3,900 ⚒ DD

A George III oak linen press, the breakfront cornice above two panelled doors flanked by fluted pilasters, the base with three drawers, 56¾in (144cm) wide.
£2,100–2,500 / €3,000–3,600
$3,500–4,200 ⚒ PFK

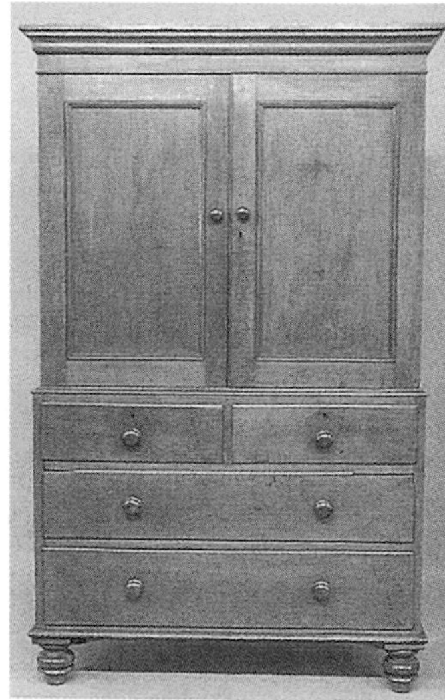

An oak linen press, the two doors enclosing shelves, above two short and two long drawers, on turned feet, Welsh, c1850, 49in (124.5cm) wide.
£440–530 / €630–760
$740–890 ⚒ PF

Cupboards

An oak and walnut cupboard, the two pairs of doors with raised panels, each carved with a lozenge, enclosing shelves, on block feet, Spanish, c1600, 47¾in (121.5cm) wide.
£5,700–6,800 / €8,200–9,800
$9,600–11,400 ⚒ S(Am)

► **An oak *cwpwrdd deuddarn*,** the doors flanked by turned supports, over two cupboard doors, Welsh, part 17thC, 52in (132cm) wide.
£1,300–1,550 / €1,850–2,200
$2,200–2,600 ⚒ HOLL

An oak wall cupboard, with a fielded panelled door, 17thC, 23¼in (59cm) wide.
£180–210 / €260–300
$300–350 ⚒ EH

A Charles II oak food cupboard, with later additions, 26in (66cm) wide.
£840–1,000 / €1,200–1,450
$1,400–1,650 ⚒ S(O)

An oak and rosewood cupboard, the panelled doors enclosing shelves and two drawers, restored, later additions, Dutch, 17thC, 57in (145cm) wide.
£1,650–1,950 / €2,350–2,800
$2,750–3,250 ⚒ S(Am)

An oak cupboard, altered, Flemish, 17thC, 50½in (128.5cm) wide.
£330–390 / €470–560
$550–650 S(O)

An oak ***cwpwrd deuddarn,*** restored, Welsh, c1700, 51in (129.5cm) high.
£4,000–4,500 / €5,800–6,500
$6,700–7,500 ANAn

An oak cupboard, with four panelled doors and two drawers, French, 18thC, 74in (188cm) high.
£2,100–2,350 / €3,000–3,350
$3,550–4,000 ANAn

An oak press cupboard, with carved rails and stiles, the upper section with two moulded doors over two narrow drawers, the lower section with a single panelled door and a matching panel, marked 'WMD', north Lancashire, c1680, 60in (152.5cm) wide.
£6,500–7,200 / €9,400–10,400
$10,900–12,100 KEY
This press cupboard belongs to a group of cupboards found in the Trough of Bowland in Westmorland, northern England, which all have characteristic finely curled, flat, strap carving. This specific carving style spans a long period from a known press cupboard dated 1658 from that area to another dated example from 1712. The duration of this style would suggest the very settled and somewhat isolated nature of the local people with a strong tradition of passing down a family trade of joinery and wood-carving through several generations. In these remote areas styles of furniture carried on unchanged long after one would expect, untouched by the latest fashions being set further south in areas with access to London.

A chestnut armoire, carved and painted, French, Brittany, c1770, 50½in (128.5cm) wide.
£5,800–6,500 / €8,400–9,400
$9,700–10,900 RYA

◄ **An oak** ***cwpwrd deuddarn,*** the projecting cornice with drop finials above two panelled doors, the lower section with three short drawers above two panelled doors, Welsh, 18thC, 44in (112cm) wide.
£2,800–3,350 / €4,000–4,800
$4,700–5,600 B(NW)

An oak press cupboard, with later carving, probably Cumbria, c1700, 52½in (133.5cm) wide.
£1,800–2,150 / €2,600–3,100
$3,000–3,600 S(O)
The Celtic entwined double heart motif is used on furniture found from areas with strong Celtic traditions, such as Wales, Cumbria and the West Country. It is also found on furniture from New England in the USA.

An oak press cupboard, the frieze carved with initials 'WSMS' and dated 1705, over two panelled doors and fixed panel, above two drawers and two panelled doors, early 18thC, 45¼in (115cm) wide.
£2,350–2,800 / €3,400–4,000
$4,000–4,700 TEN

An oak armoire, with carved decoration, the two panelled cupboard doors above two short drawers over two panelled cupboard doors, Flemish, 18thC, 51in (129.5cm) wide.
£560–670 / €800–960
$940–1,120 WW

An oak, pine and satin birch-inlaid cupboard, German, 18thC, 65in (165cm) wide.
£600–720 / €870–1,050
$1,000–1,200 ⚒ S(O)

A George III oak cabinet-on-chest, the two panelled doors over two short and three long drawers, 43½in (110.5cm) wide.
£1,300–1,450 / €1,900–2,100
$2,200–2,450 ⊞ PaA

For further information on
Cupboards see pages 191–196

An oak corner cupboard, c1800, 39in (100cm) high.
£700–800 / €1,000–1,150
$1,150–1,300 ⊞ F&F

An oak corner cupboard, with a panelled door, c1760, 37½in (95.5cm) high.
£660–740 / €950–1,050
$1,100–1,250 ⊞ F&F

An oak *cwpwrdd tridarn*, restored and altered, Welsh, c1780, 54¾in (139cm) wide.
£1,650–1,950 / €2,350–2,800
$2,750–3,250 ⚒ S(O)

A corner cupboard, the scrolled cornice over two panelled doors enclosing three shelves, above two base cupboard doors, c1800, 40½in (103cm) wide.
£640–760 / €920–1,100
$1,100–1,300 ⚒ WL

A George III oak housekeeper's cupboard, the cornice inlaid with mahogany, the panelled doors enclosing an interior with pegs, the base with real and dummy drawers, 71in (180.5cm) wide.
£3,200–3,800 / €4,600–5,500
$5,400–6,400 ⚒ L

An oak corner cupboard, with two pairs of panelled doors, Welsh, c1780, 38in (96.5cm) wide.
£4,000–4,500 / €5,800–6,500
$6,700–7,600 ⊞ KEY

A cherrywood armoire, the wire panels replaced, French, c1830, 51in (129.5cm) wide.
£1,450–1,650 / €2,100–2,350
$2,400–2,750 ⊞ GD

An oak corner cupboard, the two astragal-glazed doors enclosing serpentine-shaped shelves, over two panelled doors, Welsh, c1850, 43in (109cm) wide.
£940–1,100 / €1,350–1,600
$1,600–1,900 ⚒ PF

Early panels

In the 19th century a great deal of furniture was made in 16th- or 17th-century style, sometimes incorporating genuine early carved panels. It is therefore worth examining such pieces carefully, as their value lies mainly in these panels. Non-ecclesiastical figure-carved or 'Romayne Head' panels are particularly sought after, as well as representations of dragons and other mythological beasts. Also potentially of considerable interest and value are panels with vigorous and deeply carved floral, stylized geometric, plain linenfold and heraldic designs.

► **An oak ecclesiastical-style side cupboard,** the door and side panels moulded with figures of saints, with an open shelf below, late 19thC, 38in (96.5cm) wide.
£470–560 / €680–800
$800–940 ⚒ GAK

A Gothic-style oak low cupboard, with removable single plank top, two panels probably 16thC, 19thC, 76in (193cm) wide.
£3,950–4,750 / €5,700–6,800
$6,600–7,900 ⚒ S(O)

An elm cupboard, with two panelled doors, central European, c1895, 45in (114.5cm) wide.
£880–980 / €1,250–1,400
$1,450–1,650 ⊞ COF

Spice Cupboards

► **An oak spice cupboard,** with a single panelled door, 17thC, 12in (30.5cm) wide.
£1,300–1,450 / €1,900–2,100
$2,200–2,450 ⊞ ANAn

An oak spice cupboard, the interior with ten drawers, c1680, 21in (53.5cm) wide.
£1,050–1,250 / €1,500–1,800
$1,750–2,100 ⚒ S(O)

► **An oak spice cupboard,** the single door enclosing a shelf and 12 small drawers, 18thC, 16in (40.5cm) wide.
£210–250 / €300–360
$350–420 ⚒ G(L)

A George III oak spice cupboard, the fielded panelled door enclosing a shelf and four short and one long drawer, with later handles, on a later stand, 21in (53.5cm) wide.
£210–250 / €300–360
$350–420 ⚒ BR

Dressers

An oak dresser, Welsh, c1720, 77in (195.5cm) high.
£10,800–12,000 / €15,000–17,300 $18,100–20,100 ⊞ KEY

An oak dresser, the upper section with an inlaid frieze and shelves, the lower section with three frieze drawers and three further drawers flanked by panelled doors, Welsh, 18thC, 77in (168cm) wide.
£3,500–4,200 / €5,000–6,000 $5,900–7,000 ⚒ CGC

An oak dresser, the rack with three shelves, the base with three drawers over arcaded supports, probably Welsh, mid-18thC, 57¾in (146.5cm) wide
£2,350–2,800 / €3,300–4,000 $3,900–4,700 ⚒ Bri

An oak dresser, the frieze with iron hooks above three shelves, the base with three drawers, a pot board and pierced spandrels, rack reduced in height, early 18thC, 72in (183cm) wide.
£5,900–7,100 / €8,500–10,200 $9,900–11,900 ⚒ TEN

An oak dresser, French, 18thC, 62in (157.5cm) wide.
£3,400–3,750 / €4,900–5,400 $5,700–6,300 ⊞ MTay

An oak dresser, the associated rack with two central shelves flanked by six shelves, the lower section with three drawers above an ogee-shaped frieze, raised on block and turned legs, rear leg replaced, mid-18thC, 82in (208cm) wide.
£4,700–5,600 / €6,800–8,100 $7,900–9,400 ⚒ B(NW)

► **An oak dresser,** the rack with two spice cupboards, the base with two drawers and profile baluster supports, Welsh, c1760, 61in (155cm) wide.
£4,800–5,700 / €6,900–8,300 $8,100–9,600 ⚒ S(O)

A George II oak dresser, the associated rack with three shelves and spice drawers, on cabriole legs, 78in (198cm) wide.
£3,300–4,000 / €4,750–5,700 $5,500–6,700 ⚒ TEN

An oak dresser, Shropshire, c1750, 78in (198cm) high.
£4,300–4,800 / €6,200–6,900 $7,200–8,000 ⊞ ANAn

An oak dresser, the rack with two plate shelves supported by later brackets, the base with three frieze drawers, restorations, Welsh, mid-18thC, 73¼in (186cm) wide.
£1,750–2,100 / €2,500–3,000 $2,900–3,500 ⚒ BR

A George III oak and mahogany-crossbanded dresser, the rack flanked by cupboards, the base with seven drawers around a central cupboard with panelled doors and inlaid paterae, 84¾in (215cm) wide.
£5,400–6,500 / €7,800–9,400 $9,100–11,000 ⚒ B(EA)

A George III oak dresser, the upper section with a row of shallow dummy drawers, 60in (152cm) wide.
£2,350–2,800 / €3,400–4,000 $4,000–4,700 ⚒ L

A fruitwood dresser, the open rack above two drawers, c1790, 58in (147cm) wide.
£1,400–1,650 / €2,000–2,400 $2,350–2,750 ⚒ S(O)

► **An oak dresser,** the rack above a base with boxwood and ebony line-inlay, three frieze and three central drawers flanked by two cupboards and turned side columns, late 18thC, 65½in (166.5cm) wide.
£2,800–3,350 / €4,000–4,800 $4,700–5,600 ⚒ JM

The word dresser comes from the French *dressoir*, an item of furniture used in the main body of the house for displaying valuables or for serving wine, or in the service quarters for preparing food and storing crockery and cutlery. In Britain, the earliest dressers consisted of a side table with drawers on turned legs; the incorporation of a pot board dates from the late 17th century. Superstructures came into being after c1650 to display the tin-glazed earthenware which had become so fashionable. Dressers were particularly popular in Wales, northwest and southwest England, each type having strong regional characteristics. Examples from Wales and southwest England typically have an open rack and an open base below the pot board. Those from north Wales and northern England are nearly always 'closed' – ie with boards behind the shelves in the upper part and a cupboard base. Some mid-Wales dressers combine the northern and southern forms, having boarded racks with pot boards below.

A George III oak dresser, the rack with a shaped pediment, shelves and two panelled doors, the lower section with three long and two short drawers, 86in (218.5cm) wide.
£3,000–3,600 / €4,300–5,200 $5,000–6,000 ⚒ G(L)

An oak dresser, the reduced plate rack with four hooks above three shelves, the base with three relined frieze drawers, later feet, late 18thC, 67in (170cm) wide.
£1,750–2,100 / €2,500–3,000 $3,000–3,500 ⚒ WW

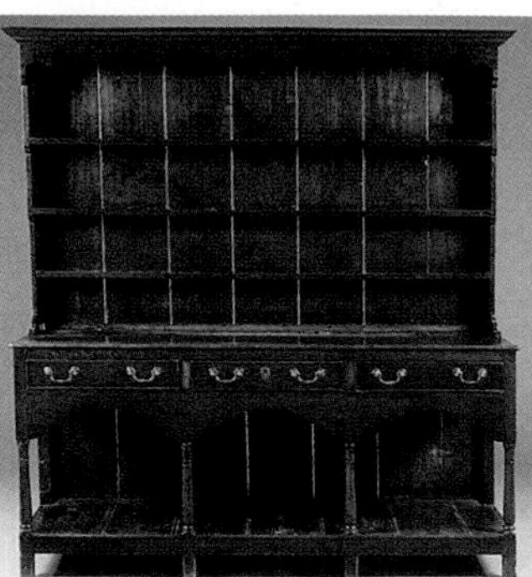

A George III oak dresser, the associated rack with a shaped frieze, 76in (193cm) wide.
£6,400–7,600 / €9,300–11,100 $10,800–12,900 ⚒ TEN

An oak and mahogany dresser, the later boarded rack with shelves flanked by cupboards, the lower section with three drawers, Shropshire, late 18thC, 72¾in (185cm) wide.
£3,000–3,600 / €4,300–5,200 $5,000–6,000 ⚒ B(NW)

An oak dresser, the rack with shelves and five short drawers, the base with three frieze and three central drawers, late 18thC, 75½in (192cm) wide.
£4,000–4,800 / €5,800–6,900 $6,700–8,000 ⚒ WW

An oak and mahogany-banded dresser, with open shelves above a base with five drawers, on turned supports, with a pot board, late 18thC, 61in (155cm) wide.
£1,650–2,000 / €2,400–2,900
$2,750–3,350 E

An oak dresser, the later rack with shelves and five spice drawers, the lower section with three drawers above two cupboard doors, late 18thC, 61¾in (157cm) wide.
£1,000–1,200 / €1,450–1,700
$1,700–2,000 B(NW)

An oak dresser, c1810, 54in (137cm) wide.
£6,100–6,800 / €8,800–9,700
$10,200–11,300 F&F

An oak, walnut and mahogany dresser, the rack with shelves above a base with six drawers and two panelled doors, stamped 'Fro D. Morgan, cabinet maker, Carnarvon', later handles, Welsh, early 19thC, 65in (165cm) wide.
£3,300–4,000 / €4,750–5,700
$5,500–6,700 SWO

An oak and elm dresser, the rack with four shelves above three frieze drawers, on turned legs joined by an undertier, some restoration, early 19th, 74¾in (190cm) wide.
£2,600–3,100 / €3,750–4,450
$4,350–5,200 Bea

An oak dresser, the upper section with hooks to the frieze above elm shelves, the lower section with three frieze drawers and later brass handles, with a pot board base, 19thC, 62½in (159cm) wide.
£1,900–2,300 / €2,750–3,300
$3,200–3,850 WW

Items in the Oak & Country Furniture section have been arranged in date order within each sub-section.

An oak dresser, the upper section with three shelves, the lower section with three drawers and a shaped alcove, with later cupboard doors, Welsh, mid-19thC, 62in (157.5cm) wide.
£880–1,000 / €1,250–1,450
$1,450–1,700 PF

An oak, pine and inlaid dresser, the rack with three shelves above a breakfront base with one real and three dummy drawers flanked by spiral columns, two drawers and panelled cupboards, Welsh, probably Caernarfonshire, mid-19thC, 63in (160cm) wide.
£3,500–4,200 / €5,000–6,000
$5,900–7,000 TEN

An oak dresser, with carved panelled doors, c1930, 48in (122cm) wide.
£1,200–1,350 / €1,700–1,900
$2,000–2,250 MTay

Low Dressers

An oak low dresser, with applied geometric mouldings, 17thC, 73½in (186.5cm) wide.
£5,600–6,300 / €8,100–9,000
$9,400–10,500 ⊞ ANAn

A yew wood serving dresser, with maker's mark 'IB', c1690, 75in (190.5cm) wide.
£19,800–22,000 / €28,500–32,000
$33,000–37,000 ⊞ RYA
Yew is the most highly prized of the indigenous English hardwoods. It is a slow growing evergreen tree that produces dense, tightly grained timber, which develops a rich honey colour and lustrous patina with the passage of time. This is a fine and important piece of William and Mary period solid yew wood furniture, with exceptional surface and patina.

Although dressers were typically made of oak, finer examples were made of elm, ash, fruitwood, yew, chestnut and walnut. Those made in Wales, the west Midlands, Derbyshire, Yorkshire and the northwest of England tended to be important show-pieces to be passed down from generation to generation.

◄ **An oak dresser base,** on cabriole legs, 18thC, 48in (122cm) wide.
£940–1,100
€1,350–1,600
$1,550–1,850
PF

An oak low dresser, with three drawers, decorated with mahogany crossbanding, 18thC, 79in (200.5cm) wide.
£1,750–2,100 / €2,500–3,000
$2,900–3,500 AG

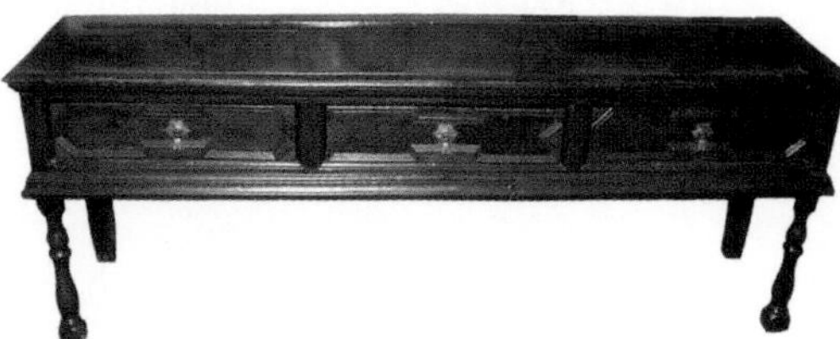

An oak low dresser, c1650, 76in (186.5cm) wide.
£7,100–7,900 / €10,200–11,300
$11,900–13,200 ⊞ ANAn

An oak low dresser, the plank top above three short drawers, applied with geometric mouldings, on turned legs with block feet, late 17thC, 76¾in (195cm) wide.
£4,100–4,900 / €5,900–7,000
$6,900–8,200 B(NW)

► **An oak dresser base,** the top above two fielded panelled drawers and cupboard doors, restored, Welsh, c1730, 45in (114cm) wide.
£1,800–2,150
€2,600–3,100
$3,000–3,600
S(O)

An oak low dresser, with three drawers flanked by two smaller drawers above two drawers and two cupboards, 18thC, 69in (175.5cm) wide.
£3,200–3,800 / €4,600–5,500
$5,400–6,400 CUN

An oak low dresser, with crossbanding and satinwood and boxwood inlay, northern England, 18thC, 75in (190.5cm) wide.
£5,400–6,000 / €7,700–8,600
$9,100–10,100 ⊞ ANAn

An oak low dresser, with three frieze drawers, on cabriole legs, mid-18thC, 77¾in (197.5cm) wide.
£2,450–2,900 / €3,500–4,150
$4,100–4,850 B(NW)

An oak dresser base, the rear legs with quadrant turning to the reverse, c1760, 77½in (197cm) wide.
£2,750–3,300 / €4,000–4,750
$4,600–5,500 S(O)

A George III oak dresser, the boarded top above three frieze drawers with mahogany banding, later handles, on cabriole legs, 72in (183cm) wide.
£2,000–2,400 / €2,900–3,450
$3,350–4,000 WW

A George III oak breakfront dresser, with one drawer above a panelled cupboard flanked by six graduated drawers, 70¾in (180cm) wide.
£1,200–1,450 / €1,750–2,100
$2,000–2,400 DD

An oak low dresser, crossbanded in plum wood, Midlands, c1750, 74½in (189cm) wide.
£8,100–9,000 / €11,700–13,000
$13,600–15,100 ANAn

A George III oak low dresser, the boarded top above seven drawers and two panelled cupboard doors, 74½in (189cm) wide.
£3,500–4,200 / €5,000–6,000
$5,900–7,000 TEN

An oak dresser, the later boarded top above two short drawers, on square tapering legs, c1810, 58¼in (148cm) wide.
£540–640 / €780–920
$910–1,100 WL

An oak and birch low dresser, the boarded top above a bank of four drawers flanked by two drawers and cupboards, early 19thC, 60¼in (153cm) wide.
£820–980 / €1,200–1,400
$1,400–1,650 TEN

◄ **An oak dresser,** the boarded top above three panelled frieze drawers and two cupboard doors with quarter panel fronts, 19thC, 59in (150cm) wide.
£1,000–1,200 / €1,450–1,700
$1,700–2,000 WW

Lowboys

An oak lowboy, the three frieze drawers above a shaped apron, on cabriole legs, late 17thC, 30in (76cm) wide.
£820–980 / €1,200–1,400
$1,400–1,650 TRM

A George III oak lowboy, 32in (81cm) wide.
£470–560 / €670–800
$790–940 L

An oak lowboy, the three drawers above a shaped apron, on cabriole legs, c1740, 30¼in (77cm) wide.
£660–790 / €950–1,150
$1,100–1,300 S(O)

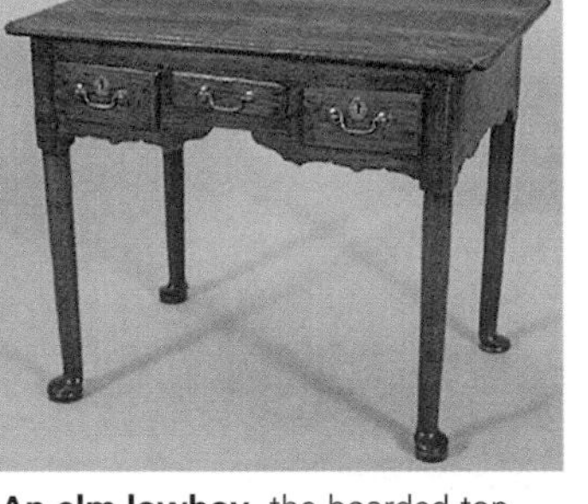

An elm lowboy, the boarded top above three frieze drawers fitted with later brass handles, above a shaped apron, on cabriole legs, 18thC, 30¾in (78cm) wide.
£800–960 / €1,150–1,400
$1,350–1,600 WW

◄ **An oak lowboy,** the three drawers above a shaped apron, early 19thC, 34in (86cm) wide.
£1,000–1,200 / €1,450–1,700
$1,700–2,000 SWO

► **A Georgian oak lowboy,** the three drawers above a shaped apron, 32¾in (83cm) wide.
£450–540 / €650–780
$760–910 WilP

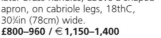

An oak lowboy, the three drawers above a shaped apron, on cabriole legs, mid-18thC, 33in (84cm) high.
£1,100–1,300 / €1,600–1,900
$1,850–2,200 NSal

An oak lowboy, the three drawers above a shaped apron, on cabriole legs, late 18thC, 29¼in (74.5cm) wide.
£2,500–2,800 / €3,600–4,000
$4,200–4,700 KEY

Racks & Shelves

A carved and painted oak and pine hanging wall shelf, with carved inscriptions and dated 'Anno 1717', Danish, 22in (56cm) wide.
£2,900–3,200 / €4,150–4,600
$4,850–5,400 RYA

A set of birchwood hanging shelves, c1825, 29¾in (75.5cm) high.
£310–350 / €440–500
$520–590 F&F

An oak Champagne fermenting rack, early 20thC, 59in (150cm) high.
£220–250 / €320–360
$370–420 HRQ

Settles

A Gothic coffer bench, the carved and pierced back above a hinged seat with one upright panelled armrest, alterations, Franco-Flemish, late 15thC, 57in (145cm) wide.
£9,600–11,500 / €13,800–16,600 $16,100–19,300 S
Towards the end of the Gothic period, because of the expense of furniture, craftsmen began to create multi-purpose items, of which this is a perfect example: integrating a coffer with a bench.

A George II oak settle, the back with four panels, on short cabriole legs, seat missing, 76in (193cm) wide.
£370–440 / €530–630 $620–740 HYD

A Charles I oak folding bench/ table, the hinged seat with an associated top, 48in (122cm) wide.
£740–890 / €1,100–1,300 $1,250–1,500 S(O)

An oak settle, the back with five arched panels, the later solid seat on cabriole legs, mid-18thC, 73¾in (187cm) wide.
£760–910 / €1,100–1,300 $1,250–1,500 DN

► **An elm enclosed settle,** West Country, c1800, 73in (185.5cm) high.
£2,350–2,600 / €3,400–3,750 $3,900–4,350 ANAn

◄ **A George III oak settle,** the panelled back with carved decoration, the loose cushioned seat above baluster tapering legs, 63in (160cm) wide.
£760–910 / €1,100–1,300 $1,250–1,500 L&E

An ebonized oak settle, carved 'IMC 1708', early 18thC, 79½in (202cm) wide.
£610–730 / €880–1,000 $1,000–1,200 L

An elm and pine settle, the panelled back above a boarded seat, 18thC, 65½in (166cm) wide.
£350–420 / €500–600 $590–700 CHTR

OAK & COUNTRY FURNITURE

Stools

A Charles I pair of oak joint stools, the moulded tops above ring-turned tapering legs, losses, 18in (45.5cm) wide.
£4,700–5,600 €6,800–8,100 $7,900–9,400 WW

An oak joint stool, 17thC, 19in (48.5cm) wide.
£1,350–1,500 €1,900–2,150 $2,250–2,500 SEA

An oak and walnut joint stool, the moulded top above turned legs and stretchers, c1660, 18in (45.5cm) wide.
£2,500–2,800 €3,600–4,000 $4,200–4,700 KEY

An oak joint stool, the two seat rails with many impressed initials, 17thC, 19in (48.5cm) wide.
£560–670 / €800–960 $940–1,100 LAY

For further information on
Stools see pages 105–107

Miller's Compares

I. A Charles I oak joint stool, the seat with a moulded edge, on turned legs united by squared stretchers, 18¼in (46.5cm) wide.
£3,800–4,550
€5,500–6,600
$6,400–7,500 ⚒ HYD

II. A Charles I oak joint stool, the seat with a moulded edge, on turned legs united by squared stretchers, 19¼in (49cm) wide.
£1,400–1,700
€2,000–2,400
$2,350–2,850 ⚒ HYD

Item I is thought to be somewhat earlier in date than Item II, but a close study of the two pieces will reveal that Item I is also more elegant in appearance. Its slightly thinner top and the flat moulding around it are both attractive features, and there was some thought that the top of Item II might have been replaced. Moreover, the legs of Item I are more pleasing than those of Item II – they are angled slightly outwards and the turning is more pronounced. The worn stretcher of Item I is also more appealing than that of Item II which shows little wear. Furthermore, Item I is of a far superior colour, which is always a major factor influencing furniture values.

A Charles II oak joint stool, the moulded top above baluster-turned tapering legs, with stretchers and turned feet, 19in (48.5cm) wide.
£2,100–2,500
€3,000–3,600
$3,500–4,200 ⚒ HYD

An oak joint stool, restored, late 17thC, 19in (48.5cm) wide.
£390–430 / €560–620
$660–720 ⊞ CHAC

A pair of oak joint stools, the moulded tops above chamfered legs and stretchers, early 18thC, 19in (48.5cm) wide.
£1,200–1,450
€1,750–2,100
$2,000–2,400 ⚒ HYD

A beech joint stool, c1720, 18in (45.5cm) wide.
£2,700–3,000
€3,900–4,300
$4,500–5,000 ⊞ SEA
This stool is unusual because it is a hybrid of a 17th-century-style joint stool, with the added desirable feature of a X-stretcher, combined with the dished seat typical of 18th- and 19th-century Windsor chairs.

A birchwood stool, c1830, 15in (38cm) high.
£70–80 / €100–115
$115–130 ⊞ F&F

An ash and elm country stool, with turned legs, c1840, 8in (20.5cm) wide.
£50–60 / €70–80
$85–100 ⊞ F&F

An ash stool, with turned legs, c1840, 14in (35.5cm) high.
£60–70 / €85–100
$100–115 ⊞ F&F

An elm milking stool, c1880, 18in (45.5cm) high.
£55–65 / €80–95
$95–110 ⊞ MIN

◄ An oak milking stool, Irish, c1880, 12in (30.5cm) high.
£30–35 / €45–50
$50–55 ⊞ Byl

► An ash and elm milking stool, Irish, c1880, 17in (43cm) wide.
£30–35
€45–50
$50–55 ⊞ Byl

An ash and elm milking stool, Irish, c1880, 11in (28cm) high.
£30–35 / €45–50
$50–55 ⊞ Byl

An oak country stool, with a rush seat, c1920, 16in (40.5cm) high.
£55–65 / €80–95
$95–110 ⊞ AMG

Tables

An oak draw-leaf extending dining table, with a plank top on four bulbous turned legs united by stretchers, Dutch, 17thC, 83in (211cm) extended.
£3,400–4,100 / €4,900–5,900
$5,700–6,900 PF

A walnut table, on two folding supports in the form of lyres joined by iron stretchers, restorations, Spanish, 17thC, 49¾in (126cm) wide.
£3,100–3,700 / €4,450–5,300
$5,200–6,200 S(Am)

An oak gateleg table, 17thC, 62¼in (158cm) wide.
£7,900–8,800 / €11,400–12,700
$13,300–14,800 NMA

A walnut side table, on ring-turned legs, with later bun feet and stretchers, Spanish, mid-17thC, 50¾in (129cm) wide.
£2,700–3,200 / €3,900–4,600
$4,500–5,300 B

► A Charles II oak credence gateleg table, the hinged leaf above a drawer, 29½in (75cm) extended.
£1,800–2,150 / €2,600–3,100
$3,000–3,600 S(O)
A credence table was originally used for storing food before serving or tasting. It has now come to denote a semi-circular table with a hinged top.

An oak gateleg table, with a drawer to one end, 17thC, 48½in (123cm) wide.
£630–750 / €910–1,100
$1,000–1,200 L

A chestnut and fruitwood side table, the top above a frieze drawer and a shaped apron, south European, 17thC, 39in (99cm) wide.
£560–670 / €800–960
$940–1,100 B(Kn)

An oak centre table, Derbyshire, 1650–1700, 29in (73.5cm) high.
£7,200–8,000 / €10,300–11,500
$12,100–13,400 KEY

An oak gateleg table, c1670, 52in (132cm) wide.
£5,000–5,500 / €7,200–8,000 $8,400–9,300 ⊞ ANAn

An oak side table, the carved frieze with a drawer, on ring-turned legs above an undertier with a central frieze drawer, alterations, late 17thC, 43in (109cm) wide.
£1,300–1,550 / €1,850–2,200 $2,200–2,600 ⚒ B(NW)

An oak side table, c1680, 27½in (70cm) wide.
£1,800–2,000 / €2,600–2,900 $3,000–3,350 ⊞ ANAn

An oak cricket table, with a single drawer, c1700, 26in (66cm) diam.
£1,550–1,850 / €2,200–2,650 $2,600–3,100 ⚒ S(O)

◄ **An oak occasional table,** with a frieze drawer, on baluster-turned legs joined by stretchers, on turned feet, top warped, early 18thC, 23in (58.5cm) wide.
£870–1,000 / €1,250–1,400 $1,450–1,700 ⚒ WW

► **An oak side table,** restored, Welsh, c1740, 31in (79cm) wide.
£1,300–1,550 / €1,850–2,250 $2,200–2,600 ⚒ S(O)

A William and Mary oak side table, with a single drawer above twist and baluster-turned legs and a flat cross stretcher, with one replaced board, 31½in (80cm) wide.
£910–1,000 / €1,300–1,550 $1,550–1,850 ⚒ SWO

An oak double gateleg dining table, the top above a shaped apron and baluster-turned legs united by stretchers, early 18thC, 68in (172.5cm) wide.
£1,650–2,000 / €2,400–2,900 $2,750–3,350 ⚒ PF

Miller's Compares

I. An oak side table, c1710, 35½in (90cm) wide.
£3,450–4,100 / €5,000–5,900 $5,800–6,900 ⚒ S(O)

II. An oak side table, the triple plank top above a later lined drawer, c1710, 32½in (81cm) wide.
£960–1,150 / €1,400–1,650 $1,650–1,900 ⚒ S(O)

Item I has very elegant proportions with a generous overhang to the top over the frame, above slender baluster-turned legs and an exceptional shaped X-stretcher. It appears to have a rich patina and possibly original brass. Item II is more solid in appearance, the plain moulded plank top has a stepped moulding beneath and little overhang. It is a plainer ginger colour and has box stretchers.

Side tables

The scale and proportion of 17th- and early 18th-century side tables can greatly influence value. A generous overhang of the top to the base is always a plus point, particularly when the outside edge has a bold shaped moulding all round. Drawers are also a desirable feature, either a single full width or, more particularly, a group of three which changes the description from side table to lowboy. In all cases a shaped frieze rail or apron is always more sought after than a plain straight one. Where replaced feet may be considered acceptable on farmhouse dining tables that have stood on damp floors, in the case of side tables it is important that the original feet remain intact in order for the piece to carry the premium value.

An oak side table, with a frieze drawer, on turned legs joined by stretchers, 18thC, 30in (76cm) wide.
£470–560 / €680–810
$790–940 CHTR

An oak drop-leaf table, with an end frieze drawer, 18thC, 41¼in (105cm) wide.
£640–770 / €920–1,100
$1,100–1,300 CGC

An oak side table, 18thC, 26in (66cm) high.
£1,350–1,500 / €1,900–2,150
$2,250–2,500 ANAn

An oak gateleg dining table, with a single drawer, on turned and squared legs with stretchers, 18thC, 48in (122cm) wide.
£330–400 / €480–580
$550–670 TRM

An oak cricket table, the plank top on three chamfered legs, 18thC, 26in (66cm) wide.
£300–360 / €430–520
$500–600 HYD

An oak gateleg dining table, the drop-leaf top with a single frieze drawer, on turned legs and stretchers, 18thC, 58in (147cm) extended.
£230–270 / €330–390
$390–450 TRM

◄ **A carved oak centre table,** the plank top above a frieze drawer flanked by two dummy drawers, French, 18thC, 102½in (260cm) wide.
£6,000–7,200
€8,600–10,300
$10,100–12,100
S

A George III oak table, 30in (76cm) diam.
£1,100–1,200 / €1,600–1,750
$1,800–2,000 KEY

A cherrywood Pembroke table, refinished, American, probably Connecticut, c1800, 35½in (90cm) wide.
£540–650 / €780–930
$910–1,100 COBB

An oak side table, the plank top above a frieze drawer and pierced bracket quatrefoils, late 18thC, 26¼in (66.5cm) wide.
£820–980 / €1,200–1,400
$1,400–1,650 WW

A fruitwood table, with a marble top, French, 19thC, 39½in (100.5cm) wide.
£450–500 / €650–720
$750–840 SIE

◄ **An oak farmhouse table,** with one real and one dummy end drawer, c1800, 67¼in (171cm) wide.
£780–930 / €1,100–1,300
$1,300–1,550 S(O)

OAK & COUNTRY FURNITURE

A Queen Anne-style oak refectory table, the plank top above an arched frieze, on baluster-turned legs, some restorations, early 19thC, 107½in (273cm) wide.
£3,100–3,700 / €4,450–5,300
$5,200–6,200 S(O)

This table was removed from Hengwrt, Merioneth, Wales, (meaning 'old court'), and was the seat of the Owen family. Their daughter Margaret was the mother of Robert Vaughan, the eminent Welsh antiquary, whose manuscript collection was housed at Hengwrt. The main body of the house was demolished after a fire in 1962 but this table was situated in what once formed the service quarters of the house and which, today, bears the name of its distinguished predecessor.

An oak side table, the top above two boxwood-strung frieze drawers, early 19thC, 34¾in (88cm) wide.
£410–490 / €590–700
$690–820 DN

An oak tripod table, the tilting top on a baluster-form splat and cabriole legs, early 19thC, 27½in (70cm) wide.
£640–770 / €920–1,100
$1,100–1,300 NOA

An oak occasional table, on turned legs, mid-19thC, 32in (81.5cm) wide.
£510–610 / €730–880
$850–1,000 NOA

A fruitwood draw-leaf table, feet retipped, French, c1860, 169½in (431cm) extended.
£1,550–1,850 / €2,250–2,650
$2,600–3,100 S(O)

◄ **An oak cricket table,** with an undertier, 19thC, 25¼in (64cm) diam.
£560–670 / €800–960
$940–1,100 EH

► **An oak cricket table,** Welsh, c1880, 18in (45.5cm) wide.
£2,000–2,250 / €2,900–3,250
$3,350–3,800 SEA

An oak country table, the plank top above two drawers, early 19thC, 53½in (136cm) wide.
£2,000–2,400 / €2,900–3,450
$3,350–4,000 Bri

An oak cricket table, with a plank top, 19thC, 28in (71cm) diam.
£470–560 / €670–800
$790–940 WW

A Victorian oak refectory dining table, with a foliate and mask carved frieze, 70in (178cm) wide.
£680–810 / €980–1,150
$1,150–1,350 B(Kn)

Cricket & tripod tables

Considerable value is attached to circular or oval country occasional table tops being formed from a single plank. A generous thick top is also usually considered desirable. Check for any sign of interference to the underside of the top – marriages are worth only a fraction of genuine untouched examples. Any old screw holes, oxidized nail holes, filler, patches or shadow marks should be treated with caution and suspicion.

An oak and ebony parquet wind-out dining table, on leaf-carved oak rails and cup and cover legs with casters, with six extra leaves in a panelled and carved oak cabinet, inscribed 'AD 1868', 141¾in (360cm) wide.
£23,500–28,200 / €34,000–41,000
$39,000–47,000 ⚒ TEN
The most unusual parquet-effect ebony top of this table combined with the rich carving and impressive size resulted in it selling for over double the top estimate.

A Victorian stained oak draw-leaf table, the carved frieze on cup and cover supports, 95¾in (243cm) wide.
£1,450–1,750 / €2,100–2,500
$2,450–2,900 ⚒ DN

A Victorian 17thC-style oak serving table, 43in (109cm) wide.
£410–490 / €590–700
$690–820 ⚒ B(Kn)

A carved oak side table, c1880, 54in (137cm) wide.
£1,550–1,750 / €2,200–2,500
$2,600–2,900 ⊞ MTay

An oak and elm refectory table, the plank top on faceted legs, restored, c1880, 93¾in (238cm) wide.
£1,000–1,200 / €1,450–1,700
$1,700–2,000 ⚒ S(O)

OAK & COUNTRY FURNITURE

A carved oak demi-lune side table, late 19thC, 32¾in (83cm) wide.
£560–670 / €800–960
$940–1,100 ⚒ B(Kn)

An oak table, the plank top on shaped end supports joined by iron stretchers, Spanish, c1900, 87in (221cm) wide.
£1,600–1,900 / €2,300–2,750
$2,700–3,200 ⚒ NOA

An oak gateleg occasional table, early 20thC, 27in (68.5cm) wide.
£760–850 / €1,100–1,200
$1,250–1,400 ⊞ ANAn

◄ **An oak gateleg occasional table,** early 20thC, 23in (58.5cm) wide.
£400–450 / €570–650
$670–750 ⊞ ANAn

A carved oak side table, c1920s, 30in (76cm) high.
£210–240 / €300–350
$350–400 ⊞ MTay

Early 20th-century gateleg tables

Copies of gateleg tables from the 1920s and 1930s generally have barley-twist legs and broad ogee mouldings around the 'egg-shaped' oval tops. They also tend to have a 'Jacobethan' dark-coloured varnish and the mortice-and-tenon joints of the stretchers are frequently inset from the stile of the leg, whereas in period examples they are flush-fitted. On 17th-century examples the joints are also pegged, and the pegs have often lifted slightly and may be uneven, or square. Also check the hinges: period examples tend to have large iron butterfly or 'H' hinges, whereas copies usually have plain brass or steel butt hinges. Furthermore, copies rarely have fitted drawers and often have high 'tulip'-shaped turned feet below the stretchers.

Pine Furniture

Beds

A pine bed, Continental, c1895, 39in (99cm) wide.
£400–450 / €580–650
$670–760 ⊞ COF

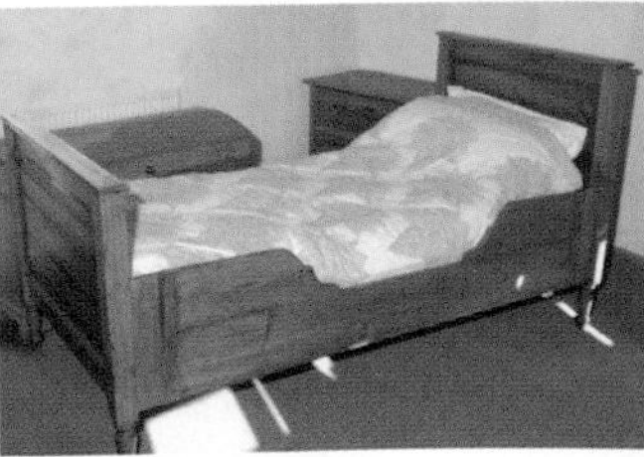

A pine bed, c1900, 40½in (103cm) wide.
£350–400 / €500–580
$590–670 ⊞ COF

◀ **A painted pine bed,** damaged, paint retouched, Austrian, c1820, 49¼in (125cm) wide, with feather mattress and three bolsters.
£2,900–3,450 / €4,200–5,000
$4,850–5,800 ⚒ DORO

Bookcases

A glazed pine bookcase, Irish, c1870, 44in (112cm) wide.
£420–470 / €600–670
$710–790 ⊞ Byl

An Oregon pine-veneered mahogany library bookcase, c1890, 96in (244cm) wide.
£1,650–1,950 / €2,350–2,800
$2,750–3,250 ⚒ TRM
This is an unusual piece. Normally the better timber would be veneered onto the inferior one, but in this case it was the other way round, with no apparent reason for it.

A glazed pine bookcase, Hungarian, c1900, 80in (203cm) high.
£500–550 / €720–800
$840–930 ⊞ MIN

Boxes

A pine box, with paper lining, c1830, 14¼in (37cm) wide.
£35–40 / €50–60
$60–70 ⊞ AL

A pine box, c1880, 20in (51cm) wide.
£50–60 / €70–85
$85–100 ⊞ HRQ

◀ **A pine box,** with iron handles, c1850, 36in (91.5cm) wide.
£230–260 / €330–370
$390–440 ⊞ P&T

A Victorian pine blanket box, 33in (84cm) wide.
£180–200 / €260–290
$300–340 ⊞ TPC

A Victorian pine box, with painted and pen work decoration, 12in (30.5cm) wide.
£370–440 / €530–630
$620–740 ⚒ G(L)

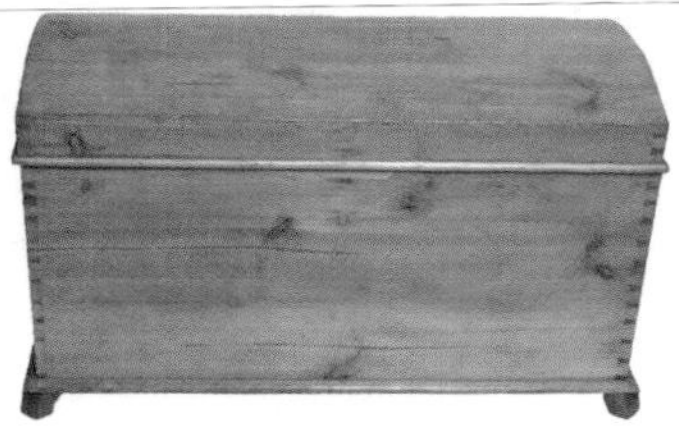

A pine box, Continental, c1880, 39in (100cm) wide.
£350–400 / €510–580
$590–670 ⊞ COF

A pine blanket box, with drawer, Irish, c1880, 56in (142cm) wide.
£180–200 / €260–290
$300–340 ⊞ Byl

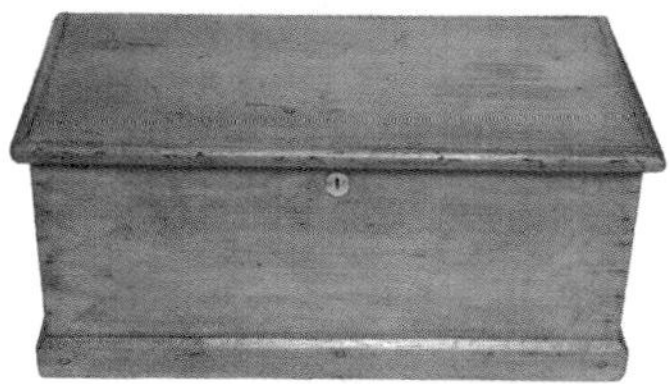

► **A pine box,** with iron handles, c1890, 31in (78.5cm) wide.
£120–135 / €170–195
$200–230 ⊞ AL

A pine blanket box, c1900, 38in (96.5cm) wide.
£110–125 / €160–180
$185–210 ⊞ DFA

A pine box, c1900, 12in (30.5cm) wide.
£35–40 / €50–60
$60–70 ⊞ AL

A pine box, Continental, c1920, 30in (76cm) wide.
£100–120 / €145–170
$170–200 ⊞ HRQ

Chairs

A pine and elm wing chair, with planked back and seat and panelled frieze on stiles, 19thC.
£1,650–1,950
€2,350–2,800
$2,750–3,250 ⚒ DN

◄ A pine Orkney chair, with beehive basketwork back, solid seat and square tapering legs, 19thC.
£910–1,090
€1,310–1,550
$1,500–1,800 ⚒ PF

► A pine country chair, Irish, c1890.
£115–130 / €165–190
$195–220 ⊞ Byl

A Victorian pine child's chair.
£110–125 / €160–180
$185–210 ⊞ COF

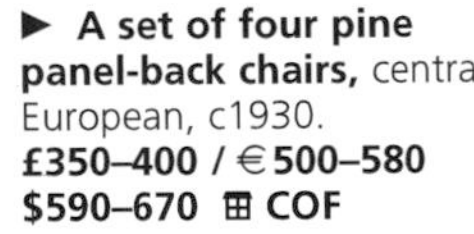

► A set of four pine panel-back chairs, central European, c1930.
£350–400 / €500–580
$590–670 ⊞ COF

A pine country chair, Irish, c1870.
£110–125 / €160–180
$185–210 ⊞ Byl

Chests & Coffers

A pine *coffor bach*, Welsh, 18thC, 17in (43cm) high.
£1,950–2,200 / €2,800–3,150
$3,250–3,700 ⊞ ANAn

A pine panelled coffer, 18thC, 44in (112cm) wide.
£400–450 / €580–650
$670–760 ⊞ HRQ

A painted pine coffer, Swiss, Tyrolean, c1800, 38in (96.5cm) wide.
£530–590 / €760–850
$890–990 ⊞ ANAn

► A stained pine blanket chest, c1800, 50in (127cm) wide.
£250–280 / €360–400
$420–470 ⊞ DFA

A pine mule chest, c1800, 35in (89cm) wide.
£440–500 / €630–720
$740–840 ⊞ TPC

◄ A pine chest, 1830, 40in (101.5cm) wide.
£540–600
€780–870
$900–1,000
⊞ COF

◄ **A painted pine chest,** American, New England, early 19thC, 19¾in (50cm) wide.
£4,650–5,600
€6,700–8,000
$7,800–9,400
S(NY)

A painted pine blanket chest, the interior fitted with a till, American, probably Pennsylvania, c1830, 48¼in (122.5cm) wide.
£5,000–6,000 / €7,200–8,600
$8,400–10,000 S(NY)

A painted pine chest, dated 1856, 48in (122cm) wide.
£350–400 / €500–580
$590–670 TPC

A painted pine blanket chest, Hungarian, c1870, 38in (96.5cm) wide.
£250–280 / €360–400
$420–470 Byl

A painted pine blanket chest, Hungarian, c1870, 40in (101.5cm) wide.
£330–370 / €470–530
$550–620 Byl

► **A pine trunk,** bound with wooden and metal slats, with leather handles, one handle damaged, c1890, 36¼in (92cm) wide.
£120–140
€170–200
$200–230
L&E

Chests of Drawers

A pine chest of drawers, c1820, 34in (86.5cm) wide.
£490–540 / €700–780
$820–910 AL

A painted pine shop bank of drawers, with three long drawers above six push/pull-through drawers, damaged, paint worn, handles replaced, two drawer fronts replaced, American, early 19thC, 75in (190.5cm) wide.
£750–900 / €1,100–1,200
$1,250–1,500 JDJ

A pine chest of drawers, with three long drawers, German, c1840, 43in (109cm) wide.
£340–380 / €490–550
$570–640 HRQ

◄ **A pine chest of drawers,** with two short over three long drawers, c1850, 40in (101.5cm) wide.
£430–480 / €620–690
$720–800 P&T

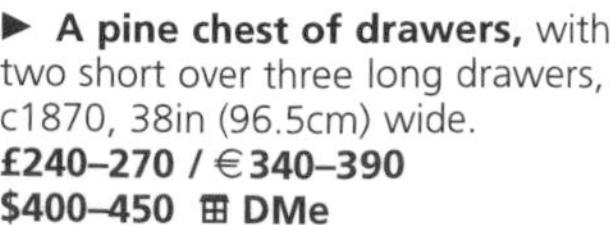

► **A pine chest of drawers,** with two short over three long drawers, c1870, 38in (96.5cm) wide.
£240–270 / €340–390
$400–450 DMe

PINE FURNITURE

A pine chest of drawers, with two short over three long drawers, c1870, 47in (119.5cm) wide.
£290–320 / €420–460
$490–540 ⊞ DFA

A pine chest of drawers, c1875, 41in (104cm) wide.
£630–700 / €900–1,000
$1,050–1,200 ⊞ COF

A pine chest of drawers, with ceramic knobs, c1880, 35in (89cm) wide.
£440–500 / €630–720
$740–840 ⊞ COF

A pine chest of drawers, c1880, 37in (94cm) wide.
£530–600 / €760–860
$890–1,000 ⊞ COF

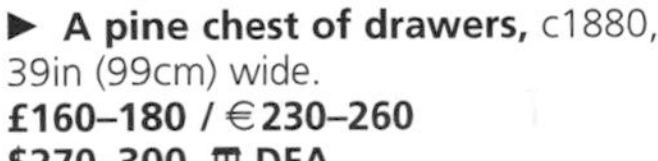

► **A pine chest of drawers,** c1880, 39in (99cm) wide.
£160–180 / €230–260
$270–300 ⊞ DFA

A pine chest of drawers, c1875, 33in (84cm) wide.
£440–500 / €630–720
$740–840 ⊞ COF

A pine chest of drawers, Romanian, c1875, 50in (127cm) wide.
£290–320 / €420–460
$490–540 ⊞ Byl

A pine chest of drawers, on turned feet, c1880, 47in (119.5cm) wide.
£350–400 / €500–580
$590–670 ⊞ HRQ

A pine chest of drawers, c1875, 47in (119.5cm) wide.
£810–900 / €1,150–1,300
$1,350–1,500 ⊞ COF

A Victorian pine chest of drawers, 32in (81.5cm) wide.
£350–400 / €500–580
$590–670 ⊞ TPC

A pine chest of drawers, with two short over three long drawers, c1880, 40in (101.5cm) wide.
£220–250 / €320–360
$370–420 ⊞ DFA

◄ **A pine chest of drawers,** c1880, 38in (96.5cm) wide.
£350–400 / €500–580
$590–670 ⊞ COF

A pine chest of drawers, on turned feet, handles replaced, c1880, 42in (106.5cm) wide.
£370–420 / €530–600
$620–700 ⊞ HRQ

◀ **A chemist's pine chest of drawers,** c1880, 15in (38cm) wide.
£180–200 / €260–290
$300–330 ⊞ AL

A pine chest of drawers, Irish, c1880, 42in (124.5cm) wide.
£290–320 / €420–460
$490–540 ⊞ Byl

A pine chest of drawers, with two short over three long drawers, Irish, c1880, 42in (106.5cm) wide.
£290–320 / €420–460
$490–540 ⊞ Byl

A pine chest of drawers, Romanian, c1880, 49in (124.5cm) wide.
£290–320 / €420–460
$490–540 ⊞ Byl

◀ **A pine chest of drawers,** on shaped feet, Hungarian, c1880, 46in (117cm) wide.
£400–450 / €580–650
$670–760 ⊞ MIN

A pine chest of drawers, c1890, 36in (91.5cm) wide.
£370–420 / €530–600
$620–700 ⊞ HRQ

A pine chest of drawers, Hungarian, c1880, 58in (147.5cm) wide.
£300–340 / €430–490
$500–570 ⊞ Byl

► **A pine chest of drawers,** Romanian, c1880, 49in (124.5cm) wide.
£290–320 / €420–460
$490–540 ⊞ Byl

◀ **A pine chest of drawers,** Irish, c1880, 38in (96.5cm) wide.
£290–320
€420–460
$490–540
⊞ Byl

PINE FURNITURE

A pine chest of drawers, c1890, 47in (119.5cm) wide.
£630–700 / €900–1,000
$1,050–1,200 ⊞ COF

A pine chest of drawers, altered, c1895, 18in (45.5cm) high.
£310–350 / €440–500
$520–590 ⊞ COF

A pine chest of drawers, central European, c1900, 48in (122cm) wide.
£530–600 / €760–860
$890–1,000 ⊞ COF

A set of pine filing drawers, c1910, 48in (122cm) wide.
£880–980 / €1,250–1,400
$1,500–1,650 ⊞ COF

A pine chest of drawers, Continental, c1910, 37in (94cm) wide.
£440–500 / €630–720
$740–840 ⊞ COF

A pine chest of drawers, the top made from a single piece of wood, c1890, 30in (76cm) wide.
£290–330 / €420–480
$490–560 ⊞ HRQ

A pine chest of drawers, with brass handles, c1900, 41in (104cm) wide.
£240–270 / €340–390
$400–450 ⊞ DFA

A pine chest of drawers, with a marble top, Continental, c1900, 43in (109cm) wide.
£530–600 / €760–860
$890–1,000 ⊞ COF

► **A pine chest of drawers,** with a marble top, German, early 20thC, 43in (109cm) wide.
£290–320 / €420–460
$490–540 ⊞ HRQ

A pine chest of drawers, c1920, 42in (106.5cm) wide.
£290–320 / €420–460
$490–540 ⊞ HRQ

► **A pine chest of drawers,** east European, c1925, 28in (71cm) wide.
£350–400 / €510–580
$590–670 ⊞ COF

A pine chest of drawers, on bun feet, Continental, c1890, 50in (127cm) wide.
£320–360 / €460–520
$540–600 ⊞ PaA

A pine chest of drawers, c1900, 46in (117cm) wide.
£400–450 / €580–650
$670–760 ⊞ MIN

An Edwardian pine chest of drawers, 35in (89cm) wide.
£440–500 / €630–720
$740–840 ⊞ P&T

PINE FURNITURE

Cupboards

A George III painted and stained pine corner cupboard, with painted stringing, the upper section with panelled cupboard door enclosing green and gilt painted shelves, on bracket feet, 84in (213.5cm) high.
£880–1,050
€1,250–1,500
$1,450–1,750 Mit

A pine corner cupboard, with two panelled doors, Irish, c1800, 54in (137cm) wide.
£1,250–1,400
€1,800–2,000
$2,100–2,350 TPC

A painted pine cupboard, the dentil cornice over four panelled doors with sunbursts, Irish, Co Galway, c1820, 60in (152.5cm) wide.
£4,700–5,200
€6,800–7,500
$7,900–8,700 DMe

A painted pine wall cupboard, upper door missing, rear feet patched, North American, possibly Canadian, c1770, 26¾in (68cm) wide.
£2,650–3,200
€3,850–4,600
$4,500–5,400 S(NY)

A pine corner cupboard, with raised and fielded panelled doors enclosing shelves, Irish, c1800, 53in (134.5cm) wide.
£850–950 / €1,200–1,350
$1,400–1,600 TPC

A painted pine linen press, the doors enclosing trays, repainted, 1775–1825, 53in (134.5cm) wide.
£1,800–2,150
€2,600–3,100
$3,000–3,600 S(O)

A painted pine corner cupboard, early 19thC, 36in (91.5cm) wide.
£1,750–1,950
€2,500–2,800
$3,000–3,300 TOP

A painted pine cupboard, with four doors, Irish, c1830, 60in (152.5cm) wide.
£5,600–6,200
€8,000–9,000
$9,400–10,500 DMe

◄ **A pine corner cupboard,** c1820, 50in (127cm) high.
£810–900 / €1,150–1,300
$1,350–1,500 COF

A painted pine corner cupboard, on a later stand, Dutch, c1800, 23¼in (59cm) wide.
£1,100–1,300
€1,600–1,900
$1,800–2,200 S(O)

A painted pine cupboard, the arched pediment and canted sides applied with carved panels of leaves and fruit, fitted with shelves, German, probably Irschenberg, early 19thC, 48¾in (124cm) wide.
£1,050–1,250
€1,500–1,800
$1,750–2,100 S(Am)

A painted pine cupboard, Swiss, Tyrolean, dated 1833, 36¾in (93.5cm) wide.
£820–980 / €1,200–1,400
$1,400–1,650 S(Am)

A pine corner cupboard, c1840, 52in (132cm) high.
£810–900 / €1,150–1,300
$1,350–1,500 ⊞ COF

A pine cupboard, the two doors with raised and fielded panels, c1860, 54in (137cm) wide.
£810–900 / €1,150–1,300
$1,350–1,500 ⊞ TPC

A painted pine cupboard, with fielded panelled doors and three drawers, Irish, Co Antrim, c1850, 61in (155cm) wide.
£870–970
€1,200–1,400
$1,500–1,600 ⊞ HON

A stained pine cupboard, the panelled doors enclosing shelves, 19thC, 74in (188cm) wide.
£1,550–1,850
€2,200–2,650
$2,600–3,100 ⚒ S(O)

A pine linen press, with a lift-up top and triple slide interior, c1860, 37in (94cm) wide.
£700–750 / €1,000–1,100
$1,200–1,300 ⊞ TPC

A pine armoire, with turned feet, German, c1860, 36in (91.5cm) wide.
£580–650 / €840–940
$980–1,100 ⊞ HRQ

A pine cupboard, with four panelled doors, Irish, c1860, 68in (172.5cm) wide.
£690–770 / €990–1,100
$1,150–1,300 ⊞ Byl

A pine cupboard, with four panelled doors, Irish, Co Tipperary, c1860, 43in (109cm) wide.
£780–870 / €1,100–1,250
$1,300–1,450 ⊞ HON

◄ **A pine cupboard,** with two panelled doors, c1870, 52in (132cm) wide.
£1,450–1,650
€2,100–2,400
$2,400–2,750 ⊞ COF

A pine cupboard, with four doors, Irish, c1865, 63in (160cm) wide.
£690–770 / €990–1,100
$1,150–1,300 ⊞ Byl

A Victorian pine cupboard, with internal drawers, 48in (122cm) wide.
£720–800 / €1,050–1,150
$1,200–1,350 ⊞ P&T

► **A pine corner cupboard,** c1870, 42in (106.5cm) high.
£720–800
€1,050–1,150
$1,200–1,350
⊞ COF

A pine bedside cupboard, c1870, 26in (66cm) high.
£95–105 / €135–150
$160–175 ⊞ DMe

A pine cupboard, with four doors, c1870, 96in (244cm) high.
£760–850 / €1,100–1,200
$1,250–1,400 ⊞ MIN

A pine cupboard, with two doors, Irish, c1870, 49in (124.5cm) wide.
£340–380 / €490–550 $570–640 ⊞ Byl

A pine cupboard, with two doors, Irish, c1875, 51in (129.5cm) wide.
£350–400 / €500–580 $590–670 ⊞ Byl

A pine corner cupboard, with four doors and two drawers, c1875, 40in (101.5cm) wide.
£460–520 / €660–750 $770–870 ⊞ Byl

A pine cupboard, with two doors, Irish, c1875, 55in (139.5cm) wide.
£350–400 / €500–580 $590–670 ⊞ Byl

A pine cupboard, with four doors, c1875, 53in (134.5cm) wide.
£690–770 / €990–1,100 $1,150–1,300 ⊞ Byl

Further reading

Miller's Pine & Country Furniture Buyers Guide, Miller's Publications, 2001

◄ **A pine cupboard,** with two part-glazed doors, Irish, c1875, 79in (200.5cm) high.
£350–400 / €500–580 $590–670 ⊞ Byl

A pine cupboard, with fitted interior, Hungarian, c1880, 72in (183cm) high.
£670–750 / €970–1,100 $1,100–1,250 ⊞ MIN

A pine chimney cupboard, with two panelled doors, c1880, 30in (76cm) wide.
£270–300 / €390–430
$450–500 ⊞ Byl

A pine hanging cupboard, with three doors, c1880, 77in (195.5cm) wide.
£580–650 / €840–940
$980–1,100 ⊞ MIN

A pine cupboard, with two doors, Irish, c1880, 52in (132cm) wide.
£340–380 / €490–550
$570–640 ⊞ Byl

A pine chimney cupboard, Irish, c1880, 37in (94cm) wide.
£260–290 / €370–410
$440–490 ⊞ Byl

A pine cupboard, with a single door, Romanian, c1880, 44in (122cm) wide.
£310–350 / €440–500
$520–590 ⊞ Byl

A pine cupboard, with four shaped panelled doors, Irish, c1880, 54in (137cm) wide.
£590–660 / €850–950
$990–1,100 ⊞ Byl

A pine cupboard, with a single door, c1890, 35in (89cm) wide.
£380–430 / €550–620
$640–720 ⊞ P&T

A pine corner cupboard, with four doors, c1885, 85in (216cm) high.
£1,750–1,950
€2,500–2,800
$3,000–3,300 ⊞ COF

A pine corner cupboard, with a glazed door, c1890, 35in (89cm) high.
£440–500 / €630–720
$740–840 ⊞ COF

A pine corner cupboard, with shaped, pedimented cornice, two glazed doors and two panelled doors, Irish, c1880, 44in (122cm) wide.
£760–850 / €1,100–1,200
$1,250–1,400 ⊞ TPC

A pine cupboard, with two doors, c1890, 6in (91.5cm) wide.
£440–500 / €630–720
$740–840 ⊞ COF

► A pine bedside cupboard, c1890, 14in (35.5cm) wide.
£220–250 / €320–360
$370–420 ⊞ COF

◄ A pine bedside cupboard, c1890, 20in (51cm) wide.
£95–105 / €135–150
$160–175 ⊞ Byl

A pine corner cupboard, with two doors over a single drawer, c1890, 36in (91.5cm) wide.
£290–330 / €420–470
$490–550 ⊞ Byl

A pine hanging cupboard, c1900, 16in (40.5cm) wide.
£70–80 / €100–115
$115–135 ⊞ HRQ

► **A pine shoe cupboard,** central European, c1900, 37in (94cm) wide.
£310–350 / €440–500
$520–590 ⊞ COF

A pine corner cupboard, with a part-glazed door, Continental, c1900, 83in (211cm) high.
£900–1,000
€1,300–1,450
$1,500–1,700 ⊞ COF

A pine cupboard, Continental, c1895, 35in (89cm) wide.
£630–700 / €900–1,000
$1,050–1,200 ⊞ COF

A pine bedside cupboard, c1900, 21in (53.5cm) wide.
£310–350 / €440–500
$520–590 ⊞ COF

► **A pine cupboard,** with a lift-up top, Continental, c1900, 25in (63.5cm) wide.
£350–400 / €500–580
$590–670 ⊞ COF

A pine bedside cupboard, Continental, c1900, 29in (73.5cm) high.
£220–250 / €320–360
$370–420 ⊞ COF

A pine hanging cupboard, c1900, 18in (45.5cm) wide.
£55–65 / €80–95
$90–105 ⊞ DFA

A pine cupboard, with shelves, central European, c1900, 33in (83.5cm) wide.
£530–600 / €760–860
$890–1,000 ⊞ COF

A pine cupboard, the two glazed doors over a drawer and two panelled doors, c1900, 41in (104cm) wide.
£310–350 / €440–500
$520–590 ⊞ Byl

A pair of pine bedside cupboards, c1900, 31in (78.5cm) high.
£270–300 / €390–430
$450–500 ⊞ HRQ

A pine cupboard, central European, c1900, 16in (40.5cm) wide.
£220–250 / €320–360
$370–420 ⊞ COF

◄ **A pine and oak wall cupboard,** central European, c1900, 19in (48.5cm) wide.
£155–175 / €220–250
$260–290 ⊞ COF

A pine corner cupboard, Continental, c1910, 76in (193cm) high.
£720–800 / €1,050–1,150
$1,200–1,350 ⊞ COF

◄ A pair of pine bedside cupboards, Continental, c1910, 19in (48.5cm) wide.
£440–500 / €630–720
$740–840 ⊞ COF

A pine glazed display cabinet, Continental, c1920, 40in (101.5cm) wide.
£900–1,000
€1,250–1,450
$1,500–1,700 ⊞ COF

A pine wall cupboard, central European, c1910, 14in (35.5cm) wide.
£155–175 / €220–250
$260–290 ⊞ COF

A pair of pine bedside cupboards, Continental, c1920, 16in (40.5cm) wide.
£400–450 / €580–650
$670–760 ⊞ COF

► A pine cupboard, with shelves, on bun feet, c1920, 32in (81.5cm) wide.
£200–220 / €290–320
$330–370 ⊞ HRQ

Desks & Bureaux

A pine bureau, Hungarian, c1860, 40in (101.5cm) wide.
£1,050–1,200 / €1,500–1,700
$1,750–2,000 ⊞ MIN

A Victorian pine pedestal desk, with leather-inset top, marked 'LCC', 51in (129.5cm) wide.
£1,950–2,200
€2,800–3,150
$3,250–3,700 ⚒ S(NY)

A pine desk, with a single drawer, altered, c1900, 24in (61cm) wide.
£220–250
€320–360
$370–420 ⊞ MIN

A pine desk/dressing table, Continental, c1910, 43in (109cm) wide.
£720–800 / €1,050–1,150
$1,200–1,350 ⊞ COF

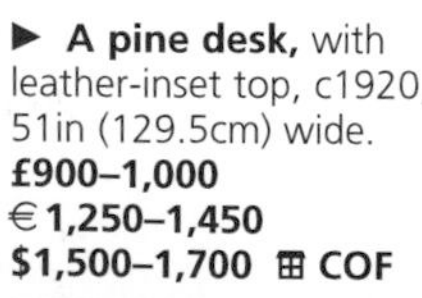

► A pine desk, with leather-inset top, c1920, 51in (129.5cm) wide.
£900–1,000
€1,250–1,450
$1,500–1,700 ⊞ COF

◄ A pine desk, Continental, c1920, 52in (132cm) wide.
£1,100–1,250
€1,600–1,800
$1,850–2,100
⊞ COF

PINE FURNITURE

Dressers

A pine *buffet à deux corps*, with original paintwork, French, c1790, 56in (142cm) wide.
£3,600–4,000
€5,200–5,800
$6,000–6,700 ⊞ TDS

A pine dresser, c1860, 75in (190.5cm) wide.
£1,600–1,800
€2,300–2,600
$2,700–3,000 ⊞ TPC

▶ **A pine dresser,** Irish, c1865, 57in (145cm) wide.
£610–680 / €880–980
$1,000–1,150 ⊞ Byl

A pine dresser, Irish, c1865, 52in (132cm) wide.
£600–660 / €860–950
$1,000–1,100 ⊞ Byl

▶ **A pine dresser,** Irish, c1870, 52in (132cm) wide.
£600–660 / €860–950
$1,000–1,100 ⊞ Byl

A pine dresser, with original paint, Irish, Co Galway, c1840, 51in (129.5cm) wide.
£770–860 / €1,100–1,250
$1,300–1,450 ⊞ HON

A pine dresser, Irish, c1860, 32in (81.5cm) wide.
£560–630 / €800–900
$940–1,050 ⊞ DMe

A pitch pine dresser, with two glazed doors over five drawers and a single door, Hungarian, c1850, 36in (91.5cm) wide.
£580–650 / €840–940
$980–1,100 ⊞ MIN

▶ **A pine dresser,** c1860, 61in (155cm) wide.
£530–600 / €760–860
$890–1,000 ⊞ DFA

A pine dresser, with herringbone panelling, c1860, 78in (198cm) wide.
£2,250–2,500
€3,250–3,600
$3,800–4,200 ⊞ TPC

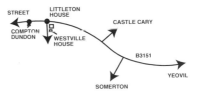

A pine dresser, with a glazed top, Irish, c1870, 49in (124.5cm) wide.
£610–680 / €880–980
$1,000–1,150 ⊞ Byl

A pine dresser, with a glazed top, Irish, c1875, 43in (109cm) wide.
£420–470 / €600–680
$700–790 ⊞ Byl

A Victorian pine dresser, the top with an arcade-pierced frieze, on turned legs, 73¾in (187.5cm) wide.
£1,900–2,250
€2,700–3,250
$3,200–3,800 ⚒ PFK

A pine dresser, c1890, 84in (213.5cm) wide.
£1,800–2,000
€2,600–2,900
$3,000–3,350 ⊞ MIN

◄ A pine dresser top, Irish, c1875, 52in (132cm) wide.
£155–175
€220–250
$260–290 ⊞ Byl

A pine dresser, with a carved and glazed top, Irish, c1880, 40in (101.5cm) wide.
£420–470 / €600–670
$710–790 ⊞ Byl

A Victorian pine dresser, the plate rack flanked by columns, above a frieze drawer and a cupboard, 47¼in (120cm) wide.
£250–280 / €360–400
$410–470 ⚒ CHTR

A pine dresser, Hungarian, c1890, 80in (203cm) high.
£580–650 / €840–940
$980–1,100 ⊞ MIN

A pine dresser, with a glazed top, Irish, c1890, 41in (104cm) wide.
£900–1,000
€1,250–1,450
$1,500–1,700 ⊞ TPC

◄ A pine dresser, with green painted glass panels, early 20thC, 45in (114.5cm) wide.
£350–400 / €500–580
$590–670 ⊞ PaA

► A pine dresser, with a glazed top, Hungarian, c1910, 48in (122cm) high.
£580–650 / €840–940
$980–1,100 ⊞ MIN

A pine dresser, with original paint, Irish, Co Mayo, c1870, 51in (129.5cm) wide.
£780–870 / €1,100–1,250
$1,300–1,450 ⊞ HON

A painted pine dresser, c1880, 80in (203cm) wide.
£880–980 / €1,250–1,400
$1,450–1,650 ⊞ DFA

A pine dresser, east European, c1900, 50in (127cm) wide.
£600–660 / €860–950
$1,000–1,100 ⊞ Byl

Low Dressers & Side Cabinets

A pine low dresser, c1800, 89½in (227.5cm) wide.
£2,850–3,200 / €4,100–4,600
$4,800–5,400 ⊞ ANAn

A Victorian low dresser, 72in (183cm) wide.
£640–720 / €920–1,050
$1,050–1,200 ⊞ TPC

◄ **A pine side cabinet,** with a single drawer, on turned feet, Continental, c1870, 40in (101.5cm) wide.
£320–360 / €460–520
$540–600 ⊞ HRQ

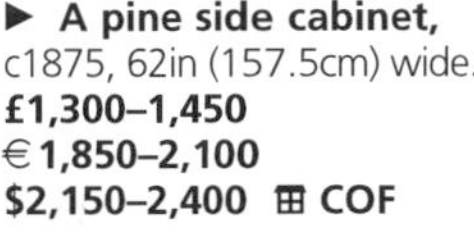

► **A pine side cabinet,** c1875, 62in (157.5cm) wide.
£1,300–1,450
€1,850–2,100
$2,150–2,400 ⊞ COF

A pine side cabinet, Irish, c1875, 42in (106.5cm) wide.
£220–250 / €320–360
$370–420 ⊞ Byl

A pine cabinet, the doors with gilt-metal trellis, 19thC, 31in (78.5cm) wide.
£760–850 / €1,100–1,200
$1,250–1,400 ⊞ HiA

A pine side cabinet, with a single drawer over two cupboard doors, Irish, c1875, 41in (104cm) wide.
£220–250 / €320–360
$370–420 ⊞ Byl

A pine side cabinet, with two drawers over two cupboard doors, Irish, c1875, 43in (109cm) wide.
£220–250 / €320–360
$370–420 ⊞ Byl

A Victorian pine sideboard, with a serpentine top, 52in (132cm) wide.
£810–900 / €1,150–1,300
$1,350–1,500 ⊞ TPC

A Victorian painted pine sideboard, the top with a shaped back and four short drawers, over three frieze drawers, a cupboard and four deep drawers, on turned legs, 61¾in (157cm) wide.
£330–390 / €470–560
$550–650 ⚒ PFK

◄ **A pine side cabinet,** with a single drawer over two cupboard doors, 19thC, 21in (53.5cm) wide.
£270–300 / €390–430
$450–500 ⊞ HRQ

► **A pine and elm low dresser,** with turned legs, c1880, 76in (193cm) wide.
£1,950–2,200
€2,800–3,150
$3,250–3,700 ⊞ MIN

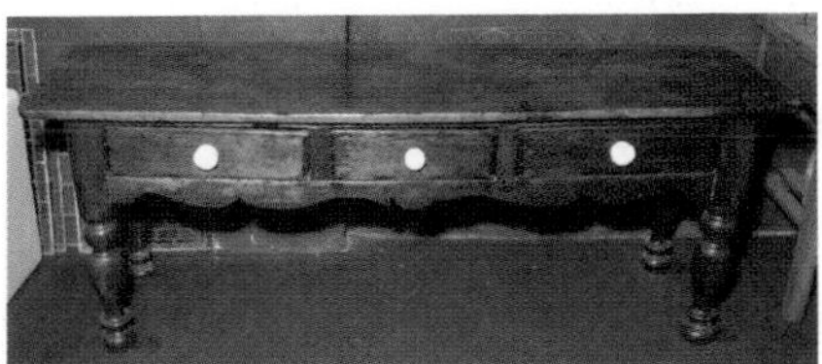

A pine low dresser, c1880, 43in (109cm) wide.
£810–900 / €1,150–1,300
$1,350–1,500 ⊞ COF

A pine side cabinet, with a splash-back top and a single drawer over two doors, c1880, 45in (114.5cm) wide.
£250–280 / €360–400
$420–470 ⊞ DFA

A pine side cabinet, with a splash-back top and single drawer over two doors, c1880, 39in (99cm) wide.
£210–240 / €300–350
$350–400 ⊞ DFA

◀ **A pine side cabinet,** c1880, 60in (152.5cm) wide.
£1,100–1,250
€1,600–1,800
$1,850–2,100
⊞ COF

A pine side cabinet, with a single drawer over two doors, Hungarian, c1880, 40in (101.5cm) wide.
£220–250 / €320–360
$370–420 ⊞ Byl

A pine side cabinet, with two drawers over two cupboard doors, Romanian, c1880, 39in (99cm) wide.
£220–250 / €320–360
$370–420 ⊞ Byl

A pine side cabinet, with a single drawer over two cupboard doors, Romanian, c1880, 40in (101.5cm) wide.
£220–250 / €320–360
$370–420 ⊞ Byl

A pine side cabinet, Irish, c1880, 47in (119.5cm) wide.
£220–250 / €320–360
$370–420 ⊞ Byl

◀ **A pine side cabinet,** c1885, 91in (31cm) wide.
£580–650
€840–940
$980–1,100
⊞ P&T

Condition

The condition is absolutely vital when assessing the value of an antique. Damaged pieces on the whole appreciate much less than perfect examples. However a rare desirable piece may command a high price even when damaged.

A pine chiffonier, c1885, 55in (139.5cm) wide.
£1,200–1,350 / €1,750–1,950
$2,000–2,250 ⊞ COF

◀ **A pine low dresser,** with elm legs, c1890, 70in (178cm) wide.
£760–850 / €1,100–1,200
$1,250–1,400 ⊞ MIN

PINE FURNITURE

A pine side cabinet, with two drawers over two cupboard doors, c1895, 42in (106.5cm) wide.
£530–600 / €760–860
$890–1,000 ⊞ COF

A pine side cabinet, with two drawers over two cupboard doors, Continental, c1900, 36in (91.5cm) wide.
£270–300 / €390–430
$450–500 ⊞ HRQ

A pine side cabinet, with two drawers over two cupboard doors, Continental, c1900, 42in (106.5cm) wide.
£290–330 / €420–480
$490–560 ⊞ HRQ

LOCATE THE SOURCE
The source of each illustration in Miller's can be found by checking the code letters below each caption with the Key to Illustrations, pages 794–800.

◄ **A pitch pine side cabinet,** central European, c1920, 26in (66cm) wide.
£310–350 / €440–500
$520–590 ⊞ COF

A pine side cabinet, c1930, 31in (78.5cm) wide.
£180–200 / €260–290
$300–340 ⊞ HRQ

Dressing Chests & Tables

A Victorian pine dressing chest, with carved mirror supports and pediment, 42in (106.5cm) wide.
£580–650 / €840–940
$980–1,100 ⊞ TPC

A Victorian pine dressing table, with ballustraded decoration, 36in (91.5cm) wide.
£440–500 / €630–720
$740–840 ⊞ TPC

A pitch pine dressing table, c1890, 48in (122cm) wide.
£110–130 / €155–185
$185–220 ⚒ BR

A pine dressing chest, with a cheval mirror supported by shelves and mirrored trinket drawers, c1890, 42in (106.5cm) wide.
£810–900 / €1,150–1,300
$1,350–1,500 ⊞ TPC

A pine dressing table, c1890, 42in (106.5cm) wide.
£530–600 / €760–860
$890–1,000 ⊞ COF

A pine dressing chest, c1900, 43in (109cm) wide.
£440–500 / €630–720
$740–840 ⊞ COF

A pine dressing table, Continental, c1910, 51in (129.5cm) wide.
£720–800 / €1,050–1,150
$1,200–1,350 ⊞ COF

A pine dressing table, Continental, c1920, 46in (117cm) wide.
£720–800 / €1,050–1,150
$1,200–1,350 ⊞ COF

Mirrors

A pair of carved pine wall mirrors, the borders carved with leaves, fruit, flowers and a crane within a C-scroll border, surmounted by a trellis panel and a crane, plates later, originally gilded, c1750, 30½in (77.5cm) high.
£2,700–3,250 / €3,900–4,650
$4,550–5,400 ⚒ LFA

A neo-classical pine mirror, decorated with gesso and traces of gilding, Swedish, c1800, 12½in (32cm) wide.
£2,500–2,800 / €3,600–4,000
$4,200–4,700 ⊞ RYA

A carved pine easel mirror, the plate flanked by cherubs, the scrolled base supported by angels, losses, Italian, late 19thC, 17in (43cm) wide.
£190–220 / €270–320
$320–370 ⚒ BR

► **A pine mirror,** with bevelled glass, c1900, 36in (91.5cm) wide.
£260–290 / €380–420
$440–490 ⊞ COF

A pine mirror, with bevelled glass, c1920, 30in (76cm) square.
£175–195 / €250–280
$300–330 ⊞ COF

Racks & Shelves

A painted pine wall shelf, with original paint, possibly Welsh, c1800, 20½in (52cm) wide.
£4,000–4,500 / €5,800–6,500
$6,700–7,500 ⊞ RYA

► **A stained pine five-tier wall shelf,** on turned supports, 19thC, 93in (236cm) wide.
£1,500–1,800 / €2,150–2,600
$2,500–3,000 ⚒ DN

A pine pot rack, Romanian, c1880, 60in (152.5cm) wide.
£125–140 / €180–200
$210–230 ⊞ HRQ

► **A pine wall shelf,** with a central cupboard, Continental, c1910, 31in (78.5cm) wide.
£270–300 / €390–430
$450–500 ⊞ COF

Further reading

Miller's Pine & Country Furniture Buyer's Guide, Miller's Publications, 2001

Settles & Sofas

A neo-classical painted pine panel back sofa, with gilt detail, Swedish, c1800, 76in (193cm) wide.
£6,700–7,500 / €9,600–10,800
$11,200–12,600 ⊞ RYA
This is a wonderful example of restrained Gustavian neo-classicism. This sofa reflects the simple harmony of line and colour associated with the finest Swedish provincial furniture of this period.

A pine settle, Irish, c1870, 72in (193cm) wide.
£510–570 / €730–820
$860–970 ⊞ Byl

A pine monk's settle/table, the box with a twin-panelled front, Welsh, late 19thC, 56in (142cm) wide.
£820–980 / €1,200–1,400
$1,400–1,650 ⚒ PF

A pine monk's settle/table, Irish, c1850, 76in (193cm) wide.
£780–870 / €1,100–1,250
$1,300–1,450 ⊞ HON

A pine settle, Irish, c1875, 72in (193cm) wide.
£380–420 / €550–610
$630–700 ⊞ Byl

A pine box settle, Continental, c1900, 78in (198cm) wide.
£720–800 / €1,050–1,150
$1,200–1,350 ⊞ COF

► **A pine box settle,** Continental, c1920, 47in (119.5cm) wide.
£630–700 / €910–1,000
$1,050–1,200 ⊞ COF

A pine settle/bed, Irish, c1865, 72in (183cm) wide.
£410–460 / €590–660
$690–770 ⊞ Byl

A pine settle, the arcaded top rail above an open gallery, the arms with turned supports, Welsh, late 19thC, 40in (101.5cm) wide.
£590–710 / €850–1,000
$1,000–1,200 ⚒ PF

Stools

A pine stool, with a carrying hole, c1880, 18in (45.5cm) wide.
£45–50 / €60–70
$75–85 ⊞ POT

Items in the Pine Furniture section have been arranged in date order within each sub-section.

A child's pine stool, with primitive decoration, on turned legs, 19thC, 10½in (26.5cm) wide.
£70–80 / €100–110
$120–135 ⊞ CHAC

A pine grotto stool, with a scallop seat and dolphin base, Italian, 19thC, 22in (56cm) high.
£700–840 / €1,000–1,200
$1,200–1,400 ⚒ G(L)

Tables

A pine cricket table, c1800, 32½in (82.5cm) diam.
£560–630 / €810–910
$940–1,050 ⊞ ANAn

A pine side table, with one drawer, French, c1850, 43½in (110.5cm) wide.
£640–770 / €920–1,100
$1,100–1,300 ⚒ NOA

A pine cricket table, with a reeded-edge frieze, 19thC, 28in (71cm) diam.
£350–420 / €500–600
$590–700 ⚒ WW

► **A pine table,** top repaired, Spanish, 19thC, 62½in (159cm) wide.
£820–980
€1,200–1,400
$1,400–1,650
⚒ DN

A painted pine tilt-top hutch table, American, possibly New England, 19thC, 48in (122cm) diam.
£3,000–3,600 / €4,300–5,100
$5,000–6,000 ⚒ S(NY)

A Victorian pine Pembroke table, 42in (106.5cm) wide.
£250–275 / €360–400
$420–460 ⊞ TPC

A Victorian pine table, with a single drawer, altered, 42in (106.5cm) wide.
£170–190 / €240–270
$280–310 ⊞ P&T

A Victorian pine tilt-top table, 20in (51cm) diam.
£440–490 / €630–700
$740–820 ⊞ COF

► **A pine table,** with one end drawer, c1870, 71in (180.5cm) wide.
£320–350
€450–500
$540–600
⊞ DFA

A pine table, c1870, 58in (147.5cm) wide.
£710–790 / €1,000–1,200
$1,150–1,300 ⊞ COF

◄ **A pine farmhouse table,** c1880, 54in (137cm) wide.
£230–260 / €330–370
$400–440 ⊞ Byl

A painted pine side table, with original paint and a single drawer, c1880, 36in (91.5cm) wide.
£100–110 / €145–160
$170–195 ⊞ DFA

◀ **A pine farmhouse table,** with a central drawer, c1880, 54in (137cm) wide.
£210–230
€300–330
$350–390
⊞ Byl

A pine drop-leaf table, Irish, c1880, 41in (104cm) diam.
£220–240 / €320–360
$370–410 ⊞ Byl

A pine occasional table, c1880, 17in (43cm) square.
£260–290 / €370–410
$440–490 ⊞ COF

A pine table, with a painted oak base, French, c1880, 69in (175.5cm) wide.
£590–650 / €850–940
$1,000–1,100 ⊞ MIN

A pine table, with two drawers, c1890, 48in (122cm) wide.
£620–690 / €890–990
$1,000–1,200 ⊞ COF

◀ **A pine drop-leaf table,** c1890, 36in (91.5cm) wide.
£250–280 / €360–400
$420–470 ⊞ TPC

A pine side table, with a drawer, c1890, 33in (84cm) wide.
£200–220 / €290–320
$330–370 ⊞ MIN

A pine table, with *faux* bamboo carving, French, late 19thC, 32in (81.5cm) wide.
£290–320 / €420–460
$490–540 ⊞ MLL

A pine butcher's table, zinc-lined, with a knife drawer, c1900, 40in (101.5cm) wide.
£310–350 / €450–500
$530–590 ⊞ MIN

A pine table, Continental, c1920, 46in (117cm) diam.
£530–590 / €760–850
$890–990 ⊞ COF

A pine table, Hungarian, c1890, 35in (89cm) wide
£160–190 / €230–270
$270–320 ⚒ DuM

A pine table, c1895, 48in (122cm) wide.
£530–590 / €760–850
$890–990 ⊞ COF

► A pine fold-out table, Hungarian, c1900, 64in (162.5cm) wide extended.
£400–450 / €580–650
$670–750 ⊞ MIN

◄ A pine kitchen table, Hungarian, c1900, 79in (201cm) wide.
£590–650
€850–940
$1,000–1,100
⊞ MIN

► A pine table, reduced in height to make a coffee table, Continental, c1920, 43in (109cm) wide.
£440–490
€630–700
$740–820
⊞ COF

A pine refectory table, 1930s, 72in (183cm) wide.
£850–950 / €1,200–1,350
$1,450–1,600 ⊞ COF

◄ A pine kitchen table, with an enamel top, c1950, 36in (91.5cm) wide.
£100–120 / €160–180
$180–200 ⊞ AL

Auction or dealer?

All the pictures in our price guides originate from auction houses ⚒ and dealers ⊞. When buying at auction, prices can be lower than those of a dealer, but a buyer's premium and VAT will be added to the hammer price. Equally, when selling at auction, commission, tax and photography charges must be taken into account. Dealers will often restore pieces before putting them back on the market. Both dealers and auctioneers can provide professional advice, so it is worth researching both sources before buying or selling your antiques.

Wardrobes

A pine two-door wardrobe, early 19thC, 76in (193cm) high.
£620–690 / €890–990 $1,000–1,200 ⊞ HRQ

A painted pine wardrobe, with original paint, Hungarian, c1870, 46in (117cm) wide.
£650–720 / €940–1,050 $1,100–1,250 ⊞ MIN

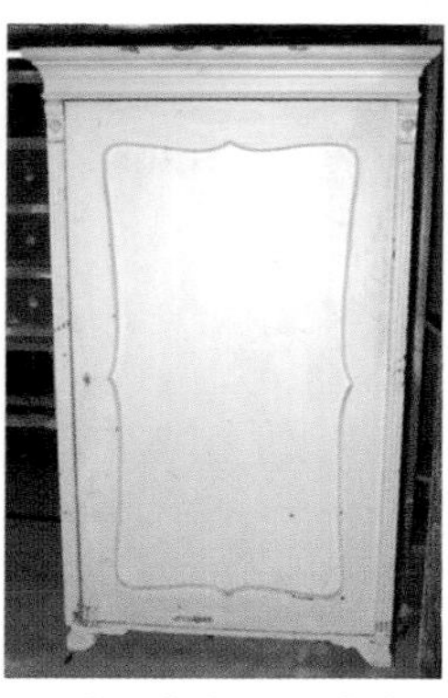
A painted pine wardrobe, with original paint, Hungarian, c1870, 44in (112cm) wide.
£680–750 / €980–1,100 $1,100–1,250 ⊞ MIN

A pair of pine wardrobes, each with two doors over a single drawer, c1870, 84in (213.5cm) high.
£1,500–1,800 €2,200–2,600 $2,500–3,000 ⊞ MIN

◄ **A pine wardrobe,** with a single drawer, c1880, 45in (114.5cm) wide.
£260–330 €370–480 $440–550 ⊞ DFA

Painted pine furniture

Pine furniture would originally have been painted, either in imitation of more expensive timbers, or simply as a protective layer and to give a more colourful appearance. These days most examples are stripped, as a result of the fashion for the simple, natural look which originated in the 1960s, but in recent years there has been a revived interest in pieces that retain their original paint and these often command a premium, particularly those with profuse decoration.

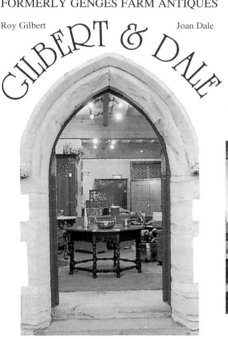

PINE FURNITURE

A pine wardrobe, c1880, 47in (119.5cm) wide.
£570–630 / €820–910
$960–1,100 ⊞ HRQ

A pine wardrobe, c1880, 52in (132cm) wide.
£260–330 / €370–480
$440–550 ⊞ DFA

A pine wardrobe, Hungarian, c1880, 46in (117cm) wide.
£420–470 / €600–680
$700–790 ⊞ MIN

A pine wardrobe, c1880, 40in (101.5cm) wide.
£710–790 / €1,000–1,100
$1,200–1,350 ⊞ COF

◄ A pine wardrobe, Continental, c1885, 88in (223.5cm) wide.
£1,550–1,750
€2,250–2,500
$2,600–2,900
⊞ COF

A pine wardrobe, with one long and four short drawers, c1890, 50in (127cm) wide.
£1,000–1,100
€1,450–1,600
$1,700–1,900 ⊞ TPC

A pine wardrobe, the doors enclosing four drawers, Hungarian, c1890, 44in (112cm) wide.
£760–850 / €1,100–1,250
$1,300–1,450 ⊞ MIN

A pine wardrobe, Continental, c1900, 60in (152.5cm) wide.
£1,100–1,250
€1,600–1,800
$1,900–2,100 ⊞ COF

A pine wardrobe, with a drawer, c1900, 72in (183cm) high.
£310–350 / €450–500
$520–590 ⊞ MIN

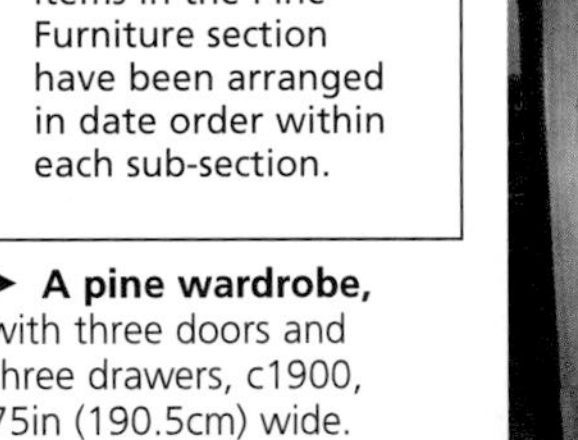

Items in the Pine Furniture section have been arranged in date order within each sub-section.

► A pine wardrobe, with three doors and three drawers, c1900, 75in (190.5cm) wide.
£890–990 / €1,300–1,450
$1,500–1,650 ⊞ HRQ

A pine wardrobe, with two drawers, central European, c1900, 59in (150cm) wide.
£1,100–1,250
€1,600–1,800
$1,900–2,100 ⊞ COF

A pine wardrobe, Continental, c1900, 55in (139.5cm) wide.
£1,050–1,150
€1,500–1,650
$1,750–1,950 ⊞ COF

◄ A pine wardrobe, Continental, c1900, 71in (180.5cm) wide.
£1,450–1,600
€2,100–2,300
$2,450–2,700
⊞ COF

PINE FURNITURE

A pine wardrobe, with three doors and two drawers, Continental, c1900, 64in (162.5cm) wide.
£1,200–1,350 / €1,700–1,900
$2,000–2,200 ⊞ COF

A pine wardrobe, Continental, c1900, 78in (198cm) wide.
£1,550–1,750 / €2,250–2,500
$2,600–2,900 ⊞ COF

A pitch pine wardrobe, with two doors, central European, c1920, 64in (162.5cm) wide.
£710–790 / €1,000–1,100
$1,200–1,350 ⊞ COF

◄ **A pine wardrobe,** with two doors over a drawer, c1920, 53in (134.5cm) wide.
£900–990
€1,300–1,450
$1,500–1,650
⊞ COF

A pine wardrobe, with original leaded lights, Continental, c1920, 59in (150cm) wide.
£1,200–1,350
€1,700–1,900
$2,000–2,200 ⊞ COF

A pine wardrobe, with three doors, German, c1930, 61in (155cm) wide.
£580–650 / €840–940
$980–1,100 ⊞ HRQ

Washstands

A pine washstand, c1850, 33in (84cm) wide.
£250–280 / €360–400
$420–460 ⊞ TPC

Insurance values

Always insure your valuable antiques for the cost of replacing them with similar items, regardless of the original price paid. Both dealers and auctioneers can provide a valuation service for a fee.

A pine washstand, Irish, c1880, 21in (53.5cm) wide.
£75–85 / €110–125
$125–140 ⊞ Byl

A pine washstand, Continental, c1890, 26in (66cm) wide.
£160–175 / €230–260
$270–300 ⊞ TPC

► **A pitch pine washstand,** the marble top inset with a wash basin, fitted with a tap, French, c1900, 46in (117cm) wide.
£1,350–1,500 / €1,950–2,150
$2,250–2,500 ⊞ C&R

Bamboo Furniture

A child's painted simulated bamboo bookcase, 19thC, 30in (76cm) wide.
£1,550–1,750 / €2,250–2,500
$2,600–2,950 ⊞ PICA

A Victorian bamboo canterbury, with floral-painted lacquered panels, the two sections over an open recess, 16in (40.5cm) wide.
£220–260 / €310–370
$370–440 ⚒ G(L)

A Victorian bamboo desk, the lacquered top with a leather inset, 35in (89cm) wide.
£420–500 / €600–720
$700–840 ⚒ LHA

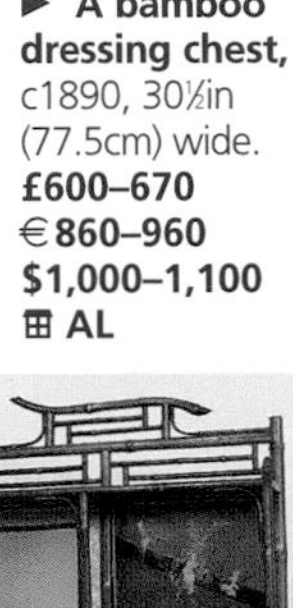

► A bamboo dressing chest, c1890, 30½in (77.5cm) wide.
£600–670
€860–960
$1,000–1,100
⊞ AL

A bamboo hall stand, with a mirror, c1880, 72in (183cm) high.
£180–200 / €260–290
$300–340 ⊞ AL

A bamboo magazine stand, c1885, 29in (73.5cm) high.
£160–180 / €230–260
$270–300 ⊞ AL

◄ A bamboo side cabinet, the upper section with lacquered panels decorated with birds, above a single drawer, the base with a glazed cupboard and shelves, 19thC, 30¾in (78cm) wide.
£1,000–1,200
€1,450–1,700
$1,700–2,000 ⚒ CHTR

► A Victorian bamboo table, with a lacquered top, 28in (71cm) wide.
£320–380 / €460–550
$540–640 ⚒ LHA

A Victorian bamboo settee and three armchairs, one mounted with a lacquer panel.
£630–760 / €950–1,100
$1,100–1,300 ⚒ LHA

A *faux* bamboo and oak three-tiered table, American, c1900, 15in (38cm) diam.
£1,000–1,100
€1,450–1,600
$1,700–1,900 ⊞ NART

A *faux* bamboo and papier-mâché whatnot, c1890, 32in (81.5cm) high.
£110–120 / €160–180
$185–200 ⊞ AL

Kitchenware

A pine barrel churn, on a stand, c1870, 34in (86.5cm) wide.
£160–175 / €230–260
$270–300 ⊞ TPC

A biscuit tin, decorated as an inlaid tea caddy, c1936, 6in (15cm) wide.
£60–70 / €90–100
$100–110 ⊞ F&F

A carved bread board, decorated with wheat, hops and grapes, c1905, 12½in (32cm) diam.
£130–140 / €190–210
$210–240 ⊞ B&R

A copper cake/roasting tin, c1880, 12½in (32cm) wide.
£70–80 / €100–110
$115–130 ⊞ F&F

A coffee tin, in three sections, inscribed 'Café', c1890, 24in (61cm) wide.
£400–450 / €580–650
$670–750 ⊞ B&R

◄ An iron cheese scoop, Welsh, c1780, 7in (18cm) long.
£430–480 / €620–690
$720–800 ⊞ SEA

◄ A mahogany cutlery tray, 19thC, 14in (35.5cm) wide.
£160–185
€230–265
$270–310
⊞ WAA

► A dairy can, with a brass plate inscribed 'W. James, Ford Farm, Newent, Glos', early 20thC, 18in (45.5cm) high.
£400–450 / €580–650
$670–750 ⊞ B&R

◄ A wooden flour barrel, 19thC, 5¾in (14.5cm) high.
£200–220 / €290–320
$330–370 ⊞ WeA

A brass fish slice, maker's mark, 1670–80, 17in (43cm) long.
£350–390 / €500–560
$600–660 ⊞ SEA

A set of wrought-iron game hooks, by Powell Edwards, Chester, 1878, 24in (61cm) wide.
£220–250 / €320–360
$380–420 ⊞ B&R

A brass goffering iron, on a knopped stem with a turned welled base, early 19thC, 7¼in (18.5cm) high.
£60–70 / €85–100
$100–120 ⚒ WW

A wrought-iron griddle, Irish, c1850, 23in (58.5cm) wide.
£760–850 / €1,100–1,250
$1,300–1,450 ⊞ STA

A cast-iron coffee grinder, by Kenrick & Sons, c1895, 7in (18cm) high.
£430–480 / €620–690
$720–810 ⊞ MFB
This coffee grinder is unusual because it is in the form of the font of York Minster.

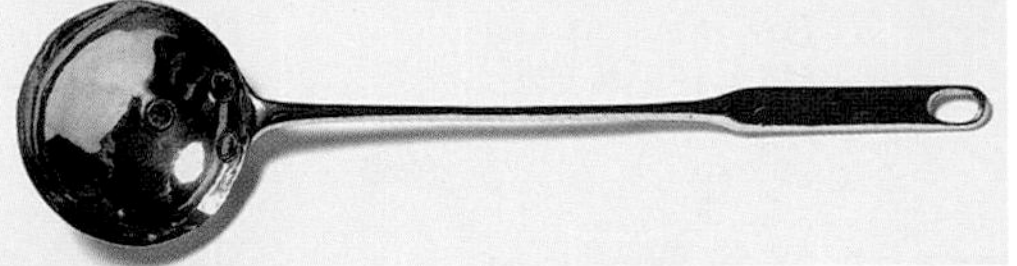

A brass ladle, with copper rivets, c1820, 14in (35.5cm) long.
£200–220 / €290–320
$340–380 ⊞ SEA

► A brass and glass mayonnaise maker, with original label, French, c1920, 10in (25.5cm) high.
£70–80 / €100–110
$115–135 ⊞ B&R

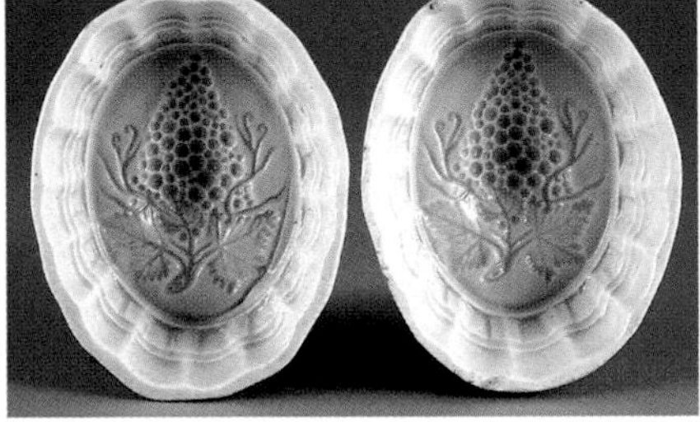

A pair of creamware moulds, decorated with bunches of grapes, late 18thC, 2¾in (7cm) wide.
£230–280 / €340–400
$400–470 ⚒ WW

◄ A copper jelly mould, 19thC, 3in (7.5cm) diam.
£160–175 / €230–260
$270–300 ⊞ SEA

A wooden cheese mould, incised with a dolphin, initialled 'M. I.' and dated 1802, 12½in (32cm) diam.
£500–600 / €720–860
$840–1,000 ⚒ L

► A copper mould, modelled as a seated lion, 19thC, 16in (40.5cm) wide.
£520–580 / €750–840
$870–970 ⊞ KEY

A copper jelly mould, with a brass seam, c1810, 13¼in (33.5cm) diam.
£90–100 / €130–145
$150–170 ⊞ F&F

A Victorian pottery milk pail, with printed and hand-painted enamel decoration, two handles, marked 'C1982', rivet repair to base, 12½in (32cm) diam.
£800–960 / €1,200–1,400
$1,350–1,600 ⚒ SWO

◄ A ceramic cream pail, by the Dairy Engineering Co, Dublin, Irish, late 19thC, 11in (28cm) diam.
£580–650 / €840–940
$980–1,100 ⊞ B&R

An oak and silver-mounted pepper mill, Birmingham 1908, 3½in (9cm) high.
£100–120 / €145–170
$170–200 SWO

A copper saucepan, with an iron handle and brass seaming, c1800, 6¼in (16cm) diam.
£90–100 / €130–145
$155–170 F&F

A set of kitchen scales, Swedish, 19thC, 21in (53.5cm) wide.
£250–280 / €360–400
$420–470 SWN

A set of Salter's ceramic kitchen scales, 1920s, 11in (28cm) high.
£90–100 / €130–145
$150–170 SMI

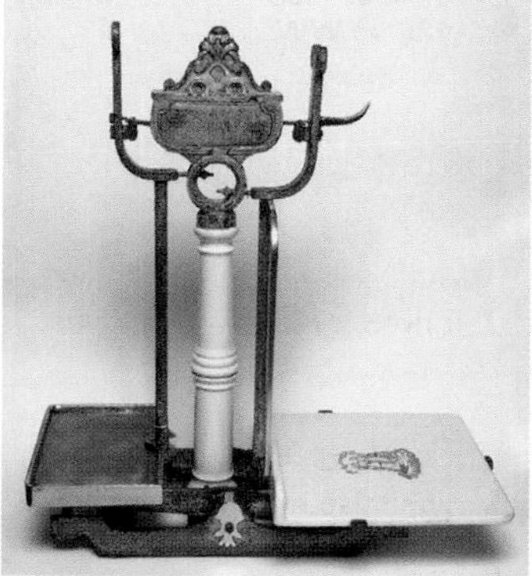

A set of cast-iron, brass and ceramic butcher's scales, c1900, 27in (68.5cm) high.
£480–530 / €690–760
$810–890 SMI

A brass bran scoop, with a turned wood handle, c1800, 16in (40.5cm) long.
£300–330 / €430–480
$500–550 MFB

A silver meat skewer, by John William Blake, London 1823, 10in (25.5cm) long.
£170–190 / €240–270
$280–310 GRe

A brass skimmer, c1780, 18in (45.5cm) long.
£90–100 / €130–145
$150–170 F&F

An iron lark spit, 18thC, 25in (63.5cm) high.
£350–390 / €500–560
$590–650 KEY

A ceramic loaf sugar barrel, c1920, 13in (33cm) high.
£250–280 / €360–400
$420–470 SMI

A brass sugar caster, c1760.
£90–100 / €130–145
$150–170 F&F

A turned boxwood spice tower, with four screwed tiers and paper labels for Mace, Cloves, Ginger and All-Spice, 19thC, 8¾in (22cm) high.
£300–360 / €440–520
$500–600 L&T

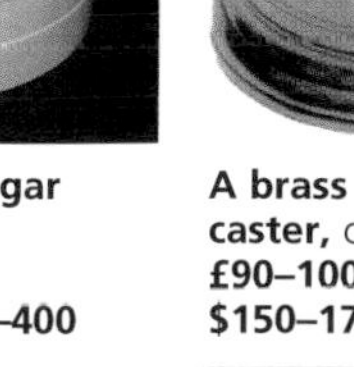

► A wrought-iron toasting fork, Welsh, c1780, 19in (48.5cm) long.
£410–450 / €590–650
$690–760 SEA

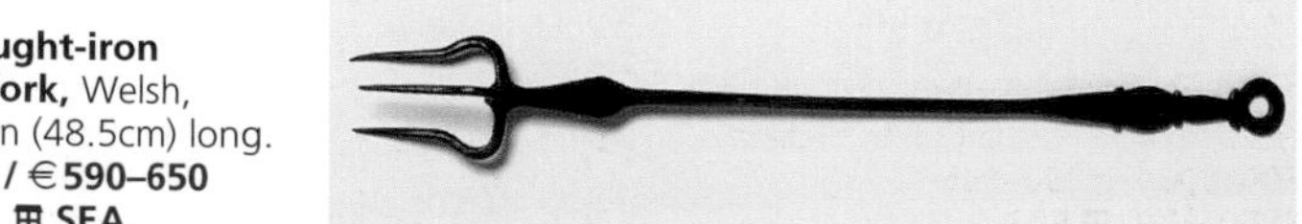

Pottery

In the past collecting was only for the rich. The Grand Tour was perhaps the 18th-century aristocratic equivalent of the modern-day backpacker, but instead of roughing it, those on tour were incredibly wealthy. They bought paintings, antiquities and artworks which they sent back to their country estates, where many of the items are still housed today. One lucky purchase was the Portland vase, a rare Roman cameo glass treasure which had been in Italy for around 1800 years. It was sold four times between 1780 and 1875 and is now in the British Museum. This is the vase which was famously copied by Josiah Wedgwood and became part of the factory's mark from 1878.

Collecting in the 18th century focused on the fine arts and antiquities but seldom included pottery. Some exceptions to this were Hispano-Moresque wares, maiolica and Iznik pottery. The 18th-century collector Horace Walpole had examples of Delft, maiolica and St Porchaire pottery, but these were impressive ornamental pieces rather than the simple domestic wares we find in modern collections. When considering important collections in the UK, the Schreiber collection in the Victoria and Albert Museum and the Glaisher collection in the Fitzwilliam Museum, Cambridge, are the first to spring to mind. Lady Charlotte Schreiber was an avid collector of both pottery and porcelain and spent much of her time scouring English and European shops in search of rarities. The wares are mainly 18th century, and include some of the very best examples of Delft, salt-glazed stoneware, Whieldon-type pieces as well as figures, creamware and transfer-printed wares.

The Glaisher collection, another showcase of European pottery, was bequeathed to the Fitzwilliam Museum in 1928 with the princely sum of £10,000 / €14,400 / $16,800 for its care, preservation and exhibition. Amassed over more than 30 years from the 1890s, and comprising over 3,000 pieces, this collection ranges from medieval jugs and mugs, 17th-century Delft and wonderful slipware dishes by Simpson, Toft and Taylor, through to red wares by the Elers brothers, early German ceramics and maiolica. Like the Schreiber collection, nearly every piece is an aficionado's dream.

Collecting today is quite a different matter. Firstly there are many more collectors than ever, and since so many of the very best pieces are now in museums, prices can soar when great rarities do arrive on the market. One consequence of this or perhaps simply of a century's evolution in collecting, is that many of the 19th- and 20th-century wares ignored by previous generations are now as popular as earlier wares.

John Axford

POTTERY

Animals & Birds

A Dutch Delft ewer and cover, modelled as a monkey, with polychrome decoration, minor damage, mid-18thC, 8¾in (22cm) high.
£1,950–2,300
€2,800–3,300
$3,300–3,900 ⚒ S(NY)

A creamware sauce boat, modelled as a dolphin, c1780, 4¾in (12cm) high.
£520–580 / €750–840
$870–970 ⊞ AUC

◄ A faïence tureen and cover, modelled as a turkey, restored, German, late 18thC, 11in (28cm) wide.
£3,350–4,000
€4,800–5,800
$5,600–6,700
⚒ S

A pair of Wedgwood basalt models of griffins, one with impressed mark, c1780, 9¾in (25cm) high.
£9,800–11,800 / €14,100–16,900
$16,500–19,800 ⚒ S

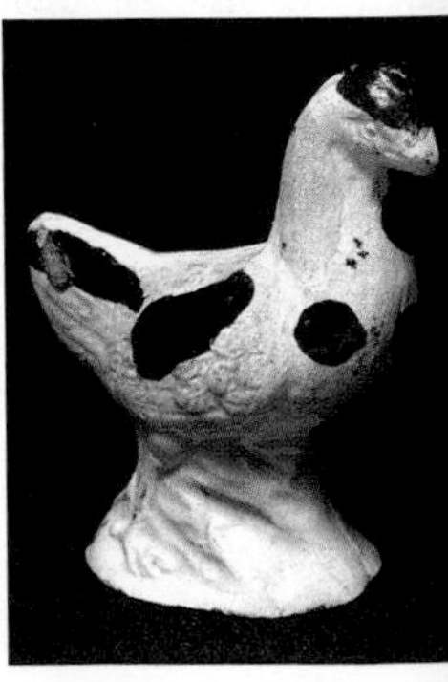

A Prattware model of a chicken, c1800, 3¼in (8.5cm) high.
£300–330 / €430–480
$500–550 ⊞ AUC

A Staffordshire bear baiting jug and cover, decorated with over-glazed enamels, slight damage, 1800–20, 12in (30.5cm) high.
£840–1,000
€1,200–1,400
$1,400–1,650 WW

A Bovey Tracey creamware model of a cat, c1810, 3¾in (9.5cm) wide.
£580–640 / €830–920
$970–1,100 RdV

A pair of Pratt-type cow groups, one with a cowherd and dog, the other with a milkmaid and calf, some restoration, c1810, 6in (15cm) high.
£2,250–2,700 / €3,250–3,900
$3,800–4,550 S(O)

A pearlware model of a dog, c1820, 4in (10cm) high.
£450–500 / €650–720
$750–840 AUC

A pair of Staffordshire models of pigeons, c1820, 4in (10cm) wide.
£1,050–1,200 / €1,500–1,700
$1,800–2,000 DAN

A salt-glazed money box, modelled as an elephant, c1820, 5in (12.5cm) high.
£810–900 / €1,150–1,300
$1,350–1,500 HOW

A pair of Staffordshire models of a ram and a ewe and lamb, with floral bocage, on hollow scrolled bases, early 19thC, 5½in (14cm) high.
£260–310 / €370–440
$440–520 PFK

◄ A Staffordshire model of a pug dog, c1825, 4in (10cm) high.
£400–440 / €570–630
$670–740 DAN

A Staffordshire model of Hercules and the bull, early 19thC, 5in (12.5cm) high.
£1,400–1,550 / €2,000–2,200
$2,350–2,600 JHo

A Staffordshire porcellaneous model of a poodle, 1835–40, 4in (10cm) high.
£340–380 / €490–550
$570–640 DAN

An agate glazed model of a cat, with a mouse in its jaw, 19thC, 5in (12.5cm) high.
£470–560 / €670–800
$790–940 TEN

A pair of Staffordshire Disraeli spaniels, with gilt collars and chains, c1850, 9in (23cm) high.
£420–500 / €600–720
$700–840 Bea
These spaniels are so-called because the kiss curls on their foreheads resemble those of the Victorian Prime Minister, Benjamin Disraeli.

A pair of Staffordshire models of spaniels, with gilt collars, c1850, 12½in (32cm) high.
£190–220 / €270–320
$320–380 DN

A pair of Victorian Staffordshire models of spaniels, highlighted with gilt, 9in (23cm) high.
£120–145 / €170–210
$200–240 SWO

A pair of Victorian Staffordshire models of spaniels, highlighted with copper lustre, 15in (38cm) high.
£1,000–1,200 / €1,450–1,700
$1,700–2,000 PF

▶ **A Staffordshire spill vase,** modelled as a leopard with cubs, c1850, 10½in (26.5cm) high.
£880–980 / €1,250–1,400
$1,500–1,650 HOW

A pair of Staffordshire models of spaniels, each seated beside a spaniel puppy, c1850, 7¾in (19.5cm) high.
£240–290 / €350–420
$400–480 G(L)

A Victorian Staffordshire group of a huntsman, fox and hounds, restored, 9¾in (25cm) high.
£440–530 / €630–760
$740–890 SWO

A pair of Victorian spill vases, modelled as sheep, 3½in (9cm) high.
£140–165 / €200–240
$240–290 G(L)

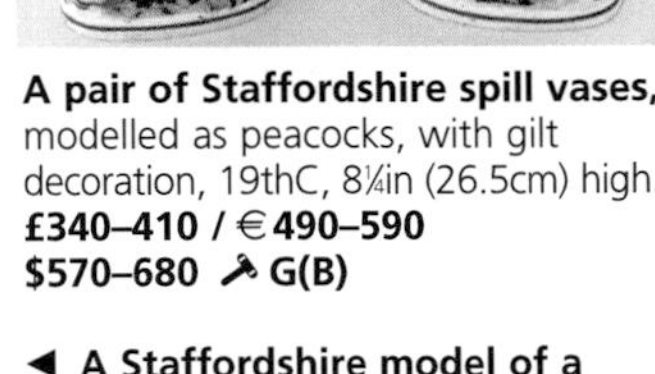

A pair of Staffordshire spill vases, modelled as peacocks, with gilt decoration, 19thC, 8¼in (26.5cm) high.
£340–410 / €490–590
$570–680 G(B)

◀ **A Staffordshire model of a parrot,** c1855, 9in (23cm) high.
£520–580 / €750–840
$870–970 DAN

A pair of maiolica models of lions, slight damage and restoration, Medici shield mark, Italian, 19thC, larger 9in (23cm) wide.
£760–910 / €1,100–1,300
$1,250–1,500 TEN

A Victorian Staffordshire model of a lion, 9in (23cm) high.
£230–270 / €330–390
$380–450 WilP

POTTERY

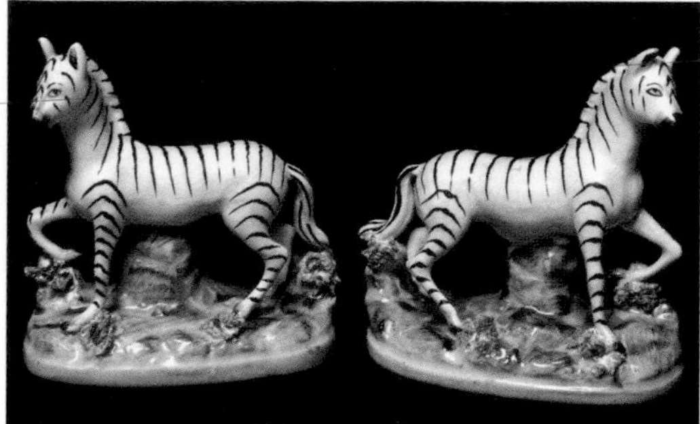

A pair of Staffordshire models of zebras, by Thomas Parr, c1860, 5in (12.5cm) high.
£730–810 / €1,000–1,150
$1,200–1,350 ⊞ HOW

A pair of Staffordshire models of poodles, c1860, 7in (18cm) high.
£380–420 / €540–600
$640–710 ⊞ DAN

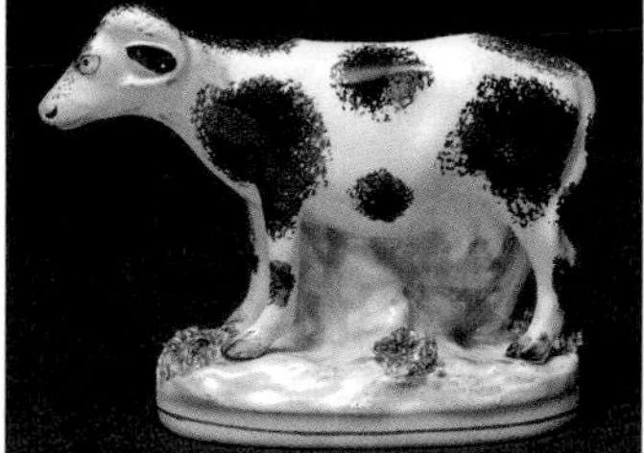

A Staffordshire model of a cow, c1860, 5in (12.5cm) wide.
£320–360 / €460–520
$540–600 ⊞ DAN

A pair of Victorian Staffordshire models of spaniels, 9½in (24cm) wide.
£165–195 / €240–290
$280–330 PF

A pair of Victorian Staffordshire models of Dalmations, with gilt collars and chains, 7½in (19cm) high.
£330–390 / €480–590
$550–660 PF

A majolica umbrella stand, attributed to Joseph Holdcroft, modelled as a heron in bullrushes, damaged, 19thC, 32½in (83cm) high.
£2,800–3,350
€4,000–4,800
$4,700–5,600 PFK

A pair of majolica wall pockets, modelled as elephant heads, with two suspension holes, incised mark, minor damage, c1872, 4in (10cm) wide.
£1,100–1,300 / €1,550–1,850
$1,850–2,200 S(O)

A Wedgwood majolica dish and cover, impressed mark, date code for 1878, 7½in (19cm) wide.
£6,400–7,700 / €9,300–11,100
$10,800–13,000 G(L)
The auctioneers had been unable to find a dish of this type offered for sale in recent times and it was therefore keenly contested in the saleroom.

A Staffordshire hen box and cover, decorated with painted enamels, minor damage, late 19thC, 9¾in (25cm) wide.
£200–240 / €290–350
$340–400 WW

◄ **A Delphin Massier stoneware model of a cockerel,** marked, early 20thC, 13½in (34.5cm) high.
£490–590 / €710–850
$820–990 G(B)
The Massier family, Clément, Delphin and Jérôme, produced ceramics at their factory in Golfe-Juan, France, during the 19th and early 20th centuries.

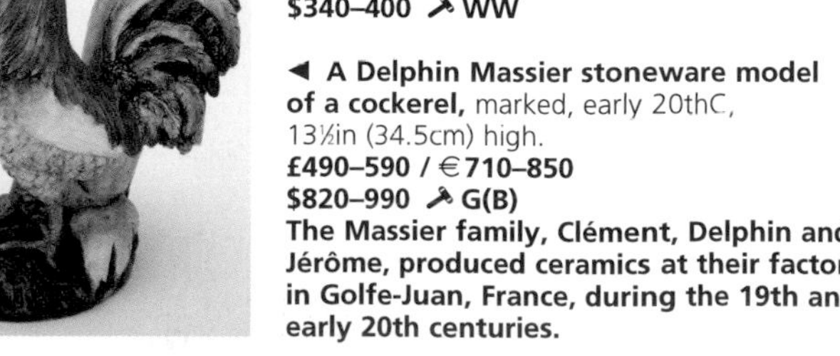

A faïence model of a rabbit, damaged, c1900, 11½in (29cm) high.
£370–440 / €530–630
$620–740 WW

POTTERY

Bowls

A Dutch Delft Bleu Persan lobed bowl, c1700, 8¼in (21cm) diam.
£940–1,100 / €1,350–1,600
$1,600–1,850 DN

An English delft bowl, probably London, c1760, 8¾in (22cm) diam.
£450–500 / €650–720
$760–840 AUC

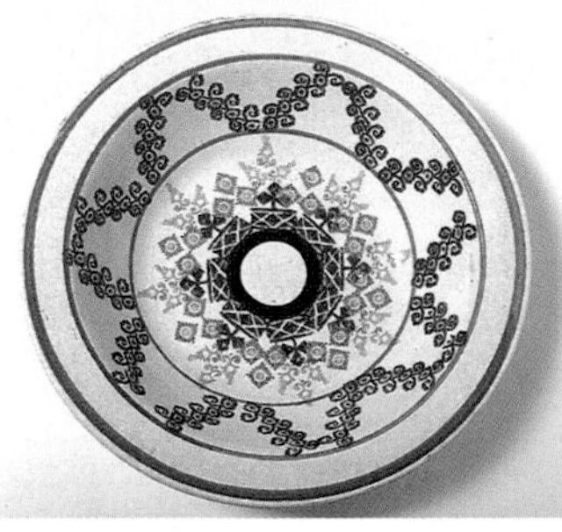

A Staffordshire spongeware bowl, c1880, 11in (28cm) diam.
£250–280 / €360–400
$420–470 HTE

► **An English delft punchbowl,** possibly Bristol, decorated with Oriental figures, 18thC, 12in (30.5cm) diam.
£420–500 / €600–720
$710–840 HYD

A Dutch Delft punchbowl, with floral decoration, minor damage, c1750, 10¼in (26cm) diam.
£620–740 / €890–1,050
$1,000–1,200 S(O)

An English delft bowl, decorated with Oriental fishermen, minor damage, c1750, 12in (30.5cm) diam.
£260–310 / €370–440
$440–520 NSal

► **A Wedgwood footed bowl,** with two handles and painted decoration, impressed mark, 19thC, 12¼in (31cm) diam.
£200–240 / €290–350
$340–400 WW

A set of six Davenport soup dishes, transfer-printed with Indian Flowers pattern, impressed maker's marks, mid-19thC, 10in (25.5cm) diam.
£150–180 / €220–260
$250–300 NOA

A Belleek spongeware bowl and mug, Irish, c1880, 6in (15cm) diam.
£155–175 / €220–250
$260–290 Byl

Covered Bowls

An English delft bowl and cover, with two handles, the interior with a pierced strainer, possibly Bristol, minor damage, 1700–25, 9¾in (25cm) wide.
£700–840 / €1,000–1,200
$1,200–1,400 DN

An English delft food warmer and cover, fitted with a candle holder, the handles modelled as leaves, minor damage, 1700–50, 5¼in (13.5cm) high.
£1,900–2,250
€2,750–3,250
$3,200–3,800 Bea

A creamware bowl and cover, probably by Neale & Wilson, c1790, 10in (25.5cm) high.
£800–880 / €1,150–1,300
$1,350–1,500 AUC

Buildings

A model of a distillery, on a stand, minor damage, Dutch, c1750, 6¼in (16cm) high.
£990–1,150
€1,400–1,650
$1,650–1,950 ⚒ S(Am)

A Pratt-style money box, modelled as a cottage flanked by two figures, early 19thC, 5¼in (13.5cm) high.
£540–650 / €780–940
$910–1,100 ⚒ AH

A stoneware tobacco jar and cover, modelled as a house, impressed 'J. C. Roper, Bristol', 19thC, 9½in (24cm) high.
£330–390 / €480–580
$550–650 ⚒ CHTR

A Staffordshire pastille burner, modelled as a cottage, restored, 19thC, 6¾in (17.5cm) high.
£45–50 / €65–75
$75–85 ⚒ L&E

Busts

◄ A Staffordshire bust of John Wesley, probably by Enoch Wood, late 18thC, 13½in (34.5cm) high.
£1,200–1,350
€1,750–1,950
$2,000–2,250 ⊞ JHo

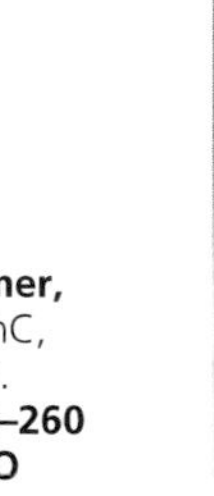

► A bust of Homer, cracked, early 19thC, 12½in (32cm) high.
£150–180 / €220–260
$250–300 ⚒ SWO

A Staffordshire bust of William Shakespeare, impressed 'shakspere', 19thC, 8½in (21cm) high.
£320–380 / €460–550
$540–640 ⚒ S(O)

Butter & Sauce Boats

◄ A Staffordshire salt-glazed sauce boat, with moulded decoration, the handle modelled as a 'Hungry Hound', some restoration, c1755, 7¾in (19.5cm) wide.
£1,900–2,250
€2,750–3,250
$3,200–3,800
⚒ B

A Staffordshire salt-glazed sauce boat, with moulded decoration, c1760, 6½in (16.5cm) wide.
£780–930 / €1,150–1,350
$1,300–1,550 ⚒ S(O)

► A pair of Wedgwood creamware butter boats, impressed marks, late 18thC, 3in (8cm) wide.
£330–390
€480–570
$560–660 ⚒ PFK

A creamware sauce boat, Staffordshire or Yorkshire, with a foliate scroll handle, c1780, 6in (15cm) wide.
£470–560 / €680–810
$790–940 ⚒ DN

Cheese Domes

A Brownfields majolica cheese dome and stand, modelled as a castle turret, impressed marks, restored, c1870, 12½in (32cm) high.
£820–980 / €1,200–1,400
$1,400–1,650 ⚒ B

A Wedgwood majolica cheese dome, moulded with a band of basket weave and wild primroses, on a similar stand, impressed mark, c1875, 10in (25.5cm) high.
£610–730 / €880–1,050
$1,000–1,200 ⚒ B

A majolica cheese dome, surmounted by a cow, moulded with blackberry branches, on a similar stand, minor damage, late 19thC, 11in (28cm) high.
£720–860 / €1,000–1,200
$1,200–1,450 ⚒ S(O)

A Victorian Brownfields cheese dome, modelled as a castle turret, with hand-painted decoration, on a turned wood base, 11in (28cm) high.
£100–120 / €145–170
$170–200 ⚒ HOLL

Comports

An earthenware comport, printed with an Adam Buck chariot and figure, moulded with vine leaves, early 19thC, 10in (25.5cm) wide.
£200–240 / €290–350
$340–400 ⚒ G(L)

► **A majolica comport,** possibly Sarreguemines, the base with three mythical fish, damaged, impressed mark, 19thC.
£110–130 / €160–190
$185–220 ⚒ AMB

► **A Minton majolica comport,** modelled as Triton holding a shell, date code for 1860, 15¼in (39cm) high.
£1,800–2,150 / €2,600–3,100
$3,000–3,600 ⚒ Bea

A Victorian majolica comport, moulded in the form of woven wicker, 12½in (32cm) wide.
£120–145 / €175–210
$200–240 ⚒ G(L)

Condiment Pots & Cruets

A pair of salts, with painted armorial decoration, on paw feet, minor damage, Italian, Faenza, c1620, 4¼in (11cm) high.
£2,350–2,800 / €3,400–4,000
$4,000–4,700 ⚒ B

A Staffordshire salt-glazed cruet, comprising six pieces, with enamelled *famille rose* decoration, losses and damage, mid-18thC, 7in (18cm) wide.
£6,600–7,900
€9,500–11,400
$11,100–13,300 ⚒ S(O)

A two-piece faïence cruet and stand, late 19thC, 6in (15cm) high.
£120–145 / €175–210
$200–240 ⚒ AMB

Cow Creamers

A Staffordshire creamware cow creamer, decorated in running glazes, c1790, 7in (18cm) wide.
£860–950 / €1,250–1,400
$1,450–1,600 ⊞ DAN

A cow creamer, North Yorkshire, early 19thC, 5½in (14cm) wide.
£1,200–1,350
€1,750–2,000
$2,000–2,250 ⊞ JHo

A lustreware cow creamer and cover, c1900, 5½in (14cm) high.
£210–250 / €300–360
$350–420 ⚒ B(W)

Cups

A London delft fuddling cup, c1650, 3½in (9cm) high.
£6,000–6,600 / €8,600–9,500
$10,000–11,000 ⊞ JHo
Fuddling cups are formed as three or more conjoined cups connected internally so that someone drinking from one cup can drain them all. They were made in the 17th and 18th centuries in England, Germany and Holland. They are usually made in delft or slipware and examples with as many as six cups are known.

A pearlware loving cup, painted 'Wm Barker', c1795, 5¾in (14.5cm) high.
£520–580 / €750–840
$870–980 ⊞ AUC

A copper lustre cup, mid-19thC, 5in (12.5cm) high.
£105–120 / €155–175
$175–200 ⊞ DAN

► **A Victorian loving cup,** with printed decoration, 5in (12.5cm) high.
£165–195 / €240–290
$280–330 ⚒ G(L)

Dishes

◄ **A maiolica *crespina*,** depicting Paris and Mercury, some restoration, Italian, Pesaro, c1540, 9¾in (24.5cm) diam.
£3,600–4,300 / €5,200–6,200
$6,000–7,200 ⚒ S(O)

► **A Dutch Delft dish,** commemorating William III, restored section to rim, late 17thC, 8½in (21.5cm) diam.
£910–1,100 / €1,300–1,550
$1,550–1,850 ⚒ DN

► **A Liverpool delft char dish,** painted with fish, slight damage, c1760, 8¾in (22cm) wide.
£1,300–1,550 / €1,850–2,200
$2,200–2,600 ⚒ S(O)
A char is a fish of the *salmonidae* family and is rarely seen today. They were made into a paste and served in dishes such as these.

A pair of creamware dishes, modelled as leaves, c1780, 6½in (16.5cm) wide.
£360–400 / €520–580
$600–670 ⊞ AUC

A slipware dish, by Harwood, Stockton-on-Tees, impressed mark, mid-19thC, 11½in (29.5cm) wide.
£260–310 / €370–440
$440–520 ⚒ PFK

A George Jones majolica strawberry dish, creamer and sugar basin missing, impressed marks, 1872, 14¾in (37.5cm) wide.
£360–430 / €520–620
$600–720 ⚒ PFK

A majolica dish, by Joseph Holdcroft, modelled as a shell on three shell feet, minor damage, impressed marks, c1880, 8in (20.5cm) wide.
£410–490 / €590–700
$690–820 ⚒ DN

A Victorian majolica bread dish, with moulded inscription 'waste not want not', 11½in (29cm) diam.
£130–145 / €185–210
$220–240 ⊞ CHAC

A pair of majolica nut dishes, moulded with holly leaves and surmounted by robins, both birds rivetted, faint registration marks, c1880, 8in (20cm) wide.
£820–980 / €1,200–1,400
$1,400–1,650 ⚒ WW

Covered Dishes

A Wedgwood Queensware entrée dish and cover, printed and enamelled with plants, repaired, late 18thC, 10in (25.5cm) wide.
£210–250 / €300–360
$350–420 ⚒ G(L)

► A Victorian dish, cover and stand, modelled as a basket, the cover with chicks emerging from eggs, with base, 9½in (24cm) diam.
£330–390 / €480–580
$550–650 ⚒ TRM

A majolica sardine dish, the cover decorated with moulded fish, minor damage, 19thC, 8in (20.5cm) wide.
£300–360 / €430–520
$500–600 ⚒ AG

A Minton majolica game pie dish and cover, No. 964, the cover surmounted by a hound, on four lion-paw feet, impressed mark, 1866, 14½in (37cm) wide.
£2,400–2,850 / €3,450–4,100
$4,000–4,800 ⚒ S(O)

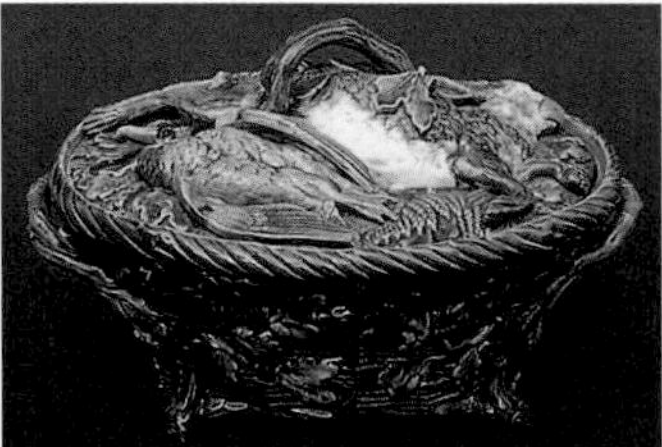

A Minton majolica game pie dish, No. 668/10, the cover with a duck, rabbit and a crow, the base with basketweave and leaves, impressed marks, minor damage, 1866, 13½in (34cm) wide.
£1,000–1,200 / €1,450–1,700
$1,700–2,000 ⚒ DD

A George Jones majolica game pie dish and cover, with a quail knop, the base moulded with rabbits, impressed marks, minor damage, c1870, 11in (28cm) wide.
£2,900–3,500 / €4,200–5,000
$4,900–5,900 ⚒ WW
Dishes of this type with chicks nesting with the quail can make around £10,000 / €14,400 / $16,800 at auction.

◄ A Minton game pie dish, with two handles, the cover with a duck, a hare and a bird, 19thC, 14in (35.5cm) wide.
£820–980 / €1,200–1,400
$1,400–1,650 ⚒ BWL

Figures

A maiolica figural group of St Benedict and St Jerome sitting before a grotto, restored, minor losses, Italian, probably Faenza, 16thC, 10¾in (27cm) high.
£7,500–9,000 / €10,800–13,000
$12,600–15,000 S(Mi)

A Nevers maiolica figure of a putto and a dolphin, minor restoration, French, 18thC, 6¾in (17cm) high.
£230–270 / €330–390
$390–470 DN

A Dutch Delft figure of a fish seller, minor damage and restoration, mid-18thC, 5in (13cm) high.
£1,950–2,350 / €2,800–3,350
$3,250–3,900 S(Am)

A Staffordshire tithe pig figural group, minor damage, c1780, 5½in (14cm) high.
£300–360 / €430–520
$500–600 G(L)

The tithe pig was a popular English ceramic subject. Examples in Derby porcelain, Staffordshire pottery and as printed scenes are found in the late 18th and early 19th centuries. The scene depicts a parson standing with a pig in each hand and a farmer and his wife. The farmer's wife is refusing to part with the tenth (or tithe) pig unless the parson takes her tenth child also.

A Prattware figure of a man with a dog, probably Yorkshire, c1790, 10in (25.5cm) high.
£760–850 / €1,100–1,250
$1,250–1,400 AUC

A Ralph Wood-type lead-glazed pearlware figure of a woman feeding birds, repaired, late 18thC, 8in (20.5cm) high.
£800–960 / €1,200–1,400
$1,350–1,600 WW

A Staffordshire pearlware figure of Jupiter and an eagle, c1795, 12in (30.5cm) high.
£800–890 / €1,150–1,300
$1,350–1,500 AUC

A pair of pearlware figures of musicians, minor restoration, c1800, 10¾in (27cm) high.
£540–650 / €780–940
$910–1,100 B(Kn)

A Wood pearlware figure of Chaucer, standing against a column with books, slight damage, c1800, 12½in (32cm) high.
£820–980 / €1,200–1,400
$1,400–1,650 B(Kn)

A Staffordshire figure of a French horn player, 1810–15, 10in (25.5cm) high.
£610–680 / €880–980
$1,000–1,100 DAN

A Staffordshire pearlware figure of a gentleman, possibly Sir Walter Raleigh, on a marbled base, some restoration, hand detached, 1810–30, 22¼in (56.6cm) high.
£850–1,000 / €1,200–1,450
$1,400–1,700 S(NY)

A Staffordshire pearlware figure of a man playing the bagpipes, 1810–15, 9in (23cm) high.
£540–600 / €780–860
$900–1,000 ⊞ DAN

A pearlware figural group of a mother and child reading, seated before bocage, minor damage and losses, 1815–25, 9in (23cm) high.
£3,000–3,600
€4,300–5,200
$5,000–6,000 ⚒ B(Kn)

A pair of Staffordshire pearlware figures of Tam O'Shanter and Souter Johnny, 1810–20, 6in (15cm) high.
£570–630 / €820–910
$950–1,050 ⊞ DAN
These figures depict characters from a poem by Robert Burns (1759–96).

A Prattware figure of St George and the Dragon, probably Yorkshire, some restoration, early 19thC, 11¼in (28.5cm) high.
£1,500–1,800
€2,150–2,600
$2,500–3,000 ⚒ WW

A pair of Obadiah Sherratt-style Staffordshire pearlware groups, entitled 'Flight to Egypt' and 'Return from Egypt', minor repairs, c1810, 8in (20.5cm) high.
£2,350–2,800 / €3,400–4,000
$4,000–4,700 ⚒ WW
The bright colouring of these figures and the design of the bases are particularly uncommon.

A Staffordshire figural group of a lady, on horseback with a dog, early 19thC, 6½in (16.5cm) high.
£3,300–3,650
€4,800–5,300
$5,500–6,100 ⊞ JHo

► A Staffordshire figural group of The Vicar and Moses, c1820, 9in (23cm) high.
£860–950 / €1,250–1,400
$1,450–1,600 ⊞ DAN

A Staffordshire pearlware spill vase, with two musicians, c1820, 7½in (19cm) high.
£1,800–2,000
€2,600–2,900
$3,000–3,350 ⊞ HOW

A Staffordshire figural group of dandies, c1820, 8½in (21.5cm) high.
£1,600–1,800
€2,300–2,600
$2,700–3,000 ⊞ JHo

A Staffordshire figure of a boy with a pipe, on a table base, early 19thC, 6in (15cm) high.
£1,000–1,100
€1,450–1,600
$1,700–1,900 ⊞ JHo

A Staffordshire pearlware figure of Diana, c1820, 12in (30.5cm) high.
£1,150–1,300
€1,650–1,850
$2,000–2,200 ⊞ HOW

◄ A figural group of a man and a woman, seated before bocage, he holding a sack, c1820, 8in (20.5cm) high.
£1,000–1,100
€1,450–1,600
$1,700–1,900 ⊞ AUC

A Staffordshire figural group of Abraham and Isaac, c1820, 10in (25.5cm) high.
£1,500–1,650
€2,150–2,400
$2,500–2,800 ⊞ JHo

A Staffordshire figural group of Peter raising the lame man, c1820, 10½in (26.5cm) high.
£3,600–4,000
€5,200–5,800
$6,000–6,700 ⊞ JHo

A Staffordshire figural group of a boy collecting nuts, early 19thC, 6½in (16.5cm) high.
£1,300–1,450
€1,900–2,100
$2,200–2,450 ⊞ JHo

A Staffordshire tithe pig figural group, early 19thC, 8½in (21.5cm) high.
£330–390 / €480–580
$550–650 ⚒ Mit

◄ **A pair of pearlware groups,** entitled 'Flight to Egypt' and 'Return from Egypt', some restoration, c1825, 9½in (24cm) high.
£1,300–1,550
€1,900–2,250
$2,200–2,600 ⚒ DN

► **A Staffordshire figure of Elijah and the ravens,** repairs, 1800–50, 11in (28cm) high.
£260–310 / €380–450
$440–520 ⚒ WW

POTTERY

A pearlware allegorical figure of Plenty, 19thC, 9¼in (23.5cm) high.
£140–165 / €200–240 $240–280 AH

A Staffordshire figural group of the King and Queen of Sardinia, 19thC, 13¾in (35cm) high.
£90–105 / €130–150 $150–175 WilP

A Staffordshire porcellaneous figure of a boy, depicted holding a bird's nest, c1840, 5in (12.5cm) high.
£290–320 / €420–460 $490–540 DAN

A Staffordshire porcellaneous figure of Winter, c1840, 10in (25.5cm) high.
£400–440 / €580–640 $670–740 DAN

A Staffordshire figural group of Uncle Tom and Eva, from *Uncle Tom's Cabin*, c1852, 8½in (21.5cm) high.
£520–580 / €750–840 $870–970 SER

A Crimean War figural group of a French soldier and a British sailor, minor damage, c1854, 13½in (34.5cm) high.
£700–840 / €1,000–1,200 $1,200–1,400 DN

► **A Staffordshire porcellaneous figure of Neptune,** c1840, 7in (18cm) high.
£340–380 / €490–550 $570–640 DAN

A Staffordshire porcellaneous figure of a man, depicted with a dog and gun, 1840–45, 7in (18cm) high.
£270–300 / €390–430 $450–500 DAN

A pair of Staffordshire figures of General Codrington and Pélissier, c1854, 13in (33cm) high.
£150–180 / €220–260 $250–300 B(Kn)
Sir William John Codrington (1804–84) succeeded Sir James Simpson in 1855 as commander-in-chief of British troops in the Crimea. He fought at Sebastopol, was MP for Greenwich and Governor of Gibralter. Jean-Jaques Pélissier, Duc de Malakoff (1794–1864) served in Spain in 1823 and succeeded François Canrobert as commander-in-chief of the French before Sebastopol. He was also French Ambassador to London.

A Staffordshire figure of Richard Cobden, 1845–50, 8in (20.5cm) high.
£430–480 / €620–690 $720–800 DAN
Richard Cobden was a politician, the 'apostle of free trade', who helped to found the Anti Corn Law League in 1838. The Corn Laws, which imposed a heavy duty on imported corn to protect the interests of British farmers, were repealed in 1846.

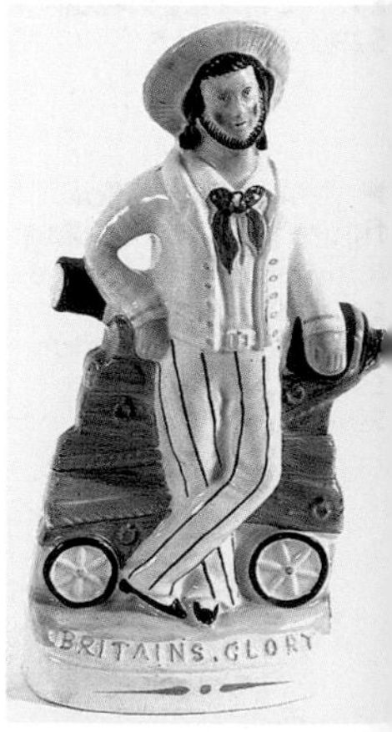

A Staffordshire figure, entitled 'Britains Glory', commemorating the Crimean War, c1854, 11in (28cm) high.
£210–250 / €300–360 $350–420 GAK

A pair of Staffordshire figures of Generals Brown and Simpson, one small crack, c1857, 12½in (32cm) high.
£1,250–1,500
€1,800–2,150
$2,100–2,500 ⚒ B(Kn)

General George Brown (1790–1865) served in the Peninsula War and commanded the Light Division in the Crimean War. Sir James Simpson (1792–1868) also fought in the Crimean War and was created a general after the capture of Sebastopol in 1855.

A Staffordshire group of Crimean War figures, late 19thC, 12¼in (31cm) high.
£175–210 / €250–300
$290–350 ⚒ LF

► A Ginori maiolica figure of a boy holding a basket, minor damage, painted mark, Italian, c1900, 8¼in (21cm) high.
£55–65 / €80–95
$90–105 ⚒ WW

◄ A pair of Staffordshire figures of a cobbler and his wife, c1900, 12in (30.5cm) high.
£360–400
€520–580
$600–670
⊞ CHAC

A Staffordshire figure of Little Red Riding Hood, c1860, 7in (18cm) high.
£120–135 / €170–195
$200–230 ⊞ DAN

A Minton majolica figure of a boy pushing a wheelbarrow, No. 413, stamped, damage and repairs, date cypher for 1868, 13in (33cm) high.
£640–770 / €920–1,100
$1,100–1,300 ⚒ TRM

A pair of Victorian Staffordshire figures of a boy and girl riding on goats, 5½in (14cm) high.
£280–330 / €400–470
$470–550 ⚒ PF

A pair of terracotta figures of a fisherman and woman, German, 19thC, 17¾in (45cm) high.
£230–270 / €330–400
$390–470 ⚒ G(L)

Flatware

A maiolica dish, possibly Casa Pirota, the underside with blue lines radiating from a loop mark, repairs, chips to rim, Italian, Faenza, 1510–20, 9¾in (25cm) diam.
£770–920 / €1,100–1,300
$1,300–1,550 ⚒ B

A pair of Dutch Delft enamelled earthenware plates, one marked 'PK', the other 'GK', chips to rim, 17thC, 13¾in (35cm) diam.
£1,050–1,250 / €1,500–1,800
$1,750–2,100 ⚒ BERN

A Lambeth delft charger, decorated with apples and pears, the upper side tin glazed, the underside lead glazed, c1680, 12in (30.5cm) diam.
£500–600 / €720–860
$840–1,000 ⚒ Mit

A majolica *istoriato* dish, with a deep cavetto, decorated with a scene depicting the abduction of Europa by the Bull, the base inscribed 'De uropa', trimmed and restored, Italian, Urbino, mid-16thC, 8¾in (22cm) wide.
£1,000–1,200 / €1,450–1,700
$1,700–2,000 ⚒ B
If this dish had not been trimmed it could have fetched £5,000–8,000 / €7,200–11,500 / $8,400–13,400.

A faïence armorial dish, decorated with a shield flanked by scrolls and fruit, the reverse with stylized foliate motifs, repaired, shield mark, Italian, Savona, 1650–1700, 14¼in (36cm) diam.
£900–1,050 / €1,350–1,600
$1,500–1,750 ⚒ S(O)

A maiolica dish, painted with a young woman holding a heart pierced with an arrow, flaked and cracked, Italian, Montelupo, 17thC, 11¾in (30cm) diam.
£1,450–1,750 / €2,100–2,500
$2,450–2,950 ⚒ SWO

◄ **A maiolica dish,** painted with a soldier carrying a long-handled axe, chipped and cracked, Italian, Montelupo, 17thC, 12½in (32cm) diam.
£1,300–1,550 / €1,900–2,250
$2,200–2,600 ⚒ SWO

A pottery charger, moulded with a central gadrooned boss within a swag border, the reverse painted in brown lustre, haircracks, some glaze loss, Hispano-Moresque, probably Valencia, mid-16thC, 16in (40.5cm) diam.
£2,900–3,500 / €4,200–5,000
$4,900–6,000 ⚒ S(O)

Italian maiolica

Tin-glazed earthenware, or maiolica, was made in Italy from at least the 13th century in the form of simple household items such as bowls, dishes, basins or jugs. By the 15th century wares had become increasingly sophisticated in both form and design, and important centres of production grew up in Faenza, Florence, Orvieto, Naples and Deruta. The high point was reached with the *istoriato* wares of the 16th century. This is the term for narrative Italian maiolica wares – that is, pieces that tell a story. The most common themes are biblical, mythological or historical. Examples are high-fired in a brilliant palette, usually with orange and blue the predominant colours. The most important centres of production were Urbino, Casteldurante and Gubbio. In Montelupo in northern Italy high-quality wares decorated with saints or single figures were produced.

A Brislington delft Adam and Eve charger, with a blue dash border, repaired, 1690–1700, 13½in (34.5cm) diam.
£1,750–2,100 / €2,500–3,000
$2,950–3,500 ⚒ B

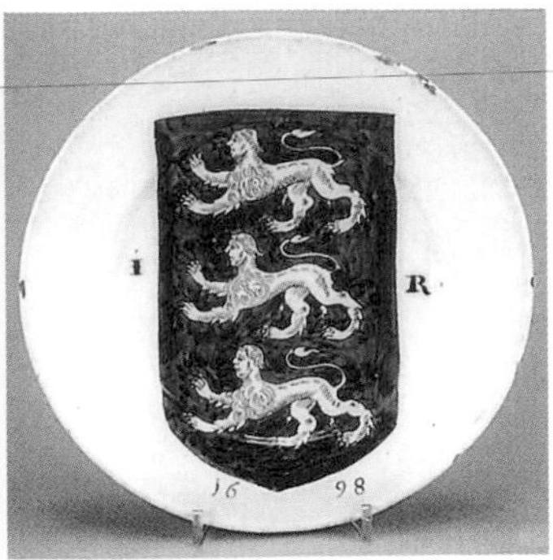

A Dutch Delft De Paeuw commemorative plate, inscribed 'IR' for James II and dated 1698, restored, 10¼in (26cm) diam.
£2,350–2,800 / €3,350–4,000
$4,000–4,700 DN

A set of ten delft plates, probably London, c1700, 8¾in (22cm) diam.
£8,800–9,800 / €12,600–14,100
$14,800–16,500 KEY

A Dutch Delft chinoiserie dish, decorated with an Oriental and a warrior on horseback, minor chips and wear, haircrack to rim, c1700, 13in (33cm) diam.
£410–490 / €590–700
$690–820 S(Am)

A Bristol delft plate, decorated with a bird, tree and floral sprays, c1710, 9in (23cm) diam.
£300–360 / €440–520
$500–600 Mit

A Lambeth delft plate, commemorating the coronation of King George II, inscribed and dated 1727, damaged, 8¾in (22cm) diam.
£8,200–9,800 / €11,800–14,200
$13,800–16,500 Bea
Commemorative delftware is rare and therefore much sought-after.

A Bristol delft plate, decorated with the initials 'I.F.' and the date 1728, 8in (20.5cm) diam.
£1,400–1,550 / €2,000–2,250
$2,350–2,600 JHo

A delft plate, decorated with a lady carrying a basket, chips and flakes, c1730, 8¾in (22cm) diam.
£380–460 / €550–660
$640–770 WW

An English delft plate, decorated with a bird in a garden, haircrack, 1700–50, 8¼in (21cm) diam.
£165–200 / €240–280
$280–330 WW

A Bristol delft plate, decorated with a peacock, c1730, 8in (20.5cm) diam.
£5,400–6,000 / €7,800–8,700
$9,100–10,100 KEY

A Bristol delft plate, decorated with a cockerel, c1730, 8¾in (22cm) diam.
£5,400–6,000 / €7,800–8,700
$9,100–10,100 KEY

A London delft plate, c1731, 8¼in (21cm) diam.
£3,300–3,650 / €4,750–5,300
$5,600–6,200 JHo

An English delft plate, probably Liverpool, decorated with a seated figure in a Chinese landscape, c1740, 9in (23cm) diam.
£380–460 / €550–660
$640–770 SWO

A delft plate, probably Bristol, decorated with Oriental figures, c1740, 8in (20.5cm) diam.
£700–780 / €1,000–1,100
$1,200–1,350 ⊞ JHo

A delft charger, probably Bristol, decorated with a mandarin beside a jardinière of flowers, 18thC, 14in (35.5cm) diam.
£820–980 / €1,200–1,400
$1,350–1,600 ⚒ G(L)

A pair of English delft plates, decorated with repeating floral sprays, the undersides glazed, 18thC, 9in (23cm) diam.
£470–560 / €680–810
$790–940 ⚒ Mit

An English delft plate, decorated with a chinoiserie garden scene, 18thC, 9in (23cm) diam.
£110–130 / €160–190
$185–220 ⚒ PFK

An English delft dish, decorated with a stylized plant, 18thC, 13¼in (33.5cm) diam.
£920–1,100 / €1,350–1,600
$1,550–1,850 ⚒ B(W)

A delft plate, possibly Lambeth, decorated with an Oriental figure under a tree, 18thC, 10¼in (26cm) diam.
£150–180 / €220–260
$250–300 ⚒ SWO

A maiolica saucer, decorated with the Virgin and Child, damaged, Italian, 18thC, 5¼in (13.5cm) diam.
£670–800 / €960–1,150
$1,100–1,300 ⚒ S(Mi)

A maiolica plate, probably after Antonia Tempesta, decorated with figures in a landscape, repaired, Italian, Siena, 18thC, 10in (25.5cm) diam.
£470–560 / €680–810
$790–940 ⚒ WW

A maiolica plate, painted with figures among ruins, Italian, Castelli, 18thC, 7in (18cm) diam.
£730–880 / €1,050–1,250
$1,250–1,500 ⚒ Bea

A maiolica dish, by Felice Clerici and Giuseppe Maria Clerici, small chips, Italian, 1756–80, 9in (23cm) diam.
£6,600–7,900 / €9,500–11,400
$11,000–13,200 ⚒ S(Mi)
The Clerici Pottery was set up in Milan in 1745 by Felice Clerici and continued in production until 1780.

A Dutch Delft plate, depicting Prince William and Princess Sophia, c1750, 9in (23cm) diam.
£470–520 / €680–750
$790–870 ⊞ KEY

A Bristol delft *bianco-sopra-bianco* plate, the centre decorated with a figure beneath a building, with a scalloped border, mid-18thC, 8¾in (22cm) diam.
£260–310 / €380–450
$440–520 ⚒ SWO

Eighteenth-century British delftware

From c1720, British delftware becomes increasingly distinctive – the decoration is less complex and looser in style. A large variety of wares was produced, including punchbowls, plates, flower bricks, wine bottles, fuddling cups, puzzle jugs and posset pots. Many examples were decorated with British landscapes, buildings and figures, but chinoiserie decoration, such as pagodas and Chinese figures, birds and flowers, was also popular. By the end of the 18th century, production had virtually ceased due to the rise in the popularity of creamware.

An English delft plate, probably Lambeth, decorated with a stylized flower bouquet, c1760, 9in (23cm) diam.
£240–290 / €350–420
$410–490 ⚒ SWO

A Lambeth delft plate, decorated with an Oriental in a landscape, c1765, 7½in (19cm) diam.
£220–250 / €320–360
$380–420 ⊞ KEY

A Dublin delft plate, Irish, 1760–80, 11in (28cm) diam.
£320–360 / €470–520
$540–600 ⊞ KEY

An English delft dish, decorated with stylized flowers, leaves and buds, rim chips, late 18thC, 13in (33cm) diam.
£880–1,050 / €1,250–1,500
$1,500–1,800 ⚒ B(W)

A faïence plate, painted with a flower spray and scattered blooms, minor damage, monogrammed, painter's mark, French, Strasbourg, c1765, 9¾in (25cm) diam.
£900–1,050 / €1,350–1,600
$1,500–1,800 ⚒ S(O)

A Bristol delft plate, depicting two ladies before a house, c1780, 9in (23cm) diam.
£800–880 / €1,150–1,300
$1,350–1,500 ⊞ JHo

An Ann Gomm-type delft plate, probably London, the spider's web decoration bordered by flower buds, c1790, 9in (23cm) diam.
£350–420 / €500–600
$600–700 ⚒ F&C
This is known as an Ann Gomm-type plate because there is a dated example that is inscribed with that name within a spider's web in the City Museum, Stoke-on-Trent.

A Whieldon-style plate, with a ribbed rim, c1765, 8¾in (22cm) diam.
£165–195 / €240–280
$280–330 ⚒ B(Kn)

A pair of Prattware plates, each decorated with an exotic bird, c1780, 8¼in (21cm) diam.
£600–720 / €850–1,000
$1,000–1,200 ⚒ Mit

A pearlware plate, with chinoiserie decoration, c1790, 9½in (24cm) diam.
£150–180 / €220–260
$250–300 ⚒ GAK

A pair of Don Pottery pearlware plates, c1800, 8in (20.5cm) diam.
£760–850 / €1,050–1,200
$1,250–1,400 ⊞ AUC

A Swansea botanical creamware plate, by Thomas Pardoe, titled 'Scarlet Azalea', impressed mark, Welsh, c1800, 8¾in (22cm) diam.
£1,100–1,300 / €1,600–1,900
$1,850–2,200 ⚒ B

A child's pearlware plate, entitled 'Perfect Innocence', decorated with Pratt colours, c1815, 7½in (19cm) diam.
£240–270 / €350–390
$400–440 ⊞ HOW

A pearlware plate, moulded with birds and butterflies and painted with flowers, c1835, 6in (15cm) diam.
£150–170 / €210–240
$250–280 ⊞ HOW

A Turner creamware plate, entitled 'Elector and Candidate', c1800, 7¾in (19.5cm) diam.
£220–250 / €320–360
$370–420 ⊞ AUC
When the plate is rotated 180°, the central portrait turns into the head of a woman.

A creamware plate, entitled 'Dr Syntax at home', c1830, 9in (23cm) diam.
£210–240 / €300–340
$350–400 ⊞ AUC

A Minton plate, commemorating the Jubilee of Queen Victoria, the reverse with printed and impressed mark, 1897, 15¼in (38.5cm) diam.
£330–390 / €470–560
$550–650 ⚒ SAS

A Spode New China meat plate, impressed mark and pattern No. 4822, c1810, 18¼in (46.5cm) wide.
£240–290 / €350–420
$400–480 ⚒ BR

A ceramic commemorative plate, entitled 'To the memory of Queen Caroline, the injured Queen of England', early 19thC, 7in (18cm) diam.
£145–170 / €200–240
$240–290 ⚒ GAK
This plate refers to Caroline of Brunswick-Wolfenbüttel, Germany, the wife of the Prince Regent, later George IV. Totally unsuited to one another, the pair had separated within two years of their marriage in 1785, and Caroline's subsequent life was often steeped in scandal. Despite that, the sympathy of the general public was with her when the Prince Regent became King in 1820 and she was put on trial in an attempt to bring about a divorce. The case was lost, but Caroline was not allowed to be crowned Queen alongside her estranged husband. On the day of the Coronation she tried, and failed, to gain admittance to the ceremony. Within a month she had died. Buried in Brunswick, her coffin was inscribed 'Caroline, the injured Queen of England.'

Flower Bricks

A London delft flower brick, glaze chips, c1720, 8¼in (21cm) wide.
£7,500–9,000 / €10,800–13,000
$12,600–15,100 ⚒ S(O)
The decoration on this flower brick is very unusual.

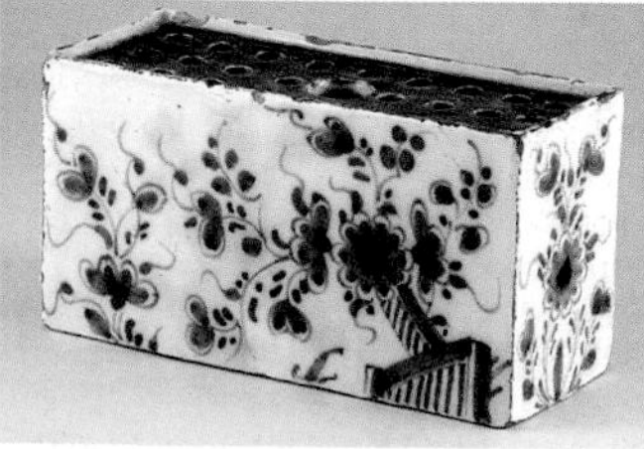

An English delft flower brick, decorated with flowers and foliage, rim chips, c1760, 6¼in (16cm) wide.
£530–640 / €770–920
$890–1,050 ⚒ WW

An English delft flower brick, painted with flowers, the top with a central aperture, flanked by smaller apertures, minor glaze flaking, c1765, 5¾in (14.5cm) wide.
£530–640 / €770–920
$890–1,050 ⚒ B

Inkstands & Inkwells

A slipware inkwell, the top with five holes surrounding a central aperture, some glaze losses, inscribed 'James Whitaker 1793', 4¼in (11cm) diam.
£660–790 / €960–1,150
$1,100–1,300 S(O)

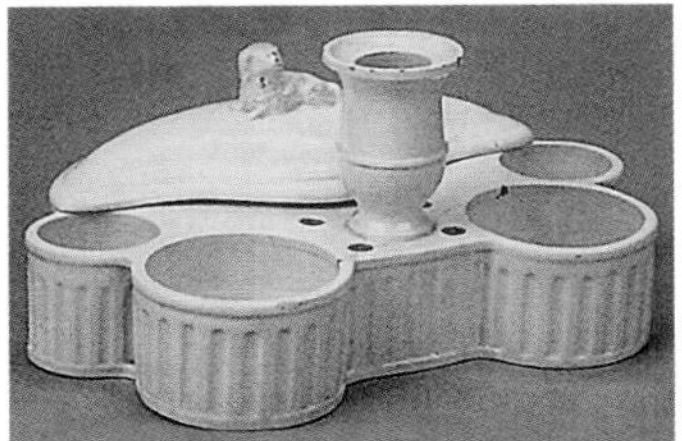

A Castleford creamware inkstand and cover, with four sections for bottles and a candle sconce, the cover with a gun dog finial, cracks, impressed marks, c1800, 8in (20.5cm) wide.
£1,400–1,650 / €2,000–2,400
$2,400–2,850 DN

A majolica inkwell, modelled as a toad with a lily pad holder and cover on its back, well missing, impressed registration number, French, c1890, 3½in (9cm) high.
£280–330 / €400–480
$470–560 SWO

Jardinières

A Nevers jardinière, decorated with shipping scenes, with snake-twist handles, French, c1660, 30in (76cm) diam.
£4,000–4,500 / €5,800–6,500
$6,800–7,600 G&G
The shape of this piece is influenced by Italian maiolica.

A majolica jardinière, by James Wardle & Co, with moulded ribbon and oak branch, impressed mark, 19thC, 18in (45.5cm) high.
£350–420 / €500–600
$590–700 AH

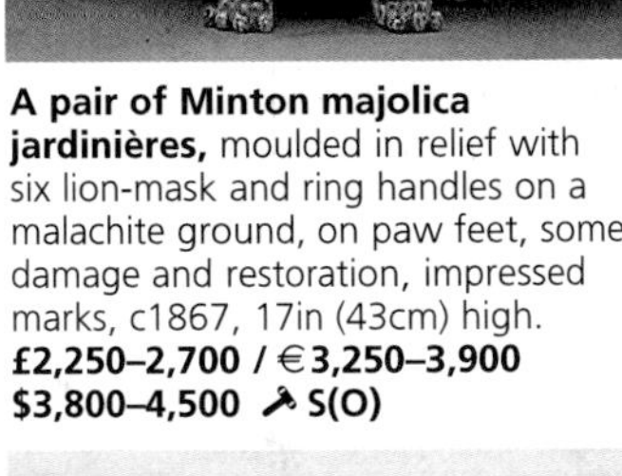

A pair of Minton majolica jardinières, moulded in relief with six lion-mask and ring handles on a malachite ground, on paw feet, some damage and restoration, impressed marks, c1867, 17in (43cm) high.
£2,250–2,700 / €3,250–3,900
$3,800–4,500 S(O)

A Minton majolica jardinière, supported by three doves on a triform base, date code for 1871, 6in (15cm) high.
£1,650–1,950 / €2,350–2,800
$2,750–3,250 G(L)

A Victorian majolica jardinière, modelled as a wooden trough, with moulded blackberries and leaves, on four stile feet, 4½in (11.5cm) high.
£110–130 / €160–190
$185–220 BR

◄ **A pair of Minton Renaissance-style jardinières,** moulded with scrolls and birds, impressed marks and dates, c1878, 11¾in (30cm) high.
£1,650–1,950 / €2,450–2,900
$2,750–3,300 RTo

A Minton majolica jardinière, No. 1400, moulded with putti and satyr masks in cartouches, on a pedestal foot, slight damage, impressed mark, c1872, 18in (45.5cm) wide.
£920–1,100 / €1,350–1,600
$1,550–1,850 DMC

A pair of Minton majolica jardinières, with bamboo and bird decoration and *bleu celeste* interiors, impressed mark, date code for 1879, 27¼in (69cm) diam.
£3,750–4,500 / €5,400–6,500
$6,300–7,600 LJ

Jars

A maiolica wet drug jar, possibly Deruta, the body decorated with stylized flowers and foliate scrolls, inscribed 'Diva Simplice', restored, Italian, early 16thC, 10in (25.5cm) high.
£1,450–1,600 / €2,050–2,300
$2,450–2,700 ⊞ G&G

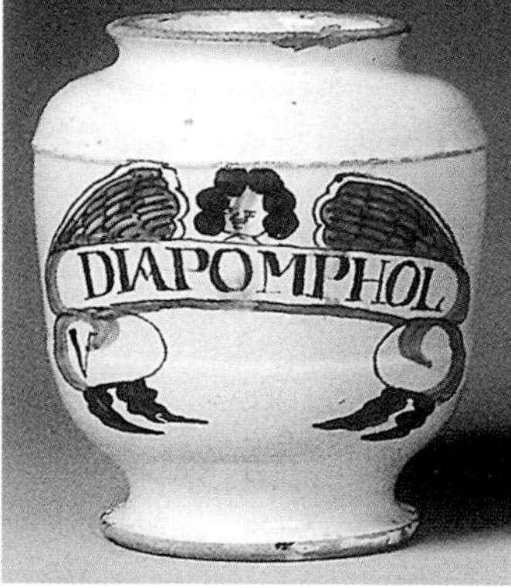

A London delft drug jar, the label inscribed 'Diapomphol', surmounted by an angel's head and wings, rim chips, c1680, 7in (17.5cm) high.
£1,550–1,850 / €2,300–2,700
$2,600–3,100 ⚒ B

A pair of *albarelli*, painted with saints and floral arbours, inscribed 'O. Nardini' and 'O. Vulpini', some restoration, Italian, Castelli, early 18thC, 7¾in (19.5cm) high.
£1,350–1,600 / €1,950–2,300
$2,250–2,700 ⚒ B

A maiolica *albarello*, possibly Deruta, painted with the inscription 'P Liri' and a pair of grotesques above an armorial device, some damage, Italian, 1500–50, 8¼in (21cm) high.
£1,550–1,850 / €2,250–2,650
$2,600–3,100 ⚒ S(O)

An *albarello*, painted with armorial bearings, scrolling foliage and animals, inscribed 'Lonfs. amech', chipped and cracked, north Italian, possibly Turin or Savona, c1700, 8in (20.5cm) high.
£1,050–1,250 / €1,500–1,800
$1,750–2,100 ⚒ DN

An *albarello*, painted with leaves beneath a banded and dotted border, some damage, Italian, Montelupo, late 16thC, 6in (15cm) high.
£760–910 / €1,100–1,300
$1,300–1,550 ⚒ B

A maiolica wet drug jar, painted with mermaid figures and 'Violt. Semp. CE. 1708', Sicilian, 8¼in (21cm) high.
£700–840 / €1,000–1,200
$1,200–1,400 ⚒ SWO
Violato simplex was a syrup of simple violets.

A bargeware tobacco jar and cover, inscribed 'Help Yourself', c1880, 7in (18cm) high.
£380–420 / €540–600
$630–700 ⊞ JBL

◄ A set of three graduated maiolica pharmacy jars and covers, chips, repaired, Italian, late 18thC, largest 10¾in (27cm) high.
£300–360 / €440–520
$500–600 ⚒ B

Jugs & Ewers

A Westerwald stoneware jug, relief-decorated with portrait medallions and heraldic lions, minor chips, German, late 17thC, 9in (23cm) high.
£940–1,100
€1,350–1,600
$1,500–1,850 B(EA)

A Westerwald stoneware pitcher, German, 18thC, 11in (28cm) high.
£800–880 / €1,150–1,300
$1,350–1,500 JHo

A creamware jug, inscribed 'Lord Weymouth success to the mines', c1780, 12in (30.5cm) high.
£1,500–1,700
€2,150–2,450
$2,500–2,850 AUC
Lord Weymouth was a lawyer and entrepreneur who lifted himself from poverty to prosperity. He reopened the Drayton Manor mines and quarries and helped many local people.

German stoneware

Stoneware, known as *Steinzeug* in German, was first made in the 12th century in the Rhine Valley, facilitated by the abundant supplies of wood for the kilns. Over the next 300 years other centres of production developed in Saxony, Cologne, Siegburg, Raeren, near Aachen, the Westerwald region and Kreussen, near Bayreuth. Wares were mainly related to drinking, in the form of tankards, drinking jugs and flasks. After c1650 a distinctive style had developed in Raeren: wares are typically in a grey-bodied stoneware covered in a lustrous brown glaze. The Westerwald region is noted for the production of grey stoneware with decoration in cobalt blue and manganese brown.

A Liverpool delft puzzle jug, c1750, 7½in (19cm) high.
£1,050–1,200
€1,500–1,700
$1,750–2,000 KEY
Puzzle jugs were first introduced in medieval times and were particularly popular in the 18th century. The nozzles around the rim are connected to a tube which runs down the handle and there is also a hole to the inside of the handle. The drinker has to cover all the holes with his fingers and suck on one of the nozzles to get his drink.

An Aynsley Lane End creamware jug, printed with the Vicar and Moses, c1780, 9½in (24cm) high.
£2,500–2,800
€3,600–4,000
$4,200–4,700 JRe
Aynsley pieces are particularly popular with collectors.

An English delft puzzle jug, possibly Liverpool, the pierced neck with a tubular rim and three pouring spouts, the double-walled body with inscription and floral decoration, losses, 1760–70, 8in (20.5cm) high.
£1,300–1,550
€1,850–2,200
$2,200–2,600 B
This jug is unusual in that the body has a double wall.

A Liverpool jug, printed with the Death of Wolfe, c1780, 7¼in (18.5cm) high.
£4,000–4,400
€5,800–6,400
$6,700–7,400 JHo
This print is copied from the famous painting by the American artist Benjamin West. General James Wolfe died at the capture of Quebec in 1759.

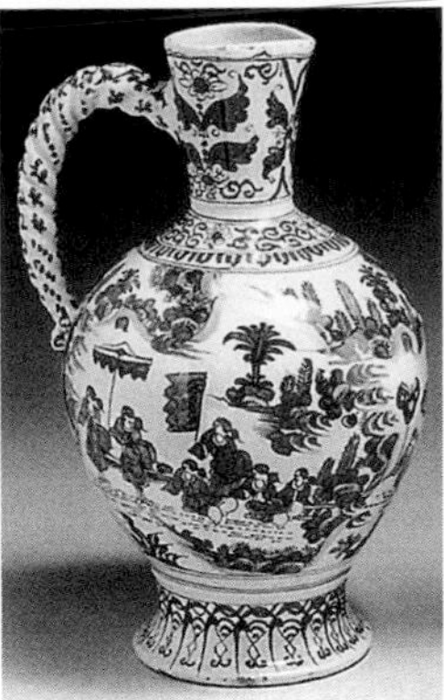

A faïence ewer, painted with Oriental figures and a stylized floral border, with a rope-twist loop handle, minor damage, German, late 17thC, 14¼in (36cm) high.
£1,250–1,500
€1,800–2,150
$2,100–2,500 S(NY)

A creamware jug and cover, painted with a monogram, c1780, 10½in (26.5cm) high.
£480–530 / €690–760
$800–890 AUC

A Prattware farmer's jug, c1790, 7in (18cm) high.
£800–880 / €1,100–1,250
$1,300–1,450 SEA

A Prattware jug, 1790–1800, 6in (15cm) high.
£400–450 / €580–650
$670–750 AUC

A creamware jug, printed with two scenes entitled 'Separation of Louis XVI from his Family' and 'Massacre of the French King', late 18thC, 7in (18cm) high.
£1,400–1,650
€2,000–2,350
$2,350–2,750 ⚒ CGC

A Yorkshire creamware jug, with painted inscription 'Samuel Webster his Pitcher 1803', early 19thC, 6½in (16.5cm) high.
£590–650 / €850–940
$990–1,000 ⊞ KEY

A jug, decorated with enamels, c1820, 6in (15cm) high.
£670–750 / €960–1,100
$1,100–1,250 ⊞ HOW

A Staffordshire jug, modelled as a thatched cottage, early 19thC, 3½in (9cm) high.
£500–550 / €710–790
$840–930 ⊞ JHo

▶ A lustre jug, printed with Masonic emblems, a ship and a verse, cracked, early 19thC, 9¼in (23.5cm) high.
£220–260 / €310–370
$370–440 ⚒ G(L)

A creamware jug, with printed decoration entitled 'Success to the Pilchard Fishery' and 'Peace and Plenty', probably Liverpool, late 18thC, 5¾in (14.5cm) high.
£1,500–1,650
€2,150–2,400
$2,500–2,750 ⊞ KEY
Liverpool was famous for printing creamware relating to shipping and this is the most likely home of this jug. However, the pilchard industry was strong around the coasts of Britain at this time and the Maritime Museum in Falmouth has a section devoted to the business in the town. This mug could have been ordered by a boat owner from the port to wish for continued good fortune in their industry.

A pearlware jug, printed with named portraits of Queen Caroline and Princess Charlotte, spout repaired, 1821, 4¾in (12cm) high.
£260–310 / €380–450
$440–520 ⚒ SAS
Caroline and Charlotte were King George IV's wife and daughter respectively. See p232 for information about Queen Caroline. Princess Charlotte died in childbirth in 1817 and was greatly mourned by the nation.

A jug, commemorating the Independence of America in 1776, late 18thC, 6¾in (17cm) high.
£1,050–1,250
€1,500–1,800
$1,750–2,100 ⚒ SWO

A pearlware jug, banded with pink lustre, printed with a portrait of Bainbridge entitled 'Hunt and Liberty, Bad Luck to the Manchester Butchers', the reverse with a vignette of trophies of rights and inscribed 'Annual Parliaments and vote by ballot', chip, c1819, 5in (13cm) high.
£560–670 / €800–960
$940–1,100 ⚒ SAS
This jug commemorates the breaking up of a radical meeting at St Peter's Fields, Manchester by a cavalry charge, which resulted in eleven deaths and many injuries. It became known as the Peterloo Massacre, as a reference to the Battle of Waterloo, in much the same way as the names of public scandals these days end in 'gate' as a reference to the American Watergate scandal.

A pottery jug, c1820, 6in (15cm) high.
£380–420 / €540–600
$640–710 ⊞ AUC

▶ A pair of relief-moulded jugs, with lustre and enamelled decoration, c1830, 4in (10cm) high.
£400–450 / €580–650
$670–760 ⊞ HOW

A pearlware jug, relief-moulded with a portrait medallion of the Duke of York and a family portrait, the loop handle with husking, c1800, 7½in (19cm) high.
£490–590 / €710–850
$820–990 ⚒ AH

A pearlware jug, hand-painted with enamels, c1820, 3in (7.5cm) high.
£75–85 / €110–125
$125–140 ⊞ HTE

A Swansea pearlware jug, transfer-printed with shells and flowers, Welsh, early 19thC, 4in (10cm) high.
£110–130 / €160–190
$185–220 ⚒ SWO

A Hylton Pottery creamware lustre jug, by J. Phillips, decorated with a view of the bridge over the River Wear at Sunderland, c1825, 9in (23cm) high.
£680–750 / €980–1,100
$1,100–1,250 ⊞ IS

POTTERY

A pearlware jug, decorated with William III, Orangemen holding up a crown and emblems of the order, c1830, 6in (15cm) high.
£340–410 / €490–590
$580–690 WW

A miniature Staffordshire jug, decorated with a transfer print and enamels, c1830, 2in (5cm) high.
£65–75 / €95–110
$110–125 HTE

An earthenware jug, printed with a view of the entrance to the Liverpool and Manchester Railway, the reverse with an early locomotive, c1835, 5¼in (13.5cm) high.
£470–560 / €680–810
$790–940 SAS

A relief-moulded jug, by Enoch Wood, with copper lustre and enamel decoration, c1830, 4in (10cm) high.
£155–175 / €220–250
$260–290 HOW

A Sunderland lustre jug, printed with the sailing ship *Northumberland 74* in full sail, c1830, 5in (12.5cm) high.
£430–480 / €620–690
$720–800 WAA

► A miniature pottery jug, c1835, 2in (5cm) high.
£45–50 / €60–70
$75–85 HTE

A Sunderland lustre jug, transfer-printed with the Mariner's Compass and Mariner's Arms, c1835, 9in (23cm) high.
£680–750 / €980–1,100
$1,150–1,250 HOW

◄ A North Shields Pottery lustre jug, decorated with 'The Sailor's Farewell', c1835, 6in (15cm) high.
£430–480
€620–690
$720–800 IS

► A Sunderland lustre jug, decorated with 'The Sailor's Farewell', and 'The Token or Jack's Safe Return to his True Love', 19thC, 7½in (19cm) high.
£300–360
€430–510
$500–600 WilP

A Goodwin & Harris jug, depicting the dissolution of Parliament, c1832, 8in (20.5cm) high.
£220–250 / €320–370
$370–420 DAN

In April 1831 Earl Grey asked William IV to dissolve Parliament so that the Whigs could secure a larger majority in the House of Commons. Grey claimed it would help carry their proposals for parliamentary reform. The King agreed, and after his speech in the House of Lords, walked back through cheering crowds to Buckingham Palace.

A Wedgwood pearlware jug, printed and painted with botanical specimens, impressed pattern No. 493, 1800–50, 5¼in (13.5cm) high.
£280–330 / €400–470
$470–550 WW

A Sunderland lustre jug, printed with the sailing ship *William IV*, c1835, 8in (20.5cm) high.
£850–950 / €1,200–1,350
$1,400–1,550 HOW

A Sunderland splash lustre jug, decorated with Masonic symbols, c1840, 7in (18cm) high.
£720–800 / €1,000–1,150
$1,200–1,350 ⊞ WAA

A Wedgwood black basalt enamelled jug, decorated in Capri enamels with scattered flowers with gilt highlights, chip to base, impressed mark, 19thC, 6in (15cm) high.
£420–500 / €600–720
$700–840 ⚒ S(O)

A lustre jug, mid-19thC, 5in (12.5cm) high.
£105–120 / €160–180
$180–200 ⊞ DAN

A Victorian Minton majolica tower jug, modelled as an ivory-clad tower with dancing medieval couples, the pewter-mounted cover with leaf decoration, impressed No. 1231, 11in (28cm) high.
£400–480 / €580–690
$670–800 ⚒ L&E

A Sunderland lustre jug, with inscription 'John Page born at the Hythe, Colchester', c1840, 10in (25.5cm) high.
£1,100–1,250
€1,600–1,800
$1,900–2,100 ⊞ WAA

A majolica jug, with a boar's head pouring lip, relief-moulded with leaves and script, French, 19thC, 9½in (24cm) high.
£95–110 / €140–160
$160–185 ⚒ G(L)

A Sunderland lustre jug, printed with the sailing ship *Star of Tasmania*, 'A Frigate in Full Sail', c1850, 7in (18cm) high.
£810–900 / €1,150–1,300
$1,350–1,500 ⊞ WAA

A sgraffito puzzle jug, the body with stylized flowering plants, incised date '1842', 11½in (29cm) high.
£730–880 / €1,050–1,250
$1,250–1,500 ⚒ PF

A Staffordshire lustre jug, decorated with a ram and greyhound interspaced with a flower basket, 19thC, 7in (18cm) high.
£105–130 / €150–180
$175–210 ⚒ SJH

A pair of Copeland Renaissance-style majolica ewers, decorated with vine fruit and leaf handles, the bodies relief-moulded with snakes, birds and scrolling vegetation, with applied winged women, damaged and repaired, impressed mark, c1860, 14½in (37cm) high.
£470–560 / €680–810
$790–940 ⚒ B(W)

A pair of Minton majolica ewers, relief-decorated with cherubs, mermen and mermaids, the foliate-moulded handle with a face mask base, one ewer damaged, impressed mark, shape No. 474, date code for 1875, 12¼in (31cm) high.
£940–1,100 / €1,350–1,600
$1,600–1,900 ⚒ SWO

A Mochaware jug, c1880, 8in (20.5cm) high.
£360–400 / €520–580
$600–670 ⊞ SMI

◄ **A Fremington Pottery harvest jug,** by Edwin Beer Fishley, the ribbed strap handle with a thumbrest and scroll terminal, the body sgraffito-decorated with an ode to the farmer, crossed pipes, a plough, a foaming jug and two ale glasses, the reverse with ears of corn and a butterfly, rim chip, incised mark, 1905, 9¾in (25cm) high.
£2,000–2,400 / €2,900–3,450
$3,350–4,000 ⚒ Bea

The Fremington Pottery was founded by George Fishley (1770–1865) in Barnstaple, Devon. Four generations of the Fishley family ran the Pottery until 1912. George was succeeded by his sons Edmund and Robert, and Edmund's son Edwin Beer Fishley (1832–1911) inherited in 1860.

Mugs & Tankards

A Westerwald stoneware tankard, German, 1650–1700, 9in (23cm) high.
£1,650–1,850
€2,400–2,650
$2,800–3,100 ⊞ JHo

A creamware mug, printed with Masonic symbols, c1790, 6in (15cm) high.
£770–850 / €1,100–1,250
$1,300–1,450 ⊞ AUC

A Liverpool creamware mug, printed with the 'East View of Liverpool Lighthouse and Signals on Bidston Hill', late 18thC, 6in (15cm) high.
£1,650–1,850
€2,350–2,600
$2,800–3,100 ⊞ KEY

LOCATE THE SOURCE

The source of each illustration in Miller's can be found by checking the code letters below each caption with the Key to Illustrations, pages 794–800.

A pewter-mounted faïence tankard, painted with Oriental figures in a chinoiserie landscape, the cover with a ball thumbpiece, incised 'J.N.' and '1805', minor glaze losses, maker's mark, German, Frankfurt, c1700, 10½in (26.5cm) high.
£600–720 / €840–1,000
$1,000–1,200 ⚒ S(O)

A Sunderland creamware mug, by Dawson & Co, Low Ford, late 18thC, 5½in (14cm) high.
£760–850 / €1,100–1,250
$1,250–1,400 ⊞ KEY

A Sunderland pearlware frog mug, printed with a view of the Iron Bridge over the River Wear at Sunderland, late 18thC, 6in (15cm) high.
£410–460 / €590–660
$690–770 ⊞ KEY

► **A pottery mug,** decorated with enamels, c1820, 5in (12.5cm) high.
£630–700 / €900–1,000
$1,000–1,150 ⊞ HOW

A creamware mug, the entwined strap handle with floret terminals, the body painted with a posy of flowers reserved on a patterned ground, Yorkshire or Derbyshire, c1775, 5½in (14cm) high.
£1,550–1,850
€2,200–2,600
$2,600–3,100 ⚒ B

A creamware mug, transfer-printed with 'The Butcher's Arms', c1790, 5¼in (13.5cm) high.
£850–950 / €1,200–1,350
$1,450–1,600 ⊞ AUC

A Leeds creamware mug, with a strap handle, inscribed, restored, double impressed marks, late 18thC, 3¾in (9.5cm) high.
£280–330 / €400–470
$470–550 ⚒ WW

A creamware mug, transfer-printed with 'The Tythe Pig', c1790, 5in (12.5cm) high.
£500–550 / €720–800
$840–930 ⊞ AUC

A creamware pint mug, printed with a harvesting scene entitled 'Autumn', late 18thC, 5in (15cm) high.
£190–220 / €280–330
$320–380 ⚒ CGC

A tin-glazed tankard, the pewter lid with a globe thumbpiece, inscribed 'I.P.F. 1782', the body decorated with stylized flowers, with a pewter base, handle cracked, German, late 18thC, 10in (25.5cm) high.
£165–195 / €240–280
$280–330 ⚒ PF

A creamware quart mug, printed and painted with a cavalry skirmish, early 19thC, 6in (15cm) high.
£470–560 / €680–810
$790–940 ⚒ CGC

A Sunderland lustre frog mug, probably by Scott of Southwick, printed with 'The Sailor's Farewell', c1820, 5in (12.5cm) high.
£450–500 / €650–720
$760–840 ⊞ WAA

A pearlware mug, celebrating the Reform Bill, printed with four figures holding a scroll inscribed 'Grey, Brougham, Russel. Althorp, Burdett, Norfolk', beneath a banner inscribed 'We are for our King and our People', printed mark, c1830, 4in (10cm) high.
£165–195 / €240–280
$290–340 ⚒ WW

The 1832 Reform Bill improved the British electoral system by disenfranchising many rotten boroughs and widening the electorate by about 50 per cent.

A Swansea mug, commemorating the Coronation of Queen Victoria, 1838, 3in (7.5cm) high.
£900–1,000
€1,300–1,450
$1,500–1,700 ⊞ WAA

A Staffordshire pottery mug, commemorating the Coronation of Queen Victoria, printed with portraits and centred by her name, crown and dates, restored, 1838, 3¼in (8.5cm) high.
£1,050–1,250
€1,500–1,800
$1,750–2,100 ⚒ SAS

A Swansea earthenware mug, commemorating the Coronation of Queen Victoria, printed with portraits, centred by her name, crown and dates, restored, 1838, 3¼in (8.5cm) high.
£940–1,100
€1,400–1,650
$1,600–1,900 ⚒ SAS

A stoneware mug, commemorating the marriage of Queen Victoria, 1840, 5¼in (13.5cm) high.
£330–400 / €480–570
$550–660 ⚒ SAS

◄ **An earthenware mug,** commemorating the Sheffield Flood, transfer-printed, c1864, 4in (10cm) high.
£100–120 / €140–165
$170–200 ⚒ G(L)

Plaques

A maiolica plaque, painted with a river scene, possibly in the Grue workshop, the rim edged in ochre, Italian, Castelli, c1750, 11¼in (28.5cm) wide, in an ebonized and giltwood frame.
£2,400–2,850 / €3,450–4,100
$4,000–4,750 ⚒ S(O)

A relief-moulded plaque, depicting St George and the Dragon, inscribed 'James Wood, 1801', 8in (20.5cm) wide.
£540–600 / €780–860
$900–1,000 ⊞ HOW

A Prattware plaque, relief-moulded, restored, early 19thC, 9½in (24cm) wide.
£370–440 / €530–630
$620–740 ⚒ WW

◄ **A Sunderland lustre plaque,** by Dixon & Co, Garrison Pottery, entitled *'Northumberland 74'*, c1830, 6½in (16.5cm) high.
£370–420 / €530–600
$620–700 ⊞ RdV

The *Northumberland 74* was the ship that took Napoleon to St Helena when he was exiled there in 1815, 74 being the number of cannons aboard.

A Staffordshire enamelled pearlware plaque, relief-moulded, incised 'J. Hall, Spotted Cow, Hanley, 1836', rim chip, 9½in (24cm) wide.
£500–600 / €720–860
$840–1,000 ⚒ RTo

POTTERY

A Sunderland lustre plaque, transfer-printed with a ship and a verse, impressed 'Dixon & Co, Garrison Pottery', c1845, 8in (20.5cm) wide.
£300–350 / €430–500
$500–580 ⊞ IS

A lustre plaque, attributed to Seaham Pottery, transfer-printed, c1850, 7½in (19cm) diam.
£220–250 / €320–360
$370–420 ⊞ IS

A Tyneside lustre plaque, c1850, 8in (20.5cm) wide.
£160–180 / €230–260
$270–300 ⊞ IS

A lustre plaque, attributed to John Carr, Low Lights Pottery, North Shields, c1850, 9in (23cm) wide.
£300–350 / €430–500
$500–580 ⊞ IS

A pair of faïence plaques, painted with figures depicting Minerva and Venus, impressed 'K', monogrammed, in wooden frames, probably Dutch, 19thC, 10 x 14in (25.5 x 35.5cm).
£600–720 / €870–1,050
$1,000–1,200 ⚒ S(O)

A Mintons plaque, painted by William Mussill with a bird on a magnolia branch, signed, impressed mark and date cypher, c1878, 22in (56cm) diam.
£780–930 / €1,100–1,300
$1,300–1,550 ⚒ S(O)

POTTERY

Items in the Pottery section have been arranged in date order within each sub-section.

◄ **A pottery plaque,** painted with a woman picking fruit attended by a winged cherub, late 19thC, 14in (35.5cm) wide.
£200–240
€290–340
$340–400
⚒ G(B)

A Wedgwood jasper ware plaque, decorated with 'The Dancing Hours' after Flaxman, impressed marks, framed, 19thC, 7½ x 2¼in (19 x 5.5cm).
£220–260 / €310–370
$360–430 ⚒ B(Kn)

A Wedgwood jasper ware plaque, decorated with 'The Dancing Hours', impressed Wedgwood mark, c1900, 15¾ x 6in (40 x 15cm).
£840–1,000 / €1,200–1,450
$1,400–1,650 ⚒ B

Pot Lids

'The Snow Drift', by F. & R. Pratt, Ball No. 276, c1840, 4¼in (11cm) diam.
£75–85 / €110–120
$125–140 ⊞ TASV

'Belle Vue Tavern', Ball No. 30, c1850, 4in (10cm) diam.
£75–90 / €110–130
$125–150 ⚒ B

'The New Houses of Parliament', Ball No. 195, c1860, 3½in (9cm) diam.
£520–620 / €750–890
$870–1,050 ⚒ SAS

'The Dentist', Ball No. 323, c1870, 4in (10cm) diam.
£360–400 / €520–580
$600–670 ⊞ JBL

'Tria Juncta in Uno', c1875, 5¼in (13.5cm) diam.
£700–780 / €1,000–1,100
$1,150–1,300 ⊞ JBL

'The Philadelphia Exhibition', by F. & R. Pratt, c1876, in a wooden frame, 6in (15cm) diam.
£75–85 / €110–120
$125–140 ⊞ TASV

Dessert, Dinner & Tea Services

A Hicks stone china part dinner service, comprising 40 pieces, heightened in gilt, minor faults, printed factory marks and pattern No. 3676, early 19thC.
£1,050–1,250 / €1,500–1,800
$1,750–2,100 ⚒ RTo

A J. & W. Ridgway 'Fancy Stone China' part dinner service, comprising 74 pieces, painted in enamels, some damage, printed marks, c1825.
£3,300–3,900 / €4,700–5,600
$5,500–6,500 ⚒ DN

A Staffordshire dessert service, comprising 20 pieces, some damage, c1835.
£260–310 / €370–440
$440–520 ⚒ B(Kn)

Items in the Pottery section have been arranged in date order within each sub-section.

An Ashworth ironstone part dinner service, comprising 20 pieces, some damage, c1870.
£260–310 / €370–440
$440–520 ⚒ B(Kn)

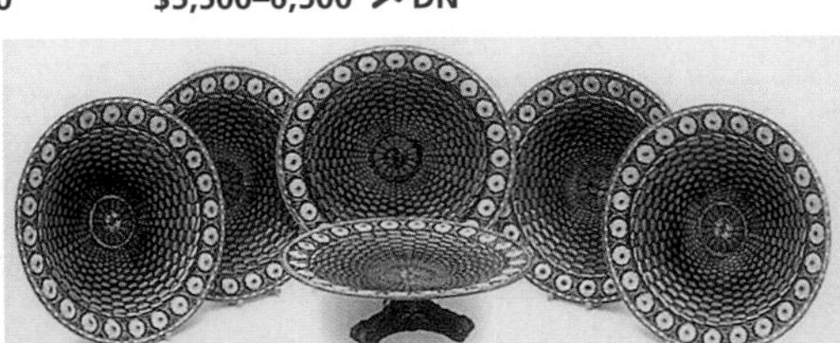

A Wedgwood majolica part dessert service, comprising six pieces, impressed marks and date code, 1894.
£730–870 / €1,050–1,250
$1,200–1,450 ⚒ Bea

► **A Booths tea service,** comprising 22 pieces, c1900.
£210–250 / €300–360
$350–420 ⚒ EH

POTTERY

Stands

A Savona stand, for four condiment bottles, chipped, Italian, late 17thC, 8½in (21.5cm) wide.
£2,600–3,100 / €3,700–4,400
$4,300–5,200 B

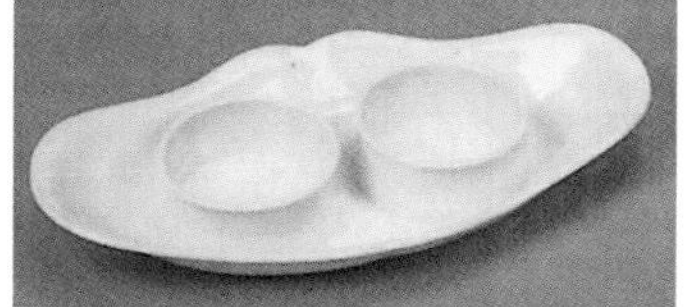

A pair of Wedgwood Queen's ware cruet bottle stands, impressed marks, c1790, 10¼in (26cm) wide.
£350–420 / €500–600
$590–700 DN

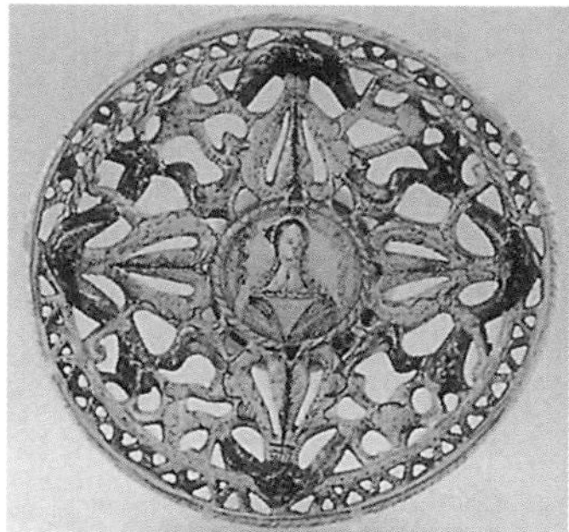

A maiolica stand, reticulated with birds and scrolls, broken and repaired, Italian, 17thC, 10¾in (27.5cm) wide.
£210–250 / €300–360
$350–420 WW

► **A majolica stand,** probably by George Jones, moulded with panels of stylized scrolls and beaded borders, impressed '760', c1870, 12¼in (31cm) wide.
£105–125 / €150–180
$175–210 WW

A Leeds pierced and moulded creamware stand, the rim pierced with panels of openwork and moulded with festoons of husks, 1780–90, 10in (25.5cm) wide.
£280–320 / €400–460
$470–540 KEY

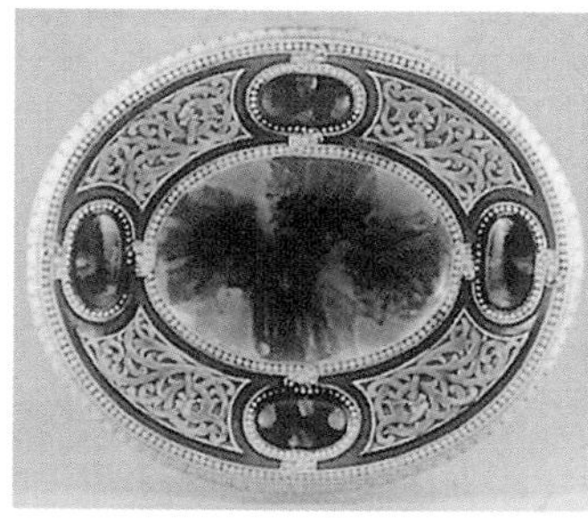

POTTERY

Tea, Coffee & Punch Pots

A Staffordshire salt-glazed stoneware coffee pot, cover missing, c1745, 6in (15cm) high.
£1,300–1,450 / €1,850–2,100
$2,200–2,450 JHo

A Staffordshire redware punch pot, decorated *en rocaille* with two panels of a Chinese figure within C-scroll foliate branches, traces of old lacquer, c1760, 6¾in (17cm) high.
£940–1,100 / €1,350–1,550
$1,550–1,850 DN

► **A Staffordshire creamware teapot,** decorated with enamels, c1765, 6in (15cm) high.
£2,500–2,850 / €3,600–4,100
$4,200–4,800 JHo

A Whieldon-style teapot, with tortoiseshell glaze, damaged, c1750, 3in (7.5cm) high.
£165–195 / €240–280
$280–330 G(L)

A Staffordshire teapot, with applied decoration and a Whieldon-style glaze, c1760, 7in (18cm) high.
£3,250–3,650 / €4,700–5,300
$5,400–6,100 JHo

A Staffordshire salt-glazed teapot, with leaf scroll moulded handle and reeded spout, cracks and chips, c1760, 5¼in (13.5cm) high.
£2,350–2,800 / €3,350–4,000
$3,950–4,700 B

A Staffordshire teapot, c1760, 6in (15cm) high.
£22,500–25,000 / €32,000–36,000
$38,000–42,000 JHo
The body and lid of this very rare teapot are double walled. This intricate work is an imitation of a Chinese technique known as Ling-Lung (the devil's) work.

Insurance values

Always insure your valuable antiques for the cost of replacing them with similar items, regardless of the original price paid. Both dealers and auctioneers can provide a valuation service for a fee.

◄ **A Robert's faïence teapot,** the cover with a rose finial, slight damage, French, Marseille, 1765–70, 4in (10cm) high.
£780–930 / €1,100–1,300
$1,300–1,550 S(O)

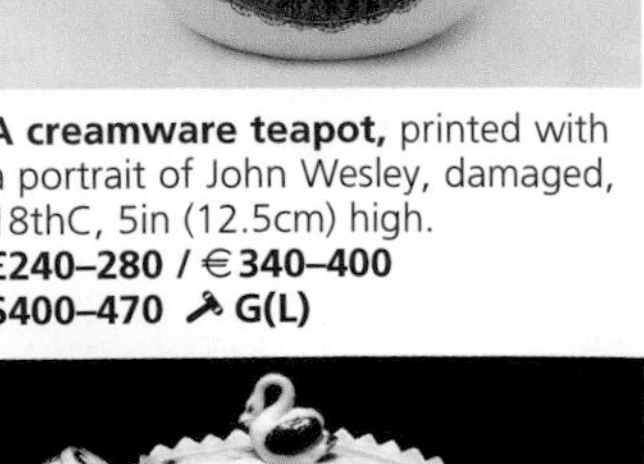

A creamware teapot, printed with a portrait of John Wesley, damaged, 18thC, 5in (12.5cm) high.
£240–280 / €340–400
$400–470 G(L)

A pearlware coffee pot, decorated with the initials 'SW' within a floral cartouche, c1790, 13in (33cm) high.
£610–680 / €880–980
$1,000–1,150 AUC

A creamware teapot, inscription rubbed, French, dated 1794, 7½in (19cm) high.
£210–250 / €300–360
$350–420 SWO

A pearlware teapot, c1795, 5in (12.5cm) high.
£340–380 / €490–550
$570–640 AUC

A Leeds creamware teapot, with stylized floral decoration, pierced rim and reeded strap handle, damaged, 18thC, 6¾in (17cm) high.
£850–1,000 / €1,200–1,450
$1,400–1,650 DMC

A creamware teapot, possibly Leeds, decorated in enamels with a sailor's farewell and a floral spray, with a leaf-moulded spout and S-scroll handle, late 18thC, 6in (15cm) high.
£4,250–5,100 / €6,100–7,300
$7,100–8,500 Mit
The Sailor's Farewell is a very rare design for a teapot. It has been suggested that this piece might have been early Wedgwood rather than Leeds.

A Castleford-style feldspathic stoneware teapot, c1800, 6in (15cm) high.
£260–290 / €370–420
$440–490 AUC

► **A Wedgwood majolica teapot,** damaged, impressed marks, 1850–1900, 8¾in (22cm) wide.
£150–180 / €210–260
$250–300 WW

◄ **A bargeware teapot,** decorated with Chinese figures and exotic flowers, c1870, 8in (20.5cm) high.
£890–990 / €1,250–1,400
$1,500–1,650 JBL

► **A majolica teapot,** in the form of a fish, the spout formed as the rear half of a smaller fish being eaten, lid damaged, c1890, 5½in (14cm) high.
£280–330 / €400–470
$470–550 PFK

A majolica teapot, in the form of a pineapple, naturalistically decorated, spout restored, marked, late 19thC, 7in (18cm) high.
£1,400–1,650 / €2,000–2,350
$2,350–2,750 GAK

POTTERY

Tiles

A stove tile, in the style of Hans Kraut of Villingen, moulded in relief with a figure of Artemesia within a columned archway surmounted by a lion mask and winged cherubs, German, c1580, 11 x 9¼in (28 x 23.5cm).
£380–450 / €550–650
$640–750 F&C

A Dutch Delft tile, 18thC, 5¼in (13.5cm) square.
£50–55 / €70–80
$85–95 AUC

A maiolica map of Italy, after Jodocus Hondius, comprising 12 tiles, chips, restored, probably south Italian, 19thC, 29½ x 39¼in (75 x 101cm).
£5,800–6,900 / €8,300–9,900
$9,700–11,600 S(Mi)

A Dutch Delft tile, depicting a Musketeer, slight wear, 1625–50, 5¼in (13.5cm) square.
£330–390 / €470–560
$550–650 S(Am)

An English delft tile, depicting the return of the prodigal son, c1740, 4¾in (12cm) square.
£60–70 / €85–100
$100–115 F&F

A Dutch Delft tile picture, comprising 12 tiles, depicting The Senses, slight damage, 19thC, each tile 5¼in (13.5cm) square.
£630–750 / €910–1,100
$1,050–1,250 VSP

◄ **A pair of Victorian earthenware tiles,** printed and enamelled with 'Touchstone, Rosalind, Celia' and 'Ferdinand, Ariel', damage and repair, 8in (20.5cm) square.
£200–240 / €290–340
$340–400 G(L)

► **A Sherwin & Cotton tile,** by George Cartlidge, depicting winter gleanings, c1905, 12 x 6in (30.5 x 15cm)
£175–195 / €250–280
$290–330 C&W

A set of nine Dutch Delft polychrome-decorated tiles, chips, Haarlem, 17thC, each tile 5¼in (13.5cm) square.
£330–390 / €470–560
$550–650 VSP

A manganese delft tile, depicting a scene from Matthew 3:13, c1750, 5in (12.5cm) square.
£70–80 / €100–115
$120–135 KEY

A Victorian Minton, Hollins & Co tile, depicting Lord William Howard of Naworth Castle, maker's mark, edge chips, 8in (20.5cm) square.
£75–90 / €110–130
$125–150 PFK

Lord William Howard (1563–1640) was the third son of Thomas, Duke of Norfolk. He served nine months in the Tower of London for refusing to renounce Catholicism.

Toby & Character Jugs

A Ralph Wood Toby jug, with a foaming jug and a glass, restored, c1780, 10in (25.5cm) high.
£1,900–2,250
€2,700–3,250
$3,200–3,800 ⚒ B

A Don Pottery Hearty Goodfellow Toby jug, decorated with enamels and pearlware glaze, maker's mark, named and dated 1830, 10in (25.5cm) high.
£800–900 / €1,150–1,200
$1,350–1,500 ⊞ JBL
Named and dated Toby jugs are scarce.

A Prattware Yorkshire Toby jug, with a pearlware glaze, marked, c1790, 10in (25.5cm) high.
£1,350–1,500
€1,900–2,100
$2,250–2,500 ⊞ JBL
This Toby is unusual in that he is holding a small Toby instead of a jug.

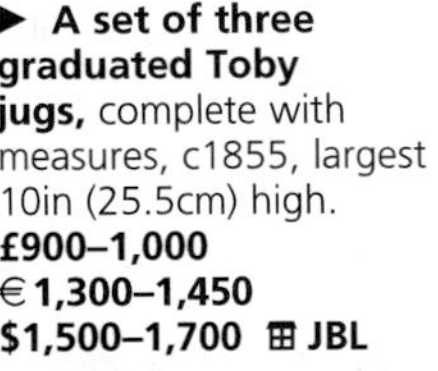

► **A set of three graduated Toby jugs,** complete with measures, c1855, largest 10in (25.5cm) high.
£900–1,000
€1,300–1,450
$1,500–1,700 ⊞ JBL

A Dutch Delft character jug, modelled as Mr Punch, with tassel hat cover, damaged, 19thC, 12½in (32cm) high.
£110–130 / €160–190
$185–220 ⚒ NSal

◄ **A Toby jug,** with measure, restored, c1870, 10in (25.5cm) high.
£110–130 / €160–190
$185–220 ⚒ SWO

A Prattware Hearty Goodfellow Toby jug, c1790, 10in (25.5cm) high.
£1,700–1,900
€2,400–2,700
$2,800–3,200 ⊞ JBL
It is unusual to find a Toby wearing long trousers.

A Yorkshire Toby jug, c1900, 10in (25.5cm) high.
£580–650 / €830–930
$970–1,100 ⊞ JBL

A pearlware Yorkshire Toby jug, c1790, 10in (25.5cm) high.
£1,950–2,200
€2,800–3,150
$3,300–3,700 ⊞ JBL
Tobys smoking pipes are seldom found.

A Judy character jug, with measure, c1860, 10in (25.5cm) high.
£540–600 / €750–850
$900–1,000 ⊞ JBL

A Tit-Bits Toby jug, by William Ault, commemorating WWI, c1917, 10in (25.5cm) high.
£360–400 / €520–580
$600–670 ⊞ JBL

Vases & Urns

A maiolica bottle vase, painted with a ship with furled sails, glaze chips, possibly Spanish, 18thC, 11in (28cm) high.
£760–900 / €1,100–1,300
$1,250–1,500 DN

► A Minton majolica potpourri vase and cover, moulded with grotesque masks, garlands and panels of arabesques, damaged, impressed maker's marks, 1868, 9¾in (25cm) high.
£1,150–1,350
€1,650–1,950
$1,900–2,250 S(O)

A pair of Wedgwood pearlware vases and covers, with slip decoration, c1790, 7½in (19cm) high.
£1,450–1,650
€2,100–2,350
$2,400–2,750 AUC

A pair of Wedgwood jasper ware vases and covers, damaged, impressed 'Wedgwood', 19thC, 10¾in (27cm) high.
£800–960 / €1,150–1,400
$1,350–1,600 WW

► A pair of faïence Gien pedestal vases, with painted decoration and serpent handles, French, 19thC, 14¼in (36cm) high.
£420–500 / €600–720
$700–840 EH

A Wedgwood jasper ware Portland vase, decorated with classical figures representing the myth of Peleus and Thetis, impressed factory mark, c1850, 8in (20.5cm) high.
£400–480 / €580–690
$670–800 RTo

POTTERY

Miscellaneous

A Bristol pearlware spirit barrel, c1820, 6in (15cm) wide.
£370–420 / €530–600
$620–700 ⊞ DAN

A majolica basket, continuously moulded with leaves, Continental, late 19thC, 9½in (24cm) wide.
£105–125 / €150–180
$175–210 ⚒ G(L)

A pearlware model of a boat, c1825, 16in (40.5cm) wide.
£670–750 / €960–1,150
$1,100–1,250 ⊞ HOW

A pair of glazed drabware bough pots, on paw feet, damaged, c1820, 8in (20.5cm) diam.
£800–960 / €1,150–1,350
$1,350–1,600 ⚒ WW

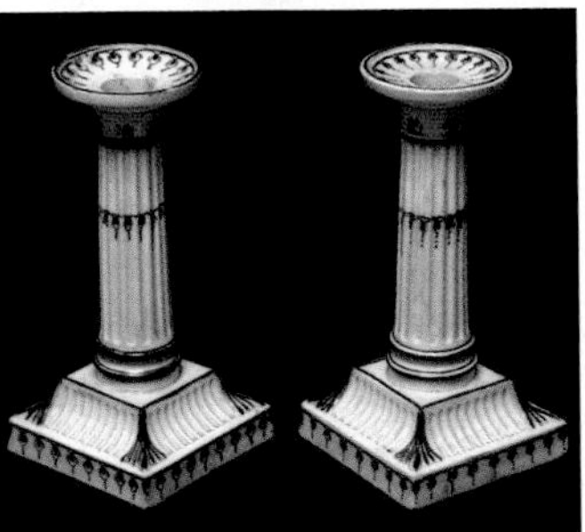

A pair of pearlware candlesticks, c1790, 8in (20.5cm) high.
£940–1,050 / €1,350–1,500
$1,550–1,750 ⊞ AUC

A pottery slabwork cradle, north country, 18thC, 7¼in (18.5cm) wide.
£490–580 / €700–830
$820–970 ⚒ SJH

A Victorian Staffordshire footbath, printed mark for Ashworth, Hanley, 19¾in (50cm) wide.
£180–210 / €260–300
$300–350 ⚒ L&E

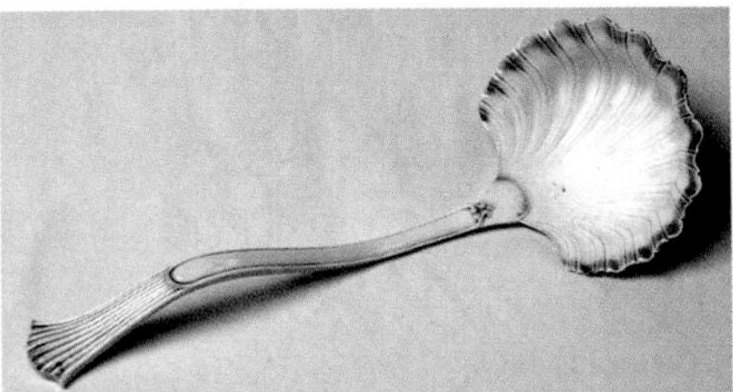

A pearlware ladle, Swansea or Staffordshire, late 18thC, 12in (30.5cm) long.
£1,300–1,450 / €1,850–2,100
$2,150–2,450 ⊞ JHo

A faïence lantern, with a glazed door and sides and a swing handle, slight damage, late 19thC, 7¾in (19.5cm) high.
£130–155 / €190–220
$220–260 ⚒ WW

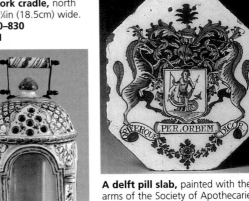

A delft pill slab, painted with the arms of the Society of Apothecaries and an inscription, wear and rim chips, 1750–1800, 10½in (26.5cm) wide.
£5,400–6,400 / €7,800–9,200
$9,000–10,700 ⚒ B

A Victorian Sunderland lustre pot and cover, painted with a sailor's lament and Masonic Arms, the cover with a mushroom finial, 5¼in (13.5cm) high.
£360–430 / €520–620
$600–720 ⚒ DD

► **A Prattware pot,** depicting the 'Charge of the Scots Greys', c1855, 3¾in (9.5cm) diam.
£360–400 / €520–580
$600–670 ⊞ JBL

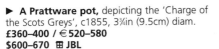

A Leeds creamware tea canister, with enamel floral decoration, c1780, 3½in (9cm) high.
£250–280 / €360–400
$420–470 ⊞ KEY

Blue & White Transfer Ware

A pearlware chestnut basket, transfer-printed with Oriental figures drying nets, impressed star mark, early 19thC, 9½in (24cm) wide.
£300–360 / €430–510
$500–600 SWO

Items in the Blue & White Transfer Ware section have been arranged in alphabetical order.

A Staffordshire openwork basket and stand, transfer-printed with a river scene and castle within floral borders, 1820–30, 11in (28cm) wide.
£600–720 / €890–1,050
$1,000–1,200 MCA

A Ridgway toilet box, transfer-printed with the Taj Mahal from the Parrot Border series, c1820, 7in (18cm) wide.
£340–380 / €490–550
$570–640 GN

A butter dish, transfer-printed with a girl and her dog, flower baskets and foliate scrolls, with lion-mask handles, chips, 1815–30, 5in (12.5cm) diam.
£260–310 / €370–440
$440–520 DN

A Spode basket, transfer-printed with Cracked Ice pattern, c1820, 5in (12.5cm) diam.
£220–250 / €310–360
$370–420 GN

A Brameld bidet, the interior transfer-printed with Boys Fishing pattern within a border of wild flowers, slight damage, 1825–50, 17in (43cm) wide.
£1,400–1,650 / €2,000–2,350
$2,350–2,750 PFK

A breakfast set, comprising four covered dishes and a stand, transfer-printed, central cover missing, impressed numbers, 19thC, on a later mahogany stand, 21in (53.5cm) wide.
£490–580 / €700–830
$820–970 SWO

A pair of Ridgway candlesticks, transfer-printed with Italian Flower Garden pattern, c1830, 9½in (24cm) high.
£900–1,000 / €1,300–1,450
$1,500–1,700 GN

► **A Brown-Westhead, Moore & Co part dinner service,** comprising 121 pieces, transfer-printed with Variete pattern, damage and staining, printed impressed marks, late 19thC.
£1,300–1,550 / €1,900–2,250
$2,200–2,600 DN

A Ridgway fruit basket, transfer-printed with Indian Temples pattern, c1825, 10in (25.5cm) diam.
£300–350 / €430–500
$500–580 GN

A Riley bowl, transfer-printed with Feeding the Chickens pattern, marked, c1820, 9in (23cm) diam.
£410–450 / €590–650
$690–760 GN
Pieces such as these have never before been found with a mark.

A Leeds butter dish, transfer-printed with The Wanderer pattern, c1810, 6½in (16.5cm) wide.
£250–280 / €360–400
$420–470 SCO

A cheese cradle, transfer-printed with flower sprays, cracked and chipped, 19thC, 12in (30.5cm) wide.
£470–560 / €680–810
$790–940 SWO

A J. & R. Riley pickle dish, transfer-printed with the Coventry Drapers armorial, 1828, 6in (15cm) wide.
£430–480 / €620–690
$720–800 GN

A Spode footbath, transfer-printed with flowers and peacocks, 19thC, 18½in (47cm) wide.
£2,000–2,400 / €2,900–3,450
$3,350–4,000 AH

A mug, transfer-printed with a view of Greenwich, c1820, 4in (10cm) diam.
£280–320 / €400–460
$470–540 GRe

A Davenport hot water plate, transfer-printed with The Villager pattern, 1815–30, 11in (28cm) diam.
£270–300 / €390–430
$450–500 GRe

A Brameld drainer, transfer-printed with Castle at Rochfort pattern, c1825, 15in (38cm) wide.
£560–630 / €800–900
$940–1,050 CoS

An inkwell/candlestick, transfer-printed with exotic birds, rim of base restored, c1830, 4in (10cm) diam.
£630–700 / €900–1,000
$1,050–1,200 GN

An Adams plate, transfer-printed with a scene from the Scripture series, restored, c1820, 7in (18cm) diam.
£200–230 / €290–330
$340–390 GN

A set of 12 plates, transfer-printed with the Drapers Arms, c1820, 9¾in (25cm) wide.
£1,350–1,500 / €1,900–2,100
$2,250–2,500 SCO

◄ **A Rogers meat plate,** transfer-printed with Tivoli pattern, impressed and printed marks, c1820, 20¾in (52.5cm) wide.
£230–270 / €330–380
$390–450 WW

A Staffordshire footbath, transfer-printed with Florentine pattern, florentine mark, c1830, 21in (53.5cm) wide.
£1,300–1,550 / €1,900–2,250
$2,200–2,600 WL

A puzzle jug, transfer-printed with sprays of flowers, c1840, 11½in (29cm) high.
£1,200–1,350 / €1,750–1,950
$2,150–2,450 SCO

A meat plate, transfer-printed with The Winemakers pattern, impressed mark, 1815–25, 15in (38cm) diam.
£1,500–1,700 / €2,150–2,450
$2,500–2,850 GRe

A John Shorthose saucer plate, transfer-printed with birds, c1820, 10in (25.5cm) diam.
£180–200 / €260–290
$300–330 SCO

A commemorative plate, transfer-printed with a figure of a monarch, probably George III, and an inscription, early 19thC, 9¾in (25cm) wide.
£280–330 / €400–470
$470–550 TRM

A Rogers & Son serving plate, transfer-printed with Elephant pattern, impressed mark, c1830, 10in (25.5cm) wide.
£150–180 / €220–260
$250–300 G(L)

A meat plate, transfer-printed, from the Tulip Border series, c1820, 17¼in (44cm) diam.
£800–900 / €1,150–1,300
$1,350–1,500 GN

Further reading

Miller's Collecting Blue & White Pottery, Miller's Publications, 2004

A Spode-style pearlware meat plate, transfer-printed with Greek pattern, early 19thC, 18½in (47cm) wide.
£260–310 / €370–440
$440–520 SWO

◄ **A dessert plate,** transfer-printed with Gunton Hall, Norfolk, printed title mark, 1820–30, 7¾in (19.5cm) wide.
£110–130
€155–185
$185–220 DN

A meat plate, transfer-printed with Craigmillar Castle, Edinburgh, from the Antique Scenery series, 1820–35, 16in (40.5cm) wide.
£590–660 / €850–950
$990–1,100 GRe
Craigmillar is now in ruins but was a favourite residence of Mary Queen of Scots.

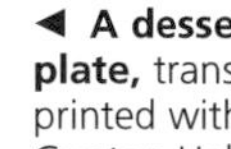

A pearlware meat plate, transfer-printed with a castle in a rural landscape, early 19thC, 20in (51cm) wide.
£940–1,100 / €1,350–1,600
$1,550–1,850 GAK

► **A pair of Spode plates,** transfer-printed, 1825–30, 10in (25.5cm) wide.
£140–155
€200–220
$230–260
DAN

◄ **A Brameld platter,** transfer-printed with Tilting at Windmills pattern, from the Don Quixote series, c1830, 19in (48.5cm) wide.
£600–670
€860–960
$1,000–1,100
GN

POTTERY

An Elkin Knight & Co meat dish, transfer-printed, from the Irish Scenery series, c1835, 20in (51cm) wide.
£270–300 / €390–430
$450–500 ⊞ STA

A meat plate, transfer-printed with an Arabian landscape, printed mark 'Manufactured for W. M. Sargeant & Co, New Orleans', slight damage, 19thC, 22½in (57cm) wide.
£110–130 / €160–190
$185–220 ⚒ FHF

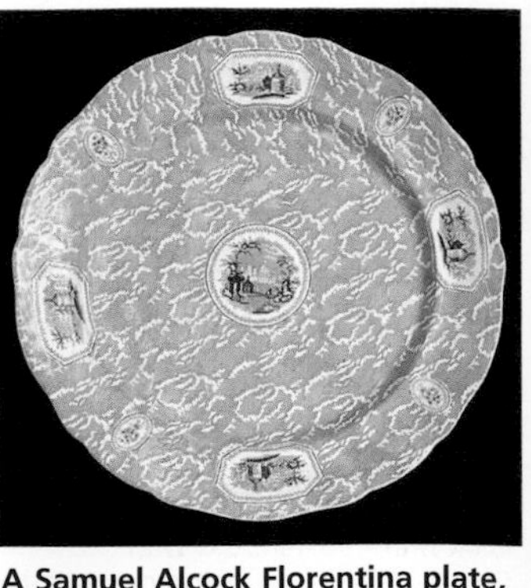

A Samuel Alcock Florentina plate, transfer-printed with Temple pattern, c1840, 17in (43cm) diam.
£540–600 / €780–860
$900–1,000 ⊞ GN

A Bovey Tracey meat plate, transfer-printed with a Staffordshire canal scene within a Wild Rose pattern border, impressed factory mark, c1850, 18in (45.5cm) wide.
£210–250 / €300–360
$350–420 ⚒ PF

► A Staffordshire meat plate, with gravy well, transfer-printed with Peking Sketches, by 'I. C.', c1850, 19½in (49.5cm) wide.
£280–330
€400–470
$470–550 ⚒ NSal

Three Victorian graduated meat plates, transfer-printed with Fonthill Abbey, Holkham Hall and Oxburgh Hall, largest 15¾in (40cm) wide.
£640–760 / €920–1,100
$1,050–1,250 ⚒ CHTR

A Wedgwood pedestal, transfer-printed with Moss Roses pattern, c1864, 31in (78.5cm) high.
£3,150–3,500 / €4,500–5,000
$5,300–5,900 ⊞ GN

A Minton pickle set, transfer-printed with Dove pattern, one segment restored, 1817–20, 6in (15cm) wide.
£470–530 / €670–760
$790–890 ⊞ GN

A spitoon, transfer-printed with grapes and flowers, c1840, 5in (12.5cm) high.
£270–300 / €390–430
$450–500 ⊞ GN

A pepper pot, transfer-printed with a rural scene, 1820–30, 3¼in (8.5cm) high.
£350–420 / €500–600
$590–700 ⚒ DN

◄ A Minton pearlware supper set segment and cover, transfer-printed with Plant pattern, c1815, 12in (30.5cm) wide.
£360–400 / €520–580
$600–670 ⊞ DSA

A Spode supper set, comprising a centrepiece with reversible segmented cover and four quadrant dishes, transfer-printed with Geranium pattern, restored, printed and impressed marks, 1818–33, 18¼in (46.5cm) diam.
£470–560 / €670–800
$790–940 DN

A part tea and coffee service, comprising 21 pieces, transfer-printed with Willow pattern, with gilt grapevine overlay, wear and browning, printed mark for Miles Mason, 1800–16.
£130–155 / €190–220
$220–260 NSal

An Enoch Wood vegetable tureen, transfer-printed with Llanercost Priory, with a lion finial, c1820, 9in (23cm) square.
£450–500 / €650–720
$750–840 GN

A two-handled urn, transfer-printed with a view of Fairmount Gardens, Catskill Moss, damaged and restored, design registration lozenge for 1844, 12in (30.5cm) high.
£350–420 / €500–600
$590–700 PFK

A tea bowl and saucer, possibly by William Smith, transfer-printed with Tea Party pattern, 1825–30, bowl 3in (7.5cm) diam.
£150–170 / €210–240
$250–280 GRe

A Spode sauce tureen stand, transfer-printed with the Cemetery of Cacamo from the Caramanian series, impressed mark, 1810–20, 7½in (19cm) wide.
£350–420 / €500–600
$590–700 DN

A Don Pottery tureen, transfer-printed with an Italian view, c1820, 12in (30.5cm) wide.
£670–750 / €960–1,100
$1,100–1,250 SCO

A Don Pottery teapot, transfer-printed with Vermicelli pattern, c1830, 11in (28cm) wide.
£540–600 / €780–860
$900–1,000 GN

A pair of Rogers sauce tureens and stands, transfer-printed with an ox being driven by the ruins of a tower, impressed marks, c1820, 8¼in (21cm) wide.
£430–510 / €620–730
$720–850 CGC

A Benjamin Adams pearlware soup tureen, transfer-printed with a pastoral scene after Claude Lorraine, the finial and handles in the form of Prince of Wales feathers, impressed mark, 1800–20, 15in (38cm) wide.
£700–840 / €1,000–1,200
$1,200–1,400 PF

A Cauldon umbrella stand, transfer-printed, c1890, 21in (53.5cm) high.
£1,250–1,400 / €1,800–2,000
$2,100–2,350 GN

◄ **A Spode spill vase,** transfer-printed with Temple pattern, c1815, 5in (12.5cm) high.
£200–230 / €290–330
$340–390 GN

POTTERY

Mason's Ironstone

The word Ironstone was introduced by the Mason family who developed the potting techniques and registered the patent name in 1813, even though other factories were already producing this type of ware. It was Miles Mason's youngest son Charles James who, at the age of 21, took out the patent for 'A process for the improvement of the manufacture of English porcelain'. The process, according to the specification, consisted of using 'Coria Slag of Ironstone' ground in water with flint, Cornwall stone, clay and blue oxide of cobalt. This greyish stoneware was extremely durable and therefore ideal for everyday domestic use.

Their patent, granted for 14 years, was never renewed, probably because the other major potters had perfected their own recipes. Ironstone was an immense success, the easily identifiable name being of paramount importance as the Masons sold directly to the public through auctions. Before this they had only disposed of surplus stock in this way.

Production reached extraordinary levels of technical and artistic excellence. The combining of strong colours such as mazarine blue, brick red and bright gilding created a rich effect. 'Felspar' porcelain and a new variety of earthenware called 'Cambrian Argil' were created. Approximately 120 patterns a year were being introduced and by 1840 the tableware numbered over 3,000 patterns. After 1840 several types of ware were introduced but none proved successful. In 1848 Charles was declared bankrupt and the golden age of Mason's Ironstone ended.

In terms of market values, dinner services of over 100 pieces of good quality, colour and mixed content have increased dramatically in price, from around £2,500 / €3,600 / $6,000 in 1985 to about £17,500 / €25,200 / $29,400 today. Large individual items such as alcove vases and bread bins, appealing to both collectors and interior decorators, are continuing to rise in value. Items produced prolifically in the early 1800s, such as jugs, mugs, toilet wares and plates, have remained static in price for the past three years unless they are of very good quality or of an unusual pattern or shape. Many such items have been restored and this is a major factor in the levelling of prices. The Art Deco-influenced Estrella and Lustrosa wares from the early 1900s appeal to new Mason's collectors. Examples are difficult to find because manufacture was severely disrupted during the two world wars, but they are worth considering as they are still reasonably priced. **Janice Paull**

A pair of Mason's Ironstone bottles and covers, painted in enamels, impressed marks, 1813–25, 4½in (11.5cm) high.
£610–680 / €880–980
$1,000–1,150 ⊞ JP

A Mason's Ironstone comport, printed and enamelled in the Oriental style with a swan, vase and flowers, on an acanthus-moulded pedestal, printed mark, c1820, 14in (35.5cm) wide.
£260–310 / €370–440
$440–520 ⚒ G(L)

A Mason's Ironstone part dessert service, comprising 11 pieces, transfer-printed and enamelled with Waterlily pattern, highlighted with gilt, minor repairs, impressed marks, 1815–20.
£1,750–1,950 / €2,500–2,800
$2,900–3,250 ⊞ JP

► A Mason's Ironstone dessert service, comprising 13 pieces, decorated in the Imari palette, 1825–50.
£1,750–2,100
€2,500–3,000
$2,950–3,500 ⚒ NOA

A Mason's Ironstone dessert service, comprising 16 pieces, transfer-printed in the Imari palette, highlighted with gilt, printed mark, c1840.
£880–1,050 / €1,250–1,500
$1,450–1,750 ⚒ TEN

◄ A Mason's Ironstone part dinner service, comprising 79 pieces, decorated with Scroll pattern, damaged and restored, impressed and printed marks, c1820.
£7,800–9,400 / €11,200–13,500
$13,100–15,800 ⚒ S(O)

► A Mason's Ironstone dinner service, comprising 38 pieces, decorated with Long Tail Pheasant pattern, 1820–30.
£1,350–1,600 / €1,950–2,300
$2,250–2,650 ⚒ G(L)

A Mason's Ironstone part dinner service, comprising 34 pieces, decorated in the Imari palette, faults, printed marks, c1830.
£2,450–2,950 / €3,550–4,250
$4,100–4,950 ⚒ WW

A pair of Mason's Ironstone dough/ bread bins and covers, decorated with Scroll pattern, impressed marks, c1820, 14¼in (36cm) high.
£12,600–15,000 / €18,000–21,600
$21,000–25,000 ⚒ S(O)

A Mason's Ironstone jug, transfer-printed and enamelled with Wheel pattern, the handle in the form of a serpent, 1815–20, 8in (20.5cm) high.
£760–850 / €1,100–1,200
$1,250–1,400 ⊞ JP

Marks

The most common early Mason's mark, used from 1813 to 1825, shows 'Mason's Patent Ironstone China' impressed in a continuous line. During the Victorian period the printed crown and banner was used, with subtle variations on the shape of the crown indicating the date of manufacture. When unmarked, pieces that cannot be definitely attributed to Mason's are simply described as Staffordshire.

A Mason's Ironstone part dinner service, comprising 22 pieces, decorated with Waterlily pattern, faults, impressed and printed marks, c1830.
£1,100–1,300 / €1,550–1,850
$1,850–2,200 ⚒ B(Kn)

A Mason's Ironstone Neapolitan ewer, painted by Samuel Bourne with a landscape, handle restored, impressed mark, c1820, 27½in (70cm) high.
£6,300–7,000 / €8,800–10,000
$10,600–11,800 ⊞ JP
This piece is unusual in that it has retained its original base – usually these have been replaced.

Further reading

Miller's Ceramics Buyer's Guide, Miller's Publications, 2000

A Mason's Ironstone jug, decorated with Butterfly pattern, impressed mark, c1820, 6¼in (16cm) high.
£150–180 / €210–260
$250–300 ⚒ G(L)

A pair of Mason's Ironstone dough/ bread bins, painted in enamels with Sacrificial Lamb pattern, one lid restored, impressed marks, 1815–20, 15¼in (38.5cm) high.
£14,800–16,500 / €21,300–23,700
$24,800–27,700 ⊞ JP

A pair of Mason's Ironstone storage jars, decorated with gilding and panels of School House pattern, the covers with crown finials, one jar restored, c1820, 15¾in (40cm) high.
£11,200–12,500 / €16,100–18,000
$18,800–21,000 ⊞ JP

A Mason's Ironstone jug, transfer-printed and enamelled with Green Mandarin pattern, impressed mark, 1815–20, 8in (20.5cm) high.
£850–950 / €1,200–1,350
$1,400–1,600 ⊞ JP

A Mason's Ironstone jug, painted with chrysanthemums, the handle in the form of a serpent, printed mark, 1820–30, 9½in (24cm) high.
£140–165 / €200–240
$230–270 ⚒ G(L)

A Mason's jug, transfer-printed and painted with Heron pattern, Fenton printed mark, 1830–40, 6in (15cm) high.
£360–400 / €520–580
$600–670 ⊞ JP

A Mason's Ironstone jug, decorated with panels of figures on a Y-diaper ground, printed mark, repaired, 1830–40, 8in (20.5cm) high.
£105–125 / €150–180
$175–210 ⚒ WW

A Mason's Ironstone mug, printed and enamelled with a Japan-style pattern, 1820–30, 4in (10cm) high.
£130–155 / €185–220
$220–260 ⚒ G(L)

A Mason's Ironstone platter, decorated with Flying Bird pattern, late 19thC, 10in (25.5cm) wide.
£80–90 / €115–130
$135–140 ⊞ HTE

► **A Mason's Ironstone tea service,** comprising 31 pieces, decorated with Jardinière pattern, c1900, teapot 7in (18cm) high.
£450–500 / €650–720
$750–840 ⊞ ANAn

► **A set of three graduated Mason's Ironstone jugs,** late 19thC, largest 9in (23cm) high.
£1,050–1,200
€1,500–1,700
$1,750–2,000
⊞ ANAn

◄ **A Mason's Ironstone mug,** decorated with School House pattern, impressed mark, c1820, 4½in (11.5cm) high.
£690–770 / €990–1,100
$1,150–1,300 ⊞ RdV

A Mason's Ironstone mug, blue printed mark, c1820, 6in (16cm) diam.
£360–400 / €520–580
$600–670 ⊞ ANAn

A Mason's Ironstone pastille burner, painted in enamels with Japan pattern, finial repaired, impressed mark, c1820, 4¼in (11cm) high.
£1,400–1,600 / €2,000–2,300
$2,350–2,700 ⊞ JP

A set of ten Mason's Ironstone plates, brown printed mark, c1835, 10in (25.5cm) diam.
£720–800 / €1,000–1,150
$1,200–1,350 ⊞ ANAn

A Mason's Ironstone slop bucket with strainer, decorated with Flying Bird pattern, late 19thC, 11in (28cm) high.
£720–800 / €1,000–1,150
$1,200–1,350 ⊞ ANAn

A Mason's Ironstone spill vase, decorated with Elephant's Foot pattern, c1818, 4in (10cm) high.
£400–450 / €580–650
$670–760 ⊞ RdV

A Mason's Ironstone toilet set, comprising four pieces, decorated with Coloured Willow pattern, late 19thC.
£130–155 / €190–220
$220–260 DMC

A Mason's Ironstone tureen and cover, decorated with a Japan-style pattern, with floral finial and pierced foot, chips, c1820, 12¼in (31cm) wide.
£520–620 / €750–890
$870–1,050 B(Kn)

A Mason's Ironstone vase and cover, decorated with various Mason's patterns, the handles in the form of sea urchins, firing crack, impressed mark, 1815–20, 26in (66cm) high.
£5,400–6,000 / €7,700–8,600
$9,000–10,000 JP

A pair of Mason's Ironstone vases, lids missing, c1820, 7in (18cm) high.
£470–530 / €670–760
$790–890 ANAn

◀ **A Mason's Ironstone vase and cover,** moulded with an exotic bird on a blossom branch issuing from rockwork, the reverse with islands and pagodas, the shoulders and pierced cover applied with dragons, wear and chips, c1825, 22in (56cm) high.
£1,550–1,850 / €2,200–2,650
$2,600–3,100 S

◀ **A Mason's Ironstone vase,** with moulded mask and ring handles, purple printed mark, c1830, 12¼in (31cm) high.
£175–210 / €250–300
$290–350 SWO

A Mason's Ironstone vase, decorated with Muscovy Duck pattern, black printed mark, lid missing, c1830, 15in (38cm) high.
£610–730 / €880–1,050
$1,000–1,200 WW

◀ **A Mason's Ironstone vase and cover,** decorated with Lyre Bird pattern, Fenton printed mark, finial restored, 1830–40, 37in (94cm) high.
£4,500–5,400
€6,500–7,800
$7,600–9,100 JP

Porcelain

For some time the trend has been that exceptional and rare porcelain will readily find buyers whereas average and plentiful items will struggle. This is particularly apparent with Continental porcelain whose collectors have become increasingly discriminating in the difficult economic climate. The best continues to be well received, particularly with Meissen and Sèvres, but the wares of the smaller German and French factories are less easy to sell. It is the British market that has generated the most excitement and growth at auction recently, and in particular pieces from before c1760. There has been no great change in demand for the products of the mid-19th century, although strong interest has been shown in Parian wares.

The highlight of the ceramics calendar was undoubtedly the delightful collection of 18th-century English porcelain formed by the late Billie Pain: examples are sprinkled throughout the following pages. As a barometer of the current market, the sale confirmed that the earliest wares of the Chelsea and Worcester factories are the most fashionable and hotly contested. It is also confirmed that single-owner collections continue to carry a cachet, the most interesting of which to be held outside London last year was the Anthony Hoyte collection of Derby porcelain sold by Neales of Nottingham. The majority of the pieces were artist-decorated wares of the late 18th and 19th centuries. Apart from the early wares and rarities, it is this period of Derby porcelain that is avidly collected at present. Prices for Derby figures of the 1760s, for instance, have generally remained static recently.

The beautiful porcelains from Swansea and Nantgarw are more sought after now than ever before. It was noticeable that new private collectors have appeared over the last year, forcing prices up to breathtaking heights. An important factor in the interest of these factories, as with Derby, is that pieces can often be attributed to particular artists by certain traits in that painter's technique and palette. Collectors love to put names to painting.

Royal Worcester has seen a surge in prices, largely due to interest from Australia. Harry Davis remains the most popular artist, although signed pieces by painters such as the Stintons, Baldwyn and Chivers have commanded high prices. Demand remained almost at fever pitch for the work of the artist Désiré Leroy at Royal Crown Derby.

Phil Howell

Animals

A Belleek Sea Horse flower holder, Irish, Second Period, 1891–1926, 3½in (9cm) high.
£250–280 / €360–400
$420–470 ⊞ DeA

A Derby model of a leopard, with one paw raised, c1756, 3in (7.5cm) wide.
£3,600–4,000 / €5,200–5,800
$6,000–6,600 ⊞ JUP

The majority of early Derby wares were left in the white, and the remainder were decorated in very pale enamels. After 1756 the colours became brighter and clearer.

◄ A 'Girl in a Swing' bonbonnière and hinged cover, modelled as a French hen sitting with her brood, gilt-metal mount, cracked and chipped, 1749–54, 2in (5cm) high.
£6,100–7,300 / €8,800–10,500
$10,300–12,300 ⚒ DN

'Girl in a Swing' wares are popular with collectors and this example is unusual.

A Fürstenberg model of a cow, with an open mouth, on a thinly potted base applied with a flower and three leaves, restoration and losses, German, c1760, 4¼in (10.5cm) wide.
£300–360 / €430–500
$500–600 ⚒ B

A Meissen model of a peacock, naturalistically coloured, on a scroll-moulded base, gilt-metal ring inserted below one wing, minor chips, crossed swords and dot mark, German, c1770, 5½in (14cm) wide.
£540–640 / €780–920
$900–1,000 ⚒ S(O)

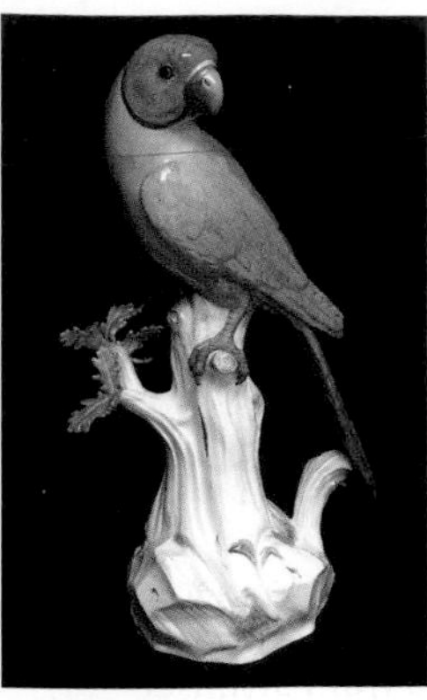

A Meissen model of a parrot, No. 63, crossed swords mark, German, c1880, 13in (33cm) high.
£2,150–2,400
€3,100–3,450
$3,850–4,350 ⊞ DAV
This design was first modelled by J. S. Kändler in 1740.

A Royal Worcester Parian vase, modelled as a dove perched on a branch, printed and impressed marks and lozenge registration, 1868, 6¼in (16cm) high.
£165–195 / €240–280
$280–330 ⚒ DD

A set of five Sitzendorf monkey orchestra figures, comprising a conductor, violinist, cellist, flautist, and bugle player, on a gilt-scrolled base, losses, maker's mark, German, early 20thC, largest 5¼in (13.5cm) high.
£420–500 / €600–720
$700–840 ⚒ BR

A pair of porcelain Aesop's fable groups, depicting the fable of the fox and the stalk, before tree spill vases, with quill holders to the backs, mid-19thC, 7in (18cm) high.
£440–530 / €630–760
$740–890 ⚒ WW

► **A porcelain model of a chicken,** beside a spill holder and foliage, crack, repairs and restoration, probably French, c1880, 10½in (26.5cm) high.
£175–210 / €250–300
$300–360 ⚒ SWO

◄ **A Meissen fish tureen,** modelled as a carp, crossed swords mark, German, 1850–1900, 12¼in (31cm) long.
£1,050–1,250 / €1,500–1,800
$1,750–2,150 ⚒ DORO

A pair of Worcester partridge tureens and covers, nesting in oval baskets, one cover glued, star crack to base of one tureen, small chips to applied foliage, painted workman's mark to one base, c1760, 5½in (14cm) wide.
£3,600–4,300 / €5,200–6,200
$6,000–7,200 ⚒ S

Baskets

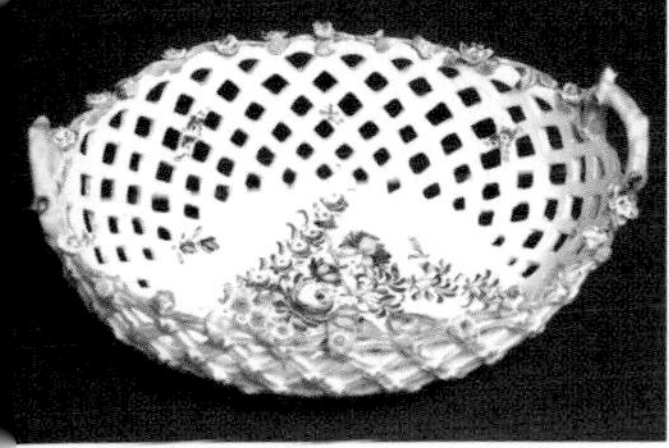

A Bow basket, painted with flower-sprays, cracks, losses and repairs to handles, c1760, 11in (28cm) wide.
£720–800 / €1,000–1,150
$1,200–1,350 ⊞ JUP

◄ **A Belleek basket,** Irish, Second Period, 1891–1926, 6in (15cm) wide.
£360–400 / €520–580
$600–670 ⊞ DeA

A Meissen basket, the interior painted with flowers, the exterior moulded in a wicker effect, German, c1750, 8½in (21.5cm) wide.
£490–580 / €700–840
$820–980 ⚒ DORO

► **A Worcester basket,** printed with Pine Cone pattern, c1775, 7in (18cm) diam.
£720–800 / €1,050–1,150
$1,200–1,350 ⊞ JUP

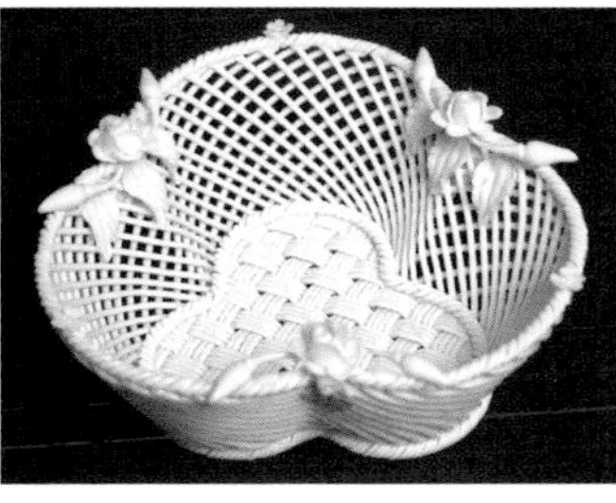

A Belleek shamrock basket, Irish, Third Period, 1926–46, 6in (15cm) diam.
£340–380 / €490–550
$570–640 ⊞ WAA

Bough Pots

Two Coalport demi-lune bough pots and covers, each painted with a frieze of flowers on a gilt ground, c1810, 8in (20.5cm) wide.
£3,100–3,700 / €4,450–5,300
$5,200–6,200 ⚒ S

A pair of Paris bough pots and covers, painted with panels of flowers, gilt marks, chip to cover, repair to one foot, French, 19thC, 8½in (21.5cm) wide.
£650–780 / €930–1,050
$1,100–1,300 ⚒ B(Kn)

A Bloor Derby *bombé* bough pot and cover, with scroll handles and feet, printed marks, minor damage, c1835, 7in (18cm) high.
£1,300–1,550 / €1,850–2,200
$2,200–2,600 ⚒ B

Bowls

A Berlin bowl, mounted with a brass rim, printed with a portrait of Kaiser Wilhelm I within a cartouche, German, c1875, 8in (20.5cm) diam.
£120–140 / €170–200
$200–240 ⚒ SAS

A Meissen *Hausmalerei* bowl, probably painted in Dresden with two panels of peasant figures in landscapes, within a *Laub-und-Bandelwerk* cartouche, restored, German, c1725, 5¼in (13.5cm) diam.
£820–980 / €1,200–1,400
$1,400–1,650 ⚒ G(L)

A Swansea sucrier, painted with 'The Blue Headed Green Flycatcher' and 'The Young Painted Finch' in a moulded panel, beneath a scroll foliate-moulded border, gilt side handles, cover missing, Welsh, early 19thC, 6½in (16.5cm) diam.
£330–390 / €480–570
$550–650 ⚒ NSal

A Coalport bowl, c1820, 7in (18cm) diam.
£130–145 / €190–210
$210–240 ⊞ DAN

A Lowestoft bowl, cracks, c1785, 6in (15cm) diam.
£260–290 / €370–410
$430–480 ⊞ JUP

A Vincennes porcelain bleu lapis bowl, with three gilt foliate-edged panels painted with birds, the interior with scattered flower sprigs and an insect, marked, French, date letter for 1756, 6½in (16.5cm) diam.
£2,150–2,550 / €3,100–3,700
$3,600–4,300 ⚒ S(NY)

► **A Worcester Barr, Flight & Barr sucrier,** painted in the Imari style with Chinese Fenced Garden pattern, c1810, 7in (18cm) wide.
£540–600 / €780–860
$900–1,000 ⊞ JUP

A Liverpool bowl, probably Gilbody or Chaffers, moulded with flowerheads and scrolls, painted with figures and leaping deer, rim chip and crack, c1760, 4¾in (12cm) diam.
£490–590 / €710–850
$820–990 ⚒ WW

A New Hall slop bowl, by Fidelle Duvivier, painted with two coastal scenes, star cracks in base, minor wear, 1782–87, 5¾in (14.5cm) diam.
£1,750–2,000 / €2,500–2,900
$2,900–3,400 ⚒ B
The service to which this slop bowl belongs does not appear to have been previously recorded.

A Worcester slop bowl, printed with floral sprays, the interior with a central rosebud and a rim frieze, c1770, 6in (15cm) diam.
£100–120 / €145–170
$170–200 ⚒ PFK

PORCELAIN

Covered Bowls

A Caughley sugar bowl and cover, transfer-printed with The Pagoda pattern, c1785, 4½in (11.5cm) high.
£175–195 / €250–280
$300–330 ⊞ WAC

A Coalport sucrier and cover, c1810, 7in (18cm) wide.
£310–350 / €450–500
$520–580 ⊞ DAN

A pair of Coalport Rose du Barry bowls and covers, with cartouches of enamel floral sprays, winged putti and fruit sprays, each emblematic of the Arts and Science, with gilt borders, flanked by moulded reeding and handles modelled as shells, marked, c1860, 9in (23cm) wide.
£590–710 / €850–1,000
$990–1,150 ⚒ Mit

A Dresden punchbowl and cover, painted with Watteauesque scenes, the cover surmounted with a bacchic putto, Berlin-type sceptre mark, German, late 19thC, 10½in (26.5cm) diam.
£590–710 / €850–1,000
$990–1,150 ⚒ DN

A Meissen pouring bowl and cover, moulded with a foliate spout and knopped faceted handle, painted with Onion Pattern, crossed swords mark and three dots, incised mark for Johann Christian Dietrich, restored chip to spout, German, 1731–36, 7½in (19cm) diam.
£3,600–4,300 / €5,200–6,200
$6,000–7,200 ⚒ S

A Meissen sucrier and cover, painted with flowers and cut sprigs, with a floral knop on the cover, German, c1750, 5in (12.5cm) diam.
£760–850 / €1,100–1,150
$1,300–1,450 ⊞ G&G

A Spode sucrier and cover, c1815, 8in (20.5cm) wide.
£290–320 / €420–470
$490–540 ⊞ DAN

A Worcester sugar bowl and cover, with a flower knop, painted in the Kakiemon style, square seal mark, hairline crack, c1770, 4¾in (12cm) diam.
£190–220 / €270–320
$320–380 ⚒ WW

A Worcester blue and white sugar bowl and cover, printed with Fence pattern, the domed cover with a flower knop, c1780, 5in (12.5cm) high.
£210–250 / €300–360
$350–420 ⚒ WL

A Worcester porcelain sucrier, with gilt detail, c1785, 5in (12.5cm) high.
£400–450 / €580–650
$670–760 ⊞ AUC

► **A sugar bowl and cover,** the ring knop reversing to form a foot, the flowerhead and leaf scroll design with later painted birds and plants, some restoration, decorated in Europe for the Western market, Chinese, 1700–20, 4½in (11.5cm) high.
£420–500 / €600–720
$710–840 ⚒ B
Ex-Bernard Watney collection. Bernard Watney was one of the foremost collectors and researchers of early English porcelain, and his extensive collection has been sold in a number of sales since 1999.

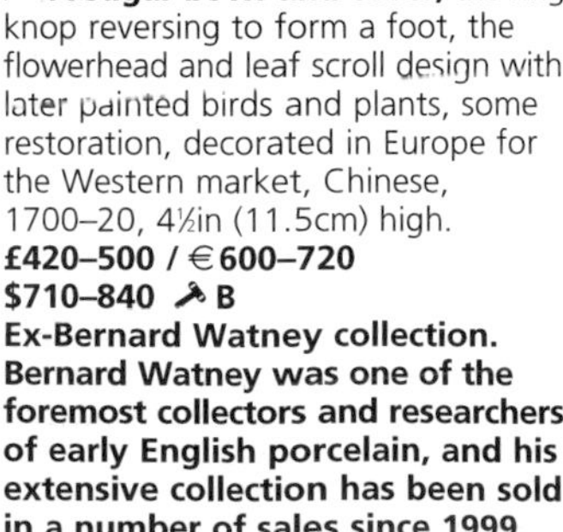

Boxes

A Meissen butter box and cover, modelled by J. J. Kändler or P. Reinicke, crossed swords mark, chips and restoration, German, c1760, 6in (15cm) wide.
£780–940 / €1,100–1,300
$1,300–1,550 ⚒ S(O)

A Mennecy bonbonnière and cover, moulded in the form of a melon, the interior cover painted with a flower spray, the rims fitted with a hinged silver mount with Paris discharge mark, French, c1755, 2¾in (7cm) diam.
£780–930 / €1,100–1,300
$1,300–1,550 ⚒ S(NY)

A Sèvres-style box, decorated with a cartouche depicting a lady and gentleman on a gilt-enriched ground, French, c1880, 4in (10cm) wide.
£400–450 / €580–640
$670–740 ⊞ MAA

Items in the Porcelain section have been arranged alphabetically in factory order, with non-specific pieces appearing at the end of each sub-section.

Busts

◄ **A Parian bust of Apollo,** by Bates Brown Westhead Moore & Co, signed C. Delpech, impressed factory marks, inscribed 'Art Union of London 1855', 14in (35.5cm) high.
£490–590 / €710–850
$820–990 ⚒ AG

A pair of Meissen portrait busts of a boy and a girl, each wearing a scarf, on gilded scroll bases, crossed swords marks and incised numeral 2744, German, late 19thC, 9¼in (23.5cm) high.
£800–960 / €1,150–1,350
$1,350–1,600 ⚒ G(L)

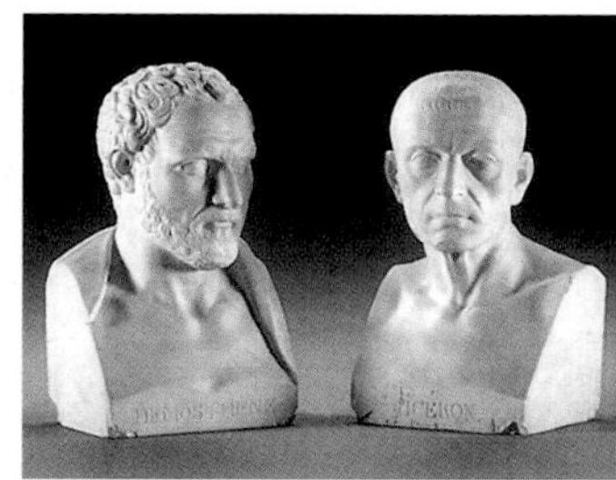

◄ **A pair of Sèvres biscuit busts of Cicéron and Démosthène,** Cicéron modelled by Alexandre Brachard, incised, chipped, French, c1820, larger 8in (20.5cm) high.
£960–1,150 / €1,400–1,650
$1,600–1,900 ⚒ S(O)

PORCELAIN

Butter, Cream & Sauce Boats

A Caughley butter boat, moulded as a leaf, the interior painted with Fisherman pattern, c1790, 3in (7.5cm) long.
£175–210 / €250–300
$290–340 ⚒ DN

The Fisherman pattern

Introduced in about 1775, both Worcester and the nearby Caughley factory produced versions of the popular printed Fisherman pattern. Although very similar, there are two main differences between the two prints. On Worcester items, the standing figure holds a long fish, while the seated fisherman holds a wavy fishing line. On Caughley examples, the standing figure holds a small fish and the seated fisherman holds a straight fishing line.

► **A Derby sauce boat,** moulded as a leaf, painted with flower sprays and sprigs, c1770, 6¾in (17cm) long.
£260–310 / €370–440
$440–520 ⚒ S(O)

A Chantilly sauce boat, with a curled stalk handle, damaged, French, 1755–60, 10in (25.5cm) wide.
£880–1,050 / €1,250–1,500
$1,450–1,700 ⚒ B

A Meissen sauce boat, with two handles and two lips, on four scroll feet, chipped foot, crossed swords mark, German, c1750, 10in (25.5cm) wide.
£730–870 / €1,050–1,250 $1,200–1,400 ⚒ G(L)

A Worcester cream boat, painted with Captive Bird pattern, c1755, 2in (5cm) high.
£1,450–1,600 / €2,050–2,300 $2,450–2,700 ⊞ JUP

A Worcester butter boat, moulded as a leaf, painted with flowering plants, painter's mark, 1751–74, 3¼in (8.5cm) wide.
£300–360 / €430–510 $500–600 ⚒ L

Candlesticks & Chambersticks

A pair of Belleek Gothic candlesticks, with gilded architectural features, gilding worn, printed marks, Irish, Second Period, 1891–1926, 9¼in (23.5cm) high.
£960–1,150 / €1,380–1,650 $1,600–1,900 ⚒ S(O)

◄ **A Nantgarw taperstick,** the gilded handle with a serpent head terminal, painted in London with a panel of flowers, small chip to foot, gilding worn, Welsh, 1818–20, 2½in (6.5cm) high.
£1,900–2,250 / €2,750–3,300 $3,200–3,800 ⚒ B

► **A Spode chamberstick,** with raised gilt exotic bird decoration, c1825, 1½in (4cm) high.
£780–860 / €1,100–1,250 $1,300–1,450 ⊞ DIA

A Jacob Petit chamberstick, with multiple applied flowerheads in the Mennecy-Vincennes style, signed 'J.P.', French, 1850–75, 3in (7.5cm) high.
£400–480 / €580–690 $670–800 ⚒ NOA

Centrepieces

A Dresden figural centrepiece, modelled as two female figures supporting a pierced basket, restored, marked, German, c1900, 19¼in (49cm) high.
£300–360 / €430–480 $500–550 ⚒ S(O)

◄ **A Meissen bowl,** encrusted with flowers, on an ormolu base, German, c1860, 17in (43cm) wide.
£3,100–3,450 €4,500–5,000 $5,200–5,800 ⊞ BROW

A Plaue centrepiece, the pierced basket above a column with two putti playing musical instruments, small chips, cross mark, German, c1900, 15¾in (40cm) high.
£370–440 / €530–630 $620–740 ⚒ DN

◄ **A Sèvres-style centrepiece,** gilt-bronze-mounted, French, c1880, 24in (61cm) wide.
£4,050–4,500 / €5,850–6,500 $6,800–7,600 ⊞ MAA

Clocks

A Jacob Petit figural clock, modelled with a man and his companion, the urn filled with flowers and painted with cherubs and flowers, highlighted with gilding, minor damage, marked 'J.P.', French, c1850, 16½in (42cm) long.
£720–860 / €1,050–1,250
$1,200–1,400 S(O)

A Meissen clock, minor losses and restoration, crossed swords mark, painted numeral 59, German, 1850–1900, 24¼in (61.5cm) high.
£5,300–6,400
€7,700–9,200
$8,900–10,700 S(NY)

A clock and stand, encrusted with flowers and mounted with putti, the pierced stand with scroll feet, some restoration, factory mark, Continental, probably French, 1850–1900, 23½in (59.5cm) high.
£900–1,050 / €1,300–1,550
$1,500–1,800 S(O)

Condiment Pots

A Berlin salt, with gilt and enamel-painted floral decoration, German, early 20thC, 4¼in (11cm) high.
£150–180 / €210–250
$250–300 EH

A set of four Sèvres table salts, each modelled with three bowls below a triple arch handle entwined with a gilt-edged ribbon and surmounted by a knot, painted with flower sprays, losses, c1774, 4in (10cm) wide.
£1,050–1,250 / €1,500–1,800
$1,750–2,100 S(O)

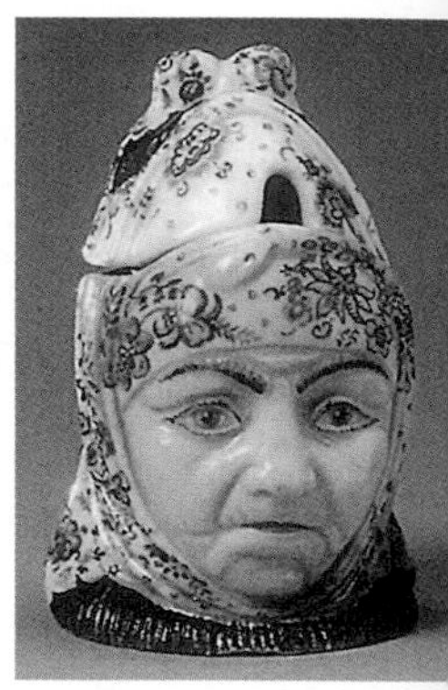

A Russian State Porcelain Factory mustard pot and cover, discolouration and minor chips, printed marks, incised initials, dated 1919, 4in (10cm) high.
£210–250 / €300–360
$350–420 B

Cups

A Belleek Tridacna cup and saucer, Irish, Second Period, 1891–1926, 8in (20.5cm) long.
£270–300 / €390–460
$450–540 MLa

► **A pair of Caughley custard cups,** printed with Cottage pattern, c1790, 2in (5cm) high.
£410–490 / €590–690
$690–820 DN

► **A KPM Berlin cup and saucer,** decorated with birds and butterflies, German, c1770, saucer 5in (12.5cm) diam.
£400–480 / €580–690
$670–800 DORO

PORCELAIN

A Coalport tea cup and saucer, c1820, saucer 6in (15cm) diam.
£145–160 / €200–230
$240–270 ⊞ DAN

A set of six Coalport coffee cans and saucers, pattern No. 3021, each with shaped gilt edges, the cans with pierced silver frames, slight staining and crazing to cans, maker's mark ESB, Birmingham 1919, in a fitted box.
£175–210 / €250–300
$300–360 BR

A Derby chocolate cup, by Zachariah Boreman, entitled 'Near Dalton, Lancashire', with borders highlighted with raised enamel, cover and stand missing, marked, c1790, 3¼in (8.5cm) high.
£2,100–2,500
€3,000–3,600
$3,500–4,200 B
The painting on this cup is particularly fine. The ground is a splendid yellow and blue with raised enamel jewelling. Blue-mark Derby attributed to named artists is a strong area of the market.

A Doccia tea cup and saucer, moulded in relief with Poseidon and his attendants, the saucer moulded with floral swags, with a rope-twist handle, Italian, 1770–80.
£300–360 / €430–510
$500–600 WW

◄ **A Doccia cup and saucer,** relief-moulded and enamelled with an allegorical chariot scene, Italian, late 19thC.
£130–155 / €185–220
$220–260 G(L)

Doccia (Italian, 1737–present)

- Founded near Florence in 1737 by the Marchese Carlo Ginori
- Earliest porcelain was a greyish hard paste with a rough surface that often cracked when fired
- After 1770 quality improved and took on a whiter, opaque appearance with the introduction of a glaze that included tin oxide
- Main output was small and decorative wares, tea and table services
- Wares are easily recognizable due to distinctive types of decoration such as *a galetto rosso* (Chinese-style cockerels painted in iron-red and gold) and *a tulipano* (iron-red Oriental-style peonies). Classical figures are moulded in low relief with strong flesh tones and gilded details
- Most prominent colours are iron-red and puce, followed by sky blue, yellow and green
- This mark was used from the late 18th century until the first half of the 19th century in blue, red or gold

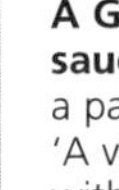

A Gardner neo-classical-style cup and saucer, the cup painted and gilt with a view of a palace across a river, entitled in cyrillic script 'A view of the town of Tatshina', the saucer with three panels showing views of houses, minor wear to gilding, impressed 'Gardner', Russian, early 19thC, saucer 6¼in (16cm) diam.
£640–770 / €920–1,100
$1,100–1,300 B

PORCELAIN

ix Gaudy Welsh tea cups nd saucers, late 19thC.
140–165 / €200–240
230–270 SWO

A Liverpool Christians' coffee can, painted with flowers, c1767, 2½in (6.5cm) high.
£450–500 / €650–720
$750–830 ⊞ JUP

A Meissen cup and saucer, encrusted with flowers, German, c1880, cup 4in (10cm) diam.
£520–580 / €750–830
$870–960 ⊞ BROW

A Minton coffee can, pattern No. 302, c1810, 2½in (6.5cm) high.
£270–300 / €390–430
$450–500 ⊞ CoS

A Nantgarw tea cup and saucer, painted in London with fruit and flower clusters within gilt bands, gilding worn, Welsh, 1818–20.
£1,100–1,300 / €1,600–1,900
$1,850–2,200 ⚒ B

A New Hall trio, pattern No. 238, 1790–95, cup 2½in (6.5cm) high.
£200–230 / €290–320
$340–380 ⊞ DSA

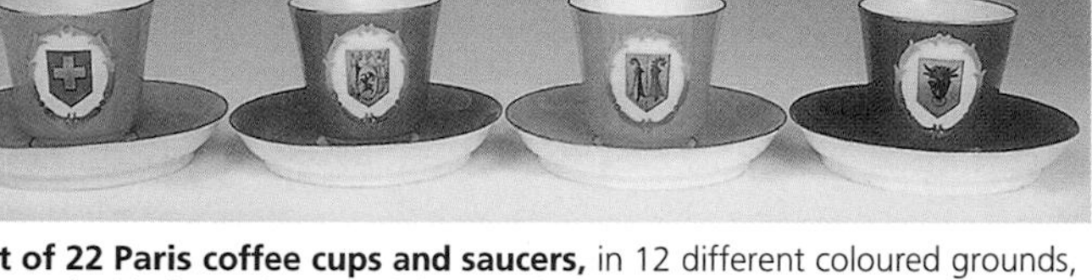

A set of 22 Paris coffee cups and saucers, in 12 different coloured grounds, decorated with framed regional shields of the Swiss Cantons, some damage, cups marked 'CH Pillivuyt & Cie, Paris', French, late 19thC.
£590–710 / €850–1,000
$990–1,150 ⚒ NSal

A pair of Rathbone tea cups and saucers, decorated with scenes featuring Dr Syntax, c1830, cup 4in (10cm) diam.
£520–580 / €750–830
$870–960 ⊞ DAN

A Ridgway trio, pattern No. 5/1598, each piece painted with a landscape in reserved panel, the ground with gilt foliage and scrollwork, c1850, saucer 5¾in (14.5cm) diam.
£190–220 / €270–320
$320–380 ⚒ DD

A Sèvres cabinet cup and saucer, painted with bands of Greek key and palmette decoration, gilt borders, marked, French, early 19thC, cup 2½in (6.5cm) high.
£540–650 / €780–940
$900–1,050 ⚒ SWO

A Royal Sèvres breakfast tea cup and saucer, from the Hunting Service of King Louis Philippe, marked, French, dated 1845, cup 3½in (9cm) high.
£370–440 / €530–630
$620–740 ⚒ NOA

The Sèvres Hunting Service of King Louis Philippe is widely regarded as one of the manufactory's most successful 19th-century neo-classical designs. Cups and saucers such as these are among the rarest pieces from the service. Pieces from the celebrated service are in the collection of the Musée des Arts Décoratifs, Paris, the Metropolitan Museum of Art, New York, the Art Institute of Chicago, and the New Orleans Museum of Art, among others.

PORCELAIN

A Spode coffee can, c1810, 2¾in (7cm) high.
£200–230 / €290–320
$340–380 ⊞ CoS

A Swansea tea cup, coffee cup and saucer, painted in London with fruit and flower clusters and gilt bows, the centres painted with tightly-packed roses, within gilt borders, minor damage, saucer marked, Welsh, 1815–17, saucer 6in (15cm) diam.
£700–840 / €1,000–1,200
$1,150–1,350 ⚒ B

◀ **A Swansea tea cup and saucer,** from the Marquis of Anglesey service, painted in London with flowers against a gilt-burnished ground within an interlocking gilt border, minor damage, Welsh, 1815–17.
£900–1,050 / €1,300–1,550
$1,500–1,800 ⚒ B

A Vauxhall coffee cup, painted with flowers and leaves and a banded hedge, c1758, 2½in (6.5cm) high.
£560–670 / €800–960
$940–1,100 ⚒ WW

A Vienna cabinet cup and saucer, rim restored, marked, Austrian, date mark for 1816, saucer 5¼in (13.5cm) diam.
£400–480 / €580–690
$670–800 ⚒ DORO

A Worcester polychrome tea cup and saucer, printed and coloured with figures in landscape ruins over a transfer outline, 1751–74.
£125–150 / €180–210
$210–250 ⚒ BWL

A 'Scratch Cross' Worcester coffee can, painted with Tamborine pattern, incised line mark, c1755, 3in (7.5cm) high.
£1,250–1,400 / €1,800–2,000
$2,150–2,400 ⊞ JUP

A Worcester blue and white tea bowl and saucer, painted with Landslip pattern, marked, 1755–65, bowl slightly later.
£420–500 / €600–720
$700–840 ⚒ WW

'Scratch Cross' Worcester

This is a term used to describe a class of Worcester porcelain produced from c1753 to 1755. Pieces were marked with a cross or an incised stroke on the base before firing. It is usually found directly beneath the handle and appears on a wide variety of wares including flared-base mugs, pear-shaped jugs, coffee cans, cream jugs, sauce boats and teapots. Items are normally decorated in colours, although blue and white and transfer-printed wares also occur.

A Worcester tea cup and saucer, painted in the Kakiemon palette with asymmetrical panels of flowers, painted marks, c1770.
£270–320 / €390–460
$450–540 ⚒ G(L)

A Chamberlain Worcester cup and saucer, c1810, cup 4in (10cm) diam.
£270–300 / €390–430
$450–500 ⊞ DAN

A Worcester Flight, Barr & Barr coffee can, c1825, 2¾in (7cm) high.
£130–145 / €190–210
$220–250 ⊞ CoS

◄ **A Worcester Flight, Barr & Barr cup and saucer,** c1825, saucer 5in (12.5cm) diam.
£340–380 / €490–540
$570–630 ⊞ DAN

A pair of Zürich tea cups and saucers, decorated with 'Pompeian decor' of fruit bowls and vases at the corners of a gilt square entwined with flowers, minor wear, marked, Swiss, c1765.
£840–1,000 / €1,200–1,450
$1,400–1,650 ⚒ S(O)

A coffee cup and saucer, decorated in Europe in *schwarzlot* or *encre de chine* style with panels pencilled in imitation of engravings, minor damage, Chinese, c1740, saucer 4½in (11.5cm) diam.
£230–270 / €330–390
$390–460 ⚒ B
Ex-Bernard Watney collection.

PORCELAIN

Dessert & Dinner Services

◄ **A Caughley part dessert service,** comprising 21 pieces, painted with Chinese riverscapes, pagodas and fenced gardens, minor damage, c1780.
£2,350–2,800
€3,400–4,000
$4,000–4,800
⚒ G(L)

A Coalport part dessert service, comprising 37 pieces, painted with Japan pattern, minor damage and repair, some wear to plates, 1805–10.
£3,600–4,300 / €5,200–6,200
$6,000–7,200 ⚒ S(O)

A Coalport part dinner service, comprising 25 pieces, decorated with flowers and highlighted in gilt, some damage and repair, impressed marks, c1815, platter 19in (48.5cm) wide.
£1,000–1,200 / €1,450–1,750
$1,700–2,000 ⚒ S(O)

A Derby part dinner service, comprising 72 pieces, decorated with Oak Leaf pattern, marked, 1800–25, oval platter 15in (38cm) wide.
£890–1,050 / €1,300–1,550
$1,500–1,800 ⚒ NOA

A Limoges part dinner service, comprising 84 pieces, decorated with Meadow Flowers pattern, retailed by P. Cellerin, Paris, marked, French, 1875–1900.
£370–440 / €530–630
$620–740 ⚒ NOA

A Meissen dinner service, comprising 12 pieces, German, c1780, vegetable dish 9¾in (25cm) high.
£3,200–3,800 / €4,600–5,500
$5,400–6,400 ⚒ HYD

A Meissen pierced dessert service, comprising 14 pieces, painted with birds, minor damage, gilding worn, marked, German, 1830–40.
£1,750–2,100
€2,500–3,000
$2,950–3,500 ⚒ B(Kn)

A Minton dessert service, comprising six pieces, painted with butterflies and foliage, with gilded borders, c1880, plates 9in (23cm) diam.
£420–500 / €600–720
$700–840 ⚒ G(L)

► **A Ridgway part dessert service,** comprising 30 pieces, each painted with a brickwork pattern within a gilt foliate border moulded in relief with gilt grape clusters, minor damage and restoration, c1815.
£2,300–2,750 / €3,300–3,900
$3,850–4,600 ⚒ S(NY)

A Paris dessert service, comprising 59 pieces, French, 19thC.
£200–240 / €290–340
$340–400 ⚒ COBB

A Ridgway dessert service, comprising 27 pieces, decorated in enamels with a basket of flowers, some wear, 1835–38.
£2,100–2,500 / €3,000–3,600
$3,500–4,100 ⚒ B(Kn)

A Chamberlain Worcester part dessert service, comprising nine pieces, painted with Japan pattern, c1800.
£700–840 / €1,000–1,200
$1,150–1,350 ⚒ G(L)

► **A set of 12 Carl Schumann dinner plates,** the cavetto centred with a bouquet of spring flowers, Lion Shield mark, German, Bavaria, c1900, 11in (28cm) diam.
£440–530 / €630–760
$740–890 ⚒ NOA

A Wedgwood part dinner service, comprising 72 pieces, each painted with a band of roses and leaves within a frame of enamelled beads, the gilt rims with flowerhead motifs, minor damage, marked, early 20thC.
£630–750 / €900–1,050
$1,050–1,250 ⚒ RTo

A set of 12 Royal Worcester Adam-style dinner plates, the borders with gilding and antique vases and leaf festoons, c1900, 10½in (26.5cm) diam.
£820–980 / €1,200–1,400
$1,400–1,650 ⚒ NOA

◄ **A dessert service,** comprising ten pieces, painted with flowers against gilded borders, c1850, plates 9½in (24cm) diam.
£1,400–1,650 / €2,000–2,400
$2,350–2,800 ⚒ G(L)

Dishes

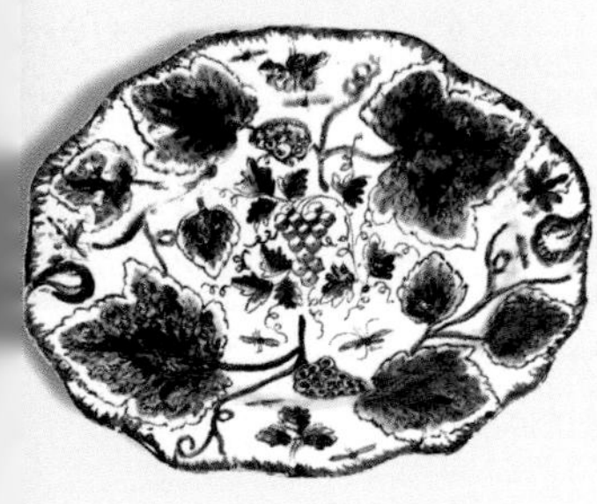

A Bow dish, moulded and painted with grapes and leaves, c1765, 9in (23cm) wide.
£350–390 / €500–560
$590–650 ⊞ JUP

A Derby dish, moulded as a peony and a leaf, repaired chip, c1760, 8in (20.5cm) wide.
£1,500–1,700 / €2,150–2,450
$2,500–2,850 ⊞ JUP

A Bow dish, c1765, 7¾in (19.5cm) diam.
£500–550 / €720–800
$840–930 ⊞ AUC

LOCATE THE SOURCE
The source of each illustration in Miller's can be found by checking the code letters below each caption with the Key to Illustrations, pages 794–800.

A Cookworthy Bristol sweatmeat dish, moulded with shells and seaweed, minor chips, 1770–72, 6¾in (17cm) wide.
£2,250–2,700 / €3,250–3,900
$3,800–4,550 ⚒ B

A pair of Derby dishes, painted with rose sprays, painted marks, late 18thC, 10in (25.5cm) wide.
£490–590 / €710–850
$820–990 ⚒ WW

◄ **A Bloor Derby dish,** decorated with a view of Windsor Castle, c1825, 11in (28cm) wide.
£500–550 / €720–800
$840–930 ⊞ DAN

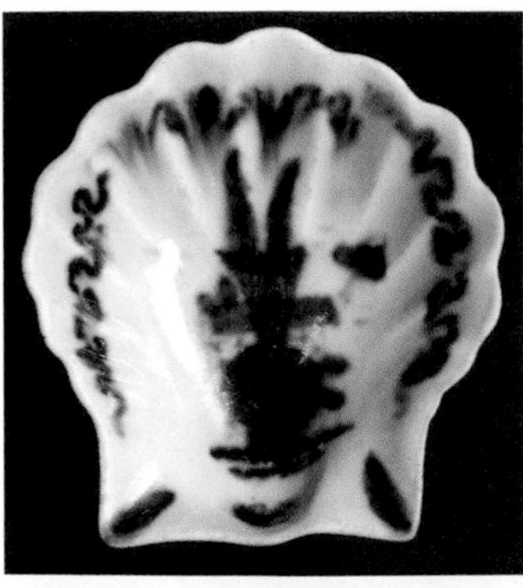

A Limehouse pickle dish, moulded in the form of a shell, painted with a Chinese vase and scroll, c1747, 3in (7.5cm) diam.
£1,600–1,800 / €2,300–2,600
$2,700–3,000 ⊞ JUP

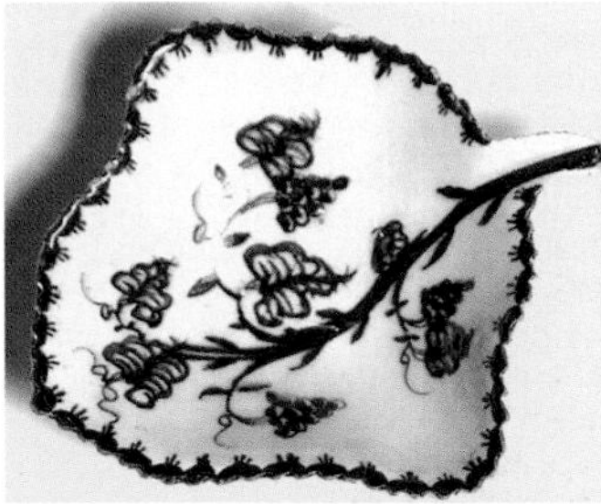

A Lowestoft pickle dish, painted with a vine, with a berry border, c1775, 4in (10cm) long.
£540–600 / €780–860
$900–1,000 ⊞ JUP
The berry border is a good indication of a Lowestoft origin.

A Worcester pickle dish, moulded in the form of a shell, with painted decoration, c1754, 3in (7.5cm) wide.
£2,600–3,100 / €3,750–4,450
$4,350–5,200 ⚒ WW

A Worcester patty pan, painted with Prunus Root pattern, c1760, 4in (10cm) diam.
£720–800 / €1,000–1,150
$1,200–1,350 ⊞ JUP

A pair of Limoges dishes, hand-painted by Charles Field Hamilton with a woman spinning and a young piper, printed marks, French, late 19thC, 12in (30.5cm) square.
£330–390 / €480–560
$550–660 ⚒ PFK

A Swansea dessert dish, painted with birds, moulded with flowers and scrolls, within gilt borders, printed mark, Welsh, 1815–17, 8¼in (21cm) square.
£2,000–2,400 / €2,900–3,450
$3,350–4,000 ⚒ B

A Worcester hors d'oeuvres dish, painted with Willow Rock Bird pattern, c1758, 3in (7.5cm) wide.
£420–470 / €600–670
$710–790 ⊞ JUP

A pair of Worcester dishes, moulded as leaves, c1760, 10in (25.5cm) wide.
£1,350–1,500 / €1,950–2,150
$2,250–2,500 ⊞ AUC

► A Worcester Blind Earl dish, moulded with a rose spray, c1765, 6½in (16.5cm) diam.
£2,450–2,950 / €3,500–4,200
$4,100–4,950 ⚒ F&C
This pattern is named after the Earl of Coventry, who lost his sight in a hunting accident. He owned a set of dishes in this pattern, which he could easily identify because the decoration is in relief.

A pair of Longton Hall dishes, 1754–57, 5½in (14cm) long.
£1,250–1,400 / €1,800–2,000
$2,100–2,350 ⊞ AUC

A Worcester pickle dish, moulded in the form of a scallop, painted in enamels, incised 'P', c1753, 2¾in (7cm) wide.
£1,900–2,250 / €2,750–3,250
$3,200–3,800 ⚒ B
An incised letter P has been noted on several early Worcester pickle dishes and cream boats. It has been suggested that the initial could relate to Robert Podmore who assisted William Davis and John Wall during the establishment of the Worcester manufactory.

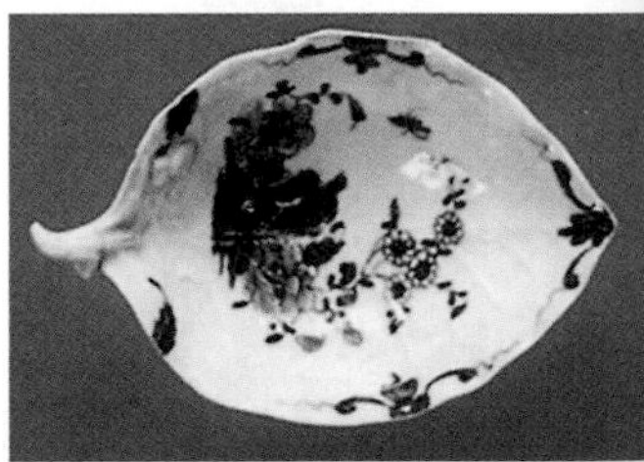

A Worcester pickle dish, moulded as a leaf, painter's mark, c1758, 4¾in (12cm) wide.
£590–710 / €850–1,000
$1,000–1,200 ⚒ TEN

PORCELAIN

A Worcester Blind Earl dish, printed with a 'Bather studying a marble frieze' after Pannini, c1772, 5½in (14cm) diam.
£810–900 / €1,150–1,300
$1,350–1,500 ⊞ JUP

A Worcester dish, painted with floral sprays, with a gilt band, open crescent mark, c1785, 8½in (21.5cm) wide.
£280–330 / €400–480
$470–550 ⚒ DN

A Worcester junket dish, transfer-printed with Pine Cone pattern, c1775, 9¾in (25cm) diam.
£530–590 / €760–850
$890–990 ⊞ AUC

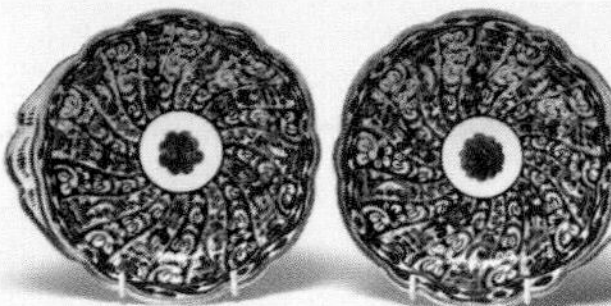

A pair of Worcester Barr Flight & Barr dishes, decorated with Queen Charlotte pattern, c1810, 8in (20.5cm) diam.
£1,000–1,150 / €1,450–1,650
$1,700–1,950 ⊞ DAN

A Worcester dish, c1775, 7¾in (19.5cm) diam.
£450–500 / €650–720
$750–840 ⊞ AUC

An Anti-Slavery dish, printed with an African kneeling in prayer, c1832, 10¼in (26cm) wide.
£190–220 / €270–320
$320–370 ⚒ SAS

◀ **A Royal Worcester dish,** moulded as a shell, date code probably for 1915, 8in (20.5cm) wide.
£220–260 / €320–370
$370–440 ⚒ L

Figures

◀ **A pair of Belleek figures of boy and girl basket-carriers,** Irish, First Period, 1863–90, 9in (23cm) high.
£900–1,000
€1,300–1,450
$1,500–1,650
⊞ MLa

A Bow figure of a flautist, restored, c1752, 4in (10cm) high.
£1,500–1,700
€2,150–2,450
$2,500–2,850 ⊞ JUP

A pair of Bow figures, entitled 'The New Dancers', 1758–60, 6in (15cm) high.
£1,600–1,800
€2,300–2,600
$2,700–3,000 ⊞ DMa

A Bow figure of Minerva, standing beside a shield, with an owl and flowers, neck restored and some cracks, c1760, 14¼in (36cm) high.
£490–590 / €710–850
$820–990 ⚒ Bea

A pair of Derby figural candlesticks, 1760–65, 8¾in (22cm) high.
£1,300–1,450 / €1,900–2,100
$2,200–2,450 ⊞ AUC

A pair of Derby figures of the Welch Tailor and his wife, after Meissen, each riding a goat, the base with applied flowers and leaves, minor repairs, 1760–70, 10½in (27cm) high.
£3,000–3,600 / €4,300–5,200
$5,000–6,000 ⚒ WW

► **A pair of Derby figures of a sailor and sailor's lass,** repairs, c1825, 7½in (19cm) high.
£1,350–1,500
€1,950–2,150
$2,250–2,500
⊞ JUP

A Derby figural group of the Hairdresser, c1800, 7in (18cm) high.
£590–650 / €850–940
$990–1,100 ⊞ DMa

A Ginori Doccia figure of a woman, arm restored, Italian, 1760–70, 5½in (14cm) high.
£620–740 / €890–1,050
$1,050–1,250 ⚒ S(Mi)

Items in the Porcelain section have been arranged alphabetically in factory order, with non-specific pieces appearing at the end of each sub-section.

A Frankenthal figural group of an old man and a young woman, by Karl Gottlieb Lück, some restoration, incised marks, restored, German, 1770–75, 6in (15cm) high.
£1,650–1,950
€2,350–2,800
$2,750–3,250 ⚒ S(O)

A Kloster Veilsdorf figural scent bottle, modelled by Fr Wilhelm Eugen Döll, modelled as a goatherd, goat and a tree, with a gilt-metal stopper, minor restoration, German, c1770, 4¾in (12cm) high.
£1,800–2,150
€2,600–3,100
$3,000–3,600 ⚒ S(O)

A pair of porcelain figures of a gentleman and a lady, losses, 'Kozloff's' factory marks, Russian, mid-19thC, 8¾in (22cm) high.
£1,300–1,550 / €1,850–2,200
$2,200–2,600 ⚒ NSal

A pair of Longton Hall figures of Harlequin and Columbine, 1754–57, 5in (12.5cm) high.
£4,000–4,450
€5,800–6,400
$6,700–7,500 ⊞ DMa

A Ludwigsburg figure of a farmer's wife, holding a basket and a chicken, marked, German, c1770, 5¾in (14.5cm) high
£400–480 / €580–690
$670–810 ⚒ G(L)

Nineteenth-century Meissen figures

The Meissen factory was in decline at the beginning of the 19th century, due to competition from other European porcelain factories and the effects of the Napoleonic Wars (1799–1815). However, mass production was growing steadily, which reduced costs and ensured that demands could be met, and from the 1820s the factory began using round kilns, resulting in a fourfold increase in production. In the late 1820s an inexpensive method of decoration using gold mixed in a solution (known as 'gloss-gliding') was introduced.

The factory's fortunes were further revived when the rococo style became fashionable again in the early 1830s. The factory began reusing their 18th-century figure moulds and these, as well as other rococo revival wares, became greatly in demand and formed the bulk of the output during the second half of the 19th century. Produced under the supervision of the chief modeller, Ernst August Leuteritz, the figures are always carefully moulded and painted to the highest standards. They represent typically 18th-century subjects such as shepherds and shepherdesses, the aristocracy and allegorical figures of the Seasons and the four Continents.

A Meissen figure of a classical maiden, probably by F. Meyer, minor damage, faintly marked, German, c1745, 4¾in (12cm) high.
£490–590 / €710–850
$820–990 ⚒ DN

A Meissen figure of The Marquis, designed by C. Huet, modelled by P. Reinicke, German, c1757, 5in (12.5cm) high.
£2,600–2,900
€3,750–4,200
$4,350–4,850 ⊞ BHa

A Meissen figure of Spanish lovers, crossed swords mark, German, c1850, 10in (25.5cm) high.
£2,500–2,750
€3,600–4,000
$4,200–4,700 ⊞ DAV

► **A Meissen figure of a boy with a lamb,** German, c1870, 5in (12.5cm) high.
£1,100–1,250
€1,600–1,800
$1,850–2,100 ⊞ BHa

► **A Meissen figure of a young woman holding grapes,** German, c1800, 5½in (14cm) high.
£1,500–1,650
€2,150–2,400
$2,500–2,750 ⊞ MAA

A Meissen figure of a flower seller, losses and minor damage, crossed swords mark, German, 19thC, 5in (12.5cm) high.
£230–270 / €330–390
$390–450 ⚒ GAK

A Meissen figure of a sleeping woman, minor damage and restoration, crossed swords mark, German, 1800–50, 7in (18cm) high.
£730–870 / €1,050–1,250
$1,200–1,450 ⚒ DORO

A Meissen figural group of Bacchus and Silenus, with a bacchante and a putto in attendance, some restoration, cancelled crossed swords mark, German, 1850–1900, 8in (20.5cm) high.
£470–560 / €680–810
$790–940 WW

A Minton spill vase group of Babes in the Wood, c1835, 6in (15cm) high.
£690–760 / €990–1,100
$1,150–1,300 DAN

For further information on
Figures see pages 223–227

A Sèvres biscuit figural group of wrestling cherubs, after a model by Falconet, slight firing cracks, marked, French, 19thC, 8in (20.5cm) high.
£165–195 / €240–280
$280–330 BR

A Meissen figure of a putto making hot chocolate, German, c1880, 5½in (14cm) high.
£1,400–1,550
€2,000–2,200
$2,350–2,600 BROW

◀ **A Meissen figure,** from a series of the Senses, modelled as a woman seated beside a table laden with food, crossed swords mark, German, late 19thC, 5in (12.5cm) high.
£1,250–1,500
€1,800–2,150
$2,100–2,500 DN

A Niderviller figure of an apple seller, restorations, marked, French, c1775, 6in (15cm) high.
£260–310 / €370–440
$440–520 G(L)

A Strasbourg allegorical figural group of a putto and a bear, by J. W. Lanz, minor damage, incised 'PH 6', French, 7in (17.5cm) high.
£2,150–2,600
€3,100–3,700
$3,600–4,300 S(O)

A Meissen figural group of a woman playing a mandolin, seated beneath a tree, with dancing putti, German, c1890, 11in (28cm) high.
£2,000–2,250
€2,900–3,250
$3,350–3,800 MAA

A Meissen figure of a cherub, from a series of 26, crossed swords mark, German, c1890, 7in (18cm) high.
£1,150–1,300
€1,650–1,850
$1,950–2,200 DAV

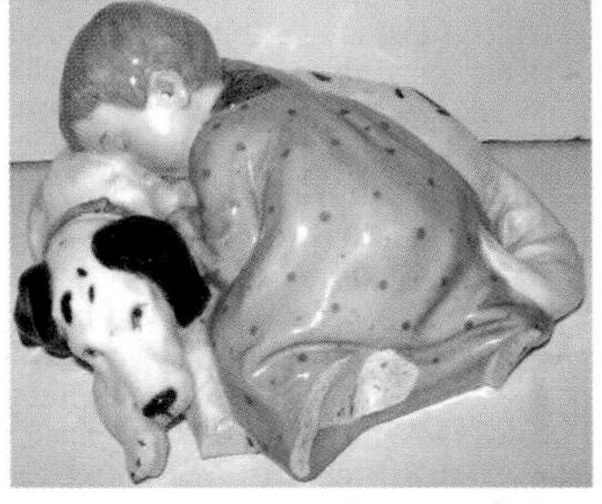

◀ **A Meissen figure of a sleeping child,** possibly by Konrad Hentschel, crossed swords mark, c1910, 6in (15cm) long.
£590–700
€850–1,000
$990–1,150
SJH

▶ **A pair of Samson figures of a shepherd and shepherdess,** after the Chelsea Derby originals, marked, 19thC, 8¾in (22cm) high.
£230–270
€330–390
$390–450 NSal

A Tournai figure of a young girl, losses, minor damage, French, c1770, 4¾in (12cm) high.
£600–720 / €860–1,000
$1,000–1,200 S(O)

A Vienna figural group of gardeners, some restoration, conjoined shields mark, Austrian, c1765, 8¾in (22cm) high.
£730–880 / €1,050–1,250
$1,250–1,500 DORO

◀ **A Royal Worcester figure of a man in Regency clothes,** c1880, 8¼in (21cm) high.
£720–800 / €1,000–1,150
$1,200–1,350 JUP

PORCELAIN

A Royal Worcester Parian figural candle snuffer, based on the Tichbourne Trial, c1880, 4in (10cm) high.
£4,500–5,000 / €6,500–7,200
$7,600–8,400 ⊞ TH

Roger Tichborne, eldest son of Lord Tichborne, was lost at sea in 1854 so his younger brother succeeded to the baronetcy in 1862. In 1867 Arthur Orton, a butcher's son from Wapping, claimed to be Roger Tichborne and was accepted by Lady Tichborne as her long-lost son. The rest of the family was not convinced, however, and went to court to protect their interests, resulting in two trials which lasted a total of 188 days – at that time the longest in English legal history. The case attracted great interest and Orton won considerable public sympathy, but was found guilty and sent to prison for ten years. This commemorative piece consists of a butcher's block with a candle holder in the centre, and figures of Arthur Orton which fits over the candle holder and a lawyer which fits over Orton, signifying the extinguishing of his claim to the Tichborne family fortune. These three components have often become separated over the years and as only the butcher's block carried the factory mark, many people are unaware that they belong together.

A Royal Worcester figural candle snuffer, entitled 'Town Girl', restored, c1881, 5in (12.5cm) high.
£1,000–1,100
€1,450–1,600
$1,700–1,850 ⊞ GGD

A pair of Hadley Worcester figural groups of schoolboys seated on benches, verses by Goldsmith printed beneath in gilt, one group repaired, c1888, 4¼in (11cm) high.
£470–560 / €680–810
$790–940 ⚒ G(L)

► A Worcester figure of a boy carrying a basket, decorated in shot enamels, impressed and printed marks, minor damage, date code for 1881, 7½in (19cm) high.
£350–420 / €500–600
$590–710 ⚒ Bea

Worcester candle snuffers

The Kerr & Binns factory (1852–62) manufactured character candle snuffers from c1855. Examples are often unmarked, perhaps because they may originally have been produced with a small base which, over the years, has become lost or broken. Monks and nuns are the most common representation.

In 1862 the company became the Worcester Royal Porcelain Company – Royal Worcester – and production of snuffers continued with an extensive range of humorous and finely observed subjects. Some examples which had been manufactured by the Kerr & Binns factory continued to be produced by Royal Worcester, but many new models were added over the years. Most of them are listed in pattern books or price lists, but occasionally an unrecorded example turns up. It appears that the models were produced on a rotation system, sometimes with a gap of a few years, although the two most popular characters, 'The Monk' and 'The Abbess', were never out of production, even during the two world wars. It is noticeable that the decoration on early snuffers is finer than on later examples, because in later years the artists were allowed less time to spend on their work.

A Royal Worcester figural candle snuffer, modelled as 'French Cook', c1885, 3in (7.5cm) high.
£290–320 / €410–460
$490–540 ⊞ GGD

A Worcester figural candle snuffer, modelled as a monk, with painted detail, c1885, 5in (12.5cm) high.
£1,650–1,850
€2,350–2,650
$2,750–3,100 ⊞ TH

◄ A pair of Royal Worcester figures of classical maidens, representing Joy and Sorrow, chip, impressed factory marks, late 19thC, 9¾in (25cm) high.
£1,100–1,300
€1,600–1,900
$1,850–2,200 ⚒ RTo

A pair of Royal Worcester figures of Bringaree Indians, c1898, 9in (23cm) high.
£450–500 / €650–720
$750–840 ⊞ GGD

A Royal Worcester figure, entitled 'Chinese', by James Hadley, from a series of Countries of the World, painted in bronzes, date code for 1904, 6¾in (17cm) high.
£470–560 / €680–810
$790–940 ⚒ DN

► A pair of Victorian Parian figures of Shakespeare and Milton, slight damage, 14in (35.5cm) high.
£190–220
€280–330
$320–380 ⚒ FHF

◄ A pair of biscuit figures of a gallant and his lady, the bases with gilt decoration, French, late 19thC, 10½in (26.5cm) high.
£300–360
€430–520
$500–600
⚒ PFK

A Victorian biscuit figure of Ceres, beside a wreath, 13in (33cm) high.
£175–210 / €250–300
$290–350 ⚒ G(L)

► A pair of figures of a gallant and his lady, minor damage, French, late 19thC, 17¾in (45cm) high.
£700–840 / € 1,000–1,200
$1,200–1,400 ⚒ Bea

A pair of figures of a lady and a gentleman, crossed swords mark, Continental, 19thC, 9¾in (25cm) high.
£330–390 / €480–560
$550–660 ⚒ WilP

PORCELAIN

Flatware

A Berlin plate, painted with a rose bush within a floral border with gilt details, sceptre mark, German, 19thC, 9½in (24cm) diam.
£140–165 / €200–240
$240–280 WW

A pair of Coalport Imari-style soup plates, c1810, 10in (25.5cm) diam.
£200–220 / €290–320
$330–370 DAN

A Bristol saucer dish, by William Cookworthy & Co, transfer-printed with a rural scene, worn, c1770, 8¼in (21cm) diam.
£1,650–1,950 / €2,350–2,800
$2,750–3,250 F&C

A Copeland plate, painted by S. Alcock with a woman holding a sheet of music within a border of 'jewelling' and gilt C-scrolls, the reverse inscribed 'I have a song to sing oh!', printed marks, date code for 1895, 9in (23cm) diam.
£470–560 / €680–810
$790–940 DN
'I have a song to sing oh!' appears in the operetta *The Yeomen of the Guard*, by W. S. Gilbert and Sir A. Sullivan.

◀ **A Derby plate,** depicting Beresford Dale, signed by Edward Trowell, c1890, 9in (23cm) diam.
£2,150–2,400 / €3,100–3,450
$3,600–4,000 BP

A Caughley plate, painted with flowers and a butterfly, crescent mark, rim chipped, c1780, 7in (18cm) diam.
£175–210 / €250–300
$290–350 G(L)

A Derby botanical plate, decorated with a gentian, the reverse inscribed 'Gentiana Acaulis, Large-flower'd Gentian', painted mark, c1800, 9¼in (23.5cm) diam.
£590–710 / €850–1,000
$1,000–1,200 WW

A Ginori Doccia plate, decorated with Diana in a rural landscape, worn, Italian, 1770–80, 9¼in (23.5cm) diam.
£1,650–1,950 / €2,350–2,800
$2,750–3,250 S(Mi)

A Meissen *Hausmalerei* saucer, decorated in the Aufenwerth workshop at Augsburg, with gilt borders, German, c1725, 5¼in (13.5cm) diam.
£780–940 / €1,150–1,350
$1,300–1,550 S(O)

Hausmalerei

This is the term given to German and Bohemian ceramics decorated by freelance decorators in their own studios or workshops from the 17th century. They were an important part of the industry, initially helping faïence factories to meet the huge demand for highly decorated pottery, but when Meissen began producing porcelain in the early 18th century, *Hausmaler* in Augsburg and elsewhere were quick to turn their attention to this desirable new medium. They bulk bought whitewares (mostly plates or tea and coffee services) from the Meissen factory and kept them in store to decorate at their leisure, so the porcelain can pre-date the decoration by up to ten years.

The palette is mainly in monochrome red, purple or black and gilding, although some polychrome decoration is also found. Subjects are typically chinoiseries, large figure scenes, landscapes, and mythological or hunting scenes. Some of the finest painting found on any German porcelain was carried out by *Hausmaler*, the most important of them being Abraham Seuter.

A Meissen armorial plate, from the Podewils Service, painted with the arms of Podewils and scattered sprigs of *indianische Blumen*, minor damage, German, c1742, 10in (25.5cm) diam.
£2,500–2,800 / €3,600–4,000
$4,200–4,700 ⊞ G&G

This plate is part of the service made for Graf Heinrich von Podewils, 1695–1760, Minister to Frederick the Great of Russia and Knight of the Prussian Order of the Eagle. He may have received the service as a diplomatic gift in connection with the second Silesian War of 1740–42, during which Saxony was allied with Prussia. The form of the service followed the design of that executed by Johann Joachim Kändler in 1741 for the Jagd Service of Clemens August, Elector of Cologne.

A pair of Minton plates, by Antonin Boullemier, painted with vignettes of girls, with tooled gilt borders, impressed and printed factory marks, dated 1875, 9½in (24.5cm) diam.
£530–640 / €770–920
$890–1,050 ⚒ B

A Paris Rue de Montmartre plate, painted with a Brazilian tree-creeper, with gilt-edged panels, inscribed 'Grimpeau du Brésil', minor rubbing, incised repairer's mark, French, early 19thC, 9¼in (23.5cm) diam.
£280–330 / €400–470
$470–550 ⚒ G(L)

A pair of Meissen plates, decorated with birds, German, c1745, 9in (23cm) diam.
£1,450–1,600 / €2,050–2,300
$2,450–2,700 ⊞ US

A Meissen plate, decorated with flowers, with a reticulated rim, German, c1860, 9in (23cm) diam.
£2,000–2,200 / €2,850–3,150
$3,350–3,700 ⊞ BROW

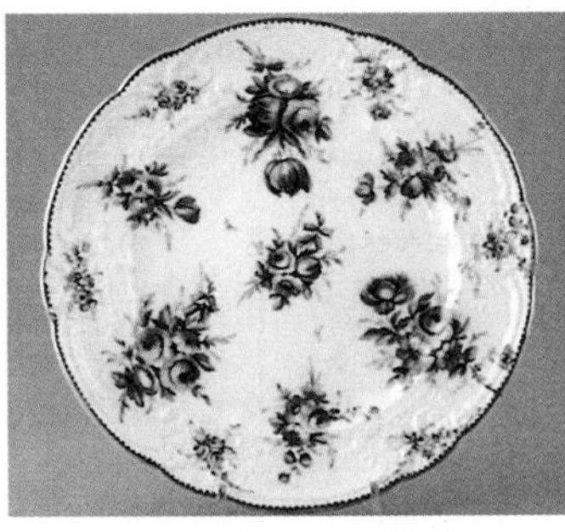

A Nantgarw plate, moulded with flowers, with a gilt rim, impressed mark, Welsh, 1814–23, 9½in (24.5cm) diam.
£1,900–2,250 / €2,750–3,350
$3,200–3,800 ⚒ WW

A pair of St Petersburg plates, the borders with eagle crests, gilt monograms and panels of flowers, damage, factory marks, Russian, 1800–50, 9½in (24cm) diam.
£700–840 / €1,000–1,200
$1,200–1,400 ⚒ WW

A Meissen plate, the centre painted with a scene of two children, crossed swords mark, German, c1840, 9½in (24cm) diam.
£760–850 / €1,100–1,200
$1,300–1,450 ⊞ DAV

A Minton dessert plate, by Henry Mitchell, painted with a terrier, c1868, 9½in (24cm) diam.
£540–600 / €780–860
$900–1,000 ⊞ JUP

A New Hall saucer dish, c1820, 9in (23cm) diam.
£230–260 / €330–370
$390–440 ⊞ DAN

A pair of Staffordshire plates, enamelled with floral sprays and sprigs, within a gilt rim, c1820, 8¾in (22cm) diam.
£50–60 / €75–85
$85–100 ⚒ WL

A pair of Cozzi plates, decorated with flowers in the Imari palette, marked, Italian, Venice, c1775, 9in (23cm) diam.
£1,550–1,850 / €2,250–2,650
$2,600–3,100 ⚒ S(Mi)

A Vienna cabinet plate, painted with a portrait of Mrs Bradyll after SIr Joshua Reynolds, within a tooled gilt border, shield mark, Austrian, 19thC, 9½in (24.5cm) diam.
£260–310 / €380–450
$440–520 ⚒ RTo

A Worcester saucer, painted with Oriental figures, minor damage, c1754, 5in (12.5cm) diam.
£630–700 / €900–1,000
$1,000–1,150 ⊞ JUP

A Worcester saucer, printed with a scene of a tea party, c1758, 5in (12.5cm) diam.
£310–350 / €450–500
$520–590 ⊞ JUP
There were several Tea Party prints produced by Robert Hancock, this one being number three.

A pair of Worcester saucer dishes, painted with exotic birds within a gilt border, crescent mark, c1775, 7½in (19cm) diam.
£610–730 / €880–1,050
$1,000–1,200 ⚒ L

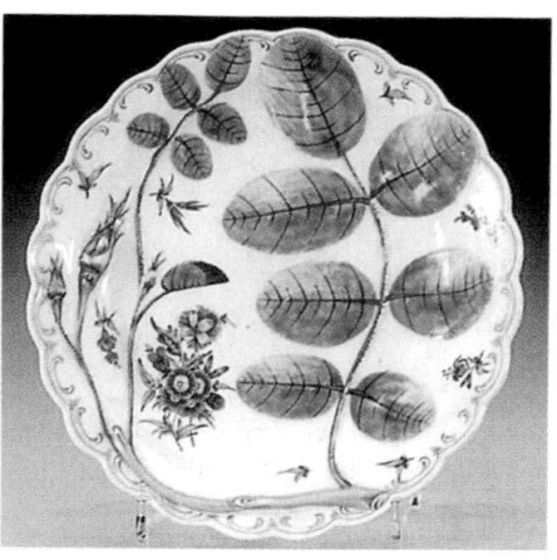

A Worcester Blind Earl plate, moulded with a branch with rose buds, some wear, 1765–70, 7½in (19cm) diam.
£1,300–1,550 / €1,900–2,250
$2,200–2,600 ⚒ S(O)

◄ **A Worcester plate,** printed and painted with a milking scene, c1768, 7in (18cm) diam.
£630–700
€900–1,000
$1,050–1,200
⊞ JUP

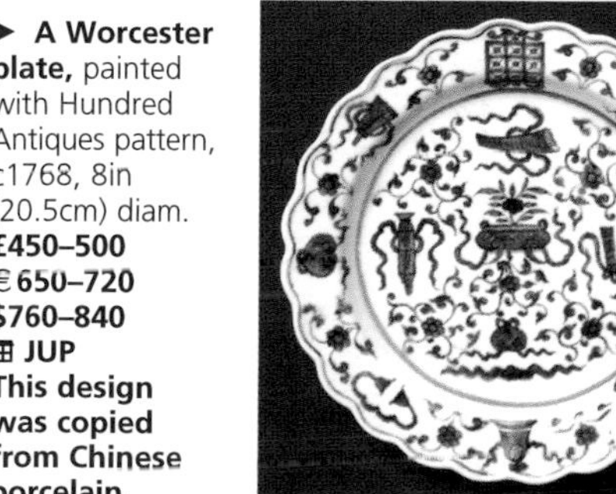

► **A Worcester plate,** painted with Hundred Antiques pattern, c1768, 8in (20.5cm) diam.
£450–500
€650–720
$760–840
⊞ JUP
This design was copied from Chinese porcelain.

◄ **A Worcester plate,** c1775, 7½in (19cm) diam.
£350–390 / €500–560
$590–660 ⊞ AUC

PORCELAIN

◀ **A Flight Worcester plate,** from the Hope and Patience service made for the Duke of Clarence, later William IV, painted *en grisaille* by John Pennington, the border with gilt medallions, marked, 1790–92, 9¾in (25cm) diam.
£530–640 / €770–920
$890–1,050 F&C
John Flight's diary records that the Duke of Clarence chose the theme for this service from three specimens provided – Arabasque, Peace and Abundance and Hope and Patience. The service comprised 296 pieces.

A Royal Worcester plate, signed 'H. Davies', 1903, 9in (23cm) diam.
£520–620 / €750–890
$870–1,050 L

◀ **A pair of Royal Worcester plates,** with gilt decoration, signed 'H. H. Price', date mark for 1925, 8½in (21.5cm) wide.
£730–880 / €1,050–1,250
$1,250–1,500 AH

A Royal Worcester plate, painted with sheep within a gilt border by Ernest Baker, c1914, 10in (25.5cm) diam.
£1,500–1,700 / €2,150–2,450
$2,500–2,850 JUP

▶ **A dish,** with a hand-painted scene, c1840, 4in (10cm) wide.
£75–85 / €105–120
$125–140 DAN

A saucer dish, minor damage, c1820, 8in (20.5cm) diam.
£290–320 / €410–460
$490–540 DAN

Inkstands & Inkwells

A Sèvres-style partners' inkstand, attributed to Coalport, c1830, 11in (28cm) diam.
£2,700–3,000 / €3,900–4,300
$4,500–5,000 DIA

A Meissen figural inkstand, on a gilt-brass dish, minor damage, marked, German, 19thC, 5¼in (13.5cm) high.
£610–730 / €880–1,050
$1,000–1,200 TEN

A Swansea inkwell, cover and liner, modelled as a shell, painted with flowers possibly by Henry Morris, minor wear, marked, Welsh, 1814–26, 4in (10cm) wide.
£4,450–5,500 / €6,800–7,900
$7,700–9,200 S(O)

A Vauxhall inkwell, minor damage, 1758–65, 3½in (9cm) diam.
£3,300–3,950 / €4,800–5,700
$5,500–6,600 B
Ex-Billie Pain collection.
Billie Pain was an enthusiastic and discerning afficionado of English porcelain, whose collection, although small due to her limited display facilities, was of excellent quality.

A Royal Worcester Ariosto inkwell, printed marks, date code for 1862, 5¾in (14.5cm) high.
£1,000–1,200 / €1,450–1,700
$1,700–2,000 DD

An inkwell and cover, modelled as a pail of flowers, with a stalk handle and gilt detailing, c1840, 2½in (6.5cm) high.
£165–195 / €240–280
$280–330 WW

Jardinières

A pair of Belleek jardinières, Irish, Second Period, c1892, 7in (18cm) high.
£3,000–3,350 / €4,300–4,800
$5,000–5,600 ⊞ DeA

A pair of KPM Berlin jardinières, painted with vignettes of riverbank scenes below ozier borders, marked, German, 1850–1900, 6¾in (17cm) high.
£980–1,150 / €1,400–1,650
$1,650–1,950 ⚒ S(Am)

A jardinière and stand, probably Coalport, painted with a goldfinch on a gilt ground, c1810, 7¼in (18.5cm) wide.
£520–620 / €750–890
$870–1,050 ⚒ WW

A pair of Davenport demi-lune bulb pots, painted with monochrome panels of landscapes between gilt columns, on ball feet, covers missing, some restoration, impressed marks, c1810, 7½in (19cm) wide.
£1,050–1,250 / €1,500–1,800
$1,750–2,100 ⚒ S(O)

A pair of Dresden jardinières, painted with Watteauesque scenes and sprays of flowers, scroll feet repaired, Berlin-type marks and a Dresden decorator's mark, German, late 19thC, 14½in (37cm) wide.
£1,300–1,550 / €1,900–2,250
$2,200–2,600 ⚒ DN

A Royal Worcester jardinière, painted with roses on a shaded ground, signed 'Sedgley', date code for 1919, 9½in (24cm) diam.
£940–1,100 / €1,350–1,600
$1,600–1,900 ⚒ L

Jugs & Ewers

A Belleek Florence jug, Irish, First Period, 1863–90, 8in (20.5cm) high.
£720–800 / €1,000–1,150
$1,200–1,350 ⊞ MLa

A ewer, possibly Coalport, the handle modelled as a swan, minor damage, 1830–40, 11in (28cm) high.
£140–165 / €200–240
$240–280 ⚒ B(Kn)

◄ **A Royal Crown Derby Sèvres-style ewer,** painted with vignettes of exotic birds, signed 'C. Harris', printed mark, date code for 1906, 9in (23cm) high.
£1,000–1,200
€1,450–1,700
$1,700–2,000 ⚒ DN

A Derby harvest jug, painted with a bird and shrubs, minor damage, c1762, 7½in (19cm) high.
£1,000–1,150
€1,450–1,650
$1,700–1,950 ⊞ JUP

A Royal Crown Derby ewer, the neck and foot with gilded stripes, printed mark, dated 1895, 7¼in (18.5cm) high.
£560–670 / €800–960
$940–1,100 ⚒ B

◄ **A Lowestoft jug,** moulded with cabbage leaves, after the Worcester original, damaged, c1775, 9in (23cm) high.
£630–760 / €910–1,100
$1,050–1,250 ⚒ SWO

A Lowestoft cream jug, moulded as a shell, painted with scattered flowers and sprigs, minor damage, c1775, 4in (10cm) wide.
£360–430 / €520–620 $600–720 S(O)

A pair of Ridgway jugs, applied with a frieze depicting a winged lion and cherubic figure, beneath a mask spout and fruiting vines, minor damage, early 19thC, 7¾in (19.5cm) high.
£330–390 / €480–560 $550–660 RTo

A Royal Worcester ewer, commemorating the Golden Jubilee of Queen Victoria, moulded with a portrait medallion, the handle with a dog's head terminal, gilt highlights, minor damage, 1887, 9¾in (25cm) high.
£360–430 / €520–620 $600–720 S(O)

A Royal Worcester jug, decorated with sprays of flowers, 1909, 5in (12.5cm) high.
£270–300 / €390–430 $450–500 GRI

A Lowestoft sparrow beak jug, painted in the *famille rose* palette with flowers and a cornucopia, c1775, 3in (7.5cm) high.
£630–700 / €900–1,000 $1,050–1,250 JUP

A Worcester jug, moulded with cabbage leaves, c1770, 9¼in (23.5cm) high.
£1,150–1,300 €1,650–1,850 $1,950–2,200 AUC

A Royal Worcester jug, decorated with flowers, dated 1889, 6½in (16.5cm) high.
£340–380 / €490–540 $570–630 GGD

A Lowestoft sparrow beak cream jug, painted with flower sprays, late 18thC, 3¼in (8.5cm) high.
£600–720 / €860–1,000 $1,000–1,200 L&E

A Royal Worcester reticulated jug, with gilt 'jewelling', c1878, 5in (12.5cm) high.
£820–980 / €1,200–1,400 $1,400–1,650 BWL

A Royal Worcester ewer, by Harry Chair, painted with a cartouche of summer flowers, heightened in gilt, signed, dated 1901, 16½in (42cm) high.
£4,900–5,900 €7,100–8,500 $8,200–9,900 B(WM)

◄ **A Royal Worcester ewer,** by John Stinton, shape No. 1587, painted with highland cattle, date code for 1910, 12½in (32cm) high.
£1,950–2,350 €2,800–3,350 $3,300–3,950 AH

► **A jug,** decorated with flowers, c1835, 6in (15cm) high.
£270–300 / €390–430 $450–500 DAN

A Naples-style ewer, moulded with putti, the handle modelled as a satyr, crossed swords mark, Continental, c1900, 14¾in (37.5cm) high.
£240–290 / €350–420 $400–480 S(O)

A Royal Worcester jug, with painted and gilt floral decoration, dated 1887, 5¼in (13cm) high.
£175–210 / €250–300 $290–350 WilP

A Royal Worcester ewer, hand-painted with poppies, the handle modelled as a dragon, signed 'Cole', dated 1909, 4¼in (11cm) high.
£470–560 / €680–810 $790–940 B(W)

PORCELAIN

Ladles

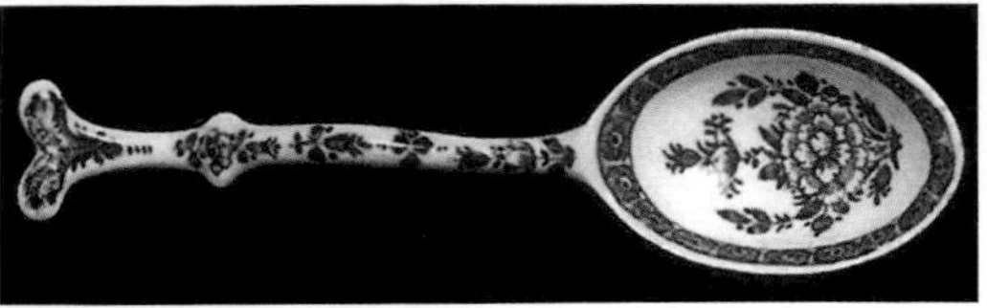

A Bow dessert ladle, the handle with a fish tail terminal, minor staining, 1765–68, 6¾in (17.5cm) long.
£490–590 / €710–850
$820–990 ⚒ B
Ex-Billie Pain collection.

► **A Worcester ladle for a honey pot,** painted with Mansfield pattern, c1758, 5in (12.5cm) long.
£1,500–1,700 / €2,150–2,450
$2,550–2,850 ⊞ JUP

A Caughley ladle, with gilded decoration, c1785, 7in (18cm) long.
£360–400 / €520–580
$600–670 ⊞ JUP

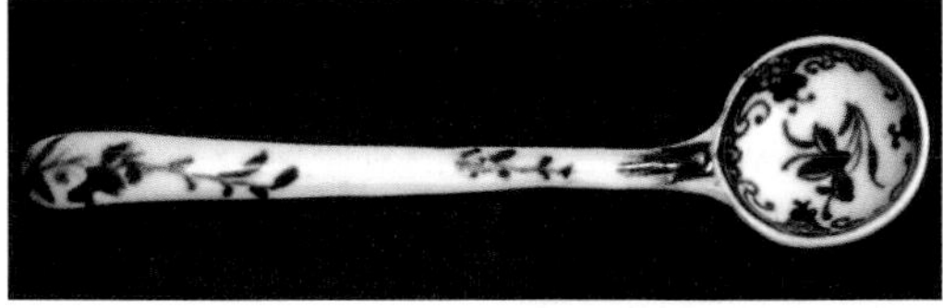

Mirrors

A Dresden-style girandole, applied with summer flowers and cherubs, the base with three candle holders, German, c1890, 36in (91.5cm) high.
£5,900–6,500
€8,500–9,300
$9,900–10,900 ⊞ NAW

A Meissen mirror frame, moulded with flower-heads and 'jewels', surmounted by two cupids, damaged, crossed swords mark, German, c1860, 13¾in (35cm) high.
£1,200–1,450
€1,750–2,100
$2,000–2,400 ⚒ B

A Plaue easel-back mirror, the hand-painted flower-encrusted frame surmounted by two winged cherubs holding a garland of flowers, slight damage, German, 19thC, 13in (33cm) high.
£140–170 / €200–250
$240–290 ⚒ FHF

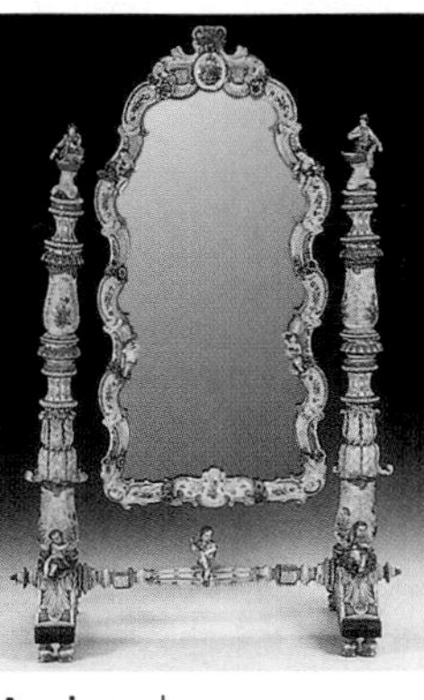

A mirror, losses, restored, German, c1900, 76¾in (195cm) high.
£9,100–10,900
€13,100–15,700
$15,300–18,300 ⚒ S(Mi)
A cheval mirror of this size would usually be made of wood. It is rare to find a porcelain example of this size and this is reflected in the price.

Mugs & Tankards

◄ **A Caughley mug,** painted in the Chamberlain workshop with 'Poor Maria', c1790, 3¼in (8.5cm) high.
£810–900 / €1,150–1,300
$1,350–1,500 ⊞ JUP
Robert Chamberlain was the chief decorator in the Worcester factory until he left in 1786 to form a rival firm, which initially decorated porcelain from Caughley but later produced their own hybrid hard paste. In 1840 Chamberlain took over the Worcester factory, which by then was trading under the names of Flight, Barr & Barr.

A Caughley mug, decorated with the arms of William, Earl of Essex, 1790–95, 5¼in (13.5cm) high.
£1,350–1,500
€1,950–2,100
$2,250–2,500 ⊞ AUC

For further information on
Mugs & Tankards see pages 239–240

► **A Davenport mug,** inscribed 'F. Thomas Lloyd', c1845, 3in (7.5cm) diam.
£95–105 / €135–150
$160–175 ⊞ DAN

◄ **A Derby cabinet mug,** painted with Japan pattern, marked, c1820, 4½in (11.5cm) high.
£350–420 / €500–600
$590–710 ⚒ G(L)

PORCELAIN

A Sèvres mug and cover, decorated with flower garlands, the cover with a chrysanthemum knop, marked, French, date letter for 1763, 5¼in (13.5cm) high.
£2,650–3,150 / €3,800–4,550
$4,450–5,300 ⚒ S(NY)

A Worcester mug, printed with Masonic arms and flanked by obelisks and globes, c1762, 5in (12.5cm) high.
£2,600–2,850 / €3,750–4,100
$4,250–4,800 ⊞ JUP

A Royal Worcester mug, painted with exotic birds and winged insects in reserve panels, signed 'G. Johnson', date code for 1919, 4¾in (12cm) high.
£420–500 / €600–720
$700–840 ⚒ DD

A Worcester mug, decorated with Red Bull pattern, 1758–60, 4¾in (12cm) high.
£1,500–1,800 / €2,150–2,600
$2,500–3,000 ⚒ WW

A Worcester mug, printed with 'La Pêche' and 'La Promenade Chinoise', 1775–80, 5¾in (14.5cm) diam.
£590–650 / €850–940
$990–1,100 ⊞ DSA

A mug, painted with a rural scene, c1830, 5in (12.5cm) diam.
£260–290 / €370–420
$440–490 ⊞ DAN

A loving cup, painted with a rural landscape, the reverse inscribed 'Frances and Joseph Davenport, Lamb Inn, Congleton', 19thC, 5¾in (14.5cm) high.
£140–165 / €200–240
$240–280 ⚒ FHF

◄ **A mug,** hand-decorated with summer flowers, c1850, 4in (10cm) high.
£80–90 / €115–130
$135–150 ⊞ HTE

A Worcester mug, transfer-printed with Plantation pattern, 1760–70, 6in (15cm) high.
£520–620 / €750–890
$870–1,050 ⚒ G(L)

A Chamberlain Worcester tankard, decorated with flowers and initials, c1822, 4in (10cm) high.
£360–400 / €520–580
$600–670 ⊞ DAN

A mug, hand-decorated with flowers, inscribed, c1840, 5in (12.5cm) diam.
£135–150 / €195–220
$220–250 ⊞ HTE

A mug, decorated and gilded with a landscape panel, c1850, 3in (7.5cm) high.
£80–90 / €115–130
$135–150 ⊞ HTE

Pastille Burners

A Royal Crown Derby pastille burner and cover, by Albert Gregory, the pierced rim applied with four satyr masks, painted with flowers, signed, marked, dated 1901, 5in (13cm) high.
£1,900–2,250 / €2,750–3,200
$3,200–3,800 B

A Royal Worcester pastille burner, decorated with a key fret pattern, with ring handles, c1874, 6in (15cm) wide.
£120–145 / €170–200
$200–240 WW

Items in the Porcelain section have been arranged alphabetically in factory order, with non-specific pieces appearing at the end of each sub-section.

◄ **A Meissen pastille burner,** by J. J. Kändler, German, c1760, 9in (23cm) high.
£4,300–4,700 / €6,000–6,700
$7,000–7,800 BHa

Plaques

A KPM Berlin wall plaque, depicting Wilhelm I in military uniform, the reverse with an impressed mark, German, c1875, 10¾in (27.5cm) high.
£800–960 / €1,200–1,400
$1,350–1,600 SAS

A Royal Worcester plaque, by Richard Sebright, decorated with fruit, signed, impressed factory mark, date mark for 1908, 11in (28cm) wide.
£8,800–10,600 / €12,700–15,300
$14,800–17,800 PF

For further information on
Plaques see pages 240–241

A KPM Berlin plaque, with hand-painted decoration, German, 19thC, 8in (20.5cm) high.
£1,300–1,550 / €1,850–2,200
$2,200–2,600 DuM

A Royal Worcester roundel plaque, by Harry Davis, signed, c1912, 4¼in (11cm) wide.
£4,700–5,200 / €6,800–7,500
$7,900–8,700 BP

A pair of Paris porcelain and ormolu-mounted wall plaques, painted in the Sèvres style, the mounts surmounted by cast and chased ribbon cresting, wear to gilding, French, c1850, 8¼in (21cm) high.
£700–840 / €1,000–1,200
$1,200–1,400 BR

A Royal Worcester plaque, by John Stinton, signed, c1928, 12in (30.5cm) diam.
£10,800–12,000 / €15,500–17,300
$18,100–20,100 BP

Sets/pairs

Unless otherwise stated, any description which refers to 'a set' or 'a pair' includes a guide price for the entire set or the pair, even though the illustration may show only a single item.

► **A plaque,** by William Dixon, inscribed 'Born September 3 1808, Eliza Ellen Dixon, Aged 4 years, Born February 28 1805, William Henry Dixon, Aged 7 years, painted by Wm Dixon, 1812, Herculaneum, near Liverpool', signed, 4½in (11cm) high.
£2,600–3,100 / €3,750–4,450
$4,350–5,200 B
William Dixon worked as an independent decorator at 9 Northumberland Street, Liverpool but later joined the staff at the Herculaneum factory.

A pair of soft paste porcelain plaques, some scratching, French, possibly c1780, 8¼in (21cm) wide.
£640–770 / €920–1,100
$1,100–1,300 B

A pair of plaques, each decorated with a mixed bouquet of flowers, 1830–40, 10¼in (26cm) high, framed.
£1,200–1,450 / €1,700–2,000
$2,000–2,400 TEN

◄ **A porcelain plaque,** after Rubens, in a giltwood frame, French, early 20thC, 18½in (47cm) wide.
£1,050–1,250 / €1,500–1,800
$1,750–2,100 DORO

Potpourri Vases

A Longton Hall potpourri vase and cover, formed as a vase of flowers, the body painted with butterflies, insects and flowers, chips and repair, c1755, 6¼in (16cm) high.
£590–710 / €850–1,000
$1,000–1,200 WW

A Meissen gilt-metal-mounted potpourri vase and cover, the cover with a lemon finial, decorated with gilding, repaired, crossed swords mark, German, c1760, 11in (28cm) high.
£600–720 / €880–1,050
$1,000–1,200 S(O)

A Jacob Petit potpourri vase and cover, the two vine-twist handles with leaf terminals, on foliate scroll feet, signed, French, 1850–75, 14½in (37cm) high.
£800–960 / €1,200–1,400
$1,350–1,600 NOA

A pair of Potschappel Sèvres-style potpourri vases and covers, decorated with musical, martial and gardening trophies and floral panels, with cone finials and handles formed as goats' masks, German, late 19thC, 15in (38cm) high.
£450–540 / €650–780
$760–910 MCA

A Wedgwood bone china potpourri vase and cover, painted with named bird studies, the cover with gilt foliage, printed factory mark, c1815, 2¾in (7cm) high.
£1,100–1,300
€1,600–1,900
$1,850–2,200 S(O)

A Royal Worcester potpourri vase and cover, marked, date code for 1892, 12in (30.5cm) high.
£610–730 / €880–1,050
$1,000–1,200 L

A pair of Grainger's Worcester potpourri vases and covers, modelled as eagles supporting urns, gilt embellished, date mark for 1897, 8¼in (21cm) high.
£1,350–1,600
€1,950–2,300
$2,250–2,700 AH

A Royal Worcester potpourri vase and cover, painted with blackberries, autumn leaves and flowers, slight damage, painted marks, rubbed date mark, probably 1908, 4in (10cm) high.
£175–210 / €250–300
$300–350 FHF

Spoons

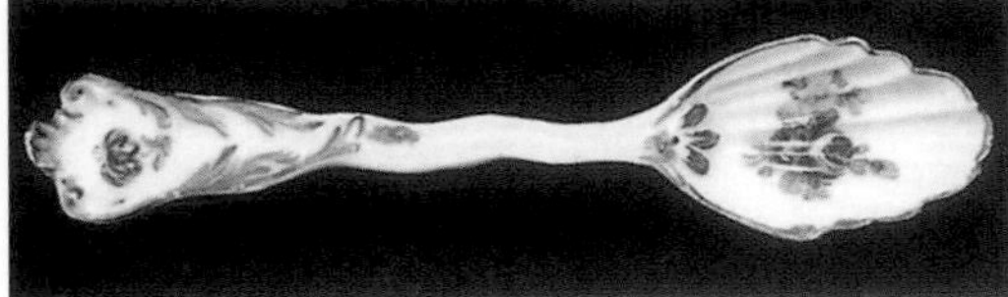

A Bristol spoon, from the Ludlow service, moulded with rococo scrolls, picked out in gold, the underside with similar decoration, c1775, 4¼in (11cm) long.
£2,600–3,100 / €3,750–4,500
$4,350–5,200 B
Ex-Billie Pain collection.

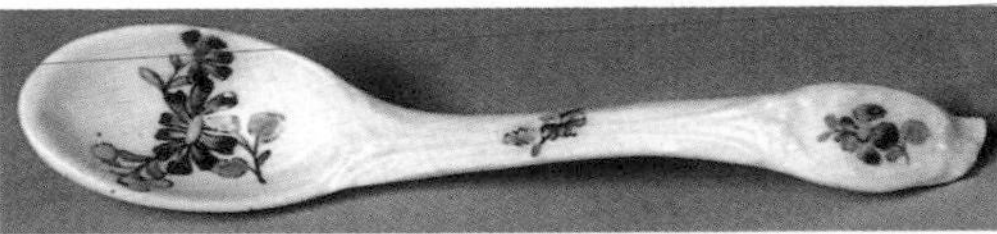

A Longton Hall spoon, painted in *famille rose* colours, the handle moulded with rococo scrollwork, c1755, 4¼in (11cm) long.
£3,200–3,800 / €4,600–5,500
$5,400–6,500 B

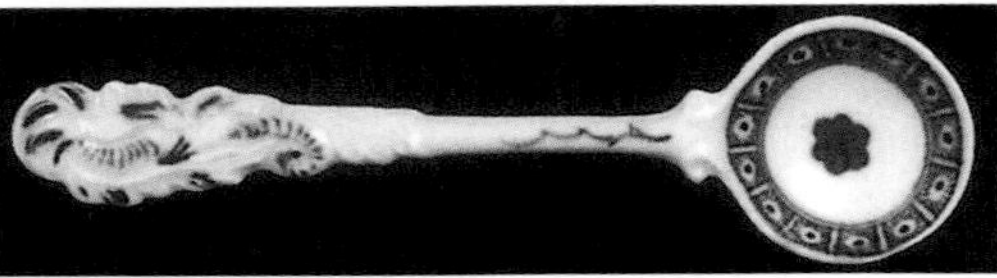

A Worcester condiment spoon, the handle moulded with leaves, the bowl painted with a cell border and central floret, 1770–75, 4in (10cm) long.
£840–1,000 / €1,200–1,400
$1,450–1,700 B
Ex-Billie Pain collection.

A West Pans caddy spoon, moulded in the form of a leaf, small chip, 1764–70, 3in (7.5cm) long.
£1,900–2,250 / €2,750–3,250
$3,200–3,800 B
Ex-Billie Pain collection.

◄ **A Worcester straining/sifter spoon,** the pierced bowl painted with flower tendrils, the handle with a scallop shell terminal, c1770, 5½in (14cm) long.
£610–730 / €880–1,050
$1,000–1,200 RTo

Stands

A Chaffer's Liverpool teapot stand, 1758–60, 5¼in (13.5cm) diam.
£1,650–1,950 / €2,350–2,800
$2,750–3,350 B

A Meissen stand, encrusted with flowers, with lattice-work sides, German, c1880, 5in (12.5cm) diam.
£1,100–1,250 / €1,600–1,800
$1,900–2,100 BROW

A Worcester finger bowl stand, transfer-printed with a river scene, 1758–60, 5¾in (14.5cm) diam.
£370–440 / €530–630
$620–740 B
Ex-Billie Pain collection.

Tea Canisters

A Meissen tea canister, with a metal cover, faint crossed swords and incised mark, German, mid-18thC, 4¼in (11cm) high.
£640–770 / €920–1,100
$1,100–1,300 WW

A set of three Paris tea canisters, comprising a pair of tea bottles and stoppers and a covered sugar/mixing bowl designed to resemble a tea bottle, all with chinoiserie decoration, damage and repair, French, c1840, bottles 5¼in (13.5cm) high, in a fitted box.
£800–960 / €1,200–1,400
$1,350–1,600 B

A Worcester tea canister, printed and painted with Borghese Vase pattern, c1765, 5in (12.5cm) high.
£630–700 / €900–1,000
$1,050–1,200 JUP

Tea & Coffee Pots

A Belleek ornamental teapot, Irish, First Period, 1863–90, 4in (10cm) high.
£2,450–2,700 / €3,500–3,900
$4,100–4,550 ⊞ DeA

A Royal Crown Derby teapot, painted in the Imari palette with pattern No. 4299, printed mark and date cypher, early 20thC, 3in (7.5cm) wide.
£165–195 / €240–280
$280–330 ⚒ GAK

A Meissen *Hausmalerei* teapot and cover, painted by Franz Ferdinand Meyer with figures by a table within a classical landscape, with a pine cone finial and silver-mounted spout, chip, crossed swords mark, German, c1745, 5¼in (13.5cm) wide.
£1,000–1,200 / €1,450–1,700
$1,700–2,000 ⚒ G(L)

A Worcester coffee pot and cover, painted in enamels with Chinese figures and animals within gilt scrolling borders, damaged, slightly later gilding, 1754–56, 7in (18cm) high.
£1,050–1,250 / €1,500–1,800
$1,750–2,100 ⚒ WW

A Bow teapot and cover, transfer-printed and painted with Oriental figures in overglaze enamels, chip and repair, c1765, 5in (12.5cm) high.
£1,350–1,500 / €1,950–2,150
$2,250–2,500 ⊞ JUP

A Liverpool teapot and cover, painted in the Kakiemon style, c1765, 5in (12.5cm) high.
£700–780 / €1,000–1,100
$1,200–1,350 ⊞ JUP

A New Hall teapot, with hand-painted decoration, 1795–1810, 10½in (26.5cm) wide.
£500–550 / €720–800
$840–930 ⊞ AUC

Items in the Porcelain section have been arranged alphabetically in factory order, with non-specific pieces appearing at the end of each sub-section.

A Worcester teapot, c1770, 6in (15cm) high.
£440–490 / €630–700
$740–820 ⊞ AUC

A Derby coffee pot and cover, painted with flowers and scattered sprigs, crack and chip, c1758, 9½in (24cm) high.
£1,800–2,000 / €2,600–2,900
$3,000–3,350 ⊞ JUP

A Lowestoft teapot and cover, painted with Chinese waterscapes, the cover with a flower knop, restored, c1780, 7½in (19cm) wide.
£280–330 / €400–480
$470–560 ⚒ WW

A Victorian Ridgway teapot, modelled as a kettle, 8½in (21.5cm) high.
£105–115 / €150–165
$175–195 ⊞ TASV

A teapot and cover, Dutch-decorated with figures in landscape panels, repaired, cover associated, German, c1770, 5¼in (13.5cm) wide.
£190–220 / €270–330
$320–380 ⚒ G(L)

Tea & Coffee Services

A Belleek tête-a-tête tea service, comprising nine pieces, Irish, Second Period, 1891–1926, tray 16in (40.5cm) diam.
£1,800–2,000 / €2,600–3,100
$3,000–3,350 ⊞ MLa

A Derby part tea and coffee service, comprising 32 pieces, decorated with blue and gilt vermiculation, some damage, red marks, c1810.
£770–920 / €1,100–1,300
$1,300–1,550 ⚒ B(Kn)

A Gaudy Welsh tea service, comprising 17 pieces, decorated in the Imari palette with copper lustre highlighting, some damage, early 19thC.
£240–290 / €350–420
$400–480 ⚒ BR

A Rockingham Old English-shape tea service, comprising 33 pieces, decorated with leaf-shaped panels of flowers, saucers marked, 1826–30.
£1,450–1,750 / €2,100–2,500
$2,450–2,950 ⚒ B

► **A Royal Worcester part Bamboo *déjeuner* service,** comprising 12 pieces, with gilt highlights, printed and impressed marks, c1905, teapot 4¼in (11cm) high.
£620–740 / €890–1,050
$1,050–1,250 ⚒ S(O)

A Berlin part tea service, comprising 11 pieces, painted with flowers, damaged, German, c1795, with original bill of sale.
£290–350 / €420–500
$490–590 ⚒ WW

A Royal Crown Derby cabaret set, comprising 10 pieces, decorated with Wilmot pattern, one cup cracked, printed and impressed marks, lozenge mark for 1883.
£280–330 / €400–480
$470–560 ⚒ DD

A Minton part tea service, comprising 20 pieces, from the Chinese Sports series, each painted with a Chinese boy engaged in a leisure activity, Sèvres-style marks, c1810.
£2,350–2,800 / €3,400–4,000
$4,000–4,700 ⚒ B

A Staffordshire tea and coffee service, comprising 33 pieces, enamelled with floral sprays within gilt panels, c1845.
£165–195 / €240–290
$280–330 ⚒ WL

A Coalport cabaret service, comprising nine pieces, decorated with rose sprays on a ground of stylized buds, the rims gilt, 1820–25, tray 16½in (42cm) wide.
£2,600–3,100 / €3,750–4,500
$4,350–5,200 ⚒ B

A Frankenthal solitaire, from the workshop of Carl Theodor, comprising eight pieces, decorated with scenes of bathing women or cupids on a ground decorated with gilt sprays of flowers and geometrical borders, coffee pot cover associated, minor restoration, marked, German, c1778, tray 12¾in (32.5cm) wide.
£2,050–2,450 / €2,950–3,500
$3,450–4,100 ⚒ S(Am)

A New Hall London-shape part tea service, comprising 37 pieces, painted with panels of floral sprays on an ozier-moulded ground, damaged and restored, c1825.
£560–670 / €810–960
$920–1,100 ⚒ DN

A Wiltshaw & Robinson tea and breakfast service, comprising 43 pieces, with gilt decoration, some marked 'B. G. Wiltshaw' with a crown and some with an earlier monogram, c1890.
£330–390 / €480–570
$550–660 ⚒ NSal

A cabaret set, comprising eight pieces, teapot cover missing, Continental, 19thC.
£520–620 / €750–890
$880–1,050 G(L)

◄ **A Royal Worcester tea service,** by James Hadley, comprising 43 pieces, three pieces signed by Kitty Blake, some damage, marked, c1907.
£700–840 / €1,000–1,200
$1,200–1,400 B(Kn)

A bone china part tea service, comprising 33 pieces, painted with flowers against leaf-scroll borders, c1840.
£210–250 / €300–360
$350–420 G(L)

Trays

A Dresden tray, erased factory mark, printed decorator's mark, German, early 20thC, 20in (51cm) wide.
£1,600–1,900 / €2,300–2,750
$2,700–3,200 S(NY)

A John Pennington Liverpool spoon tray, c1785, 6½in (16.5cm) wide.
£540–600 / €780–860
$900–1,000 ⊞ JUP

► **A Naples-style tray,** with scroll handles, marked, Continental, 19thC, 14in (35.5cm) wide.
£470–560 / €680–810
$790–940 B

A Spode tray, decorated with hand-painted roses, c1825, 6in (15cm) wide.
£130–145 / €190–210
$220–250 ⊞ DAN

Tureens

A pair of Bloor Derby sauce tureens, covers and stands, decorated with lion's-head masks and flowers, printed marks, c1830, 8¾in (22cm) wide.
£610–730 / €880–1,050
$1,000–1,200 WW

A pair of Meissen tureens, covers and stands, moulded with Neubrandenstein pattern and painted with flowers and scattered blooms, the covers with a seated boy or girl finial, gilt rims, small chip and repair, crossed swords and dot mark to one tureen, traces of crossed swords on the other, the stands marked and impressed 'H', German, 1755–65, 17¼in (44cm) wide.
£6,000–7,200 / €8,700–10,400
$10,100–12,100 S

The fact that these are a pair rather than a single tureen make them particularly desirable. They are highly decorative and in good overall condition.

◄ **A Spode feldspar tureen, cover and stand,** c1830, 7in (18cm) high.
£520–580 / €750–830
$870–970 ⊞ HA

A Meissen soup tureen and cover, painted with flower sprays, the cover with a fruit finial, with scroll handles, repaired, crossed swords mark, German, 19thC, 17in (43cm) wide.
£420–500 / €600–720
$700–840 WW

A pair of tureens, c1820, 8in (20.5cm) diam.
£1,000–1,150 / €1,450–1,650
$1,700–1,950 ⊞ DAN

Vases

A Belleek Turnip vase, chips, printed and impressed marks, Irish, First Period, 1863–90, 11½in (29cm) high.
£1,200–1,450
€1,700–2,000
$2,000–2,400 S(O)

A Coalport vase and cover, with hand-painted floral decoration and gilded borders, with a ball finial, mid-19thC, 16in (40.5cm) high.
£4,500–5,000
€6,500–7,200
$7,600–8,400 ⊞ Man

A Belleek Double Fish vase, Irish, First Period, 1863–90, 8in (20.5cm) high.
£2,600–2,900
€3,800–4,200
$4,400–4,900 ⊞ MLa

A set of three Derby vases, decorated with riverside landscapes and gilt foliage, with scrolling serpent handles, some damage, painted marks, c1800, largest 8¼in (21cm) high.
£400–480 / €580–690
$670–800 Bea

A pair of Derby vases, decorated in the Imari palette, late 19thC, 5in (12.5cm) high.
£280–330 / €400–480
$470–560 WW

◄ **A Royal Crown Derby vase,** by W. E. J. Dean, painted with a landscape, signed, c1919, 4½in (11.5cm) high.
£540–600 / €780–860
$910–1,000 ⊞ JUP

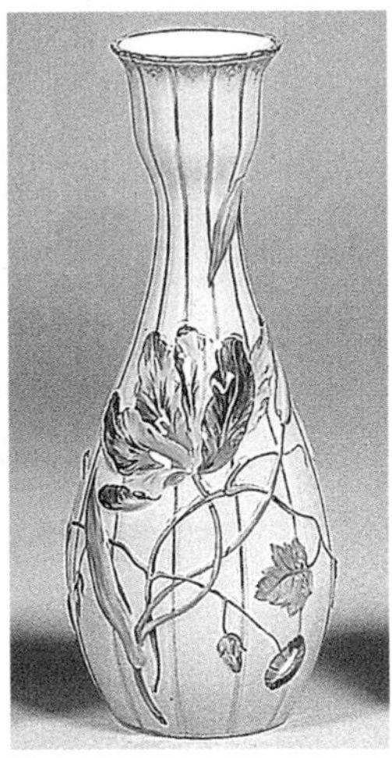

A Berlin vase, relief-decorated with flowers and leaves, marked, German, 1849–70, 12¼in (31cm) high.
£400–480 / €580–690
$670–800 DORO

For further information on antique porcelain see the full range of Miller's books at **www.millers.uk.com**

A pair of Dresden jars and covers, painted with scenes of couples in a garden and flower sprays, pseudo Augustus Rex mark, 1850–1900, 12¼in (31cm) high.
£530–640 / €760–910
$1,000–1,100 RTo

A set of three spill vases, probably by Charles Bourne of Fenton, painted with flowers, with gilt borders of trailing ivy, c1825, largest 5½in (14cm) high.
£165–195 / €240–280
$290–340 NSal

A pair of Derby rococo-moulded vases of flowers, each painted with figures in a landscape, the reverse painted with flowers, chips, restored, c1760, 5¾in (14.5cm) high.
£660–790 / €950–1,100
$1,100–1,300 S(O)

A Dresden vase and cover, painted after Watteau with figural panels and flowers, on a plinth, cracked, German, late 19thC, 18½in (47cm) high.
£350–420 / €500–600
$590–700 G(L)

PORCELAIN

A Longton Hall vase, painted with flowers, c1758, 3½in (9cm) high.
£1,350–1,500
€1,950–2,150
$2,250–2,500 ⊞ JUP
This piece was formerly in the Rous Lench collection.

A pair of Paris vases, decorated with buildings in landscapes on a gilt ground, French, c1820, 12¾in (32.5cm) high.
£1,000–1,200
€1,450–1,700
$1,700–2,000 ⚒ S(P)

A Vauxhall vase, printed and painted with flowers, c1758, 5in (12.5cm) high.
£3,600–4,000
€5,100–5,700
$6,000–6,700 ⊞ JUP

A pair of Meissen vases, with stiff-leaf-moulded borders and scroll handles heightened with gilding, damaged and restored, crossed swords marks, German, late 19thC, 24¼in (61.5cm) high.
£960–1,150
€1,400–1,650
$1,600–1,900 ⚒ S(O)

A pair of Sèvres porcelain and ormolu vases and covers, each decorated with figural reserves, cast cupid and foliate handles, with hoof feet, on socle bases with disc feet, French, 19thC, 15in (38cm) high.
£2,100–2,500
€3,000–3,600
$3,500–4,200 ⚒ JAd

A pair of Meissen vases, decorated with cartouches of pastoral scenes, German, c1880, 11½in (29cm) high.
£6,200–6,900
€8,900–9,900
$10,400–11,600 ⊞ MAA

A pair of Spode spill vases, c1820, 5in (12.5cm) high.
£800–880 / €1,100–1,250
$1,350–1,500 ⊞ DAN

A pair of Meissen automobile vases, painted with panels of summer flowers, with gilt foliate borders, gilt-metal clip mounts, crossed sword marks, German, c1920, 5in (12.5cm) high.
£210–250 / €300–360
$350–420 ⚒ B
These vases were designed to hang in the early automobiles.

A Spode vase, painted with flowers in a cartouche, c1825, 6½in (16.5cm) high.
£720–800 / €1,000–1,150
$1,200–1,350 ⊞ JUP

◄ **A Worcester vase,** decorated with floral bouquets, with gilt-highlighted rococo handles, c1770, 9½in (24cm) high.
£1,150–1,400
€1,700–2,000
$2,000–2,350 ⚒ Bri

► **A pair of Worcester Flight, Barr & Barr vases,** probably painted by Thomas Baxter, minor damage, 1813–40, 6½in (16.5cm) high.
£4,700–5,600
€6,800–8,100
$7,900–9,400
⚒ SERR

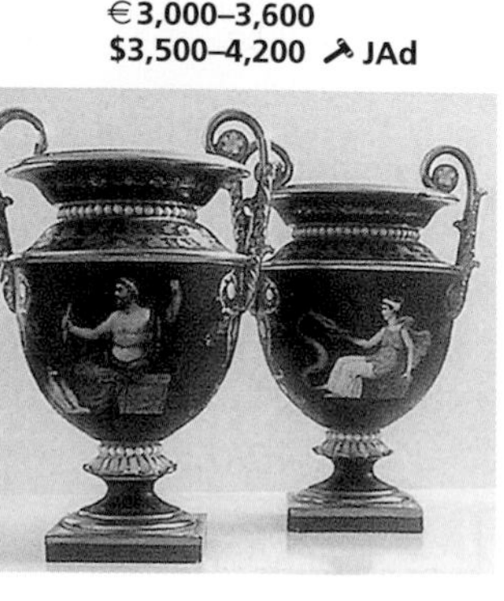

► **A Grainger's Worcester porcelain vase and cover,** the pierced cover with a leafy knop, the body with foliate moulding, the handles formed as displaying swans, painted with botanical specimens, painted marks, 1800–50, 13in (33cm) high.
£910–1,100
€1,350–1,600
$1,550–1,850 ⚒ Bea

A pair of Worcester Kerr & Binns bottle vases, each painted with two putti in reserves, one with small chip, printed mark, c1857, 7in (18cm) high.
£720–860 / €1,050–1,250
$1,200–1,400 ⚒ S(O)

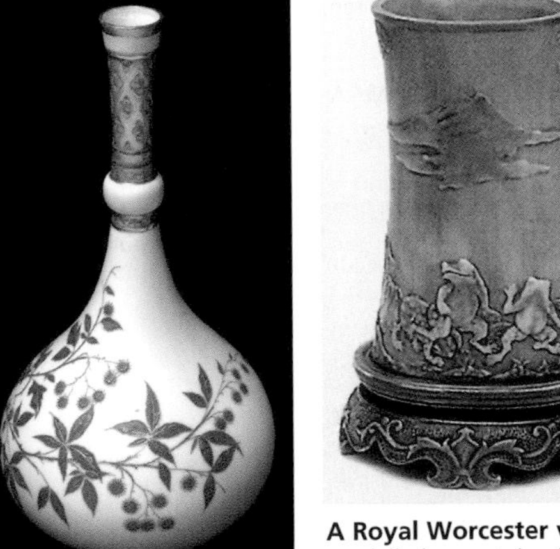

A pair of Royal Worcester vases, with gilt decoration, c1883, 12in (30.5cm) high.
£1,100–1,250
€1,600–1,800
$1,900–2,100 ⊞ WAC

A Royal Worcester vase, hand-painted with Highland cattle by J. Stinton, signed, date code for 1918, 5in (13cm) high.
£650–780 / €920–1,100
$1,100–1,300 ⚒ SWO

A Royal Worcester vase, painted with a view entitled 'Pallanza Laco Maggiore', within a tooled gilt border, printed marks, c1863, 11¾in (30cm) high.
£1,900–2,250
€2,750–3,300
$3,200–3,850 ⚒ WW

A Royal Worcester vase, modelled as a stained ivory tusk, with raised decoration depicting a serpent, the reverse with a group of dancing frogs, minor chips, impressed and printed marks with date code for 1886, 7¾in (20cm) high.
£230–270 / €330–390
$390–460 ⚒ Bea

A pair of Royal Worcester vases, decorated with gilt and enamels by James Henry Liseron Lewis, with twin gilt handles, signed, dated 1920, 13in (33cm) high.
£530–640 / €770–920
$950–1,100 ⚒ LAY

A pair of Royal Worcester vases and covers, painted with figures and children in a garden on a gilt-decorated ground, covers restored and damaged, date code for 1865, 14½in (37cm) high.
£1,100–1,350
€1,600–1,900
$1,900–2,250 ⚒ B(L)

For further information on
Vases see page 247

A Royal Worcester Parian vase, decorated with humming birds and a parrot, with entwined scroll handles, marked, c1865, 12¼in (31cm) high.
£135–160 / €195–230
$230–270 ⚒ NSal

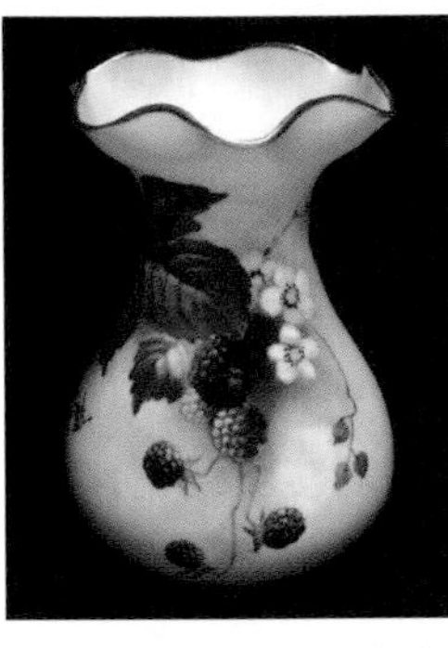

► **A Royal Worcester vase,** painted with leaves and berries probably by Kitty Blake, c1913, 4½in (11.5cm) high.
£340–380 / €490–540
$570–640 ⊞ JUP

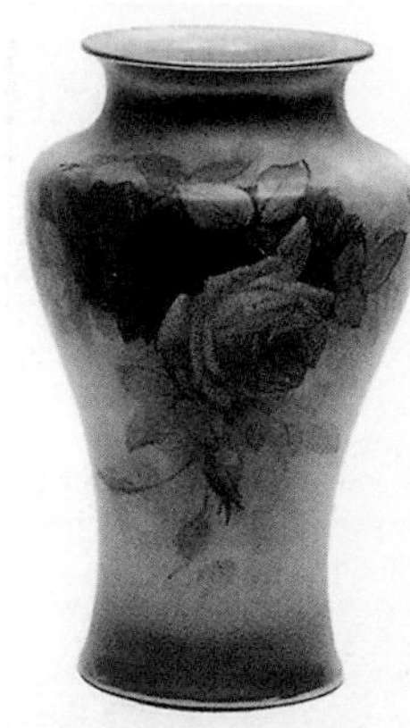

A Royal Worcester vase, painted by Walter Sedgley with a bouquet of roses, printed marks, date code for 1925, 7¾in (19.5cm) high.
£450–540 / €650–780
$760–910 Bea

A vase, enamelled in 18thC style with a woman and a cat, with gilt ram's-head handles, enamelled marks, French, c1870, 17in (43cm) high.
£330–400 / €470–580
$560–670 WL

A pair of vases and covers, painted with classical figures within flower-swag borders supported by cherubs and urns, the covers with putto finials, one finial repaired, Italian, late 19thC, 12¼in (31cm) high.
£480–580 / €700–840
$810–970 S(O)

A vase, decorated in Europe for the Western market, carved with *anhua* flowers and scrolls, enamelled with deer and a flying bird within dentil borders, cracked, restored, Chinese, 1720–30, 10½in (26.5cm) high.
£400–480 / €580–690
$670–800 B
Ex-Bernard Watney collection.
This piece was shown at the British Museum East Meets West exhibition. The catalogue noted how the Dutch painter did not understand Chinese imagery and has given the bird a crane's head and the tail of a phoenix.

A pair of vases, painted with bouquets of flowers against a gilt ground, with two gilt swan-neck handles, restoration and repair, c1820, 12in (30.5cm) high.
£1,800–2,150
€2,600–3,100
$3,000–3,600 S(O)

A pair of vases, c1835, 4in (10cm) high.
£290–320 / €390–460
$490–540 DAN

► **A pair of vases and covers,** with relief-moulded female and male masks, the reserves painted with women and children at a well feeding chickens, and a landscape view, the covers with acanthus knops, wear to gilding, pseudo Sèvres marks, one impressed 'C411', late 19thC, 10½in (26.5cm) high.
£840–1,000
€1,200–1,400
$1,450–1,700 S(O)

◄ **A pair of rococo-style vases,** each decorated with a Turkish figure, the bases with moulded lily blooms, foliage and berry clusters, Franco-Bohemian, late 19thC, 17in (43cm) high.
£950–1,100 / €1,350–1,600
$1,600–1,850 NOA

A pair of vases, decorated with garlands of flowers, French, late 19thC, 13in (33cm) high.
£500–600 / €720–860
$840–1,000 S(P)

◄ **A porcelain vase and cover,** applied with masks and flower swags, painted with two landscape panels, impressed '5768', knop repaired, Continental, c1900, 14¼in (36cm) high.
£350–420 / €500–600
$590–700 WW

PORCELAIN

Miscellaneous

A Meissen bell push, decorated with a flower, crossed swords mark, German, c1900, 4½in (11.5cm) wide.
£760–850 / €1,050–1,200
$1,250–1,400 ⊞ DAV

A *bordalou*, decorated with posies of flowers, c1840, 11in (28cm) wide.
£270–300 / €390–430
$450–500 ⊞ CuS

A pair of Imperial Porcelain Manufactory egg cups, decorated in enamels with the crowned cipher of Nicholas II, chipped, Imperial marks, Russian, dated 1906, 2½in (6.5cm) high.
£470–560 / €670–800
$790–940 ⚒ B

Items in the Miscellaneous section have been arranged in alphabetical order.

► **A Belleek flask,** of Jewish interest, Irish, First Period, 1863–90, 6in (15cm) long.
£800–900 / €1,150–1,300
$1,350–1,500 ⊞ MLa

A pair of Sèvres wine glass coolers, incised marks and blue stamps for 1828 and 1830, 14¼in (36cm) wide.
£7,900–9,500 / €11,400–13,700
$13,300–16,000 ⚒ S(P)

A pair of Worcester guglets, painted with The Lange Lijzen pattern, one with rim chips, 1753–55, 9½in (24cm) high.
£28,000–33,000
€40,000–47,000
$47,000–55,000 ⚒ Bri
This is a very rare item and only a few examples are known to exist.

A Bow guglet, painted with chrysanthemum and bamboo, damage and repair, c1760, 11in (28cm) high.
£800–900 / €1,150–1,300
$1,350–1,500 ⊞ JUP

A pair of Derby ice pails, painted *en grisaille* with urns and a border of scrolls and swags, covers and liners missing, marked, c1790, 5¾in (14.5cm) wide.
£1,000–1,200
€1,450–1,700
$1,700–2,000 ⚒ B

A Copeland inkstand and letter rack, decorated with flower sprays, with gilt detail, c1895, 9in (23cm) high.
£720–800 / €1,000–1,150
$1,200–1,350 ⊞ DIA

◄ **A pair of jars and covers,** painted with reserved panels of courting couples, restored, crossed swords marks, German, 19thC, 17¾in (45cm) high.
£590–700 / €850–1,000
$1,000–1,200 ⚒ RTo

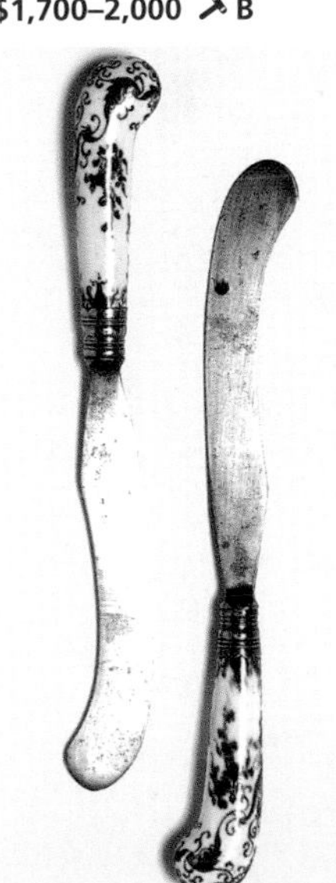

► **A pair of Worcester knives,** with original steel blades, c1760, 11in (28cm) long.
£490–550 / €700–790
$820–920 ⊞ AUC

A Mennecy pomade pot and cover, decorated with flower sprays, the cover with flower bud knop, slight damage, incised mark, French, c1765, 3¾in (9.5cm) high.
£230–270 / €330–390
$380–450 ⚒ B

Chelsea

The Chelsea factory was founded c1744 by Nicholas Sprimont. He was a Flemish silversmith, and many early Chelsea wares such as the goat and bee jugs, salt cellars and small vases were modelled from original silver shapes. Unlike the other English porcelain manufacturers, Chelsea concentrated on the luxury end of the market – the products were expensive and in limited supply.

The earliest Chelsea pieces often bear an incised triangle mark, the alchemists' sign for fire. When the factory moved to larger premises in 1749, the mark changed to a raised anchor. Sprimont employed Joseph Willems, a Belgian sculptor, who modelled a fine series of birds based on the engravings of George Edwards. Wares depicting scenes from Aesop's Fables were also introduced, probably painted by Jefferyes Hamett O'Neale, an artist who later produced similar work at Worcester.

From 1752, wares were marked with a red anchor. A wide range of figures was produced, mostly copies of Meissen originals, as well as the famous 'Hans Sloane' pieces featuring finely executed botanical studies – these are currently attracting huge interest.

During the gold anchor period, from c1756, the influence of Meissen was superseded by the exuberant rococo style of the Sèvres factory and, by adding bone ash to strengthen the paste, it was now possible to produce large and more elaborate wares. The decoration is usually on a richly-coloured ground inspired by Sèvres. The high-quality gilding is thought to have been effected by an amalgam of finely ground gold and honey.

Due to Sprimont's failing health, the Chelsea factory closed in 1769. It was purchased the following year by William Duesbury, the proprietor of the Derby factory, who ran the two concerns together until 1784.

Chelsea is currently the most fashionable and hotly contested of all the 18th-century English porcelain factories. The most sought-after pieces are those produced up to the mid-1750s – the highest price in the Billie Pain collection was for a Chelsea milk jug c1750, painted by the highly-regarded Jefferyes Hamett O'Neale.

The fever for Chelsea porcelain reached a peak late in 2003, when a tureen c1755 modelled in the form of a hen and chicks sold for a staggering £195,000 / €281,000 / $328,000 at Christie's, setting a new auction record for English porcelain. In the 18th century, Chelsea was the most luxurious and expensive porcelain, and remains so today.

Phil Howell

PORCELAIN

A pair of Chelsea models of Chinese pheasants, probably decorated in the workshop of William Duesbury, damaged and repaired, raised red anchor marks, 1750–52, 8¼in (21cm) high.
£16,500–19,800 / €23,700–28,500 $27,700–33,300 Bea

Although one of these pheasants was extensively damaged, they were keenly contested because pairs are scarce and these are very well decorated, probably in the workshop of William Duesbury. As the pheasant was quite crudely repaired, it would be relatively simple to take it apart and restore it to professional standards.

A Chelsea model of a parakeet, repaired, raised red anchor mark, 1751–53, 4¾in (12cm) high.
£7,800–9,300 €11,200–13,400 $13,100–15,600 S(NY)

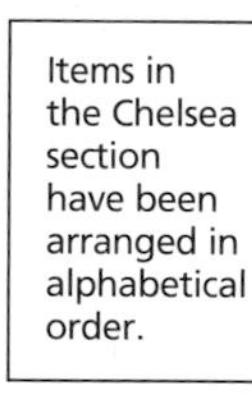

Items in the Chelsea section have been arranged in alphabetical order.

► **A Chelsea model of a pheasant,** repaired, raised red anchor mark, c1752, 6in (15cm) high.
£3,150–3,500 €4,500–5,000 $5,300–5,900 JUP

Further reading

Miller's Ceramics Buyer's Guide, Miller's Publications, 2000

A pair of Chelsea baskets, with reticulated sides, the interiors painted with rose sprays, one damaged and repaired, red anchor mark, c1755, 5¼in (13.5cm) wide.
£1,750–2,100 / €2,500–3,500 $2,900–3,500 WW

A Chelsea-Derby basket, 1769–75, 7½in (19cm) diam.
£630–700 / €900–1,000 $1,050–1,200 AUC

A Chelsea teaplant beaker, in the white, relief-moulded with spirals of flowers and leaves, slight damage, 1744–49, 2¾in (7cm) high.
£2,600–3,100
€3,750–4,450
$4,350–5,200 B
Ex-Billie Pain collection.

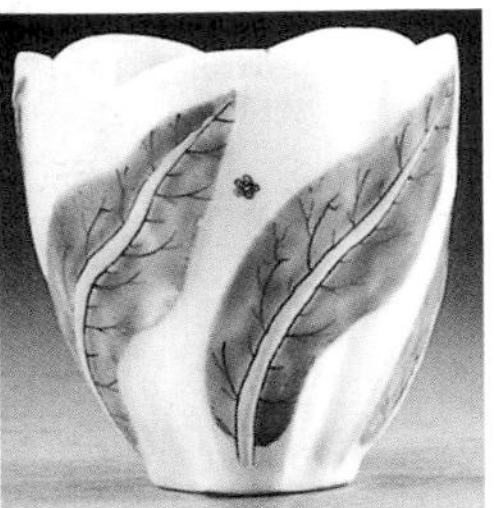

A Chelsea beaker, decorated with fern leaves, the interior with an insect, flowerheads and leaves, chipped, raised anchor mark, c1750, 2¾in (7cm) high.
£2,600–3,100
€3,750–4,450
$4,350–5,200 S(O)

► **A Chelsea box and cover,** modelled as a rosebud, restored, c1755, 3½in (9cm) high.
£660–790 / €950–1,100
$1,100–1,300 WW

A Chelsea-Derby box and cover, painted with cherubs and musical instruments on a gilt-decorated ground, the cover with a flower knop, damaged, double gold anchor mark, 1770–75, 2¾in (7cm) high.
£200–240 / €290–350
$340–400 WW

► **A Chelsea dish,** painted in *famille rose* enamels, damage and repair, c1752, 8¾in (22cm) diam.
£740–880 / €1,050–1,250
$1,250–1,450 S(O)

A Chelsea teaplant beaker, relief-moulded, the interior with scattered flowerheads, slight damage, 1745–49, 3in (7.5cm) high.
£780–930 / €1,100–1,300
$1,300–1,550 S(O)

A Chelsea bowl, decorated in gilt with a peacock, a pheasant and other birds, hairline crack, gold anchor mark, c1760, 3¾in (9.5cm) high.
£400–480 / €580–690
$670–800 WW

A Chelsea dish, decorated in the Kakiemon style with Tiger and Dragon pattern, raised anchor mark, 1750–52, 9½in (24cm) wide.
£4,450–5,300
€6,400–7,600
$7,500–8,900 B

Chelsea periods

Production at the Chelsea factory falls into five periods, four of which are named after marks used at the time:

Triangle Period (1744–49)
Mark usually incised or painted in underglaze blue. White, glassy, transluscent body, often left uncoloured, the shape based on British silverware shapes.

Raised anchor period (1749–52)
Mark embossed on a raised pad. Milky white, silky body, containing impurity specks. Decoration based on Japanese porcelain, Vincennes and Meissen.

Red anchor period (1752–56)
Very small mark in red enamel on the backs of figures and bases of plates and cups. Creamy white body with dribbling glaze, often decorated with Meissen-style flowers. When held up to a strong light, so-called Chelsea 'moons' can be seen – bubbles trapped in the paste, that appear as lighter spots in the body.

Gold anchor period (1756–69)
Mark painted in gold. Creamy body, prone to staining. Clear, thickly applied glaze that tends to craze. Rococo decoration, influenced by Sèvres. Use of gilding significantly increased.

Chelsea-Derby period (1770–84)
Mark of a D with an anchor conjoined, usually in gold. Gold anchor mark also continued to be used. Chelsea factory bought and run by William Duesbury & Co, owners of the Derby porcelain factory, until it was closed in 1784. Predominantly neo-classical decoration with a new French look.

A Chelsea-Derby chocolate cup, cover and saucer, decorated with spirally moulded flutes, highlighted in gilt, c1775, 4in (10cm) high.
£760–850 / €1,050–1,200
$1,250–1,400 JUP

A set of eight Chelsea-Derby custard cups and covers, enamelled with leaf and berry swags, some damage, gold anchor mark, c1775, 3¾in (9.5cm) high.
£2,000–2,400 / €2,900–3,450
$3,350–4,000 S(O)

► **A Chelsea dish,** moulded as a flowerhead with leaves, painted with flower sprays, the handle moulded as a flower stalk, restored, red anchor mark, c1755, 9in (23cm) wide.
£540–640 / €770–920
$900–1,050 WW

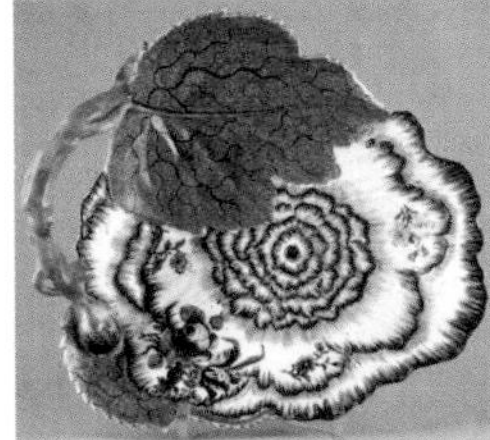

PORCELAIN

A Chelsea 'Hans Sloane' dish, painted with a lemon, bean flowers and insects, hair cracks, red anchor mark, c1755, 10½in (26.5cm) wide.
£2,150–2,550 / €3,100–3,700
$3,600–4,300 ⚒ S(O)
These wares are so-called because their decoration is said to represent botanical specimens from Sir Hans Sloane's Chelsea Physic garden and is based on engravings by the curator, Philip Miller, and Georg Dionysus Ehret.

A Chelsea sunflower dish and cover, naturalistically coloured, repaired, c1755, 5in (12.5cm) wide.
£2,100–2,350 / €3,000–3,350
$3,500–3,900 ⊞ JUP

A Chelsea leaf dish, painted with flower sprays, c1756, 10¾in (27.5cm) wide.
£610–680 / €870–980
$1,000–1,100 ⊞ AUC

A pair of Chelsea dishes, painted with fruit and insects, slight damage, gold anchor marks, c1760, 9¾in (25cm) wide.
£1,300–1,550 / €1,850–2,200
$2,200–2,600 ⚒ S(O)

A pair of Chelsea leaf dishes, c1756, 9½in (24cm) wide.
£1,350–1,500 / €1,950–2,150
$2,250–2,500 ⊞ AUC

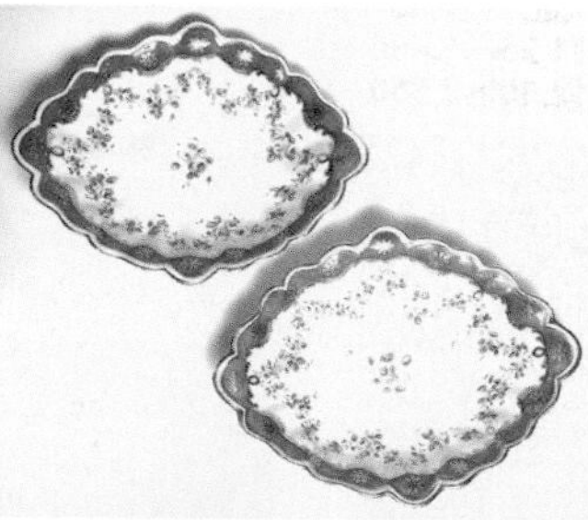

A Chelsea sunflower dish, damaged, c1758, 8in (20.5cm) diam.
£760–850 / €1,100–1,250
$1,250–1,400 ⊞ AUC

◀ **A pair of Chelsea-Derby fluted dishes,** painted with garlands of roses, highlighted with gilt, some wear and regilding, c1775, 12½in (32cm) wide.
£720–800 / €1,000–1,150
$1,200–1,350 ⊞ JUP

PORCELAIN

A Chelsea figure of Pierrot, c1755, 6in (15cm) high.
£5,400–6,000
€7,800–8,600
$9,000–10,000 ⊞ DMa

A Chelsea masquerade figure, c1760, 8½in (21.5cm) high.
£2,250–2,500
€3,250–3,600
$3,750–4,200 ⊞ DMa

◀ **A Chelsea reeded milk jug,** painted by Jefferyes Hamett O'Neale, minor rim chips, c1750, 3¼in (8cm) high.
£36,500–44,000
€53,000–63,000
$62,000–74,000
⚒ B
Ex-Billie Pain collection.

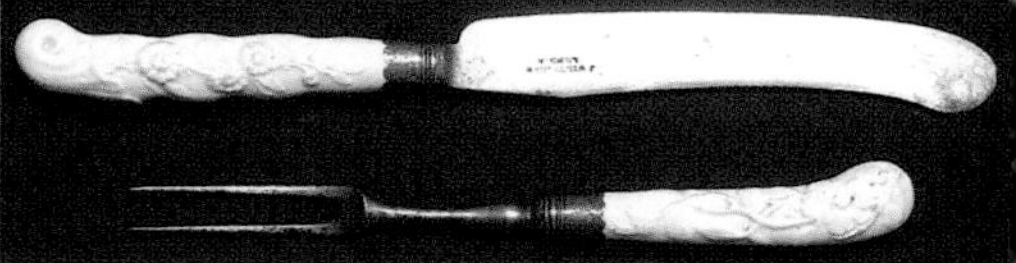

A Chelsea knife and fork, c1755, knife 11in (28cm) long.
£340–380 / €490–550
$570–640 ⊞ AUC

◀ **A Chelsea plate,** the border painted and gilt with landscape vignettes and moulded with scrolls, restored, red anchor mark, c1755, 9½in (24cm) diam.
£165–195 / €240–280
$270–320 ⚒ SWO

▶ **A Chelsea plate,** painted with flower sprays, red anchor mark, 1755–60, 8¼in (21cm) wide.
£420–500 / €600–720
$700–840 ⚒ WW

A Chelsea plate, moulded and decorated with flowers, c1756, 9¼in (23.5cm) diam.
£520–580 / €750–840
$870–970 ⊞ AUC

A Chelsea sauce boat, moulded as a leaf, raised anchor mark, 1751–52, 7¼in (18.5cm) wide.
£1,600–1,800 / €2,300–2,600
$2,700–3,000 ⊞ AUC

A Chelsea soup plate, painted with enamels in the Kakiemon style with Quail pattern, highlighted with gilt, 1752–56, 9¼in (23.5cm) diam.
£840–1,000 / €1,200–1,400
$1,400–1,650 ⚒ PFK

A Chelsea tea bowl, painted in the Vincennes style, raised anchor mark, 1752–53, 2½in (6.5cm) high.
£4,100–4,900 / €5,900–7,000
$6,800–8,200 ⚒ B
Ex-Billie Pain collection.

► **A pair of Chelsea vases,** gold anchor marks, one vase damaged, c1765, 8½in (21cm) high.
£840–1,000 / €1,200–1,400
$1,400–1,650 ⚒ S(O)

Three Chelsea plates, comprising a meat plate and two dessert plates, with gilt and scalloped borders, c1765, largest 14¼in (36cm) wide.
£3,300–3,900 / €4,750–5,600
$5,500–6,500 ⚒ B(EA)

A Chelsea sauce boat, moulded as a leaf, on moulded strawberry leaf feet, repaired, c1754, 7in (18cm) wide.
£1,250–1,400 / €1,800–2,000
$2,100–2,350 ⊞ JUP

A Chelsea saucer, gold anchor mark, c1760, 5½in (14cm) diam.
£1,100–1,300 / €1,600–1,900
$1,850–2,150 ⚒ WW

A Chelsea tea bowl, painted in the Meissen style, red anchor mark, c1755, 3in (7.6cm) diam.
£960–1,150 / €1,400–1,650
$1,600–1,900 ⚒ B
Ex-Billie Pain collection.

A Chelsea saucer, painted in the Kakiemon style, with gilt highlights, raised anchor mark, 1750–52, 4¼in (10.5cm) wide.
£1,500–1,800 / €2,150–2,600
$2,500–3,000 ⚒ B
Ex-Billie Pain collection.

A Chelsea seal pendant, inscribed 'Si j'avais des yeux' (If I had eyes), c1770, ¾in (2cm) high.
£1,550–1,750 / €2,250–2,500
$2,600–2,950 ⊞ NBL

A garniture of five Chelsea vases and covers, comprising a vase with applied goats' heads, on three hoof feet, a pair of vases with coiled handles and a pair of vases decorated with swags and lions' masks, gold anchor and patch marks, c1768, largest 9in (23cm) high.
£1,500–1,800 / €2,200–2,600
$2,500–3,000 ⚒ B

PORCELAIN

A Selection of Chinese Dynasties & Marks

Early Dynasties

Neolithic	10th – early 1st millennium BC
Shang Dynasty	16th century–c1050 BC
Zhou Dynasty	c1050–221 BC
Warring States	480–221 BC
Qin Dynasty	221–206 BC
Han Dynasty	206 BC–AD 220
Six Dynasties	222–589
Wei Dynasty	386–557
Sui Dynasty	581–618
Tang Dynasty	618–907
Five Dynasties	907–960
Liao Dynasty	907–1125
Song Dynasty	960–1279
Northern Song	960–1127
Southern Song	1127–1279
Xixia Dynasty	1038–1227
Jin Dynasty	1115–1234
Yuan Dynasty	1279–1368

Ming Dynasty Marks

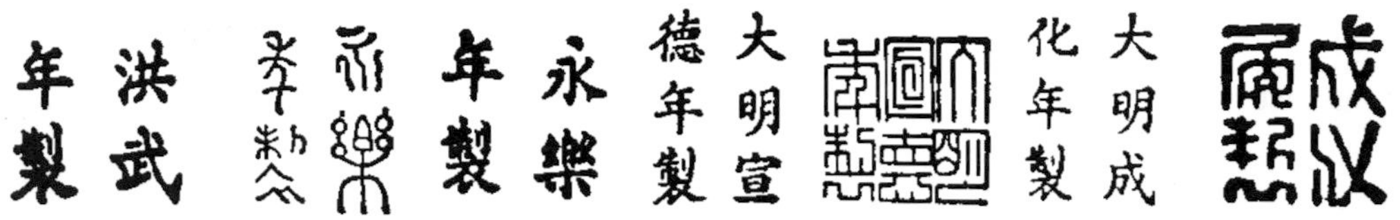

Hongwu 1368–1398

Yongle 1403–1424

Xuande 1426–1435

Chenghua 1465–1487

大明弘治年製
Hongzhi 1488–1505

大明正德年製
Zhengde 1506–1521

大明嘉靖年製
Jiajing 1522–1566

大明隆慶年製
Longqing 1567–1572

大明萬曆年製
Wanli 1573–1619

大明天啟年製
Tianqi 1621–1627

崇禎年製
Chongzhen 1628–1644

Qing Dynasty Marks

大清順治年製
Shunzhi 1644–1661

大清康熙年製
Kangxi 1662–1722

大清雍正年製
Yongzheng 1723–1735

大清乾隆年製
Qianlong 1736–1795

嘉慶年製
Jiaqing 1796–1820

大清道光年製
Daoguang 1821–1850

大清咸豐年製
Xianfeng 1851–1861

大清同治年製
Tongzhi 1862–1874

大清光緒年製
Guangxu 1875–1908

Xuantong 1909–1911

Hongxian 1916

Chinese Ceramics

Animals

A pottery model of a horse, Oxford T/L tested, repair to one leg, Han Dynasty, 206 BC–AD 220, 22in (56cm) high.
£4,500–5,000 / €6,500–7,200
$7,600–8,400 ⊞ GLD

A painted pottery Tomb Guardian, Tang Dynasty, AD 618–907, 11½in (29cm) high.
£600–720 / €880–1,050
$1,000–1,200 ⚒ S(O)

A pair of biscuit models of parrots, Kangxi period, 1662–1722, 3in (7.5cm) high.
£280–330 / €400–480
$470–560 ⚒ WW

T/L test

Oxford T/L test refers to a test certificate awarded by Oxford Authentication Ltd to those genuine pieces of ceramics which have passed their thermoluminescence test which is accurate to plus or minus 200 years.

A sancai-glazed model of a camel, Oxford T/L tested, Tang Dynasty, AD 618–907, 22in (56cm) high.
£7,650–8,500 / €11,000–12,300
$12,800–14,300 ⊞ GLD

A pottery model of a pony, tail repaired, Six Dynasties, AD 222–589, 20¾in (52.5cm) high.
£6,500–7,800 / €9,400–11,200
$11,000–13,100 ⚒ B

A pottery model of a bull, Tang Dynasty, AD 618–907, 10½in (26.5cm) wide.
£240–290 / €350–420
$400–480 ⚒ S(O)

Tang Dynasty

Tang Dynasty (AD 618–907) wares are typically made of low-fired buff-coloured earthenware decorated with runny lead glazes tinted blue, green or amber by the addition of copper, cobalt or iron pigments. Vessels such as jars, vases and bowls are usually squat and rounded with moulded or painted spotted decoration based on contemporary textile designs. Models include Tomb Guardians (often with unglazed faces that were painted with coloured pigments after firing), horses and camels. Tang horses have been widely copied, so it is inadvisable to buy without a T/L test certificate.

A pair of porcelain models of doves, one beak repaired, c1775, 7in (18cm) wide.
£6,000–7,200 / €8,700–10,400
$10,100–12,100 ⚒ BUK

◄ **A pair of glazed porcelain models of dogs,** one leg restored, 18thC, 8in (20.5cm) high.
£9,400–11,300 / €13,500–16,200
$15,800–19,000 ⚒ B

A *famille rose* model of a bridled pony, 19thC, 10½in (26.5cm) high.
£7,200–8,600 / €10,400–12,400
$12,100–14,500 ⚒ S

Bowls

A Yaozhou bowl, the interior carved with a flower spray and a geometric combed pattern, Northern Song/Jin Dynasty, 960–1127, 5½in (14cm) diam.
£2,900–3,500 / €4,200–5,000
$4,900–5,900 B
Ex-du Boulay collection. Anthony du Boulay was, until 1976, Director of the Ceramics department at Christie's. He then went to New York to help establish auction sales for Christie's there, and retired in 1980. He is the author of *Chinese Porcelain* and *Christie's Pictorial History of Chinese Ceramics*. His lifetime collection was sold by Bonhams in November 2003.

A *famille verte* bowl, decorated with three standing figures and a procession of banner men in a rocky wooded landscape, the interior with fish and shellfish among water plants, repaired, Kangxi period, 1662–1722, 13¼in (33.5cm) diam.
£3,000–3,600 / €4,350–5,200
$5,000–6,000 WW

A bowl and cover, decorated with a pair of phoenix among cloud and fire scrolls, divided by two lotus heads, the cover with a lotus finial, Kangxi period, 1662–1722, 7in (18cm) high.
£1,400–1,650 / €2,000–2,400
$2,350–2,800 B

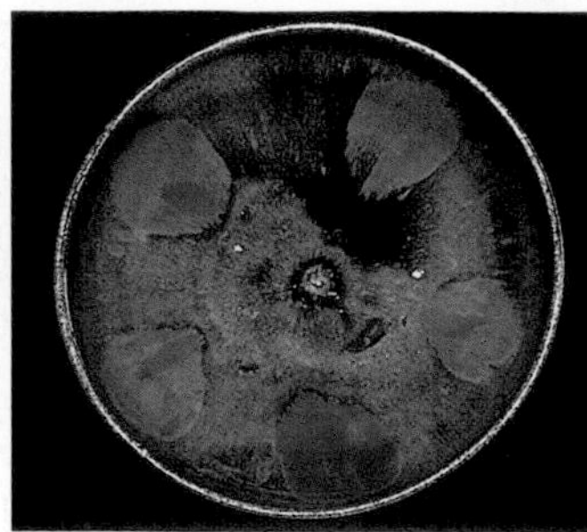

A Henan bowl, glazed with hare's fur markings, Northern Song Dynasty, 960–1127, 6½in (16.5cm) diam.
£2,400–2,900 / €3,500–4,200
$4,050–4,850 S
Henan is a province in central China where this distinctive type of stoneware was produced.

A lotus celadon bowl, with a gold lacquer repair, Southern Song Dynasty, 1127–1279, 8in (20.5cm) diam.
£850–950 / €1,200–1,350
$1,450–1,600 GLD

A bowl, Kangxi period, 1662–1722, 8½in (21.5cm) diam.
£420–500 / €600–720
$700–840 L

A bowl, from the Vung Tau cargo, c1690, 5in (12.5cm) diam.
£90–100 / €130–145
$150–165 RBA
The Vung Tau cargo was the haul from a Chinese junk that foundered off the coast of Vietnam, south of Vung Tau, c1960.

Song Dynasty

The Song Dynasty (960–1279) is regarded as the classic period of Chinese ceramic production. The simple, elegant pieces are typically decorated with attractive monochrome glazes; Jun wares are splashed with purple derived from copper oxide on an opaque lavender-blue ground. Most products are stonewares, although Ding and Qingbai are porcellaneous. The five 'classic wares' – Ding, Jun, Ru, Guan and Ge – were produced for Imperial use, while wares such as Cizhou and some of the northern celadons were made for a much wider market. Pieces are generally unmarked, although a few stoneware moulds have been found with 12th- or 13th-century dates incised on the surface.

A dragon bowl, from the Hatcher cargo, minor damage, Transitional period, c1640, 7in (18cm) diam.
£1,400–1,650 / €2,000–2,400
$2,350–2,800 B
Ex-du Boulay collection.

◄ **A helmet bowl,** Kangxi period, 1662–1722, 8in (20.5cm) diam.
£3,400–3,800 / €4,900–5,500
$5,700–6,400 GLD

A pair of *doucai* bowls, painted with a scholar taking tea, his attendants nearby, the interior with a floral spray, pseudo Chenghua mark, Kangxi period, 1662–1722, 3½in (9cm) diam.
£1,800–2,150 / €2,600–3,100
$3,000–3,600 S(NY)

A bowl, decorated with three *lingzhi* sprays, hairline crack, Yongzheng period and mark, 1723–35, 6in (15cm) diam.
£3,750–4,500 / €5,400–6,500
$6,300–7,500 B
Ex-du Boulay collection.

A Batavian glazed bowl, the interior with a cracked ice and prunus border and decorated in *famille verte* enamels, the exterior decorated in raised enamel, chips, marked with a Cash symbol, one of the Eight Precious Things, 1700–10, 6¼in (16cm) diam.
£500–600 / €720–860
$840–1,000 B
Ex-Bernard Watney collection. The *famille verte* enamelling inside this bowl is original Chinese decoration made for the Mogul or Middle-Eastern market. The exterior was enamelled in England at the beginning of the 18th century.

The Eight Precious Things

The Jewel — The Cash — The Open Lozenge — The Pair of Books

The Solid Lozenge — The Musical Stone — The Pair of Horns — The Artemisia Leaf

Eight is considered to be the perfect Yin and Yang and is the basis of Tai Chi. These devices often occur as decorative motifs and occasionally individually as marks. The Artemisia Leaf is particularly common as a mark on Kangxi export porcelain.

A *famille verte* bowl, enamelled with flowering plants, restored, Yongzheng mark and period, 1723–35, 6in (15cm) diam.
£4,700–5,600 / €6,800–8,100
$7,900–9,400 B
By tradition, this bowl was taken in 1860 from the Summer Palace, Beijing, by Lord Loch of Drylaw, aide-de-camp to the British Plenipotentiary leading the Anglo-French expedition of 1856–60 which sacked the palace in 1860.

A *famille rose* armorial punch bowl, decorated with flowering plants and a coat-of-arms on either side, the interior with gilt fruit and flowers, damaged and restored, Qianlong period, 1736–95, 12in (30.5cm) diam.
£740–820 / €1,050–1,200
$1,250–1,400 G&G

A Canton export *famille verte* bowl, decorated with panels of figures, c1850, 15¾in (40cm) diam, on a hardwood stand.
£900–1,050 / €1,350–1,550
$1,500–1,750 HOK

A milk bowl, from the Nanking cargo, the body decorated with a figure in a landscape, c1750, 6in (15cm) diam.
£850–950 / €1,200–1,350
$1,450–1,600 RBA
The Nanking cargo was named after the type of porcelain it contained. It was salvaged in 1985 from the Dutch East India Company's ship *Geldermalsen*, which sank near Java in 1751.

A bowl, with gilt line decoration, c1780, 6in (15cm) diam.
£135–150 / €200–220
$230–260 DAN

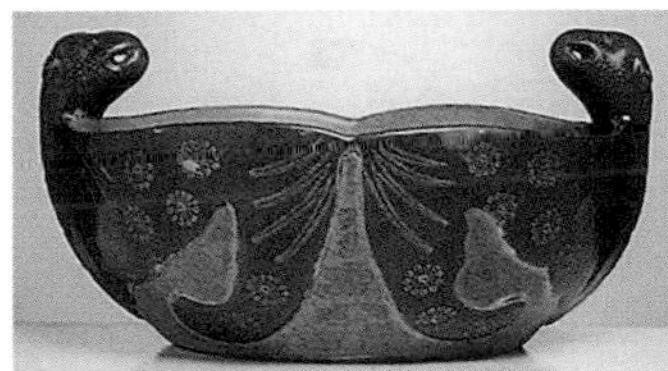

A 'bat' bowl, with gilt detail, Daoguang mark and period, 1821–50, 7¼in (18.5cm) wide.
£2,250–2,700 / €3,200–3,800
$3,700–4,450 B

► **A fish bowl,** decorated with chinoiserie scenes with a cherry blossom and Greek key border, late 19thC, 15in (38cm) diam.
£230–280 / €330–390
$390–470 Mit

A Chinese export porcelain armorial bowl, hairline crack, c1755, 10¼in (26cm) diam.
£1,100–1,300 / €1,600–1,900
$1,850–2,200 EH

A bowl, from the *Tek Sing* cargo, decorated with a figure of a boy, c1822, 6in (15cm) diam.
£220–250 / €320–360
$380–420 RBA
The *Tek Sing* sank in the Gaspar Straits in 1822.

A Canton bowl, with panelled decoration of figures, birds and flowers, 19thC, 16¼in (41.5cm) wide.
£260–310 / €380–450
$440–520 G(L)

Boxes

A stationery box and cover, the cover painted with a cloud-capped mountainous landscape scene with a figure beside a waterfall, the sides with ten ribbon-tied Buddhist symbols, some damage, Tianqi period, 1621–27, 8in (20.5cm) long.
£3,300–3,950 / €4,750–5,700
$5,500–6,600 B
This piece was produced for the Japanese market.

A box and cover, painted with a woman and three children beside a pavilion enclosed by a border of stylized flowers and *ruyi* heads, Transitional period, c1650, 8in (20.5cm) diam.
£5,000–6,000 / €7,200–8,600
$8,400–10,100 S(O)
Transitional wares have trebled in price recently as the mainland Chinese dealers have come into the market.

Further reading

Miller's Chinese & Japanese Antiques Buyer's Guide, Miller's Publications, 2004

A blue and white box and cover, the cover depicting boys at play, the base painted with garden scenes, 19thC, 6¼in (16cm) diam.
£1,300–1,550 / €1,900–2,250
$2,200–2,600 S(O)

A *famille rose* box and cover, decorated with flowers, Guangxu period and mark, 1875–1908, 9in (23cm) diam.
£2,000–2,400 / €2,900–3,450
$3,350–4,000 BUK

Brushpots

A brushpot, depicting two figures watching fishermen in a boat, restored, Kangxi period, 1662–1722, 8in (20.5cm) diam.
£1,200–1,450 / €1,750–2,100
$2,000–2,400 B

A *famille rose* brushpot, enamelled with a seated scholar and a woman in a garden, Yongzheng period, 1723–35, 4¾in (12cm) high.
£2,400–2,900
€3,500–4,200
$4,000–4,800 S(O)

A brushpot, the 'gunpowder' glaze with silver metallic streaks, 18thC, 5¼in (13.5cm) high.
£3,850–4,600
€5,500–6,600
$6,400–7,700 S(O)
This is quite a rare glaze, and of particular appeal to the Chinese.

Miller's Compares

I. A brushpot, depicting scholars seated in a rocky landscape, below a hatched chevron border, Transitional period, c1650, 5¼in (13.5cm) high.
£9,000–10,800
€13,000–15,500
$15,100–18,100 S(O)

II. A brushpot, depicting a boy on a buffalo, with *anhua* borders, Transitional period, c1650, 5¾in (14.5cm) high.
£6,000–7,200
€8,600–10,300
$10,100–12,100 S(O)

Item I, although the same height as Item II, is much wider and has more exciting painting. It is overall a more desirable pot to the Chinese taste.

Transitional wares

Between 1620 and 1683 there was a period of political upheaval in China during the transition from the Ming to the Qing Dynasties. Imperial orders diminished and the potters of Jingdezhen had to search for new markets. New shapes, exceptionally good glazes and a high standard of painting were hallmarks of a new and exciting production aimed at the Western market. These wares are currently the subject of a collecting vogue in China and the price for the better pieces has quadrupled in two years.

Brush Rests & Stands

A brush rest, Kangxi period, 1662–1722, 3¾in (9.5cm) wide.
£280–340 / €400–480
$470–560 L

Yixing pottery

The Yixing pottery culture originated in the 11th century and reached maturity in the 16th century. The area became particularly famous for purple clay teapots and scholars' tableware. The high kaolin content of the clay used meant that pieces could be fired to a high temperature to give a strong stone-like quality.

A Yixing stoneware enamelled brush stand, modelled as a pierced seedpod on a leaf base, with a lotus flower water reservoir to one side, 18thC, 4½in (11.5cm) diam.
£3,000–3,600 / €4,350–5,200
$5,000–6,000 S

Brush Washers

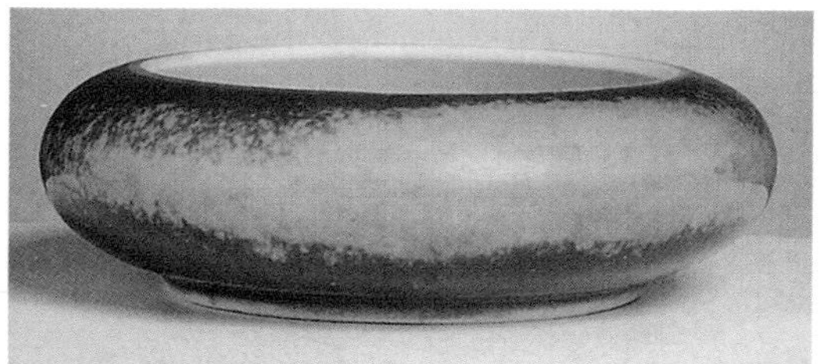

A brush washer, decorated with a peachbloom glaze, the interior glazed white, cracks and chips, Kangxi mark and period, 1662–1722, 4½in (11.5cm) diam.
£2,000–2,400 / €2,900–3,450
$3,350–4,000 B
Ex-du Boulay collection.
The condition of this piece has adversely affected the price.

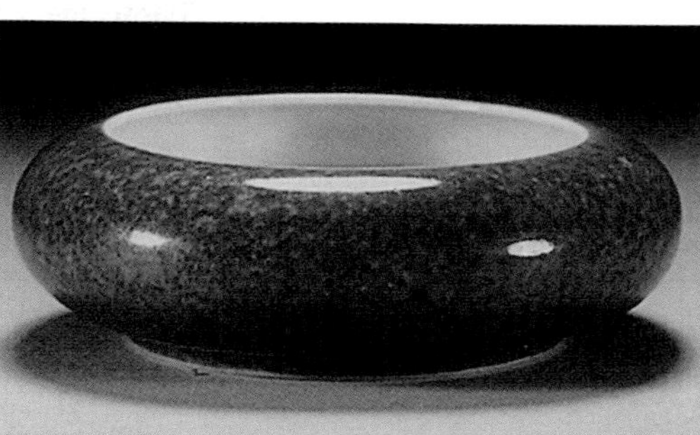

A brush washer, decorated with a peachbloom glaze, Kangxi mark and period, 1662–1722, 4¾in (12cm) diam.
£7,800–9,300 / €11,200–13,400
$13,100–15,600 S(O)
This piece achieved a high price because of its perfect condition.

◄ **A *faux* bamboo porcelain brush washer,** moulded in relief with bamboo sprigs, 19thC, 4in (10cm) wide, on a wooden stand.
£1,200–1,450
€1,750–2,100
$2,000–2,400 S(O)

A brush washer, modelled as a conch shell, the interior glaze mottled in iron-red and gilt splashes, Daoguang period, 1821–50, 3½in (9cm) wide.
£1,500–1,800 / €2,150–2,550
$2,500–3,000 B
Ex-du Boulay collection.

Candlesticks & Holders

◄ **A Longquan celadon taper holder,** with biscuit-moulded decoration of the Eight Immortals, Ming Dynasty, 15th/16thC, 9½in (24cm) high, on a wooden stand.
£3,600–4,300
€5,200–6,200
$6,000–7,200 S(O)

A candle holder, from the Vung Tau cargo, 1690–1700, 2in (5cm) high.
£155–175 / €220–250
$270–300 McP

◄ **A porcelain candlestick,** surmounted by a gilt-bronze sconce, Transitional period, c1640, 10½in (26.5cm) high.
£940–1,100
€1,400–1,650
$1,600–1,900 B

Censers

A Longquan celadon censer, carved with foliage, on three feet, restored, Ming Dynasty, 14thC, 11¾in (30cm) diam.
£320–380 / €460–550
$540–640 WW

A Longquan celadon censer, incised with stylized foliage and horizontal lines, on three animal-head feet, early Ming Dynasty, c1400, 8in (20.5cm) diam.
£990–1,100 / €1,450–1,600
$1,650–1,850 ⊞ G&G

A censer and cover, modelled as a two-tiered pagoda, the cover moulded as the roof and surmounted by a lotus finial, minor damage, finial restored, Wanli period, 1573–1619, 8¼in (21cm) high.
£4,450–5,300 / €6,400–7,600
$7,500–8,900 B
This piece was produced for the Japanese market.

A *blanc-de-Chine* censer, Kangxi period, 1662–1722, 6in (15cm) diam.
£630–700 / €900–1,000
$1,000–1,200 ⊞ GLD

◄ **A tripod censer,** 18thC, 7½in (19cm) diam.
£1,100–1,300 / €1,600–1,900
$1,850–2,200 S(O)

Condiment Pots

A mustard pot, the foot with a trefoil band, some fritting, Transitional period, c1640, 4¾in (12cm) high.
£700–840 / €1,100–1,200
$1,200–1,400 B
Ex-du Boulay collection.

A pair of salts, on three feet, Qianlong period, 1736–95, 3in (7.5cm) diam.
£630–700 / €900–1,000
$1,000–1,200 ⊞ G&G

A salt, painted with a lady and a boy in a garden, the sides decorated with flowers, on a pedestal foot, Kangxi period, 1662–1722, 3in (7.5cm) wide.
£540–650 / €790–940
$920–1,100 S(O)

Cups

A Jianyao hare's fur tea bowl, Southern Song Dynasty, 1127–1279, 5in (12.5cm) diam.
£1,750–2,100 / €2,500–3,000
$2,950–3,500 B
Ex-du Boulay collection.
Markings known as 'hare's fur' result from iron oxides formed in the firing and the type of crystals that develop as the glaze cools.

A stem cup, painted with groups of officials playing *weiqi*, with later refired iron-red ground, Jiajing mark and period, 1522–66, 5½in (14cm) diam.
£3,100–3,700 / €4,500–5,300
$5,200–6,200 S(O)

A stem cup, painted with winged dragons among waves and scrolls, crack and repair, Wanli period, 1573–1619, 3in (7.5cm) high.
£1,500–1,800 / €2,200–2,600
$2,500–3,000 B
Ex-du Boulay collection.

A pair of *famille verte* cups, decorated with butterflies among flowers and grasses, the interior with a chrysanthemum, Kangxi period, 1662–1722, saucers 4½in (11.5cm) diam.
£720–860 / €1,050–1,250
$1,200–1,400 S(O)

A stem cup, decorated with scrolling lotus, Kangxi period, 1662–1722, 4¾in (12cm) high.
£1,000–1,200
€1,600–1,800
$1,800–2,000 G&G

A cup, cover and saucer, from the Vung Tau cargo, c1690, 5in (12.5cm) diam.
£470–520 / €680–750
$790–870 RBA

A tea bowl and saucer, Yongzheng period, 1723–35, cup 2½in (6.5cm) diam.
£210–240 / €320–360
$370–410 McP

► **A Chinese export *famille rose* coffee cup,** c1760, 3in (7.5cm) diam.
£65–75 / €95–110
$115–130 DAN

Ewers & Kendi

A lobed Yingqing ewer, Song Dynasty, 960–1279, 7in (18cm) high.
£480–570 / €690–820
$810–960 S(O)
Yingqing, also known as Qingbai, is a type of porcelain first produced during the Song Dynasty from Jingdezhen, Jiangxi Province.

A milk jug and cover, with contemporary northern European silver-gilt mounts, Kangxi period, 1662–1722, 5¼in (13.5cm) high.
£1,200–1,450
€1,750–2,100
$2,000–2,400 B
Ex-du Boulay collection.

A Chinese Imari jug and cover, Qianlong period, 1736–95, 8½in (21.5cm) high.
£1,650–1,850
€2,350–2,650
$2,750–3,100 G&G

A milk jug and cover, c1760, 5in (12.5cm) high.
£390–430 / €560–620
$650–720 DAN

Figures

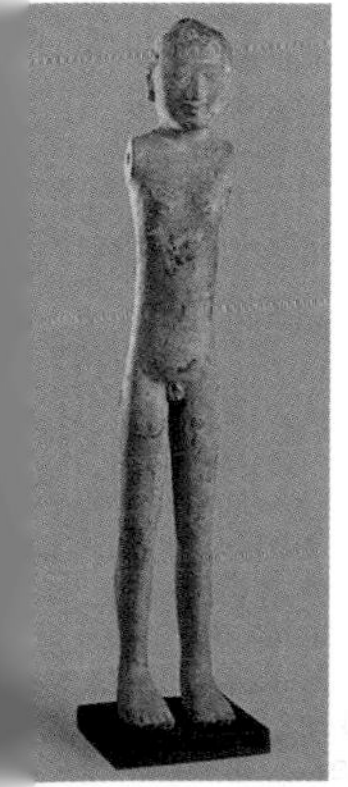

◄ **A pottery 'stickman' figure,** traces of pigment, Han Dynasty, 206 BC–AD 220, 24in (61cm) high.
£240–290
€350–420
$400–480 S
Hundreds of these figures have come out of China in recent years, keeping the price low for pieces of such antiquity.

◄ **A pair of soldiers,** Oxford T/L tested, rejoined at the waist, repair to one hand, Tang Dynasty, AD 618–907, 25in (63.5cm) high.
£3,600–4,000
€5,200–5,800
$6,000–6,700 GLD

► **A *famille verte* figure of a boy,** on a raised base, Kangxi period, 1662–1722, 11in (28cm) high.
£1,100–1,250
€1,600–1,800
$1,900–2,100 G&G

A biscuit *famille verte* waterpot, modelled as Zhong Kui reclining against a hawthorn jar, decorated with enamels, Kangxi period, 1662–1722, 7¼in (18.5cm) wide.
£4,000–4,800 / €5,800–6,900
$6,700–8,000 B
Zhong Kui is a legendary Chinese figure who is considered to be a demon-queller, usually depicted as a large, ugly man wearing a scholar's hat, a green robe and large boots, with which he stamps on offensive imps.

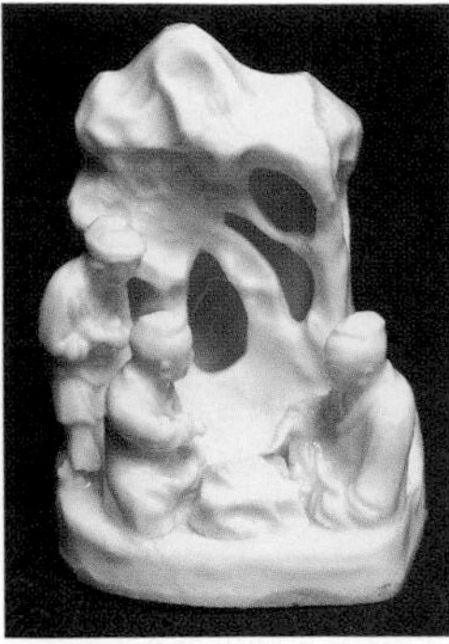

A *blanc-de-Chine* group, modelled as three figures outside a cave, c1700, 4½in (11.5cm) high.
£1,000–1,150
€1,450–1,650
$1,700–1,950 G&G

A pair of celadon figures, each holding a flower, c1750, 5¾in (14.5cm) high.
£850–950 / €1,200–1,350
$1,450–1,600 G&G

Flatware

A Longquan celadon dish, incised with stylized flowers, c1500, 12¼in (31cm) diam.
£850–950 / €1,200–1,350
$1,450–1,600 G&G

A *kraak porselein* dish, the centre decorated with birds, rockwork and flowers, some fritting, Wanli period, 1573–1619, 11¼in (28.5cm) diam.
£1,250–1,400 / €1,800–2,000
$2,100–2,350 G&G

Kraak porselein

Production of porcelain for export increased greatly during the reign of the Emperor Wanli (1573–1619). Pieces were predominantly blue and white, much of it *kraak porselein*, so-called because a cargo of such pieces was captured by the Dutch from a Portuguese carrack (*kraak* in Dutch) in 1603 and subsequently auctioned in Amsterdam amid great excitement. The decoration on this type of porcelain is enclosed in panels and the most common themes found are floral, precious objects or symbols tied with ribbons, crickets, beetles and butterflies.

◄ **A *wucai* dish,** painted with sages in a mountainous landscape, the base with a six character Chenghua mark, Tianqi period, 1621–27, 8in (20.5cm) diam.
£2,900–3,200 / €4,150–4,600
$4,900–5,400 G&G
This piece was made for the Japanese market.

A *kraak porselein* dish, Wanli period, 1573–1619, 14in (35.5cm) diam.
£1,650–1,850 / €2,400–2,650
$2,800–3,100 GLD

A set of four plates, each decorated with gilt flowers within a fretwork border set with four vignettes containing fruit and flowers, marked, Kangxi period, 1662–1722, 10¾in (27.5cm) diam.
£3,000–3,600 / €4,350–5,200
$5,000–6,000 S

A *famille verte* saucer dish, enamelled with a lady standing between a scholar's table and a stand, hairline crack, Hongzhi six character mark, Kangxi period, 1662–1722, 8¾in (22cm) diam.
£1,050–1,250 / €1,500–1,800
$1,750–2,100 B
Ex-du Boulay collection.

A spirally fluted dish, Kangxi period, 1662–1722, 10½in (26.5cm) diam.
£900–1,000 / €1,300–1,450
$1,500–1,700 ⊞ G&G

A pair of Chinese export porcelain armorial plates, each painted with a coat-of-arms surrounded by flower sprays and a demi-lion rampant, some damage, c1720, 9in (23cm) wide.
£3,000–3,600 / €4,300–5,100
$5,000–6,000 TEN

A set of six plates, Qianlong period, c1750, 9in (23cm) diam.
£1,500–1,650 / €2,150–2,400
$2,500–2,750 ⊞ McP

famille rose plate, c1760, in (23cm) diam.
270–300 / €390–430
450–500 ⊞ DAN

A dish, enamelled in Master of the Rocks style, the reverse with two *wucai* floral sprays, restored, rim cracks, Xuande six character mark, Kangxi period, c1670, 11in (28cm) diam.
£2,800–3,350 / €4,000–4,800
$4,700–5,600 B
Ex-du Boulay collection.

A *rouge de fer* armorial plate, painted with a central coat-of-arms within a diaper border, the rim with flower sprays and a crest of a fired beacon, c1722, 9½in (24cm) diam.
£780–940 / €1,100–1,300
$1,300–1,550 S

► **A pair of armorial plates,** c1750, 9in (23cm) diam.
£1,300–1,450 / €1,900–2,100
$2,200–2,450 ⊞ McP

A pair of *famille verte* plates, Kangxi period, c1700, 9in (23cm) diam.
£700–780 / €1,000–1,100
$1,200–1,300 ⊞ McP

A soup dish, from the Nanking cargo, decorated with Willow Terrace and Peony pattern, c1750, 9in (23cm) diam.
£360–400 / €520–580
$600–660 ⊞ RBA

Miller's Compares

I. A chrysanthemum dish, moulded with forty fluted petals, with *café-au-lait* glaze on a white-glazed base, repaired, Qianlong mark and period, 1736–95, 7¼in (18.5cm) diam.
£3,750–4,500 / €5,400–6,500
$6,300–7,600 B
Ex-du Boulay collection.

II. A saucer dish, moulded with lobed sides, with coral glaze on a white-glazed base, some over-painting and wear, Yongzheng six character mark, 1723–35, 6¼in (16cm) diam.
£1,900–2,250 / €2,750–3,300
$3,200–3,850 B
Ex-du Boulay collection.

There is very little difference in date between these dishes and they both came from the famed du Boulay collection. However, a *café-au-lait* glaze, as seen on Item I, is much rarer than a coral glaze (Item II) on porcelain which bears the correct mark for the period.

A pair of moulded dishes, Dutch-decorated, Qianlong period, 1736–95, 9in (23cm) diam.
£2,700–3,000 / €3,900–4,300
$4,500–5,000 ⊞ GLD

A *famille rose* dish, decorated with a gilt nude figure enclosed by a flower garland, the border with three men and three cockerels interspersed with flowers, slight damage, Qianlong period, 1736–95, 11¾in (30cm) diam.
£4,000–4,500 / €5,800–6,500
$6,850–7,600 ⊞ G&G

A dish, decorated with a pagoda landscape, 18thC, 15in (38cm) diam.
£230–270 / €330–390
$390–460 ⚒ WW
This dish achieved a comparatively high price owing to its large size.

► A set of four *famille rose* plates, each decorated with an artemesia leaf, antiquities and flowering peonies, the border decorated with a similar pattern reserved on a trellis diaper background, some damage, 18thC, 9in (23cm) diam.
£570–680 / €820–980
$960–1,150 ⚒ S(Am)

A soup plate, c1775, 9in (23cm) diam.
£110–125 / €160–180
$190–210 ⊞ DAN

A starburst dish, from the *Diana* cargo, 1817, 11in (28cm) diam.
£310–350 / €450–500
$540–600 ⊞ RBA
The *Diana* sank off the coast of Malacca in 1817 and the cargo was recovered in 1985.

A Canton *famille rose* dish, the centre gilded with Persian script framed by six panels alternating with figures, birds and flowers, heightened in gilt, restored, 19thC, 12¾in (32.5cm) diam.
£520–620 / €750–890
$880–1,050 ⚒ RTo

◄ A Canton porcelain dish, painted with butterflies and insects, late 19thC, 15in (38cm) diam.
£260–310 / €380–450
$440–520 ⚒ CGC

A European subject dish, after a contemporary engraving, with shipwrecked figures on a rocky shore, with two children nearby, repaired, 18thC, 8in (20.5cm) diam.
£330–390 / €470–560
$550–650 ⚒ S(Am)

A meat plate, painted with a pagoda in a lake landscape, 19thC, 10½in (26.5cm) wide.
£220–260 / €310–370
$370–440 ⚒ SWO

A pair of *famille rose* plates, each decorated with characters, two butterflies and sprays of flowers, the rims with a border of butterflies and characters, chips and cracks, Guangxu seal mark and period, 1875–1908, 9½in (24cm) diam.
£490–590 / €700–840
$820–980 ⚒ S(Am)
These plates were probably made at the order of the Guangxu Emperor to celebrate the marriage of one of his generals.

Garden Seats

◄ **A Longquan celadon garden seat,** Ming Dynasty, 14th/15thC, 15in (38cm) high.
£3,750–4,500
€5,400–6,500
$6,400–7,600 B
Ex-du Boulay collection.

► **A pair of *famille rose* garden seats,** c1890, 18½in (47cm) high.
£4,500–5,400
€6,500–7,800
$7,600–9,100 BUK
Matching pairs always command a premium.

A porcelain garden seat, decorated with enamels, damaged, late 19thC, 18½in (47cm) high.
£450–540 / €650–780
$760–910 SWO

Jardinières

A jardinière, the body decorated with two dragons chasing the flaming pearl, 17thC, 9½in (24cm) diam.
£570–680 / €820–980
$960–1,150 S(Am)

A ***famille rose* jardinière,** decorated with flowers and scrolls, on four stylized dragon-scroll feet, Qianlong period, 1736–95, 11¾in (30cm) diam.
£9,700–11,600 / €14,000–16,700
$16,300–19,500 S(HK)
This jardinière is very much to the Hong Kong taste and therefore achieved a high price.

A ***famille rose* jardinière,** enamelled with figures in a garden landscape, the interior with a lady playing a stringed instrument and another seated on a bench, Jiaqing seal mark and period, 1796–1820, 10½in (26.5cm) wide.
£2,800–3,350 / €4,000–4,800
$4,700–5,600 B

◄ **A jardinière,** painted with a landscape of fishermen in boats and figures on bridges, below a key-fret band, 19thC, 15½in (39.5cm) diam.
£1,400–1,650 / €2,000–2,350
$2,350–2,750 B

► **A jardinière,** hairline cracks, late 19thC, 15½in (39.5cm) diam, with root-wood stand.
£330–400 / €480–570
$550–670 SWO

Jars

A glazed jar and cover, Oxford T/L tested, Song Dynasty, 11thC, 18in (45.5cm) high.
£4,000–4,500 / €5,800–6,500
$6,700–7,600 GLD

► **A jar,** decorated with squirrels and vines, chip, c1600, 5½in (14cm) high.
£1,050–1,200 / €1,500–1,700
$1,800–2,000 G&G

◄ **A *fahua* jar,** restored, cracks, c1500, 12½in (32cm) high.
£4,000–4,800 / €5,800–6,900
$6,700–8,100 B
***Fahua* is a type of *sancai*, or three-colour ware. It usually has a turquoise or purple-blue ground and dates from the late 15th/early 16th centuries.**

A jar, metal lid later, Transitional period, c1640, 2in (5cm) high.
£2,900–3,200
€4,150–4,600
$4,900–5,400 ⊞ GLD

A Chinese export porcelain jar and cover, c1760, 6in (15cm) high.
£300–340 / €430–500
$500–570 ⊞ DAN

A jar, the body painted with flying bats among *ruyi*-head cloud scrolls, Qianlong period, 1736–95, 7in (18cm) high.
£2,000–2,400
€2,900–3,450
$3,350–4,000 ⚒ B

An Imperial jar, hairline crack, Daoguang seal mark and period, 1821–50, 9¼in (23.5cm) high.
£3,750–4,500
€5,400–6,500
$6,400–7,600 ⚒ B

Mugs & Tankards

A pair of porcelain mugs, painted in the Imari palette with prunus and flowers within scrolled borders, marked, early 18thC, larger 3¾in (10.5cm) high.
£140–165 / €200–240
$230–270 ⚒ BR

A pair of Chinese Imari chocolate mugs, each decorated with birds in a flowering rocky landscape, Qianlong period, 1662–1722, 5¼in (13.5cm) high.
£1,550–1,750 / €2,200–2,500
$2,600–2,950 ⊞ G&G

A Dehua mug, with embossed borders of stiff leaves, painted in enamel with scrolling plants, with gilded highlights, cracks and chips, 1700–20, 3¾in (9.5cm) high.
£730–880 / €1,050–1,250
$1,250–1,500 ⚒ B
Dehua is a town in Southern China where much *blanc-de-Chine* was produced.

◀ **A *famille rose* mug,** decorated with peonies and chrysanthemums, Qianlong period, 1736–95, 5in (12.5cm) high.
£790–880 / €1,150–1,300
$1,350–1,500 ⊞ G&G

▶ **An armorial tankard,** decorated with sprigs of flowers surrounding the arms, beneath a border of gilt stars, with a double strap handle, c1790, 5½in (14cm) high.
£720–860 / €1,050–1,250
$1,200–1,450 ⚒ S

Sauce Boats

A *famille rose* sauce boat, Qianlong period, 1736–95, 7¾in (19.5cm) long.
£790–880 / €1,150–1,300
$1,350–1,500 ⊞ G&G

A pair of *famille rose* sauce boats, decorated with antiques and flowers, one repaired, Qianlong period, 1736–95, 9¼in (23.5cm) wide.
£1,200–1,400 / €1,700–2,000
$2,000–2,400 ⚒ BUK

A sauce boat, from the Nanking cargo, decorated with a pine tree and peonies, c1750, 7in (18cm) wide.
£1,650–1,850 / €2,350–2,600
$2,800–3,100 ⊞ RBA

Snuff Bottles

◄ **A porcelain snuff bottle,** painted with stylized flowers and scrolling foliage, 1780–1850, 3in (7.5cm) high.
£1,600–1,800
€2,300–2,600
$2,700–3,000 ⊞ RHa

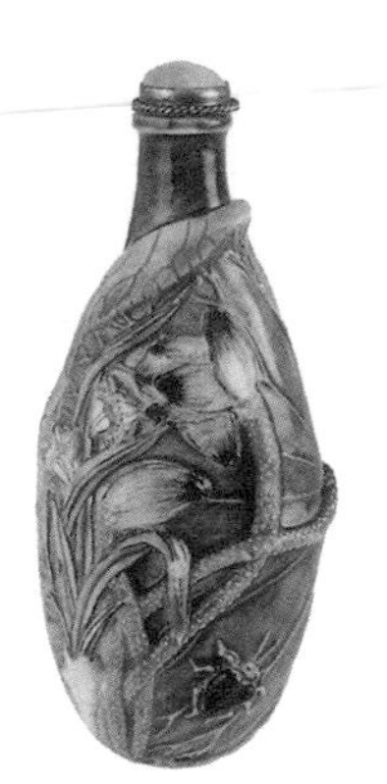

► **A *famille rose* snuff bottle,** relief-moulded as a lotus leaf wrapped around a bottle, 1840–1900, 3¼in (8.5cm) high.
£600–720 / €850–1,000
$1,000–1,200 ⚒ S(O)

A porcelain snuff bottle, 1800–80, 3in (7.5cm) high.
£1,050–1,200
€1,500–1,700
$1,750–2,000 ⊞ RHa

Tea Canisters

◄ **A *famille rose* tea canister,** painted with a lady by a fence, flowers growing from a rock and precious objects with a vase, replacement silver cover and neck, Kangxi period, 1662–1722, 7in (18cm) high.
£1,100–1,250
€1,600–1,800
$1,850–2,050 ⊞ G&G
This piece would originally have had a porcelain neck and cover.

A tea canister, with later silver mount, leaf mark to base, Kangxi period, 1662–1722, 5½in (14cm) high.
£660–790 / €950–1,100
$1,100–1,300 ⚒ S(O)

A pair of Chinese Imari tea canisters, the grooved surfaces decorated with prunus, with wooden lids, one with rim and glaze cracks, Kangxi period, 1662–1722, 4in (10cm) high.
£740–880 / €1,050–1,250
$1,250–1,500 ⚒ BUK

Teapots

A *famille noire* teapot and cover, Yongzheng period, 1723–35, 4½in (11.5cm) high.
£780–870 / €1,100–1,250
$1,350–1,450 ⊞ McP

A Chinese Imari teapot and cover, from the Nanking cargo, c1750, 5in (12.5cm) high.
£430–480 / €620–690
$720–800 ⊞ RBA

A *famille rose* Cadogan teapot, modelled as a dog of *Fo* clutching a ball, spout reglued, late 18thC, 5¾in (14.5cm) high.
£1,400–1,650 / €2,000–2,400
$2,350–2,800 ⚒ WW
This type of teapot derives its name from the Earl of Cadogan, who was the first Englishman to own one. When shipped from China in the 18th century, they were filled with tea to avoid damage and were therefore presumed to be teapots, although strictly speaking they are wine pourers. They are lidless pots into which liquid is poured through a hole in the bottom and which is then quickly turned the right way up. An interior funnel prevents the liquid from leaking out through the hole. This particular example is a very rare shape.

A *sancai*-glazed Cadogan teapot, 19thC, 5½in (14cm) high.
£310–370 / €450–540
$520–620 ⚒ S(O)

A tortoiseshell-veneered teapot and cover, faint seal mark, Guangxu period, 1875–1908, 5¼in (13.5cm) wide.
£1,400–1,650 / €2,000–2,400
$2,350–2,800 ⚒ WW
This is a very rare teapot.

Tureens

A *famille rose* tureen, cover and stand, decorated with panels of figures on a scale ground, small chips, stand associated, 18thC, 7¾in (19.5cm) wide.
£700–840 / €1,000–1,200
$1,150–1,350 WW

A *famille rose* armorial tureen and cover, decorated with flower sprays and a coat-of-arms, cracks, cover handle damaged, c1755, 14¼in (36cm) wide.
£1,700–2,000 / €2,450–2,900
$2,850–3,400 WW

A tureen, cover and stand, decorated with sprays of flowers beneath a border of enclosed panels, symbols and horns with flowers, stand associated, Qianlong period, 1736–95, stand 15½in (39.5cm) wide.
£650–780 / €950–1,100
$1,100–1,300 S(Am)

Further reading

Miller's Porcelain Antiques Checklist, Miller's Publications, 2000

A tureen and cover, from the Nanking cargo, decorated with Lattice Fence pattern, with pagodas and flowering trees, the cover with a pomegranate finial, c1750, 9in (23cm) diam.
£5,800–6,500 / €8,400–9,300
$9,700–10,700 RBA

A Chinese export tureen and cover, decorated with a landscape, applied mask handles, 19thC, 11½in (29cm) wide.
£540–640 / €780–930
$900–1,050 SWO

Vases

A neolithic vase, Oxford T/L tested, 3000 BC, 14in (35.5cm) high.
£2,000–2,500
€2,900–3,600
$3,400–4,200 GLD

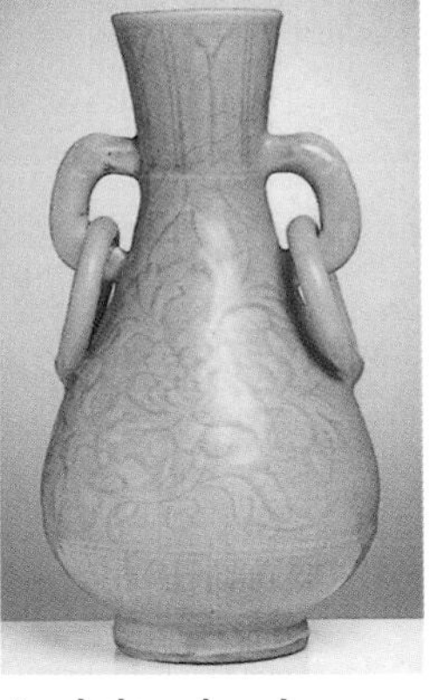

A celadon-glazed vase, applied with two elephant-mask handles suspending fixed rings, 14thC, 11¾in (30cm) high.
£1,600–1,900
€2,300–2,750
$2,700–3,200 B

◄ **A vase,** decorated with panels of flowers in watery landscapes on a diaper ground, base cracked and repaired, Kangxi period, 1662–1722, 20in (51cm) high.
£960–1,150
€1,400–1,650
$1,600–1,900 WW

A vase, decorated with panels of flowers, birds, geometric and diaper panels, the neck and foot with conforming panelled borders, Wanli period, 1573–1619, 13¾in (35cm) high.
£3,000–3,600
€4,300–5,100
$5,000–6,000 HYD

A bottle vase, painted with herons in flight among stylized clouds, Wanli period, 1573–1619, 12½in (32cm) high.
£4,900–5,900
€7,100–8,500
$8,300–9,900 Bea

◄ **A *wucai* vase and cover,** painted with two lion dogs among flowers and foliage, the cover and neck marked with six-character Xuande marks, 17thC, 5in (12.5cm) high, with wooden stand and case.
£530–630 / €760–910
$890–1,050 WW

Asian symbols

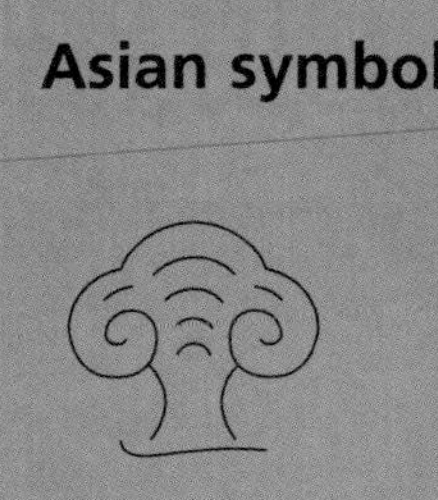
Lingzhi – the sacred fungus

Shou – the symbol for long life

Lotus – there are many variations of this device, which is used as a repetitive decoration

Fuku – based on the Chinese character for good fortune and happiness, this symbol appears on Japanese porcelain of the 17thC

A vase and cover, from the Vung Tau cargo, c1690, 7in (18cm) high.
£530–590 / €760–840
$890–980 ⊞ RBA

A *flambé*-glazed beaker vase, modelled as an archaic bronze vessel, the interior moulded with a raised square carved with a seal mark, Yongzheng/Qianlong period, 1723–95, 12½in (32cm) high.
£11,000–13,200
€16,000–19,200
$18,500–22,200 S(HK)

A glazed bottle vase, on a spreading foot, Yongzheng mark and period, 1723–35, 11in (28cm) high.
£3,600–4,300
€5,200–6,200
$6,000–7,200 S

A pair of vases and covers, with moulded outlined cartouches painted with river landscapes, reserved on a moulded cod's roe ground, Qianlong period, 1736–95, 10½in (26.5cm) high.
£260–310 / €370–440
$430–510 L

◄ **A 'robin's egg' glazed vase,** with applied elephant-head handles, on a spreading foot, chips to rim and foot, 18thC, 4in (10cm) high.
£1,050–1,250
€1,500–1,800
$1,750–2,100 B
Ex-du Boulay collection.

A vase, decorated with flowering tendrils, with Ming-style 'heaping' and 'piling', Yongzheng mark within a double circle, paper labels, 1723–35, 10in (25.5cm) high.
£120,000–144,000
€173,000–207,000
$200,000–240,000 HYD
This is an Imperial piece made for the Emperor, and therefore of exceptional quality.

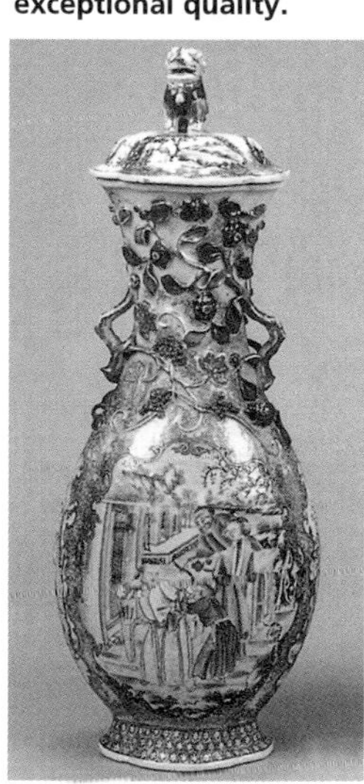

A pair of *famille rose* vases and covers, the sides decorated with panels of figures on a gilt flower scroll ground, the covers with dog of *Fo* finials, firing crack, gilding rubbed, Qianlong period, 1736–95, 14¼in (36cm) high.
£3,200–3,800
€4,600–5,500
$5,400–6,400 DN

A pair of glazed biscuit wall vases, applied with a *taotie* mask holding a ring handle, moulded with shaped chrysanthemum and foliage, Kangxi period, 1662–1722, 6in (15cm) high.
£660–790 / €950–1,100
$1,100–1,300 S(Am)

A porcelain *famille verte* vase, decorated with birds among rockwork and prunus blossom, restored, 18thC, 13¾in (35cm) high.
£1,400–1,650
€2,000–2,400
$2,350–2,800 S

A vase, the neck decorated with a foliate scroll of stylized lotus blooms, above a medallion of three phoenix surrounded by tufts of clouds between a band of lappets and a border of pendant *ruyi* heads, the sides with handles, 18thC, 14in (35.5cm) high.
£3,550–4,250
€5,100–6,100
$6,000–7,200 S(NY)

Miller's Compares

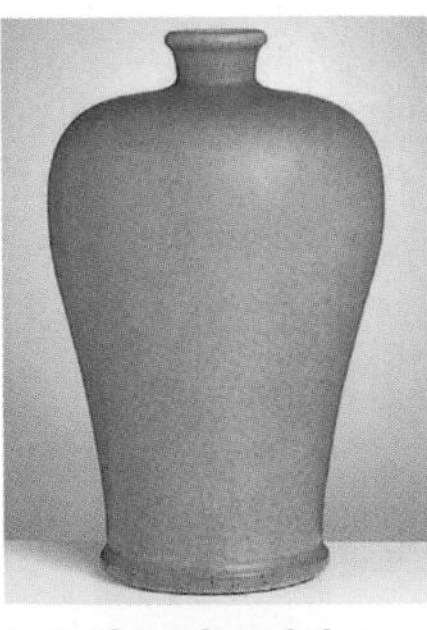

I. A glazed *meiping*, with everted rim, 18thC, 8½in (21.5cm) high.
£2,100–2,500
€3,000–3,600
$3,500–4,200 B
Ex-du Boulay collection.

II. A glazed vase, on a tapering foot, white-glazed interior, 18thC, 4½in (11.5cm) high.
£590–700
€850–1,000
$990–1,100 B
Ex-du Boulay collection.

These vases are of a similar colour and date, but Item I has a much better and more even crackle glaze. As well as being larger in size, Item I is also a more pleasing shape than Item II.

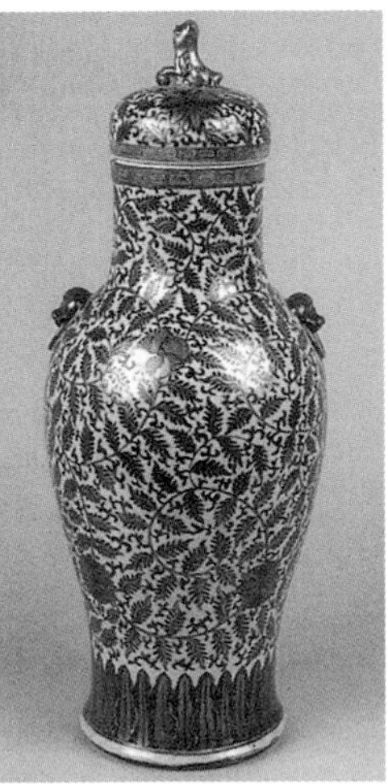

A pair of gilded vases, and one cover, painted with stylized peony scrolling foliage, the shoulders with lion mask handles, Daoguang period, 1821–50, 26in (66cm) high.
£540–640 / €780–930
$910–1,050 L

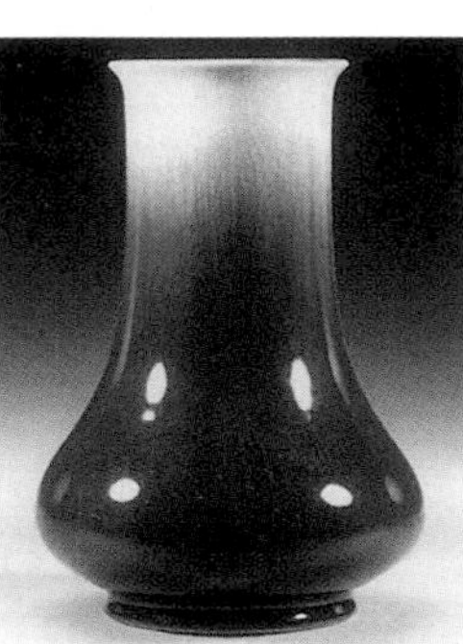

A *flambé*-glazed vase, with stand, 19thC, 9½in (24cm) high.
£540–640 / €780–930
$910–1,050 S(O)

A pair of crackle-glazed vases, decorated with dragons among flowers, moulded lion ring handles, impressed mark, 19thC, 13¾in (35cm) high.
£500–600 / €720–860
$840–1,000 TRM

◄ **A glazed vase,** carved with flowers and archaic symbols, 19thC, 22¾in (58cm) high.
£630–750 / €900–1,050
$1,050–1,250 WW

A *flambé*-glazed vase, with white-glazed interior, c1800, 14¾in (37.5cm) high.
£500–600 / €720–860
$840–1,000 S(Am)

A *famille verte* bottle vase, decorated with mythological beasts on a ground carved with waves and enamelled with flames, six-character Kangxi mark, 19thC, 18½in (47cm) high, with a wooden stand.
£1,750–2,000
€2,500–3,000
$2,950–3,500 DN

A celadon *kong* vase, 19thC, 11in (28cm) high.
£200–240 / €290–340
$340–400 SWO
***Kong* is the term for the shape of this vase.**

► **A bottle vase,** with white rim and interior, late 19thC, 15¾in (40cm) high.
£1,650–1,950
€2,400–2,850
$2,800–3,350 S(Am)

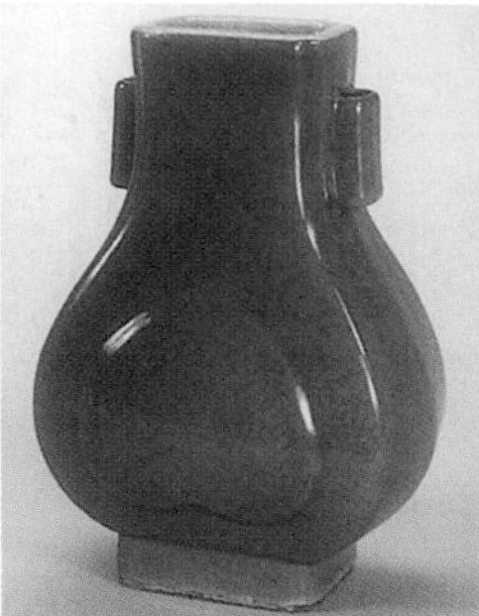

A crackle-glazed vase, Yongzheng seal mark, early 19thC, 11¾in (32.5cm) high.
£750–900 / €1,100–1,300
$1,250–1,500 NOA

A *famille verte* vase, decorated with figures and deities in a landscape, with a carved wood cover, 19thC, 16in (40.5cm) high.
£190–220 / €270–320
$320–380 G(L)

A flower vase, in five lobed sections with six necks, decorated with birds among flowers and foliage 19thC, 8in (20.5cm) high.
£420–500 / €600–720
$700–840 WW

Miscellaneous

A pair of Canton *famille rose* bough pots, painted with panels of figures, birds, flowers and butterflies on a gilt ground applied with squirrels, fruit and leaves, with pierced covers and rope-twist handles, repaired, mid-19thC, 9in (23cm) high.
£2,700–3,200 / €3,900–4,650
$4,650–5,500 ⚒ WW
These bough pots are very popular with interior designers, particularly when in pairs.

A flask, decorated with figures and landscapes, small chips and frits, Kangxi period, 1662–1722, 11in (28cm) high.
£1,200–1,400
€1,700–2,000
$2,000–2,400 ⚒ WW
Chinese rice wine flasks are rare.

A near pair of *famille verte* guglets, decorated with stemmed chrysanthemums and lotus, the necks decorated with bands of stylized flowerheads, one with rim chips, Kangxi period, 1662–1722, 10in (25.5cm) high.
£3,150–3,500
€4,500–5,000
$5,300–5,900 ⊞ G&G
Originally these would have sat in a matching round basin, and are the 18th-century version of the 19th-century jug and basin set for bedrooms.

A lidded jar, from the Vung Tau cargo, 1690–1700, 6in (15cm) high.
£130–145 / €190–210
$220–250 ⊞ McP

A *famille verte* plaque, decorated with figures in buildings within a floral and foliate border, in a wooden frame, 19thC, 14½ x 11½in (37 x 29cm).
£350–420 / €500–600
$600–720 ⚒ WW

Items in the Miscellaneous section have been arranged in alphabetical order.

A pair of *famille rose* strainers, decorated with floral sprays, Qianlong period, 1736–95, 8in (20.5cm) diam.
£670–750 / €970–1,100
$1,100–1,250 ⊞ G&G

A tray, the sides painted with a lotus-lappet band, the everted rim centred with a bat flanked by stylized lotus and a *ruyi* head at each corner, on four *ruyi*-scroll feet, Qianlong seal mark and period, 1736–95, 10in (25.5cm) wide.
£2,100–2,500
€3,000–3,600
$3,500–4,200 ⚒ B

A Chinese export armorial tea service, comprising eight pieces, Qianlong period, 1736–95, teapot 5in (14cm) high.
£1,800–2,150 / €2,600–3,100
$3,000–3,600 ⚒ G(L)

▶ **A pair of *famille rose* wine pots,** modelled as Buddhistic lions crouched on balls, the hollow bodies with flattened loop handles and short spouts, one spout restored, mid-18thC, 5½in (14cm) high.
£2,900–3,450 / €4,200–5,000
$4,900–5,800 ⚒ B

A *famille rose* fluted spoon tray, painted with leaf and scroll motifs, Qianlong period, 1736–95, 5in (12.5cm) wide.
£230–270 / €330–390
$380–450 ⚒ WW

A wrist rest, with marbled glaze, minor restoration, Song Dynasty, 11th/12thC, 5½in (14cm) wide.
£1,600–1,800
€2,300–2,600
$2,700–3,000 ⊞ GLD

Japanese Ceramics

Unlike the vibrant Chinese economy, Japan is still in a depression that has lasted for ten years. With few buyers from Japan, consignors are reluctant to offer goods to a weakened market but this could therefore be an opportune time to consider starting a collection of Japanese antiques.

The mainstay of the Japanese ceramic trade is the traditional Imari pattern exported to the West for 200 years or more. The prices of wares from the early Genroku period (1688–1703), in such demand ten years ago, seem to have levelled out to about a third of previous values. However, interior designers still go after pairs of large, decorative pieces, made evident by the £7,200 / €10,300 / $12,100 paid recently for a pair of 18th-century hexagonal jardinières. Early 17th-century Imari figures are also down in price although, again, large pairs are still popular in the decorators' market.

Satsuma wares have a strong following in the West. The painstakingly detailed decoration is much appreciated and the gap between poor and excellent quality is obvious. The best pieces still find a ready market although prices are down: a Meiji period Imperial vase by Satsuma Yaki (see page 323) sold for considerably less than could have been expected four or five years ago.

Early Kutani is among the most sought-after Japanese porcelain. The kiln was established in Kutani, Kaga Province, in 1656 and is generally known as Ao-kutani (green Kutani) because of the predominance of a dark green enamel. These pieces rarely appear on the market and are notoriously difficult to authenticate. Late 19th-century Kutani is often dismissed as being unworthy of collecting but some of the output was exceptional, such as the large baluster vase by Hyoyu, pictured on page 323.

The attraction of Kakiemon continues, with collectors still willing to pay high prices for the best pieces. A well documented 17th-century jar in perfect condition recently fetched £13,200 / €19,400 / $22,200 (see page 322).

High-quality Hirado wares, which have some of the best underglaze blue painting in Japan, are increasing in value. This is illustrated by the beautifully painted lidded jar shown on page 322. Such pieces are still undervalued and worth consideration by collectors.

The current fashion for 20th-century art and design is reflected in the continued rise in prices for Japanese studio ceramics. It is important to retain the original fitted wooden boxes with which these pieces are sold: being signed, they help to confirm the provenance of the piece. **Peter Wain**

Animals

An Arita model of a cockerel, the wing and tail feathers with incised detail, probably late 17thC, 8½in (21.5cm) high.
£1,200–1,400 / €1,700–2,000
$2,000–2,400 ⚒ B

A Hirado model of a rabbit, with engraved details, Meiji period, 1868–1911, 7½in (19cm) long.
£960–1,150 / €1,400–1,650
$1,600–1,900 ⚒ S(O)

A Satsuma earthenware model of a *shishi*, resting on a textured ball, decorated in gilt and coloured enamels, Meiji period, 1868–1911, 21¼in (54cm) long.
£960–1,100 / €1,400–1,650
$1,600–1,900 ⚒ S(O)

A Kutani hanging flower vase, modelled as a duck, with enamelled and gilded plumage, Meiji period, 1868–1911, 12¼in (31cm) long.
£1,200–1,400 / €1,750–2,100
$2,000–2,400 ⚒ S(O)

A Tsuboya *yaki* model of a dragon, seated and coiled, clutching the sacred pearl in its claws, Meiji period, 1868–1911, 6¾in (17cm) long.
£360–430 / €520–620
$600–660 ⚒ S(O)

A pair of Imari models of dogs, with comical faces, decorated with flowers and leaves, c1900, 4¾in (12cm) high.
£200–240 / €300–360
$350–420 ⚒ WW

Bottles

An Imari bottle, decorated with sprays of peony, chrysanthemums and foliage, late 17thC, 11in (28cm) high.
£1,550–1,850
€2,250–2,700
$2,600–3,100 S(O)
In 1964 this bottle was purchased for £7 / €10 / $12.

A Kakiemon-style sake bottle, painted with two children, late 17thC, 10in (25.5cm) high.
£7,800–9,400
€11,200–13,400
$13,100–15,700 S(O)
In 1966 this bottle was purchased for £20 / €29 / $33.

An Imari bottle, with an everted rim, decorated with scrolling *karakusa* above a band of lappets, 18thC, 12¾in (32.5cm) high.
£600–720 / €860–1,000
$1,000–1,200 S(O)

A sake bottle, decorated in the Imari palette with a basket of flowers, Meiji period, c1890, 5½in (14cm) high.
£400–450 / €580–650
$670–760 AUA

Bowls

An Arita enamelled bowl, decorated with a branch of pomegranates below panels of flowering branches with peach and prunus growing from rockwork, the exterior with three flower sprays, 1675–1725, 5½in (14cm) diam.
£410–490 / €590–700
$690–820 S(Am)

A pair of Kakiemon-style bowls, decorated in enamels and gilt with bamboo and plum emerging from rockwork and fences, the rims with a continuous peony flower spray, the reverse with birds perched on blossoming branches, early 18thC, 5in (12.5cm) diam.
£780–930 / €1,100–1,300
$1,300–1,550 S(O)

A Kakiemon-style bowl, the centre decorated with bell flowers and chrysanthemums behind rockwork, the exterior with pomegranates and flowering peony, *Fuku* mark, late 17thC, 8¾in (22cm) diam.
£2,400–2,850 / €3,450–4,100
$4,000–4,800 S(O)

An Imari porcelain 'Dutch ship' bowl, the interior painted with four panels containing sailing ships and mythological creatures around a floral medallion, the exterior with two phoenix and scrolling foliage, Meiji period, 1868–1911, 14¾in (37.5cm) diam.
£1,450–1,700 / €2,100–2,500
$2,500–3,000 Bea

► **A Satsuma bowl,** painted with figures in a mountainous landscape, signed, early 20thC, 7¼in (18.5cm) diam.
£130–150 / €190–220
$220–250 G(L)

An Imari barber's bowl, c1700, 10½in (26.5cm) diam.
£2,050–2,300 / €3,000–3,300
$3,500–3,850 G&G

A porcelain bowl and cover, decorated with a flock of birds, signed in seal form 'Makuzu Kozan sei', pierced wood cover, Meiji period, 1868–1911, 6in (15cm) diam.
£1,500–1,800 / €2,150–2,550
$2,500–2,800 S(O)

Dishes

An Imari dish, moulded in relief with maple leaves floating on swirling waters beside a basketwork breakwater, the reverse with sprays of peach, *Fuku* mark, 17thC, 6¼in (16cm) diam.
£1,650–1,950 / €2,400–2,850
$2,800–3,350 S(O)

A Satsuma earthenware dish, by Senzan, decorated in enamels and gilt with three priests at the Tosho Daigongen shrine in Nikko, bordered by swirling brocade and chrysanthemum blossoms, signed, Meiji period, 1868–1911, 12in (30.5cm) wide.
£1,550–1,850 / €2,250–2,700
$2,600–3,100 S(O)

A pair of Imari dishes, painted with a central flower-filled vase within a raised segmented border filled with panels of *ho-o* birds and landscapes, one with hairline crack to rim, Meiji period, 1868–1911, 17¼in (44cm) wide.
£600–720 / €860–1,000
$1,000–1,200 RTo

Ewers & Jugs

An Arita jug, restored haircrack and chip, c1680, 9in (23cm) high.
£990–1,100
€1,400–1,550
$1,650–1,850 G&G

A Kakiemon-style ewer, moulded with four panels of stylized wave design, the shoulder with *kiri-mon*, painted in enamels with stylized leaves and flowers, replacement wooden handle, late 17thC, 7½in (19cm) high.
£2,300–2,750
€3,300–3,950
$3,850–4,600 S(O)

A Kakiemon jug, decorated with panels of floral sprays in overglaze enamels, restored crack and minor chips, c1680, 5½in (14cm) high.
£860–960 / €1,250–1,400
$1,450–1,600 G&G

An Arita ewer, painted with a butterfly among flowers and foliage, with a grooved strap handle, drilled at side of foot, c1700, 10¼in (26cm) high.
£610–730 / €880–1,050
$1,000–1,200 WW

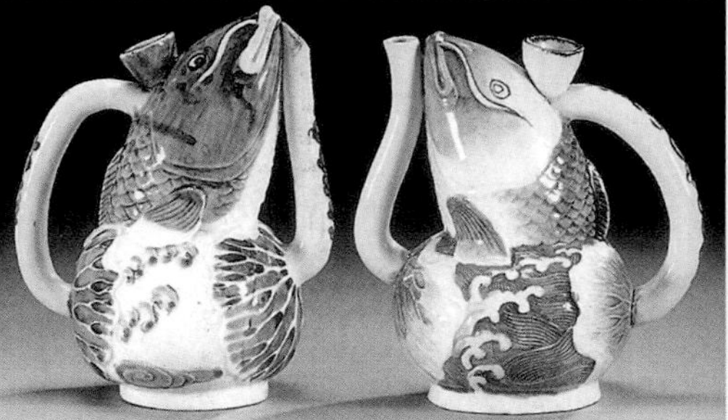

A pair of Imari ewers, modelled as leaping carp emerging from waves from between lotus leaves, the loop handle and spout painted with *karakusa*, late 17thC, 8¼in (21cm) high.
£4,100–4,900 / €5,900–7,000
$6,900–8,200 S(O)

Miller's Compares

I. An Imari wine ewer, decorated in enamels and gilt with sprays of meandering chrysanthemums, the handle painted with tendril scrolls with moulded flowerheads to either side, 1675–1725, 6½in (16.5cm) high.
£2,400–2,850
€3,450–4,100
$4,000–4,800 S(O)

II. An Imari wine ewer, painted with a repeated pattern of a *bijin* and three children, the spout with floral scrolls, the handle with cloud scrolls, with applied moulded chrysanthemums, 1675–1725, 6¾in (17cm) high.
£1,800–2,150
€2,600–3,100
$3,000–3,600 S(O)

Both of these wine ewers are from the same factory and the same mould, and were made during the same period. However, Item I has a much more unusual pattern than that of item II, and therefore fetched the higher price.

Figures

A pair of Arita figures of actors, minor damage, Genroku period, 1688–1703, 18½in (47cm) high.
£8,200–9,800
€11,800–14,100
$13,800–16,500 ⚒ BUK

An Imari figure of a *bijin*, decorated in enamels and gilt, 1675–1725, 19¼in (49cm) high.
£3,600–4,300
€5,200–6,200
$6,000–7,200 ⚒ S(O)

An Imari figure of an actor, his kimono decorated in enamels, c1700, 12¼in (31cm) high.
£1,000–1,200
€1,450–1,700
$1,700–2,000 ⚒ S(O)

A Satsuma figure, hand-painted and gilded, late 19thC, 10in (25.5cm) high.
£160–180 / €230–260
$270–300 ⊞ BAC

Flatware

An Arita saucer dish, decorated with iris, marked, probably 18thC, 8¾in (22cm) diam.
£380–450 / €550–660
$640–760 ⚒ WW

For an explanation of Japanese terms see the Glossary p760–763

An Imari dish, after an 18thC original, painted with a vase of flowers within an elaborate border, marked *fuki kaki*, c1880, 16in (40.5cm) diam.
£250–300 / €360–430
$420–500 ⚒ SWO
***Fuki kaki* means 'wealth and honour, beautiful vessel'.**

An Imari charger, the centre enamelled with a fruiting tree and a jardinière of flowers, 19thC, 22in (56cm) diam.
£540–640 / €780–940
$910–1,050 ⚒ Bea

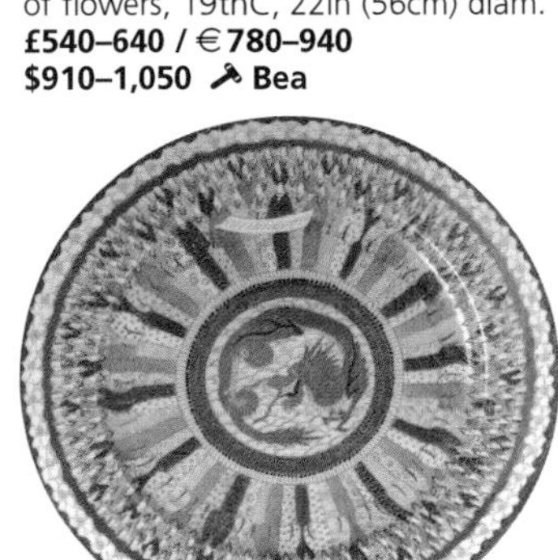

A Kutani plate, the central roundel with a dragon, the rim decorated with 1000 Faces pattern, signed, 1900, 9½in (24cm) diam.
£150–170 / €220–260
$250–300 ⊞ BAC

► **A Satsuma plate,** decorated with Bird in Tree pattern, Meiji period, 1868–1912, 10in (25.5cm) diam.
£80–90 / €115–130
$135–150 ⊞ BAC

An Imari dish, Meiji period, 1868–1911, 15in (38cm) diam.
£350–420 / €500–600
$590–700 ⚒ B&L

A charger, painted in the Imari palette, gilt-enriched, signed, 19thC, 15in (38cm) diam.
£190–210 / €270–320
$320–380 ⚒ PFK

Jars

A Kakiemon jar, decorated in enamels with a pair of *ho-o* birds, the shoulder with cherry blossoms reserved on *karakusa*, 17thC, 8in (20.5cm) high.
£13,200–15,800
€19,000–22,800
$22,000–26,400 S(O)

A Kyoto ware jar, decorated in enamels and gilding with pine and bamboo, with a wooden cover, c1700, 3in (7.5cm) high.
£840–1,000
€1,200–1,400
$1,400–1,650 S(O)

A Hirado jar and cover, painted with figures examining a scroll beneath a pine tree, the cover with a pine cone knop, 18th/19thC, 8in (20.5cm) high.
£1,250–1,500
€1,800–2,150
$2,100–2,500 WW

A pair of Imari jars and covers, painted with two roundels of stylized floral motifs, the covers surmounted by a tear knop, c1900, 17¼in (44cm) high.
£600–720 / €860–1,000
$1,000–1,200 S(O)

Koros

A Kakiemon koro and cover, decorated with stylized sprays of chrysanthemums, with a persimmon finial, on three incised feet, c1700, 6½in (16.5cm) high.
£2,900–3,450 / €4,200–5,000
$4,900–5,800 S(O)

A Hirado koro, painted with scrolls, with mask handles, reticulated sides and cover, 19thC, 4in (10cm) wide.
£190–220 / €270–320
$320–380 WW

A Satsuma koro and cover, decorated with pine trees, with a *shishi* knop and terrapin handles, signed, Meiji period, 1868–1911, 3¼in (8.5cm) wide.
£610–730 / €880–1,050
$1,000–1,200 WW

◄ **A Satsuma earthenware koro and cover,** by Gyokushozan, decorated in enamels and gilt, the cover pierced and surmounted by a knop in the form of the priest Doryo, with applied handles, impressed signatures, Meiji period, 1868–1911, 17in (43cm) high.
£1,150–1,350 / €1,650–1,950
$1,950–2,300 S(O)

► **A koro,** decorated with 12 figures beneath a band of stylized clouds, the finial modelled as a *shishi*, signed 'Fukyuen', Meiji period, 1868–1911, 26½in (67.5cm) high.
£900–1,050 / €1,300–1,550
$1,500–1,800 S(O)

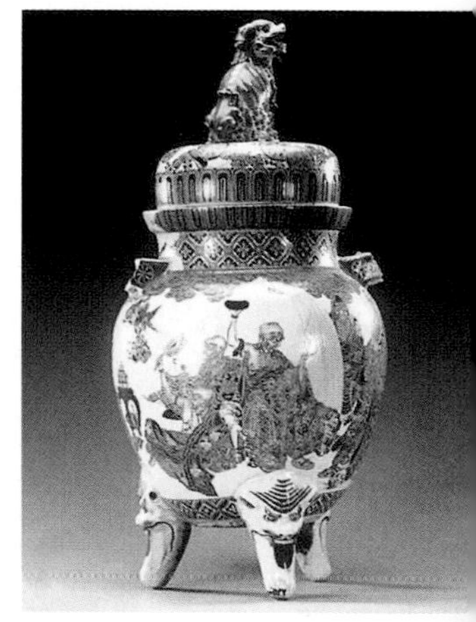

Japanese chronology chart

Jomon (Neolithic) period	c10,000–100 BC
Yayoi period	c200 BC–AD 200
Tumulus (Kofun) period	200–552
Asuka period	552–710
Nara period	710–794
Heian period	794–1185
Kamakura period	1185–1333
Muromachi (Ashikaga) period	1333–1568
Momoyama period	1568–1600
Edo (Tokugawa) period	1600–1868
Genroku period	*1688–1703*
Meiji period	1868–1911
Taisho period	1912–1926
Showa period	1926–1989

Vases

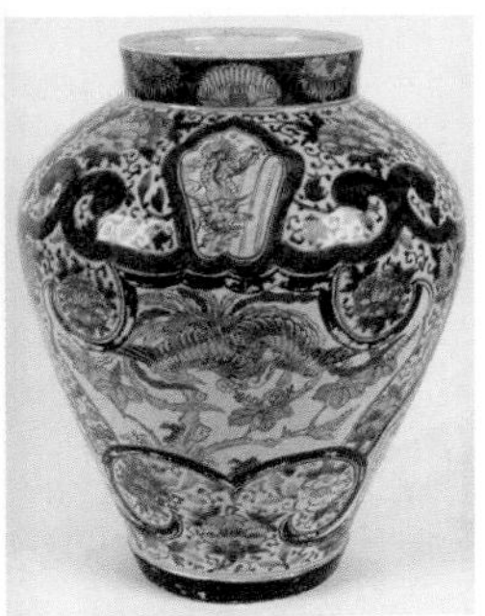

An Imari vase, decorated with panels depicting exotic birds, carp and dragons within rich scrolling floral borders, late 17thC, 16in (40.5cm) high.
£1,050–1,250
€1,500–1,800
$1,750–2,100 FHF

An Imari vase, decorated with a band of birds and flowers within decorative borders, 18thC, 12¼in (31cm) high.
£350–420 / €500–600
$590–700 DN

An Imperial Satsuma vase and cover, decorated in gilt and enamels with two panels depicting a *ho-o* bird above peony and flowers beside a garden fence, the base signed 'Satsuma Yaki' beneath the *mon* of Lord Shimazu, Meiji period, 1868–1911, 14in (35.5cm) high.
£2,350–2,800
€3,400–4,000
$4,000–4,800 B

A Kakiemon *hanaike*, decorated with rockwork and flowering plum, an incised band around the centre, a scrolling handle to each side, the back pierced for wall hanging, late 17thC, 7½in (19cm) high.
£1,800–2,150
€2,600–3,100
$3,000–3,600 S(O)
A *hanaike* is a flower vase, often used in the tea ceremony room.

A Kutani vase, by Hyoyu, decorated with scholars and their pupils engaged in the Four Accomplishments within the grounds of a temple, between bands of stylized floral motifs, signed 'Kutani Kineido Hyoyu ga', c1900, 18½in (47cm) high.
£2,650–3,150
€3,800–4,550
$4,500–5,400 S(O)
The Four Major Arts of Chinese tradition practised by scholars and members of the ruling élite consist of the cultivation of musical talents (*Koto*), chess-playing (*go*), calligraphy and painting. In Japan, this theme was especially popular in Edo-period literati painting that typically depicted the Four Gentlemanly Accomplishments being practised in outdoor settings.

Kakiemon

In the mid-17th century, the potter Sakaida Kakiemon, with the help of other potters and the guidance of Chinese teachers, succeeded in producing the first true Japanese porcelain decorated in on-glaze enamels. The style of wares he produced is known by the generic term 'Kakiemon'. His descendants and various pupils have carried on the tradition to this day. This distinctive porcelain has a palette of red, green, yellow and a purple-blue, often in combination with a finely-drawn underglaze blue. Kakiemon is known for its sparsity of decoration and general lack of borders or repeat decoration, and wares are often of geometric form.

A pair of Fukagawa Imari vases, decorated with panels of flowers on geometric and foliate grounds, Meiji period, 1868–1911, 9¾in (25cm) high.
£800–960 / €1,150–1,350
$1,350–1,600 RTo
The Fukagawa factory was founded in Arita in the late 19th century. Wares were always marked with a leaf spray and/or an image of Mount Fuji. It is still in production today.

A pair of Satsuma vases, decorated with figures in panels, the shoulders applied with masks, seal marks, signed 'Hotoda', Meiji period, 1868–1911, 5in (12.5cm) high.
£140–165 / €200–240
$230–270 HOLL

A Satsuma vase, by Yabu Meizan, the neck with three vignettes of blossoming branches, the body painted with groups of men, women and children admiring works of art, impressed and gilt-painted signatures, Meiji period, 1868–1911, 5¼in (13.5cm) high.
£4,700–5,600
€6,700–8,000
$7,900–9,400 RTo
This vase is of superb quality and therefore very desirable.

A Satsuma pottery vase, decorated with figures, heightened with gilding, marked, Meiji period, 1868–1911, 5¾in (14.5cm) high.
£100–120 / €140–165
$170–200 SWO

A pair of Satsuma earthenware vases, modelled as bamboo buckets, decorated in enamels with sprays of flowers on a *karakusa* ground, signed 'Senzan', Meiji period, 1868–1911, 9¾in (25cm) high.
£600–720 / €860–1,000
$1,000–1,200 S(O)

◄ A pair of Satsuma vases, decorated with panels of children, Meiji period, 1868–1911, 9½in (24cm) high.
£120–145
€170–200
$200–240
SWO

A pair of Satsuma vases, decorated with Geishas in panels, Meiji period, 1868–1911, 6in (15cm) high.
£220–250 / €320–360
$370–410 BAC

A Satsuma vase, decorated with panels of figures in gardens, gilt slightly worn, Meiji period, 1868–1911, 9¾in (25cm) high.
£370–440 / €530–630
$620–740 WW

◄ A Hirado vase, c1880, 11½in (29cm) high.
£1,050–1,200
€1,500–1,700
$1,750–1,950 G&G

A Satsuma vase, by Kinkozan, with millefiori decoration, c1890, 9½in (24cm) high.
£370–440 / €530–630
$620–740 SWO

► A Satsuma vase, marked, c1911, 6¼in (16cm) high.
£150–180 / €210–250
$250–300 SWO

Miscellaneous

A Satsuma earthenware canister and cover, by Ryozan, depicting a festival procession of figures and a temple scene, signed, Meiji period, 1868–1911, 10in (25.5cm) high.
£2,750–3,300
€4,000–4,800
$4,700–5,600 S(O)

A Satsuma earthenware sweetmeat box, decorated with Yamabushi in a forest and Benton and her acolytes, signed 'Senzan', Meiji period, 1868–1911, 6¼in (15.5cm) diam.
£650–780 / €930–1,100
$1,100–1,300 S(O)
Yamabushi is a demon and Benton is the Japanese Dragon Goddess – the Queen of the sea.

► A Satsuma earthenware tea canister, by Shoun, painted with panels of a pheasant, ducks and garden scenes, the shoulder and cover with a variety of shell fish, signed, Meiji period, 1868–1911, 4in (10cm) high.
£4,300–5,200 / €6,200–7,400
$7,200–8,600 S(O)
This piece is of excellent quality.

A Kutani jardinière, decorated with dragons and birds, signed, Meiji period, 1868–1911, 8in (20.5cm) high.
£180–200 / €260–290
$300–330 BAC

East Asian Ceramics

An earthenware jar, with vertical ribs and three lug handles, Burmese, c1500, 23½in (59.5cm) high.
£4,100–4,900 / €5,900–7,000
$6,900–7,200 S(O)

A bowl, from the Hoi An hoard, Vietnamese, 1450–1500, 6in (15cm) diam.
£160–180 / €230–260
$270–300 McP

A stoneware jar and cover, from the Hoi An hoard, decorated with a lotus pattern, Vietnamese, late 15thC, 6in (15cm) high.
£670–750 / €960–1,100
$1,100–1,250 AWI

A porcelain water dropper, painted with a leaf motif, Korean, 19thC, 2½in (6cm) diam.
£120–145 / €170–200
$200–240 WW

A stoneware bottle, from the Hoi An hoard, Vietnamese, late 15thC, 3¾in (9.5cm) high.
£90–100 / €130–140
$150–170 AWI

This huge cargo of late 15th-century Vietnamese ceramics was found in the early 1990s by fishermen off Hoi An in central Vietnam. The pieces are from kilns in the northern province of Hai Duong and were being transported to markets in South East Asia.

A pot and cover, from the Hoi An hoard, Vietnamese, 1450–1500, 2½in (6.5cm) wide.
£120–140 / €170–190
$200–220 McP

A bowl, from the Hoi An hoard, Vietnamese, 1450–1500, 9in (23cm) diam.
£1,100–1,250 / €1,550–1,750
$1,850–2,050 McP

An inkwell, from the Hoi An hoard, Vietnamese, 1450–1500, 3½in (9cm) wide.
£70–80 / €100–110
$120–140 McP

A porcelain jar, painted with auspicious emblems, peony and stylized clouds, Korean, 19thC, 4½in (11.5cm) diam.
£900–1,050 / €1,300–1,550
$1,500–1,800 S(O)

A celadon stemcup, decorated with chrysanthemum sprays, Korean, Koryo Dynasty, c1300, 2¾in (7cm) diam.
£1,800–2,150 / €2,600–3,050
$3,000–3,600 S(O)

◄ **A celadon vase,** Korean, 13thC, 10½in (26.5cm) high
£760–850 / €1,100–1,250
$1,300–1,450 G&G

Glass

Growing interest in glass has helped it to avoid the depression that has afflicted other areas of antiques. Indeed, the greatest problem facing dealers and collectors of classic glass is not falling demand but a shortage of fresh pieces. The era when the major London auction houses held several glass sales each year is a distant memory, and in fact these days none can manage to stage even one.

One of the reasons for the shortage is that a great many collectors are looking for the same pieces. Economic prosperity and improving health have led to collections remaining with their owners far longer than before, and many of the finest and rarest pieces have been donated to museums. During the 1950s, for instance, the work of George Ravenscroft, who perfected the formula for lead crystal in 1678, appeared at auction every few months. However, not a single example has been offered for sale in nearly 30 years.

Traditionally, collections were slowly assembled over a lifetime before being dispersed when their guardians died or became too infirm to handle them. The average span of this cycle was around 20 years, but has now grown to over 30. So, when a fresh collection does appear on the market, it attracts great interest. The dispersal of the contents of Harvey's Wine Museum (many examples from which are pictured on the following pages) provides a perfect case in point, with the prices fetched by unusual items going through the roof and even those of standard forms fetching high prices.

There are many types, forms and colours of inexpensive but potentially collectable glass. An exhibition mounted by the Glass Circle at the Wallace Collection, London, entitled Palace to Parlour, A Celebration of Victorian Glass, provided potential newcomers to the field with an excellent snapshot of some 19th-century alternatives. The display of around 300 objects, mostly drawn from the collections of the Circle's members, showcased some of the extraordinary variety available, ranging from priceless pieces to inexpensive pressed glass.

A visit to any sizeable antiques fair will confirm the abundant availability of interesting glass, often at prices lower than modern equivalents. The key for the collector is the willingness to devote the time and energy to acquire the knowledge necessary to discern the desirable from the ordinary.

Andy McConnell

GLASS

Ale, Spirit & Wine Glasses

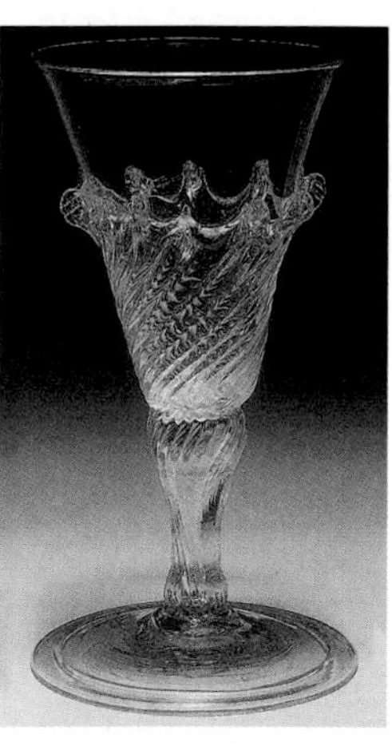

◄ **An Anglo-Venetian ale flute,** the bowl with flammiform pincered fringe and spirally-moulded lower section, on a baluster stem and a conical folded foot, losses, c1690, 6in (15cm) high.
£3,600–4,300 / €5,200–6,200
$6,000–7,200 ⚒ B
Ex-Harvey's Wine Museum sale.
Harvey's Wine Museum was founded by the Bristol sherry company in the late 1960s to fill its historic cellars after its maturing and bottling operations were moved to new premises. The museum's contents were sold in 2003 after Harvey's was bought by the drinks giant Allied Domecq.

Many of the museum's drinking glasses were acquired at the sales that dispersed the collection of Walter Smith in 1967 to 1968. A large number of Smith's purchases had previously been in other notable collections and it is estimated that former ownership by Smith added around 10 to 15 per cent to prices at auction.

A römer, the stem applied with raspberry prunts, on a hollow stem and a conical ribbed foot, Dutch/German, c1700, 6in (15cm) high.
£530–640 / €760–910
$890–1,050 ⚒ S(Am)
The römer is one of the oldest forms of wine glass and is present in illustrations of contemporary German life dating from the 15th century. Intended for drinking white Rhineland wines, early römers were made in green *Waldglas* (forest glass), which was inadvertently tinted by the potash on which it is based. Antique römers can be difficult to date accurately, although more modern versions often have moulded lower sections.

► **A champagne/ale flute,** the funnel bowl wrythen-moulded to the base, the inverted baluster stem with a basal knop, on a conical foot, 1690–1720, 6¾in (17cm) high.
£810–970 / €1,150–1,350
$1,350–1,600 ⚒ B
Flute-shaped glasses have been produced since the Renaissance and were used in 17th- and 18th-century Britain for consuming sparkling drinks such as champagne, ale, cider and perry.

The first specific reference to flutes may date to 1773 when London merchant Colebron Hancock invoiced the historian Edward Gibbon for '1 doz Champain Flutes, 8/-'. The pattern books of most European glassworks show that flutes of various types have been in almost continuous production over the past four centuries.

A heavy baluster wine glass, with a tulip bowl and a solid base, on a domed and folded foot, c1700, 7in (18cm) high.
£2,650–3,200
€3,850–4,600
$4,500–5,400 B
Ex-Harvey's Wine Museum sale.

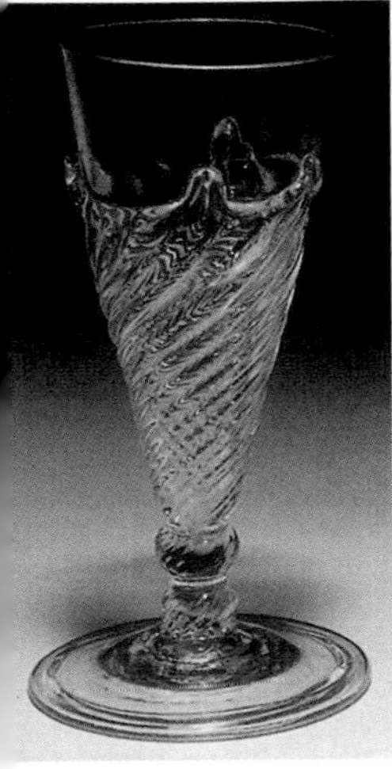

A wrythen dwarf ale flute, the bowl spirally-moulded with a flammiform fringe, the double knopped stem also wrythen-moulded, on a conical folded foot, c1720, 4¾in (12cm) high.
£440–530 / €640–760
$740–890 B
Ex-Harvey's Wine Museum sale.

► A baluster wine glass, the waisted bell bowl with a solid base above an annulated knop, on a conical foot, c1730, 8¼in (21cm) high.
£810–970 / €1,250–1,400
$1,350–1,600 B
Ex-Harvey's Wine Museum sale.

A heavy baluster goblet, engraved with trophies and an inscription, the inverted baluster stem with a tear, on a folded conical foot, Dutch, c1710, 6¾in (17cm) high.
£2,100–2,500
€3,000–3,600
$3,500–4,200 DN

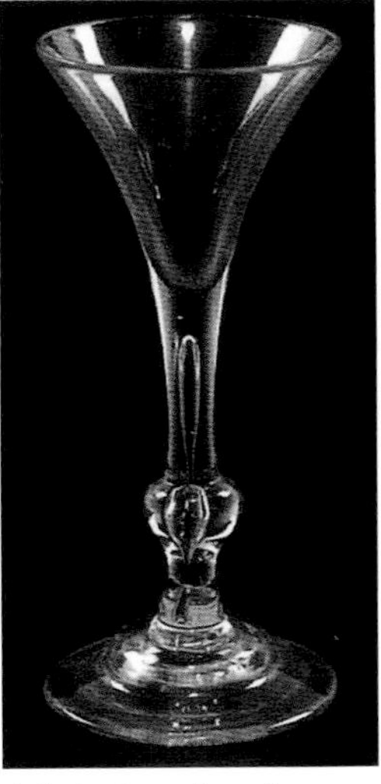

A baluster wine glass, with a drawn trumpet bowl, the stem with a tear, on a domed foot, c1720, 7in (17.5cm) high.
£700–840 / €1,000–1,200
$1,200–1,400 DN

A mead glass, the bowl with a gadrooned base supported on a double knop, on a folded conical foot, c1710, 5¼in (13.5cm) high.
£3,350–4,000
€4,850–5,800
$5,600–6,700 B
Ex-Harvey's Wine Museum sale.

A baluster wine glass, engraved with an allegorical vignette of a cockerel and hen, the pedestal stem with a tear, on a domed and folded foot, minor damage, Dutch, c1725, the engraving c1745, 6¾in (17cm) high.
£1,650–1,950
€2,350–2,800
$2,750–3,300 B
Ex-Harvey's Wine Museum sale.
The precise meaning of the mating cockerel and hen motifs is not known, but it occurs on English delftware with anti-Jacobite subject matter.

► A baluster wine glass, the waisted bell bowl with a solid base above an annular knop, on a conical foot, c1730, 8¼in (21cm) high.
£810–970 / €1,250–1,400
$1,350–1,600 B
Ex-Harvey's Wine Museum sale.

An armorial goblet, engraved with the arms of Shaw of Eltham Bt and a motto, on a knopped stem and domed folded foot, the cover with a faceted knop and engraved with a crest of six crossed arrows, c1720, 18¾in (47.5cm) high.
£11,500–13,800
€16,600–19,900
$19,300–23,200 WW
The massive Shaw Goblet is one of the most extraordinary examples of British glass to reach the market in recent years. It was probably made to commemorate the wedding of a member of the Shaw family and is likely to have been made for the guests to drink from in turn. The lower section, formed as a gigantic baluster drinking glass typical of the period, is capped by a cover, which is a feature more common to German than English glass. Accompanying this lot are a number of letters of correspondence and a Westminster Bank cheque for £120 / €170 / $200 dating from 23 November 1926 relating to the purchase of the goblet.

A heavy baluster wine glass, with a knopped stem and folded foot, c1730, 7¾in (19.5cm) high.
£1,000–1,200
€1,450–1,700
$1,700–2,000 WW

A pair of wine glasses, the funnel bowls over double-knopped hollow stems, c1740, 6in (15cm) high.
£590–710 / €850–1,000
$960–1,150 DN

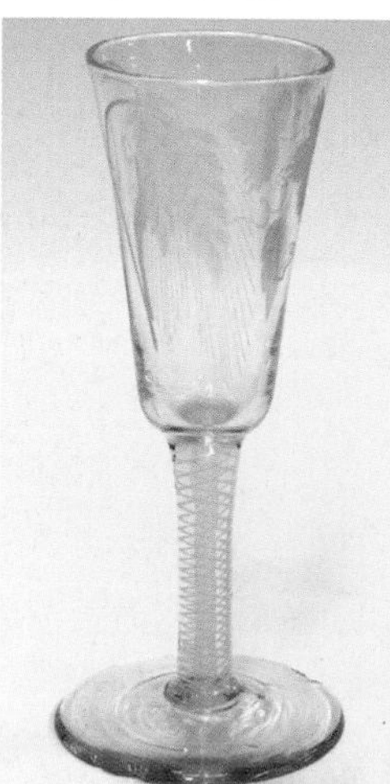

An ale flute, on an opaque twist stem and conical foot, minor damage, 18thC, 7in (18cm) high.
£200–240 / €300–350
$350–410 G(L)

Folded feet

A high proportion of the glassware produced by Venetian glassmakers from the Renaissance period onwards had the outer rims of their feet folded back, either upwards or downwards, and flattened against the disc of the foot. This was done to strengthen the foot and help to prevent chipping. While it is physically possible to chip a folded foot, it is rare to see one. The practice was adopted by English glassmakers, who continued to fold the feet of drinking glasses and bowls until c1750. Suggestions that the practice ceased after the introduction of the weight-related Glass Excise Duty in 1745 cannot be substantiated.

Miller's Compares

I. A cordial glass, the drawn trumpet bowl engraved with fruiting vines and an inscription, the stem with a tear terminating in a basal knop, on a domed and folded foot, 1730–40, 6¾in (17cm) high.
£2,650–3,200
€3,850–4,600
$4,450–5,300 B
Ex-Harvey's Wine Museum sale.

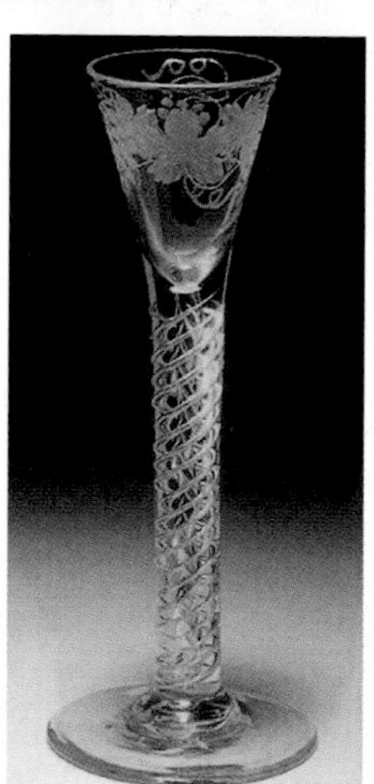

II. An air-twist cordial glass, the drawn trumpet bowl engraved with a frieze of fruiting vines, the stem with a spiral cable enclosed by spiral threads, on a conical foot, c1760, 7in (18cm) high.
£1,000–1,200
€1,450–1,700
$1,700–2,000 B
Ex-Harvey's Wine Museum sale.

These two 18th-century English cordial glasses are both engraved with fruiting vines, but Item I is earlier in date, of a more interesting form and is additionally engraved with the toast 'Trade and Navigation'. These differences resulted in a price almost three times higher than that of Item II.

Crizzling

'Glass disease' or 'weeping', also termed 'crizzling' or crystalization of salts, causes webs of tiny silvery vein-like cracks within the body of the glass, resulting from an inadequacy of fluxing alkali in the glass 'metal'. Given time, crizzled vessels will theoretically crumble to dust, although innumerable heavily crizzled 17th-century vessels have survived intact.

► **A goblet and cover,** engraved with David and Jonathan and an inscription, the lappet-cut cover with a facet-cut baluster knop, crizzled, German, 18thC, 15¾in (40cm) high.
£700–840
€1,000–1,200
$1,200–1,400
WW

A light baluster goblet, the rim with a band of engraving, the stem with an annulated shoulder knop and dum-bell ball knops, on a domed foot, 1730–40, 7¼in (18.5cm) high.
£1,050–1,200
€1,550–1,700
$1,800–2,000 Som

A light baluster wine glass, engraved with a flower and an insect, c1740, 7in (18cm) high.
£850–940 / €1,200–1,350
$1,450–1,600 BrW

GLASS

A 'Newcastle' light baluster wine glass, the drawn trumpet bowl engraved with a broad band of fruiting vines, the stem with cushion and teared knops, on a conical foot, c1745, 7in (17.5cm) high.
£1,200–1,450
€1,750–2,100
$2,000–2,400 B
Ex-Harvey's Wine Museum sale.

A wine glass, the trumpet bowl on a drawn stem with a multiple spiral air-twist stem, on a folded conical foot, c1745, 7in (18cm) high.
£340–380 / €490–550
$570–640 ⊞ Som

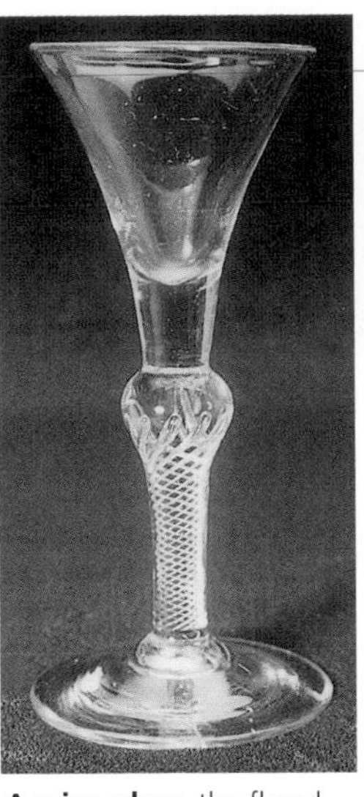

A wine glass, the flared trumpet bowl and shoulder knop supported on a multiple spiral air-twist stem, c1745, 6¾in (17cm) high.
£540–600 / €780–860
$900–1,000 ⊞ Som

A wine glass, the bell bowl above a shoulder and a central knop, on a multiple spiral air-twist stem, c1750, 7¼in (18.5cm) high.
£540–600 / €780–860
$900–1,000 ⊞ Som

A Bohemian-style goblet, with cut decoration, the knop with a ruby thread, Russian, c1750, 8¾in (22cm) high.
£370–440 / €530–630
$620–740 BUK
Encased ruby threads in knops and decanter stoppers have been common in Bohemian glass since c1720.

Russian Bohemian style

Over the centuries, Bohemia's craftsmen have proved themselves to be the world's master glass-makers and decorators, through both the quality and the diversity of their work. However, with the abundance of skills in their homeland, thousands moved abroad to make their fortune. During most of the 18th century, glass made in the Bohemian style, or the *façon de Bohême*, proved virtually ubiquitous across most of Europe. The Bohemian influence was felt especially in Russia and Spain, where its migrants provided the direction and specialist skills at the Imperial glassworks and decorating shops. As a result, it can be difficult to distinguish between glassware made in Bohemia and glass made in foreign countries by Bohemian craftsmen.

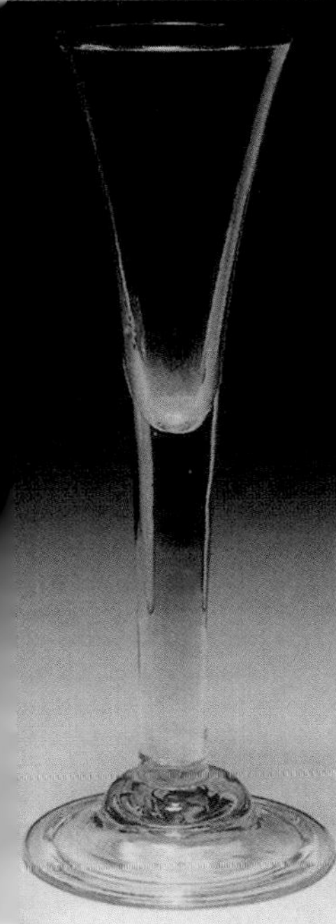

A Champagne flute, the drawn trumpet bowl on a plain stem with a domed and folded foot, c1750, 8¼in (21cm) high.
£630–750 / €910–1,100
$1,050–1,250 B
Ex-Harvey's Wine Museum sale.

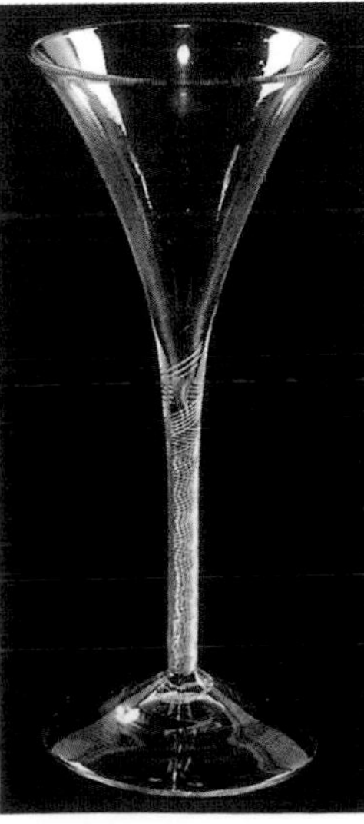

► A toasting glass, the drawn trumpet bowl on an air-twist stem, c1750, 7¼in (18.5cm) high.
£440–520 / €630–750
$740–870 DN

A wine glass, the funnel bowl engraved with a floral meander, on an incised twist stem and a domed foot, c1750, 6½in (16.5cm) high.
£1,250–1,400
€1,800–2,000
$2,100–2,350 ⊞ RAP
This glass has an unusual domed foot.

A light baluster wine glass, the bell bowl on a plain stem with a swelling knop, a basal knop and a beaded knop, on a domed foot, c1750, 7¼in (18.5cm) high.
£1,200–1,350
€1,750–1,950
$2,000–2,200 ⊞ GS

Engraved 'Jacobite' roses

The addition of the romantic and value-enhancing word 'Jacobite' to describe all mid-18th century British glassware engraved with roses should be treated with caution. The London glass merchant-decorator Jerom Johnson advertised such 'Flower'd glasses' in 1742, three years before the 1745 revolt. Of all the flowers in question, the rose had the broadest appeal with the English for its link to the Tudors, with the Catholics for its association with the exiled Stuarts, and with the Hanoverians who combined it with a horse to symbolize the House of Hanover. Many English towns still have at least one pub named 'The Rose & Crown'. Rustic, bold, heraldic six- or eight-petalled roses, often supported by stems, leaves and one or two buds, were applied to thousands of wine glasses and decanters between 1740 and 1760, although few were associated with the Jacobite cause.

A glass, the bell bowl on a plain stem, c1750, 6in (15cm) high.
£260–290 / €380–420
$440–490 ⊞ GGD
English 18th-century drinking glasses such as this have increased in price from £75 / €110 / $125 ten years ago to nearly £300 / €430 / $500 today.

A glass, with a moulded foot, c1750, 3½in (9cm) high.
£290–320 / €410–460
$490–540 ⊞ GGD
The foot of this glass is moulded with an unusual series of steps.

A glass, with a plain foot, c1750, 4½in (11.5cm) high.
£115–130 / €165–185
$200–220 ⊞ GGD

A wine glass, with Bohemian-style engraving, the trumpet bowl above a folded foot, 1760, 4½in (11.5cm) high.
£70–80 / €100–110
$115–130 ⊞ GGD

A Jacobite wine glass, the funnel bowl engraved with a seven-petal rose spray and a flying insect, on a stem with a spiral cable and a conical foot, c1750, 7in (18cm) high.
£1,800–2,150
€2,600–3,100
$3,050–3,600 ⚒ B
Ex-Harvey's Wine Museum sale.
According to Geoffrey B. Seddon's, *The Jacobites and their Drinking Glasses*, the engraved butterfly or moth may represent the 'return of the soul' in the form of Prince Charles Edward, or may just be a decorative motif typical of the naturalism of the period. It is relatively unusual to find the rose engraved with seven petals.

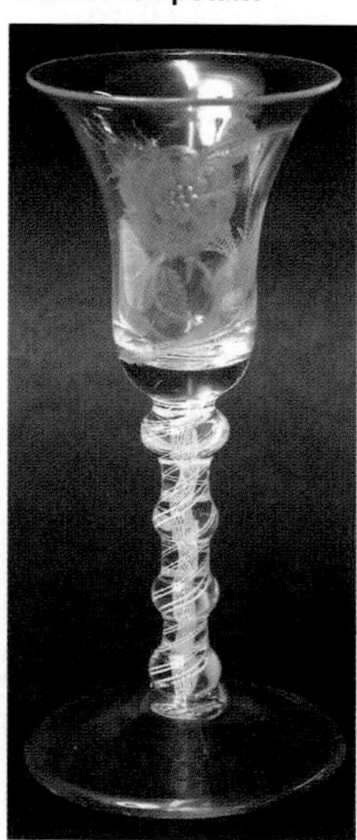

A wine glass, the bell bowl engraved with a rose and a single bud, on a double-series opaque-twist stem with four knops, c1760, 7in (18cm) high.
£630–750 / €920–1,100
$1,050–1,250 ⚒ G(L)

A wine glass, the bowl engraved with a moth and a flower, the shoulder knopped stem with spiral threads, c1750, 6¼in (16cm) high.
£1,000–1,200
€1,450–1,700
$1,700–2,000 ⚒ DN
This glass is of Jacobite significance.

A mead goblet, the cup bowl with a multiple spiral air-twist stem, on a domed conical foot, c1750, 6½in (16.5cm) high.
£1,000–1,200
€1,450–1,700
$1,700–2,000 ⚒ B
Ex-Harvey's Wine Museum sale.
The suggestion that large-bowled 18th-century glasses of this form were used for drinking mead remains unproven, and it seems likely that they were more generally used for Champagne. Mead, or honey wine, is an ancient drink, reputedly the first alcoholic beverage. Said to have been the ambrosia of the gods on Mount Olympus and the favoured beverage of Vikings, it is now regarded as more of a drink favoured by medieval monks.

A glass, with a double spiral opaque-twist stem, c1760, 5in (12.5cm) high.
£200–230 / €300–330
$340–380 ⊞ GGD

A goblet, the bowl supported on a swollen-knopped stem moulded with vertical flutes, on a domed foot with spiral decoration, c1760, 6¼in (16cm) high.
£820–980 / €1,200–1,400
$1,400–1,650 ⚒ DN
This is an English derivative of the römer shape.

A wine glass, the bell bowl above a triple-knopped opaque-twist stem with vertical gauze enclosed by three-ply spiral bands, on a conical foot, c1765, 6¾in (17cm) high.
£710–790 / €1,050–1,150
$1,200–1,350 ⊞ RAP

A glass, the moulded bowl with an engraved lip, on an air-twist stem, c1760, 5¾in (14.5cm) high.
£810–900 / €1,150–1,300
$1,350–1,500 ⊞ CHAC

A cider flute, the tapering funnel bowl engraved with an apple branch and an insect, on a multiple spiral air-twist stem with knops, on a conical foot, rim chip to foot, c1760, 7¾in (19.5cm) high.
£1,400–1,650
€2,000–2,400
$2,300–2,750 ⚒ B
Ex-Harvey's Wine Museum sale.
The small chip to the foot reduced the value of this glass by at least a half, even though it is a rare piece with superb quality engraving.

► **A wine glass,** the lower bowl and stem cut with graduated facets, with a swollen knop, c1770, 6in (15cm) high.
£570–630 / €820–910
$950–1,050 ⊞ BrW

A wine glass, the bell bowl and shoulder knop on an air-twist stem and a conical foot, c1760, 6¼in (16cm) high.
£330–390 / €470–560
$560–660 ⚒ G(L)

A wine glass, decorated by James Giles with gilt floral spray sprigs, with a gilt rim, on a plain stem and conical foot, minor wear, c1765, 6¼in (16cm) high.
£3,050–3,650
€4,400–5,200
$5,100–6,100 ⚒ B
Ex-Harvey's Wine Museum sale.

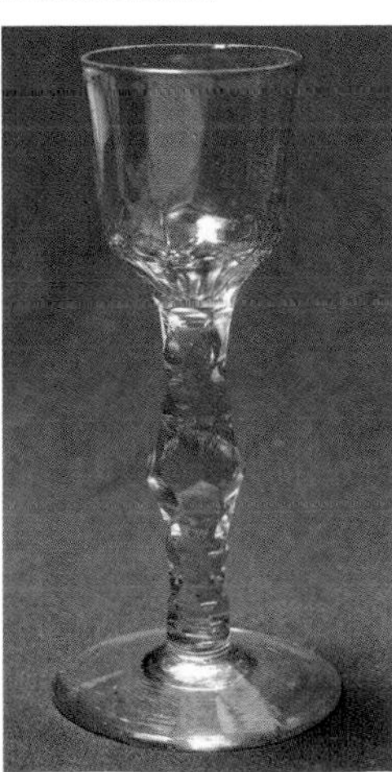

A glass, the ogee bowl engraved with birds and flowers, on a folded foot, c1760, 5in (12.5cm) high.
£200–220 / €290–320
$330–370 ⊞ GGD

A firing glass, of trumpet form with opaque double-series twist and a thick foot rim, 18thC, 4¼in (11cm) high.
£165–195 / €240–280
$280–330 ⚒ TRM

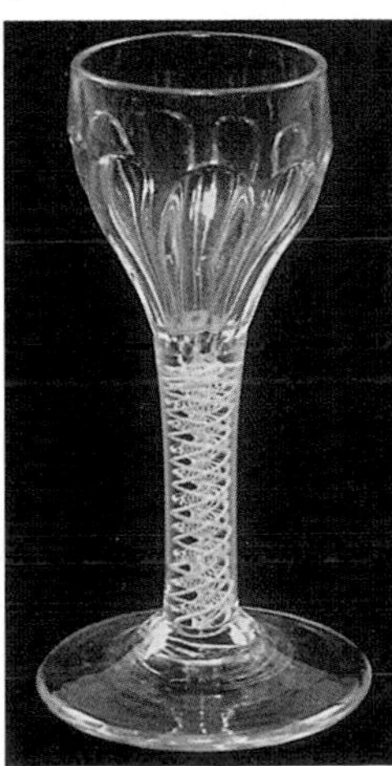

A wine glass, the petal-moulded ogee bowl on a double-series opaque-twist stem and conical foot, c1770, 5¼in (13cm) high.
£370–440 / €530–630
$620–740 ⚒ DN

Miller's Compares

I. A tartan-twist wine glass, the bell bowl on a stem with a white gauze enclosed by spiralling white, red, blue and green threads, with three knops, on a conical foot, c1770, 6¾in (17cm) high.
£6,400–7,700
€9,200–11,000
$10,900–13,000 B
Ex-Harvey's Wine Museum sale.

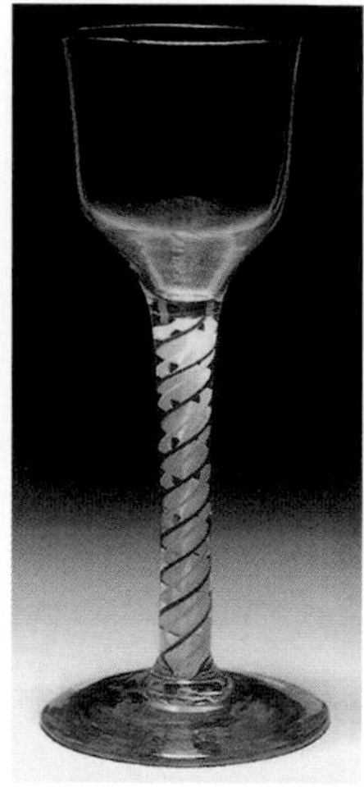

II. A wine glass, the ogee bowl on a stem with a white spiral edged with red, enclosed by a pair of spiral tapes, on a conical foot, c1770, 6in (15.5cm) high.
£2,800–3,350
€4,000–4,800
$4,700–5,600 B
Ex-Harvey's Wine Museum sale.

These two mid-18th century drinking glasses are of similar capacity, height and with twisted stems, but Item I sold for more than twice the price of Item II. The reason is entirely due to the colour of their twists. The rarest form of colour twist is tartan, enclosing white, red, blue and green threads around a central opaque-white gauze. They seldom reach the market, which is why Item I, enhanced by a Smith Collection provenance, fetched the highest price. The order of rarity of twist colours, in descending order, are canary yellow, green and red, and red.

A glass, the ogee bowl on a diamond facet stem with a knop, c1770, 6in (15cm) high.
£240–270 / €350–390
$400–440 GGD

A wine glass, the drawn trumpet bowl with a plain stem, c1790, 4in (10cm) high.
£175–195 / €250–280
$290–320 BrW

Toasting

Toasting is one of the world's oldest social customs. It is thought that the ancient Greeks believed that the sound of drinking vessels being tapped together warded off evil spirits, and the Romans added pieces of burnt toast to their wines as the carbon counteracted the bitter taste. Toasting etiquette differs from country to country. In China, for instance, the standard toast *ganbei* literally means 'dry glass', or perhaps 'bottoms up', whereas in Korea a guest's glass should never be emptied.

Guests have been toasted in Britain since at least AD 450, when King Vortigen drank the health of his guests at a banquet. The practice developed through the centuries and had arrived in the Americas by 1639 when the Massachusetts General Court banned the 'abominable practice of drinking healths'.

By the 18th century, after-dinner toasting sometimes required guests to offer a salutation, a ritual that required the presence of footmen to loosen the neckcloths of diners as they eventually collapsed to the floor in a stupor.

An ale flute, the funnel bowl engraved with ears of barley and a stylized floral sprig, supported on a double-series opaque-twist stem and a conical foot, c1770, 7¾in (19.5cm) high.
£440–530 / €640–760
$740–890 DN

A Loyalist firing glass, the flute-moulded bowl engraved with the toast 'The King & The Friends of His Majestys American Loyalists', the double-series opaque-twist stem on a conical foot, c1770, 4in (10cm) high.
£4,300–5,200
€6,300–7,500
$7,300–8,700 B
Ex-Harvey's Wine Museums sale.

► **A rummer,** with later grapevine engraving, c1800, 5½in (14cm) high.
£105–120 / €155–170
$180–200 GGD

Further reading

Miller's Glass Buyer's Guide, Miller's Publications, 2001

A set of three wine glasses, c1820, 5¼in (13.5cm) high.
£680–750 / €1,000–1,100 $1,100–1,250 ⊞ JAS

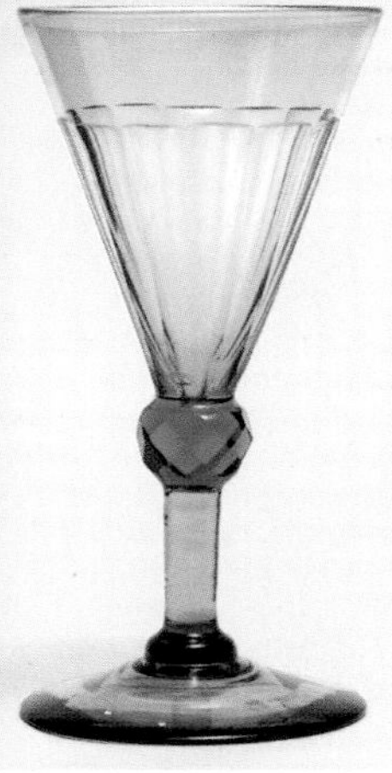

A pair of wine glasses, by Richardsons of Stourbridge, 1835–45, 6in (15cm) high.
£155–175 / €220–250 $260–290 ⊞ GGD

A goblet, decorated with gilt bands of Cupid and Psyche among scrolling foliage, the foot with an inscription, Venetian, c1900, 14½in (36.5cm) high, with matching dish.
£490–590 / €710–850 $830–990 ⚒ WW

This huge goblet and its supporting dish were made c1900, probably by Antonio Salviati's son Giulio. Decorated in the Renaissance revival, or Historismus, style it is covered in elaborate gilding and enamelling.

Coloured glasses & decanters

It is a strange fact that while cobalt, or so-called 'Bristol' blue decanters are far more common than green, green wine glasses outnumber blue ones by hundreds-to-one. The reason is uncertain, but possibly because red wine appears muddy in blue glass, and green has been the traditional colour for white wine glasses since the 15th century. Green decanters are consequently more valuable than blue ones, with early amethyst, 'peacock', ultramarine, aquamarine and amber versions progressively rarer. In the case of drinking glasses, blue are the most expensive, being three or four times the price of green examples.

A Bohemian goblet, with gilt decoration of a couple taking tea, c1840, 6in (15cm) high.
£120–145 / €175–210 $200–240 ⚒ SWO

A Bohemian goblet and cover, decorated with enamelled and gilt flowers, c1840, 14½in (37cm) high.
£1,100–1,300 €1,600–1,900 $1,850–2,200 ⚒ WW

► A set of eight Champagne coupes, engraved with fruiting vines, with flute-cut stems, c1895, 5in (12.5cm) high.
£700–770 / €1,000–1,100 $1,150–1,300 ⊞ JAS

◄ A Baccarat wine goblet, decorated with Renaissance-style engraving and a bee, French, c1875, 6in (15cm) high.
£65–75 / €95–105 $110–125 ⊞ GGD

Venetian revival

Venetian glass, one of the wonders of the Renaissance, became internationally unfashionable to such a degree after c1700 that by 1840 the number of glassmakers on the island of Murano had considerably reduced. However, a growing appetite for hand-made glass in Britain led two aristocrats, Sir Austin Layard and Sir Henry Drake, to finance a new glassworks on Murano in the 1860s, run by their partner Dr Antonio Salviati. The reaction to the arrival in London of Salviati's glassware was electric and it rapidly became established as the epitome of good taste.

A pair of rummers, the cup bowls on plain stems and reinforced conical feet, 1820–30, 4½in (11.5cm) high.
£125–140 / €180–200 $210–240 ⊞ Som

A set of six wine glasses, engraved with fruiting vines and leaves, c1870, 5¼in (13.5cm) high.
£500–550 / €720–790 $830–920 ⊞ JAS

A pair of wine glasses, the tulip bowls with intaglio-cut flowers and foliage on stems with cut knops, c1910, 6in (15cm) high.
£60–70 / €90–100 $105–115 ⊞ GGD

Beakers & Tumblers

A beaker, engraved with a crowned coat-of-arms and a bouquet of flowers, German, 1760–80, 6in (15cm) high.
£270–320 / €390–460
$450–540 BUK

A beaker, possibly by Johann Ludwig Mohn, decorated with a gilt bands and views of the Polytechnic Institute and the Carlskirche in Vienna, Austrian, 1840–50, 4¼in (10.5cm) high.
£2,900–3,500
€4,200–5,000
$4,900–5,900 DORO
Beakers such as this are highly sought after. The Mohn family (father and brothers) and Anton Kothgasser were among the best decorators and executed their designs in tranpsarent enamels.

A commemorative tumbler, engraved with a monogram, c1790, 4¾in (12cm) high.
£300–360 / €430–520
$500–600 DN
Tumblers are a specific collecting field. This is a good example decorated with fine neo-classical engraving.

A tumbler, commemorating Louis Napoleon, French, dated 1848, 3¼in (8.5cm) high.
£55–65 / €80–95
$95–100 BrW
This glass dates from the very short period of Louis Napoleon's elected tenure of office as Prince President of France. On the establishment of the Second Empire in 1852 he became Emperor Napoleon III.

A beaker, with rococo-style floral decoration, Dutch or German, early 19thC, 7¼in (18.5cm) high.
£490–590 / €710–850
$820–990 S(Am)

A beaker, with enamelled and engraved decoration, Bohemian, c1900, 6½in (16.5cm) high.
£115–130 / €165–185
$195–220 GGD

A tumbler, engraved for a member of the Atthill Family of Essex, 1800–15, 4in (10cm) high.
£520–580 / €750–840
$870–970 BrW
The engraving on this glass may be by William Absolom, who began his career in Market Row, Yarmouth, in 1783. Judging by his surviving trade cards, he started as a retailer but began decorating Wedgwood porcelain and glass, probably shipped from London's Whitefriars Glasshouse, from 1789 until his death in 1815. Unlike most of his predecessors and contemporaries, Absolom often signed his gilding on glass, typically applied to tumblers and rummers. His naive engraving and gilding falls into four principal categories: souvenirs, farming, commemoratives and military/naval themes.

Condition

The condition is absolutely vital when assessing the value of an antique. Damaged pieces on the whole appreciate much less than perfect examples. However a rare desirable piece may command a high price even when damaged.

GLASS

Bottles, Carafes & Decanters

◄ **A shaft and globe wine bottle,** with a string rim, c1660, 8¾in (22cm) high.
£3,350–4,000
€4,800–5,800
$5,600–6,700 B
Ex-Harvey's Wine Museum sale.

► **A sack bottle,** Dutch, 18thC, 8in (20.5cm) high.
£330–390 / €470–560
$550–660 HOLL
This typical Dutch portrait bottle is cold-painted and gilded and wears easily. It is inadvisable to wash such pieces.

An 'onion' bottle, with a string rim, minor damage, c1720, 11½in (29cm) high.
£1,650–1,950
€2,350–2,800
$2,750–3,250 B
Ex-Harvey's Wine Museum sale.

◄ **A pair of shoulder decanters,** engraved 'Port' and 'Mountain', with cut spire stoppers, c1765, 10in (25.5cm) high.
£3,600–4,000
€5,200–5,800
$6,000–6,700 ⊞ CB
Mountain was a type of wine that came from Malaga in Spain. Decanters from this period are rare.

A pair of club-shaped decanters, engraved 'Brandy' and 'Rum', with flattened disc stoppers, late 18thC, 9in (23cm) high.
£470–560 / €680–810
$790–940 ⚒ DN

A taper decanter, engraved 'Brandy', some wear, late 18thC, 11¾in (30cm) high.
£230–270 / €330–390
$380–450 ⚒ DN

◄ **A taper decanter,** cut with flutes and eight stars, with a bevelled lozenge stopper, c1780, 9¾in (25cm) high.
£310–350 / €440–500
$520–590 ⊞ Som

A 'Rodney' or ship's decanter, cut with elliptical flutes, the neck with stepped facets, with a moulded target stopper, late 18thC, 7½in (19cm) high.
£1,250–1,500
€1,800–2,150
$2,100–2,500 ⚒ B
Ex-Harvey's Wine Museum sale.
Arguably the most popular of all decanter shapes, the ship's decanter coincided with Britain's naval supremacy. It was popularly dubbed the 'Rodney' in honour of Admiral Lord Rodney's victories, most notably over the French at the Battle of the Saints off Guadeloupe in 1781. 'Rodneys' appear in contemporary records perhaps more often than all other types combined.

A pair of ship's decanters, 1800–30, 10½in (26.5cm) high.
£1,350–1,500
€1,950–2,150
$2,250–2,500 ⊞ JAS

A pair of amethyst glass decanters, c1820, 10½in (26.5cm) high.
£1,800–2,150
€2,600–3,100
$3,000–3,600 ⚒ B
Ex-Harvey's Wine Museum sale.
These decanters are of an unusual colour.

Three decanters, with silver-plated mounts, in a silver-plated pierced stand with handle, c1850, 13¾in (35cm) high.
£560–670 / €810–960
$940–1,100 ⚒ DN

A pair of Prussian-shaped decanters, cut with flutes, with faceted neck rings, 1810–20, 10in (25.5cm) high.
£1,350–1,500
€1,950–2,150
$2,250–2,500 ⊞ Del

A pair of Prussian-shaped decanters, with diamond cutting below fan-cut shoulders and three neck rims, with cut mushroom stoppers, c1830, 7in (18cm) high.
£500–550 / €720–790
$830–920 ⊞ Som

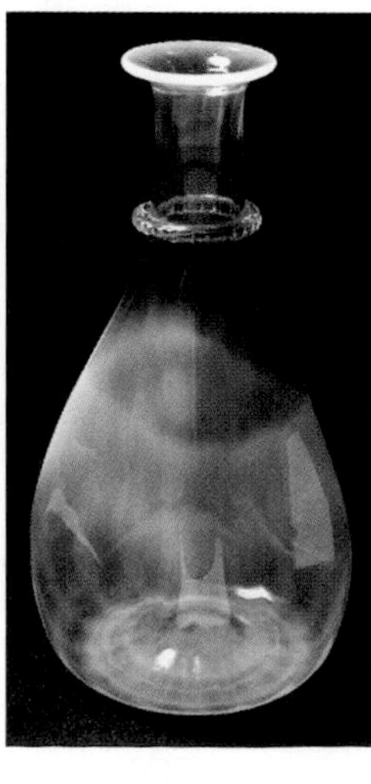

Flagon decanters

Flagon decanters appeared in all colours between 1835 and 1870. They had oval-sectioned bodies, short necks and often featured neck-mounted finger-rings. The earliest examples were *Bocksbeutel*, literally 'goatbag', made in the Spessart forest, near Würzburg, Germany, and imported into Britain containing Frankish wines. Their unusual shape inspired a local silversmith to start a fashion when he embellished one with a mount. Fine quality flagons, based on the original shape, were later made across Britain and in the United States.

Converted *Bocksbeutels* and flagon decanters were usually fitted with silver or silver-plated collars and stoppered with metal-fitted corks. The metal-makers Elkington produced at least 11 different stopper types for flagons, with finials including silver or plated balls, pull-rings, fruiting vines and a figure of Bacchus.

◀ **An amber glass flagon,** with a loop handle, metal mount and cork and metal stopper, c1830, 7½in (19cm) high.
£180–200 / €260–290
$300–330 ⊞ Som

A globe-and-shaft decanter, gilded with roses, French, c1840, 11in (28cm) high.
£790–880 / €1,100–1,250
$1,300–1,500 ⊞ BrW

◀ **A pair of straw opal tint carafes,** by Whitefriars, c1890, 6in (15cm) high.
£400–450 / €580–650
$670–750 ⊞ SHa
This 'Poppy Head' carafe is from a service designed by the Whitefriars Glass Works in 1880 and produced by the firm into the 1930s.

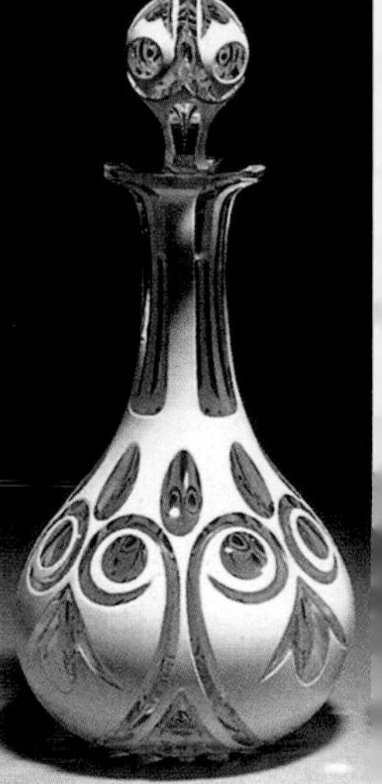

A pair of decanters, probably by Richardson of Stourbridge, cased in white glass cut away in swirling foliate designs, with stoppers, minor damage, 1845–50, 6½in (16.5cm) high.
£500–600 / €720–860
$840–1,000 ⚒ B
Ex-Harvey's Wine Museum sale.
W. H., B. & J. Richardson was established in 1829 by William Haden Richardson, his brother Benjamin and Thomas Webb in Wordsley, near Stourbridge. Webb was bought out for £7,000 / €10,100 / $11,800 in 1836 when the Richardson's younger brother Jonathan joined the firm. The company is known for its patented designs and high quality.

Bowls

A punch bowl, on a folded pedestal foot, c1730, 8¾in (22.5cm) wide.
£1,400–1,650 / €2,000–2,400
$2,350–2,750 B
Ex-Harvey's Wine Museum sale. Punch became a favourite beverage among the English after the capture of Jamaica from the Spanish in 1655, after which rum became more widely available. Eighteenth-century glass punch bowls remain remarkably common, probably because they were reserved for special occasions and put away after use.

A canoe-shaped bowl, cut with a band of star and diamond decoration beneath a waved rim, on an inverted baluster stem and a moulded lobed foot, minor damage, Irish, possibly Cork, c1790, 13¾in (35cm) wide.
£1,500–1,800 / €2,200–2,600
$2,500–3,000 DN

A honeycomb-moulded finger bowl, c1740, 4in (10cm) wide.
£480–530 / €690–760
$800–890 BrW
Bowls such as these were used for rinsing fingers after handling food during the course of a meal.

A Kosta butter dish and cover, the knop in the form of a crown, late 18thC, 6½in (16.5cm) high.
£810–970 / €1,200–1,400
$1,350–1,600 BUK
The presence of a crown suggests a royal association and boosts its value.

◀ **A set of eight cut-glass finger/dessert bowls,** c1880, 5in (12.5cm) diam.
£210–240 / €300–340
$350–400 BrW

▶ **A footed bowl,** 19thC, 9½in (24cm) diam.
£320–380 / €460–540
$540–640 SWO

A blue glass sugar bowl, c1790, 4½in (11cm) high.
£180–200 / €260–290
$300–330 BrW
Supplies of cobalt oxide – the agent that tints glass blue – became far more available after Bristol porcelain-maker William Cookworthy bought a vast supply of it in 1763.

A finger bowl, rib-moulded, c1830, 3¼in (8cm) high.
£90–100 / €130–145
$150–170 Som

GLASS

Boxes

A cut-glass box, with ormolu edges, French, 1825–50, 6½in (16.5cm) high.
£5,000–6,000 / €7,200–8,600
$8,400–10,000 S(NY)

A crystal jewellery casket, with ormolu decoration, central European, c1880, 8in (20.5cm) wide.
£400–450 / €580–650
$670–750 HTE

A casket, enamelled with fleurs-de-lys pendants and beaded garlands, heightened in gilt, with gilt-metal scrolled feet, Continental, late 19thC, 6½in (16.5cm) high.
£410–490 / €590–710
$690–820 RTo

Candlesticks & Candelabra

A pair of lustre candelabra, the lacquered-brass arms hung with icicle drops, c1820, 14in (35.5cm) high.
£2,700–3,000 / €3,900–4,300
$4,500–5,000 ⊞ Del

A pair of ruby-flashed candlesticks, Bohemian, 19thC, 11¼in (28.5cm) high.
£520–620 / €750–890
$870–1,000 ⚒ AG

A pair of lustre candlesticks, c1840, 8in (20.5cm) high.
£360–430 / €520–620
$600–720 ⚒ SWO

◀ **A pair of lustre candlesticks,** hung with cut-glass drops, late 19thC, 24in (61cm) high.
£1,500–1,650 / €2,150–2,400
$2,500–2,750 ⊞ JSt

▶ **A set of four candle holders,** cut with stylized bands of flowers, with brass collars, Continental, c1910, 19in (48cm) high.
£1,600–1,900 / €2,300–2,700
$2,700–3,200 ⚒ HOK

Centrepieces

◀ **A tazza,** the moulded pedestal stem on a domed base with a folded foot, c1750, 11½in (29cm) diam.
£190–220
€270–320
$320–370
⚒ GAK

A two-tier two-part epergne, the trumpet vase and two dishes engraved with ferns, c1870, 18in (45.5cm) high.
£450–500 / €650–720
$760–840 ⊞ CB
Ferns are an archetypal motif of Victorian engraving.

A cranberry glass epergne, with crimped rims, the two hanging baskets supported by glass canes, c1880, 21in (53.5cm) high.
£1,800–2,000
€2,600–2,900
$3,000–3,350 ⊞ CB

A Victorian cranberry glass epergne, the two hanging baskets supported by wrythen-moulded canes, 22in (56cm) high.
£550–660 / €790–950
$920–1,100 ⚒ FHF

A Victorian cranberry glass epergne, the two hanging baskets supported by wrythen-moulded green glass canes, 17in (43cm) high.
£150–180 / €220–260
$250–300 ⚒ WilP

▶ **An epergne,** the barley-twist branches supporting two hanging baskets, late 19thC, 22in (56cm) high.
£440–520 / €630–750
$740–870 ⚒ Bea

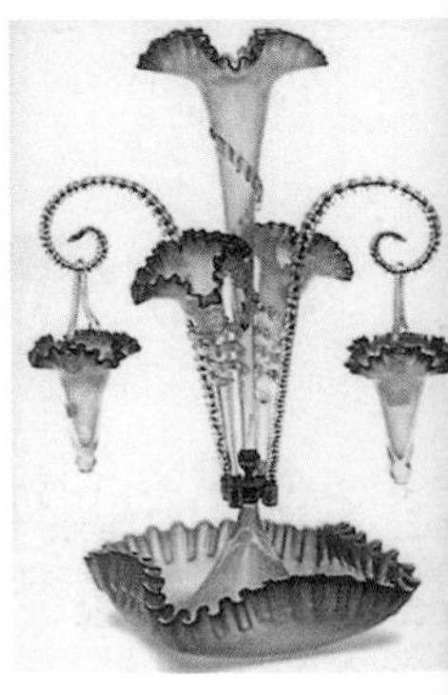

GLASS

Jars

A silver-mounted jar and cover, on a pedestal foot, the cover with a knop finial, c1790, 8¾in (22cm) high.
£210–250 / €300–360
$350–420 WW

A silver-mounted jar and cover, the silver collar by Paul Storr, engraved with trailing flowers and leaves, glass damaged, London 1800, 9in (23cm) high.
£560–670 / €800–960
$940–1,100 TEN

A pair of jars and covers, diamond-cut with slice-cut fans, on stepped bases, 19thC, 12½in (32cm) high.
£1,900–2,250
€2,750–3,250
$3,200–3,800 S

A pair of Regency cut-glass *bonbonnières,* on pedestal feet, slight damage, 9in (23cm) high.
£820–980 / €1,200–1,400
$1,400–1,650 F&C

Items in the Glass section have been arranged in date order within each sub-section.

◄ **A pair of cut-glass silver-mounted ginger jars and a tureen,** with covers, the tureen with a stand, slight damage, south Netherlands/French, 1830–60, ginger jars 11in (28cm) high.
£1,950–2,350 / €2,800–3,350
$3,300–3,950 S(Am)

Jugs

A cut-glass water jug, with prismatic and diamond cutting, c1815, 7½in (19cm) high.
£140–165 / €200–240
$240–280 G(L)

A cream jug, with a star-cut base, c1820, 4in (10cm) high.
£450–500 / €650–720
$760–840 CB

A pair of opaline glass jugs, decorated with gilt flowers and foliage, with scroll handles, 19thC, 12in (30.5cm) high.
£230–270 / €330–390
$390–450 AG

A Victorian glass claret jug, gilded with leaves and fitted with a silver-plated handle and cover, 10½in (26.5cm) high.
£460–550 / €660–790
$770–920 G(L)

A cream jug, with a ruby overlay rim, on a star-cut base, c1870, 6in (15cm) high.
£450–500 / €650–720
$760–840 CB

A silver-mounted claret jug, slight damage, Russian, Gratsev, 1896–1907, 10¾in (27cm) high.
£650–780 / €930–1,100
$1,100–1,300 BUK

► **A night jug and tumbler,** with intaglio-cut flowers, c1900, 8½in (21.5cm) high.
£250–300 / €360–430
$420–500 CB

GLASS

Lustres

A pair of cranberry glass lustres, decorated with enamel and gilt floral panels, on fluted stems and domed feet, drops missing, 19thC, 13¾in (35cm) high.
£1,650–1,950 / €2,350–2,800
$2,800–3,350 ⚒ AMB

These lustres are of a good colour and the casing, gilding and enamelling are all of the finest quality, resulting in a realized price in excess of the estimate.

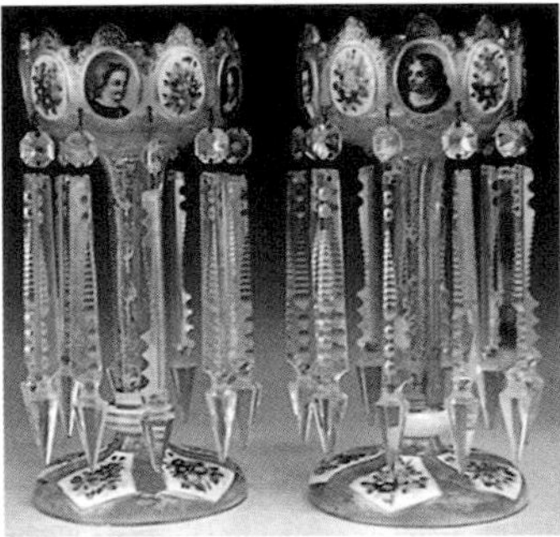

A pair of lustres, each overlaid with gilt foliate scrolls and enamel-painted panels of portraits and flowers, with cut-glass spear drops, slight damage, Bohemian, 1860–80, 12¼in (31.5cm) high.
£1,150–1,350 / €1,650–1,950
$1,950–2,250 ⚒ RTo

A pair of cut-glass lustres, each with prismatic-cut drops and a multi-faceted knopped stem on a facet-cut foot, slight damage, 1840–45, 13½in (34cm) high.
£640–770 / €920–1,100
$1,100–1,300 ⚒ BR

A pair of lustres, with crimped rims, decorated in cold enamels with clear prismatic drops, Bohemian, c1880, 9½in (24cm) high.
£175–210 / €250–300
$290–350 ⚒ GAK

► **A pair of lustres,** with cobalt-blue overlay, the lobed rims each hung with ten clear drops, on gilt-metal bases, Bohemian, c1880, 13¾in (35cm) high.
£940–1,100 / €1,350–1,600
$1,600–1,850 ⚒ PFK

A pair of frosted opaline glass lutres, with gilt decoration and cut and faceted drops, slight damage, Bohemian, c1860, 10¾in (27cm) high.
£120–145 / €170–200
$200–240 ⚒ L&E

A pair cranberry glass lustres, decorated with enamel and gilt, with prismatic drops, c1880, 14in (35.5cm) high.
£760–910 / €1,100–1,300
$1,250–1,500 ⚒ PF

GLASS

Paperweights

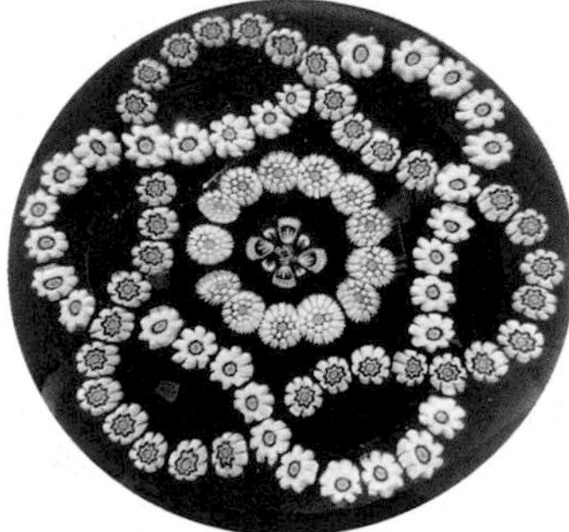

A Baccarat concentric paperweight, with interlaced trefoils, French, 1845–60, 3in (7.5cm) high.
£1,400–1,550 / €2,000–2,200
$2,350–2,600 ⊞ SWB

A Baccarat paperweight, with a double clematis, French, c1848, 2½in (6.5cm) diam.
£1,100–1,250 / €1,600–1,800
$1,850–2,100 ⊞ DLP

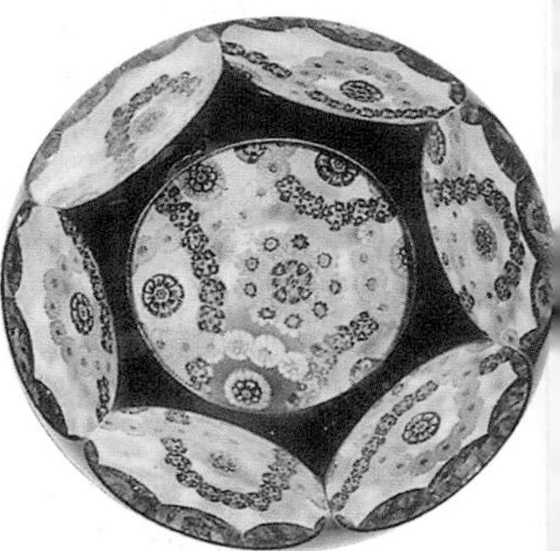

A Baccarat ruby overlay paper-weight, facet-cut with intersecting trefoil garlands formed of stardust canes and arrowhead canes, with 12 deep facets cut around the base, slight damage, French, c1850, 3in (7.5cm) diam.
£350–420 / €500–600
$590–700 ⚒ B

A paperweight, probably Baccarat, facet-cut with a flower spray, minor damage, French, 19thC, 3¼in (8cm) diam.
£320–380 / €460–550
$540–640 WW

A Clichy scattered millefiori paperweight, French, c1850, 2½in (6.5cm) diam.
£420–500 / €600–720
$700–840 G(L)

► **A Clichy millefiori paperweight,** French, 19thC, 1¾in (4.5cm) diam.
£280–330 / €400–480
$470–550 G(L)

A Baccarat close-pack millefiori mushroom paperweight, with a star-cut base, French, c1850, 3¼in (8cm) diam.
£610–730 / €880–1,050
$1,000–1,200 RTo

Items in the Paperweights section have been arranged alphabetically in factory order, with non-specific pieces appearing at the end.

A Clichy barber-pole paperweight, with a 'C' cane, French, 1845–60, 2½in (6.5cm) diam.
£3,500–3,900 / €5,000–5,600
$5,900–6,500 SWB

A Clichy millefiori paperweight, the canes divided by *latticinio* threads, French, c1880, 3¼in (8cm) diam.
£370–440 / €530–630
$620–740 B&L

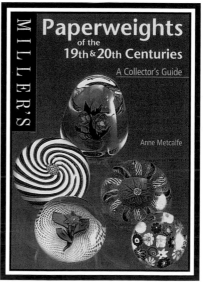

GLASS

A New England Glass Co paperweight, with a floral sheath, American, c1860, 4in (10cm) diam.
£3,850–4,300 / €5,500–6,200
$6,500–7,200 ⊞ DLP

A St Louis concentric amber-flash paperweight, facet-cut, French, 1845–60, 2¼in (3cm) diam.
£1,800–2,000 / €2,600–2,900
$3,000–3,350 ⊞ SWB

A St Louis paperweight, with a double dahlia, on a star-cut base, French, 1845–60, 2½in (6.5cm) diam.
£2,100–2,350 / €3,000–3,400
$3,500–3,900 ⊞ SWB

A St Louis paperweight, the *latticinio* staves radiating from a central millefiori cane, French, c1850, 3in (7.5cm) diam.
£1,500–1,800 / €2,200–2,600
$2,500–3,000 ⚒ DORO

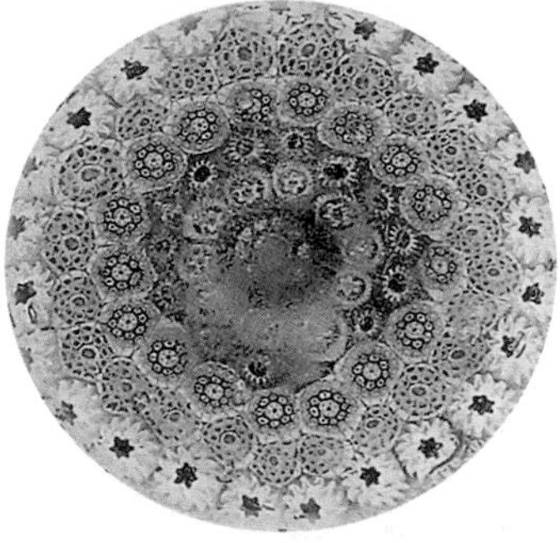

A St Louis concentric millefiori paperweight, slight damage, French, c1850, 2½in (6.5cm) diam.
£400–480 / €580–690
$670–800 ⚒ B

A Val St Lambert paperweight, with a flower, Belgian, c1850, 3¼in (8.5cm) diam.
£1,500–1,650 / €2,150–2,400
$2,500–2,750 ⊞ DLP

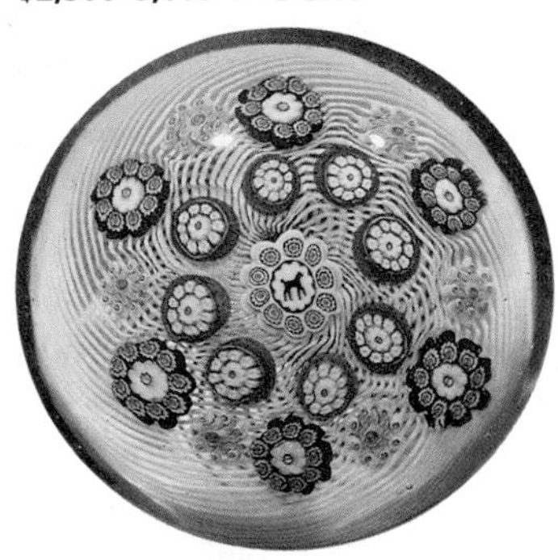

◄ **A concentric millefiori paperweight,** with spiral filigree, Bohemian, c1850, 2¼in (7cm) diam.
£940–1,050 / €1,350–1,500
$1,550–1,750 ⊞ DLP

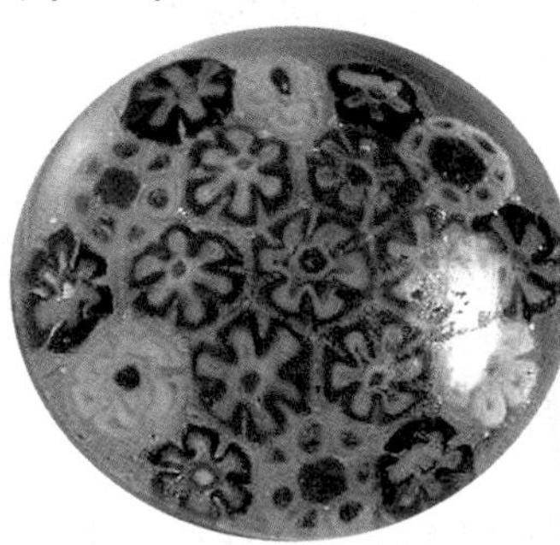

► **A pair of paperweights,** c1870, 2in (5cm) diam.
£135–150 / €195–220
$220–250 ⊞ HTE

Scent Bottles

A pair of gold-mounted scent bottles, atttributed to James Giles, 1765–70, 1¾in (4.5cm) high, in a shagreen étui.
£1,000–1,200 / €1,450–1,700
$1,700–2,000 ⚒ B

James Giles' decorations on glass, between 1760 and 1775, are remarkable for their diversity. Apart from pairs and sets, virtually no two pieces appear to share precisely the same design.

A pair of gilded scent bottles, c1840, 3in (7.5cm) high.
£270–300 / €390–430
$450–500 ⊞ BrW

Further reading

Miller's Perfume Bottles: A Collector's Guide, Miller's Publications, 1999

A gold-mounted opaline glass scent bottle, by Hunt Roskell, with a 'jewelled' monogram, 1860, 4in (10cm) high, in original case.
£1,100–1,250 / €1,600–1,800
$1,850–2,100 ⊞ CoS

Hunt Roskell, successors to Storr, Mortimer & Hunt, were among the finest Victorian silversmiths. Their shop was in New Bond Street, London. Collectors are usually prepared to pay a premium for examples by the best makers.

GLASS

A gilt-brass-mounted opaline glass scent bottle coffer, fitted with two cut-glass scent bottles with *verre églomisé* stoppers, the lid inlaid with a mother-of-pearl *verre églomisé* reserve of La Madeleine, French, c1870, 4¾in (12cm) high.
£410–490 / €590–700
$690–820 ⚒ NOA

A silver-mounted opaque glass scent bottle, probably Stourbridge, decorated with gilt and enamel prunus sprigs, stopper missing, maker's mark 'CM', silver cap Birmingham 1886, 3¼in (8cm) high.
£120–145 / €170–200
$200–240 ⚒ BR

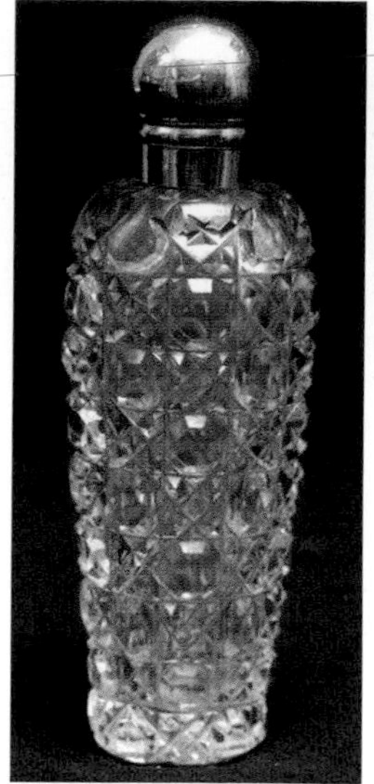

A silver-mounted cut-glass scent bottle, 1889, 5½in (14cm) high.
£105–120 / €150–170
$175–200 ⊞ GGD

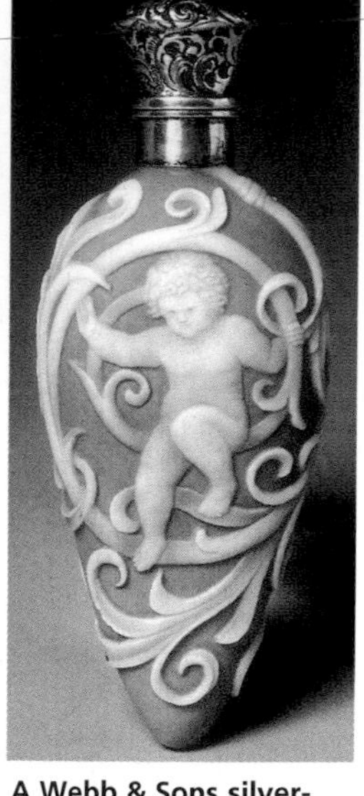

A Webb & Sons silver-mounted cameo glass scent bottle, attributed to George or Tom Woodall, relief-carved with a putto and scrolling foliage, the mounts embossed with scrolling leaves, with an inner glass stopper, slight damage, c1890, 5in (12.5cm) high.
£6,400–7,700
€9,200–11,100
$10,700–12,900 ⚒ B
The quality of the carving on this scent bottle would suggest an attribution to the Woodalls' workshop at Webb's. In addition, the treatment of the figure, similar to other putti found in signed Woodall pieces, is consistent with the high level of artistry associated with their work.

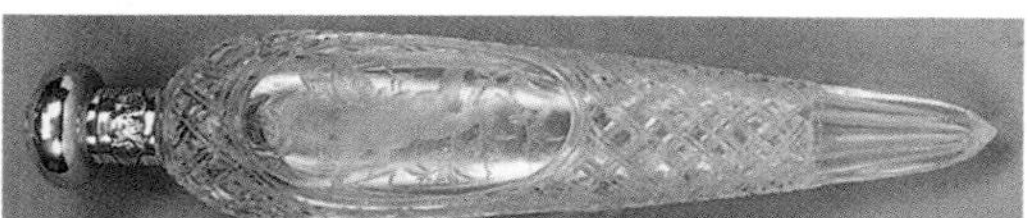

A Stourbridge silver-mounted scent bottle, the diamond-cut ground with an engraved panel, the mount with chased putti, with an inner stopper, silver probably William Comyns, London 1897, 9in (23cm) high.
£420–500 / €600–720
$700–840 ⚒ S(O)

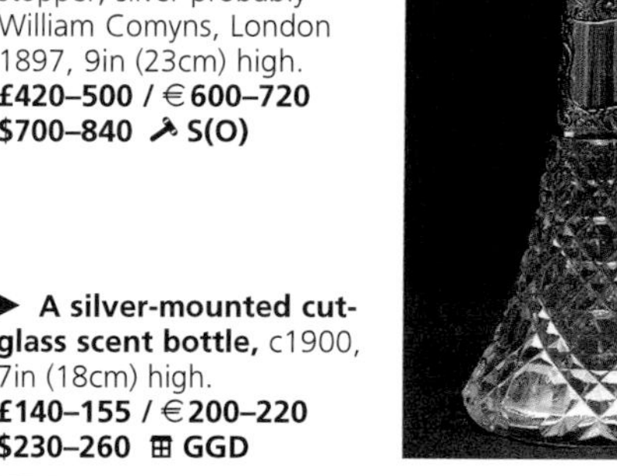

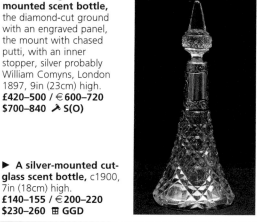

► **A silver-mounted cut-glass scent bottle,** c1900, 7in (18cm) high.
£140–155 / €200–220
$230–260 ⊞ GGD

A silver-mounted scent bottle, cut with hobnail diamonds on a star-cut base, silver Birmingham 1905, 4½in (11.5cm) high.
£165–185 / €240–270
$280–310 ⊞ GGD

Sweetmeat Glasses

◄ **A sweetmeat dish,** the ogee bowl with a crimped dentil rim, on a knopped stem and domed foot, 1730–40, 3½in (9cm) high.
£440–530
€630–760
$740–890 ⚒ DN

While collectors of 18th-century drinking glasses are prepared to pay four-figure sums for one example, sweetmeat dishes have failed to attract attention, with the result that these 250-year-old examples of English glass are often available for approximately £200 / €290 / $340.

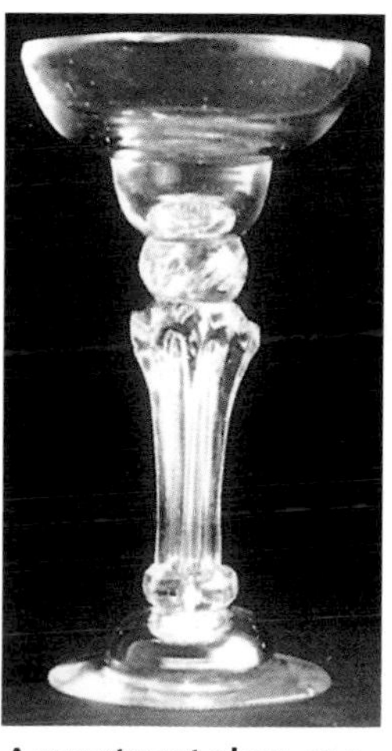

A sweatmeat glass, on a hollow stem and domed foot, chip to footrim, c1740, 6in (15cm) high.
£260–310 / €380–450
$440–520 ⚒ WW

A sweetmeat glass, the ogee bowl with a cupped rim, on a pedestal stem and domed foot, minor damage, c1745, 6¾in (17cm) high.
£210–250 / €300–360
$350–420 ⚒ TEN

Vases

A Staffordshire opaque glass bottle vase, enamel-painted with scattered floral sprays, c1760, 4¼in (11cm) high.
£560–670 / €800–960
$940–1,100 ⚒ DN

English 18th-century opaque-white glass was made to resemble porcelain. Changes to the rates of the Glass Excise Duty in 1777 made opaque-white glass more expensive at a time when the price of porcelain was falling, which greatly reduced the market for this type of glass.

A Stourbridge cameo glass vase, carved in relief with insects and flowers, the neck with a lappet band, minor damage, c1880, 15in (38cm) high.
£1,650–1,950
€2,350–2,800
$2,800–3,300 ⚒ DN

► **A pair of opaline glass vases,** painted with flower sprays, Continental, c1880, 8¾in (22cm) high.
£520–620 / €750–890
$870–1,050 ⚒ RTo

A cranberry glass vase, with white overlay and gilt Arabesque decoration, Bohemian, 1845–55, 11½in (29cm) high.
£260–310 / €370–440
$430–520 ⚒ FHF

A ruby-flashed vase, engraved with a stag and a doe, leaves and a fruiting vine, on a knopped stem and faceted foot, slight damage, Bohemian, c1860, 19in (48cm) high.
£820–980 / €1,200–1,400
$1,400–1,650 ⚒ B

A pair of glass vases, with white overlay and gilt decoration, 1845–50, 14¼in (36cm) high.
£940–1,100
€1,350–1,600
$1,550–1,850 ⚒ SWO

A pair of vases, probably Baccarat, French, 19thC, 14¼in (36cm) high, with giltwood pedestals.
£610–730 / €880–1,050
$1,000–1,200 ⚒ RTo

Items in the Glass section have been arranged in date order within each sub-section.

A ruby-flashed vase, engraved with Prague Cathedral, Bohemian, c1850, 9in (23cm) high.
£390–430 / €560–630
$650–720 ⊞ BrW

A vase, with blue overlay enamel decorated with flowers, probably Bohemian, c1880, 16½in (42cm) high.
£220–260 / €310–370
$370–440 ⚒ TRM

◄ **A pair of turquoise glass vases,** hand-painted in enamels with birds and flowers, the rims and handles with gilt decoration, slight wear, c1880, 9in (23cm) high.
£280–330 / €400–480
$470–550 ⚒ B(W)

Miscellaneous

A bell, c1870, 11in (28in) high.
£450–500 / €650–720
$760–840 ⊞ CB

An opaque bell, with a colourless handle, c1880, 9¾in (25cm) high.
£165–195 / €240–280
$280–330 ⚒ DN

► **A ruby glass bonbon dish,** with cover and stand, c1880, 6¼in (16cm) wide.
£150–180
€220–260
$250–300 ⚒ WilP

◄ **A pair of egg cups,** with gilt rims, minor wear, c1780, 3in (7.5cm) high.
£420–500
€600–720
$700–840 ⚒ B
Ex-Harvey's Wine Musuem Sale.

► **A Hyalith plate,** by Count Von Buquoy Glassworks, Bohemian, c1830, 6in (15cm) diam.
£230–270
€330–390
$380–450
⚒ DORO
Hyalith is opaque black glass resembling basalt, formulated by Count Von Buquoy in 1817.

A Nailsea-type pocket flask, decorated with spiralling stripes, early 19thC, 4in (10.5cm) high.
£160–190 / €230–270
$270–320 ⚒ PFK

A Nailsea-type flask, decorated with trailing, 19thC, 4in (10cm) high.
£120–145 / €170–200
$200–240 ⚒ WW

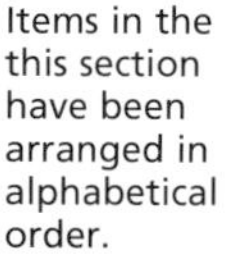

Items in the this section have been arranged in alphabetical order.

A Nonsuch wine glass rinser, gilded by Isaac Jabobs, inscribed 'I. Jacobs, Bristol', c1805, 3¾in (9.5cm) high.
£2,250–2,700 / €3,250–3,900
$3,750–4,500 ⚒ B
Ex-Harvey's Wine Museum sale.
While little blue glass was made in Bristol, the city's association with cobalt-blue glassware is reinforced by a small number of pieces with gilt decoration that bear the signature of I. Jacobs, Bristol. These were produced locally at Isaac Jacobs' Nonsuch Glassworks, and probably gilded by Michael Edkins. Jacobs' signature has been found on just three types of glassware: decanters, wine glass rinsers and a series of plates gilded with a stag's head, the heraldic symbol of the Earls of Verulam. However, blue glass was made in numerous other glassmaking centres, including Warrington, Sunderland and London, and most British cobalt-blue glassware was not made in Bristol.

A Salviati commemorative plate, minor damage, Venetian, c1900, 13½in (34.5cm) diam.
£570–680 / €820–980
$960–1,150 ⚒ S(Am)

A Pellatt & Green sulphide, signed, c1820, 4in (10cm) diam.
£570–630 / €820–910
$950–1,050 ⊞ BrW
Sulphides are small opaque-white medallions made of china clay or glass paste enclosed in transparent glass. They usually feature busts or figures embedded in the side or base of a clear glass object. The technique originated in the mid-18th century in Bohemia but was developed after 1775 by the Frenchman Barthélemy Desprez.

◄ **A tankard,** on a pedestal foot, c1780, 4¼in (11cm) high.
£450–500 / €650–720
$760–840 ⊞ Som

GLASS

Silver

Animals

A silver cow creamer, monogrammed, maker's mark possibly John Schuppe, London 1761, 6in (15cm) wide, 4½oz.
£5,300–6,300 / €7,600–9,100
$8,900–10,600 ⚒ Bea

A silver hedgehog toothpick holder, by Levi & Salaman, Birmingham 1903, 1¾in (4.5cm) long, ¼oz.
£210–250 / €300–360
$350–420 ⚒ WW

A silver pig pincushion, Birmingham 1905, 3½in (9cm) long.
£200–240 / €280–330
$340–400 ⚒ G(L)

A silver articulated fish patch box, set with turquoise eyes, c1880, 3in (7.5cm) long.
£280–320 / €400–440
$470–520 ⊞ LBr

A silver partridge scent bottle, by Berthold Muller, Chester 1903, 2½in (6.5cm) long.
£180–210 / €260–310
$300–360 ⚒ BR

A silver articulated model of a fish, by Neresheimer & Co, import mark for 1908, German, Hanau, 14in (35.5cm) long, 8oz.
£1,550–1,850 / €2,200–2,600
$2,600–3,100 ⚒ S(O)

► **A silver model of a peacock,** by Berthold Muller, London 1911–12, 16½in (42cm) diam, 37¼oz.
£4,000–4,500 / €5,700–6,300
$6,700–7,400 ⊞ NS

A silver model of a pig, Chester 1901, 1½in (4cm) high.
£240–270 / €340–380
$400–440 ⊞ BLm

A silver dachshund pepper caster, London 1904, 4in (10cm) long.
£730–870 / €1,000–1,200
$1,250–1,500 ⚒ RTo

Baskets

A silver sugar basket, by Edward Aldridge, with swing handle and glass liner, initialled, London 1771, 4¼in (11cm) diam, 3¾oz.
£430–520 / €630–750
$740–880 ⚒ Bea

A silver sugar basket, by Peter and Ann Bateman, with reeded borders and swing handle, on a pedestal foot, London 1794, 5½in (14cm) wide, 5oz.
£500–600 / €720–860
$840–1,000 ⚒ WW

A silver sweetmeat basket, embossed with a band of scrolling foliage, on a pedestal foot, Irish, Dublin 1805, 6½in (16.5cm) wide, 8oz.
£540–640 / €780–930
$900–1,050 ⚒ GH

A silver pierced basket, with gilt interior, Assay Master's mark AJ, Russian, St Petersburg, c1830, 10¾in (27.5cm) wide.
£1,300–1,550 / €1,850–2,200
$2,200–2,600 DORO

A silver basket, by Henry Wilkinson & Co, with cast and pierced foliate scroll swing handle, the body chased and embossed with putti among vines and tendrils within a rim cast with fruiting vines, on a lobed foot, Sheffield 1836, 9¾in (25cm) diam.
£500–600 / €720–860
$840–1,000 RTo

A silver bread basket, by Alexander Kordes, Russian, St Petersburg 1859, 13in (33cm) wide.
£740–900 / €1,100–1,300
$1,250–1,500 BUK

A silver repoussé basket, with rope-twist swing handle, repaired, maker's mark JB, London 1884, 6in (15cm) wide.
£120–140 / €170–200
$200–240 PF

A silver pierced fruit basket, with swing handle, on four scroll feet, maker's mark rubbed, Birmingham 1905, 11¾in (30cm) wide, 13½oz.
£140–160 / €200–240
$230–270 BR

A pair of silver baskets, Birmingham 1907, 5in (12.5cm) high.
£240–270 / €350–390
$400–440 BLm

Beakers

A silver beaker, by Anders Carlborg, with engraved decoration, Finnish, Turku 1780, 3¼in (8.5cm) high.
£500–600 / €720–860
$840–1,000 BUK

A silver beaker, with everted rim, the body engraved with foliate decoration and 'Orange', on a pedestal foot, rim split, maker's mark IJT below a crown, French, 19thC, 4in (10cm) high.
£190–220 / €270–310
$320–380 TEN

A silver-gilt and niello beaker, the frosted sides decorated with two panels, one depicting Falconet's statue of Peter the Great, the other a ruined building, scrolling foliage between, maker's mark TT, later Soviet marks, Russian, Moscow 1839, 3in (7.5cm) high, 3½oz.
£820–980 / €1,150–1,350
$1,350–1,600 B

A niello beaker, Russian, Moscow 1840, 3¼in (8.5cm) high.
£1,100–1,250
€1,600–1,800
$1,850–2,050 SHa

Items in the Silver section have been arranged in date order within each sub-section.

◄ **A silver-gilt beaker,** by George Fox, chased with a chinoiserie vignette and the inscription 'H.F.H.P. Clinton from his Godfather F.E.C. Byng March 6th 1866', London 1865, 3½in (9cm) high, 4¾oz.
£420–500 / €600–720
$700–840 WW

► **A silver quatrefoil beaker,** retailed by Mappin & Webb, with scaled sides, maker's mark LNM, London 1890, 4½in (11.5cm) high.
£230–280 / €350–420
$400–480 SWO

Bowls

A silver porringer, by Marmaduke Best, the body chased with flowers, beneath engraved initials 'I F', York 1667, 5in (12.5cm) wide, 3½oz.
£6,400–7,800 / €9,400–11,200
$10,900–13,000 ⚒ TEN

A silver porringer, the rope-style band flanked by struck foliate decoration above a part-wrythen gadrooned base with vacant cartouche, framed scrolls, maker's mark and date mark rubbed, lion head and Britannia mark, early 18thC, 3½in (9cm) high.
£230–280 / €350–420
$400–480 ⚒ SWO

A silver porringer, by Thomas Whipham, modelled as a loving cup, the body chased and embossed with a scrolling and chased cartouche, with rope-twist band, London 1774, 4¼in (11cm) high, 9½oz.
£470–560 / €680–810
$790–940 ⚒ BR

A silver sugar bowl, by Martin & Hall, with a beaded rim, the body with embossed floral festoons suspended from applied masks with engraved festoons in the background, gilt interior, Sheffield 1864, 5in (12.5cm) diam, 8oz.
£240–300 / €360–430
$420–500 ⚒ WW

A silver armorial bowl, by Edward Workman, Irish, Dublin 1717, 7in (18cm) diam.
£18,900–21,000 / €27,000–32,000
$32,000–36,000 ⊞ WELD
This bowl is highly desirable because of the attractive armorial device, early date and Irish origin.

A silver bowl, by John Swift, engraved with a rococo armorial cartouche flanked by military trophies and with motto scroll below, on a tucked-in foot, 1732, engraving c1750, 8½in (21.5cm) diam, 23½oz.
£13,000–15,500 / €18,700–22,400
$21,800–26,000 ⚒ B
Although the armorial is later in date than the actual bowl, it is still contemporary and has not adversely affected the price, as the piece is an example of fine craftsmanship.

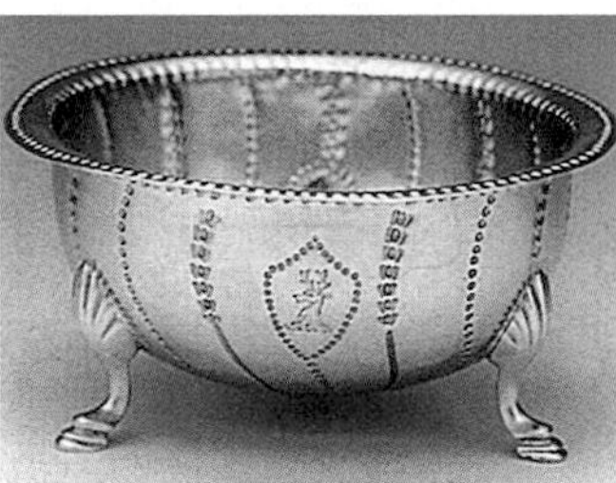

A silver sugar bowl, by Thomas Harman, the rim chased in geometric designs with a punched bead rim, above a shield cartouche enclosing a family crest, on three hoof feet with shell knees, Irish, Cork, c1785, 5½in (14cm) diam, 6¼oz.
£3,150–3,500 / €4,600–5,100
$5,300–5,900 ⊞ NS

A silver bowl, by Henry Wilkinson, Sheffield 1867, 4½in (11.5cm) high.
£230–260 / €330–370
$390–430 ⊞ GRe

A Britannia standard silver porringer, by Thomas Mason, with beaded scroll handles, engraved with initials, three further pairs of initials on base, London, c1718, 3in (7.5cm) high.
£800–960 / €1,150–1,350
$1,350–1,600 ⚒ F&C

A silver sugar bowl, probably by Robert Glanville, embossed with birds holding fruit and flower pendants, on shell feet headed by female masks, underside initialled 'JJR', Irish, Dublin, c1760, 5in (12.5cm) diam, 8oz.
£3,850–4,600 / €5,500–6,600
$6,400–7,600 ⚒ S

A silver sauce bowl and dish, by Erik Adolf Zethelius, with gilt interior, Swedish, Stockholm 1837, dish 6¾in (17.5cm) diam.
£600–720 / €860–1,000
$1,000–1,200 ⚒ BUK

A silver sugar bowl, by John and Henry Lias, decorated with a chased frieze and beading, gilt interior, London 1872, 4½in (11.5cm) diam.
£120–140 / €170–200
$200–240 ⚒ WW

LOCATE THE SOURCE
The source of each illustration in Miller's can be found by checking the code letters below each caption with the Key to Illustrations, pages 794–800.

A silver bowl, London 1889, 4½in (11.5cm) wide.
£160–180 / €230–260
$270–300 ⊞ EXC

For further information on
Tiffany & Co see pages 473–474

A silver bowl, by Daniel and John Wellby, with cast floral and foliate rim, the body embossed with floral swags against a pierced trellis ground, on a domed foot, London 1896, 13¼in (33.5cm) wide.
£900–1,050 / €1,300–1,750
$1,500–1,800 ⚒ RTo

A silver bowl, by Tiffany & Co, maker's mark, American, c1895, 8in (20.5cm) wide.
£850–950 / €1,200–1,350
$1,400–1,550 ⊞ SHa

A silver sweet/sauce bowl, with chased, pierced and repoussé decoration, London 1896, 7in (18cm) wide.
£400–450 / €570–650
$670–750 ⊞ CoHA

A silver rose bowl, by Charles Stuart Harris, with wrythen fluted and punched decoration, London 1896, 9in (23cm) diam.
£500–600 / €720–860
$840–1,000 ⚒ GAK

A silver hand-raised bowl, by Heming & Co, London 1912, 4in (10cm) diam.
£140–160 / €200–220
$230–260 ⊞ CoHA

Covered Bowls

A silver sugar bowl and cover, by Marthinus Lourens Smith, South African, late 18thC, 6¾in (17cm) high, 12oz.
£4,700–5,600 / €6,800–8,000
$7,900–9,400 ⚒ BR

A silver sugar bowl, with indistinct maker's marks, Swedish, Stockholm 1801, 8¼in (21cm) high.
£1,050–1,250 / €1,500–1,800
$1,750–2,100 ⚒ BUK

A silver rococo sugar bowl and cover, the cover engraved with flowers, Assay Master's mark IGG, German, c1780, 5½in (14cm) diam.
£480–570 / €690–820
$800–960 ⚒ DORO

A silver sugar bowl, the cover with a tooled band of acanthus leaves, Assay Master's mark FH for Franz Hellmayer, Austrian, Vienna 1807, 6¾in (17cm) wide.
£700–840 / €1,000–1,200
$1,150–1,350 ⚒ DORO

► **A silver sugar bowl,** by Fredrik Tiander, Finnish, Lovisa 1842, 10¾in (27.5cm) high.
£1,800–2,150 / €2,600–3,200
$3,000–3,600 ⚒ BUK

Sugar containers

In the late 17th and early 18th centuries, sugar was kept in boxes – there are still many to be found in America, as much of the sugar came from the West Indies. Bowls with reversible covers, probably for holding a spoon, began to appear in the early 18th century, and by the middle of the century the covers generally had cone finials. The vase shape then became fashionable, the covers sometimes cut to hold a spoon. In the 1770s, the vases no longer had covers, and bowls were eventually replaced by larger, open sugar baskets.

Boxes

A silver presentation box, by Richard Stevens, Irish, Cork, c1795, 3in (7.5cm) wide.
£2,200–2,450 / €3,150–3,500
$3,700–4,100 ⊞ WELD

A silver snuff/dressing table box, Birmingham 1888, 5in (12.5cm) diam.
£200–230 / €290–330
$330–380 ⊞ EXC

► **A silver trinket box,** London 1894, 2in (5cm) wide.
£140–155 / €200–220
$230–260 ⊞ CoHA

A silver repoussé-decorated box, French, c1895, 5½in (14cm) diam.
£850–950 / €1,200–1,350
$1,450–1,600 ⊞ SHa

A silver nutmeg grater, by Thomas Phipps and Edward Robinson II, London 1801, 2¼in (5.5cm) wide, 2oz.
£880–1,050 / €1,250–1,500
$1,550–1,750 ⚒ Bea

A silver ring box, the cartouche with inscription, on four paw feet, Birmingham 1902, 6½in (16.5cm) wide.
£300–360 / €430–510
$500–600 ⚒ TMA

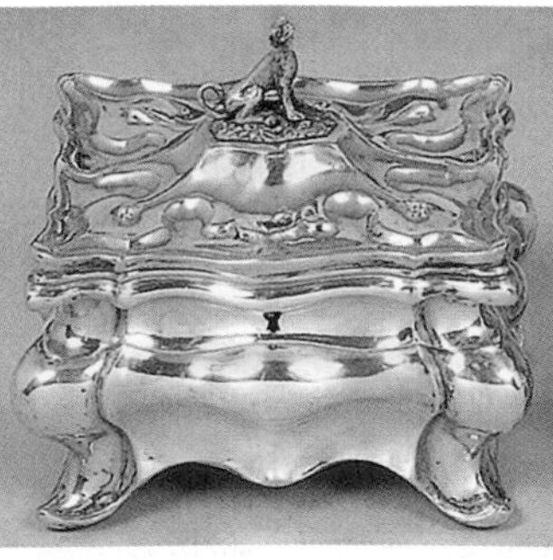

A silver sugar box, with gilt interior, Assay Master's mark CS, Austrian, Vienna 1854, 5½in (14cm) wide, 11½oz.
£690–830 / €1,000–1,200
$1,150–1,350 ⚒ DORO

A silver repoussé-decorated dressing table box, Chester 1901, 5½in (14cm) wide.
£120–140 / €170–200
$200–230 ⚒ WilP

A silver playing cards box, Birmingham 1909, 3¼in (8.5cm) high.
£330–370 / €470–530
$550–620 ⊞ BLm

Caddy Spoons

A silver caddy spoon, by Samuel Pemberton, the fluted bowl inset with a filigree panel, with a ring handle, Birmingham 1804, 1¾in (4.5cm) long.
£270–320 / €390–460
$450–540 ⚒ WW

► **A silver caddy spoon,** by Henry Ellis, with a fluted bowl, the handle relief-decorated with a leaf, stamped registered design number, Exeter 1849, 3¾in (9.5cm) long, ½oz.
£120–140 / €170–200
$200–230 ⚒ WW

A silver caddy spoon, by Joseph Willmore, with bright-cut handle, the bowl inset with a filigree panel, Birmingham 1808, 3¼in (8.5cm) long.
£270–320 / €390–460
$450–540 ⚒ AH

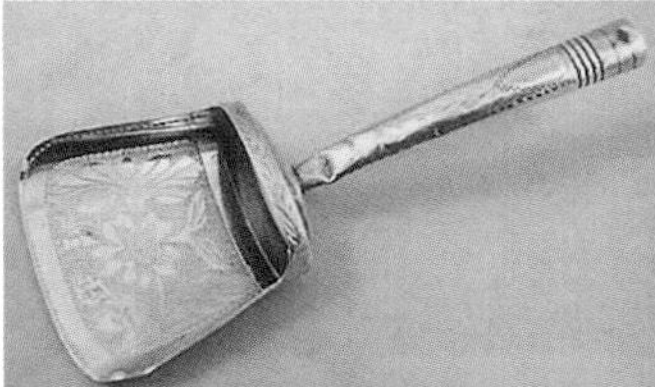

A George IV silver caddy spoon, by John Lawrence & Co, Birmingham 1829, 3¼in (8cm) long.
£150–180 / €220–260
$250–300 ⚒ BR

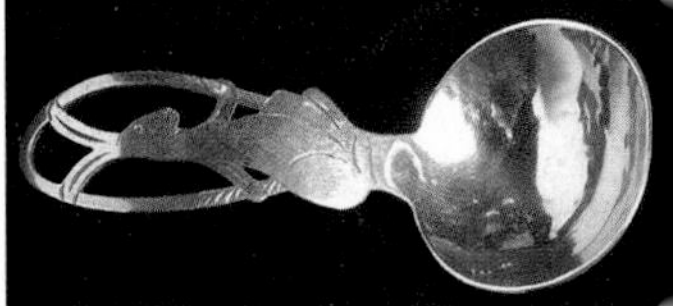

A silver caddy spoon, Birmingham 1936, 3in (7.5cm) long, with box.
£100–110 / €145–160
$170–190 ⊞ BLm

SILVER

Candlesticks & Chambersticks

A silver chamberstick, by John Boddington, with a reeded border and ring handle, the pan engraved with an armorial and the sconce with a double crest, London 1697, 5½in (14cm) diam, 7oz.
£720–860 / €1,050–1,250
$1,200–1,450 ⚒ S(O)

◄ **A set of four silver candlesticks,** by David King, after a design by Joseph Bird of London, Irish, Dublin 1702, 10in (25.5cm) high, 112oz.
£234,000–260,000 / €337,000–375,000
$390,000–440,000 ⊞ WELD
These candlesticks were among the most important pieces of Irish silver to come onto the market in over 50 years. A set of four in this very desirable style is a great rarity.

A cast silver candlestick, with a knopped baluster column, scratchweight marks, Irish, Dublin 1727, 6in (15cm) high, 10oz.
£1,350–1,600
€1,950–2,300
$2,250–2,700 ⚒ WW

A set of four candlesticks, by James Gould, London 1743, 8in (20.5cm) high.
£11,000–12,500
€15,800–18,000
$18,500–21,000 ⊞ TSC

A pair of silver candlesticks, by Gilles Berryer, with fluted baluster columns, Belgian, Liège, 1747–48, 9in (23cm) high, 30oz.
£7,300–8,700
€10,500–12,500
$12,200–14,600 ⚒ B

A pair of cast silver candlesticks, with knopped stems and embossed bases, maker's mark possibly IC, London 1767, 10in (25.5cm) high.
£2,350–2,800
€3,350–4,000
$3,950–4,700 ⚒ GAK

A silver chamberstick, relief-decorated with stylized leaves, the handle with wooden grip, Assay Master's mark GF for Giovanni Fina, Italian, Turin, c1780, 5¼in (13.5cm) diam, 11½oz.
£1,950–2,350 / €2,800–3,350
$3,300–3,950 ⚒ DORO

A pair of silver candlesticks, embossed with swags, the feet with stylized leaves, French, late 18thC, 10¼in (26cm) high.
£2,100–2,500 / €3,000–3,600
$3,500–4,200 ⚒ BERN

A silver chamberstick, by Richard Sawyer, Irish, Dublin 1816, 3½in (9cm) high.
£1,150–1,300 / €1,650–1,850
$1,950–2,200 ⊞ WELD

A pair of silver candlesticks, Birmingham 1898, 8in (20.5cm) high.
£450–500 / €650–720
$750–840 ⊞ HTE

◄ **A set of four silver candlesticks,** by Reed & Barton, decorated with rococo scrolls and flowers and monogrammed cartouches, American, Massachusetts, c1900, 10½in (26.5cm) high.
£1,100–1,300 / €1,550–1,850
$1,850–2,200 ⚒ NOA

SILVER

Candle Snuffers & Trays

A silver candle snuffer tray, by William Archdall, with a crest, the handle with a bifurcated scroll, on four button feet, Irish, Dublin 1717, 7¼in (18.5cm) wide, 8½oz.
£3,300–3,950 / €4,750–5,700
$5,500–6,600 WW

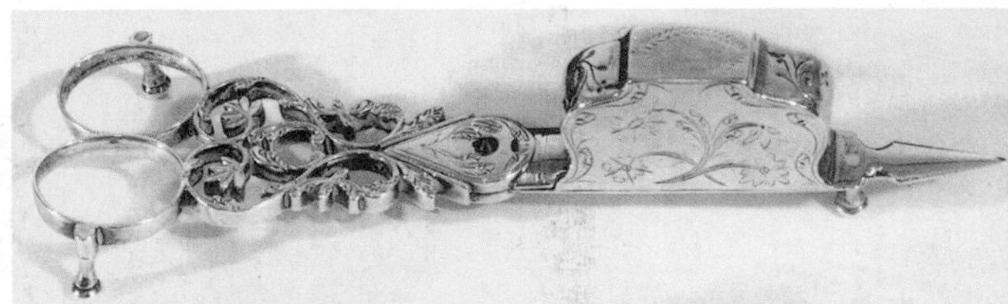

A pair of silver candle snuffers, London 1759, 6½in (16.5cm) long, 3oz.
£470–560 / €670–800
$790–940 AH

► A pair of silver candle snuffers, by William Bayley, London 1795, 6½in (16.5cm) long.
£720–800 / €1,000–1,150
$1,200–1,350 BLm

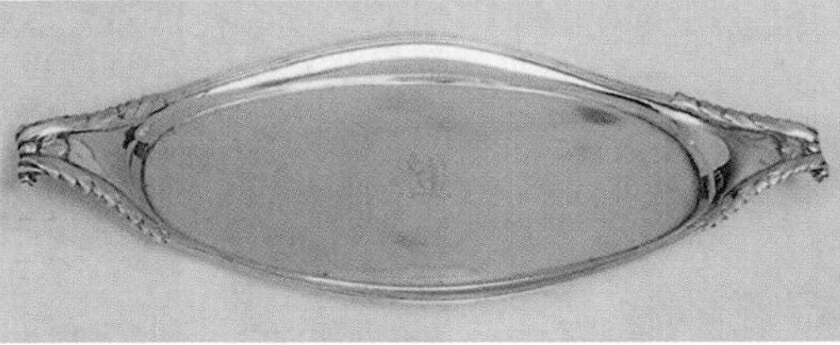

A silver candle snuffer tray, by Robert and David Hennel, engraved with a squirrel crest, London 1796, 10in (25.5cm) wide, 5oz.
£230–280 / €350–420
$400–480 NSal

A silver candle snuffer tray, by J. Le Bass, Irish, Dublin 1813, 8½in (21.5cm) wide.
£1,050–1,200 / €1,500–1,700
$1,750–2,000 SIL

Card Cases

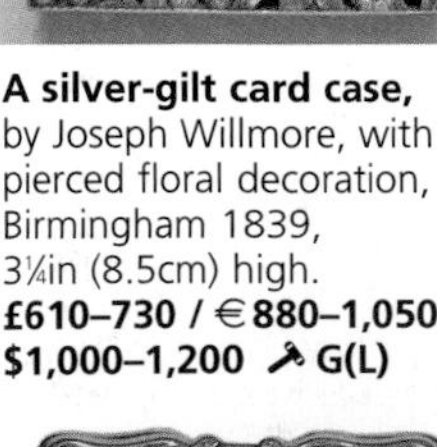

A silver-gilt card case, by Joseph Willmore, with pierced floral decoration, Birmingham 1839, 3¼in (8.5cm) high.
£610–730 / €880–1,050
$1,000–1,200 G(L)

A silver castle top card case, by Nathaniel Mills, decorated with Windsor Castle, with engraved coronet and initials, Birmingham 1843, 4in (10cm) high.
£1,300–1,550
€1,850–2,200
$2,200–2,600 HYD

A silver castle top card case, by Frederick Marsden, with a vignette of Warwick Castle, Birmingham 1845, 4in (10cm) high, 2oz.
£590–700 / €850–1,000
$990–1,150 WW

A silver card case, with bright-cut foliate decoration, Birmingham 1849, 4in (10cm) high, in a leather case.
£210–250 / €300–360
$350–420 GAK

Items in the Silver section have been arranged in date order within each sub-section.

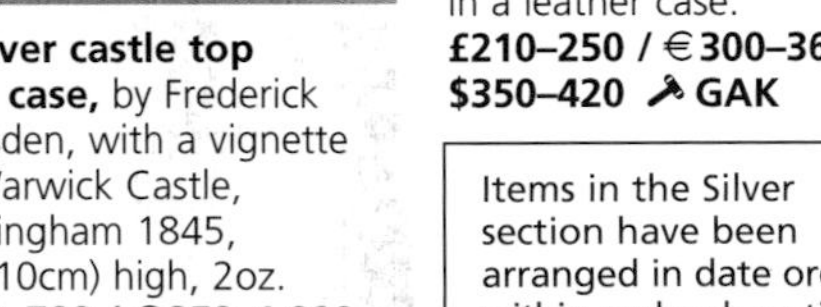

Castle top card cases are so-called because they are embossed or engraved with a view of a tourist attraction such as the castles of Windsor, Kenilworth or Warwick.

◄ A silver castle top card case, by Nathaniel Mills, relief-decorated with a view of Abbotsford, Birmingham 1850, 4in (10cm) high, 2oz.
£1,300–1,550
€1,850–2,200
$2,200–2,600 Bri

► A silver castle top card case, by Edward Smith, relief-decorated with Crystal Palace, Birmingham 1850, 4in (10cm) high, 2½oz.
£1,100–1,300
€1,550–1,850
$1,850–2,200 Bri

A silver card case, by A. Thomason, engraved coat-of-arms, motto and initials, maker's mark, Birmingham 1853, 4in (10cm) high, 2oz.
£200–240 / €290–340
$340–400 BR

A silver card case, engraved with foliate scrolls, maker's mark CC, Birmingham 1867, 4in (10cm) high.
£120–140 / €170–200
$200–240 BR

A silver-gilt filigree card case, French, c1875, 2¾in (7cm) high.
£270–300 / €390–430
$450–500 JTS

A silver card case, by George Unite, with chased foliate decoration and an initialled cartouche, Birmingham 1879, 5in (12.5cm) wide, 2oz.
£200–240 / €290–340
$340–400 AH

◄ **A silver card case,** decorated with cherubs, with a chain, Birmingham 1901, 4¼in (11cm) wide.
£340–380
€490–550
$570–640
BLm

◄ **A silver card case,** the interior with green watered silk lining, an ivory *aide-memoire* and a pencil, Chester 1906, 4in (10cm) high.
£105–125 / €150–180
$180–210 AH

Casters

◄ **A silver sugar caster,** by William Gamble, the cover with bayonet fitting, the base with a gadrooned border, London 1697, 6¾in (17cm) high, 6½oz.
£4,100–4,900
€5,900–7,000
$6,900–8,200 TEN

A silver caster, by Charles Adam, London 1713, 4¾in (12cm) high, 2¾oz.
£610–730 / €880–1,050
$1,000–1,200 Bea

A silver caster, by Zachariah Bridgen, engraved with a monogram, American, Boston, c1760, 5½in (13.5cm) high, 2½oz.
£2,200–2,650
€3,200–3,800
$3,700–4,500 NOA
This piece represents an extremely rare example of pre-Revolutionary American table silver. Zachariah Brigden (1734–87) was an accomplished and well-recorded silversmith in 18th-century Boston. Although prolific and known to have been a supplier to the trade, perhaps fewer than 100 examples of his work survive, many of them in churches in Massachusetts, Maine and Connecticut.

A silver pepper caster, by Thomas Daniel, London 1775, 5in (12.5cm) high.
£320–360 / €460–520
$540–600 GRe

A silver caster, by Reily & Storer, London 1839, 5in (12.5cm) high.
£165–185 / €240–270
$280–310 CoHA

► **A Britannia Standard silver sugar caster,** by Charles Stuart Harris, with wrythen-fluted body, London 1894, 6½in (16.5cm) high, 7oz.
£370–440 / €530–630
$620–740 BR

Centrepieces

A silver centrepiece, by Joseph Scammel, the pierced sides with vacant cartouches and a chased band of stiff leaves, the centre engraved with a coat-of-arms, with ram's-mask drop-ring handles, on four ball feet, cranberry glass liner, London 1795, 13½in (34.5cm) wide.
£3,400–4,000 / €4,900–5,700
$5,700–6,700 WW

A pair of silver tazzas, by Robert Garrard, with basketweave borders and knopped pedestal bases, London 1850, 9½in (24cm) high, 89¾oz.
£2,150–2,550 / €3,100–3,650
$3,600–4,300 S(O)

A silver centrepiece, embossed with flowers and foliage and two detachable enamel plaques, one with a crest, the other with the American flag surmounted by an eagle, with scrolling foliage and mask handles, London 1889, 23in (58.5cm) wide, 128oz.
£2,700–3,250 / €3,850–4,650
$4,500–5,400 E

Items in the Silver section have been arranged in date order within each sub-section.

A silver rococo revival-style centrepiece, by P. Bruckmann & Söhne, the latticework sides decorated with C-scrolls, acanthus leaves and flowers, the dolphin handles with putti mounts, with gilt-metal liner, German, Heilbronn, c1890, 11½in (29cm) wide, 16oz.
£1,100–1,300 / €1,600–1,900
$1,850–2,200 NOA

A silver epergne, the central stem with lobed and pierced rim, Birmingham 1913, 10½in (26.5cm) high.
£350–420 / €500–600
$590–700 AH

A silver epergne, the pierced central basket supporting three pierced baskets with swing-loop handles, Birmingham 1924, 12¼in (31cm) high, 44oz.
£640–760 / €920–1,100
$1,050–1,250 CDC

Cigar & Cigarette Cases

A silver and niello tobacco/cheroot case, the cover decorated with a floral spray, the base bordered by scrolls, probably Russian Provincial/Caucasian, 1850–70, 4¼in (11cm) wide.
£140–165 / €195–230
$230–280 WW

A silver and niello cigarette case, with gilt interior, Russian, Moscow 1877, 3½in (9cm) wide.
£330–390 / €470–560
$550–650 BUK

► **A silver cigarette case,** celebrating the Moscow to St Petersburg air race, decorated with a cartouche depicting a monoplane, Russian, 1911–12, 4½in (11.5cm) wide.
£850–950 / €1,200–1,350
$1,450–1,600 AU

◄ **A silver and niello cheroot case,** the cover decorated with an architectural scene, maker's mark partially distorted, Russian, Moscow 1888, 4in (10cm) wide.
£190–220 / €270–320
$320–370 WW

A silver and niello cigarette case, the cover decorated with a view of St Petersburg within chased borders, St Petersburg hallmark, Russian, 19thC, 3¾in (9.5cm) wide.
£280–330 / €400–470
$470–550 RTo

Coffee, Chocolate & Teapots

A silver chocolate pot, by R. Wouldham, Irish, Dublin, c1735, 9in (23cm) high.
£15,600–17,400 / €22,500–25,000 $26,000–29,200 ⊞ WELD
Irish antiques are still keenly collected in Ireland and America, and chocolate pots are scarcer than coffee pots.

A silver coffee pot, with spiral finial, foliate spout and ivory handle, London 1767, 10¾in (27.5cm) high.
£1,250–1,500 / €1,800–2,150 $2,100–2,500 ⚒ HOK

A Gustavian-style silver coffee pot, by Petter Eneroth, with a rose finial and ebony handle, Swedish, Stockholm 1782, 8¾in (22.5cm) high.
£2,350–2,800 / €3,400–4,050 $3,950–4,700 ⚒ BUK

► A silver coffee biggin, by William Eaton, London 1824, 8½in (21.5cm) high.
£900–1,000 / €1,300–1,450 $1,500–1,650 ⊞ GRe

A silver coffee pot, by Richard Bayley, with scrolled wood handle, London 1736, 9in (23cm) high, 21oz.
£960–1,150 / €1,400–1,650 $1,600–1,900 ⚒ S(O)

A silver coffee pot, by John King, with a twisted fluted finial, leaf-moulded spout and composition handle, London 1773, 12¼in (31cm) high, 29oz.
£2,050–2,450 / €2,950–3,500 $3,400–4,000 ⚒ Bri

An Empire-style silver teapot, by Adolf Zethelius, one side decorated with the head of Medusa, minor dents, later handle, Swedish, Stockholm 1814, 5½in (14cm) high.
£910–1,100 / €1,300–1,550 $1,500–1,800 ⚒ BUK

A silver coffee pot, by Alexis Peze Pilleau, chased with masks, shells and scrolls, with a crest, London 1737, 9¼in (23.5cm) high.
£1,900–2,250 / €2,750–3,250 $3,200–3,800 ⚒ LAY

A silver saffron pot, by John Wakelin and William Taylor, London 1776–77, 3in (7.5cm) high.
£3,400–3,750 / €4,900–5,400 $5,700–6,300 ⊞ NS
This very attractive pot is rare because of its small size. It would have been used to make infusions of saffron for medicinal purposes.

A silver teapot, by John Walton, later monogram, Newcastle 1816, 7in (18cm) high.
£380–450 / €540–650 $630–750 ⚒ SWO

A silver teapot, by Richard Garde, with a flower bud finial, embossed with flowers, fruit and scrolls, Irish, Dublin 1831, 8¼in (21cm) high.
£590–710 / €850–1,000 $1,000–1,200 ⚒ RTo

SILVER

A coin silver coffee pot, by William V. Moore & Co, decorated with chased panels and bouquets, the cover decorated with oak leaves, the handle with acanthus scrolls and grapevines, on a cast acanthus scroll foot, American, Mobile, c1855, 9in (23cm) high, 28½oz.
£1,650–2,000 / €2,400–2,850
$2,800–3,350 NOA
Moore was in partnership in Mobile, Alabama with William Steadman in 1844 and with his more prolific and better-known contemporary J. Conning in 1852. By 1854, however, he had established his own shop which operated until the outbreak of the Civil War. His work is much rarer than that of Conning or the l'Hommedieu brothers, the major Mobile silversmiths.

A silver teapot, engraved with foliate scrolls and a cartouche, on four cast foliate feet, London 1863, 8in (20.5cm) high, 25oz.
£350–420 / €500–600
$590–700 L&E

A silver teapot, by Charles Stuart Harris, the cover with an urn finial, the body with a flowerhead-decorated frieze above twin-beaded bands and a reeded lower body, London 1878, 5½in (14cm) high, 19oz.
£240–290 / €350–420
$400–480 PFK

A silver coffee pot, by E. & J. Barnard, the cover with a scrolled finial, the body diaper-engraved with rosettes, London 1866, 9in (23cm) high, 24oz.
£380–460 / €550–660
$640–770 CGC

A silver teapot, London 1925, 6½in (16.5cm) high.
£540–600 / €780–860
$900–1,000 BLm

Coffee & Tea Services

◄ **A silver three-piece tea and coffee service,** by Carl Johann Berg, with a gilt interior, engraved with garlands of flowers and medallions, ebony handles, Russian, St Petersburg 1802, coffee pot 8in (20.5cm) high.
£3,000–3,600 / €4,300–5,100
$5,000–6,000 BUK

A silver three-piece tea and coffee service, by Wolfers, decorated in high relief with garlands of flowers, the tea and coffee pot with lion-head spouts and wooden handles, the sugar bowl with lion-head ring handles, Belgian, Brussels, 1831–68, teapot 11½in (29cm) high.
£2,400–2,850 / €3,450–4,100
$4,050–4,800 DORO
This service is fine quality work by the Belgian court jewellers Wolfers.

A silver three-piece tea service, chased and engraved with scroll and foliate motifs enclosing a central crested cartouche, gilt interior, Irish, Dublin 1824.
£2,500–3,000 / €3,600–4,300
$4,200–5,000 JAd

Irish silver

Recently Irish silver has become extremely popular, particularly in Ireland and America. The largest quantities come from Dublin, with Cork silver being about five times scarcer than Dublin silver, and Limerick silver being 20–30 times scarcer than Cork silver. Items from Galway or Kinsale are extremely rare. Collectors should choose pieces of typical Irish style and of good authentic colour with original armorials or crests when possible. There should be no added treatments such as flagellation or plating. Missing date letters are quite common in the Dublin hallmark from 1738 to 1785.

A silver three-piece tea service, by R. Smith, with chased, engraved foliate and scallop decoration to the rims, the bodies on foliate and scroll-decorated feet, Irish, Dublin 1844 and 1846.
£1,600–1,900 / €2,300–2,750
$2,700–3,200 JAd

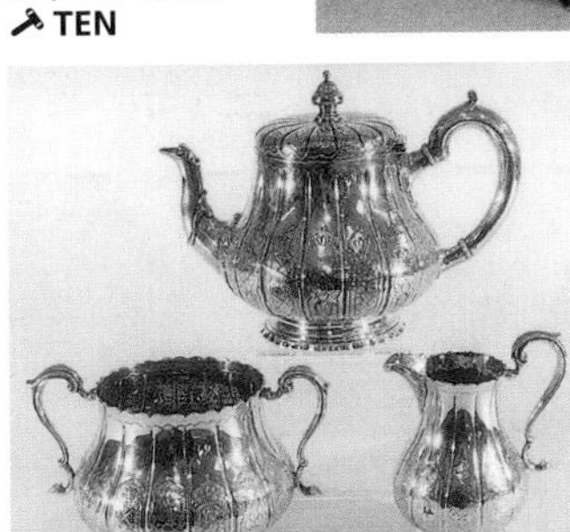

► **A silver four-piece tea service,** by George Richards, engraved with scrolling foliate decoration, the tea and coffee pots with hinged lids and moulded knops, London 1846, 77oz.
£700–840
€1,000–1,200
$1,200–1,400
TEN

A silver three-piece coffee service, with gilt interiors, decorated in relief with roses and rocaille, the coffee pot and jug with ivory handles, marked 'T u. Co' for Triesch & Co, Austrian, Vienna 1860, coffee pot 6½in (16.5cm) high, 30oz.
£900–1,100 / €1,350–1,600
$1,500–1,800 DORO

◄ **A silver three-piece tea service,** the teapot with an acorn finial, London 1868, teapot 6¾in (17cm) high, 41oz.
£610–730
€880–1,050
$1,000–1,200
AH

A silver four-piece tea and coffee service, by Samuel Smily, part-fluted, with floral swags, London 1875, 67oz.
£840–1,000 / €1,200–1,400
$1,400–1,650 B(L)

A silver three-piece tea service, by Robert Harper, the teapot with a melon finial, decorated with panels of repoussé scrollwork, 1875, 37¾oz.
£320–380 / €460–550
$540–640 L

A batchelor's silver tea service, by Heath & Middleton, the jug and bowl with gilt interiors, maker's mark, Registered No. 18367, London 1886, 13½oz, in a presentation box.
£290–350 / €420–500
$490–590 DD

A silver three-piece tea service, by Charles Stuart Harris, London 1893–4, teapot 8in (20.5cm) high.
£710–790 / €1,000–1,100
$1,200–1,350 GRe

A silver coffee pot and hot water jug, by Fordham & Faulkner, 1894, 9½in (24cm) high.
£370–440 / €530–630
$620–740 SWO

A silver three-piece tea service, by Peter L. Krider & Co, the teapot with wooden handle, American, Philadelphia, c1900, teapot 7in (18cm) high.
£270–320 / €390–460
$450–540 NOA

A silver four-piece tea and coffee service, by Holland, Aldwinckle & Slater, engraved with initials, London 1901, matching hot water jug by Charles Clement Pilling, London 1905, 89oz.
£530–640 / €760–910
$890–1,100 B(L)

Condiment Pots

A silver trencher salt, with moulded corded borders, maker's mark IM, London 1694, 3½in (9cm) diam, 2oz.
£610–730 / €880–1,050
$1,000–1,200 WW

A silver salt, with gilt interior, maker's marks VA and PSI, Russian, Moscow 1769, 2¾in (7cm) diam.
£440–530 / €630–760
$740–890 BUK

◄ **A set of silver salts,** with reeded rims and gilt interiors, maker's mark JD, London 1794, 3¼in (8.5cm) diam.
£410–490 / €590–700
$690–820 GAK

A set of four silver salts, by W. Ward, with pierced and bright-cut decoration, Irish, Dublin 1793, 4in (10cm) wide.
£3,000–3,300 / €4,300–4,800
$5,000–5,500 SIL

Bright cutting

This technique was popular at the end of the 18th century, mainly for neo-classical ornament. It is effected by cutting with a graver at an angle to create facets that reflect the light. The facets can be easily worn by heavy polishing and this will affect the value.

A pair of silver salts, by Eric Holmberg, with gilt interiors, Swedish, Lund 1795, 4¾in (12cm) long.
£810–970 / €1,200–1,400
$1,350–1,600 BUK

A pair of silver salts, by John Andrews II, London, 1825–26, 3in (7.5cm) diam.
£410–460 / €590–660
$690–770 GRe

A silver mustard pot, by G. F. Pinnell, London 1845, 3in (7.5cm) high.
£330–370 / €470–530
$550–620 HTE

A silver mustard pot, by George Richards and Edward Brown, with pierced strapwork and engraved decoration, London, 1860–61, 2½in (6.5cm) high, 3oz.
£880–980 / €1,250–1,400
$1,500–1,650 NS

► **A pair of silver salts,** by James Dixon & Sons, London 1863, 3¼in (8.5cm) wide, 9½oz.
£280–330 / €400–480
$470–550 TEN

A pair of silver salts, by Albert Savory, London 1864, 3in (7.5cm) high.
£340–380 / €490–550
$570–640 BLm

A set of four silver salts and two spoons, by Winder & Lamb, Irish, Dublin 1886, in original case, 10in (25.5cm) wide.
£900–1,000 / €1,300–1,450
$1,500–1,700 SIL

A pair of silver pepper shakers, by Vale Bros & Sermon, Birmingham 1891, 3½in (9cm) high.
£120–135 / €170–195
$200–230 CoHA

◄ **A silver salt,** by A. Lyubavin, in the form of a birch bark hod, Russian, St Petersburg, 1896–1908, 1½in (4cm) high
£150–180 / €210–250
$250–300 WW

Cruets

◀ **A silver cruet,** by Samuel Wood, with silver-mounted cut-glass oil and vinegar bottles, London 1748, 9½in (24cm) high, 55oz.
£3,350–4,000 / €4,800–5,700
$5,600–6,700 ⚒ S

A George III silver-gilt cruet, by the widow of Edward Aldridge Snr, with five silver-gilt-mounted glass bottles, London 1766, 5¼in (13.5cm) high.
£590–700 / €850–1,000
$990–1,150 ⚒ WW

A silver cruet, maker's mark CC, possibly Charles Chesterman, one stopper missing, London 1806, 9in (23cm) high.
£490–590 / €710–850
$820–990 ⚒ SWO

◀ **A silver cruet,** by Thomas Robinson, with four bottles, London 1815, 7in (18cm) high, 11oz.
£630–700 / €900–1,000
$1,050–1,200 ⊞ GRe

A silver condiment set, with blue glass liners to mustard pots, Birmingham 1911, in original case, 8in (20.5cm) wide.
£130–145 / €185–210
$220–240 ⊞ EXC

Cups & Goblets

A silver-gilt chalice, probably Belgian, early 18thC, 10¾in (27.5cm) high, 30oz.
£1,000–1,200
€1,450–1,700
$1,700–2,000 ⚒ S(Mi)

A silver vodka cup, by Adrej Ivanov, with chased and fluted decoration, Russian, Moscow 1761, 1½in (4cm) high, ¾oz.
£350–420 / €500–600
$590–710 ⚒ WW

◀ **A silver wager cup,** London 1836, 3in (7.5cm) high.
£165–185 / €240–270
$280–310 ⊞ BLm

▶ **A silver-gilt chalice,** marked TS for Thomas Scheidel, Austrian, Vienna 1859, 11¼in (28.5cm) high, 26½oz.
£1,250–1,500
€1,800–2,150
$2,100–2,500 ⚒ DORO

A silver loving cup, by John Moore, Irish, Dublin, c1765, 5in (12.5cm) high.
£1,750–1,900
€2,500–2,700
$2,950–3,200 ⊞ WELD

A silver-mounted coconut cup, by T. Phipps & E. Robinson, London, 1792–93, 7in (18cm) high.
£1,500–1,650
€2,150–2,400
$2,500–2,750 ⊞ NS

A set of six Tiffany & Co silver cups and saucers, by John C. Moore, American, c1910, cup 2in (5cm) high.
£1,550–1,750
€2,250–2,500
$2,600–2,900 ⊞ SHa

Cutlery

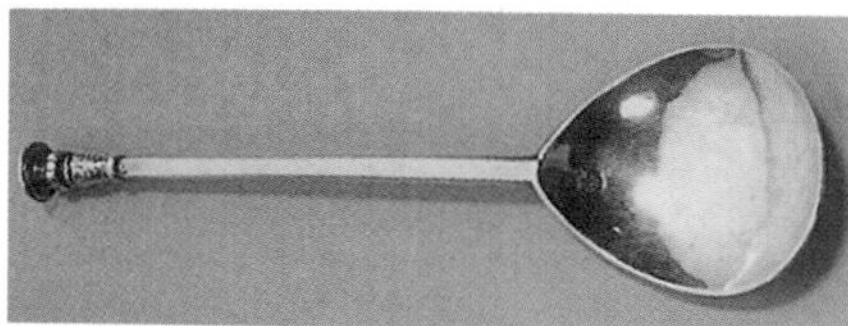

A silver seal top spoon, by Daniel Cary, with inscription, London 1628, 6¼in (16cm) long, 1oz.
£810–970 / €1,150–1,400
$1,350–1,600 S(O)

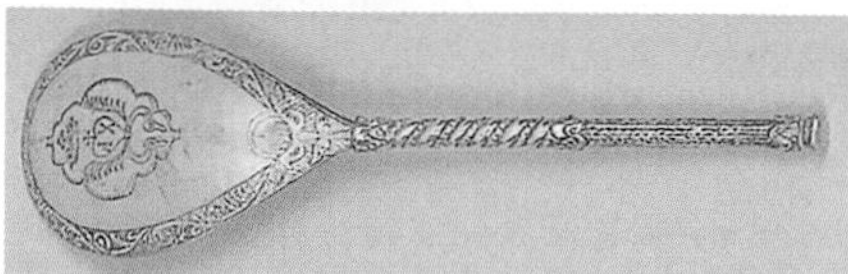

A baroque silver spoon, with silver-gilt decoration, engraved with a monogram, German, c1700, 7in (18cm) long, 1½oz.
£490–590 / €710–850
$820–990 DORO

A pair of silver scroll-back spoons, by Benjamin Cartwright II, London 1762, 8in (20.5cm) long.
£170–190 / €240–270
$290–320 GRe

A silver basting spoon, London 1810, 11in (28cm) long.
£155–175 / €220–250
$260–290 HTE

► **A silver tablespoon,** by Josiah Low, Irish, Dublin 1838, 9in (23cm) long.
£85–95 / €120–135
$140–155 CoHA

A silver dog nose spoon, by Lawrence Cole, initialled 'W. M.', 1696, 7½in (19cm) long.
£770–920 / €1,100–1,300
$1,300–1,550 G(L)

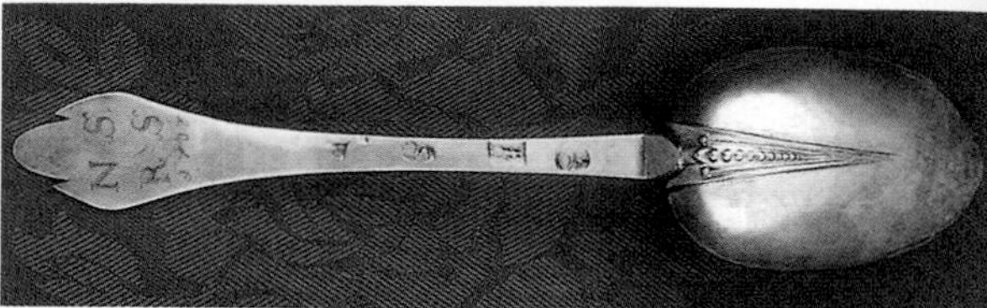

A silver trefid spoon, by Peter Jouet, the bowl with a rat-tail, initialled 'NS' and 'RS', Exeter/Topsham, dated 1707, 1¼oz.
£460–550 / €660–790
$770–920 Bea

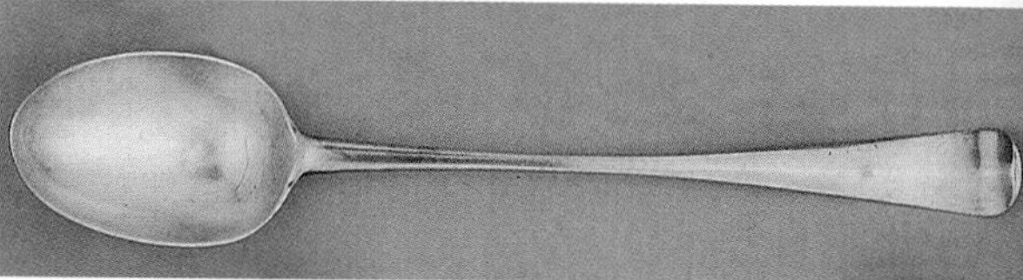

A silver hash spoon, by Daniel Popkins, engraved 'RBA', Irish, Dublin, 1758–59, 15¾in (40cm) long.
£3,600–4,000 / €5,200–5,800
$6,000–6,700 NS

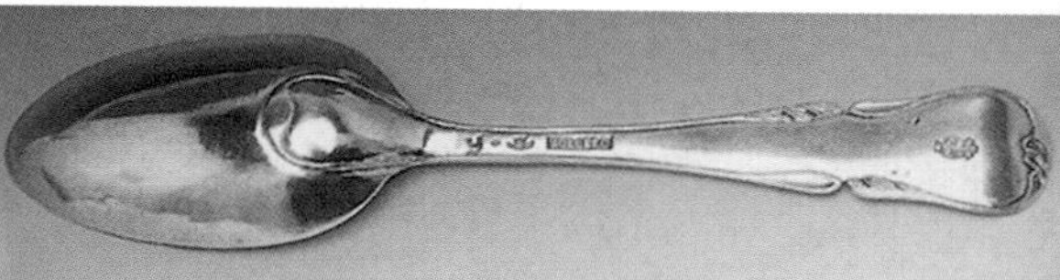

A silver spoon, by Henrik Johan Sohlberg, engraved with a coat-of-arms, Finnish, Helsinki 1781.
£420–500 / €600–720
$710–840 BUK

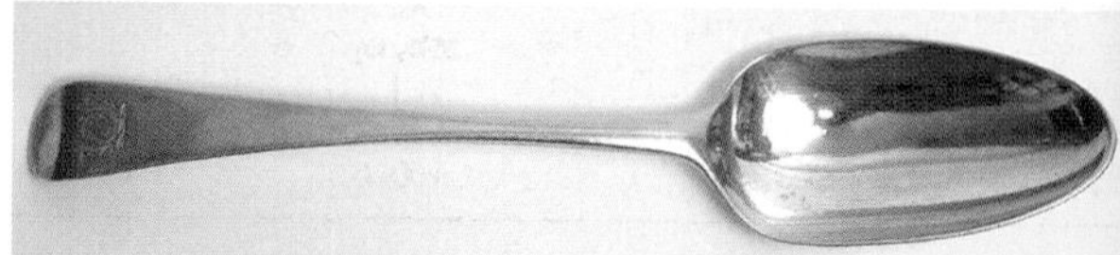

A silver-gilt presentation set, by Nichols & Plinke, Russian, St Petersburg 1848, 9in (23cm) long.
£1,300–1,450
€1,850–2,100
$2,200–2,450 SHa

A set of six silver dessert spoons, by George Angell, each engraved 'J', London 1877.
£100–120 / €145–170
$170–200 SWO

► **A selection of table silver,** by Samuel Kirk & Son, comprising 180 pieces, American, New York, c1910, 273oz.
£1,200–1,450 / €1,750–2,100
$2,000–2,400 S(O)

A silver child's knife, fork and spoon, by Tiffany & Co, American, c1890, fork 7in (18cm) long.
£450–500 / €650–720
$760–840 BEX

Dishes

A silver sweetmeat dish, with traces of gilding and S-scroll handles, Continental, 17thC, 2½in (6.5cm) wide.
£95–110 / €135–155
$160–185 WW

A silver strawberry dish, by Charles Edwards, with monogram for Queen Victoria below a crown, London 1890, 7¼in (18.5cm) diam, 5½oz.
£300–360 / €430–520
$500–600 WW

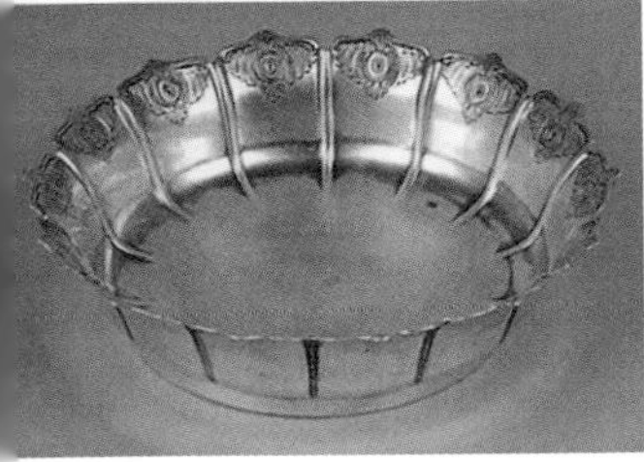

A silver dish, embossed with a bird surrounded by flowerheads and vines, maker's mark SM, Portuguese, Porto, c1760, 13¾in (35cm) diam, 16oz.
£1,800–2,150 / €2,600–3,100
$3,000–3,600 S(O)

A silver sweetmeat dish, by Nikolai Kemper, with a gilt interior, Russian, St Petersburg, 1890s, 8¼in (21cm) wide.
£490–590 / €710–850
$820–990 BUK

► A pair of Tiffany & Co silver bonbon dishes, by John C. Moore, c1910, 6in (15cm) diam.
£860–950 / €1,200–1,350
$1,450–1,600 ⊞ SHa

◄ A George I-style silver strawberry dish, by D. & J. Wellby, with engraved panels, 1903, 9in (23cm) wide, 22¼oz.
£400–480 / €580–690
$670–800 L

A silver strawberry dish, by William Smith, Irish, Dublin 1715, 9in (23cm) diam.
£28,200–31,300 / €40,000–45,000
$47,000–52,000 ⊞ WELD
This dish is of unusually large size, is in superb condition and is by a rare maker.

A silver repoussé dish, by Finley & Taylor, the interior with rococo-style floral, foliate and C-scroll decoration, London 1891, 9½in (24cm) wide, 8oz.
£95–110 / €135–155
$160–185 PF

Covered Dishes

A silver entrée dish and cover, by John Scofield, engraved with a Royal coat-of-arms, London, c1790, 13¼in (33.5cm) wide, 31oz.
£470–560 / €670–800
$790–940 WW

Further reading

Miller's Silver & Plate Buyer's Guide, Miller's Publications, 2002

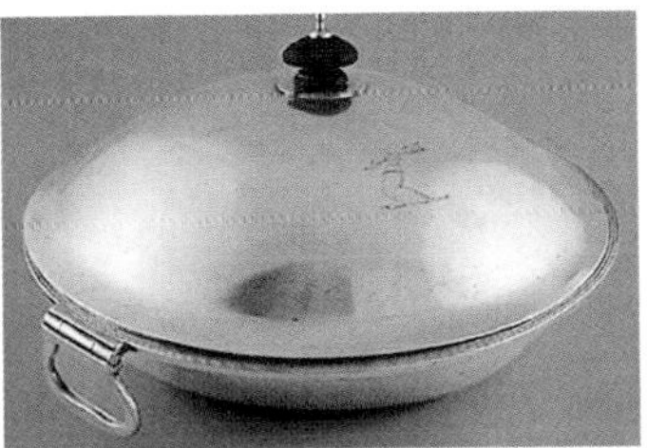

A silver chafing dish and cover, probably by Henry Nutting, crested, London 1800, 9in (23cm) diam, 27½oz.
£460–550 / €660–790
$770–920 WW
A chafing dish is used for cooking at the table.

► A silver entrée dish and cover, 1905, 10¾in (27cm) wide.
£240–290 / €350–420
$400–480 SWO

A silver chafing dish, cover and stand, with burner, maker's mark SW, London 1869, 15¾in (40cm) wide.
£390–470 / €560–670
$660–790 SWO

Dish Rings

A silver dish ring, decorated with chased figures, liner replaced, c1755, 8in (20.5cm) diam.
£9,400–10,400 / €13,500–15,000
$15,700–17,500 ⊞ WELD

A silver dish ring, by James Wakely & Frank Clarke Wheeler, with pierced decoration, Irish, Dublin 1904, 8in (20.5cm) diam, 15oz.
£1,200–1,450
€1,750–2,100
$2,000–2,400 ⚒ S(O)

A silver dish ring, by C. Lambe, Irish, Dublin 1926, 9in (23cm) diam.
£3,750–4,150 / €5,400–6,000
$6,300–7,000 ⊞ SIL

► **A pair of George III-style silver dish rings,** by J. W., each chased and pierced with mythical reptiles and birds, with inscription, Irish, Dublin, c1930, 8in (20.5cm) diam, 28oz.
£2,850–3,400 / €4,100–4,900
$4,800–5,700 ⚒ MEA

Dredgers

A set of three silver spice dredgers, by George Greenhill Jones, with pierced detachable covers, 1728, 3in (8cm) high, 7oz.
£3,350–4,000
€4,800–5,800
$5,600–6,700 ⚒ S

A silver dredger, by John Gorham, with an engraved cover, London 1753, 3¼in (8.5cm) high, 2oz.
£730–880 / €1,050–1,250
$1,200–1,450 ⚒ WW

A Georgian-style silver dredger, by Garrards, with a double scroll handle, London 1881, 4¼in (11cm) high.
£220–260 / €310–370
$370–440 ⚒ TMA

A silver dredger, by J. Wilmont, Birmingham 1901, 2½in (6.5cm) high.
£65–75 / €95–110
$110–125 ⊞ CoHA

Items in the Silver section have been arranged in date order within each sub-section.

Egg Cups

A silver egg cruet, possibly John Angell, each egg cup with a gilt interior, London 1821, 7¾in (19.5cm) wide, 52oz, with matched spoons, 1820.
£1,700–2,000 / €2,450–2,900
$2,900–3,500 ⚒ AH

A silver three-handled egg cup and spoon, by Wakely & Wheeler, egg cup Dublin 1915, spoon London 1915, in original case, 6in (15cm) wide.
£420–470 / €600–690
$710–790 ⊞ SIL

A silver egg cup, napkin ring and spoon, Birmingham 1936, in original case, 5½in (14cm) wide.
£200–230 / €290–330
$340–390 ⊞ BLm

Ewers & Jugs

A cast silver cream jug, by Peter Taylor, London, 1750–51, 4in (10cm) high.
£3,350–3,750
€4,800–5,400
$5,600–6,300 ⊞ NS

A silver cream jug, by Hester Bateman, London 1780, 5in (12.5cm) high.
£1,250–1,400
€1,800–2,000
$2,100–2,350 ⊞ TSC

A silver cream jug, with bright-cut decoration and reeded handle, maker's mark rubbed, London 1790, 6½in (16.5cm) high.
£240–290 / €350–420
$400–480 ⚒ GAK

A silver cream jug, London 1800, 4in (10cm) high.
£310–350 / €450–500
$520–590 ⊞ HTE

A silver cream jug, Irish, 1812, 5in (12.5cm) high.
£470–520 / €680–750
$790–880 ⊞ WELD

A silver milk jug, by William Bond, Irish, Dublin 1804, 5in (12.5cm) high.
£1,050–1,200
€1,500–1,700
$1,750–2,000 ⊞ SIL

◄ **A silver cream jug,** by Peter and William Bateman, London 1806, 4½in (11.5cm) high.
£310–350 / €450–500
$520–590 ⊞ GRe

► **A silver jug,** London 1837, 5in (12.5cm) high.
£210–240 / €300–350
$350–400 ⊞ LaF

Claret jugs

Silver-mounted glass claret jugs became fashionable in the middle of the 19th century. The silver was often elaborately decorated but quality varies and those made from thin metal can become easily worn. The glass body is often elegantly shaped and usually has etched or engraved decoration – a plain example is likely to be a replacement. A silver base might be a later addition to hide a chipped glass base, so check before purchasing that the jug does not leak. The two standard all-silver claret jug designs are the Cellini and Armada patterns, made throughout the second half of the 19th century. All follow the same shape and can have self-opening lids. They tend to be marked in a line close to the neck. Solid-bodied claret jugs tend to be less popular than glass-bodied examples where the colour of the wine can be seen.

A silver-mounted glass claret jug, maker's mark C&Co, Sheffield 1866, 9¾in (25cm) high.
£2,000–2,400
€2,900–3,500
$3,350–4,000 ⚒ TEN

A silver claret jug, by W. & G. Sissons, Sheffield 1868, 11in (28cm) high.
£1,800–2,000
€2,600–2,900
$3,000–3,350 ⊞ TSC

A silver water pitcher, by Gorham Manufacturing Co, American, Providence, c1874, 10in (25.5cm) high, 30oz.
£1,650–2,000
€2,400–2,850
$2,800–3,350 NOA

A silver sparrow beak beer jug, by Walter & John Barnard, the handle with heart-shaped terminal, London 1891, 8in (20.5cm) high.
£240–290 / €350–420
$400–480 MCA

A silver hot water jug, by Aldwinkle & Slater, London 1892, 6¾in (17cm) high.
£165–195 / €240–280
$280–330 SWO

A silver hot water jug, with a hinged cover and wooden handle, Sheffield 1915, 7¾in (19.5cm) high.
£120–145 / €175–210
$200–240 WilP

Flatware

A silver meat dish, by Matthew Boulton & John Fothergill, engraved with two crests, Birmingham 1777, 17in (43cm) wide, 30oz.
£540–650 / €780–940
$910–1,100 WW

Paul Storr

Paul Storr, the most prolific of the early 19th-century silversmiths, was a master of the heavy neo-classical styles. In association with Philip Rundell and John Bridge, his workshop produced enormous quantities of silver and silver-gilt, the designs so heavy and robust that many pieces have survived in excellent condition. His patrons included both George III and the Prince Regent and his wares were highly sought after and remain so today.

A set of twelve silver dinner plates, by Paul Storr, with gadrooned borders, each engraved with a crest, London 1827, 10in (25.5cm) diam, 203oz.
£12,600–15,100 / €18,100–21,700
$21,200–25,400 S

Frames

◄ **A silver frame,** by William Comyns, with pierced decoration of putti, London 1899, 14½in (37cm) square.
£200–230 / €290–330
$340–390 RICC

A silver-mounted stand with two frames, minor damage, 1901, stand 8 x 7in (20.5 x 18cm).
£370–440 / €530–630
$620–740 GAK

A silver double frame, Birmingham 1900, 5½ x 7in (14 x 18cm).
£240–270 / €350–390
$400–450 BrL

◄ **A silver frame,** in the form of an easel, Birmingham 1904, 5½in (14cm) wide.
£200–240 / €290–350
$340–400 B(NW)

► **A silver frame,** Birmingham 1920, 6½ x 8½in (16.5 x 21.5cm).
£150–165 / €210–240
$250–280 FOX

Grape Scissors

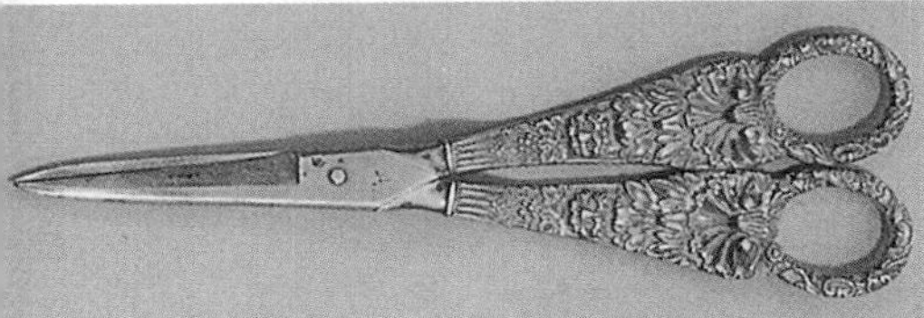

A pair of silver-gilt grape scissors, by William Snooke Hall, London 1818, 7in (18cm) long, ¼oz.
£360–430 / €520–620
$600–720 S(O)

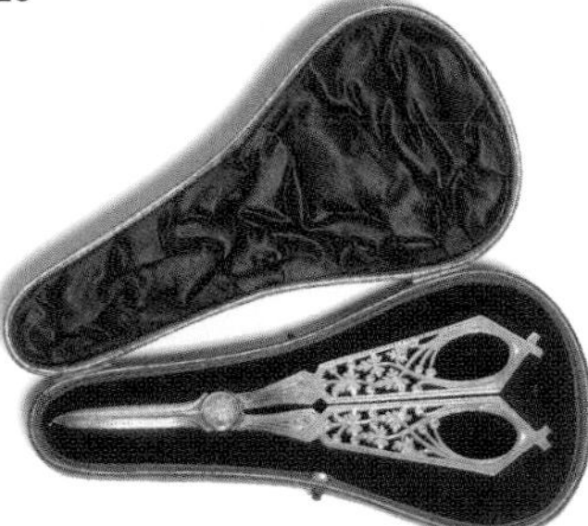

► A pair of silver grape scissors, by Hutton & Sons, London 1905, in original case, 7in (18cm) long.
£500–550
€720–790
$840–920
⊞ BLm

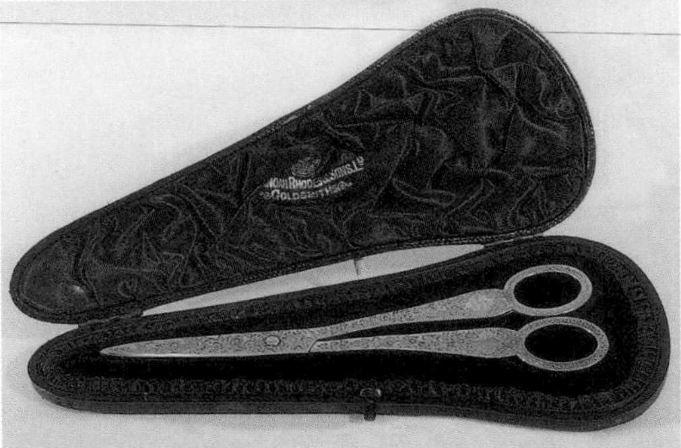

A pair of silver grape scissors, inscribed 'F. E. Coates', London 1891, in a case, 8¼in (21cm) wide, 2½oz.
£290–350 / €420–500
$490–580 AH

Insurance values

Always insure your valuable antiques for the cost of replacing them with similar items, regardless of the original price paid. Both dealers and auctioneers can provide a valuation service for a fee.

Inkstands & Inkwells

A silver inkstand, by Andrew Fogelberg, London 1770, 10¼in (26cm) wide, 23oz.
£880–1,050 / €1,250–1,500
$1,500–1,800 HOLL

A silver presentation inkstand, by Hawksworth, Eyre & Co, fitted with a taperstick and two silver-mounted cut-glass ink bottles, Sheffield 1844, 10½in (26.5cm) wide.
£940–1,100 / €1,350–1,600
$1,600–1,900 BWL

◄ A silver inkstand, with two silver-mounted glass bottles, 1909, 8½in (21.5cm) wide, 11oz.
£280–330 / €400–470
$470–550 G(L)

A silver novelty inkwell, by Samuel Jacob, modelled as a hot air balloon, London, 1900–01, 5in (12.5cm) high.
£1,550–1,750
€2,250–2,500
$2,600–2,900 ⊞ NS

Lamps

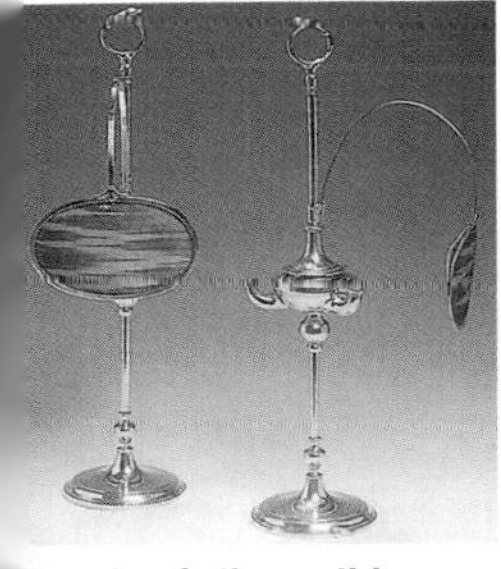

A pair of silver oil lamps, the oil reservoirs with three spouts, Italian, c1820, 24in (61cm) high, 84oz.
£5,600–6,700
€8,000–9,600
$9,400–11,200 B

A silver sanctuary lamp, with an openwork gallery of fleur-de-lys, maker's mark JS, Irish, Dublin 1891, 14½in (37cm) high, 99oz.
£1,300–1,550
€1,850–2,200
$2,200–2,600 S(O)

► A silver lamp, drilled for electricity, with later detached Victory figure, maker's mark F&S, loaded, Sheffield 1913, 22½in (57cm) high.
£1,300–1,550
€1,850–2,200
$2,200–2,600
S(O)

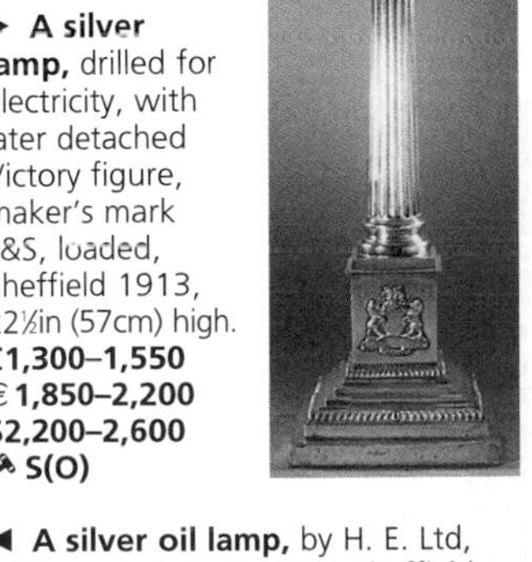

◄ A silver oil lamp, by H. E. Ltd, with a cut-glass reservoir, Sheffield 1903, 29¼in (74cm) high.
£750–900 / €1,100–1,300
$1,250–1,500 Bea

Menu Holders

A set of four silver owl menu holders, by Sampson Mordan & Co, with glass eyes, Chester 1905, 2in (5cm) high, in a fitted case.
£800–960 / €1,150–1,350
$1,350–1,600 SWO

A near pair of silver butterfly menu holders, with mother-of-pearl wings, maker's mark W&C, Birmingham 1910 and 1912.
£560–670 / €810–960
$940–1,100 B

A set of four silver and tortoiseshell menu holders, by Asprey, decorated with game, London 1927, 1½in (4cm) wide.
£1,050–1,250 / €1,500–1,800
$1,750–2,100 G(L)

Mirrors

A silver mirror, by William Comyns, London 1898, 18in (45.5cm) high.
£1,750–1,900
€2,500–2,750
$2,900–3,200 WELD

A silver dressing table mirror, by Henry Matthews, Chester 1900, 19in (48.5cm) high.
£440–530 / €630–760
$740–890 WW

A silver mirror, surmounted by a Prince's coronet, Italian, c1900, 27in (68.5cm) high.
£2,000–2,400
€2,900–3,450
$3,350–4,000 S(O)

A silver-backed hand mirror, Chester 1907, 11in (28cm) long.
£180–200 / €260–290
$300–330 GRe

Mugs & Tankards

A silver tankard, with a twisted scroll thumbpiece and a contemporary armorial shield, maker's mark SL, 1689, 6¼in (16cm) high, 20oz.
£4,700–5,600
€6,800–8,100
$7,900–9,400 B

A Britannia Standard silver tankard, by Nathaniel Lock, with a scroll thumb-piece and a contemporary armorial, London 1711, 8¼in (21cm) high.
£3,100–3,700
€4,450–5,300
$5,200–6,200 F&C

◄ **A silver tankard,** by Thomas Whipham, London 1754, 8in (20.5cm) high, 26¾oz.
£1,400–1,650
€2,000–2,400
$2,350–2,750 S(O)

A silver tankard, by Humphrey Payne, London 1713, 7¾in (19.5cm) high, 30oz.
£2,250–2,700
€3,250–3,900
$3,750–4,500 CGC

LOCATE THE SOURCE

The source of each illustration in Miller's can be found by checking the code letters below each caption with the Key to Illustrations, pages 794–800.

A silver mug, by Thomas Mason, engraved with initial 'F', London 1723, 10½in (26.5cm) high, 10oz.
£700–840 / €1,000–1,200
$1,200–1,400 TEN

A silver mug, by Joseph Sanders, London, 1754–55, 5in (12.5cm) high.
£1,200–1,350
€1,700–1,950
$2,000–2,250 NS

A silver mug, by Sebastian Crespell, London 1820, 4in (10cm) high.
£220–250 / €320–360
$370–420 ⊞ GGD

A silver christening mug, by J. & N. Creswick, London 1854, 4½in (11.5cm) high.
£260–310 / €370–440
$440–520 ⚒ GAK

A silver mug, by J. S. Hunt, with a gilt interior, embossed and chased with fruiting vines, initialled, London 1859, 3in (7.5cm) high, 6¼oz.
£390–470 / €560–670
$660–790 ⚒ WW

A silver mug, repoussé decorated, London 1882, 5½in (14cm) high.
£420–470 / €600–670
$710–790 ⊞ HTE

A silver mug, by Edward Charles Brown, London 1894, 4in (10cm) high.
£430–480 / €620–690
$720–810 ⊞ SHa

Further reading
Miller's Silver & Plate Antiques Checklist, Miller's Publications, 2001

◄ **A silver tankard,** c1903, 2¼in (5.5cm) high.
£220–250 / €320–360
$370–420 ⊞ BLm

A silver christening mug, with cut-card decoration, Birmingham 1906, 4in (10cm) high.
£250–280 / €360–400
$420–470 ⊞ HTE

Napkin Rings

A silver napkin ring, by Messrs Williams, with engraved decoration, Exeter 1869, 1in (2.5cm) wide, 1oz.
£140–165 / €200–240
$240–280 ⚒ WW

A pair of silver napkin rings, Birmingham 1870, in original case, 3¾in (9.5cm) wide.
£250–280 / €360–400
$420–470 ⊞ BLm

A silver napkin ring, London 1880, 1¾in (4.5cm) wide.
£75–85 / €105–120
$125–140 ⊞ BLm

Items in the Silver section have been arranged in date order within each sub-section.

Rattles

◄ **A Victorian baby's silver rattle,** by A. H., with six bells, engraved 'S. H.', 5½in (14cm) long.
£260–310 / €370–440
$440–520 ⚒ BWL

► **A child's silver rattle,** possibly by May & Co, with a whistle, four bells and a coral teether, Birmingham 1900, 3½in (9cm) long.
£200–240 / €290–340
$340–400 ⚒ WW

A child's silver rattle, by H. Matthews, with a mother-of-pearl handle and two bells, Birmingham 1924, 4¼in (11cm) long.
£100–120 / €145–170
$170–200 ⚒ GAK

Salvers & Trays

A silver footed salver, by Benjamin Pyne, with a gadrooned border, the centre later engraved with armorial shields within a wreath, 1692, 7½in (19cm) diam, 15¾oz.
£7,500–9,000 / €10,800–13,000
$12,600–15,100 B

A silver card tray, with an engraved cartouche surrounded by a shell and scrolled border, on three feet, London 1762, 6¾in (17cm) diam.
£200–240 / €290–350
$340–400 WilP

A silver dressing table tray, Chester 1896, 12in (30.5cm) wide.
£200–230 / €290–330
$340–390 EXC

A silver waiter, by Bartholomew Mosse, Irish, Dublin 1750, 6in (15cm) diam.
£900–1,000 / €1,300–1,450
$1,500–1,700 WELD

A pair of silver waiters, by John Carter, engraved with the Agincourt crest, the raised moulded borders with a gadrooned edge, the feet with knurled toes, London 1774, 7in (18cm) diam, 18½oz.
£820–980 / €1,200–1,400
$1,400–1,650 NSal

A silver dressing table tray, Sheffield 1899, 10½in (26.5cm) wide.
£180–200 / €260–290
$300–330 FOX

A silver salver, by Dorothy Mills, chased with an armorial crest and motto inside a shell and S-scroll border, on four leafy feet, London 1753, 14½in (37cm) diam, 40oz.
£1,300–1,550 / €1,900–2,250
$2,200–2,600 MEA

A silver salver, by Hands & Sons, with a shell and scrolled border, the centre with foliate engraving, on four cast acanthus feet, London 1880, 12in (30.5cm) diam.
£540–650 / €780–930
$920–1,100 GAK

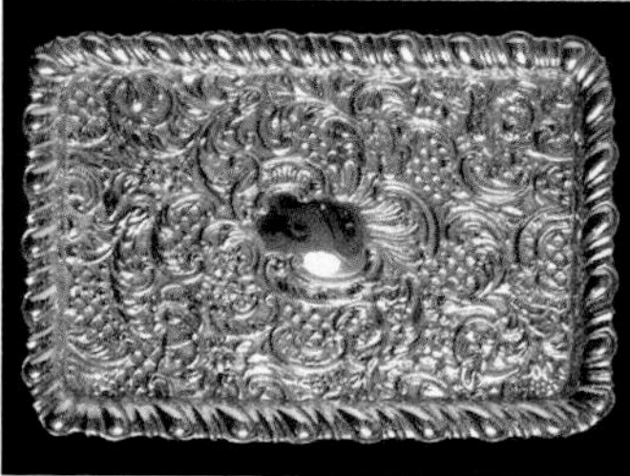

A silver dressing table tray, by Lyner & Bedoes, Birmingham 1901, 12in (30.5cm) wide.
£270–300 / €390–430
$450–500 GRe

Borders

The borders of silver can often provide a clue to the date of the article, although the collector should bear in mind that many 18th-century styles were reproduced in the 19th century. Similar decoration can also appear around the feet.

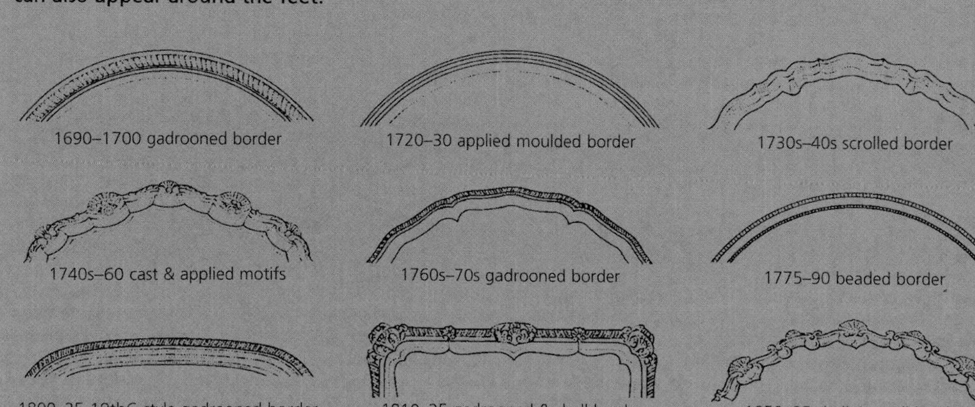

SILVER

Sauce & Cream Boats

A pair of silver sauce boats, by John Pollock, London 1742, 7in (18cm) wide.
£3,600–4,000 / €5,200–5,800
$6,000–6,700 ⊞ PAY

A pair of silver sauce boats, by John Schuppe, London, 1766–67, 7in (18cm) wide.
£6,800–7,500 / €9,800–10,800
$11,400–12,600 ⊞ NS

A silver double-lipped sauce boat, by Guillaume-Gaspar Velez, with bifurcated scroll handles, Belgian, Liège, 1748–49, 8½in (21.5cm) wide, 12½oz.
£9,400–11,300 / €13,500–16,200
$16,000–19,000 ⚒ B

A silver sauce boat, by Thomas Walshe, with female mask legs, Irish, Limerick 1775, 7in (18cm) wide.
£11,500–12,800 / €16,800–18,700
$19,300–21,500 ⊞ WELD
This sauce boat was made for the Duke of Ormonde. Limerick silver is rare and very desirable.

A silver sauce boat, by William Robertson, London 1753, 4in (10cm) high.
£4,500–5,000 / €6,500–7,200
$7,600–8,400 ⊞ MCO

A silver sauce boat, with a shaped edge, on three feet, London 1895, 6¾in (17cm) wide.
£190–220 / €280–320
$320–370 ⚒ SWO

Scent Bottles

A silver-mounted cranberry glass scent bottle, by Sampson Mordan, the lid formed as an owl's head with glass eyes, damaged, London 1849, 3in (7.5cm) high.
£560–670 / €820–980
$940–1,100 ⚒ GAK

A silver-mounted ruby cut-glass scent bottle, by G. E. W. Ltd, with a screw cover, Birmingham 1880, 2¾in (7cm) high.
£175–210 / €250–300
$290–340 ⚒ WW

◀ **A silver-mounted cut-glass scent bottle,** by Mappin & Webb, London 1899, 6in (15cm) high.
£120–140 / €175–200
$200–230 ⊞ TOP

A silver scent bottle, by Hilliard & Thomason, Chester 1897, 2½in (6.5cm) high.
£120–135 / €170–190
$200–220 ⊞ CoHA

For further information on
Scent Bottles see pages 342–343

A silver scent bottle case, by William Comyns, decorated with cherubs, containing a glass scent bottle labelled 'W. E. Clarke, Pharmacist, Strood', London 1898, 3¾in (9.5cm) high.
£320–350 / €460–510
$530–590 ⊞ BLm

▶ **A silver scent bottle,** Chester 1901, 3in (7.5cm) high, in original case.
£420–470 / €610–680
$710–790 ⊞ HTE

Serving Implements

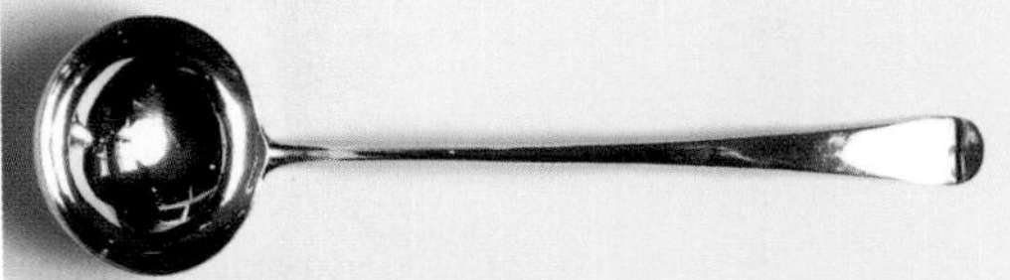

A silver ladle, by Wildman Smith, London 1784, 12in (30.5cm) long.
£300–340 / €440–500
$500–570 ⊞ GRe

A pair of silver asparagus tongs, by Simon Harris, engraved with a coat-of-arms, London 1810, 9¾in (25cm) long, 5oz.
£260–310 / €380–450
$440–520 🔨 BR

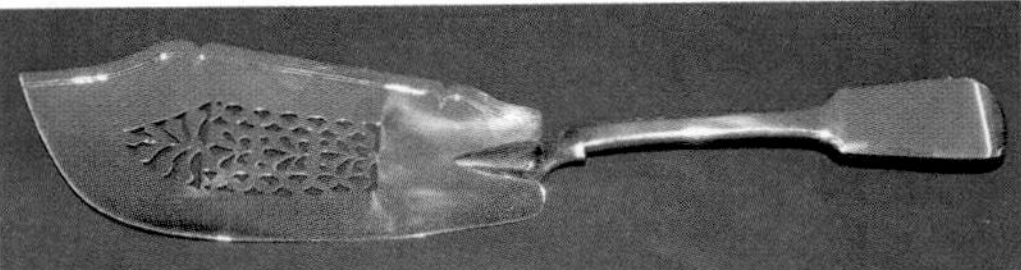

A silver fish slice, Exeter 1834, 12in (30.5cm) long.
£130–145 / €190–210
$220–250 ⊞ TASV

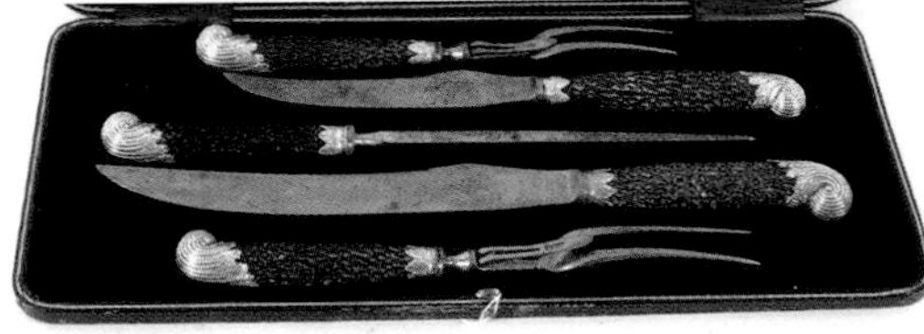

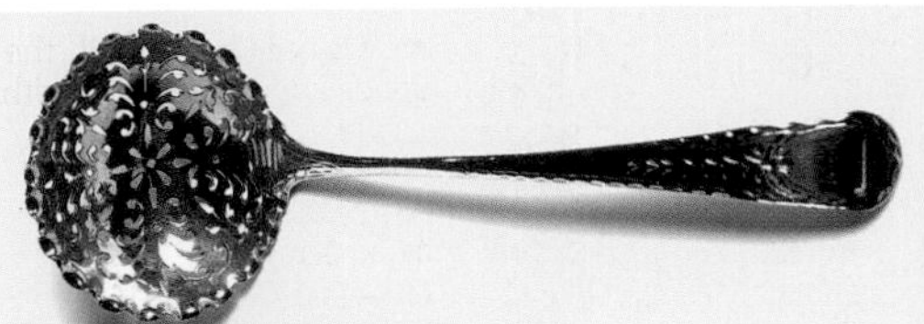

A silver sugar sifter spoon, London 1796, 8in (20.5cm) long.
£150–165 / €210–240
$250–280 ⊞ HTE

A silver-mounted blue john condiment ladle, by Samuel Pemberton, with a fiddle stem and round bowl, some damage, Birmingham 1810, 5in (12.5cm) long.
£100–120 / €145–170
$170–200 🔨 WW

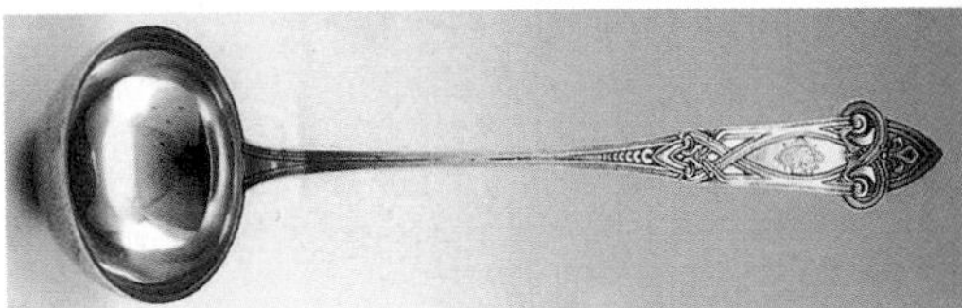

A silver ladle, with an embossed and monogrammed handle, hallmarked 'Thune', Norwegian, c1895, 14in (35.5cm) long, 9oz.
£170–200 / €250–290
$290–340 🔨 NOA

◄ **A Victorian silver-mounted five-piece carving set,** with horn handles, in a fitted case, 13in (33cm) wide.
£135–160 / €195–230
$230–270 🔨 GAK

Snuff Boxes

A silver snuff box, with a gilt interior, engraved with a scene from an Aesop's fable, maker's mark EI, c1720, 2¾in (7cm) wide, 2oz.
£320–380 / €460–550
$540–640 🔨 WW

A silver snuff box, with a gilt interior, hinged lid repaired, Birmingham 1808, 5¼in (13.5cm) wide.
£210–250 / €300–360
$350–420 🔨 BR

A silver and hardstone snuff box, by B. Stokes, Irish, Dublin, c1750, 3in (7.6cm) diam.
£4,000–4,500 / €5,800–6,500
$6,800–7,600 ⊞ WELD

A silver snuff box, London 1804, 2¾in (7cm) wide.
£590–650 / €850–940
$1,000–1,100 ⊞ BEX

A silver snuff box, by Thomas Eley, with engine-turned decoration and a floral foliate thumbpiece, London 1824, 2¼in (5.5cm) wide.
£230–270 / €330–390
$380–450 🔨 FHF

◄ **A silver snuff box,** decorated in relief with a panel depicting a man seated on a log, Russian, St Petersburg 19thC, 3¾in (9.5cm) wide.
£210–250 / €300–360
$350–420 🔨 RTo

Table Bells

◄ **A silver hand bell,** the upper body embossed with foliate and floral scrolls, below a handle cast as a putto, Birmingham 1893, 4in (10cm) high, 1¾oz.
£95–110 / €140–160
$160–185 ⚒ CGC

► **A silver table bell,** by Charles Fox, London 1897, 5in (12.5cm) high.
£360–400 / €520–580
$600–660 ⊞ BLm

A silver table bell, Continental, import marks for London 1899, 3¾in (9.5cm) high, 4¼oz.
£150–180 / €220–260
$250–300 ⚒ WW

Tea Caddies

A silver tea caddy, by Henry Green, London 1792, 6in (15cm) high, 14oz.
£2,000–2,400
€2,950–3,500
$3,350–4,000 ⚒ WW

A silver-gilt and niello tea caddy, by Fedor Kirillovich Yatsev, decorated with four views of Moscow, Russian, Moscow 1884, 4in (10cm) high.
£3,600–4,000
€5,200–5,800
$6,000–6,700 ⊞ MIR

◄ **A silver tea caddy,** by Bradbury, London 1898, 5¾in (14.5cm) high.
£700–780 / €1,000–1,100
$1,150–1,300 ⊞ BLm

A tea caddy, by Edward Moore for Tiffany & Co, c1885, 5in (12.5cm) high.
£2,450–2,750
€3,550–4,000
$4,100–4,600 ⊞ SHa

► **A silver tea caddy,** chased with Dutch-style panels of figures in landscapes, London 1909, 5in (12.5cm) high.
£320–380 / €460–550
$540–640 ⚒ GAK

A silver tea caddy, Birmingham 1896, 4in (10cm) high.
£270–300 / €390–430
$450–500 ⊞ HTE

Toast Racks

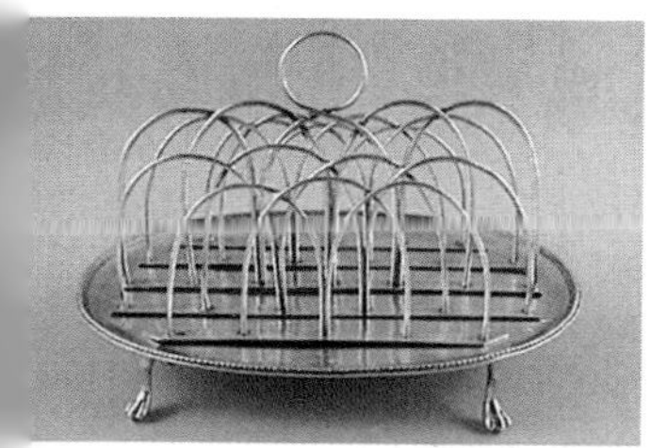

A silver bannock/toast rack, by John Hampston and John Prince, the wirework bars removable for cleaning, on four paw feet, York 1780, 7½in (19cm) wide, 11½oz.
£1,700–2,050 / €2,450–2,900
$2,850–3,400 ⚒ WW

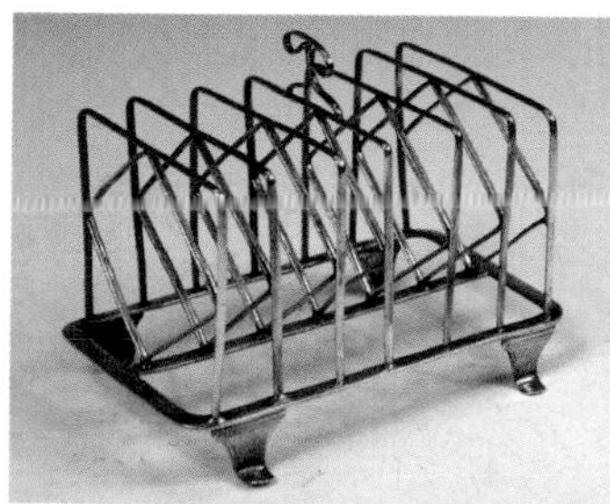

A silver toast rack, by Alex Goodman & Co, Sheffield 1805, 6½in (16.5cm) wide.
£220–260 / €320–380
$370–440 ⚒ SWO

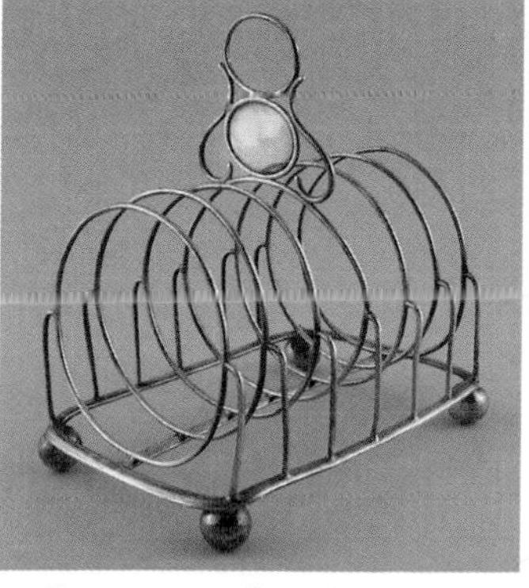

A silver toast rack, probably by Thomas Hayter, some damage, London 1811, 6½in (16.5cm) wide, 8oz.
£200–240 / €290–350
$340–400 ⚒ WW

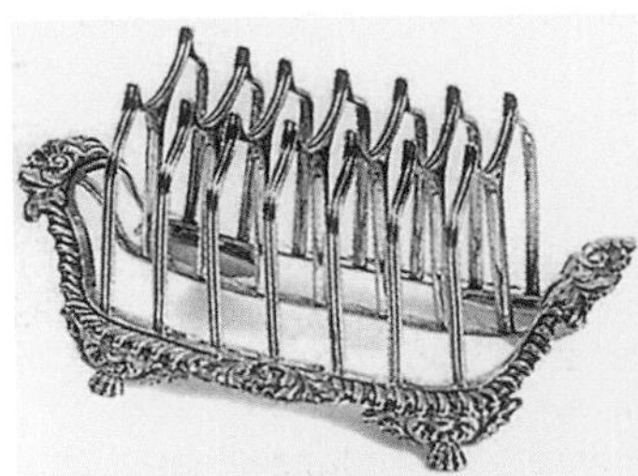

A silver toast rack, by Charles Fox II, London 1823, 9¾in (25cm) wide, 22oz.
£730–880 / €1,050–1,250
$1,250–1,500 Bea

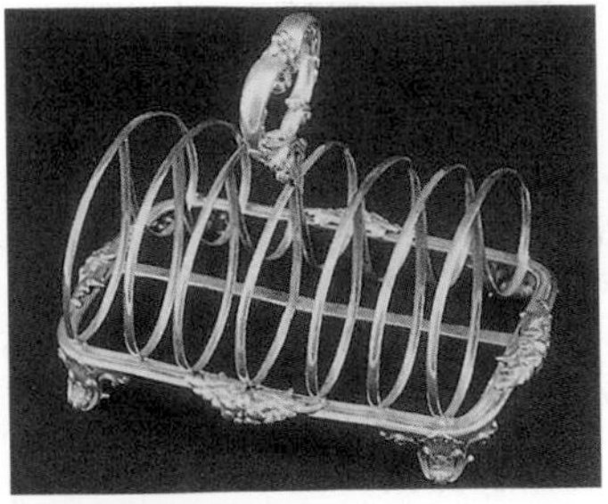

A silver toast rack, by Charles Reilly and George Storer, London 1837, 7in (18cm) wide, 11oz.
£420–500 / €600–720
$700–840 BR

A silver toast rack, possibly by R. Smith, Irish, Dublin, c1840, 5½in (14cm) wide, 8½oz.
£165–195 / €250–290
$280–330 WW

A silver toast rack, by Henry Wilkinson & Co, Sheffield 1840, 6in (15cm) wide.
£290–350 / €420–500
$490–590 GAK

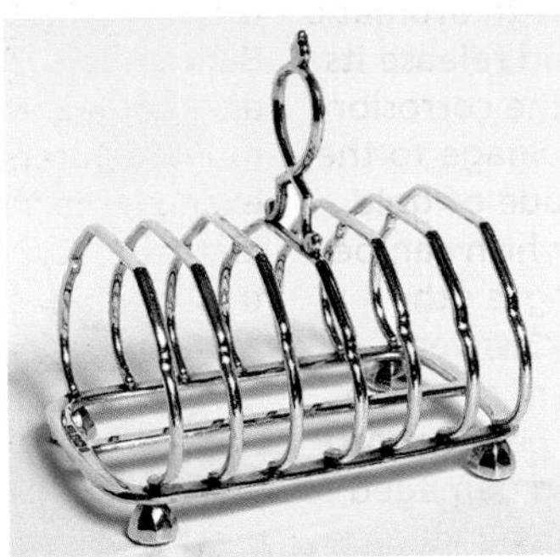

A silver toast rack, by George Harrison, London 1897, 4½in (11.5cm) wide.
£165–185 / €240–270
$280–310 GRe

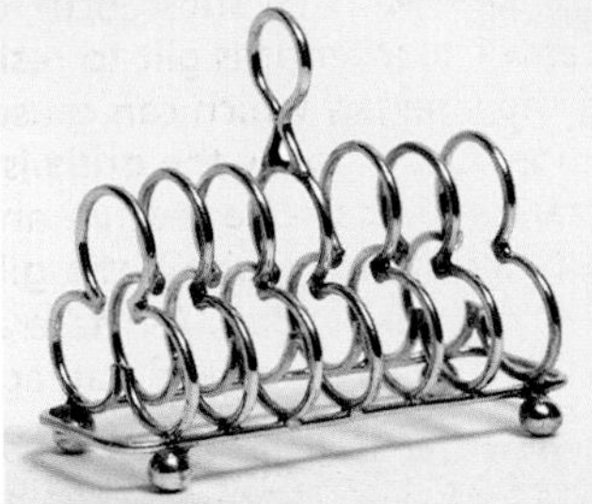

A silver toast rack, by T. H. Hazlewood & Co, Birmingham 1903, 3in (7.5cm) wide.
£55–65 / €80–95
$90–100 CoHA

Tureens

A silver soup tureen and cover, by Thomas Heming, with a detachable plate liner, crested, with a presentation inscription, London 1781, 17in (43cm) wide, 146½oz.
£4,100–4,900 / €5,900–7,000
$6,900–8,200 S(O)

A silver soup tureen and cover, by L. N. N. Naudin, the cover initialled 'AB', French, Paris, 1819–38, 9in (23cm) diam, 33oz.
£720–860 / €1,050–1,250
$1,200–1,400 S(O)

A silver soup tureen and cover, by James Dixon & Son, with a presentation inscription, Sheffield 1909, 16in (40.5cm) wide, 67¾oz.
£860–1,000 / €1,250–1,450
$1,450–1,700 S(O)

For further information on
Tureens see page 290

Vesta Cases

A silver vesta case, the foliate scrollwork decoration centred by an enamel panel depicting a walrus, maker's mark WJD, Birmingham 1896, 1½in (4cm) high.
£800–960 / €1,200–1,400
$1,350–1,600 B

A silver vesta case, by The Goldsmiths & Silversmiths Co, inset with a compass London 1913, 2in (5cm) high, 1oz.
£230–270 / €330–390
$380–400 WW

◄ **A silver vesta case,** Birmingham 1902, 2in (5cm) high.
£105–125 / €150–190
$175–210 GAK

SILVER

Vinaigrettes

It is hard to imagine a world where it was necessary to disguise odours caused by poor hygiene and drainage. The vinaigrette came into being for this purpose, enjoying its heyday from c1780 to 1850.

Vinaigrettes are found in many forms, such as handbags, watches, animals, shells and nuts. The most common type, however, is rectangular, usually engraved, with a hinged cover enclosing a decorative pierced grille through which a sponge, soaked with aromatic vinegar and other substances, could release its scent. The interior is gilt to resist the corrosion of the vinegar, which can cause damage to the hinge. Occasionally the grille is made of gold, a rare and desirable feature and which can be difficult to distinguish if the gilding is otherwise generally good. As these articles were made for use, wear and damage are common and should be avoided. Splits and perforation at the corners, worn engraving and damaged grilles and joints are the usual faults.

Vinaigrettes can be found in almost every material: precious stone and metal, agates, pearl, shell, ivory, enamel and combinations of all these. Silver examples were the most popular, however, and by the 1790s they were being mass-produced, particularly in the Birmingham area.

Small rectangular silver vinaigrettes can be bought at auction for under £200 / €290 / $340 depending on condition; larger and better specimens can be twice as expensive. Collectors usually, however, aspire to the more decorative examples with an accordingly higher price tag. Of these the castle top, depicting a building of note on the cover, is the most popular. Nathaniel Mills of Birmingham was the most prolific maker, although identical pieces by a variety of manufacturers can be found. Look for examples in their original velvet-lined morocco leather case, as this should have protected them from wear, unless much used.

The finest vinaigrettes are often of hollowed hardstone, faceted citrine or other gemstones, with gold grilles and mounts set with small rubies, pearls or turquoise. Prices for the best pieces continue to escalate, but beware of fakes. A castle top can very convincingly be set into the top of an otherwise plain box and snuff boxes can have grilles inserted. The hallmarks must be carefully examined: all parts should be marked. **Hugh Gregory**

A silver vinaigrette, the lower part engraved and pierced with swirling scrolls and foliage, probably Dutch/German, c1700, 1½in (4cm) diam.
£190–220 / €280–320
$320–370 ⚒ WW

A silver pomander vinaigrette, German, c1760, 1¼in (3cm) long.
£310–350 / €450–500
$530–590 ⊞ LBr
This pomander vinaigrette has a small ring at one end to attach to a chain.

A George III silver-gilt and agate vinaigrette, with stamped star decoration and engraved floral grille, 1¼in (3cm) diam, in a red leather case.
£630–750 / €910–1,100
$1,050–1,250 ⚒ G(L)

A silver vinaigrette, by Gervase Wheeler, in the form of a basket, with vermicular engraving and a gilt foliate grille, Birmingham 1802, 1¼in (3cm) wide.
£520–620 / €750–890
$850–1,000 ⚒ G(L)

A silver-gilt vinaigrette, by Henry Tippen, with a hardstone cover, the grille with flowerhead and scroll piercing, maker's mark, London 1818, 1¼in (3cm) diam.
£530–640 / €760–910
$880–1,050 ⚒ LFA

A silver vinaigrette, by Thomas & William Shaw, the cover with wrigglework decoration, the liner with foliate piercing, maker's mark, Birmingham 1824, 1½in (4cm) wide.
£140–165 / €200–240
$240–280 ⚒ PFK

◄ **A silver vinaigrette,** by Lea & Co, maker's mark, 19thC, ½in (1.5cm) wide.
£160–180 €230–260 $270–300 ⊞ LBr

A silver vinaigrette, by William Spooner, with a floral edge and engine-turned decoration, Birmingham, c1825, 1½in (4cm) wide.
£175–210 / €250–300 $295–350 ⚒ TRM

A silver vinaigrette, by William Steen, Birmingham 1829, 1½in (4cm) wide.
£270–300 / €390–430 $450–500 ⊞ GGD

A George IV silver vinaigrette, by William Ellerby, 1½in (4cm) wide.
£770–850 / €1,100–1,250 $1,250–1,400 ⊞ BEX

A silver vinaigrette, by Nathaniel Mills, with moulded edges and engine-turned decoration, Birmingham 1833, 1½in (4cm) wide.
£260–310 / €380–450 $440–520 ⚒ TRM

A silver viniagrette, with relief decoration of a musician and his companion, Birmingham 1833, 1½in (4cm) wide, on a later chain.
£820–980 / €1,200–1,400 $1,400–1,650 ⚒ CHTR

A cast silver vinaigrette, by William Simpson, the cover decorated with a view of Abbotsford, Birmingham 1835, 1¾in (4.5cm) wide.
£1,550–1,750 / €2,250–2,550 $2,600–2,950 ⊞ BEX
Abbotsford, in Roxburghshire, was the home of Sir Walter Scott.

A silver vinaigrette, the cover decorated with a castle, Birmingham 1839, 1½in (4cm) wide.
£1,050–1,200 / €1,500–1,750 $1,750–2,000 ⊞ WELD

A silver pendant vinaigrette, c1840, 1in (2.5cm) diam.
£180–200 / €260–290 $300–330 ⊞ LBr

A silver vinaigrette, in the form of a hunting horn, with a hinged cover and chain handle, London 1871, 4in (10cm) wide.
£360–430 / €520–620 $600–720 ⚒ GAK

A silver vinaigrette, by Nathaniel Mills, engraved with a view of the Scott Memorial in Edinburgh, Birmingham 1853, 2in (5cm) high.
£610–680 / €880–980 $1,000–1,100 ⊞ CoHA

A silver-gilt vinaigrette, by Edward Smith, with a foliate scroll grille, maker's mark, Birmingham 1856, 1½in (4cm) wide.
£300–360 / €430–510 $500–600 ⚒ G(L)

► **A silver vinaigrette,** engraved 'HH', c1880, 1½in (4cm) wide.
£250–275 / €360–400 $420–460 ⊞ CVA

A silver vinaigrette, engraved 'June 1937', Birmingham 1882, 1½in (4cm) wide.
£250–275 / €360–400 $420–460 ⊞ CVA

Miscellaneous

A silver *aide-mémoire*, London 1874, 2¾in (7cm) long.
£150–170 / €210–240
$250–280 ⊞ BLm

Items in the Miscellaneous section have been arranged in alphabetical order.

A pair of silver-mounted dressing table jars, by Judah Rosenthal & Samuel Jacob, London 1888, 5½in (14cm) high.
£500–560 / €720–800
$850–940 ⊞ GRe

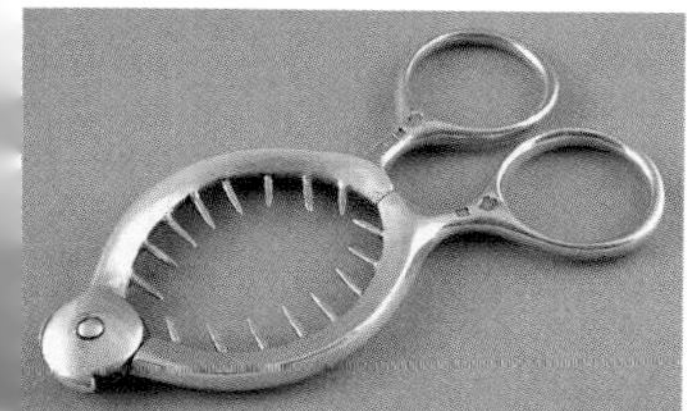

A silver egg topper, by Messrs Hutton, Sheffield 1901, 4in (10cm) long, 2oz.
£260–310 / €380–450
$440–520 ⚒ WW

A silver-gilt and ivory baton, by William Neale, London 1869, 22in (56cm) long, in original case.
£1,250–1,400 / €1,800–2,000
$2,100–2,350 ⊞ PAY

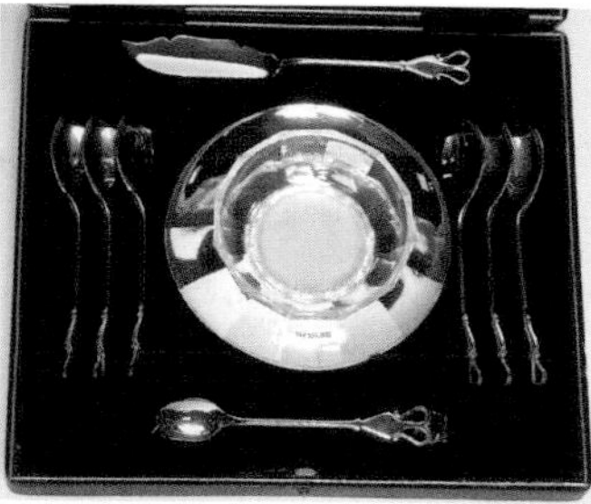

A silver breakfast set, Sheffield 1909, in original case, 8in (20.5cm) wide.
£340–380 / €500–550
$570–640 ⊞ BLm

A silver, tortoiseshell and mother-of-pearl dressing table set, Birmingham 1914, in an inlaid mahogany box, 15in (38cm) wide.
£370–440 / €530–630
$620–740 ⚒ Mit

A silver spirit kettle, burner and stand, by The Goldsmiths & Silversmiths Co, London 1910, 10in (25.5cm) high.
£350–420 / €500–600
$590–710 ⚒ GAK

◄ **A silver sugar scuttle,** Sheffield 1899, 6in (15cm) high.
£1,100–1,250 / €1,600–1,800
$1,900–2,100 ⊞ BLm

A silver cream pail, by William Comyns, decorated with a latticework of flowers, fruit and leaves, London 1902, 4¼in (11cm) high.
£155–185 / €230–270
$260–310 ⚒ EH

A silver-mounted tortoiseshell string dispenser, by William Comyns, London 1915, 3¼in (8.5cm) high.
£1,700–1,900 / €2,450–2,750
$2,850–3,200 ⊞ JTS

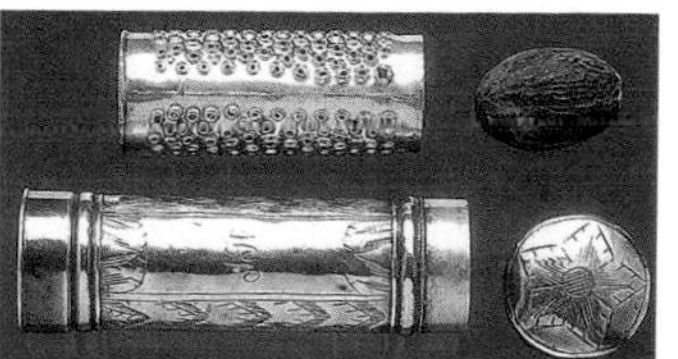

A silver nutmeg grater/tobacco rasp, probably by Thomas Kedden, engraved with a leaf and floral design, initialled 'IH', with detachable covers at each end, c1700, 3in (7.5cm) long.
£1,050–1,250 / €1,500–1,800
$1,750–2,100 ⚒ AG

Silver Plate

A silver-plated biscuit barrel, with engraved decoration and inscription, 19thC, 7in (18cm) diam.
£140–165 / €200–240
$240–280 SWO

A Sheffield plate coffee pot, with a vase finial, decorated with beaded borders, engraved with a cypher, c1785, 12in (30.5cm) high.
£175–210 / €250–300
$290–350 WW

A silver-plated and cut-glass cruet set, with six bottles, c1900, 6in (15cm) wide.
£180–200 / €260–290
$300–340 FOX

A Sheffield plate dish cross, c1790, 11in (28cm) wide.
£390–430 / €560–620
$650–720 GRe

A pair of Sheffield plate candlesticks, by Matthew Boulton, c1810, 12¼in (31cm) high.
£960–1,150 / €1,400–1,650
$1,600–1,900 NOA

A Victorian silver-plated comport stand, with a glass liner, 12½in (32cm) high.
£220–260 / €320–380
$370–440 WilP

Items in the Silver Plate section have been arranged in alphabetical order.

A child's silver-plated musical drinking cup, by Girod of Paris, inscribed 'Au Clair de la Lune', signed, c1910, 3½in (9cm) high, in original box.
£630–700 / €900–1,000
$1,100–1,250 JTS

► **A William IV silver-plated wine ewer,** with applied fruiting vine and foliage, 13½in (34.5cm) high.
£130–155 / €195–230
$220–260 EH

A silver-plated chatelaine, pierced and cast in Indian style, with seven accessories, c1895, 15in (38cm) long.
£210–250 / €300–360
$350–420 WL

A silver-plated novelty donkey cruet, c1870, 4½in (11cm) wide.
£260–290 / €380–420
$440–490 GRe

A Victorian silver-plated desk stand, the two cut-glass inkwells mounted with stags'-head covers, a seated stag mounted on the box, with a presentation inscription, 12½in (32cm) wide.
£360–430 / €520–620
$600–720 SWO

A silver-plated and cut-glass claret jug, with a standing lion thumbpiece, late 19thC, 11in (28cm) high.
£400–480 / €580–690
$680–810 Mit

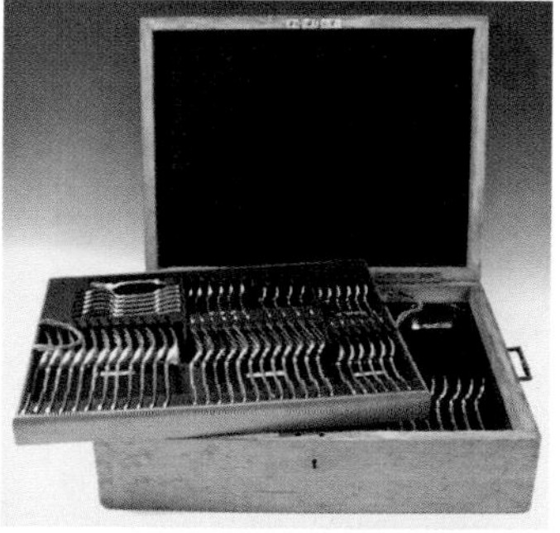

A Victorian silver-plated Fiddle pattern table service, by James Dixon & Son, comprising 82 pieces, in an oak case.
£610–730 / €880–1,050
$1,000–1,200 SWO

A silver-plated spoon warmer, in the form of a shell, with a hinged cover, 19thC, 5½in (14cm) high.
£130–155 / €185–220
$220–260 HOLL

A Victorian silver-plated tray, on four scrolling feet, 24in (61cm) wide.
£140–165 / €200–240
$240–280 SWO

A silver-plated kettle, stand and spirit burner, engraved with foliate designs and crests, on curved legs with shell feet, 19thC, 16in (40.5cm) high.
£420–500 / €620–740
$730–870 GAK

A silver-plated supper set, by Walker & Hall, comprising four dishes and covers and a central dish and cover, all with volute finials, 1900–20, 17½in (44.5cm) diam.
£350–420 / €500–600
$590–710 WW

A pair of silver-plated sugar cutters/ tongs, c1890, 6in (15cm) long.
£50–60 / €75–85
$85–100 CoHA

A Sheffield plate beehive hot water urn and burner, possibly by Roberts, Cadman & Co, on a plinth base with ball feet, c1800, 9in (23cm) high.
£640–770 / €920–1,100
$1,100–1,300 NOA

A silver-plated mug, by Elkington & Co, relief-decorated with Pan and cherubs within arcade and floral-cast borders, the S-scroll handle with a cherub thumbpiece, detachable silver-gilt liner, date code for 1896, 4½in (11.5cm) high.
£175–210 / €250–300
$290–350 DD

A Victorian silver-plated tea caddy, 3¾in (9.5cm) high.
£150–180 / €220–260
$250–300 G(L)

A Gothic-style silver-plated four-piece tea and coffee service, by Elkington & Co, with engraved decoration, c1862.
£340–410 / €490–590
$580–690 B(NW)

A pair of Victorian Sheffield plate two-handled wine coolers, with bands of scrolling acanthus, with scroll handles, 12in (30.5cm) high.
£880–1,050 / €1,250–1,500
$1,500–1,800 HOLL

Wine Antiques

An oak copper-banded coopered ale/cider jug, early 19thC, 7in (18cm) high.
£120–135 / €170–190
$200–220 ⊞ F&F

An oak and silver-plated ale set, comprising a jug and two goblets, carved with a band of oak leaves and acorns, 19thC, jug 10½in (26.5cm) high.
£590–710 / €850–1,000
$1,000–1,200 ⚒ GH

Items in the Wine Antiques section have been arranged in alphabetical order.

A pair of silver wine bottle grips, by Walker & Hall, the fluted collars with leaf-capped scroll handles, on a beaded base, Sheffield 1911, 38oz.
£2,350–2,800 / €3,350–4,000
$3,900–4,650 ⚒ B(NW)

A set of six silver-plated and cork bottle stoppers, the ivory inserts engraved in black with wine varieties, 19thC.
£330–390 / €480–570
$560–670 ⚒ B

A silver-plated bottle stopper, in the form of a top hat, c1880.
£120–135 / €170–190
$200–220 ⊞ JAS

◄ **A silver brandy saucepan,** with an ivory handle, London 1825, 2in (5cm) diam.
£220–260
€330–390
$380–450
⚒ GAK

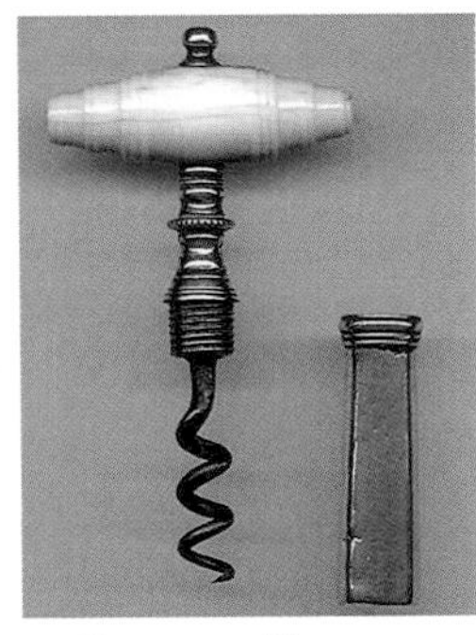

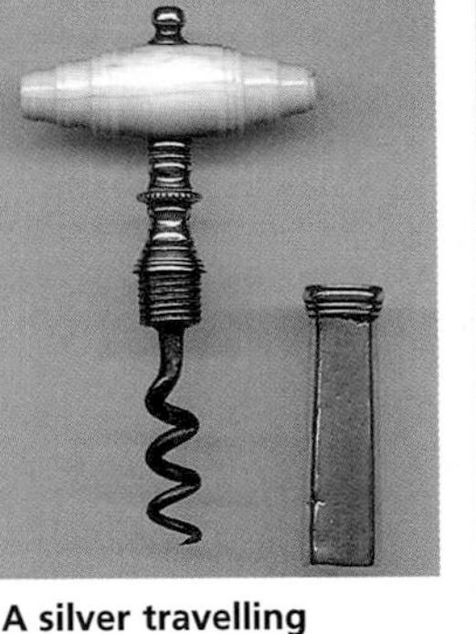

A silver travelling corkscrew, with a turned ivory handle, maker's mark IR, c1790, 3½in (9cm) long.
£310–350 / €450–500
$520–580 ⊞ CS

A double-action corkscrew, with a bone handle, the brass barrel applied with a royal coat-of-arms, c1820, 7in (18cm) long.
£135–150 / €200–220
$230–260 ⊞ CS

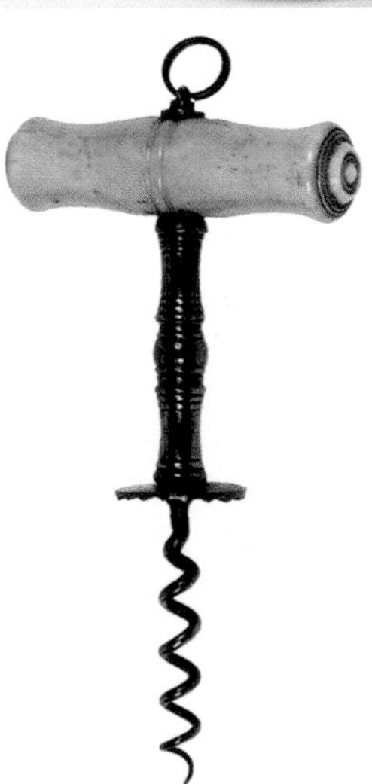

A steel Henshall-type corkscrew, with a bone handle, c1830, 7in (18cm) long.
£160–175 / €230–250
$270–300 ⊞ WAA

A cast-iron Kings-type corkscrew, possibly by Hatleigh, with a four pillar rack and screw, brush replaced, 1860–70, 11¼in (28.5cm) extended.
£350–420 / €500–600
$590–710 ⚒ SWO

Further reading

Miller's Corkscrews & Wine Antiques: A Collector's Guide, Miller's Publications, 2001

◄ **A brass double corkscrew,** with a bone handle and fitted brush, 19thC, 7in (18cm) closed.
£140–165 / €200–240
$240–280 ⚒ BWL

A mahogany decanter box, fitted with twelve glass decanters, c1790, 14in (35.5cm) wide.
£540–600 / €780–860
$900–1,000 ⊞ WAA

A Karelian birch and ebony-strung drinks box, by N. Rodriguez, with three decanters and two tester glasses, Bramah lock, signed, c1880, 13¾in (35cm) wide.
£1,750–1,950 / €2,500–2,800
$2,950–3,250 ⊞ JTS

An inlaid mahogany decanter box, containing six glass decanters with original gilding, 19thC, 11in (28cm) wide.
£620–690 / €890–990
$1,000–1,200 ⊞ MB

A pair of walnut decanter driers, the backboard with a suspension hole and a carrying handle, on three bun feet, 19thC, 11¼in (28.5cm) high.
£1,650–1,950 / €2,350–2,800
$2,800–3,350 ⚒ B

A liqueur set, comprising four cut-glass decanters and 16 glasses gilded with stylized flowerheads, in an amboyna and ebony case crossbanded with brass stringing, the hinged lid with brass and mother-of-pearl paterae, on turned feet, French, 19thC, 13¼in (3.5cm) wide.
£940–1,100 / €1,350–1,600
$1,600–1,900 ⚒ AH

A Victorian silver-plated and glass spirit barrel wagon, with an engraved inscription, 7¾in (19.5cm) high.
£590–710 / €840–1,000
$1,000–1,200 ⚒ SWO

WINE ANTIQUES

A silver toddy ladle, with a rosewood handle, c1740, 13¾in (35cm) long.
£230–260 / €330–370
$400–440 ⊞ JAS

A pair of silver wine coasters, by John Roberts & Co, with gadrooned sides and rims, the inset wooden bases with a silver disc engraved with initials, Sheffield 1809, 6in (15cm) diam.
£880–1,050 / €1,250–1,500
$1,500–1,800 ⚒ TEN

A silver wine funnel, by R. & S. Hennell, the bowl engraved with a lion crest, London 1807, 4½in (11.5cm) high.
£520–620 / €740–880
$850–1,000 ⚒ EH

A silver wine funnel, by William Chawner, London 1827, 6½in (16.5cm) high.
£1,150–1,300 / €1,650–1,850
$2,000–2,200 ⊞ BLm

A silver vine leaf wine label, by C. Reily and G. Storer, decorated with veins and malting, pierced 'Moselle', London 1837.
£120–145 / €170–200
$200–240 ⚒ WW

Clocks

British Bracket, Mantel & Table Clocks

Miller's Compares

I. A red-lacquered chinoiserie-decorated bracket clock, by Ben Ward, London, the brass dial with date aperture, alarm set disc and strike/silent dial, twin fusee movement, later anchor escapement and alarm striking on a bell, c1750, 20in (51cm) high.
£6,300–7,600
€9,100–11,000
$10,600–12,800 B

II. A mahogany bracket clock, by Thomas Horsley, London, the silvered dial with mock pendulum, date aperture and strike/silent dial, twin fusee movement, later anchor escapement striking the hours on a bell and the quarters on bells and hammers, 1750–1800, 20½in (52cm) high.
£3,500–4,200
€5,000–6,000
$5,900–7,000 B

Both these clocks have the same basic shape, strike/silent subsidiaries in the arch and date apertures. However, Item II has a silvered flat dial whereas Item I has a raised chapter ring and spandrels. Item I also has a red-lacquered case which is far more unusual than the mahogany case of Item II, making it interesting to decorators as well as horologists, and hence it fetching nearly double the price. It is worth noting that both these clocks have had their escapements changed from verge to anchor.

A mahogany bracket clock, by Richard Wilson, London, the brass dial with mock pendulum and date aperture, strike/silent and slow/fast dials, the eight-day twin fusee movement with verge escapement, c1750, 21in (53.5cm) high.
£10,300–12,300
€14,800–17,800
$17,300–20,700 G(L)

A George III mahogany and ormolu-mounted bracket clock, by William Fox, London, the silvered brass dial with a strike/silent dial, the twin-train movement and anchor escapement mounted with a bell, 17¾in (45cm) high.
£7,300–8,700
€10,500–12,500
$12,300–14,600 BR

A fruitwood bracket clock, the brass dial with calender aperture, strike/silent and inscribed 'Abel Panchaud, London', the eight-day twin fusee movement with five pillars, striking on a bell, case formerly ebonized, c1765, 15in (38cm) high.
£2,050–2,450
€2,950–3,500
$3,450–4,100 Bri
Abel Panchaud appears to be unrecorded working in London but recorded in Britten's *Old Clocks and their Makers* as working in Oxford as Panchaud & Co from 1765 to 1785.

A mahogany bracket clock, the dial with perpetual calendar and strike/silent dial, the five-pillar twin fusee movement with anchor escapement and striking on a bell, c1795, 15½in (39.5cm) high.
£3,000–3,600
€4,300–5,200
$5,000–6,000 Bri

A mahogany clock, by John Taylor, London, with strike/silent dial and concentric calendar, with five pillar, trip-repeating fusee movement striking on a bell, signed, case probably Russian, c1785, 17in (43cm) high.
£2,600–3,100
€3,700–4,400
$4,400–5,200 S(O)

A mahogany musical bracket/table clock, by De Lasalle, London, the silvered brass dial with date and strike/silent dials, the eight-day movement with verge escapement striking on a bell, the quarters on eight bells, the sides with carrying handles, c1795, 20in (51cm) high.
£13,300–14,800
€19,100–21,300
$22,300–24,800 PAO

◄ **A George III mahogany bracket clock,** by John May Southampton, the silvered dial with a strike/silent dial, eight-day striking double fusee movement, 22in (56cm) high.
£4,250–5,100
€6,100–7,300
$7,100–8,500 LFA

A George III mahogany bracket clock, the dial with secondary dial, with eight-day twin fusee movement, marked 'Baggs, London', with original bracket, 24in (61cm) high.
£6,700–8,000
€9,600–11,500
$11,300–13,400 HOLL

The prices realized at auction may reflect the fact that the clocks have sometimes undergone alterations to their movements, or are in unrestored condition.

A Regency mahogany and brass-inlaid bracket clock, by Lacey, Bristol, with an enamel dial, the fusee movement with replacement bell, 17in (43cm) high.
£1,750–2,100
€2,500–3,000
$2,900–3,500 CGC

A walnut bracket time-piece, the silvered brass dial with mock pendulum aperture, the single fusee movement with verge escapement, signed 'Saml Whichcote, London', 18thC, 18½in (47cm) high.
£7,000–8,400
€10,100–12,100
$11,700–14,100 Bea

Clocks with walnut cases were cheaper to buy than ebony-veneered examples and, as only the rich could afford a bracket clock, more ebony examples were produced. The result is that walnut clocks are now the scarcer of the two and generally command twice the price.

A Regency mahogany and brass-inlaid bracket clock, by Richard Webster, London, 19in (48.5cm) high.
£6,800–7,500
€9,800–10,800
$11,400–12,600 JeF

◄ **A Regency mahogany bracket clock,** with a painted dial, the twin fusee movement with anchor escapement striking on a bell, 18½in (47cm) high.
£1,750–2,100
€2,500–3,000
$2,900–3,500 HAM

Signatures

Most clocks are signed by the maker and in most instances this will help to date it. However, the appearance of a signature does not guarantee that the clock was made by the man whose name it bears, nor that it is of the period in which he was working. Clocks dating from the 19th century are often signed by the retailer rather than the maker. The location of the signature can vary depending on the type of clock, but usually appears on the dial and/or the backplate.

A George III mahogany repeater bracket clock, the dial with pendulum aperture and seconds dial, with a gilt operated fusee movement, dial signed 'Buchanan, Dublin', Irish, 15½in (39cm) high.
£4,300–5,100
€6,200–7,400
$7,200–8,600 MEA

A mahogany and brass-inlaid bracket clock, by Hardy, Truro, with a painted dial, the twin-chain fusee movement with anchor escapement striking on a bell, early 19thC, 18½in (47cm) high.
£1,400–1,650
€2,000–2,400
$2,400–2,800 B

◄ **A Regency rosewood bracket clock,** by Hirst, Leeds, with eight-day twin-train fusee movement, restored, 20in (51cm) high.
£2,000–2,400
€2,900–3,450
$3,350–4,000
Mit

A patinated and gilt-bronze mantel clock, with an enamel dial, on a stepped base with applied mounts, the single gut fusee movement with anchor escapement, 1800–50, 14¼in (36.5cm) high.
£3,000–3,600 / €4,300–5,200
$5,000–6,000 B

A mahogany bracket clock, by John Tunnell, London, with eight-day movement, c1820, 19in (48.5cm) high.
£7,200–8,000
€10,400–11,500
$12,100–13,400 JeF

A George IV mahogany bracket clock, with a trade label of George G. Cocks, Bristol, 11in (28cm) high.
£2,250–2,700
€3,250–3,900
$3,800–4,500 LAY

A mahogany bracket clock, with an enamel dial, the fusee movement with anchor escapement striking on a later gong, with a plain bracket, c1820, 14¼in (36cm) high.
£1,800–2,150
€2,600–3,100
$3,000–3,600 S(O)

A mahogany bracket clock, by Hampston, Prince & Cattles, York, the painted dial with strike/silent dial, the twin fusee movement with adjustable pendulum striking on a bell, c1820, 18¼in (46.5cm) high.
£2,800–3,350
€4,000–4,800
$4,700–5,600 PFK

A George IV mahogany bracket clock, with a painted dial, the twin chain fusee movement with anchor escapement striking on a bell, 20in (51cm) high.
£1,050–1,250
€1,500–1,800
$1,750–2,100 Bea

A William IV mahogany bracket clock, with a painted enamel dial, the twin fusee movement with rack strike, pull-repeating on one bell, signed 'Wright, London', with associated bracket, 21¾in (55cm) high.
£4,950–5,900
€7,100–8,500
$8,300–10,000 TEN

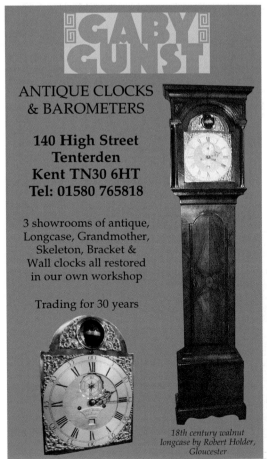

A mahogany mantel clock, the painted dial inscribed 'Johnston, London', 19thC, 13in (33cm) high.
£760–910 / €1,100–1,300
$1,250–1,500 SWO

Further reading

Miller's Clocks & Barometers Buyer's Guide, Miller's Publications, 2001

An oak mantel clock, with a silvered dial, the twin fusee movement striking on a gong, 19thC, 19¾in (50cm) high.
£1,250–1,500
€1,800–2,150
$2,100–2,500 ⚒ Bea

A mahogany mantel clock, by E. J. Dent, London, with a silvered dial, the fusee and chain movement with five pillars striking on a bell, feet missing, c1840, 19in (48.5cm) high.
£2,150–2,550
€3,100–3,700
$3,600–4,300 ⚒ S(O)

A bird's-eye maple bracket clock, with an enamel dial, the eight-day twin-train fusee movement striking on a bell, c1850, 14½in (37cm) high.
£680–820 / €980–1,150
$1,150–1,350 ⚒ DN

A rosewood bracket clock, with an enamel dial, the eight-day twin fusee movement striking on a bell, c1850, 21in (53.5cm) high.
£1,750–2,100
€2,500–3,000
$2,900–3,500 ⚒ WW

◀ **A Gothic-style oak bracket clock,** with a silvered dial, the triple-train movement striking on eight bells and a coiled gong, pendulum missing, signed 'Loveday, Wakefield', c1850, 30in (76cm) high.
£1,400–1,650
€2,000–2,400
$2,350–2,800 ⚒ B(L)

◀ **A Victorian Gothic revival brass mantel clock,** the design attributed to Bruce James Talbert, mounted with cabochon-set roundels, 11½in (29cm) high.
£1,650–1,950
€2,350–2,800
$2,750–3,250 ⚒ LAY

A walnut mantel clock, the silvered dial with strike/silent dial, the twin fusee movement with anchor escapement and striking on a gong, signed 'Clerke, 1 Royal Exchange, London, No. 5020', 1850–75, 16in (41cm) high.
£1,700–2,000
€2,450–2,900
$2,850–3,350 ⚒ TEN

A Victorian figured walnut bracket clock, the silvered dial signed 'J. & J. Thristle, Williton', the twin fusee movement with anchor escapement striking on a bell, bell inscribed 'P. B. Bristol', minor losses, 17¼in (44cm) high.
£1,200–1,450
€1,750–2,100
$2,000–2,400 ⚒ BR

◄ A rosewood and brass-inlaid table clock, with chime/silent, chime selection and regulation dials, the triple-train fusee and chain movement with anchor escapement chiming on eight bells and striking on a gong, c1890, 29½in (75cm) high.
£2,650–3,150
€3,800–4,500
$4,400–5,300 ⚒ S(O)

An ebonized and gilt-mounted table clock, with chime/silent, chime selection and regulation dials, the fusee and chain movement with anchor escapement chiming on eight bells and striking on a gong, c1880, 22½in (57cm) high.
£2,500–3,000
€3,600–4,300
$4,200–5,000 ⚒ S(O)

A figured mahogany bracket clock, with a painted dial, the eight-day twin fusee movement striking on a bell, late 19thC, 19¼in (49cm) high.
£440–530 / €630–760
$740–890 ⚒ RTo

► A mahogany library clock, by H. Kyze, Brighton, with eight-day fusee movement, c1890, 17in (43cm) high.
£880–980
€1,250–1,400
$1,500–1,650
⊞ PTh

Backplates

From the late 17th century the backplates of English bracket and table clocks were profusely engraved with flowers and foliage, often including birds and figures as well. The maker's name might also be engraved amid the decoration. By 1770 the engraving had become simpler and, by 1800, had been reduced to a border, often with a matching border to the pendulum bob and a signature to the centre. By 1820 all decoration had ceased, leaving the signature only.

A walnut bracket clock, the silvered dial with subsidiary dials, the eight-day triple-train movement striking on eight bells and five gongs, late 19thC, 27¾in (70.5cm) high.
£2,100–2,500
€3,000–3,600
$3,500–4,200 ⚒ MAR

◄ An ebonized and brass-mounted table clock, the dial with enamel cartouches, the triple-train fusee and chain movement with anchor escapement chiming on nine bells and striking on a further bell, losses, late 19thC, 34¾in (88.5cm) high.
£3,500–4,200
€5,000–6,000
$5,900–7,000 ⚒ TEN

A walnut bracket clock, with eight-day quarter-chiming movement, late 19thC, 14½in (36.5cm) high.
£820–980 / €1,200–1,400
$1,400–1,650 SWO

Chimes

Many quarter-chiming mantel clocks are only twin-train and strike the quarters on two gongs, known as 'ting-tang'. These should not be confused with triple-train clocks which chime on a series of bells or gongs, and are generally considerably more expensive than twin-train quarter chimers.

A tortoiseshell and silver-mounted bedside clock, by William Comyns, London, 1908, 4in (10cm) high.
£1,000–1,200
€1,450–1,700
$1,700–2,000 RTo

► **An Edwardian mahogany and brass-inlaid clock and barometer compendium set,** by Thomas & William Armstrong, Manchester and Liverpool, dials signed, with eight-day movement, replacement platform, 10¾in (27cm) high.
£610–680 / €880–980
$1,000–1,100 FOF

Thomas and William Armstrong, Mathematical and Philosophical Instrument Makers, worked from 1875 to c1900 and were renowned for their aneroid barometers. Philosophical instruments were items such as compasses, globes and barometers etc.

◄ **A rosewood mantel clock,** with subsidiary chime/silent, chime selection and regulation dials, the triple-train fusee and chain movement with deadbeat escapement chiming on eight bells or four gongs and striking on a further gong, signed 'Russells Ltd, Liverpool', c1900, 22½in (57cm) high.
£3,000–3,600
€4,300–5,200
$5,000–6,000 S(O)

► **An inlaid mahogany mantel clock and pedestal,** the silvered dial with chime/silent, chime selection and regulation subsidiary dials, the triple-train fusee and chain movement chiming on four gongs and a further gong, c1905, 71½in (181.5cm) high.
£1,250–1,500
€1,800–2,150
$2,100–2,500 S(O)

A tortoiseshell desk clock, by William Comyns, London, inlaid with 9ct gold foliate swags and a flower-filled vase, 1906, 5¾in (14.5cm) high.
£2,400–2,900
€3,450–4,150
$4,000–4,800 S(O)

Almost all small tortoiseshell and silver timepieces have French carriage movements and the cases were made and hallmarked in the United Kingdom. Both items shown here, with gold and silverwork assayed by William Comyns, are typical examples.

◄ **An oak military mess clock,** by Elliott & Co, London, with eight-day movement, c1910, 14in (35.5cm) high.
£790–880 / €1,100–1,250
$1,350–1,500 PTh

CLOCKS

Continental Bracket, Mantel & Table Clocks

A gilt-brass and glass table clock, by Elias Weckerlin, Augsburg, the fusee movement with verge escapement striking on a bell, chain damaged, with an associated silvered dial, losses from case, movement signed, German, late 17thC, 5½in (14cm) diam.
£3,300–3,950 / €4,750–5,700
$5,500–6,600 ⚒ S(Am)

► A boulle bracket clock, with an enamel dial, movement signed 'Charles Voisin à Paris', French, early 18thC, 47in (119cm) high, with bracket.
£5,800–6,900
€8,400–10,000
$9,700–11,600
⚒ S(P)
Charles Voisin was received Master in 1710.

A boulle and ormolu-mounted bracket clock, by Gudin, Paris, with enamel numerals and a bell-striking movement, damaged, case stamped 'J. Pecourt', French, 18thC, clock 28in (71cm) high, with bracket.
£1,100–1,300
€1,600–1,900
$1,850–2,200 ⚒ CGC

A painted bracket clock, restored, Swiss, 18thC, 33in (84cm) high, with bracket.
£1,750–2,100
€2,500–3,000
$2,900–3,500 ⚒ S(NY)

A rococo-style lacquered and bronze mantel clock, by Petter Ernst, Stockholm, Swedish, 1753–84, 21in (53cm) high.
£4,750–5,700
€6,800–8,200
$8,000–9,600 ⚒ BUK

A rococo-style lacquered bracket clock, by Johan Nyberg, with gold decoration, Swedish, c1761, 40¼in (102cm) high.
£4,350–5,200
€6,300–7,500
$7,300–8,700 ⚒ BUK
Johan Nyberg was received Master in 1761.

An oak bracket clock, by Klaas Johannes Andriese Grouw, with an engraved brass dial, the five-pillar fusee and chain movement with verge escapement, with a pull wind alarm on a bell and quarter striking on two bells, case probably associated, Dutch, late 18thC, 20½in (52cm) high.
£6,500–7,800
€9,400–11,200
$10,900–13,100 ⚒ S(Am)

A *vernis Martin* and gilt-metal-mounted bracket clock, the dial signed 'Boucheret à Paris', the eight-day twin-train movement striking on a bell, French, c1770, 19½in (50cm) high.
£1,200–1,450
€1,750–2,100
$2,000–2,400 ⚒ Bri

A giltwood clock, with an enamel dial, the associated movement with verge escapement, Flemish, probably Liège, late 18thC, 32in (81.5cm) high.
£5,000–6,000
€7,200–8,600
$8,400–10,000 ⚒ S

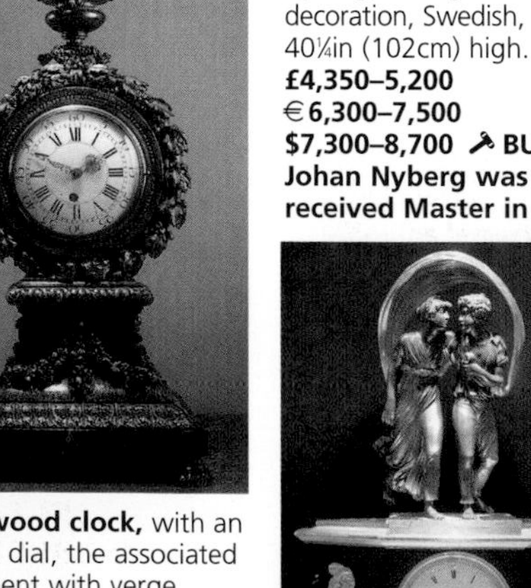

◄ A patinated-bronze and ormolu clock, the eight-day movement striking on a bell, French, c1800, 21in (53cm) high.
£18,000–20,000
€26,000–29,000
$30,000–33,000 ⊞ GDO
This clock illustrates part of the story of *Paul et Virginie* by Bernadin de Saint-Pierre. Clocks such as this are seldom seen.

An ormolu mantel clock, with a figure of Diana the Huntress, the dial with a calendar hand, with eight-day striking movement, signed 'Bausse au Meridien Bvd D'Antin', French, c1805, 17¼in (44cm) high.
£5,300–5,900
€7,600–8,500
$8,900–9,900 ⊞ GDO

An ormolu desk clock, by Gallé, with original inkwells, French, Paris, 1810–15, 15in (38cm) high.
£6,500–7,200
€9,400–10,400
$10,900–12,000 ⊞ KK

A gilt-metal mantel clock, in the form of a chariot drawn by two goats and a putto, with an enamel dial signed 'M. Gentilhomme, Palais Royale', French, early 19thC, 9¾in (25cm) high.
£1,900–2,250
€2,700–3,200
$3,200–3,800 ⚒ G(L)

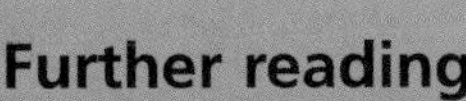

Further reading

Miller's Clocks Antiques Checklist, Miller's Publications, 2000

A gilt-bronze clock, 'La Partie de Dames', French, c1810, 18¼in (46.5cm) high.
£12,900–14,300
€18,600–20,600
$21,700–24,000 ⊞ KK

An ormolu clock, with a figure of The Muse of Science, with eight-day movement striking the hours and half-hours on a bell, steel suspended pendulum, the gilt dial signed 'Lepaute à Paris', French, c1813, 18½in (47cm) high.
£6,100–6,800
€8,800–9,800
$10,200–11,400 ⊞ GDO

A cut-crystal and gilt-bronze portico mantel clock, the ormolu dial with enamel chapter ring, the movement with anchor escapement striking on a bell, French, c1830, 17in (43cm) high.
£1,300–1,550
€1,900–2,250
$2,200–2,600 ⚒ S(Am)

An Empire mantel clock, the enamel chapter ring signed 'Chopin à Paris', surmounted by a reclining Bacchante, the base applied with lions, French, c1810, 16in (40.5cm) high.
£9,900–11,000
€14,200–15,800
$16,600–18,500 ⊞ RPA

An ormolu-mounted marble clock, the enamel dial with Roman numerals and Arabic quarters, signed 'Voisin à Paris', the twin-barrel movement rack-striking on two bells, French, early 19thC, 19¾in (50cm) high.
£1,750–2,100
€2,500–3,000
$2,900–3,500 ⚒ TEN

◄ **A gilt-metal mantel clock,** with a chased and embossed dial and eight-day drum movement, French, c1820, 12½in (32cm) wide.
£730–880 / €1,050–1,250
$1,200–1,450 ⚒ AH

A slate mantel clock, by Vincent & Co, the black slate chapter ring with gilt numerals, the half-hour striking movement chiming on a coiled gong, decorated with cast-brass panels, stamped, French, 19thC, 20¼in (51.5cm) high.
£130–155 / €185–220
$220–260 ⚒ PFK

A marble table clock, with an enamel dial and eight-day movement, surmounted with a Parian figure of a classical maiden, French, 19thC, 19in (48.5cm) high.
£370–440 / €530–630
$620–740 ⚒ AH

► A gilt-metal mantel clock, with an enamel dial, French, 19thC, 8¼in (21cm) high.
£170–200 / €250–290
$290–340 ⚒ TRM

◄ An ormolu and *champlevé* enamel mantel clock, the eight-day movement striking on a bell, stamped 'Japy Frères et Cie', French, 19thC, 17½in (44.5cm) high.
£1,400–1,650
€2,000–2,400
$2,350–2,800 ⚒ WW

An ormolu mantel clock, with a striking movement, French, 19thC, 11¾in (30cm) high.
£330–390 / €480–560
$550–650 ⚒ WilP

An inlaid rosewood mantel clock, with an enamel dial, the movement with double hour cylinder escapement striking on a bell, pull-wind alarm, French, Morbier, c1840, 11¼in (28.5cm) high.
£960–1,150
€1,400–1,650
$1,600–1,900 ⚒ S(O)

A tortoiseshell and brass-inlaid mantel clock, with a gilt-metal dial, the twin-barrel movement striking on a bell, stamped 'Z & Co Paris', French, 19thC, 21¼in (54cm) high.
£910–1,100
€1,300–1,550
$1,550–1,850 ⚒ Bea

A ormolu mantel clock, the enamel dial signed 'C. Taylor & Son, à Paris', the eight-day movement striking on a bell, French, c1840, 16½in (42cm) high.
£2,450–2,950
€3,500–4,200
$4,100–4,900 ⚒ Bri

A *petite sonnerie* mantel clock, with a gilt dial, the movement with square plates striking on twin gongs, the base with a musical movement, Austrian, c1850, 22½in (57cm) high.
£370–440 / €530–630
$620–740 ⚒ B(Kn)

◄ A gilt-metal mantel clock, with a painted porcelain dial and panel, French, c1875, 17in (43cm) high.
£680–820 / €980–1,150
$1,150–1,350 ⚒ SWO

A marble mantel clock, by Potonie, Paris, with visible Brocot escapement, the eight-day movement with a pendulum and striking the hours and half-hours on a bell, French, c1875, 13in (33cm) high.
£510–570 / €730–820
$860–960 ⊞ K&D

A marble and malachite-inlaid mantel clock, the marble dial with gilt numerals, the month-going movement with a gridiron pendulum and rack-striking on a bell, French, late 19thC, 19in (48.5cm) high.
£1,600–1,900
€2,300–2,750
$2,700–3,200 ⚒ S(Am)

A brass-mounted mock boulle mantel clock, the cast dial with enamel cartouche chapters, the twin-barrel movement striking on a bell, French, c1890, 20½in (52cm) high.
£700–840 / €1,000–1,200
$1,200–1,400 ⚒ TEN

A Gothic-style porcelain-mounted ormolu mantel clock, with a half-hour striking movement by Japy Frères, French, mid-19thC, 12in (30.5cm) high.
£1,000–1,200
€1,450–1,700
$1,700–2,000 ⚒ PF

A walnut and ebonized mantel clock, the eight-day movement striking on a bell, French, c1880, 10in (25.5cm) high.
£420–470 / €600–670
$710–790 ⊞ PTh

An ormolu and *champlevé* enamel mantel clock, with an enamel dial, the eight-day movement striking on a bell, French, c1880, 16½in (42cm) high.
£3,600–4,000
€5,200–5,800
$6,000–6,700 ⊞ GDO

LOCATE THE SOURCE

The source of each illustration in Miller's can be found by checking the code letters below each caption with the Key to Illustrations, pages 794–800.

► **An ormolu and marble mantel clock,** by Morgin, Paris, the movement striking on a bell, French, mid-19thC, 18in (45.5cm) wide.
£1,250–1,500
€1,800–2,150
$2,100–2,500
⚒ TMA

A tortoiseshell and ormolu-mounted mantel clock, with an enamel dial, the eight-day movement by Japy Frères striking the hours and half-hours on a bell, French, c1885, 15in (38cm) high.
£760–870 / €1,100–1,250
$1,250–1,400 ⊞ K&D

A lacquered-brass and silvered mantel clock, by Etienne Maxant, Paris, with an enamel dial, gong striking movement and patent winding system, French, late 19thC, 15¼in (39cm) high.
£1,650–1,950
€2,350–2,800
$2,750–3,250 ⚒ B
Etienne Maxant is listed as working from Rue de Saintonge, Paris from 1880 to 1905.

CLOCKS

A brass mantel clock, with a drum striking movement, French, late 19thC, 11½in (29cm) high.
£610–730 / €880–1,050
$1,000–1,200 SWO

An ormolu and *champlevé* enamel mantel clock, with a gilt dial, the eight-day movement striking on a bell, French, late 19thC, 10¾in (27cm) high.
£470–560 / €680–810
$790–940 EH

A Black Forest carved wood mantel clock, surmounted by a stag, the base with a recumbent doe, the twin-drum movement striking on a gong, German, late 19thC, 33½in (85cm) high.
£1,550–1,850
€2,250–2,650
$2,600–3,100 Bea

A carved oak mantel clock, by Winterhalder & Hofmeier, with subsidiary chime/silent, chime selection and regulation dials, the triple-train movement chiming on eight bells or four gongs and striking on a further gong, German, c1890, 25in (63.5cm) high.
£1,400–1,650
€2,000–2,400
$2,350–2,750 S(O)

An ebonized and gilt-bronze mantel clock, in the form of a globe supported by cherubs, with a lever escapement, on a marble base, French, late 19thC, 8in (20.5cm) high.
£330–390 / €470–560
$550–660 G(L)

An enamel strut clock, with eight-day movement, the case signed 'Chevron', the enamel panel signed 'Albin', Swiss, early 20thC, 5in (13cm) high.
£350–420 / €500–600
$590–700 B(Kn)

A slate, gilt-brass and marble-mounted mantel clock, French, 1875–1900, 18½in (47cm) high.
£230–270 / €330–390
$390–460 NOA

A tortoiseshell and gilt-bronze mantel clock, the porcelain dial inscribed 'Edwards & Sons, Paris', French, late 19thC, 13in (33cm) high.
£260–310 / €370–440
$440–520 SWO

A marble and spelter figural clock, by Garnier, French, c1900, 32in (81.5cm) high.
£1,350–1,500
€1,950–2,150
$2,250–2,500 ASP

A brass and onyx four-glass mantel clock, with an enamel dial, the eight-day movement with a pendulum and striking on a gong, French, late 19thC, 11¾in (30cm) high.
£320–380 / €470–550
$550–640 Oli

A Charles X-style mahogany and gilt-metal-mounted portico clock, with a gilt-metal dial, the eight-day twin-train movement with a bimetallic pendulum and striking on a bell, French, late 19thC, 19in (48.5cm) high.
£530–630 / €760–910
$890–1,050 DN

A carved wood cuckoo clock, the twin fusee movement sounding on the hour and half-hour, stamped 'G. H. S.', German/Swiss, c1900, 21½in (54.5cm) high.
£470–560 / €680–810
$790–940 PFK

Carriage Clocks

French carriage clocks were mass-produced – particularly in their simplest form – and were the standard wedding present from the 1880s to the start of WWI. Prices for these have remained stable over the last year, while those for the more substantial English examples have strengthened.

Carriage timepieces (non-strikers) can often be bought in fairly rough condition at auction for under £150 / €215 / $250. These examples will never be scarce so do not expect a quick return. It should also be remembered that the cost of restoration can amount to three figures. Striking clocks start at around £280 / €400 / $470 and repeaters from £350 / €500 / $650. These have a button on the top which, when pushed, makes the clock strike to the preceding hour – very useful for telling the time at night before gas or electric light came into regular domestic use.

All carriage clocks had travelling cases – few have now. When buying this is not of great importance, but good makers such as Henri Jacot always provided a numbered case and key. To find these with your clock is an added bonus.

With French clocks look for additional features such as engraved gorge cases, porcelain or enamel panels, *grande sonneries* or subsidiary dials. These indicate that the clock would have been very expensive when new, and therefore well cared for. They seldom appear in poor condition and are always hotly contested at auction by collectors and dealers. An increasingly aware public assures that good examples rarely slip through as 'sleepers'. No major single-owner sales of these have occurred recently in the UK, but when they do, demand soars. Collectors worldwide compete for the best examples and drive up prices.

English carriage clocks are far more substantial and mechanically of a much higher grade than Continental examples. They always had chain fusee movements and the most superb and substantial platform escapements. A two-train movement with chronometer escapement is a work of wonder. Produced by the best makers and retailed by them or fine jewellers, these clocks have always been sought after. Prices have firmed this year as a result of fewer offerings at auction and the realization that they are getting much scarcer.

The carriage clock market is strong at present, but any drop might result in lower grade items losing value much quicker than top of the range pieces.

Richard Price

A gilt-brass carriage timepiece, the engraved silvered dial signed 'Grafton, Barbican', the eight-day movement with replaced lever escapement, c1840, 6in (15cm) high.
£690–830 / €1,000–1,200
$1,150–1,350 ⚒ S(O)

A brass rococo carriage clock, the movement with divided lift escapement and outside countwheel probably by Jules, striking on a bell, French, c1840, 7in (18cm) high.
£1,500–1,700
€2,150–2,450
$2,500–2,850 ⊞ ROH

A brass carriage clock, by Bolviller, Paris, with a porcelain dial, French, c1845, 7½in (19cm) high.
£600–720 / €870–1,050
$1,000–1,200 ⚒ ROSc

A brass carriage clock, with an enamel dial and repeating movement, French, 1845–50, 6in (15cm) high.
£2,000–2,250
€2,900–3,200
$3,350–3,800 ⊞ CPC

◄ **A gilt-brass carriage clock,** by Guierot Frères, the enamel dial with subsidiary alarm dial, the single lever platform escapement striking on a bell, stamped mark, minor damage, French, c1850, 5¼in (14cm) high.
£700–840 / €1,000–1,200
$1,200–1,400 ⚒ EH

◄ **A gilt-brass carriage clock,** by Bolviller, Paris, the twin-train movement with lever platform escapement striking on a bell, the handle in the form of two intertwined bronzed mermaids, each canted corner with a niche containing a bronzed female figure, French, c1850, 8½in (21.5cm) high
£820–980 / €1,200–1,400
$1,400–1,650 ⚒ TMA

A gilt-brass carriage timepiece, with fusee movement, c1850, 5½in (14cm) high, with original travelling case.
£3,600–4,000 / €5,200–5,800
$6,000–6,700 ⊞ JeF

A rosewood carriage clock, by Payne, with a gilt dial, the triple-chain fusee movement with five pillars and lever platform escapement striking on a gong, c1850, 8¼in (21cm) high, with original tooled leather travelling case.
£24,500–29,400 / €35,000–42,000
$41,000–49,000 B
William Payne moved from South Molton Street to 163 New Bond Street, London, in 1825. The firm continued to make and retail clocks and watches into the 20th century. This clock has three trains, which is exceptional in a case as small as this, and hence the exceptional price.

A gilt-brass carriage clock, the enamel dial signed 'J. W. Benson, London', the movement with platform lever escapement striking on a gong, French, c1870, 6¾in (17.5cm) high, with a travelling case.
£2,300–2,750
€3,300–3,950
$3,850–4,600 S(Am)

► **A gilt-brass carriage clock,** the dial and side panels with decorated enamel panels, with a repeating movement alarm, French, c1880, 7½in (19cm) high.
£4,300–4,800
€6,200–6,900
$7,200–8,000
⊞ BELL

► **A gilt-brass *grande sonnerie* carriage clock,** by Leroy, Paris, the silvered guilloche mask with subsidiary dials for day, date and alarm, repeating movement with lever platform, French, c1880, 8in (20.5cm) high.
£7,200–8,000
€10,400–11,500
$12,100–13,500 ⊞ CPC

A gilt-brass porcelain-mounted miniature carriage timepiece, by Drocourt, the panels decorated with rural scenes, French, c1880, 4in (10cm) high.
£4,300–4,800
€6,200–6,900
$7,200–8,000 ⊞ BELL

A gilt-brass porcelain-mounted carriage clock, the repeating movement by Brunelot, the gorge case with panels decorated with rural scenes, French, c1880, 7in (18cm) high.
£6,300–7,000
€9,100–10,100
$10,600–11,800 ⊞ BELL

A gilt-brass carriage clock, by Drocourt, with a repeating movement and an engraved gorged case, French, c1880, 6in (15cm) high, with original travelling case and key.
£2,700–3,000
€3,900–4,300
$4,500–5,000 ⊞ CPC

CLOCKS

A gilt-brass *petite sonnerie* carriage clock, retailed by Lewis & Son, with a silvered dial, in an engraved gorge case, French, c1880, 5½in (14cm) high.
£4,400–4,900
€6,300–7,000
$7,400–8,200 ⊞ ROH

A brass carriage clock, the enamel dial above a subsidiary alarm dial within a silver panel, the eight-day repeating movement with alarm, in a gorge case, c1880, 5½in (14cm) high.
£1,300–1,550
€1,850–2,200
$2,200–2,600 ⚒ SWO

A brass carriage clock, by Henri Jacot, Paris, with an enamelled dial, the eight-day twin-train movement with lever escapement striking the hours on a gong, with half-hour passing strike, French, 1880s, 6¾in (17cm) high.
£700–840 / €1,000–1,200
$1,200–1,400 ⚒ DN

A brass carriage time-piece, with a silvered dial, compass and crescent thermometer, French, 19thC, 8in (20.5cm) high.
£280–330 / €400–480
$470–550 ⚒ EH

A gilt-metal carriage clock, by Dent, Paris, the enamel dial with subsidiary seconds dial, the lever platform escapement striking on a gong, French, 19thC, 4¾in (12cm) high, with a leather travelling case.
£820–980 / €1,200–1,400
$1,400–1,650 ⚒ B(EA)

A brass miniature carriage timepiece, 1880–1900, 2½in (6.5cm) high, with a leather travelling case.
£230–270 / €330–390
$380–450 ⚒ GAK

A brass carriage clock, with strike, repeat and alarm movement, French, c1890, 6¾in (17cm) high, with original velour-lined case.
£2,500–3,000 / €3,600–4,300
$4,200–5,000 ⚒ ROSc

A brass carriage clock, with an enamel dial, the twin-barrel movement with lever platform escapement striking on a bell, signed 'Bolviller à Paris', French, c1890, 6in (15.5cm) high.
£880–1,050 / €1,250–1,500
$1,450–1,750 ⚒ TEN

A brass carriage clock, retailed by The Goldsmiths & Silversmiths Co, London, the eight-day movement striking the hours and half-hours on a gong, in a corniche case, French, c1895, 5½in (14cm) high.
£590–650 / €850–940
$990–1,100 ⊞ K&D

A *champlevé* enamel-decorated carriage clock, with gilt floral-decorated dial, lever platform escapement striking and repeating on a gong, in a corniche case, late 19thC, 6¾in (17.5cm) high.
£1,350–1,600 / €1,950–2,300
$2,250–2,700 ⚒ B

A gilt-brass carriage clock, with painted and 'jewelled' dial, the lever platform escapement striking on two gongs, with alarm, dial cracked, inscribed, French, c1900, 8¼in (21cm) high, with a leather travelling case.
£800–960 / €1,150–1,350
$1,350–1,600 WW

A brass carriage timepiece, by Duverdry & Bloquel, the dial with pierced and engraved foliate mask, French, c1900, 5½in (14cm) high.
£850–940 / €1,200–1,350
$1,400–1,550 CPC

A silver carriage clock, with a French movement, maker's mark 'G. B.', Birmingham 1901, 2¾in (7cm) high.
£420–500 / €600–720
$700–840 DMC

A brass carriage clock, with an enamel dial and half repeating eight-day movement, minor damage, French, early 20thC, 5in (13cm) high.
£280–330 / €400–470
$470–550 EH

A brass and tortoiseshell-veneered carriage clock, with an enamel dial and earlier fusee movement, marked 'B. Schalfino, Taunton', early 20thC, 5in (12.5cm) high.
£290–350 / €420–500
$490–590 FHF

A brass carriage clock, French, early 20thC, 5¾in (14.5cm) high.
£290–350 / €420–500
$490–590 FHF

► **A carriage timepiece,** the enamel dial above a subsidiary alarm dial, stamped 'B.T.G.', early 20thC, 8½in (21.5cm) high, with a fitted case.
£175–210
€250–300
$290–350
SWO

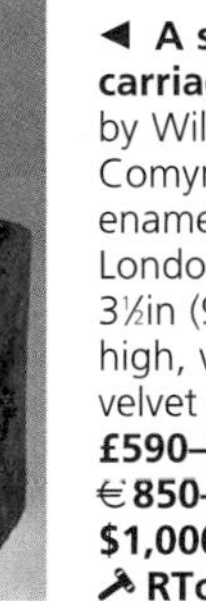

◄ **A silver carriage clock,** by William Comyns, with enamel dial, London 1901, 3½in (9cm) high, with a velvet case.
£590–700
€850–1,000
$1,000–1,200
RTo

A miniature silver carriage clock, retailed by William Ogden, with a Swiss eight-day 'jewelled' movement, 1910, 3½in (9cm) high, in original presentation case.
£1,300–1,450 / €1,850–2,100
$2,200–2,450 GDO

CLOCKS

Electric Clocks

An electric clock, by Eureka Clock Co, London, on a gilt-metal base, with presentation inscription, dial inscribed 'S. Fisher Ltd', c1906, 11½in (29cm) high.
£680–810 / €980–1,150
$1,150–1,350 SWO

A mahogany electric timepiece, by Eureka Clock Co, London, with an enamel dial and brass movement, signed, c1920, 11in (28cm) high.
£650–780 / €940–1,100
$1,100–1,300 S(Am)

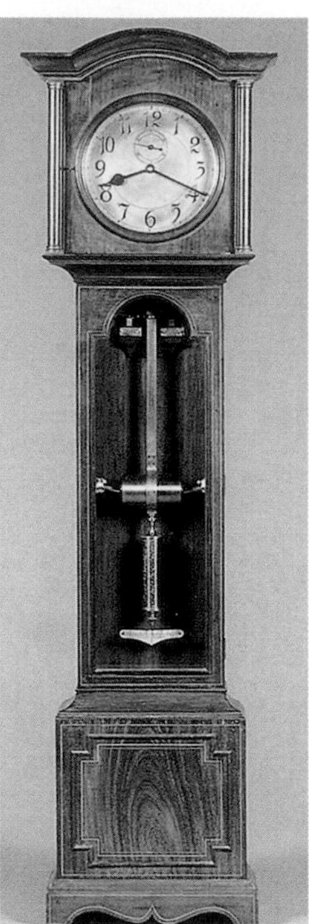

A mahogany Bentley's patent electric longcase clock, the silvered dial with subsidiary seconds, the pendulum with a steel rod, with a modern transformer, c1910, 82½in (209.5cm) high.
£6,600–7,900
€9,500–11,400
$11,100–13,300 S(O)
According to company records very few of these clocks were produced – probably no more than about 70. The scarcity increased when a consignment bound for America was lost with the sinking of the *Titanic*.

A gilt-metal electric timepiece, by G. S. Tiffany Electric Co, with an enamel dial, American, c1910, 9¾in (25cm) high.
£570–680 / €820–980
$960–1,150 S(Am)

A brass Bulle patent electric mantel clock, with a cut-glass dome, on an ebonized plinth, 1920s, 14¼in (36cm) high.
£680–810 / €980–1,150
$1,150–1,350 SWO

A brass four-glass electric mantel timepiece, by Brillié Frères, French, c1920, 21¼in (54cm) high.
£3,600–4,300
€5,200–6,200
$6,000–7,200 S(O)

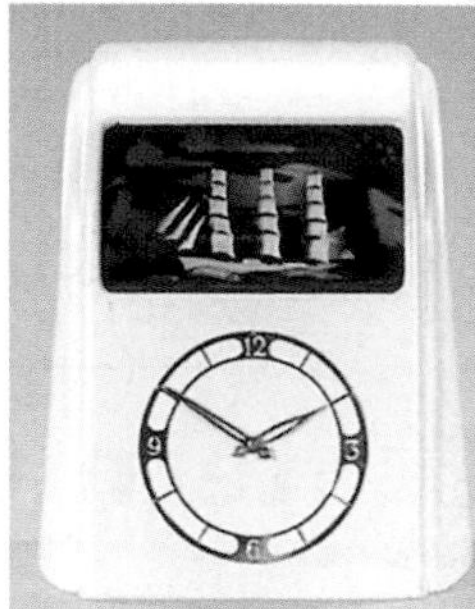

A painted Bakelite synchronous electric automaton mantel timepiece, by Vitascope Industries, Isle of Man, the glazed aperture revealing a rocking ship against a changing sky, c1950, 12½in (32cm) high.
£380–450 / €550–650
$640–760 S(O)

Garnitures

A marble and gilt-brass-mounted mantel clock garniture, the clock with an enamelled dial signed 'Marti', the twin-drum movement striking on a bell, 19thC, clock 13½in (34.5cm) high.
£820–980 / €1,200–1,400
$1,400–1,650 Bea

An Egyptian revival-style slate and marble clock garniture, the clock with eight-day movement striking on a gong, surmounted by a bronze and gilt sphinx, 19thC, clock 17½in (44.5cm) high.
£840–1,000 / €1,200–1,450
$1,400–1,650 NSal

A brass and *champlevé* enamel clock garniture, the clock with eight-day movement striking the hours and half-hours on a gong, c1895, clock 16in (40.5cm) high.
£880–970 / €1,250–1,400
$1,500–1,650 ⊞ K&D

A gilt-bronze clock garniture, the clock mounted with porcelain vases and plaques, late 19thC, clock 15¾in (40cm) high.
£230–270 / €330–390
$390–460 ⚒ SWO

A gilt-metal and marble timepiece garniture, the clock with ivorine dial and barrel movement, side pieces associated, French, late 19thC, clock 18½in (47cm) high.
£340–410 / €490–590
$580–690 ⚒ B(Kn)

A porcelain-mounted gilt-metal clock garniture, the clock with a porcelain dial and half-hour striking movement, painted with Watteauesque lovers, French, 19thC, clock 17in (43cm) high.
£1,650–1,950 / €2,350–2,800
$2,750–3,250 ⚒ PF

A porcelain-mounted gilt-metal clock garniture, with glass domes, the clock with a painted dial, the movement striking on a bell and stamped 'Vincenti & Cie', at fault, French, 19thC, clock 13in (33cm) high.
£1,650–1,950 / €2,350–2,800
$2,750–3,250 ⚒ B(Kn)

An 18thC-style marble, glass and gilt-metal clock garniture, the clock with an enamelled dial signed 'Leroy, Paris', with a bell-striking movement, French, late 19thC, 17in (43cm) high.
£2,000–2,400 / €2,900–3,450
$3,350–4,000 ⚒ S(O)

Lantern Clocks

◄ **A hoop and spike wall clock,** by George Prior, London, for the Turkish market, with a brass dial and bell-striking movement with verge escapement, 18thC, dial 8in (20.5cm) diam.
£1,650–1,950
€2,350–2,800
$2,750–3,250 ⚒ CGC

A brass lantern clock, the eight-day movement striking on a bell, early 20thC, 15in (38cm) high.
£350–420 / €500–600
$590–710 ⚒ AMB

◄ **A brass lantern clock,** with eight-day platform movement, French, c1920, 10in (25.5cm) high.
£400–440 / €580–640
$670–740 ⊞ PTh

Miller's Compares

I. A brass lantern clock, signed 'John Waklin Fecit', the weight-driven movement with anchor escapement and countwheel striking on a bell, with later side doors, 17thC, 15in (38cm) high.
£3,400–4,050
€4,900–5,800
$5,700–6,800 ⚒ B

II. A brass lantern clock, by Henry Spendlove, with a silvered and engraved dial, the later twin-chain ting-tang fusee movement with anchor escapement quarter-chiming on a bell, early 18thC, 15in (38cm) high.
£1,500–1,800
€2,150–2,600
$2,500–3,000 ⚒ B

Item II is not a great deal later in date than Item I, but it sold for less than half as much. Item I has replaced side doors, but it does retain its original movement which is of prime importance when assessing the value of a clock. Item II has been fitted with a Victorian twin-train fusee movement and later hands which makes it less attractive to collectors.

Longcase Clocks

◄ **A walnut marquetry longcase clock,** by Christoph Gould, with a brass dial, chiming on a single bell, the hood and case inlaid with floral marquetry panels, repairs to base, late 17thC, 83in (211cm) high.
£15,200–18,200
€21,800–26,200
$25,600–30,500 HOLL

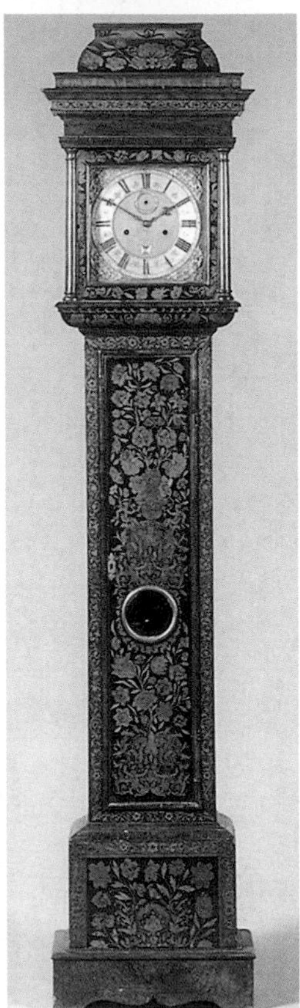

A walnut marquetry longcase clock, by Isaac Thompson, London, with a brass dial and a seconds dial, the movement with five pillars, the case inlaid with floral marquetry on an ebony ground, the door with a lenticle, alterations and replacements, c1700, 90in (228.5cm) high.
£9,000–10,800
€13,000–15,500
$15,100–18,100 S(O)

◄ **An ebonized longcase clock,** by James Hagger, London, the brass dial with subsidiary seconds, the eight-day movement striking on a bell, movement restored, case later ebonized, reduced and altered, early 18thC, 88in (223.5cm) high.
£940–1,100
€1,400–1,600
$1,600–1,850 WW

A walnut longcase clock, by Joseph Windmills, London, with a brass dial, the movement with five pillars and anchor escapement striking on a bell, the case door with a brass-bound lenticle, plinth and base replaced, late 17th/early 18thC, 84in (214cm) high.
£6,800–8,200
€9,800–11,800
$11,500–13,800 B
Joseph Windmills was a very fine maker of clocks and watches who worked from Tower Street, London. He was free of the Clockmakers Company in 1671 and was Master of the Clockmakers Company from 1702 to 1723.

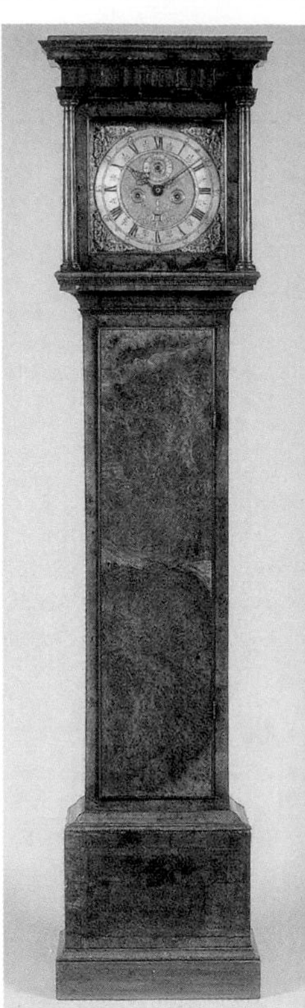

A burr-walnut longcase clock, by Richard Hautin, London, the engraved brass dial with subsidiary seconds, the movement with five pillars and later deadbeat escapement with maintaining power, striking on a bell, alterations to base, early 18thC, 86in (218.5cm) high.
£3,750–4,500
€5,400–6,500
$6,300–7,600 B

► **An oak longcase clock,** by Thomas Richards, Newport Pagnell, with a brass dial, the 30-hour posted movement with anchor escapement and striking on a bell, plinth reduced, restored, early 18thC, 74½in (189cm) high.
£760–910 / €1,100–1,300
$1,300–1,550 B(Kn)

CLOCKS

An oak and walnut longcase clock, by William Moore, London, the brass dial with subsidiary dial, eight-day movement, early 18thC, 82in (208.5cm) high.
£8,200–9,800
€11,800–14,100
$13,800–16,500 AH

A burr-walnut longcase clock, by Claude Viet, the dial with silvered chapter ring and subsidiary seconds dial, the eight-day movement striking on a bell, c1725, 98¾in (251cm) high.
£11,400–13,700
€16,400–19,700
$19,100–23,000 B(Ed)

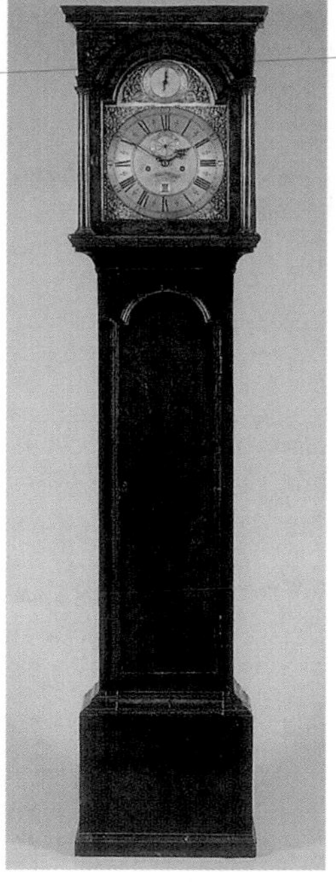

A walnut longcase clock, by Henry Massam, London, the brass dial with subsidiary seconds and strike/silent dial, the five-pillar movement with anchor escapement and rack striking on a bell, 1725–50, 87½in (222.5cm) high.
£6,300–7,600
€9,100–10,900
$10,600–12,800 B

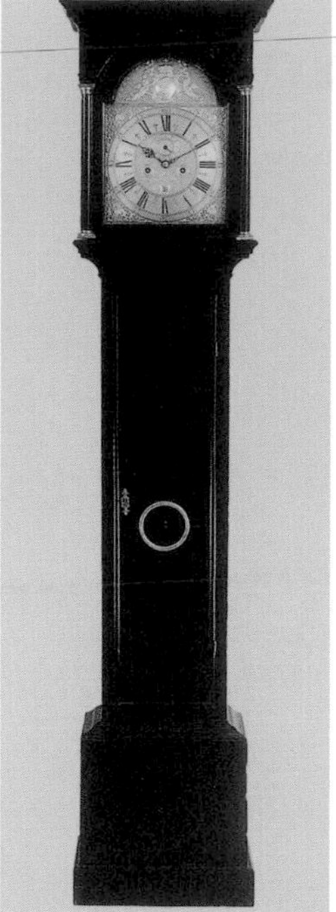

An ebonized longcase clock, by Edward Moore, Oxford, the brass dial with subsidiary seconds, the eight-day movement with four pillars and anchor escapement striking on a bell, c1725, 90in (228.5cm) high.
£7,500–8,300
€10,800–12,000
$12,600–13,900 PAO

The prices realized at auction may reflect the fact that the clocks have sometimes undergone alterations to their movements, or are in unrestored condition.

◀ **A burr-walnut and marquetry-inlaid alarm longcase clock,** by Willem van Dadelbeek, the engraved brass dial with subsidiary seconds, the four-pillar movement with anchor escapement and Dutch half-hour rack striking on two bells, alarm on a bell, restorations, marquetry probably later, on later ball feet, Dutch, dated 1739, 108¼in (275cm) high.
£4,900–5,900
€7,100–8,500
$8,200–9,900 S(Am)
Willem van Dadelbeek was born in 1707 in Utrecht and probably first started working around 1733. He is recorded as a clockmaker in 1747, with a workshop in the 'Schoutensteeg'.

CLOCKS

A George II oak longcase clock, by Thomas Dadswell, Burwash, the brass dial with subsidiary seconds, the twin-train movement with five pillars and anchor escapement striking on a bell, 88¼in (224cm) high.
£1,750–2,100
€2,500–3,000
$2,950–3,500 BR

A lacquered longcase clock, by John Ellicott, London, the brass dial with subsidiary seconds, the eight-day five-pillar movement striking on a bell, c1740, 94in (239cm) high.
£17,500–19,500
€25,000–28,000
$29,400–33,000 PAO

A George II figured walnut longcase clock, by Joseph Duke, London, the brass dial with strike/silent and subsidiary seconds dial, eight-day movement, 91in (231cm) high.
£6,600–7,900
€9,500–11,400
$11,100–13,300 G(L)

A japanned longcase clock, by R. Henderson, Scarborough, the dial with subsidiary seconds, automaton ship in the arch, the eight-day movement with rack striking on a bell, hands and ship automaton replaced, c1740, 94in (239cm) high.
£6,000–7,200
€8,600–10,300
$10,100–12,100 S

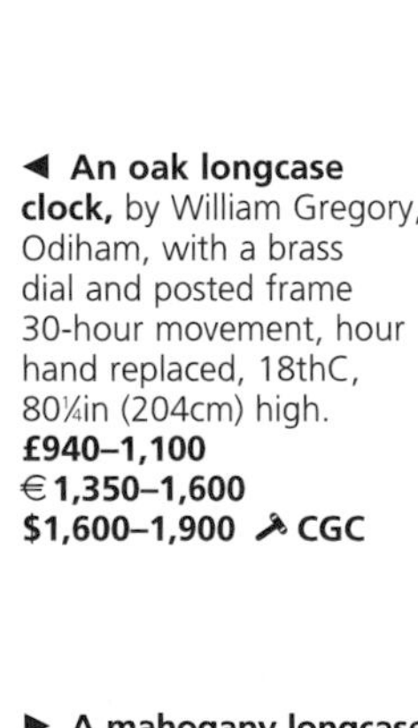

◄ **An oak longcase clock,** by William Gregory, Odiham, with a brass dial and posted frame 30-hour movement, hour hand replaced, 18thC, 80¼in (204cm) high.
£940–1,100
€1,350–1,600
$1,600–1,900 CGC

► **A mahogany longcase clock,** by J. Mayo, London, with a brass dial and eight-day striking movement, 18thC, 86¼in (219cm) high.
£4,450–5,300
€6,400–7,600
$7,500–8,900 B(NW)

A mahogany longcase clock, by Henry Rendell, Tiverton, the brass dial with subsidiary seconds, the twin-train movement striking on a bell, 18thC, 87in (221cm) high.
£1,800–2,150
€2,600–3,100
$3,000–3,600 Bea

A mahogany longcase clock, by Jonson, London, the dial with seconds dial and later arch, the five-pillar movement with rack striking on a bell, case associated, 18thC, 79½in (202cm) high.
£1,100–1,300
€1,600–1,900
$1,900–2,250 ⚒ S(O)

A lacquered longcase clock, by George Neale, Gloucester, the brass dial with subsidiary seconds and strike/silent, with twin-train movement, mid-18thC, 96in (244cm) high.
£3,650–4,400
€5,300–6,300
$6,200–7,400 ⚒ PF

An oak longcase clock, by Jas Hopper, Stockport, the brass dial with silvered chapter ring and subsidiary seconds, the eight-day movement striking on a bell, 18thC, 86in (218.5cm) high.
£1,500–1,800
€2,150–2,550
$2,500–3,000 ⚒ M

An ormolu-mounted and ebonized inlaid longcase clock, by Verdier, Paris, with a signed and engraved brass dial, similarly signed movement with baluster pillars, the pinwheel escapement with spring-driven countwheel striking on a bell, at fault, French, 1725–50, 82¼in (209cm) high.
£6,200–7,400
€8,900–10,400
$10,400–12,400 ⚒ S(Am)

◄ **A mahogany longcase clock,** by Andrew Hewlett, Bristol, the brass dial with subsidiary seconds, high water and phases of the moon, the eight-day movement striking on a bell, c1750, 87in (221cm) high.
£12,800–14,300
€18,400–20,500
$21,500–24,000 ⊞ PAO

► **An oak longcase clock,** by Wilson, Askrigg, the brass dial with rolling moon mechanism, 30-hour movement, mid-18thC, 76in (193cm) high.
£2,000–2,400
€2,900–3,450
$3,350–4,000 ⚒ PFK

An inlaid walnut longcase clock, with a brass dial, the wood-posted Black Forest movement with anchor escapement striking on a gong, movement and case associated, German, 1725–50 and later, 103½in (263cm) high.
£660–790 / €950–1,100
$1,100–1,300 ⚒ S(Am)

A lacquered and chinoiserie-decorated longcase clock, by John Johnson, Walton, with a brass dial and five-pillar movement with anchor escapement striking on a bell, dial associated, hood reduced, mid-18thC, 91¾in (233cm) high.
£1,400–1,650
€2,000–2,400
$2,350–2,800 ⚒ B(Kn)

A walnut longcase clock, by James Weston, Lewes, with a brass dial and five-pillar movement with rack striking on a bell, fret missing, plinth possibly associated, c1750, 93¾in (238cm) high.
£3,600–4,300
€5,200–6,200
$6,000–7,200 ⚒ S(O)

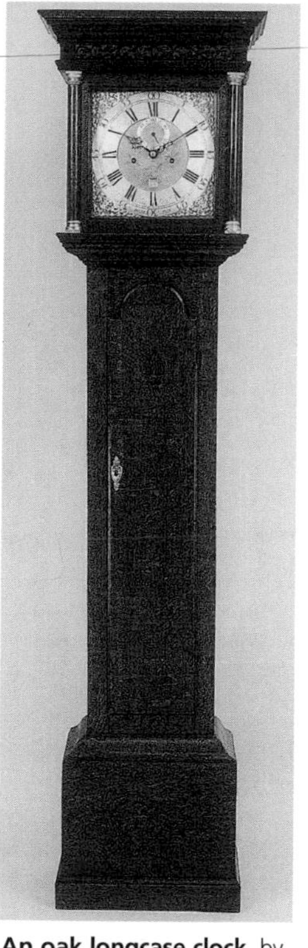

An oak longcase clock, by Francis Pile, Honiton, with a brass dial and eight-day movement striking on a bell, c1750, 81in (205.5cm) high.
£6,500–7,250
€9,300–10,300
$10,900–12,000 ⊞ PAO

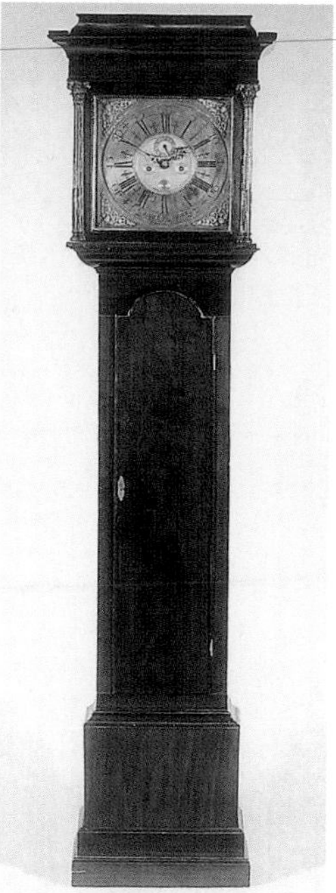

A mahogany longcase clock, by Martin Kirkpatrick, Dublin, with a brass dial and four-pillar movement with anchor escapement rack striking on a bell, case possibly associated, Irish, mid-18thC, 89in (226cm) high.
£3,000–3,600
€4,300–5,100
$5,000–6,000 ⚒ B

A mahogany longcase clock, by Edmund Prideaux, London, with a brass dial, the eight-day five-pillar movement with thick plates, deadbeat escapement, Harrison maintaining power and calibrated pendulum, c1760, 101in (256.5cm) high.
£15,100–16,800
€21,700–23,900
$25,300–27,900 ⊞ PAO

◀ **An oak longcase clock,** by Manister Baxter, St Neots, with a brass dial and eight-day five-pillar movement striking on a bell, c1760, 83in (211cm) high.
£6,500–7,200
€9,300–10,300
$10,900–12,000 ⊞ PAO

CLOCKS

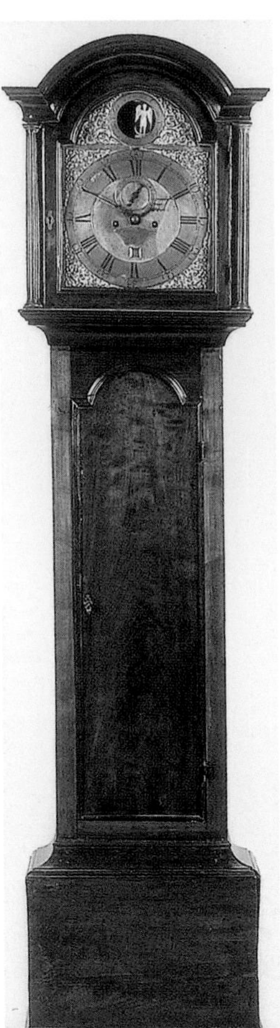

◀ **A mahogany longcase clock,** by James Jones, London, with a brass dial, the eight-day four-pillar movement with rack striking on a bell, at fault, c1760, 82¾in (210cm) high.
£2,700–3,200
€3,900–4,600
$4,500–5,400 ⚒ Bri

The pendulum

- Introduced to regulate timekeeping in the mid-17th century by the Dutch scientist Christiaan Huygens
- As a pendulum swings in a regular arc, accuracy can be controlled to within a few seconds a week
- Consists of a metal rod, usually brass or steel, with a metal disc (bob) at the end – by altering the height of the bob, the pendulum swings faster or slower, altering the speed of the clock
- The disadvantage is that the length of the pendulum alters with temperature changes, altering the swing rate and therefore the accuracy of the clock, and so in the 18th century two types of temperature-compensating pendulums were invented
- The mercurial pendulum, designed by Graham in 1726, had a glass jar of mercury for a bob – the expansion of the mercury with heat countered that of the steel rod
- John Harrison (1693–1776) invented the gridiron pendulum, which has up to nine alternating steel and brass rods. As these metals expand at different rates, the length of the pendulum remains constant

A lacquered longcase clock, by Daniel Keele, Sarum, with a brass dial and eight-day movement striking on a bell, date feature to arch, c1765, 85in (216cm) high.
£9,200–10,200
€13,200–14,600
$15,400–17,000 ⊞ PAO

An oak longcase clock, by Richard Holland, Coventry, with a brass dial and eight-day movement, c1770, 79in (200.5cm) high.
£1,750–2,100
€2,500–3,000
$2,950–3,500 ⚒ WL

A mahogany longcase clock, by Conyers Dunlop, London, with a brass dial and eight-day five-pillar movement striking on a bell, c1770, 91in (231cm) high.
£14,800–16,500
€21,300–23,500
$24,800–27,300 ⊞ PAO

A mahogany longcase clock, by Richard Grove, London, the brass dial with phases of the moon, the eight-day five-pillar movement striking on a bell, c1770, 101in (256.5cm) high.
£21,100–23,500
€30,000–33,000
$35,000–39,000 ⊞ PAO

A mahogany longcase clock, by Charles Packer, Reading, the dial with an annual calendar with signs of the zodiac and engraved with a rural scene, the five-pillar movement with anchor escapement rack striking on a gong, seconds hand missing, movement later, c1775, 93½in (237.5cm) high.
£12,600–15,100
€18,200–21,800
$21,200–25,400 ⚒ S(O)

CLOCKS

◄ **A George III mahogany longcase clock,** the silvered and engraved dial with moonphase, the eight-day movement striking on a bell, arch plaque missing inscription, 95in (241.5cm) high.
£8,000–9,600 / €11,500–13,800
$13,500–16,200 ⚒ B(Ed)

A George III longcase clock, by Richard Gilks, Devizes, with a painted dial and eight-day movement, 92¼in (234.5cm) high.
£1,750–2,100
€2,500–3,000
$3,000–3,600 ⚒ SWO

A mahogany longcase clock, by Edmund Wills, Salisbury, with a brass dial and eight-day movement striking on a bell, c1780, 83in (211cm) high.
£7,400–8,300
€10,700–11,800
$12,400–13,700 ⊞ PAO

An oak longcase clock, by Thomas Stripling, Bamell, with a silvered dial and 30-hour movement, c1780, 77½in (197cm) high.
£770–920 / €1,100–1,300
$1,300–1,550 ⚒ WL

A mahogany longcase clock, by Thomas Nevitt, Bristol, the brass dial with moonphase and 'High Water at Bristol Key', eight-day four-pillar rack striking movement, c1780, 91¼in (232cm) high.
£4,500–5,400
€6,500–7,800
$7,600–9,100 ⚒ Bri

◄ **A longcase clock,** by Benjamin Anns, Highworth, with a silvered dial and 30-hour movement, c1780, 85in (216cm) high.
£650–780 / €940–1,100
$1,100–1,300 ⚒ WL

Insurance values

Always insure your valuable antiques for the cost of replacing them with similar items, regardless of the original price paid. Both dealers and auctioneers can provide a valuation service for a fee.

► **A longcase clock,** by William Fenton, with brass dial and eight-day five-pillar movement striking on a bell, c1784, 94in (239cm) high.
£7,100–7,900
€10,200–11,300
$11,900–13,100 ⊞ K&D

CLOCKS

In ancient Egypt, Greece and Rome time was measured using sundials or water clocks. The first mechanical weight-driven clocks were made in Europe for monasteries and churches from the late 13th century, and these were scaled down to smaller domestic versions by the late 14th century. In the 17th century the lantern clock became an important part of the furnishings of the middle or upper class British home, with longcase, bracket, mantel and table clocks replacing them in popularity from the 18th century onwards.

A mahogany longcase clock, by Samuel Robson, South Shields, the brass dial with painted moon-phase above globes, eight-day movement, c1785, 90in (228.5cm) high.
£3,500–4,200
€5,000–6,000
$5,900–7,000 TRM

An oak longcase clock, by T. Gragg, with 30-hour movement, c1785, 84in (213.5cm) high.
£2,000–2,400
€2,900–3,400
$3,400–4,000 SWO

A mahogany longcase clock, by John Spendlove, Brandon, with a brass dial and eight-day five-pillar movement striking the hours on a bell, c1785, 86in (218.5cm) high.
£13,300–14,800
€19,100–21,100
$22,300–24,600 PAO

A mahogany longcase clock, by John Day, Wakefield, the dial with calendar and seconds dial, movement with rack striking on a bell, at fault, c1785, 86½in (219.5cm) high.
£1,450–1,700
€2,100–2,500
$2,450–2,900 S(O)

◄ **A George III mahogany longcase clock,** by Thomas Richardson, Weverham, the dial with moonphase, inscribed 'The appointed, the moon, four seasons', 91¼in (232cm) high.
£7,600–9,100
€11,000–13,200
$12,800–15,300 B(Ed)

A mahogany longcase clock, by William Cox, Devizes, the white dial with seconds and date aperture, the eight-day movement striking on a bell, c1790, 86in (218.5cm) high.
£8,200–9,200
€11,800–13,000
$13,800–15,200 ⊞ PAO

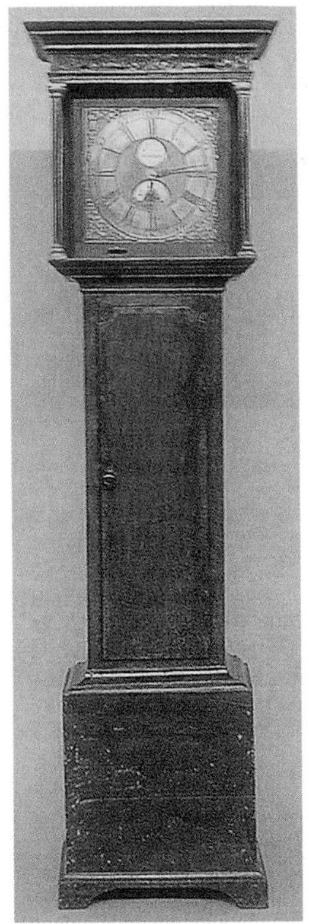

A George III oak longcase clock, by Francis Bayley, Uttoxeter, with a brass dial and 30-hour movement, 80in (203cm) high.
£750–900 / €1,100–1,300
$1,300–1,550 ⚒ PF

A George III mahogany longcase clock, by Latham, Wigan, the brass dial with a tune-selecting dial, the quarter-repeating movement striking with 20 hammers on 13 graduated bells, 98½in (250cm) high.
£9,400–11,200
€13,500–16,200
$15,800–18,900 ⚒ B(Ed)

A George III oak and mahogany-banded longcase clock, by Tanner & Son, Lewes, with a painted dial, the 30-hour single train movement with anchor escapement with passing strike on a bell, at fault, 79¼in (201.5cm) high.
£750–900 / €1,100–1,300
$1,300–1,500 ⚒ BR

A George III mahogany longcase clock, by Clements, Oxford, with a silvered dial and eight-day striking movement, 100½in (255cm) high.
£3,000–3,600
€4,300–5,100
$5,000–6,000 ⚒ B(O)

◄ A George III mahogan longcase clock, by Eardle Norton, St John's Street, wit a brass dial and eight-day movement with deadbeat escapement striking on a bell, 83in (211cm) high.
£14,000–16,800
€20,200–24,200
$23,500–28,200 ⚒ HYD

CLOCKS

A George III oak longcase clock, by Sam Lomas, Poolton, the brass dial with date aperture, 30-hour movement, 78in (198cm) high.
£2,250–2,700
€3,200–3,850
$3,700–4,400 Mit

A George III oak and mahogany-crossbanded longcase clock, the painted dial indistinctly inscribed, the 30-hour movement striking on a bell, 78¼in (199cm) high.
£530–630 / €760–910
$890–1,000 RTo

An oak and mahogany-crossbanded longcase clock, inscribed 'In Chaffey, Sherbourne', with a brass dial and eight-day movement, c1790, 77in (195.5cm) high.
£950–1,100
€1,400–1,650
$1,600–1,900 WL

A George III mahogany longcase clock, by Peter Conqueror, Berwick, with a painted dial and eight-day striking movement, 88¼in (224cm) high.
£1,650–1,900
€2,400–2,850
$2,800–3,300 RTo

. George III mahogany ›ngcase clock, by Lawrence Wood, Bath, the brass ˈal with moonphase, ght-day movement, 9½in (227.5cm) high.
2,800–3,350
4,000–4,800
4,700–5,600 B&L

A George III mahogany-veneered and inlaid long-case clock, by J. M. Thomas, Redruth, with a brass dial and eight-day movement, 78in (198cm) high.
£2,450–2,900
€3,500–4,200
$4,000–4,800 LAY

CLOCKS

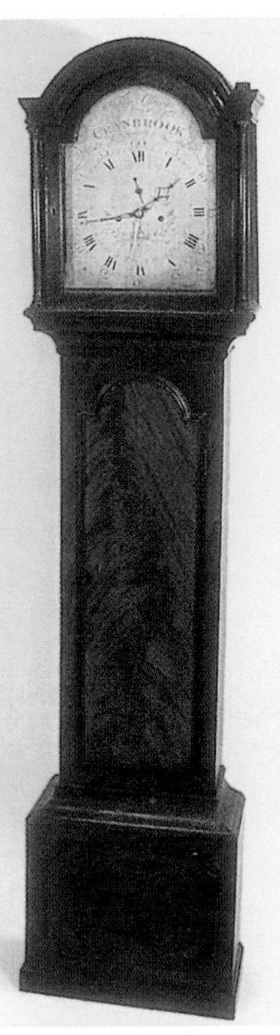

A George III mahogany longcase clock, by Thomas Ollive, Cranbrook, with a silvered dial and eight-day striking movement, 81in (205.5cm) high.
£2,350–2,800
€3,400–4,000
$4,000–4,800 E

A George III figured mahogany longcase clock, by Thomas Lees, Bury, the dial with moonphase, eight-day striking movement, 90¼in (229cm) high.
£1,200–1,400
€1,700–2,000
$2,000–2,400 RTo

A George III mahogany longcase clock, by T. Richardson, Weaverham, with a painted dial and twin-train movement, 90in (228.5cm) high.
£2,250–2,700
€3,250–3,900
$3,750–4,500 CDC

◄ **A George III mahogany longcase clock,** by W. Lastell, Toxteth Park, the dial painted with a lady seated in a landscape, the eight-day movement striking on a bell, 93¾in (238cm) high.
£4,700–5,600
€6,800–8,200
$7,900–9,400 B(Ed)

A George III mahogany and brass-mounted longcase clock, the associated painted dial inscribed 'Dowsett, Margate', the twin-train movement with anchor escapement, striking works and bell removed, alterations, 83½in (212cm) high.
£2,500–3,000
€3,600–4,300
$4,200–5,000 BR

Items in the Clocks section have been arranged in date order within each sub-section.

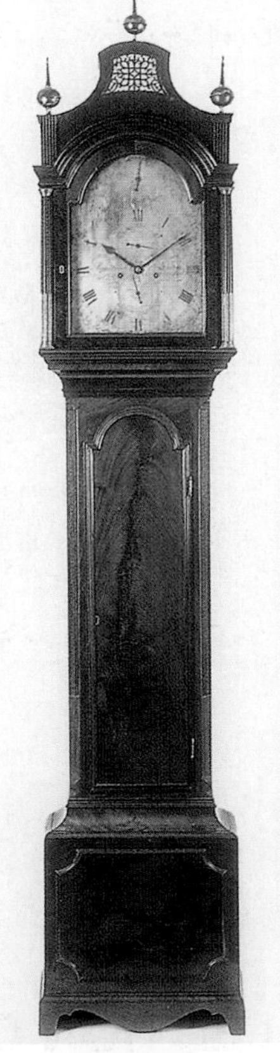

A George III mahogany longcase clock, by Leplastrier, London, with a silvered dial and twin-train movement with anchor escapement striking on a bell, 96in (244cm) high.
£6,200–7,400
€8,900–10,600
$10,400–12,400 Bea

A George III mahogany longcase clock, by Jones, Warwick, the painted dial with moonphase, the eight-day movement striking on a bell, 91¾in (233cm) high.
£1,300–1,550
€1,900–2,200
$2,200–2,400 RTo

A George III mahogany longcase clock, by J. Pearce, Stratford, with a painted dial, 90in (228.5cm) high.
£1,450–1,700
€2,100–2,500
$2,450–2,900 B(O)

CLOCKS

A George III mahogany longcase clock, by Thomas Honey, Launceston, with a brass dial and eight-day twin fusee movement, 85in (216cm) high.
£1,300–1,550
€1,900–2,250
$2,200–2,600 B&L

An oak longcase clock, by Richardson Bubwith, with a brass dial and eight-day movement, plinth missing, 18thC, 86in (218.5cm) high.
£1,300–1,550
€1,900–2,250
$2,200–2,600 WW

A George III oak longcase clock, by Bromley, Horsham, with a painted dial and eight-day movement striking on a bell, 84¼in (214cm) high.
£2,100–2,500
€3,000–3,600
$3,500–4,200 RTo

► **An oak longcase clock,** by James Irish, Brighthelmstone, with a silvered dial, the associated 30-hour four-pillar movement striking on a bell, late 18thC, 72½in (184cm) high.
£880–1,050
€1,250–1,500
$1,500–1750 B(Kn)

A mahogany and boxwood-strung longcase clock, by Hugh Knight, Stone, with a painted dial, the four-pillar movement striking on a bell, c1795, 94in (239cm) high.
£1,500–1,800
€2,200–2,600
$2,500–3,000 B

A Louis XVI carved oak longcase clock, by Villeret à Londinières, with an enamel dial, the weight-driven movement striking on a bell, movement probably associated, French, c1790, 96½in (245cm) high.
£580–700 / €840–1,000
$1,000–1,200 S(Am)

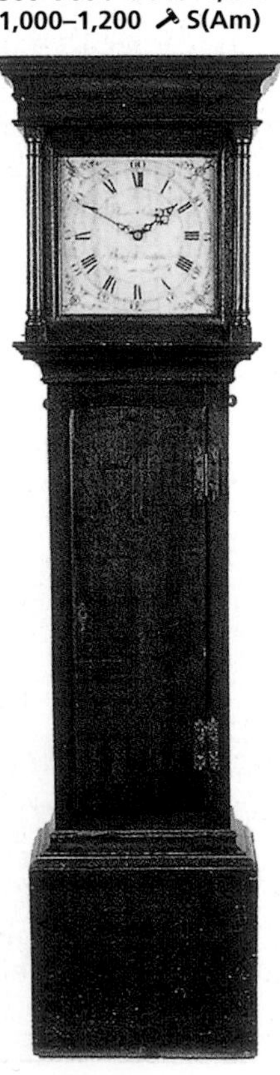

An oak longcase clock, by Richard Thomas, with a painted dial, the numerals replaced with the letters of the maker's name, 30-hour birdcage movement, Welsh, c1790, 75½in (192cm) high.
£900–1,100
€1,350–1,600
$1,500–1,800 S(O)

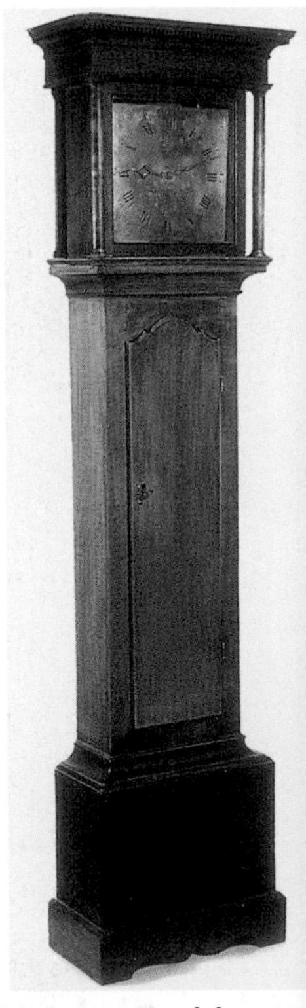

A George III oak longcase clock, by Thomas Crofts Junior, Newbury, with a brass dial and 30-hour movement striking on a bell, case partially stripped 82¼in (209cm) high.
£530–640 / €770–920
$890–1,050 DN

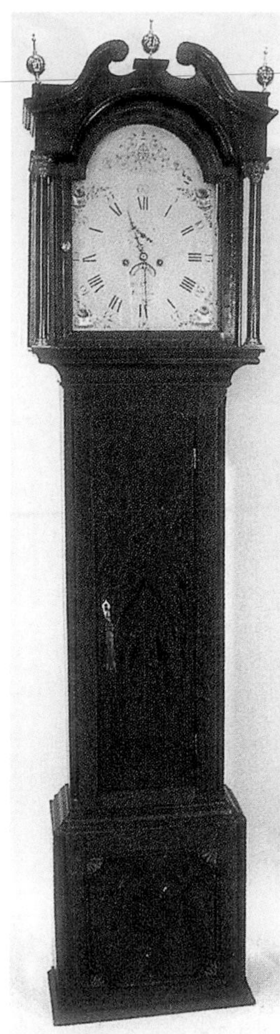

An oak and mahogany-crossbanded longcase clock, by Thomas Bradford, Leeds, the brass dial with painted moonphase, the four-pillar movement striking on a bell, late 18thC, 91¾in (233cm) high.
£3,500–4,200
€5,000–6,000
$5,900–7,100 ⚒ B

A mahogany longcase clock, by Dan Saunders, Knightsbridge, with a silvered dial and eight-day four-pillar movement, late 18thC, 90¼in (229cm) high.
£3,500–4,200
€5,000–6,000
$5,900–7,100 ⚒ AMB

◄ A mahogany longcase clock, by William Johnson, Evesham, with a painted dial and eight-day striking movement, late 18thC, 96in (244cm) high.
£1,750–2,100
€2,500–3,000
$2,950–3,500 ⚒ E

A mahogany longcase clock, by Giscard, Ely, with a painted dial and four-pillar eight-day movement striking on a bell, case damaged, late 18thC, 83in (211cm) high.
£1,300–1,550
€1,900–2,250
$2,200–2,600 ⚒ CGC

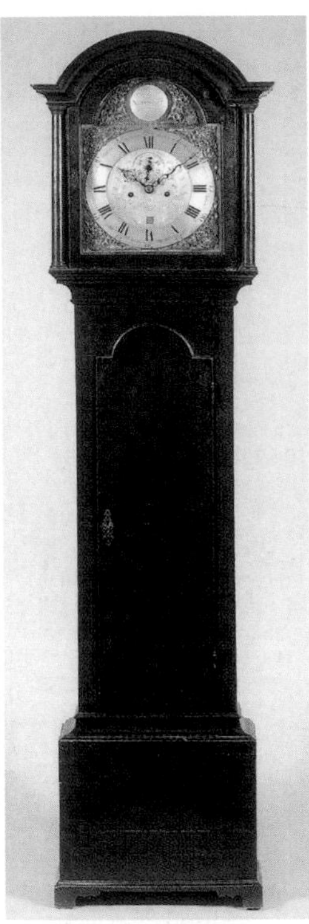

An oak longcase clock, by Robert Trattle, Newport, Isle of Wight, with a brass dial and five-pillar movement striking on a bell, base reduced, late 18thC, 81in (205.5cm) high.
£1,550–1,850
€2,200–2,700
$2,600–3,100 ⚒ B

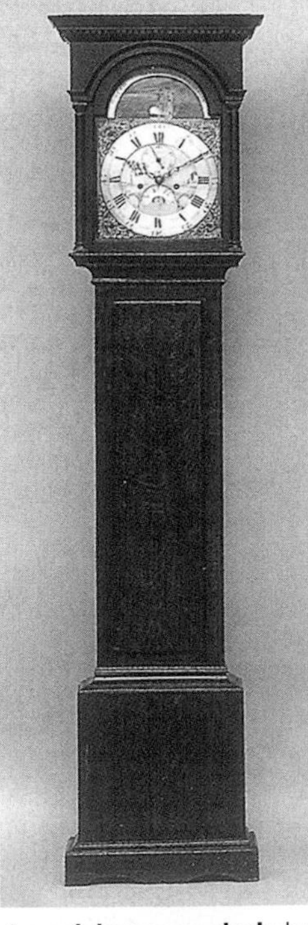

An oak longcase clock, by Joseph Miles, Shaston, the brass dial with a painted automaton ship at sea, c1800, 85in (216cm) high.
£1,500–1,800
€2,200–2,600
$2,500–3,000 ⚒ B(O)

An oak and mahogany longcase clock, by James Newby, Kendal, with a painted dial and 30-hour movement, late 18thC, 84in (213.5cm) high.
£820–980 / €1,200–1,400
$1,400–1,650 ⚒ PFK

An inlaid walnut longcase clock, with a brass dial and automaton scene of Bellerophon riding Pegasus across the sky, above five rocking ships, the eight-day movement striking on a bell, case associated, Dutch, late 18thC, 102in (259cm) high.
£3,400–4,100
€4,900–5,900
$5,700–6,800 ⚒ TMA
If this clock had been in its original case it could have realized three times as much.

◄ A mahogany longcase clock, by Sykes, Malton, with a painted dial and eight-day striking movement, early 19thC, 82¾in (210cm) high.
£660–790 / €950–1,100
$1,100–1,300 ⚒ B(O)

► A mahogany longcase clock, by James Clarke, Bristol, the painted dial with a moonphase, the eight-day four-pillar rack movement striking on a bell, c1810, 89¾in (228cm) high.
£4,300–5,100
€6,200–7,300
$7,200–8,600 ⚒ Bri

A pine longcase clock, by C. Boney, Padstow, with a painted dial and automaton depicting Adam and Eve, the eight-day twin-train movement striking on a bell, suspension of pendulum broken, c1800, 81½in (207cm) high.
£730–880 / €1,050–1,250
$1,250–1,500 ⚒ DN

A mahogany longcase clock, by John Buckley, Ashton-under-Lyne, the painted dial with a moon-phase, eight-day movement, c1810, 96in (244cm) high.
£6,700–7,500
€9,700–10,800
$11,300–12,500 ⊞ MHA

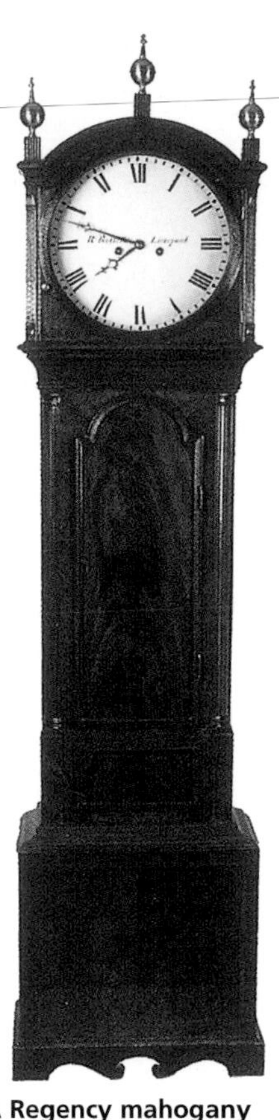

A Regency mahogany longcase clock, by R. Roskell, Liverpool, with eight-day striking movement, 85in (216cm) high.
£2,200–2,650
€3,150–3,750
$3,700–4,450 Mit

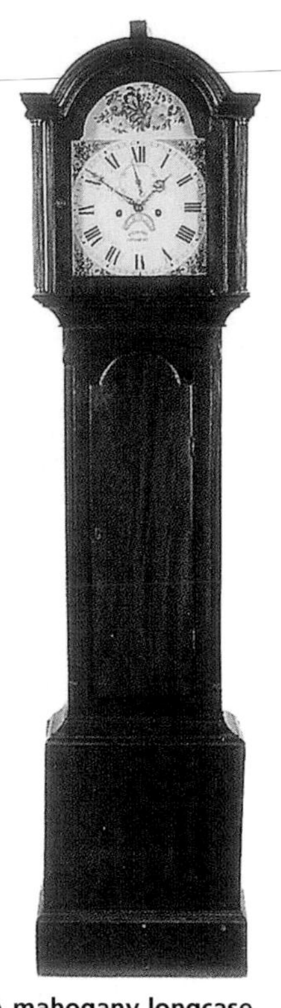

A mahogany longcase clock, by A. Rawlings, Devonport, with a painted dial and four-pillar movement striking on a bell, early 19thC, 81½in (207cm) high.
£820–980 / €1,200–1,400
$1,400–1,650 B(Kn)

An oak longcase clock, by Blakeborough, Pateley Bridge, with a painted dial and 30-hour movement, early 19thC, 86in (218.5cm) high.
£1,050–1,250
€1,500–1,800
$1,750–2,100 PFK

A mahogany longcase clock, by A. Thwaites, London, with a gilt dial and triple-train movement striking eight graduated bells and a gong, early 19thC, 87¾in (223cm) high.
£3,200–3,850
€4,600–5,500
$5,400–6,500 B(Ed)

An oak longcase clock, by J. Moore, Warminster, with a painted dial, the single-train brass movement with four pillars, anchor escapement and outside countwheel striking on a bell, early 19thC, 78¾in (200cm) high.
£580–700 / €840–1,000
$1,000–1,200 BR

CLOCKS

An oak and mahogany-banded longcase clock, by W. Stephenson, Dorchester, with a painted dial and eight-day movement striking on a bell, early 19thC, 80in (203cm) high.
£1,200–1,450
€1,750–2,100
$2,000–2,400 ⚒ WW

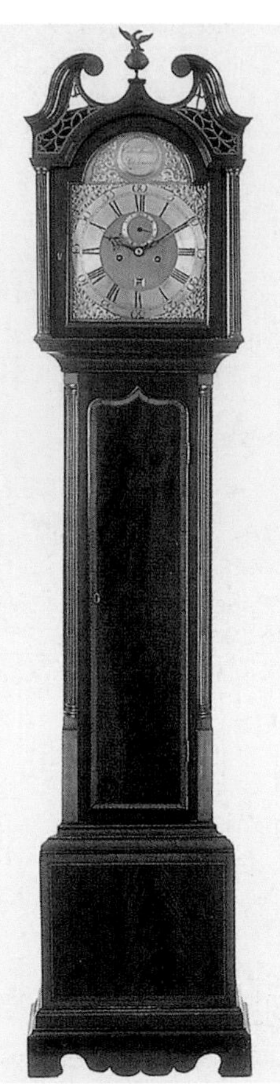

A mahogany and satinwood-banded long-case clock, by Edward Smith, Richmond, with a brass dial and twin-train movement striking on a bell, early 19thC, 90¼in (229cm) high.
£3,300–3,950
€4,750–5,700
$5,500–6,600 ⚒ Bea

A mahogany longcase clock, by R. Fletcher, Chester, with a painted dial and eight-day movement, early 19thC, 86½in (220cm) high.
£1,500–1,800
€2,200–2,600
$2,500–3,000 ⚒ CHTR

◄ A mahogany longcase clock, by John Bates, Kettering, with a brass dial and eight-day five-pillar movement, early 19thC, 82in (208.5cm) high.
£2,900–3,500
€4,200–5,000
$4,900–5,900 ⚒ SWO

An oak longcase clock, by Barry, Marlborough, with a painted dial and 30-hour movement, early 19thC, 72¼in (183.5cm) high.
£820–980 / €1,200–1,400
$1,400–1,650 ⚒ WW

An oak, bird's-eye maple and rosewood longcase clock, with a painted dial and twin-train movement, early 19thC, 92in (233.5cm) high.
£820–980 / €1,200–1,400
$1,400–1,650 ⚒ PF

A mahogany longcase clock, by S. Fort, the painted dial with moonphase, eight-day movement, early 19thC, 94¼in (240cm) high.
£2,600–3,100
€3,750–4,500
$4,400–5,200 ⚒ B&L

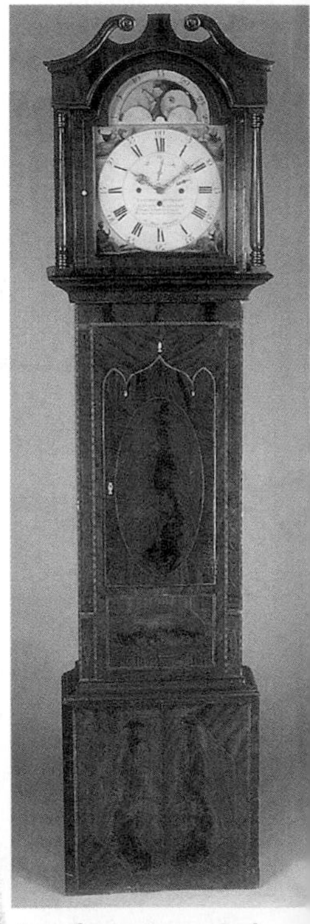

A mahogany musical longcase clock, by James Shaw, Halifax, the painted dial with a selection dial for six psalms, the triple-train eight-day movement playing the psalms on eight bells and striking the hour with two bells, c1820, 111in (282cm) high.
£2,350–2,800
€3,350–4,000
$3,900–4,650 ⚒ TEN

CLOCKS

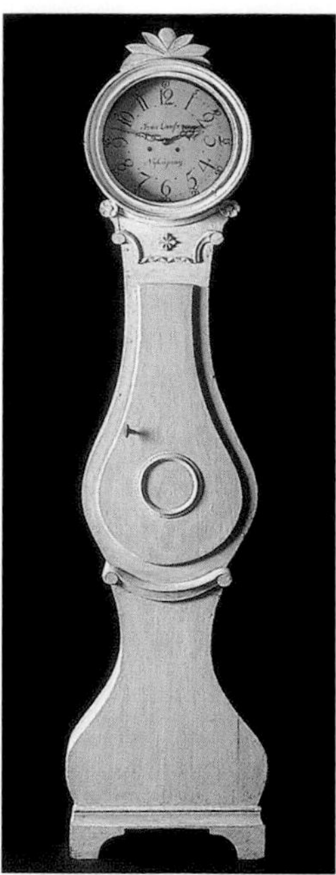

A painted pine longcase clock, with a painted dial and eight-day movement, Swedish, c1820, 90in (228.5cm) high.
£4,900–5,500
€7,000–7,900
$8,200–9,200 ⊞ RYA

A mahogany longcase clock, by B. Swinerton, Newcastle-under-Lyme, the painted dial with moonphase, the eight-day movement striking the hours on a bell, c1830, 92in (233.5cm) high.
£3,800–4,200
€5,400–6,000
$6,400–7,000 ⊞ K&D

A flame mahogany-veneered longcase clock, by Thomas Sykes, Leeds, with a painted dial and eight-day movement, some restoration, c1820, 92in (233.5cm) high.
£4,450–4,950
€6,400–7,100
$7,300–8,200 ⊞ GGD

A George IV mahogany longcase clock, by W. Wain, Burslem, with a painted enamel dial and eight-day movement, 94in (239cm) high.
£2,100–2,500
€3,000–3,600
$3,500–4,200 ⚒ WL

A mahogany longcase clock, by Richard Alexander, Chippenham, the painted dial with moonphase, the eight-day movement striking the hours on a bell, c1830, 87in (221cm) high.
£8,000–8,800
€11,500–12,700
$13,400–14,800 ⊞ PAO

◄ **A mahogany-crossbanded oak longcase clock,** by Martin Roper, Penrith, with a painted dial and 30-hour movement, 1825–50, 78½in (199.5cm) high.
£820–980 / €1,200–1,400
$1,400–1,650 ⚒ PFK

A George IV oak and marquetry-inlaid longcase clock, by Alex Simpsons, Warwick, with a painted dial and 30-hour movement, 84in (213.5cm) high.
£1,200–1,450
€1,700–2,000
$2,000–2,400 ⚒ G(L)

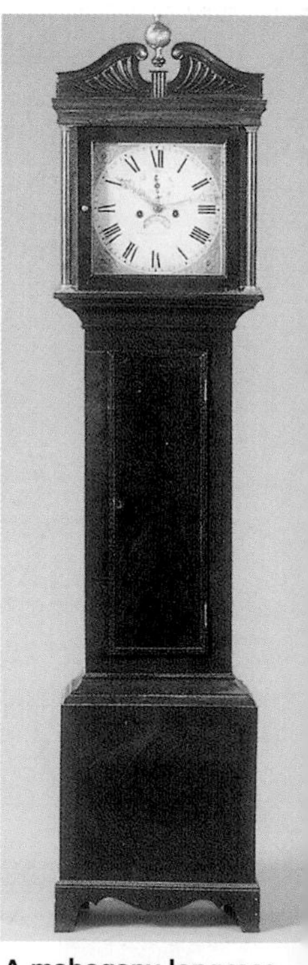

A mahogany longcase clock, by Birch & Masters, Tenterden, with a painted dial and rack and bell-striking movement, c1835 80in (203cm) high.
£1,800–2,150
€2,600–3,100
$3,000–3,600 ⚒ S(O)

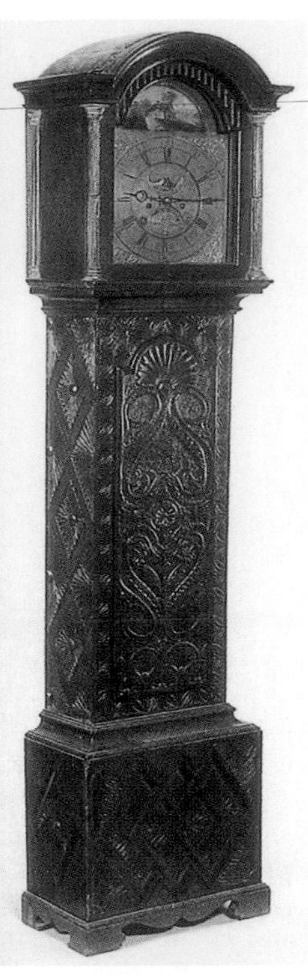

A carved oak longcase clock, by Samuel Fletcher, Dewsbury, with a brass dial and twin-train eight-day movement striking on a bell, 19thC, 83½in (212cm) high.
£1,100–1,300
€1,600–1,900
$1,850–2,200 DN

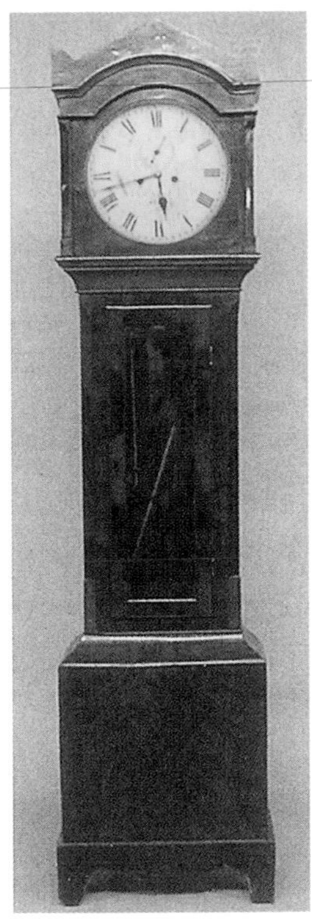

A mahogany longcase clock, by H. H. Curtis, Neath, with a silvered dial and twin-train movement, Welsh, 19thC, 82in (208.5cm) high.
£1,400–1,700
€2,000–2,400
$2,350–2,800 PF

A mahogany longcase clock, by Stevenson, Leicester, with a painted dial and eight-day movement striking on a bell, 19thC, 85in (216cm) high.
£1,100–1,300
€1,600–1,900
$1,850–2,200 WW

A mahogany longcase clock, by J. Pearce, St Austell, the painted dial with rocking ship automaton, eight-day movement, 19thC, 89½in (227.5cm) high.
£3,500–4,200
€5,000–6,000
$5,900–7,100 B(Pr)

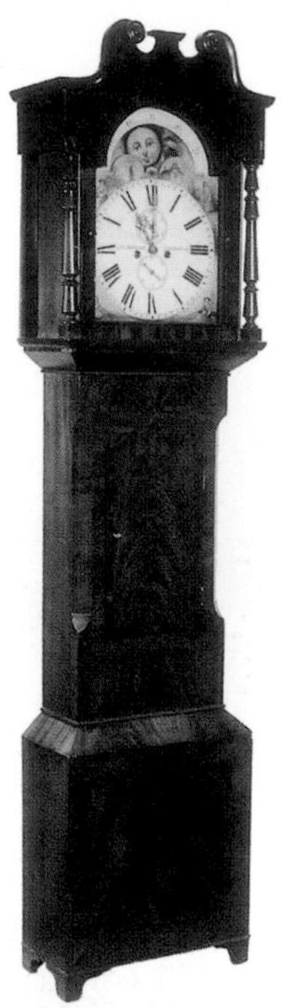

A mahogany longcase clock, by J. E. Armson, Leebrooks, the painted dial with moonphase, the eight-day twin-train movement striking on a bell, pediment damaged, 19thC, 89½in (227.5cm) high.
£1,650–2,000
€2,400–2,850
$2,750–3,300 ⚒ DN

An oak and crossbanded longcase clock, by J. Weare, Wincanton, with a painted dial and eight-day movement striking on a bell, 19thC, 82½in (209.5cm) high.
£1,300–1,550
€1,900–2,250
$2,200–2,600 ⚒ WW

An oak and mahogany longcase clock, by Briggs, Skipton, with a painted dial and 30-hour movement striking on a bell, suspension broken, 19thC, 85in (216cm) high.
£760–910 / €1,100–1,300
$1,300–1,550 ⚒ DN

A mahogany longcase clock, with a painted dial and eight-day twin-train movement striking on a bell, some wear to dial, 19thC, 89¾in (228cm) high.
£1,000–1,200
€1,500–1,750
$1,700–2,000 ⚒ DN

An oak longcase clock, by T. Cooper, Newport, with a painted dial and eight-day movement, 19thC, 82¼in (209cm) high
£1,400–1,700
€2,000–2,400
$2,350–2,800 ⚒ CHTR

◀ **An oak *comtoise* clock,** with an enamel dial and eight-day movement striking on a bell, French, 19thC, 90in (228.5cm) high
£350–420 / €500–600
$590–700 ⚒ WW

CLOCKS

A mahogany and boxwood-strung musical clock, by William Carter, Ampthill, the associated twin-train movement striking on a gong, the organ with wooden pipes, the cylinder with weight-driven bellows action, 19thC, 93¾in (238cm) high.
£2,400–2,900
€3,550–4,200
$4,050–4,850 Bea

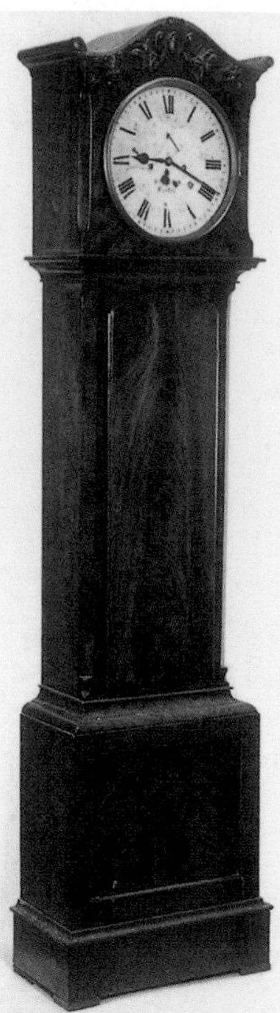

A mahogany longcase clock, by UpJohn, Exeter, with a painted dial and eight-day twin-train movement striking on a bell, wear to dial, c1835, 78¾in (200cm) high.
£1,750–2,100
€2,500–3,000
$2,950–3,500 DN

A flame mahogany, ebonized and boxwood-strung longcase clock, by Collings of Thornbury, the painted dial with moonphase, the eight-day movement striking on a bell, c1840, 88in (223.5cm) high.
£4,350–4,850
€6,200–7,000
$7,300–8,200 ⊞ K&D

An inlaid mahogany and rosewood longcase clock, by Dobbings, Leeds, the movement striking on a gong, dial and movement later, c1840, 92½in (235cm) high.
£1,400–1,700
€2,000–2,400
$2,350–2,800 S(O)

Wooden cases

In order to give a clock a neater appearance, wooden cases were introduced c1660 to house the movement, pendulum and weights. In the case of longcase clocks, the carcass is usually of oak, overlaid with veneers. Early veneers are hand-sawn and vary in thickness, while modern machine-sawn veneers are thin and of uniform thickness. The most common woods used are walnut, oak, mahogany, rosewood, ebony, or pale fruitwoods if the case was to be ebonized. Ebonized cases are generally less desirable than ebony examples. In the USA, walnut or cherry was often used as a less expensive alternative to mahogany.

◄ **A mahogany longcase clock,** by Lazarus Samuels, Newport, the painted dial with moonphase, the eight-day movement striking the hours on a bell, Welsh, c1845, 89in (226cm) high.
£7,200–8,000
€10,400–11,500
$12,100–13,400 ⊞ PAO

► **An oak and mahogany-veneered longcase clock,** by Bothamley, Boston, with a painted dial, the eight-day movement striking on a bell, mid-19thC, 80in (203cm) high.
£1,200–1,450
€1,750–2,100
$2,000–2,400 WW

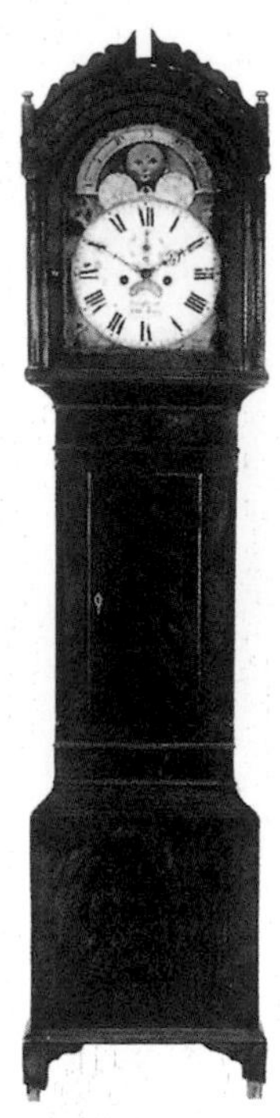

A crossbanded mahogany longcase clock, by John Thristle, Stogursey, the painted dial with moonphase, the four-pillar movement striking on a bell, finials missing, mid-19thC, 85½in (217cm) high.
£2,450–2,950
€3,500–4,200
$4,100–4,900 B(Kn)

A mahogany longcase clock, by William Jones, Tredegar, with a silvered-brass dial and eight-day movement striking the hours on a bell, Welsh, c1850, 90in (228.5cm) high.
£4,750–5,300
€6,800–7,600
$7,900–8,900 ⊞ PAO

The prices realized at auction may reflect the fact that the clocks have sometimes undergone alterations to their movements, or are in unrestored condition.

A pine longcase clock, the eight-day *comtoise* movement with a repeating chime, French, mid-19thC, 84in (213.5cm) high.
£1,500–1,650
€2,150–2,400
$2,500–2,750 ⊞ COF

An oak and mahogany longcase clock, by Ness Kirby-Moorside, with a painted dial and 30-hour movement, mid-19thC, 87½in (222.5cm) high.
£1,200–1,450
€1,750–2,100
$2,000–2,400 DD

CLOCKS

A Louis XV-style ebonized boulle longcase clock, with ormolu mounts and enamel dial, the twin-train *comtoise* movement double-striking the hour, French, c1860, 90in (228.5cm) high.
£6,000–7,200
€8,600–10,300
$10,100–12,100 S

A Victorian oak and mahogany-crossbanded longcase clock, by J. Blackhurst, Weaverham, with an enamel painted dial and eight-day striking movement, 85¾in (218cm) high.
£940–1,150
€1,400–1,650
$1,600–1,900 B(NW)

A carved mahogany longcase clock, with a brass dial, the quarter-chiming movement with maintaining power, Continental, late 19thC, 98in (249cm) high.
£6,000–7,200
€8,600–10,300
$10,100–12,100 B

An Edwardian carved mahogany longcase clock by Waring & Gillow, with a brass dial, the five-pillar triple train movement striking on gongs, 94½in (240cm) high
£6,800–8,200
€9,800–11,800
$11,500–13,800 B(EA)

An Edwardian mahogany longcase clock, with a brass dial, the triple-train movement with nine hammers striking on nine tubular bells, 92in (233.5cm) high.
£3,500–4,200
€5,000–6,000
$5,900–7,100 TEN

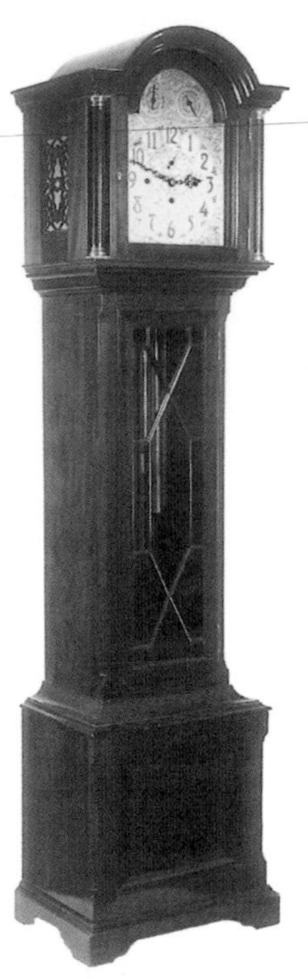

An Edwardian mahogany longcase clock, retailed by Harrods, with a silvered dial, the eight-day twin-train movement striking and chiming on nine tubular gongs, 88½in (225cm) high.
£4,250–5,100
€6,100–7,300
$7,200–8,600 DN

A mahogany longcase clock, by Leonard Hall & Son, Grimsby, the triple-train movement striking on eight tubular bells, c1910, 92½in (235cm) high.
£3,400–4,100
€4,900–5,900
$5,800–6,900 TEN

A chinoiserie-style longcase clock, with a brass dial, the triple fusee movement striking on ten rods, early 20thC, 80¼in (204cm) high.
£660–790 / €960–1,150
$1,100–1,300 B(Kn)

Mystery Clocks

An ormolu and glass mystery timepiece, in the manner of Robert Houdin, with a glass dial, the movement with platform lever escapement enclosed in an ebonized plinth, restored, French, c1900, 15in (38cm) high.
£5,300–6,400
€7,700–9,200
$8,900–10,700 S(Am)

A bronzed-spelter mystery clock, by the Hamburg American Clock Co, modelled as an elephant supporting the pendulum, with an enamel dial, crossed arrows mark, German, early 20thC, 11¾in (30cm) high.
£530–630 / €760–910
$890–1,050 PFK
The crossed arrows device is the trademark of the Hamburg American Clock Co, Württemberg, Germany.

The series of small German mystery clocks (often signed on the dial by Junghans) include various female figures, the elephant and the kangaroo. They were all made c1900 in spelter, and hold the swinging movement on the arm or trunk. A number of copies have recently appeared on the market. The movements are reasonably convincing, but the castings of the figures are in bronze or brass and weigh more than twice as much as the originals.

A bronzed-spelter mystery timepiece, modelled as a figure of Diana holding the movement, the enamel dial with Junghans trademark, on an ebonized base, German, c1910, 13¾in (35cm) high.
£900–1,050
€1,300–1,500
$1,500–1,750 S(O)

Novelty Clocks

CLOCKS

◄ A bronze novelty mantel clock, in the form of Rheims Cathedral, with enamelled numbered reserves, on an inlaid rosewood base, inscribed 'Richond Paris', French, c1840, 28in (71cm) high.
£1,950–2,350 / €2,800–3,350
$3,300–3,950 IM

A brass automaton clock, by Guilmet, modelled as a ship's deck, the rocking helmsman linked to the pendulum, on a marble base, French, c1885, 11¾in (35cm) high.
£5,300–6,400 / €7,700–9,200
$8,900–10,700 G(L)
This example of the 'helmsman' by Guilmet fetched a standard price as it is in unrestored condition. An example in superb original condition fetched £10,000 / €14,400 / $16,800 at Sotheby's. All French industrial and marine automaton clocks made from 1880 to 1900 have performed well at auction. Lighthouses, steam hammers, boilers and beam engines have all proved highly desirable to collectors.

A carved giltwood shadowbox novelty wall clock, with an enamel dial, French, 1850–75, 17in (43cm) high.
£300–360 / €430–520
$510–610 NOA

A cast-iron turret novelty clock, with a cast-iron dial, the twin-train weight-driven movement with ten cast-iron weights, the lead pendulum bob cast with an owl above a cogwheel and JWF, Welsh, Caerphilly, 19thC, 45in (114.5cm) high.
£1,700–2,000 / €2,450–2,900
$2,850–3,350 PF

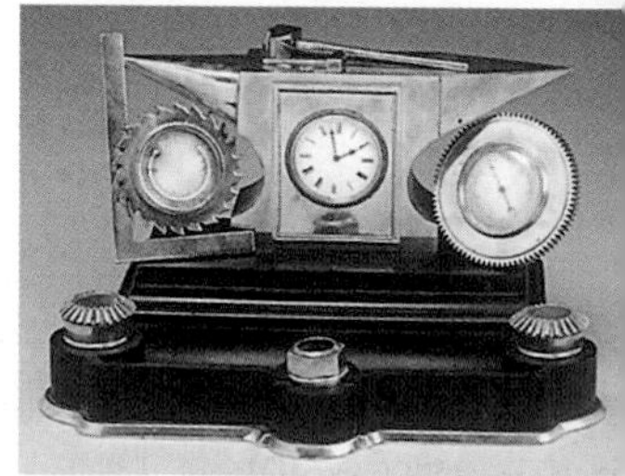

► A lacquered-brass and nickel-plated industrial novelty desk compendium, cast as an anvil, the clock with an enamel dial, flanked by a silvered-dial aneroid barometer and a mercury thermometer within a saw blade and a set square, the base in the form of a pen tray with inkwells, French, c1880, 12½in (32cm) high.
£1,900–2,250 / €2,750–3,250
$3,200–3,800 B

Skeleton Clocks

A brass skeleton timepiece, with an open dial, single fusee movement, on a walnut base beneath a glass dome, with brass presentation label, mid-19thC, 15½in (39.5cm) high.
£1,050–1,250
€1,500–1,800
$1,750–2,100 PF

A brass skeleton clock, with a single fusee movement striking on a bell, on a marble plinth beneath a glass dome, mid-19thC, 18in (45.5cm) high.
£1,000–1,200
€1,450–1,700
$1,700–2,000 G(L)

► A Victorian brass skeleton clock, by H. Palmer, Birmingham, the twin-train chain fusee movement striking on a gong, on a marble plinth, signed, 24¾in (63cm) high.
£2,350–2,800
€3,400–4,000
$3,950–4,700 CGC

◄ A Victorian brass skeleton clock, with a silvered dial and single fusee movement, on a rosewood base, 16in (40.5cm) high.
£480–570 / €690–820
$810–960 HYD

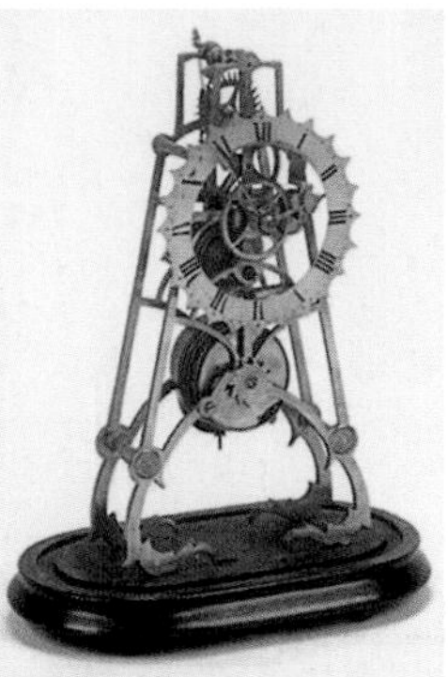

A Victorian brass skeleton clock, with an eight-day movement and a bob pendulum, on an ebonized stand beneath a glass dome, 15¼in (38.5cm) high.
£560–670 / €810–960
$940–1,100 DN

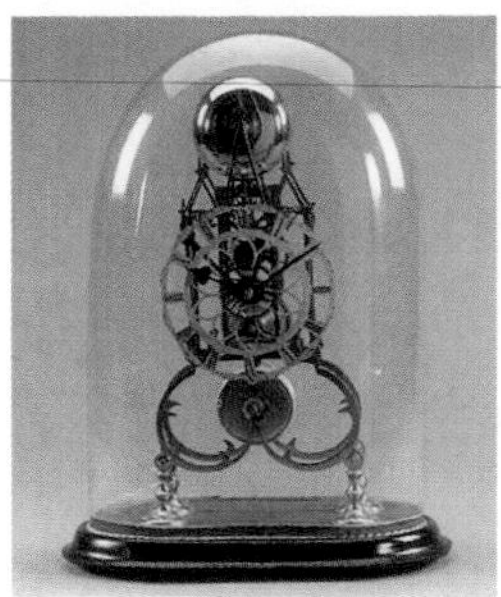

A brass skeleton timepiece, the fusee movement with anchor escapement striking on a bell, on an ebonized base beneath a glass dome, c1870, 15in (38.5cm) high.
£620–740 / €890–1,050
$1,050–1,250 S(O)

A brass skeleton timepiece, the eight-day single-train fusee movement with anchor escapement, on an ebonized stand beneath a glass dome, late 19thC, 13¾in (35cm) high.
£470–560 / €680–810
$790–940 DN

Wall Clocks

A painted wall clock, with an engraved brass dial, the iron weight-driven movement with verge escapement striking on a bell, with alarm front-mounted pendulum detached, restored, German, mid-17thC, 6¼in (16cm) high.
£5,400–6,500
€7,800–9,400
$9,100–10,900 S(O)

◄ A painted wood 'Zaanse' wall clock, by Cornelius van Roosen, with a velvet-covered dial and weight-driven movement, surmounted by cast-brass figures of Faith, Hope and Charity, Dutch, Zaandam, c1700, 32in (80cm) high.
£2,000–2,400
€2,900–3,450
$3,350–4,000 B
Cornelius van Roosen was a known maker of 'Zaanse' clocks in the late 17th century. By the 1720s this style of clock had largely fallen out of fashion.

A rococo iron and chased-brass wall timepiece, with a copper chapter ring, the movement with verge escapement and front pendulum, minor imperfections, German, 1725–50, 19in (48cm) high.
£740–890 / €1,050–1,250
$1,250–1,500 S(Am)

Insurance values

Always insure your valuable antiques for the cost of replacing them with similar items, regardless of the original price paid. Both dealers and auctioneers can provide a valuation service for a fee.

A *comtoise* wall clock, the brass relief dial with enamel cartouches, the iron and brass posted movement with verge escapement repeat striking on a bell, with alarm and a wire pendulum, signed 'Gaillard à Charchillat', French, c1740, 14¼in (36cm) high.
£2,050–2,450
€2,950–3,550
$3,450–4,100 ⚒ S(Am)

A mahogany and bronze-inlaid wall clock, by Eric Pettersson Öhman, Swedish, Stockholm, c1770, 25½in (65cm) square.
£1,650–1,950
€2,350–2,800
$2,750–3,250 ⚒ BUK

A carved giltwood wall clock, by Johan Fredrik Cedergren, Stockholm, Swedish, early 19thC, 34¼in (87cm) high.
£1,350–1,600
€1,950–2,300
$2,250–2,700 ⚒ BUK

► A mahogany wall clock, the painted dial inscribed 'Massey, London', the single train fusee movement with bob pendulum, 1825–50, 14¼in (36cm) high.
£1,900–2,250
€2,750–3,250
$3,200–3,800 ⚒ PFK

A Norwich-style mahogany and line-inlaid wall timepiece, by Benjamin Neeves, Wrentham, the engraved brass dial with minute hand and date aperture, 18thC, 55¼in (140cm) high.
£2,100–2,500
€3,000–3,600
$3,500–4,200 ⚒ B(Pr)

An oak wall clock, by George Duncan, the brass dial with seconds dial and date aperture, with eight-day movement, dial probably associated, early 19thC, 80¾in (205cm) high.
£880–1,050
€1,250–1,500
$1,450–1,750 ⚒ B(Ed)

A George III japanned tavern clock, by Josh Gurney, Bristol, with a painted dial, the month-going twin-train five-pillar movement striking on a bell, 58¾in (149cm) high.
£7,000–8,400
€10,100–12,100
$11,800–14,100 ⚒ DN

A mahogany wall clock, by Chas. Frodsham & Co, with an enamelled and painted dial and five-pillar twin fusee striking movement, inscribed, early 19thC, dial 11¾in (30cm) diam.
£3,300–3,950
€4,750–5,700
$5,500–6,600 ⚒ SWO

Items in the Clock section have been arranged in date order within each sub-section.

A giltwood *petite sonnerie* musical picture frame wall clock, the dial with an engine-turned gilt centre, the triple-train movement with silk suspension and striking on two gongs, Austrian, c1830, 22in (56cm) high.
£2,250–2,700
€3,250–3,900
$3,800–4,500 ⚒ S

A painted wood and gilt-lead *stoelklok*, by Aleva, the painted dial with date aperture, the brass movement with twisted pillars, verge escapement and Dutch half-hour rack striking on two bells, with alarm, restored, Dutch, Friesland, 1750–75, 29½in (75cm) high.
£3,100–3,700
€4,500–5,300
$5,200–6,200 ⚒ S(Am)

A giltwood and lacquered wall clock, the dial painted with a coastal scene above a pendulum aperture, the weight-driven movement with four pillars and anchor escapement, Maltese, 19thC, 41¾in (106cm) high.
£7,600–9,100
€10,900–13,100
$12,800–15,300 ⚒ B

A rosewood wall time-piece, by Johnson, Liverpool, with a painted dial and eight-day fusee movement, c1830, 17in (43cm) high.
£870–970 / €1,250–1,400
$1,450–1,600 ⊞ K&D

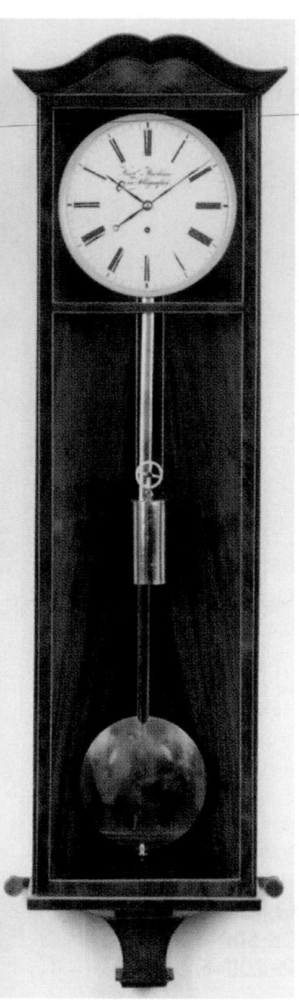

A mahogany and maplewood strung *Dachluhr*, with a milk-glass dial, signed 'Karl Martinis in Klagenfurl', the eight-day movement with a steel pendulum, German, c1835, 38in (96.5cm) high.
£6,800–7,500
€9,800–10,800
$11,400–12,600 ⊞ C&A

A mahogany drop-dial wall timepiece, by John Lownds, London, the fusee movement with anchor escapement, the base with a door, c1850, 27½in (70cm) high.
£1,000–1,200
€1,450–1,700
$1,700–2,000 ⚒ S(O)

A gilt-bronze cartel clock, with an enamel dial, signed 'T. Martin, Paris', the twin-barrel movement striking on a bell, French, 19thC, 20½in (52cm) high.
£400–480 / €580–690
$670–800 ⚒ Bea

A mahogany drop-dial wall timepiece, by Godden, Malling, the painted wooden dial with cast-brass locking bezel, single fusee movement with four pillars, early 19thC, 24in (61cm) high.
£4,000–4,800
€5,800–6,900
$6,800–8,100 ⚒ B

A Vienna-style mahogany wall clock, by Gustav Becker, the enamel dial with subsidiary seconds dial and marked GB, German, 19thC, 52in (132cm) high.
£410–490 / €590–700
$690–820 ⚒ FHF

An oak alarm wall timepiece, with a painted dial, inscribed 'Geo. Bradshaw, Whitchurch', the 30-hour movement with verge escapement, minor damage, 19thC, 32¼in (82cm) high.
£760–910 / €1,100–1,300
$1,300–1,550 ⚒ DN

An early Victorian mahogany drop-dial wall timepiece, the painted dial signed 'Thomas Whithill, Hotham Sand', the single fusee movement with anchor escapement, 27½in (70cm) high.
£1,900–2,250
€2,750–3,250
$3,200–3,800 ⚒ TEN

A Victorian wall clock, by A. Faller, Battersea, with a single fusee movement, 15½in (39cm) diam.
£210–250 / €300–360
$350–420 ⚒ AMB

A coromandel and mother-of-pearl-inlaid timepiece, with a painted dial, 19thC, 21in (53cm) high.
£520–620 / €750–890
$870–1,050 ⚒ TRM

The prices realized at auction may reflect the fact that the clocks have sometimes undergone alterations to their movements, or are in unrestored condition.

A Biedermeier rosewood *grande sonnerie* wall clock, the dial with gilt decoration, the eight-day movement striking the quarters on gongs, signed 'Franz Niewelt', Austrian, c1850, 58in (147cm) high.
£11,700–13,000
€16,900–18,700
$19,700–21,900 ⊞ C&A

LOCATE THE SOURCE

The source of each illustration in Miller's can be found by checking the code letters below each caption with the Key to Illustrations, pages 794–800.

CLOCKS

An oak wall clock, by William Potts, Leeds, with a brass-mounted glass-panelled trunk door, dated 1867, 135¾in (345cm) high.
£6,300–7,500
€9,100–10,800
$10,600–12,600 B(Ed)

William Potts set up a clock making business in 1833 in Pudsey, West Yorkshire. Initially they made domestic clocks and then expanded into making turret clocks for churches and public buildings. Potts moved to Leeds in 1862. Later his three sons joined the business and it became known as William Potts & Sons.

A japanned tavern time-piece, the painted dial inscribed 'Ralph Soleson, London', the eight-day single-train movement with anchor escapement, c1900, 59in (150cm) high.
£2,700–3,200
€3,900–4,600
$4,500–5,400 DN

A Louis XVI-style gilt-bronze cartel wall timepiece, the enamel dial signed 'Humbert, Paris', the movement with Brocot escapement, stamped 'Vincenti & Cie', French, c1870, 16½in (42cm) high.
£780–930 / €1,150–1,350
$1,300–1,550 S(Am)

A rococo-style gilt-brass cartel clock, with an enamel dial, the twin-barrel movement striking on a bell, stamped 'Japy Frères & Cie', French, late 19thC, 24in (61cm) high.
£350–420 / €500–600
$590–700 WW

An Empire-style giltwood clock, signed 'E. G. Eriksson', Swedish, 1910–20, 24in (61cm) high.
£1,800–2,000
€2,600–2,900
$3,000–3,350 CAV

A mahogany alarm timepiece, with a painted dial, the 30-hour movement with anchor escapement and a separate alarm train, Dutch, late 19thC, 55¼in (140cm) high.
£530–640 / €770–920
$890–1,050 DN

A gilt and patinated-bronze *oeil-de-boeuf* wall clock, the enamel dial signed 'Lepaute à Paris', the eight-day movement striking on a bell, French, c1875, 15¾in (40cm) high.
£1,650–1,950
€2,350–2,800
$2,750–3,250 S(O)

An ebonized walnut Vienna-style wall timepiece, the movement driven by a single brass weight, German, late 19thC, 40in (101.5cm) high.
£350–420 / €500–600
$590–700 PF

A mahogany clock, thermometer and aneroid barometer, by the Hamburg American Clock Co, German, early 20thC, 25½in (65cm) high.
£280–330 / €400–470
$470–550 PFK

◄ **A mahogany wall clock,** by Wm Lister & Sons, Newcastle-upon-Tyne, with eight-day fusee movement, c1920, 14in (35.5cm) diam.
£880–980 / €1,250–1,40
$1,500–1,650 PTh

American Clocks

A mahogany shelf clock, by Silas Headly, with a wooden movement, c1820, 29¾in (75.5cm) high.
£1,650–2,950
€2,350–2,800
$2,750–3,250 ⚒ **LHA**

A mahogany-veneered ottage timepiece, by Henry Sperry & Co, New York, with later hands nd pendulum, c1855, 2in (30.5cm) high.
210–250 / €300–360
360–420 ⚒ **ROSc**

walnut parlour No. 5 alendar clock, by Seth homas, with eight-day novement, calendar novement and lower ial replaced, c1880, 0in (51cm) high.
800–890 / €1,150–1,300
1,350–1,500 ⊞ **SET**

A walnut-veneered shelf alarm clock, by David Dutton, the 30-hour wooden movement striking on a bell, with later glass, mirror and veneer, Mount Vernon, New Hampshire, c1838, 31½in (80cm) high.
£150–180 / €220–260
$250–300 ⚒ **ROSc**

A walnut double-dial calendar clock, The Cottage No. 7, by Ithaca Calendar Clock Co, c1874, 22in (56cm) high.
£900–1,000
€1,300–1,450
$1,500–1,650 ⊞ **SET**

A rosewood cottage clock, by Atkins, c1880, 17in (43cm) high.
£120–145 / €170–210
$200–240 ⚒ **DuM**

A mahogany wall clock, by Elisha Hotchkiss, Nassau Hall, Princeton, New Jersey, c1840, 34in (86.5cm) high.
£320–380 / €460–550
$540–640 ⚒ **DuM**

A bronze-patinated spelter mantel clock, by Ansonia Clock Co, the ebonized embossed brass dial with enamel plaques, signed, late 19thC, 25½in (65cm) high.
£950–1,100
€1,350–1,600
$1,600–1,850 ⚒ **NOA**

A painted wood and mother-of-pearl-inlaid shelf clock, by Terry & Andrews, with eight-day movement, c1848, 15¼in (38.5cm) high.
£320–380 / €460–550
$540–640 ⚒ **ROSc**

A brass floor-standing timepiece, by Lewis Paul Juvet, with an enamel dial, the movement contained in a terrestrial globe, c1880, 54¾in (139cm) high.
£10,000–12,000
€14,400–17,300
$16,800–20,100 ⚒ **S(NY)**

Lewis Paul Juvet received patents for his globe timepieces in January and May of 1867. A partnership was formed with James Arkell and A. G. Richmond of Canajoharie, New York in 1879 to manufacture these clocks. Table and floor standing models of various sizes were produced until 1886, when a fire destroyed the factory.

◄ **A mahogany drop-dial wall clock,** 19thC, 32in (81.5cm) high.
£630–700 / €900–1,000
$1,050–1,200 ⊞ **RTW**

British Regulators

An ebonized and mahogany table regulator, by Ellicott, London, the silvered dial with subsidiary seconds dial, the movement with six pillars, maintaining power and deadbeat escapement, striking on a bell, signed, late 18thC, 22½in (57cm) high.
£4,950–5,900
€7,100–8,500
$8,300–9,900 B

◄ A mahogany mantel regulator, by Thearle, London, the silvered minute dial with hours and seconds dial with astronomer's marks, the fusee movement with deadbeat escapement, signed, c1850, 19¾in (50.5cm) high.
£4,500–5,400
€6,500–7,800
$7,600–9,100 S(O)

◄ A satinwood and mahogany-banded longcase regulator, by Josiah Emery, London, the silvered minute dial with hours and seconds dials, the movement with five pillars, maintaining power and deadbeat escapement, signed, late 18thC, 84in (213cm) high.
£17,500–21,000
€25,200–30,000
$29,400–35,000 B
Josiah Emery (1725–97) was an eminent Swiss watchmaker who settled in London. Respected as a watchmaker rather than a clockmaker, it is possible that this regulator was a commissioned item.

A Victorian oak regulator, by Wm Tunnell, Sunderland, the painted dial above a glazed pendulum, the eight-day movement driven by two brass-covered weights and striking on a bell, 63in (160cm) high.
£2,100–2,500
€3,000–3,600
$3,500–4,200 CGC

◄ An oak table regulator, by J. Grant, London, the dial with an open seconds dial revealing the detent escapement, with a single chain fusee movement, 19thC, 17¾in (45cm) high.
£1,400–1,650
€2,000–2,350
$2,350–2,750 B

Continental Regulators

A mahogany and ormolu-mounted table regulator, the enamel dial with a calendar inscribed '*Montassier à Vannes*', the striking movement and pendulum within a glazed case, French, late 18thC, 24in (61cm) high.
£7,100–8,500
€10,200–12,200
$11,900–14,300 S(NY)

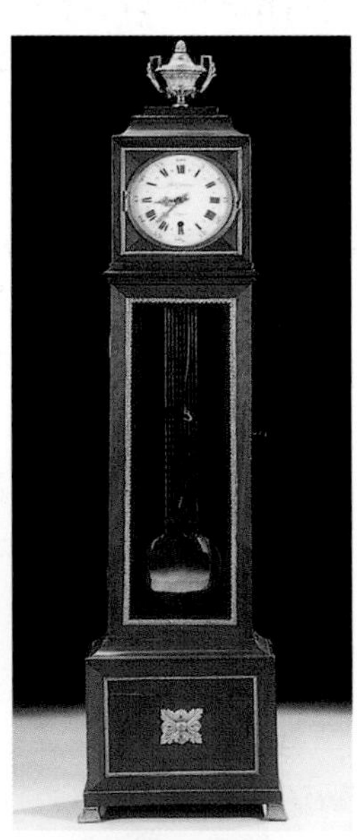

A mahogany and gilt-bronze-mounted regulator, signed 'D. F. Dubois à Paris', French, late 18thC, 82¾in (210cm) high.
£5,800–6,900
€8,300–9,900
$9,700–11,600 S(P)

A Biedermeier rosewood wall regulator, with an eight-day movement, Austrian, c1845, 41in (104cm) high.
£1,300–1,450
€1,900–2,100
$2,200–2,450 K&D

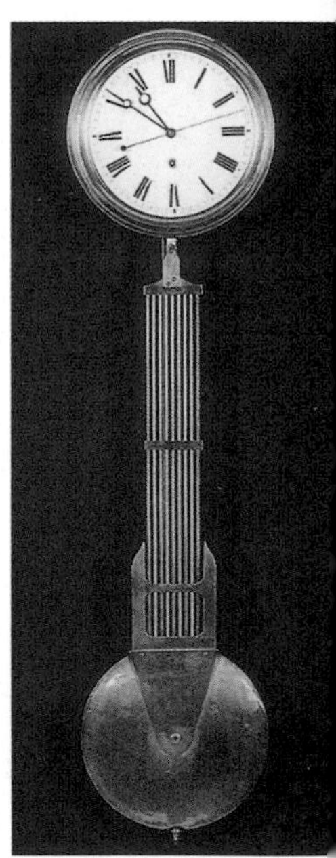

A brass *comtoise* wall regulator, with an enamel dial, the brass movement with pinwheel escapement and maintaining power, French, mid-19thC, 54¼in (138cm) high.
£1,450–1,750
€2,100–2,500
$2,450–2,950 S(Am)

Watches

Pocket Watches

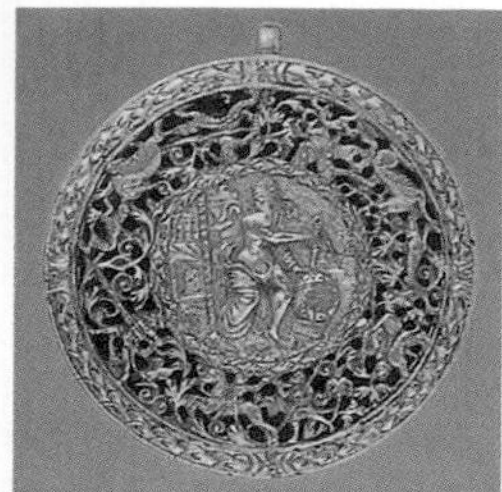

A gilt tambour watch case and dial, the case chased, pierced and engraved, the edge depicting a boar and stag hunt, the base engraved with a further hunting scene and a depiction of astronomy, German, c1540, 2¼in (6cm) diam.
£2,350–2,600
€3,350–3,750
$3,950–4,350 ⊞ PT

An 18ct gold pocket watch, by F. Jones, London, with a gold chased dial and winding key, London 1823, 1¾in (4.5cm) diam.
£370–440 / €530–630
$620–740 ⚒ BR

A silver pair-cased verge pocket watch, by W. Roberts, Long Marton, c1825, 2½in (6.5cm) diam.
£290–320 / €410–460
$480–540 ⊞ TIC

► **A silver open-faced pocket watch,** by F. T. Johnson of Dublin, the movement with a diamond endstone and bosley regulator, Irish, hallmarked London 1842, 2in (5cm) diam.
£660–730 / €950–1,050
$1,100–1,250 ⊞ FOF

► **A four-case pocket watch,** by Edward Prior, London, the chain-driven fusee movement with pierced pillars, with two silver cases, a tortoiseshell and piqué case and a Turkish silver outer case, c1859.
£940–1,100
€1,350–1,600
$1,600–1,900 ⚒ BWL

A silver 'slow-beat' pocket watch, by Thomas Yates of Preston, with a signed ivorine enamel dial, the fusee lever movement with diamond endstone and bosley regulator, the double-bottomed case by Samuel Quilliam, Chester 1863, 2in (5cm) diam.
£850–950 / €1,200–1,350
$1,450–1,600 ⊞ FOF

Yates obtained patents in 1864 for two watches with slower beats: 7,200 or 10,800 instead of the normal 14,400. The theory was that this slower escapement would be more adept at handling the shock sustained when used by people with an active lifestyle. In fact, the complete opposite was true.

A silver pocket watch, the silver and gold engine-turned and hand-chased dial with applied gold numerals, with chain-driven fusee movement, London 1886.
£160–180 / €230–260
$270–300 ⊞ Bns

A silver open-faced 24-hour dial lever pocket watch, signed 'Heloisa', with a keyless movement, in an engine-turned case, the cuvette engraved with medals and 'Ancre de Précision', Swiss, c1895, 1¾in (4.5cm) diam.
£510–570 / €740–820
$860–960 ⊞ PT

◄ An 18ct gold and enamel diamond-set pocket watch, c1900, 1½in (4cm) diam, in original box.
£850–950 / €1,200–1,350
$1,400–1,550 ⊞ SGr

A 14ct pink gold open-faced pocket watch, signed 'Eppner, Berlin', the enamel dial with gilt lever movement, the cuvette with a profile and the back with the monogram and crown of Kaiser Wilhelm II, German, c1910, 2in (5cm) diam.
£1,100–1,300
€1,600–1,900
$1,850–2,200 ⚒ S(O)

An 18ct gold and enamel watch, with a matching enamel chain, 1920s, 1in (2.5cm) diam.
£880–980 / €1,250–1,400
$1,500–1,650 ⊞ EXC

A gunmetal calendar pocket watch, the dial with subsidiary dials for month, day and seconds containing moonphase and date, late 19thC, 2½in (6.5cm) diam.
£590–710 / €850–1,000
$1,000–1,200 ⚒ B(Kn)

A gold, diamond and opal pocket watch, with an enamel dial and keyless cylinder movement, the back set with an opal surrounded by rose-cut diamonds, with a diamond-set bow, c1910, 1in (2.5cm) diam.
£940–1,100
€1,400–1,600
$1,600–1,850 ⚒ TEN

A silver and enamel fob watch, with an enamel dial, the case set with half seed pearls, suspended from a matching bow brooch, Swiss, early 20thC 2¾in (7cm) high.
£175–210 / €250–300
$290–350 ⚒ BR

Wristwatches

A Glashütte chronograph wristwatch, with a twin register dial and rotating bezel, German, c1945, 1½in (4cm) diam.
£2,250–2,700
€3,250–3,900
$3,800–4,550 ⚒ FHF

Further reading

Miller's Wristwatches: How to Compare & Value, Miller's Publications, 2004

► **An Omega 14ct white gold wristwatch,** Swiss, 1930s.
£810–900 / €1,150–1,300
$1,350–1,500 ⊞ TEM

A Harwood 9ct gold automatic wristwatch, Swiss, 1929.
£760–850 / €1,050–1,200
$1,250–1,400 ⊞ TIC

A Jolus 18ct gold chronograph wristwatch, with subsidiary seconds and 30-minute marker, Swiss, 1940s, 1½in (4cm) diam.
£175–210 / €250–300
$290–350 ⚒ B(Kn)

A Longines silver pilot's wristwatch, movement and Borgel case by Baume & Co, case, dial and movement signed, Swiss, hallmarked London 1917, 3¼in (8.5cm) diam.
£610–680 / €880–980
$1,000–1,100 ⊞ FOF

The Borgel case was an early attempt at water/dust-proofing, and allowed the movement to be screwed into the case from the front.

◄ **An Omega 10ct gold automatic wristwatch,** with a coppered and silvered dial, Swiss, 1960s.
£410–490 / €580–700
$690–820 ⚒ SWO

A Patek Philippe 18ct gold wristwatch, with a gilt dial, Swiss, 1930s.
£330–390 / €480–570
$550–660 G(L)

A Rolex silver wristwatch, the engine-turned sunburst dial with subsidiary seconds, Swiss, Glasgow import marks for 1922.
£540–600 / €780–860
$900–1,000 Bns

A Rolex stainless steel and gilt driver's wristwatch, the silvered dial with subsidiary seconds, Swiss, c1930, 1½in (4cm) wide.
£740–890 / €1,100–1,300
$1,250–1,500 S(O)
The top of the case is higher than the bottom, for use when driving.

A Rolex steel and gold Oyster Viceroy wristwatch, Swiss, 1940s.
£1,500–1,650
€2,150–2,400
$2,500–2,750 TEM

A Rolex stainless steel Oyster Perpetual Bubble-back wristwatch, with automatic chronometer movement, Swiss, c1945.
£990–1,100
€1,400–1,550
$1,650–1,850 Bns

◄ A Rolex 9ct gold Oyster Precision wristwatch, with an associated 18ct gold bracelet, Swiss, c1950.
£910–1,100
€1,350–1,600
$1,550–1,850 TEN

A diamond-set wristwatch, the dial bordered by single-cut diamonds, the shoulders of Greek key pattern, 1920s, strap c1970, 6¼in (16cm) long.
£660–790 / €1,000–1,150
$1,100–1300 S(O)

A Zenith 18ct pink gold wristwatch, with a silvered dial, signed, Swiss, 1950s, 1½in (4cm) diam.
£460–550 / €660–790
$770–920 B(Kn)

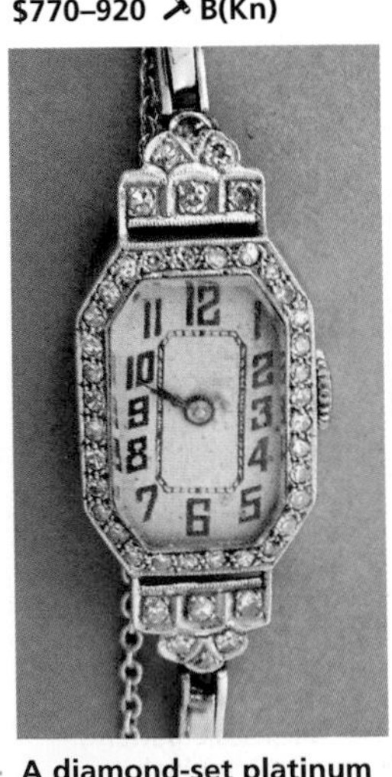

A diamond-set platinum cocktail wristwatch, 1930s.
£290–350 / €420–500
$490–590 G(L)

A diamond bracelet wristwatch, the centrepiece detachable for conversion to a brooch, the dial set in a surround of pavé-set petals extending to diamond articulated bracelet sections with leaf-style shoulders, c1940.
£5,300–6,400
€7,600–9,100
$9,200–11,000 WW

Barometers

Stick Barometers

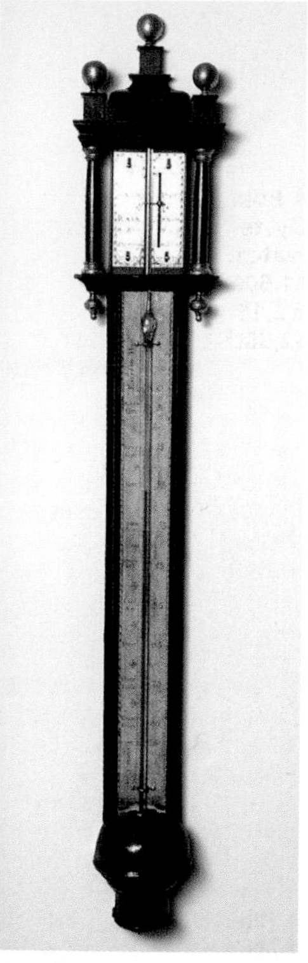

A walnut stick barometer, with paper thermometer scale, c1720, 41in (104cm) high.
£13,500–15,000
€19,400–21,500
$22,700–25,200 ⊞ RAY

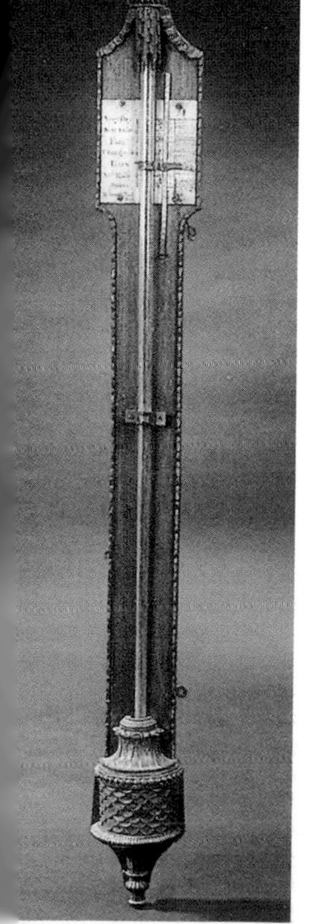

A George III mahogany stick barometer, by T. Blunt, London, the silvered dial with vernier, the case with a circular cistern cover, signed, 38¼in (97cm) high.
£2,100–2,500
€3,000–3,600
$3,500–4,200 ⚒ TEN
Thomas Blunt was in business from 1760 to 1822.

The prices realized at auction may reflect the fact that some barometers have undergone alterations, or are in unrestored condition.

◄ A George III mahogany barometer, by B. Storr, York, with a painted dial, the cistern cover carved with a fishscale pattern, 41¼in (105cm) high.
£6,400–7,700
€9,200–11,000
$10,800–13,000 ⚒ B(Ed)

► A mahogany stick barometer, by Benjamin Martin, London, with mercury thermometer, hygrometer and vernier, signed, c1760, 38in (96.5cm) high.
£7,200–8,600
€10,400–12,400
$12,100–14,500 ⚒ S(O)
Benjamin Martin, a farmer's son from Worplesdon Surrey, was born in 1704. After some years of teaching in Chichester, lecturing on scientific subjects and publishing essays, he moved to London and by 1756 had set up as an optician and instrument maker in Fleet Street. This barometer is of the type Martin named a triple weather barometer, as it has a barometer, thermometer and hygrometer. Indeed, he may have been the first maker to include a hygrometer in his instruments. In 1780 his son Joshua joined the business but within two years it was bankrupt and Benjamin had died.

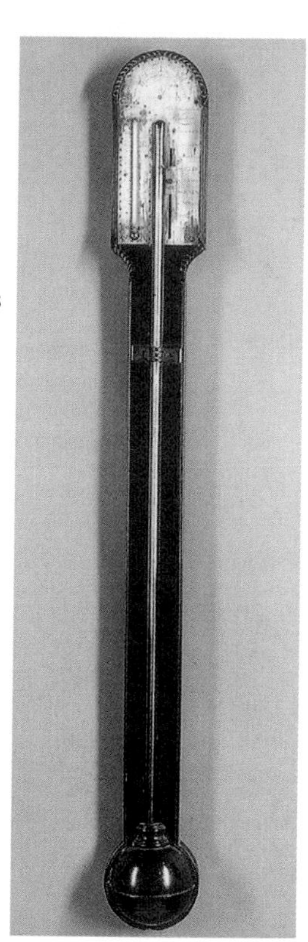

An inlaid mahogany stick barometer, by Joseph Gatty, New York, American, c1795, 44½in (113cm) high.
£7,900–9,500
€11,400–13,700
$13,300–16,000 S(NY)

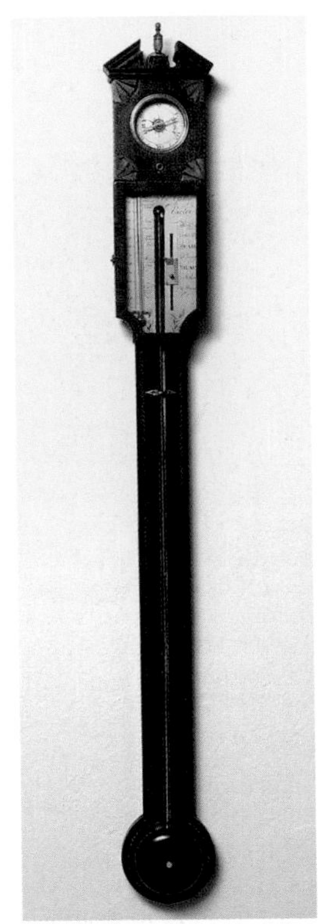

An inlaid mahogany stick barometer, with hygrometer, signed 'Gally, Exeter', c1820, 43in (109cm) high.
£6,700–7,500
€9,600–10,800
$11,300–12,600 ⊞ RAY

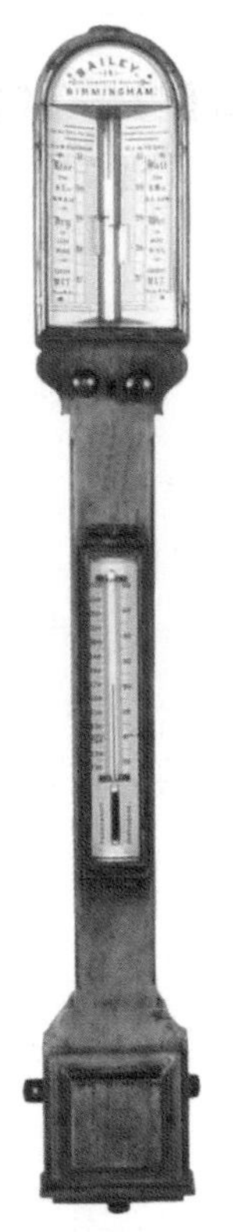

A mahogany stick barometer, by Bailey, Birmingham, with painted white opaque scales, 19thC, 39½in (100.5cm) high.
£540–650 / €780–930
$920–1,100 FHF

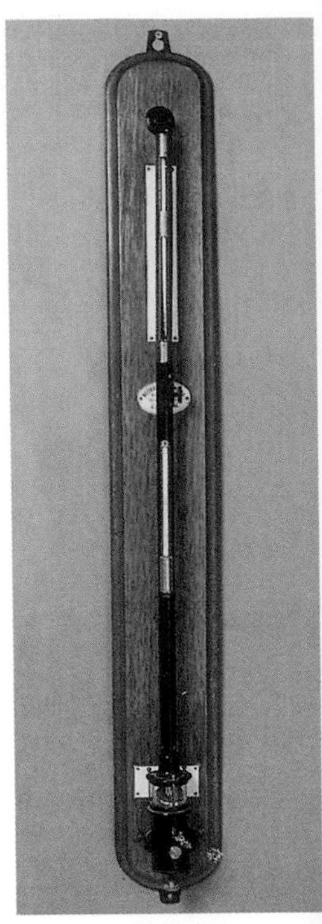

A Fortin-type metal stick barometer, by Negretti & Zambra, London, with a brass register, the thermometer tube numbered 1809 and signed, early 20thC, 40½in (103cm) high.
£470–560 / €680–810
$790–940 TEN

Admiral Fitzroy Barometers

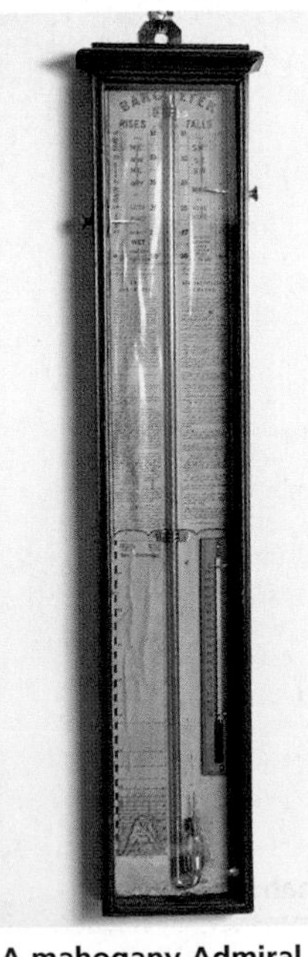

A mahogany Admiral Fitzroy barometer, c1880, 36in (91.5cm) high.
£850–950 / €1,200–1,350
$1,450–1,600 ⊞ TRI

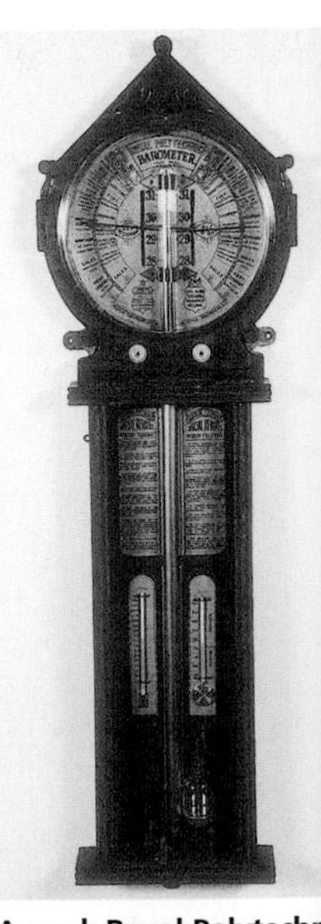

An oak Royal Polytechn Admiral Fitzroy baromet with silvered card scales, c1880, 41in (104cm) high
£1,650–1,800
€2,350–2,600
$2,700–3,000 ⊞ RAY

Wheel Barometers

A George III mahogany wheel barometer, by P. Cetti, Kendal, with a silvered brass dial, the case boxwood- and ebony-strung and inlaid with shell medallions, 39in (99cm) high.
£820–980 / €1,200–1,400
$1,400–1,650 ⚒ Mit

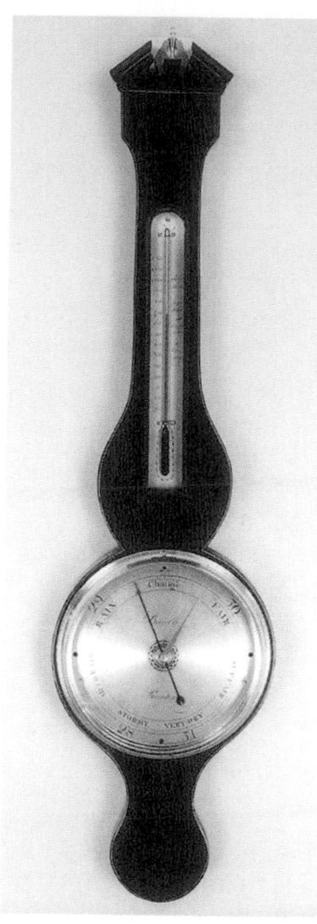

A partridge wood wheel barometer, by Barelli, Reading, with silvered brass barometer and thermometer scales, the case with boxwood stringing, c1810, dial 8in (20.5cm) diam.
£1,500–1,650
€2,150–2,400
$2,500–2,750 ⊞ PAO

A mahogany boxwood- and ebony-strung wheel barometer, by John Smith, London, with silvered dials, the barometer with brass bezel and ivory setting knob, restored, c1830, 39¼in (99.5cm) high.
£1,100–1,250
€1,600–1,800
$1,900–2,100 ⊞ JC

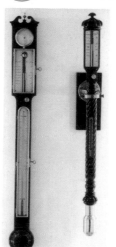

A giltwood wheel barometer, by Negretti & Zambra, London, with silvered barometer and thermometer dials, carved with a mask of the Duke of Wellington, naval trophies, ribbons, tassels and foliage, crested with Wellington's hat, inscribed 'Salimanci Piloria, Waterloo & Tolusse', 19thC, 47in (119.5cm) high.
£4,150–5,000
€6,000–7,200
$7,000–8,400 ⚒ MEA

mahogany wheel rometer, by Braham, istol, c1830, in (96.5cm) high.
,700–1,900
2,450–2,700
,850–3,200 ⊞ RAY

A mahogany wheel barometer, by Reader, Cranbrook, c1830, 41in (104cm) high.
£1,100–1,250
€1,600–1,800
$1,850–2,100 ⊞ RAY

An ebony and satinwood-strung wheel barometer, by H. Cattanio & Co, York, with four silvered dials, convex mirror, 19thC, 38½in (98cm) high.
£410–490 / €590–710
$690–820 ⚒ DD

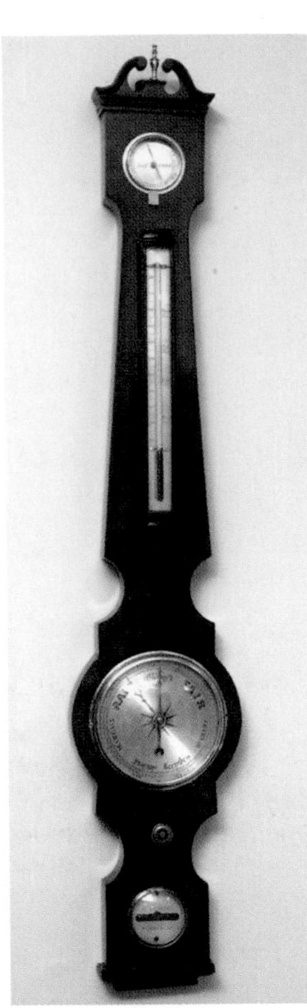

A mahogany wheel barometer, by Pearce, Cirencester, c1850, 35in (89cm) high.
£2,000–2,200
€2,900–3,200
$3,350–3,700 ⊞ DJH

A mahogany wheel barometer, by P. Carnova, Halesworth, with silvered dial, convex mirror, thermometer, hygrometer and spirit level, mid-19thC, 38¼in (97cm) high.
£470–560 / €680–810
$790–940 ⚒ DN

A carved stained oak wheel barometer, by Ronchetti Brothers, London, with a signed silvered dial, knob missing, mid-19thC, 45in (114.5cm) high.
£450–540 / €650–780
$760–910 ⚒ S(Am)

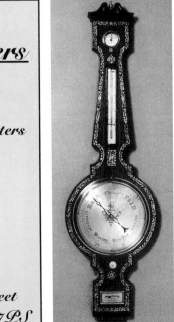

A rosewood and mother-of-pearl-inlaid wheel barometer, by Grisbrook, Tenterden, with silvered dial, hygrometer, thermometer and spirit level, signed, some restoration, c1860, 45¼in (115cm) high.
£680–820 / €1,000–1,200
$1,200–1,400 ⚒ TEN

A Victorian rosewood-veneered wheel barometer, the silvered dial with a turned bone adjuster knob, with a hygrometer, thermometer and convex mirror, 38in (96.5cm) high.
£300–360 / €440–520
$500–600 ⚒ WW

Continental Barometers

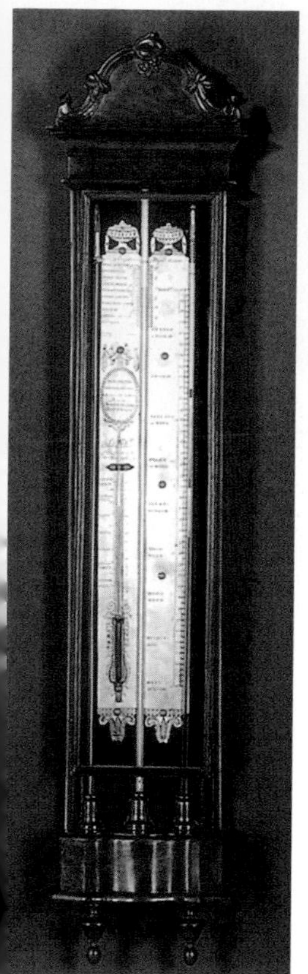

A carved giltwood barometer, by Goyou, Paris, some losses to carving, French, c1785, 49½in (125.5cm) high.
£5,000–6,000 / €7,200–8,600
$8,400–10,100 S

A carved giltwood wheel barometer, some paint and gesso losses, French, late 18thC, 40in (101.5cm) high.
£960–1,150
€1,400–1,650
$1,600–1,900 JAA

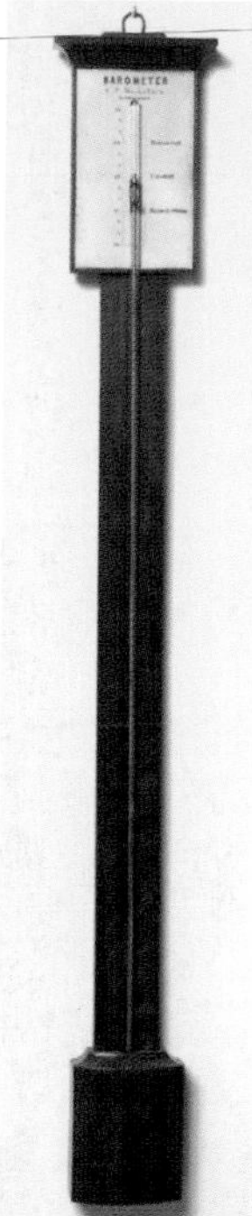

A stick barometer, Danish, Copenhagen, c1860, 39in (99cm) high.
£1,350–1,500
€1,950–2,150
$2,250–2,500
RAY

◄ **A carved mahogany bakbarometer,** by A. Reballio, Rotterdam, the barometer and thermometer with pewter plates, possible alterations, Dutch, c1770, 44in (112cm) high.
£1,650–1,950 / €2,350–2,800
$2,800–3,350 S(Am)

Aneroid Barometers

Victorian aneroid **arometer,** with exposed echanism, mounted on n electrotype group of vo greyhounds and a are, after Moigniez, l in (28cm) wide.
320–980 / €1,200–1,400
1,400–1,650 G(B)

► **A Victorian brass aneroid barometer,** by Lewis Dixey, Brighton, 3¾in (9.5cm) diam.
£310–340 / €450–500
$520–570 FOF
George and Charles Dixey were twin sons of Edward Dixey, optician to King George IV and King William IV.

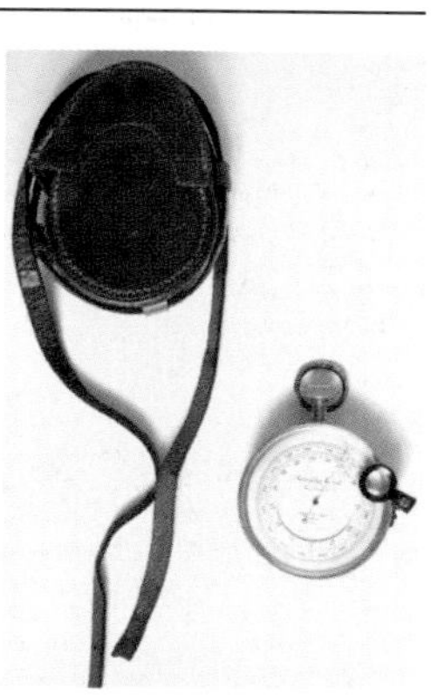

An aluminium-cased compensated surveying aneroid barometer, by Negretti & Zambra, London, the silvered dial with raised chapter ring and scale, altimeter, rackwork adjustment to vernier and rotating magnifier, c1890, 3¼in (8.5cm) long, in a leather sling case.
£590–650 / €850–940
$1,000–1,100 FOF

A carved oak aneroid **arometer and clock,** with rcelain dials, the clock th eight-day movement, 890, 23in (58.5cm) diam.
90–650 / €850–940
,000–1,100 PTh

◄ **An oak aneroid barometer,** signed 'Chadburn's, Opticians, Liverpool', with a silvered dial and silvered mercurial thermometer, early 20thC, 28¼in (72cm) high.
£290–350 / €420–500
$490–590 B(Kn)

An aneroid barometer, by D. McGregor & Co, London, Makers to the Royal Navy, with a subsidiary thermometer, some damage to case, early 20thC, 7in (18cm) diam.
£80–90 / €115–130
$135–150 ⊞ RTW

◄ An aneroid thermometer, by Harrison & Co, Montreal, Canadian, c1920, 11in (28cm) diam, in a lacquered case.
£400–440 / €580–640
$670–740 ⊞ RTW

► A carved oak aneroid barometer, with a copper bezel, c1920, 8in (20.5cm) diam.
£105–120 / €160–180
$190–210 ⊞ PTh

A mahogany aneroid barometer, retailed by Harrods, Opticians, c1930, 7in (18cm) diam.
£210–240 / €310–360
$350–400 ⊞ RTW

Desk Barometers

A cast-metal and chrome desk compendium, by Negretti & Zambra, London, comprising an eight-day clock, mercury thermometer and barometer, 1930s, 11in (28cm) high.
£340–380 / €490–550
$570–640 ⊞ RTW

◄ A Victorian engraved gilt-brass desk barometer/ thermometer, with a steel dial, on an ebonized stand, 5½in (14cm) high.
£240–290 / €350–420
$410–490 ⚒ EH

An Art Deco-style metal barometer, by C. P. Goertz, Berlin, German, 1930s, 9in (22cm) diam.
£360–400 / €520–580
$600–670 ⊞ RTW

Pocket Barometers

A walker's compendium barometer, compass and thermometer, by F. Barker & Son, London, c1880, 2in (5cm) diam, in original case.
£410–460 / €600–660
$700–770 ⊞ ETO

► A silver pocket barometer, maker's mark LD, London 1882, 2in (5cm) diam.
£200–240 / €300–350
$340–400 ⚒ FHF

A brass-cased pocket barometer, by Negretti & Zambra, London, with a silvered register, late 19thC, 2in (5cm) diam, in a leather case.
£350–420 / €500–600
$590–700 ⚒ DN

Barographs

► **A mahogany-cased barograph,** with subsidiary aneroid barometer and thermometer dials, late 19thC, 14in (35.5cm) wide.
£1,750–1,950 / €2,500–2,800
$3,000–3,300 ⊞ DJH

An Edwardian oak-cased barograph, with an engraved steel scale, over a chart drawer, 15¾in (40cm) wide.
£1,350–1,600 / €1,950–2,300
$2,250–2,700 ⚒ EH

A mahogany-cased barograph, by Thomas Armstrong & Brother, Manchester, the recording drum with a French timepiece movement, over a chart drawer, c1910, 14¼in (36cm) wide.
£500–600 / €720–860
$840–1,000 ⚒ S(O)

An oak-cased barograph, c1900, 14in (35.5cm) wide.
£540–600 / €780–860
$910–1,000 ⊞ RTW

A mahogany-cased barograph, by C. W. Dixey & Son, London, the base with a chart drawer, the cover with ebonized mouldings, c1910, 14¼in (36cm) wide.
£540–650 / €780–930
$920–1,100 ⚒ S(O)

A walnut-cased barograph, by Dollond, London, with a chart drawer, early 20thC, 14¾in (37.5cm) wide.
£720–860 / €1,050–1,250
$1,200–1,400 ⚒ S(O)

► **An oak-cased barograph,** by Short & Mason, with a chart drawer, c1910, 15in (38cm) wide.
£1,250–1,400 / €1,800–2,000
$2,100–2,350 ⊞ RTW

Items in the Barographs section have been arranged in date order.

► **An oak-cased brass-mounted barograph,** retailed by Harrods, London, with a chart drawer, early 20thC, 14½in (37cm) wide.
£350–420
€500–600
$590–700 ⚒ GAK

◄ **An oak-cased baro-thermograph,** by Negretti & Zambra, London, with a hinged cover, c1920, 17in (43cm) wide.
£1,250–1,400
€1,800–2,000
$2,100–2,350
⊞ RTW

► **An oak-cased barograph,** with bevelled gass and chart drawer, 1930s, 15in (38cm) wide.
£1,800–2,000
€2,600–2,900
$3,000–3,350
⊞ RTW

Decorative Arts

Aesthetic Movement Ceramics

A Burgess & Leigh teapot, printed with a Japanese figure holding a parasol, c1894, 8¾in (22cm) high.
£120–145 / €170–200
$200–240 ⚒ G(L)

A Minton pottery washstand jug, possibly by Christopher Dresser, decorated with Blenheim pattern, printed marks, c1875, 12¼in (31cm) high.
£420–500 / €600–720
$700–840 ⚒ S(O)

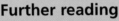

A barbotine Bretby vase, decorated with Grecian-style handles and raised impasto flower bouquets, c1891, 9¾in (25cm) high.
£155–175 / €220–250
$260–290 ⊞ HUN

Barbotine is a type of slip used to make small floral and other decorations on the rims of flat dishes and is applied by piping or trailing. Impasto is the technique of applying paint thickly so that the brush or palette knife marks are visible.

Further reading

Miller's Art Nouveau & Art Deco Buyers Guide, Miller's Publications, 1999

► **A Minton Japanese-style earthenware vase,** decorated with butterflies and grasses, possibly designed by Christopher Dresser, in a stand, c1870, 5½in (14cm) high.
£1,200–1,450 / €1,750–2,100
$2,000–2,400 ⚒ B

Christopher Dresser visited the 1862 International Exhibition in London, which displayed a large number of Japanese items, and made detailed drawings of many exhibits. Apart from the Japanese pieces, Dresser was also impressed with the Minton stand and made drawings of some of their exhibits.

A William de Morgan Persian-style bottle vase, by James Hersey, decorated with stylized motifs and a band of birds, glaze chip, impressed mark 'J. H.' and '7½', 1888–97, 8¾in (22cm) high.
£800–960 / €1,150–1,350
$1,350–1,600 ⚒ SWO

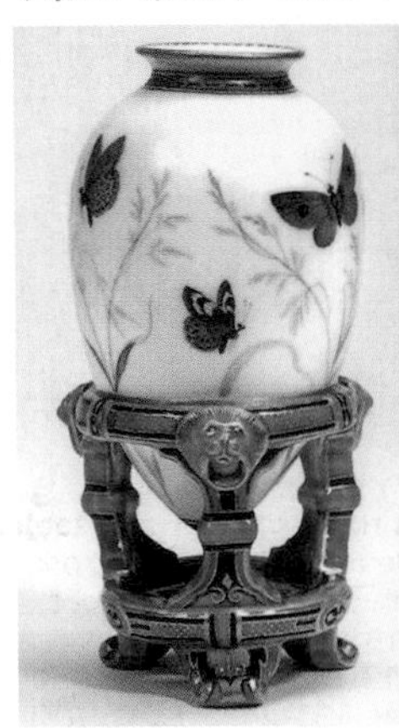

Aesthetic Movement Furniture

◄ **A rosewood corner cabinet,** with mirrored and fabric-covered panels and open shelves, late 19thC, 27in (68.5cm) wide.
£230–270 / €330–390
$380–450 ⚒ MCA

► **A walnut and parcel-gilt side cabinet,** attributed to Morris & Co, the pierced three-quarter gallery and glazed doors with silk and woolwork panels of flowers, late 19thC, 20½in (52cm) wide.
£1,400–1,650
€2,000–2,350
$2,350–2,750 ⚒ DN

A set of twelve mahogar dining chairs, by Smith & Co, Bristol, each with a slat back and upholstered seat, legs retipped, stamped, late 19thC.
£1,500–1,800
€2,150–2,600
$2,500–3,000 ⚒ DN

DECORATIVE ARTS

An Anglo-Japanese-style burrwood and rosewood fireplace surround, the upper section with a mirrored plate flanked by galleried shelves, the lower section with fluted columns enclosing shelves, the whole decorated with floral marquetry, American, 1875–1900, 76in (193cm) wide.
£4,600–5,500 / €6,600–7,900 $7,700–9,200 NOA

An oak and ebonized sideboard, in the manner of A. Jonquet or Wyman & Sons, London, the upper section with a balustrade above a mirror plate, the lower section with a central drawer flanked by short drawers above cupboards, one enclosing a shelf, the other a revolving three-bottle cellaret, 1880–85, 87in (221cm) wide.
£1,300–1,550 / €1,850–2,200 $2,200–2,600 PFK

An ash bedroom suite, comprising triple wardrobe, twin pedestal dressing table, washstand, bedside cabinet and chair, c1870, dressing table 60in (152.5cm) wide.
£1,700–2,050 / €2,450–2,950 $2,850–3,400 M

▶ **An ebonized salon suite,** comprising a settee, one armchair, one upholstered chair and six side chairs, American, c1880, settee 48in (122cm) wide.
£3,000–3,600 / €4,300–5,200 $5,100–6,100 S(NY)

A Victorian satinwood two-tier occasional table, with pierced galleries and painted decoration, on simulated bamboo supports, 29¼in (74.5cm) high.
£630–750 / €910–1,100 $1,050–1,250 SWO

A rosewood writing table, by Herter Brothers, New York, with inlaid decoration, stamped, American, c1875, 37¾in (96cm) wide.
£10,000–12,000 / €14,500–17,300 $16,800–20,100 S(NY)

◀ **An oak table,** with two real and two dummy drawers, with inlaid ebonized decoration, late 19thC, 42¼in (107cm) wide.
£230–270 / €330–390 $390–450 SWO

Aesthetic Movement Metalware

A locket and chain, probably silver, cast with a flowering rose, 19thC, locket 2½in (6.5cm) long.
£100–120 / €145–170 $170–200 FHF

A silver three-piece tea set, engraved with chinoiserie-style birds and insects within foliage, with bamboo-moulded handles and spouts, the pot by Johnson & Springthorpe, 1883, the jug and basin by Edward Brown, London 1880, pot 8in (20.5cm) high.
£900–1,050 / €1,300–1,500 $1,500–1,750 S(O)

A silver-plated and glass claret jug, by Hukin & Heath, the design attributed to Christopher Dresser, c1880, 7in (18cm) high.
£860–950 / €1,250–1,400 $1,450–1,600 SHa

Arts & Crafts Ceramics

An Ault jug, by Christopher Dresser, marked, late 19thC, 10in (25.5cm) high.
£230–270 / €330–390
$380–450 HOLL

◄ **A pair of Ault candlesticks,** c1900, 7in (18cm) high.
£110–125 / €160–180
$185–210 ⊞ SHa

► **A Brannam pottery three-handled vase,** decorated with a griffin and scrolling foliage, signed, 1899, 18in (45.5cm) high.
£300–360 / €430–520
$500–600 NSal

A Brannam pottery vase, with sgraffito decoration, rim restored, decorator's mark for William Baron, signed, 1893, 11¾in (30cm) high.
£590–710 / €850–1,000
$990–1,150 Bea

A pottery jardinière, attributed to Bretby, with boss decoration, c1900, 4in (10cm) high.
£120–135 / €170–195
$200–220 ⊞ HUN

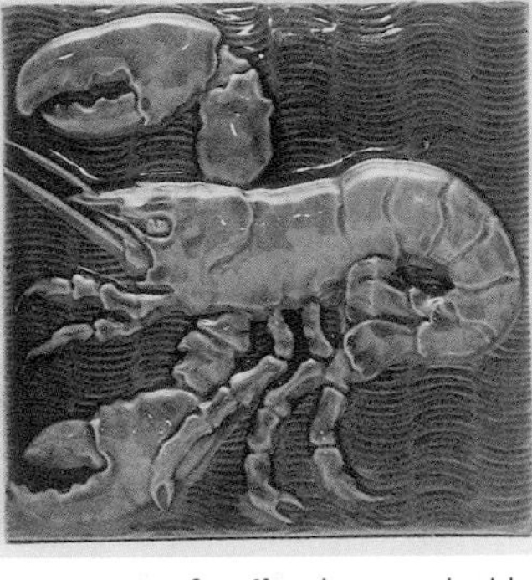

A Burmantofts tile, decorated with a lobster, c1880, 6in (15cm) square.
£210–240 / €300–340
$350–400 ⊞ KMG

A Burmantofts faïence wall plaque, relief-decorated with a farmer, marked, late 19thC, 28in (71cm) high.
£590–700 / €850–1,000
$990–1,150 M

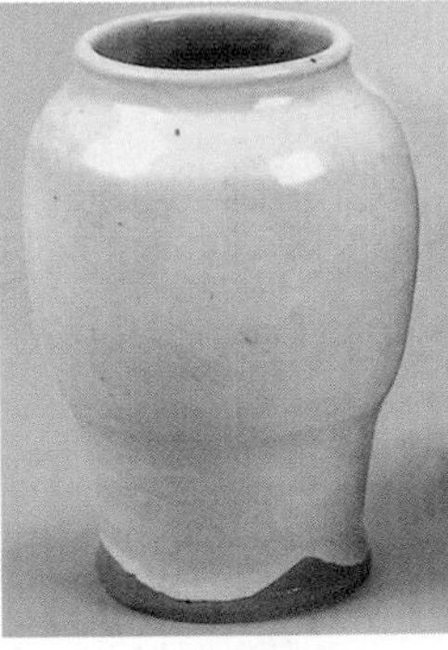

A Mortlake vase, by George Cox, signed, 1913, 6¾in (17cm) high.
£175–210 / €250–300
$290–350 DN

A ceramic vase, by Bruno Emmel, decorated with running glazes, impressed mark, Austrian, Vienna, 1900–02, 6in (15.5cm) high.
£820–980 / €1,200–1,400
$1,400–1,650 DORO

Ewenny ceramics

There has been a thriving ceramics business around the village of Ewenny near Bridgend in South Wales since medieval times, due to the abundance of red clay in the area. Two of these potteries, that have survived to the present day, are the Claypits Pottery, established in the 18th century and the Ewenny Pottery, founded in 1815. The latter was set up by a Claypits apprentice, Evan Jenkins, and it is still owned by the Jenkins family. The potteries produced simple, traditional pieces for everyday use and in the late 19th century, with the popularity of the Arts & Crafts movement, these wares began to attract a wider interest. London designer and dealer Horace Elliot would make annual visits to Ewenny to purchase stock for his showrooms, and a three-handled vase, thrown by David Jenkins and decorated by Elliot, was exhibited at the Arts & Crafts Exhibition in London in 1893. Ewenny wares are usually in the local red earthenware with slip or mottled glaze decoration, although some white-bodied pieces were made using kaolin clay imported from Cornwall.

◄ **A Ewenny pottery dog bowl,** inscribed in Welsh 'Love me: Love my dog', signed, Welsh, 1900, 7¼in (18.5cm) diam
£490–590 / €710–850
$820–990 PF

◄ **A Ewenny pottery loving cup,** by Evan Jenkins, commemorating the General Election, with inscription, minor damage, 1895, 6in (15cm) high.
£155–185
€220–260
$260–310 S(O)

► **A Ewenny slipware three-handled vase,** by Horace Elliot, decorated with foliate motifs and inscription 'A & C 1893', 6¼in (15.5cm) high.
£1,750–2,100 / €2,500–3,000
$2,900–3,500 PF
A three-handled vase thrown by David Jenkins and hand-finished and decorated by Horace Elliot was exhibited at the Arts & Crafts Exhibition in 1893.

LOCATE THE SOURCE
The source of each illustration in Miller's can be found by checking the code letters below each caption with the Key to Illustrations, pages 794–800.

A Saturday Evening Girls earthenware plate, decorated with pigs, with monogram medallion for Helen Osborne Storrow, American, dated 1910, 8½in (21.5cm) diam.
£8,600–10,300 / €12,400–14,800
$14,500–17,300 S(NY)
Trained in pottery-making while at summer school on Chestnut Hill, a group of young Italian and Jewish immigrant girls began creating their own style of glaze and colour under the patronage of Mrs James J. Storrow. Their designs were sometimes based upon children's book decorations, but flowers and landscape patterns proved to be most popular. The pig plates are among the most famous creations, with each member of the group creating only two examples.

A Linthorpe plaque, with a central motif and stylized floral band, Christopher Dresser facsimile signature and Henry Tooth monogram, c1880, 15¾in (40cm) high.
£1,500–1,650 / €2,150–2,400
$2,500–2,750 HUN

A Pilkington vase, 1905–10, 5½in (13.5cm) high.
£85–95 / €120–135
$140–160 RUSK

DECORATIVE ARTS

Arts & Crafts Clocks

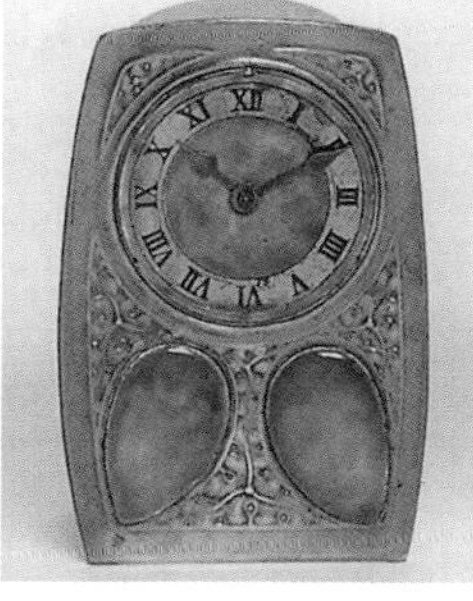

A Liberty & Co Tudric pewter timepiece, the enamel and copper face above enamel plaques, c1905, 5½in (14cm) high.
£1,050–1,250
€1,500–1,800
$1,750–2,100 B

◄ **A mahogany longcase clock,** the pewter dial embossed with butterflies and foliage, flanked by two open shelves, the movement striking on a gong, c1900, 71¼in (181cm) high.
£4,800–5,700
€6,900–8,200
$8,100–9,600 S(O)

► **A Liberty & Co Cymric silver carriage clock,** the enamel dial above two cabochons, one hand replaced, stamped, Birmingham 1905, 4in (10cm) high.
£2,700–3,000
€3,900–4,300
$4,500–5,000 DAD

A Liberty & Co Tudric pewter mantel timepiece, the enamel dial with a copper band, stamped, c1920, 7¾in (19.5cm) high.
£1,400–1,650 / €2,000–2,350
$2,350–2,750 S(O)

Arts & Crafts Furniture

An oak bureau bookcase, with a glazed top, c1890, 29in (73.5cm) wide.
£630–700 / €900–1,000
$1,050–1,200 ⊞ ASP

An oak bookcase, in the style of Liberty, with glass-panelled doors and the motif 'Choose an author as you choose a friend', c1900, 54in (137cm) wide.
£1,300–1,550
€1,850–2,200
$2,200–2,600 ⚒ L

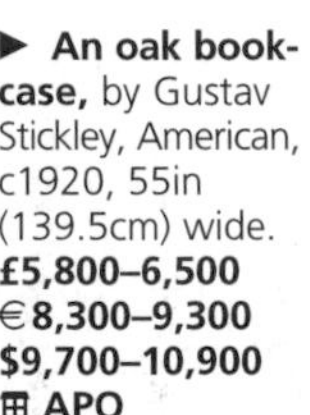

► **An oak bookcase,** by Gustav Stickley, American, c1920, 55in (139.5cm) wide.
£5,800–6,500
€8,300–9,300
$9,700–10,900
⊞ APO

An oak bureau, the fall-front with chequer inlay above a drawer, c1900, 28in (71cm) wide.
£790–880 / €1,150–1,300
$1,350–1,500 ⊞ APO

An ash ladder-back armchair, by Gordon Russell, c1925.
£580–650 / €830–930
$970–1,100 ⊞ APO

A mahogany high-back armchair, c1900.
£1,150–1,300
€1,650–1,850
$1,950–2,200 ⊞ APO

A mahogany chair, by James S. Henry, probably designed by George Walton, the concave back with Art Nouveau motifs, signed, c1900.
£1,400–1,650
€2,000–2,350
$2,350–2,750 ⚒ LAY

Liberty & Co

Arthur Lasenby Liberty established Liberty & Co in Regent Street, London in 1875, selling Oriental goods such as Indian silks, Arabian furniture and Chinese porcelain. The craze for art furniture of the Aesthetic Movement led him to open a design studio in 1883, directed by Leonard F. Wyburd and their own cabinet-making workshops four years later. The store stocked furniture from outside designers including Baillie Scott, Voysey and George Walton, as well as producing their own, toned-down versions of pieces by these designers. Fabrics were designed by the Silver Studio and Walter Crane, among others, and printed by Thomas Wardle. In 1899 the Cymric line of gold and silverware was launched, made by the Birmingham-based company W. H. Haseler. The Tudric line of pewter wares followed a year later. Archibald Knox, Jessie M. King, Arthur Gaskin and Bernard Cuzner produced designs for a wide range of jewellery, candlesticks, boxes, clocks and mirror frames. Apart from Knox, who was occasionally permitted to sign his work, all designers had to accept Liberty's rule of anonymity. Such was the influence of Liberty that in Italy the style was called 'Stile Liberty.'

◄ **A Liberty & Co stained oak dresser,** the raised back with a glass door by James Powell flanked by pierced panels, the base with two drawers above a recess and two panelled doors, stamped, c1900, 71¾in (182cm) wide.
£2,100–2,500
€3,050–3,600
$3,500–4,200
⚒ DN

Items in the Decorative Arts section have been arranged in date order within each sub-section.

► **A mahogany and copper fire screen,** decorated with pomegranates, c1890, 40in (101.5cm) high.
£450–500 / €650–720
$760–840 ⊞ ASP

n oak linen press, by mbrose Heal, with two anelled doors enclosing anging hooks and later helves, gilt-metal label for leal & Son, London, c1900, 7¼in (120cm) wide.
1,400–1,650
2,000–2,350
2,350–2,750 B

► **A brass mirror,** c1900, 28in (71cm) wide.
£360–400
€520–580
$600–670
⊞ TDG

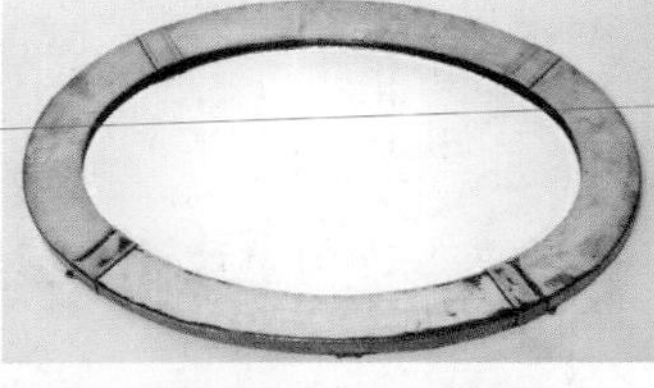

A repoussé copper mirror, c1900, 27in (68.5cm) wide.
£1,800–2,000
€2,600–2,900
$3,000–3,350
⊞ AFD

◄ **An oak purdonium,** with a repoussé copper panel, c1890, 25in (63.5cm) high.
£200–220
€290–320
$340–380
⊞ SAT

A carved wood mirror, inset with a marquetry panel depicting a village scene, with a paper label marked 'Salcot, The Rowley Gallery, Kensington', c1925, 13in (33cm) wide.
£270–300 / €390–430
$450–500 ⊞ DAD

◄ **A mahogany sideboard,** by Shapland and Petter, with a mirror and two glazed doors over two drawers and four doors, c1890, 76in (193cm) wide.
£2,700–3,000
€3,900–4,300
$4,500–5,000 ⊞ APO

An oak and rosewood sideboard, c1900, 65in (165cm) wide.
£540–600 / €780–860
$900–1,000 ⊞ APO

A walnut sideboard, the mirror back above two drawers and two cupboards enclosing shelves and a cellaret, with carved stylized floral decoration, c1900, 60in (152.5cm) wide.
£590–690 / €850–1,000
$990–1,150 ⚒ PFK

An oak sideboard, the mirror back above two drawers and two cupboards c1900, 75in (190.5cm) wide.
£3,350–3,750 / €4,800–5,400
$5,600–6,300 ⊞ MTay

◄ **A mahogany-stained beech easy stool,** by Arthur W. Simpson, with a leather seat, on tapering legs, stamped plaque, c1925, 15¾in (40cm) wide.
£200–240 / €290–340
$340–400 ⚒ PFK

An oak table, by Stickley Brothers, with 'Quaint Furniture' label, 1891–1941, 18¾in (47.5cm) wide.
£310–370 / €440–530
$520–620 ⚒ BB(L)

A pokerwork tripod table, painted with butterflies, c1890, 19in (48.5cm) diam.
£270–300 / €390–430
$450–500 ⊞ ASP

A Liberty & Co oak library table, by Leonard Wyburd, c1895, 32¾in (83cm) high.
£440–490 / €630–700
$740–820 ⊞ TDG

A Liberty & Co occasional table, with label, c1895, 24in (61cm) wide
£105–125 / €150–180
$175–210 ⚒ MCA

A mahogany table, by J. S. Henry, c1900, 36in (91.5cm) wide.
£1,050–1,200 / €1,500–1,700
$1,750–2,000 ⊞ APO

An oak centre table, in the style of Ambrose Heal, inlaid with chevron banding, c1910, 30in (76cm) wide.
£360–430 / €520–620
$600–720 ⚒ DMC

► **A carved oak torchère,** c1890, 61in (155cm) high.
£720–800
€1,000–1,150
$1,200–1,350
⊞ ASP

Arts & Crafts Jewellery

An opal, emerald, pink tourmaline and mother-of-pearl brooch/pendant, by Arthur and Georgie Gaskin, set with a cabochon opal, early 20thC.
£1,750–2,100
€2,500–3,000
$2,950–3,550 B(NW)

A silver morse, by the Birmingham Guild of Handicraft, the stylized floral plaque flanked by fleur-de-lys motifs, Birmingham 1900, 6½in (16.5cm) wide.
£240–290 / €340–410
$400–480 DN
A morse is a clasp or fastening on a cloak.

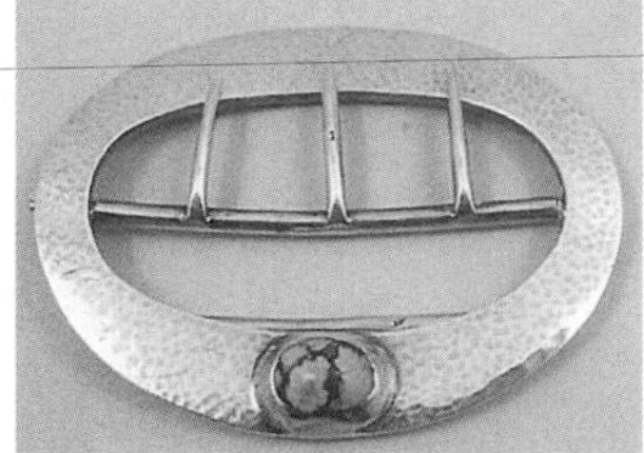

A Liberty & Co silver belt buckle, set with a turquoise matrix cabochon, Birmingham 1909, 3in (8cm) wide.
£175–210 / €250–300
$290–350 BR

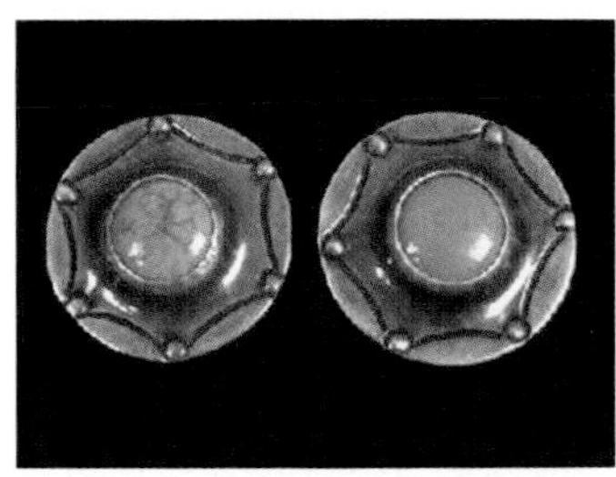

► A set of six silver buttons, by A. E. Jones, Birmingham 1903, 1¼in (3cm) diam, in a fitted case.
£200–240
€290–340
$340–400 FHF

A silver pendant, in the style of Edward Spencer, in the form of a pectoral cross, set with amethysts within chased borders of leafy grape clusters, c1915, 4in (10cm) long.
£630–700 / €910–1,000
$1,000–1,150 DAD

A necklace, by Arthur and Georgie Gaskin, set with a blister pearl surrounded by turquoise and moonstone collets, the wirework links applied with birds and leaves, signed 'G', early 20thC, in a case.
£3,300–3,950
€4,750–5,700
$5,500–6,600 B(NW)

Arthur & Georgie Gaskin

Arthur Gaskin (1862–1928) was born in Birmingham, educated at Wolverhampton Grammar School and in 1883 became a student at Birmingham School of Art, where he met his future wife, Georgie Evelyn Cave France (1866–1934). During the early years of his career Gaskin concentrated on his interest in book illustration and painting, turning towards jewellery and metalwork in the few years before his appointment as Headmaster of Birmingham School of Jewellery in 1903.

Georgie's output at college varied widely, but by the turn of the century she was concentrating purely on jewellery and its design and, from 1900, she and Arthur executed pieces together. Many of the pieces they produced were unsigned, but those pieces shown here were offered for sale by direct descent through the family and many are illustrated in the catalogue of the 1982 exhibition that Arthur and Georgie Gaskin held at the Birmingham Museum and Art Gallery.

Arts & Crafts Lighting

An Old Mission Kopper Kraft table lamp, with four slag glass panels, base plate missing, American, early 20thC, 11¾in (30cm) high.
£210–250 / €300–360
$350–420 BB(L)
Slag glass is a term used for opaque pressed glass with coloured streaks.

◄ A Hinks copper and brass lamp, the glass shade engraved with sunflowers, c1900, 37in (94cm) high.
£800–890 / €1,150–1,300
$1,350–1,500 TDG

A copper and brass wall light, modelled as flowerheads and leaves, c1900, 15in (38cm) high.
£330–390 / €420–560
$550–650 S(O)

◄ A Josef Hoffmann bronze table lamp, with later shade, Austrian, c1912, 23in (58.5cm) high.
£1,150–1,300
€1,650–1,850
$1,950–2,200 JSG

Arts & Crafts Metalware

A Walker & Hall silver-plated sugar bowl, designed by Christopher Dresser, c1880, 4½in (11.5cm) high.
£400–440 / €570–630
$670–740 ⊞ JSG

A hammered silver bowl, the foot with a pierced band, retailer's mark for 'Schwarz & Steiner', German, c1900, 11¾in (30cm) wide, 23½oz.
£1,150–1,350 / €1,650–1,950
$1,950–2,300 ⚒ DORO

A hammered silver sugar bowl, by Sibyl Dunlop, set with four cabochons and applied with Celtic knotwork, maker's mark, London 1922, 5in (12.5cm) high.
£2,700–3,000 / €3,900–4,300
$4,500–5,000 ⊞ DAD

A silver vesta box, in the style of William Burges, the sides collet-set with cabochon chrysoprase and baroque pearls, the top with enamel decoration of a bird, gilt interior, on four cushion feet, c1880, 3in (7.5cm) wide.
£940–1,100 / €1,350–1,600
$1,600–1,900 ⚒ B

Sibyl Dunlop (1889–1968)

Sibyl Dunlop was born in Scotland. After training as a jewellery designer in Brussels she established a shop in Kensington Church Street, London, specializing in silver jewellery set with a range of gems and hardstones, such as sapphires, amethyst, chalcedony, fire opals, malachite and lapis-lazuli. Enamelling featured in some pieces and Dunlop also produced silver boxes and bowls. Her work is similar to that of Dorrie Nossiter.

A pair of Liberty & Co Tudric pewter candlesticks, moulded with stylized foliage, with detachable sconces, early 20thC, 5in (12.5cm) high.
£350–420 / €500–600
$590–700 ⚒ G(L)

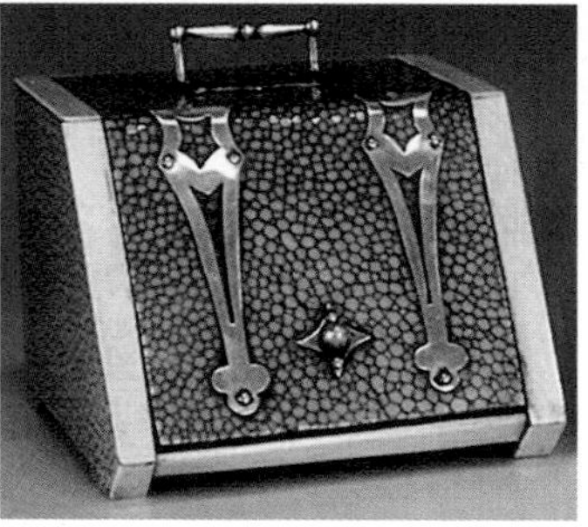
A silver-mounted shagreen box, by Hilliard & Thomason, in the form of a coal scuttle, the hinged front with silver strapwork hinges and ivory banding, damaged, Birmingham 1904, 3½in (9cm) high.
£750–900 / €1,050–1,250
$1,250–1,500 ⚒ RTo

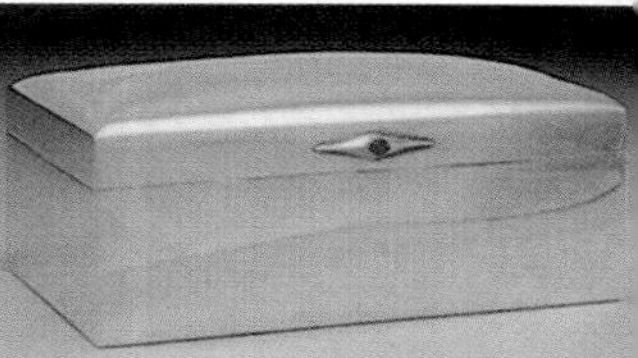
A silver box, by the Goldsmiths Company, with a gold thumbpiece and wooden interior, Swedish, Stockholm 1917, 8¾in (22cm) wide.
£460–550 / €660–790
$770–920 ⚒ BUK

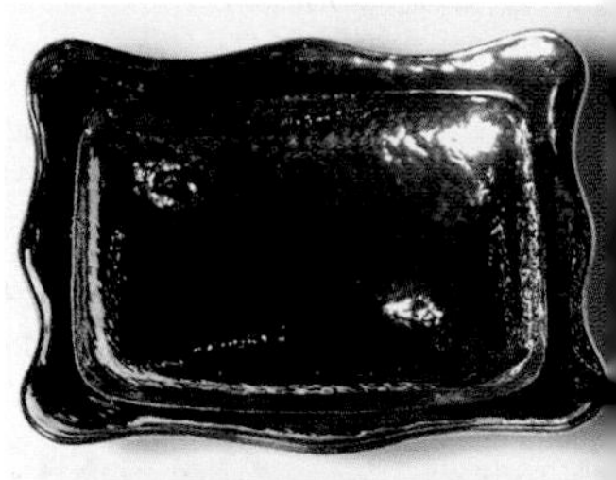
► **A silver dish,** by Omar Ramsden, London 1900, 4in (10cm) wide.
£590–650 / €850–940
$990–1,100 ⊞ SHa

A silver dish, with an embossed border of acorns and oak leaves, marked 'P. F. A.', London 1905, 11½in (29cm) diam, 16½oz.
£470–560 / €680–810
$790–940 ⚒ LAY

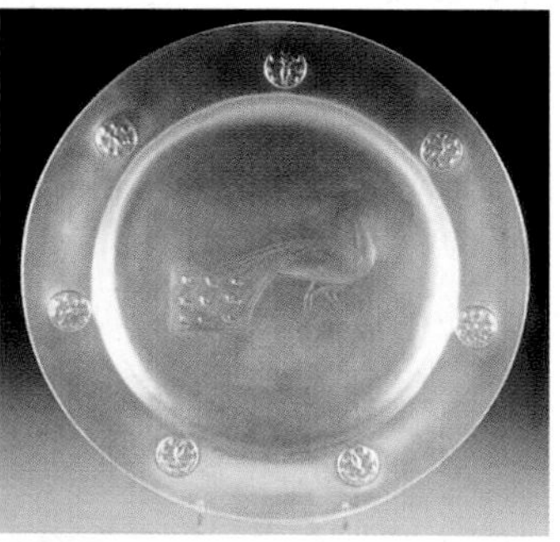
A Liberty & Co Tudric pewter dish, with embossed decoration of a peacock, the rim with embossed roundels, stamped, early 20thC, 13in (33cm) diam.
£720–860 / €1,050–1,250
$1,200–1,450 ⚒ S(O)

A repoussé copper jardinière, by John Pearson, decorated with Viking longboats and mythical creatures, incised signatures, 1894, 10½in (26.5cm) high.
£1,650–1,950 / €2,350–2,800
$2,750–3,250 ⚒ F&C

A silver-plated milk jug, by Edward Spencer for the Artificer's Guild, applied with stylized grape clusters and wirework bands, stamped, c1910, 4in (10cm) high.
£540–600 / €780–860
$900–1,000 ⊞ DAD

A Beldray copper kettle and stand, stamped, c1900, 11in (28cm) high.
£120–135 / €175–195
$200–220 ⊞ TDG

A silver pepperette, by Omar Ramsden, with rope-twist bands, signed, London 1927, 3½in (9cm) high.
£270–320 / €390–460
$450–540 ⊞ HOLL

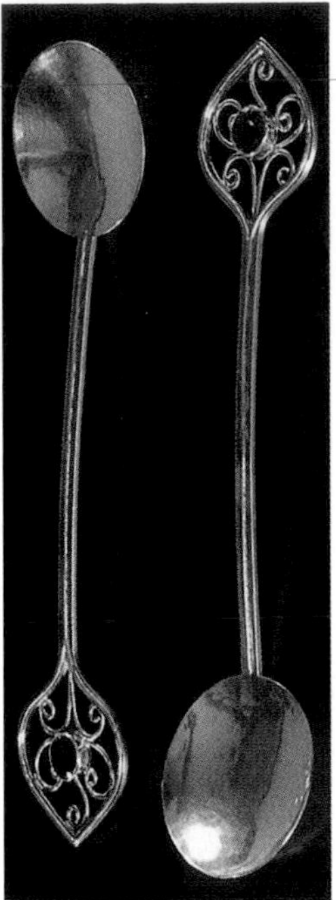

► A pair of silver spoons, by Albert Edward Bonner, the pierced finials set with amethysts within a scrolled surround, London 1909, 8¾in (22cm) long, 4oz.
£590–700 / €850–1,000
$990–1,150 ⚒ TEN

A Liberty & Co Cymric silver spoon, attributed to Oliver Baker, Birmingham 1908, 8in (20.5cm) long.
£800–880 / €1,150–1,350
$1,350–1,500 ⊞ AFD

A Newlyn copper tea caddy, with repoussé decoration, stamped, c1890, 6in (15cm) high.
£570–630 / €820–910
$950–1,050 ⊞ TDG

► A Liberty & Co Tudric vase, possibly by Archibald Knox, the quatrefoil base with enamel heart-shaped 'jewels', early 20thC, 8in (20.5cm) high.
£360–430 / €520–620
$600–720 ⚒ TMA

A hammered silver tea caddy, by Philip Frederick Alexander, the detachable cover with a ball finial applied with beads, maker's mark, London 1923, 5in (12.5cm) high.
£630–700 / €900–1,000
$1,050–1,200 ⊞ DAD

A Newlyn copper vase, with repoussé decoration, signed, c1900, 8in (20.5cm) high.
£680–750 / €980–1,100
$1,100–1,250 ⊞ SHa

Arts & Crafts Rugs & Carpets

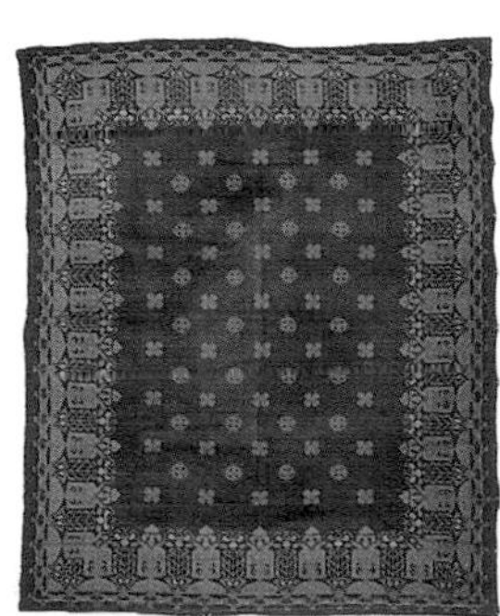

A hand-tufted carpet, European, early 20thC, 203 x 156in (575 x 396cm).
£1,900–2,250 / €2,750–3,250
$3,200–3,800 ⚒ S(O)

A carpet, Irish, Donegal, 1900–10, 120½ x 143¼in (306 x 364cm).
£1,400–1,650 / €2,000–2,350
$2,350–2,750 ⚒ S(O)

A rug, probably by C. F. A. Voysey, the central panel decorated with lotus palmettes, worn, Irish, Donegal, c1900, 98½ x 53½in (250 x 136cm).
£5,300–6,300
€7,600–9,100
$8,900–10,600 ⚒ SH

DECORATIVE ARTS

Doulton

The Doulton factory was established in 1815 in Lambeth, south London by John Doulton, who had previously been employed at the nearby Fulham Pottery. John's son Henry joined the company in 1835 and the production of stoneware items such as inkwells and ginger beer bottles was expanded to include laboratory articles, sanitary ware and drainpipes, which were sold worldwide. From c1860, Doulton began to revive earlier types of stoneware, such as copies of 18th-century vessels. The famous salt-glazed wares with blue decoration first appeared in 1862.

From 1866 the pottery was associated with the Lambeth School of Art, directed by John Sparkes. He trained George Tinworth who joined Doulton as the first resident sculptor in 1867. Tinworth enjoyed a long career at the Lambeth studio, producing a wide range of figures, vases, jugs, tankards and reliefs, as well as fountains and monumental sculptures. The international popularity of the art pottery produced at Lambeth led to the number of art potters increasing from six in 1873 to 345 in 1890, including such famous names as Frank Butler, Eliza Simmance, Arthur Barlow and his sisters Hannah and Florence Barlow.

In 1877, Henry Doulton invested in a pottery on Nile Street, Burslem, Staffordshire, to manufacture tableware and ornamental ware. Charles Noke, an experienced modeller, joined in 1889 and, convinced that the development of figure production would benefit the Doulton studio, he invited well-known independent sculptors to submit designs. The range of figures was launched during a visit by King George and Queen Mary to the factory in 1913 and it was the Queen's comments, on seeing a study of a child in a nightgown, 'isn't he a darling!' that led to naming it Darling in her honour. It was given the first number in the collection, HN1, the HN referring to Harry Nixon who was in charge of the new figure painting department. This system of numbering is still used today and the company has issued over 4,000 numbers, although these are not all new models, with some numbers being assigned to colourways.

The company was granted the Royal Warrant by Edward VII in 1901. Production continued at the Lambeth factory until 1956, after which Doulton concentrated on their activities at Burslem, where they remain today.

John Masters and Chrissie Painell

A Doulton Lambeth group, by George Tinworth, entitled 'Play Goers', c1886, 5¼in (13.5cm) high.
£5,800–6,400
€8,300–9,200
$9,700–10,700 ⊞ POW

A Doulton Lambeth barrel, by Francis E. Lee, with silver-plated cover and stand, c1878, 8in (20.5cm) diam.
£630–700 / €900–1,000
$1,050–1,200 ⊞ JE

A Doulton beaker, commemorating the Diamond Jubilee of Queen Victoria, 1897, 4in (10cm) high.
£170–190 / €240–270
$280–310 ⊞ WAA

A Royal Doulton beaker commemorating the Coronation of Edward VII, printed and inscribed mark 1902, 4in (10cm) high.
£1,750–2,100
€2,500–3,000
$2,900–3,500 ⚒ SAS

► A Doulton Lambeth stoneware bottle, with four panels bordered with laurel wreaths and surmounted by monkeys, the stopper surmounted by an owl, minor restoration, incised marks C. A. O. and Fc, 1876, 7½in (19cm) high.
£420–500
€600–720
$710–840
⚒ Bea

A Doulton Lambeth bowl, by Edith Lupton, Edward Eggleton & Letitia Rosevear, 1876, 7in (18cm) diam.
£520–580 / €750–830
$870–970 ⊞ CANI

A Doulton Lambeth stoneware bowl, with a silver-plated rim, decorated with incised stylized foliate, scroll and flowerhead motifs and borders, impressed marks, inscribed with initials FEB and RB for Florence Barlow and Rosina Brown, 1879, 10¾in (27.5cm) diam.
£110–130 / €160–190
$185–220 ⚒ TRM

A Royal Doulton stoneware bowl, by Mark V. Marshall, supported on three winged lions, impressed factory mark and 'Art Union of London', c1902, 9in (23cm) high.
£900–1,050
€1,300–1,500
$1,500–1,750 S(O)

The Art Union of London was an organization whose members purchased the right to take part in an annual draw. The prizes ranged from paintings which had been exhibited at the Royal Academy to smaller pieces including Parian wares.

A Royal Doulton sculpture of Beethoven, by Richard Garbe, No. 6 of limited edition of 25, crazing, 1933, 24¾in (63cm) high.
£2,700–3,200
€3,900–4,600
$4,500–5,300 B

► **A Doulton Lambeth mantel clock,** in the form of a moonflask, c1900, 12in (30.5cm) high.
£770–920 / €1,100–1,300
$1,300–1,550 BWL

◄ **A pair of Doulton Lambeth candlesticks,** by Francis E. Lee, assisted by Fanny Clark and Mary Butterton, 1876, 6in (15cm) high.
£720–800 / €1,000–1,150
$1,200–1,350 CANI

A pair of Doulton candlesticks, by Frank Butler, c1885, 8in (20.5cm) high.
£680–750 / €980–1,100
$1,150–1,300 HTE

◄ **A Royal Doulton Kingsware clock case,** by Charles Noke, decorated with a friar, printed mark and impressed signature, c1913, 7½in (19cm) high.
£180–210 / €260–300
$300–350 DMC

A Royal Doulton dinner service, by Frank Brangwyn, comprising 29 pieces, c1930.
£175–210 / €250–300
$290–350 BR

A Doulton Burslem tripartite dish, printed with Norfolk pattern, printed mark, early 20thC, 12in (30.5cm) wide.
£430–520 / €620–750
$720–870 GAK

A Royal Doulton Lambeth salt-glazed stoneware spirit flask, modelled as Lloyd George, impressed marks, c1910, 8in (20.5cm) high.
£175–210 / €250–300
$290–350 G(L)

A Royal Doulton Toby ash pot, by Harry Simeon, 1924–27, 4in (10cm) high.
£200–230 / €290–330
$340–390 CANI

◄ **A Royal Doulton figure,** entitled 'The Bather', model No. HN687, 1924–49, 7¾in (19.5cm) high.
£820–980
€1,200–1,400
$1,400–1,650 G(L)

HN numbers

The HN numbers on Royal Doulton figures refer to Harry Nixon, the first manager of the factory's Figure Painting Department. HN1 is 'Darling', first issued in 1912.

A Royal Doulton figure, by Leslie Harradine, entitled 'Marietta', model No. HN1446, base damaged, printed and painted marks, 1931–49, 8¼in (21cm) high.
£350–420 / €550–600
$590–700 WW

A Royal Doulton figure, by Leslie Harradine, entitled 'Windflower', model No. HN1920, minor damage, printed and painted marks, 1939–49, 11in (28cm) high.
£820–980 / €1,200–1,400
$1,400–1,650 SWO

► **A pair of Royal Doulton figures of Jack and Jill,** model Nos. HN2060 and 2061, impressed mark, 1950s, 5½in (14cm) high.
£130–155
€185–220
$220–260 NSal

A Royal Doulton stoneware ice cream drum, the inner compartment and base with a wooden cover, impressed mark, c1910, 10¾in (27.5cm) high.
£130–155 / €185–220
$220–260 SWO

A Doulton Lambeth lemonade jug, by Louisa E. Edwards, assisted by Mary Ann Thomson, Elisa Bowen and Kate Everett, c1878, 9½in (24cm) high.
£690–770 / €990–1,100
$1,150–1,300 CANI

A Doulton metal-mounted stoneware jug, by George Tinworth, incised and applied with scrolls, beading and stiff leaves, marked, 1879, 9½in (24cm) high.
£480–570 / €690–820
$800–960 S(O)

A Doulton Lambeth simulated blackjack water jug, the silver rim with presentation inscription, minor repair, c1893, 7½in (19cm) high.
£50–60 / €75–90
$85–100 TRM
A blackjack is a tarred-leather tankard or jug.

A pair of Royal Doulton ewers, with stylized floral decoration, impressed marks, c1910, 11½in (29cm) high.
£370–440 / €530–630
$620–740 WL

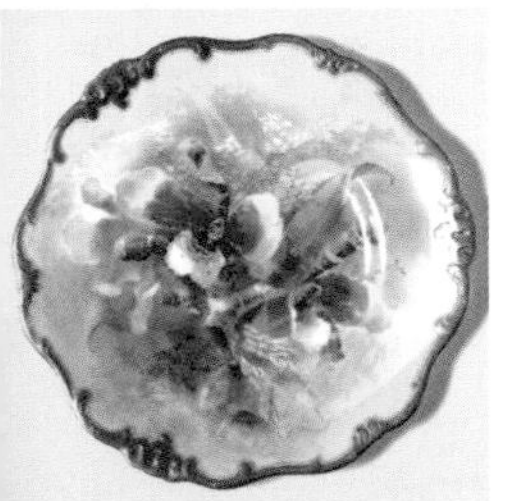

A Royal Doulton plate, by David Dewsberry, decorated with orchids, 1905, 9½in (24cm) diam.
£400–450 / €580–650
$670–750 JE

A Doulton Lambeth faïence vase, painted with flowers, monogrammed 'MMA', 1879, 7in (18cm) high.
£270–320 / €390–460
$450–530 G(L)

A Royal Doulton jug, commemorating the Coronation of King George V and Queen Mary, with embossed cameos and floral decoration, 1911, 10in (25.5cm) high.
£165–195 / €240–280
$280–330 AMB

A Doulton tankard, decorated by E. Violet Hayward with the head of Bacchus, 1929, 8in (20.5cm) high.
£270–300 / €390–430
$450–500 CANI

◄ **A Doulton Lambeth water filter,** designed by John Broad, assisted by Alice Cooke, decorated with bands of foliage, 1884, 15½in (39.5cm) high.
£300–360 / €430–520
$500–600 CGC

Sets/pairs

Unless otherwise stated, any description which refers to 'a set' or 'a pair' includes a guide price for the entire set or the pair, even though the illustration may show only a single item.

► **A Doulton Lambeth faïence vase,** by Emily Gilman, c1880, 14¼in (36cm) high.
£2,000–2,200
€2,900–3,200
$3,350–3,700 POW

A Royal Doulton Lambeth stoneware jug, 1921–23, 7in (18cm) high.
£110–125 / €160–180
$185–210 PGO

A pair of Doulton stoneware vases, by Florence Barlow, each with four roundels decorated with deer, 1877, 10in (25.5cm) high.
£1,400–1,650
€2,000–2,350
$2,350–2,750 LAY

A Doulton Lambeth stoneware tyg, relief-decorated with flowers and motifs, with a silver collar, incised mark for Mary Ann Thomson and 'F. S.', maker's mark CP, silver Sheffield 1877, 6½in (16.5cm) high.
£390–470 / €560–670
$660–790 MCA

◄ **A Doulton Lambeth silver-mounted tea canister,** inscribed 'honest tea is the best policy', c1885, 4in (10cm) high.
£620–690 / €890–990
$1,000–1,150 POW

A Doulton Lambeth Silicon ware amphora vase, by Edith Lupton, incised and enamelled with three cusped panels of flowers, artist's signature and painter's initials 'R. W.' and 'M. D.', 1885, 10¾in (27.5cm) high, on a wrought-metal tripod.
£230–270 / €330–390
$380–450 G(L)

Silicon ware was mainly produced from 1880 to 1912, although examples exist up to 1930. It consists of a very hard high-fired stoneware body in light brown and blue, covered in a barely perceptible matt glaze known as 'smear'. Wares are usually decorated with applied beads, rosettes and medallions, sometimes by major Doulton artists such as Eliza Simmance, Florence Barlow and Edith Lupton. Silicon ware is currently less sought after than other ranges and so is relatively inexpensive to collect.

A pair of Doulton Slater patent vases, with fruiting foliate and C-scroll decoration, monogrammed 'J. H.', c1900, 11¾in (30cm) high.
£150–180 / €220–260
$250–300 ⚒ EH

Slater patent was a decorative process in which lace and other materials were impressed into the ware.

A Doulton Holbein ware vase, by George Fernyhough, painted with a man riding a mare and leading another through a woodland, signed, c1900, 25¼in (64cm) high.
£3,500–4,200
€5,000–6,000
$5,900–7,100 ⚒ B

Invented in 1895 by C. J. Noke, Holbein ware has underglaze painting in coloured slips, which gives an impressive depth and canvas-like quality to the body of this vase. The artist George Fernyhough was renowned for his horse subjects.

A Royal Doulton vase, c1902, 7in (18cm) high.
£140–160 / €200–230
$240–270 ⊞ PGO

A pair of Royal Doulton spill vases, by Bessie Newberry, 1906–11, 7in (18cm) high.
£200–230 / €290–330
$340–390 ⊞ CANI

A Royal Doulton vase, decorated with flowers, 1906–11, 8½in (21.5cm) high.
£180–200 / €260–290
$300–330 ⊞ PGO

A Royal Doulton earthenware vase, decorated with a woodland scene, some damage, printed factory mark, early 20thC, 8¼in (21cm) high.
£110–130 / €160–190
$185–220 ⚒ FHF

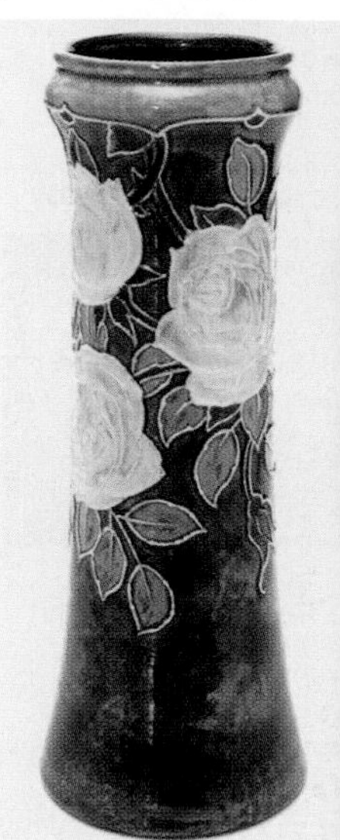

A Royal Doulton vase, by Christine Abbott, 1912–20, 13in (33cm) high.
£200–230 / €290–330
$340–390 ⊞ PGO

A Royal Doulton Sung vase, c1925, 7in (18cm) high.
£1,700–1,900
€2,450–2,750
$2,850–3,200 ⊞ POW

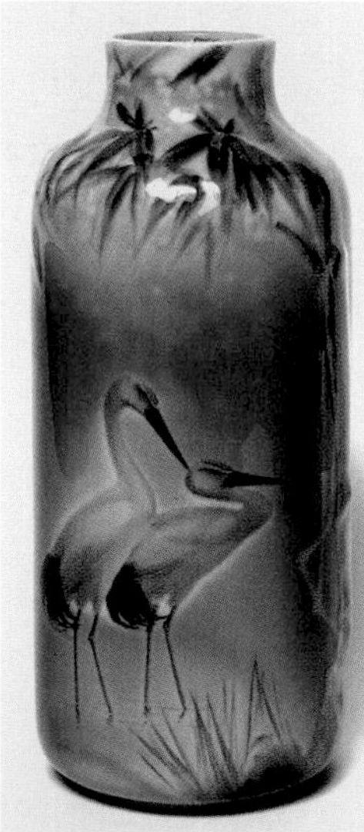

◄ A Royal Doulton Titanian ware vase, by Harry Allen, c1915, 10½in (26.5cm) high.
£2,500–2,800 / €3,600–4,000
$4,200–4,700 ⊞ POW

Titanian ware, produced from 1915 to 1930, used titanium oxide in the glaze to give a blue colouration, ranging in tone from pale grey to dark royal blue. It was used to provide a background for fine porcelain pieces decorated by artists such as Harry Allen and F. Henri.

► A Royal Doulton Chang vase, by Fred More, c1925, 9in (23cm) diam.
£3,400–3,800
€4,900–5,500
$5,700–6,400
⊞ POW

Imitation Chinese glazes

The Burslem studio at Doulton began to experiment with the production of high-temperature glazes from the late 1890s, in imitation of early Chinese wares. The Sung range, introduced in 1920, developed from these flambé glazes. Chang ware, identified by its crackled surface formed from thick, richly coloured glazes that have run and reacted against each other, was produced in relatively large numbers from 1925 until WWII.

Martin Brothers

A Martin Brothers clock case, 1875, 16in (40.5cm) high.
£11,300–12,500
€16,300–18,000
$19,000–21,000 ⊞ POW

A Martin Brothers jardinière, painted with pomegranates and leaf scrolls, incised marks, 1896, 9in (23cm) diam.
£730–870 / €1,050–1,250
$1,200–1,450 ⚒ BWL

A Martin Brothers stoneware vase, decorated with medieval musicians, incised mark, 1899, 9½in (24cm) high.
£2,150–2,600
€3,100–3,750
$3,600–4,350 ⚒ S(O)

► **A Martin Brothers vase,** decorated with fantastic birds among grass, 1903, 7in (18cm) high.
£5,400–6,000
€7,800–8,600
$9,100–10,100 ⊞ POW

◄ **A Martin Brothers ewer,** moulded with grotesque smiling faces, incised mark, 1903, 6in (15cm) high.
£2,800–3,350
€4,000–4,800
$4,700–5,600 ⚒ GAK

► **A Martin Brothers stoneware figure of a seated woman,** incised mark, 1880, 6½in (16.5cm) high.
£420–500 / €600–720
$710–840 ⚒ S(O)

A Martin Brothers plate, decorated with scrolling flowers and foliage, 1886, 10in (25.5cm) diam.
£3,050–3,400 / €4,400–4,900
$5,100–5,700 ⊞ POW

A Martin Brothers stoneware teapot, with a copper cover and spout, incised with flowers, stamped mark, c1890, 6in (15cm) high.
£520–620 / €750–890
$870–1,050 ⚒ AH

A pair of Martin Brothers salt-glazed stoneware vases, decorated with carved birds, inscribed marks, 1883, 11¾in (30cm) high.
£7,100–8,500
€10,200–12,200
$11,900–14,300 ⚒ S(NY)

◄ **A Martin Brothers stoneware vase,** incised and painted with beasts and scrolling foliage, kiln damage, inscribed marks, 1892, 9½in (24cm) high.
£1,550–1,850
€2,200–2,650
$2,600–3,100 ⚒ Bea

A Martin Brothers posy vase, incised marks, 1907, 3¼in (8.5cm) high.
£470–560 / €680–810
$790–950 ⚒ G(L)

A Martin Brothers stoneware vase, with sgraffito decoration of spine-backed fish, an eel and jelly fish, inscribed mark, 1908, 9in (23cm) high.
£1,200–1,450
€1,750–2,100
$2,000–2,400 ⚒ BR

DECORATIVE ARTS

Moorcroft

A Moorcroft ashtray, with silver-plated mounts, decorated with Pomegranate pattern, with a 'turn-over' ashtray, impressed marks, c1920, 4¾in (12cm) high.
£350–420 / €500–600
$590–700 G(L)

A Moorcroft tobacco bowl and cover, decorated with Cornflower pattern, early 20thC, 5½in (14cm) diam.
£590–700 / €850–1,000
$990–1,150 WilP

► A Moorcroft jardinière, decorated with Wisteria pattern, c1920, 13in (33cm) high.
£2,250–2,500 / €3,250–3,600
$3,800–4,200 JSG

A pair of Moorcroft candlesticks, decorated with fruit and flowerheads, impressed Burslem marks and painted initials, c1915, 3¼in (8.5cm) high.
£400–480 / €580–690
$670–810 G(L)

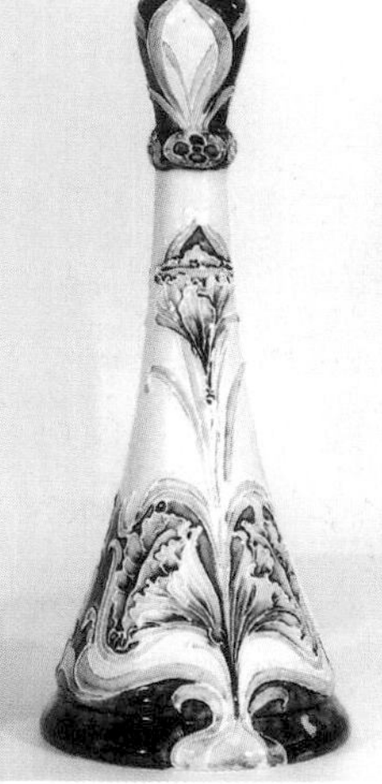

A Moorcroft Florian ware lamp base, tube-lined with irises, c1900, 12in (30.5cm) high.
£820–960 / €1,200–1,400
$1,400–1,650 AH

A Walter Moorcroft tankard, commemorating the coronation of King Edward VII and Queen Alexandra, 1902, 9½in (24cm) high.
£300–360 / €430–520
$500–600 WilP

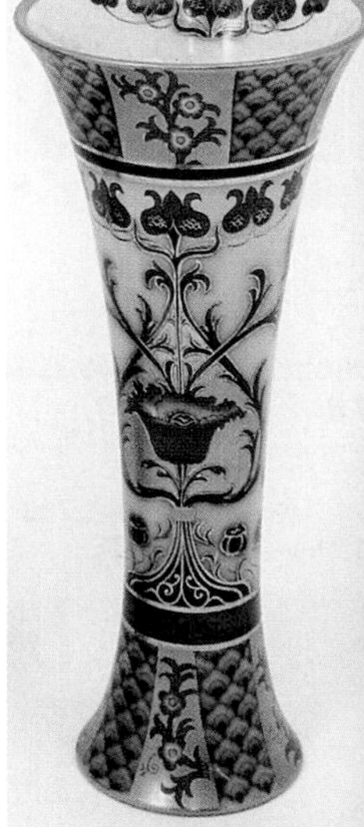

► A pair of Moorcroft Macintyre Aurelian ware vases, decorated with floral panels and segmented bands, with gilt highlights, printed mark, c1904, 10in (25.5cm) high.
£1,300–1,550
€1,900–2,250
$2,200–2,600
G(L)

A Moorcroft vase, decorated with Orchid pattern, impressed and painted marks, c1920, 10¾in (27cm) high.
£1,650–1,950
€2,350–2,800
$2,750–3,250 S(O)

A Moorcroft stem vase, decorated with Moonlit Blue pattern, signed 'William Macintyre', c1920, 8in (20.5cm) high.
£1,700–1,900
€2,450–2,700
$2,850–3,200 MPC

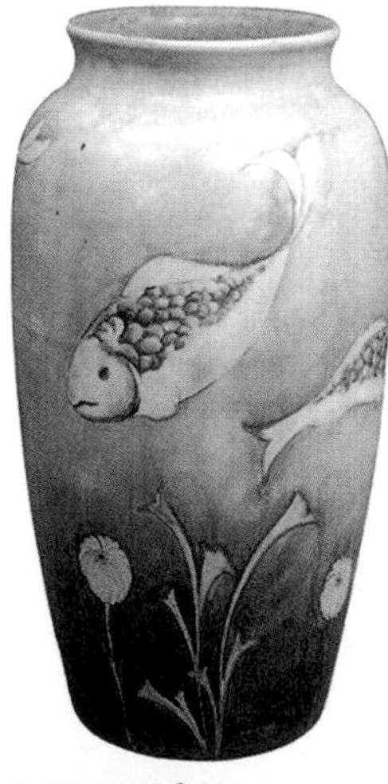

A Moorcroft vase, decorated with Fish pattern, painted signature, dated 1931, 18¼in (46.5cm) high.
£3,650–4,350
€5,200–6,200
$6,100–7,300 DD

A Moorcroft flambé vase, decorated with Anemone pattern, c1930, 5½in (14cm) high.
£670–750 / €960–1,100
$1,100–1,250 PGO

Art Nouveau Ceramics

An Amphora vase, Bohemian, c1910, 18in (45.5cm) high.
£450–500 / €650–720
$760–840 ⊞ DSG

\ Holland Pottery vase, ›y Jan Willem Mijulief, ›utch, Utrecht, 1893–1920, 4in (35.5cm) high.
:740–830 / €1,050–1,200
›1,250–1,400 ⊞ HTE

Minton tile panel, y Léon V. Solon, relief- ioulded, depicting a iaiden against a back- round of rhododendron ossom and leaves, ipressed factory iarks, 1889, 18 x 12in 5.5 x 30.5cm).
5,900–7,100
8,500–10,200
9,900–11,900 ⚒ B

A pair of Mettlach vases, German, 1904, 15in (38cm) high.
£1,500–1,700
€2,100–2,450
$2,500–2,850 ⊞ POW

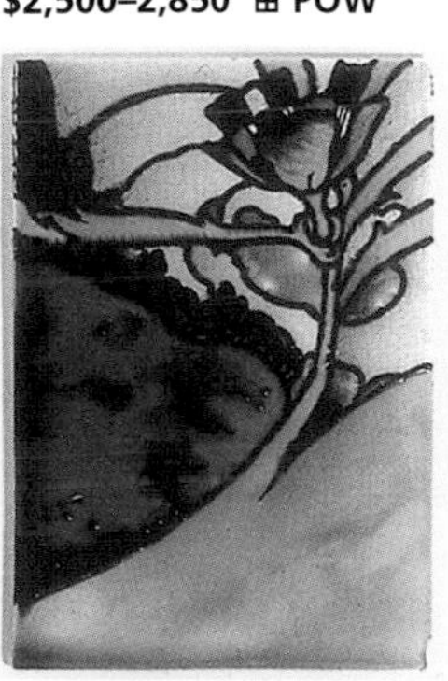

A Minton ceramic tile, tube-lined with a stylized plant, minor damage, 1901, 15 x 10in (38 x 25.5cm).
£760–910 / €1,100–1,300
$1,250–1,500 ⚒ B

◄ A Bretby jardinière and pedestal, with applied cabochons, impressed marks, early 20thC, 37½in (95.5cm) high.
£560–670 / €810–960
$940–1,100 ⚒ BB(L)

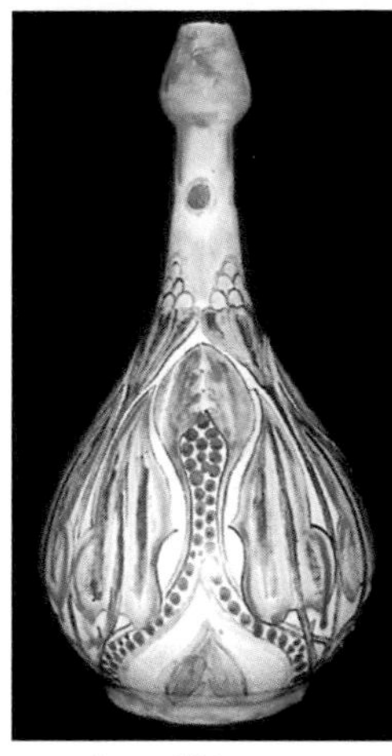

A Della Robbia pottery vase, painted with stylized flowers and foliage, marked, late 19thC, 13¾in (35cm) high.
£1,200–1,450
€1,750–2,100
$2,000–2,400 ⚒ MAR

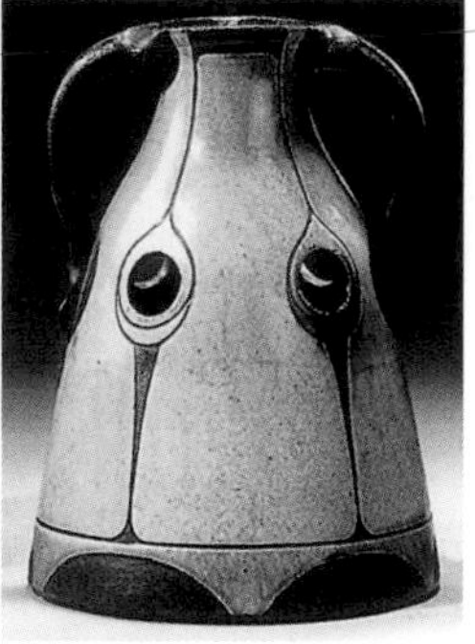

A Brouwer earthenware two-handled vase, with four pierced holes, stamped factory mark, Dutch, 1913, 7¾in (19.5cm) high.
£1,650–1,950
€2,350–2,800
$2,750–3,250 ⚒ S(Am)

A Hutschenreuther plate, with silver overlay, German, c1900, 8in (20.5cm) diam.
£250–280 / €360–400
$420–470 ⊞ ANO

Minton

Established in 1793 by Thomas Minton, the firm's reputation was boosted in the 19th century by the success of the new majolica glazes. In 1835, Minton produced the first pattern book of encaustic tiles which was highly praised by Augustus Pugin. Pugin designed encaustic and majolica tiles for the company from around 1840 until the early 1850s.

Minton's output was strongly influenced by the Aesthetic Movement and Art Nouveau. Minton, Hollins & Co was established as a subsidiary of Minton in 1845 and transfer-printed tiles were produced for the walls and floors of the Houses of Parliament. In 1871, Minton set up an art pottery, also producing tiles, in Kensington Gore, London. The design director was W. S. Coleman and designers included Dr Christopher Dresser, John Moyr Smith, Henry Stacy Marks, E. J. Poynter, Walter Crane and Hannah Barlow, who later joined Doulton. Coleman also produced a series of aesthetic-style wall plaques.

In 1875, fire broke out in the factory and it never reopened. However, this did not signal the end of the production of Minton Art Pottery. In 1897, Léon V. Solon was employed as an artist and art director and a range of Art Nouveau vases was produced, followed by the Secessionist wares inspired by Continental Art Nouveau, designed around 1902 to 1904 by Solon and John Wadsworth.

◀ **A Minton Secessionist bowl,** tube-lined with flowers, printed factory marks, c1900, 8¼in (21cm) diam.
£140–165
€200–240
$240–280
PFK

A Pilkington's Lancastrian vase, by William D. Mycroft, decorated with Tudor roses and heart motifs, printed and impressed marks, 1907, 5in (13cm) high.
£350–420 / €500–600
$590–700 B(W)

A Rookwood vase, by Sallie Coyne, with silver overlay, restored, American, 1900, 8½in (21.5cm) high.
£2,250–2,700
€3,250–3,900
$3,750–4,500 TREA

A Royal Worcester Sabrina ware vase, c1910, 11in (28cm) diam.
£630–700 / €910–1,000
$1,050–1,200 DSG

◀ **A Villeroy & Boch ceramic tray,** decorated with water lilies, German, c1900, 20in (51cm) wide.
£450–500 / €650–720
$760–840 JSG

▶ **A Zsolnay acid-etched earthenware jardinière,** with an iridescent glaze, impressed factory marks, Hungarian, c1900, 13¼in (33.5cm) high.
£7,800–9,400 / €11,200–13,500
$13,100–15,800 S(NY)

A Zsolnay lustre pot and cover, at fault, Hungarian, 1907–10, 4in (10cm) high.
£450–500 / €650–720
$760–840 ANO

Zsolnay (Hungarian, 1862 to present)

- Established at Pêcs, Hungary in 1862, producing stonewares decorated in traditional Hungarian styles, this factory became a leading producer of Art Nouveau ceramics in eastern Europe
- From the 1870s it produced wares in Islamic or Italian neo-Renaissance styles
- After the appointment in 1893 of a new artistic director, Vinsce Wartha, the factory began to make wares of organic form with iridescent glazes in the style of Clément Massier
- Vases, often thickly potted, were sometimes decorated with low relief-moulded detail. Motifs included tree silhouettes, female figures and dark ruby skies
- Other wares were often of a somewhat pod-like naturalistic form, with moulded leaves and branches picked out in contrasting iridescent colours
- All pieces are marked with variations of a medallion showing the five church towers of Pêcs

A ceramic charger, Austrian, c1910, 11in (28cm) diam.
£180–200 / €260–290
$300–340 ASP

DECORATIVE ARTS

Art Nouveau Figures & Busts

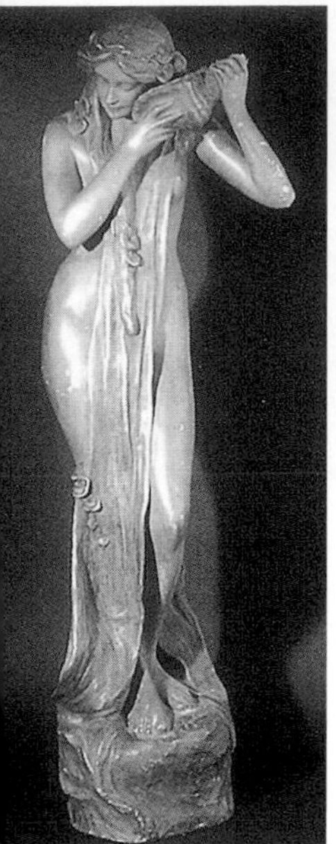

∖ Goldscheider earthenware figure of a maiden, holding conch shell, slight amage, impressed marks, igned, Austrian, c1900, 6in (66cm) high.
490–590 / €710–850
820–990 WW

◀ **A Goldscheider terracotta bust of a young woman,** impressed marks, signed, Austrian, c1900, 21in (53.5cm) high.
£700–840 / €1,000–1,200
$1,200–1,400 TEN

▶ **A bronze bust,** by Emmanuel Villanis, entitled 'Moe', inscribed and stamped marks, French, early 20thC, 10¾in (27cm) high.
£1,550–1,850
€2,250–2,650
$2,600–3,100 S(O)

Goldscheider

Founded in Vienna by Friedrich Goldscheider, the company produced ceramic and stone reproductions of classical figures from local museums. By the 1920s, under the direction of Marcel and Walter Goldscheider, designs in bronze and ivory by sculptors Bruno Zach and Josef Lorenzl were produced in brightly-painted porcelain. African-inspired pottery wall masks were also produced to Lorenzl's designs.

The pre-WWI mark is a rectangular pad featuring a kneeling Greek figure. Pieces produced after 1918 have a transfer-printed mark: 'Goldscheider Wien. Made in Austria'. Arthur Goldscheider ran the company's Parisian foundry, producing pieces by sculptors such as Pierre L. Faguays under the 'La Stele' foundry seal. Marcel Goldscheider moved to England in 1939 and manufacturers such as Myott, Son & Co produced figures for him. Myott's wares have the mark 'Goldscheider. Made in England'. Marcel established a pottery in Hanley, Staffordshire c1946, where he produced new models in earthenware and china until 1959. Pieces made there bear a signature mark.

DECORATIVE ARTS

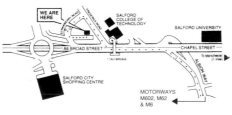

A Daum *pâte-de-verre* figure of a mermaid, by Almaric Walter, French, c1890, 5¼in (13.5cm) high.
£6,200–6,900
€8,900–9,900
$10,400–11,600 ⊞ MI
Almaric Walter was chief artist at the Daum factory for many years.

◄ A patinated-metal *torchère*, modelled as a nymph among reeds, fitted for electricity, on a marble base, early 20thC, 55in (139.5cm) high.
£950–1,100
€1,350–1,600
$1,600–1,900 ⚒ NOA

► A Goldscheider painted and bronzed terracotta bust of young girl, by Montenave, the hairband set with glass stones, some restoration, Austrian, c1905, 26½in (67cm) high.
£1,500–1,800
€2,150–2,600
$2,500–3,000 ⚒ BUK

Art Nouveau Furniture

A bentwood bed, by Thonet or Kohn, restored, Austrian, Vienna, c1900, 53½in (136cm) high.
£900–1,050 / €1,100–1,300
$1,500–1,750 ⚒ DORO

A revolving bookcase, by Edwards & Sons, London, with marquetry panels, labelled, c1900, 15in (38cm) wide.
£810–900 / €1,150–1,300
$1,350–1,500 ⊞ DAD

A mahogany and marquetry display cabinet, the glazed doors with stained glass and floral marquetry panels, c1900, 43in (109cm) wide
£1,500–1,800
€2,150–2,600
$2,500–3,000 ⚒ B

A rosewood-veneered secretaire cabinet, by Louis Majorelle, with a leather-covered top, the back panel lined with pleated silk, the fall-front inlaid with precious woods and enclosing shelves and small drawers, restored, French, c1900, 35½in (90cm) wide.
£9,800–11,700
€14,100–16,800
$16,500–19,600 ⚒ DORO

A mahogany bowfronted display cabinet, inlaid with mother-of-pearl, c1905, 41½in (105.5cm) wide.
£950–1,100
€1,350–1,600
$1,600–1,900 ⚒ JM

► A mahogany and inlaid bowfronted display cabinet, by Shapland & Petter, c1905, 53in (134.5cm) wide.
£7,500–8,300
€10,800–12,000
$12,600–13,900 ⊞ MTay

◄ An inlaid mahogany cabinet, the leaded and stained glass doors enclosing shelves, the lower section with an open shelf above two cupboards, c1900, 43in (109cm) wide.
£640–770 / €920–1,100
$1,100–1,300 ⚒ WW

A walnut music cabinet the carved panelled doors enclosing four shelves, late 19thC, 21in (53.5cm) wide.
£320–380 / €460–550
$540–640 ⚒ DMC

A bentwood armchair, by Thonet, Model No. 4, with a later canework seat, restored, impressed mark, Austrian, Vienna, c1850.
£490–590 / €710–850
$820–990 DORO

► **A set of six mahogany chairs,** with padded leather cresting rails above flower- and tendril-carved splat backs, above leather drop-in seats, c1900.
£470–560 / €680–810
$790–940 BR

A Secessionist oak and leather chair, c1900.
£420–500 / €600–720
$710–840 S(O)

A mahogany elbow chair, the cresting rail inlaid with floral decoration, c1900.
£540–650 / €780–940
$910–1,100 BWL

Further reading

Miller's Art Nouveau & Art Deco Buyer's Guide, Miller's Publications, 2001

► **A J. & J. Kohn stained beechwood armchair,** by Koloman Moser, Model No. 413, minor damage, Austrian, designed 1901.
£5,700–6,800
€8,200–9,800
$9,600–11,400 DORO

A set of four J. & J. Kohn stained bentwood armchairs, by Gustav Siegel, Austrian, c1900.
£380–450 / €550–650
$640–760 S(O)

An Edwardian oak box seat, with pokerwork motifs, the hinged seat on a carved front and bracket feet.
£590–700 / €850–1,000
$990–1,150 PFK

A pair of Meroni & Fossati stained wood armchairs, by Carlo Bugatti, the *faux* leather backrests held by sisal stringing, with geometric and stylized floral pewter inlays, slight damage, signed, Italian, Milan, 1912–18.
£6,500–7,800
€9,300–11,200
$10,900–13,100 DORO

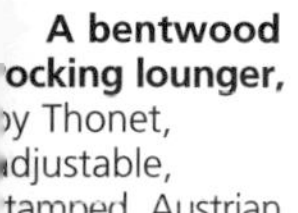

A bentwood rocking lounger, by Thonet, adjustable, stamped, Austrian, Vienna, c1900.
£210–250
€300–360
$350–420
B(Kn)

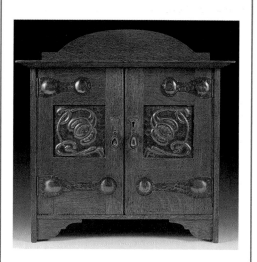

A lady's rosewood writing desk, by Louis Majorelle, impressed mark, French, c1900, 44½in (113cm) wide.
£6,100–7,300
€8,800–10,500
$10,200–12,200 ⚒ S(NY)

A blackwood desk, set with a copper repoussé panel depicting gumtrees, Australian, c1900, 36¼in (92cm) wide.
£2,650–3,150
€3,800–4,550
$4,450–5,300 ⚒ SHSY

A lady's mahogany writing desk, possibly by Shapland & Petter, with a raised shelf above an inset leather writing surface, with two frieze drawers, c1905, 32¾in (83cm) wide.
£640–770 / €920–1,100
$1,100–1,300 ⚒ B

A marquetry three-tier *étagère*, by Emile Gallé, each tier inlaid with a bird and foliage, marked, restorations, French, c1905, 33½in (85cm) wide.
£2,150–2,550
€3,100–3,700
$3,600–4,300 ⚒ S(O)

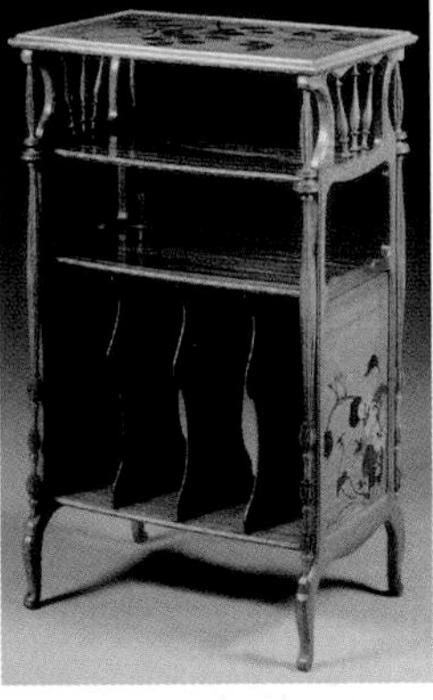

A walnut and marquetry *étagère*, by Louis Majorelle, the top and sides inlaid with foliage, signed, French, c1905, 23¼in (59cm) wide.
£4,550–5,500
€6,600–7,800
$7,600–9,100 ⚒ S(O)

◄ A fruitwood and marquetry mirror, by Emille Gallé, signed, French, c1900, 20in (51cm) wide.
£6,400–7,700
€9,200–11,100
$10,800–12,900 ⚒ S(NY)

► A mahogany and brass mirror, Nancy School, French, c1900, 32in (81.5cm) high.
£530–590
€760–850
$890–990 ⊞ MI

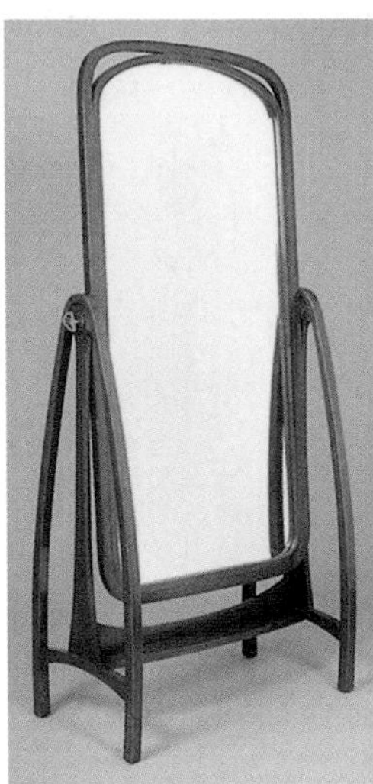

A stained beechwood cheval mirror, by Thonet, Model No. 4, with bevelled glass, Austrian, Vienna, c1904, 70in (178cm) high.
£2,400–2,850
€3,450–4,100
$4,050–4,800 ⚒ DORO

An oak hanging shelf, with bronze panels, c1910, 27in (68.5cm) wide.
£720–800 / €1,050–1,200
$1,200–1,350 ⊞ ASP

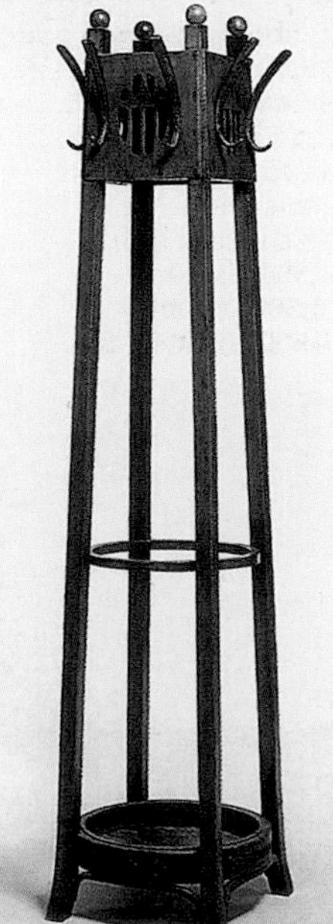

◄ A J. & J. Kohn beech hat and coat stand, by Josef Hoffmann, with plywood panels, Austrian, c1908, 79½in (202cm) high.
£820–980 / €1,200–1,400
$1,400–1,650 ⚒ B

A bentwood luggage stand, by Thonet, upholstered with *faux* leather, some wear, Austrian, Vienna, c1888, 31¼in (79.5cm) wide.
£1,150–1,350 / €1,650–1,950
$1,950–2,300 ⚒ DORO

A bentwood newspaper stand, by Thonet, some wear, Austrian, Vienna, c1904, 21¼in (54cm) wide.
£570–680 / €820–980
$960–1,150 ⚒ DORO

A Shapland & Petter mahogany three-piece bedroom suite, by Maurice Adams, comprising a dressing table, wardrobe and chest of drawers, inlaid with mother-of-pearl and fruitwood, stamped, c1900, wardrobe 71¾in (182.5cm) wide.
£15,300–17,400 / €22,000–25,000
$26,000–29,000 ⊞ MI

A bentwood centre table, Austrian, 1850–1900, 50½in (128.5cm) wide.
£3,250–3,900 / €4,700–5,600
$5,500–6,600 ⚒ NOA

A beechwood and marquetry occasional table, by Emile Gallé, the top with Hungarian ash and rosewood inlay of a magpie and foliage, signed, French, early 20thC, 24½in (62cm) wide.
£3,700–4,400 / €5,300–6,300
$6,200–7,400 ⚒ S(O)

► A fruitwood marquetry and gilt-bronze two-tier lily pad table, by Louis Majorelle, minor imperfections, marked, French, c1900, 19¾in (50cm) wide.
£6,200–7,400 / €8,900–10,600
$10,400–12,400 ⚒ S(Am)

Shapland & Petter

Shapland & Petter was established in Barnstaple, Devon in 1864. The firm was a major manufacturer of furniture in the Arts & Crafts and Art Nouveau styles, supplying retailers such as Liberty and Waring & Gillow. The workers were highly skilled, serving seven-year apprenticeships and attending classes at the Barnstaple School of Art. The company's archives are deposited at the Museum of Barnstaple and North Devon.

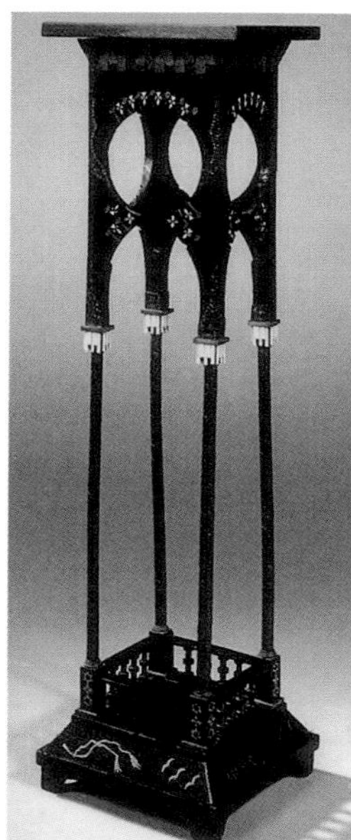

An ebonized wood and fruitwood pedestal table, by Carlo Bugatti, decorated with ivory, pewter inlay and chased copper mounts, restored, Italian, c1900, 38½in (98cm) high.
£4,500–5,400
€6,500–7,800
$7,600–9,100 ⚒ S(Am)

An oak six-piece salon suite, by Louis Majorelle, comprising a settee, table, two armchairs and two side chairs, upholstered in leather, French, c1900, settee 46½in (118cm) wide.
£9,300–11,100 / €13,400–16,000
$15,600–18,700 ⚒ S(NY)

A stained beechwood five-piece salon suite, by Thonet, comprising a settee, two armchairs and two chairs, upholstered in leather, restored, impressed marks, Austrian, Vienna, c1904, settee 50½in (128cm) wide.
£2,300–2,750 / €3,300–3,950
$3,850–4,600 ⚒ DORO

A nest of four fruitwood and marquetry tables, by Emile Gallé, signed, French, c1900, 29in (73.5cm) high.
£6,800–8,200 / €9,800–11,800
$11,400–13,700 ⚒ S(NY)

► A cast-iron and marble table, by Hector Guimard, damaged, French, c1900, 21in (53.5cm) diam.
£5,700–6,800
€8,200–9,800
$9,600–11,400
⚒ S(NY)

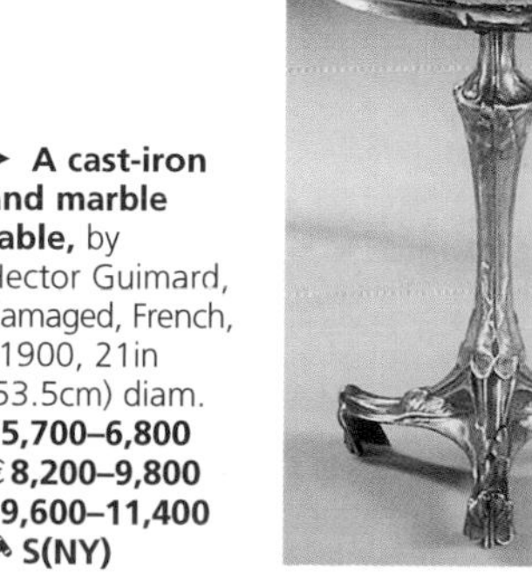

DECORATIVE ARTS

Art Nouveau Glass

A Burgun & Schverer cameo glass vase, with wheel-carved and enamel decoration, signed, French, c1900, 9in (23cm) high.
£4,300–5,100
€6,200–7,300
$7,200–8,600 ⚒ S(NY)

A Daum silver-mounted glass scent bottle, with etched and enamelled decoration, signed, hallmarked, French, Nancy, c1895, 5in (12.5cm) high.
£3,450–3,800
€4,950–5,500
$5,800–6,400 ⊞ MI

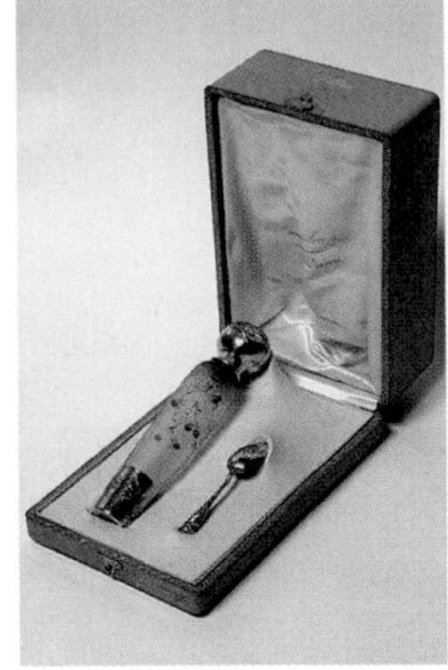

A Daum silver-mounted glass bottle, with a silver spoon, signed and hallmarked, French, Nancy, c1895, in original box, 6in (15cm) high.
£3,750–4,150
€5,400–6,000
$6,300–7,000
⊞ MI

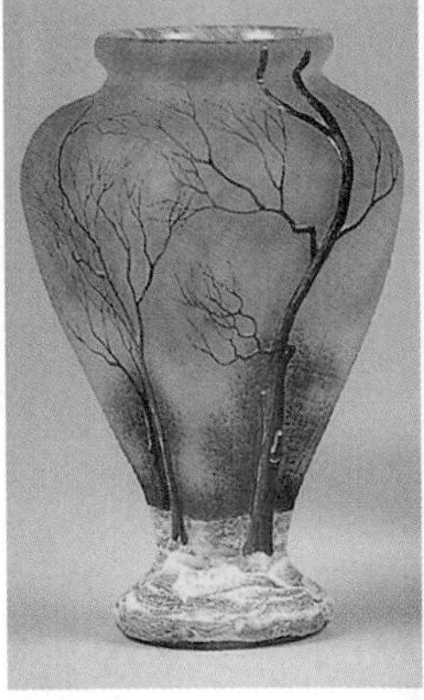

A Daum glass vase, acid-etched and painted with a winter landscape, signed, cross of Lorraine, French, Nancy, c1900, 5¼in (13.5cm) high.
£1,800–2,150
€2,600–3,100
$3,000–3,600 ⚒ DORO

► A Daum cameo glass Peacock vase, signed, cross of Lorraine, French, Nancy, c1900, 6in (15cm) high.
£3,200–3,800
€4,600–5,500
$5,300–6,300
⚒ S(NY)

► A Daum glass vase, acid-etched and painted with a landscape, signed, cross of Lorraine, French, Nancy, c1900, 4½in (11.5cm) high.
£2,300–2,750
€3,300–3,950
$3,850–4,600
⚒ DORO

A Daum cameo glass vase, etched and carved with foliage and fruit, cameo mark with cross of Lorraine, French, Nancy, c1910, 5½in (14cm) high.
£4,300–4,800 / €6,200–6,900
$7,200–8,100 ⊞ MI

A Daum glass vase, etched and gilt with a duck among irises, Daum mark and cross of Lorraine, French, Nancy, early 20thC, 3¼in (8.5cm) high.
£1,100–1,300
€1,600–1,850
$1,850–2,200 ⚒ S(O)

A Daum cameo glass vase, enamelled with thistles, signed, cross of Lorraine, dated 1914, 4¼in (11cm) high.
£920–1,100
€1,300–1,550
$1,550–1,850 ⚒ JDJ
The date on this vase may signify the closure of the factory in 1914. It reopened in 1919.

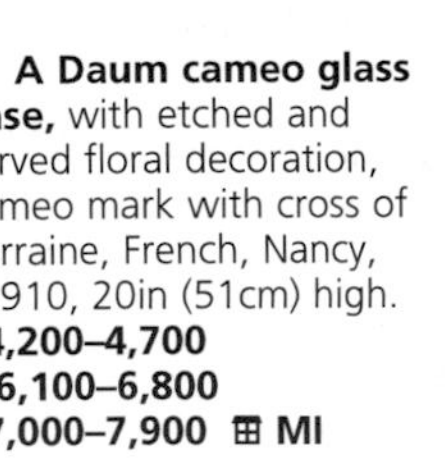

◄ A Daum cameo glass vase, with etched and carved floral decoration, cameo mark with cross of Lorraine, French, Nancy, c1910, 20in (51cm) high.
£4,200–4,700
€6,100–6,800
$7,000–7,900 ⊞ MI

◄ An Emile Gallé glass dressing table box, signed, French, c1900, 7½in (19cm) wide.
£2,800–3,100
€4,050–4,500
$4,700–5,200 ⊞ MI

DECORATIVE ARTS

An Emile Gallé cameo glass bowl, etched with sycamore leaves and seeds, cameo mark, French, c1900, 7½in (19cm) wide.
£660–790 / €950–1,100
$1,100–1,300 ⚒ S(O)

► An Emile Gallé overlaid glass bowl, decorated with Bleeding Hearts, the bronze socle on a figural shaft and glass base, signed, French, 1908–14, 8in (20.5cm) high.
£1,950–2,350
€2,800–3,350
$3,300–3,950
⚒ DORO

An Emile Gallé cameo glass vase, decorated with lilies, signed, French, c1900, 7in (18cm) high.
£1,350–1,600
€1,950–2,300
$2,250–2,650 ⚒ WW

An Emile Gallé cameo glass vase, carved with pansies and leaves, signed, French, c1900, 4in (10cm) high.
£260–310 / €370–440
$440–520 ⚒ S(O)

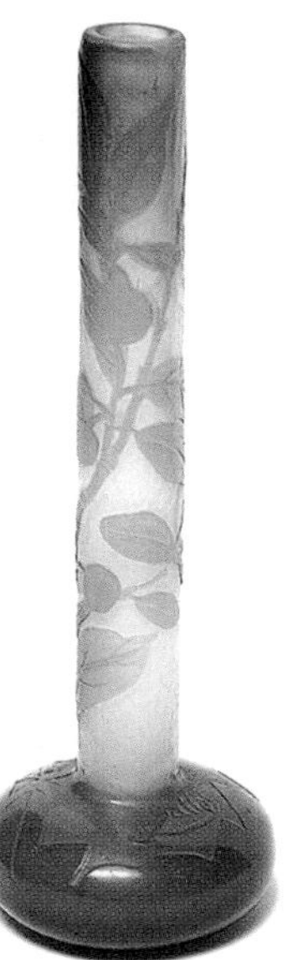

An Emile Gallé cameo glass vase, French, c1900, 7in (18cm) high.
£700–780 / €1,000–1,100
$1,150–1,300 ⊞ AFD

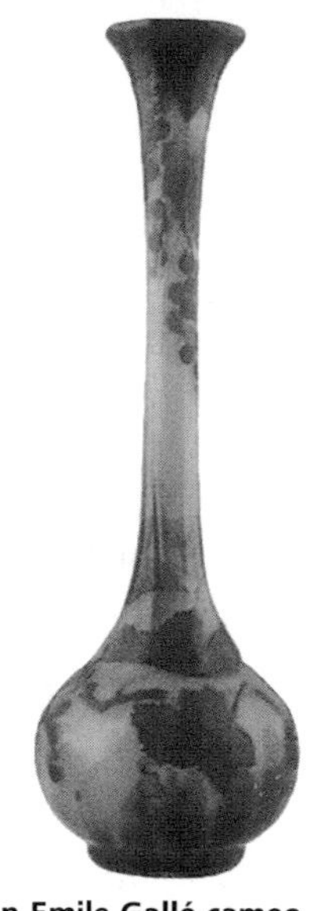

An Emile Gallé cameo glass vase, etched with berries and leaves, signed, French, c1900, 18in (45.5cm) high.
£3,400–4,050
€4,900–5,800
$5,700–6,800 ⚒ WL

. Legras Solifleur glass ase, acid-etched and namelled, French, c1910, 0in (51cm) high.
1,250–1,400
1,800–2,000
2,100–2,350 ⊞ AFD
his vase is designed to ake a single flower.

An Emile Gallé glass vase, signed, French, Nancy, c1905, 6in (15cm) high.
£1,200–1,350
€1,750–1,950
$2,000–2,250 ⊞ MI

A Loetz iridescent glass vase, Austrian, c1898, 10in (25.5cm) high.
£860–950 / €1,200–1,350
$1,450–1,600 ⊞ HTE

A Legras Mont Joye glass vase, French, c1900, 10in (25.5cm) high.
£880–980 / €1,250–1,400
$1,500–1,650 ⊞ AFD

► A Loetz iridescent glass vase, with three applied handles, Austrian, c1900, 5¼in (13.5cm) high.
£2,100–2,500
€3,000–3,600
$3,500–4,200 ⚒ DORO

A Loetz Candia Papillon silver-mounted vase, Austrian, c1900, 5in (12.5cm) high.
£1,250–1,500
€1,800–2,150
$2,100–2,500 ⚒ S(O)

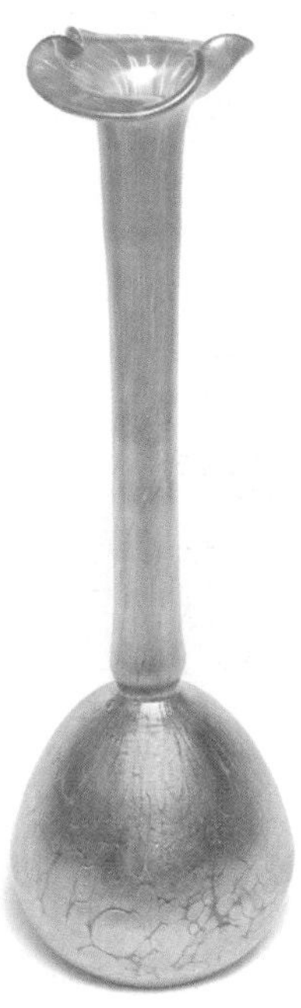

A Loetz Solifleur glass vase, Austrian, c1900, 13in (33cm) high.
£770–850 / €1,100–1,250
$1,300–1,450 ⊞ HTE

A Loetz iridescent cased glass vase, signed, Austrian, c1901, 5in (12.5cm) high.
£1,250–1,500
€1,800–2,150
$2,100–2,500 ⚒ DORO

A Loetz iridescent cased glass vase, signed, Austrian, c1902, 6¼in (16cm) high.
£3,300–3,950
€4,750–5,700
$5,500–6,600 ⚒ DORO

A Muller Frères cameo glass vase, enamelled with poppies and trees, signed, French, c1900, 12¾in (32.5cm) high.
£2,250–2,700
€3,250–3,900
$3,800–4,500 ⚒ BB(L)

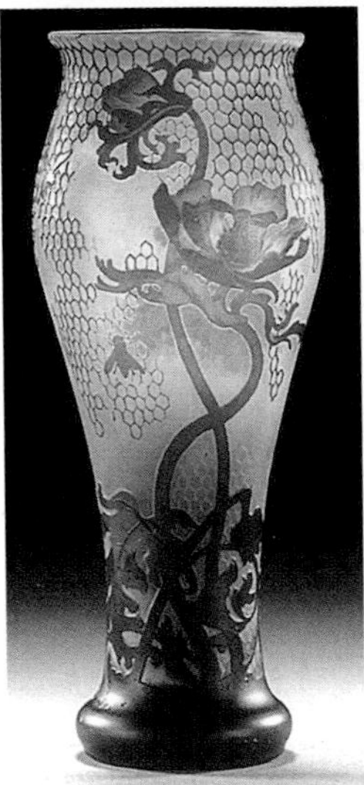

► **A Muller Frères cameo glass vase,** decorated with anemones, honeycomb and bees, engraved mark, French, early 20thC, 10in (25.5cm) high.
£1,800–2,150
€2,600–3,100
$3,000–3,600 ⚒ S(O)

A Quezal iridescent glass vase, after the Tiffany model 'Jack in the Pulpit', signed, American, c1900, 8in (20.5cm) high.
£1,750–2,100
€2,500–3,000
$2,900–3,500 ⚒ B

A Quezal silver-mounted iridescent glass vase, the mount cast as flowers and leaves, engraved marks, mounts marked for Alvin Corporation, American, c1900, 6in (15cm) high.
£1,600–1,900
€2,300–2,750
$2,700–3,200 ⚒ S(O)

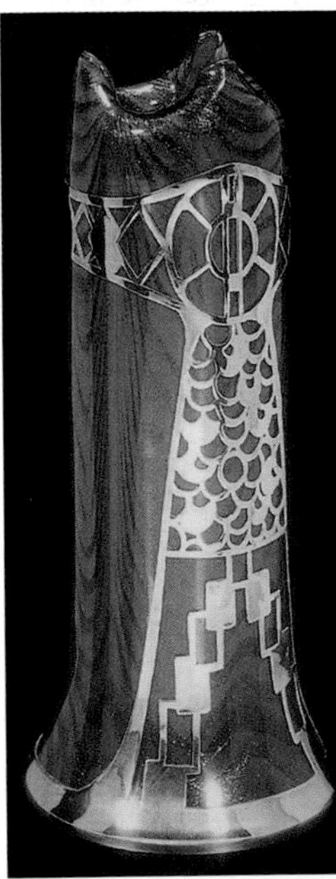

A silver-mounted iridescent glass vase, possibly by Rindskopf Söhne, the Secessionist-style mount cast with geometric motifs, Austrian, early 20thC, 13in (33cm) high.
£1,550–1,850
€2,250–2,650
$2,600–3,100 ⚒ S(O)

A silver-mounted glass vase, the mount cast as flowers and entwined tendrils, probably American, c1900, 6in (15cm) high.
£500–550 / €720–800
$840–930 ⊞ DAD

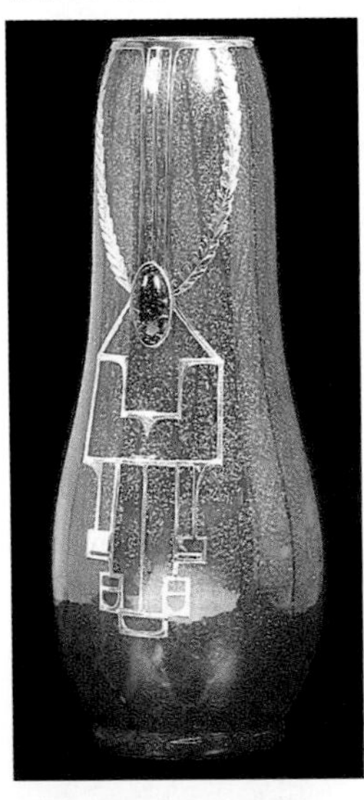

◄ **A silver-mounted glass vase,** with Secessionist-style decoration, early 20thC, 10in (25.5cm) high.
£900–1,050
€1,300–1,500
$1,500–1,750 ⚒ S(O)

► **An iridescent glass bowl,** Austrian, c1900, 6in (15cm) diam.
£240–270
€340–390
$400–450
⊞ HTE

A silver metal-mounted iridescent glass vase, the mount cast as a stylized thistle, c1900, 5in (13cm) high.
£330–390 / €470–560
$550–660 ⚒ S(O)

Art Nouveau Jewellery

A 15ct gold and turquoise brooch, c1890, 3in (7.5cm) wide.
£410–450 / €590–650
$690–760 ⊞ ANO

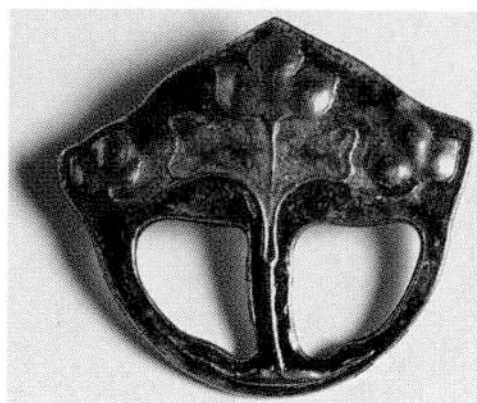

A Liberty & Co enamel and silver brooch, hallmarked, 1900, ½in (1.5cm) wide, with original case.
£500–550 / €720–790
$840–920 ⊞ SHa

An enamel and silver brooch, by Charles Horner, Chester 1908, 1¼in (3cm) wide.
£150–170 / €220–250
$260–290 ⊞ HTE

Plique à jour

Developed in Russia in the 17th century, *plique à jour* was adopted by French and English jewellers of the Art Nouveau period to produce pieces of very distinctive style. The method, similar to the production of stained glass, involves placing a structure of metal strips on a metal background, which is then filled with translucent enamel powder. After the powder has been fired, the backing is removed and the reverse of the enamel is polished, achieving a 'stained glass' effect.

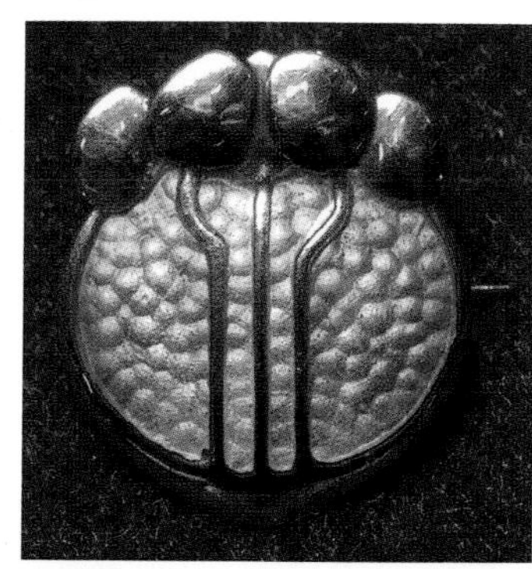

► **A silver and enamel brooch,** by J. Fenton, Birmingham 1909, 1in (2.5cm) diam.
£270–300 / €390–430
$450–500 ⊞ ANO
J. Fenton was a Birmingham-based jewellery designer and maker who produced items similar to those made by Charles Horner.

A Liberty & Co silver and enamel set of six buttons, by Archibald Knox, Birmingham 1903, 1in (2.5cm) diam, in original fitted case.
£1,650–2,000 / €2,450–2,850
$2,750–3,300 ⚒ WW

An 18ct gold necklace, French, c1900, 16in (40.5cm) long.
£630–700 / €910–1,000
$1,050–1,200 ⊞ ANO

. gold wisteria pendant, y Fred Partridge, with *lique à jour* leaves, the lossom set with nine ıoonstones, maker's mark, 1900, 2¾in (7cm) long, ith a gold chain.
5,300–6,300
7,600–9,100
8,900–10,600 ⚒ LAY
red Partridge worked or the Guild of Handi-aft and also produced number of pieces of wellery for Liberty.

A 15ct gold pendant, set with aquamarines, seed pearls and a diamond, c1910, 2in (5cm) long.
£800–880 / €1,150–1,300
$1,350–1,500 ⊞ EXC

An enamel and silver pendant, c1910, 1in (2.5cm) diam.
£200–220 / €290–320
$340–380 ⊞ SGr

DECORATIVE ARTS

Art Nouveau Lighting

A terracotta lamp, modelled as a lady under a tree by a mirrored pool, marked 'Clemens', Austrian, c1910, 23in (58.5cm) high.
£1,800–2,000
€2,600–2,900
$3,000–3,350 ⊞ ASP

A Loetz glass and nickel-plated metal table lamp, worn, shade fixing damaged, Austrian, c1900, 18½in (47cm) high.
£6,100–7,300
€8,800–10,500
$10,300–12,400 ⚒ DORO

► A copper and glass hanging lantern, c1900, 24in (61cm) high.
£540–600 / €780–860
$900–1,000 ⊞ ASA

A Daum glass ceiling lamp, with coloured inclusions and acid-etched blackberries, suspended on cords from a patinated iron mount, signed, cross of Lorraine, French, c1900, 15¾in (40cm) diam.
£4,850–5,800
€7,000–8,400
$8,100–9,700 ⚒ DORO

A Muller Frères cameo glass table lamp, with a wrought-iron mount, etched with a lakeside view, French, c1910, 11½in (29cm) high.
£2,450–2,950
€3,550–4,200
$4,150–4,900 ⚒ S(Am)

◄ A brass three-arm ceiling light, with vaseline glass shades, c1900, 16in (40.5cm) wide.
£1,150–1,300
€1,650–1,850
$2,000–2,200
⊞ CHA

A Daum glass and brass table lamp, the glass with coloured inclusions, the base moulded with foliate motifs, signed, cross of Lorraine, French, c1910, 10¾in (27.5cm) high.
£1,150–1,350
€1,650–1,950
$1,950–2,300 ⚒ DORO

A Palme, König & Habel glass and bronze table lamp, the opalescent shade with applied green threads, fitted for three lights, Bohemian, 1900–10, 24in (61cm) high.
£2,200–2,650
€3,250–3,800
$3,700–4,450 ⚒ DORO

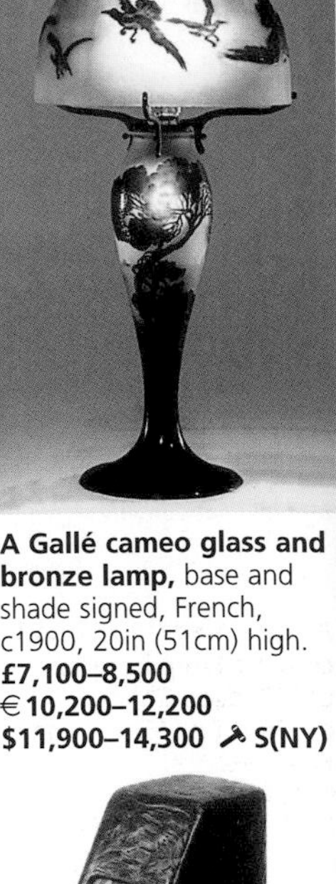

A Gallé cameo glass and bronze lamp, base and shade signed, French, c1900, 20in (51cm) high.
£7,100–8,500
€10,200–12,200
$11,900–14,300 ⚒ S(NY)

A bronze and glass lamp, by Paul Tereszczuk, modelled as a girl with sheep standing in front of a tower, signed, c1910, 14in (35.5cm) high.
£3,000–3,300
€4,300–4,750
$5,000–5,500 ⊞ MI

A brass three-arm light fitting, with origina glass shades, early 20thC, 20in (51cm) high.
£450–500 / €650–720
$760–840 ⊞ EAL

◄ A pair of gilt-bronze and iridescent glass wall lights, c1900, 12½in (32cm) high.
£840–1,000
€1,200–1,400
$1,400–1,650 ⚒ S(O)

A pair of gilt-metal and ceramic lamps, French, c1900, dogs Chinese c1865, 17in (43cm) high.
£2,450–2,700
€3,500–3,900
$4,100–4,550 ⊞ MI

A reverse-painted glass table lamp, American, c1910, 23in (58.5cm) high.
£650–780 / €920–1,100
$1,100–1,300 ⚒ DuM

A brass and iridescent glass bedside lamp, some wear, Bohemian, c1900, 16in (40.5cm) high.
£1,400–1,650
€2,000–2,400
$2,350–2,800 ⚒ DORO

A brass three-arm ceiling light, with vaseline glass shades, c1910, 20in (51cm) wide.
£1,150–1,300
€1,650–1,850
$2,000–2,200 ⊞ CHA

► A patinated-bronze and mottled glass table lamp, American, early 20thC, 21¼in (54cm) high.
£1,450–1,700
€2,100–2,450
$2,450–2,850 ⚒ S(O)

A gilt-bronze four-arm ceiling light, French, c1900, 19in (48.5cm) high.
£1,850–2,200
€2,650–3,150
$3,100–3,700 ⚒ S(O)

A patinated-metal and leaded glass table lamp, American, early 20thC, 26½in (67.5cm) high.
£1,600–1,900
€2,300–2,750
$2,700–3,200 ⚒ BB(L)

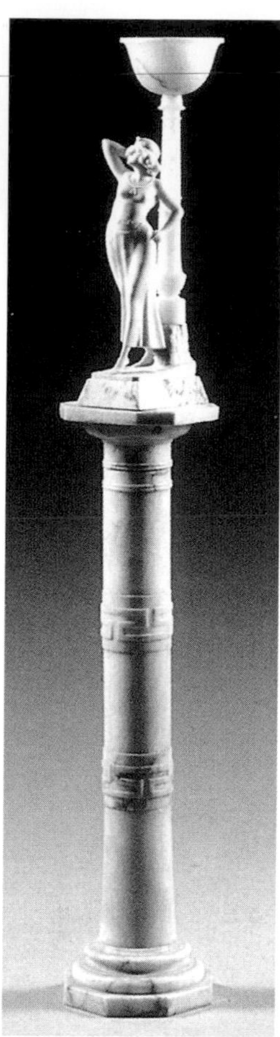

An alabaster figural lamp, carved as a woman standing by a lamppost, on a pedestal, early 20thC, 42½in (108cm) high overall.
£840–1,000
€1,200–1,400
$1,400–1,650 ⚒ S(O)

Tiffany & Co

A Tiffany silver bowl, decorated with chased arabesques, American, c1907, 9¼in (23.5cm) diam, 21oz.
£2,000–2,250 / €2,900–3,200
$3,350–3,750 ⊞ KK

A Tiffany opaque glass and pierced brass desk set, comprising letter rack, inkwell, perpetual calendar and pen tray, each piece stamped, American, 1930s.
£530–640 / €760–920
$890–1,100 ⚒ B&L

A Tiffany Favrile glass flower bowl, decorated with lily pads, frog missing, inscribed '6838K', American, c1916, 10in (25.5cm) diam.
£520–620 / €750–890
$880–1,050 ⚒ BB(L)

A Tiffany Furnaces Favrile glass bowl, wheel-carved, on a gilt-bronze foot, impressed 'Louis C. Tiffany Furnaces, Inc./37', American, 1918–28, 12in (30.5cm) diam.
£2,850–3,400 / €4,100 4,900
$4,750–5,700 ⚒ S(NY)

Tiffany

Charles Louis Tiffany (1812–1902) founded Tiffany, Young & Ellis which later became Tiffany & Co. After Charles's death in 1902 his son Louis Comfort Tiffany (1848–1933) became a Director of the company. He also founded Louis C. Tiffany & Assoc Artist (1879), Tiffany Glass Co (1855), Stourbridge Glass Co (1890), Tiffany Furnaces (1892) and Tiffany Studios (1902).

A Tiffany Favrile glass and gilt-bronze Pomegranate lamp, sockets, cap and finial associated, impressed marks to shade and base, American, 1899–1920, 25in (63.5cm) high.
£4,900–5,900
€7,100–8,500
$8,300–9,900 BB(L)

A Tiffany glass and metal Bellflower lamp, impressed marks, c1925, 21¾in (55.5cm) high.
£15,500–17,200
€22,300–24,800
$26,000–28,900 LUA

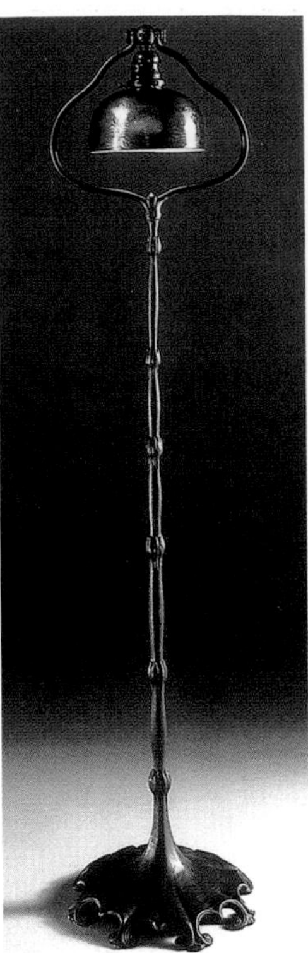

A Tiffany Favrile glass and bronze Harp lamp, inscribed and impressed marks, American, 1899–1920, 54¾in (139cm) high.
£5,700–6,800
€8,200–9,800
$9,600–11,400 S(NY)

► **A set of six Tiffany silver teaspoons,** by John C. Moore, c1910, 6in (15cm) long.
£340–380 / €500–550
$580–640 SHa

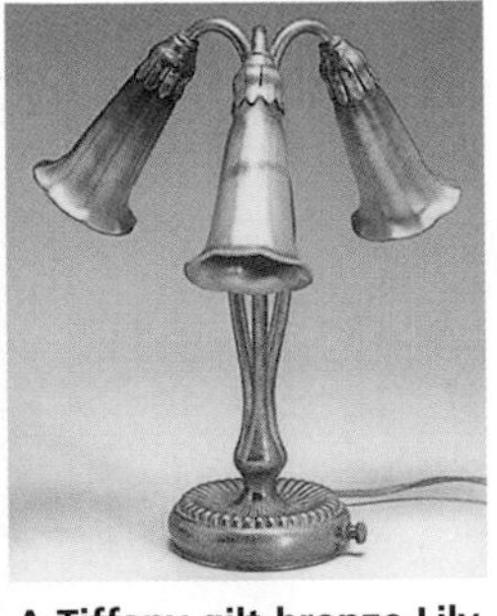

A Tiffany gilt-bronze Lily lamp, with later associated shades, base stamped 'Tiffany Studios/New York 319', 1902–18, 13in (33cm) high.
£980–1,150
€1,400–1,650
$1,650–1,850 BB(L)

A Tiffany Favrile glass and gilt-metal lampshade, on a patinated-bronze base, impressed marks, 1902–18, base 25in (63.5cm) high.
£10,500–12,600
€15,100–18,100
$17,600–21,200 BB(L)

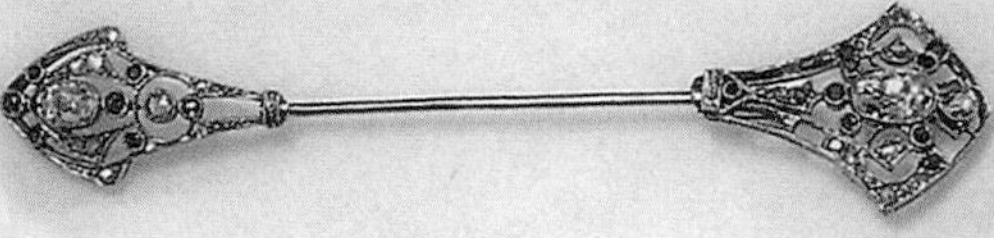

A Tiffany ruby and diamond *sûreté* pin, set with cushion-shaped and rose-cut diamonds and circular-cut rubies, signed, c1920.
£3,600–4,300 / €5,200–6,200
$6,100–7,200 S(O)

Prices

The price ranges quoted in this book reflect the average price a purchaser might expect to pay for a similar item. The price will vary according to the condition, rarity, size, popularity, provenance, colour and restoration of the item, and this must be taken into account when assessing values. Don't forget that if you are selling it is quite likely that you will be offered less than the price range.

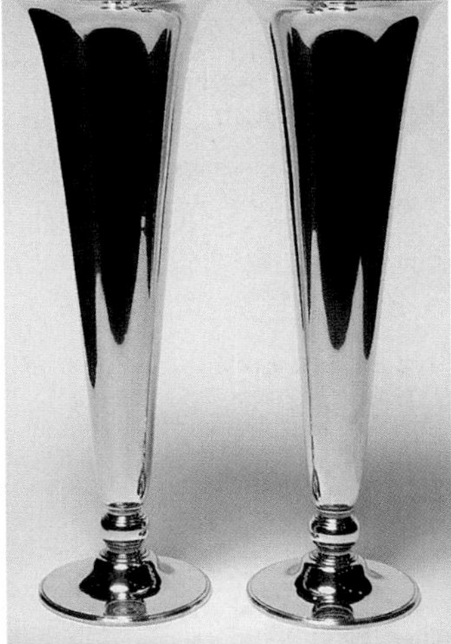

A pair of Tiffany silver vases, by John C. Moore, c1910, 12in (30.5cm) high.
£2,450–2,750 / €3,550–3,900
$4,100–4,600 SHa

◄ **A Tiffany Favrile pottery vase,** inscribed marks, 1902–14, 9in (23cm) diam.
£4,600–5,500 / €6,600–7,900
$7,700–9,200 S(NY)

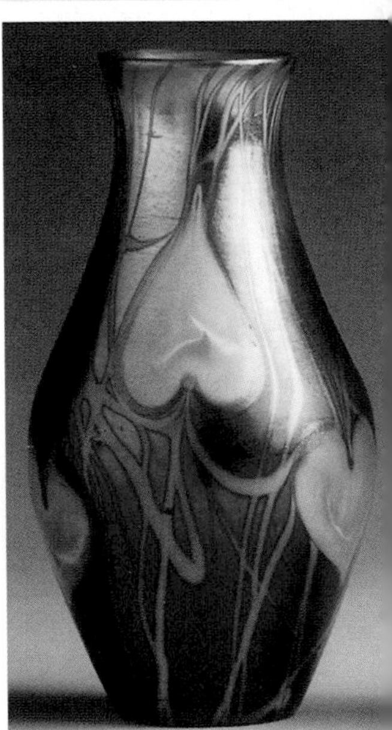

A Tiffany Furnaces Favrile glass vase, inscribed 'Louis C. Tiffany Furnaces Inc. Favrile 1667', original paper label, c1918, 9in (23cm) high
£5,700–6,800 / €8,200–9,800
$9,600–11,400 S(NY)

DECORATIVE ARTS

Art Nouveau Metalware

A silver-coloured metal basket, by A. K. & Co, with a whiplash scroll handle and glass liner, French, c1890, 7in (18cm) diam.
£900–1,050 / €1,300–1,500
$1,500–1,750 ⚒ S(O)

A WMF Secessionist-style glass punchbowl, with silver-plated mounts and ladle, German, c1910, 15in (38cm) high.
£1,300–1,450 / €1,900–2,100
$2,200–2,450 ⊞ TDG

Items in the Art Nouveau Metalware section have been arranged in alphabetical order.

A pair of pewter candelabra, cast with stylized foliage, c1905, 11¾in (30cm) high.
£840–1,000 / €1,200–1,450
$1,400–1,700 ⚒ S(O)

A silver and enamel dish, by S. L. Connell, the border embossed with enamelled seedpods, maker's mark, London 1902, 4½in (11.5cm) diam.
£500–550 / €720–800
$840–930 ⊞ DAD

A Liberty & Co pewter two-handled bowl, the pierced sides set with eight iridescent enamelled motifs, stamped, early 20thC, 7¾in (19.5cm) diam.
£370–440 / €530–630
$620–740 ⚒ PF

An electroplated jewellery box, German, c1900, 6¼in (16cm) wide.
£1,050–1,200 / €1,500–1,700
$1,750–2,000 ⊞ JSG

A brass and rosewood bridge box, by Erhart, Austrian, 1900–10, 9in (23cm) wide.
£390–430 / €560–620
$650–720 ⊞ ANO

A painted bronze centrepiece, by Charles Korschann, signed, foundry stamp, French, Paris, c1895, 15in (38cm) diam.
£5,600–6,200 / €8,000–8,900
$9,400–10,400 ⊞ MI

A silver bowl, by the Guild of Handicraft, with *martelé* decoration, the rim pierced and engraved with stems, berries and leaves, on three ball feet, London 1905, 6in (15cm) diam.
£1,300–1,550 / €1,900–2,250
$2,200–2,600 ⚒ RTo

A silver box, with enamel decoration by H. Levinger, Birmingham 1900, 1½in (4cm) diam.
£680–750 / €980–1,100
$1,100–1,250 ⊞ ANO

A silver dish, by Gilbert Marks, decorated with tulips, maker's mark, London 1895, reverse with incised signature and dated 1896, 8¾in (22cm) diam.
£1,000–1,200 / €1,450–1,700
$1,700–2,000 ⚒ B

A WMF silver-plated fruit dish, with pierced whiplash handles, the sides embossed with a maiden, the glass liner etched with foliage motifs, maker's mark, German, c1910, 12in (30.5cm) wide.
£540–600 / €780–860
$900–1,000 ⊞ DAD

A lead figural ewer, by Emmanuel Villanis, cast with a grotesque mask and reclining nudes, French, early 20thC, 14½in (37cm) high.
£2,050–2,450 / €2,950–3,500
$3,450–4,100 S(O)

An embossed silver photograph frame, by William Comyns, rebacked, London 1908, 8¾in (22cm) high.
£330–390 / €490–560
$560–660 EH

A silver mirror, embossed with a pair of kingfishers, Chester 1903, 12in (30.5cm) high.
£610–730 / €880–1,050
$1,000–1,200 AH

A Liberty & Co Tudric three-piece pewter tea service, by Archibald Knox, cast with stylized leaves, c1905.
£470–560 / €680–810
$790–940 B

A silver and enamel photograph frame, by William Hutton & Sons, London 1903, 9¾in (25cm) high.
£2,250–2,500 / €3,250–3,600
$3,800–4,200 RICC

A Liberty & Co Tudric pewter inkwell, by Archibald Knox, c1900, 2½in (6.5cm) high.
£680–750 / €980–1,100
$1,100–1,250 SHa

A brass wall-hanging post box, with repoussé decoration, c1900, 10in (25.5cm) wide.
£450–500 / €650–720
$760–840 DAD

A silver bread tray, by Unger Brothers, repoussé-decorated with irises, monogrammed 'N', American, New Jersey, c1895, 12½in (32cm) wide.
£240–290 / €350–420
$400–480 NOA
All the Art Nouveau silver produced by Unger Brothers was designed by Eugene Unger's wife, Emma L. Dickinson.

► **A gilt-bronze tray,** by Albert Marionnet, La Société des Artistes Français, c1905, 8in (20.5cm) diam.
£1,200–1,350 / €1,750–1,950
$2,000–2,200 MI

A silver photograph frame, by W. Neal & Sons, Birmingham 1907, 12½in (32cm) high.
£1,050–1,200 / €1,500–1,700
$1,750–2,000 RICC

A silver jug, repoussé-decorated with carnations and hydrangeas, American, c1890, 11½in (29cm) high.
£2,750–3,300 / €3,950–4,700
$4,600–5,500 NOA

A Liberty Cymric silver lidded tankard, by Archibald Knox, thumbpiece missing, Birmingham 1900, 7¾in (19.5cm) high.
£8,200–9,800 / €11,800–14,100
$13,800–16,500 CHTR

Art Deco Ceramics

An Altrohlauer Porzellanfabriken hand-painted charger, Bohemian, c1920, 13in (33cm) diam.
£270–300 / €390–430
$450–500 ⊞ ASP

A Carlton Ware bowl, decorated with Leaves pattern, c1925, 9in (23cm) diam.
£360–400 / €520–580
$600–660 ⊞ TDG

A Carlton Ware comport tray, decorated with Fantasia pattern, hairline crack, c1925, 12in (30.5cm) wide.
£500–550 / €720–800
$840–930 ⊞ TDG

A Carlton Ware baluster vase, decorated with Fan pattern, c1920, 10in (25.5cm) high.
£2,250–2,500 / €3,250–3,600
$3,800–4,200 ⊞ TDG

A Boch Frères earthenware vase, Belgian, c1924, 9¼in (23.5cm) high.
£910–1,100 / €1,350–1,600
$1,500–1,800 ⚒ DuM

A Carlton Ware charger, decorated with Floral Comets pattern, c1920, 15in (38cm) diam.
£2,250–2,500 / €3,250–3,600
$3,800–4,200 ⊞ TDG

A Carlton Ware ginger jar, decorated with Heron and Magical Tree pattern, c1920, 13in (33cm) high.
£4,500–5,000 / €6,500–7,200
$7,600–8,400 ⊞ TDG

A Boch Frères earthenware vase, by Charles Catteau, signed, model No. D984, printed factory mark, Belgian, c1925, 13½in (34.5cm) high.
£4,650–5,600 / €6,700–8,000
$7,800–9,400 ⚒ S(NY)

Carlton Ware

The Carlton Works were set up c1890 by Wiltshaw & Robinson in Stoke-on-Trent. During the 1920s, the company became renowned for its Art Deco lustre wares, which are highly sought after today. Many of the patterns were of imaginative, geometric and stylized floral designs, some using Egyptian and Oriental influences.

Also at this time a 'floral embossed' range was introduced to be used as tableware. Other later collectable areas of Carlton Ware are the advertising wares, particularly items displaying the Guinness name and the Walking Ware range of the 1970s.

A Carlton Ware vase, decorated with Spangled Tree pattern, minor chip, printed, painted and impressed marks, 1930s, 6½in (16.5cm) high.
£190–220 / €280–320
$320–370 ⚒ PFK

◀ **A Carter, Stabler & Adams pottery vase,** by Truda Adams, decorated with Blue Bird pattern, c1930, 7in (18cm) high.
£220–250 / €320–360
$380–420 ⊞ BEV

A Crown Devon cake stand, decorated with Fairy Castle pattern, c1920, 10in (25.5cm) diam.
£810–900 / €1,150–1,300
$1,350–1,500 ⊞ TDG

A Crown Devon wall charger, with stylized floral decoration, c1930, 12in (30.5cm) diam.
£630–700 / €900–1,000
$1,050–1,200 ⊞ RH

A pair of Hancock Rubens Ware vases, by F. X. Abraham, decorated with Pomegranate pattern, c1922, 8in (20.5cm) high.
£290–320 / €410–460
$490–540 ⊞ PIC

A Hancock Corona ware bowl, by Molly Hancock, decorated with Cherry Ripe pattern, c1924, 9½in (24cm) diam.
£240–270 / €350–390
$400–450 ⊞ PIC

A René Herbst earthenware decanter and plate, painted marks, French, c1930, decanter 11in (28cm) high.
£3,200–3,850 / €4,600–5,500
$5,400–6,400 ⚒ S(NY)

A Longwy enamelled and gilded earthenware vase, printed factory mark, French, c1925, 14¾in (37.5cm) high.
£5,300–6,400 / €7,600–9,100
$8,900–10,700 ⚒ S(NY)

◄ A Longwy ceramic charger, made for Primavera, French, c1930, 15in (38cm) diam.
£2,350–2,600
€3,400–3,750
$3,950–4,400
⊞ MI

A pair of Auguste Mouzin ceramic vases, signed and stamped, Belgian, c1920, 15in (38cm) high.
£1,800–2,000
€2,600–2,900
$3,000–3,350 ⊞ MI

A Newcomb College ceramic vase, decorated by Anna F. Simpson, impressed marks, American, 1895–1940, 9½in (24cm) high.
£10,500–12,600
€15,200–18,200
$17,600–21,200 ⚒ BB(L)

The pottery at Newcomb College, New Orleans, has produced some of the rarest and most valuable American art pottery.

A Pilkington's Royal Lancastrian lustre vase, by William Mycock, dated 1930, 8in (20.5cm) high.
£560–620 / €800–890
$940–1,050 ⊞ HTE

A Ram earthenware Luchtig vase, by T. A. C. Colenbrander, painted by Roelof Sterken, hairline crack, Dutch, 1924, 8¾in (22cm) high.
£1,400–1,650
€2,000–2,350
$2,350–2,800 ⚒ S(Am)

A pair of Ram earthenware Los plates, by T. A. C. Colenbrander, painted by Adriaan Kool, stamped factory mark, painted model number, date code and painter's monogram, Dutch, 1925, 9¾in (25cm) diam.
£3,950–4,750
€5,700–6,800
$6,600–7,900 ⚒ S(Am)
The Ram factory was founded by T. A. C. Colenbrander in Arnhem and was in production from 1920 to 1928.

A Rookwood vase, decorated by Elizabeth Lincoln with flowerheads and berries, impressed factory mark and artist's initials, American, 1923, 8¼in (21cm) high.
£520–620 / €750–900
$870–1,050 ⚒ BB(L)

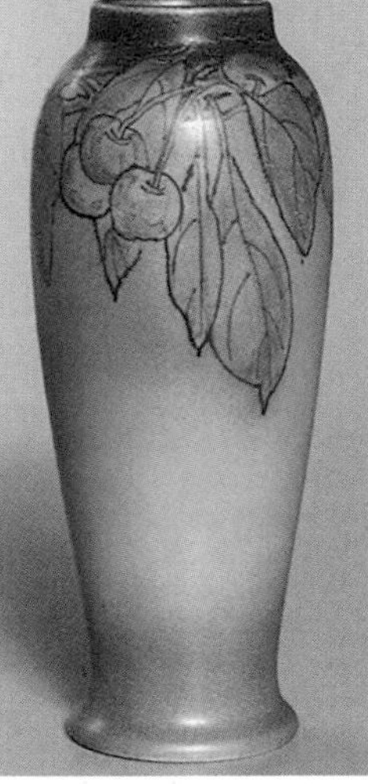

A Rookwood vase, by S. E. Coyne, decorated with cherries and leaves, American, 1927, 11in (28cm) high.
£770–920 / €1,100–1,300
$1,300–1,550 ⚒ TREA

Rookwood Pottery (American 1880–1960)

The Rookwood Pottery was established by Maria Longworth Nichols in 1880. It was situated in Cincinnati in the Ohio valley and was able to take advantage of the rich clay deposits and easy access to major water routes.

The factory employed many artists and expert technicians and imposed very high production standards. Wares were hand-painted with designs such as indigenous flora and fauna, landscapes, Native Americans and Oriental flowers on a naturalistic underglaze slip. 'Standard' glaze wares, featuring brown, yellow and ochre slips on dark grounds and covered with a clear, glossy glaze, were produced from 1883. 'Vellum' wares, produced from 1904, were typically decorated with stylized flora or forest landscapes and covered in a matt glaze.

A Rookwood ceramic jardinière, by Lorinda Epply, impressed and painted marks, American, c1930, 5¾in (14.5cm) high.
£670–800 / €960–1,150
$1,100–1,300 ⚒ LHA

A Shelley Queen Anne trio, decorated with Sunrise and Tall Trees pattern, 1930s, plate 7in (18cm) square.
£75–85 / €105–120
$125–140 ⊞ RH

A Shelley Eve part tea service, decorated with Blocks pattern, 1932–33.
£1,300–1,550 / €1,900–2,250
$2,200–2,600 ⚒ AMB

◄ **A pair of Wedgwood Fairyland lustre vases,** by Daisy Makeig-Jones, decorated with Imps on a Bridge pattern, c1920, 13in (33cm) high.
£10,800–12,000 / €15,500–17,300
$18,100–20,200 ⊞ POW
Fairyland lustre pieces are currently attracting high prices.

► **A ceramic vase,** by A. Villiers, with bronze mounts, signed, French, c1925, 10in (25.5cm) high.
£1,850–2,050
€2,650–2,950
$3,100–3,450
⊞ MI

► **A Zsolnay ceramic model of a bird,** by Lajos Mack, Hungarian, c1914, 10in (25.5cm) high.
£1,800–2,000
€2,600–2,900
$3,000–3,300 ⊞ POW

Clarice Cliff

A Clarice Cliff Bizarre Gaiety flower basket, decorated with Berries pattern, 1930–31, 14in (35.5cm) high.
£1,400–1,550
€2,000–2,200
$2,350–2,600 MI

A Clarice Cliff biscuit barrel, decorated with Acorn pattern, with a wicker handle, printed mark and shape No. 335, 1934, 6in (15cm) diam.
£420–500 / €600–720
$700–840 GAK

► **A Clarice Cliff bowl,** decorated with Pink Pearls I pattern, on a cross-form base, black printed marks, c1935, 4½in (11.5cm) diam.
£200–240 / €290–350
$340–400 SWO

◄ **A Clarice Cliff bowl,** decorated with Tulips pattern, c1935, 9in (23cm) diam.
£680–820
€980–1,150
$1,150–1,350
LAY

A pair of Clarice Cliff Fantasque Bizarre candlesticks, painted with Melon pattern, slight damage, c1930, 8in (20.5cm) high.
£490–590 / €720–850
$820–980 TRM

A Clarice Cliff Bizarre candle holder, decorated with Blue Chintz pattern, c1932, 4½in (11.5cm) diam.
£760–840 / €1,050–1,200
$1,250 1,400 MI

► **A Clarice Cliff cigarette and match holder,** decorated with Rudyard Honolulu pattern, c1933, 3in (7.5cm) high.
£680–750 / €980–1,100
$1,150–1,300 TDG
Rudyard is the name for the blue and green colourway of the Honolulu pattern. It was named after the village of Rudyard, Stoke-on-Trent.

A Clarice Cliff bowl, decorated with Mondrian pattern, black printed marks, 1929–30, 9½in (24cm) diam.
£660–790 / €950–1,100
$1,100–1,300 S(O)

A Clarice Cliff bowl, decorated with Blue W pattern, c1930, 9in (23cm) square.
£4,000–4,500 / €5,800–6,500
$6,800–7,600 BD

A Clarice Cliff bowl, decorated with Autumn Crocus pattern, c1935, 8¼in (21cm) diam.
£150–180 / €220–260
$250–300 CHTR

A Clarice Cliff Bizarre condiment trio, decorated with Solomon's Seal pattern, c1930.
£230–270 / €330–400
$390–460 G(L)

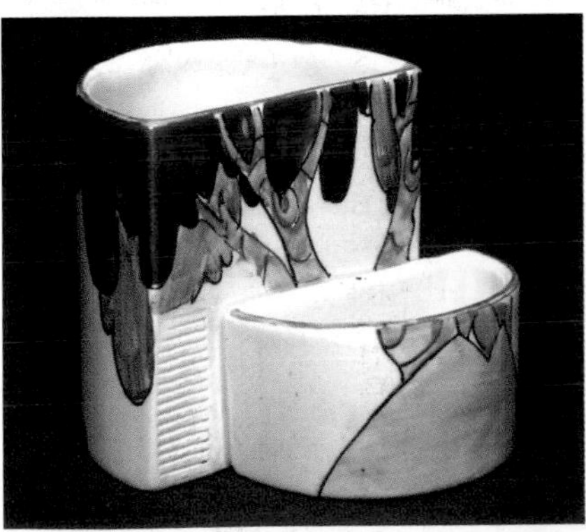

A Clarice Cliff cup and saucer, decorated with Mondrian pattern, c1930, 3in (7.5cm) high.
£720–800 / €1,000–1,150
$1,200–1,350 ⊞ TDG

A Clarice Cliff Bizarre Fantasque jug, decorated with Secrets pattern, small chip, c1933, 7½in (19cm) high.
£460–550 / €660–790
$770–920 ⚒ EH

A Clarice Cliff Biarritz plate, decorated in Blue Firs pattern, printed mark and date code, 1933–37, 12in (30.5cm) wide.
£210–250 / €300–360
$350–420 ⚒ SWO
This is the more unusual colourway of Coral Firs and was only produced in small quantities. Early pieces may feature a cottage.

A Clarice Cliff Beehive honey pot, decorated with Liberty pattern, c1930, 4in (10cm) high.
£430–480 / €620–690
$720–800 ⊞ TDG

A Clarice Cliff Fantasque jardinière, decorated with Lily pattern, c1930, 11in (28cm) diam.
£370–440 / €530–630
$620–740 ⚒ BWL

A Clarice Cliff Bizarre plate, hand-enamelled with flowers, signed, c1930, 8¾in (22cm) diam.
£240–290 / €350–420
$400–480 ⚒ WW

A Clarice Cliff Newport plate, decorated with Pine Grove pattern, black printed mark, c1935, 9in (23cm) diam.
£350–420 / €500–600
$590–700 ⚒ GAK

A Clarice Cliff jam pot, decorated with Secrets pattern, c1930, 4in (10cm) high.
£580–650 / €840–940
$980–1,100 ⊞ RH

A Clarice Cliff Athens jug, decorated with Alton pattern, c1933, 7in (18cm) high.
£810–900 / €1,150–1,300
$1,350–1,500 ⊞ TDG
This pattern was inspired by Alton Towers, the ornamental park near Stoke, Staffordshire.

A Clarice Cliff plate, decorated with Applique Idyll pattern, c1932, 9in (23cm) wide.
£900–1,000 / €1,300–1,450
$1,500–1,700 ⊞ BD

A Clarice Cliff Bizarre Fern Heath pot, decorated with Trees and Hous pattern, c1930, 4in (10cm) high.
£680–750 / €980–1,100
$1,150–1,300 ⊞ MI

A Clarice Cliff Fantasque sandwic set, comprising seven pieces, decorate with Solomon's Seal pattern, some damage, gilt retailer's mark, 1930s.
£280–330 / €400–480
$470–560 ⚒ BR

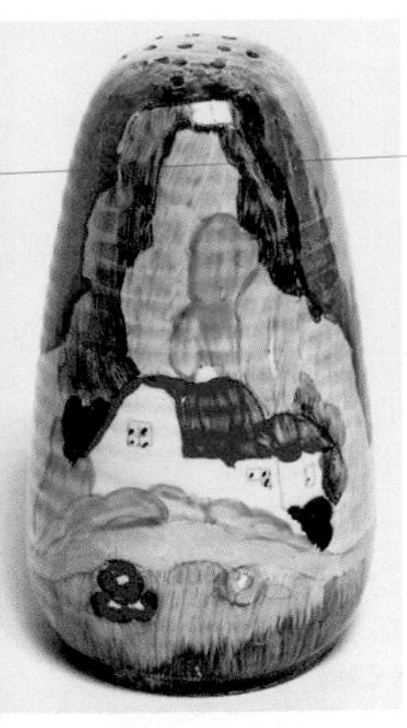

A Clarice Cliff Lynton sugar caster, decorated with Newlyn pattern, c1935, 5in (12.5cm) high.
£720–800 / €1,000–1,150
$1,200–1,350 ⊞ BD

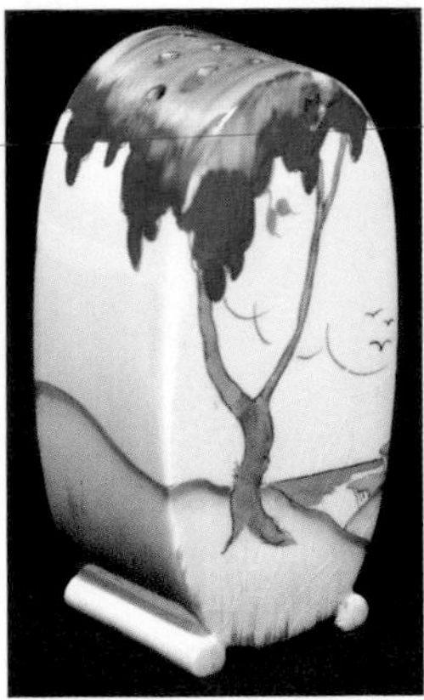

A Clarice Cliff Bon Jour sugar caster, decorated with Taormina pattern, c1936, 5in (12.5cm) high.
£500–550 / €720–800
$840–930 ⊞ TDG

► A Clarice Cliff Bizarre teapot, designed by Dame Laura Knight, decorated with Circus pattern, printed factory marks and 'First Edition 1934', 7in (18cm) high.
£1,450–1,750
€2,100–2,500
$2,450–2,950
RTo

A Clarice Cliff Bizarre part tea service, comprising 15 pieces, c1930.
£270–320 / €390–460
$450–540 BWL

A Clarice Cliff miniature vase, decorated with Applique Lucerne pattern, c1930, 3in (7.5cm) high.
£2,450–2,950
€3,500–4,200
$4,100–4,900 WW

A Clarice Cliff vase, decorated with Diamonds pattern, shape No. 358, c1930, 8in (20.5cm) high.
£3,150–3,500
€4,500–5,000
$5,300–5,900 ⊞ BD

DECORATIVE ARTS

Charlotte Rhead

A Charlotte Rhead Burleigh Ware pottery wall plaque, tube-lined with a maiden in profile, with a stylized floral border, c1930, 10in (25.5cm) diam.
£3,400–4,100 / €4,900–5,900
$5,800–6,900 AH

The price realized for this charger, which had been found in a house clearance, set a new auction record for Charlotte Rhead. The design had previously only been known from pattern books dating from c1928.

A Charlotte Rhead vase, tube-lined with stylized flowers, painted signature and pattern No. 5623, c1930, 5¾in (14.5cm) high.
£65–75 / €100–115
$115–135 G(L)

A Charlotte Rhead Crown Ducal ceramic plaque, tube-lined and decorated with Manchu pattern, printed and applied marks, c1935, 17¾in (45cm) diam.
£520–620 / €750–890
$870–1,050 DD

A Charlotte Rhead Crown Ducal vase, tube-lined and enamelled with stylized flowers, c1930, 6¾in (17cm) high.
£120–145 / €175–210
$200–240 G(L)

Insurance values

Always insure your valuable antiques for the cost of replacing them with similar items, regardless of the original price paid. Both dealers and auctioneers can provide a valuation service for a fee.

Art Deco Clocks

A hardstone timepiece, the onyx frame surmounted by jade elephants, supported by two fluted rock crystal columns above an onyx tray, movement inscribed 'Frank Hyams', c1910, 5¼in (13cm) high.
£960–1,150 / €1,400–1,650
$1,600–1,900 🔨 S(O)

Frank Hyams, who came from Dunedin in New Zealand, registered a limited company as 'artistic jewellers, gold and silversmiths, and dealers in gems of rarity', at 128 New Bond Street, London in 1902. The firm specialized in retailing objects incorporating New Zealand jade; their jewellery made a stir at the Imperial International Exhibition in London in 1909. They closed around 1914 but the business was continued by Hyam's associate, Ernest J. Lowe.

A Hermès clock, by Jaeger-le-Coultre, modelled as a ship's porthole, Swiss, c1925, 6in (15cm) diam.
£2,700–3,000 / €3,900–4,300
$4,500–5,000 ⊞ JTS

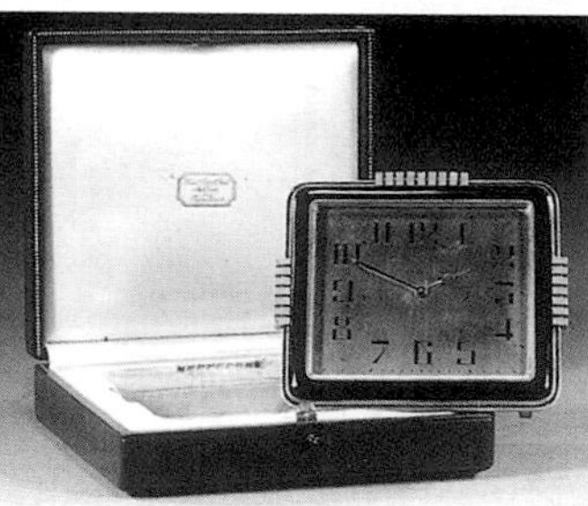

An enamelled and silver cased desk timepiece, by P. Jacot Guillarmod, stamped, French, c1930, 3½in (9cm) high, with a leather velvet-lined case.
£480–580 / €690–830
$810–970 🔨 S(O)

A marble and slate mantel clock, the dial inscribed 'Goldsmiths and Silversmiths Company', c1930, 6¾in (17.5cm) high.
£220–260 / €320–380
$370–440 🔨 SWO

A bronze and onyx figural clock, by Josef Lorenzl, signed, Austrian, c1930, 21¼in (54cm) high.
£4,950–5,900 / €7,100–8,500
$8,300–9,900 🔨 WW

Art Deco Figures & Busts

A *pâte-de-cristal* figure, by G. Argy-Rousseau, entitled 'Danceuse', after a model by Marcel Bouraine, signed, French, c1928, 12in (30.5cm) high.
£21,000–25,000
€30,000–36,000
$35,000–42,000 🔨 BB(L)

A silver and patinated-bronze female figure, by M. Bouraine, signed, French, 1920s, 15in (38cm) high.
£10,800–12,000 / €15,500–17,300
$18,000–20,000 ⊞ TDG

A patinated-spelter figure of a woman and a parrot, by Demêtre Chiparus, on a marble base, inscribed mark, French, c1925, 14½in (36.5cm) high.
£1,000–1,200 / €1,450–1,700
$1,700–2,000 🔨 S(Am)

► A crackle ware figure of a guitar player, signed 'G. Conde', French, c1930, 10in (25.5cm) high.
£470–520 / €680–750
$790–870 ⊞ MI

Further reading

Miller's Art Deco Antiques Checklist, Miller's Publications, 2000

► A Crown Devon group of a lady and a Borzoi, impressed and printed marks, c1935, 10¼in (26cm) high.
£700–840 / €1,000–1,200
$1,200–1,400 🔨 Bea

Specialist in Art Nouveau & Art Deco
AUDREY STERNSHINE
AS
Antique Galleries
26 Broad St
Pendleton, Salford
Manchester M6 5BY
Tel: 0161 737 5938
Fax: 0161 737 6626
as@sternshine.demon.co.uk

A Goldscheider figure, by Dakon, impressed marks, restored, signed, Austrian, c1930, 15¾in (40cm) high.
£1,050–1,250
€1,500–1,800
$1,750–2,100 WW

A patinated-bronze and ivory figure, by G. Gori, entitled 'The Charmer', bird missing, restored, signed, French, 1920s, 15½in (39.5cm) high.
£830–990 / €1,200–1,400
$1,400–1,650 BB(L)

A patinated-bronze figure of a female nude, by Josef Lorenzl, on an onyx socle, signed, Austrian, 1920s–30s, 14¼in (36cm) high.
£1,400–1,650
€2,000–2,350
$2,350–2,750 BUK

A Goldscheider figure, by Dakon, impressed marks, Austrian, c1930, 9in (23cm) high.
£750–900 / €1,100–1,300
$1,250–1,500 DMC

A Goldscheider figure of a dancer, by Thomasch, signed and numbered, Austrian, c1930, 15in (38cm) high.
£3,000–3,300
€4,300–4,750
$5,000–5,500 MI

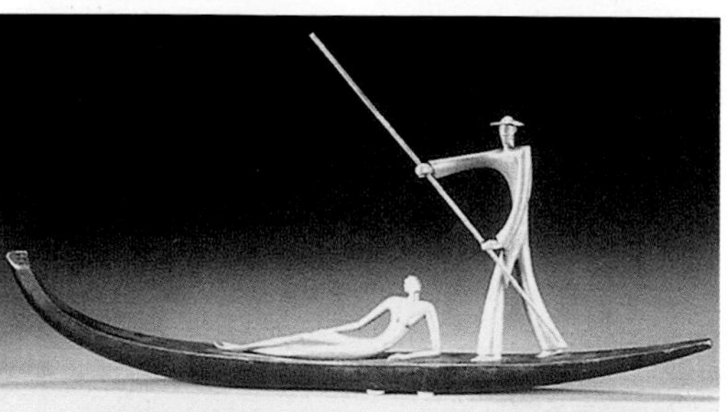

A Hagenauer brass figure, Austrian, c1930, 4in (10cm) high.
£300–330 / €430–480
$500–550 JSG

A silvered- and patinated-bronze figure of a dancer, by Josef Lorenzl, on an onyx base, signed, Austrian, c1930, 10½in (26.5cm) high.
£800–960 / €1,150–1,350
$1,350–1,600 G(L)

A patinated-bronze figure, by Pierre le Faguays, entitled 'Warrior Girl', signed, French, c1920, 22in (56cm) high.
£2,200–2,450
€3,150–3,500
$3,700–4,100 TDG

A Goldscheider group of a girl and a dog, by Dakon, factory marks, Austrian, c1939, 12¾in (32.5cm) high.
£1,250–1,500
€1,800–2,150
$2,100–2,500 DORO

◄ **A Hagenauer nickel-plated group of figures on an ebonized wood gondola,** stamped, Austrian, c1930, 8¾in (22.5cm) high.
£1,300–1,550
€1,900–2,250
$2,200–2,600 S(O)

A Lenci figure of a girl, standing beside a vase, painted marks, Italian, dated 1936, 17¾in (45cm) high.
£480–570 / €690–820
$810–960 S(O)

The Lenci Workshops in Turin (established 1919) produced a mixture of stylish and kitsch glazed earthenware and porcelain figures in the 1920s and '30s. They are hand-painted and usually depict women with serene, coy or coquettish expressions and exaggerated painted eyebrows.

◄ **A silvered and enamel-painted gilt cigar lighter,** after Lorenzl, in the form of a young woman leaning on a column, inscribed mark, Austrian, c1930, 8in (20.5cm) high.
£280–330 / €400–470
$470–550 PF

A porcelain figure of a lady, by Metzler and Ortloff, German, 1930s, 8in (20.5cm) high.
£130–155 / €185–220
$220–260 BR

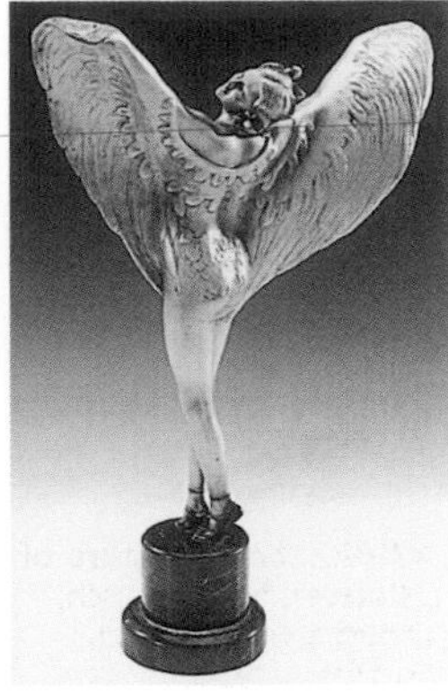

A patinated-bronze figure, by Otto Poertzel entitled 'Bird Dancer', on a marble pedestal, inscribed 'Prof. Poertzel', German, c1928, 16¼in (41.5cm) high.
£3,850–4,600
€5,500–6,600
$6,500–7,700 SHSY

A cold-painted bronze and carved ivory figure of a female swimmer, by Ferdinand Preiss, on an onyx and marble base, signed, German, c1925, 9½in (24cm) high.
£4,450–5,300
€6,400–7,600
$7,500–8,900 B

A Royal Dux group of a woman and a deer, Bohemian, c1930, 14in (35.5cm) high.
£540–600 / €780–860
$900–1,000 ASP

► **An Alméric Walter *pâte-de-verre vide poche,*** by A. Finot, signed 'A. Walter/Nancy', French, c1925, 8¾in (22cm) long.
£4,650–5,600 / €6,700–8,000
$7,800–9,300 S(NY)
Initially a ceramicist, Walter joined Daum in 1908 to make *pâte-de-verre* wares. In 1919, he set up his own glassworks.

A patinated-bronze figure of a dancer, by Bruno Zach, on a stone base, some wear, Austrian, c1930, 16½in (42cm) high.
£2,450–2,950
€3,550–4,250
$4,100–4,900 DORO

A gilded-spelter figure of a dancer, on a stepped base, c1930, 11in (28cm) high.
£370–440 / €530–630
$620–740 AH

A bronze and gilt-bronze group of Ballet Russe dancers, on a stepped marble base, French, c1913, 19in (48.5cm) wide.
£3,700–4,100 / €5,300–5,900
$6,200–6,900 MI

Art Deco Furniture

An amboyna cabinet, by Paul Follot, with ivory handles and inlay, stamped, French, c1925, 55in (139.5cm) wide.
£13,500–15,000 / €19,400–22,000
$22,000–25,000 ⊞ TDG
The French designer Paul Follot created fine quality furniture, being one of the few designers to move from Art Nouveau to Art Deco.

A cocktail cabinet, with scalloped doors and fall-front, 1930s, 60in (152cm) wide.
£470–560 / €680–800
$790–940 ⚒ SWO

A rosewood, aluminium and chromium-plated metal revolving record cabinet, French, 1930s, 24in (61cm) wide.
£3,550–4,250
€5,100–6,100
$6,000–7,100 ⚒ S(NY)

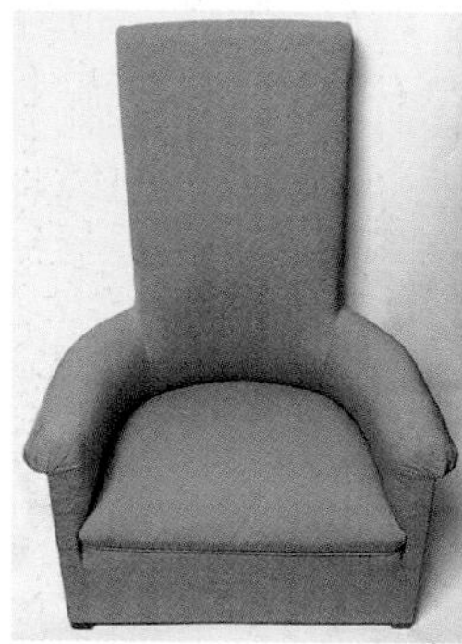

A chair, by Pierre Chareau, French, 1924–27.
£8,100–9,000
€11,700–13,000
$13,600–15,100 ⊞ MI
Pierre Chareau (1883–1950) belongs to a small group of designers of furniture, carpets and earthenware who stood out from the general mass of designers of that period. The works have only recently been saluted by the art market and prices have increased three-fold over the past ten years.

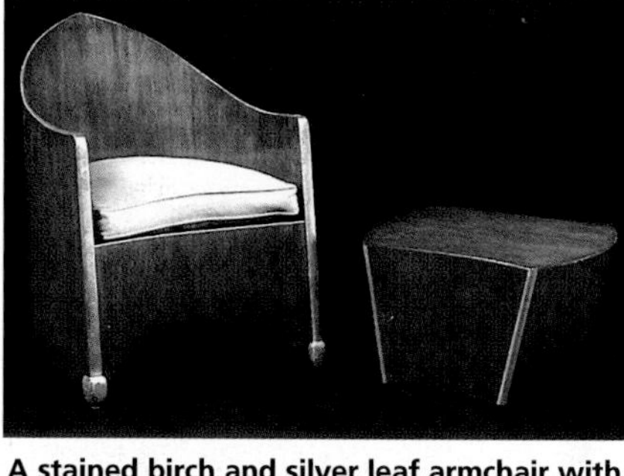

A stained birch and silver leaf armchair with ottoman, by Walter von Nessen, American, c1929.
£6,000–7,200 / €8,600–10,300
$10,100–12,100 ⚒ S(NY)
This armchair and ottoman were acquired by Mr and Mrs Glendon Allvine of Long Beach, New York to furnish their Modernist home designed in 1929 by architect Warren Shepard Matthews. This house was praised at the time as 'America's First Modernistic Home'. Following their passion for Modernism, the Allvines commissioned some of the most avant-garde designers working in the United States to execute furnishings for their new home including Donald Deskey, Paul Frankl, Walter von Nessen and K. E. M. Weber.

A pair of Fautehouse sycamore chairs, by André Domin, with silvered toe caps, upholstered with doe-skin, Austrian, c1930.
£4,300–4,800 / €6,200–6,900
$7,200–8,100 ⊞ MI

A pair of mahogany and leather club armchairs, French, c1930.
£1,150–1,350
€1,650–1,950
$1,900–2,250 ⚒ NOA

A pair of leather armchairs, with later upholstery, French, c1930.
£2,800–3,350 / €4,000–4,800
$4,700–5,600 ⚒ BB(L)

A set of ten dining chairs, by Dimea, 1930s.
£2,100–2,500
€3,000–3,600
$3,500–4,200 ⚒ BB(L)

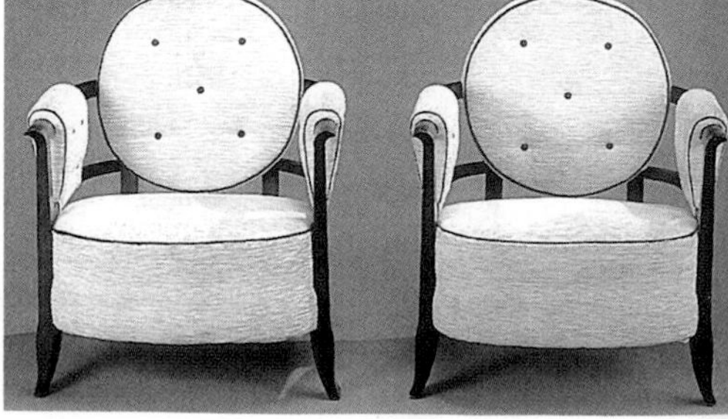

► A pair of stained beech armchairs, upholstered in velvet, French, 1930.
£3,750–4,500
€5,400–6,500
$6,300–7,500 ⚒ S(P)

An Airline Chair Co birch and ash armchair, by K. E. M. Weber, upholstered in oilcloth, painted mark, American, Los Angeles, c1935.
£5,300–6,400 / €7,700–9,200
$9,000–10,800 ⚒ S(NY)

A shagreen and ivory table mirror, c1925, 14in (35.5cm) high.
£2,250–2,500 / €3,250–3,600
$3,800–4,200 ⊞ BBo

A wrought-iron illuminated floor mirror, with frosted-glass lamps, French, c1930, 70in (178cm) high.
£1,050–1,250 / €1,500–1,800
$1,750–2,100 ⚒ BB(L)

An oak desk, by Betty Joel, the leather inset top above a frieze drawer and a kneehole flanked by six graduated drawers, later handles and inset, c1938, 69¼in (176cm) wide.
£2,350–2,800 / €3,400–4,050
$3,950–4,700 ⚒ B

A walnut mirror, with Macassar ebony and walnut banding, c1930, 15¼ x 27in (38.5 x 68.5cm).
£165–195 / €240–280
$280–330 ⚒ NSal

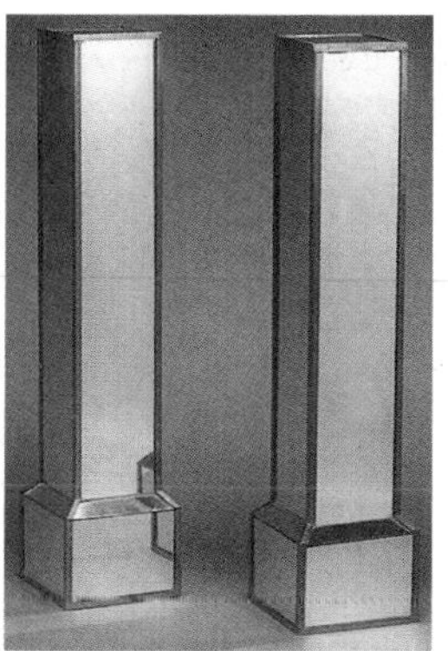

A pair of mirror pedestals, slight damage, French, 1940s, 50¾in (129cm) high.
£4,600–5,500
€6,600–7,900
$7,700–9,200 ⚒ S(P)

◄ **An oak folding screen,** with engraved and enamelled mirror panels decorated with jungle animals, French, 1940s, 56¼in (143cm) high.
£7,900–9,500
€11,400–13,700
$13,300–16,000 ⚒ S(P)

◄ **A sycamore and ebonized kneehole desk,** by Maurice Adams, the frieze drawer above a recess flanked by a cupboard and four short drawers, one foot missing, inscribed label, 1930s, 54in (137cm) wide.
£470–560 / €680–810
$790–940 ⚒ BR

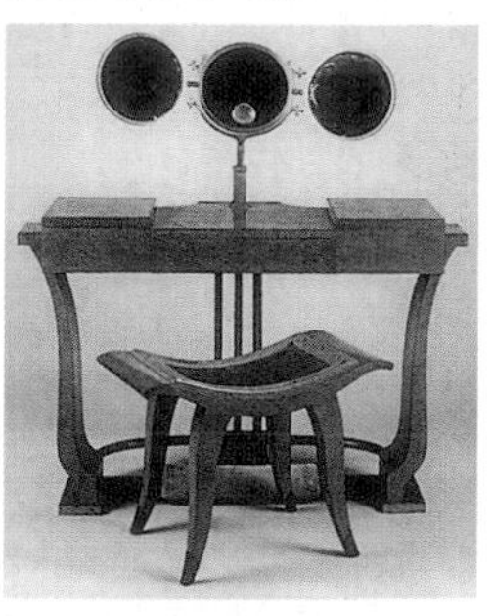

A *loupe d'amboine*-veneered dressing table and stool, attributed to Jules Leleu, French, c1925, 45¾in (116cm) wide.
£21,000–23,000
€30,000–33,000
$35,000–38,000 ⊞ MI

► **An inlaid mahogany pedestal,** French, c1930s, 41in (104cm) high.
£1,350–1,600
€1,950–2,300
$2,250–2,650
⚒ BB(L)

An oak sideboard, by Betty Joel, the stepped top above two drawers and two cupboard doors enclosing glass shelves, signed and dated 1925, 71¾in (182.5cm) wide.
£1,200–1,450 / €1,750–2,100
$2,000–2,400 ⚒ B

This sideboard was commissioned by the vendor's parents who met Betty Joel while living in China. Betty Joel (then Betty Stewart Lockhart) was born in Hong Kong where her father was the Colonial Secretary. She founded Betty Joel Ltd with her husband David Joel in the years following the end of WWII.

DECORATIVE ARTS

An ebonized wood and upholstered settee, with foliate-capped terminals and gilt highlights, French, c1930, 55¼in (140.5cm) wide.
£1,400–1,650 / €2,000–2,350
$2,350–2,800 S(O)

A set of four oak stools, by Betty Joel, with drop-in cane seats and tapering legs, three stools with painted marks, 1925, 17¼in (44cm) wide.
£530–630 / €760–910
$890–1,050 B

An oak bedroom suite, comprising wardrobe, kneehole dressing table, tallboy and stool, with painted and mother-of-pearl decoration, c1930, dressing table 36¼in (92cm) wide.
£300–360 / €430–510
$500–600 DD

◄ A burr-walnut dining suite, by Ray Hille, comprising a dining table and 12 chairs, c1930, table 120in (305cm) long.
£22,000–25,000
€31,000–35,000
$37,000–42,000 ⊞ MI

A mahogany and beechwood dining suite, comprising a dining table and six beechwood dining chairs, French, c1930, table 95in (241cm) extended.
£2,850–3,400 / €4,100–4,900
$4,800–5,700 S(O)

A Cloud lounge suite, comprising a settee, pair of armchairs and footstool, c1930, settee 76¾in (195cm) wide.
£2,250–2,700 / €3,250–3,900
$3,800–4,500 S(O)

A stained beechwood plant stand, by Thonet, with label, restored, Austrian, Vienna, c1922, 32¼in (82cm) high.
£970–1,150
€1,400–1,650
$1,650–1,950 DORO

A palisander and tooled leather two-tier table, by Clément Mère, French, c1925, 27½in (70cm) wide.
£6,100–7,300 / €8,800–10,500
$10,200–12,200 S(NY)

A wrought-iron console table, with a later marble top, c1930, 39¾in (101cm) wide.
£1,400–1,650
€2,000–2,350
$2,350–2,750 S(O)

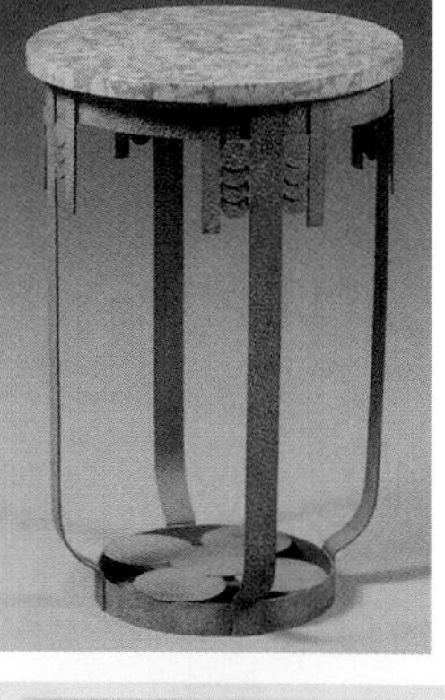

◄ An iron and marble occasional table, c1930, 16in (40.5cm) diam.
£540–650
€780–930
$920–1,100
S(O)

► A wrought-iron and travertine console table, by Gilbert Poillerat, French, 1930s, 53in (134.5cm) wide.
£2,900–3,500
€4,150–5,000
$4,900–5,900 BB(L)

A chrome-plated steel and glass centre table, attributed to Dexter Industries, Philadelphia, American, c1935, 60¾in (154.5cm) wide.
£24,000–27,000 / €35,000–39,000
$40,000–45,000 ⊞ NART
This example of American Modernism is of an excellent design and therefore highly desirable.

Art Deco Glass

◄ **A glass candelabra,** by Jacques Adnet, with chromed-bronze mounts, French, 1930s, 5¼in (13.5cm) high.
£2,600–3,100
€3,750–4,450
$4,350–5,200
S(O)

A Vetreria Artistica Barovier & Co Primavera glass vase, by Ercole Barovier, with applied handles, Italian, c1930, 12¾in (32.5cm) high.
£6,300–7,550
€9,100–10,900
$10,600–12,700 BB(L)
This is an example of one of the most innovative techniques created by Ercole Barovier, which involved dipping the glass in a specific chemical to produce the desired effect. It was invented accidentally in 1929 but due to depletion of the chemical source, the series was short-lived.

A Daum acid-etched glass vase, French, Nancy, 1920s, 12in (30.5cm) high.
£2,000–2,200
€2,850–3,150
$3,350–3,700 TDG

An Emile Gallé cameo glass vase, decorated with blossoms and leaves, signed, stamped, French, c1920, 8in (20.5cm) high.
£1,250–1,500
€1,800–2,150
$2,100–2,500 BB(L)

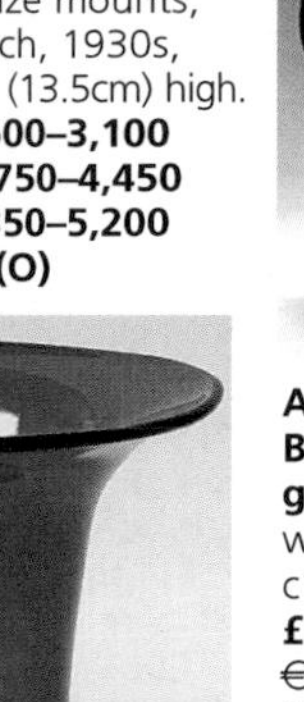

A Loetz glass vase, attributed to Michael Powolny, Austrian, c1930, 8in (20.5cm) high.
£250–280 / €360–400
$420–470 MI

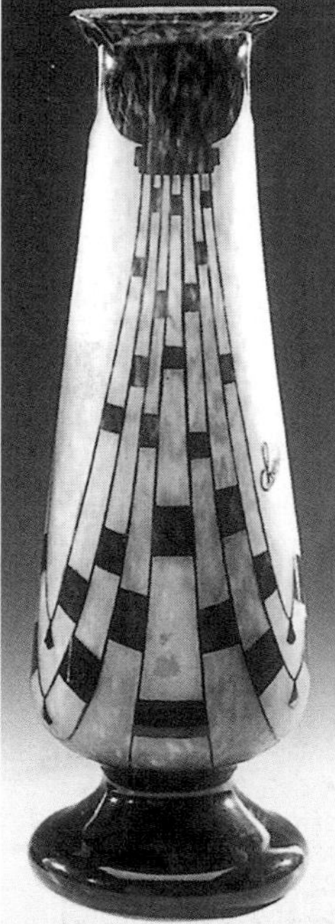

► **A Le Verre Français cameo glass vase,** signed 'Charder', French, c1920, 23½in (59.5cm) high.
£2,200–2,650
€3,200–3,800
$3,700–4,450 SHSY
Charles Schneider founded the Cristallerie Schneider in Epinay-sur-Seine near Paris in 1913. Many wares are signed Le Verre Français or Charder.

A Moser cut-glass vase/bowl, by Josef Hoffmann, Czechoslovakian, Karlsbad, c1920, 8in (20.5cm) wide.
£450–500 / €650–720
$760–840 JSG

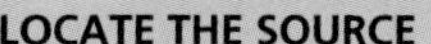

LOCATE THE SOURCE
The source of each illustration in Miller's can be found by checking the code letters below each caption with the Key to Illustrations, pages 794–800.

Quezal glass vase, igned, American, c1930, in (20.5cm) high.
1,550–1,850
2,250–2,650
2,600–3,100 BB(L)

► **A Sabino etched glass bowl,** 1920s, French, 7¾in (19.5cm) high.
£2,900–3,200
€4,150–4,600
$4,850–5,400
KK

◄ **A set of six glass napkin rings,** c1930, 3in (7.5cm) wide.
£135–150
€200–220
$220–250 HTE

A Webb's acid-etched cameo fleur vase, decorated with stylized lilies, slight damage, marked, c1930, 9¾in (25cm) high.
£330–390 / €470–560
$550–660 DN

DECORATIVE ARTS

Lalique

A René Lalique opalescent glass ashtray, 'Chien', French, c1930, 2½in (6.5cm) high.
£440–490 / €630–700
$740–820 ⊞ AFD

A René Lalique glass bowl, 'Chiens', decorated with opalescent greyhounds, French, c1921, 9½in (24cm) wide.
£590–650 / €850–940
$990–1,100 ⊞ GGD

A René Lalique opalescent and stained glass bowl, 'Anvers', moulded with fish and seaweed, etched mark, French, designed 1930, 15½in (39.5cm) wide.
£2,450–2,950 / €3,550–4,250
$4,150–4,950 ⚒ B

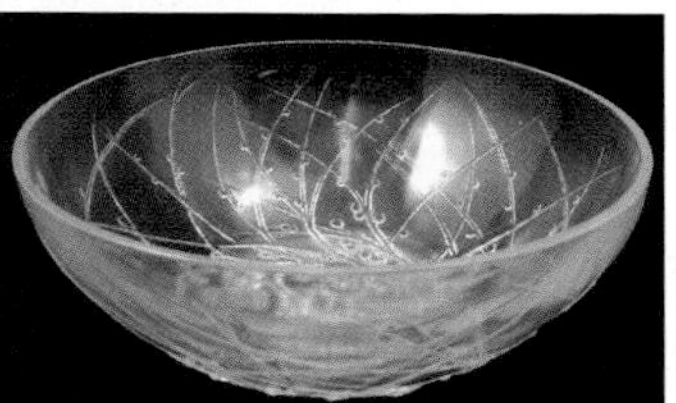

A René Lalique opalescent glass bowl, 'Graines d'Asperges', press-moulded with twigs and berries, moulded mark, French, c1935, 9½in (24cm) wide.
£470–560 / €680–810
$790–940 ⚒ G(L)

A René Lalique opalescent glass box and cover, 'Tokio', moulded with a flower, moulded mark, French, designed 1921, 6¾in (17cm) wide.
£640–770 / €920–1,100
$1,100–1,300 ⚒ B

A René Lalique glass powder box, 'Le Lys', produced for D'Orsay, the flower-decorated cover with sepia patina, French, c1925, 4in (10cm) diam.
£270–300 / €390–430
$450–500 ⊞ GGD

► **A René Lalique glass desk clock,** 'Cinq Hirondelles', moulded and enamelled with swallows, marked, French, designed 1920, 6in (15cm) high.
£1,900–2,250
€2,750–3,250
$3,200–3,800 ⚒ BB(L)

A René Lalique glass timepiece, 'Moineaux', moulded with sparrows, with internal light bulb and ATO movement, moulded mark, French, designed 1924, 6¼in (15.5cm) high.
£2,450–2,950 / €3,550–4,200
$4,100–4,850 ⚒ B

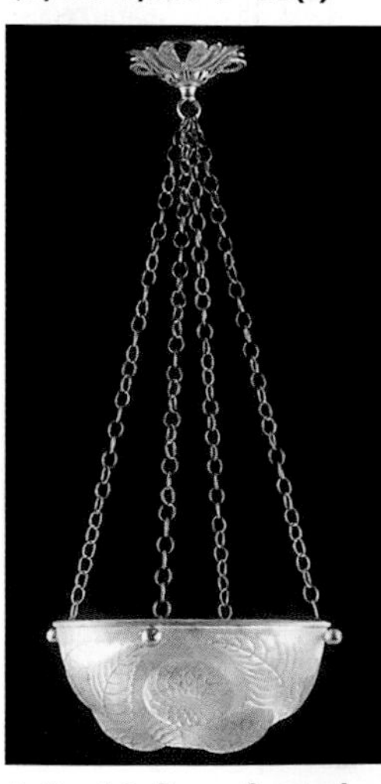

A René Lalique frosted glass chandelier, 'Dahlias', signed, French, designed 1921, 11¾in (30cm) diam.
£3,300–3,950
€4,800–5,700
$5,500–6,600 ⚒ S(P)

A René Lalique glass scent bottle, French, c1930, 2½in (6.5cm) high.
£400–450 / €580–650
$670–760 ⊞ LaF

A René Lalique frosted glass vase, 'Perruches', inscribed mark, French, designed 1919, 10in (25.5cm) high.
£9,300–11,200
€13,400–16,000
$15,600–18,700 ⚒ S(NY)

A René Lalique glass vase, 'Moissac', moulded with overlapping leaves, engraved mark, French, post-1927, 5¼in (13.5cm) high.
£1,850–2,200
€2,650–3,150
$3,100–3,700 ⚒ S(O)

Art Deco Jewellery

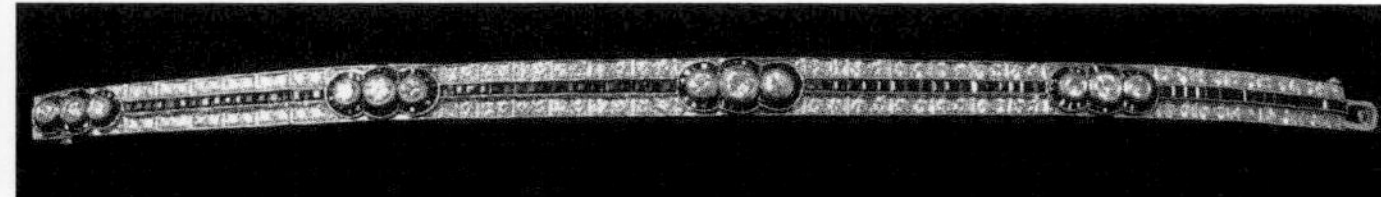

A sapphire and diamond bracelet, c1930, 7½in (19cm) long.
£13,100–14,500 / €18,700–21,000
$22,000–25,000 ⊞ NBL

A platinum and gold bar brooch, set with diamonds, c1920, 3in (7.5cm) long.
£3,100–3,450 / €4,450–4,950
$5,200–5,800 ⊞ WIM

► An 18ct white gold and platinum double clip brooch, set with diamonds and calibre-cut sapphires, c1930.
£1,250–1,500
€1,800–2,150
$2,100–2,500 ⚒ LJ

A platinum clip brooch, set with diamonds and carved emeralds and rubies, c1925, 1½in (4cm) long.
£11,100–12,200 / €15,800–17,600
$18,500–20,500 ⊞ NBL

A platinum brooch, in the form of a stylized lion's face, set with diamonds, c1930, 1in (2.5cm) high.
£2,900–3,250 / €4,150–4,650
$4,950–5,500 ⊞ WIM

◄ A diamond plaque brooch, with original fitted case, c1935.
£2,700–3,250
€3,900–4,600
$4,500–5,400 ⚒ WW

A pair of enamel and mother-of-pearl :ufflinks,** set with diamonds, ½in (1cm) wide.
€810–900 / €1,150–1,300
$1,350–1,500 ⊞ WIM

◄ A paste clip brooch, with fitted case by Jourado, 1930s.
£210–250 / €300–360
$350–420 ⚒ S(O)

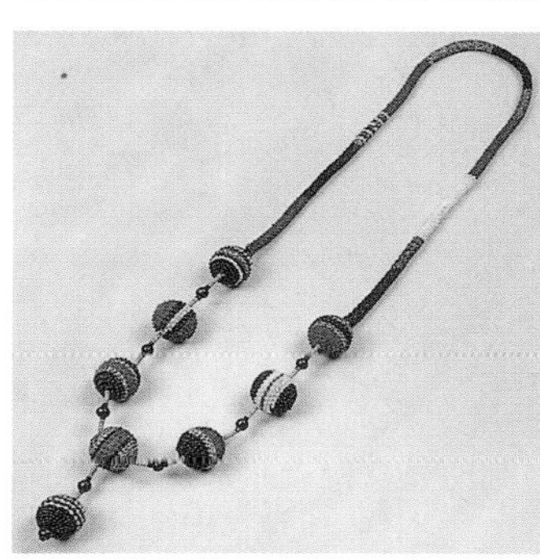

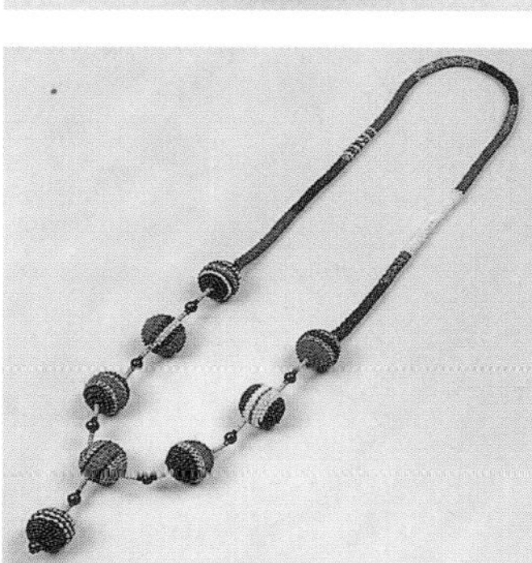

A Wiener Werkstätte glass bead necklace, Austrian, 1925–30, 16½in (42cm) long.
£2,300–2,750 / €3,300–3,950
$3,850–4,600 ⚒ DORO

A gold and platinum ring, set with onyx and diamonds, c1915.
£2,450–2,750
€3,550–3,950
$4,100–4,600 ⊞ WIM

\ platinum ring, set with sapphires and iamonds, c1920.
2,900–3,250 / €4,200–4,700
4,850–5,500 ⊞ WIM

· A platinum ring, set with diamonds, \merican, c1925.
9,400–10,500 / €13,500–15,100
15,800–17,600 ⊞ NBL

An 18ct white gold and platinum ring, set with a diamond within a border of carré set diamonds, c1930.
£940–1,100
€1,350–1,600
$1,600–1,850 ⚒ G(L)

DECORATIVE ARTS

Art Deco Lighting

An Albert Cheuret bronze and alabaster lamp, alabaster replaced, inscribed mark, French, c1925, 16in (40.5cm) high.
£8,600–10,300
€12,400–14,800
$14,400–17,300 S(NY)

A Muller Frères wrought-iron and glass chandelier, moulded with motifs, signed, French, c1930, 37in (94cm) high.
£360–430 / €520–620
$600–720 S(O)

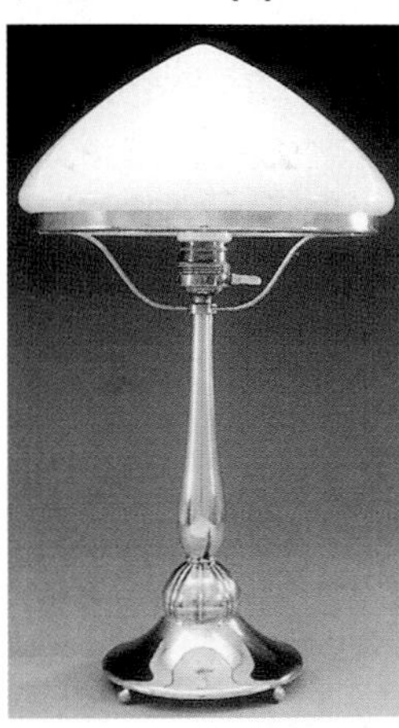

A Silverware Factory silver table lamp, by J. Grönroos, Swedish, Kristianstad 1929, 14in (35.5cm) high.
£630–750 / €920–1,100
$1,050–1,250 BUK

A Desny chrome and plate glass lamp, French, Paris, c1930, 5¼in (13.5cm) high.
£900–1,000
€1,300–1,450
$1,500–1,700 JSG

A pair of steel and brass wall sconces, attributed to Gilbert Poillerat, with frosted glass shades, French, c1940, 16½in (42cm) high.
£6,600–7,400
€9,500–10,600
$11,200–12,500 NART

A bronzed-spelter and glass table lamp, the base modelled as a female figure, on a marble base, c1930, 27in (68.5cm) high.
£540–650 / €790–940
$920–1,100 G(L)

A copper, bronze and earthenware hanging lamp, by Jan Eisenloeffel, the shade lined in silk, damaged, losses, Dutch, 1920s, 43¼in (110cm) diam.
£2,750–3,300
€4,000–4,800
$4,600–5,500 S(Am)
This lamp was one of several important commissions for various lamps, light fixtures and decorative metalwork given by A. J. M. Goudriaan to Jan Eisenloeffel between 1916 and 1928.

A Sabino nickel-plated bronze and glass bedside lamp, fitted for electricity, impressed mark, French, Paris, c1930, 27½in (70cm) high.
£1,400–1,650
€2,000–2,400
$2,300–2,750 DORO

A brass boudoir lamp, sand-finished and painted with a landscape, marked, American, early 20thC, 11in (28cm) high.
£280–330 / €400–480
$470–550 BB(L)

A patinated spelter lamp, 'Pluie', after a model by Max Le Verrier, sockets replaced, signed, stamped, French, 1920s, 21in (53.5cm) high.
£620–740 / €890–1,050
$1,050–1,250 BB(L)

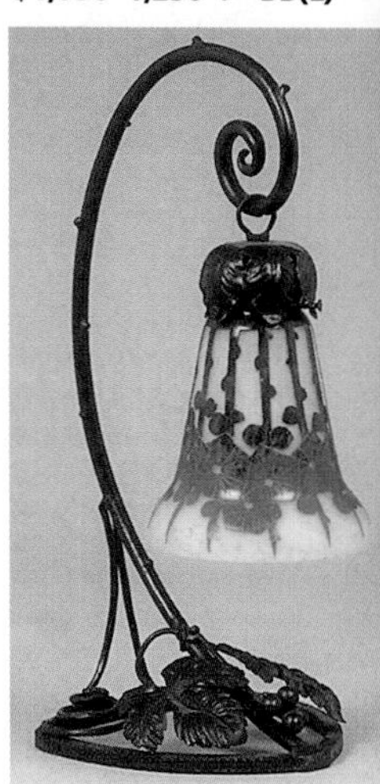

A Le Verre Français patinated wrought-iron and glass bedside lamp, the shade decorated with an acid-etched geometric floral pattern, the base decorated with vine leaves, French, c1925, 17¼in (43.5cm) high.
£1,300–1,550
€1,850–2,200
$2,200–2,600 DORO

A pair of carved wood and metal table lamps, American, 1930s, 26½in (67.5cm) high.
£380–450 / €550–650
$640–750 BB(L)

Art Deco Metalware

◀ **A hammered-silver bowl,** Austrian, Vienna, c1930, 13¼in (33.5cm) wide.
£830–1,000
€1,200–1,400
$1,400–1,650
DORO

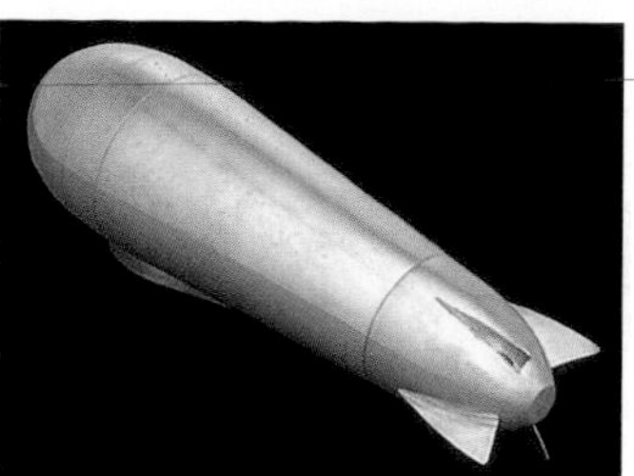

A J. A. Henckels Twin Works chromium-plated brass Zeppelin travelling bar, comprising 17 components, stamped and marked, German, Solingen, c1928, 12in (30.5cm) long.
£1,300–1,550 / €1,850–2,200
$2,200–2,600 S(NY)

A silver footed bowl, by Johan Rohde, with Swedish import marks, Danish, Copenhagen, 1925–33, 9¾in (25cm) diam, 41½oz.
£4,000–4,800 / €5,800–6,900
$6,700–8,000 BUK

A Puiforcat silver and rosewood bowl, signed, French, Paris, c1930, 4in (10.5cm) high.
£1,300–1,550 / €1,850–2,200
$2,200–2,600 S(O)

A silver and Bakelite desk calendar, with engine-turned decoration, London 1931, 3¼in (8.5cm) diam.
£175–210 / €250–300
$300–350 TMA

A silver and enamel cigarette case, the central cartouche surrounded by diamonds, c1920, 3in (7.5cm) wide.
£1,100–1,250 / €1,600–1,800
$1,900–2,100 ⊞ SHa

◀ **An enamelled-silver and eggshell-lacquered cigarette case,** by Gerard Sandoz, depicting a view of Notre Dame, impressed and inscribed marks, French, c1925, 5in (12.5cm) high.
£6,400–7,700 / €9,200–11,100
$10,800–13,000 S(NY)

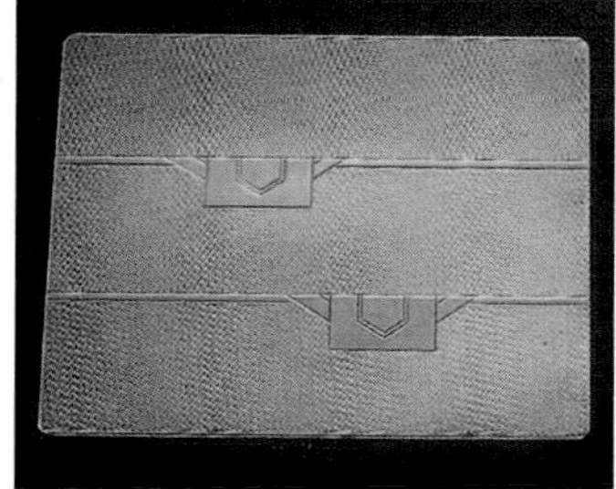

An 18ct gold cigarette case, with engine-turned decoration and a concealed push clasp, c1930, 4in (10cm) long.
£1,150–1,350 / €1,650–1,950
$1,950–2,300 LJ

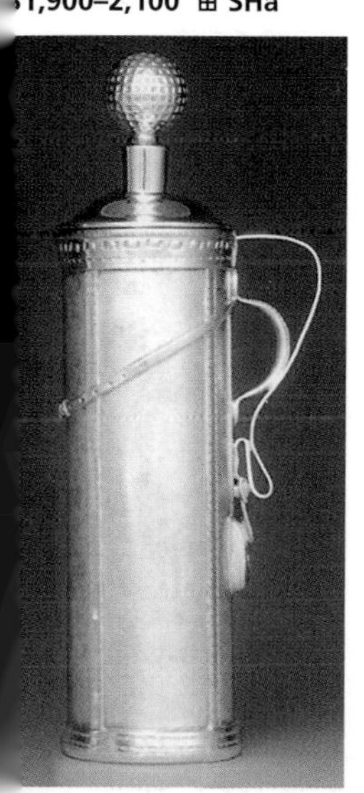

◀ **A Standard Silver Co silver-plated cocktail shaker,** by George Berry, in the form of a golf bag, the cover and cap probably later, stamped, American, c1926, 13½in (34.5cm) high.
£1,450–1,700
€2,100–2,450
$2,400–2,800
S(NY)

A J. M. van Kempen silver and ebony coffee set, by Christa Ehrlich, comprising coffee pot, sugar basin and cream jug, the latter by Kempen Begeer en Vos, Dutch, 1920–22, coffee pot 4¾in (12cm) high.
£1,400–1,650
€2,000–2,400
$2,350–2,750 S(Am)

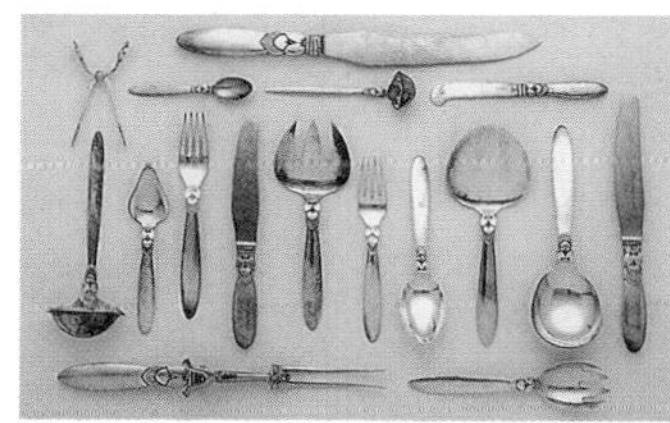

A set of Georg Jensen silver Cactus cutlery, by Gundorph Albertus, comprising 81 pieces, maker's mark, hallmarked London, Danish, 1930s.
£4,250–5,100 / €6,100–7,300
$7,100–8,500 B

A Walker & Hall silver-plated muffin dish and cover, with a frosted-glass liner, marked, c1925, 9in (23cm) diam.
£360–400 / €520–580
$600–670 ⊞ DAD

► **A silver fruit dish,** with plastic handles, Birmingham 1937, 14in (35.5cm) wide, 18oz.
£230–270
€330–390
$380–450 ⚒ G(L)

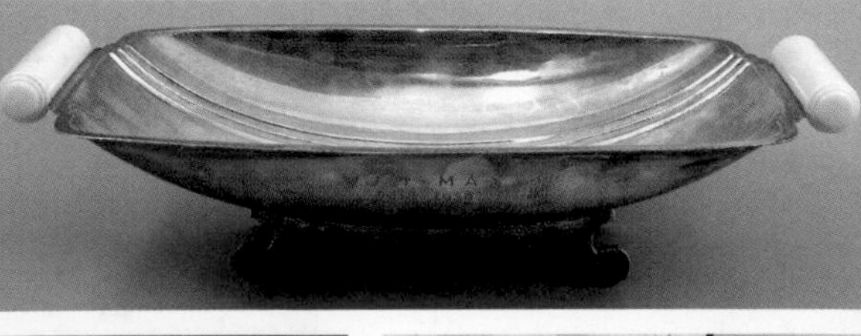

An R. E. Stone silver-mounted glass dish, signed, London 1937, 5¼in (13cm) wide.
£480–570 / €690–820
$810–960 ⚒ S(O)

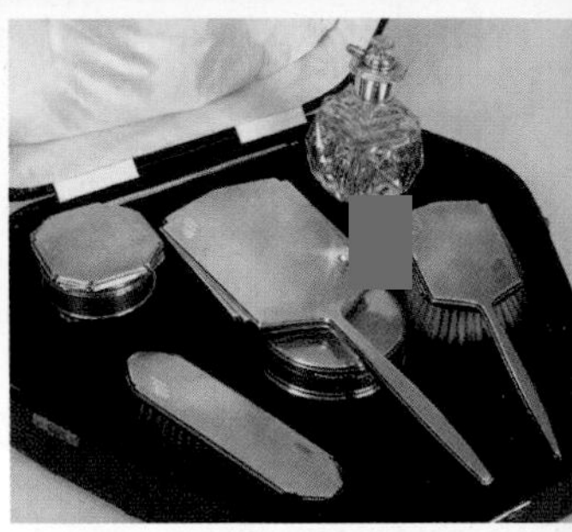

A Walker & Hall silver six-piece dressing table set, comprising mirror, hairbrush, clothes brush, pot, atomizer and jewellery box, with engine-turned decoration, Sheffield 1934, in a fitted case.
£330–390 / €480–560
$550–650 ⚒ FHF

An enamelled silver snuff box, depicting a car, English import marks, sponsor's mark of George Stockwell, Continental, 1926, 3in (7.5cm) wide.
£2,350–2,800 / €3,400–4,000
$3,950–4,700 ⚒ B

◄ **An Elkington & Co silver tankard,** the hinged cover with ivory finial, Birmingham 1932, 7½in (19cm) high, 25oz.
£1,200–1,450 / €1,750–2,100
$2,000–2,400 ⚒ TEN

A Wiener Werkstätte silver teapot, by Josef Hoffmann, with later finial and handle, initialled 'MSW', Austrian, Vienna, c1922, 6in (15cm) high.
£2,150–2,600 / €3,100–3,700
$3,600–4,300 ⚒ S(O)

A George Keller silver-gilt six-piece tea service, with a matching tray, French, c1922, urn 21½in (54.5cm) high.
£9,600–10,700
€13,800–15,400
$16,200–18,000 ⊞ KK

A silver four-piece tea service, comprising a teapot, hot water jug, two-handled sugar basin and milk jug with ivory handles and finials, maker's mark 'S.W.', Sheffield 1932, 52oz.
£330–390 / €480–560
$550–650 ⚒ CDC

A Puiforcat silver four-piece tea and coffee service, comprising a teapot, coffee pot, cream jug and covered sugar bowl, with rosewood handles and finials, marked and stamped, French, Paris, c1937, coffee pot 6in (15cm) high, 68oz.
£2,850–3,400 / €4,100–4,900
$4,800–5,700 ⚒ S(NY)

A Camille Fauré enamelled metal vase, damaged, French, c1930, 12½in (32cm) high.
£2,000–2,400
€2,900–3,450
$3,350–4,000 ⚒ SHSY

A dinanderie vase, 'Evolution', by Paul Louis Mergier, signed and marked French, c1925, 10¾in (27cm) high.
£3,200–3,800 / €4,600–5,500
$5,400–6,500 ⚒ S(NY)
Dinanderie is the term for work in non-precious metals.

Twentieth-Century Design

Ceramics

A Ruskin Pottery high-fired vase, marked and dated 1923, 7¼in (18.5cm) high.
£700–840 / €1,000–1,200
$1,200–1,400 L

Ruskin Pottery

This art pottery was founded in 1898 in West Smethwick, Birmingham, by William Howson Taylor, who a few years later named it Ruskin Pottery in honour of the artist John Ruskin. The range included high-fired stonewares, which are particularly sought after today, as well as lustre-decorated or mottled monochrome 'soufflé' earthenwares and crystalline glazed wares in eggshell-thin bone china.

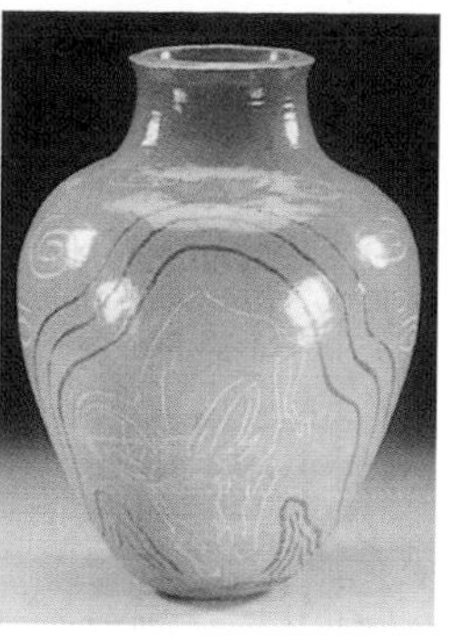

A William Staite Murray stoneware vase, decorated with a stylized ox, impressed mark, c1927, 11¾in (30cm) high.
£1,200–1,450
€1,750–2,100
$2,000–2,400 S(O)
William Staite Murray (1881–1962) is regarded as one of the foremost British ceramicists of the 20th century. He set up a pottery in Rotherhithe, London in 1919 and produced simple pots and vases with monochrome glazes, sometimes with splashed or brushed decoration showing a strong influence from the East. In 1939, Staite Murray settled in Zimbabwe (then Southern Rhodesia) and stopped potting, although he became Trustee of the National Arts Council of Southern Rhodesia.

A stoneware tankard, by Charles Vyse, decorated with a foliate motif and inscribed 'George Edmund Barlow', incised 'Vyse 1935', 5½in (14cm) high.
£140–165 / €200–240
$250–290 WW
Charles Vyse (1882–1971) was born in Staffordshire and apprenticed to Doulton as a modeller in 1896. His talent won him a scholarship to the Royal College of Art in 1905 and by 1911 he had become a member of the Royal Society of British Sculptors. In 1919, Vyse set up a studio with his wife in Cheyne Walk, London and they produced high-fired wares inspired by Chinese and Japanese ceramics, as well as a range of cast pottery figures of local characters. The studio was bombed in 1940 and Vyse became a modelling and pottery instructor at Farnham School of Art, while continuing to produce his own wares.

A Wedgwood vase, by Keith Murray, printed signature and impressed marks, c1930, 7¼in (18.5cm) high.
£240–290 / €350–420
$400–480 SWO
Keith Murray (1892–1981) was a New Zealander who spent most of his working life in Britain. A trained architect, he was one of the few designers in Britain to actively promote Modernist principles in his designs. From 1933, he worked part-time for Wedgwood, designing several ranges of hand-thrown and hand-turned tablewares and other functional pieces. The vase shown here is typical of his work.

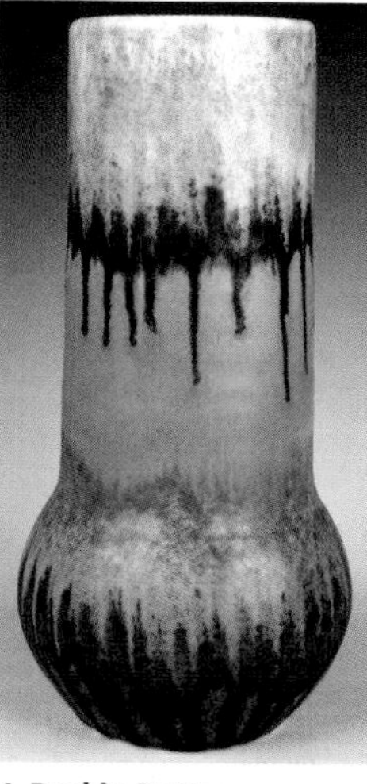

A Ruskin Pottery vase, by William Howson Taylor, impressed marks, signed and dated 1930, 11¾in (30cm) high.
£240–290 / €350–420
$400–480 SWO

► **A Ruskin Pottery vase,** with impressed marks, 1932, 6in (15cm) high.
£130–155 / €185–220
$220–260 FHF

A pair of Carter, Stabler & Adams vases, impressed marks, c1950, 11in (28cm) high.
£440–530 / €630–750
$740–890 CGC

◄ **A set of six tiles,** by Salvador Dali, each painted with a different geometric or figural motif, c1954, 7¾in (19.5cm) wide.
£320–380 / €460–550
$540–640 L&E

Condition

The condition is absolutely vital when assessing the value of an antique. Damaged pieces on the whole appreciate much less than perfect examples. However, a rare desirable piece may command a high price even when damaged.

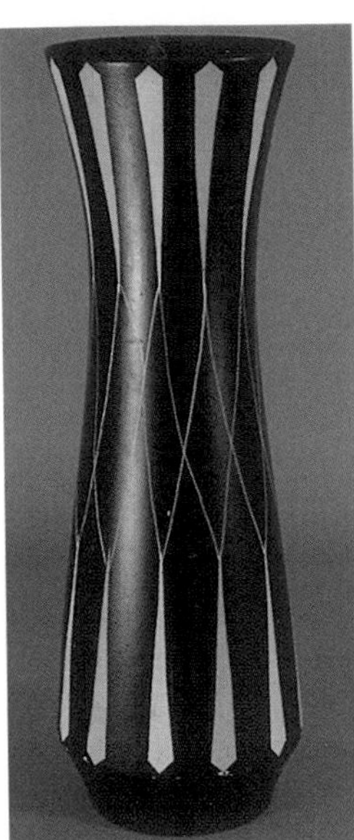

A Ranleigh vase, decorated with Sandown pattern, 1950s, 18½in (47cm) high.
£35–40 / €50–60
$60–70 WilP

A set of six porcelain plates, by Piero Fornasetti, with printed decoration of a female face, marked, Italian, 1950–60, 10in (25.5cm) diam.
£400–480 / €580–690
$680–810 BUK
Piero Fornasetti (1913–88) worked from his house in Milan, where his son continues the studio today. His whimsical, dramatic decorations were based on the trompe l'oeil techniques of stage scene painters. They were used to cover every surface of his designs for furniture, ceramics and a host of other household objects.

A Polia Pillin vase, decorated with a figure with a bird, signed, American, 1950s, 6¾in (17cm) high.
£170–200 / €240–280
$290–340 BB(L)

A Madoura pottery Têtes jug, by Pablo Picasso, signed and impressed mark, limited edition of 500, French, 1956, 5in (12.5cm) high.
£1,500–1,800 / €2,200–2,600
$2,500–3,000 BUK
Madoura is a pottery and gallery in Vallauris in the south of France, which exhibits and sells Picasso's ceramics.

► A Höganäs earthenware bowl, by Åke Holm, signed, Swedish, 1950s, 21in (53.5cm) diam.
£430–520 / €620–740
$730–870 BUK

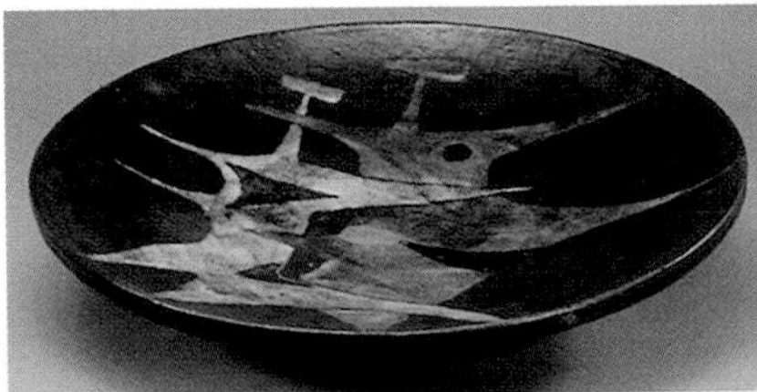

► A Saxbo ceramic bowl, impressed makers marks and 'Saxbo/Denmark', Danish, c1950, 4¼in (11cm) high.
£230–270
€330–390
$390–460
BB(L)

► A William and Polia Pillin ceramic vase, signed, American, 1950s, 7in (18cm) diam.
£140–170
€200–240
$240–280
BB(L)

◄ A Palshus ceramic bowl, inscribed 'Palshus/Denmark 1132B' and artist's initials, Danish, c1950, 2¾in (7cm) high.
£120–145
€175–210
$200–240 BB(L)

A Rörstrand part service, by Hertha Bengston, comprising five pieces, printed factory marks, Swedish, c1955, jug 9in (23cm) high.
£195–230 / €280–330
$330–390 SHSY
Hertha Bengston worked for Rörstrand from 1941 to 1964 and then went to Höganäs as a designer from 1965 to 1969. From there she moved to Rosenthal and finally designed for Ideal-Standard from 1976 to 1981.

◄ A stoneware boulder vase, by Marea Gazzard, Australian, c1972, 18½in (47cm) diam.
£6,300–7,600 / €9,100–10,900
$10,600–12,700 SHSY
Marea Gazzard studied ceramics at the National Art School, East Sydney and then at the Central School of Arts and Crafts in London. After a period of travelling, she returned to Australia in 1960 to set up her own workshop. Working in both clay and metal, her designs are influenced by Aboriginal culture.

A stoneware plate, by Peter Voulkos signed, American, dated 1973, 19in (48.5cm) diam, in a Plexiglass case.
£10,000–12,000 / €14,400–17,300
$16,800–20,200 S(NY)
Peter Voulkos (b1924) is considered one of the foremost American ceramicists of the late 20th century. His expressionistic, sculptural work is highly respected and very collectable, but very few of his pieces exist outside America.

Furniture

A Heal's walnut-veneered corner unit, the drawer above a cupboard door, trade label, 1930s, 27½in (70cm) wide.
£190–230 / €280–330
$320–380 NSal

► **A chrome table,** American, 1930s, 21½in (54.5cm) high.
£175–210 / €250–300
$300–350 BB(L)

An enamelled aluminium and pine Cloud bookshelf, by Charlotte Perriand for Les Ateliers Jean Prouvé, French, c1954, 82¾in (210cm) wide.
£5,700–6,800 / €8,200–9,800
$9,700–11,500 SHSY

Charlotte Perriand attended the Ecole Central des Arts Décoratifs in Paris from 1920 to 1925. In October 1927, she joined the architect Le Corbusier and together they designed modern furniture using tubular steel, sheet metal and aluminium. Perriand was inspired by the Machine Age and developed a great interest in creating furniture using industrial materials. She is well known for creating space-saving and storage furniture.

◄ **A Descon Laminates formed plywood Kone chair,** by Roger McLay, on an iron frame, Australian, designed 1948.
£790–950 / €1,150–1,350
$1,350–1,600 SHSY

A teak armchair, by Finn Juhl for Niels Vodder, No. 53, Danish, 1953.
£880–980 / €1,250–1,400
$1,500–1,650 MARK

TWENTIETH-CENTURY DESIGN

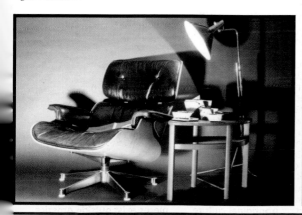

A leather Swan chair, by Arne Jacobsen, Danish, 1956.
£1,500–1,650 / €2,150–2,400
$2,500–2,750 ⊞ MARK

A pair of Pierre Paulin-style Lip chairs, with metal legs, French, 1950s.
£1,300–1,450 / €1,900–2,100
$2,200–2,450 ⊞ DeP

A Fler enamelled metal and aluminium Shell chair, by Fred Lowen, with vinyl upholstery, Australian, c1957.
£920–1,100 / €1,350–1,600
$1,550–1,850 ⚒ SHSY

A maple desk, American, 1950s, 54in (137cm) wide.
£1,250–1,500 / €1,800–2,150
$2,100–2,500 ⚒ BB(L)

◄ A Mouseman-style oak sideboard, by Frank Christian, the top with a raised back above four short drawers flanked by panelled doors, on stile feet, with beehive mask, 1950s, 59¾in (152cm) wide.
£490–590 / €700–840
$820–980 ⚒ DN
Frank Christian worked in Newby Clapham, Yorkshire in the 1950s.

► A glazed earthenware low table, by Roger Capron, signed 'L/L', French, c1950, 38½in (98cm) wide.
£2,200–2,450 / €3,150–3,500
$3,700–4,100 ⊞ MI
Roger Capron is one of France's most distinguished ceramicists, based in Vallauris in the south of France.

A Heal's iron, brass and glass Atom table, 1950s, 26¼in (66.5cm) diam.
£330–390 / €480–570
$560–670 ⚒ SWO

A foam and vinyl Superronda sofa, by Archizoom Associati, Italian, 1966, 93in (236cm) wide.
£580–700 / €840–1,000
$1,000–1,200 ⚒ S(Am)
Archizoom began as an avant-garde architectural group in Florence in 1966, the name being an amalgam of the British architectural group Archigram and their journal Zoom. They produced kitsch artworks that played with people's perceptions of what was 'good' and 'bad' design, as a form of revolt against what they considered the pretensions of Modernist designers from earlier in the century. The Superronda foam seating unit is the epitome of Pop design. Although it looks like a sofa, it can be rearranged to form a variety of different types of furniture, such as a flat bed or a chaise longue. Designed in 1966, it came in a variety of colours and is still being produced today.

An enamelled metal, vinyl and laminate Scape dining suite, by Grant Featherston for Aristoc, comprising a table and six chairs, Australian, designed 1960.
£630–760 / €910–1,100
$1,050–1,250 ⚒ SHSY

A chrome and glass dining suite, comprising a dining table and six chairs, c1960, table 59in (150cm) diam.
£2,900–3,200 / €4,150–4,600
$4,850–5,400 ⊞ DeP

► A Lucite coffee table, with original glass top, American, c1965, 61in (155cm) wide.
£1,800–2,000
€2,600–2,900
$3,000–3,300
⊞ AGO

A hanging chrome Parrot chair, by Ib Arberg, Swedish, c1970, 64in (162cm) high.
£880–1,050
€1,250–1,500
$1,500–1,800 SWO

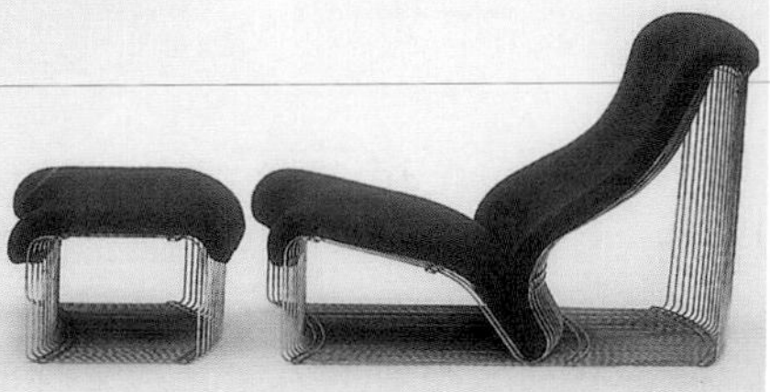

A chrome-plated and wool Pantonova relaxer and stool, by Verner Panton for Fritz Hansen, Danish, designed 1971.
£1,150–1,350 / €1,650–1,950
$1,950–2,250 SHSY

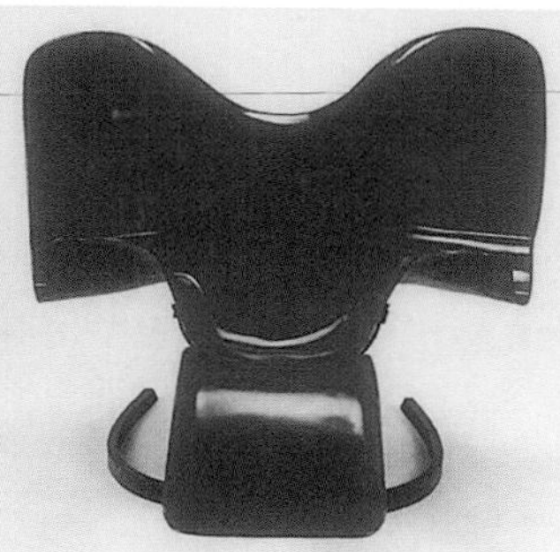

A moulded fibreglass and steel chair, by B. Rancillac, No. 45/100, French, 1970s, 56in (142cm) wide.
£1,300–1,550 / €1,900–2,250
$2,200–2,600 BB(L)

◄ **A set of six goatskin and chrome-plated tubular steel cantilever chairs,** by Peter Wigglesworth for Plush Kicker, c1970.
£330–390 / €480–560
$560–670 SWO

A rosewood and chrome nest of three tables, by Archie Shine, c1970, 48½in (123cm) wide.
£500–600 / €720–860
$840–1,000 SWO

A painted wood four-fold screen, by Cyril Fradan, with pierced circles and crosses within a divisional framework, dated 1972, 72in (183cm) high.
£320–380 / €460–550
$540–640 RTo

A Ghost Chair, by Cini Boeri for Fiam, limited edition, Italian, c1987.
£2,000–2,200 / €2,900–3,200
$3,350–3,700 ⊞ DeP

A pair of painted and laminated Polar occasional tables, by Michele de Lucchi for Memphis, Italian, designed 1984, 27½in (70cm) wide.
£660–790 / €1,000–1,150
$1,100–1,300 S(O)

The Memphis group was founded in Milan following a gathering held at the house of Ettore Sottsass in December 1980. With the purpose of discussing their ideas for a new creative approach to design, it was attended by many of the up-and-coming designers of the day, including Michele de Lucchi, Barbara Radice (Sottsass' wife) and Martine Bedin. The group derived its name from the Bob Dylan song 'Stuck Inside of Mobile with the Memphis Blues Again', which was playing for much of the evening, and its work was shown for the first time in Milan in September 1981. Memphis designers used new materials, particularly patterned laminated plastics, to achieve brightly-coloured and often kitsch effects and the group dominated Italian avant-garde design throughout the 1980s. Most pieces are marked, and some also bear the designer's name and the date and place of manufacture. Condition is important – once plastic cannot be restored, damage can affect the value of a piece.

► **An enamelled metal and wool Embryo chair,** by Marc Newson for Idee, Japan, designed 1988.
£2,650–3,200
€3,850–4,600
$4,500–5,400 SHSY

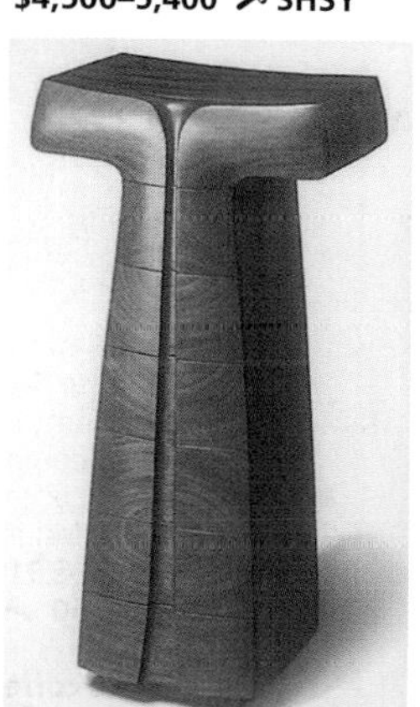

A Honduran mahogany lingerie chest, by David D. Ebner, signed, American, dated 1986, 24in (61cm) wide.
£7,100–8,500
€10,200–12,200
$11,900–14,300 S(NY)

A bent and woven laminated wood Powerplay armchair, by Frank Gehry, stamped 'Gehry/Knoll/made in USA/4/16/93, American, 1990–92.
£1,050–1,250 / €1,500–1,800
$1,750–2,100 S(NY)

Glass

An Orrefors Turkos Selena glass bowl, by Sven Palmqvist, with manufacturer's exhibition label, engraved 'Orrefors PU3090/14', Swedish, 1950, 9½in (24cm) diam.
£730–880 / €1,050–1,250
$1,250–1,500 SHSY

An Orrefors Melon glass vase, by Ingeborg Lundin, signed, Swedish, c1955, 13in (33cm) high.
£1,700–2,050 / €2,450–2,900
$2,900–3,450 BUK

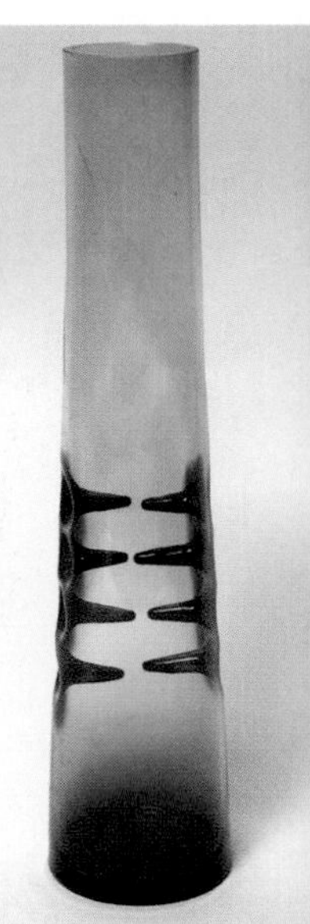

A Cesky glass vase, by Pavel Hlava, decorated with punctured hollow spikes, Czechoslovakian, c1950, 14in (35.5cm) high.
£1,400–1,550
€2,000–2,200
$2,350–2,600 MI

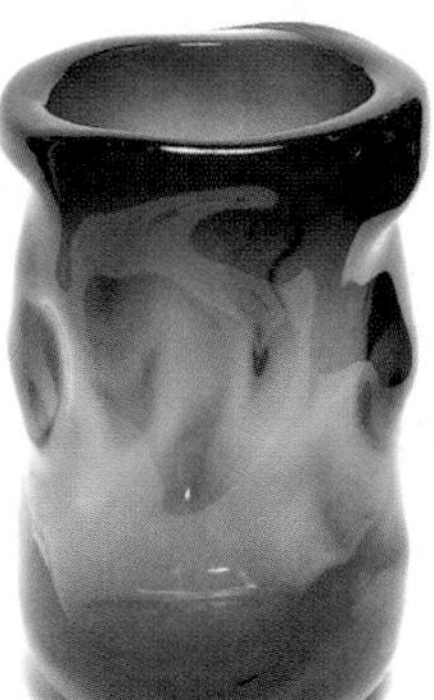

A Whitefriars Nobbly glass vase, 1960s, 8in (20.5cm) high.
£75–85 / €105–120
$125–140 LUNA

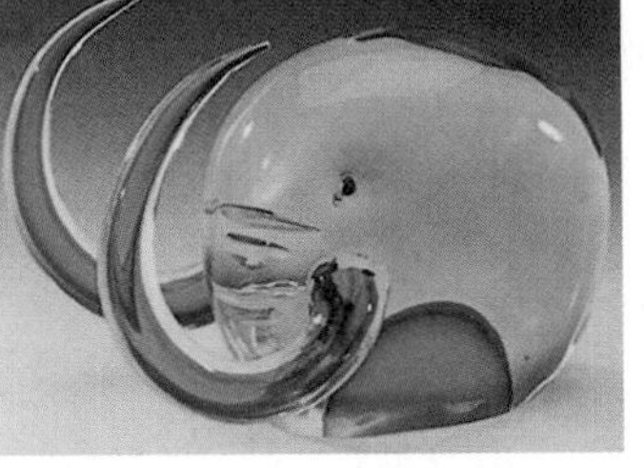

A Cenedese glass sculpture of a mammoth, by Antonio da Ros, manufacturer's label, Italian, c1960, 8in (20.5cm) wide.
£1,050–1,250 / €1,500–1,800
$1,750–2,100 SHSY

An Orrefors glass vase, by Sven Palmqvist, Swedish, c1960, 11½in (29cm) high.
£80–90
€115–130
$135–150
MARK

A Whitefriars Drunken Bricklayers glass vase, by Geoffrey Baxter, c1970, 8¼in (21cm) high.
£230–270 / €330–390
$390–460 NSal

A Whitefriars glass Banjo vase, by Geoffrey Baxter, c1970, 12½in (32cm) high.
£1,350–1,600
€1,950–2,300
$2,250–2,700 WW

A Murano glass dish, with label, Italian, c1960, 12½in (32cm) diam.
£290–350 / €420–500
$490–590 SHSY

► **A Salviati glass vase,** by Claire Falkenstein, with three applied opalescent tubes terminating in short feet, signed to base '14/24, Claire Falkenstein 1973 Salviati', with paper label, Italian, 17¼in (44cm) high.
£1,750–2,100
€2,500–3,000
$2,950–3,550 DORO

An Emergence glass sculpture, by Dominick Labino, enclosing an air-trapped bubble and two dichroic veils with gold aventurine, signed 'Labino 11-1979', American, 7¾in (19.5cm) high.
£4,100–4,900
€5,900–7,000
$6,900–8,200 JAA

A sculptured glass vase by Howard Ben Tré, American, 1980s, 7in (18cm) high.
£620–740 / €880–1,050
$1,000–1,200 JAA

Jewellery

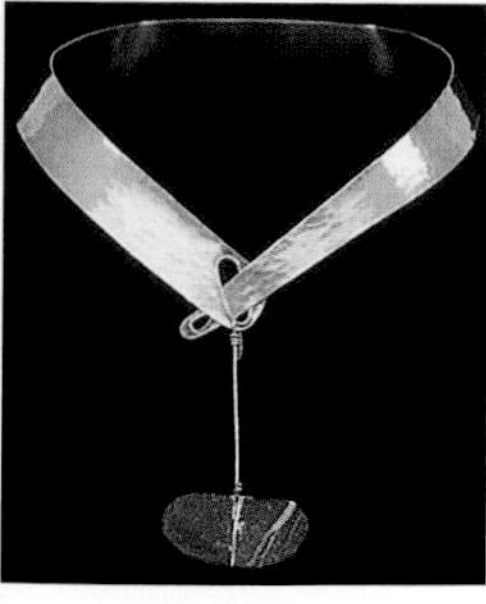

◄ **A silver necklace,** by Vivianna Torun Bülow Hübe, with a detachable Mediterranean stone pendant, Swedish, Stockholm 1953.
£1,800–2,150 / €2,600–3,100
$3,000–3,600 ⚒ BUK

A silver brooch, by Wiwen Nilsson, in the form of a flying peacock, Swedish, Lund 1969, 3¼in (8.5cm) wide.
£600–720 / €860–1,000
$1,000–1,200 ⚒ BUK

A silver Signatures brooch, by Ivan Tarratt for Geoffrey Bellamy, in the form of two bellflowers amid scrolled foliage, Birmingham 1962, 1½in (4cm) wide, with case.
£60–70 / €70–80
$100–115 ⚒ CDC

An opal pendant and ring, on a chain, c1970, 22¾in (58cm) long.
£460–550 / €660–790
$770–920 ⚒ S(O)

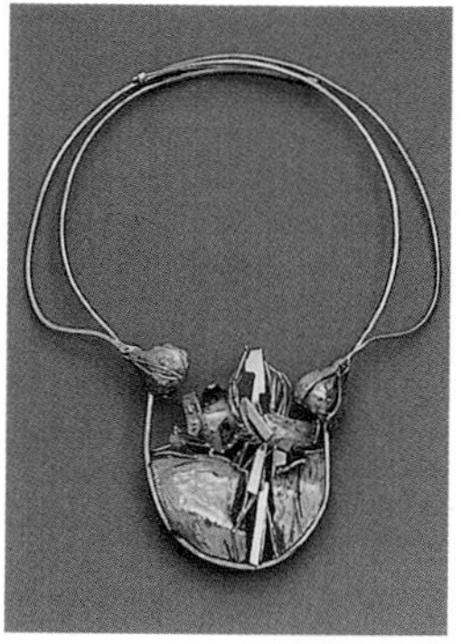

► **A tourmaline and gold necklace,** the tourmaline plaque pendant within a wirework surround, on a gold torque necklace, maker's mark 'GGM', London 1972.
£280–330 / €400–470
$470–550 ⚒ TEN

◄ **A 14ct gold necklace,** by Glenda Arentzen, with inscription, American, 1976, 7½in (19cm) wide.
£4,650–5,600
€6,700–8,000
$7,900–9,400 ⚒ S(NY)

Lighting

. **chiselled glass and hrome hanging lamp,** y Fontana Arte, Italian, 930s, 15¾in (40cm) high.
1,100–1,200
1,600–1,800
1,800–2,000 ⊞ DeP

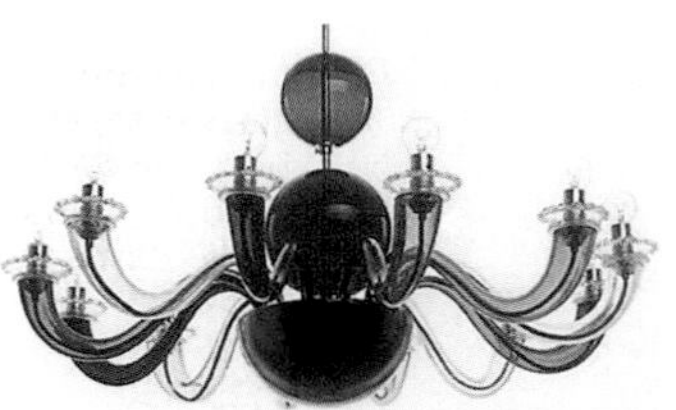

A glass and brass twelve-light chandelier, by Gio Ponti for Venini, fitted for electricity, Italian, c1950, 34¾in (88.5cm) diam.
£5,100–6,100 / €7,300–8,700
$8,600–10,200 ⚒ SHSY

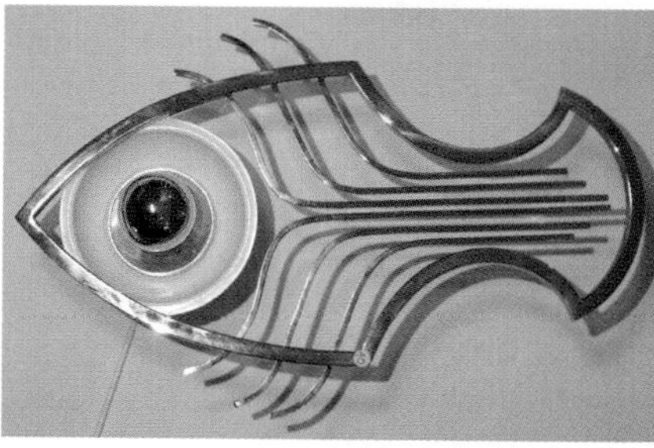

A pair of chrome wall lamps, Italian, 1960s, 20in (51cm) wide.
£540–600
€780–860
$900–1,000
⊞ DeP

A Plexiglass and metal ye lamp, by Nicola, edition /50, signed, Italian, dated 968, 60in (155cm) high.
340–1,000
1,200–1,400
,450–1,700 ⚒ BB(L)

A pair of Lucite table lamps, American, c1970, 10in (25.5cm) high.
£810–900 / €1,150–1,300
$1,350–1,500 ⊞ AGO

A painted metal Treetops standard lamp, by Ettore Sottsass for Memphis, Italian, designed 1981, 75½in (192cm) high.
£1,200–1,450
€1,750–2,100
$2,000–2,400 ⚒ S(O)

Metalware

◀ **A silver dish,** by Tiffany, with fluted scroll handles, American, 1950s, 16in (40.5cm) wide, 27oz.
£1,700–1,900 / €2,450–2,750
$2,850–3,200 ⊞ KK

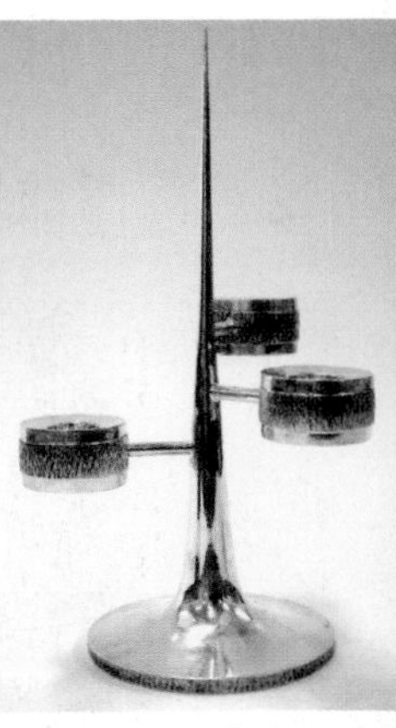

A silver three-light candelabrum, by Gerald Benney, with a central spike and textured decoration, 1957, 11in (28cm) high, 15oz.
£700–840 / €1,000–1,200
$1,200–1,400 ⚒ G(L)

A silver-plated four-piece Pride tea service, by David Mellor for Walker & Hall, 1959.
£450–500 / €650–720
$760–840 ⊞ JSG

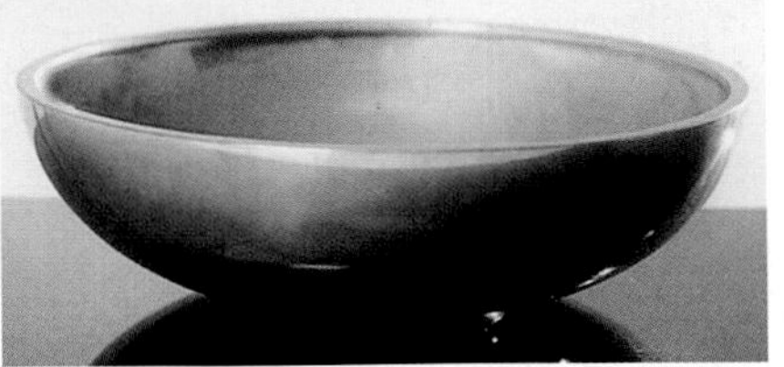

A pewter bowl, by Henning Koppel for Georg Jensen, impressed marks, Danish, c1980, 10½in (26.5cm) diam.
£820–980 / €1,200–1,400
$1,400–1,650 ⚒ SHSY

Sculpture

A bronze figure of a clarinet player, by Mane-Katz, signed 'MK', French, c1952, 11in (28cm) high.
£2,200–2,450
€3,150–3,500
$3,700–4,100 ⊞ MI

A lacquered-iron sculpture, by Antoni Milkowski, entitled 'Untitled Sketch', American, 1966, 8in (20.5cm) high.
£390–470 / €560–670
$650–780 ⚒ LHA

A chromed-steel sculpture, by Eduardo Paolozzi, entitled 'Ety', inscribed, maker's mark, 1967, 16½in (42cm) high.
£1,100–1,300
€1,600–1,900
$1,850–2,200 ⚒ LHA

A lacquered-bronze sculpture, by Robert Adams, entitled 'Link', numbered 1/6, American, 1973, 10½in (26.5cm) high.
£1,550–1,850
€2,250–2,650
$2,600–3,100 ⚒ LHA

LOCATE THE SOURCE

The source of each illustration in Miller's can be found by checking the code letters below each caption with the Key to Illustrations, pages 794–800.

Miscellaneous

A glass and bronze clock, by Fontana Arte, Italian, 1940s, 16in (40.5cm) square.
£1,050–1,200
€1,500–1,700
$1,750–2,000 ⊞ DeP

Items in the Twentieth-Century Design section have been arranged in date order within each sub-section.

◀ **A Bakelite New World Globe radio,** by Colonial Radio Corp, model No. 700, with gilt decoration, maker's mark and design patent No. 90586, American, c1933, 16in (40.5cm) high.
£710–850 / €1,000–1,200
$1,200–1,450 ⚒ S(NY)

A mirrored-glass and chrome-plated metal Bluebird radio, by Walte Dorwin Teague for the Sparton Corporation, printe paper label, American, c1934, 14½in (37cm) diar
£3,100–3,700
€4,500–5,300
$5,200–6,200 ⚒ S(NY)

TWENTIETH-CENTURY DESIGN

Lamps & Lighting

Ceiling & Wall Lights

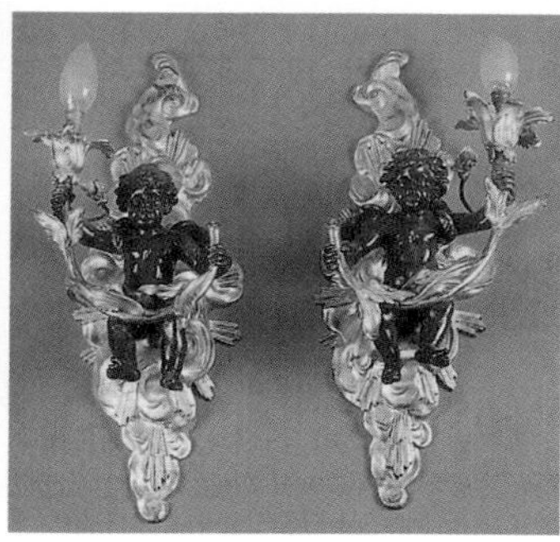

A pair of gilt-brass and bronze wall sconces, with putti holding torches, fitted for electricity, French, 19thC, 19in (48cm) high.
£1,100–1,300 / €1,600–1,850
$1,850–2,200 JAd

A glass lustre chandelier, the four candle branches with glass drip trays, Swedish, 19thC, 27in (68.5cm) high.
£540–650 / €780–940
$910–1,100 G(L)

A pair of Victorian Gothic-style brass ceiling lights, in the manner of John Hardman, with lion-mask tops, converted for electricity, slight damage, 32in (81cm) wide.
£3,300–3,950 / €4,750–5,700
$5,500–6,600 WW

John Hardman & Co, founded in Birmingham in 1838, described themselves as medieval metal-workers. They produced ecclesiastical and domestic plate to designs by A. W. N. Pugin and William Burges, among others. From the 1840s, they extended their output to include brasswork, embroidery and stained glass.

A Victorian brass and leaded glass hall lantern, 18½in (47cm) high.
£220–260 / €310–370
$370–440 CHTR

◄ **A Victorian Gothic revival brass hanging light fitting,** lacquered to simulate gilt, 19in (48cm) wide.
£200–240 / €290–350
$340–410 PFK

A rococo revival gilt-lacquered bronze and brass six-arm gasolier, by Cornelius & Baker, fitted for electricity, marked, shade associated, American, Philadelphia, 1850–75, 37in (94cm) high.
£7,200–8,600
€10,300–12,400
$12,100–14,400 NOA

An ormolu three-branch gas lamp, with handmade frosted glass shades, c1870, 32in (81.5cm) high.
£450–500 / €650–720
$760–840 EAL

A gas pendant lamp, with original glass shade, c1880, 37in (94cm) diam.
£490–550 / €700–790
$820–920 CHA

A late Victorian oxidized copper and cut-glass ceiling lamp, decorated with a ram's head and swag motif, fitted for electricity, 12in (30.5cm) wide.
£310–350 / €450–500
$520–590 ⊞ EAL

◄ **A silver-plated brass six-arm ceiling lamp,** with cut-glass shades, 1890–1900, 25in (63.5cm) wide.
£680–750
€980–1,100
$1,100–1,250
⊞ EAL

A brass three-branch rise and fall gasolier, with cranberry glass shades, c1894, 42in (106.5cm) high.
£1,500–1,650
€2,150–2,400
$2,500–2,750 ⊞ CHA

A pair of gilt-metal three-branch wall lights, cast with foliate scrolls and a flower finial, early 20thC, 23¼in (59cm) high.
£3,400–4,100
€4,900–5,900
$5,700–6,800 ⚒ DN

An Edwardian oxidized copper rise and fall lamp, with etched glass shades, 44in (112cm) high.
£360–400 / €520–580
$600–670 ⊞ EAL

An Edwardian cast-brass hall lantern, with a cut-glass shade, 49¼in (125cm) high.
£520–620 / €740–890
$870–1,050 ⚒ TRM

A brass lantern, with a vaseline glass liner, c1910, 16in (40.5cm) diam.
£580–650 / €830–930
$970–1,100 ⊞ CHA

An Edwardian gilded-brass three-branch ceiling light, with original opaque glass shades, 21in (53.5cm) high.
£290–320 / €410–460
$490–540 ⊞ EAL

◄ **An Edwardian cut-glass and silver-plated ceiling bowl,** in the manne of Osler, minor damage, 16½in (42cm) wide.
£1,100–1,300
€1,600–1,850
$1,850–2,200 ⚒ B(Kn)

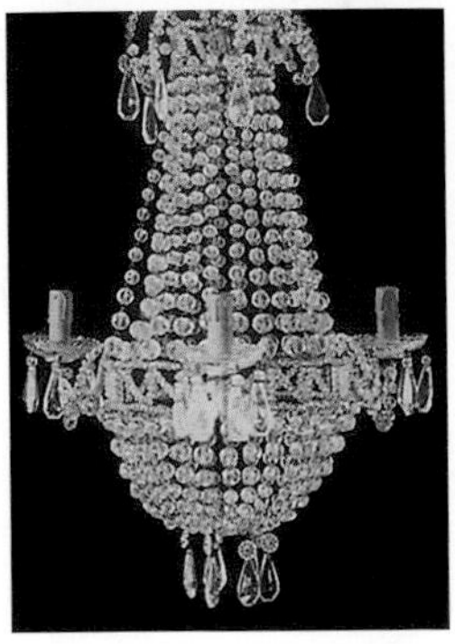

◄ **A three-light cut-glass chandelier,** fitted for electricity, Italian, 1900–25, 25in (63.5cm) high.
£680–810 / €980–1,150
$1,150–1,350 ⚒ NOA

► **A four-tier chandelier,** with staged hanging lustres terminating in a prismatic cut finial, early 20thC, 31in (80cm) high.
£440–520 / €630–750
$740–870 ⚒ HOLL

A cast-brass hanging lamp, with original shades, French, c1920, 18in (45.5cm) wide.
£670–750 / €960–1,100
$1,100–1,250 ⊞ CHA

Table & Standard Lamps

A gilt-bronze *lampe à bouillotte*, fitted for electricity, Swedish, 1800–20, 19¾in (50cm) high.
£2,900–3,500
€4,150–5,000
$4,850–5,800 BUK

A silver travel/carriage lamp, by Thomas Johnson, London 1862, 5¾in (14.5cm) high.
£1,100–1,250
€1,600–1,800
$1,850–2,100 ChC
To use this lamp, the lid is lifted enabling the two bowfronted doors to be opened, revealing the candle holder. The base is then extended down and twisted on its bayonet fitting to stay in place. The matches, which are contained in a compartment below the grille, can be struck on the serrated underside of the lamp base. The candle is replaced by unscrewing the base, giving access to the leg of the lamp which holds the candle. The holder has a spring which pushes the candle up as it burns. A removable bowfronted piece of glass would originally have been placed behind the two doors to protect the flame from the wind.

A patinated-bronze Argand lamp, fitted for electricity, early 19thC, 17½in (44.5cm) high.
£240–290 / €340–410
$400–480 COBB
An Argand lamp, named after an 18th-century French physicist, is fitted with a cylindrical burner which allows air to pass both the inner and outer surfaces of the flame.

A pair of Burmese glass and brass oil lamps, the shades moulded with scrolling foliage, on Corinthian columns, 19thC, 20in (51cm) high.
£800–960 / €1,150–1,350
$1,350–1,600 GAK
Burmese glass, characterized by a body colour which graduates from yellow to pale pink, was originally produced in the US in 1886 by the Mount Washington Glass Company. In Britain, in the same year, this style of glass was patented by Thomas Webb & Sons under the name 'Queen's Burmese', so-called because it was favoured by Queen Victoria.

► **A Victorian brass oil lamp,** with a cut-glass oil well and etched-glass shade, 25in (63.5cm) high.
£340–380 / €490–550
$570–640 EAL

A gilt-iron lamp base, early 19thC, 14¼in (36cm) high.
£1,650–1,950
€2,400–2,800
$2,750–3,250 S(P)

A brass-mounted marble and cut-glass kerosene lamp, Anglo-American, 1850–75, 31in (78.5cm) high.
£200–240 / €290–340
$340–400 NOA

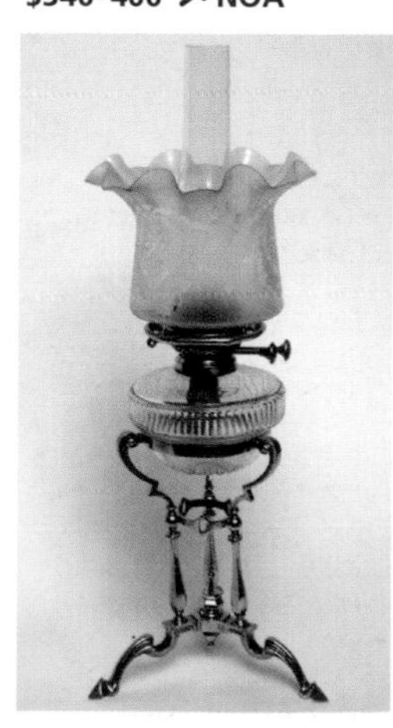

A pair of brass spirit lamps, the Corinthian columns with vented hand-warming capitals and flame finials, 19thC, 19½in (49.5cm) high.
£330–390 / €470–560
$550–650 TMA

A gilt-mounted porcelain table lamp, fitted for electricity, 19thC, 18½in (47cm) high.
£230–270 / €330–390
$380–450 SWO

A bronze table lamp, fitted for electricity, with moulded cranberry glass font and shade, late 19thC, 16in (40.5cm) high.
£720–850 / €1,050–1,250
$1,200–1,450 JAA

A brass adjustable standard lamp, c1890, 70in (178cm) high.
£670–750 / €960–1,100
$1,100–1,250 ⊞ CHA

A pair of brass-mounted, enamelled and parcel-gilt lamps, the cranberry glass hurricane shades with diamond-cut reserves, fitted for electricity, Bohemian, 1875–1900, 28½in (72.5cm) high.
£410–490 / €590–700
$690–820 ⚒ NOA

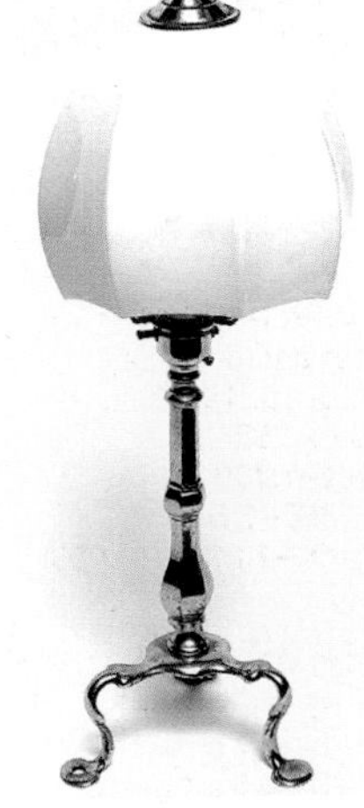

A chrome-plated Pullman lamp, with original glass shade, 1910–20, 20in (51cm) high.
£90–100 / €130–145
$150–170 ⊞ EAL

A brass portable table lamp, with an etched-glass shade, c1890, 18in (45.5cm) high.
£530–590 / €760–850
$890–990 ⊞ CHA

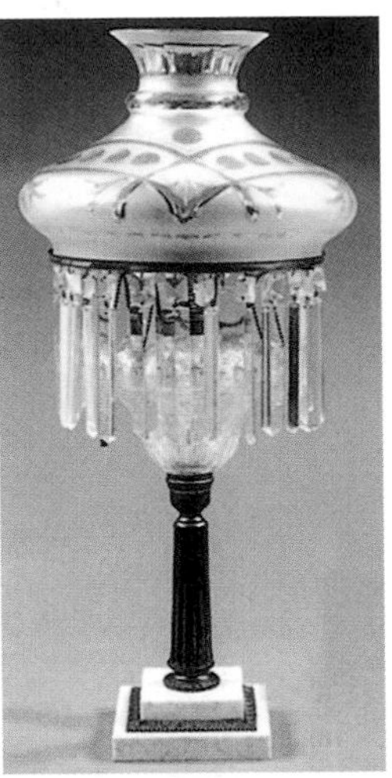

A late Victorian silver library oil lamp, by J. N. Mappin, engraved inscription, fitted for electricity, London 1890, 20in (51cm) high.
£7,500–9,000
€10,800–13,000
$12,600–15,100 ⚒ WW
This lamp was given by Queen Victoria to Lord Edward Pelham Clinton, Master of the Household (1894–1901), in remembrance of Her Majesty's Diamond Jubilee.

◀ **A gilt-brass and cut-glass lamp,** with a marble base, American, 1875–1900, 28in (71cm) high.
£2,050–2,450
€2,950–3,500
$3,450–4,100 ⚒ NOA

An Edwardian brass desk lamp, embossed with scrolls, repairs and alterations, 15½in (39.5cm) high.
£200–240 / €290–340
$340–400 ⚒ BR

A leaded glass and patinated-metal table lamp, American, early 20thC, shade 25in (63.5cm) square.
£2,800–3,350
€4,000–4,800
$4,700–5,600 ⚒ BB(L)

► **A cold-painted bronze table lamp,** possibly Viennese School, in the form of an Arabian house, on a marble base, early 20thC, 15in (38cm) high.
£900–1,050
€1,300–1,500
$1,500–1,750
⚒ S(Am)

A gilt-spelter lamp, modelled as a young girl seated on a tree stump, late 19thC, 46in (117cm) high.
£890–1,050
€1,300–1,500
$1,500–1,750 ⚒ Bea

A brass table lamp, with a cranberry glass shade, the gas mantle with later conversion, c1910, 22in (60cm) high.
£490–550 / €710–790
$820–920 ⊞ CHA

A cut-glass electric tabl lamp, the two lights with chain-pull switches, 1920 16in (40.5cm) high.
£350–420 / €500–600
$590–700 ⚒ CDC

Rugs & Carpets

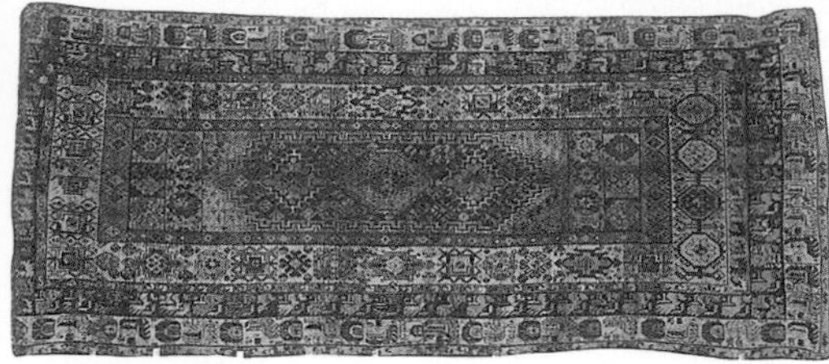

A Rabat carpet, Moroccan, mid-19thC, 63¾ x 150in (161 x 381cm).
£1,650–1,950 / €2,350–2,800
$2,750–3,250 ⚒ B(Kn)
Most Moroccan carpets are comparable in their layout and proportions to the so-called 'Safavid Portuguese' carpets and their motifs are primarily influenced from the 18th-century Anatolian, specifically Konya, rugs. In this piece it can be seen predominantly in the Konya-type borders of serrated flowerheads. The shape of this carpet suited the room sizes of Moroccan houses, which were based around a central courtyard until fashions in architecture changed in the late 19th century.

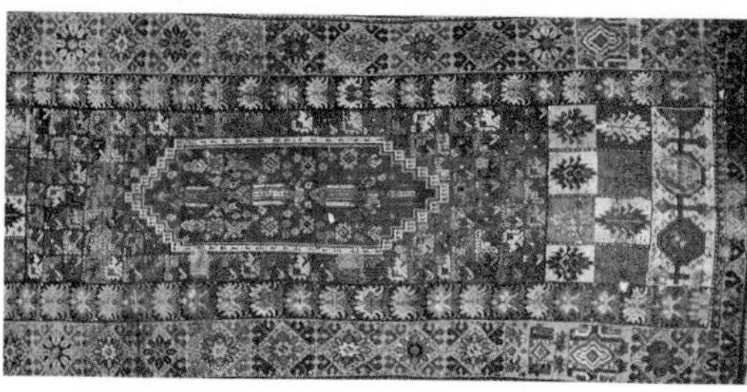

A Rabat carpet, some wear and damage, Moroccan, 1850–75, 71 x 162in (180.5 x 411cm).
£1,250–1,500 / €1,800–2,150
$2,100–2,500 ⚒ WW
Rabat carpets of good age and free of synthetic dyes are now extremely rare. They have never been common in Europe.

European carpet production

The most highly prized European carpets are those from the great factory known as Savonnerie, in France, established in the 17th century. The workshops produced magnificent floral pile weavings in vibrant colours – the first carpets produced in the west that are typically European in design. These were pile weavings. By the mid-18th century, demand outstripped the capabilities of the factory. Carpets with similar designs were then produced using the tapestry technique known as *tapis-ras* at workshops at Aubusson. Production was prolific until the early part of the 20th century.

English carpet-weaving centres were established in the 18th century to compete with France, and their designs tended to imitate French styles, Axminster and Wilton being the most well known centres of manufacture. Belgium and Austria copied the French Savonnerie styles too, but products tend to be of inferior quality. Spain is the only European country to have an indigenous carpet industry, and their designs owe much to the influence of Moorish culture. Spanish carpets of the Moorish period up to the 15th century were similar to early Anatolian designs: from the mid-18th century their designs were inspired by French examples.

A Cuenca rug, some wear and restoration, Spanish, c1700, 78 x 50¾in (198 x 129cm).
£3,000–3,600
€4,300–5,200
$5,000–6,000 ⚒ S

A carpet, some wear and damage, Spanish, signed and dated 1901, 200 x 162in (520 x 405cm).
£700–840 / €1,000–1,200
$1,200–1,400 ⚒ WW
A fully signed and dated Spanish carpet is most unusual and of considerable documentary interest.

A Savonnerie-style carpet, stained, Belgian, c1920, 200 x 154in (508 x 391cm).
£5,700–6,800
€8,200–9,800
$9,600–11,500 ⚒ S(NY)

A Wilton carpet, slight wear and damage, 1820–40, 198¾ x 59¾in (497 x 152cm).
£940–1,100
€1,350–1,600
$1,600–1,850 ⚒ WW

◄ **An Aubusson carpet,** French, 1850–1900, 230 x 228in (584 x 578cm).
£4,550–5,500 / €6,600–7,900
$7,700–9,200 ⚒ S(O)

► **A Bessarabian kilim,** Romanian, probably Pirot, c1900, 109 x 75in (277 x 190.5cm).
£3,600–4,000
€5,200–5,800
$6,000–6,700 ⊞ WADS
Pirot in Romania is known for making particularly fine kilims.

A Bergama carpet, some damage and repairs, Turkish, c1800, 111½ x 57in (283 x 145cm).
£4,200–5,000
€6,000–7,200
$7,000–8,400 ⚒ S

A Kula prayer rug, Turkish, c1800, 85¾ x 58in (218 x 157cm).
£1,300–1,550
€1,900–2,250
$2,200–2,600 ⚒ S(O)

An Isparta carpet, Turkish, early 20thC, 226 x 145¾in (574 x 370cm).
£840–1,000 / €1,200–1,400
$1,400–1,650 ⚒ S(O)

A Smyrna carpet, damage and minor repairs, Turkish, 18th/19thC, 132¼ x 116in (337 x 295cm).
£1,200–1,400 / €1,750–2,000
$2,000–2,350 ⚒ BUK
Smyrna carpets tend to include large blue medallions in the design.

◄ **An Isparta carpet,** Turkish, 1900–20, 188 x 115in (478 x 292cm).
£1,050–1,250 / €1,500–1,800
$1,750–2,100 ⚒ WW

A Kum Kapi silk pictorial rug, minor wear, partially faded, Turkish, c1910, 55 x 82¾in (140 x 210cm).
£6,000–7,200 / €8,600–10,400
$10,100–12,100 ⚒ S
Rugs woven by the Armenian weavers of the so-called Kum Kapi workshops in Istanbul usually derived their inspiration from Safavid designs. This rug is unusual, however, due to its pictorial subject matter, arranged in a landscape format and influenced by 19th-century European Orientalist pictures. The scene depicts a group of travellers and their mules in front of the mosque of Sultan Ahmed II, with the Blue Mosque in the distance.

The rugs in this section have been arranged in geographical sequence from west to east, in the following order: Europe, Turkey, Anatolia, Caucasus, Persia, Turkestan, India and China.

A Yürük kilim, minor damage, probably central Anatolian, 1850–1900, 37 x 48in (94 x 122cm).
£280–330 / €400–470
$470–550 ⚒ WW

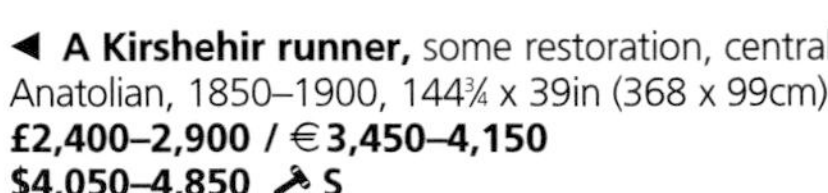

◄ **A Kirshehir runner,** some restoration, central Anatolian, 1850–1900, 144¾ x 39in (368 x 99cm).
£2,400–2,900 / €3,450–4,150
$4,050–4,850 ⚒ S

► **A Bezalel carpet,** slight wear and repairs, Israeli, Jerusalem, early 20thC, 86½ x 65in (220 x 165cm).
£6,600–7,900 / €9,500–11,400
$11,100–13,300 ⚒ S
Founded in Jerusalem by Boris Schaatz in the early 20th century, the Bezalel school of Arts and Crafts was established to forge a Jewish National style that would unify Jews with their European counterparts to promote Zionist ideas. Output in the early days included a wide range of objects from tiles to jewellery, but this period is most associated with the production of rugs and carpets. Material used were silk, wool and cotton and designs often incorporated religious themes and a curious blend of symbols and styles from the home countries of the rug designers.

A Gendje Kazak rug, southwest Caucasian, c1880, 87 x 53in (221 x 134.5cm).
£2,700–3,000
€3,900–4,300
$4,500–5,000 WADS

A Gendje runner, some wear, slight loss, southwest Caucasian, c1880, 92¼ x 40½in (234.5 x 102cm).
£1,200–1,400
€1,750–2,000
$2,000–2,350 S

A Gendje Kazak rug, southwest Caucasian, c1900, 63¾ x 41¾in (162 x 106cm).
£660–790 / €950–1,100
$1,100–1,300 S(O)

A Karabagh runner, south Caucasian, c1890, 132 x 41in (335.5 x 104cm).
£850–950 / €1,200–1,350
$1,450–1,600 WADS

A Kazak rug, wear and damage, west Caucasian, 1850–75, 97¼ x 44in (247 x 112cm).
£1,400–1,650
€2,000–2,400
$2,350–2,750 S

A Kazak Lori Pambak rug, wear, southwest Caucasian, c1880, 80¾ x 55½in (205 x 141cm).
£2,000–2,400
€2,900–3,450
$3,350–4,050 S

A Kazak rug, southwest Caucasian, c1900, 89¾ x 61½in (228 x 156cm).
£1,300–1,550
€1,850–2,200
$2,200–2,600 S(O)

A Baku Chila carpet, minor repiling, northeast Caucasian, c1880, 150 x 53¼in (381 x 135cm).
£2,850–3,400
€4,100–4,900
$4,800–5,700 S(NY)

A Kuba rug, northeast Caucasian, c1890, 41 x 73in (104 x 185.5cm).
£7,200–8,000 / €10,400–11,500
$12,100–13,400 WADS

A Kuba Chi Chi runner, northeast Caucasian, c1890, 159 x 42½in (404 x 108cm).
£2,450–2,950
€3,550–4,250
$4,100–4,950 RTo

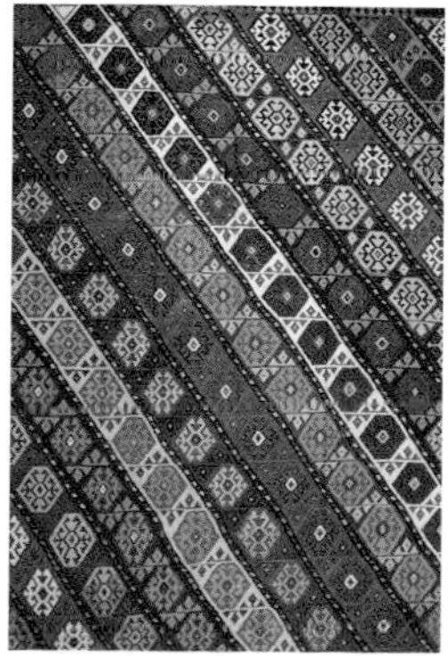

A Kuba kilim, northeast Caucasian, c1900, 219½ x 108¼in (549 x 275cm).
£1,000–1,200
€1,450–1,700
$1,700–2,000 WW

◄ **A Kuba rug,** northeast Caucasian, c1900, 47 x 82in (119.5 x 208.5cm).
£175–210 / €250–300
$290–350 G(L)

◄ **A Kuba rug,** reduced in size, northeast Caucasian, c1900, 59¾ x 100½in (152 x 255cm).
£420–500
€600–720
$710–840
⚒ S(O)

A Marasali prayer rug, minor restoration, east Caucasian, late 19thC, 61½ x 46in (156 x 117cm).
£2,400–2,900 / €3,450–4,150
$4,050–4,850 ⚒ S

A Moghan rug, minor losses, south Caucasian, c1900, 42½ x 85½in (108 x 217cm).
£2,400–2,900 / €3,450–4,150
$4,050–4,850 ⚒ S
White ground examples are particularly popular and more sought after than other coloured fields, particularly in this type of rug.

A Perepedil prayer rug, minor wear and repiling, selvages replaced, east Caucasian, c1890, 67 x 45¼in (170 x 115cm).
£2,150–2,600 / €3,100–3,700
$3,600–4,350 ⚒ S

A Moghan runner, overall wear, some restoration, south Caucasian, c1900, 128 x 39¼in (335 x 100cm).
£210–250 / €300–360
$350–420 ⚒ WW

A Shirvan rug, east Caucasian, c1900, 78 x 50in (198 x 127cm).
£910–1,100 / €1,300–1,550
$1,550–1,850 ⚒ LHA

A Shirvan rug, east Caucasian, early 20thC, 114 x 45in (289.5 x 114.5cm).
£2,800–3,350 / €4,050–4,800
$4,700–5,600 ⚒ G(L)

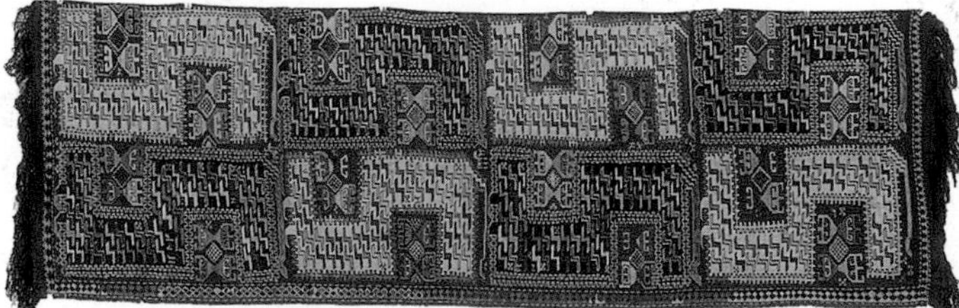

A Sileh panel, south Caucasian, dated AH1284 (1866), 41 x 123¼in (104 x 313cm).
£2,850–3,400 / €4,100–4,900
$4,800–5,700 ⚒ S

► **A runner,** south Caucasian, dated AH1314 (1897), 41 x 143¾in (104 x 365cm).
£730–870 / €1,050–1,250
$1,250–1,450 ⚒ B(Kn)

‹n Afshar rug, with flowerhead
notifs, southwest Persian, late
9thC, 70 x 48½in (178 x 123cm).
540–650 / €780–940
910–1,100 AMB

Bakshaish carpet, northwest
ersian, c1880, 161½ x 137in
10 x 348cm).
14,000–18,600 / €20,000–24,000
24,000–28,000 RTo
his carpet, with its pale ackground and decorative overall esign in popular colours of pale ue and terracotta, is extremely ought after in today's market.

Feraghan cushion, west Persian,
370, 18in (45.5cm) square.
5–85 / €105–120
25–140 DNo

Heriz carpet, northwest Persian,
380, 120 x 86in (305 x 218.5cm).
400–6,000 / €7,800–8,600
100–10,100 WADS

An Isfahan rug, central Persian,
00, 83¾ x 52¼in (213 x 133cm).
650–1,950 / €2,350–2,800
750–3,250 S

An Afshar rug, southwest Persian, c1900,
32 x 33in (81.5 x 84cm).
£630–700 / €900–1,000
$1,050–1,200 WADS
Rugs of this size are rare and their function is unknown. This example is made with exceptionally soft lustrous wool.

A Bakhtiari rug, some wear and losses, west
Persian, 1920–30, 63 x 118in (160 x 300cm).
£175–210 / €250–300
$290–350 WW

A Bidjar rug, with Herati design, some wear,
staining and damage, northwest Persian, early
20thC, 216 x 130in (548.5 x 330cm).
£3,400–4,100 / €4,900–5,900
$5,700–6,800 COBB

► **A Hamadan rug,**
west Persian, c1900,
52 x 74in (132 x 188cm).
£400–450 / €580–650
$670–750 DNo

◄ **A Joshagan carpet,**
central Persian,
early 20thC,
163½ x 142½in
(415 x 362cm).
£1,100–1,300
€1,600–1,850
$1,850–2,200
S(O)

A Seichur Ardebil rug,
northwest Persian, 1920–30,
78 x 52in (198 x 132cm).
£220–260 / €320–380
$370–440 WW

A Garrus Bidjar carpet,
with Harshang design,
northwest Persian,
19thC, 220½ x 131½in
(560 x 334cm).
£14,000–18,600
€20,000–24,000
$24,000–28,000 SH
Harshang is a design often seen in northwest Persian and south Caucasian carpets and rugs, and refers to the repeat stylized floral design as seen in the blue field of this carpet.

A Kamo *soffreh*, central Persian, 1875–1900, 37 x 50in (94 x 127cm).
£1,300–1,450 / €1,850–2,100
$2,200–2,450 ⊞ SAM

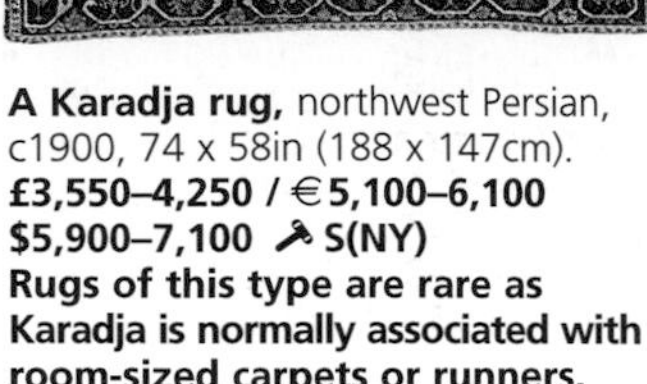

A Karadja rug, northwest Persian, c1900, 74 x 58in (188 x 147cm).
£3,550–4,250 / €5,100–6,100
$5,900–7,100 ⚒ S(NY)
Rugs of this type are rare as Karadja is normally associated with room-sized carpets or runners.

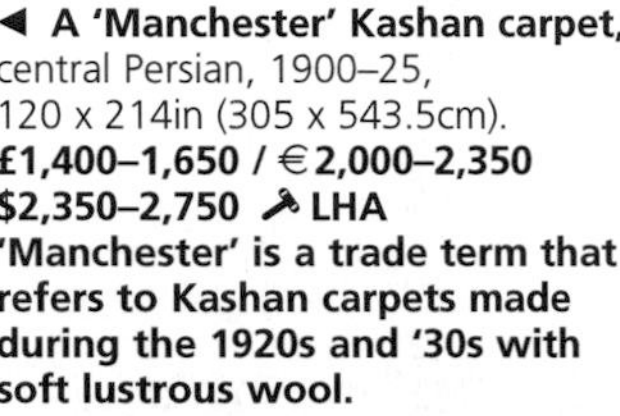

A Karadja runner, northwest Persian, c1910, 133 x 36in (338 x 91.5cm).
£670–750 / €960–1,200
$1,100–1,250 ⊞ WADS

◄ A 'Manchester' Kashan carpet, central Persian, 1900–25, 120 x 214in (305 x 543.5cm).
£1,400–1,650 / €2,000–2,350
$2,350–2,750 ⚒ LHA
'Manchester' is a trade term that refers to Kashan carpets made during the 1920s and '30s with soft lustrous wool.

A Kashan prayer rug, slight wear and minor damage, central Persian, 1900–20, 80 x 53¼in (203 x 135cm).
£300–360 / €430–510
$500–600 ⚒ WW

A Kashan rug, central Persian, c1910, 35 x 25in (89 x 63.5cm).
£540–600 / €780–860
$900–1,000 ⊞ WADS

► A Kashgai rug, southwest Persian, c1870, 90 x 62in (228.5 x 157.5cm).
£2,150–2,400
€3,100–3,450
$3,600–4,050
⊞ WADS

A Khamseh carpet, southwest Persian, c1890, 116 x 73in (294.5 x 185.5cm).
£1,800–2,000 / €2,600–2,900
$3,000–3,350 ⊞ WADS

A Khorasan *kelleh*, northeast Persian, late 19thC, 72 x 171in (183 x 434.5cm).
£1,050–1,250 / €1,500–1,800
$1,750–2,100 ⚒ G(L)

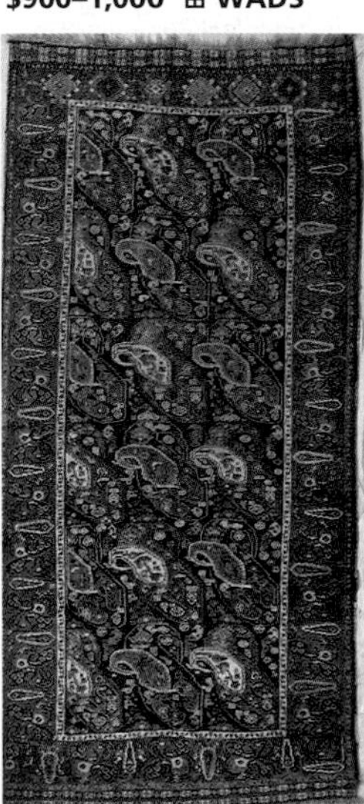

◄ A Khamseh rug, some wear, southwest Persian, 1850–1900, 137 x 65in (348 x 165cm).
£1,750–2,100
€2,500–3,000
$2,900–3,500 ⚒ WW

► A Kurdish rug, northwest Persian/south Caucasian, c1870, 51 x 93in (129.5 x 236cm).
£1,800–2,000
€2,600–2,900
$3,000–3,350 ⊞ WADS

A set of four Lori
3akhtiari bags, west
'ersian, c1910, 55 x 41¼in
140 x 105cm).
:1,050–1,250
€1,500–1,800
;1,750–2,100 B(Kn)

Meshad rug, northeast
ersian, Khorasan, c1930,
0¾ x 54in (205 x 137cm).
280–330 / €400–470
470–550 WW

Sarouk Fereghan rug,
est Persian, c1900,
x 49in (183 x 124.5cm).
,000–3,300
,300–4,750
,000–6,000 WADS

A Mahal runner, west Persian, c1900, 121 x 42in (307.5 x 106.5cm).
£720–800 / €1,050–1,150
$1,200–1,350 WADS

A Sarab runner, northwest Persian, c1890, 197 x 38in (500.5 x 96.5cm).
£1,100–1,250
€1,600–1,800
$1,850–2,100 WADS

A Sarouk rug, west Persian, c1920, 37¾ x 25½in (96 x 65cm).
£650–780 / €940–1,100
$1,100–1,300 DORO
The open, uncluttered design of this rug is popular in today's market.

◄ A Tabriz rug, northwest Persian, c1920, 108¼ x 75½in (275 x 192cm).
£1,350–1,500
€1,950–2,150
$2,250–2,500 WADS

A Mahal carpet, substantial wear and damage, repairs, west Persian, 1920–30, 248 x 169¼in (630 x 430cm).
£2,450–2,900
€3,550–4,200
$4,100–4,850 DORO

A Malayer rug, slight wear, west Persian, late 19thC, 77¼ x 48in (196 x 122cm).
£530–630 / €760–900
$890–1,050 WW

► A Sarouk rug, west Persian, late 19thC, 79 x 52in (200.5 x132cm).
£1,300–1,550
€1,900–2,250
$2,200–2,600
LHA

◄ An 'American' Sarouk rug, slight wear and losses, west Persian, c1930, 80 x 51¼in (203 x 130cm).
£120–145 / €170–200
$200–240 WW
'American' is a trade name and refers to Sarouk rugs of this type made during the 1930s. They often have a thick, long pile.

A Senneh rug, with *herati* pattern, west Persian, c1900, 82¾ x 50¾in (210 x 129cm).
£1,000–1,200
€1,450–1,700
$1,700–2,000 B(Kn)

A runner, northwest Persian, c1910, 133 x 36in (338 x 91.5cm).
£1,200–1,350
€1,700–1,950
$2,000–2,250 WADS

A Beshir *chuval*, wear and losses, west Turkestani, c1880, 33¾ x 49¼in (86 x 125cm).
£1,050–1,250 / €1,500–1,800
$1,750–2,100 DORO

► **A Beshir *khelleh*,** west Turkestani, c1890, 202¾ x 86½in (515 x 220cm).
£690–820 / €990–1,150
$1,150–1,350 S(O)

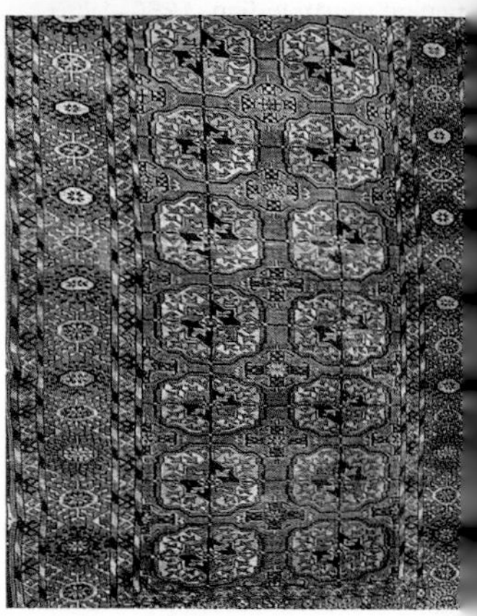

A Chodor carpet, Turkestani, c1880 100½ x 77½in (255 x 197cm).
£1,300–1,550 / €1,850–2,200
$2,200–2,600 RTo

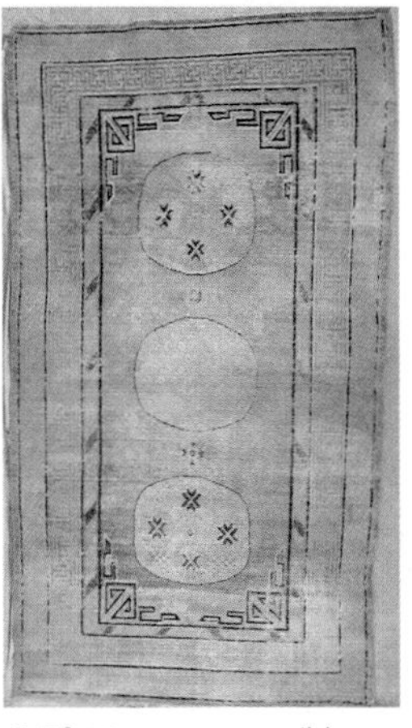

A Khotan rug, possibly silk, heavy wear, east Turkestani, 1850–1900, 85 x 47in (216 x 119.5cm).
£1,200–1,400
€1,750–2,000
$2,000–2,350 WW

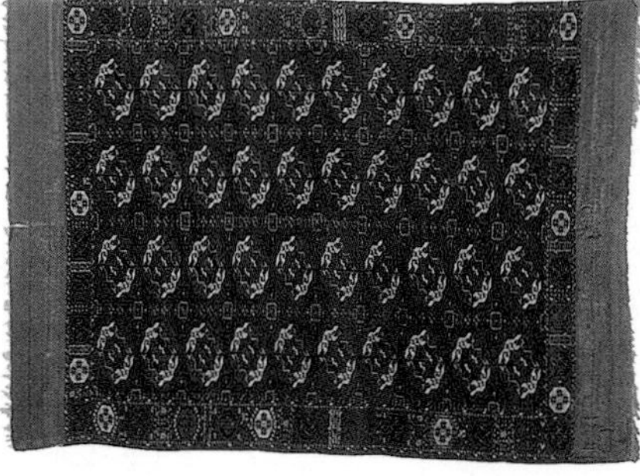

A Tekke carpet, wear and staining, rewoven section, west Turkestani, 1850–75, 77¼ x 114¼in (196 x 290cm).
£2,150–2,600 / €3,100–3,700
$3,600–4,300 S

A Tekke Turkman rug, west Turkestani, c1910, 63 x 34in (160 x 86.5cm).
£165–195 / €240–280
$280–330 G(L)

A Kizil Ayak Turkman carpet, west Turkestani, late 19thC, 108 x 75½in (274 x 192cm).
£820–980 / €1,200–1,400
$1,350–1,600 NSal

A Balouch prayer rug, Afghani, 1850–1900, 55 x 31in (139.5 x 78.5cm).
£850–950 / €1,200–1,350
$1,450–1,600 SAM

A Balouch rug, Afghani, c1880, 53 x 38in (134.5 x 96.5cm).
£650–720 / €940–1,050
$1,050–1,200 WADS

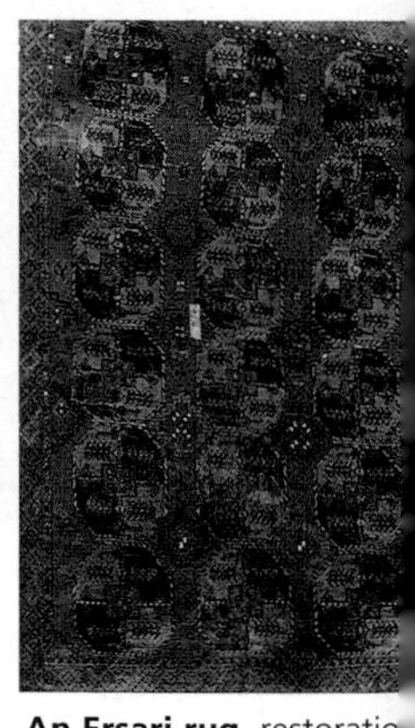

An Ersari rug, restoratio and wear, northwest Afghani, c1900, 121 x 93 (307 x 236cm).
£530–630 / €760–900
$890–1,050 LCM

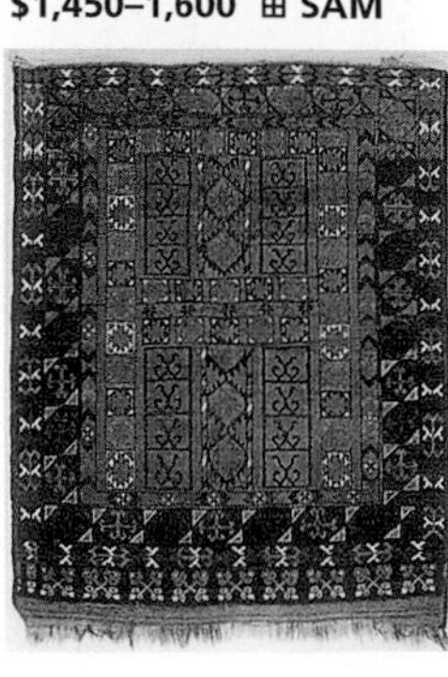

► **An Ersari *ensi*,** minor damage, northwest Afghani, 1920–30, 70 x 56¼in (178 x 143cm).
£730–870 / €1,050–1,250
$1,250–1,450 DORO

◄ **A Timuri tr saddlebag fa** west Afghani, 1850–1900, 2 (73.5cm) squa
£2,000–2,250
€2,900–3,200
$3,350–3,800
SAM

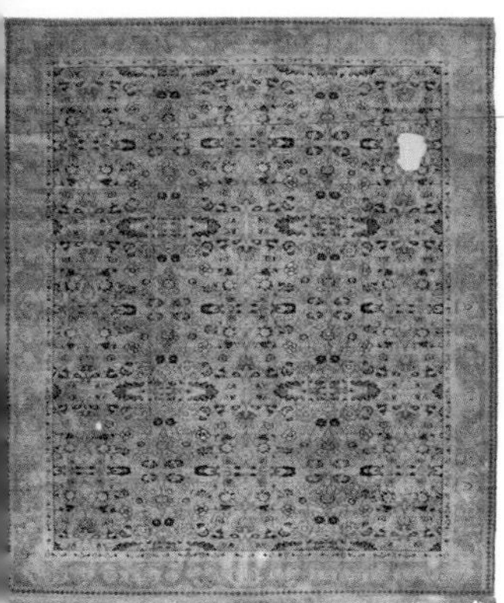

An Agra carpet, damage and
taining, north Indian, 1850–1900,
76 x 139in (447 x 353cm).
17,500–21,000 / €25,000–30,000
29,000–35,000 WW
he knotting on this carpet is xceptionally fine.

Jail carpets from India

Before the middle of the 19th century, carpets in India were chiefly made for royal or aristocratic commissions and were produced in small Imperial workshops. Carpet production then became a more commercially orientated activity and originated from the country's jails. The most renowned of these jails were Lahore and Agra and they produced carpets of particularly high quality. The earliest jail products copied designs used in classical Persian carpets of the 16th and 17th centuries. Such carpets are highly sought after in today's market, popular for their decorative appearance and for the fine quality of workmanship. Large carpets are usually easy to find, but smaller rugs are scarce.

An Agra carpet, north Indian, late 19thC, 188 x 142½in (478 x 362cm).
£2,850–3,400
€4,100–4,900
$4,800–5,700 S(O)

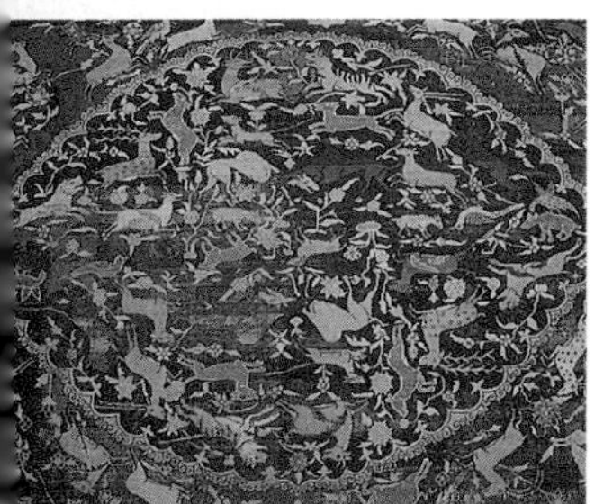

n Agra carpet, north Indian,
1900, 169 x 174in (429 x 442cm).
3,850–4,600 / €5,500–6,600
6,500–7,700 LHA

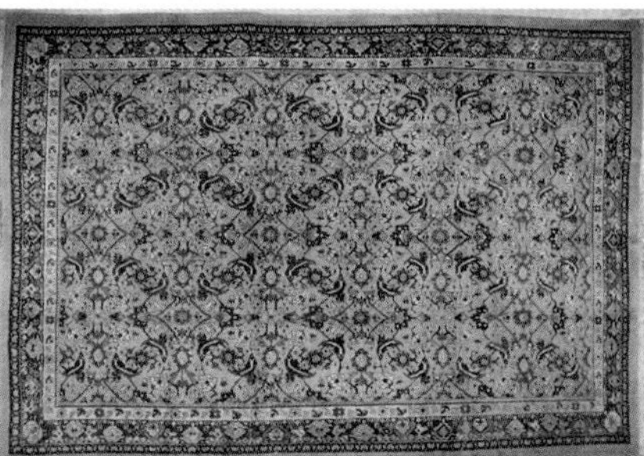

An Agra carpet, slight wear, north Indian, c1900, 85 x 122in (216 x 310cm).
£1,900–2,250 / €2,750–3,250
$3,200–3,800 WW

An Amritsar carpet, wear and losses, north Indian, late 19thC, 161 x 121¼in (409 x 308cm).
£6,000–7,200
€8,600–10,300
$10,100–12,100 S

pair of Amritsar rugs, one with slight wear,
rth Indian, late 19thC, 55¼ x 77¼in (140 x 196cm).
,100–1,300 / €1,600–1,850
,850–2,200 WW

An Amritsar carpet, minor damage, losses and repairs, north Indian, c1910, 105¼ x 111in (267 x 282cm).
£4,600–5,500 / €6,600–7,900
$7,700–9,200 S(NY)

An Amritsar carpet, some wear, losses and repairs, north Indian, 1900–20, 161 x 124in (409 x 315cm).
£1,100–1,300
€1,600–1,850
$1,850–2,200 WW

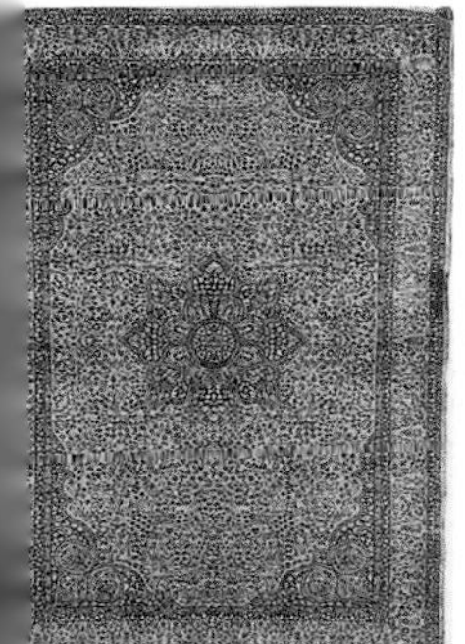

Lahore carpet, north
ian, early 20thC,
2 x 174in (665 x 442cm).
,700–2,000
,450–2,900
,850–3,400 S(O)

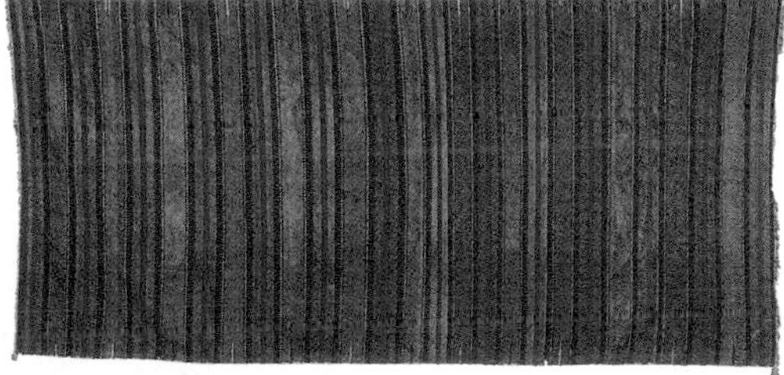

A *dhurrie*, minor stains, Indian, early 20thC, 99½ x 204in (253 x 518cm).
£1,550–1,850 / €2,200–2,650
$2,600–3,100 S(O)

► **A *dhurrie*,** minor stains, Indian, c1900, 120 x 83½in (305 x 212cm).
£1,550–1,850 / €2,200–2,650
$2,600–3,100 S

A Ninghsia rug, northwest Chinese, mid-19thC, 26 x 51in (66 x 129.5cm).
£1,300–1,450 / €1,850–2,100
$2,200–2,450 ⊞ PCA

A Ninghsia rug, some wear and damage, northwest Chinese, late 19thC, 106 x 139in (269 x 353cm).
£300–360 / €430–520
$500–600 WW

A carpet, probably Tianjin, depicting a pair of *Fo* dogs and the 12 animals of the Chinese zodiac, slight wear, northeast Chinese, c1930, 94¾ x 129in (241 x 328cm).
£210–250 / €300–360
$350–420 WW

Further reading

Miller's Antiques Encyclopedia, Miller's Publications, 2004

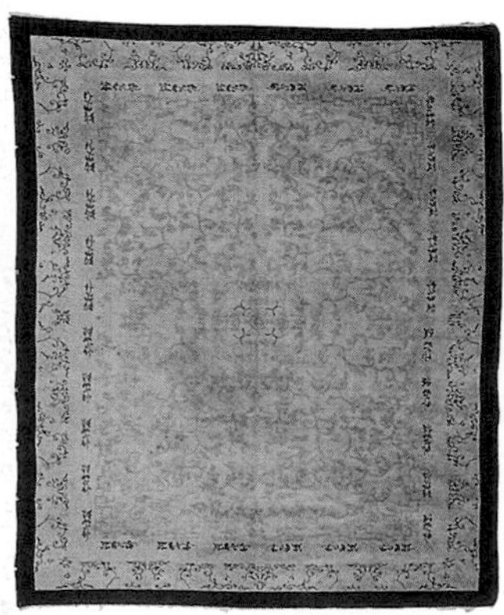

A carpet, slight wear, stains and reweaving, Chinese, c1900, 141 x 109¾in (358 x 278cm).
£4,800–5,700 / €6,900–8,200
$8,100–9,600 S

A Ninghsia rug, northwest Chinese, 1850–1900, 76 x 52in (193 x 132cm).
£700–840 / €1,000–1,200
$1,200–1,400 WW

A pillar rug, probably Ninghsia, Chinese, 1920–30, 124 x 49¼in (315 x 125cm).
£190–220 / €270–320
$320–370 WW

A carpet, Chinese, c1900, 117 x 96¾in (297 x 246cm).
£8,400–10,100 / €12,100–14,500
$14,100–17,000 S

► **A carpet,** Chinese, c1920, 159½ x 152¾in (405 x 388cm).
£6,600–7,900 / €9,500–11,300
$11,100–13,300 S(O)

A Ninghsia rug, northwest Chinese 1850–1900, 115¾ x 96¾in (294 x 246cm).
£1,800–2,150 / €2,600–3,100
$3,000–3,600 S(O)

A carpet, heavily worn and restored Chinese, c1900, 161½ x 149½in (410 x 380cm).
£5,600–6,700 / €8,100–9,700
$9,400–11,200 S(P)

A carpet, Chinese, late 19thC, 116¼ x 97¾in (295 x 248cm).
£1,800–2,150 / €2,600–3,100
$3,000–3,600 S(O)

Textiles

Covers & Quilts

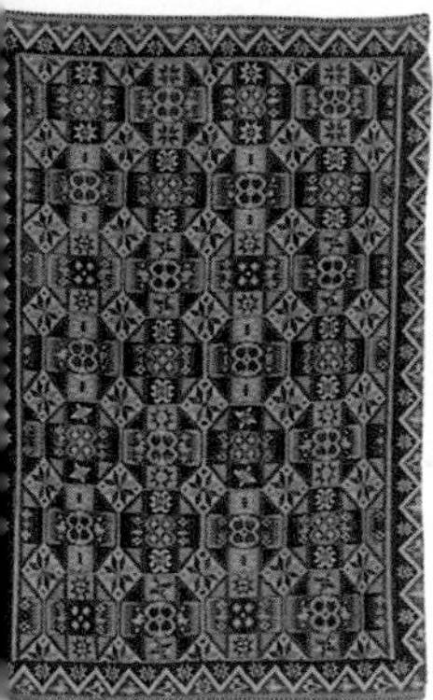

Skåne quilt, with initials 'IS', some wear, damage nd repair, Swedish, ated 1827, 81½ x 49½in 07 x 125.5cm).
580–820 / €980–1,150
1,150–1,350 BUK

A Birds in the Bushes appliqué cotton quilt, with diagonal line quilting, American, 19thC, 72 x 88in (183 x 223.5cm).
£1,600–1,900 / €2,300–2,750
$2,700–3,200 S(NY)

A patchwork coverlet, merican, 19thC, x 79½in (201 x 202cm).
300–360 / €430–520
500–600 PFK

A candlewick bedspread, by Harry Tyler, decorated with American eagles with shields, berry trees, stars and roses, the corners with lions, three sides with original tatted fringe, some discolouration to fringe, American, 19thC, 120 x 96in (305 x 244cm).
£2,850–3,400 / €4,100–4,900
$4,800–5,700 S(NY)
This is an exceptional quilt by a known American quilter. In Britain a similar quilt without this attribution can be purchased for £50–150 / €70–220 / $85–250.

A Princess Feather appliqué cotton quilt, heightened with diamond quilting, minor wear, American, 19thC, 88 x 80in (223.5 x 203cm).
£1,200–1,400 / €1,700–2,000
$2,000–2,350 S(NY)

A Star of the East cotton quilt, the field heightened with cubes and outline stitching, American, probably Pennsylvania, 19thC, 100 x 92in (254 x 233.5cm).
£640–770 / €920–1,100
$1,100–1,300 S(NY)

A trapunto album and appliqué cotton quilt, the motifs outlined with wool embroidery and seed stitching, the blossoms with trapunto, heightened with shell and outline stitching, some losses and discolouration, American, probably Maryland, c1850, 96in (244cm) square, mounted on a stretcher.
£7,100–8,500 / €10,200–12,200
$11,900–14,300 S(NY)
Trapunto was developed in Italy and is a form of quilting that involves stuffing raised designs. Album quilts were appliquéd wi individual blocks often made by different quilters.

► **A Victorian Log Cabin patchwork coverlet,** unbacked, 80½ x 83in (207 x 211cm).
£260–310 / €380–450
$440–530 PFK

A cotton Bokhara *susani*, with silk tambour stitching, laid down on linen, central Asian, mid-19thC, 46 x 19in (117 x 48.5cm), mounted on a stretcher.
£420–500 / €600–720
$700–840 WW
The fact that this item has been laid down on linen would suggest that the original condition was poor and it has had to be appliquéd. *Susanis* often sell for in excess of £1,000 / €1,450 / $1,700, so in this case an attractive wall hanging has been acquired at a fraction of the cost.

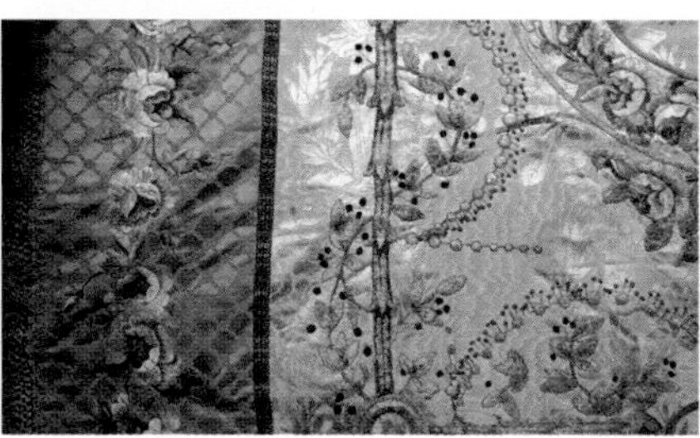

A coverlet, embroidered with bees and flowers, late 19thC, 88 x 68in (223.5 x 172.5cm).
£1,100–1,250 / €1,600–1,800
$1,850–2,100 JPr

A cotton frame coverlet, with a hexagon centre, 1850–1900, 88½ x 91¼in (225 x 232cm).
£210–250 / €300–360
$350–420 DN

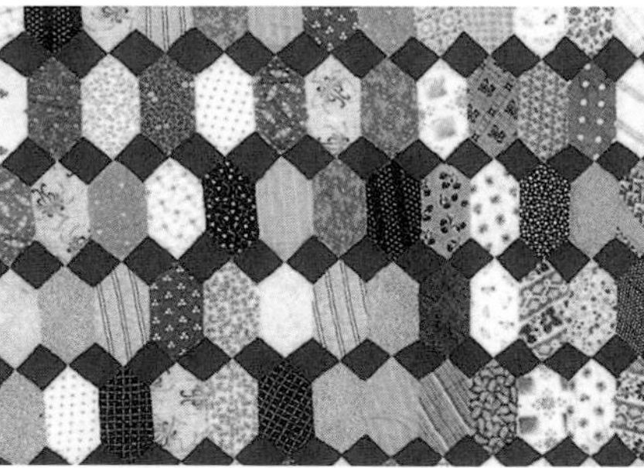

A patchwork quilt, possibly Manx or Irish, late 19thC, 73¾ x 92½in (187.5 x 235cm).
£280–330 / €400–470
$470–550 DN

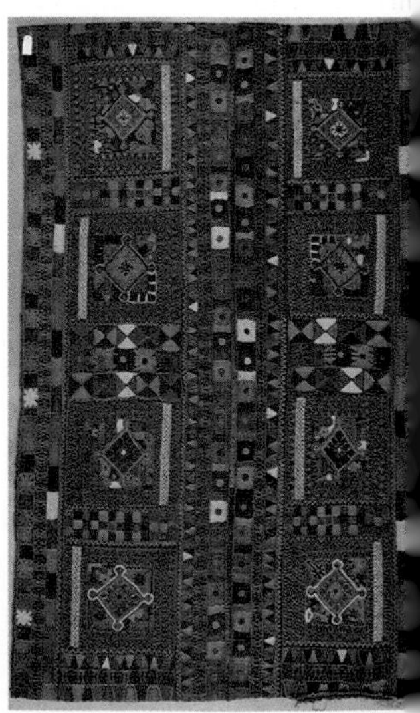

A needlework cover, Middle East probably Syrian or Iraqi, early 20th 100 x 64in (254 x 162.5cm).
£105–125 / €150–180
$175–210 WW

► **A crewelwork bed cover,** 1920s, 56 x 85in (142 x 216cm).
£430–480 / €620–690
$720–800 JPr

:mbroidery & Needlework

The recent appearance on the market of several single-owner collections has added to the appreciation and understanding of ıl types of antique textiles. The embroidery nd textile collection of the late Cora insburg, offered for sale by Sotheby's in ovember 2003, will be a benchmark in this eld for many years to come. Among the ighlights were a 17th-century embroidered nd painted silk picture by Elena Stefanini ıat sold for £13,200 / €19,000 / $22,200, and 17th-century embroidered feast scene that ːalized £16,800 / €24,200 / $28,200. The prices :hieved for single-owner collections sold by ajor auction houses may appear distorted ıt the rarity, quality and provenance of the ems usually result in prices that stand the st of time.

There has been a great revival of interest wall decorations of all types, from 17th- late 19th-century tapestries to those of a ore manageable size in the form of samplers ıd needlework pictures. As always, quality, ndition, subject matter and fashion trends must all be taken into consideration when attempting to predict values.

The current popularity of French culture coupled with the export of large quantities of French furniture to the USA, Japan and the rest of Europe has led to the increased use of pale-coloured French toiles and faded embroideries in interior design. Dark, rich and voluptuous coloured fabrics are out of fashion at present and prices for these strong-coloured materials are lower than for many years.

One of the more dramatic changes to be seen in the somewhat staid and archaic field of antique textiles has been the increased use of the internet by collectors to source items. Also, the many fine film and television dramas that have been produced recently have allowed the aspiring collector to see authentic recreations of domestic furnishings and costume, thanks to the academic expertise of the production companies involved in these projects. This has had an advantageous effect on the antique textiles trade as new collectors have been introduced to this fascinating field. **Joanna Proops**

ı ecclesiastical ıbroidery, from a est's maniple, French, e 16th/early 17thC, x 11¼in (33 x 28.5cm), med and glazed.
90–650 / €850–940
,000–1,100 ⊞ ACAN

maniple is a vestment ɔrn by a priest ebrating the Eucharist.

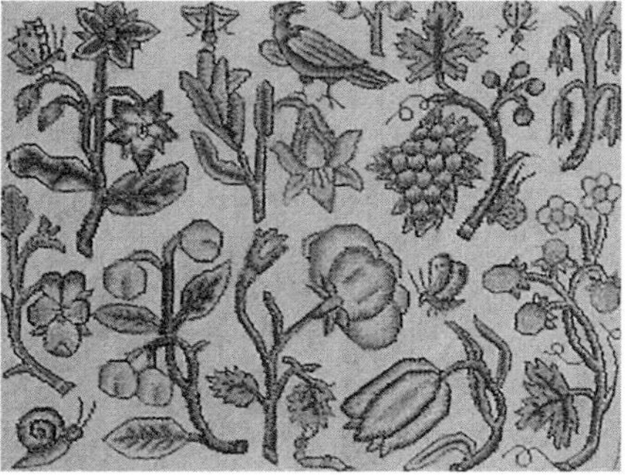

An embroidered spot motif panel, worked in tent stitch with wool and silk, mounted on to a later cushion panel, early 17thC, 8 x 10½in (20.5 x 26.5cm).
£720–860 / €1,050–1,250
$1,200–1,400 ⚒ S(O)

An embroidered picture, worked in satin stitch, mid-17thC, 11 x 9¾in (28 x 25cm).
£4,500–5,000 / €6,500–7,200
$7,600–8,400 ⊞ HIS

An embroidered :ture, depicting Esther and ɔsuerus, worked in tent :h with wool and silk, with aised silver thread throne, 50–60, 8¼ x 12¼in x 31cm), framed.
400–2,900
,500–4,200
050–4,850 ⚒ S(O)

Items in the Textiles section have been arranged in date order within each sub-section.

◄ An embroidered silk raised-work picture, depicting Daphne, worked in silk on a satin ground, c1660, 4¼ x 5¼in (11 x 13.5cm).
£1,050–1,250 / €1,500–1,800
$1,750–2,100 ⚒ S(O)

A raised stumpwork picture, c1660, 9½ x 9in (24 x 23cm).
£2,700–3,000 / €3,900–4,350
$4,550–5,000 ⊞ HIS

A giltwood and embroidery casket, worn, Italian, 17th/18thC, 12½ x 18in (32 x 46cm).
£3,350–4,000 / €4,800–5,700
$5,600–6,700 S(Mi)

An embroidered wool-covered casket, worked in flame stitch with wool, with *pointe d'Hongrie* needlework and green silk over paper lining to the interior, embroidery c1700, 10¼in (26cm) wide.
£240–290 / €350–420
$400–480 S(O)

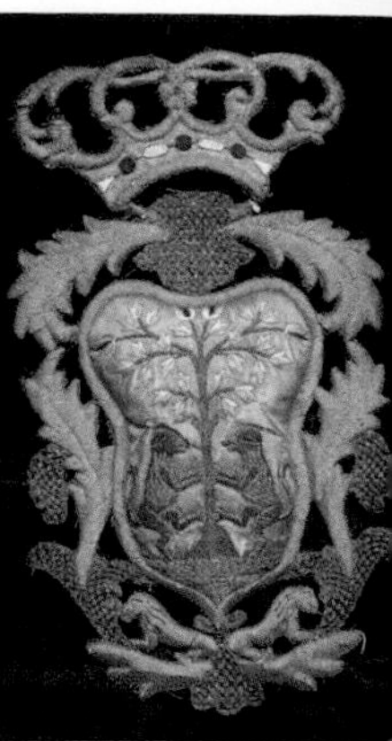

An embroidered silk an[d] bullion-work crest, earl[y] 18thC, 13in (33cm) high.
£310–350 / €450–500
$520–580 JPr

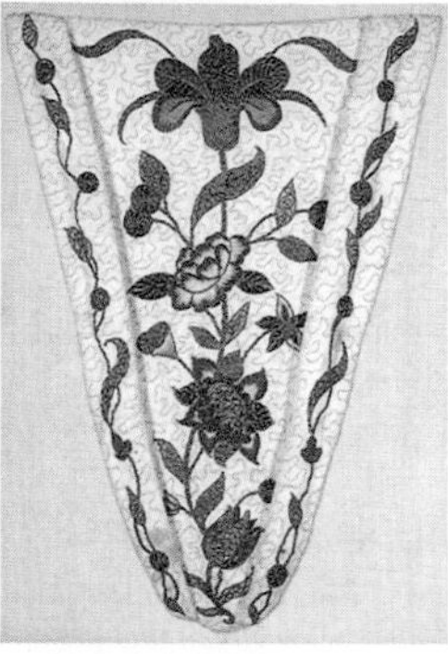

◄ **An embroidered stomacher panel,** the linen ground with couched silver thread patterns, c1710, 13in (33cm) long, in a glazed frame.
£1,900–2,300
€2,750–3,300
$3,200–3,850 S
Ex-Cora Ginsburg collection. Cora Ginsburg was a renowned New York dealer and collector of antique textiles and costume.

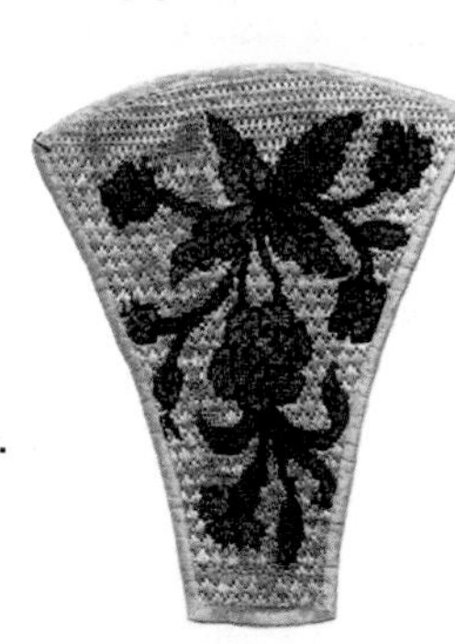

◄ **A silkwork stomache[r],** worked in cushion and tent stitch, early 18thC, 10in (25.5cm) long.
£180–200 / €260–290
$300–330 JPr

An embroidered panel, depicting a figure with animals and an angel, early 18thC, 6½ x 10in (16.5 x 25.5cm), framed and glazed.
£460–550 / €660–790
$770–920 DMC

Condition

By their very nature, textiles are fragile items and vulnerable to a large variety of attacks from nature, so if the piece in question has survived in a better state of preservation than one could normally expect, this will add a premium to its value. With needlework, good condition is essential: fading is a major problem, especially with the aniline dyes used after 1850, and worn or damaged fabric will also reduce the value. The colours on samplers should also be bright; check as well for moth or mould damage and for run-stained grounds.

An embroidered panel depicting dolphins, Portuguese, early 18thC, converted into a table runner late 19thC, 38 x 11in (96.5 x 28cm).
£220–250 / €320–360
$370–410 JPr

An embroidered chair/firescreen panel, worked in tent stitch with silks, English/French, 1740–50, 27½ x 20½in (70 x 52cm), mounted on a stretcher.
£900–1,050 / €1,350–1,500
$1,500–1,750 S
Ex-Cora Ginsburg collection.

◄ **An embroidered apron front,** worked wi[th] silks, 1760–70, 20 x 36i[n] (51 x 91.5cm).
£150–165 / €220–250
$250–280 JPr

► **An embroidery,** on a lawn ground, 1770–1800, 9 x 13in (23 x 33cm).
£85–95 / €120–140
$140–155 JPr

A George III silkwork, tears to backing, 17 x 1[5in] (43 x 38cm), in a glaze[d] gilt frame.
£260–310 / €380–450
$440–520 PFK

A George III wool and silkwork cushion cover, 16 x 18in (40.5 x 45.5cm), framed and glazed, with label tracing its history to 1764.
£120–145 / €180–210
$200–240 G(L)

A silkwork picture, depicting a shepherdess and her beau, American, Mrs Folwell's School, Philadelphia, late 18thC, 24½ x 27½in (62 x 70cm).
£6,100–7,300 / €8,800–10,500
$10,200–12,200 S(NY)

An embroidered picture, depicting Mary Magdalene and Christ in the Garden of Gethsemane, worked in satin and split stitch with silks on a silk ground, the figures with painted details, English/French, late 18th/early 19thC, 11 x 15½in (28 x 39.5cm).
£660–790 / €960–1,150
$1,100–1,300 S
Ex-Cora Ginsburg collection. Embroideries depicting religious scenes often sell for less than other types.

◄ **An embroidered table runner,** Italian, late 18thC, 60 x 15in (152.5 x 38cm).
£270–300 / €390–430
$450–500 JPr

◄ **A Georgian silk-embroidered picture,** depicting a maiden placing flowers on Shakespeare's tomb, 9¼ x 12in (23.5 x 30.5cm), in a *verre églomisé* mount, framed and glazed.
£140–165
€200–240
$240–280 AH

A silk-embroidered picture, c1810, 11 x 15in (28 x 38cm).
£1,050–1,200 / €1,500–1,800
$1,750–2,000 HIS

TEXTILES

A Regency silk-embroidered picture, 18 x 15in (45.5 x 38cm).
£580–650 / €840–940
$970–1,100 ⊞ JPr

A Regency woolwork picture, worked in gros point, 16¾ x 16½in (42.5 x 42cm).
£400–480 / €580–690
$680–810 ⚒ BR

A silk and woolwork picture, the boy's face and hair painted, early 19thC, 17 x 14in (43 x 35.5cm), framed and glazed.
£290–350 / €420–500
$490–590 ⚒ TMA

This is a potentially valuable picture with good subject matter. However, the colour is poor, the frame is not in good condition and there appears to be damage to the silk background, hence the low price.

LOCATE THE SOURCE

The source of each illustration in Miller's can be found by checking the code letters below each caption with the Key to Illustrations, pages 794–800.

A pair of Regency woolwork and silk needlework pictures, 10½ x 9in (26.5 x 23cm).
£470–560 / €680–810
$790–940 ⚒ SWO

A pair of Regency felt appliqué floral pictures, 15 x 13in (38 x 33cm), in carved wood and gesso frames.
£3,750–4,500 / €5,400–6,500
$6,300–7,500 ⚒ TEN

An embroidered mourning picture, attributed to Samuel Folwell, face, hands and some foliage painted, some fraying, inscribed 'Charlotte' and 'Werter', American, early 19thC, 17 x 24in (43 x 61cm), in original gilt frame.
£3,900–4,700 / €5,600–6,700
$6,600–7,900 ⚒ S(NY)

In the late 18th century, Johann Wolfgang von Goethe published *The Sorrows of Young Werter*, a novel relating the tragic tale of a young German nobleman. On holiday, he meets and falls hopelessly in love with the coquettish Charlotte, daughter of a local dignitary. To his despair, Charlotte is already engaged; during the course of the book she marries, but continues to flirt with and tease Werter to the point of madness. At last, no longer able to endure the torment of his unrequited love for her, he dramatically commits suicide.

A Regency needlework and painted silk picture, label verso inscribed 'Worked by Matilda Cockburn', 13½ x 11½in (34.5 x 29cm), with a *verre églomisé* mount and gilt frame.
£1,300–1,550
€1,900–2,250
$2,200–2,600 ⚒ AH

The subject matter of a child and animals, combined with vibrant colours and excellent condition, make this picture a desirable and collectable item.

◄ A beadwork picture, depicting a Poussinesque landscape, inscribed 'Iulie Croul a Sophie Barwinski en 1827', early 19thC, 8¾ x 12½in (22 x 32cm).
£410–490 / €590–710
$690–820 ⚒ DN

An ecclesiastical embroidered silk panel, Italian, early 19thC, 22½ x 17½in (57 x 44.5cm), framed and glazed.
£750–830 / €1,100–1,2
$1,250–1,400 ⊞ ACAN

A woolwork picture, depicting St Francis, 19th 11¾in (30cm) high, in a *verre églomisé* mount.
£160–190 / €230–270
$270–320 ⚒ SWO

An embroidered panel, worked in silks on a quilted silk ground, 19thC, 18 x 82in (45.5 x 208.5cm), mounted and framed as a triptych.
£150–180 / €220–260
$250–300 TRM

An early Victorian petit point embroidery, worked on net, 8in (20.5cm) square, in a maple frame.
£180–200 / €260–290
$300–340 ACAN

A Berlin woolwork picture, of an 18thC scene, probably during the American War of Independence, mid-19thC, 35 x 42in (89 x 106.5cm).
£190–220 / €270–320
$320–370 WW

mid-Victorian silk cushion, with a late 7thC appliqué panel, 16 x 20in (40.5 x 51cm).
310–350 / €450–500
520–580 JPr

beadwork panel, depicting water lilies and rds, c1890, 16 x 55in (40.5 x 139.5cm).
300–340 / €450–500
510–570 JPr

Victorian silk and velvet cushion, applied th a silk and bullion-work crest, cushion late thC, crest mid-18thC, 17 x 20in (43 x 51cm).
00–450 / €580–650
70–760 JPr

A Victorian cut velvetwork panel, with silk embroidered detail, mounted on net, 87 x 10in (221 x 25.5cm).
£120–140 / €170–200
$200–240 NSal

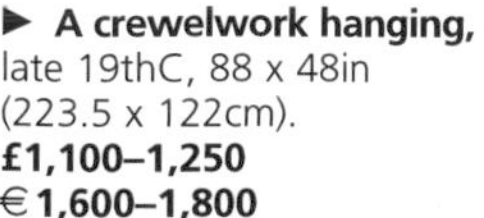

► **A crewelwork hanging,** late 19thC, 88 x 48in (223.5 x 122cm).
£1,100–1,250
€1,600–1,800
$1,900–2,100 JPr

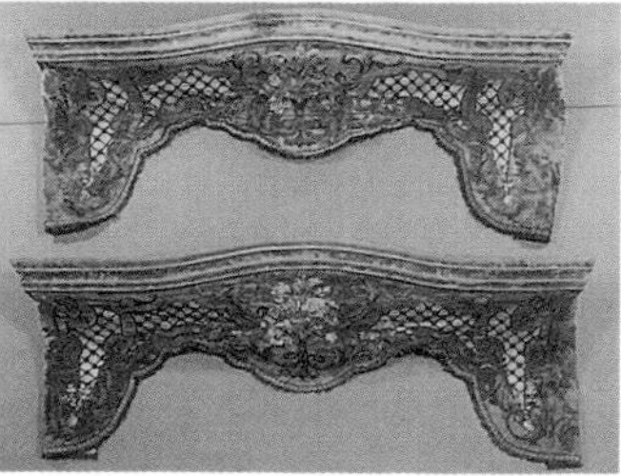

A pair of velvet-covered pelmets, with plain mouldings, worked in silver wire silk with a spray of flowers within leaf, flower and trellis borders, French, 19thC, 9¾ x 69in (24.5 x 175cm).
£1,900–2,250 / €2,750–3,250
$3,200–3,800 TEN

A tufted embroidery, of birds, nests and fruit on a linen ground, on a stretcher frame, mid-19thC, 24in (61cm) square.
£550–660 / €790–950
$920–1,100 COBB

◄ **A Victorian needlework picture,** 16½ x 13½in (42 x 34.5cm), framed and glazed.
£190–220 / €270–320
$320–370 NSal

A Victorian beaded centrepiece and teacosy, the centrepiece with a lacquered and gilt-metal border, some beads missing, centrepiece 23¾in (60.5cm) wide.
£170–200 / €240–280
$290–340 SWO

TEXTILES

Lace

A lacis lace square, with stylized geometric flowers and mythical beasts, bordered with reticella lace, possibly of earlier date, Italian, late 16th/early 17thC, 33½in (85cm) square.
£410–490 / €590–700
$690–820 DN
Lacis or fillet lace dating from the 15th and 16th centuries is fine knotted net with darned needle rim patterns. Nineteenth-century examples appear in French table linen and can be quite beautiful. For true lacis look for knots at the corner of each square.

A Honiton lace collar, worked with roses, thistles and shamrocks, c1850, 18in (45.5cm) long.
£30–35 / €45–50
$50–60 ⊞ JPr
This collar incorporates all the most desirable motifs of Honiton lace.

A lace collar, Irish, c1880, 13in (33cm) long.
£20–25 / €30–35
$35–40 ⊞ JPr

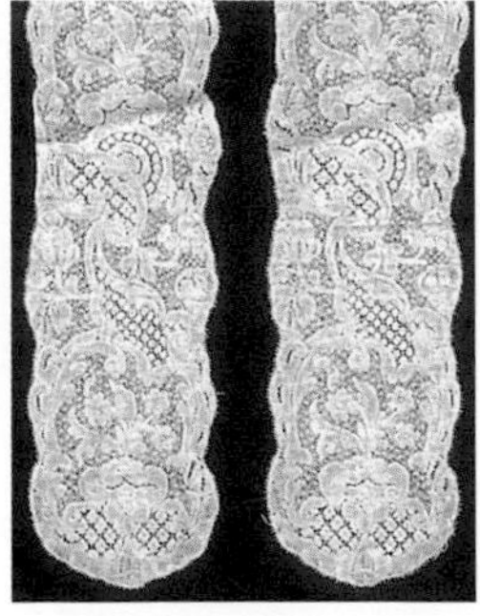

A pair of Mechlin lace lappets, with a later picot edge, Flemish, mid-18thC, longer 20in (51cm) long.
£280–330 / €400–480
$470–560 DN
Mechlin lace has always been collectable and this is a very reasonable price for a good pair of lappets. They are very desirable when complete: in the 19th century they were often cut in half to make collars.

A Honiton lace collar, 1850–60, 29in (74cm) long.
£180–200 / €260–290
$300–340 ⊞ HL

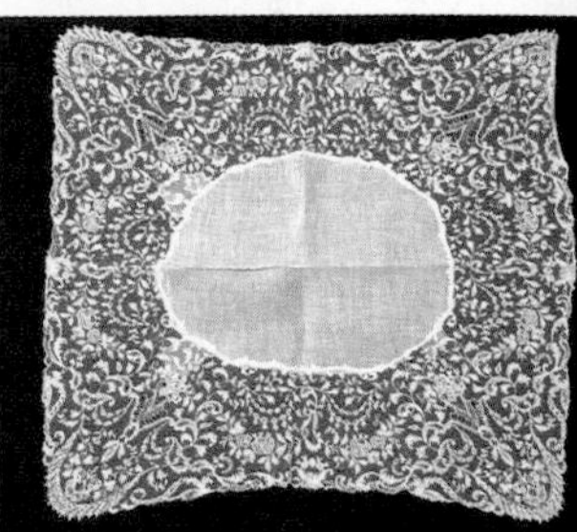

A Victorian lace handkerchief, 10in (25.5cm) square.
£105–120 / €150–180
$185–210 ⊞ MARG

Hand-made lace

Hand-made lace has always been expensive to buy because of the time it takes to produce such highly skilled work. Consequently, from the 16th to the 18th centuries it was seen as a status symbol, and fortunes were spent on it by those who were rich enough to be able to commission it. Today, museum quality 17th- and 18th-century pieces and large dress flounces of 19th-century *point de gaze* command high prices, but generally this area is undervalued and some beautiful examples of exquisite work can be picked up relatively inexpensively. If possible, pieces should be in original condition – that is, unwashed and unaltered. Handkerchiefs must be in perfect condition with no damage to the centre. Important centres of production were Brussels and Bruges in Belgium, Honiton and Nottingham in England, Chantilly and Valenciennes in France, Youghal in Ireland and Genoa and Venice in Italy.

Samplers

◄ **A sampler,** with a boxer motif, dated 1668, 22¼ x 12½in (56.5 x 32cm).
£1,100–1,250
€1,600–1,800
$1,900–2,100 ⊞ PSC

► **A sampler,** by Ellenor Dickinson, aged 11, dated 1749, 13 x 9in (33 x 23cm), in a giltwood frame.
£2,350–2,800
€3,400–4,000
$3,950–4,700 G(L)
This sampler realized a high price because of its overall good condition, the strong colours, the unusual layout for a 'Tree of Life' sampler, and the early, readable date.

It is very important when buying unframed samplers that they are correctly stretched before reframing.

A sampler, by Ann Gardner, worked with the Ten Commandments, 1750, 17¾ x 12in (45 x 30.5cm).
£980–1,150
€1,400–1,650
$1,650–1,850 L

◀ **A silkwork sampler,** by Susanna Tomplon, c1750, 20in (51cm) high, framed and glazed.
£1,800–2,000
€2,600–2,900
$3,000–3,350 ⊞ **CB**

◀ **An embroidered sampler,** by Amy Sarah Blake, aged 10, 1784, 18½ x 12½in (47 x 32cm), framed and glazed.
£480–580 / €690–830
$810–970 ⚒ **DMC**

A sampler, by Grace Ann Richards, aged 11, worked in silks, American, probably Pennsylvania, 1786, 15¼ x 13in (38.5 x 33cm).
£6,800–8,100 / €9,800–11,700
$11,400–13,600 ⚒ **S(NY)**
American samplers from this period are rare. The massive growth in the population of the USA has resulted in many collectors chasing a limited supply, hence the apparently disproportionately high prices for American samplers from all periods, compared to those from Europe and the UK.

pair of samplers, c1800, 8 x 6in
0.5 x 15cm), framed.
200–220 / €290–320
330–370 ⊞ **HTE**

A sampler, by Mary Ann Mason Turner, dated 1802, 13 x 12½in (33 x 32cm), framed and glazed.
£770–920 / €1,100–1,300
$1,300–1,550 ⚒ **AMB**
This is a very reasonable price for this sampler, as it has all the plus points of condition, colour, visible date and subject matter. Animals and houses are popular motifs.

darning sampler, 1805,
x 12½in (33 x 32cm).
,050–1,200
1,600–1,800
,750–2,050 ⊞ **HIS**
is example is a type not
ten seen. The addition
a bouquet of flowers
unusual as most stitch
mplers contain only
fferent examples
darns.

A sampler, by M. Joy, embroidered with silk and linen, some insect holes, dated 1816, 14¼ x 11in (36 x 28cm), framed and glazed.
£1,650–1,950
€2,400–2,800
$2,750–3,300 ⚒ **WW**

A mahogany
le screen
ounted with
ilkwork
ivas
npler, dated
16, sampler
¼ x 12¾in
.5 x 32.5cm).
50–670
10–960
30–1,100
ON

TEXTILES

A sampler, by Sarah Griffin, dated 1818, 12 x 13in (30.5 x 33cm).
£520–620 / €750–890
$880–1,050 ⚒ GH

A sampler, by Margaret Morton, aged 14, dated 1823, 15 x 14¼in (38 x 36cm).
£1,400–1,650 / €2,000–2,400
$2,350–2,800 ⚒ TEN

A sampler, by Hannah Stickney Johnson, 'Born August 12 1814 Age 12 years', frayed, American, c1826, 15¼ x 17¼in (38.5 x 44cm).
£580–700 / €840–1,000
$980–1,150 ⚒ JDJ

A sampler, by 'EJ, 1827', 16 x 11in (40.5 x 28cm), framed.
£910–1,100 / €1,350–1,600
$1,550–1,850 ⚒ BWL

A sampler, by Henry Sicklen, dated 1818, 12 x 9½in (30.5 x 24cm), framed.
£1,050–1,200 / €1,600–1,800
$1,750–2,000 ⊞ HIS

A sampler, by Hannah Oster, 1824, 24 x 21in (61 x 53.5cm), framed.
£530–640 / €760–910
$890–1,050 ⚒ HYD

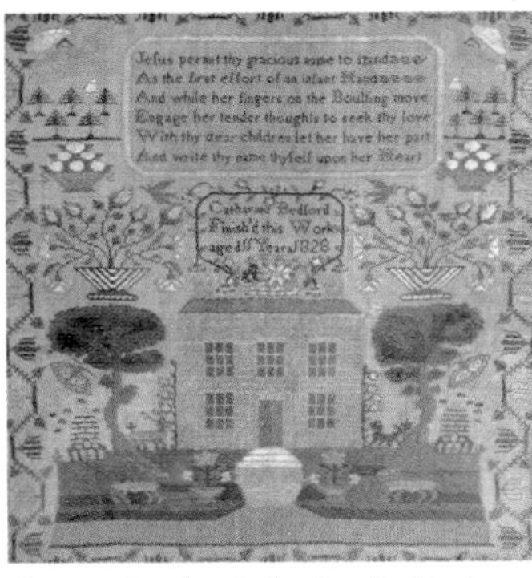

A sampler, by Catherine Bedford, aged 11 years, dated 1828, 15½ x 12½in (39.5 x 32cm).
£1,450–1,750 / €2,100–2,500
$2,450–2,950 ⚒ SWO

A sampler, signed 'Mary Moody's Work' and dated 1823, 17¼ x 15in (44.5 x 38cm), in a maple frame.
£420–500 / €600–720
$710–840 ⚒ FHF

A sampler, by Sarah Cookson, Didsbury, dated 1825, 25¼in (64cm) square, framed and glazed.
£1,400–1,650 / €2,000–2,400
$2,350–2,800 ⚒ MAR

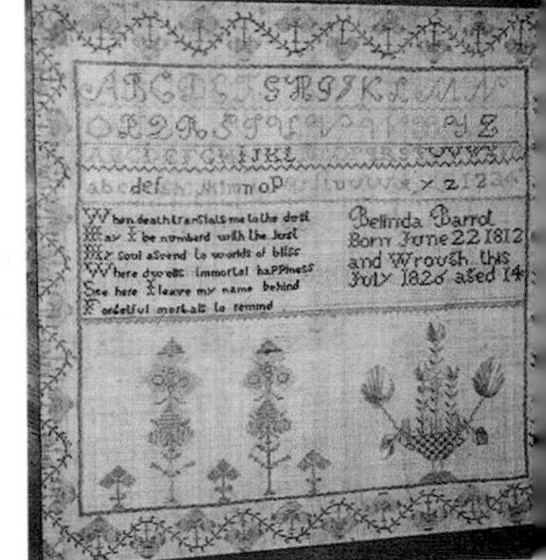

A sampler, by Belinda Barrot, American, dated 1826, 19in (48.5cm) square, framed.
£1,000–1,150 / €1,450–1,650
$1,650–1,900 ⊞ HCFA

Condition

The condition is absolutely vital when assessing the value of an antique. Damaged pieces on the whole appreciate much less than perfect examples. However, a rare desirable piece may command a high price even when damaged.

◄ **A sampler,** by Ellen Gregson, aged 9, dated 1828, 19½ x 17½in (49.5 x 44.5cm).
£630–760 / €920–1,100
$1,050–1,250 ⚒ WL

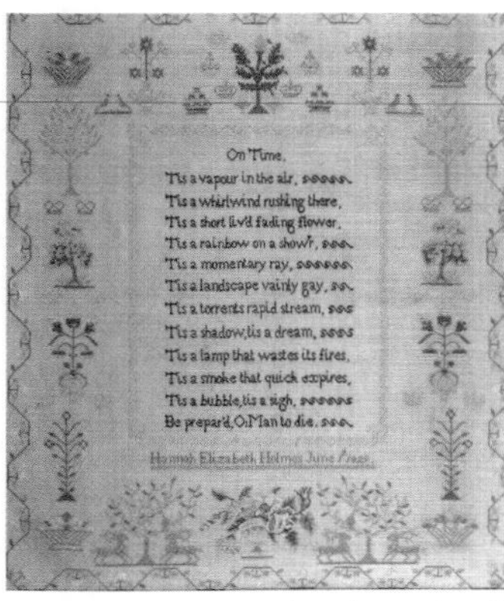

A sampler, by Hannah Holmes, dated 1829, 27 x 23½in (68.5 x 59.5cm), in a maple frame.
£700–840 / €1,000–1,200
$1,200–1,400 G(L)

A sampler, worked with a central hidden message 'I die to live forever', and 'Cheltenham Female Orphan Asylum', on a linen ground, 19thC, 3½in (9cm) square, in an oak frame.
£4,950–5,900 / €7,100–8,500
$8,300–9,900 G(L)
This is a very rare type of sampler and the price realized reflects this.

Further reading

Miller's Collecting Textiles, Miller's Publications, 2000

► **A sampler,** by Jane Barber, aged 10, dated 1839, 17 x 12¾in (43 x 32.5cm), framed.
£350–420 / €500–600
$590–700 MCA

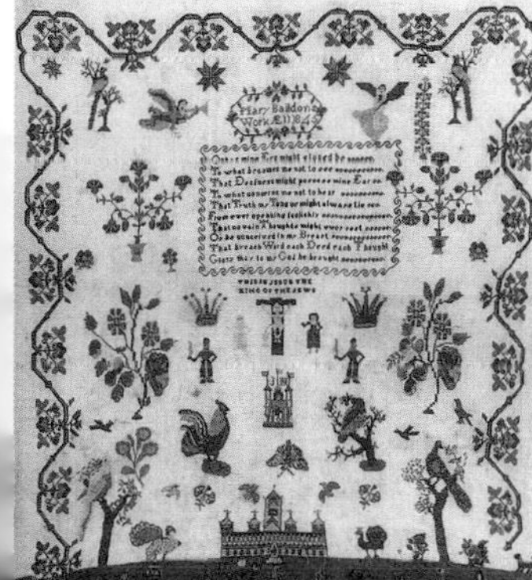

A woolwork sampler, by Mary Baildon, dated 1845, 24 x 22in (61 x 56cm).
£1,200–1,450 / €1,750–2,100
$2,000–2,400 AH

A sampler, by Eliza Husband, aged 9, dated 1829, 18 x 13in (45.5 x 33cm), framed.
£2,250–2,500
€3,200–3,600
$3,750–4,200 HIS

A sampler, by Miriam Parslow, dated 1831, 19¼ x 14¾in (49 x 37.5cm), framed and glazed.
£520–580 / €750–840
$870–970 PSC

► **A sampler,** worked in silks on a linen ground, 19thC, 14 x 19½in (35.5 x 49.5cm).
£700–840 / €1,000–1,200
$1,200–1,400 F&C

A multiplication table sampler, by Ann Nimmo, aged 8, c1830, 8 x 12in (20.5 x 30.5cm), framed.
£1,800–2,000 / €2,600–2,900
$3,000–3,350 HIS
This is a very rare sampler.

Researching a sampler

The story behind a sampler can often add to its value, even when the design is quite plain and would perhaps otherwise cause it to be overlooked. The samplers shown on these pages that have been worked by inmates of orphanages are a case in point. A little research on the internet or local Records Offices can add a whole new dimension to the appeal of these pieces, and at the same time enhance the value.

A sampler, worked with figures of Adam and Eve beneath the Tree of Knowledge, surrounded by various spot motifs, with text below, 19thC, 11½ x 9½in (29 x 24cm), framed and glazed.
£230–270 / €340–400
$390–460 DMC

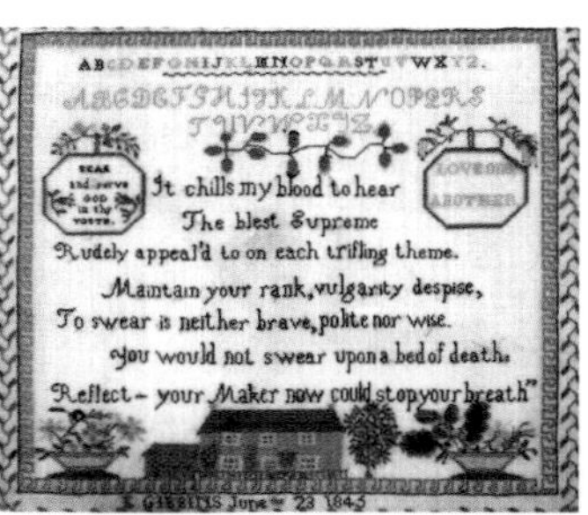

◄ **A sampler,** by E. Gibbons, dated 1845, 12½ x 13in (32 x 33cm), framed.
£1,050–1,250 / €1,500–1,800
$1,750–2,100 BWL

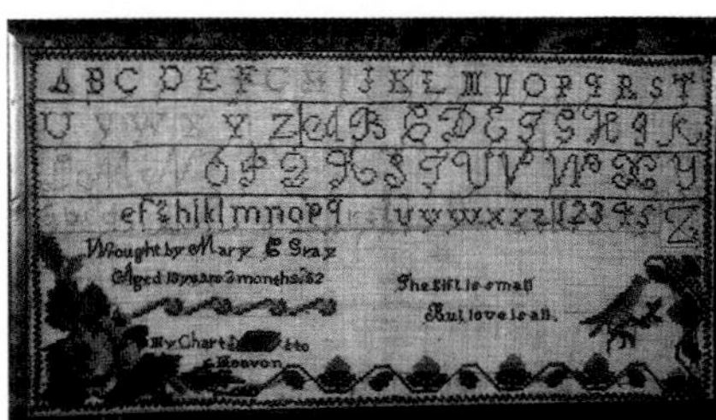

◀ **A sampler,** by Mary Gray, American, dated 1852, 10 x 18in (25.5 x 45.5cm), framed.
£810–900 / €1,150–1,300
$1,350–1,500 ⊞ HCFA

◀ **A woolwork sampler,** by Maria Louisa Thurston, aged 12, dated 1859, 14¼ x 12¼in (36 x 31cm), framed.
£210–250
€300–360
$350–420 ⚒ EH

A silkwork sampler, by Adeline Bourdon, dated 1862, 8 x 10in (20.5 x 25.5cm), in an ebonized frame.
£280–330 / €400–480
$470–560 ⚒ G(L)

A silkwork sampler, by Sarah Beebee, dated 1859, 15 x 13in (38 x 33cm), in a rosewood frame.
£410–450 / €590–650
$690–760 ⊞ JPr

A silkwork sampler, by Jane Munday, dated 1871, 18in (45.5cm) high, framed.
£1,800–2,000
€2,600–2,900
$3,000–3,350 ⊞ CB

A sampler, by Jane Casilda Tendall, aged 11, dated 1853, 14¼ x 13¼in (36 x 33.5cm), set in a fire screen.
£95–110 / €140–160
$160–190 ⚒ CHTR

A sampler, by Mary Bishop, of the New Orphan House, Ashley Down, Bristol, 1860–80, 12 x 9in (30.5 x 23cm), framed.
£2,700–3,000 / €3,900–4,300
$4,550–5,050 ⊞ HIS

Tapestries

A tapestry fragment, depicting classical figures playing musical instruments, Flemish, early 17thC, 82 x 49in (208.5 x 124.5cm).
£1,100–1,300
€1,600–1,900
$1,850–2,200 ⚒ G(L)
The presence of contemporary musical instruments in this tapestry has added interest and increased the value.

A tapestry fragment, depicting the preparations for sacrificing a bull before a feast, Flemish, 17thC, 99¼ x 174in (252 x 442cm).
£1,150–1,350 / €1,650–2,000
$1,950–2,350 ⚒ Bea

A wool and silk tapestry fragment, depicting quivers, arrows and flowers, later border, French, mid-18thC, 78¾in (200cm) high.
£740–890 / €1,100–1,300
$1,250–1,500 ⚒ S(Am)

◀ **An Aubusson verdure tapestry,** after Jean Baptiste Oudry, depicting a bird being pursued by a dog, French, 1725–50, 86¼ x 134in (219 x 340.5cm).
£3,750–4,500
€5,400–6,500
$6,300–7,600 ⚒ DN

Costume

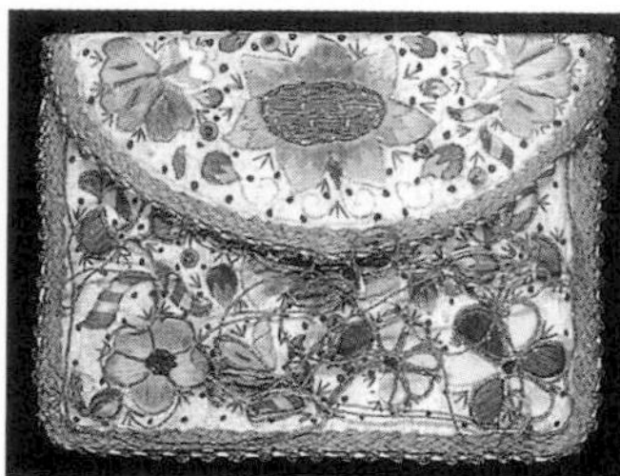

An embroidered satin purse, worked with flowerheads edged in couched gold threads, the reverse with a starfish-like medallion with purl wire sections, spotted with spangles, 17thC, 6in (15cm) wide.
£420–500 / €600–720
$700–840 ⚒ S(O)

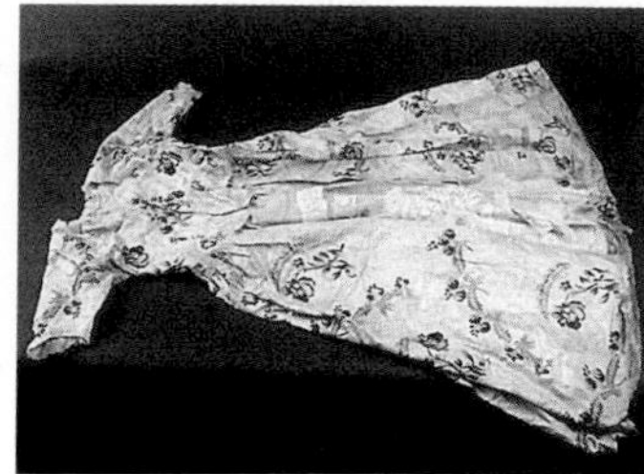

A brocaded silk open robe, woven with ferns and foliage, embroidered with sprigs and garlands, linen-lined bodice, some damage, mid-18thC, in a domed tin trunk.
£530–640 / €770–920
$920–1,100 ⚒ M

A lady's feather hat, covered in tinted and natural feathers, lined in pale blue silk, mid-18thC, 14½in (37cm) diam.
£1,200–1,450 / €1,750–2,100
$2,000–2,400 ⚒ S(O)
Ex-Castle Howard collection. The extensive collection of period costume housed at Castle Howard in Yorkshire contained many rarities. It was started by George Howard in the mid-1960s and was sold recently due to the rising cost of upkeep.

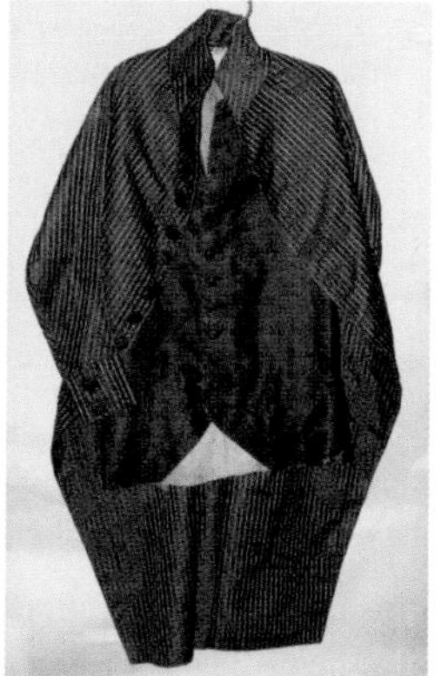

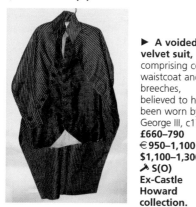

A silk coat and waistcoat, French, 18thC.
£1,350–1,500
€1,950–2,150
$2,250–2,500 ⊞ JPr

► **A voided velvet suit,** comprising coat, waistcoat and breeches, believed to have been worn by George III, c1760.
£660–790
€950–1,100
$1,100–1,300
⚒ S(O)
Ex-Castle Howard collection.

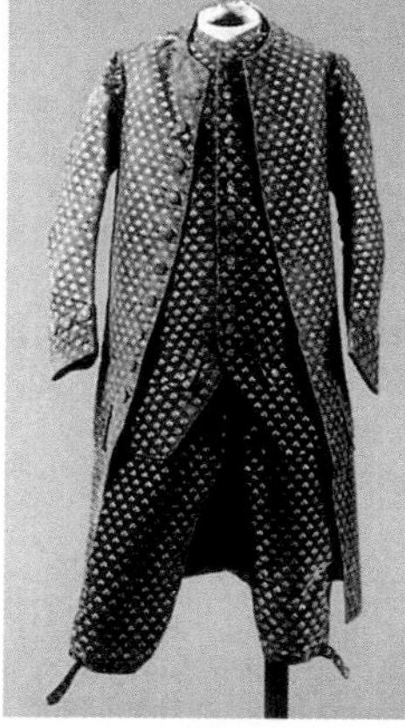

An embroidered silk purse, late 18thC, 10in (25.5cm) high.
£260–290 / €380–420
$440–490 ⊞ JPr

Collecting tips

Brightly coloured dresses and waistcoats are more collectable than sober greys and browns, although 18th-century black dresses are greatly sought after. Beware of later alterations on 18th-century dresses as these will reduce the value. Nineteenth-century black mourning wear and white bridal wear are surprisingly common and can still be purchased very reasonably, as can Victorian gowns from the mid-19th century, even those in perfect condition. Look for a label in the waistband of 19th-century dresses – those made by Worth can command a high price if undamaged. Late 19th-century camisole tops and petticoats are abundant, but examples with fine embroidery or lace detail will generally sell for a premium. As with all textiles, good condition is crucial.

An early Victorian embroidered silk court dress, with a cream brocade underdress.
£500–550 / €720–780
$830–920 ⊞ VICT

► **A Midlands Paisley shawl,** c1840, 64in (162.5cm) square.
£340–380 / €500–550
$570–630 ⊞ JPr

A Victorian silk day dress.
£200–230 / €290–330
$340–390 ⊞ Ech

A silk dress, with an apron front, 1870s.
£175–195 / €250–280
$290–320 ⊞ L&L

A Victorian silk waistcoat.
£135–150 / €200–220
$230–260 ⊞ OH
Late Victorian waistcoats are mainly sold to young people to wear. They therefore have to be in good condition, colourful, and of a size that can be worn by people who are larger than our Victorian ancestors.

A Worth satin and lace ball gown, embroidered with papyrus blooms and decorated with sequins and pearlized beads, French, c1900.
£1,100–1,300
€1,600–1,900
$1,850–2,200 ⚒ S(O)

A Victorian lady's velvet cape, embroidered with floral designs, with a feathered fringe.
£120–145 / €175–210
$200–240 ⚒ SWO
Garments such as this tend to fetch higher prices because they are wearable today – particularly if the colour and condition are right. This is a black cape, but if the colour had been grey it could have fetched double this amount.

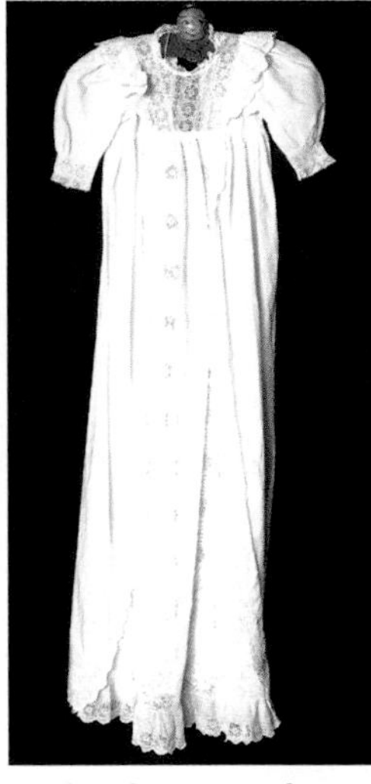

A Victorian cotton lawn christening gown.
£135–150 / €200–220
$230–260 ⊞ MARG

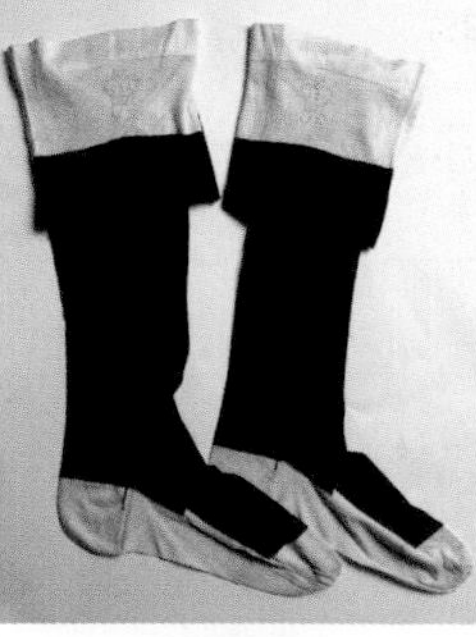

A pair of Victorian silk stockings, monogrammed with a crest and the initial 'VR', denoting Queen Victoria, with numbers at the top and embroidered devices at the ankles, in original box.
£1,500–1,750
€2,100–2,500
$2,500–2,950 ⊞ CFSD

A Victorian silk and crochet cape.
£140–160 / €200–220
$240–270 ⊞ MARG

A Victorian child's braided wool coat, decorated with black beads.
£180–200 / €260–290
$300–340 ⊞ Ech

A tapestry bag, with a silver frame, c1900, 10in (25.5cm) high.
£175–195 / €250–280
$300–330 ⊞ LBe
This is a pretty bag and prices for similar items have risen dramatically over the last three years. They have become 21st-century fashion accessories and as such can fluctuate greatly in price, like other types of antique clothing that have become fashionable again. Prices may drop in the short term, but exceptional items will hold their value, backed by demand from true collectors.

A Victorian two-piece silk costume.
£220–250 / €320–360
$370–410 ⊞ Ech

A silk and wool Paisley shawl, 1870–80, 36 x 64in (91.5 x 162.5cm).
£400–450 / €580–650
$670–750 ⊞ JPr
The price of Paisley shawls has been very volatile over the last ten years and at present they are at a low point. A similar shawl to that illustrated would have been worth at least double ten years ago. The price will rise again and this is a good time to buy. Look for shawls in good condition with strong colours and sensibly priced.

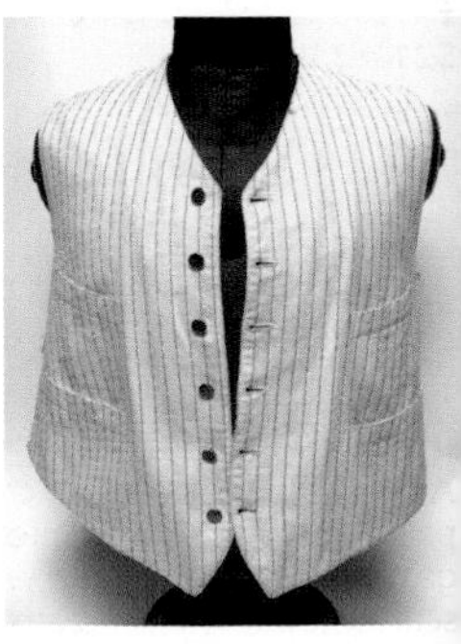

An Edwardian cotton waistcoat.
£90–100 / €130–145
$150–170 ⊞ OH

Fans

A dismounted fan leaf, decorated with a mythological scene, extended to form a painting, c1720, 21in (53.5cm) wide, framed.
£2,700–3,000 / €3,900–4,300
$4,550–5,000 ⊞ LDC

An ivory fan, the paper leaf painted with female classical figures, with pierced and painted sticks and guards, French, 18thC, 7in (18cm) long.
£270–320 / €390–460
$450–540 ⚒ Bri

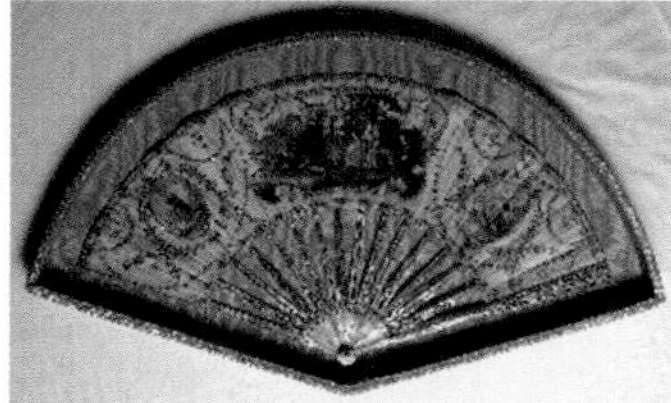

A mother-of-pearl fan, the silk leaf painted with a gentleman dreaming of his love, the carved sticks pierced and gilt, French, c1785, 19½in (49.5cm) wide, framed.
£540–600 / €780–860
$910–1,000 ⊞ LDC

An ivory fan, with gilt foliate scroll decoration, the leaf painted with Regency figures, signed 'J. Besnard', early 19thC, 12in (30.5cm) long.
£125–150 / €190–220
$210–250 ⚒ AG

A mother-of-pearl fan, the leaf painted with figures in a formal garden, the sticks carved with ladies seated at a table and pierced with oval panels, 19thC, 20in (51cm) wide, in a gilt-framed case.
£280–330 / €400–480
$470–560 ⚒ GH

An ivory fan, painted with a chinoiserie design, the sticks and guards pierced and carved with mythological subjects, possibly Flemish, c1750, 9½in (24cm) long.
£780–940 / €1,100–1,300
$1,300–1,550 ⚒ S(O)

A painted double-sided fan leaf, with a female goddess seated in a cloud being offered a basket of flowers by two putti, the reverse with four figures in a wooded landscape, within a border of painted and gilded flowers, paint rubbed, probably French, 18thC, 15in (38cm) wide, in a giltwood frame, damaged.
£230–270 / €330–390
$390–460 ⚒ WW

A mother-of-pearl fan, the silk gauze leaf decorated with a maiden in a wooded river landscape, the sticks and guards decorated with floral garlands, at fault, signed 'T. Houghton', 19thC, 13in (33cm) wide, in a glazed case.
£200–240 / €290–350
$340–400 ⚒ G(L)

Items in the Fans section have been arranged in date order.

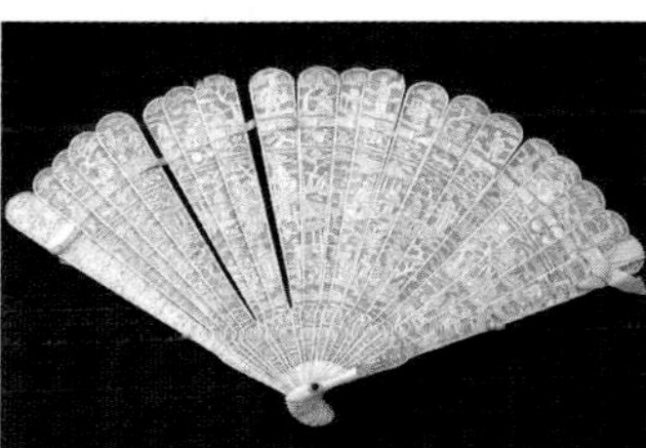

An ivory brisé fan, carved with figures at various pursuits, Chinese, Canton, 19thC, 7½in (19cm) long.
£150–180 / €220–260
$250–300 ⚒ G(L)
A brisé fan is one that consists of pierced sticks of ivory, horn or tortoiseshell.

An ivory fan, the paper leaf painted with a group of musicians, the guards painted and pierced, 18thC, 21in (53.5cm) wide, in a gilt case.
£420–500 / €600–720
$710–840 ⚒ HYD

A mother-of-pearl fan, the skin leaf painted with a mother and her children, the guards and sticks carved, painted, silvered and gilded with a vignette of Adonis taking leave of Venus, Italian, c1770, 11¾in (30cm) long, with associated case.
£1,200–1,450 / €1,750–2,100
$2,000–2,400 ⚒ S(O)

An ivory fan, the silk leaf appliquéd with three vignettes, the reserves with vignettes of sequins, the sticks pierced with classical motifs and musical trophies enriched with silvered paste, a *faux* diamond stud at the rivet, c1790, 9½in (24cm) long.
£290–350 / €420–500
$490–590 ⚒ TEN

A Chinese export lacquered gilt fan, the leaf painted and inlaid with ivory, the sticks and guards painted with figures seated in a garden, 19thC, 20½in (52cm) wide, in original fitted box.
£610–730 / €880–1,050
$1,000–1,200 ⚒ B(Ed)

A mother-of-pearl fan, the skin leaf depicting an outdoor entertainment, signed 'Malay Dubois Davernes', the guards and sticks pierced, carved and gilded, French, c1849, 10½in (26.5cm) long.
£300–360 / €440–520
$500–600 ⚒ S(O)

A fan, the hand-painted leaf decorated with sequins, with wooden sticks and guards, mid-19thC, 9in (23cm) wide.
£75–85 / €110–125
$125–140 ⊞ JPr

A fan, the leaf of Flemish bobbin lace, with hand-carved ivory sticks, c1880, 8in (20.5cm) long.
£85–95 / €125–140
$145–160 ⊞ JPr

A fan, the paper leaf painted with 118 characters, each with a painted ivory face, the papier-mâché sticks with gilt decoration, Japanese, late 19thC, 11in (28cm) long, in a fitted lacquered case.
£420–500 / €600–720
$710–840 ⚒ G(L)

A fan, with lace leaf and wooden sticks, Spanish, c1900, 14in (35.5cm) long.
£75–85 / €110–125
$125–145 ⊞ JPr

A fan, with a hand-painted leaf, the mother-of-pearl sticks and guards inlaid with silver, c1850, 10in (25.5cm) long.
£210–240 / €300–350
$350–400 ⊞ JPr

A fan, with a hand-painted silk leaf and ivory brisé sticks and guards, damaged, c1860, 9in (23cm) long.
£80–90 / €115–130
$135–150 ⊞ JPr

An ivory brisé fan, with silk satin leaf, c1880, 9in (23cm) long.
£85–95 / €125–140
$145–160 ⊞ JPr

A silk and ebony fan, belonging to the Empress Elisabeth of Austria, the ebony sticks with a gilt monogram of Emperor Franz Joseph of Austria and the Imperial arms, with a silk tassel, Austrian, c1890, 17in (43cm) wide.
£1,700–2,050 / €2,450–2,950
$2,850–3,400 ⚒ Herm
This fan originates from the mourning period following the Mayerling tragedy when Crown Prince Rudolf committed suicide with his lover in 1889. It was a present from Emperor Franz Joseph, c1890.

► **A fan,** the silk leaf decorated with sequins, the sticks and guards engraved and inlaid with metal, French, early 20thC, 21½in (54.5cm) wide.
£95–110 / €140–165
$160–185 ⚒ BR

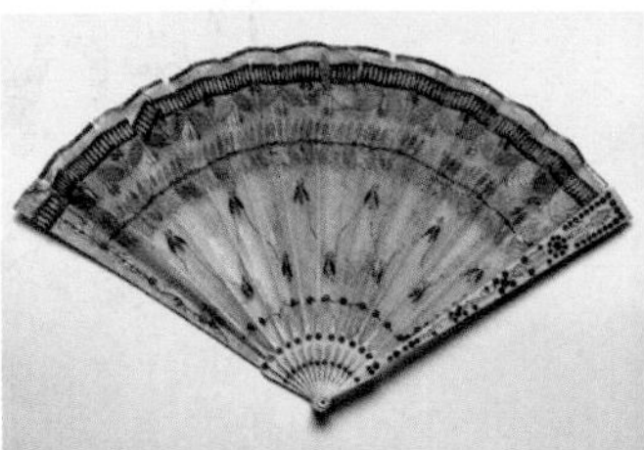

An ivory and net fan, decorated with bees and sequins, c1850, 8in (20.5cm) long.
£75–85 / €110–125
$125–145 ⊞ JPr

A fan, with a Brussels duchesse lace leaf and tortoiseshell sticks and guards, c1870, 9in (23cm) long.
£105–120 / €150–170
$175–200 ⊞ JPr
Duchesse lace is a type of Brussels lace that has bold floral patterns worked with a fine thread.

A fan, the leaf of Brussels lace, with tortoiseshell sticks, one end applied with a gold ducal coronet and monogram, Belgian, late 19thC, 10in (25.5cm) long, with original box.
£230–270 / €330–390
$390–460 ⚒ NSal

A lacquered ivory fan, with coral and agate inlay, depicting cranes in a bamboo grove and plovers in flight, Japanese, c1900, 12in (30.5cm) long, in a lacquered box.
£4,550–5,400 / €6,500–7,800
$7,600–9,000 ⚒ S(O)

Jewellery

Bangles & Bracelets

A paste bracelet, with seven glass plaques and metal mounts, c1720.
£910–1,100 / €1,300–1,550
$1,550–1,850 ⚒ WW

A Berlin ironwork bracelet, with scrolled panels, German, c1830.
£530–630 / €760–900
$890–1,050 ⚒ WW

Berlin ironwork

This type of black cast-iron jewellery in lacy designs was made in Berlin and Silesia from the early 19th century; the Royal Berlin Factory was founded in 1804. It was particularly popular during the Napoleonic wars (1800–15) when wealthy Prussians donated their valuable jewellery in support of the war effort and wore ironwork instead. Early designs were neo-classical in style: later, crosses became fashionable. Ironwork was also popular until the mid-19th century in France and Britain, where it was an acceptable form of mourning jewellery.

A bloomed gold bracelet, the repoussé clasp decorated with scrolls and fern leaves, 19thC.
£520–620 / €750–890
$870–1,050 ⚒ G(L)
Bloom is the frosted or matt surface on many types of gold jewellery, especially Victorian examples.

◄ A gold hinged bangle, set with turquoise stones, French, 19thC.
£260–310
€370–440
$440–520 ⚒ EH

A gold mesh bracelet, set with amethyst and diamond clusters within beadwork borders and spacers, with a mesh bracelet, c1840.
£540–640 / €780–920
$910–1,100 ⚒ TEN

► A gold ribbed mesh bracelet, with pearl and enamel slide and terminal, c1840.
£330–390
€470–560
$550–650
⚒ TRM

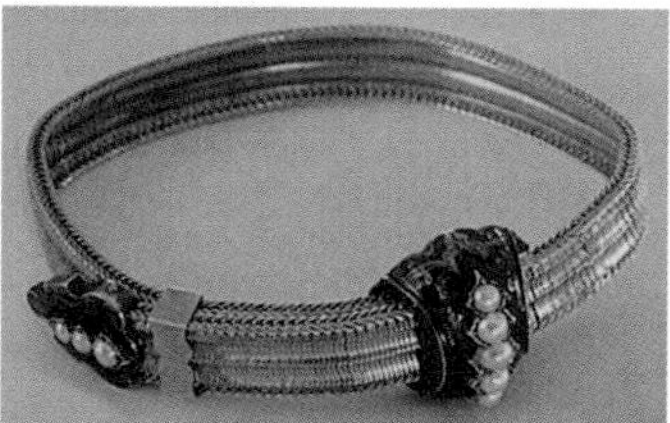

An enamelled snake bracelet, set with opals and a cabochon garnet, the eyes with peridots, c1850, 2¼in (5.5cm) wide.
£690–820 / €1,000–1,200
$1,150–1,350 ⚒ S(O)

◄ A pair of gold bracelets, with enamel strapwork, c1860.
£350–420 / €500–600
$590–710 ⚒ TEN

A Victorian 9ct rose gold bracelet, the padlock in the shape of a heart, 7in (18cm) long.
£165–195 / €240–280
$280–330 ⚒ SWO

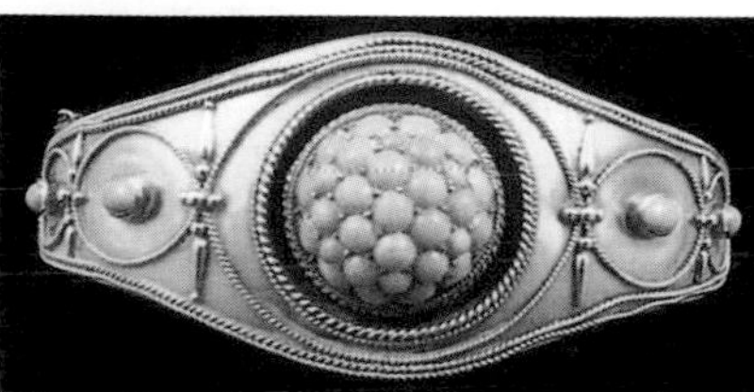

► A Victorian gold hinged bangle, set with turquoise stones, with ropetwist borders.
£370–440 / €530–630
$620–750 ⚒ BR

A jet bangle, set with a shell cameo, c1870.
£340–380 / €490–540
$570–640 ⊞ SAY

Jet jewellery

Jet jewellery was produced in great quantities in the 19th century, mostly in Whitby in North Yorkshire. It was an obvious medium for mourning jewellery, which had become so popular in Victorian times after the death of Prince Albert. Jet can become dull and acquire a bloomed surface through age – pieces that retain their original shiny appearance are more desirable, as are those that are particularly well-carved or engraved.

A Victorian gold and enamel bracelet, the heart-shaped pendant set with a pearl.
£370–440 / €530–630
$620–740 ⚒ G(L)

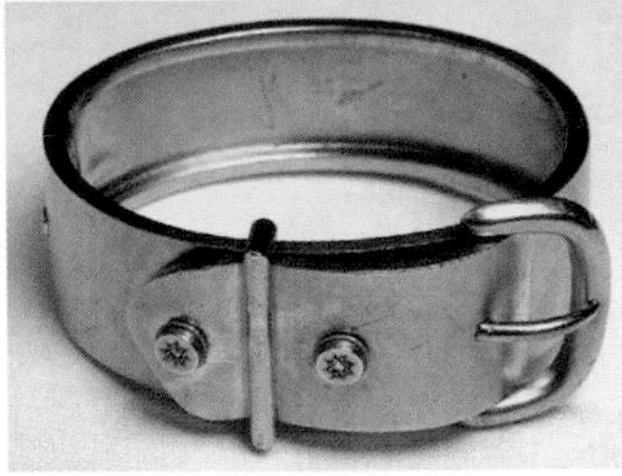

A Victorian 15ct gold buckle bangle, 2½in (6.5cm) diam.
£810–900 / €1,150–1,300
$1,350–1,500 ⊞ WIM

An 18ct gold bracelet, set with a garnet and diamonds, French, 1850–1900, 2¾in (7cm) diam.
£1,750–1,950 / €2,500–2,800
$2,900–3,250 ⊞ WIM

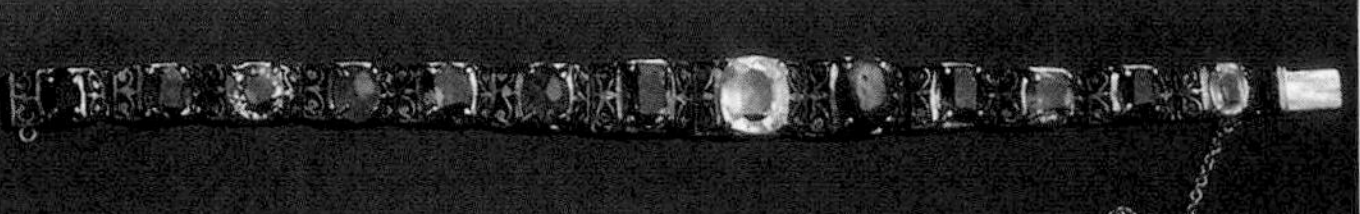

A gold bracelet, set with vari-coloured cut sapphires, late 19thC.
£1,050–1,250 / €1,500–1,800
$1,750–2,100 ⚒ TEN

◄ **A Victorian gold hinged bangle,** surmounted by a floral motif with an enamel and split-pearl locket.
£400–480 / €570–690
$670–800 ⚒ FHF

A 15ct gold bracelet, set with pearls and a ruby, c1890, 5in (12.5cm) wide.
£850–950 / €1,200–1,350
$1,450–1,600 ⊞ EXC

► **A Victorian bangle,** set with garnets, 2¼in (5.5cm) diam.
£300–360
€430–520
$500–600
⚒ CGC

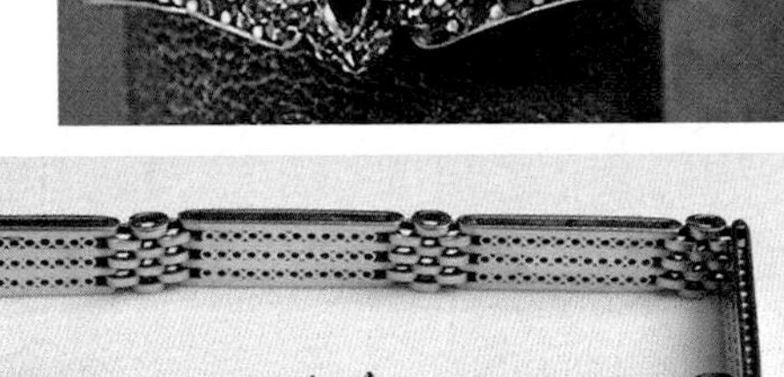

An 18ct gold gate bracelet, c1900, 4in (10cm) long.
£810–900 / €1,150–1,300
$1,350–1,500 ⊞ WIM

A 15ct gold gate bracelet, c1890, 3in (7.5cm) diam.
£810–900 / €1,150–1,300
$1,350–1,500 ⊞ WIM

A pair of gold bangles, the enamel peacocks set with half pearls, emeralds and rubies, c1900, 2¼in (5.5cm) diam.
£1,100–1,300 / €1,600–1,900
$1,850–2,200 ⚒ S(O)

► **A pair of gold bangles,** one set with a pearl and diamond cluster on a bar with a pearl to either end, the other with a sapphire and diamond cluster on a bar with a diamond to either end, marked, Austrian, c1910.
£1,750–2,100
€2,500–3,000
$2,900–3,500 ⚒ B(Ed)

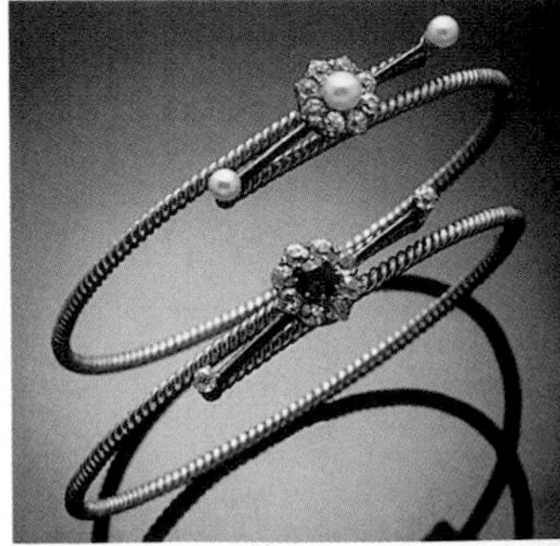

Brooches

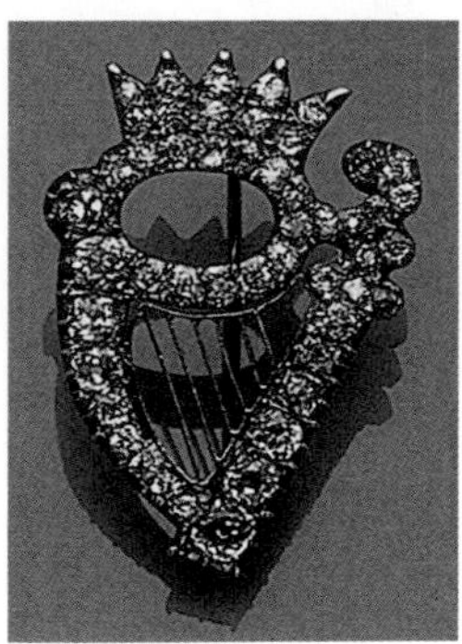

A gold brooch, in the shape of a lyre, set with diamonds, c1810.
£1,500–1,800
€2,150–2,600
$2,500–3,000 WW

◄ **A Masonic gold brooch,** with engraved decoration and inscribed 'Charles Eyfe, Jamaica, AD 1816', 2¾in (7cm) high.
£760–910
€1,100–1,300
$1,250–1,500
F&C

A Cavan brooch, by West & Son, Irish, Dublin, c1849, 2¾in (7cm) diam.
£240–270 / €350–390
$400–450 STA
This is a replica of a 9th-century brooch found in County Cavan in Ireland. The original, sometimes known as the Queen's brooch because it was given to Queen Victoria, is now in the National Museum of Ireland.

A silver scent bottle brooch, with a cranberry glass horn suspended from a bow, c1860, 2in (5cm) high.
£430–480 / €620–690
$720–800 CoS

Snake jewellery

Snake jewellery was fashionable throughout most of the 19th century. Necklaces and bracelets generally consist of a snake-like chain of interlocking scales with a gem-set or enamelled head at one end which 'bites' the tail at the other end, forming a circle, which was seen as a symbol of eternity. The snakes often had a jewel suspended from their mouths and garnets or rubies for the eyes. Unlike necklaces, brooches tended to be rigid. Snake rings became particularly popular after Prince Albert presented Queen Victoria with a snake engagement ring in 1839. The body of the snake is generally represented by a single, double or triple gold band, sometimes with a jewelled head or eyes.

A 15ct gold, garnet and citrine snake brooch, 1860–70, 1½in (4cm) high.
£540–600 / €780–860
$900–1,000 WIM

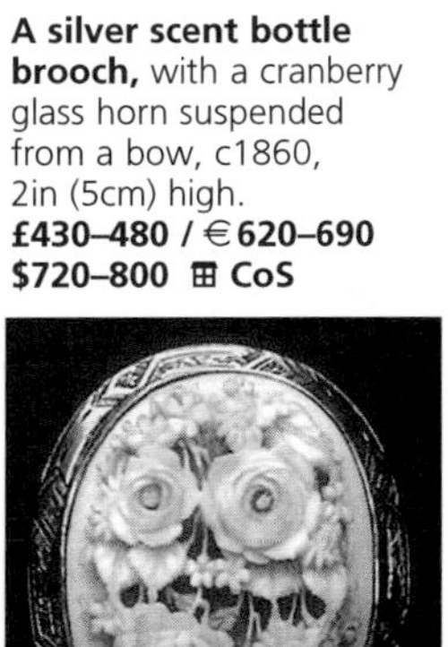

A mid-Victorian engraved silver brooch, set with an ivory plaque carved with flowers.
£280–330 / €400–470
$470–550 TEN

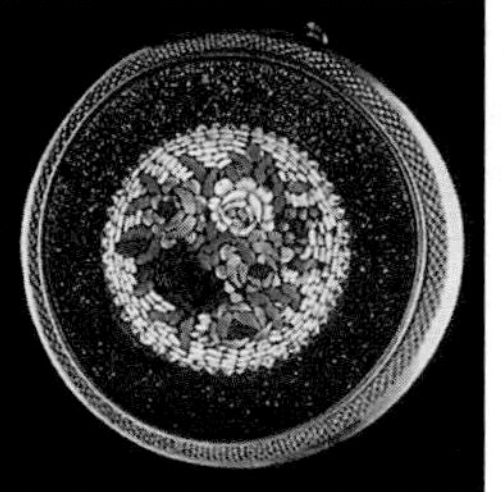

An 18ct gold brooch/ pendant, by A. G. Björkman, with a micro-mosiac and aventurine glass centre, Swedish, Stockholm, 1873.
£270–320 / €390–460
$450–540 BUK

A Victorian diamond brooch, in the shape of a spider, the pin suspending a fly, set with emeralds and rubies.
£640–760 / €920–1,100
$1,100–1,300 BWL

A Whitby jet brooch, c1890, 1¾in (4.5cm) diam.
£65–75 / €95–110
$110–125 AM

A gold and silver brooch, set with sapphires and diamonds, c1895, 3in (7.5cm) diam, in a case.
£4,000–4,500 / €5,800–6,500
$6,800–7,600 EXC

A ruby and diamond pin brooch, in the shape of a butterfly, c1900, 2in (5cm) wide.
£1,150–1,300 / €1,650–1,850
$1,950–2,200 SGr

An Edwardian platinum and gold brooch/pendant, set with diamonds, 1½in (4cm) high.
£2,700–3,000
€3,900–4,300
$4,500–5,000 NBL

Cameos

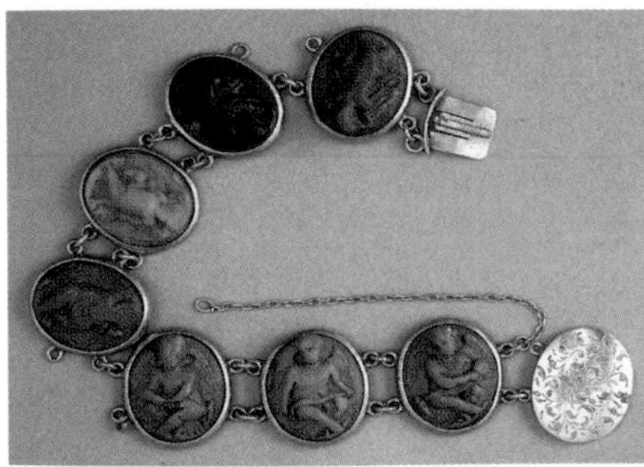

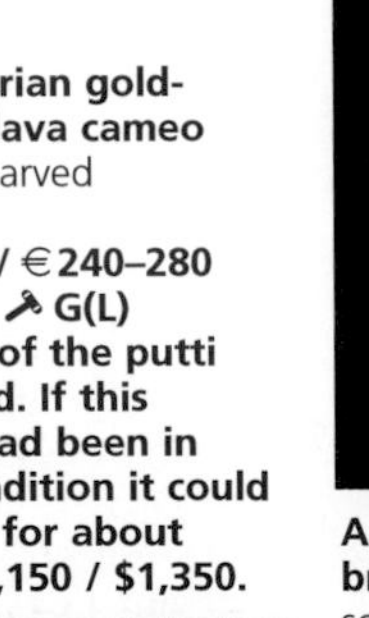

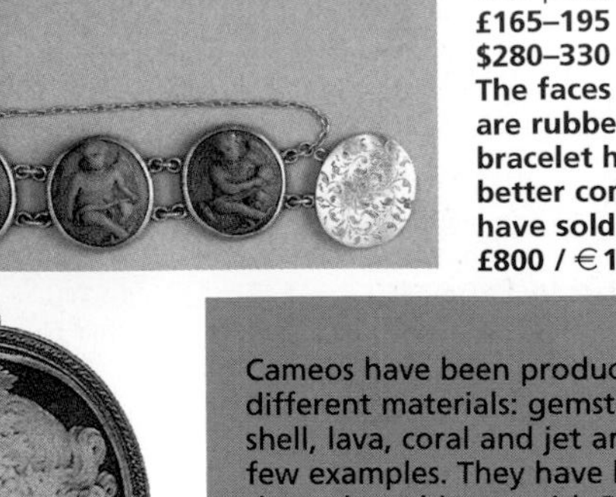

◀ **A Victorian gold-mounted lava cameo bracelet,** carved with putti.
£165–195 / €240–280
$280–330 ⚒ G(L)
The faces of the putti are rubbed. If this bracelet had been in better condition it could have sold for about £800 / €1,150 / $1,350.

An early Victorian gold cameo brooch, carved with Medusa, with scroll mounts, 2¼in (5.5cm) long.
£670–750 / €960–1,100
$1,100–1,250 ⊞ AMC

A gold and shell cameo brooch, carved with a woman, 19thC, 1¾in (4.5cm) long.
£330–390 / €470–560
$550–660 ⚒ Bea

Cameos have been produced in many different materials: gemstones, agates, shell, lava, coral and jet are just a few examples. They have been made throughout history with Roman and Greek examples influencing Renaissance, Georgian and Victorian jewellers and carvers. The subjects vary from portraits, through mythology to historical figures, biblical scenes and even battles. There have also been many copies, from the 18th-century copies of Roman hardstone cameos, now very collectable themselves, to glass moulded to look like a gemstone and plastic moulded to look like jet.

An early Victorian cameo brooch, carved with a warrior, set in a pinchbeck mount, 2¼in (5.5cm) long.
£540–600 / €780–860
$900–1,000 ⊞ AMC
Four faces are hidden in the carving on this cameo brooch.

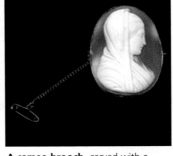

A Victorian ivory cameo brooch, carved with a bacchante, in a gold frame.
£590–710 / €850–1,000
$1,000–1,200 ⚒ WW

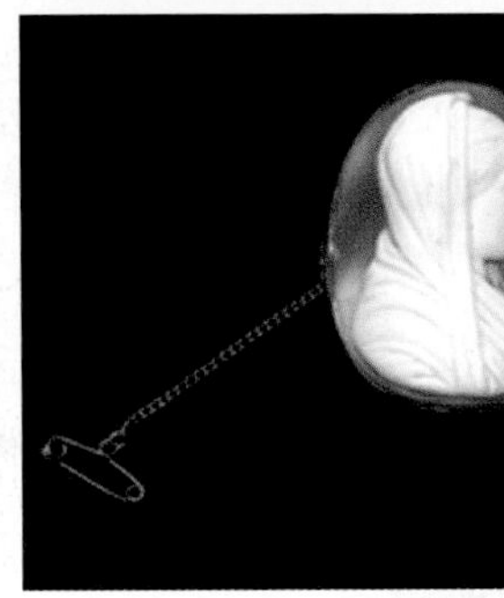

A cameo brooch, carved with a lady's head and shoulders draped in a shawl, in a gold mount, c1900, 1½in (4cm) high.
£270–300 / €390–430
$450–500 ⊞ AMC

A Victorian shell cameo brooch, carved with the Virgin Mary and Christ child being offered gifts by a man and a woman, the gold frame with a twisted border, 2½in (6.5cm) long.
£80–95 / €115–135
$135–160 ⚒ JDJ

A pair of Victorian 15ct gold shell cameo earrings, c1860, 2¼in (5.5cm) long.
£1,350–1,500
€1,950–2,150
$2,250–2,500 ⊞ WIM

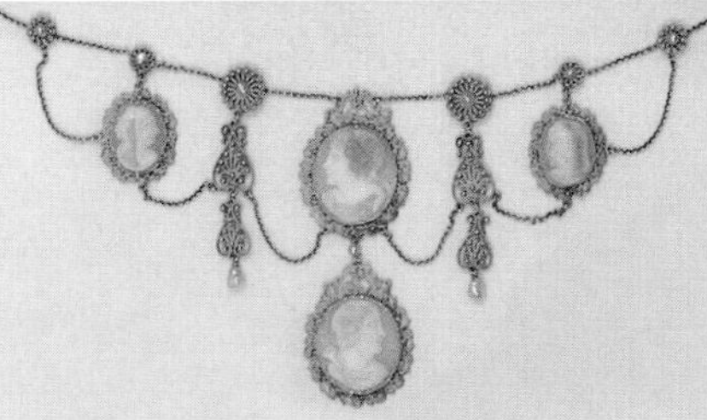

A shell cameo necklace, the four panels depicting classical busts in wirework surrounds linked by chains and pearl-set palmette spacers, 19thC.
£800–950 / €1,150–1,350
$1,350–1,600 ⚒ B(L)

▶ **A Victorian cameo stick pin,** in an engraved gold mount, 1in (2.5cm) long.
£130–155 / €185–220
$220–260 ⚒ SWO

Cufflinks

A pair of Victorian 15ct gold and turquoise cufflinks, ½in (1.5cm) wide.
£430–480 / €620–690
$720–800 ⊞ SPE

A pair of 14ct gold cufflinks, set with gemstones, Austrian, c1900, ½in (1.5cm) wide, in original case.
£720–800 / €1,050–1,150
$1,200–1,350 ⊞ WIM

A pair of 18ct gold and enamel cufflinks, decorated with a star motif, c1905.
£125–150 / €180–210
$210–250 ⚒ LCM

◄ **A pair of cufflinks,** with carved amethyst and emerald intaglios, within ropework mounts and beaded borders, c1910.
£1,800–2,150
€2,600–3,100
$3,000–3,600 ⚒ LFA

A pair of 14ct gold and citrine cufflinks, Austrian, c1910, ½in (1.5cm) wide.
£810–900 / €1,150–1,300
$1,350–1,500 ⊞ WIM

Earrings

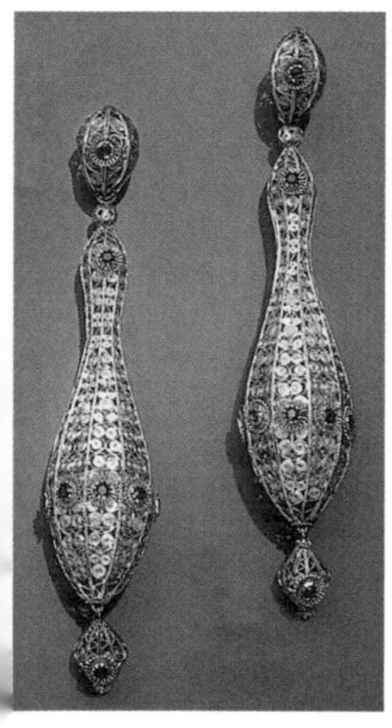

A pair of gold earrings, decorated with spun gold cannetille and set with garnet collets, with later fittings, c1800, with original fitted case by E. & W. Smith.
£2,800–3,350
€4,000–4,800
$4,700–5,600 ⚒ WW

LOCATE THE SOURCE

The source of each illustration in Miller's can be found by checking the code letters below each caption with the Key to Illustrations, pages 794–800.

A pair of early Victorian earrings, set with old-cut diamonds, with hook fittings.
£1,500–1,800
€2,150–2,600
$2,500–3,000 ⚒ B(Ed)

A pair of Egyptian-style earrings, by Carl Bacher, the pharoahs' heads carved in amethyst, with ruby, diamond and sapphire highlights and enamel detail, converted c1870.
£2,900–3,500
€4,200–5,000
$4,800–5,800 ⚒ TEN

A pair of Victorian gold earrings, set with garnets and peridots, with later snake fittings.
£190–220 / €270–320
$320–370 ⚒ G(L)

A pair of Victorian 15ct gold earrings, with enamel decoration, set with pearls and diamonds, 2in (5cm) long.
£1,500–1,700
€2,150–2,450
$2,500–2,850 ⊞ WIM

A pair of jet earrings, c1870, 2¼in (5.5cm) long.
£400–450 / €570–650
$670–760 ⊞ SAY

A pair of platinum earrings, set with diamonds and emeralds, c1910, 1½in (4cm) long.
£7,600–8,500
€10,900–12,200
$12,700–14,300 ⊞ NBL

Mourning Jewellery

There was a general obsession with mortality in 17th-century England – by the latter half of the century it had become customary to leave money to pay for memorial rings to be distributed at one's funeral. Much of the mourning jewellery of the time depicts enamelled or gold skulls or skeletons, sometimes with the name of the deceased and date on the reverse.

By the 18th century, mourning rings usually bore an enamel band inscribed with the name and date on the outside, rather than the inside as previously. Generally, black enamel was used for married people and white for unmarried. Brooches and rings with a central hair locket surrounded by diamonds or paste and coloured stones had become fashionable by c1750, while towards the end of the century a more romantic and allegorical style was introduced. Pieces were usually painted in sepia on ivory with the addition of tiny pieces of hair and typically depicted a woman weeping over a tomb beside a willow tree. Colour was occasionally used, usually in a pale wash. The more important sepia pendants were often decorated on the reverse with elaborate hairwork in the form of beautiful, sometimes bejewelled, combed plumes, wheat sheaves or cornucopias laid on opaline glass. A typical inscription was 'not lost but gone before'. Some of these pieces were surrounded by engraved gold or enamel, others by paste, garnets or pearls. Examples framed with diamonds are rare and would have been expensive in their time.

Mourning jewellery dating from the early 19th century often incorporated enamelled urns and snakes (symbolizing eternity), reflecting the taste for the neo-classical. Wide enamelled band rings replaced the narrow rings of the 18th century and many of the mourning rings from this period are hallmarked. From Victorian times, the rise of middle-class prosperity resulted in a much greater selection of styles, the heart, bow and snake starting to replace the skull and skeleton. Towards the end of the century large brooches made in jet (or its simulants), onyx or black enamel proliferated. The more expensive pieces were set with pearls or diamonds, but in general people were demanding more inexpensive jewellery. By the 1880s photographs were being incorporated into lockets and rings, following a fashion set by Queen Victoria who included a photograph of Prince Albert in the mourning ring she wore in his memory.

Charlotte Sayers

An 18ct gold bangle, with three double-photograph lockets, each set with a cultured pearl, two photographs and a lock of hair, c1863, 2¼in (5.5cm) diam.
£490–590 / €710–850
$820–990 ⚒ SWO

A gold and enamel brooch, set with hair in the form of Prince of Wales feathers, c1860, 1½in (4cm) long.
£175–195 / €250–280
$290–330 ⊞ AMC

► An 18ct gold ring, set with enamel and Stuart crystal, 1710.
£1,200–1,300 / €1,700–1,850
$1,950–2,150 ⊞ CVA

A slide, the enamel eternal flame flanked by skulls and set on a base of hair, with a rose-cut rock crystal cover, converted to a brooch, 1680–1700.
£2,600–2,900 / €3,700–4,250
$4,400–4,900 ⊞ SAY

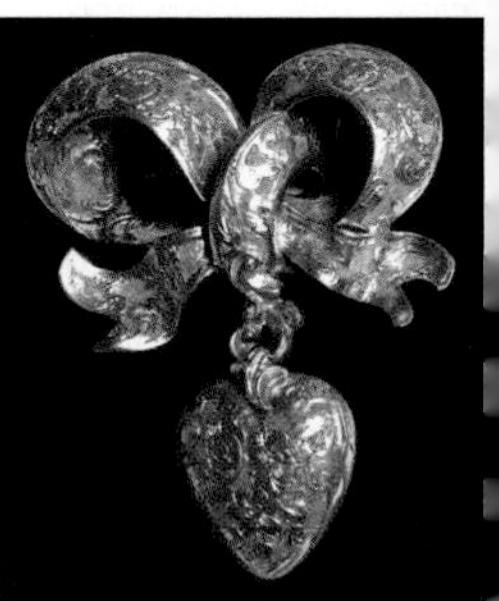

A 15ct gold brooch, inscribed 'L. W. Little, 19 months', c1858, 2½in (6.5cm) long.
£1,600–1,800
€2,300–2,600
$2,700–3,000 ⊞ WIM

◄ An enamel brooch, set with seed pearls, commemorating the death of Queen Victoria, 1901, 1¼in (3cm) wide.
£1,250–1,400
€1,800–2,000
$2,100–2,350 ⊞ SAY

Further reading

Miller's Jewellery Antiques Checklist, Miller's Publications, 1998

An 18ct gold ring, set with rock crystal, decorated with a skull and crossbones, inscribed, c1758.
£2,000–2,250 / €2,900–3,200
$3,350–3,700 ⊞ WIM

A gold, enamel and ivory ring, inscribed 'Dorothy Hopkinson 29th Jan 1788 aged 73', 1788, 1in (2.5cm) diam.
£1,050–1,200 / €1,500–1,750
$1,750–2,000 ⊞ WELD

◄ **An enamel ring,** set with seed pearls, initialled, 1810–25.
£500–550 / €720–800
$840–930 ⊞ SAY

A gold and enamel ring, the hinged heart containing a lock of hair, inscribed and dated 1860.
£760–850 / €1,100–1,250
$1,300–1,450 ⊞ SAY

Further reading

Miller's Encyclopedia,
Miller's Publications, 2003

An 18ct gold ring, set with crystal, with enamel decoration, inscribed 'Un seul me tient', c1790.
£1,200–1,350 / €1,750–1,950
$2,000–2,250 ⊞ CVA

A gold ring, set with a pearl and diamond cluster, one pearl missing, inscribed and dated 1833.
£260–310 / €370–440
$440–520 ⚒ G(L)

An 18ct gold ring, set with old- and rose-cut diamonds and a lock of hair, with enamel decoration, 1906.
£150–180 / €220–260
$250–300 ⚒ SWO

A gold and enamel ring, inscribed 'in memory of', London 1841.
£175–210 / €250–300
$290–350 ⚒ Bea

A pendant, set with Stuart crystal and a later pearl, decorated with a skull and two cherubs, inscribed and dated 1707, ¾in (2cm) long.
£2,800–3,350 / €4,000–4,800
$4,700–5,600 ⊞ SAY

◄ **An 18ct gold pendant,** depicting angels above an urn, the reverse set with hair, inscribed and dated 1788.
£1,450–1,600
€2,050–2,300
$2,450–2,700 ⊞ CVA

Mourning miniatures such as these have increased greatly in price over the last two years. The larger and more expensive the miniature, the higher the price will be.

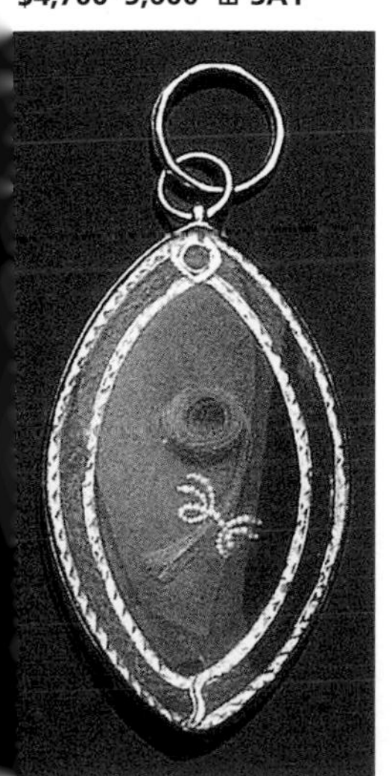

◄ **A pendant,** set with a lock of hair tied with seed pearls, on an enamel ground within a border of plaited hair, early 19thC.
£210–250
€300–360
$350–420 ⚒ TEN

► **A 9ct gold and enamel pendant brooch,** with inscription, the reverse set with hair, 1830s, 2in (5cm) diam.
£190–210
€270–300
$310–350 ⊞ SIL

An enamel locket, set with a butterfly and a chrysalis, inscribed 'Not lost but gone before', 1845, 1¼in (3cm) diam.
£2,500–2,800
€3,600–4,000
$4,200–4,700 ⊞ CVA

Necklaces

A paste necklace, foil-backed in collet settings, early 19thC.
£410–490 / €590–710
$690–820 TEN

A gold and turquoise serpent necklace, the head set with diamonds and garnets, c1845.
£3,900–4,700 / €5,600–6,700
$6,600–7,900 WW

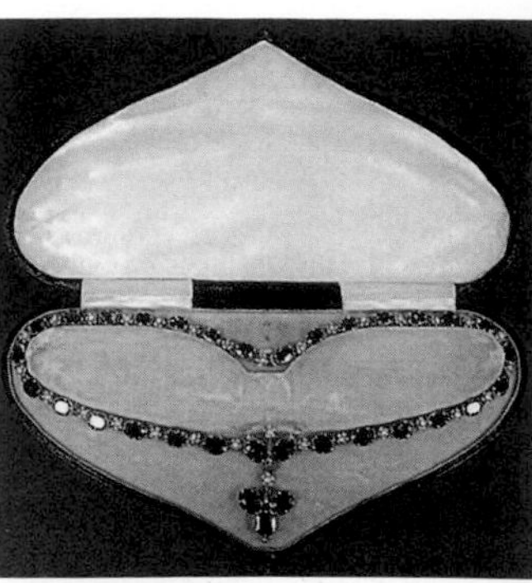

► **A Victorian garnet necklace,** the stones interspersed with flowerheads each set with a seed pearl, cased.
£1,000–1,200
€1,450–1,700
$1,700–2,000 DD

A gold and amethyst necklace, c1850, 14in (35.5cm) long.
£2,700–3,000 / €3,900–4,300
$4,500–5,000 WIM

A 'French jet' elasticated choker, c1870.
£520–580 / €750–840
$870–970 SAY

► **A gold, diamond and seed pearl fringe necklace,** with a detachable star pendant brooch, late 19thC.
£730–870 / €1,050–1,250
$1,250–1,450 Bea

A Victorian 15ct gold collar.
£1,400–1,650 / €2,000–2,400
$2,300–2,750 WW

A diamond and natural pearl necklace, c1890.
£4,100–4,600 / €5,900–6,600
$6,900–7,700 SGr

A peridot and seed pearl necklace, with a trace link back chain, c1900.
£910–1,100 / €1,300–1,600
$1,550–1,850 B(L)

A turquoise and seed pearl necklace, with a detachable pendant/brooch, c1890, 18½in (47cm) long. in a fitted case.
£840–1,000
€1,200–1,400
$1,400–1,650 S(O)

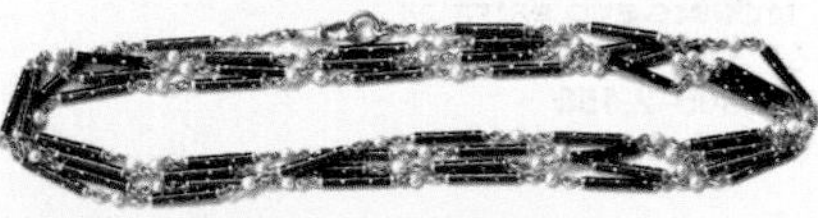

A gold, pearl and enamel necklace, c1900.
£3,900–4,400 / €5,600–6,300
$6,500–7,400 SGr

An Edwardian 15ct gold and amethyst necklace, collet-set with amethysts, on a belcher link chain, 16in (41cm) long.
£1,400–1,650 / €2,000–2,350
$2,350–2,750 FHF

◄ **An Edwardian gold, turquoise and pearl necklace,** on a trace link back chain.
£300–360 / €430–520
$500–600 G(L)

Parures & Sets

A gold, silver and diamond necklace and pendant, Portuguese, 18thC, pendant 3¼in (8.5cm) long.
£2,150–2,600 / €3,100–3,750
$3,600–4,350 S
This style is generally known as Iberian jewellery.

A silver-gilt and micro-mosaic suite, comprising necklace and bracelet, the filigree panels set with glass micro-mosaic depicting flowers, damaged, possibly Italian, c1860, cased.
£1,200–1,400 / €1,750–2,000
$2,000–2,350 B(Ed)

A silver collar and locket, with enamel floral sprays, late 19thC, in fitted case.
£620–740 / €890–1,050
$1,050–1,250 Bea

An almandine garnet necklet and matching brooch, early 19thC.
£420–500 / €600–720
$710–840 WL

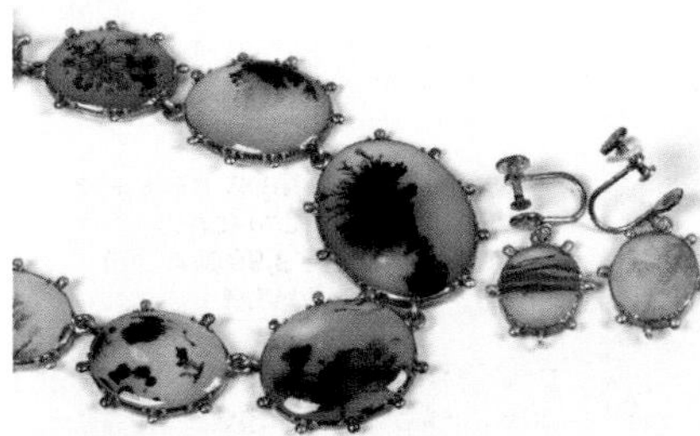

A 15ct gold demi-parure, comprising a brooch and earrings, modelled as fuchsias, possibly Australian, c1860, in original fitted case.
£1,550–1,850 / €2,250–2,650
$2,600–3,100 LJ

◄ **A Victorian gold, emerald and rose diamond necklace and earrings.**
£1,250–1,500
€1,800–2,150
$2,100–2,500 F&C

► **A 15ct gold brooch and earring set,** each set with a central diamond, c1890, brooch 2in (5cm) wide.
£670–750 / €970–1,100
$1,100–1,250 EXC

◄ **An opal and diamond demi-parure,** comprising necklace, brooch and earrings, c1900, necklace 15¾in (40cm) long.
£2,600–3,100
€3,750–4,450
$4,350–5,200
S(O)

A silver and gold brooch, pendant and earrings, set with diamonds and almandine garnets, c1850.
£10,400–12,500
€15,000–18,000
$17,500–21,000 BUK

◄ **A Victorian gold-mounted fern agate necklace and earrings.**
£1,250–1,500
€1,800–2,150
$2,100–2,500 FHF

An ivory demi-parure, comprising necklace with locket and a pair of earrings, carved with leaves and flowers, c1860.
£400–480 / €570–690
$670–800 TEN

Pendants

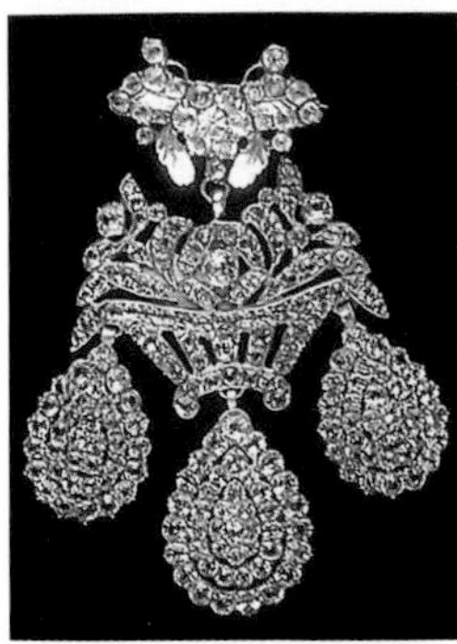

A George III silver and paste brooch/pendant, 3¼in (8cm) long, in a later case.
£940–1,100
€1,350–1,600
$1,600–1,850 L

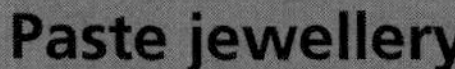

Paste jewellery

Paste jewellery originated in the late 17th and 18th centuries with the invention of lead glass. This was a more translucent type of glass that could be polished and faceted to imitate precious stones. The girandole brooch pendant in this section and the necklace on page 542 are typical of the designs of the period. The finest 18th-century pieces were made of stones cut into unusual shapes with the thinnest sliver of metal between each one, and then backed with foil to enhance the colour of the glass. Precise settings ensured that humidity did not get behind the glass and spoil the bright reflection. Sometimes a black painted spot can be seen at the bottom of the culet to make the stone look brighter. Generally, colourless glass was set in silver and coloured pieces set in gold or metal settings that were sometimes gilded. From the early 19th century the settings were opened up at the back when jewellers realized that the reflection was just as bright from unbacked glass.

A gold cross pendant, c1820.
£410–490 / €590–700
$690–820 TEN

◄ **A Victorian 14ct gold and enamel locket,** depicting a woman in a headdress set with rose-cut diamonds, losses, 1¾in (4.5cm) long.
£1,300–1,550
€1,850–2,200
$2,200–2,600 JDJ

A 15ct gold pendant, with micro-mosiac decoration and a locket compartment, c1870, 2½in (6.5cm) long.
£1,500–1,650
€2,100–2,350
$2,500–2,750 EXC

A diamond cross pendant, Continental, c1820, 1¾in (4.5cm) high.
£500–550 / €720–800
$840–930 NBL

An 18ct gold, pearl and simulated sapphire pendant, with enamel decoration, 1850–1900.
£1,500–1,800
€2,150–2,600
$2,500–3,000 BUK

A silver-gilt and enamel cross pendant, set with aquamarines and garnets, Continental, late 19thC, 3½in (9cm) long.
£340–380 / €490–550
$570–640 G(L)

◄ **A diamond, ruby and agate pendant,** with a trace link chain, c1890.
£350–420 / €500–600
$590–700 B(Ed)

A 10ct gold and pearl pendant, the three flowers set with rubies, one missing, c1900.
£75–90 / €110–130
$125–150 LCM

Insurance values

Always insure your valuable antiques for the cost of replacing them with similar items, regardless of the original price paid. Both dealers and auctioneers can provide a valuation service for a fee.

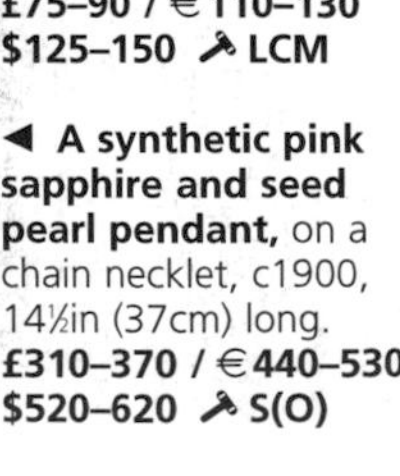

◄ **A synthetic pink sapphire and seed pearl pendant,** on a chain necklet, c1900, 14½in (37cm) long.
£310–370 / €440–530
$520–620 S(O)

JEWELLERY

Rings

A 22ct gold posy ring, inscribed 'Wee loyne our Hartes in God', 1600–50.
£940–1,050 / €1,350–1,500
$1,550–1,750 ⊞ WELD

Posy is a corruption of the word poesie, and refers to a short inscription often found engraved on the inside of gold hoop rings dating from the late 16th to the early 18th centuries. Sometimes a skull or extended skeleton would be added after a loved one had died, converting the piece into a mourning ring.

A George III enamel and diamond ring, with floral engraved shoulders, three stones missing and some replaced simulated diamonds.
£470–560 / €670–800
$790–940 ⚒ B(Ed)

A ring, inscribed 'Deus Nos lunxit', c1790.
£1,500–1,650
€2,150–2,400
$2,500–2,750 ⊞ SGr

► A Victorian gold, opal and diamond ring.
£490–590
€710–850
$820–990
⚒ G(L)

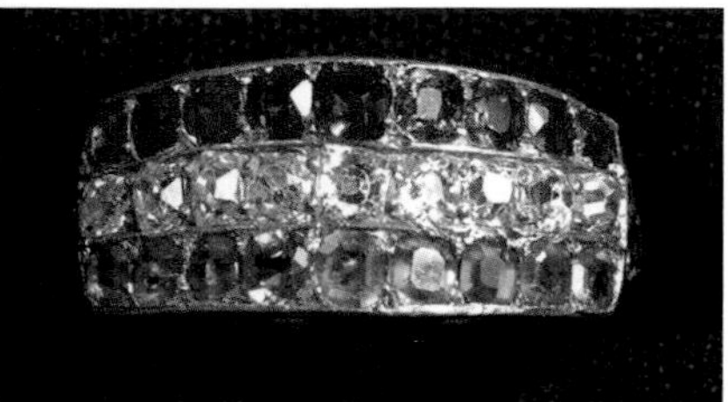

An 18ct gold, ruby, diamond and emerald ring, c1885.
£2,500–2,800 / €3,600–4,000
$4,200–4,700 ⊞ EXC

A gold, silver and diamond ring, late 19thC.
£730–870 / €1,050–1,250
$1,250–1,450 ⚒ Bea

A Victorian diamond and ruby ring.
£1,250–1,400 / €1,800–2,000
$2,100–2,350 ⊞ WIM

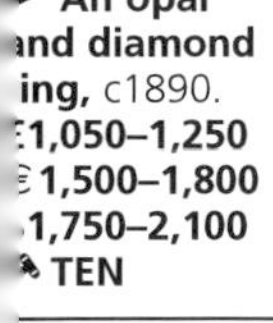

► An opal and diamond ring, c1890.
£1,050–1,250
€1,500–1,800
$1,750–2,100
⚒ TEN

◄ A gold, sapphire and diamond ring, c1900.
£960–1,150 / €1,400–1,650
$1,600–1,900 ⚒ G(L)

Stick Pins

A late Victorian gold stick pin, set with an amethyst entwined by a coiled snake with amethyst cabochon-set eyes.
£120–145 / €175–210
$200–240 ⚒ PFK

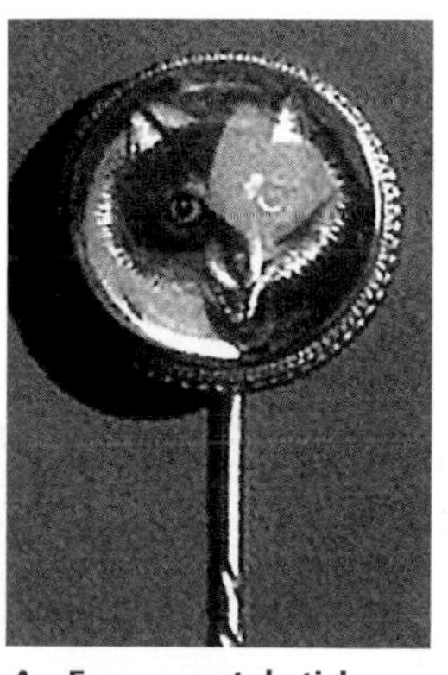

An Essex crystal stick pin, depicting a fox's head within a collet mount and ropework border, c1900.
£175–210 / €250–300
$290–350 ⚒ TEN

A gold and diamond stick pin, c1900, in original fitted case.
£500–600 / €720–860
$840–1,000 ⚒ LJ

A gold and diamond hat pin, set with a star sapphire, French, c1905.
£880–1,050
€1,250–1,500
$1,450–1,750 ⚒ WW

Enamel

An enamel patch box, painted with a three-masted man-o'-war, inscribed 'A Trifle from New York', the hinged cover with a mirrored interior, 18thC, 2in (5cm) wide.
£2,700–3,200 / €3,900–4,600
$4,500–5,300 TMA

An 18th-century-style enamel patch box, the cover with a portrait of a mythical figure making an offering, c1910, 1½in (4cm) diam.
£220–250 / €320–360
$370–410 LBr

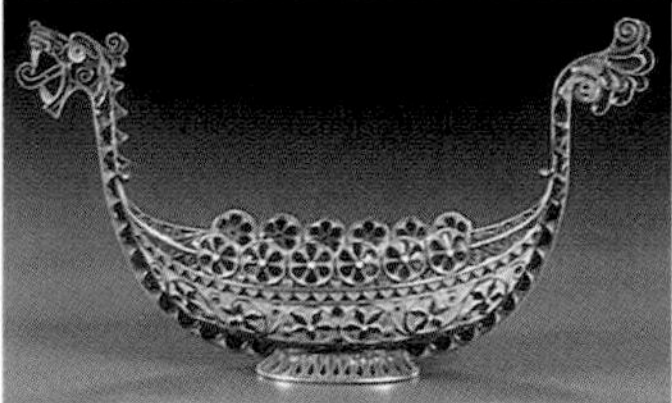

A silver-gilt and *plique à jour* enamel model of a Viking longboat, with an enamelled interior, Norwegian, c1900, 6in (15cm) long.
£1,900–2,250 / €2,750–3,300
$3,200–3,850 S(O)

◄ **An enamel box,** the hinged cover inscribed 'A Present from Bristol', early 19thC, 2½in (6.5cm) wide.
£140–165 / €200–240
$240–280 SWO

A silver and enamel box, with a gilt interior, Master's mark 'Malcz', Polish, Warsaw, c1870, 4¼in (11cm) wide.
£490–590 / €700–840
$830–990 DORO

A silver-gilt and cloisonné enamel *kovsh*, by Ivan Khlebnikov, Russian, Moscow, c1908, 3in (7.5cm) wide.
£1,350–1,500 / €1,950–2,150
$2,250–2,500 MIR

A set of six silver and enamel napkin rings, Birmingham, 1927–28, in a fitted case, 8in (20.5cm) wide.
£2,400–2,650 / €3,450–3,800
$4,000–4,400 NS

◄ **A Limoges enamel-on-copper plaque,** by Restoueix, French, c1900, 12 x 10in (30.5 x 25.5cm).
£1,600–1,800 / €2,300–2,600
$2,700–3,000 ANO

► **A lady's silver and enamel toilet set,** by Drew & Sons, comprising 15 items, Birmingham 1935, in a pigskin travelling case, 21in (53.5cm) wide.
£700–840 / €1,000–1,200
$1,200–1,400 M

An enamel double scent box/*bonbonnière*, paintec with classical figures, each end fitted with silver-gilt hinged covers inset with cameos designed as Europea bust portraits, Continental, 19thC, 2¾in (7cm) high.
£1,250–1,500
€1,800–2,150
$2,100–2,500 RTo

An enamel scent flask, painted with flowers, the metal stopper modelled as a bird, 18thC, 3¼in (8.5cm) high.
£260–310 / €380–450
$440–520 WW

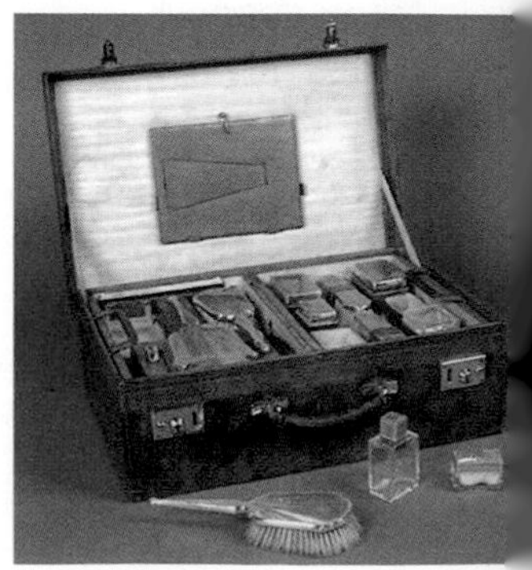

Fabergé

A Fabergé gold, ruby and diamond brooch, Russian, c1900, 1in (2.5cm) diam.
£1,550–1,750
€2,250–2,500
$2,600–2,900 ⊞ ICO

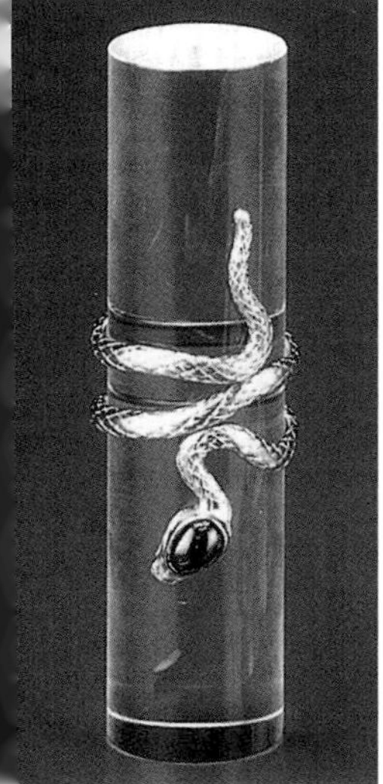

A Fabergé rock crystal and gold desk seal, encircled by a serpent with a sapphire-set head, small chip, workmaster E. Kollin, Russian, St Petersburg, c1890, 3¾in (9.5cm) high.
£5,400–6,500
€7,800–9,300
$9,100–10,900 ⚒ S

A Fabergé silver tea-glass holder, cast and chased with bands of leaves and wreaths, maker's mark beneath Imperial warrant, Russian, Moscow, 1899–1908, ¼in (8.5cm) high.
2,650–3,200
3,850–4,600
4,500–5,400 ⚒ S(O)

A Fabergé silver-mounted vase, Russian, 1900, 6¼in (16cm) high.
,500–2,750
3,600–4,000
4,200–4,650 ⊞ ICO

A Fabergé silver cigarette case, with repoussé and chased decoration of a bearded *boyar*, with a cabochon sapphire thumbpiece, marked, Russian, Moscow, c1900, 3½in (9cm) wide.
£3,550–4,250
€5,100–6,100
$5,900–7,100 ⚒ S(NY)
A *boyar* is a member of an old order of Russian nobility.

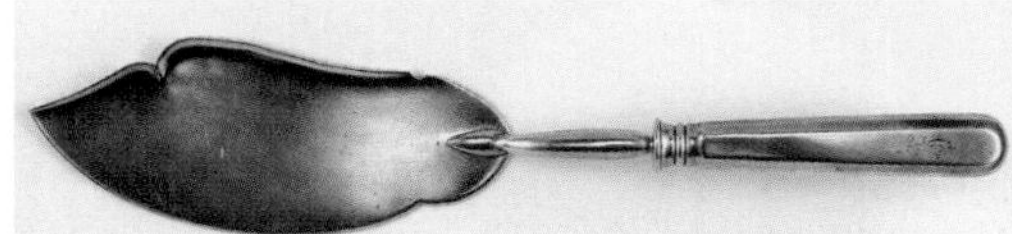

A Fabergé silver fish slice, with a shaped blade and panelled handle, initialled 'F', Russian, Moscow, 1908–17, 12¾in (32.5cm) long.
£590–710 / €850–1,000
$1,000–1,200 ⚒ WW

A Fabergé two-colour gold and nephrite paper knife/page turner, the blade decorated with an engraved Imperial double-headed eagle, the hilt with fluted chevrons and a reeded central section, inscribed 'October 1896, Lord Edward Pelham Clinton from the Emperor of Russia', workmaster Michael Perchin, Russian, St Petersburg, c1896, 19¾in (50cm) long.
£47,000–56,000 / €68,000–81,000
$79,000–94,000 ⚒ WW
Lord Edward Pelham Clinton (1836–1907), younger brother of the 6th Duke of Newcastle, was Master of Queen Victoria's household from 1894 to 1901.

◄ **A Fabergé gold, silver and enamel taperstick,** slight damage, Russian, c1900, 2½in (6.5cm) high.
£4,450–5,300 / €6,400–7,600
$7,500–8,900 ⚒ CHTR

Gold

A gold and enamel snuff box, French, c1770, 2in (5cm) diam.
£2,500–2,750 / €3,600–4,000
$4,200–4,600 ⊞ SHa

A two-colour gold box, the cover chased between red gold straps, the sides and base turned and engraved with key plate and simulated handles, Swiss, probably Geneva, early 19thC, 2in (5cm) wide.
£720–860 / €1,050–1,250
$1,200–1,400 ⚒ S

A jewelled gold snuffbox, engraved and decorated with applied floral scrollwork, the cover applied with a diamond monogram 'W' for Emperor Wilhelm II, the interior inscribed 'Presented to Lord Edward Pelham Clinton by the German Emperor William II at Windsor Castle November 24th 1899', the base engraved with the German Imperial eagle, some stones missing, German, late 19thC, 3¾in (9.5cm) wide, 7oz.
£7,100–8,500 / €10,200–12,250
$11,900–14,300 ⚒ WW

◄ **A gold and enamel chatelaine,** French, c1800, 5½in (14cm) long.
£3,400–3,750 / €4,900–5,400
$5,700–6,300 ⊞ SHa

◄ **A gold and blonde tortoiseshell scent bottle *étui*,** comprising two scent bottles and matching wax holder, French, 18thC, *étui* 3in (7.5cm) high.
£3,150–3,500 / €4,500–5,000
$5,300–5,900 ⊞ LBr

A gold-mounted cornelian miniature scent bottle, c1880, 1in (2.5cm) high.
£250–280 / €360–400
$420–470 ⊞ CoS

A gold thimble, 'Piercy's Patent' with trellis piercing around the base, the cartouche with initials 'EH', liner missing, 1815–20, 1¾in (4.5cm) high.
£1,400–1,650
€2,000–2,350
$2,350–2,750 ⚒ WW

A gold-mounted and garnet-set scent bottle, with a flip top, c1900, 3¼in (8.5cm) high.
£580–650 / €840–940
$970–1,100 ⊞ LBr

A gold and quartz fob seal, decorated with entwined snakes and scallop shells, the quartz intaglio carved with a crest, early 19thC, 2in (5cm) high.
£230–270 / €300–390
$390–460 ⚒ G(L)

A gold combination seal, vesta case and compass, modelled as a post box, the hinged base set with a bloodstone matrix with intaglio crest and monogram, the glazed domed base set with a compass, c1880, 1¼in (3cm) high.
£3,000–3,600
€4,300–5,100
$5,000–6,000 ⚒ B

◄ **An early Victorian gold viniagrette,** with scroll engraving and a foliate-scroll grille, 1¼in (3cm) wide.
£280–330 / €400–470
$470–560 ⚒ G(L)

Asian Works of Art

Cloisonné & Enamel

A pair of Canton enamel bowls, painted with bats among flowers and plants, the interior enamelled, foot and seal gilded, seal marks, Chinese, Qianlong period, 1736–95, 5in (12.5cm) diam.
£9,200–11,000 / €13,200–15,800
$15,500–18,500 ⚒ S(HK)
It is rare to find Canton enamel bowls painted in this manner, which may be inspired by coral or ruby-ground imperial porcelain bowls bearing the *'yuzhi'* mark.

A Canton *famille rose* European-style enamel inkstand, the three containers enamelled with lotus strapwork, the tops with floral scrolls, on a trefoil tray, Chinese, Qianlong period, 1736–95, 6in (15cm) wide.
£2,350–2,800 / €3,400–4,000
$4,000–4,700 ⚒ B
Ex-du Boulay collection.

A cloisonné *koro* and cover, decorated with floral sprays, the cover with exotic flowers and tendrils surmounted by a chrysanthemum knop, Japanese, Meiji period, 1868–1911, 10½in (26.5cm) high.
£960–1,150 / €1,400–1,650
$1,600–1,900 ⚒ S(O)

A cloisonné enamel charger, decorated with a *qilin* bearing a peach on a saddle cloth, some wear and damage, Chinese, late Ming Dynasty, 17thC, 18¾in (47.5cm) diam.
£490–590 / €700–840
$820–980 ⚒ B(Kn)

Chinese cloisonné

Cloisonné is considered to have reached its peak in terms of quality during the reign of the Ming Emperor Jingtai (1450–57). Objects were mostly of a blue (*lan*) colour, so cloisonné is known in China as *jingtailan*.

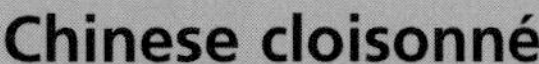

► **A cloisonné plate,** decorated with scrolls and a band of lotus, Chinese, Ming Dynasty, 17thC, 9in (23cm) diam.
£1,050–1,200 / €1,500–1,800
$1,750–2,000 ⊞ G&G

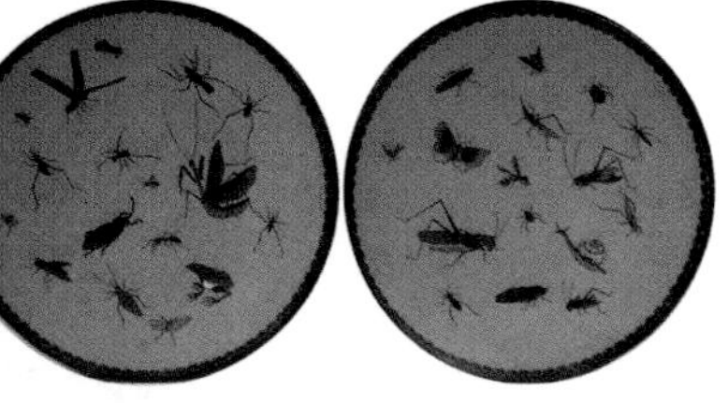

► **A pair of cloisonné plates,** decorated with insects, late 19thC, 11¾in (30cm) diam.
£280–330 / €400–480
$470–560 ⚒ SWO

A cloisonné holy water stoup, the bowl decorated with a crucifix rising above a heart entwined with thorns, Chinese, 19thC, 5in (15cm) high.
£530–640 / €770–920
$890–1,050 ⚒ WW

\ cloisonné enamel vase, lecorated with pigeons eeding among flowers, the houlder decorated with appet-shaped motifs and rocade patterns, Japanese, Aeiji period, 1868–1911, 0in (51cm) high, with a itted wooden stand.
.2,350–2,800
3,400–4,050
3,900–4,650 ⚒ B

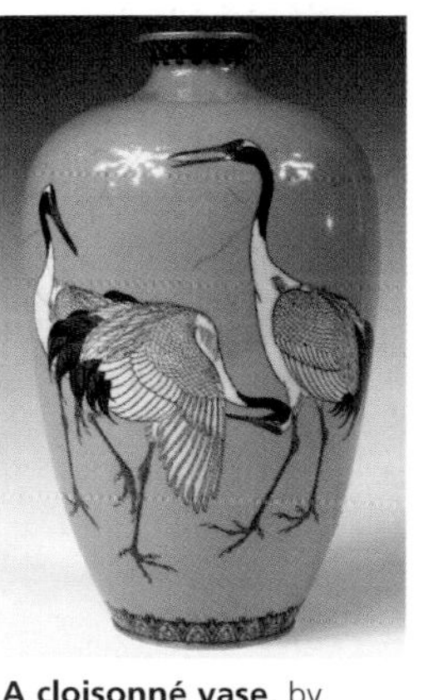

A cloisonné vase, by Hyashi Kodenji, decorated with cranes, with a silver rim and base, some crazing, signed, Japanese, late 19thC, 7¼in (18.5cm) high.
£260–310 / €380–450
$440–530 ⚒ SWO

◄ **A cloisonné vase,** by Ota, decorated with flowers and bamboo, signed, Japanese, Meiji period, 1868–1911, 12in (30.5cm) high.
£1,100–1,300
€1,600–1,900
$1,850–2,200 ⚒ S(O)

A pair of *champlevé* enamelled archaistic bronze vases, with mask-and-tongue handles, raised foundry marks, Japanese, late 19thC, 18in (45.5cm) high.
£420–500 / €600–720
$710–850 RTo

A pair of bronze and cloisonné vases, signed, Japanese, 19thC, 10¾in (27.5cm) high.
£470–560 / €680–810
$790–940 MAR

A cloisonné vase and cover, decorated with hawks, prunus flowers and cranes, with 'ear' handles, domed cover and ball knop, Japanese, c1880, 24in (1cm) high.
£1,650–1,950
€2,350–2,800
$2,800–3,300 SWO

Glass

A rock crystal brushpot, carved in relief with two bearded figures on horseback in a pine forest, with a seated sage and his attendant, Chinese, c1900, 5¼in (13.5cm) high, with a wooden stand and fitted box.
£840–1,000 / €1,200–1,400
$1,400–1,650 S(O)

► **A carved red and green overlay translucent white glass vase,** the neck carved with overlapping stiff plantain leaves, key-fret band at the shoulder, the body carved with panels of flowers and birds representing the Four Seasons between lotus lappets, Chinese, Beijing, Qianlong period, 1736–95, 7½in (19cm) high.
£2,350–2,800 / €3,400–4,050
$3,950–4,700 B

◄ **A reverse painting on glass,** Chinese, 1800–50, 17¼ x 25½in (44 x 65cm), in original wooden frame.
£1,200–1,450
€1,750–2,100
$2,000–2,400 BUK

Jade

◄ **A jade boulder carving,** depicting a bearded scholar attended by a servant boy under a pine tree, the celadon stone with russet calcified inclusions, Chinese, 18thC, 4½in (11.5cm) high, with wooden stand and fitted box.
£2,150–2,600
€3,100–3,700
$3,650–4,350 S(O)

► **A pair of jade openwork cricket cages and covers,** each carved with scroll flanges of leafy lotus stems, on four cabriole legs, the domed covers similarly pierced, Chinese, Qianlong period, 1736–95, 3¾in (9.5cm) high, with wooden stands.
£3,750–4,500 / €5,400–6,500
$6,300–7,500 B

A white jade openwork pomander and cover, carved and pierced with two carp on a reticulated ground, with a brass hinge, hairline crack, Chinese, Qianlong/Jiaqing periods, late 18th/early 19thC, 2in (5cm) diam.
£3,000–3,600
€4,300–5,100
$5,000–6,050 B

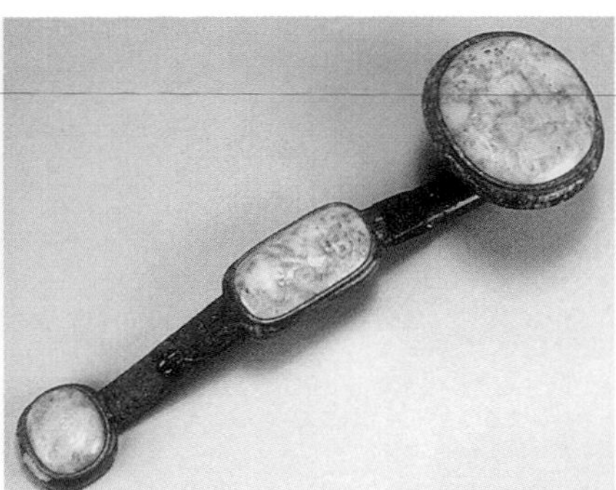

A green jade *ruyi* sceptre, applied with grey panels carved with auspicious symbols, Chinese, 19thC, 18½in (47cm) long.
£500–600 / €720–860
$840–1,000 DN
According to the vendor's family tradition, this was acquired during the Boxer Rebellion, an uprising in 1900 by nationalistic Chinese against foreign interests in China.

◄ **A celadon jade dragon and magnolia vase,** carved and pierced in high relief, Chinese, 19thC, 10½in (26.5cm) high, with a carved and pierced wooden stand.
£2,100–2,500 / €3,000–3,600
$3,500–4,200 B

A jade dragon-handled vessel, the body divided into three bands carved in archaistic style, a carp head under the spout, Chinese, late 19th/early 20thC, 9in (23cm) wide.
£480–580 / €690–830
$810–970 S(O)

Lacquer

A pair of lacquer, painted and parcel-gilt doors, decorated with animals, figural scenes and butterflies, the reverse with figures amid a pagoda and river landscape, above exotic enamel panels, Chinese, 19thC, 84½in (214.5cm) high.
£2,500–3,000
€3,600–4,300
$4,200–5,000 LHA

A *guri* lacquer *zhadou*, carved with three rows of *ruyi*-head scrolls, on a foot with a lotus lappet band, some cracks and chips, Chinese, Ming Dynasty, 14th/15thC, 4½in (11.5cm) high.
£2,900–3,500 / €4,200–5,000
$4,900–5,900 B

A pair of lacquer jars, damage to rim interiors, slight flaking to lacquer, Chinese, Qianlong period, 1736–95, 5in (15cm) diam.
£2,500–3,000 / €3,600–4,300
$4,200–5,000 BUK

A pair of lacquered ostrich eggs on Chinese silvered mounts, the eggs decorated in gold, silver and *iroe hiramakie* and *takamakie*, depicting a lady and gentleman in a garden with Imperial cranes and plovers in flight, the stands embossed in the form of dragons, signature rubbed, mounts stamped, Japanese, Meiji period, 1868–1911, 10½in (26.5cm) high.
£1,900–2,250 / €2,750–3,300
$3,200–3,850 S(O)

Lacquer is obtained from the sap of the *Rhus vernici flua* tree and has to be built up in layers, normally applied every two days. Thickly carved lacquer will require up to 60 coats before carving can commence.

A lacquer jar and cover, Burmese, 19thC, 26in (66cm) high.
£360–400 / €520–580
$600–670 QM

A lacquered *shishi* mask, decorated in gesso and lacquer, with moveable ears and jaw, Chinese, 19thC, 12¼in (31cm) high.
£600–720 / €870–1,000
$1,000–1,200 S(O)

A mother-of-pearl-inlaid lacquer tray, decorated with two birds perched on prunus branches, the sides decorated with floral sprays, Japanese, Ryükyü Islands, 16th/17thC, 17in (43cm) wide.
£1,200–1,450 / €1,700–2,000
$2,000–2,400 B

Metalware

A silver beaker, by Hamilton & Co, Indian, Calcutta, late 19thC, 4½in (11.5cm) high, 8oz.
£175–210 / €250–300
$300–360 WW

A pair of bronze candlesticks, by Mitsuaki, with iris blossom candle holders, dragons twining around the stems, each clutching the sacred pearl set in glass, signed, Japanese, Meiji period, 1868–1911, 12½in (32cm) high.
£1,450–1,750
€2,100–2,500
$2,450–2,950 S(O)

A silver flask, Chinese, c1900, 6in (15cm) high.
£1,550–1,750
€2,250–2,500
$2,600–2,950 SHa

► **A pair of wire lanterns,** Chinese, 19thC, 31in (78.5cm) high.
£175–195 / €250–280
$300–330 QM

A bronze buffalo bell, Burmese, 19thC, 7in (18cm) diam.
£210–240 / €300–350
$350–400 QM

A Chinese Export silver rose bowl, with chased floral decoration below an applied foliate rim, Chinese character mark, Chinese, late 19thC, 8½in (21.5cm) diam, 53oz.
£1,900–2,250
€2,750–3,250
$3,200–3,800 WW

A bronze censer, on a lotus-shaped stand, Chinese, 17thC, 7½in (19cm) diam.
£150–180 / €220–260
$250–300 WW

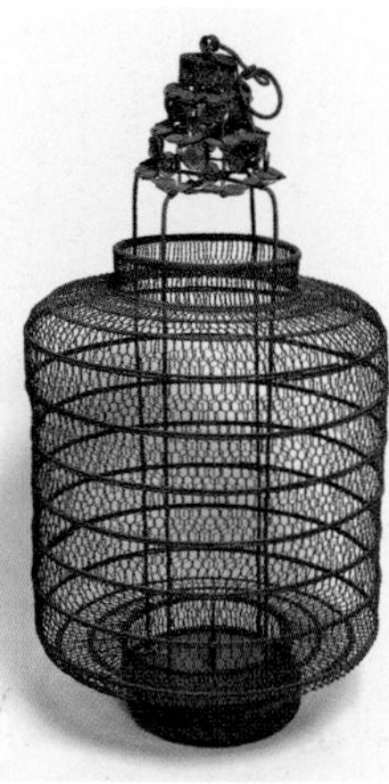

A white metal inlaid belt hook, Chinese, Warring States Period, 480–221 BC, 4in (10cm) wide.
£580–650 / €840–940
$970–1,100 GLD

A bronze bowl, decorated with gilt splashes, the two *chilong* handles with tails decorating the sides, on four *ruyi*-style feet, Xuande six-character mark, Chinese, 17thC, 6¾in (17cm) wide.
£1,500–1,800 / €2,200–2,600
$2,500–3,000 B
Ex-du Boulay collection. For information on Anthony du Boulay see page 302.

► **A bronze brush rest,** Chinese, 17thC, 6in (15cm) long.
£350–420
€500–600
$590–700 B
Ex-du Boulay collection.

A silver curry pan and cover, by Hamilton & Co, the handle with a slide fitting, Indian, Calcutta, c1800, 5in (12.5cm) diam, 21½oz.
£1,450–1,750 / €2,100–2,500
$2,450–2,950 L

A silver jar and cover, inlaid with coral, turquoise and enamel, depicting birds and blossoming branches, the cover with a filigree finial, Chinese, early 20thC, 7¼in (18.5cm) high.
£280–330 / €400–480
$470–560 LHA

A silver and enamel *koro* the pierced cover with a flor knop, the body pierced in filigree with cherry blossor chrysanthemums and stylize foliage, with two inset ivory panels decorated in *Shibayama* style with flowe and birds, the handles form as *ho-o* birds, with a silver liner, Japanese, 1868–191 5¾in (14.5cm) high.
£2,500–3,000
€3,600–4,300
$4,200–5,000 S(O)

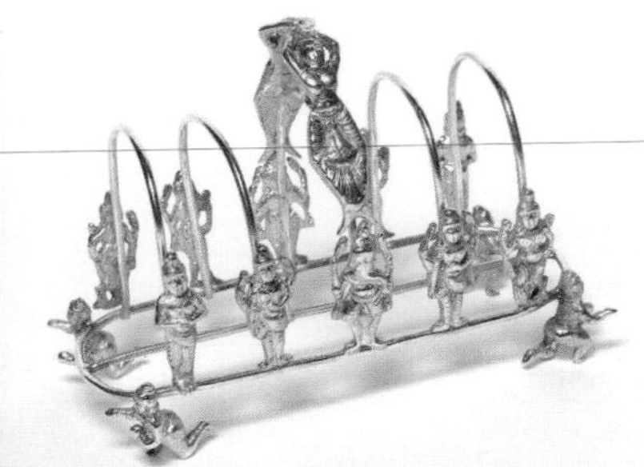

A silver toast rack, Indian, c1890, 6in (15cm) wide.
£220–250 / €320–360
$370–420 ⊞ BLm

► **A *Shibayama* vase,** with silver and enamel mounts, signed, late Meiji period, 1900, 11in (28cm) high.
£3,800–4,200 / €5,400–6,000
$6,400–7,100 ⊞ LBO

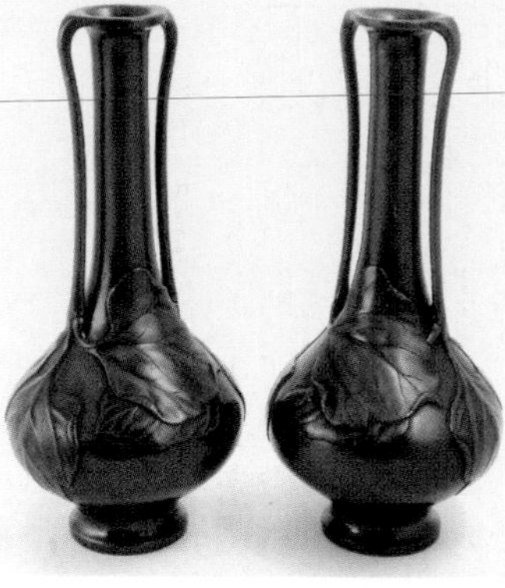

A pair of bronze vases, with twin-handled necks, the bodies cast in relief with leaves, Japanese, late Meiji period, 1900, 11in (28cm) high.
£290–350 / €420–500
$490–590 ⚒ G(L)

Wood

A sandalwood and rosewood bookstand, inlaid with ivory, with a pierced porcupine quill gallery, Indian, possibly Vizagapatam, mid-19thC, 16¼in (41.5cm) wide.
£540–650 / €780–930
$920–1,100 ⚒ SWO

A woodroot brushpot, carved as an aged tree trunk, Chinese, 17thC, 5¾in (14.5cm) high, with a carved and lacquered stand.
£3,700–4,450
€5,300–6,400
$6,300–7,500 ⚒ S(HK)

A bamboo brushpot, carved with a scholar's rock, a Buddha's hand and calligraphy, with a hardwood rim and base, Chinese, 18thC, 8¼in (21cm) high.
£700–840 / €1,000–1,200
$1,200–1,400 ⚒ B
A Buddha's hand is a citrus fruit that has five pointed stems resembling a hand. It is regarded as a lucky symbol.

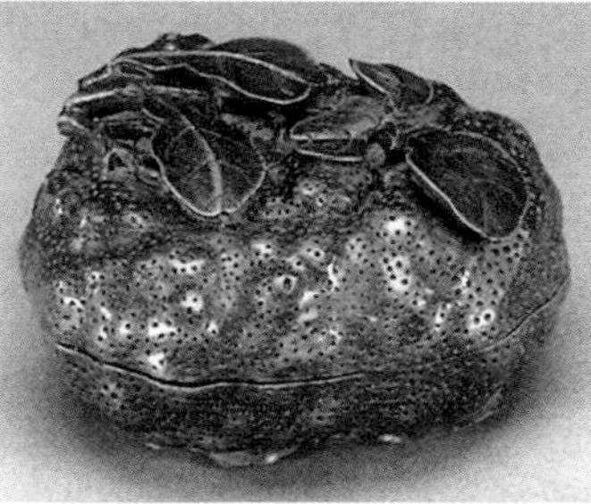

► **A bamboo box and cover,** carved as a lychee and leafy branch, Chinese, 18thC, 3¼in (8.5cm) wide.
£780–940
€1,100–1,300
$1,300–1,550
⚒ S(O)

► **An elm rice carrier,** Chinese, 19thC, 29in (73.5cm) wide.
£220–250
€320–360
$370–420 ⊞ QM

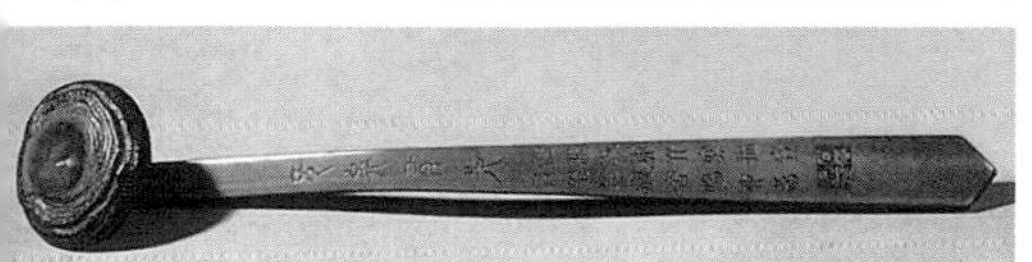

A carved and inscribed bamboo *ruyi* sceptre, with a *lingzhi*-style head, the underside incised with a three-character name, Chinese, 17th/18thC, 10¼in (26cm) long.
£7,800–9,400 / €11,200–13,400
$13,200–15,800 ⚒ S(HK)

Ruyi sceptres

On court celebration days in China, *ruyi* sceptres would be presented to the Emperor who would then give them to favoured ministers or subjects. The form of these ceremonial objects evolved from the humble back-scratcher and examples are found in many materials including jade and wood. They usually carry auspicious symbols such as 'pine and crane' (longevity) or 'phoenix and peony' (prosperity). Depictions of these sceptres can also often be seen on ceramics, carvings etc.

◄ **A wooden silk winder,** Chinese, 19thC, 7in (18cm) wide.
£50–55 / €70–80
$85–95 ⊞ JCH

Arms & Armour

A suit of iron and fabric armour, of brigandine construction, the helmet with damascened steel fittings and decorated with gilt lotus buds, the plume tube with three gilt flaming devices, the velvet-edged fabric embroidered with dragons, the damascened shoulder and cuff plates with gilt tailed scrolls, some restoration and cleaning, fabric worn, Chinese, Kangxi period, c1650.
£9,100–10,900
€13,100–15,500
$15,300–18,000 ⚒ WAL
The vendor, a leading academic of Oriental armour, has supplied research notes concerning this armour. It appears that the armour can be no earlier than 1635, and no later than the reign of the Qing Emperor Kangxi (1662–1722); the likelihood is that it was made close to the earlier date.

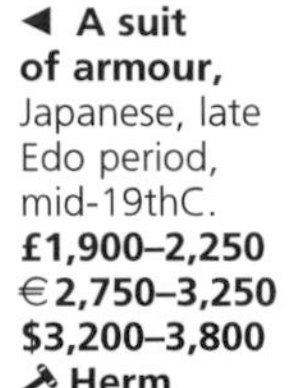

◄ A suit of armour, Japanese, late Edo period, mid-19thC.
£1,900–2,250
€2,750–3,250
$3,200–3,800
⚒ Herm

A lacquered iron, brass and leather suit of armour, with bronze overlay, covered with laced printed leather, Japanese, Taisho period, 1912–26, on a wooden stand.
£5,900–7,100
€8,500–10,200
$9,900–11,900 ⚒ B(Kn)

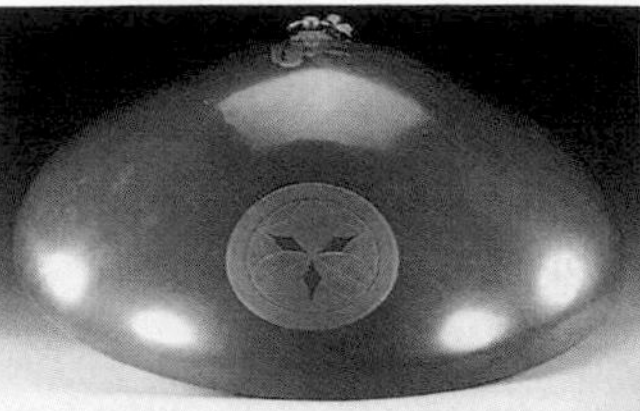

A lacquer war hat, with gold *takamakie* decoration, Japanese, 19thC, 16½in (42cm) diam.
£900–1,050 / €1,300–1,500
$1,550–1,750 ⚒ S(O)

A cloisonné enamel warrior's helmet, modelled after a Korean original from the Choson Dynasty, decorated with dragons, flaming pearls and waves, the finial decorated with dragons and scrolling motifs, some restoration, Japanese, Meiji period, 1868–1911, 17in (43cm) high, on a display stand.
£10,000–12,000 / €14,400–17,300
$16,800–20,200 ⚒ B

◄ A cloisonné-mounted *aikuchi*, decorated with butterflies among leaves, chrysanthemum and other flowers, Japanese, Meiji period, 1868–1911, blade 8¾in (22cm) long.
£1,650–1,950 / €2,400–2,800
$2,800–3,300 ⚒ B(Kn)

A lacquer sword, the blade decorated with a dragon, some losses, signed 'Kaga no Kuni Katsuiye', 18th/19thC, 40¼in (102cm) long.
£2,600–3,100 / €3,750–4,500
$4,400–5,200 ⚒ B

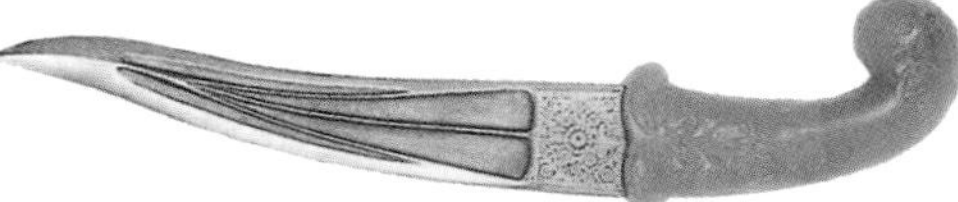

A jade khanjar, the double-edged blade cut with three converging ridges on either side, the forte damascened with a panel of flowering gold foliage on each side, the jade hilt carved with lotus blossoms in low relief, Indian, 18th/19thC, 9¼in (23.5cm) long.
£1,400–1,650 / €2,000–2,350
$2,350–2,750 ⚒ B(Kn)

A *katana*, with a pierced *tsuba*, Japanese, 18thC, blade 29in (73.5cm) long.
£610–730 / €880–1,050
$1,000–1,200 ⚒ SWO

An ivory-mounted *tanto*, the grip carved as a dragon's head, the *tsuba* decorated with geometric patterns and foliage, the scabbard carved with village scenes, some splits, Japanese, Meiji period, 1868–1911, blade 8¾in (22cm) long.
£530–640 / €760–910
$890–1,050 ⚒ B(Kn)

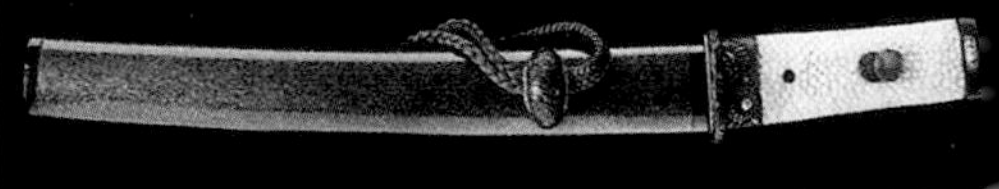

An armour-piercing *tanto*, with an impressed seal of Hosogawa Masamori, Japanese, 19thC, 8¾in (22cm) long
£1,550–1,850 / €2,250–2,650
$2,600–3,100 ⚒ S(O)

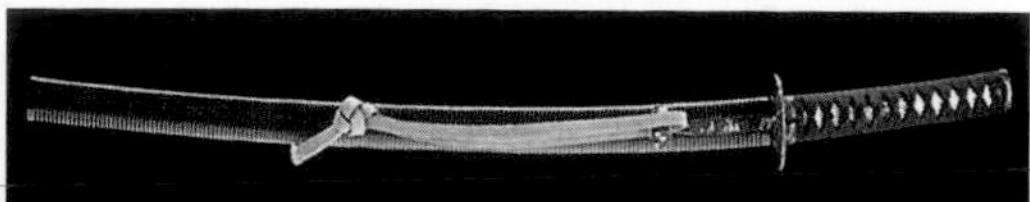

A **wakizashi,** with Goto School mounts, Japanese, blade 16thC, mounts 19thC, 18¼in (46.5cm) long.
£3,350–4,000 / €4,800–5,750
$5,600–6,700 S(O)

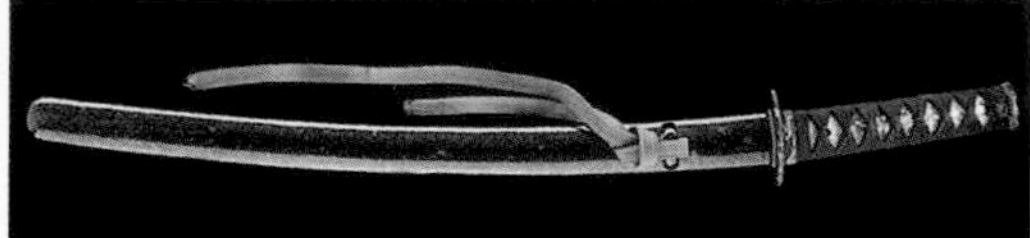

A **wakizashi,** the hilt decorated with dragons, with gilt *tsuba* and dragon *menuki*, Japanese, 19thC.
£2,400–2,900 / €3,500–4,200
$4,000–4,800 S(O)

A dagger, the jade hilt set with gems, Indian, 19thC, 14in (35.5cm) long.
£12,000–14,400 / €17,300–20,800
$20,200–24,300 S

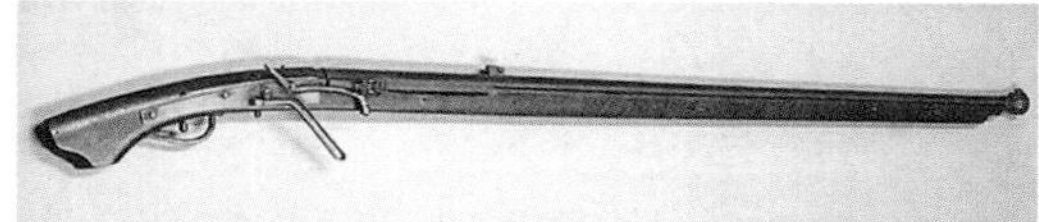

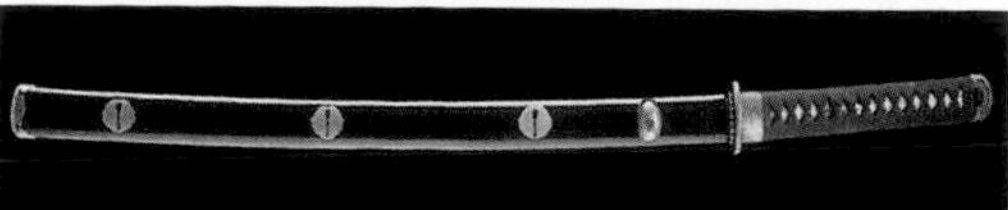

A **wakizashi,** with a lacquer scabbard, *shakudo* and gilt *tsuba* decorated with cranes and pines with a silver rope rim, *kozuka* missing, Japanese, probably 17thC, mounts 19thC, 22¼in (56.5cm) long.
£1,900–2,250 / €2,750–3,250
$3,200–3,800 S(O)

A **wakizashi,** Japanese, c1850, 26in (66cm) long.
£3,400–3,750 / €4,900–5,400
$5,700–6,300 MDL

A **katana,** with military mounts, Japanese, early 20thC, blade 25½in (65cm) long.
£390–470 / €570–680
$660–790 SWO

◄ **A matchlock gun,** with a wooden stock and distorted brass lock, signed 'Koshu (no) Kuni taro Masakata', Japanese, 19thC, 54¼in (138cm) long.
£660–790 / €960–1,150
$1,100–1,300 S(O)

Tsuba

A Choshu School **tsuba,** carved in relief with *shishi* among clouds, Japanese, 18thC, 3¼in (8.5cm) high.
£840–1,000 / €1,200–1,400
$1,400–1,650 S(O)

A **tsuba,** carved with waves and clouds and inlaid with a gilt dragon and spray drops, Japanese, late 18th/early 19thC, 3½in (9cm) high.
£660–790 / €960–1,150
$1,100–1,300 S(O)

◄ **A brass tsuba,** by Yasunao, carved and inlaid in soft metals with a horseman plunging into waves, Japanese, 19thC, 2¾in (7cm) high.
£380–450 / €550–650
$640–760 WAL

► A **shakudo tsuba,** decorated with a tiger drinking from a stream beneath a pine tree, with gilt details and a gilt copper rim, the centre carved with a seal, Japanese, 19thC, 2¾in (7cm) high.
£370–440 / €530–630
$620–740 WAL

An iron tsuba, by Choshu Tomokata, carved in relief with a dragon among clouds, signed, Japanese, late 18th/early 19thC, 3in (7.5cm) high.
£660–790 / €960–1,150
$1,100–1,300 S(O)

Boxes

A cinnabar and painted lacquer treasure box and stand, the box cover carved with flowers and floral sprigs, the sides carved with flowering sprays and foliate designs, the two interior tiered boxes painted with diapers, the top tier containing two boxes flanking a diamond-shaped box, all with painted exteriors, Chinese, Qianlong Period, 1736–95, 8in (20.5cm) high.
£9,200–11,000 / €13,200–15,800 $15,500–18,500 S(HK)

A horn workbox, Anglo-Indian, c1820, 5½in (14cm) high.
£3,150–3,500 / €4,500–5,000 $5,300–5,900 HAA

A rosewood and ivory-inlaid workbox, inlaid inside and out with trailing foliage, the interior with tortoiseshell panels, lidded compartments and drawers surrounding a well, Indian, Vizagapatam, 19thC, 18in (45.5cm) wide.
£3,750–4,500 / €5,400–6,500 $6,300–7,500 L&T

A leather hat box, Chinese, 19thC, 14in (35.5cm) diam.
£250–280 / €360–400 $420–470 QM

An ivory-veneered and ebony-moulded table desk, the interior with pigeonholes and drawers, ivory cracked, some losses, Indian, Vizagapatam, late 18thC, 17½in (44.5cm) wide.
£410–490 / €590–710 $690–820 WW

Vizagapatam

Vizagapatam, also known as Vishakhapatnam, is situated on the Bay of Bengal, half-way between Madras and Calcutta. From the late 18th century it was a thriving centre of production of furniture and small objects made of local hardwoods and elaborately inlaid with ivory. Initially these items were mainly bought by the Indian ruling classes and officials of the East India Company, but when India came under British rule in Victorian times a wider market opened up and a fashion for such pieces soon developed in the west. Export was facilitated because Vizagapatam was an important trading port for southeast Asia and also European trading vessels stopped there on their way to and from Canton.

An ivory casket, carved with pierced and undercut figurative scenes and panels of flowers, the interior with a velvet-lined tray, Chinese, mid-19thC, 6¼in (16cm) wide.
£1,250–1,400 / €1,800–2,000 $2,100–2,350 G&G

► **A *shakudo*-decorated iron box and cover,** with a silver-lined interior, signed, Japanese, Meiji period, 1868–1911, 6in (15cm) wide.
£2,000–2,400 / €2,900–3,450 $3,350–4,000 RTo

A Chinese export padouk and soapstone double tea caddy, the front and sides carved in shallow relief with chinoiserie figures among temples, traces of original colouring and mahogany banding, Chinese, c1775, 10in (25.5cm) wide.
£1,800–2,000 / €2,600–2,900 $3,000–3,300 JTS

Soapstone (steatite) was much favoured by the 18th-century Chinese export market. The relative softness of the stone enabled intricate carving to be carried out, making full use of the different colours and the soft, soap-like finish of the polished surface.

An ivory sewing cask, with tools, Indian, Vizagapatam, c1820, 8in (20.5cm) wide.
£900–1,000 / €1,300–1,450 $1,500–1,650 RdeR

A Chinese export lacquer desk box, with gilded chinoiserie decoration, the interior fitted with a lacquer tray, rubbed, 1825–50, 12¼in (31cm) wide.
£580–700 / €840–1,000 $1,000–1,200 NOA

Figures & Models

A marble torso of a bodhisattva, repairs, Chinese, Northern Dynasty, AD 420–589, 8in (20.5cm) high.
£4,050–4,500
€5,800–6,500
$6,800–7,600 ⊞ GLD

A stone head of a guardian warrior, Chinese, Jin Dynasty, 1115–1234, 16½in (42cm) high.
£4,900–5,500
€7,000–7,900
$8,200–9,200 ⊞ LOP

A carved grey schist stele, depicting Ganesh, Pala Dynasty, Indian, 12thC, 12¾in (32.5cm) high.
£1,250–1,500
€1,800–2,150
$2,100–2,500 ⚒ B(Kn)
Ganesh is the Hindu god of prophecy. Pala was the ruling dynasty in northeastern India from the 8th to the 12th century.

A stone figure of a lohan, Chinese, 12th–13thC, 37¾in (96cm) high.
£5,400–6,000
€7,700–8,600
$9,100–10,100 ⊞ LOP

► A carved grey jade model of a pony, Chinese, 14thC, 3¼in (8.5cm) long.
£2,100–2,500
€3,000–3,600
$3,500–4,200
⚒ B
Ex-du Boulay collection.

A cast-bronze incense burner, in the form of a female dog of *Fo* on a carved wooden base, Chinese, Ming Dynasty, c1600, 16½in (42cm) high.
£2,850–3,400 / €4,100–4,900
$4,800–5,700 ⚒ NOA

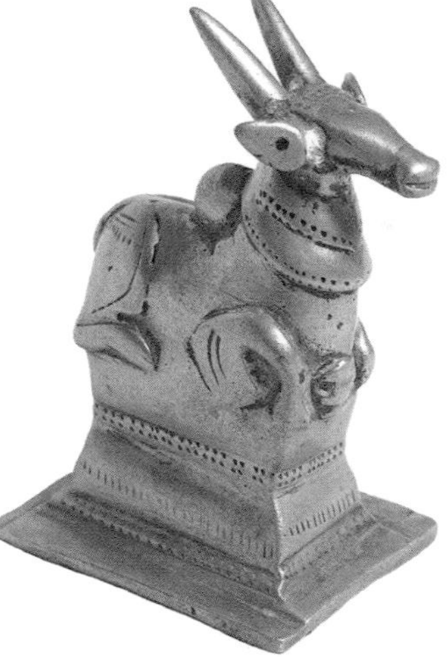

A marble figure of an official, Chinese, 16th–17thC, 39in (99cm) high.
£9,000–10,000
€13,000–14,400
$15,100–16,800 ⊞ LOP

A gilt-lacquer figure of a Buddha, Burmese, 17th–18thC, 8in (122cm) high.
£9,900–11,000
€14,200–15,800
$16,600–18,500 ⊞ LOP

A bronze model of a Nandi bull, Indian, late 17thC, 4in (10cm) high.
£270–300 / €390–430
$450–500 ⊞ HEL
In Hindu mythology, Nandi is a bull which is ridden by the god Shiva and symbolizes fertility.

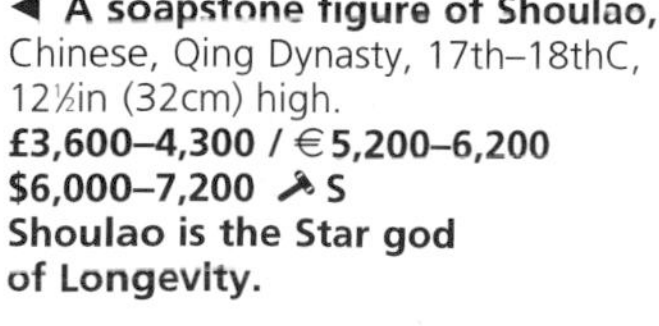

◄ A soapstone figure of Shoulao, Chinese, Qing Dynasty, 17th–18thC, 12½in (32cm) high.
£3,600–4,300 / €5,200–6,200
$6,000–7,200 ⚒ S
Shoulao is the Star god of Longevity.

► A marble head of Buddha, Burmese, 18thC, 13¾in (35cm) high.
£2,700–3,000 / €3,900–4,300
$4,500–5,000 ⊞ LOP

A carved soapstone model of a lion dog, Chinese, 18thC, 6½in (16.5cm) wide.
£2,400–2,900 / €3,450–4,150
$4,000–4,800 S(O)

An ivory pietà, heightened in gilt, Indo-Portuguese, 18thC, 7¼in (18.5cm) high, on a wooden base.
£3,000–3,600
€4,300–5,200
$5,000–6,000 S

A carved and lacquered wood figure of Buddha, Japanese, 18thC, 31in (78.5cm) high.
£1,100–1,300
€1,600–1,850
$1,850–2,200 Gam

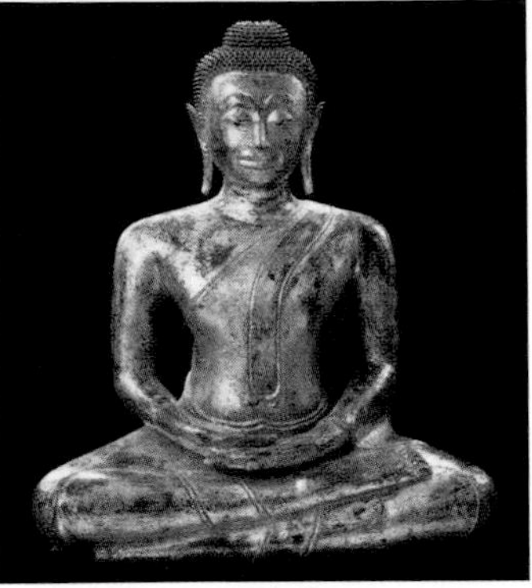

◄ **A gilt-bronze figure of Buddha,** Thai, 18thC, 20½in (52cm) high.
£8,500–9,500
€12,200–13,700
$14,300–16,000
LOP

A carved jade model of a lion dog, Chinese, c1800, 2¾in (7cm) wide.
£1,050–1,250 / €1,500–1,800
$1,750–2,100 S(O)

◄ **A bronze figure of Buddha,** Thai, c1800, 26in (66cm) high.
£2,550–2,850
€3,650–4,100
$4,300–4,800
QM

A bronze figure of a sage holding a *vajra* and a sceptre, inlaid with silver and gold, some damage, Chinese, 18th–19thC, 14½in (37cm) high.
£940–1,100
€1,350–1,600
$1,600–1,850 WW
This is a figure of Vajrapani, the Great Protector and Giver of Rain. He was one of the Lokapala (the Guardian Kings). The *vajra* he carries represents the thunderbolt. The word *vajra* also means a diamond, and thus hardness and indestructibility.

A wooden head of Guanyin, Chinese, 19thC, 20¾in (53cm) high.
£850–950 / €1,200–1,350
$1,400–1,600 LOP
Guanyin is the Buddhist bodhisattva of Compassion.

A giltwood figure of a dancer, Burmese, Mandalay, 19thC, 28¼in (72cm) high.
£2,250–2,500
€3,250–3,600
$3,800–4,200 LOP

◄ **A carved soapstone figure of Shoulao,** holding a staff and a peach, with a crane at his feet, Chinese, 19thC, 8in (20.5cm) high.
£150–180 / €220–260
$250–300 WW

A soapstone figure of Guanyin, seated next to a Buddhist lion dog, Chinese, 19thC, 2¾in (7cm) high.
£600–720 / €860–1,000
$1,000–1,200 S(O)

A bronze model of an elephant, by Seiya, with ivory tusks, signed, Japanese, Meiji period, 1868–1911, 14½in (37cm) high.
£1,000–1,200 / €1,450–1,750
$1,750–2,000 S(O)

Japanese ivory

In 1887 the Tokyo Chokokkai (Tokyo Sculpture Association) was established. This revitalized the ivory-carving industry, setting new standards. Exceptional carvings were created, mainly for the export market to Europe and North America. Where possible the figures were carved from a single piece of ivory and these have a greater value.

► **An enamelled parcel-gilt silver model of an elephant and a howdah,** set with gems, Indian, Jaipur, 19thC, 9¾in (25cm) high.
£1,800–2,150
€2,600–3,100
$3,000–3,600 B(Kn)

A wooden figure of Buddha, Thai, 19thC, 57½in (146cm) high.
£3,100–3,500
€4,450–5,000
$5,200–5,900 LOP

A stained ivory *okimono* of a chicken farmer, by Soko, signed, Japanese, Meiji period, 1868–1911, 5in (12cm) high.
£3,000–3,600 / €4,300–5,200
$5,000–6,000 B

► **A Tokyo School ivory group of a male and female peasant and a child,** Japanese, Meiji period, 1868–1911, 6in (15cm) high.
£1,650–1,950
€2,350–2,800
$2,750–3,250 FHF

◄ **An ivory *okimono* of a fisherman carrying a basket of fish,** Japanese, Meiji period, 1868–1911, 6½in (16.5cm) high.
£1,250–1,400 / €1,800–2,000
$2,100–2,350 AMC

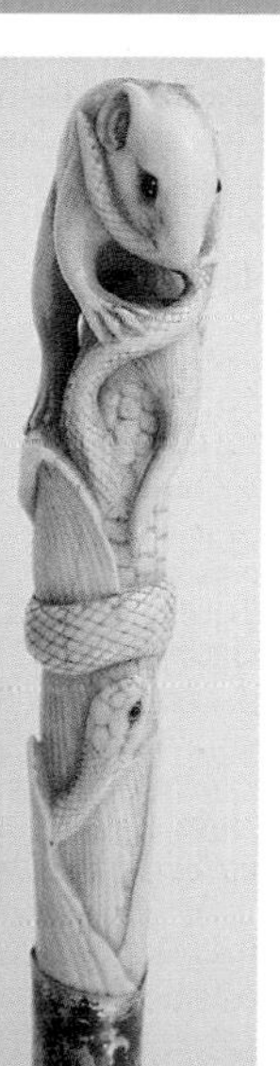

An ivory figure of a seated man drinking sake, signed 'Seitei', Japanese, Meiji period, 1868–1911, 2½in (6.5cm) high.
£2,150–2,400
€3,100–3,450
$3,600–4,000 LBO

◄ **An ivory-handled walking stick,** carved as a mouse nibbling corn, a snake around the stem, Japanese, Meiji period, 1868–1911, 38in (96.5cm) high.
£490–590 / €710–850
$820–990 G(L)

A marine ivory *okimono* of a basket-maker and seller, signed 'Masatoshi', Japanese, Meiji period, 1868–1911, 5in (12.5cm) high.
£1,250–1,400 / €1,800–2,000
$2,100–2,350 AMC

A bronze figure of a Samurai warrior holding his sword, Japanese, Meiji period, 1868–1911, 7in (18cm) high.
£3,050–3,400 / €4,400–4,900
$5,100–5,700 ⊞ LBO

A carved coral group of a lady and two boys, Chinese, c1900, 10¼in (26cm) high.
£4,550–5,400 / €6,500–7,700
$7,600–9,100 ⚒ S(O)

A bronze model of a hare, signed 'Bizan', Japanese, c1900, 2½in (6.5cm) high.
£1,500–1,700 / €2,150–2,450
$2,500–2,850 ⊞ LBO

◀ **A pair of silver-plated models of Manchurian cranes,** by Hidenao, with gilt legs, on a carved wood stand, one signed, Japanese, Meiji period, 1868–1911, taller 23in (59cm) high.
£2,600–3,100 / €3,750–4,250
$4,350–5,200 ⚒ B

An ivory group of musicians and geishas, Chinese, late 19thC, 14in (35.5cm) wide.
£1,800–2,150 / €2,600–3,100
$3,000–3,600 ⚒ BERN

◀ **A bronze model of an eagle,** Japanese, c1890, 28¼in (72cm) high.
£960–1,150 / €1,400–1,650
$1,600–1,900 ⚒ S(O)

A carved ivory figure, with sgraffito decoration, on a wooden base, Chinese, c1900, 19½in (49.5cm) high.
£1,100–1,300
€1,600–1,850
$1,850–2,200 ⚒ LCM

An ivory *okimono* of a fisherman, the base carved with crabs, Japanese, c1900, 10½in (26.5cm) high.
£360–400
€520–570
$600–670
⊞ AMC

A carved coral group of a maiden and four children, losses to extremities, Chinese, c1900, 12¼in (31cm) high, on a wooden stand.
£3,750–4,500
€5,400–6,500
$6,300–7,500 ⚒ B

▶ **A Tokyo School ivory figure of a fisherman with cormorants,** signed 'Masayuki', Japanese, c1900, 12in (30.5cm) high.
£4,300–4,800
€6,200–6,900
$7,200–8,100
⊞ LBO

An ivory *okimono* of rats, on a wooden stand, Japanese, early 20thC, 5¼in (13.5cm) wide.
£590–710 / €850–1,000
$990–1,150 ⚒ BR

▶ **An ivory figure of a boy holding a fish,** signed, Japanese, early 20thC, 5½in (14cm) high.
£290–350 / €420–500
$480–590 ⚒ EH

Furniture

A lacquer bed, carved in relief with foliage and a bird, Chinese, early 20thC, 44in (112cm) wide.
£160–190 / €230–270
$270–320 DMC

An elm and fruitwood cabinet, with 19thC painted panels, Chinese, Shanxi Province, 16thC, 60in (152.5cm) wide.
£5,400–6,000 / €7,700–8,600
$9,100–10,100 ⊞ QM

A lacquer cabinet, decorated with plants and insects, the pair of doors enclosing shelves, on a later stand, Japanese, early 18thC, 40½in (102.5cm) wide.
£420–500 / €600–720
$710–840 L&E

A painted and giltwood cupboard, with two pairs of panelled doors decorated with Chinese characters, flower vases and fruit baskets, above two smaller panelled doors carved with flowers and scrolling foliage, Chinese, 19thC, 43¼in (110cm) wide.
£1,150–1,350
€1,650–1,950
$1,950–2,250 S(Am)

Chinese woods

Much Chinese furniture sold in Britain is described as being made of hardwood. The main timbers used in the construction of Chinese furniture are:

- *huanghuali*, the most sought-after because of its fine colour and grain
- *jichi*, purplish-brown in colour, the grain can resemble chicken feathers
- *ju* (southern elm), a large-grained wood of which most provincial furniture is made, greatly enhanced by cleaning and waxing
- *tieli*, the most readily available and least expensive of all the hardwoods, it is often used for back panels of cabinets and bases of drawers
- *zitan*, the most expensive and since ancient times considered the most precious of woods. Purplish-black in colour and with a grain so dense it is virtually invisible

Zitan can usually only be obtained in quite narrow strips and so it is rare to find large pieces of furniture made from this wood. True Chinese rosewood is a variety of *zitan* and is very rare. Most Asian rosewood furniture is made in Hong Kong and Guangdong of imported Indo-Chinese rosewood, a type of mahogany.

A lacquer console cabinet, the two pairs of panelled doors decorated with figures of children in landscapes, Chinese, 19thC, 46¾in (119cm) wide.
£330–390 / €470–560
$550–650 BR

A pair of lacquer cupboards, Chinese, mid-19thC, 32in (81.5cm) wide.
£2,400–2,700 / €3,450–3,900
$4,000–4,500 ⊞ GRG

A lacquer table cabinet, the silk panels decorated with *ho-o* birds within borders of gilt scrolling foliage and flowers, on a hardwood base, Chinese, late 19thC, 20in (51cm) wide.
£230–270 / €330–390
$380–450 AH

A pair of padouk open armchairs, decorated with roudels, Anglo-Indian, early 19thC.
£2,800–3,350 / €4,000–4,800
$4,700–5,600 F&C

► **An elm chair,** carved with a key pattern and a dragon's head, cane seat, with later foot ends and foot rest, Chinese, early 19thC.
£540–600 / €780–860
$900–1,000 ⊞ OE

A carved ebony armchair, Indo-Dutch, 19thC.
£2,150–2,600
€3,000–3,600
$3,600–4,300 S(O)

A lacquer chair, decorated with birds and blossom, Chinese, 19thC.
£240–290 / €340–410
$400–480 L&E

A pierced hardwood chair, the supports carved with animal masks and foliage, Anglo-Indian, 19thC.
£500–600 / €720–860
$840–1,000 WW

A child's lacquered elm chair, with carved panels, Chinese, 19thC.
£170–190 / €240–270
$280–310 OE

A set of six peachwood chairs, with rattan seats, Chinese, c1860.
£8,000–8,900
€11,500–12,800
$13,400–14,900 GRG
It is unusual to find sets of chairs in China, especially in this rare and desirable wood.

A rosewood chair, carved with dragons, Chinese, c1900.
£510–610 / €730–880
$850–1,000 NOA

A set of four carved hardwood doors, Chinese, 18thC.
£3,600–4,000
€5,200–5,800
$6,000–6,700 LOP

A carved and stained rosewood dumb waiter, with three galleried shelves, probably Indo-Burmese, 19thC, 35¾in (91cm) wide.
£490–590 / €710–850
$820–990 HOK

A pair of lacquer screens, decorated with landscapes, figures, insects, deer and palatial buildings, Chinese, 17th–18thC, each panel 18¾in (47.5cm) wide.
£12,000–14,400
€17,400–21,000
$20,000–24,000 HYD
A photograph of these screens from Glemham Hall, Suffolk appeared in an article about the house published on 1 January 1910 in *Country Life*. In the article, the screens are described as having belonged to Elihu Yale, the founder of the eponymous American university.

A lacquer dressing table mirror, with four drawers, Chinese, c1800, 17in (43cm) wide.
£900–1,000
€1,300–1,500
$1,500–1,750 S(O)

A pair of brocade six-fold screens, Japanese, 17th–18thC each panel 24¾in (63cm) wide.
£11,900–14,300 / €17,400–21,000
$20,000–24,000 LHA

◄ **A pair of lacquer screens,** with three leaves, painted in gilt with figures, buildings and river landscapes, some cracks, Chinese, 19thC, each panel 23¾in (60.5cm) wide.
£8,400–10,100
€12,100–14,500
$14,100–17,000
DN

A two-fold paper screen, with ink decoration of blossoming branches, Japanese, Meiji period, 1868–1911, 37¾in (96cm) wide.
£630–750 / €910–1,100
$1,050–1,250 LHA

A cherrywood two-fold screen, with *Shibayama* decoration of birds in landscapes, Japanese, 19thC, each panel 32½in (82.5cm) wide.
£620–740 / €890–1,050
$1,050–1,250 JAd

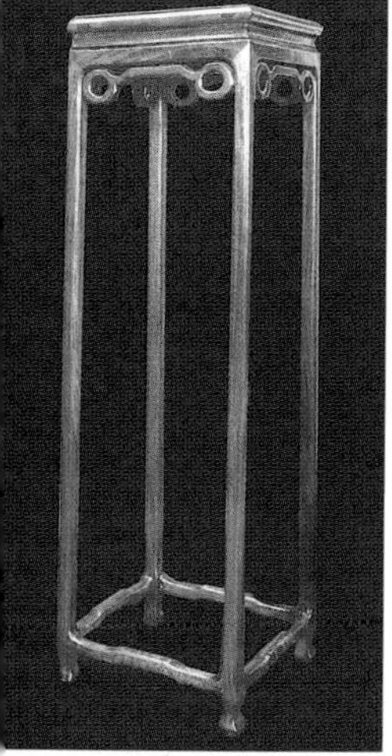

A pair of stained elm jardinière stands, Chinese, 19thC, 44in (112cm) high.
£680–750 / €980–1,100
$1,150–1,300 LOP

A ten-fold screen, decorated with narrative scenes and inscriptions, severe damage, Korean, Choson Dynasty, 19thC, each panel 18in (45.5cm) wide.
£2,100–2,500 / €3,000–3,600
$3,500–4,200 B(Kn)
The late Choson Dynasty saw an increase in screen painting, produced for Korea's court and aristocracy; narrative scenes of diplomatic missions and Royal banquets were popular. The story depicted here is a typical pictorial biography, Confucian in principle, showing the suggested ideal for a Sadaebu (Scholar bureaucrat) from the cradle to wise old age. Each panel represents a significant step in the Scholar's career of birth, marriage and success at climbing the Civil Service ladder. The last panel commemorates the Sadaebu's long and fruitful marriage.

► **A pair of stained elm stools,** Chinese, 19thC, 42in (106.5cm) wide.
£590–650 / €850–940
$990–1,100 QM

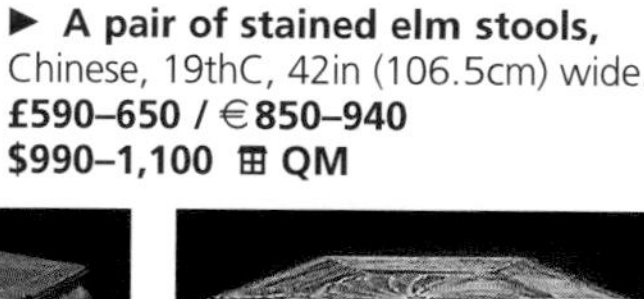

A hardwood *kang*, Chinese, 19thC, 37¾in (96cm) wide.
£1,350–1,500 / €1,950–2,150
$2,250–2,500 LOP
A *kang* is a bed of chair height which is also used for daytime seating.

◄ **A carved hardwood nest of four tables,** with pierced panels and simulated bamboo legs, Chinese, late 19thC, 19¾in (50cm) wide.
£440–520 / €630–750
$740–870 EH

► **A lacquer side table,** with two drawers and carved decoration, Chinese, late 19thC, 62in (157.5cm) wide.
£1,050–1,200 / €1,500–1,700
$1,750–2,000 OE

A carved hardwood settee, with seven drawers, Chinese, 19thC, 43½in (110.5cm) wide.
£480–570 / €690–820
$810–960 NOA

A burr-elm opium bench, with a moulded back panel, Chinese, c1880, 39in (99cm) wide.
£1,100–1,250 / €1,600–1,800
$1,850–2,100 GEO

◄ **A carved ebony and calamander occasional table,** the top with central roundels inlaid with segments of various woods, Singhalese, 1825–50, 19¼in (49cm) diam.
£2,000–2,400 / €2,900–3,450
$3,350–4,000 B
These tables were manufactured in the Galle district in southwest Ceylon. Sir Henry Charles wrote in 1850 that at Galle 'are also manufactured those exquisite inlaid articles, which far surpass any specimen of Tunbridge ware that has yet been produced – ivory and various coloured native woods are inlaid upon ebony and, as the designs are well defined, the effect produced is magnificent'.

Inro

A *takamakie* and inlaid-silver four-case *inro*, decorated with branches and vines, Japanese, 17thC, 3½in (9cm) high.
£360–430 / €520–620
$600–720 S(O)

A lacquer four-case *inro*, decorated in gold and coloured lacquers with toys, signed, Japanese, 19thC, 3in (7.5cm) high.
£130–150 / €190–220
$220–250 Mit

A lacquered wood five-case *inro*, by Jokasai, decorated with a cockerel on a drum, the reverse decorated with a hen and a chick, signed, Japanese, 19thC, 3in (7.5cm) high.
£2,150–2,600
€3,100–3,750
$3,600–4,350 S(O)

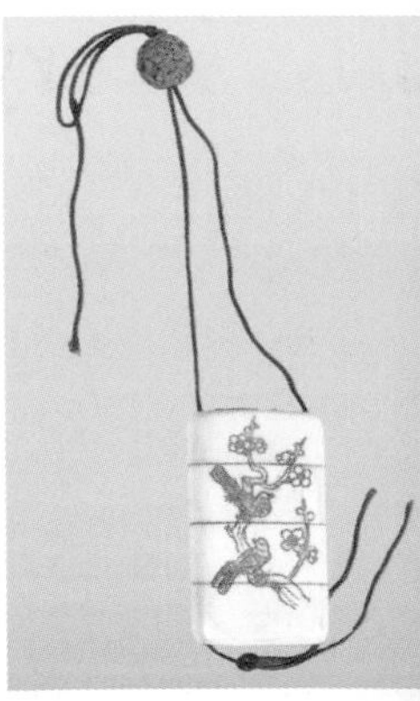

An ivory three-case *inro*, carved with birds on branches, signed, Japanese, 19thC, 2¾in (7cm) high.
£220–260 / €320–370
$370–440 Mit

Inro

The quantity and artistry of *inro*, combined with the names of certain key artists, determine value. Among the most popular artists are Ogawa Haritsu, known as Ritsuo (1767–1857), and Shibata Zeshin (1812–92).

► A lacquer single case *inro*, Japanese, late 19thC, 3¼in (8.5cm) high, with a *netsuke* of a squat male figure carrying a sack, and a carved ivory *ojime*.
£150–180 / €220–260
$250–300 Mit

Netsuke

A wood *netsuke* of a horse, by Meiroku, slightly worn, signed, Japanese, c1800, 2in (5cm) high.
£960–1,150
€1,400–1,650
$1,600–1,900 S(O)

An ivory *netsuke* of an *oni* carrying a ball, Japanese, early 19thC, 1½in (4cm) high.
£310–350 / €440–500
$520–590 AMC

An ivory *netsuke* of a *shishi*, Japanese, Meiji period, 1868–1911, ¾in (2cm) high.
£310–350 / €440–500
$520–590 AMC

Netsuke

Netsuke are generally made of wood or ivory. Old *netsuke* acquire a distinctive patina after years of handling. This patina is very desirable and great care must be taken when cleaning *netsuke* so as not to degrade it. A wipe with a soft cloth is normally sufficient.

An ivory *netsuke* of a basket seller, signed 'Nasatoshi', Japanese, Meiji period, 1868–1911, 2¼in (5.5cm) high.
£850–950 / €1,200–1,350
$1,450–1,600 AMC

A lacquered wood *netsuke* of two dancers dressed as a *shishi*, by Chikusai, signed, Japanese, late 19thC, 1½in (4cm) high.
£720–860 / €1,050–1,250
$1,200–1,450 S(O)

► An ivory *netsuke* of a man with an abacus, Japanese, Meiji period, 1868–1911, 1¼in (3cm) high.
£400–450
€570–640
$670–750
AMC

Jewellery

► **A gold buckle,** set with diamonds, emerald and citrine, Indian, c1900, 3¼in (7.5cm) wide.
£2,100–2,500
€3,000–3,600
$3,500–4,200 B(Kn)

◄ **A 9ct gold brooch,** set with carved ivory, Chinese, c1930, 1½in (4cm) high.
£130–145 / €185–210
$210–240 AMC

An 18ct gold necklace, set with enamel, diamonds, pearls and emeralds, Indian, late 19thC.
£5,400–6,400 / €7,700–9,200
$9,100–10,800 BUK

► **A glass court necklace,** Chinese, 19thC, 47in (119.5cm) long.
£1,550–1,850 / €2,250–2,650
$2,600–3,100 S(O)

A gold pendant, set with rose diamonds and rubies, with natural pearl drops, Indian, 18thC, 3in (7.5cm) high.
£670–800 / €960–1,150
$1,100–1,300 F&C

obes & Costume

◄ **A mandarin's hat,** Chinese, late 19thC, 10in (25.5cm) diam.
£220–250
€320–360
$370–420 JCH

► **A child's hat,** Chinese, late 19thC, 11in (28cm) long.
£220–250
€320–360
$370–420 JCH

A glass and metal rank hat finial, Chinese, 19thC, 2in (5cm) high.
£120–135 / €170–195
$200–230 JCH

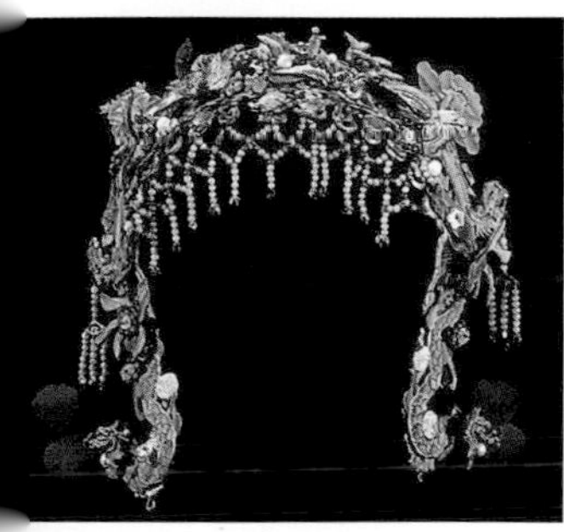

gilt-metal and silvered-glass eaddress, mounted with beads d kingfisher feathers, hung with agon motifs, Chinese, 19thC, n (23cm) diam.
,800–5,700 / €6,900–8,200
,100–9,600 S
is was probably used in inese theatre.

Further reading

Miller's Chinese & Japanese Antiques Buyer's Guide, Miller's Publications, 2004

◄ **A child's kimono,** Japanese, c1880, 20in (51cm) long.
£65–75 / €95–105
$110–125 JCH

► **A Daoist priest's robe,** in a plexi-glass mount, Chinese, c1800, 52¾ x 68½in (134 x 174cm).
£1,400–1,650
€2,000–2,350
$2,350–2,750
S(O)

◄ **A printed silk kimono,** Japanese, c1900.
£175–195 / €250–280
$290–330 TIN

A silk robe, with embroidered decoration, Chinese, 1880–90.
£200–220 / €290–320
$330–370 MARG

A lady's silk surcoat, embroidered with panels of acolytes and peony blossoms, framed in a velvet-lined box, Chinese, 19thC, 33½in (84cm) wide.
£1,050–1,250
€1,500–1,800
$1,750–2,100 NOA

A Kashmir shawl, with embroidered signature, Indian, c1860.
£660–790 / €950–1,150
$1,100–1,300 S(O)
Ex-Castle Howard collection.

A brocade robe, woven with flower sprays in gold and silver thread, lined in silk, Indian, 19thC.
£1,000–1,200
€1,450–1,700
$1,700–2,000 S(O)

A pair of shoes for bound feet, Chinese, c1900,
£175–195 / €250–280
$290–320 JCH

Snuff Bottles

A Duan stone snuff bottle, carved with phoenix scrolls, the reverse with a later inscription, Chinese, 1750–1800, 2¼in (5.5cm) high.
£1,200–1,450
€1,750–2,100
$2,000–2,400 S(O)
Duan stone is a hard smooth stone often used for artists' ink stones or blocks.

A *laque burgauté* snuff bottle and stopper, inlaid with figures in gardens, Chinese, 1821–50, 3¼in (8.5cm) high.
£720–860 / €1,050–1,250
$1,200–1,450 S(O)

► **A jadeite snuff bottle,** carved in relief with *chilong* handles, with stopper, Chinese, 1880–1940, 2in (5cm) high.
£840–1,000
€1,200–1,450
$1,400–1,650 S(O)

► **A glass snuff bottle,** the overlay carved with a carp, Chinese, 19thC, 3in (7.5cm) high.
£270–300 / €390–430
$450–500 LBr

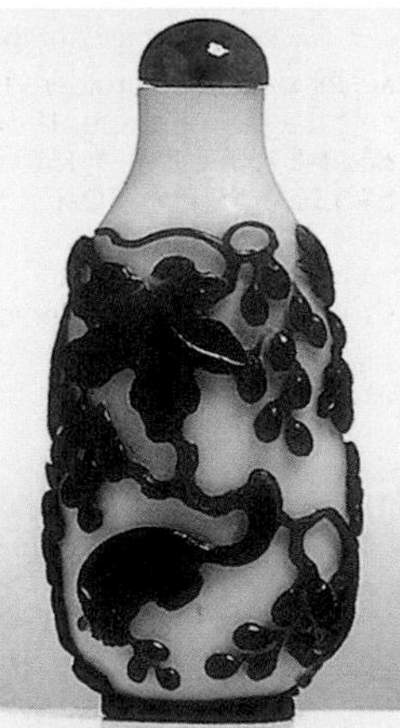

A glass snuff bottle, the overlay carved with a squirrel and a fruiting grapevine, with a hardstone stopper, Chinese, early 19thC, 2¾in (7cm) high.
£3,500–4,200
€5,000–6,000
$5,900–7,000 B

A carved ivory snuff bottle, carved in relief with Immortals, the shoulders with lion-mask handles, Japanese, Meiji period, 1868–1911, 2½in (6.5cm) high.
£660–790 / €950–1,100
$1,100–1,300 S(O)

Textiles

An embroidered panel, Chinese, c1720, 19in (48.5cm) square, framed and glazed.
£440–500 / €650–720
$750–830 ⊞ ACAN

A velvet panel, embroidered with gilt and silver-metal thread with floral patterns, worn, Indian, c1800, 191 x 98½in (485 x 250cm).
£7,400–8,900 / €10,600–12,800
$12,400–14,900 ⚒ S(Am)

A brocade banner, Chinese, c1800, 1½ x 1¾in (4 x 4.5cm).
£850–950 / €1,200–1,350
$1,450–1,600 ⊞ WRi
This banner would have been hung from a pillar or from the ceiling in a temple. It is made from silks that were provided by a wealthy family, to pave their path into the after life with silken treasures. Banners such as this warded away the evil spirits by dancing in the breeze.

An embroidered silk wall hanging, depicting a phoenix hovering over an incense burner, with later brocade borders, Japanese, c1830, 68 x 43½in (172.5 x 110.5cm).
£4,250–5,100
€6,100–7,300
$7,100–8,500 ⚒ NOA

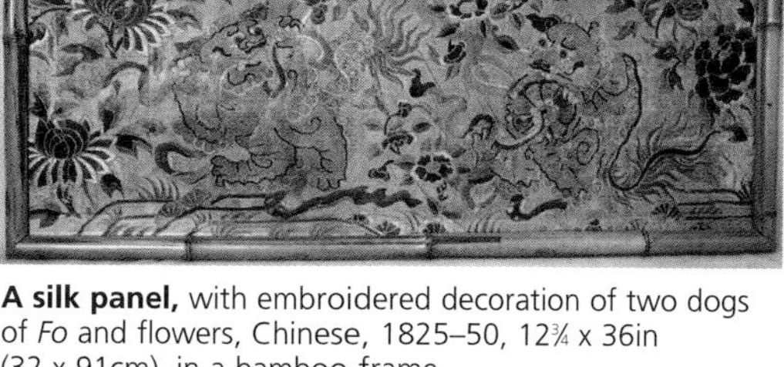

A silk panel, with embroidered decoration of two dogs of *Fo* and flowers, Chinese, 1825–50, 12¾ x 36in (32 x 91cm), in a bamboo frame.
£60–70 / €85–100
$100–115 ⚒ WW

A silk panel, embroidered with 24 Buddhist symbols and nine dragons, Chinese, 19thC, 38½ x 45¼in (98 x 115.5cm).
£680–810 / €980–1,150
$1,150–1,350 ⚒ NOA

A silk roundel, decorated with the Eight Buddhist symbols, Chinese, mid-19thC, 11½in (29cm) diam.
£380–430 / €550–620
$640–720 ⊞ JCH

► **A pair of satin sleevebands,** embroidered with ladies in a garden scene, with a silk border, Chinese, c1860, sleevebands 20½ x 8¼in (52 x 21cm).
£450–500 / €650–720
$750–840 ⊞ WRi

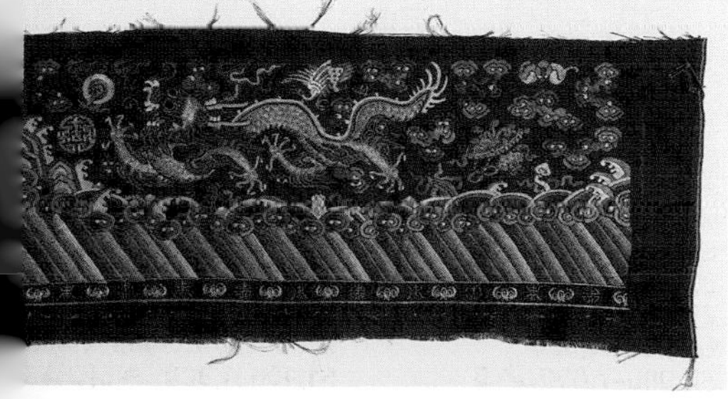

◄ **A silk panel,** with embroidered decoration, Chinese, late 19thC, 11 x 26in (28 x 66cm).
£150–165 / €210–240
$250–280 ⊞ JCH

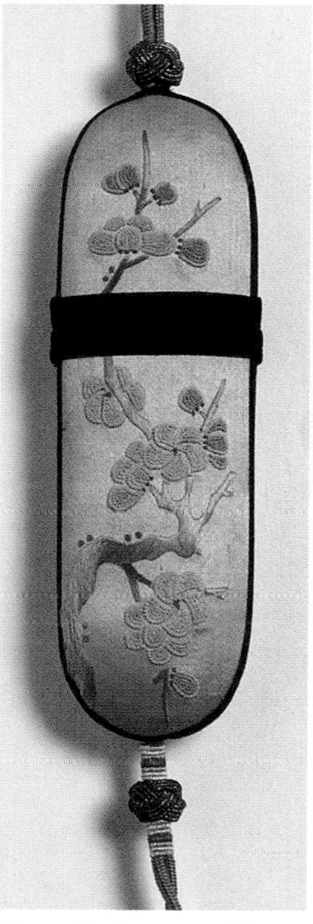

A spectacle case, with hand-embroidered decoration, late 19thC, 6in (15cm) long.
£130–145 / €185–210
$210–240 ⊞ JCH

Islamic Works of Art

Arms & Armour

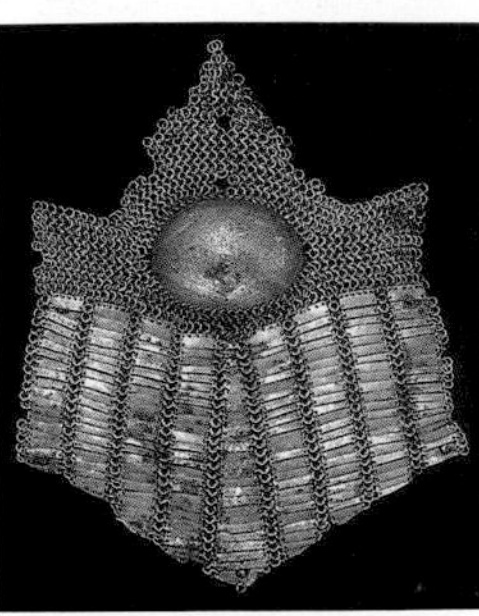

An Ottoman gold- and silver-decorated steel kneeguard, c1500, 24½in (62cm) long.
£4,500–5,400
€6,500–7,800
$7,500–9,000 S

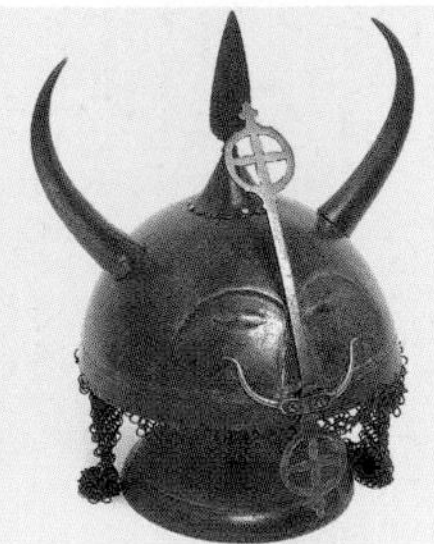

A *khulah khud,* with embossed devil mask, damascened with silver and gold, damage to mail skirt, Indo-Persian, early 19thC, 10in (25.5cm) high.
£390–430 / €560–620
$650–720 ⊞ MDL

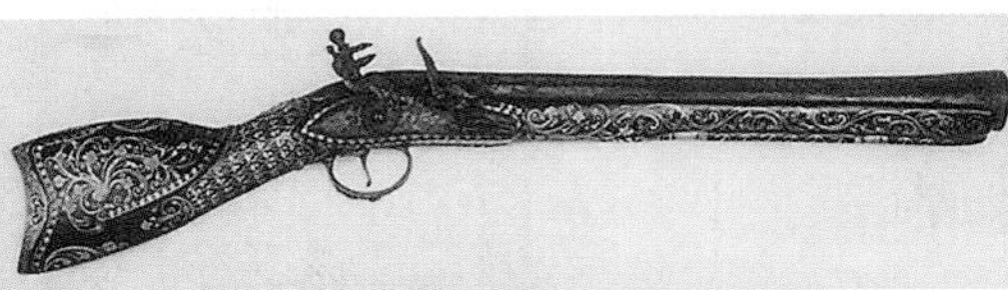

A silver-mounted flintlock blunderbuss, the ebony full stock inlaid with silver wire and engraved silver foliage, steel parts with rust, silver marks, Turkish, early 19thC, barrel 15¼in (38.5cm) long.
£2,000–2,400 / €2,900–3,450
$3,350–4,000 B(Kn)

A silver *jambiya,* with a silver-mounted horn hilt, Omani, c1870, blade 12½in (32cm) long.
£430–480 / €620–690
$720–800 ⊞ TLA

A steel shield, the central sunburst mask within four domed mounts, with outer border of script cartouches and gilt decoration, Persian, 19thC, 15in (38cm) diam.
£375–450 / €540–650
$630–750 TMA

Miller's Compares

I. An iron *khulah khud,* decorated with silver and gold *koftgari* and chiselled calligraphy, with sliding nasal piece and twin plume holders, Persian, 18thC.
£1,900–2,150
€2,700–3,100
$3,200–3,600 ⊞ FAC

II. An iron *khulah khud,* with etched calligraphy and panels depicting mounted nobles in various pursuits, with sliding nasal piece and twin plume holders, Persian, 18thC.
£1,450–1,650
€2,100–2,350
$2,450–2,750 ⊞ FAC

***Khulah khuds* are of standard design, but the quality of the decoration will differ. Item I is not only in better condition than Item II, but it is also decorated with *koftgari*. This is a process where the surface of the object is roughened and the artisan, with a small hammer in one hand and a wire of precious metal (usually gold or silver) in the other, hammers the wire into the other surface while manipulating it to form the design. Item II has interesting panels depicting sporting and mythological scenes, but a piece with the type of superior decoration as seen on Item I will invariably command a premium.**

Ceramics

A pottery tile, Persian or Mesopotamian, c10thC, 8½ x 9in (21.5 x 22.5cm).
£1,050–1,250 / €1,500–1,800
$1,750–2,100 B(Kn)

A Kubachi pottery dish, Persian, 15th–16thC, 13½in (34.5cm) diam.
£3,600–4,300 / €5,200–6,200
$6,000–7,200 S

An Iznik dish, decorated with tulips and carnations, the reverse with leaf motifs, damaged, Turkish, 1550–1600, 11¾in (30cm) diam.
£1,900–2,250 / €2,750–3,250
$3,200–3,800 WW

An Iznik pottery *ming*, painted with sprigs of campanulas and asters, Turkish, c1590, 6¾in (17cm) high.
£2,400–2,900
€3,450–4,150
$4,000–4,800 S

A Kutahya pottery dish, painted with a courtesan and flowers, Turkish, 18thC, 6in (15cm) diam.
£2,250–2,700
€3,250–3,900
$3,800–4,550 S

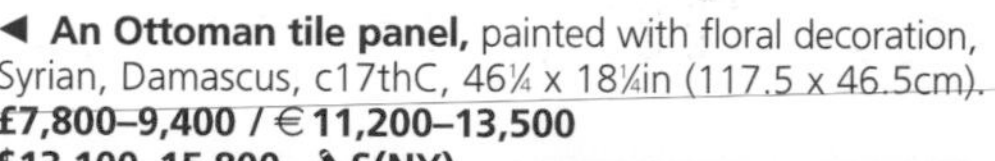

◄ **An Ottoman tile panel,** painted with floral decoration, Syrian, Damascus, c17thC, 46¼ x 18¼in (117.5 x 46.5cm).
£7,800–9,400 / €11,200–13,500
$13,100–15,800 S(NY)

A Safavid *cuerda seca* pottery tile, decorated with flowers, Persian, 17thC, 9in (23cm) square.
£2,800–3,350
€4,000–4,800
$4,700–5,600 B(Kn)

A Safavid pottery dish, decorated with peonies and vines, Persian, c1700, 15in (38cm) diam.
£880–1,050
€1,250–1,500
$1,450–1,750 B(Kn)

A Chanakkale pottery dish, slip-painted with floral sprays, Turkish, 18th/19thC, 10¼in (26cm) diam.
£470–560 / €680–810
$790–940 B(Kn)

An Iznik charger, painted with scrolling flowers and leaves, glaze flakes, Turkish, early 19thC, 18in (45.5cm) diam.
£350–420 / €500–600
$590–700 TMA

A tile, depicting a nobleman on horseback with a hovering peacock, cracked, Persian, 19thC, 13¼ x 10¼in (33.5 x 26cm).
£290–350 / €420–500
$490–590 NSal

Furniture

[A] wooden mirror, with [a]canthus sprays and gilt [d]ecoration, Turkish, [Ur]dine, early 19thC, [4]3¼in (110cm) high.
[£]4,100–4,900
[€]5,900–7,100
[$]6,900–8,200 B(Kn)
[T]his mirror is an Ottoman [v]ersion of the rococo [s]tyle that was popular in [E]urope in the mid- and [la]te 18th century.

A rosewood chair, inlaid with mother-of-pearl and ivory, with a leather seat and back, Persian, 19thC.
£940–1,100
€1,350–1,600
$1,600–1,850 BWL

► **A hardwood side chair,** the back formed by interlocking spindles and balls, inlaid with mother-of-pearl, the underside with inscription in a Persian dialect, Persian, late 19thC.
£560–670 / €800–960
$940–1,100 NOA

► **A walnut and ebony dressing table,** inlaid with bone and ivory, the bevelled mirror flanked by a pair of small drawers, above a frieze drawer and panelled doors, Hispano-Moresque, 19thC, 48in (122cm) wide.
£1,750–2,100
€2,500–3,000
$2,950–3,500 L&T

An occasional table, inlaid with shell and ebony decoration, Moorish, early 20thC, 18½in (47cm) high.
£175–210 / €250–300
$290–350 G(L)

Metalware

A bronze model of a bird, with incised detail, Syria, probably Umayyad, 9thC, 2½in (6.5cm) high.
£500–600 / €720–860
$840–1,000 B(Kn)

A silver box, the enamelled lid depicting two seated figures in a landscape, damaged, marked, Persian, 19thC, 6½in (16.5cm) wide.
£105–125 / €150–180
$175–210 SWO

A Qajar gold-damascened steel flask and cover, decorated with chiselled and raised floral motifs, Persian, 19thC, 18½in (47cm) high.
£3,100–3,700
€4,450–5,300
$5,200–6,200
S

A Mamluk-style silver-inlaid brass vase, decorated with inscriptions and floral patterns, Egyptian or Syrian, 19thC or earlier, 12½in (31.5cm) high.
£1,200–1,450
€1,750–2,100
$2,000–2,400 B(Kn)
This vase appears to be a continuation of Mamluk metalwork produced after the Ottoman conquest of Egypt and Syria in the 16th century, rather than an example of so-called Mamluk revival wares.

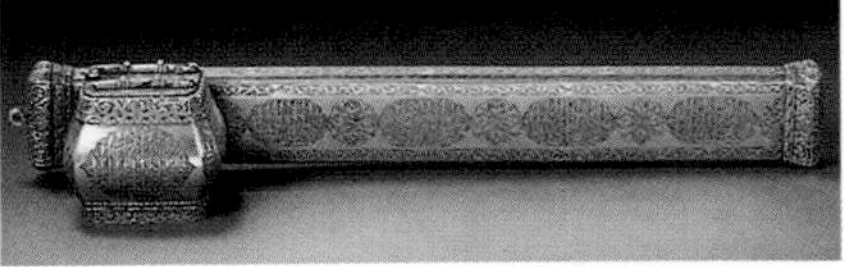

An Ottoman scribe's silver pen box, decorated with cursive script, with traces of gilding, silver pen enclosed, stamped, marked, Egyptian, 1861–76, 11½in (29.5cm) long.
£4,550–5,400 / €6,600–7,800
$7,600–9,100 S

A Safavid or Mughal bronze ewer, the hollow handle with a funnel, the curved spout in the form of a dragon's head, with engraved decoration, Persian or Indian, early 17thC, 10¼in (26cm) high.
£2,800–3,350 / €4,000–4,800
$4,700–5,600 B(Kn)

An Ottoman tombak tray, engraved with a vine with eight blossoms, Turkish, early 19thC, 10½in (26.5cm) diam.
£8,400–10,100 / €12,100–14,500
$14,100–17,000 B(Kn)
Baroque and rococo European styles made a strong impact on 18th- and early 19th-century Ottoman art.

A silver tea urn, decorated with stamped trelliswork borders, with a later Egyptian liner, on a later plated stand, Turkish, c1860, 18in (45.5cm) high, 193oz excluding stand.
£2,400–2,850
€3,450–4,100
$4,050–4,800 S(O)

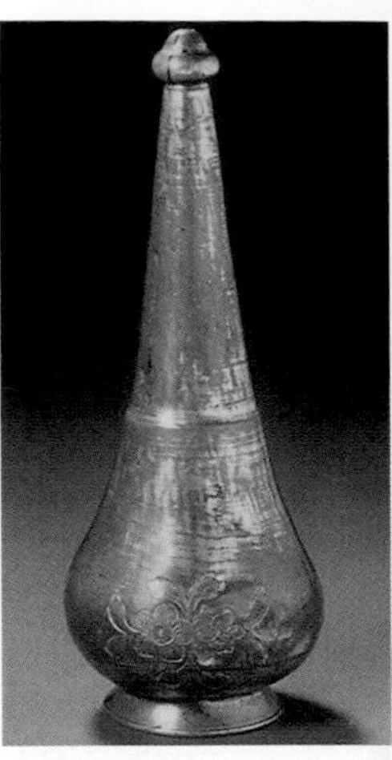

An Ottoman tombak rosewater sprinkler, decorated with floral sprays, Turkish, c1800, 7¼in (18.5cm) high.
£840–1,000
€1,200–1,450
$1,400–1,650 S
Tombak is an alloy of copper, zinc and other base metals.

A gold goblet, set with amethyst and turquoise bands, the stem chased with figures, animals and leaves, Persian, 1850–1900, 3¼in (8.5cm) high.
£2,100–2,500
€3,000–3,600
$3,500–4,200 Bri

For further information on
Metalware see pages 589–596

A silver dish, in the form of a leaf, stamped with Tughra mark, Turkish c1900, 2½in (6.5cm) diam, 5¼oz.
£200–240 / €290–340
$340–400 WW

Textiles

An Ottoman wool purse, embroidered in silks with a vase of flowers and a vine border, with braided edges, Turkish, c1800, 7¾in (20cm) high.
£2,350–2,800
€3,400–4,000
$3,950–4,700 B(Kn)

◄ **A pair of Ottoman velvet boots,** embroidered with flowers in orange metal thread, lined with ikat, with leather soles and heels, Turkish, early 19thC, 22½in (57cm) high.
£3,500–4,200
€5,000–6,000
$5,900–7,100 B(Kn)

A silk panel, formed from six panels, Uzbekistan, 19thC, 77¼ x 51½in (196 x 131cm), in an oak frame.
£720–860 / €1,050–1,250
$1,200–1,450 S(O)

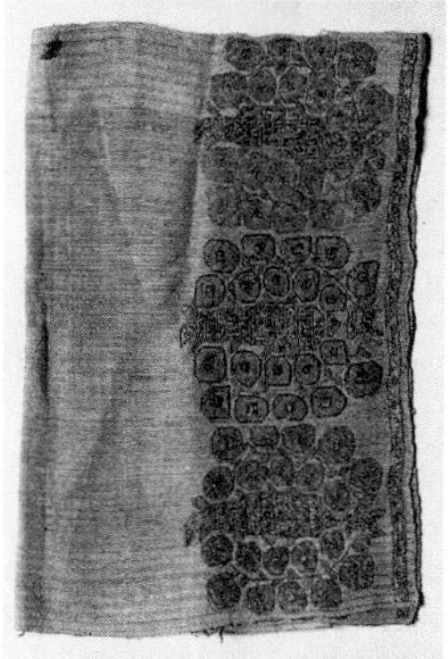

► **A linen towel,** with embroidered decoration, Turkish, c1870, 42 x 17in (106.5 x 43cm).
£75–85 / €110–125
$125–140 JPr

A Rasht panel, with embroidered decoration, Persian, 19thC, 95¼ x 63in (242 x 160cm).
£1,300–1,550
€1,900–2,250
$2,200–2,600 S(O)

A towel, with embroidered decoration, Turkish, c1890, 43 x 20in (109 x 51cm).
£75–85 / €110–125
$125–140 JPr

Miscellaneous

◄ **A glass bottle,** in the form of a camel with a tall receptacle on its back, Syrian, 7th–9thC, 3½in (9cm) high.
£2,350–2,800 / €3,400–4,000
$3,950–4,700 B(Kn)

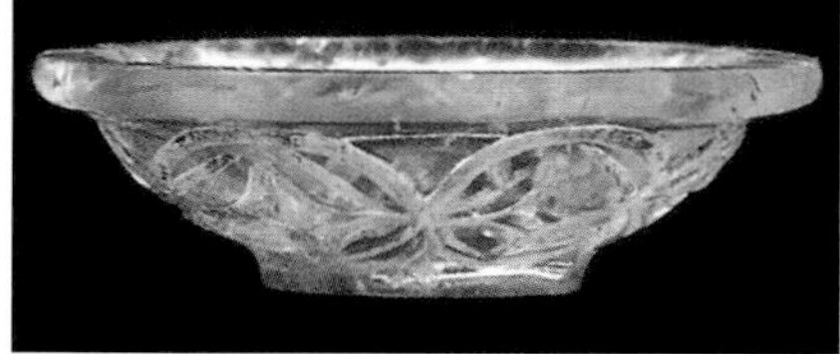

An Abbasid rock-crystal vessel, relief-cut with seven roundels, Persian or Mesopotamian, 9th–10thC, 1¼in (3.5cm) diam.
£3,000–3,600 / €4,300–5,200
$5,000–6,000 B(Kn)

A scribe's ivory-inlaid wood box, decorated with stylized tulips and small florets on split-palmette tendrils, with later lock and handle, Egyptian or Turkish, 17thC, 10½in (26.5cm) wide.
£8,100–9,700 / €11,600–14,000
$13,600–16,300 S

A lacquer book cover, decorated with birds and flowers, signed 'Amin', some damage and restoration, with inscription, Persian or Indian, 1650–1700, 10in (25.5cm) wide.
£3,600–4,300 / €5,200–6,200
$6,000–7,200 S

gold cross, set with a abochon beryl, probably yrian or Egyptian, 1th–13thC, 2in (5cm) high.
3,900–4,700
5,600–6,700
5,600–7,900 S(NY)

An Ottoman leather-covered wood ceremonial saddle, c1900, 21½in (54.5cm) long.
£1,450–1,750 / €2,100–2,500
$2,450–2,950 Herm

LOCATE THE SOURCE

The source of each illustration in Miller's can be found by checking the code letters below each caption with the Key to Illustrations, pages 794–800.

Architectural Antiques

Bronze

A set of four gilt-bronze curtain ties, each cast in the form of a lily, c1860, 8¾in (22cm) high.
£960–1,150
€1,400–1,650
$1,600–1,900 ⚒ S(O)

A bronze fountain head, in the form of a lion's head, north European, 17thC, 12in (30.5cm) high.
£1,750–2,100
€2,500–3,000
$2,950–3,550 ⚒ HYD

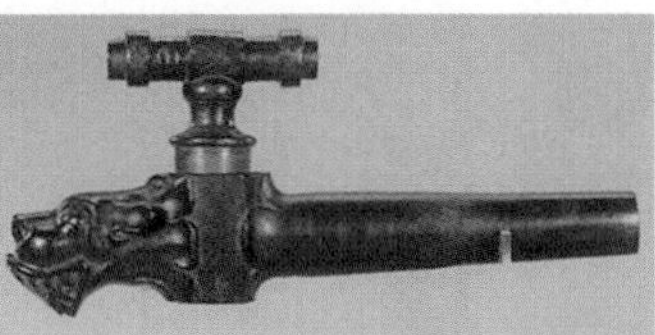

◄ **A bronze spigot,** French, late 18thC, 14½in (37cm) long.
£420–500
€600–720
$700–840 ⚒ S(O)

► **A marble and bronze noonday gun sundial,** with bronze gnomon, American, 1875–1900, 13in (33cm) diam.
£6,600–7,900
€9,500–11,400
$11,100–13,300
⚒ S(S)

Ceramics

A stoneware pineapple finial, c1860, 48in (122cm) high.
£3,600–4,300
€5,200–6,200
$6,000–7,200 ⚒ S(S)

A pottery planter, modelled as a tree trunk, late 19thC, 34¾in (88.5cm) high.
£900–1,050
€1,300–1,500
$1,500–1,750 ⚒ SWO

◄ **A terracotta gnome,** Austrian, c1820, 33in (84cm) high.
£2,150–2,400 / €3,100–3,450
$3,600–4,000 ⊞ GGD

A pair of terracotta garden urns, on raised plinths, early 20thC, 33½in (85cm) high.
£280–330 / €400–480
$470–550 ⚒ SWO

Glass

A Victorian leaded, stained and painted glass window panel, with the Scarborough coat-of-arms, in a timber frame, 20 x 47¼in (78 x 120cm).
£270–320 / €390–460
$450–540 ⚒ DD

► **A pair of stained glass windows,** depicting a knight and an angel, c1920, 48 x 25in (122 x 63.5cm).
£2,350–2,800 / €3,400–4,000
$3,950–4,700 ⚒ TEN
These windows commemorate parishioners who died in WWI. They were possibly made in the West Riding of Yorkshire or Lancashire as a pair, or as part of a series of church windows.

◄ **A hand-painted and leaded glass window,** c1890, 20 x 36in (51 x 91.5cm).
£310–350
€440–500
$520–590 ⊞ OLA

Iron

A cast-iron boot scraper, cast as two winged beasts, 19thC, 10in (25.5cm) wide.
£70–85 / €100–120
$120–140 SWO

A cast-iron fountain, cast as a flowerhead, weathered, 19thC, 42½in (108cm) high.
£1,950–2,350
€2,800–3,350
$3,300–3,950 PFK

◄ **A pair of Regency cast-iron gateposts,** decorated with anthemia and foliage, 80¾in (205cm) high.
£290–350 / €420–500
$490–590 SWO

An iron garden gate, 19thC, 47in (119.5cm) wide.
£340–380 / €490–550
$570–640 DRU

An iron garden gate, 19thC, 36in (91.5cm) wide.
£390–440 / €560–630
$660–740 DRU

A cast-iron jardinière, early 19thC, 36in (91.5cm) wide.
£3,150–3,500 / €4,500–5,000
$5,300–5,900 WRe

◄ **A zinc and cast-iron jardinière,** 19thC, 45½in (115.5cm) high.
£1,800–2,000 / €2,600–2,900
$3,000–3,350 PAS

A cast-iron jardinière, moulded with foliate arabesques, c1900, 33in (84cm) wide.
£290–350 / €420–500
$490–590 NOA

A cast-iron jardinière, c1900, 20in (51cm) wide.
£1,800–2,000 / €2,600–2,900
$3,000–3,350 OLA

◄ **A pair of cast-iron lampposts,** with associated copper tops, late 19thC.
£1,400–1,650 / €2,000–2,350
$2,350–2,750 S(S)

ARCHITECTURAL ANTIQUES

◄ **A pair of cast-iron armorial lions,** 1850–1900, 18in (46cm) high.
£1,800–2,150
€2,600–3,100
$3,000–3,600
S(S)

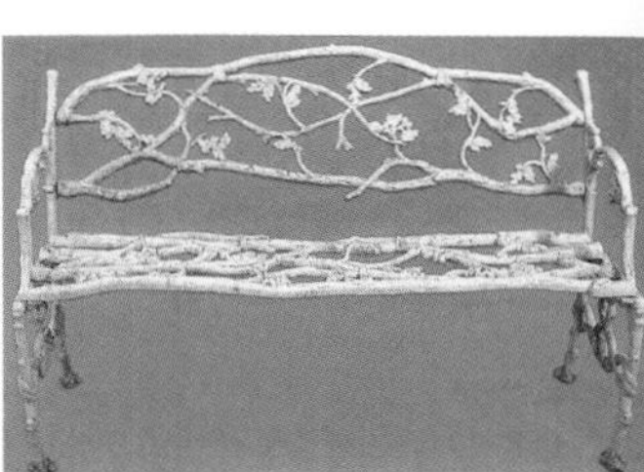

A Deane, Dray & Deane cast-iron garden seat, the entwined branches with oak leaves and acorns, 19thC, 52in (132cm) wide.
£1,200–1,400 / €1,750–2,000
$2,000–2,350 WilP

A Victorian Coalbrookdale-style painted garden seat, with a slatted wooden seat, 72in (183cm) wide.
£1,000–1,200 / €1,450–1,700
$1,700–2,000 HYD

A Victorian metal garden seat, with mesh seat and back.
£45–50 / €65–75
$75–85 L&E

An Edwardian Coalbrookdale cast-iron seat, 33½in (85cm) high.
£990–1,100 / €1,400–1,600
$1,650–1,850 PAS

◄ **A painted cast-iron garden seat,** by Edward Bawden RA, the back pierced with geometric patterns representing a cobweb and two spiders, above a slatted wooden seat, damaged and repaired, 1952–55, 47¾in (121.5cm) wide.
£1,000–1,200 / €1,450–1,700
$1,700–2,000 RTo

A cast-iron umbrella and stick stand, the back cast in the form of a knight, with spiral-twisted supports, inscribed 'Cap a Pied', registration marks for 1881, 36in (91.5cm) high.
£530–640 / €770–920
$890–1,050 BWL

An iron urn and cover, with Renaissance-style decoration, damaged, stamped 'John Crowley & Co, Sheffield', 19thC, 33½in (85cm) high.
£130–155 / €185–220
$220–260 SWO

A pair of cast-iron urns, on pedestals, 19thC, 56in (142cm) high.
£1,200–1,400 / €1,700–2,100
$2,000–2,400 WW

A cast-iron paraffin stove, by Canon, Bilston, 19thC, 36¼in (92cm) high.
£120–145
€170–200
$200–240
WilP

◄ **A pair of painted cast-iron urns,** cast with floral swags and scroll handles, on plinths, c1900, 31½in (80cm) high.
£230–270
€330–390
$390–460 WL

◄ **A painted cast-iron water hopper,** decorated with flowers, c1880, 24in (61cm) high.
£310–350
€440–500
$520–590
WRe

Lead

◄ **A lead figure of Mercury,** 19thC, 52in (132cm) high.
£1,350–1,500
€1,950–2,150
$2,250–2,500 ⊞ PAS

A pair of lead urns, c1900, 21in (53cm) high.
£2,400–2,850 / €3,450–4,100
$4,000–4,800 ⚒ S(S)

◄ **A lead Customs and Excise plaque,** depicting the City of London coat-of-arms and a panel inscribed 'Port 164', 18thC, 15in (38cm) high.
£320–380 / €460–550
$540–640 ⚒ B
Plaques of this type were issued by Customs and Excise for external display on buildings designated as being bonded warehouses.

Marble

A marble bust of Flora, early 18thC, 33in (85cm) high.
£2,850–3,400
€4,100–4,900
$4,800–5,700 ⚒ S(S)

A Regency marble bust of a gentleman, 25in (63.5cm) high.
£700–840 / €1,000–1,200
$1,200–1,400 ⚒ HYD

A carved marble head of Neptune, 19thC, 18in (45.5cm) high.
£590–700 / €850–1,000
$990–1,150 ⚒ WW

A marble figure of an angel, 19thC, 32in (81.5cm) high.
£680–750 / €970–1,100
$1,150–1,300 ⊞ PAS

Stone

◄ **A pair of Japanese-style carved limestone *shishi*,** 19thC, 42in (106cm) high.
£6,200–7,400 / €8,900–10,700
$10,400–12,400 ⚒ S(S)

A carved sandstone figure of a greyhound, slight damage, 19thC, 42in (106.5cm) wide.
£1,750–2,100 / €2,500–3,000
$2,950–3,550 ⚒ PFK

pair of Art Deco-style stone lions, by . Demanges, 1930s, 43in (109cm) wide.
9,700–10,800 / €14,000–15,600
16,300–18,100 ⊞ DRU

► **A pair of Caen stone columns,** 19thC, 81½in (207cm) high.
£2,500–3,000 / €3,600–4,300
$4,200–5,000 ⚒ S(S)

A gritstone allegorical figure of America, Low Countries, c1700, 54½in (138cm) high.
£14,400–17,300
€21,000–25,000
$24,200–29,000 S(S)

► **A limestone well top,** c1770, 40in (101.5cm) wide.
£360–400 / €520–580
$600–670 DOR

A pair of composition stone figures of gardeners, Belgian, c1900, taller 74in (188cm) high.
£4,800–5,700 / €6,900–8,200
$8,100–9,600 S(S)

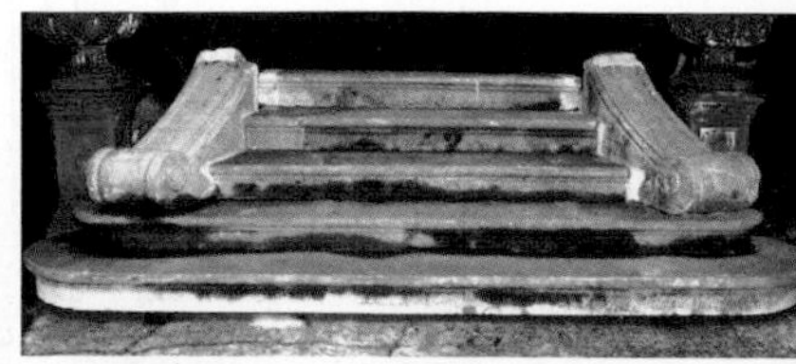

A set of stone steps, 19thC, 130in (330cm) wide.
£8,300–9,200 / €11,900–13,300
$13,900–15,500 DRU

A bronze sundial, on a limestone pedestal base, 1850–1900, 54¼in (138cm) high.
£3,000–3,600
€4,300–5,200
$5,000–6,000
NOA

A George III stone garden urn, carved with a fruiting vine and a band of gadrooning, on a plinth, 35in (89cm) wide.
£2,000–2,400
€2,900–3,450
$3,350–4,050 HYD

Wood

An Edwardian butler's electric bell, in a wooden case, 10in (25.5cm) high.
£400–450 / €570–650
$670–760 DRU

A set of four carved pine corbel figures, late 19thC, 59in (150cm) high.
£1,800–2,150
€2,600–3,100
$3,000–3,600 S(S)

A pair of painted and parcel-gilt columns, carved with cherub heads, possibly Italian, c1700, later platforms and socles.
£4,300–5,100
€6,200–7,300
$7,200–8,600 B

► **A carved pine frieze,** the medallion motif flanked by coffered panels with gilt decoration, slight damage, possibly Spanish, 16thC, 48in (122cm) wide.
£105–125 / €150–180
$175–210 BR

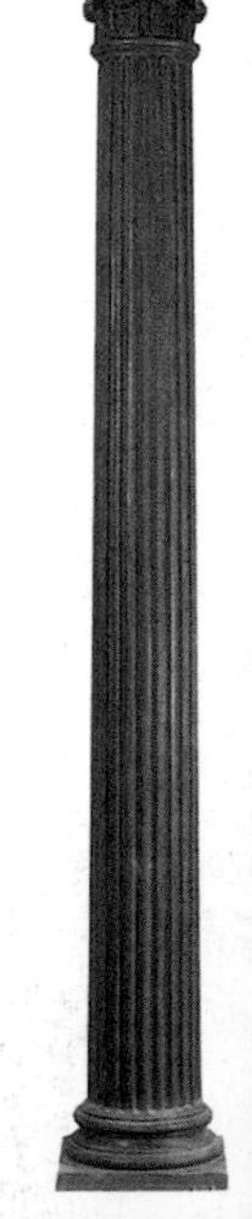

► **A pair of Edwardian oak columns,** with carved Corinthian capitals, on moulded bases, early 20thC, 139in (353cm) high.
£2,000–2,400 / €2,900–3,450
$3,350–4,000 S(S)

A giltwood crest, carved with stylized clouds and putti, 19thC, 44¾in (113.5cm) wide.
£1,000–1,200 / €1,450–1,700
$1,700–2,000 DN
This was probably the crest to a mirror.

◀ **A carved oak frieze,** depicting a hunting scene, Dutch, 17thC, 22in (56cm) wide.
£680–750 / €980–1,100
$1,100–1,250 ⊞ SEA

A pair of carved oak panels, Flemish, 16thC, 15in (38cm) square.
£1,500–1,700 / €2,150–2,450
$2,500–2,850 ⊞ SEA

A carved oak panel, with entwined initials 'CE' and 'AE', some rails replaced, early 17thC, 46½in (118cm) wide.
£2,250–2,700 / €3,250–3,900
$3,800–4,550 ⚒ S(O)

A George III giltwood and gesso pelmet, the centre pediment above an egg-and-dart moulded frieze with repeating medallion decoration flanked by a shell and flower ornament to each drop terminal, 86in (218.5cm) wide.
£630–750 / €910–1,100
$1,050–1,250 ⚒ Mit

An oak wall carving, Flemish, 16thC, 60in (152.5cm) wide.
£220–250 / €320–360
$370–420 ⊞ SEA

A wood plaque, carved with winged angels' heads, leaf husks and scrolls, Italian, 18thC, 30in (76cm) wide.
£3,300–3,950
€4,750–5,700
$5,500–6,600 ⚒ SWO

A carved oak fragment of a pulpit, 18thC, 42½in (108cm) wide.
£1,450–1,750
€2,100–2,500
$2,450–2,950 ⚒ BERN

A pair of carved walnut panels, depicting male and female figures, c1600, 35in (89cm) high.
£3,800–4,200
€5,400–6,000
$6,400–7,100 ⊞ KEY
These carvings came from a house in West Yorkshire and were part of a fireplace overmantel but may have been made originally for a panelled room in a grand late Elizabethan house.

A pair of carved oak wall ornaments, each depicting Eve holding an apple above a winged cherub, 17thC, 40in (101.5cm) high.
£610–730 / €880–1,050
$1,050–1,250 ⚒ HYD

A pair of carved and painted Palladian-style niche frames, Italian, 19thC, 58in (148cm) wide.
£1,800–2,150
€2,600–3,100
$3,000–3,600 ⚒ S(S)

A carved wood panel, depicting a profile bust of a military officer, the reverse incised 'W. Afbridge 1817', 19thC, 11½ x 8¾in (29 x 22cm).
£750–900 / €1,100–1,300
$1,250–1,500 ⚒ Bea

A pair of 18thC-style giltwood and gesso wall appliqués, 19thC, 64¼in (163cm) high.
£1,650–1,950
€2,400–2,800
$2,800–3,300 ⚒ S(O)

Bathroom Fittings

A Shanks & Co basin, with a marble top, on a brass stand, c1900, 32in (81.5cm) wide.
£4,050–4,500
€5,800–6,500
$6,800–7,600 ⊞ DRU

► A Shanks & Co cast-iron and enamel canopy bath and shower, with a mahogany surround, c1890, 82in (208.5cm) long.
£11,500–12,800
€16,600–18,500
$19,300–21,500 ⊞ DRU

A pedestal basin, French, c1900, 28in (71cm) wide.
£1,800–2,000
€2,600–2,900
$3,000–3,350 ⊞ C&R

A Victorian copper bath, with a concealed heating element, 61¾in (157cm) long.
£960–1,150 / €1,400–1,650
$1,600–1,900 ⚒ BR

A Victorian roll-top plunger bath, 76in (193cm) long.
£3,600–4,000 / €5,200–5,800
$6,000–7,200 ⊞ WRe

An enamelled bath, with soap dishes, c1900, 72in (183cm) long.
£1,600–1,800
€2,300–2,600
$2,700–3,000 ⊞ DOR

► An enamelled plunger bath, French, c1900, 63in (160cm) long.
£2,500–2,800
€3,600–4,050
$4,200–4,700 ⊞ DOR

► A cast-iron bateau bath, c1900, 65in (165cm) long.
£2,700–3,000
€3,900–4,200
$4,500–5,000 ⊞ C&R

A cast-iron slipper bath, c1900, 60in (152.5cm) long.
£900–1,000 / €1,300–1,450
$1,500–1,700 ⊞ C&R

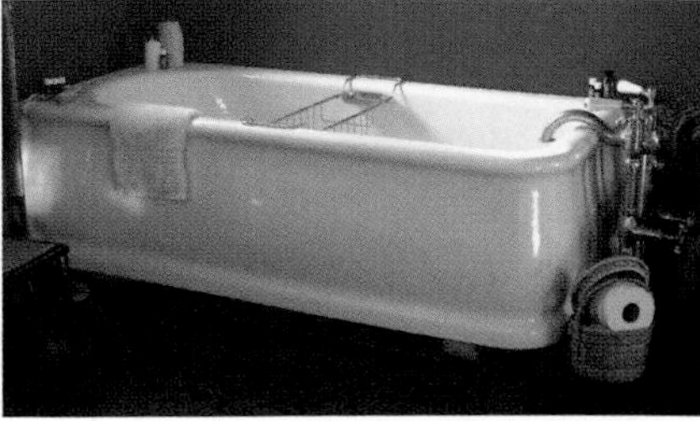

A Twyfords ceramic bath, with brass floor-mounted mixer taps, c1920, 66in (167.5cm) long.
£3,150–3,500 / €4,500–5,000
$5,300–5,900 ⊞ DOR

A corner bath, 1920s, 64in (162.5cm) long.
£1,250–1,400 / €1,800–2,000
$2,100–2,350 ⊞ WRe

A copper bath, French, c1860, 65in (165cm) long.
£3,000–3,400
€4,300–4,900
$5,000–6,000 ⊞ L(r)

A Victorian Pickups ceramic high level cistern and cover, 21in (53.5cm) wide.
£710–790 / €1,000–1,150
$1,200–1,350 ⊞ DRU

A walnut commode, 19thC, 16in (40.5cm) wide.
£150–165 / €210–240
$250–280 ⊞ NoC

A lavatory pan, printed with a classical scene, 19thC, 44in (112cm) wide.
£140–165 / €200–240
$240–280 ⚒ SWO

◄ An earthenware 'Waterfall' lavatory pan, with floral decoration, early 20thC, 16in (40.5cm) high.
£300–360
€430–520
$500–600
⚒ AMB

A Lucania lavatory pan, c1890, 16in (40.5cm) high.
£720–800 / €1,050–1,200
$1,200–1,350 ⊞ OLA

'The Burrator' lavatory pan, c1895, 16in (40.5cm) high.
£670–750 / €960–1,100
$1,100–1,250 ⊞ NOST

► A John Bolding stoneware lavatory pan, c1900, 16in (40.5cm) high.
£900–1,000
€1,300–1,450
$1,500–1,700
⊞ WRe

ARCHITECTURAL ANTIQUES

Doors & Door Furniture

An iron door, with a later lock and possibly a later small door inserted into the lower part, heavy rusting, 16thC, 87¼in (221.5cm) high.
£900–1,100
€1,300–1,550
$1,500–1,800 DORO

An oak and ebony door, c1880, 42in (106.5cm) wide.
£1,100–1,250
€1,600–1,800
$1,850–2,100 ⊞ SAW

A pair of silver door knobs and plates, c1895, 8in (20.5cm) long.
£135–150 / €195–220
$220–250 ⊞ Penn

▶ A Victorian Kenrick cast-iron door knocker, in the form of a goat's head, 11in (28cm) long.
£145–160 / €200–230
$240–270 ⊞ OLA

A studded pine door, 18thC, 89in (226cm) high.
£400–450 / €570–650
$670–760 ⊞ PAS

A pair of parcel-gilt beechwood salon doors, painted with foliate scrolls and floral sprays, with gilt-bronze door pulls, c1900, 45½in (115.5cm) wide.
£2,300–2,750
€3,300–4,000
$3,900–4,600 NOA

An inner hall fanlight and doors, the dentil-moulded border crested with an acanthus leaf, above stained and leaded glass doors, early 19thC, 102½in (260cm) wide.
£3,300–4,000
€4,750–5,700
$5,500–6,600 MEA

A brass bell pull, c1890, 5in (12.5cm) long.
£175–195 / €250–280
$290–330 ⊞ SAT

A brass door knocker, in the form of a dolphin, c1860, 5in (12.5cm) wide.
£310–350 / €440–500
$520–590 ⊞ RGe

An oak panelled front door, with linenfold carving, French, 19thC, 43in (109cm) wide.
£1,350–1,500
€1,950–2,150
$2,250–2,500 ⊞ DRU

A brass and mahogany door handle, 19thC, 9in (23cm) wide.
£90–100 / €130–145
$150–170 ⊞ DRU

A Regency-style ormolu door knocker, cast with a mask of Neptune and acanthus leaves, probably 19thC, 9½in (24cm) high.
£1,200–1,400
€1,750–2,000
$2,000–2,350 SGA

◀ A steel lock, with Gothic motifs, 15thC, 9¼in (23.5cm) high.
£1,400–1,650
€2,000–2,350
$2,350–2,750 S

Fireplaces

A rococo-style carved pine fire surround, c1750, 79½in (202cm) wide.
£4,200–5,000 / €6,000–7,200
$7,000–8,400 S(O)

A Georgian painted pine and gesso fire surround, with applied figural scrolling decoration, 69¾in (178cm) wide.
£560–670 / €800–960
$940–1,100 SWO

A pine fire surround and overmantel, the frieze carved with flowerheads, the jambs carved with egg, dart and foliate mouldings, c1760 and later, 67in (170cm) wide.
£4,800–5,700
€6,900–8,200
$8,100–9,600 S(S)

LOCATE THE SOURCE
The source of each illustration in Miller's can be found by checking the code letters below each caption with the Key to Illustrations, pages 794–800.

A George III marble fire surround, the moulded cornice above a carved frieze depicting classical maidens, Irish, 74in (188cm) wide.
£11,400–13,500 / €16,400–19,500
$19,000–23,000 JAd

A marble fire surround, early 19thC, 57in (145cm) wide.
£2,950–3,550 / €4,250–5,100
$4,950–5,900 WRe

◄ **A Carrara marble fire surround,** on scroll-form legs with acanthus carving, c1835, 59in (150cm) wide.
£2,200–2,600
€3,200–3,800
$3,700–4,400
NOA

A French-style Carrara marble fire surround, the shaped frieze centred by a scrolling foliate cabochon, 19thC, 74in (188cm) wide.
£4,950–5,900
€7,100–8,500
$8,300–9,900
L&T

A Victorian pine fire surround, set with 22 Copeland blue and white tiles, 85½in (217cm) wide.
£1,300–1,550 / €1,850–2,200
$2,200–2,600 SWO

ARCHITECTURAL ANTIQUES

A George II-style carved walnut fire surround, restored, c1880, 94½in (240cm) wide.
£19,000–21,500 / €28,000–31,000
$32,000–36,000 ⊞ W&C

A Georgian-style painted pine and gesso fire surround, the tablet mounted in relief with griffins, flanked by paterae and bellflower festoons, early 20thC, 67in (170cm) wide.
£1,650–1,950 / €2,350–2,800
$2,750–3,250 ⚒ S(S)

A Regency cast-iron basket grate, in the manner of George Bullock, with gilt-metal anthemia mounts and paw feet, 33¾in (85.5cm) wide.
£3,300–3,950 / €4,750–5,700
$5,500–6,600 ⚒ HYD

A cast-iron hob grate, c1830, 31½in (80cm) wide.
£1,900–2,250 / €2,750–3,250
$3,200–3,800 ⚒ S(S)

A late Victorian mahogany fire surround, the carved frieze flanked by pillars with rams' mask mounts, 77in (195.5cm) wide.
£610–730 / €880–1,050
$1,050–1,250 ⚒ JM

A steel fire grate, c1780, 32¾in (83cm) wide.
£1,900–2,250 / €2,750–3,250
$3,200–3,800 ⚒ S(O)

A cast-iron register grate, c1820, 36in (91.4cm) wide.
£1,450–1,600 / €2,100–2,300
$2,450–2,700 ⊞ WRe

A cast-iron fire grate, in the style of Robert Adam, 19thC, 37¼in (94.5cm) wide.
£840–1,000 / €1,200–1,400
$1,450–1,700 ⚒ S(O)

◄ **A Crichley's Improved Patent cast-iron fire grate,** with adjustable fire cheeks, c1870, 38in (96.5cm) wide.
£900–1,000 / €1,300–1,450
$1,500–1,700 ⊞ WRe

A Georgian-style marble fire surround, with a marble hearth, early 20thC, 66in (167cm) wide.
£4,800–5,700 / €6,900–8,200
$8,100–9,600 ⚒ S(S)

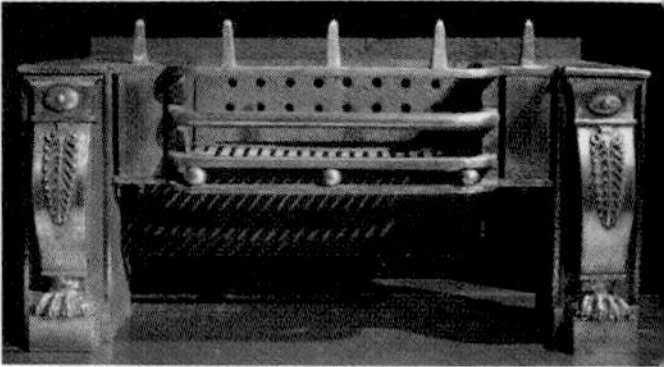

A cast-iron hob grate, c1800, 42in (106.5cm) wide.
£7,200–8,000 / €10,400–11,500
$12,100–13,400 ⊞ L(sm)

An iron fire grate, in the style of George Bullock, c1820, 34in (86.5cm) wide.
£2,700–3,000 / €3,900–4,300
$4,500–5,000 ⊞ WRe

A cast-iron and bronze fire grate, c1840, 31¾in (80.5cm) wide.
£540–650 / €780–940
$910–1,100 ⚒ S(O)

A brass-fronted dog grate, in the style of Robert Adam, late 19thC, 36in (91.5cm) wide.
£1,800–2,000 / €2,600–2,900
$3,000–3,350 ⊞ OLA

Fireplace Accessories

An iron-bound ash cistern, with pierced carrying handles, 56in (142cm) wide.
£7,800–9,300 / €11,200–13,400
$13,100–15,600 ⚒ S

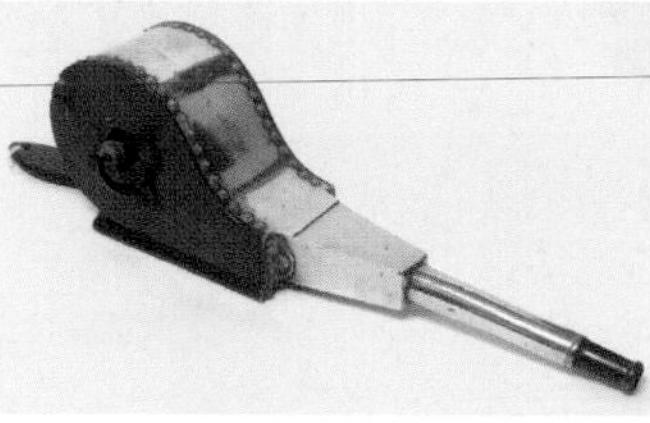

► **A set of mechanical brass and wood bellows,** 19thC, 22in (56cm) long.
£75–85 / €105–120
$125–140 ⊞ TOP

A pair of engraved steel ember tongs, c1780, 16in (40.5cm) long.
£580–650 / €840–940
$970–1,100 ⊞ SEA

A Regency bronze and iron fender, 53in (134.5cm) long.
£760–850 / €1,100–1,250
$1,300–1,450 ⊞ NOST

A brass fender, with tool rests, c1860, 54in (137cm) wide.
£510–570 / €730–820
$860–960 ⊞ ASH

A late Victorian brass club fender, with a leather-pholstered seat, on spiral turned supports, 7¾in (146.5cm) wide.
775–930 / €1,100–1,300
1,300–1,550 ⚒ B(WM)

An extending brass-mounted cast-iron fender, French, c1880, 60in (152.5cm) extended.
£580–650 / €830–930
$970–1,100 ⊞ ASH

cast-iron fireback, cast with a mily coat-of-arms and inscriptions, arly 17thC, 30in (76cm) wide.
1,650–1,850 / €2,350–2,650
2,750–3,100 ⊞ KEY

A pair of brass fire dogs, stamped mark, c1870, 11½in (29cm) high.
£150–180 / €220–260
$250–300 ⚒ SWO

A pair of cast-brass and wrought-iron andirons, with later sections to billet bars, probably American, New York, 18thC, 12½in (32cm) high.
£1,350–1,600 / €1,950–2,300
$2,250–2,700 ⚒ S(NY)

pair of brass andirons, n claw-and-ball feet, merican, 1800–25, 7½in (70cm) high.
500–600 / €720–860
840–1,000 ⚒ LHA

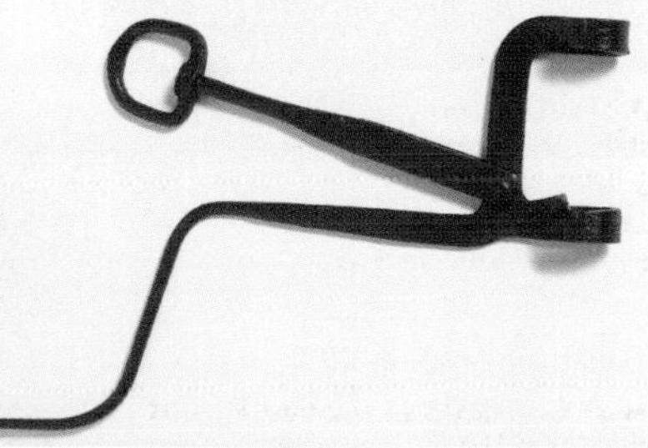

A wrought-iron kettle tilt, early 19thC, 19in (48.5cm) high.
£150–170 / €210–240
$250–290 ⊞ KEY

A wrought-iron and brass trammel, c1750, 39in (99cm) long.
£520–580 / €750–840
$870–970 ⊞ SEA

Sculpture

An alabaster plaque, in the form of a scallop shell enclosing a female figure holding a branch, and a dragon, Flemish, late 15thC, 4in (10cm) wide.
£540–650 / €780–930
$920–1,100 BWL

A carved bust of Benjamin Franklin, damage to nose, on an associated marble socle, possibly American, 1775–1825, 11¾in (30cm) high.
£470–560 / €680–810
$790–940 B(Kn)

A carved wood figure of St Anthony of Padua, inset with glass eyes, Peruvian, early 19thC, 19¼in (49cm) high.
£560–670 / €810–960
$960–1,150 LHA

A carved oak figure of the Madonna and Child, a serpent at her feet, damage to limbs, blackened varnished patina, probably Flemish, 17thC, 17½in (44.5cm) high.
£370–440 / €530–630
$620–740 F&C

► **A bronze, ormolu and marble sculpture,** probably by Boizot, modelled as a classical lamp, French, c1780, 14½in (37cm) wide.
£5,800–6,500
€8,400–9,400
$9,700–10,900 RGa

A carved ivory group of a woman and a boy, on an ebony socle, 19thC, 9½in (24cm) high.
£260–310 / €380–450
$440–520 AMB

► **A Carrara marble bust of Apollo,** by Ferdinando Vichi, signed, Italian, 19thC, 13in (33cm) high.
£1,200–1,450
€1,750–2,100
$2,000–2,400 LHA

A carved wood figure of a priest, fingertips damaged, 17thC, 23¼in (59cm) high.
£1,500–1,800
€2,200–2,600
$2,500–3,000 BERN

A marble head of a classical philosopher, Italian School, tip of nose restored, 1800–50, 22¼in (56.5cm) high.
£3,000–3,600
€4,300–5,100
$5,000–6,000 TEN

A carved wood male figure, decorated with foliate motifs, minor restorations, Spanish, 18thC, 31in (78.5cm) high.
£1,550–1,850
€2,250–2,650
$2,600–3,100 S(Am)

A Regency Carrara marble bust of a gentleman, 30½in (77.5cm) high, with a marble column.
£2,250–2,700
€3,250–3,900
$3,800–4,550 HYD

A bronze figure of an admiral, by F. Hamar, 19thC, 21in (53.5cm) hig
£3,400–3,800
€4,900–5,500
$5,700–6,400 RAN

A carved marble bust of a judge, by Matthew Noble, signed and dated 1845, 15¾in (40cm) high, with associated plinth.
£1,200–1,450
€1,750–2,100
$2,000–2,400 B
Born in Hackness in South Yorkshire, Noble studied under John Francis and first exhibited at the Royal Academy in 1845. He came to public prominence with his monument to Wellington erected in Manchester in 1856. Noble continued to exhibit at the Royal Academy until his death in 1876, and many of his most famous works were copied in unglazed Parian-type porcelain by Copeland.

A marble figure of a maiden, by Sommer, Italian, Naples, 19thC, 33in (84cm) high.
£900–1,050
€1,300–1,500
$1,500–1,750 DMC

A bronze Grand Tour classical figure, 19thC, 27in (68.5cm) high.
£1,800–2,000
€2,600–2,900
$3,000–3,350 DJH

A bronze sculpture of 'The Standing Sappho', by Jean-Jacques, called James, Pradier, foundry stamp, Swiss, signed and dated 1848, 17¾in (45cm) high.
£5,000–6,000
€7,200–8,600
$8,400–10,100 S

◄ **A marble figure,** by Harriet Goodhue Hosmer, entitled 'The Sleeping Faun', signed and inscribed, American, c1865, 37in (94cm) wide, on a later *faux* marble base.
£26,500–31,000 / €38,000–45,000
$44,000–52,000 S

► **A plaster group,** by Joseph Edgar Boehm, entitled 'Captain Anstruther-Thomson on Rainbow', signed and inscribed 'To Mr. John Perry from the Artist 1867', 21½in (54.5cm) wide.
£1,200–1,400 / €1,750–2,050
$2,000–2,350 S
Boehm was Sculptor in Ordinary to Queen Victoria and a regular exhibitor at the Royal Academy.

A bronze figure, by Jean-Alexander-Joseph Falguière, entitled 'Winner of the Cock Fight', foundry mark for the Baut Frères, French, Paris, c1880, 31½in (80cm) high.
£5,100–5,700
€7,300–8,200
$8,600–9,600 G&H
Jean-Alexander-Joseph Falguière was one of the leading lights of the Toulouse School. He made his debut in 1857 and was awarded the Medal of Honour in 1868.

A cold-painted bronze figure of a North African man, by Bergman, some losses and repairs, Austrian, 19thC, 10¼in (26cm) high.
£200–240 / €300–350
$340–400 SWO

A silvered bronze model of a cock and hen, by Auguste Nicolas Cain, entitled 'Coq et Poule', signed, stamped 'Christofle & Cie', French, c1870, 7½in (19cm) high.
£2,150–2,400
€3,100–3,450
$3,600–4,000 BeF

A carved marble figure of a classical maiden, by Emile Carlier, the base with cast ormolu mounts, 19thC, 34in (86.5cm) high.
£5,700–6,800
€8,200–9,800
$9,600–11,400 JAd

SCULPTURE

A bronze model of a lion, by Paul Edouard Delabrierre, French, c1875, 17in (43cm) wide.
£2,400–2,700 / €3,500–3,900
$4,050–4,550 ⊞ G&H

At an early stage in his career Delabrierre concentrated on animal sculpture and he made his debut at the Paris Salon in 1848. His model lions were imbued with a spirit of realism.

A bronze group, by Pierre Jules Mêne, known as 'The Good Companions', signed, French, c1850, 18½in (47cm) wide.
£4,350–5,200 / €6,200–7,400
$7,300–8,700 ⚒ JNic

A bronze model of a retriever with a rabbit, by Jules Moigniez, French, 19thC, 12in (30.5cm) wide.
£1,050–1,250 / €1,500–1,800
$1,750–2,100 ⚒ PBA

A Highland hunting group, by Pierre Jules Mêne, entitled 'Chausseur Ecossain avec deux chiens', French, 19thC, 20in (51cm) high.
£8,900–9,900
€12,800–14,300
$15,000–16,600 ⊞ BHa

A pair of bronze models of hounds, by Alfred Dubucand, signed, French, c1850, 12½in (32cm) high.
£3,500–4,200 / €5,000–6,000
$5,900–7,100 ⚒ HAM

A bronze model of a Highland terrier, by Thomas François Cartier, on a marble base, French, 19thC, 14in (35.5cm) wide.
£1,650–1,850 / €2,400–2,650
$2,800–3,100 ⊞ RAN

A pair of bronze figures of Anthony Van Dyck and his companion, after Jean-Jules Salmson, signed, 19thC, 22in (56cm) high.
£1,500–1,800 / €2,200–2,600
$2,500–3,000 ⚒ M

Items in the Sculpture section have been arranged in date order.

A cast metal model of a dog, damaged, American, 19thC, 62in (157.5cm) wide.
£3,900–4,700 / €5,600–6,700
$6,600–7,900 ⚒ SGA

A bronze figure of a child and cockerel, by E. Laporte, 19thC, 19¾in (50cm) high.
£1,050–1,250
€1,500–1,800
$1,750–2,100 ⚒ LAY

A carved, stained and giltwood figure of an angel, French, 19thC, 32¼in (82cm) high.
£1,150–1,350
€1,700–2,000
$1,950–2,300 ⚒ BERN

A bronzed spelter figure inscribed 'Mignon', Frenc 19thC, 22½in (57cm) hig
£420–500 / €600–720
$700–840 ⚒ SWO

A terracotta model of a bronze group, depicting bacchanalian putti with a goat, the base inscribed 'Toinet', 19thC, 16½in (42cm) wide.
£590–700 / €850–1,000
$1,000–1,200 NSal

A bronze model of striding lion, by Ernst Julius Hähnel, signed, German, 19thC, 13½in (34.5cm) wide.
£1,300–1,550 / €1,900–2,250
$2,200–2,600 S

A bronze figure, by Henri Emile Allouard, French, c1885, 21¾in (55.5cm) high.
£3,400–3,800
€4,900–5,500
$5,700–6,400 ⊞ G&H
From 1865 to 1928, Allouard exhibited paintings and sculpture, including a number of busts in plaster, marble and bronze, at the Salon, Paris. Many of his works have been produced in porcelain by the Sèvres factory and in bronze by a number of founders.

A Carrara marble figure of a girl, by Pietro Lazzerini, Italian, dated 1887, 41in (104cm) high.
£6,900–8,300
€10,000–12,000
$11,700–14,000 DuM

A bronze figure of General Gordon, by Sir William Hamo Thornycroft, signed and dated 1888, 14½in (37cm) high.
£2,250–2,700
€3,250–3,900
$3,800–4,550 B(Kn)

◄ **A Victorian spelter figure of a gladiator,** 25½in (65cm) high.
£300–360 / €440–520
$500–600 SWO

A gilt-bronze model of a pug dog, c1890, 3in (7.5cm) high.
£360–400 / €520–580
$600–660 ⊞ RdeR

A figure of a female harlequin, by Mestais, French, c1890, 18¼in (46.5cm) high.
£1,900–2,100
€2,700–3,000
$3,150–3,500 ⊞ BeF

A pair of bronze models of foxes, by Pierre Jules Mêne, French, late 19thC, 6in (15cm) high.
£3,600–4,000 / €5,200–5,800
$6,000–6,700 ⊞ BHa

◀ **A model of a thoroughbred stallion,** by Heinrich Hussmann, German, late 19thC, 16in (40.5cm) wide.
£4,850–5,400
€7,000–7,800
$8,100–9,100
⊞ RGa

An alabaster group, carved as the heads of two children embracing, Italian, late 19thC, 18½in (47cm) high.
£440–530 / €630–750
$740–890 ⚒ G(L)

A bronze figure, by Bessie Potter Vonnoh, entitled 'Girl Dancing', signed, American, c1900, 13in (33cm) high.
£6,400–7,700
€9,200–11,000
$10,800–12,900 ⚒ JAA

A bronze sculpture of a horse, by Pierre Tourgueneff, entitled 'Cheval Anglais', signed, French, late 19th–early 20thC, 18½in (47cm) high.
£2,400–2,900
€3,500–4,200
$4,100–4,900 ⚒ S(O)
Tourgueneff was born in Paris to Russian parents. He studied with Frémiet and became well known for his equestrian and military sculptures. He exhibited at the Salon between 1880 and 1911 and was awarded a 'Grand Prix' at the Exposition Universelle in 1889 and the Légion d'Honneur in 1903.

A marble and alabaster bust of a young lady, inscribed 'Bessier', signed, c1900, 13in (33cm) high.
£420–500 / €600–720
$700–840 ⚒ WL

▶ **A bronze figure,** by Comte d'Astanière, entitled 'Flower of the Water', French, c1900, 16¾in (42.5cm) high, on a marble socle.
£3,400–3,750
€4,900–5,400
$5,700–6,300 ⊞ MI

A pair of carved and painted wood figures, early 20thC, 70in (178cm) high.
£2,250–2,500
€3,250–3,600
$3,800–4,200 ⊞ NoC

▶ **A cast-lead model of a Newfoundland dog,** carrying three fox cubs in a canvas bag, late 19th/early 20thC, 8¾in (22cm) wide.
£190–220 / €270–320
$320–370 ⚒ DD

An equestrian group, by Thomas Cartier, French, c1920, 21¼in (54cm) wide.
£3,400–3,800 / €4,900–5,500
$5,700–6,400 ⊞ G&H
Trained by George Gardet, Cartier exhibited at the Salon des Artistes Français in 1900. He is particularly known for his sculptures of animals.

A bronze plaque, by Heinnach Kantsch, on a marble base, French, Paris, 1910, 11in (28cm) wide.
£1,400–1,550 / €2,000–2,200
$2,350–2,600 ⊞ MI

▶ **A cold-painted bronze model of a grouse,** with original paint, marked 'Bergman', Austrian, Vienna, c1910, 9in (23cm) high.
£1,800–2,000 / €2,600–2,900
$3,000–3,350 ⊞ RdeR

Metalware

Brass

An embossed brass alms dish, the centre depicting Adam and Eve, 17th/18thC, 18½in (47cm) diam.
£720–860 / €1,050–1,250
$1,200–1,450 ⚒ S(O)

A brass candlestick, c1720, 7¼in (18.5cm) high.
£145–165 / €210–240
$250–280 ⊞ F&F

A brass caster, the cover pierced with a flower-filled basket, with applied foliate cut-card work below the baluster finial, on a gadrooned foot, c1700, 7½in (19cm) high.
£1,900–2,250
€2,750–3,250
$3,200–3,800 ⚒ S

A brass candle mould, 19thC, 13in (33cm) high.
£450–500 / €650–720
$750–840 ⊞ SEA

A pair of brass telescopic candlesticks, 18thC, 9in (23cm) extended.
£520–580 / €750–840
$870–970 ⊞ KEY

► **A brass dog collar,** German, late 18thC, 6¾in (17cm) diam.
£400–450
€580–650
$670–760
⊞ GGv

◄ **A studded brass dog collar,** c1850, 8in (20.5cm) diam.
£540–600
€780–860
$900–1,000
⊞ RGe

► **A gilt-brass easel frame,** with stamped and applied foliate decoration, velvet-lined interior, with a hook, French, early 19thC, 8¼in (21cm) high.
£220–260 / €320–380
$370–440 ⚒ G(L)

A brass candle sconce, with a cut and engraved scrolling back panel, early 19thC, 9in (23cm) high.
£330–390 / €470–560
$550–660 ⚒ TMA

A brass candle holder, c1840, 18in (45.5cm) high.
£580–650 / €840–940
$970–1,100 ⊞ RGe

A brass candlestick, with a ridged stem and drip pan, 1670–80, 5½in (14cm) high.
£1,750–1,950
€2,500–2,800
$2,950–3,250 ⊞ KEY

A pair of Victorian brass candlesticks, modelled as a pair of sword hilts, the bases as three spurs, 12½in (31.5cm) high.
£440–530 / €630–750
$740–890 ⚒ L&E

A brass fob seal, with four matrices depicting a stag, a ship, a bird and a heart with arrows, 17thC, 1¼in (3cm) wide.
£410–490 / €590–710
$690–820 ⚒ F&C

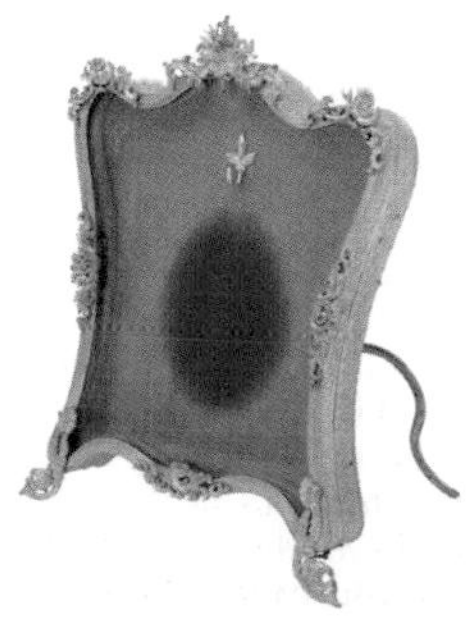

A brass easel triple photograph frame, with three folding sections, the front with a *pietra dura* foliate-inlaid panel, with a pierced foliate stand, 19thC, 11in (28cm) high.
£470–560 / €680–810
$790–940 ⚒ L&E

► **A brass inkstand,** mounted with mask heads, grotesque figures and fans, the two glass inkwells with hinged brass covers and Oriental figural finials, the stamp box with a hinged cover and eagle finial, late 19thC, 21in (53.5cm) wide.
£290–350 / €420–500
$490–590 ⚒ AG

◄ **A brass jardinière,** decorated in relief with fruit and fleur-de-lys motifs, the handles with ring terminals, on claw-and-ball feet, late 19th/early 20thC, 20½in (52cm) wide.
£130–155 / €190–220
$220–260 ⚒ PFK

A brass Hanukkah lamp, in the form of the temple in Jerusalem, surmounted by birds flanked by stylized lions, with associated candle branches, Polish, 18thC, 13¼in (33.5cm) high.
£2,100–2,500 / €3,000–3,600
$3,500–4,200 ⚒ DORO

A brass samovar, with turned wood bail handles and a spout, Russian, late 19thC, 24in (61cm) high.
£230–270 / €330–390
$380–450 ⚒ WW

► **A brass shaving mug,** 19thC, 5½in (14cm) high.
£250–280
€360–400
$420–470
⊞ SEA

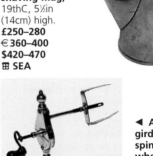

◄ **A brass girdle flax-spinning wheel,** Dutch, c1760, 8in (20.5cm) high.
£1,050–1,200
€1,600–1,800
$1,800–2,000
⊞ SEA

Bronze

A pair of bronze ewers, moulded with mythological animals, scrolls and designs, with applied putto handles, 19thC, 18in (45.5cm) high, on marble socles.
£680–820 / €1,000–1,200
$1,200–1,400 ⚒ GAK

A pair of bronze and ormolu ewers, decorated with cherubs portraying the Arts and Sciences, ormolu fruiting vines and acanthus leaves, late 19thC, 22¾in (58cm) high.
£940–1,100 / €1,350–1,600
$1,600–1,900 ⚒ SWO

A gilt-bronze inkstand, modelled as a cherub seated between two hinged drums, one an inkwell, the other a sander, French, 19thC, 8in (20.5cm) wide.
£240–280 / €340–400
$400–470 ⚒ HOLL

► **A bronze mortar,** bearing the coat-of-arms of Charles I, c1640, 6in (15cm) high.
£1,350–1,500
€1,950–2,150
$2,250–2,500
⊞ SEA

A bronze mortar, 17thC, 3½in (9cm) high.
£160–180 / €230–260
$270–300 ⊞ KEY

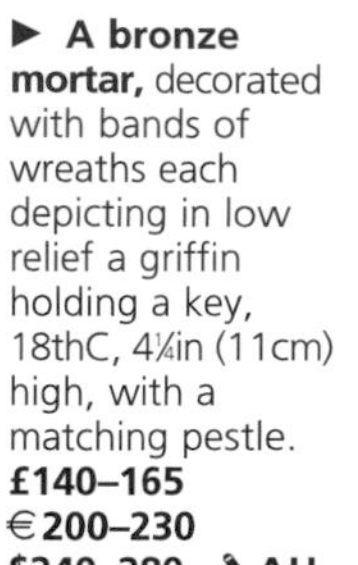

► **A bronze mortar,** decorated with bands of wreaths each depicting in low relief a griffin holding a key, 18thC, 4¼in (11cm) high, with a matching pestle.
£140–165
€200–230
$240–280 ⚒ AH

A George III bronze 7lb wool weight, cast with a royal coat-of-arms and GIIIR, stamped in the margin with a royal cypher, dagger stamp, two avoirdupois A and a ewer stamp, the top with a loophole, with a hollow back, 4¼in (11cm) wide.
£2,100–2,500
€3,000–3,600
$3,500–4,200 ⚒ B(L)
Wool weights date back to Edward IV and were used to check the accuracy of the 'trone', a beam used to weigh wool for tax purposes. Their flat shape allowed them to be carried easily by a horse. The marks stamped in the margin of weights were similar to those used in hallmarking silver. Wool was weighed by the 'tod' (28lbs). Most wool weights are, therefore, quarter tods (7lbs), although they can also be found in half tods and, very rarely, a full tod. Their rarity is due to the fact that, once they had passed their useful life, they were supposed to have been returned to Founders Hall in London, to be replaced by new weights.

A bronze tazza, by Ferdinand Levillain, with central relief decoration of a classical market scene within a border of palmettes and baskets of fruit, signed, inscribed 'F. Barbedienne', French, 19thC, 22½in (57cm) diam.
£2,150–2,600 / €3,100–3,700
$3,600–4,300 ⚒ S(O)
The central medallion on this tazza is typical of Levillain's work. Born in Passy in 1837, Levillain began his career under the tutelage of the sculptor Jouffroy and quickly developed a personal interest in working with bas-reliefs, plaques and medallions, using a mixture of historical, classical and genre subjects.

A pair of bronze campana urns, decorated with fire-gilded laurel wreaths and stylized mask mounts, c1820, 12½in (32cm) high.
£3,000–3,400 / €4,300–4,900
$5,000–5,700 ⊞ GDB

► **A pair of bronze vases and covers,** decorated with hunting trophies, c1870, 18in (45.5cm) high.
£2,650–2,950 / €3,900–4,300
$4,400–4,900 ⊞ RGa

Copper

◄ **A Baroque silvered-copper baptismal chalice,** with repoussé decoration, chased with foliage and scrolls, inscribed 'Hans Philips Finckel v Weinheim war getavft den 12. aug. Ao 1651', 'm' mark, base probably associated, German, dated 1651, 6¾in (17cm) high.
£820–980 / €1,200–1,400
$1,400–1,650 ⚒ S(Am)

A copper kettle, c1890, 10½in (26.5cm) high.
£100–115 / €145–165
$165–195 ⊞ AL

◄ **A copper jug,** with a brass seam, c1790, 8½in (21.5cm) high.
£165–185 / €240–270
$280–310 ⊞ F&F

A copper half-gallon 'haystack' measure, with a brass seam, c1840, 8in (20.5cm) high.
£130–145 / €190–210
$220–250 ⊞ F&F

A copper quart measure, c1850, 5½in (14cm) high.
£150–165 / €210–240
$250–280 ⊞ MFB

A copper watering can, 18thC, 15½in (39.5cm) high.
£260–310 / €380–450
$440–530 ⚒ DMC

Iron

◄ A wrought-iron candle and rush holder, 18thC, 4½in (11.5cm) high.
£360–400 / €520–580
$600–670 ⊞ SEA
This is an unusual form of candlestick as it can also hold a lighted rush. The rushes would have been collected from ditches, then cut to length and dried. The skin would have been pulled off all of it but the back strip, to give support, then passed through a grisset (a type of pan) containing tallow, and then dried again. The rushlight would have been gripped by the flange on the side of the candlestick. This piece allows you the choice of using a rushlight or a candle. Rushlighting was dirty and smelly, but was cheaper than using candles.

A cast-iron doorstop, cast as a pug dog, c1890, 10in (25.5cm) wide.
£175–195 / €250–280
$290–320 ⊞ WAA

► A cast-iron medallion of the State Seal of New York, with the arms of New York within a Latin inscription, c1930, 17½in (44.5cm) diam.
£1,000–1,200
€1,500–1,750
$1,700–2,000 ⚒ S(NY)

► A painted iron sign, for a gentleman's hat shop, c1850, 46in (117cm) wide.
£960–1,150
€1,400–1,650
$1,600–1,900
⚒ S(O)

Ormolu

► An ormolu jewellery casket, the cover engraved and cast with flowers and scrolls, surmounted by an angel holding a vacant shield for a picture, suspended with floral swags, the body set with four porcelain plaques, the corners set with leaf scrolls and ram's-head masks, on scrolled feet, velvet-lined interior, French, late 19thC, 11½in (29cm) wide.
£800–960 / €1,200–1,400
$1,350–1,600 ⚒ BR

An ormolu and rock crystal model of a sledge, on a malachite plinth, Russian, 19thC, 5in (12.5cm) wide.
£470–560 / €680–810
$790–940 ⚒ G(L)

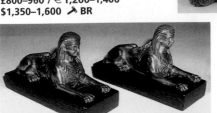

◄ A pair of ormolu sphynx paperweights, on later mahogany plinths, 19thC, 5in (13cm) wide.
£200–240 / €300–350
$340–400 ⚒ Bri

Sets/pairs

Unless otherwise stated, any description which refers to 'a set' or 'a pair' includes a guide price for the entire set or the pair, even though the illustration may show only a single item.

Pewter

Pewter is an alloy of tin hardened with small amounts of other metals such as copper, lead or antimony. The craft of pewtering started in antiquity – the earliest known item, a flask dating from c1350 BC, was found in Egypt. Pewter is believed to have been introduced to Britain by the Romans, who exploited the main source of tin in Europe at the time, which was in Cornwall. The craft fell into decline after the Romans withdrew from Britain but it is thought that the Cistercian monks reintroduced it after the Norman Conquest in AD 1066. Production spread throughout the country with a wide range of mainly domestic goods being made.

In 1348 articles granted to the Worshipful Company of Pewterers in London enabled them to control the quality of pewter and, to facilitate this, each maker had to strike a unique mark, called a touchmark, on his goods.

Collecting pewter became popular in the late 19th century. The Society of Pewter Collectors was formed in 1918 which today, under the name of the Pewter Society, has worldwide membership. Pewter has always been scarce as it was traditionally recycled and, with its low melting point, was easily lost in fires. When demand exceeds supply, such as in the 1920s and '30s, fakes as well as bona fide reproductions entered the market, but through the work of the Pewter Society these can now be more easily identified.

Many fine items can be seen in museums, particularly the Museum of British Pewter at Harvard House, Stratford-on-Avon, Warwickshire. Many more, however, are in private collections, and these tend to re-enter the market every 20 years or so, although previously unknown pieces also surface regularly. Pewter is still very affordable – 250 year-old plates with makers' marks can sell for under £100 / €145 / $170 although exceptional items can command four-figure sums. While many collectors concentrate on the golden age of English pewter production from c1660 to 1710, others prefer perhaps 19th-century tankards or Georgian spoons. In the last decade Art Nouveau pewter, especially Liberty's Tudric range, has become very sought after.

The craft still flourishes, particularly in Birmingham and Sheffield, where both traditional and contemporary wares are being produced. Modern designers are recognizing the inherent beauty and versatility of this lovely metal. **David Moulson**

A baby's pewter feeding bottle, c1850, 6in (15cm) high.
£310–350 / €450–500
$520–580 ⊞ CuS

A pair of 17thC-style pewter candlesticks, 19thC, 16¼in (41.5cm) high.
£600–720 / €880–1,050
$1,000–1,200 ⚒ S(O)

A pewter centrepiece, decorated with cast acanthus scrolls, with opposing cartouches depicting a nude female and a putto, the handles in the form of nude females, with a silvered-metal liner, probably German, c1895, 11½in (29cm) wide.
£750–900 / €1,100–1,300
$1,250–1,500 ⚒ NOA

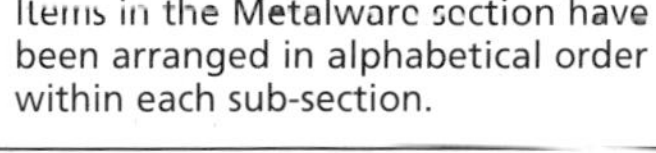
Items in the Metalware section have been arranged in alphabetical order within each sub-section.

A pewter charger and strainer, both with ownership initials on front rims, touchmark of A. Nicholson, c1750, 22½in (57cm) wide.
£1,750–1,950 / €2,500–2,800
$2,950–3,300 ⊞ HWK

◄ **A pewter coffee pot,** with rococo wrythen decoration, German, c1780, 10½in (26.5cm) high.
£580–650 / €850–940
$980–1,100 ⊞ HWK

A pewter dish, by Richard King Jnr, London, with an engraved crest to the front rim, c1760, 17in (43cm) wide.
£150–180 / €220–260
$250–300 ⚒ G(L)

A pewter ewer, German, mid-18thC, 8in (20.5cm) high.
£580–650 / €850–940
$1,000–1,100 ⊞ HWK

◄ A pewter flagon, the heart-shaped lid with a twin acorn thumbpiece, crown GR mark to neck, Channel Islands, 18thC, 11¼in (28.5cm) high.
£700–840
€1,000–1,200
$1,200–1,400
B(NW)

A pewter lidded flagon, decorated with wriggle-work, the initials 'JGE' and date '1832' within a heart, probably Swiss, early 19thC, 8in (20.5cm) high.
£850–950 / €1,200–1,350
$1,450–1,600 ⊞ HWK

► A pewter inkstand, possibly Continental, c1800, 9in (23cm) wide.
£540–600 / €780–860
$910–1,000 ⊞ HWK

A pair of pewter loving cups, early 19thC, 6¼in (16cm) high.
£580–650 / €850–940
$950–1,050 ⊞ HWK

► A pewter half-pint baluster measure, by John Fasson, London, with a double volute thumbpiece, c1740, 4in (10cm) high.
£580–650
€850–940
$950–1,050
⊞ SEA

A pewter spouted gallon measure, the handle with a lug and initials 'IFC', the body inscribed 'J. Francis Coach & Horses Mount Strt', touchmarks to base, 18thC, 11¼in (28.5cm) high.
£640–770 / €920–1,100
$1,050–1,250 B(NW)

A Jersey-style pewter half-pint measure, 19thC, 4¾in (12cm) high.
£220–250 / €320–360
$370–420 ⊞ DML

A pewter quart measure, Jersey, early 19thC, 8in (20.5cm) high.
£760–850 / €1,100–1,250
$1,300–1,450 ⊞ HWK

◄ A set of four pewter 'haystack' measures, by Joseph Austen & Son, Cork stamped on base, Irish, 19thC, largest 7½in (19cm) high.
£1,700–1,900 / €2,450–2,750
$2,850–3,150 ⊞ HWK
These measures are so-called because they resemble haystacks.

A pewter lidded measure, with a shell thumbpiece and decorated spout, French, 1800–20, 10in (25.5cm) high.
£630–700 / €910–1,000
$1,050–1,150 ⊞ HWK

A pewter plate, by John French, with triple reeding, hallmarked, late 17thC, 17in (43cm) diam.
£440–490 / €640–710
$740–820 ⊞ KEY

A set of four pewter plates, by Johan Caspar Ritter, with rococo-style edges, Austrian, Innsbruck, late 18thC, 9¾in (25cm) diam.
£1,000–1,100 / €1,450–1,600
$1,650–1,850 ⊞ HWK

► A pewter plate, with a gadrooned edge, late 18thC, 9½in (24cm) diam.
£310–350 / €450–500
$520–580 ⊞ HWK

A matched set of six Georgian pewter plates, by William Fasson and another maker, all with an engraved crest to the rim, largest 10in (25.5cm) diam.
£190–220 / €280–320
$320–370 ⚒ G(L)

A pewter porringer, early 18thC, 5½in (14cm) diam.
£810–900 / €1,150–1,300
$1,350–1,500 ⊞ DML

A pewter cup salt, late 18thC, 2in (5cm) high.
£135–150 / €195–220
$220–250 ⊞ DML

► A pewter spice pot, 1720–50, 4in (10cm) high.
£400–450
€570–650
$670–750
⊞ DML

A pewter tankard, with a double domed top and open chair thumbpiece, possibly Bristol, c1780, 7½in (19cm) high.
£1,300–1,450 / €1,900–2,100
$2,200–2,450 ⊞ HWK

A pewter urn, with a lift-off cover and filter, lion-mask ring handles and brass tap, on a stepped column with compressed ball feet, 19thC, 12½in (32cm) high.
£150–180 / €220–260
$250–300 ⚒ TMA

A pewter spouted wine pot, the body initialled 'IBK' and decorated with flowers, German, Munich, dated 1724, 8½in (21.5cm) high.
£700–780 / €1,000–1,100
$1,200–1,350 ⊞ HWK

Steel

A steel box, with loops at the sides and pendants at either end, one side decorated with flower scrolls, the other inscribed 'When thes ye sie remembre Dawid Bellie A.M. 1678', 4in (10cm) long.
£960–1,150 / €1,400–1,650
$1,600–1,900 ⚒ B(L)

► **A steel casket,** inlaid with Indian-style gold and silver damascening, the cover inscribed 'E. Arnall', possibly Spanish, Toledo, 19thC, 8½in (21.5cm) wide.
£140–165 / €200–230
$240–280 ⚒ G(L)

► **A steel sewing clamp,** with a sliding drawer, Russian, Tula, 18thC, 5½in (14cm) high.
£2,000–2,250
€3,000–3,300
$3,400–3,800
⊞ ICO

The Tula ironworks

The Tula ironworks were founded in central Russia by Peter the Great to make small arms, but by 1725 had been partly converted into a factory making steel furniture and small ornaments. By 1736, the factory was producing large quantities of decorative objects and later in the 18th century was greatly patronized by Catherine the Great. At the time, Tula pieces were very expensive, and because of their rarity and desirability they still command a premium today.

Toleware

A toleware box, inscribed 'May we always have a friend...', c1790, 5in (12.5cm) wide.
£400–450 / €580–650
$670–750 ⊞ RdeR

A pair of toleware seated cats, on painted oak bases, early 19thC, 8¼in (21cm) high.
£2,150–2,550 / €3,100–3,700
$3,600–4,300 ⚒ S(O)

A japanned toleware tea caddy, the hinged cover and side panels painted with birds and butterflies within gilt foliate scroll cartouches, with an integral lock, c1840, 6in (15cm) wide.
£105–125 / €150–180
$175–210 ⚒ BR

A painted toleware tray, losses, possibly Welsh, Pontypool, c1760, 29in (74cm) diam.
£1,400–1,650 / €2,000–2,350
$2,350–2,750 ⚒ S(NY)

Toleware is japanned tin-plated ironware, made in imitation of the imported Chinese lacquer wares that were popular in the 18th century. The most desirable toleware comes from Pontypool in South Wales, produced at a factory founded in the 18th century by Thomas Allgood, who discovered that a by-product of the coal that was mined locally could be applied as a varnish to objects made of thinly-rolled iron plates. This varnish was applied in several layers, each being fired at high temperature, which rendered the finished object extremely durable. The factory remained in operation until 1820, but a rival concern in nearby Usk owned by two of Allgood's grandsons, continued until the mid-19th century. Another member of the family founded a japanning factory in Birmingham, which became the main centre of the industry during the 19th century.

◄ **A toleware tray,** with leaf decoration, c1825, 26in (66cm) wide.
£1,100–1,250 / €1,600–1,800
$1,900–2,100 ⊞ RGe

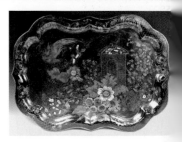

► **A toleware tray,** decorated with mother-of-pearl and painted with a bird and flowers, 19thC, 29½in (75cm) wide.
£260–310 / €370–440
$440–520 ⚒ SWO

Leather

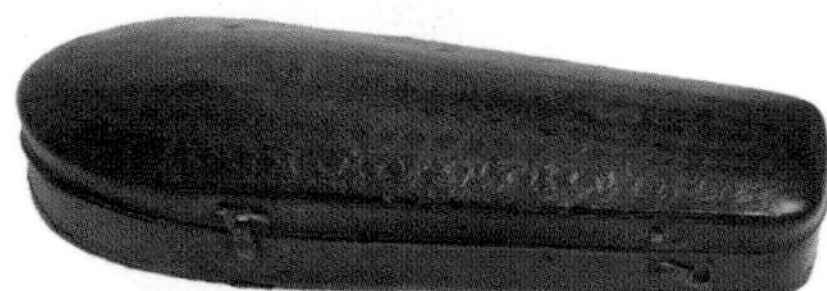

◄ **A leather coffin-shaped box,** c1800, 6in (15cm) long.
£90–100 / €130–145
$150–170 MB
These boxes are sometimes called cabinet maker's finger coffins.

A tooled leather-covered casket, with metal handles, Italian, late 18th/early 19thC, 12¼in (31cm) wide.
£260–310 / €380–450
$440–520 HOLL

A set of decorated leather chair-backs, four singles and two armchairs, naively painted with figures, beasts and landscapes, unmounted, 1600–50, 21in (53.5cm) square.
£2,600–3,100 / €3,700–4,400
$4,350–5,200 GH

A Victorian leather dog collar, with engraved steel mounts.
£230–270 / €330–390
$380–450 Bri

► **A painted leather fire bucket,** with a padded collar and leather-covered rope handle, some repairs, American, Massachusetts, c1811, 14in (35.5cm) high.
£1,400–1,650 / €2,000–2,350
$2,350–2,800 SK

► **A painted leather fire bucket,** some wear, American, early 19thC, 17¾in (45cm) high.
£660–790
€950–1,100
$1,100–1,300
SK

◄ **A Victorian leather fire bucket,** with a copper border, printed with the royal coat-of-arms, 12¼in (31cm) high.
£290–350 / €420–500
$490–590 DN

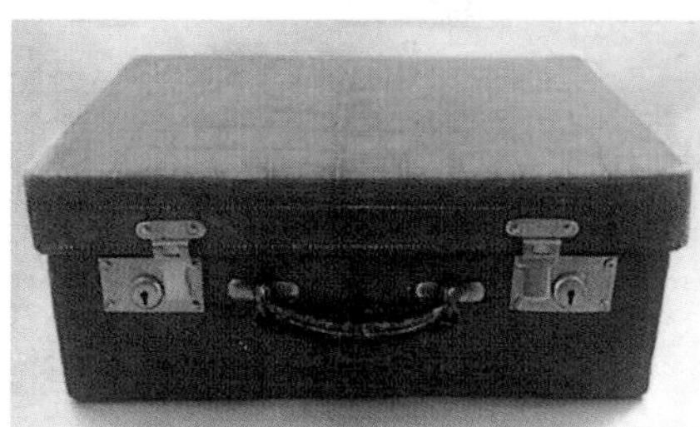

A crocodile skin suitcase, with chrome-plated fittings and locks, enclosing a watered silk interior, early 20thC, 18in (45.5cm) wide.
£200–240 / €300–350
$340–400 BR

A gilt tooled leather postal pouch, the interior with four compartments, dated 1743, 7in (18cm) wide.
£540–650 / €780–930
$920–1,100 S(O)

A leather vessel, applied with arched handles and a decorative band, damage to rim, 17thC, 9¾in (25cm) high.
£360–430 / €520–620
$600–720 B

◄ **A Louis Vuitton leather suitcase,** early 20thC, 26in (66cm) wide.
£760–910 / €1,100–1,300
$1,300–1,550 EH

A Victorian morocco leather stationery and writing case, by Castrell & Co, the lid with a white metal monogram, with a fitted interior and Bramah lock, 24¾in (63cm) wide.
£200–240 / €300–350
$340–400 WilP

Papier-Mâché

A Victorian papier-mâché *aide mémoire*, the floral-painted covers containing six ivory fillets, 4in (10cm) wide.
£220–260 / €320–380
$370–440 TMA

► **A papier-mâché dish,** hand-painted with a scene entitled 'Return from the Warren', c1840, 13in (33cm) diam.
£270–300 / €390–430
$450–500 HTE

A papier-mâché snuff box, painted with the goddess Diana, French, c1830, 4in (10cm) diam.
£450–500 / €650–720
$760–840 RdeR

A pair of Victorian papier-mâché snuffer trays, decorated in gilt with a peacock and insects, 10in (25.5cm) wide.
£410–490 / €590–700
$690–820 WW

An early Victorian lacquered papier-mâché box, by Jennens & Bettridge, inlaid with mother-of-pearl, stamped and numbered 29, 6½in (16.5cm) wide.
£130–155 / €185–220
$220–260 PFK

A papier-mâché tea tray, by Walton & Co, painted with a view of the river at Cork enclosed by a vermicular and acanthus leaf gilt border, impressed mark and painted title to reverse, mid-19thC, 25½in (65cm) wide.
£2,900–3,500 / €4,200–5,000
$4,900–5,900 B

Benjamin Walton took over the running of the firm of Walton & Co at Old Hall in Wolverhampton (previously known as Ryton & Walton) in 1842 when William Ryton, his partner, died. Under his direction the firm produced a wide range of decorative papier-mâché wares until his death in 1847. Walton & Co are associated with a series of these so-called 'gothic' trays, which were well painted with all-over landscapes. These trays are seldom, if ever, signed by the artist but generally bear the company's impressed mark. Most have survived in very good condition which suggests that they were looked upon as decorative pictures and rarely used as tea trays.

◄ **A Victorian papier-mâché tray,** painted with flowers, with a gilt-decorated border, damaged, stamped 'B. Walton Warranted', 27in (68.5cm) wide.
£190–220 / €280–320
$320–380 NSal

A Victorian papier-mâché writing box, the cover painted with Crystal Palace within a gilt and mother-of-pearl-inlaid reserve, the interior with a writing surface, inkwell and pen rest, 10¼in (26cm) wide.
£270–320 / €390–460
$450–540 Bri

A pair of painted papier-mâché panels, by Jennens & Bettridge, each entitled 'The Mask' and depicting a different lady, both titled and inscribed, c1860, 11½ x 8¾in (29 x 22cm).
£470–560 / €680–810
$790–940 TEN

Jennens & Bettridge (1816–64) was founded when the firm took over the Birmingham factory of Henry Clay. They also had a showroom in Belgrave Square, London. By 1825, they had been appointed Japanners in Ordinary to George IV, and in later years they received commissions from William IV and Queen Victoria. They exhibited a variety of wares at the Great Exhibition in 1851.

A papier-mâché tray, by Vishniakov depicting children at play, medal of merit mark, Russian, c1889, 7in (18cm) square.
£450–500 / €650–720
$760–840 RdeR

Treen

A carved pine and birch ceremonial ale jug, Norwegian, c1800, 15¾in (40cm) high.
£2,700–3,000 / €3,900–4,300
$4,500–5,000 ⊞ RYA

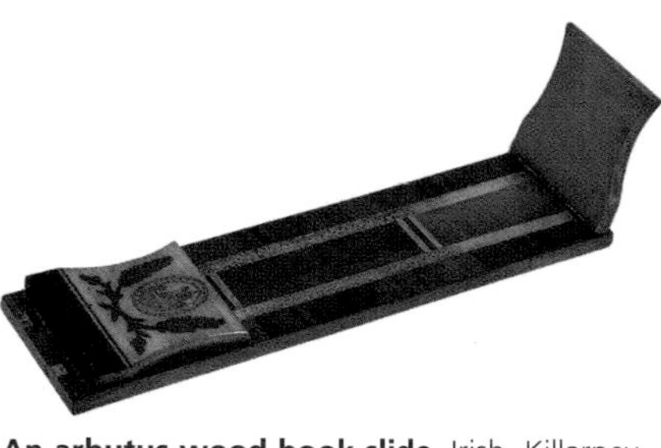

An arbutus wood book slide, Irish, Killarney, c1870, 15in (38cm) wide.
£430–480 / €620–690
$730–800 ⊞ STA

A pair of Victorian turned fruitwood candle stands, by Edmund Nye, Tunbridge Wells, with adjustable tops, label to underside, 9¼in (23.5cm) high.
£2,150–2,600 / €3,100–3,700
$3,600–4,300 ⚒ S(NY)

Edmund Nye (1797–1863), the son of Tunbridge ware manufacturer James Nye, formed a partnership on his father's death with William Fenner, which was dissolved in 1817. Although Fenner proved to be the more successful of the two, Nye took advantage of the latter's retirement in 1840 and later advertised himself as 'Manufacturer...to the Queen and the Royal Family'.

An oak ballot box, c1890, 9in (23cm) wide.
£720–800 / €1,050–1,200
$1,200–1,350 ⊞ GEO

◄ **A mahogany book tray,** c1830, 16¾in (42.5cm) wide.
£270–300 / €390–430
$450–500 ⊞ F&F

A lignum vitae wassail bowl, cracked, 17thC, 8¾in (22cm) high.
£4,250–5,100
€6,100–7,300
$7,100–8,550 ⚒ F&C

A coconut shell box, the cover with a pineapple finial, the body carved with a royal coat-of-arms, hares and monkeys, on ball feet, c1790, 6in (15cm) high.
£1,100–1,250
€1,600–1,800
$1,850–2,100 ⊞ JTS

► **A carved birch and pine butter jar and cover,** inscribed, initialled 'ICDN' and dated 1869, Norwegian, 10in (25.5cm) high.
£680–750 / €970–1,100
$1,150–1,250 ⊞ RYA

A fretwork fruitwood birdcage, French, late 19thC, 36¾in (93.5cm) wide.
£720–860 / €1,050–1,250
$1,300–1,450 ⚒ S(O)

A pair of oak candlesticks, late 18thC, 9in (23cm) high.
£1,200–1,400 / €1,800–2,000
$2,100–2,350 ⊞ SEA

A coquilla nut box, with turned and incised decoration, the centre unscrewing to reveal a miniature china-headed doll, mid-19thC, 3in (7.5cm) high.
£380–450 / €550–660
$640–770 ⚒ PFK

A wooden cheese coaster, c1810, 16¼in (41.5cm) wide.
£540–600 / €780–860
$900–1,000 ⊞ F&F

◄ A Regency mahogany candlestick, with an acid-etched storm glass, 24in (61cm) high.
£420–500 / €600–720
$700–840 ⚒ G(B)

A turned mahogany coaster, early 19thC, 9¾in (25cm) diam.
£130–155 / €185–220
$220–260 ⚒ WW

A carved walnut inkstand, with animal and serpent-carved handles, the centre with a nib/wafer box with a cherub surmount flanked by glass inkwells, late 19thC, 19in (48.5cm) wide.
£200–240 / €290–350
$340–400 ⚒ DMC

A Black Forest wooden inkwell, carved as a hinged dog's head, with inset glass eyes, enclosing a compartment for tobacco or an inkwell, German, late 19thC, 6¾in (17cm) high.
£1,150–1,350 / €1,650–1,950
$1,950–2,250 ⚒ Bea

An oak signpost desk calendar, with ivory markers, impressed registration stamp, some losses and damage, late 19thC, 12½in (32cm) high.
£530–590 / €770–850
$890–990 ⚒ SWO

◄ A dug-out and carved birchwood double horse-head *kasa*, inscribed '1803', Norwegian, 10¾in (27.5cm) wide.
£2,250–2,500 / €3,250–3,600
$3,800–4,200 ⊞ RYA

A carved fruitwood knife case, by Thomas Smith, the front decorated with panels depicting figures, insignia and inscriptions, the reverse with panels depicting a figure and a dog, signed 'Thomas Smithe Made me Anno 1600', 9½in (24cm) long.
£2,350–2,800 / €3,400–4,100
$3,950–4,700 ⚒ B(Kn)

A pair of stained sycamore love spoons, one dated 1837 with twin spoon bowls, the other with four fig-shaped bowls, damaged and repaired, Welsh, larger 17½in (44.5cm) long.
£880–1,050
€1,250–1,500
$1,500–1,800 ⚒ PF

An Edwardian mahogany lazy Susan, 15in (38cm) diam.
£100–115 / €145–165
$170–195 ⊞ WAA

► A wooden mangling board, the handle in the form of a lion, the board decorated with scrolling acanthus, traces of polychrome paint, Norwegian, late 18thC, 28in (71cm) long.
£840–1,000
€1,200–1,400
$1,400–1,650 ⚒ S(O)

◄ **A Regency painted boxwood nutmeg grater,** modelled as a cottage with a central chimney, 2¾in (7cm) high.
£390–400 / €530–630
$620–740 ⚒ AH

A Black Forest carved walnut pipe bowl, in the form of an eagle's head with glass inset eyes and ivory beak, on a stag horn base, German, early 20thC, 3½in (9cm) high.
£260–310 / €380–450
$440–520 ⚒ BR

A burrwood pipe, 18thC, 8¾in (22cm) long.
£220–260 / €310–370
$370–440 ⚒ S(O)

◄ **A boxwood pokerwork pin box,** 1860–70, 3½in (9cm) high.
£135–150 / €200–220
$230–260 ⊞ RdeR

A carved bog oak pot, c1860, 1in (2.5cm) high.
£40–45 / €55–65
$65–75 ⊞ STA

A coconut shell snuff box, French, c1780, 3in (7.5cm) diam.
£450–500 / €650–720
$760–840 ⊞ AEF

A carved coquilla nut snuff box, French, c1790, 5in (12.5cm) long.
£850–950 / €1,200–1,350
$1,400–1,550 ⊞ AEF

A coquilla nut powder jar, with engine-turned decoration, containing a feather puff, c1880, 2¼in (5.5cm) high.
£70–80 / €100–110
$115–130 ⊞ MB

A fruitwood snuff box, with a sliding cover, c1800, 3in (7.5cm) diam.
£180–200 / €260–290
$300–330 ⊞ MB

An ebonized wood snuff box, carved as a monkey's head, c1800, 3in (7.5cm) wide.
£850–950 / €1,200–1,350
$1,450–1,600 ⊞ AEF

A coquilla nut snuff box, carved as a laughing monkey, French, c1800, 4in (10cm) high.
£1,100–1,250
€1,600–1,800
$1,900–2,100 ⊞ AEF

A burr-walnut snuff box, the cover carved with three crania, the box lined with tortoiseshell, French, c1810, 4in (10cm) diam.
£880–980
€1,250–1,400
$1,500–1,650 ⊞ RdeR
The underside of this box is inscribed with information relating to phrenology, the study of the shape and size of the cranium as a supposed indicator of characteristic traits, first promulgated by Dr Franz Gall at the end of the 18th century.

◄ **A carved coquilla nut snuff box,** French, c1820, 3in (7.5cm) wide.
£160–180 / €230–260
$270–300 ⊞ MB

TREEN

A maple snuff box, with traces of original paint, 19thC, 3in (7.5cm) wide.
£105–120 / €150–170
$175–200 ⊞ SEA

A sycamore spoon, inscribed 'AR', Welsh, dated 1796, 7in (18cm) long.
£350–390 / €500–550
$590–650 ⊞ SEA

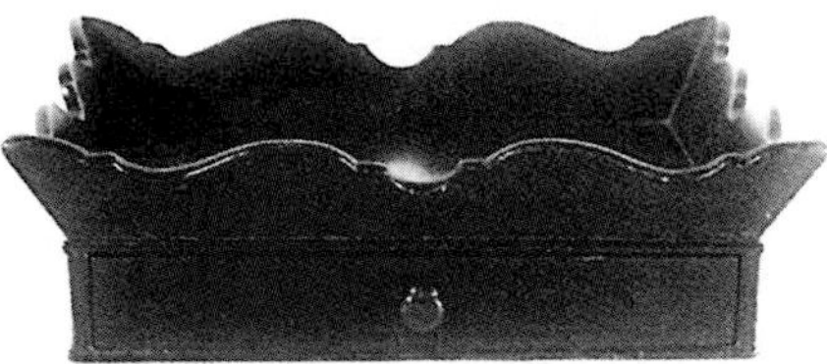

A George III mahogany stationery tray, with a waved gallery and a frieze drawer, 9½in (24cm) wide.
£490–590 / €710–850
$820–990 ⚒ L&E

► A lignum vitae tobacco box, c1850, 9in (23cm) high.
£70–80 / €100–110
$115–130 ⊞ MB

An oak table snuff box, c1830, 4¼in (11cm) diam.
£135–150 / €200–220
$220–250 ⊞ MB
This box was made from oak retrieved from the fire at York Minster in 1829.

A mahogany and pin-work snuff shoe, the cover inscribed 'Reform' in pin-work, slight losses, early 19thC, 4in (10cm) wide.
£170–200 / €240–290
$280–330 ⚒ BR
The inscription on this item possibly refers to the 1832 Reform Bill. For more information on this see page 240.

◄ A turned fruitwood spice jar and cover, the cover with an acorn finial, the body with two applied prunts, early 19thC, 7½in (19cm) high.
£350–420 / €500–600
$590–700 ⚒ WW

A birch love token washing bat, with carved and painted decoration, initialled 'KJED', dated 1821, 13½in (34.5cm) high.
£680–750 / €970–1,100
$1,150–1,250 ⊞ RYA

Miller's Compares

I. A George III fruitwood tea canister, carved as a melon with a stalk, 5¾in (14.5cm) high.
£4,100–4,900 / €5,900–7,000
$6,900–8,200 ⚒ L&T

II. A George III fruitwood tea canister, carved as a pear with a stalk, 7in (18cm) high.
£2,350–2,800 / €3,400–4,000
$3,950–4,700 ⚒ L&T

These two fruitwood tea canisters are of similar date and have both been restored. The melon shape, however, is seen far less commonly than the pear, which resulted in Item I selling for almost twice as much as Item II, even though the latter is larger.

► A walnut watch stand, the inlaid sunburst face inset with a fixed watch movement, 18thC, 14in (35.5cm) high.
£220–260
€320–380
$370–440
⚒ TMA

An inlaid mahogany watch stand, the upper section with a hinged lid and fall-front, 19thC, 9½in (24cm) wide.
£165–195 / €240–280
$280–330 ⚒ TRM

Tunbridge Ware

A Tunbridge ware work basket, printed with views of the Royal Mews and Donaldson's Library, Brighton, c1810, 8¼in (21cm) wide.
£1,350–1,550 / €1,950–2,250
$2,250–2,600 ⊞ AMH

A pair of Tunbridge ware bonnet stands, attributed to Thomas Barton, c1880, 12in (30.5cm) high.
£1,950–2,200 / €2,800–3,150
$3,250–3,700 ⊞ AMH

A Tunbridge ware rosewood book stand, with floral mosaic borders and panels, c1860, 10in (25.5cm) wide.
£440–490 / €630–710
$740–820 ⊞ GGD

A Tunbridge ware box, c1810, 10½in (26.5cm) wide.
£440–490 / €630–710
$740–820 ⊞ F&F

A Tunbridge ware ebony games box, possibly by Thomas Barton, inlaid with mosaic flower sprays, with a fitted interior, 19thC, 27in (68.5cm) wide.
£520–620 / €750–890
$870–1,050 ⚒ BR

A Tunbridge ware box, painted with flower garlands, with an enamel plaque inscribed 'A present from Bath', c1820, 6½in (16.5cm) wide.
£450–500 / €650–720
$750–840 ⊞ RdeR

A Victorian Tunbridge ware rosewood glove box, the hinged cover decorated with a bullfinch within cubework borders, lined with silk, 9½in (24cm) wide.
£360–430 / €520–620
$600–720 ⚒ TMA

A Tunbridge ware box, c1880, 6in (15cm) square.
£150–165 / €220–250
$250–280 ⊞ HTE

A Tunbridge ware rosewood jewellery box, inlaid with a stag, lined with silk, 19thC, 6in (15cm) wide.
£120–145 / €175–210
$200–240 ⚒ SWO

A Tunbridge ware glove darner, c1880, 5¾in (14.5cm) long.
£105–125 / €150–180
$175–210 ⊞ VB

A Tunbridge ware needlecase, painted with scenes of Brighton, c1820, 3in (7.5cm) wide.
£270–300 / €390–430
$450–500 ⊞ RdeR

Early Tunbridge ware consisted of simple wood wares which were often painted or decorated with printed paper labels.

A Tunbridge ware turned tambour holder, containing implements, c1850, 3¼in (8.5cm) high.
£310–350 / €440–500
$520–590 ⊞ VB

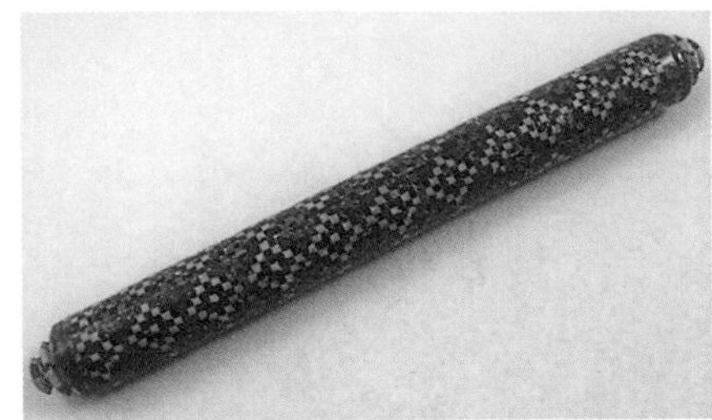

A Tunbridge ware needlecase, with tesserae mosaic shaft and turned ends, 19thC, 4in (10cm) long.
£260–310 / €370–440
$440–520 ⚒ BR

A Tunbridge ware tea caddy, inlaid with St George and the Dragon and a geometric mosaic, with compressed shavings veneer, c1845, 12in (30.5cm) wide.
£2,500–2,750 / €3,600–4,000
$4,200–4,650 ⊞ AMH

A Tunbridge ware whitewood nutmeg grater, printed with a view of Brighton Pavilion, 19thC, 2¾in (7cm) diam.
£350–420 / €500–600
$590–710 ⚒ BR

◄ **A Tunbridge ware paperweight,** c1880, 2¾in (7cm) diam.
£220–250 / €320–360
$370–420 ⊞ VB

A Tunbridge ware double tea caddy, decorated with flowers, containing four canisters and two mixing bowls, mid-19thC, 16½in (42cm) wide.
£3,000–3,600 / €4,300–5,200
$5,000–6,000 ⚒ CGC

A Tunbridge ware rosewood writing slope, c1825, 11in (28cm) wide.
£1,250–1,400 / €1,800–2,000
$2,100–2,350 ⊞ HAA

A Tunbridge ware tea caddy, the cover decorated with roses, c1860, 5¼in (13.5cm) wide.
£450–500 / €650–720
$750–840 ⊞ JTS

A Tunbridge ware tea caddy, c1860, 6in (15cm) high.
£1,500–1,650 / €2,150–2,400
$2,500–2,750 ⊞ PGO

A Victorian Tunbridge ware rosewood writing slope, depicting a castle within a floral border, with a fitted interior comprising two inkwells and a stamp box, one marked 'Thomas Barton, Tunbridgeware Manufacturer, Mount Ephraim, Tunbridge Wells', 14½in (37cm) wide.
£940–1,100 / €1,350–1,600
$1,550–1,850 ⚒ WilP

► **A Victorian Tunbridge ware rosewood writing slope,** with a fitted interior, c1860, 12¼in (31cm) wide.
£840–1,000
€1,200–1,450
$1,400–1,650 ⚒ S(O)

Boxes

A velvet-covered and gilt-metal-mounted casket, with swing handles, damaged, Italian, 15thC, 7½in (19cm) wide.
£1,450–1,750 / €2,100–2,500
$2,450–2,950 ⚒ S(Am)

A lacquer tea caddy, decorated in gold leaf with Chinese figures, with a lead lining, 18thC, 8in (20.5cm) wide.
£310–350 / €450–500
$520–590 ⊞ LBr

A mahogany tea caddy, with a brass rococo-style handle and escutcheon, c1770, 10in (25.5cm) wide.
£290–320 / €410–460
$480–540 ⊞ GGD

An inlaid satinwood tea caddy, c1875, 4in (10cm) square.
£1,050–1,200 / €1,500–1,750
$1,750–2,000 ⊞ WAA

An oysterwork and walnut-veneered lace box, inlaid with stained ivory flowers within a crossbanded surround, damaged, c1700, 19½in (49.5cm) wide.
£1,500–1,800 / €2,200–2,600
$2,500–3,000 ⚒ B(WM)

An oak tea caddy, with laburnum crossbandings and a secret spoon drawer, c1760, 9in (23cm) wide.
£1,150–1,300 / €1,650–1,850
$1,950–2,200 ⊞ JTS

A padouk wood tea caddy, with brass mounts, c1775, 10in (25.5cm) wide.
£260–290 / €370–420
$440–490 ⊞ WAA

A satin birch and marquetry tea caddy, the hinged top enclosing a foil-lined interior, c1785, 4½in (11.5cm) wide.
£720–860 / €1,050–1,250
$1,200–1,450 ⚒ S(O)

A walnut and featherbanded table bureau, the oak interior with three drawers and four pigeonholes, c1705, 15¾in (40cm) wide.
£1,800–2,150 / €2,600–3,100
$3,000–3,600 ⚒ S(O)

A George III mahogany work box, in the form of a house, the hinged cover and watch holder forming the roof, the interior with a lift-out tray, 13¼in (33.5cm) wide.
£7,700–9,200 / €11,100–13,300
$13,000–15,500 ⚒ SWO

A mahogany tea caddy, the cover inlaid with a satinwood and rosewood medallion and burr-yew spandrels, containing two canisters, c1785, 8½in (22cm) wide.
£1,900–2,250 / €2,750–3,250
$3,200–3,800 ⚒ WL

A harewood and sycamore tea caddy, c1790, 5½in (14cm) high.
£1,400–1,600 / €2,000–2,300
$2,350–2,700 ⊞ HAA

A mid-Georgian Chippendale-style mahogany tea caddy, inlaid with floral motifs and crossbanding, 7in (18cm) wide.
£550–660 / €790–950
$920–1,100 TMA

An ivory tea caddy, with tortoiseshell edging and silver handle, escutcheon and plate, c1790, 4¾in (12cm) high.
£3,600–4,000 / €5,200–5,800
$6,000–6,700 HAA

A George III stained tortoiseshell tea caddy, with ivory stringing and a metal loop handle and escutcheon, 6in (15cm) high.
£4,950–5,900 / €7,100–8,500
$8,300–9,900 LFA

A harewood tea caddy, inlaid with a shell and fan, yew medallions and flutes, c1790, 5in (12.5cm) high.
£1,700–1,900 / €2,450–2,750
$2,850–3,200 HAA

A tortoiseshell tea caddy, on silvered ball feet, c1800, 7in (18cm) wide.
£2,600–2,900
€3,750–4,200
$4,350–4,850 BBo

A wooden box, inlaid with mother-of-pearl and tooled in gilt-metal, the interior decorated with St Dominic, St Francis and Fray Bartolomé de las Casas, minor losses, Mexican, late 18thC, 31¾in (80.5cm) wide.
£5,000–6,000 / €7,200–8,600
$8,400–10,100 LCM

A mahogany knife box, inlaid with a cartouche depicting Britannia, c1800, 14½in (37cm) high.
£1,150–1,300
€1,650–1,850
$1,950–2,200 HAA

A Georgian fruitwood tea caddy, with rolled paper panels depicting ears of wheat and flowers, 7½in (19cm) wide.
£570–680 / €820–980
$960–1,150 AH

A mahogany work box, with boxwood stringing, c1810, 10in (25.5cm) wide.
£140–155 / €200–220
$230–260 F&F

A Regency penwork tea caddy, decorated with flowers and insects, with a canister and a cut-glass bowl, on brass feet, 12in (30.5cm) wide.
£760–910 / €1,100–1,300
$1,300–1,550 G(L)

A Regency japanned work box, decorated with Chinoiserie figures and scenes, the hinged cover enclosing a velvet-lined interior, some damage, 11¾in (30cm) wide.
£220–260 / €320–370
$370–440 BR

A Regency rosewood and cut-brass sewing box, with a hinged cover and turned spindle sides, 8¾in (22cm) wide.
£1,000–1,200
€1,450–1,700
$1,700–2,000 SWO

► **A Regency wooden work box,** painted with flowers and fretwork borders, 15in (38cm) wide.
£590–700 / €850–1,000
$990–1,150 G(L)

◄ **A Regency boxwood work box,** transfer-printed with views of the Royal Pavilion, Steyne and the beach at Brighthelmstone, with a partially fitted interior, 8½in (21.5cm) high.
£680–810 / €980–1,150
$1,150–1,350 G(L)

A wooden sewing box, with Chinoiserie decoration, containing sewing implements, c1820, 7in (18cm) wide.
£270–300 / €390–430
$450–500 ⊞ RdeR

A satinwood and rosewood écarté box, with counters, decorated with cut steel, c1820, 8in (20.5cm) wide.
£270–300 / €390–430
$450–500 ⊞ RdeR
Ecarté is a card game for two players; it originates in France.

A rosewood tea caddy, inlaid with brass decoration, with two lidded canisters and a mixing bowl, c1820, 12in (30.5cm) wide.
£400–440 / €570–630
$670–740 ⊞ GGD

A painted ivory pins and needles case, inscribed 'A trifle from Leamington', French, c1820, 2in (5cm) wide.
£180–200 / €260–290
$300–330 ⊞ RdeR

A tortoiseshell dressing table box, decorated with *piqué* work and applied classical motifs, damaged, early 19thC, 8in (20.5cm) wide.
£3,300–3,950 / €4,750–5,700
$5,500–6,600 TMA

A pine and straw-work casket, decorated with a landscape and floral panels, lined with silk, damaged, early 19thC, 11in (28cm) wide.
£240–280 / €340–400
$400–470 HOLL

A work box, attributed to Turnbull of Jamaica, inlaid with exotic woods, with brass handles and feet, early 19thC, 11¾in (30cm) wide.
£470–560 / €670–800
$790–940 NSal

A painted metal wig box, by Ede & Son, London, with wig, early 19thC, 10in (25.5cm) high.
£190–220 / €270–310
$320–370 GAK

A carved wood casket, mounted with medieval and classical figures, south German, early 19thC, 18in (45.5cm) wide.
£820–980 / €1,200–1,400
$1,400–1,650 B(NW)

◄ **A George IV rosewood writing box,** inset with a ducal crest and inlaid with cut brass, with a fitted writing drawer, 20in (51cm) wide.
£590–700 / €850–1,000
$990–1,150 G(B)

A coromandel sewing casket, in the form of a piano, incomplete, c1830, 12in (30.5cm) wide.
£900–1,000 / €1,300–1,450
$1,500–1,700 RdeR

A satinwood and painted tea caddy, inlaid with acanthus leaf decoration and a medallion, painted with floral swags, with two lidded canisters and a mixing bowl, c1825, 14½in (37cm) wide.
£2,450–2,900 / €3,550–4,200
$4,100–4,850 WL

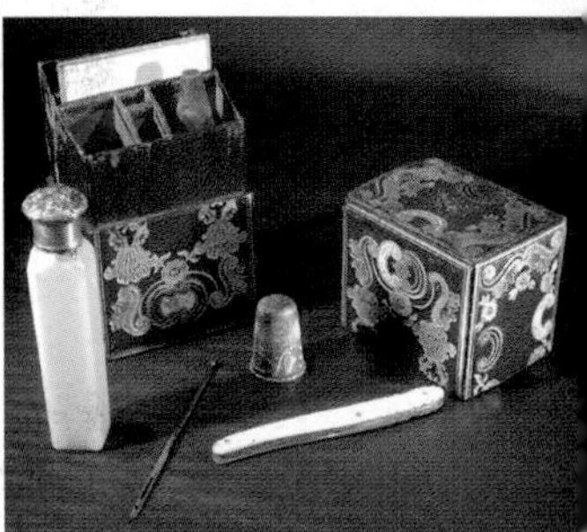

A leather-bound *nécessaire*, decorated with silver leaf, containing a silver-mounted scent bottle, thimble, pen knife, needle and scissors, c1830, 4in (10cm) high.
£900–1,000 / €1,300–1,450
$1,500–1,700 JTS

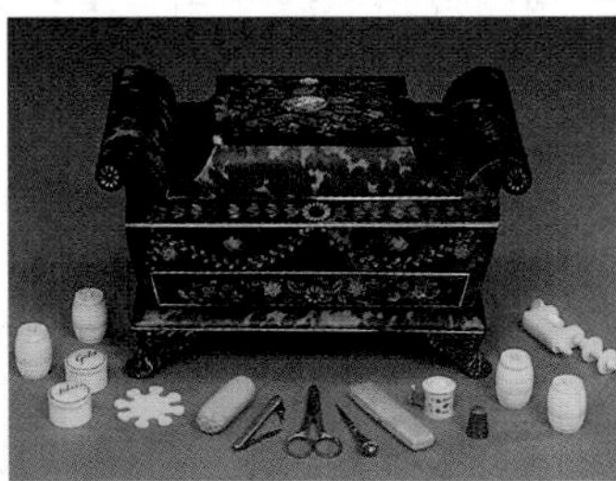

◄ **A William IV tortoiseshell-veneered and mother-of-pearl-inlaid work box,** decorated with flowers and leaves, with original contents, lined with silk, 11¾in (30cm) wide.
£3,750–4,500 / €5,400–6,500
$6,300–7,500 TEN

A William IV rosewood and parquetry tea caddy, with ebony, palm, burr-yew and satinwood inlay, 14½in (37cm) wide.
£530–630 / €760–900
$890–1,050 DN

► **A tortoiseshell and ivory tea caddy,** 19thC, 4in (10cm) high.
£380–430 / €550–620
$640–720 LBr

A William IV kingwood and brass bound writing slope, by I. Turrill, with a leather writing surface, the interior with a removable tray, music stand and compartments, with brass label, minor damage, 21¾in (55.5cm) wide.
£2,450–2,950 / €3,550–4,250
$4,100–4,950 RTo

An ebony and brass-inlaid tea caddy, with two canisters and original glass bowl, c1835, 14in (35.5cm) wide.
£2,400–2,650 / €3,450–3,800
$4,000–4,450 ⊞ JTS

A boulle stationery box, the interior lined with silk, stamped 'J. G. Vickery, Regent Street', 19thC, 8½in (21.5cm) wide.
£940–1,100 / €1,350–1,600
$1,600–1,850 ⚒ TMA

A carved ivory box, decorated with a floral spray, 19thC, 3½in (9cm) wide.
£390–460 / €560–660
$660–770 ⚒ GAK

A painted tea caddy, modelled as a cottage, with a drawer to the rear, 19thC, 6in (15cm) high.
£10,700–12,800 / €15,400–18,400
$18,000–21,500 ⚒ BWL
There is a strong market, particularly in the USA, for quaint, naïvely decorated pieces such as this.

◄ **An ormolu casket,** with enamel decoration of cherubs and foliate engraving, the interior with five cut-glass scent bottles and covers, 19thC, 7in (18cm) square.
£140–165 / €200–240
$240–280 ⚒ TRM

A rosewood tea caddy, 19thC, 8in (20.5cm) wide.
£210–240 / €300–340
$350–400 ⊞ WAA

A painted lacquer snuff box, 19thC, 3in (7.5cm) diam.
£100–110 / €145–160
$165–185 ⊞ HTE

A jewellery box, modelled as a Georgian house, with a fitted interior and a drawer to the side, rear roof, chimney and gables missing, 19thC, 5in (13cm) wide.
£1,000–1,200 / €1,450–1,750
$1,700–2,000 ⚒ SWO

A parquetry tea caddy, decorated with trompe l'oeil blocks, with two canisters and a glass well, 19thC, 12in (30.5cm) wide.
£590–700 / €850–1,000
$990–1,150 ⚒ TRM

A mahogany-veneered double money box, modelled as a house, sliding base missing, 19thC, 10in (25.5cm) high.
£460–550 / €660–790
$770–920 ⚒ BWL

A burr-amboyna, brass, ivory and marquetry stationery box, the fall-front enclosing a lined and fitted interior, French, 19thC, 16in (40.5cm) wide.
£520–620 / €750–890
$880–1,050 ⚒ HYD

◄ **A *pietra dura*-mounted casket,** decorated with birds in branches, lined in velvet, French, 19thC, 9¼in (23.5cm) wide.
£910–1,100 / €1,300–1,550
$1,550–1,850 ⚒ WW

A boulle glove box, the interior with bird's-eye maple veneer, French, 19thC, 10in (25.5cm) wide.
£165–185 / €240–270
$280–310 ⊞ GGD

A rosewood-veneered jewellery box, inlaid with mother-of-pearl floral decoration, c1840, 12in (30.5cm) wide.
£270–300 / €390–430
$450–500 ⊞ GGD

An early Victorian tea caddy, chequer-veneered with mother-of-pearl and abalone-banded, with a silver-plated shield cartouche, the interior with two lidded compartments, minor damage, 9in (23cm) wide.
£600–720 / €860–1,000
$1,000–1,200 ⚒ B

A Victorian walnut tea caddy, inset with a marquetry picture of a boat and a harbour, the interior fitted with two compartments, inscribed 'Cork', 9in (23cm) wide.
£800–960 / €1,150–1,350
$1,350–1,600 ⚒ GAK

A palmwood tea caddy, with a glass-lined interior, French, c1840, 6in (15cm) high.
£1,300–1,450 / €1,850–2,100
$2,200–2,450 ⊞ JTS

A mahogany money box, with a brass *piqué* design of harps, initialled 'G. J.', Irish, dated 1849, 9½in (24cm) wide.
£470–560 / €670–800
$790–940 ⚒ BWL

A burr-walnut tea caddy, inlaid with silver, ivory and mother-of-pearl, mid-19thC, 9in (23cm) wide.
£360–400 / €520–580
$600–670 ⊞ CoHA

A walnut-veneered box, with decorative banding, c1860, 12in (30.5cm) wide.
£130–145 / €185–210
$210–240 ⊞ GGD

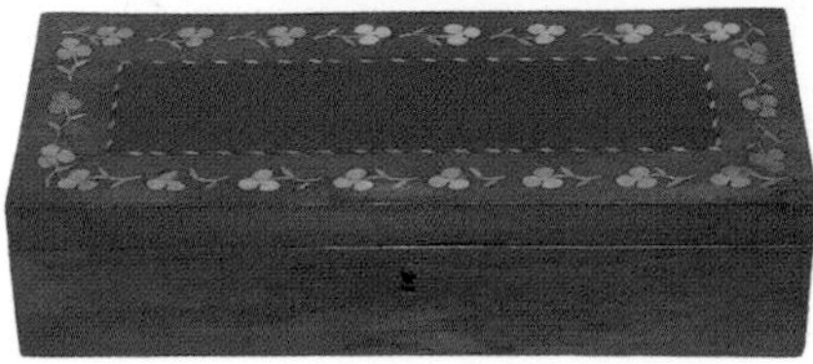

◄ **An arbutus wood box,** inlaid with shamrocks, Irish, Killarney, c1860, 10in (25.5cm) wide.
£390–430 / €560–620
$650–720 ⊞ STA

A satinwood tea caddy, with tulipwood crossbanding and ebony stringing, brass handles, c1840, 14in (35.5cm) wide.
£450–500 / €650–720
$750–840 ⊞ WAA

An early Victorian coromandel travelling box, with 12 glass bottles and jars, some with silver-plated mounts, seven mother-of-pearl-handled manicure implements, with removable tray and concealed drawer, 12¼in (31cm) wide.
£210–250 / €300–360
$350–420 ⚒ CGC

An ebonized glove box, with boulle decoration and brass inlay, French, mid-19thC, 10in (25.5cm) wide.
£165–185 / €240–270
$280–310 ⊞ GGD

A tea caddy, with a glass-lined interior, French, c1870, 5in (12.5cm) wide.
£720–800 / €1,000–1,150
$1,200–1,350 ⊞ JTS

A Victorian burr-walnut and brass-mounted letter box, inset with a porcelain panel of a bird, with two openings labelled in bone 'Answered' and 'Unanswered', 9in (23cm) wide.
£230–270 / €330–390
$380–450 TMA

► A lacquer box, by Vishniakov, Russian, c1880, 5in (12.5cm) diam.
£760–850 / €1,100–1,250
$1,300–1,450 SHa

\ Victorian rosewood tea caddy, ılaid with mother-of-pearl, the interior vith two canisters initialled for black ınd green tea and and a moulded ılass bowl, 14in (35.5cm) wide.
'370–440 / €530–630
620–740 Oli

n ivory casket, carved in relief with ınels of deer and fretwork, surmounted / a huntsman and a deer, Swiss, ıte 19thC, 6½in (16.5cm) wide.
1,900–2,250 / €2,750–3,250
3,200–3,800 G(L)

◄ A Mongolian ash tea caddy, with engraved brass decoration, the interior with two compartments marked 'Black & Green', signed 'Howell & James Regent St', c1870, 9½in (24cm) wide.
£1,750–1,950
€2,500–2,800
$2,950–3,250 JTS

A tortoiseshell *étui*, with a silver thimble, scissors, tape measure, penknife and note pad, dated 1870, 4in (10cm) high.
£620–740 / €890–1,050
$1,050–1,250 Mit

An ivory box, decorated with a portrait of a young woman, c1900, 4in (10cm) diam.
£310–350 / €450–500
$520–590 LBr

A Victorian walnut and brass-bound travelling writing desk, 15in (38cm) high.
£990–1,100 / €1,450–1,600
$1,650–1,850 GEO

A stained wood tea caddy, the lid inset with a needlework floral pattern on silk, with a glass cover, French, c1870, 6in (15cm) high.
£450–500 / €650–720
$750–840 JTS

A lacquer box, depicting troikas, Russian, c1880, 8in (20.5cm) diam.
£720–800 / €1,000–1,150
$1,200–1,350 F&F

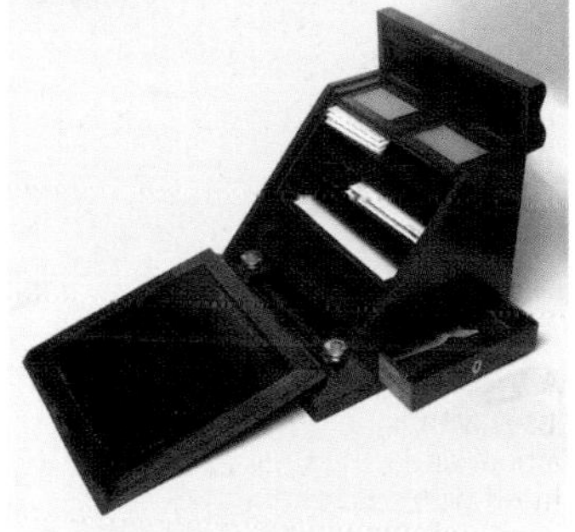

A burr-walnut stationery cabinet and writing slope, by Asprey, with drawers, slates, penholders and inkwells, 1900–10, 14in (35.5cm) wide.
£760–850 / €1,100–1,250
$1,300–1,450 PEZ

◄ An inlaid parquetry box, c1910, 13in (33cm) wide.
£145–160 / €200–230
$240–270 CoHA

Music

Cylinder Musical Boxes

A cylinder musical box, by Nicole Frères, playing 12 airs, restored, Swiss, c1860, 20in (51cm) wide.
£4,950–5,500 / €7,100–7,900
$8,300–9,200 ⊞ KHW

A cylinder musical box, playing ten airs, accompanied by a drum, castanet and six saucer bells with bee strikers, in a rosewood case with marquetry inlay of birds, 19thC, 29¾in (75.5cm) wide.
£2,100–2,500 / €3,000–3,600
$3,550–4,200 ⚒ LHA

A Victorian cylinder musical box, playing six airs, within a rosewood inlaid and strung box, 18in (45.5cm) wide.
£1,000–1,200
€1,450–1,700
$1,700–2,000 ⚒ PBA

A cylinder Concerto Piccolo, by Samuel Troll, restored, Swiss, Geneva, c1870, 24in (61cm) wide.
£3,400–3,800 / €4,900–5,500
$5,700–6,400 ⊞ KHW

► **A miniature cylinder musical box,** the tortoiseshell case inlaid with a metal plaque, with external winding mechanism, in need of restoration, French, 19thC, 3½in (9cm) wide.
£210–250 / €300–360
$350–420 ⚒ FHF

◄ **A cylinder musical box,** the movement with drum and three bells, in a floral-inlaid rosewood-veneered case, Swiss, 19thC, 22in (56cm) wide
£630–750
€910–1,100
$1,050–1,250
⚒ HOLL

► **A cylinder musical box,** with original tune sheet, movement restored, Swiss, 1870–80, 20in (51cm) wide.
£2,150–2,400
€3,100–3,450
$3,600–4,000
⊞ PGO

◄ **A cylinder musical box,** playing six airs, in a fruitwood case, Swiss, c1880, 7in (18cm) wide.
£1,550–1,750
€2,250–2,500
$2,600–2,950
⊞ AUTO

MUSIC

A cylinder musical box, playing eight airs, with drum and castanets in sight, the amboyna-veneered case with bird's-eye maple crossbanding and an ebonized rim, Swiss, c1880, 35½in (90cm) wide.
£4,000–4,800 / €5,800–6,900
$6,700–8,100 ⚒ TEN

A cylinder musical box, by Mojon Manger, with two Mandarin figures striking four bells, restored, c1885, 17in (43cm) wide.
£3,150–3,500
€4,500–5,000
$5,300–5,900 ⊞ KHW

A painted metal cylinder musical box, decorated with a lake scene depicting buildings and trees, stamped 'E. Reymond à Genève', Swiss, late 19thC, 3½in (9cm) wide.
£290–350 / €420–500
$490–590 ⚒ G(L)

A cylinder musical box, by L'Epee, playing six airs, in a Brazilian rosewood-veneered case, refinished case, movement restored, French, c1885, 16¾in (42.5cm) wide.
£1,700–1,900 / €2,450–2,750
$2,850–3,200 ⊞ PGO

A cylinder musical box, playing eight airs, in a crossbanded walnut case, the lid inlaid with marquetry musical trophies, Swiss, late 19thC, 18in (45.5cm) wide.
£1,000–1,200 / €1,450–1,700
$1,700–2,000 ⚒ PF

A cylinder musical box, by B. Abrahams, with three bells, restored, Swiss, c1900, 18in (45.5cm) wide.
£1,950–2,200 / €2,800–3,150
$3,300–3,700 ⊞ PGO

MUSIC

Disc Musical Boxes

◄ **A Polyphon disc musical box,** with 8in (20.5cm) metal discs, contained in a walnut case with line inlay, German, late 19thC, 10½in (25.5cm) wide.
£420–500 / €600–720
$700–840 ⚒ BWL

A Victorian Polyphon disc musical box, in the form of an organ, with 15 discs, 19in (48cm) wide.
£540–650 / €780–940
$910–1,100 ⚒ AMB

◄ **A Kalliope coin-operated disc musical box,** with 37 discs, German, c1900, 87in (221cm) high.
£6,600–7,900
€9,500–11,300
$11,100–13,300 ⚒ S(O)

Gramophones

An Edwardian mahogany Operaphone gramophone, in the form of a piano, with lift-up lid and tapering legs, 31½in (80cm) wide.
£420–500 / €600–720
$700–840 AMB

An HMV gramophone, with painted tin horn, early 20thC, 21¾in (55.5cm) high.
£400–480 / €580–690
$670–800 SWO

A gramophone, with a mahogany case and painted horn, c1910, 15½in (39.5cm) wide.
£140–165 / €200–240
$230–270 L&E

Mechanical Music

A hand-cranked barrel organ, the 11½in (29cm) barrel playing eight airs, the mahogany case pierced with simulated organ pipes, c1840, 22in (56cm) high.
£380–450 / €550–650
$640–760 S(O)

A Cabinetto 25-note organette, by George Wright, American, c1898, 17in (43cm) wide.
£2,250–2,500 / €3,250–3,600
$3,800–4,200 KHW

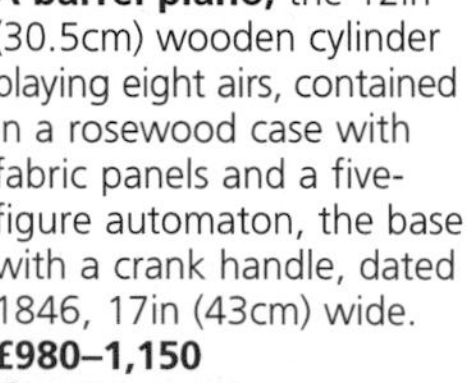

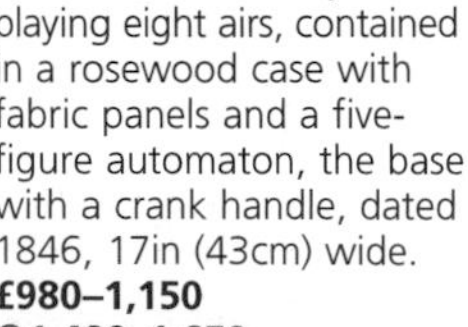

A barrel piano, the 12in (30.5cm) wooden cylinder playing eight airs, contained in a rosewood case with fabric panels and a five-figure automaton, the base with a crank handle, dated 1846, 17in (43cm) wide.
£980–1,150
€1,400–1,650
$1,650–1,950 Bri

A Little Dot Orguinete hand-operated barrel organ, with seven punched rolls, contained in a pine case, printed with imitation inlay, c1890, 14in (35.5cm) high.
£120–145 / €170–210
$200–240 BWL

An automatic upright piano, by Steinway & Sons, the iron-framed overstrung movement with seven-octave 86-note keyboard fitted wit Pianotist roll player, c1905, 61¾in (157cm) wid
£1,900–2,250 / €2,750–3,250
$3,200–3,800 Bri

◄ **A bone and ivory singing bird box,** carved with figures, the hinged cover revealing a gilt-meta screen and a feathered singing bird, late 19thC, 4¾in (12cm) wide.
£1,950–2,300
€2,800–3,300
$3,300–3,900 LFA

Musical Instruments

◄ **An accordion,** by Hohner, German, c1912, 13in (33cm) wide.
£70–80 / €100–120
$120–140 ⚒ BERN

An English School cello, with a bow by Grimm, probably 19thC, length of back 29in (73.5cm), cased.
£1,650–1,950 / €2,350–2,800
$2,750–3,250 ⚒ JM

A double bass, 19thC, length of back 44in (112cm).
£1,750–2,100
€2,500–3,000
$2,950–3,550 ⚒ PF

A brass Improved Cornet, by Chas Pace, Westminster, stamped, c1860, 10½in (26.5m) long, in original fitted pine box.
£1,400–1,650 / €2,000–2,350
$2,350–2,750 ⚒ B

A boxwood and ivory clarinet in B, by C. Mahillon, Belgian, Brussels, c1830, 22½in (57cm) long.
£1,000–1,200 / €1,450–1,700
$1,700–2,000 ⚒ B

► **A Victorian ebony flute,** with silver metal keys, in three parts, stamped 'Sold by Besson & Co, 198 Euston Road, London', minor damage, cased.
£280–330 / €400–480
$470–560 ⚒ NSal
Besson & Co were at 198 Euston Road from 1862 to 1873.

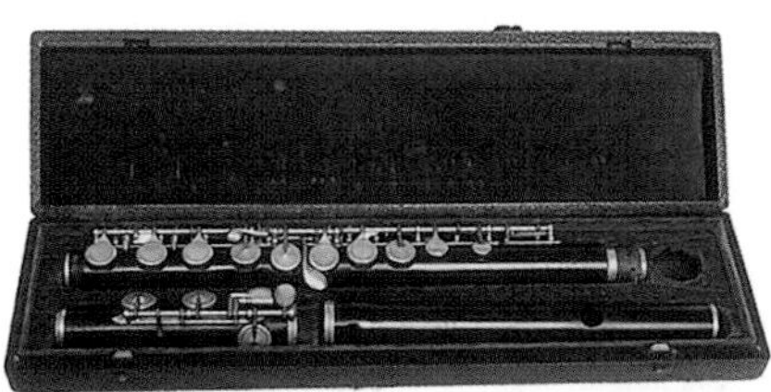

MUSIC

Miller's Compares

I. A rosewood and gold 46-string Gothic-type harp, by Erard, Paris, French, c1896, 67in (170cm) high.
£14,000–15,600
€20,000–22,000
$23,000–26,000 ⊞ RBM

II. A black and gold 43-string Grecian-type harp, by Erard, c1821, 46in (117cm) high.
£8,600–9,600
€12,400–13,800
$14,500–16,100 ⊞ RBM

Item I is a Gothic harp, produced by Erard from circa 1825 as a more powerful version of the smaller Grecian type such as Item II, which is lighter and has a simpler mechanism. Item I is more sought after because of its increased complexity and because it was made in Paris – consequently fewer of them are found in Britain. Erard had factories in both France and Britain – the country of manufacture can be determined from the language of the inscription on the face plates.

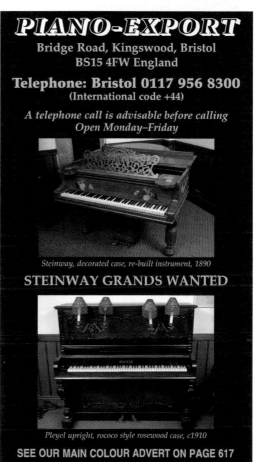

A mahogany harpischord, c1950, 90in (228.5cm) wide.
£760–850 / €1,100–1,200
$1,300–1,450 ⊞ PEx

A rococo revival rosewood melodian, labelled 'Austin C. Chase, Syracuse, New York', American, mid-19thC, 49in (124.5cm) wide.
£510–610 / €730–870
$850–1,000 ⚒ NOA

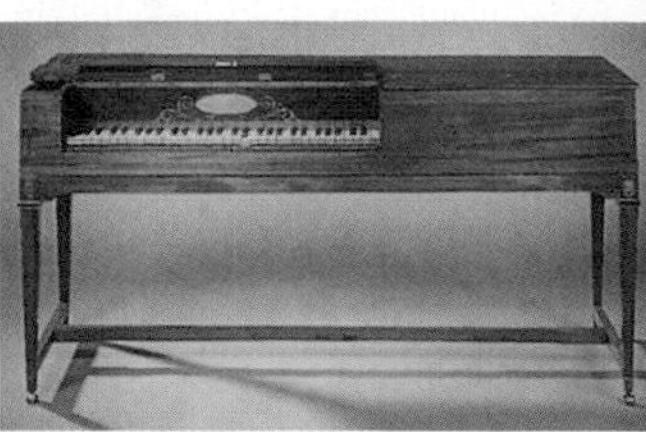

A mahogany square piano, by Schoene & Co, with parquetry inlay and ivory-covered keys, inscribed mark, dated 1788, 64¼in (163cm) wide.
£1,650–1,950 / €2,350–2,800
$2,750–3,250 ⚒ S(Am)

A mahogany square piano, by Longman & Broderip, the name-board inlaid with husks, in need of restoration, 1796, 62½in (159cm) wide.
£660–790 / €950–1,100
$1,100–1,300 ⚒ L

A mahogany piano, by John Broadwood & Son, the stand reduced, inscribed mark, dated 1797, 62½in (159cm) wide.
£1,050–1,250 / €1,500–1,800
$1,750–2,100 ⚒ S(NY)

A mahogany fortepiano, by John Broadwood & Son, c1807, 45¾in (116cm) wide.
£27,000–30,000 / €39,000–43,000
$45,000–50,000 ⊞ RBM

► A mahogany and boxwood square piano, by James Ball, marked 'By appointment to the Prince Regent', early 19thC, 67in (170cm) wide.
£610–730 / €880–1,050
$1,000–1,200 ⚒ E

► A cabinet piano, with six-octave 73-note keyboard, with Dutch marquetry decoration of a vase and flower trails, early 19thC, 48¾in (123.5cm) wide.
£3,500–4,200
€5,000–6,000
$5,900–7,000
⚒ Bri

◄ A rococo revival rosewood parlour grand piano, the case labelled 'Weber N. Y.', American, mid-19thC, 83in (211cm) wide.
£1,200–1,400
€1,750–2,000
$2,000–2,350
⚒ NOA

► A rosewood boudoir grand piano, by John Broadwood & Son, c1868, 81¾in (207.5cm) wide.
£3,150–3,500
€4,500–5,000
$5,300–5,900
⊞ RBM

A painted wood grand piano, by Erard, decorated by Thomas Matthew Rooke, with artist's monogram, c1880, 55¼in (140.5cm) wide.
£19,600–23,300 / €28,000–33,000
$33,000–39,000 ⚒ S(NY)
After training at the Royal College of Art and the Royal Academy, Thomas Matthew Rooke was hired by the design firm Morris & Co where he was appointed assistant to Edward Burne-Jones. For several years Rooke executed preliminary sketches and variations on Burne-Jones' works, transferring his highly detailed pencil drawings onto canvas. Rooke also worked for John Ruskin, for whom he executed many architectural designs which are now in the collection of the Ruskin Museum at Sheffield.

A rosewood and maple grand piano, by Schindler, French, 1930–40, 56in (142cm) wide.
£10,700–12,800 / €15,400–18,400
$18,000–21,500 ⚒ DuM

A walnut upright piano, by Morley, c1937, 57in (145cm) wide.
£2,250–2,500 / €3,250–3,600
$3,800–4,200 ⊞ RBM

► **A spinet,** by Arnold Dolmetsch, with a painted interior by Omega Workshop, dated 1919, 46in (117cm) wide.
£6,300–7,000 / €9,100–10,100
$10,600–11,800 ⊞ RBM
The design of this spinet was developed from an Italian example and it was small enough to fit into an early 20th-century London taxi.

A mahogany baby grand piano, inlaid in brass 'Challen', c1900, 56½in (143.5cm) wide.
£1,550–1,850 / €2,250–2,650
$2,600–3,100 ⚒ S

A Klassic piano, by Bechstein, c1910, 71½in (181.5cm) wide.
£8,900–9,900 / €12,800–14,300
$15,000–16,600 ⊞ RBM

An Art Deco lacquered baby grand piano, by Monington & Weston, restored, relacquered, inlaid brass mark, c1930, 56in (142cm) wide.
£19,200–23,000 / €28,000–33,000
$32,000–38,000 ⚒ S(NY)

A mahogany piano, by Bechstein, c1904, 71½in (181.5cm) wide.
£8,400–9,400 / €12,000–13,500
$14,100–15,800 ⊞ RBM

A rosewood baby grand piano, by Erard, French, c1922, 70¾in (179.5cm) wide.
£530–630 / €760–910
$890–1,050 ⚒ SWO

A mahogany piano, by Bechstein, c1936, 56in (142cm) wide.
£8,800–9,800 / €12,600–14,100
$14,800–16,800 ⊞ RBM

A rosewood spinet, by Arnold Dolmetsch, stamped 'L. Ward 513', dated 1948, 39½in (100.5cm) wide.
£400–480 / €580–690
$670–800 ⚒ RTo

A viola, by Alfred Vincent, 1931, length of back 16in (40.5cm), in a later case.
£5,200–6,200
€7,500–8,900
$8,700–10,400 B

A patent violin, by Thomas Howell, stamped, c1835, length of back 12in (30.5cm), in a wooden case.
£360–430 / €520–620
$600–720 Bri

A violin, labelled 'Copie De Lofredus Cappa In Saluzzo, Fecit Anno 1640', possible maker's/repairer's label 'A. Sarson – Thurmaston, 1887', 19thC, length of back 14¼in (36cm).
£530–630 / €760–900
$890–1,050 CDC

A violin, labelled 'Leopold Widhalm Lauten-und Geigen-Macher in Nurenburg Fecit A 1774', stamped initials 'L. W.', late 19thC, length of back 14in (35.5cm).
£2,000–2,400
€2,900–3,450
$3,350–4,000 CDC

◄ **A violin,** labelled 'Jacobus Stainer', late 19thC, length of back 14in (35.5cm), with case.
£190–220 / €270–320
$320–370 G(L)

◄ **A violin,** labelled 'Paolo Fiorini, Taurini Faciebat Anno 1924', probably French, length of back 14¼in (36cm), cased.
£1,250–1,500
€1,800–2,150
$2,100–2,500 MAR

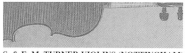

A violin, by G. Wulme-Hudson, after Antonio Stradivarius, labelled, dated 1925, length of back 14¼in (36cm).
£4,800–5,700
€6,900–8,200
$8,000–9,600 B

A violin, labelled 'Guiseppe Fiorini', the bow stamped 'Hill', dated 1929, 22¾in (58cm) long.
£200–240 / €290–340
$340–400 SWO

Icons

A pair of icons of the Annunciation, north Italian, Umbria, 15thC, 53½ x 30¼in (136 x 76.5cm).
£13,500–15,000
€19,400–22,000
$22,000–25,000 ⊞ RKa

An icon of the Resurrection and Descent into Hell, some losses and later restorations, Russian, 1550–1600, 9¾ x 8¼in (25 x 21cm).
£2,050–2,450 / €2,950–3,500
$3,450–4,100 ⚒ JAA

An icon of the Calendar for the month of April, Russian, 16thC, 13 x 10¾in (33 x 27.5cm).
£4,950–5,500 / €7,100–7,900
$8,300–9,200 ⊞ RKa

An icon of Christ 'Man of Sorrows', with a later painted and tooled gilt surround, Greek, early 17thC, 13¼ x 10½in (34 x 26.5cm).
£2,600–3,100 / €3,750–4,450
$4,350–5,200 ⚒ S(O)

◄ A triptych, depicting the Deisis and 10 saints, Greek, probably Mount Athos, late 17thC, 10 x 12½in (25.5 x 32cm).
£5,000–6,000 / €7,200–8,600
$8,400–10,100 ⚒ S(O)

► An icon of the Virgin with the Playful Child, Russian, c1700, 13½ x 11in (34.5 x 28cm).
£3,400–3,750 / €4,900–5,400
$5,700–6,300 ⊞ ICO

An icon of St Luke the Evangelist, in a cloisonné-decorated gilt-metal oklad, Russian, late 17thC, 4 x 3¼in (10 x 8.5cm).
£1,300–1,550 / €1,850–2,200
$2,200–2,600 ⚒ S(O)

An icon of the Smolensk Hodigitria Mother of God, Russian, c1700, 12 x 10½in (30.5 x 26.5cm).
£890–1,050 / €1,300–1,500
$1,500–1,750 ⚒ JAA

◄ An icon of St Arsenius and St Michael of Tver, Russian, early 18thC, 12¼ x 10½in (31 x 26.5cm).
£1,250–1,400 / €1,800–2,000
$2,100–2,350 ⊞ TeG
Saint Arsenius was a man of great prayer and a peace maker. He played a key role in the affairs of the Russian Church in the turbulent 14th century and was caught up in lengthy political affairs and disputes that involved Prince Michael, one of the most powerful men in Russia at the time. Arsenius died in 1409 and was buried in the Zheltikov monastery of the Dormition of the Most Holy Mother of God which he founded and which is represented in this icon.

◀ **A bronze triptych of the Nativity and the Fools in Christ,** Russian, 18thC, 2½ x 5½in (6.5 x 14cm).
£3,100–3,450
€4,450–4,950
$5,200–5,800
⊞ ICO

A brass and enamel icon of St Nicholas with saints and apostles, Russian, 18thC, 5¾ x 5in (14.5 x 12.5cm).
£400–450 / €570–650
$670–760 ⊞ RKa

A painted icon of the Pokrov Mother of God, Russian, 18thC, 29 x 22½in (73.5 x 57cm).
£750–900 / €1,100–1,300
$1,250–1,500 ⚒ JAA

A quadripartite icon, depicting the Holy Mother of God, the life of St John the Baptist, the Hodigitria Mother of God and saints, a roundel to the centre depicting the Holy Trinity, some damage, Russian, 18thC, 20¾ x 17¼in (52.5 x 44cm).
£1,050–1,250 / €1,500–1,800
$1,750–2,100 ⚒ DORO

An icon of the Mother of God, also depicting the Deisis, Russian, 18thC, 14 x 11¾in (35.5 x 30cm).
£590–700 / €850–1,000
$990–1,150 ⚒ BERN

An icon of the Transfiguration on Mount Tabor, Russian, 18thC, 37 x 28in (94 x 71cm).
£1,300–1,550 / €1,900–2,250
$2,200–2,600 ⚒ BERN

An icon of St John in Silence, late 18thC, 14 x 12in (35.5 x 30.5cm).
£1,300–1,450 / €1,850–2,100
$2,200–2,450 ⊞ ICO

An icon of the Guardian Angel and Saints, with an oklad, Russian, late 18thC, 12½ x 10¾in (32 x 27.5cm).
£1,500–1,700 / €2,150–2,450
$2,500–2,850 ⊞ TeG
The detailed miniature work is of high quality and suggests one of the principal workshops in Moscow or St Petersburg. On the left are Saints Evdokia, Natalia and Boniface, a bishop and Miron. On the right are Saints Pelagia, Stephan, Laura, Demian and a monk.

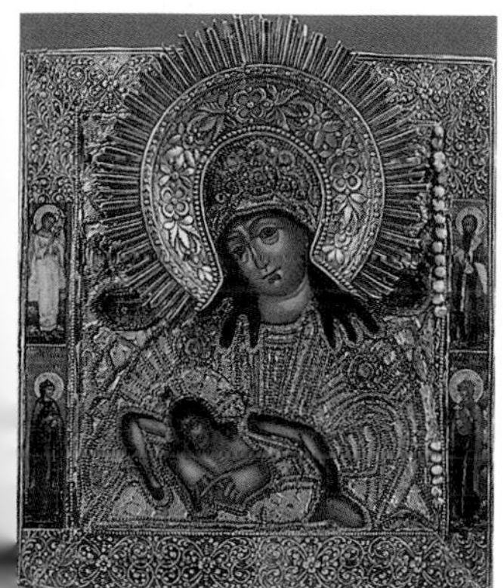

An icon of the Mother of God Plachushaya, with an oklad of paste stones, with a later silver-gilt halo dated 1841, Russian, c1800, 12¾ x 11½in (32.5 x 29cm).
£1,750–2,100 / €2,500–3,000
$2,950–3,550 ⚒ JAA

◀ **An icon of the All-Seeing Eye of God,** Russian, early 19thC, 12¼ x 10½in (31 x 26.5cm).
£2,250–2,500 / €3,250–3,600
$3,800–4,200 ⊞ TeG

An icon of the Kazan Mother of God, within a beadwork covering, applied with seed pearls and mother-of-pearl, in a glazed display case, early 19thC, 14¼ x 11¾in (36 x 30cm).
£4,050–4,850 / €5,800–7,000
$6,800–8,100 S(O)

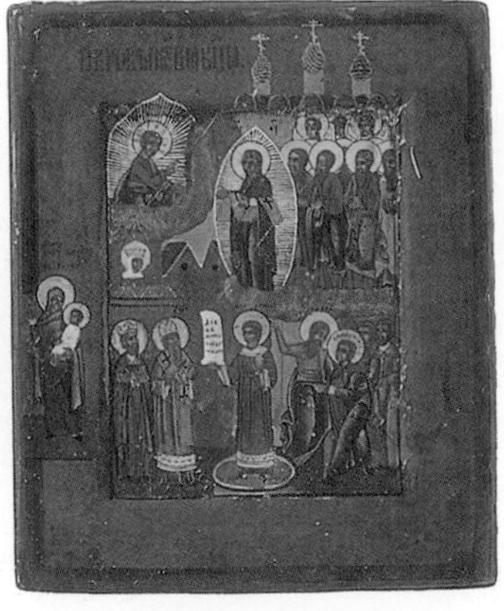

An icon of the Protecting Veil, Russian, early 19thC, 6 x 5in (15 x 12.5cm).
£300–340 / €430–490
$500–570 TeG

An icon of the Ascension of Christ, Russian, early 19thC, 23 x 16in (58.5 x 40.5cm).
£620–740 / €890–1,050
$1,050–1,250 BERN

An icon of St Nicholas, Christ and Mary, with a chased silvered-metal oklad, damaged, Russian, early 19thC, 12½ x 10½in (32 x 26.5cm).
£210–250 / €300–360
$350–420 DORO

An icon of the Vladimir Mother of God, with a silver oklad, damaged, marked 'Moscow 1815', Russian, 12¼ x 9½in (31 x 24cm).
£1,650–1,950 / €2,350–2,800
$2,750–3,250 BUK

A painted quadripartite icon, depicting Jesus on the cross, the Madonna and Child and various saints, Greek, 19thC, 15 x 12in (6 x 30.5cm).
£350–420 / €500–600
$590–700 LHA

◄ **A triptych,** depicting the Descent into Hell and saints, Russian, 19thC, 3½ x 9¼in (9 x 23.5cm) open.
£890–1,050 / €1,300–1,500
$1,500–1,750 JAA

An icon of the Synaxis of the Archangel Michael, Russian, 19thC, 12¼ x 10¼in (31 x 26cm).
£2,150–2,400 / €3,100–3,450
$3,600–4,000 RKa

An icon of the saints and the Mother of God, minor damage, Russian, 19thC, 9¾ x 8¾in (25 x 22cm).
£490–590 / €710–850
$820–990 DORO

An icon of the Holy Prince Alexander Nevski, flanked by four scenes depicting his life, Russian, 19thC, 12¼ x 10½in (31 x 26.5cm).
£105–125 / €150–180
$175–210 SWO

A painted and gilded icon of six saints, the silver oklad engraved with scrolling foliage, Russian, 19thC, 4in (10cm) high.
£230–270 / €330–390
$380–450 RTo

A painted icon of a male saint, with a silver oklad, Russian, 19thC, 11½ x 9¼in (29 x 23.5cm).
£280–330 / €400–470
$470–550 DuM

An icon of the Annunciation, minor losses, Russian, 19thC, 11½ x 9½in (29 x 24cm).
£440–520 / €630–750
$740–870 DORO

An icon of the Ascension of the prophet Elias, Russian, mid-19thC, 37¼ x 14¾in (94.5 x 37.5cm).
£730–870 / €1,050–1,250
$1,200–1,450 BERN

An icon of the Virgin of Vladimir, Russian, mid-19thC, 10½ x 9in (26.5 x 23cm).
£810–900 / €1,150–1,300
$1,350–1,500 ⊞ TeG
The composition follows that of the great icon painted in Constantinople in the late 11th century and taken to Russia shortly after, since when it has been chief palladium of the Russian state – protecting the Russian people, delivering them from enemies and performing many miracles. The Virgin's glance varies; sometimes it is down towards her son, sometimes outwards towards the onlooker. The composition, in the embrace of the two figures, characterizes tenderness.

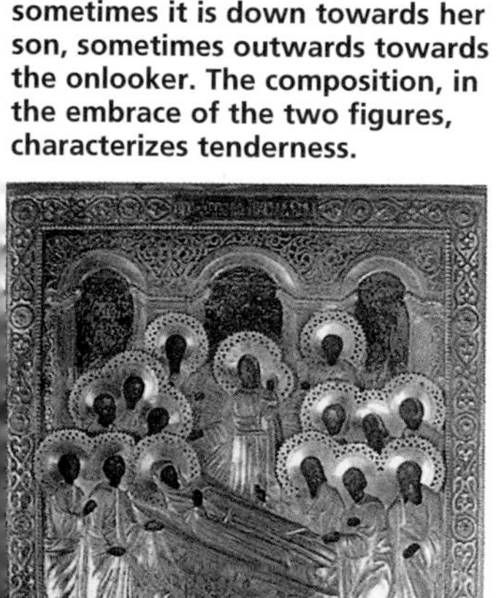

An icon of the Death of the Mother of God, also depicting the Apostles of Christ receiving her soul in the form of a child, damaged, Greek, c1900, 12¼ x 10½in (31 x 26.5cm).
£260–310 / €370–440
$440–520 DORO

A painted icon of a saint, possibly St Nicholas, Greek, dated 1867, 12¾ x 9¾in (32.5 x 25cm).
£260–310 / €370–440
$430–520 L

► **An icon of Metropolitan Alexei,** Russian, late 19thC, 7 x 5½in (18 x 14cm).
£350–390 / €500–560
$590–660 ⊞ TeG
The painted border, simulating Russian enamel work of the 17thC, is typical of the late 19thC.

An icon of the Iverskaya Mother of God, with a gilded silver and enamel oklad by Feodor Ovchinnikov, Russian, c1890, 7 x 5¾in (18 x 14.5cm).
£3,900–4,700 / €5,600–6,700
$6,600–7,900 S(NY)
Ovchinnikov was a leading Moscow silversmith.

► **An icon of St Seraphim of Sarov,** Russian, c1903, 12¼ x 10½in (31 x 26.5cm).
£440–520 / €630–750
$740–870 JAA

A brass icon of the Ascension of the Mother of God, with enamel decoration, inscribed, Russian, dated 1872, 11½ x 9½in (29 x 24cm).
£490–590 / €710–850
$820–990 F&C

Portrait Miniatures

A portrait miniature of a gentleman, English School, in a gilt-metal frame, c1680, 2½in (6.5cm) high.
£590–700 / €850–1,000
$990–1,150 TEN

► **A portrait miniature of a military gentleman,** watercolour on ivory, in a gilt-metal frame, mid-18thC, 1½in (4cm) high.
£140–165 / €200–230
$230–270 PFK

A portrait miniature of a young lady, by William Wood, on ivory, signed, 1780, 4¼in (11.5cm) high.
£840–1,000 / €1,200–1,450
$1,400–1,650 BWL

A portrait miniature of a gentleman, English School, watercolour on ivory, in a gilt-metal mount and a papier-mâché frame, signed and inscribed, late 18thC, 2½in (6.5cm) high.
£280–330 / €400–470
$470–550 B(EA)

A portrait miniature, oil on copper, Continental, 17thC, 5½in (14cm) high.
£500–550 / €720–790
$840–920 RGa

A portrait miniature of a naval officer, by Philippe Jean, watercolour on ivory, late 18thC, 3in (7.5cm) high.
£5,600–6,700 / €8,200–9,600
$9,400–11,300 B&L

A portrait miniature of a girl, English School, watercolour on ivory, in a gold locket frame, 18thC, 2in (5cm) high.
£700–840 / €1,000–1,200
$1,200–1,400 G(L)

A portrait miniature of a lady, possibly Peg Woffington, by Thomas Frye of Dublin, in a gold frame, Irish, c1760, 2in (5cm) high.
£2,700–3,000 / €3,900–4,300
$4,500–5,000 SIL
Peg Woffington was a celebrated Irish actress.

A portrait miniature of Mrs Mills, by George Engleheart, in a diamond frame, engraved, details on reverse, c1790, 2½in (6.5cm) high.
£15,300–17,000 / €22,000–25,000
$25,000–29,000 BHa

◄ **A portrait miniature of a young man,** on ivory, in a gilt-metal frame, c1800, 1½in (4cm) high.
£300–360 / €430–520
$500–600 DMC

◄ **A portrait miniature of a young lady,** English School, c1800, 2¾in (7cm) high.
£350–420 / €500–600
$590–700 Bea

A portrait miniature of a young lady, on ivorine, the reverse with a lock of hair and initials, the reverse inscribed 'Died 1811, Aged 28', 19thC, 3in (7.5cm) high, in a leather case.
£220–260 / €310–370
$370–440 FHF

A portrait miniature of a young gentleman, Circle of Frederic Millet, watercolour on ivory, in a gilt mount and wooden frame, Continental, early 19thC, 2in (5cm) diam.
£175–210 / €250–300
$290–350 RTo

A portrait miniature of a foot soldier of the Royal American 60th Regiment, by Frederick Buck, with hair panel and monogram to reverse, in a gold locket frame, Irish, 1808, 3in (7.5cm) high.
£1,800–2,000 / €2,600–2,900
$3,000–3,350 BHa

► **A portrait miniature of a gentleman,** watercolour, c1810, 4½in (11.5cm) high.
£210–240 / €300–340
$400–400 PSC

A portrait miniature of a young man, by George Engleheart, watercolour on ivory, signed and inscribed, dated 1813, 3¼in (8.5cm) high.
£4,950–5,900
€7,100–8,500
$8,300–9,900 L
This is a late example dating from the year in which Engleheart retired to his country house, Bedfont, near Hounslow.

A portrait miniature of a gentleman, attributed to Frederick Bude, watercolour on ivory, c1820, 5in (12.5cm) high.
£350–390 / €500–560
$590–660 PSC

► **A portrait miniature of John Blayes,** by Thomas Hargreaves, the reverse with an interwoven hair panel, in a gilt-metal frame, c1830, 3½in (9cm) high.
£2,500–2,800
€3,600–4,000
$4,200–4,700 BHa

A portrait miniature of John Hare, c1831, 4in (10cm) high.
£440–520 / €630–750
$740–870 ⚒ L&E

A portrait miniature of Oliver Cromwell, by W. Essex, inscribed, in a gilt-metal frame, signed and dated 1832, 2¾in (7cm) high.
£1,500–1,800 / €2,150–2,600
$2,500–3,000 ⚒ FHF

A portrait miniature of J. Gibson Reeves, by Frederick Cruickshank, watercolour on ivory, signed and dated 1833, 4in (10cm) high, in a leather case.
£880–1,050 / €1,250–1,500
$1,500–1,750 ⚒ B(EA)

A portrait miniature of a lady, on ivory, in a burr-maple-veneered frame, c1835, 3½in (9cm) high.
£100–120 / €145–170
$170–200 ⚒ NSal

A portrait miniature of a gentleman, watercolour on paper, in a gilt-metal frame, American, 1830–40, 3in (7.5cm) high, in original velvet-lined folding case.
£330–390 / €470–560
$550–650 ⊞ GFA

A portrait miniature of a girl holding a doll, American School, watercolour on ivory, in a leather-covered hinged case, 19thC, 2½in (6.5cm) high.
£1,500–1,800 / €2,150–2,600
$2,500–3,000 ⚒ SK

► **A portrait miniature of a lady,** on ivory, 19thC, 2in (5cm) high.
£200–240 / €290–350
$340–400 ⚒ LHA

A portrait miniature of James H. Lawton, by Doyle, watercolour on ivory, signed, 1830s, 3in (7.5cm) high.
£1,100–1,300 / €1,600–1,900
$1,850–2,200 ⚒ COBB

A portrait miniature of Mr Bellew, on ivory, in a yellow metal case, the reverse with a lock of hair, 19thC, 2½in (6.5cm) high.
£230–270 / €330–390
$390–450 ⚒ CHTR

► **A portrait miniature of a flower seller,** Anglo-Indian School, on ivory, signed 'B. R.', in an ormolu mount, c1838, 6¾in (17cm) high.
£370–440 / €530–630
$620–740 ⚒ F&C

A portrait miniature of a gentleman, European School, oil on ivory, 19thC, 2¼in (5.5cm) diam.
£280–330 / €400–470
$470–550 ⚒ LCM

A portrait miniature of the Marquis of Angelsea, by Samuel Lover, in a papier-mâché frame, signed, Irish, c1840, 6in (15cm) high.
£1,000–1,150
€1,450–1,650
$1,700–1,950 ⊞ SIL

A portrait miniature, after Boucher, watercolour on ivory, French, 19thC, 3½in (9cm) high, in a gilt-brass mount and leather case.
£230–270 / €330–390
$390–450 ⚒ PFK

A portrait miniature of a lady, Continental School, watercolour on ivory, 19thC, 3in (7.5cm) high.
£260–310 / €370–440
$440–520 ⚒ G(L)

A portrait miniature of Francis Bruce, in the style of Reginald Easton, on ivory, c1840, 4in (10cm) high.
£1,600–1,900
€2,300–2,750
$2,700–3,200 ⚒ L

A portrait miniature of a boy, attributed to Augustus Fuller, watercolour on ivory, in an embossed leather case, American, 19thC, 2¾in (7cm) high.
£2,950–3,500
€4,250–5,000
$4,950–5,900 ⚒ SK

A portrait miniature of the Marquise Visconti, on ivory, signed 'Heller', Continental, c1854, 1½in (4cm) high.
£200–240 / €290–350
$340–400 ⚒ LHA

A pair of portrait miniatures of Mr and Mrs Morier, by Mrs Henry Moseley, in an enamel locket frame, initialled, one signed and dated 1855, 2in (5cm) high.
£1,300–1,550 / €1,850–2,250
$2,200–2,600 ⚒ S(O)

A portrait miniature of David Garrick, by W. Essex, after Gainsborough, in an ebonized frame, signed and dated 1856, 3¾in (9.5cm) high.
£1,350–1,600
€1,950–2,300
$2,250–2,700 ⚒ FHF

◀ A portrait miniature of a boy, by Augustus Fuller, watercolour on ivory, American, signed and dated 1860, 2in (5cm) high, mounted in an embossed leather case.
£2,600–3,100 / €3,750–4,450
$4,350–5,200 ⚒ SK
Augustus Fuller was born in Brighton, Massachusetts in 1912, and was both deaf and dumb. He was educated at the American Asylum in West Brookfield, Connecticut. In 1832 he was painting portraits for £6 / €8 / $10 each and miniatures for £1/ €1.5 / $2 in Chatham, Connecticut. He also worked in Massachusetts, New Hampshire and Vermont.

A pair of Edwardian portrait miniatures of young ladies, on ivory, in ivory and gilt-metal frames, with easel supports, 3½in (9cm) high.
£300–360 / €430–510
$500–600 ⚒ SWO

◀ A portrait miniature of a girl holding a canary, on porcelain, in a stamped brass frame, late 19thC, 3¼in (8.5cm) high.
£230–270 / €330–390
$390–450 ⚒ FHF

A portrait miniature of a lady, watercolour on ivory, in a brass glazed frame, early 20thC, 2½in (6.5cm) high.
£120–145 / €170–200
$200–240 ⚒ PFK

Silhouettes

A silhouette of a group of figures and a dog, by Francis Torond, labelled, 14½ x 19¼in (37 x 49cm).
£5,400–6,500 / €7,800–9,300
$9,100–10,900 ⚒ L
The label on the reverse of this silhouette is inscribed 'Mr Stanley the celebrated blind organist who conducted the Oratorio in Westminster Abbey at the commencement of the reign of George III'.

A George III silhouette of a gentleman, watercolour on card, signed 'T. B.', in a lacquered-brass, beaded and gadrooned frame, 4¾in (12cm) high.
£105–125 / €150–180
$175–210 ⚒ PFK

A silhouette of a young woman, English School, c1800, 3in (7.5cm) high, in a *verre églomisé* bordered, glazed and papier-mâché frame.
£350–420 / €500–600
$590–700 ⚒ TEN

A bronzed silhouette, by Miers or Field, on paste, c1810, 5¼in (13.5cm) high.
£500–550 / €720–800
$830–920 ⊞ PSC

A bronzed silhouette of a woman, c1840, 4 x 3in (10 x 7.5cm).
£200–220 / €290–320
$330–370 ⊞ HTE

A silhouette of a gentleman, labelled 'by Wm Hamlet of Bath', c1825, 4¾in (12cm) high.
£210–240 / €300–340
$350–400 ⊞ PSC

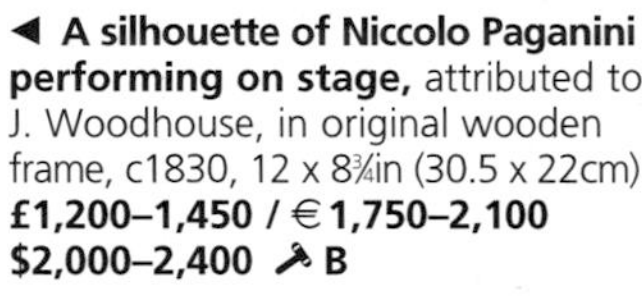

◀ **A silhouette of Niccolo Paganini performing on stage,** attributed to J. Woodhouse, in original wooden frame, c1830, 12 x 8¾in (30.5 x 22cm).
£1,200–1,450 / €1,750–2,100
$2,000–2,400 ⚒ B

A double silhouette of Mr and Mrs Henry Lilley Smith, by Augustin Edouart, inscribed, dated 1837, 8½ x 7in (21.5 x 18cm), in a bird's-eye maple-veneered frame.
£410–490 / €590–700
$690–820 ⚒ WW

A group of three silhouettes, depicting a lady, a gentleman and a girl, with gilt highlights, early 19thC, 4in (10cm) high, in mahogany frames.
£230–270 / €330–390
$380–450 ⚒ TRM

A cut-paper silhouette of a group of figures, by Letitia Louisa Kerr, inscribed, signed and dated 1832, 7¼ x 8¾in (18.5 x 22cm).
£910–1,100 / €1,300–1,600
$1,550–1,850 ⚒ L

A double silhouette of a gentleman and a lady, American School, with stencilled and watercoloured details, inscribed, in original frame, 19thC, 7 x 10½in (18 x 26.5cm).
£2,100–2,500 / €3,000–3,600
$3,550–4,200 ⚒ S(NY)

Antiquities

An alabaster vase, slight damage and repair, Egyptian, 6th Dynasty, 2345–2195 BC, 2¾in (7cm) high.
£300–340 / €430–500
$500–570 ⊞ MIL
One side of this vase is almost perfect, but the other was probably facing upwards in the ground and has suffered some damage. When illuminated, the stone is translucent.

A composition amuletic necklace, the tubular beads interspersed with disc beads and flat amulets, restrung, Egyptian, New Kingdom, 1567–1085 BC, 20in (51cm) long.
£280–330 / €400–480
$470–560 ⚒ B(Kn)

The items in this section have been arranged chronologically in sequence of civilizations, namely Egyptian, Near Eastern, Greek, Roman, Byzantine, western Europe, British, Anglo-Saxon and Medieval.

A limestone bust of a goddess, Egyptian, 1085–730 BC, 1½in (4cm) high.
£540–600 / €780–860
$900–1,000 ⊞ HEL

◄ A bronze model of a cat, with an incised beaded collar and Greek gold earring, a votive inscription engraved on the base, Egyptian, 26th/30th Dynasty, 664–342 BC, 4in (10cm) high.
£6,400–7,700 / €9,200–11,000
$10,800–12,900 ⚒ S(NY)

◄ A faïence fragment of a figure of the god Thoth, Egyptian, 730–332 BC, 2¼in (5.5cm) high.
£360–400
€520–580
$600–660 ⊞ HEL

Egyptian gods

The classical world hated the idea of the Egyptian gods, who were often portrayed as humans with animal or bird heads. The major deities in human form were in families of three. Chief of the gods was Amun, with his wife Mut and son Khonsu, the moon god. Osiris, god of the dead, had as his wife Isis, the protective mother, and son Horus (later named Harpocrates). Ptah of Memphis, creator god and god of workmen, was seen as a tightly-wrapped mummiform with close cap. His wife, Sekhmet, was the lioness-headed goddess, and his son, Nefertum, was often shown emerging from a lotus flower. Other important gods were jackal-headed Anubis, god of embalming, and Thoth, ibis-headed god of wisdom.

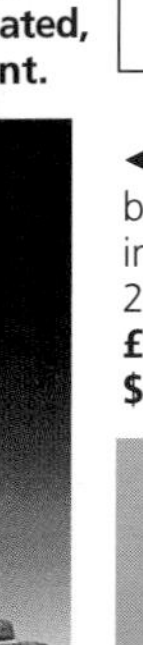

A bronze model of a ram of Amun, worn, Egyptian, Ptolemaic Period, 664–30 BC, 3¼in (8.5cm) wide.
£820–980 / €1,200–1,400
$1,400–1,650 ⚒ B(Kn)

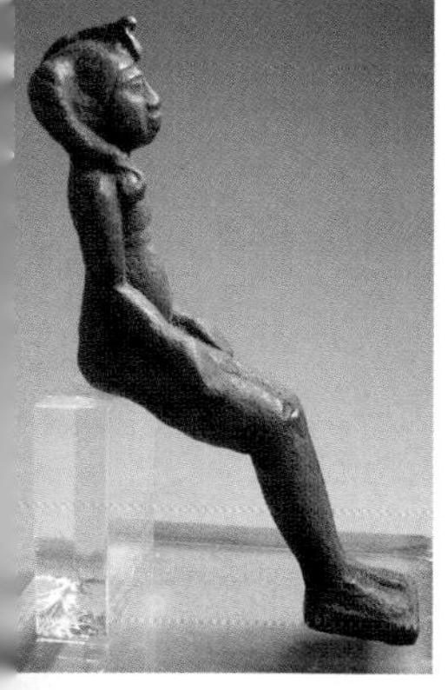

A bronze seated figure of Harpocrates, Egyptian, c600 BC, 3½in (9cm) high.
£560–620 / €800–890
$950–1,050 ⊞ MIL
Harpocrates, the child Horus, was the son of the goddess Isis and the god of the dead, Osiris. As Harpocrates, he is depicted in human form with the sidelock of youth, wearing a uraeus on a skull cap with a tie fastening, clearly visible at the back.

◄ A bronze herm, with the head of a Ptolemaic ruler, Greek/Egyptian, 3rd/2ndC BC, 3¼in (8.5cm) high.
£440–490 / €630–700
$740–820 ⊞ ANG
Originally, herms were statues of Hermes with short square stubs for arms and the legs tapering to a narrow base, with drapery on the shoulders and chest. In this case, the head of Hermes is replaced by the head of a Ptolemaic ruler.

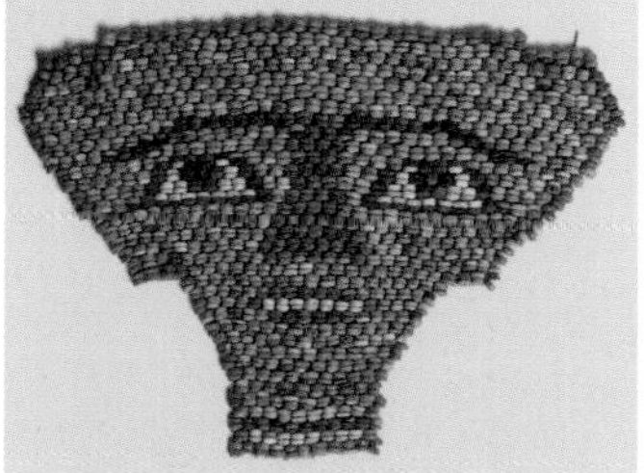

A mummy bead mask, restrung, late Ptolemaic/Roman, 200 BC–100 AD, 8in (20.5cm) wide.
£400–450 / €590–650
$670–760 ⊞ LBr

A pottery vase, Ancient Near East, 3000–2500 BC, 11½in (29cm) high.
£220–250 / €320–360
$370–420 ⊞ HEL

A terracotta stirrup jar, decorated with sea urchin motifs and encircling bands, repaired, Mycenaean, 1350–1300 BC, 7½in (19cm) high.
£1,650–1,950 / €2,400–2,850
$2,800–3,300 ⚒ B(Kn)

A gold appliqué, the high relief repoussé decoration depicting a griffin, with bosses and attachment holes to the border and part of the original wood lining, Graeco-Scythian, c5thC BC, 2¾in (7cm) wide.
£2,850–3,400 / €4,100–4,900
$4,800–5,700 ⚒ S(NY)

A bronze bracelet, Greek, 5thC BC, 3in (7.5cm) diam.
£310–350 / €450–500
$520–580 ⊞ HEL

► **A bronze mount,** in the form of the head of a satyr, Greek, 5thC BC, 1¼in (3cm) wide.
£175–195 / €250–280
$300–330 ⊞ ANG

A bronze or copper figure of a warrior, Syrian/Canaanite, mid-2nd millennium BC, 5¾in (14.5cm) high.
£3,600–4,300
€5,200–6,200
$6,000–7,200 ⚒ S(NY)

A painted pottery jug, Cypriot, 1050–650 BC, 9in (23cm) high.
£310–350 / €450–500
$520–580 ⊞ HEL

◄ **A terracotta *rhyton*,** modelled emerging from the forequarters of a horse, the surface covered in a polished slip, southwest Caspian area, 1000–800 BC, 10½in (26.5cm) high.
£1,600–1,900
€2,300–2,750
$2,700–3,200
⚒ S(NY)

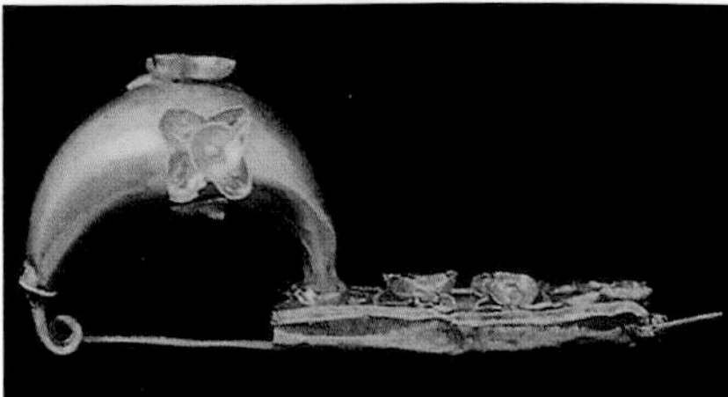

A gold fibula, the high bow applied with floral rosettes, the foot with wire plait-work, the end applied with a sphinx, Etruscan, c6thC BC, 1½in (3.5cm) long.
£820–980 / €1,200–1,400
$1,400–1,650 ⚒ B(Kn)

Etruscans

The Etruscans were pre-Roman people who mainly inhabited central and part of north Italy. With the increasing importance of Rome they were virtually wiped out, for Rome would not tolerate a competitive civilization. Many Etruscan rituals and aspects of their culture were taken over by Rome: Etruscan funeral games became the Roman gladiatorial combats and the science of divination came from the Etruscans. They were also incredible craftsmen in precious metals. It was said that the famous Etruscan Sibylline books of received wisdom were burnt by Rome and that the emperor Claudius was the last person who could read Etruscan, a language that is still largely undeciphered.

◄ **A terracotta female head,** with plug earrings, Etruscan, 5th–4thC BC, 3¾in (8.5cm) high.
£160–180 / €230–260
$270–300 ⊞ HEL

A *kotile*, with incised decoration depicting animals, the field with rosettes, the base with dashes below the rim, repaired and restored, Corinthian, c580–560 BC, 7½in (19cm) diam.
£820–980 / €1,200–1,400
$1,400–1,650 ⚒ B(Kn)

An Attic Black-Figure skyphos, decorated with dancing bacchic revellers among vine tendrils, with two handles, repaired and restored, Greek, 6th–5thC BC, 9¾in (25cm) diam.
£1,200–1,450 / €1,750–2,100
$2,000–2,400 B(Kn)

◄ **A Red Figure kantharos,** decorated with the head of a Lady of Fashion, slight damage, Greek South Italy, Apulia, late 4thC BC, 8in (20.5cm) high.
£680–750
€980–1,100
$1,150–1,300
A&O

A Red-Figure terracotta hydria, the front decorated with female figures, restored, Greek South Italy, Apulia, 4thC BC, 26¾in (68cm) high.
£3,300–3,950
€4,750–5,700
$5,600–6,700 S(Am)

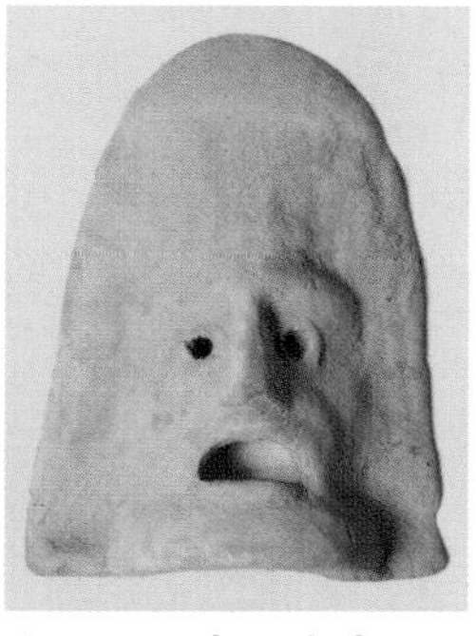

A pottery theatrical tragedy mask, Greek, c4thC BC, 3¾in (9.5cm) high.
£400–450 / €580–650
$670–760 HEL

A parcel-gilt silver bowl, the border decorated with dots and scrolling above a frieze of laurel leaves with buds and flowers, with four lotus petals alternating with four leaves at the base, some restoration, Hellenistic, 2nd–1stC BC, 3½in (9cm) high.
£2,100–2,500
€3,000–3,600
$3,550–4,200 B(Kn)

A terracotta figure of a boy with a cockerel, on a separate reel-shaped plinth, damaged, Hellenistic, Asia Minor, c3rdC BC, 3¾in (9.5cm) high.
£880–1,050 / €1,250–1,500
$1,500–1,800 B(Kn)

► **A pottery bowl,** with moulded decoration, Hellenistic, Megara, 3rd–2ndC BC, 5in (12.5cm) diam.
£145–160 / €210–230
$245–270 HEL

An oinochoe, with a trefoil mouth, Greek, 5thC BC, 8¾in (22cm) high.
£4,300–5,100
€6,200–7,300
$7,200–8,600 S(NY)

A terracotta figure of a closely-draped seated woman, damaged, Hellenistic, 3rd–2ndC BC, 13¾in (35cm) high.
£3,350–4,000
€4,800–5,700
$5,700–6,700 S(P)

A Red-Figure bell-krater, decorated on one side with a figure of Eros in flight, the reverse decorated with the head of a Lady of Fashion, light wear, Greek South Italy, 4thC BC, 9in (23cm) high.
£1,650–1,850
€2,400–2,650
$2,750–3,100 A&O

◄ **An amphora,** one side decorated with a woman presenting a casket to a seated man, the reverse with two youths, the neck with panels of laurel, neck repaired, Greek South Italy, c340–320 BC, 18in (45.5cm) high.
£2,550–2,850
€3,700–4,100
$4,200–4,700 A&O

A pottery female head, wearing a *polos*, Greek, c3rdC BC, 4½in (11.5cm) high.
£400–450 / €580–650
$670–760 HEL

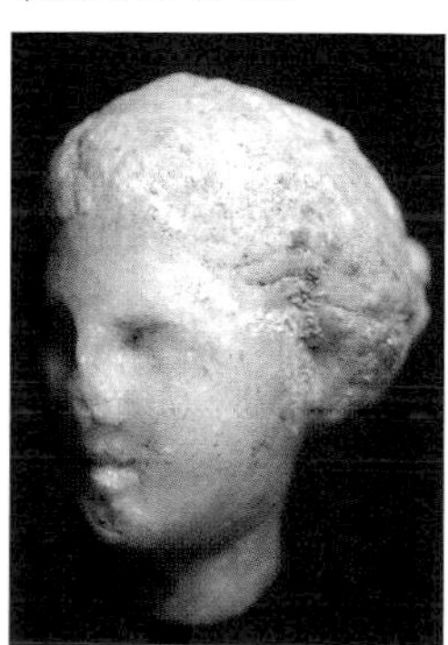

A marble head of Aphrodite, Hellenistic, 2nd–1stC BC, 1¾in (4.5cm) high.
£630–700 / €900–1,000
$1,050–1,200 HEL

A bronze horse-head appliqué, the eyes inlaid with silver, traces of original lead infill, some damage, Roman, c1stC BC/AD, 2¼in (5.5cm) wide.
£410–490 / €590–700
$690–820 ⚒ B(Kn)

A bronze serving dish, decorated with two goats on rocky ground, 1stC AD, 7¼in (18.5cm) diam.
£350–390 / €500–560
$600–660 ⊞ ANG

A bronze pin, the terminal in the form of a boar's head, with a woad grinder to the underside, Roman, 1stC AD, 8½in (21.5cm) long.
£250–280 / €360–400
$420–470 ⊞ HEL

A glass beaker, decorated with wheel-cut horizontal bands, with iridescence and some encrustation, Roman, mid–late 1stC AD, 4in (10cm) high.
£440–530 / €630–750
$740–890 ⚒ B(Kn)

An ivory cosmetic spoon, engraved with a centurion, Roman, 1stC AD, 5¼in (13.5cm) long.
£630–700
€900–1,000
$1,050–1,200
⊞ HEL

A bronze figure of Zeus, the navel and nipples inlaid with silver, Gallo-Roman, c1stC AD, 6¼in (16cm) high.
£5,000–6,000
€7,200–8,600
$8,400–10,100 ⚒ S(NY)

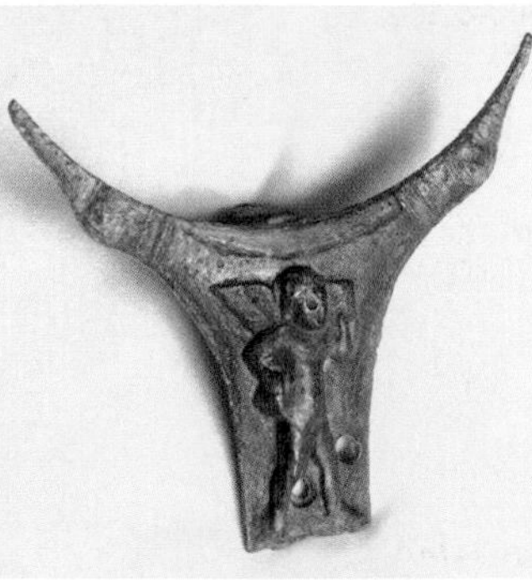

A skillet/*patera* handle, decorated with a figure of Cupid moulded in high relief, the terminals in the form of ravens' heads, Roman, 1stC AD, 3¼in (8.5cm) wide.
£350–390 / €500–550
$600–660 ⊞ ANG
***Paterae* were flat dishes that were used in the sacrificial ceremonies observed when offering libations to the gods.**

A marble inscription fragment, Roman, 2nd–3rdC AD, 6½in (16.5cm) wide.
£220–250 / €320–360
$370–410 ⊞ HEL

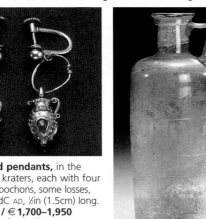

A pair of gold pendants, in the form of volute kraters, each with four garnet/glass cabochons, some losses, Roman, 1st/2ndC AD, ½in (1.5cm) long.
£1,150–1,350 / €1,700–1,950
$1,950–2,300 ⚒ S(NY)

◄ **A glass ewer,** with an applied handle, some wear, Roman, 2nd/3rdC AD, 12¼in (31cm) high.
£2,450–2,950 / €3,500–4,200
$4,100–4,900 ⚒ S(Am)

A double-edged short sword, water-damaged, Roman, 2nd/3rdC AD, 21¾in (55.5cm) long.
£3,200–3,850 / €4,600–5,500
$5,400–6,500 ⚒ Herm

◄ **A bronze roundel from a horse's harness or vehicle,** decorated with three pelta motifs around a central roundel, Romano-British, 3rdC AD, 3½in (9cm) diam.
£175–195 / €250–280
$290–330 ⊞ ANG

► **A bronze flagon,** with an applied rim, handle and base, slight damage, Roman, 3rd–4thC AD, 10½in (26.5cm) high.
£440–490 / €640–710
$740–820 ⊞ A&O

A sea-encrusted terracotta amphora, Roman, 3rd–4thC AD, 35½in (90cm) high, with fitted iron wall mount.
£1,100–1,300
€1,600–1,900
$1,850–2,200 B

► A bronze dish, with incised decoration, Roman, 4thC AD, 4¼in (11cm) diam.
£180–200 / €260–290
$300–330 HEL

◄ A mould-blown glass bottle, with an indistinct inscription around the base, iridescence and some interior encrustation, late Roman/Byzantine, 4th–6thC AD, 9¼in (23.5cm) high.
£3,500–4,200 / €5,000–6,000
$5,900–7,100 B(Kn)

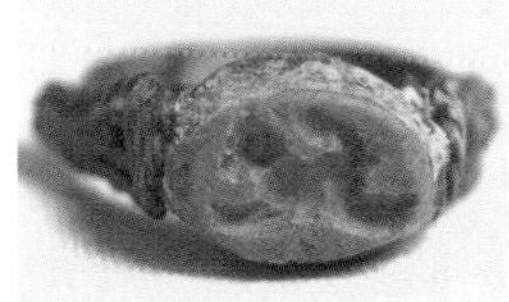

► A glass intaglio, carved with a running dog, set in a later mount, Sasanian, 4th–5thC AD, 5½in (14cm) wide.
£70–80 / €100–110
$120–135 HEL

◄ A silver bowl, the silver-inlaid *tondo* depicting a pheasant holding a cloth and pendant in its beak, within a decorative border, worn, Sasanian, 6th–7thC AD, 5½in (14cm) diam.
£700–840 / €1,000–1,200
$1,200–1,400 B(Kn)

A pair of gold, onyx, amethyst and pearl earrings, each with an onyx head of Medusa set to the centre of an openwork disc, with three beaded pendants hung from a crossbar of stylized birds, Roman, 3rd/4thC AD, 2in (5cm) long.
£3,200–3,850 / €4,600–5,500
$5,400–6,400 S(NY)

A bronze eagle finial, with incised feather detail, some losses, late Roman/early Byzantine, 5th–7thC AD, 3½in (9cm) high, mounted.
£1,900–2,250
€2,750–3,300
$3,200–3,850 B(Kn)

A mosaic fragment, depicting a wounded horse named Theba, Roman, 3rd/4thC AD, 27 x 36in (68.5 x 91.5cm).
£7,100–8,500 / €10,200–12,200
$12,000–14,300 S(NY)

A glass carafe, with mould-blown striations and indented base, Roman, 4thC AD, 7in (18cm) high.
£260–310 / €380–450
$440–520 B(Kn)

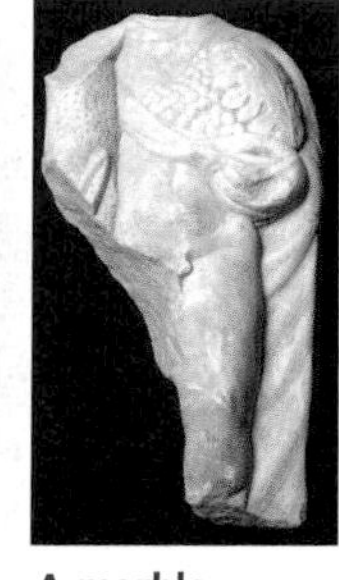

A marble torso of Priapus, holding grapes, Roman, 4th–5thC AD, 13in (33cm) high.
£1,600–1,800
€2,350–2,600
$2,700–3,000
HEL

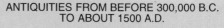

A bronze door hasp, decorated with a head of Christ flanked by Latin crosses, Byzantine, pre-10thC, 6½in (16.5cm) wide.
£7,900–8,800 / €11,400–12,700
$13,300–14,800 ICO

◄ **A pair of gold earrings,** with repoussé and incised decoration of two confronted peacocks flanking a Maltese cross, with three glass beads around the perimeter, Byzantine, 6th/7thC AD, 2in (5cm) wide.
£3,550–4,250
€5,100–6,100
$5,900–7,100 S(NY)

A Neolithic stone axe head, Scandinavian, c2000 BC, 5¼in (13.5cm) wide.
£70–80 / €100–110
$120–135 HEL

A double-edged bronze dagger, with patination, Middle-European, Bronze Age, c1100 BC, 9½in (24cm) long.
£2,100–2,500 / €3,000–3,600
$3,550–4,200 Herm

A broadsword, Celtic, c400 BC–AD 100, blade 25in (63.5cm) long.
£2,900–3,250 / €4,200–4,650
$4,850–5,400 FAC

A bronze torque, with bud-shaped terminals, Celtic, c6thC BC, 7½in (19cm) diam.
£1,950–2,350
€2,850–3,400
$3,300–3,900 S(NY)

A pottery urn, the shoulder decorated with geometric patterns, the body with four bosses and incised vertical lines, section of rim missing, Saxon, 6thC AD, 4½in (11.5cm) high.
£1,350–1,600 / €1,950–2,300
$2,250–2,700 F&C

A buckle, with linear decoration, decorated pin and buckle plate, southeast European, 5th/6thC AD, 2½in (6.5cm) wide.
£65–75 / €95–105
$110–125 ANG

A latch key, the latch lifter with an open fretwork pattern, East Anglia, Viking, 9–11thC, 2in (5cm) long.
£65–75 / €100–110
$110–125 ANG

◄ **A bronze stirrup mount,** depicting a lion with an open mouth, East Anglia, Viking, early 11thC, 2in (5cm) high.
£65–75
€100–110
$110–125
ANG

A single-edged sword, the hilt inlaid with flat silver roundels on each side, the pommel incised with pairs of lines and decorated *en suite* with the cross-piece around the base, Viking, 10thC, blade 31in (78.5cm) long.
£20,000–24,000 / €28,800–29,500
$34,000–40,000 B(Kn)

A single-edged dagger, with a bronze quillon and pommel and iron blade, 14th/15thC, 11in (28cm) long.
£480–530 / €690–760
$800–890 A&O
This dagger was found in the River Thames in London.

Tribal Art

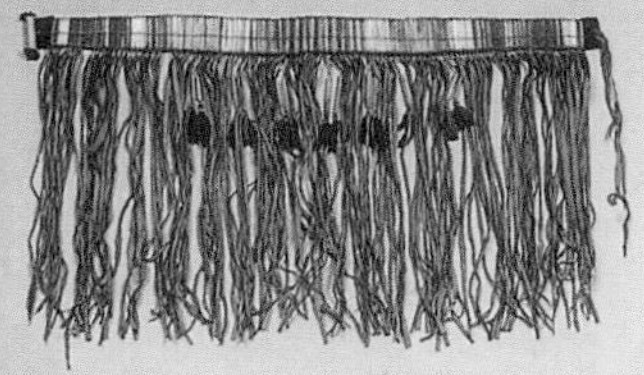

A buckskin and quill belt, with bone fastener and hide fringes, Native American, Northern Athabascan.
£3,500–4,200 / €5,000–6,000
$5,900–7,000 B(Kn)
Ex-James Hooper collection.

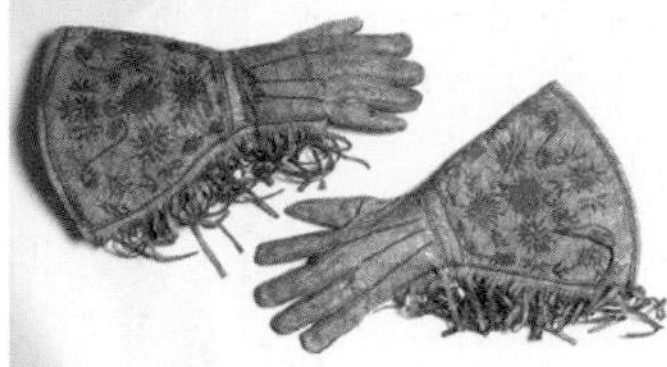

A pair of embroidered buckskin gauntlets, with monogrammed initials, probably Cree, Native American, c1840, 16in (40.5cm) long.
£1,700–1,900 / €2,450–2,750
$2,850–3,200 TLA

A birch box and cover, embroidered with moose hair and lined in grosgrain silk, possibly Huron, Native American, 1850–75, 8½in (21.5cm) wide.
£370–440 / €530–630
$620–740 G(B)

The James Hooper collection

James Hooper (1897–1917) began collecting tribal art in 1912, by visiting flea markets and small antique shops in Britain. As his collection grew he began to exchange pieces with other collectors and dealers and purchased some items from auctions. His fascination with ethnographic objects predominantly from Melanesia, Polynesia and North America resulted in one of the finest and most comprehensive private collections.

Art and Artefacts of the Pacific, Africa and the Americas: The James Hooper Collection, compiled by Steven Phelps, and published in 1976, catalogues 1,927 pieces. This book has become the 'bible' of ethnographic art from these regions and itself commands a price of approximately £1,000 / €1,450 / $1,700. The collection was sold in the 1970s through a number of high profile auctions.

A Navajo rug, some repairs and fraying, Native American, 51 x 84in (127 x 213.5cm).
£550–660 / €790–950
$920–1,100 JDJ

A Navajo textile panel, slight damage, Native American, early 19thC, 92½ x 81½in (235 x 207cm).
£1,150–1,350
€1,650–1,950
$1,900–2,250 BUK

A rug, Native American, Southern United States, early 20thC, 76 x 56in (193 x 142cm).
£220–260 / €320–370
$370–440 WW

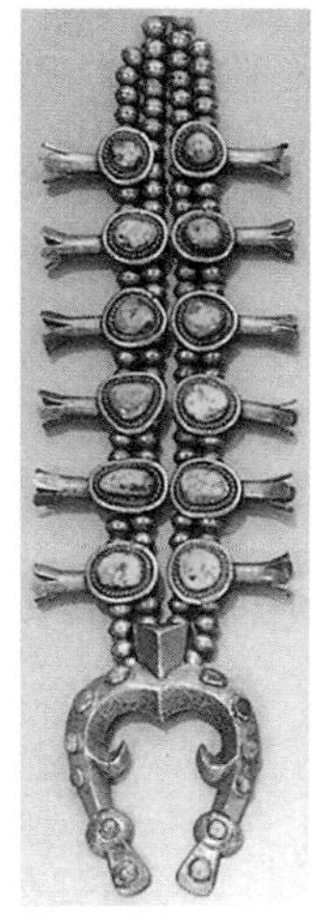

A Navajo silver necklace, with 12 squash blossoms each set with a turquoise cabochon, Native American, 25½in (65cm) long.
£530–630
€750–900
$890–1,050
B(Kn)

A Salish woven spruce root basket, Native American, 8¼in (21cm) high.
£2,350–2,800 / €3,400–4,000
$3,950–4,700 B(Kn)
Ex-James Hooper collection.

A Tlingit alderwood grease bowl, in the form of a seal, set with six ivory medallions, with ivory teeth and abalone shell eyes and nose, Native American, c1900, 15in (38cm) long.
£1,750–2,100 / €2,500–3,000
$2,950–3,500 B(Kn)

◀ **A hand-woven basket,** Native American, c1900, 12½in (32cm) diam.
£280–330
€400–470
$470–550
DuM

A Salish wooden comb, carved in the form of an owl and surmounted by a pair of eagles' heads forming spouted channels, Native American, 6in (15cm) long.
£19,000–22,800
€27,500–33,000
$32,000–38,000 B(Kn)
Ex-James Hooper collection.
Combs rarely survive in this condition especially one which has obviously been used so much – evident from the fine patina. It is very beautiful and has the added advantage of having been in the James Hooper collection with the catalogue number inscribed in ink on the back.

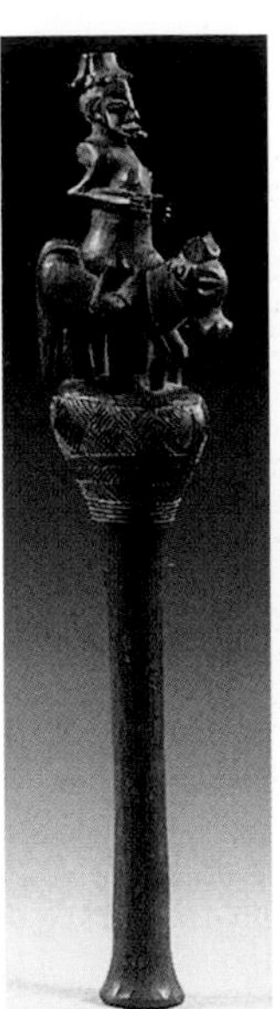

◀ **A Songo staff,** surmounted by a man on an animal, slight damage, African, Angola, 17¼in (43.5cm) high.
£1,650–1,950 / €2,350–2,800
$2,750–3,250 ⚒ S(P)

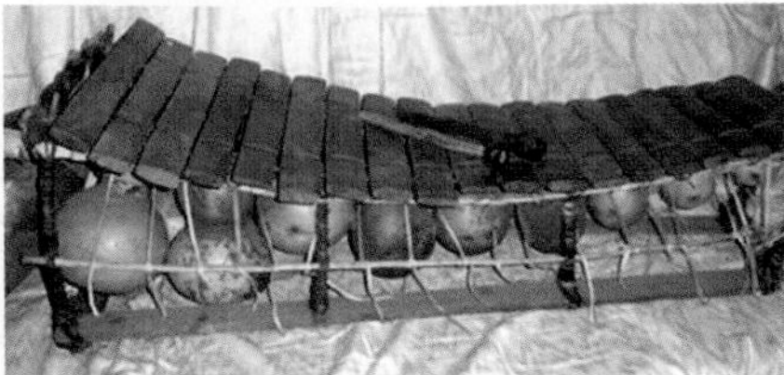

A wood, leather and paper *balafon*, African, Burkina Faso, c1960, 60in (152.5cm) long.
£290–330 / €420–470
$490–550 ⊞ ARTi
A *balafon* is a xylophone constructed from wooden keys above gourd resonators with holes covered by membranes to create a buzzing sound. The word *balafon* is said to come from the Mandingo word *baza* meaning to speak.

A Bamum bronze and basketwork helmet mask, African, Cameroon, c1950, 20in (51cm) high.
£430–480 / €620–690
$720–800 ⊞ ARTi
The Bamum are a group of people living in the grasslands area of western Cameroon. Before colonialization the Bamum had their own kingdom but today they are citizens of the Republic of Cameroon.

A ceremonial staff, restored, African, Cameroon, 64¼in (163cm) long.
£620–740
€890–1,050
$1,050–1,250
⚒ S(P)

▶ **An iron sword,** African, Democratic Republic of Congo, 23½in (59.5cm) high.
£1,350–1,500 / €1,950–2,150
$2,250–2,500 ⊞ HUR
Straight-bladed swords are rare among the corpus of African weapons. The figural aspect created by the pommels, with expanded hand-like termini, give this type of weapon a distinctive appearance. These swords were presented only to men of nobility who had inherited the right to rule particular branches of the Congo people. More than just an insignia of office, the sword was considered to be the actual repository of the leader's power; the authority of the ruler was forfeited if his sword was stolen or lost.

It has been suggested that the derivation of this weapon form can be traced to the straight-bladed swords of the European crusaders of the medieval period whose influence may have spread to Africa.

This sword is slightly shortened and missing its ivory grip. The rusted surfaces and eroded edges are testimony to the practice of leaving swords exposed to the elements on the grave of an unsucceeded ruler.

A Kuba wood and raffia cloth mask, decorated with beads and cowrie shells, African, Democratic Republic of Congo, 10¼in (26cm) high.
£900–1,050
€1,300–1,500
$1,500–1,750 ⚒ BERN
These masks are also known as Royal Masks as they represent figures in mythological history.

A Lega raffia hat, decorated with elephant hair, buttons, tusks and seashells, African, Democratic Republic of Congo, 1940s, 8in (20.5cm) high.
£320–360
€460–520
$540–600
⊞ Trib
When a hat such as this is surmounted with elephant hair it signifies that the wearer is of the highest level in the Bwami Association.

A Suku painted wood and raffia helmet mask, African, Democratic Republic of Congo, early 20thC, 24in (61cm) high.
£1,300–1,450
€1,850–2,100
$2,200–2,450 ⊞ Trib

A Yaka fetish, African, Democratic Republic of Congo, 1940s, 21¼in (54cm) high.
£210–250
€300–360
$350–420
⚒ BERN

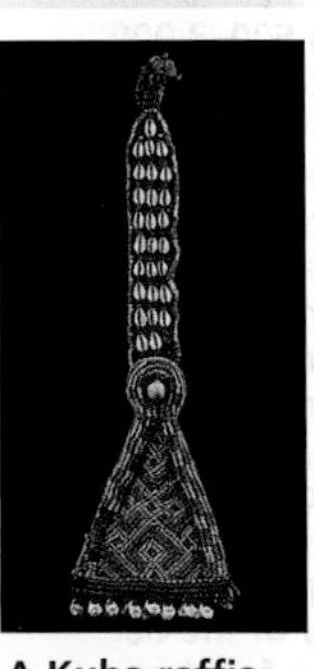

A Kuba raffia body ornament, woven with glass beads and cowrie shells, some beads missing, African, Democratic Republic of Congo, 18in (45.5cm) long.
£250–300
€360–430
$420–500
⚒ S(P)

A carved wood chair, African, Ethiopia, 19thC, 40in (101.5cm) high.
£3,150–3,500
€4,500–5,000
$5,300–5,900 ⊞ Trib

An Ashanti fertility doll, with five glass bead necklaces on the base, African, Ghana, 13¼in (33.5cm) high.
£1,350–1,600
€1,950–2,300
$2,250–2,700 S(P)
To aid fertility young women carry these dolls around on their backs and care for it as they would a child.

A Baga wooden male figure, African, Guinea, c1960, 50in (127cm) high.
£450–500 / €650–720
$760–840 ⊞ ARTi
These figures were kept in sacred houses that could only be entered by officials of the men's association or by tribal elders. Similar figures are seen in Nimba head-dresses and represent the Baga vision of goodness.

◄ **An Akye terracotta anthropomorphic vessel,** African, Ivory Coast, 12¼in (31cm) high.
£1,500–1,800
€2,150–2,600
$2,500–3,000 S(P)
The Akye people abandoned the practice of placing a funerary vessel on tombs of their dead, at the beginning of the 20th century. This piece was collected by the vendor in the Ivory Coast in 1962.

A Baule wooden model of a leopard, African, Ivory Coast, 4½in (11.5cm) high.
£1,050–1,200 / €1,500–1,750
$1,750–2,000 ⊞ HUR
Depictions of animals are abundant in African art, perhaps because particular attributes of certain animals lend themselves to comparison with human behaviour. Due to its intelligence, courage and predatory behaviour, the leopard is often associated with political authority. As a symbol of royal kingship, the qualities of aggression, cunning and speed, associated with the leopard, are transferred to the leader himself. This simple yet animated Baule carving appears to have been carved as a free-standing sculpture to be noticed and admired.

A Dan wooden gameboard, with incised decoration, African, Ivory Coast, 20¼in (51.5cm) long.
£2,850–3,400 / €4,100–4,900
$4,800–5,700 S(NY)
This gameboard was probably for playing wari – a game played with cowrie shells.

◄ **A Dogon wood, fibre and iron mask,** African, Mali, 22in (56cm) high.
£2,450–2,700 / €3,500–3,900
$4,100–4,500 ⊞ HUR
Masks are worn in dances as part of an elaborate funerary ritual, the final ceremony performed two to three years after a person's death to officially end the mourning period. The performances can last several days and include hundreds of masked dancers, each wearing a brightly coloured costume of cloth, fibre and shells. In performance, the masks acts as the physical locus of the spiritual energy of the deceased, providing a vehicle for the disembodied forces to move from the village realm of the living into the ancestral world, thereby restoring order to the universe. The mask pictured here represents the antelope and the hare. The Dogon associate antelopes with masculine strength, virility and courage, as well as with agricultural cultivation. The hare symbolizes craftiness and intelligence and is recognized as a trickster figure in Dogon folklore.

A Dogon wooden ladder, African, Mali, c1930, 72in (183cm) long.
£640–720
€920–1,050
$1,050–1,200
⊞ ARTi

A Dogon wooden helmet mask, African, Mali, c1900, 26in (66cm) high.
£700–780 / €1,000–1,100
$1,150–1,300 ⊞ Cas

A Makonde chieftain chair, African, Mozambique, early 20thC, 32in (81.5cm) high.
£490–550 / €710–790
$820–920 ⊞ Trib

A Benin carved coconut, depicting a king and two attendants, the reverse with a royal priest, damage and repair, African, Nigeria, 5½in (14cm) high.
£610–730 / €880–1,050
$1,000–1,200 ⚒ B(Kn)

A Benin bronze model of a leopard, African, Nigeria, c1950, 26in (66cm) long.
£650–720 / €930–1,050
$1,050–1,200 ⊞ ARTi

A Tutsi woven basket and cover, African, Rwanda, early 20thC, 14in (35.5cm) high.
£760–850 / €1,100–1,250
$1,250–1,450 ⊞ Trib

A Xhosa glass bead necklace, South African, 110¼in (280cm) long.
£540–650 / €780–940
$910–1,100 ⚒ S(P)
This collar was bought in Cape Town in the 1930s.

A Zulu wooden headrest, decorated with zigzag motifs, South African, 13in (33cm) long.
£5,700–6,800 / €8,200–9,800
$9,600–11,400 ⚒ S(NY)
Headrests were utilitarian, protecting the head and coiffure of the sleeper. Over extended periods of ownership and use they became invested with complex spiritual associations. It is known that headrests were often buried with their owners, but in some cases were retained as vehicles through which the late owner might be contacted in the ancestral realm. This piece was collected in Kwazulu in the 1930s.

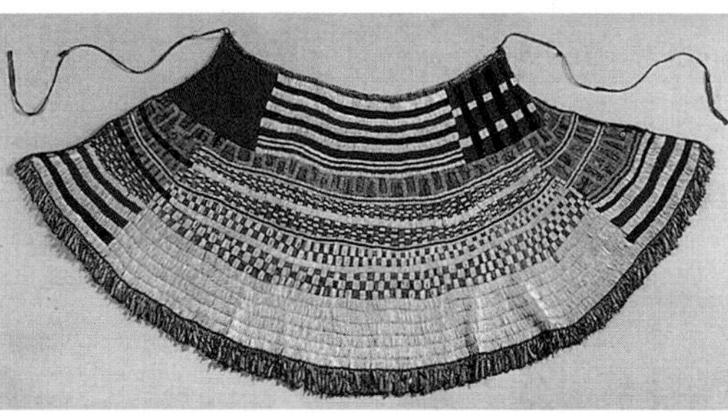

An Iraqw hide skirt, decorated with glass beads, African, Tanzania, 70in (177.5cm) long.
£7,100–8,500 / €10,200–12,200
$12,000–14,300 ⚒ S(NY)

A Dinka carved wood and aluminium stool, African, southern Sudan, early 20thC, 8in (20.5cm) high.
£760–850 / €1,100–1,250
$1,250–1,450 ⊞ Trib

LOCATE THE SOURCE

The source of each illustration in Miller's can be found by checking the code letters below each caption with the Key to Illustrations, pages 794–800.

◄ **A wooden milk container,** with cover, African, Uganda, 1950–60, 11in (28cm) high.
£135–150 / €195–220
$220–250 ⊞ Trib

A Lozi carved wooden bowl and cover, in the form of a rabbit, African, Zambia, 1950s, 11in (28cm) wide.
£90–100 / €130–145
$150–165 ⊞ Trib
The Lozi live in and around the flood plain of the Zambezi river in western Zambia. They used ornamental bowls for food storage and serving meat and vegetables.

A Bongo woode staff, with aluminium eyes, African, Sudan, 1940–50s, 23in (58.5cm) high.
£660–740
€950–1,050
$1,100–1,250
⊞ Trib

A Dyak *mandau*, with a carved bone handle and mounted scabbard, Borneo, 19thC, blade 22¾in (58cm) long.
£200–240 / €290–340
$340–400 WW

◄ **A Dyak *mandau*,** the carved hardwood handle with rattan grip, in a wood scabbard decorated with abstract panels and a woven mount, Borneo, 19thC, blade 15¾in (40cm) long.
£480–540 / €690–780
$810–910 FAC

A carved wood zoomorphic head, Indonesian, Flores Island, 17¾in (45cm) high.
£260–310 / €370–440
$440–520 SHSY

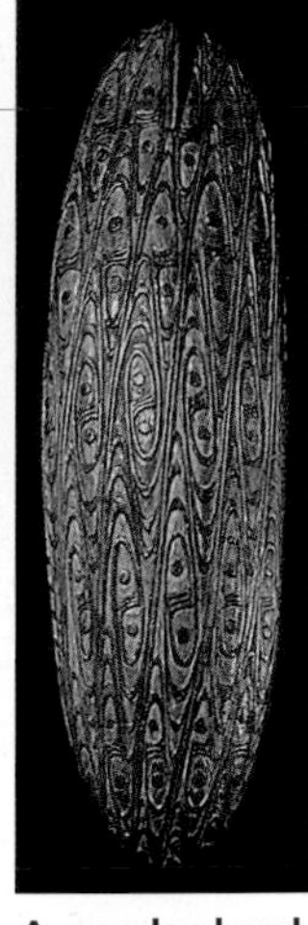

A wooden bowl, carved in low relief, Indonesian, Irian Jaya, Lake Sentani, 26¾in (68cm) long.
£1,400–1,650
€2,000–2,350
$2,350–2,750
S(NY)

A Lombok executioner's *kris*, the wooden hilt carved as a stylized figure, Indonesian, 19thC, 29½in (75cm) long, in a wooden sheath.
£380–450 / €540–640
$640–750 WAL

◄ **A carved wood Leti female figure,** Indonesian, 20in (51cm) high.
£690–820 / €990–1,150
$1,150–1,350 BERN

A wood, polished stone and vegetable fibre adze, handle split, New Guinea, 23¼in (59cm) long.
£1,050–1,250 / €1,500–1,800
$1,750–2,100 S(P)
This item was collected in the 1920s.

◄ **An Iatmul clay *mei* mask,** decorated with cowrie shells and boar's tusks, Papua New Guinea, Sepik River, 32in (81.5cm) long.
£540–650 / €780–930
$910–1,100 S(O)
These masks represent ancestral spirits and are worn in ceremonies to instruct initiates.

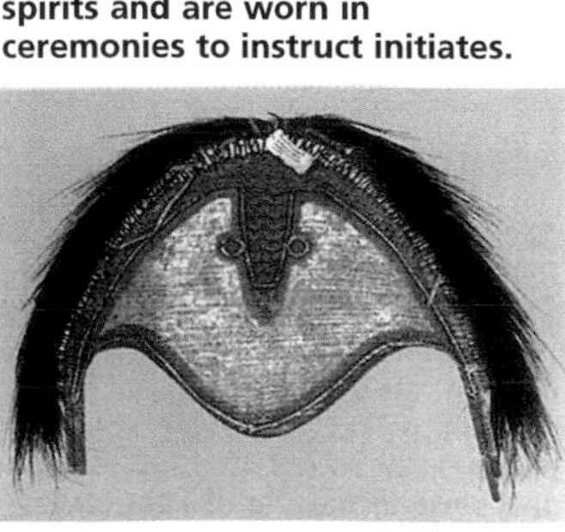

► **A woven headpiece,** applied with feathers, possibly Papua New Guinea, 11½in (29cm) wide.
£3,350–4,000
€4,800–5,700
$5,600–6,700
S(O)

A carved wood door, Indonesian, Timor, 76¾ x 19¾in (195 x 50cm).
£870–1,000
€1,250–1,500
$1,450–1,750 SHSY

► **A payback doll,** made of tightly bound vegetable matter decorated with cassowary feathers, seeds and shells, New Guinea, Mendi, 21¼in (54cm) long.
£290–340 / €420–490
$480–570 SHSY
These dolls symbolize a vengeance for a war death. They are usually destroyed once recompense has been made by way of an agreed payment of money, or the death of a member of the enemy tribe.

A wooden canoe splash board, Papua New Guinea, Massim, 30¾in (78cm) wide.
£720–860 / €1,050–1,250
$1,200–1,450 SHSY
Large sea-going canoes still play an important part in local trading and are richly decorated. The most distinctive features are the canoe prow boards which include splash boards. Massim objects are instantly recognizable by their intricate carved flat surfaces.

A Tiwi carved wood female figure, decorated with natural pigments and feathers, Australian, Bathurst Island, 17in (43cm) high.
£360–430 / €520–620
$600–720 SHSY

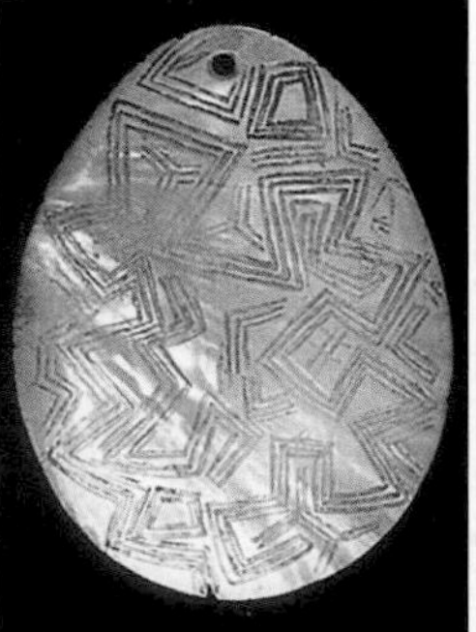

An Aboriginal shell pendant, decorated with an incised geometric motif, Australian, 6¼in (16cm) high.
£1,350–1,600
€1,950–2,300
$2,250–2,700 S(NY)

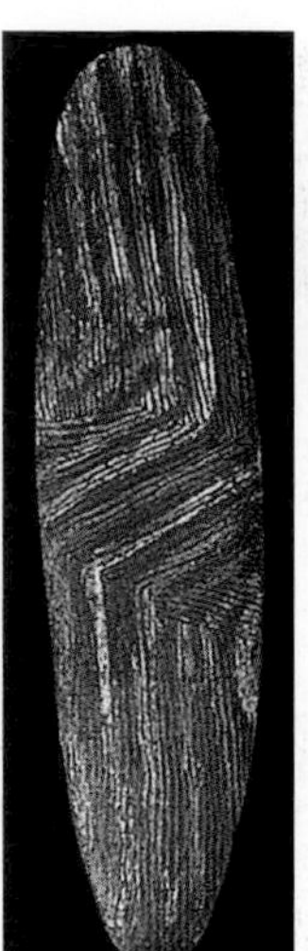

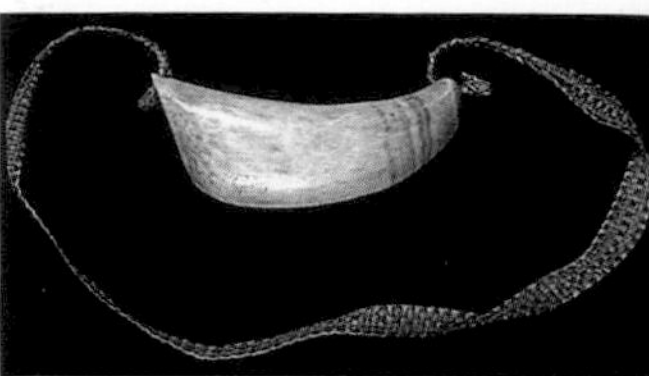

A *tambua*, the sperm whale tooth suspended on a fibre necklace, Fijian, tooth 6in (15cm) long.
£1,050–1,250 / €1,500–1,800
$1,750–2,100 S(NY)
Ex-James Hooper collection.

◄ **A wunda,** incised with linear striations, West Australian, 25¼in (64cm) long.
£530–630 / €760–900
$890–1,050 SHSY
Wunda is the Aboriginal name for this type of shield.

A rootwood club, split, Fijian, early 19thC, 44½in (113cm) long.
£500–600 / €720–860
$840–1,000 F&C

A throwing club, slight damage, Fijian, 19thC, 16¾in (42.5cm) long.
£390–430 / €560–620
$650–720 ⊞ FAC
These throwing clubs were used as missiles in combat. They were thrown underarm with great precision.

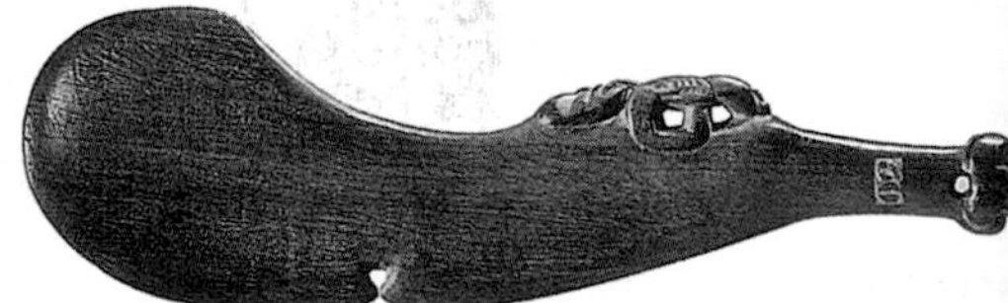

A hardwood club, carved with bands of zigzag and serrated decoration, reduced in length, head chipped, Fijian, 19thC, 38¼in (97cm) long.
£125–150 / €180–210
$210–250 WAL

A Maori wooden *wakahuia*, New Zealand, 18¾in (47.5cm) long.
£3,300–3,900
€4,800–5,700
$5,500–6,600 S(P)
These *wakahuia*, or treasure boxes, were used for storing small valuables such as ornaments or feathers. They were originally suspended from rafters and viewed from below, hence the elaborate decoration on the underside.

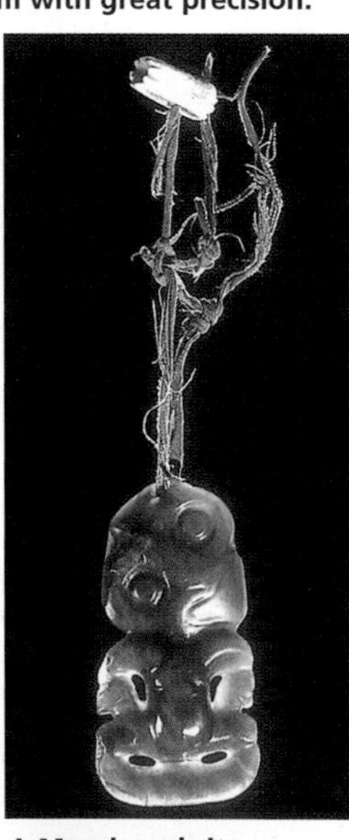

A Maori nephrite pendant (*hei tiki*), damaged, New Zealand, 4in (10cm) high.
£2,500–3,000
€3,600–4,300
$4,200–5,000 S(P)
The *hei tiki* figures could represent either an ancestral figure or Hineteiwaiwa, the goddess of childbirth, and were considered fertility symbols.

A Maori wooden hand club (*wahaika*), the outer edge and the pommel decorated with stylized *tiki*, New Zealand, 15½in (39.5cm) long.
£3,000–3,600
€4,300–5,200
$5,000–6,000 S(NY)

A Maori flax bag, decorated with shells, New Zealand, 1860–80, 9in (23cm) wide.
£490–550 / €700–790
$820–920 ⊞ FAC

A Mangaia ceremonial club, Cook Islands, 16in (40.5cm) high.
£1,000–1,200
€1,450–1,700
$1,700–2,000 S(P)

Books & Book Illustrations

Richard Adams, *Watership Down*, published by Rex Collings, first edition, 1972, 8°, presentation copy signed by the author, folding map, original cloth, dust jacket.
£1,300–1,550
€1,900–2,250
$2,200–2,600 ⚒ BBA

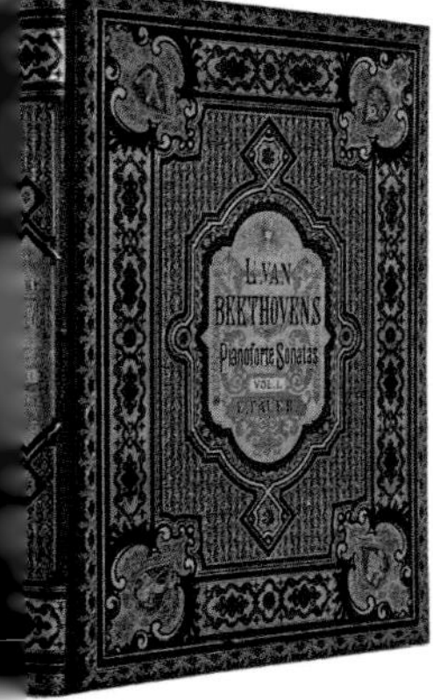

Ludwig van Beethoven, *Piano Sonatas*, c1870, 2 vols, 13½in (34.5cm) high.
£430–480 / €620–690
$720–800 ⊞ TDG

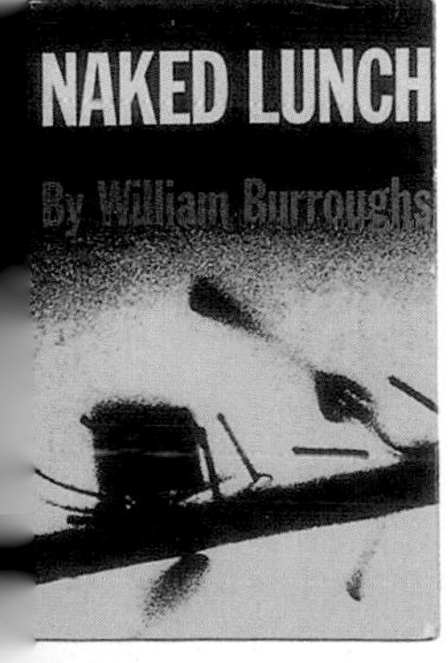

William Burroughs, *Naked Lunch*, published in New York, 1959, 8°, cloth-backed boards, dust jacket, some chips and fading.
£280–330 / €400–470
$470–550 ⚒ BBA

Sir James Edward Alexander, *Transatlantic Sketches, Comprising Visits to the Most Interesting Scenes in North and South America, and The West Indies,* 1833, 8°, 2 vols, engraved map and 10 etched plates by William Heath, bookplates for Joseph Feilden, calf with gilt decoration.
£540–650 / €780–930
$920–1,100 ⚒ L

Enid Bagnold, *National Velvet*, published by Heinemann, first edition, 1935, 8°, illustrated by Laurian Jones, original cloth, dust jacket, some repairs.
£450–540 / €650–780
$760–910 ⚒ BBA

Book of Hours, published by Guillaume Anabat for Giffet et Germain Hardouyn, c1520, 8°, illuminated and coloured woodcut illustrations on vellum with gold leaf, including coloured and gold engravings with some initial letters highlighted, later purple suede binding.
£8,900–10,700
€12,800–15,400
$15,000–18,000 ⚒ G(L)

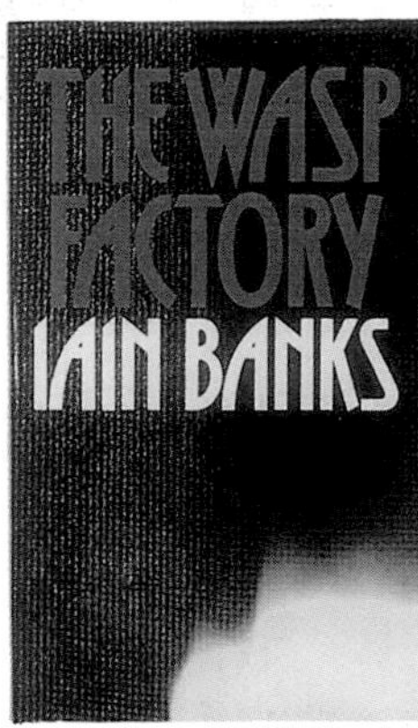

John James Audubon and John Bachman, *The Quadrupeds of North America*, published by Nagel & Weingartner, first 8° edition, 1849–54, 8°, 3 vols, hand-coloured plates by W. E. Hitchcock and R. Trembly after J. J. and J. W. Audubon, modern polished calf with morocco lettering pieces, some staining and browning.
£4,250–5,100
€6,100–7,300
$7,100–8,600 ⚒ S(NY)

◄ **Iain Banks,** *The Wasp Factory*, published by Macmillan, 1984, 8°, first edition, signed by the author, cloth gilt with dust jacket.
£195–230 / €280–330
$330–390 ⚒ DW

Book of Common Prayer, 1704, 12°, tortoiseshell binding with engraved silver medallions, endpieces and clasps, with contemporary leather pouch.
£1,600–1,900 / €2,300–2,750
$2,700–3,200 ⚒ B(B)

Lord George Gordon Byron, *The Works*, 1832–33, small 8°, 17 vols, 16 engraved frontispieces and 16 engraved titles, contemporary blue calf, gilt, some browning.
£260–310 / €380–450
$440–530 ⚒ RTo

Lewis Carroll (Reverend Charles Lutwidge Dodgson), *Alice's Adventures in Wonderland*, published by Macmillan & Co, first edition, 1872, 7¼ x 5in (18.5 x 12.5cm).
£2,700–3,000
€3,900–4,300
$4,500–5,000 BIB

Lewis Carroll, (Reverend Charles Lutwidge Dodgson), *The Hunting of the Snark, An Agony in Eight Fits,* published by Macmillan, first edition, 1876, 8°, illustrations by Henry Holiday, original gilt-decorated red cloth, rubbed and worn.
£440–530 / €630–750
$740–890 DW

Basil Hall Chamberlain, *Japanese Fairy Tales*, published by Griffith Farran & Co, 1890, 8°, 4 vols, colour woodblock illustrations on *crepe-de-chine*, bound in contemporary red cloth gilt, fading to spines.
£740–890 / €1,100–1,300
$1,250–1,500 DW

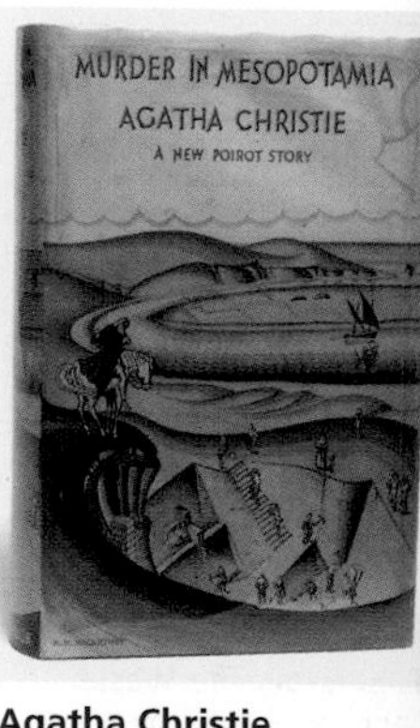

Agatha Christie, *Murder in Mesopotamia*, published by Collins Crime Club, first edition, 1936, 8 x 5½in (20.5 x 14cm).
£2,900–3,200
€4,150–4,600
$4,850–5,400 BIB

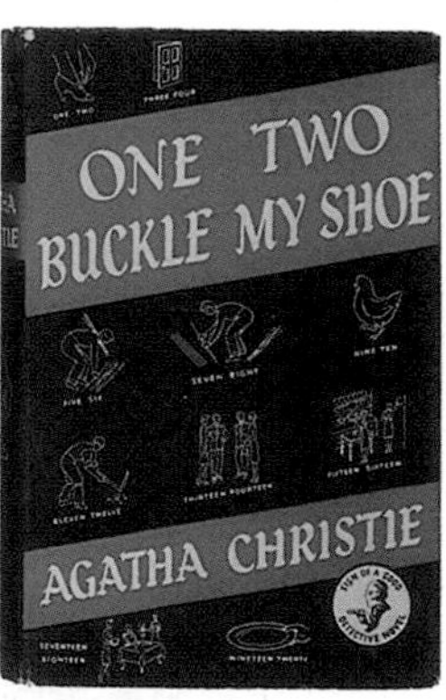

Agatha Christie, *One, Two, Buckle My Shoe,* published by Collins, first edition, 1940, 8°, original red cloth and pictorial dust jacket, light foxing, rubbed corner.
£1,600–1,800
€2,350–2,600
$2,700–3,000 JON

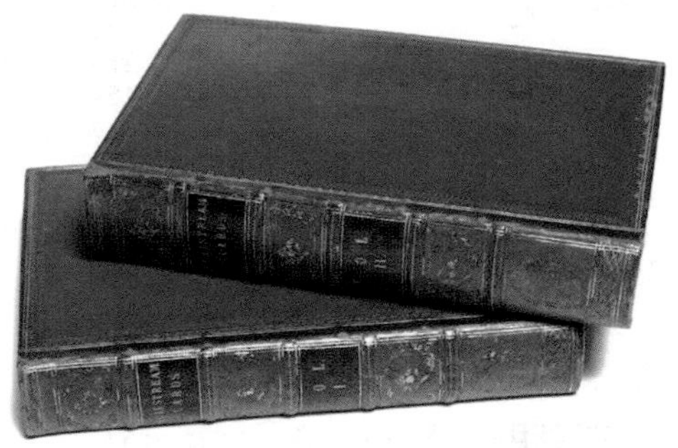

***Coldstream Guards*,** 1833, 2 vols, 8½ x 5½in (21.5 x 14cm), printed by A. J. Valpy, leather bound.
£200–230 / €290–330
$340–390 TLA

Confucius, *The Morals*, 1691, 8°, engraved portrai frontispiece, contemporary sheep, light staining, spotting and water-staining, small tear, rubbed, joints cracked.
£630–760 / €920–1,100
$1,100–1,300 BBA

► **Captain James Cook,** *Third Voyage – A Voyage to the Pacific Ocean,* 1784, large folio, 1 folding chart, 1 double-page chart, 61 engraved plates, contemporary marbled calf, some spotting and repairs, cover worn.
£3,000–3,600
€4,300–5,100
$5,000–6,000 RTo

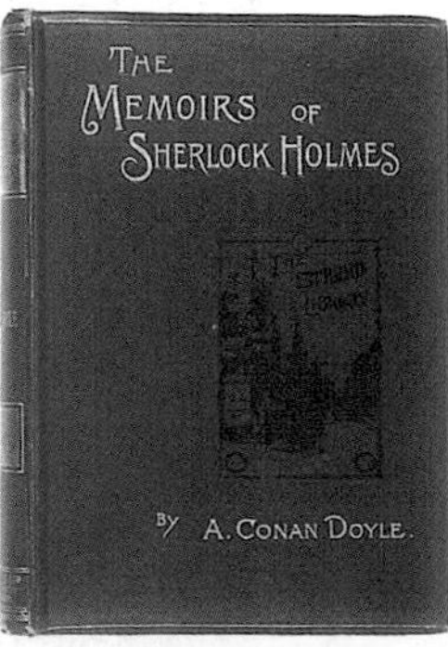

Sir Arthur Conan Doyle, *The Memoirs of Sherlock Holmes*, published by Newnes, first edition, 1894, tall 8°, illustrations by Sidney Paget, original gilt cloth, some damage and losses.
£430–510 / €620–740
$720–860 DW

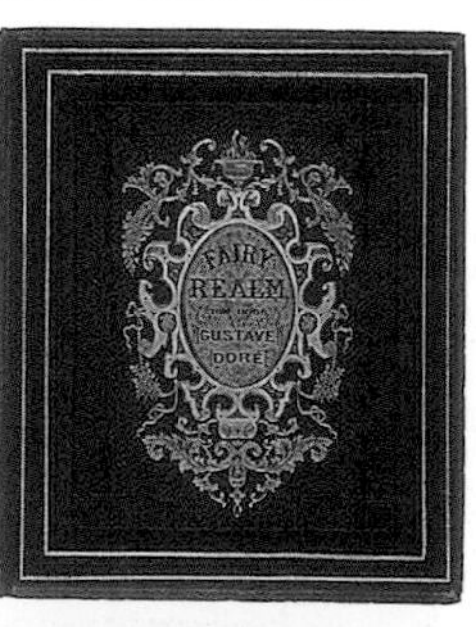

Gustave Doré (illustrator), *Fairy Realm*, verse by Tom Hood, published by Ward Locke and Tyler, large 4°, 1865, original gilt-decorated brown cloth, slight rubbing.
£540–650 / €780–930
$910–1,100 DW

Edwin James, *Account of an Expedition from Pittsburg to the Rocky Mountains...compiled from the notes of Major Long, Mr. T. Say and other Gentlemen of the Part* first edition, 1823, 8°, 3 vols, folding engraved map and plan and 8 plates, 3 hand-coloured, brown cloth with roan spine labels, cover soiled and worn.
£1,050–1,250 / €1,500–1,800
$1,750–2,100 L

T. S. Eliot, *The Waste Land*, published by Hogarth Press, first UK edition, 1923, 8°, spine defective, light spotting, wear to boards.
£820–980 / €1,200–1,400 $1,400–1,650 DW
About 460 copies of this book were printed.

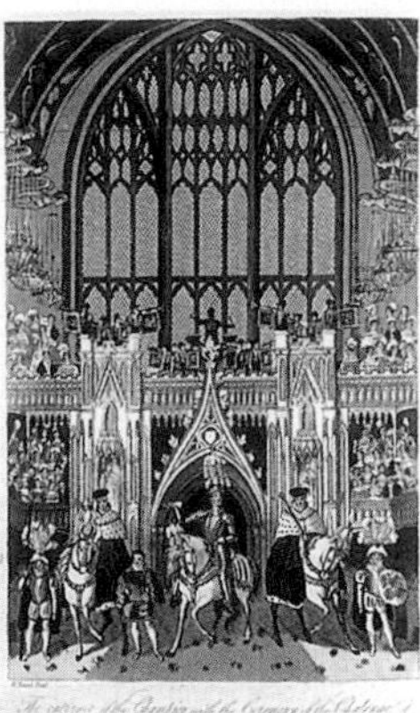

George IV, King of England, 1821, 8°, 8 engraved plates including 6 hand-coloured aquatints, uncut, rebacked.
£610–730 / €880–1,050 $1,000–1,200 BBA

◄ **Jane Elizabeth Geraud,** *The Flowers from Shakespeare*, published by Day & Haghe, 1846, 4°, hand-coloured title and 29 plates by Geraud, contemporary tooled and gilt green morocco cover, some damage.
£370–440 / €530–630 $620–740 RTo

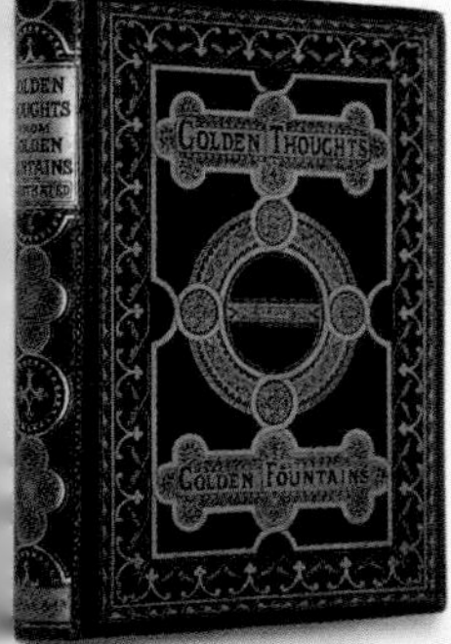

Further reading

Miller's Collecting Modern Books, Miller's Publications, 2003

◄ ***Golden Thoughts from Golden Fountains,*** engravings by Dalziel Bros, c1870, 10in (25.5cm) high.
£150–175 / €230–260 $250–290 TDG

Moses Harris, *The Aurelian, or Natural History of English Moths and Butterflies,* published by John O'Westwood, 1840, 4°, hand-coloured frontispiece and additional title, colour key plate, 44 hand-coloured plates, contemporary half-morocco gilt cover, lower cover detached.
£3,300–3,950 €4,750–5,700 $5,500–6,600 DW

Paul Kane, *Wanderings of An Artist Among the Indians of North America,* first edition, 1859, 8°, folding engraved hand-coloured map, 8 chromolithographic plates and 16 woodcuts, half calf.
£1,050–1,250 €1,500–1,800 $1,750–2,100 L

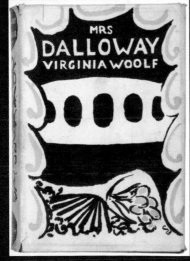

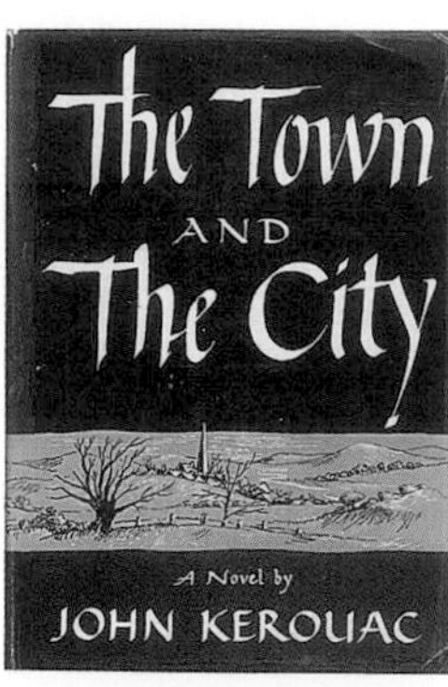

Jack Kerouac, *The Town and the City*, published by Harcourt, Brace & Co, first edition, signed by the author, 1950, 8°, red cloth gilt, minor wear, half brown morocco folding case with marbled boards.
£2,700–3,250
€3,900–4,650
$4,600–5,500 ⚒ S(NY)

James Merigot, *A Select Collection of Views and Ruins in Rome*, part 2 only, published by J. Whatman, 1797, 2°, 32 hand-coloured plates, text in English and French, half calf gilt-decorated spine, worn.
£430–520 / €610–720
$720–860 ⚒ DW

A. A. Milne, *Little Bo Peep, Little Boy Blue and Other Poems*, c1930, 2°, original manuscript on 9 vellum paper leaves, in red, green, black, blue and brown ink, 5 illustrations, 1 pencil illustration, some soiling.
£240–290 / €350–420
$400–480 ⚒ DW

Jack Kerouac, *Big Sur*, published in New York, first edition, 1962, 8°, original cloth-backed boards, dust jacket.
£250–300 / €360–430
$420–500 ⚒ BBA

Lena Lowis (illustrator), *Familiar Indian Flowers*, published by L. Reeve & Co, 1885, 12 x 9in (30.5 x 23cm), coloured plates.
£180–200 / €260–290
$300–330 ⊞ BAY

Reverend F. O. Morris, *The History of British Birds*, published by Zaehnsdorf, first edition, 1851–57, 8°, 6 vols, 358 hand-coloured plates, black gilt morocco cover, rubbed.
£640–770 / €920–1,100
$1,050–1,250 ⚒ L

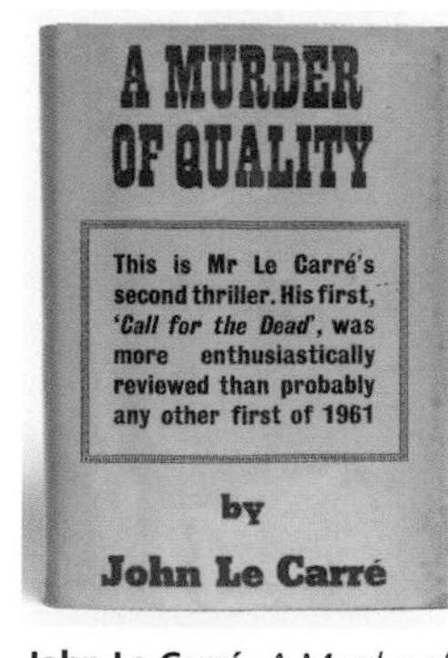

John Le Carré, *A Murder of Quality*, published by the Camelot Press Ltd, signed, 1962, 7½ x 5½in (19 x 14cm).
£2,700–3,000
€3,900–4,300
$4,500–5,000 ⊞ BIB

A. A. Milne, *The Christopher Robin Verses*, published by Methuen, first edition, 1932, 8°, colour plates by E. H. Shepard, original cloth, dust jacket.
£240–290 / €350–420
$410–490 ⚒ LAY

National Nursery Rhymes, published by Novello & Co, c1890, 10½in (26.5cm) high, engravings by the Dalziel Bros after Arthur Hughes, Pinwell and A. B. Houghton.
£120–140 / €170–200
$200–240 ⊞ TDG

John Linley and Sir Joseph Paxton, *Paxton's Flower Garden*, Vols 2 & 3, 1851–5[illegible] 4°, 72 hand-coloured plate[illegible] illustrated by L. Constans, cloth and spines gilt.
£1,100–1,300
€1,600–1,900
$1,850–2,200 ⚒ L

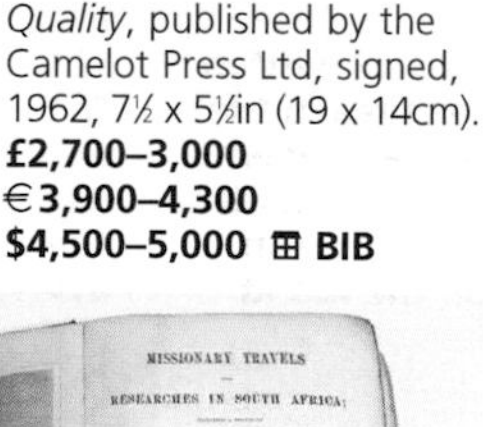

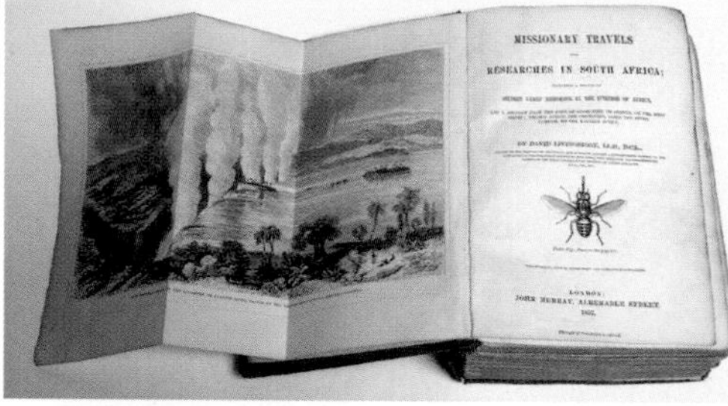

◄ **David Livingstone,** *Missionary Travels and Researches in South Africa*, published by John Murray, first edition, 1857, 9in (23cm) high, inscribed by author, original detail map
£90–100 / €130–145
$150–165 ⊞ HTE

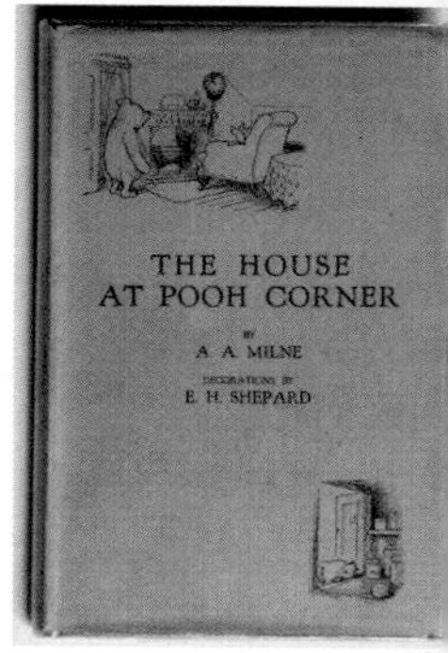

A. A. Milne, *The House a[illegible] Pooh Corner*, published by Methuen, first edition, 192[illegible] 8 x 6in (20.5 x 15cm), illustrated by E. H. Shepard.
£450–500 / €650–720
$760–840 ⊞ ADD

Elsie J. Oxenham, *Joy's New Adventure, A Romance of the Abbey Girls*, published by Chambers, first edition, 1935, 8°, 4 black and white plates, cloth, dust jacket, tear and chip.
£800–960 / €1,200–1,40[illegible]
$1,350–1,600 ⚒ DW

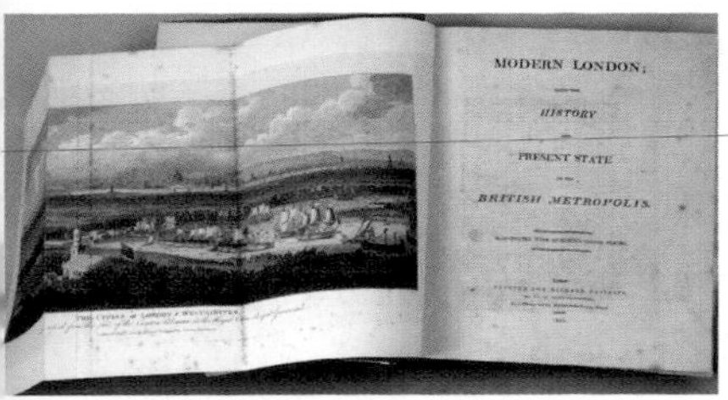

Richard Philips, *Modern London; Being the History and Present State of the British Metropolis*, published by the author, 1805, 10¼ x 7¾in (26 x 19.5cm), illustrations, fold-out maps, ¾ leather bound.
£420–500 / €600–720
$710–840 SWO
This book accompanied by a hand-written note: 'This book was for some time in the possession of Capt. Ross, the well-known navigator to the North Pole, who presented it to Dr O'Meara, physician to Napoleon Bonaparte during his exile on the island of St Helena.'

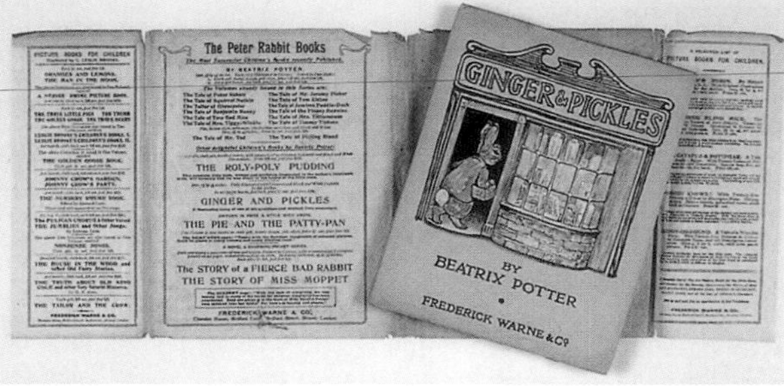

Beatrix Potter, *Ginger & Pickles*, published by Frederick Warne & Co, c1913, small 4°, colour illustrations, dust jacket with chipped edges, spine darkened.
£1,250–1,500 / €1,800–2,150
$2,100–2,500 DW
The printed dust jacket records the publisher's list of works written by Beatrix Potter to date. The list announces the latest titles of *The Tale of Mr Tod*, published in 1912, and *The Tale of Pigling Bland*, published in 1913. The price reflects that it is an early copy with its original dust jacket.

Beatrix Potter, *The Tale of Peter Rabbit*, published by Frederick Warne & Co, first edition, 1902, 12°, coloured frontispiece, 30 coloured illustrations, original paper-covered boards.
£2,450–2,950
€3,500–4,200
$4,100–4,900 RTo

Arthur Rackham (illustrator), *Peter Pan in Kensington Gardens,* published by Hodder & Stoughton, 1912, 4°, 50 tipped-in colour prints, black and white illustrations, green gilt cloth, some spotting and minor wear.
£700–840 / €1,000–1,200
$1,200–1,400 DW
This was a reprint of the 1906 edition with a new coloured frontispiece and seven additional pages of black and white illustrations.

◄ **Christina Rossetti,** *Goblin Market and Other Poems,* first edition, published by Macmillan, 1862, 8°, original gilt-decorated cloth, slightly rubbed and faded.
£540–650 / €780–930
$920–1,100 DW
This was the author's first published book.

Saint Gertrude the Great, *Insinuacion de la Divina Piedad*, published by the Press of the Widow of Francisco de Hierro, 1732, 4°, 2 vols, each with 2 engravings, leather-bound.
£190–220 / €280–320
$320–370 LCM

◄ ***Regulations & Instructions relating to His Majesty's Service at Sea,*** named to the Officer Lt Edward Augustus Frankland, HMS *Curaçoa*, 1815, 10½ x 8½in (26.5 x 21.5cm), leather-bound.
£810–900 / €1,150–1,300
$1,350–1,500 TLA

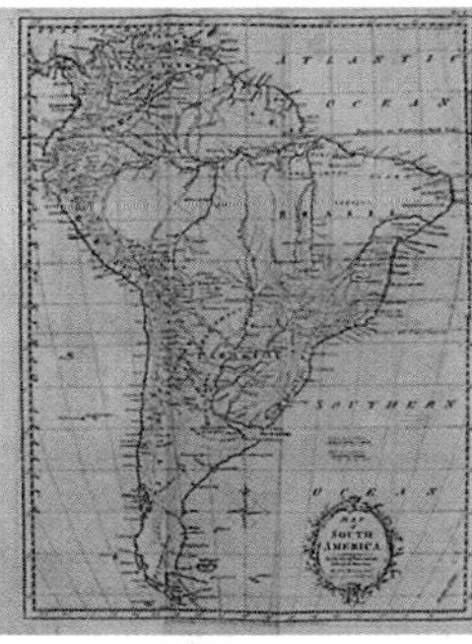

William Robertson, *History of America*, first edition, 1777, 8°, 2 vols, 4 folding engraved maps and folding plate, contemporary calf, rebacked and recornered, foxing and rubbing.
£300–360 / €430–510
$500–600 BBA

F. St J. Gore, *Lights & Shades of Hill Life in the Afghan and Hindu Highlands of the Punjab,* published by John Murray, first edition, 1895, 9 x 6¼in (23 x 16cm), 72 photo plates, 21 illustrations and 2 fold-out coloured maps, red calf binding with gilt tooling.
£140–165 / €200–230
$240–280 SWO

Victoria Sackville-West, *The Heir*, published by leinemann, first edition, No. 93 of 100, 1922, 8°, presentation copy signed by the author on the frontispiece and signed by the author's mother on half-title, inscribed To Miss Alice Warrender in anticipation of the much-valued prize given to young writers through her great generosity from the author's mother (B. M.) – Victoria Sackville', cloth-backed decorated boards.
210–250 / €300–360
350–420 BBA
he oldest of the major British literary prizes, the Hawthornden Prize, was founded in 1919 by Miss Alice Warrender. It is awarded annually to an English writer for 'the best work of imaginative literature'.

BOOKS & BOOK ILLUSTRATIONS

Sakoontala, or The Lost Ring; An Indian Drama, translated by Monier Williams, printed and published by Stephen Austin, 1855, small 4°, colour frontispiece, colour and gold-print part-titles, gilt edges, gilt-decorated full morocco binding designed and signed by T. Sulman, light foxing and rubbing.
£370–440 / €530–630
$620–740 DW
This deluxe issue was awarded both the silver and gold medals at the Paris Exposition Universelle in 1855, as well as a gold medal from Queen Victoria.

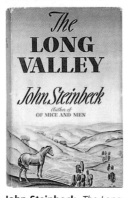

John Steinbeck, *The Long Valley*, published by Viking, first edition, 1938, 4°, original cloth, dust jacket rubbed and slightly marked.
£135–160 / €195–230
$230–270 DW

YOUNG MEN IN SPATS
P.G. WODEHOUSE

P. G. Wodehouse, *Young Men in Spats,* published by Herbert Jenkins, 1936, 8°, original orange cloth, dust jacket, slightly rubbed and chipped.
£165–195 / €240–280
$280–330 DW

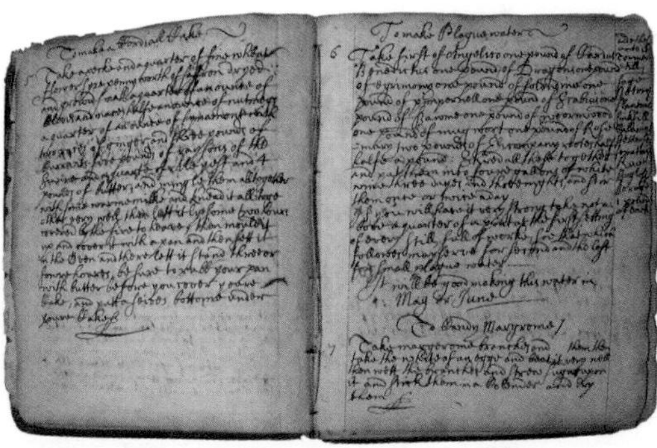

Sir Edwin Sandys, *Manuscript of Medical and Cookery Receipts*, 16th/17thC, 4°, closely written on 212 pages, leather boards now detached, missing backstrip, first few leaves detached.
£7,700–9,200 / €11,100–13,300
$12,900–15,500 F&C

Dr Seuss, *The Seven Lady Godivas*, published by Random House, first edition, 1939, 4°, illustrated, original cloth, dust jacket rubbed and slightly damaged.
£260–310 / €380–450
$440–520 DW

► H. G. Wells, *The Research Magnificent*, published by Macmillan, first edition, presentation copy, 1915, 8 x 6in (20.5 x 15cm).
£220–250 / €320–360
$370–410 ADD

N. P. Willis & W. H. Bartlett (illustrator), *American Scenery; or Land, Lake and River Illustrations of Transatlantic Nature*, published by George Virtue, 1840, 2°, 2 vols, frontispiece portrait of Bartlett, plates, calf gilt, extremities rubbed.
£370–440 / €530–630
$620–740 DN

◄ Reverend G. N. Wright, *China, In A Series of Views*, published by Fisher, Son & Co, 1843, 4°, 4 vols, pictorial cloth gilt, engraved titles, 124 plates by Thomas Allom, slight wear.
£400–480 / €580–690
$670–800 L

Scotson-Clark (illustrator), *The Halls*, published by T. Fisher Unwinn, c1910, 11 x 8in (28 x 20.5cm).
£360–400 / €520–580
$600–660 ADD

◄ George Smith, *The Cabinet-Maker's and Upholsterer's Guide: Being a Complete Drawing Book*, published by Jones & Co, 1826, 2°, hand-coloured frontispiece, 145 plates, 33 hand-coloured, leather half-calf, spotting and browning.
£280–330 / €400–470
$470–550 DN

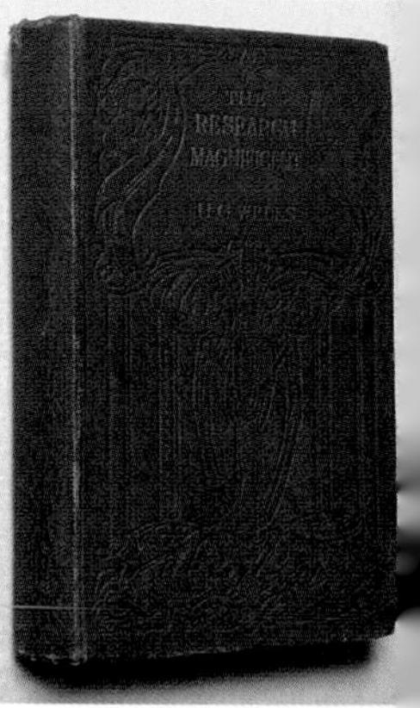

Virginia Woolf, *On Being Ill*, published by Hogarth Press, first separate edition, 1930, 8°, No. 104 of 250, signed by the author, untrimmed and unopened, publisher's vellum-backed green cloth, dust jacket.
£6,400–7,700
€9,200–11,000
$10,800–13,000 B

Maps & Atlases

World

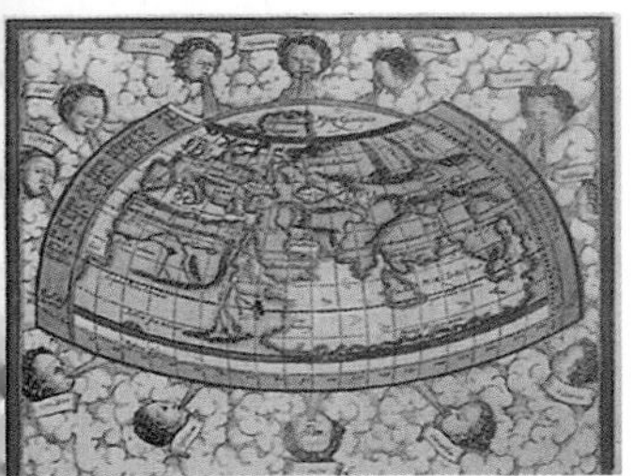

Sebastian Munster, a woodcut Ptolemaic map of the world, with old hand colouring, relaid onto archival tissue, slight damage, German, 12¼ x 14¼in (31 x 36cm).
£680–810 / €980–1,150
$1,150–1,350 DW

► Antonio Zatta, a copperplate map, Venetian, 1774, 12 x 15in (30.5 x 38cm).
£900–1,000 / €1,300–1,450
$1,500–1,700 ⊞ JOP

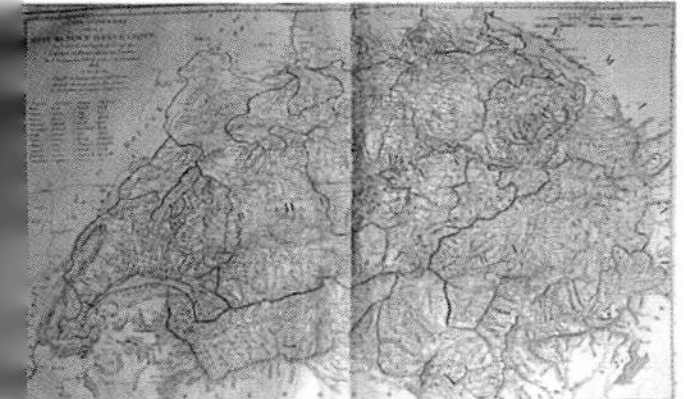

Robert de Vaugondy, *Atlas D'Eude pour L'Instruction de la Jeunesse*, published by Delamarche & Les Dien, Paris, 36 maps, 1819, damaged, spine and lining missing.
£850–1,000 / €1,200–1,400
$1,450–1,700 LCM

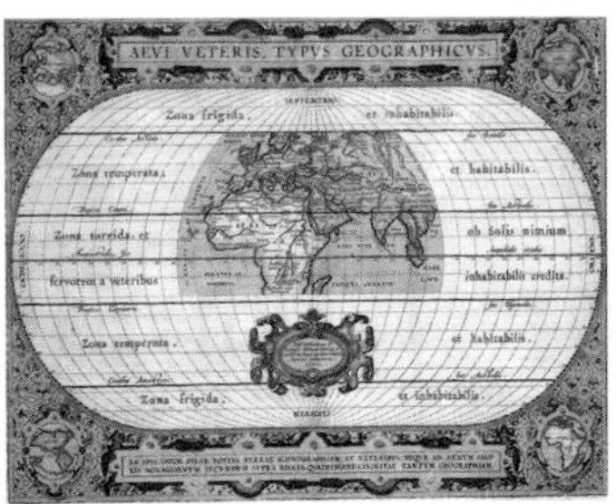

Abraham Ortelius, a copperplate map of the world, Flemish, Antwerp, 1590, 13 x 18in (33 x 45.5cm).
£810–900 / €1,150–1,300
$1,300–1,500 ⊞ JOP

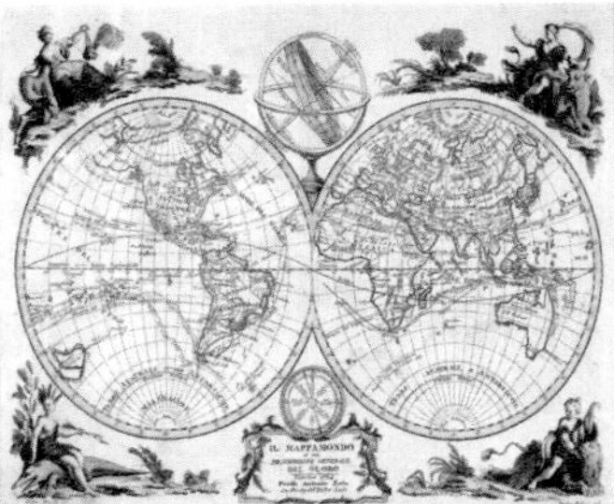

Pierre du Val, *La Géographie Universelle, Vol 1*, 40 double-page engraved maps, seven full-page engraved plates of flags, French, Paris, 1663, 8°.
£1,900–2,250 / €2,750–3,250
$3,200–3,800 S

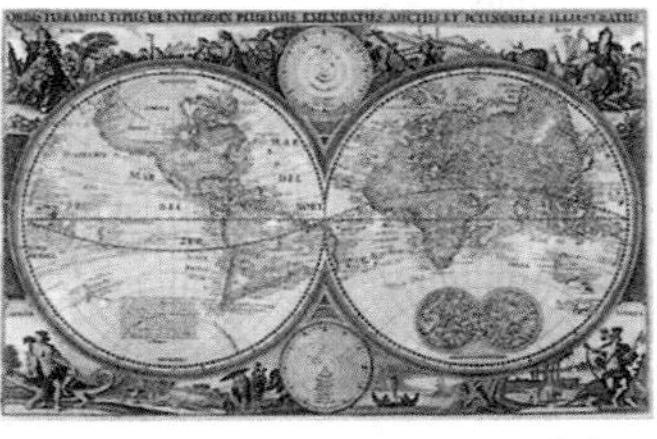

Frederick Houtmann, a map of the world, hand-coloured and engraved, decorated with celestial charts and figures, c1700, 12½ x 18¾in (32 x 47.5cm)
£940–1,100 / €1,350–1,600
$1,600–1,850 DW

◄ George W. Colton, *Colton's Atlas of the World*, published by J. H. Colton, New York, 1856, 2°, loose pages, one plate missing.
£2,200–2,600 / €3,150–3,750
$3,700–4,350 JAA

Africa & Arabia

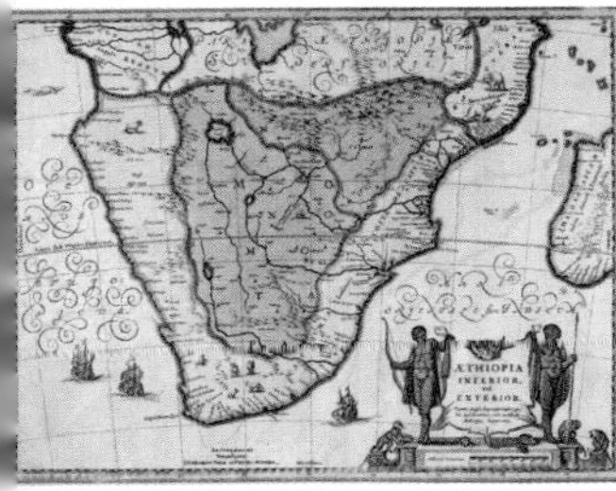

Johannes Jansson, Pieter Schenk and Gerard Valk, a copperplate map of southern Africa, original colour, Dutch, 1636–1720, 15 x 20in (38 x 51cm).
£580–650 / €830–940
$970–1,100 ⊞ JOP
In the late 17th century the plates of some of the Jansson's maps were bought at auction by Gerard Valk and Pieter Schenk.

Items in the Maps & Atlases section have been arranged in date order within each sub-section.

John Speed, a hand-coloured engraved map of Africa, published by Roger Rea, with figures in costume and eight miniature views, some restoration, 1662, 15¾ x 20in (40 x 51cm).
£1,150–1,350 / €1,650–1,950
$1,950–2,250 DW

► John Senex, a copperplate map of Turkey, Arabia and Persia, original outline colour, 1711–20, 20 x 23in (51 x 58.5cm).
£400–450 / €580–650
$670–760 ⊞ JOP

Tobias Conrad Lotter, a copperplate map of southern Africa, original colour, German, Augsburg, c1750, 19 x 22in (48.5 x 56cm).
£540–600 / €780–860
$900–1,000 ⊞ JOP

Americas

Giacomo Gastaldi, *La Nvova Francia* and *Terra Nvova*, a double-page woodcut map of New England and maritime Canada, Venetian, 1556, 10¾ x 14¾in (27.5 x 37.5cm).
£2,600–3,100 / €3,750–4,450
$4,350–5,200 S

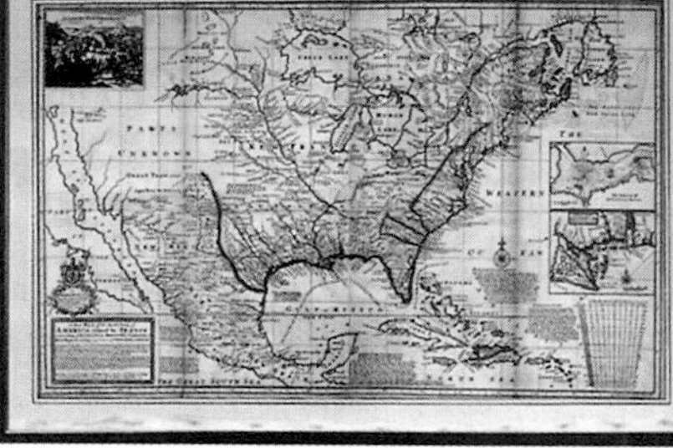

► **Jodocus Hondius,** a double-page engraved map of the Americas, depicting Brazilian natives making alcohol from mandioca roots, Dutch, Amsterdam, dated 1606 but 1623, 14¾ x 19¾in (37.5 x 50.5cm).
£3,350–4,000 / €4,800–5,800
$5,600–6,700 S

Johann Baptist Homann, a map of the Mississippi delta, Louisiana, 1687, framed, 19¼ x 22½in (49 x 57cm).
£1,100–1,300 / €1,600–1,850
$1,850–2,200 BERN

Pierre Mortier, *Archipelague du Mexique*, an engraved map of the Eastern West Indies, original hand colouring, slight damage, Dutch, Amsterdam, c1700, 23¼ x 20in (59 x 51cm).
£370–440 / €530–630
$620–740 BBA

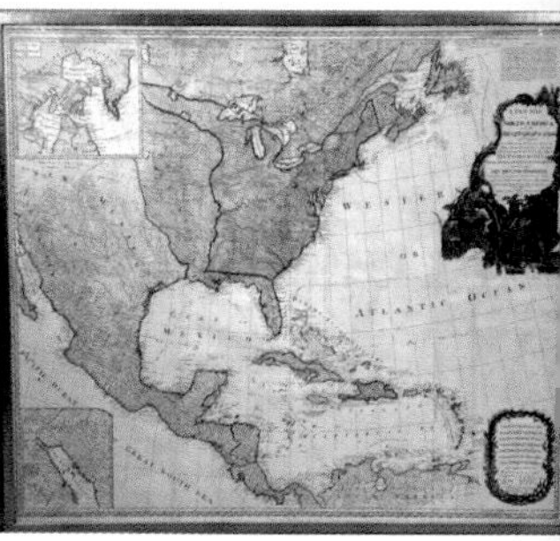

Herman Moll, an engraved map of Canada and the United States, hand-coloured, c1720, 24¼ x 40¼in (61.5 x 103cm), in a giltwood frame.
£1,600–1,900 / €2,300–2,750
$2,700–3,200 NOA

► **Matthäus Seutter and Tobias Conrad Lotter,** a copperplate map of Canada, original outline colour, German, Augsburg, 1750–57, 23 x 20in (58.5 x 51cm).
£1,250–1,400 / €1,800–2,000
$2,100–2,350 JOP

A map of North America and the West Indian Islands, published by Laurie & Whittle, hand-coloured, 1794, 39¾ x 45¾in (101 x 116cm).
£940–1,150 / €1,350–1,600
$1,600–1,850 SWO

Asia

John Speed, a hand-coloured engraved map of Asia and the Islands, the margins with figures in costume and eight vignettes, slight damage and repair, 1626, 15¾ x 20½in (40 x 52cm).
£830–990 / €1,200–1,400
$1,400–1,650 DW

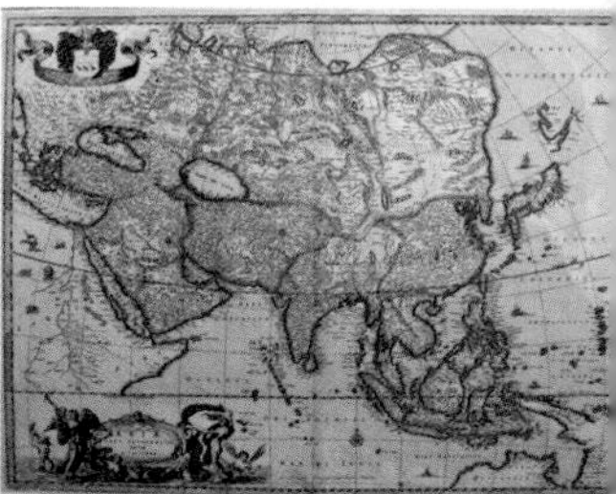

► **Nicolaus Vischer,** a copperplate map of Asia, original colour, Dutch, Amsterdam, c1683, 17 x 22in (43 x 56cm).
£610–680 / €880–980
$1,000–1,150 JOP

► **John Cary,** *A New Map of Hindoostan*, 1806, 19 x 21in (48.5 x 53.5cm).
£230–260 / €330–370
$390–440 JOP

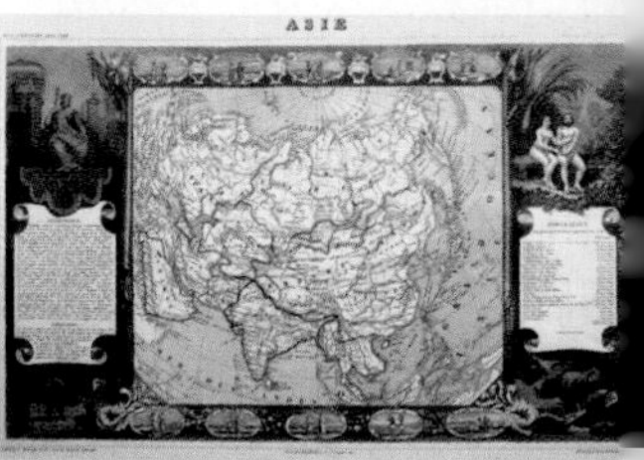

Victor Levasseur, a steelplate map of Asia, 1845, 13 x 17½in (33 x 44.5cm).
£190–220 / €270–310
$320–370 JOP

Europe

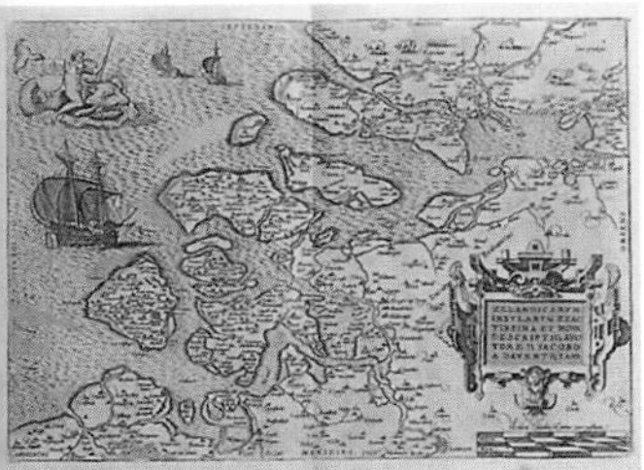

Jacob van Deventer, a map of Zeeland, Dutch, late 16thC, 13¼ x 18¼in (33.5 x 46.5cm).
£570–680 / €820–980
$960–1,150 ⚒ BERN

Joannes Jansson, a copperplate map of Europe, Dutch, Amsterdam, c1680, 14 x 19in (35.5 x 48.5cm).
£490–550 / €710–790
$820–920 ⊞ JOP

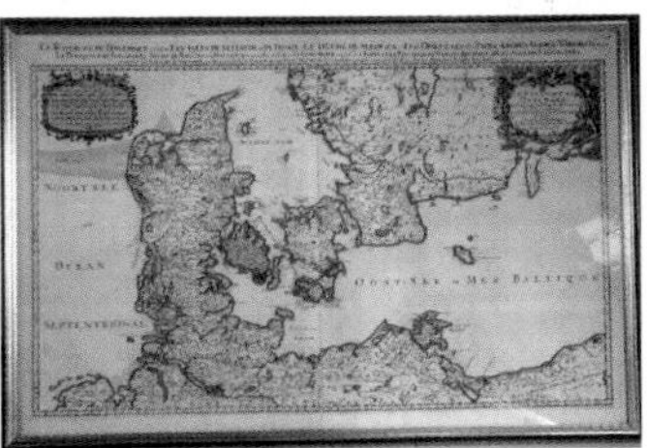

Alexis Hubert Jaillot, *Le Royaume de Danemark*, a coloured map of Denmark, French, c1692, 23¼ x 35in (59 x 89cm).
£330–390 / €470–560
$550–660 ⚒ SWO

Christopher Weigel, *Regnum Sveciae*, German, 1712–40, 12½ x 15¼in (32 x 38.5cm).
£330–390 / €470–560
$550–650 ⚒ BUK

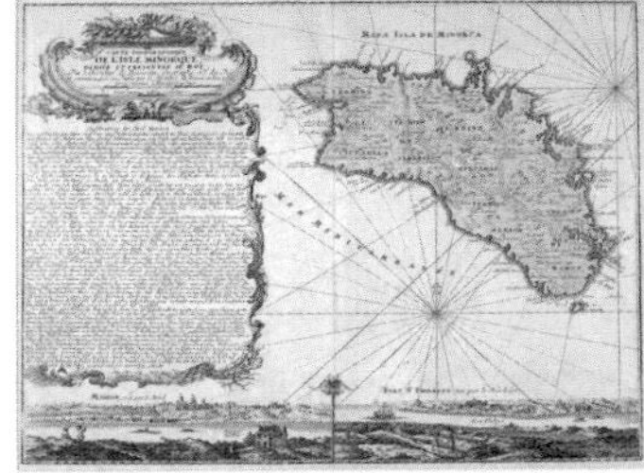

Le Chevalier de Beaurain and Homanns' Heirs, a copperplate map of Minorca, German, Nuremberg, 1757, 17 x 21in (43 x 53.5cm).
£590–650 / €850–930
$990–1,100 ⊞ JOP

A copperplate map of Tyrol, published by J. Walch, Augsburg, slight damage, German, 1797, 18¾ x 22½in (47.5 x 57cm).
£200–240 / €290–340
$340–400 ⚒ DORO

Great Britain & Ireland

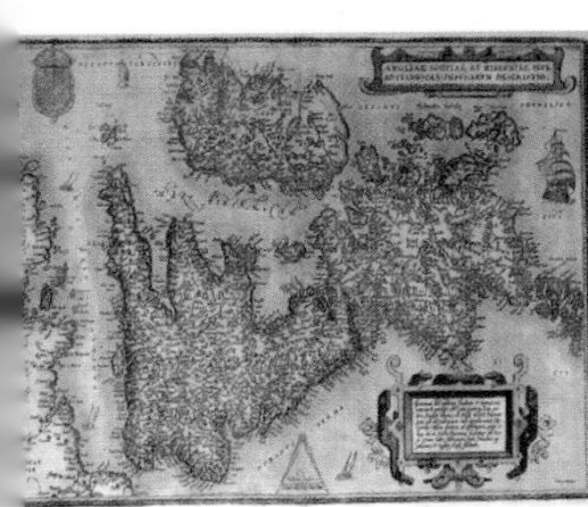

Abraham Ortelius, a copperplate map of the British Isles, hand-coloured, Flemish, 1579, 13½ x 19in (34.5 x 48.5cm).
£2,700–3,000 / €3,900–4,300
$4,500–5,000 ⊞ APS

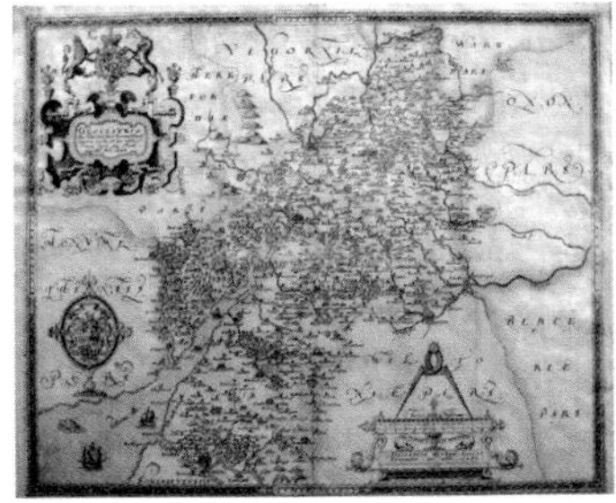

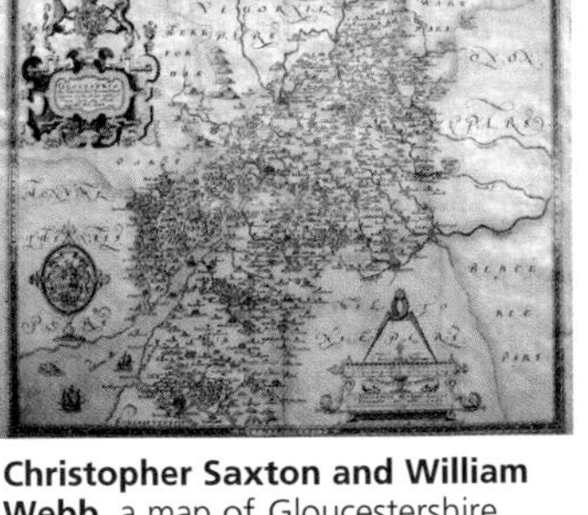

Christopher Saxton and William Webb, a map of Gloucestershire, 1579–1645, 16 x 20in (40.5 x 51cm).
£2,350–2,600 / €3,400–3,750
$3,950–4,350 ⊞ JOP

John Speed, *The Countye of Monmouth with Shiretowne described anon 1610*, an engraved map, with later hand colouring, 17thC, 16½ x 20¾in (42 x 52.5cm), mounted in an ebonized free-standing swivel frame.
£240–280 / €340–400
$400–470 ⚒ HOLL

John Speed, a copperplate map of Great Britain, coloured, 1611–12, 15 x 20in (38 x 51cm).
£1,950–2,200 / €2,800–3,150
$3,250–3,700 ⊞ JOP

John Speed, an engraved map of the Isle of Wight, hand-coloured, inset with plans of Southampton and Newport, slight damage and repair, 1611, 15 x 20in (38 x 51cm), framed and glazed.
£480–570 / €690–820
$800–960 ⚒ DW

John Speed, an engraved map of Yorkshire, with original hand colouring, slight damage, 1614, 15¼ x 20¼in (38.5 x 51.5cm), framed and glazed.
£230–270 / €330–390
$390–450 ⚒ BBA

Gerard Mercator, a map of England, 1630, 16 x 22in (40.5 x 56cm).
£1,050–1,200 / €1,500–1,750
$1,750–2,000 ⊞ APS

Gerard Mercator, an engraved map of northwest England and North Wales, hand-coloured, with an ornamental title cartouche, 1633, 14¼ x 16in (36 x 40.5cm).
£230–270 / €330–390
$390–450 ⚒ DW

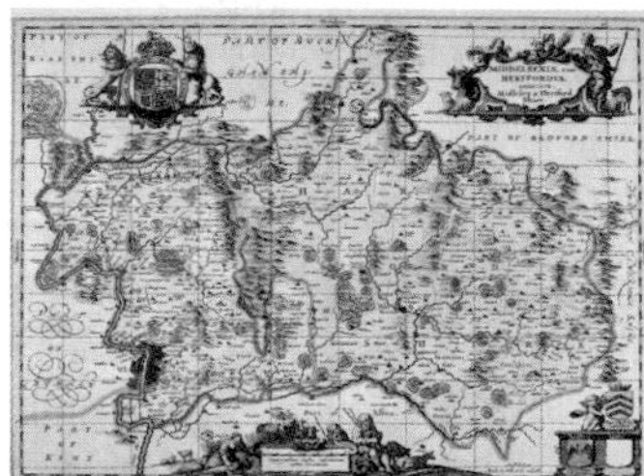

Johannes Jansson, Gerard Valk and Pieter Schenk, a copperplate map of Middlesex and Hertfordshire, coloured, Dutch, Amsterdam, 1646–1710, 17 x 21in (43 x 53.5cm).
£580–650 / €830–930
$970–1,100 ⊞ JOP

Johann Baptist Homann, an engraved map of England and Wales, with an engraved view of the royal court, slight damage, 1730s, 22¾ x 19¼in (58 x 49cm).
£210–250 / €300–360
$350–420 ⚒ DW

Miller's Compares

I. **John Speed,** *The Kingdome of England*, published by Abraham Goos, an engraved map of England and Wales, hand-coloured, the side margins inset with figures, some restoration, 1646, 15¼ x 20in (38.5 x 51cm).
£770–920 / €1,100–1,300
$1,300–1,550 ⚒ DW

II. **Jan Blaeu,** an engraved map of England and Wales, hand-coloured, with ornamental cartouche and royal arms, 1645, 15¼ x 19¾in (38.5 x 50cm).
£240–290 / €350–420
$400–480 ⚒ DW

These maps are of a similar date and size, but Item I, the example by John Speed, sold for three times as much as Item II by Jan Blaeu.

John Speed's maps replaced Christopher Saxton's as the benchmark standard of British county maps when they were first published in 1610–11 (Item I is a later edition of 1646). They were more up-to-date and in the eyes of many people more attractive, with inset town plans, vignette views and figures in contemporary costume.

Blaeu's county maps were first published in 1645 and, while still finely engraved, are much more simplistic and lack some of the charm of Speed's work. His maps are mostly based on Speed's although he also borrowed from other map makers. However, Speed in turn had borrowed heavily from Christopher Saxton.

Generally maps became less decorative through the 17th, 18th and 19th centuries as functionality and a more scientific approach became more entrenched. Earlier maps are sought after not just because of their historical importance but because they retain some of the Elizabethan charm of the earliest British cartographers.

John Overton, a copperplate map of Sussex, coloured, c1672, 13 x 19¼in (33 x 49cm).
£1,350–1,500 / €1,950–2,150
$2,250–2,500 ⊞ JOP

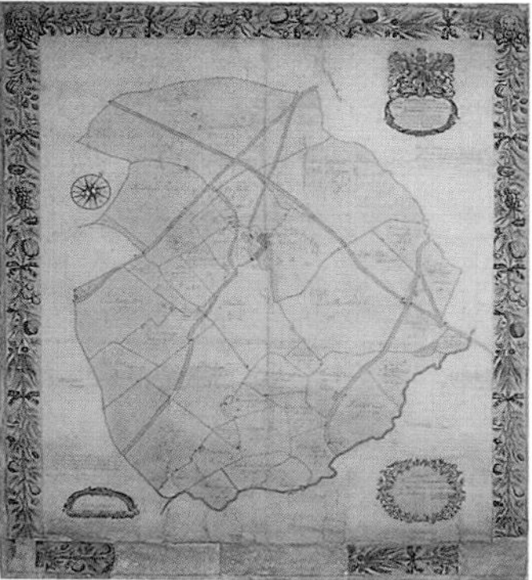

J. Maud, an estate plan of Lenborough, Buckinghamshire, in ink, vellum on linen, with an engraved border, losses and restoration, 18thC, 38½ x 47in (98 x 119.5cm).
£900–1,050 / €1,300–1,500
$1,500–1,750 ⚒ S

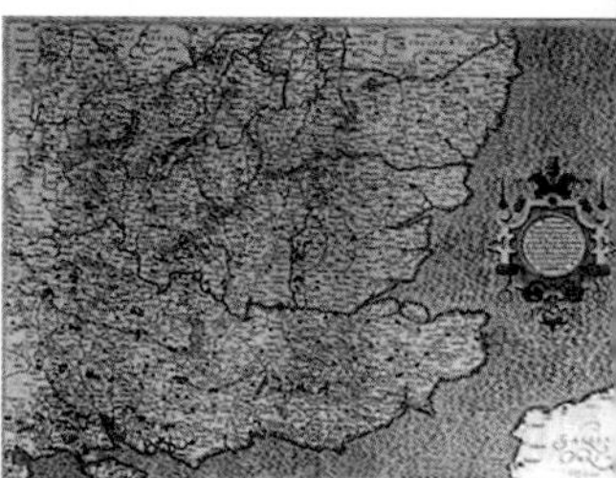

An engraved map of the southeast of England, hand-coloured, 17thC, 14½ x 15¾in (37 x 40cm), framed and glazed.
£90–105 / €130–150
$150–175 ⚒ WilP

Matthäus Seutter, a copperplate map of the southeast of England and part of France, German, Augsburg, c1740, 20 x 23in (51 x 58.5cm).
£540–600 / €780–860
$900–1,000 ⊞ JOP

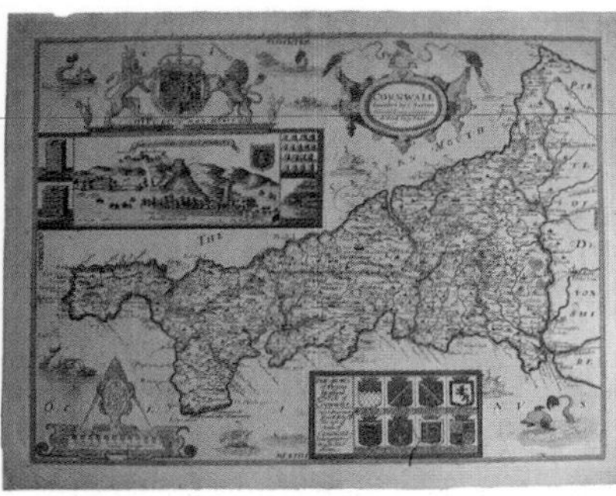

Christopher Saxton and Jeffreys, a map of Cornwall, 1746, 17 x 21in (43 x 53.5cm).
£1,800–2,000 / €2,600–2,900
$3,000–3,350 ⊞ APS

Bernard Scale, *An Hibernian Atlas; or General Description of the Kingdom of Ireland,* with 37 hand-coloured county maps, 1776, 4°.
£1,950–2,350
€2,800–3,350
$3,250–3,900 ⚒ BBA

Samuel Lewis, *Atlas to the Topographical Dictionaries of England and Wales*, 55 engraved maps, all but one hand-coloured, 14 folding, slight damage, 1844, 9½ x 12¾in (24 x 32.5cm).
£300–360 / €430–520
$500–600 ⚒ RTo

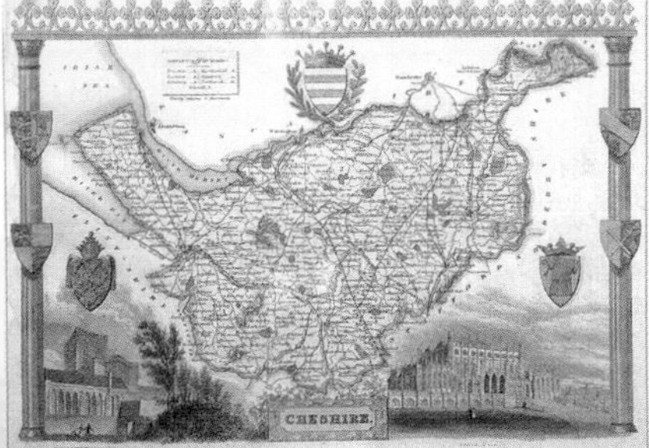

Thomas Moule, a map of Cheshire, 1845, 8 x 10in (20.5 x 25.5cm).
£115–130 / €165–185
$195–220 ⊞ APS

► **Ruben Ramble,** a map of Oxfordshire, 1845, 7 x 6in (18 x 15cm).
£180–200 / €260–290
$300–330 ⊞ SAT

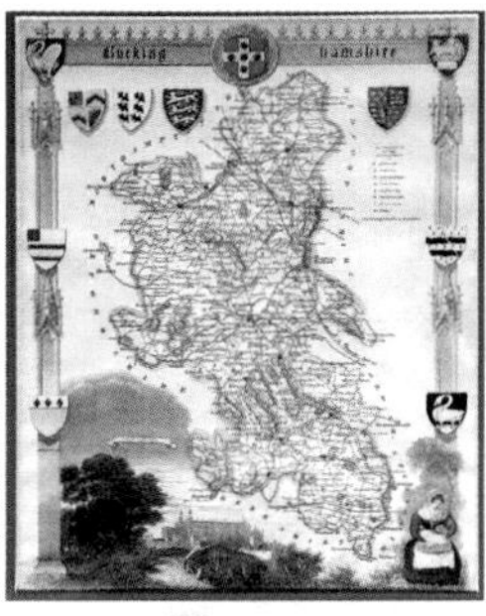

Thomas Moule, a map of Buckinghamshire, mid-19thC, 11 x 8in (28 x 20.5cm).
£140–160 / €200–230
$230–270 ⊞ SAT

Town & City Plans

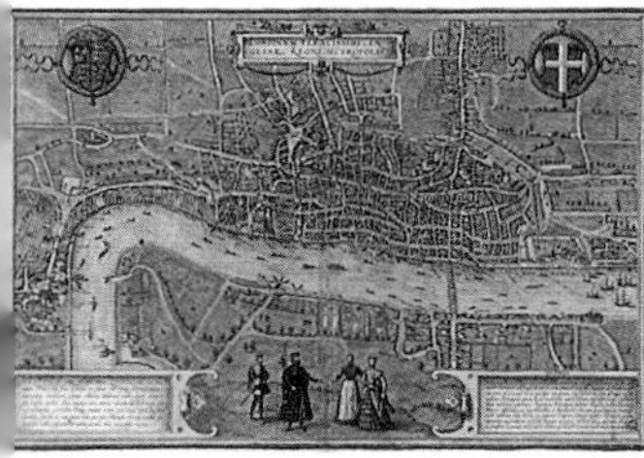

Georg Braun and Frans Hogenberg, a double-page engraved map of London, hand-coloured, minor damage, German, 1572, 13¼ x 19in (33.5 x 48.5cm).
£3,800–4,550 / €5,500–6,600
$6,400–7,600 ⚒ S
This is the earliest known printed plan of London.

Claude du Bosc, a copperplate map of Antwerp, coloured, c1750, 13½ x 17¼in (34.5 x 44cm).
£270–300 / €390–430
$450–500 ⊞ JOP

Joannes Jansson, a copperplate map of Lucerne, coloured, Dutch, Amsterdam, 1657, 13 x 19½in (33 x 50cm).
£1,350–1,500 / €1,950–2,150
$2,250–2,500 ⊞ JOP

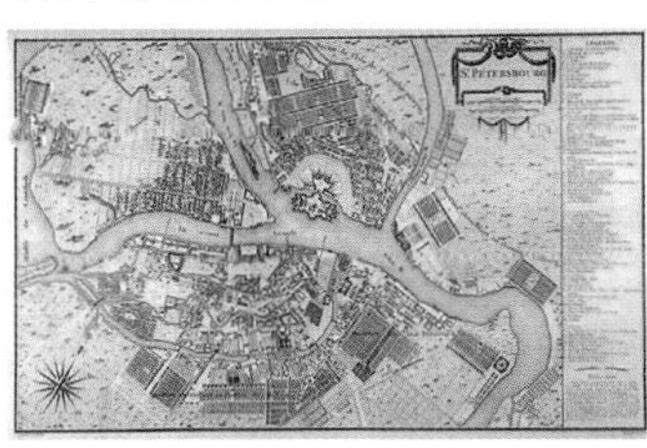

► **P. F. Tardieu,** a map of St Petersburg, 1785, 17¾ x 29½in (45 x 75cm).
£810–970 / €1,150–1,400
$1,350–1,600 ⚒ BUK

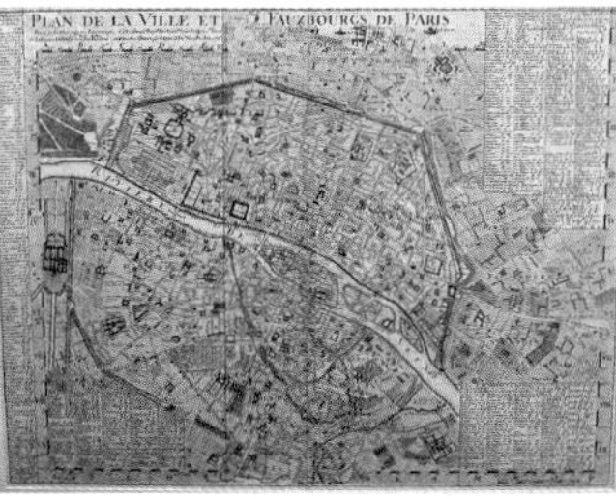

Guillaume de l'Isle, a copperplate map of Paris, coloured, French, 1716, 19 x 25½in (48.5 x 65cm).
£540–600 / €780–860
$900–1,000 ⊞ JOP

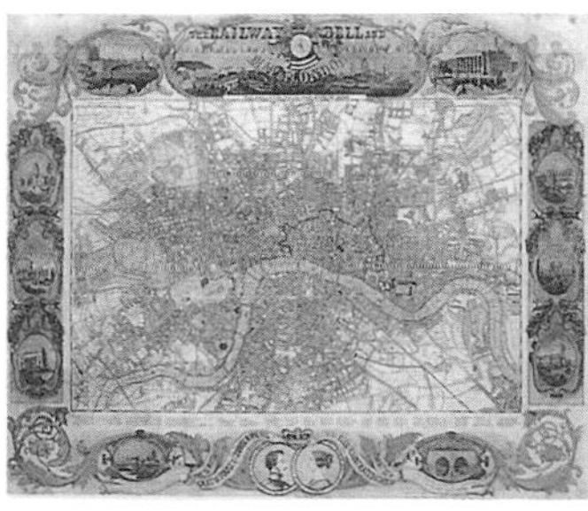

◄ **Measom,** *The Railway Bell*, published by George Biggs, a wood-engraved map of London, bordered with vignette views of various mainline stations, hand-coloured, linen-backed, slight damage and repairs, 1845, 29 x 36¼in (73.5 x 92cm).
£700–840 / €1,000–1,200
$1,200–1,400 ⚒ BBA
This was presented to the subscribers of the *Railway Bell* and *Illustrated London Advertiser*.

Dolls

Selected Makers

A Madame Alexander Scarlet O'Hara doll, with composition body, original clothing, American, c1936, 18in (45.5cm) high.
£310–370 / €440–530
$520–620 ⚒ JAA

An Alt, Beck & Gottschalck china shoulder-headed doll, mould 1008, with moulded hair, German, c1890, 11in (28cm) high.
£160–180 / €230–260
$270–300 ⊞ BaN

A Bähr & Pröschild doll, mould 309, with kid body, original clothes and wig, German, c1890, 26in (66cm) high.
£400–450 / €580–650
$670–760 ⊞ DOL

A bisque-headed fashion doll, possibly by E. Barrois, with fixed eyes, closed mouth, mohair wig and leather body, with a gilt mirror, watch and brooch, French, c1870, 20in (51cm) high.
£1,750–2,100
€2,500–3,000
$2,950–3,500 ⚒ B(Kn)

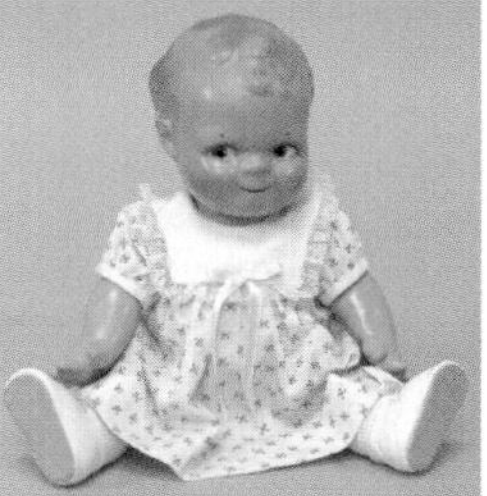

A Cameo Doll Co Scootles doll, by Rose O'Neill, with painted eyes and painted and moulded hair, arms and legs repainted, 1925, 12½in (32cm) high.
£130–150 / €190–220
$220–260 ⚒ Bert

A Porzellanfabrik Burggrub bisque-headed doll, mould 169, with original wig, bent-limbed toddler body and Victorian clothes, German, c1930, 24in (61cm) high.
£470–530 / €670–760
$790–890 ⊞ POLL

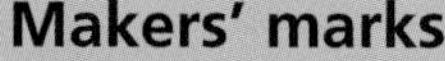

Makers' marks

Early bisque dolls were often unmarked and it is therefore difficult to attribute them to a particular maker. By the late 19th century most examples had the makers' initials or the mould number stamped on the back of the head. Occasionally, the maker's name is stamped on the doll's body.

A Greiner doll, with papier-mâché head and shoulders and moulded hair, wearing original linen dress with apron, net jacket and hand-stitched oilcloth boots, replaced leather arms and legs, labelled shoulder plate, American, c1860, 17in (43cm) high.
£980–1,150
€1,400–1,650
$1,650–1,950 ⚒ Bert

◄ **A Chad Valley Snow White and the Seven Dwarfs,** with moulded and painted felt heads, stuffed fabric bodies and limbs and cotton clothing, c1935, Snow White 15in (38cm) high.
£630–750 / €900–1,050
$1,050–1,250 ⚒ AH

◄ **A Cuno & Otto Dressel bisque-headed doll,** with cloth body and composition lower arms and legs, German, c1920, 18in (45.5cm) high.
£250–280 / €360–400
$420–470 ⊞ BaN

► **A Max Handwerck *bébé* Elite doll,** German, c1920, 25in (63.5cm) high.
£450–500 / €650–720
$750–840 ⊞ DOL

A Hertel, Schwab & Co bisque-headed character doll, mould 201, German, c1910, 21in (53.5cm) high.
£450–500 / €650–720
$750–840 ⊞ BaN

► An Ernst Heubach bisque-headed doll, mould 342, German, c1920, 19in (48.5cm) high.
£210–240 / €300–340
$350–400 ⊞ BaN

An Edward Horsman composition crawling baby doll, American, c1930, 12in (30.5cm) high.
£360–400 / €520–580
$600–670 ⊞ DOL

A bisque-headed fashion doll, possibly Jumeau, with fixed glass eyes, closed mouth, pierced ears, leather body, jointed wooden and bisque lower arms, one finger broken, French, c1860, 16in (41cm) high.
£840–1,000
€1,200–1,400
$1,400–1,650 ⚒ B(Kn)

A Jumeau doll, with closed mouth, marked ED for Emile Douillet, French, 1892–99, 30in (76cm) high.
£2,500–2,800
€3,600–4,000
$4,200–4,700 ⊞ BaN

◄ A Gebrüder Heubach bisque-headed doll, mould 2/142, with painted hair and intaglio eyes, jointed composition body, early 20thC, 11in (28cm) high, with an assortment of whitework clothes.
£220–260 / €310–370
$370–440 ⚒ G(L)

An Ernst Heubach character doll, mould 399, German, c1912, 17in (43cm) high.
£450–500 / €650–720
$750–840 ⊞ DOL

LOCATE THE SOURCE

The source of each illustration in Miller's can be found by checking the code letters below each caption with the Key to Illustrations, pages 794–800.

◄ A Jeune bisque-headed Julienne doll, with composition and wood body, wearing original clothes, French, Paris, c1900, 34in (86.5cm) high, with original box.
£2,250–2,500 / €3,250–3,600
$3,800–4,200 ⊞ BaN
Jeune of Paris (1875–1904) amalgamated with S. F. B. J. in 1904.

► A Jumeau fashion doll, wearing original clothes, French, c1870, 10½in (26.5cm) high.
£670–750
€960–1,100
$1,100–1,250
⊞ DOL

◄ A Tête Jumeau doll, with fixed glass eyes, closed mouth, feather brows, pierced ears, mohair wig and cork pate, fully jointed composition body, wearing a fur coat and muff, ermine stole, marked, French, c1880, 19in (48cm) high.
£2,600–3,100
€3,750–4,450
$4,350–5,200 ⚒ B(Kn)

A Tête Jumeau bisque-headed doll, with original wig, French, c1890, 25in (63.5cm) high.
£940–1,050
€1,350–1,500
$1,550–1,750 ⊞ DOL

A Kämmer & Reinhardt doll, German, c1900, 34in (86.5cm) high.
£1,100–1,250
€1,600–1,800
$1,850–2,100 ⊞ DOL

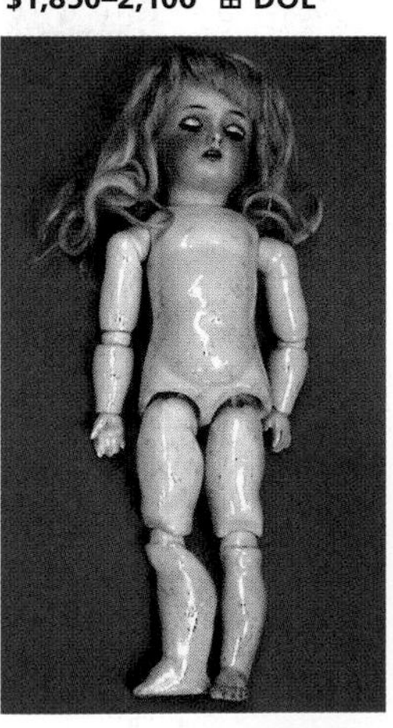

A Kämmer & Reinhardt bisque-headed doll, with sleeping eyes and jointed composition body, German, early 20thC, 12in (30.5cm) high.
£300–360 / €430–520
$500–600 ⚒ TMA

A Tête Jumeau bisque-headed *bébé* doll, with paperweight eyes, closed mouth, feather brows, pierced ears, mohair wig and fully jointed composition body, wearing original clothes, incised mark Déposé, French, c1890, 20in (51cm) high.
£2,150–2,550
€3,100–3,650
$3,600–4,300 ⚒ B(Kn)

A Kämmer & Reinhardt doll, wearing original clothes, German, c1900, 17in (43cm) high, in box.
£580–650 / €830–930
$970–1,100 ⊞ DOL

A Kämmer & Reinhardt character doll, mould 126, with flirty eyes and original clothes, German, c1920, 24½in (62cm) high.
£580–650 / €830–930
$970–1,100 ⊞ DOL

A Tête Jumeau bisque-headed doll, with paperweight eyes, applied ears, French, c1890, 29in (73.5cm) high.
£2,000–2,200
€2,900–3,200
$3,350–3,700 ⊞ BaN

A Kämmer & Reinhardt doll, with twill-covered body, wearing original clothes, shoes later, German, c1900, 15in (38cm) high.
£450–500 / €650–720
$750–840 ⊞ DOL

A J. D. Kestner bisque-headed doll, with weighted eyes, closed mouth, mohair wig and fully jointed composition body with fixed wrists, German, c1880, 15in (38cm) high.
£1,100–1,300
€1,600–1,900
$1,850–2,200 ⚒ B(Kn)

A Jumeau doll, with original wig, marked DEP, c1910, 33in (84cm) high.
£1,250–1,400
€1,800–2,000
$2,100–2,350 ⊞ BaN

A Kämmer & Reinhardt/ Simon & Halbig bisque-headed character doll, mould 117, with weighted glass eyes, closed mouth, mohair wig and fully jointed composition body, two fingers repaired, German, c1910, 19in (48.5cm) high.
£1,350–1,600
€1,950–2,300
$2,250–2,700 ⚒ B(Kn)

A J. D. Kestner celluloid-headed character doll, with sleeping eyes, the leather body with celluloid arms and legs, German, c1920, 13in (33cm) high.
£310–350 / €440–500
$520–590 ⊞ POLL

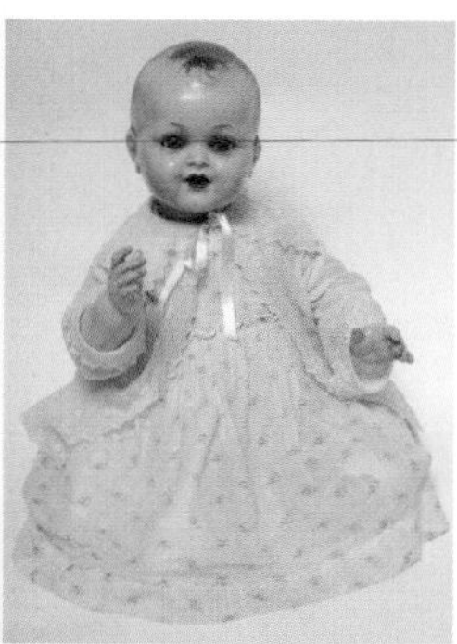

A König & Wernick character doll, with composition body, German, 1930s, 22in (56cm) high.
£220–250 / €320–360
$370–420 ⊞ DOL

◄ **A pair of Lenci felt flapper display dolls,** with painted faces and leather shoes, Italian, 1920s, 24in (61cm) high.
£4,000–4,800
€5,800–6,900
$6,700–8,000
SH

A Lenci cloth doll, with painted features, right foot stamped 'I6', Italian, c1930, 18in (45.5cm) high.
£330–390 / €470–560
$550–650 G(L)

Lenci (1918–present)

In 1918, Elena and Enrico Scarini began designing dolls near their home in Turin. They exhibited 100 models at the Leipzig Show in 1921 and received high praise. Among the various ranges they produced Indians, ethnic groups, cowboys, soldiers and policemen. The factory was destroyed during WWII but the company is still in production.

◄ **A pair of Lenci fabric dolls of a Tyrolean couple,** in traditional dress, Italian, c1930, 11¼in (28.5cm) high.
£120–145 / €170–200
$200–240 L&E

A Lenci felt doll, Italian, c1930, 17in (43cm) high.
£360–400 / €520–570
$600–670 ⊞ DOL

◄ **A Lenci cloth doll,** with painted features, Italian, c1930, 14in (35.5cm) high.
£330–390 / €470–560
$550–650 G(L)

Cloth dolls

Cloth dolls were first manufactured on a commercial basis in the late 19th century, particularly in America, where Martha Chase and Izannah Walker both produced life-like dolls covered in a fabric called stockinette, which was then painted in oils. Very few early examples of these have survived and they are consequently highly valued. More attainable are the cloth dolls made in the 1920s and '30s by the leading manufacturers of the day such as Lenci in Italy, Käthe Kruse in Germany and Chad Valley, Dean's and J. K. Farnell in Britain. These are still relatively affordable and therefore it is important that they should be in as good condition as possible, since cloth can get marked and blemishes will reduce the value.

An Armand Marseille marotte, in original costume, German, 1890s, 13in (33cm) high.
£360–400 / €520–570
$600–670 ⊞ DOL
A marotte is a doll's head mounted on a stick which often plays music when twirled.

An Armand Marseille bisque-headed doll, with sleeping eyes, open mouth and leather body with jointed composition limbs, impressed marks and 'No. 3200', c1910, 21½in (54.5cm) high.
£190–220 / €270–320
$320–370 DD

Magiuzin felt doll, alian, 1930s, 2in (30.5cm) high.
250–280 / €360–400
420–470 ⊞ DOL

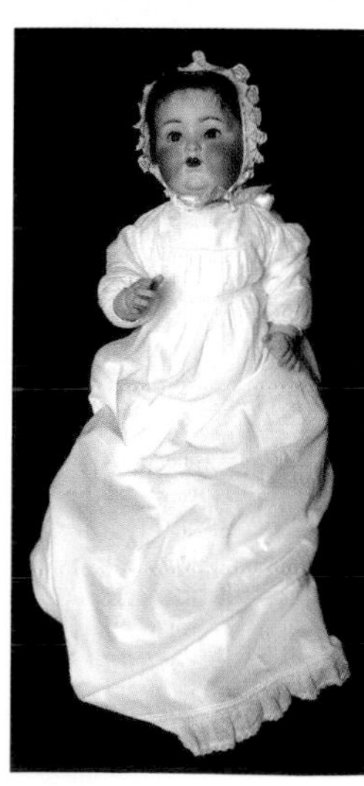

◄ **An Armand Marseille bisque-headed doll,** mould 990, with sleeping eyes, original wig and bent-limbed toddler body, German, c1920, 22in (56cm) high.
£390–430 / €560–620
$650–720 ⊞ POLL

DOLLS

An Armand Marseille bisque-headed doll, mould 990, with bent limbed body, German, c1925, 17in (43cm) high.
£350–390 / €510–560
$590–660 ⊞ POLL

An Armand Marseille doll, with mohair wig and bent limbed toddler body, German, c1925, 14in (35.5cm) high.
£300–340 / €430–480
$500–550 ⊞ POLL

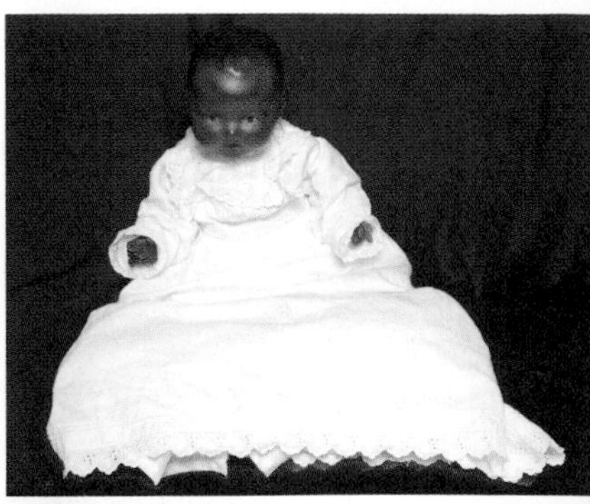

An Armand Marseille Dream Baby doll, mould 351/6K, German, c1925, 18in (45.5cm) high.
£270–300 / €390–430
$450–500 ⊞ DOL

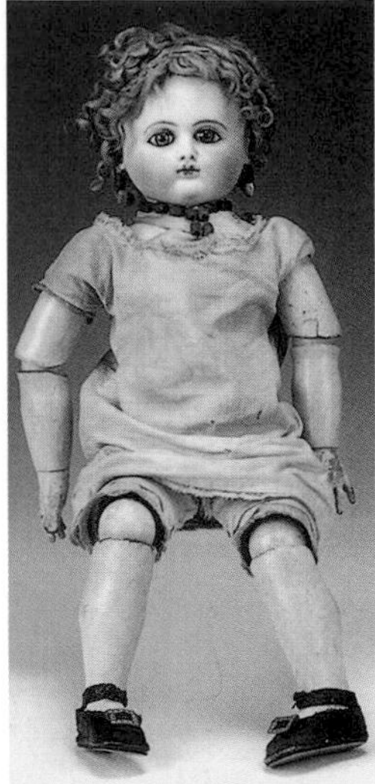

A Petit Dumortier bisque-headed doll, with open eyes and closed mouth, marked, French, c1900, 18in (45.5cm) high.
£2,900–3,450
€4,150–4,950
$4,850–5,800 ⚒ BERN

► A Pierotti poured wax doll, with fixed glass eyes, painted mouth and moulded ears, the cloth body with wax lower arms and legs, her trousseau including flannel skirt and blouse, muslin dress and cape, silk nightdress, fur-trimmed cape, knitted bonnet, velvet hat, tortoiseshell combs and brush, left lower leg damaged and detached, c1860, 20in (51cm) high.
£680–810 / €980–1,150
$1,150–1,350 ⚒ B(Kn)

A Victorian poured wax doll, probably Pierotti, with fixed paperweight eyes, wearing hand-sewn silk clothes, 18½in (47cm) high.
£300–360 / €430–520
$500–600 ⚒ G(L)

Wax dolls

Wax was used by doll makers from the 17th to the 20th centuries. It enabled facial expressions to be skillfully captured, and Victorian wax dolls often represented children in the sentimental manner typical of those times. However, due to the fragile nature of the medium, wax dolls have not survived in large numbers. The most well-known makers of the 19th century are Charles Marsh, Lucy Peck, Pierotti and Montanari – the latter two were Italian immigrants living in London who often vied against each other to produce the best dolls of that era.

A Grace Putnam Bye-Lo bisque-headed baby doll, with cloth body, marked, American, early 20thC, 12in (30.5cm) high.
£135–160 / €195–230
$230–270 ⚒ JAA

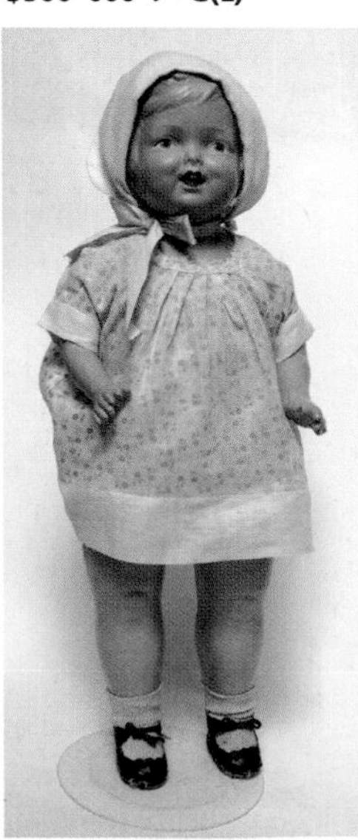

► A Regal Doll Inc Kiddie Pal doll, Canadian, c1920, 23in (58.5cm) high.
£135–150 / €195–220
$220–250 ⊞ DOL

A Rheinische Gummi und Celluloid Fabrik Co doll, German, c1920, 27in (68.5cm) high.
£250–280 / €360–400
$420–470 ⊞ UD

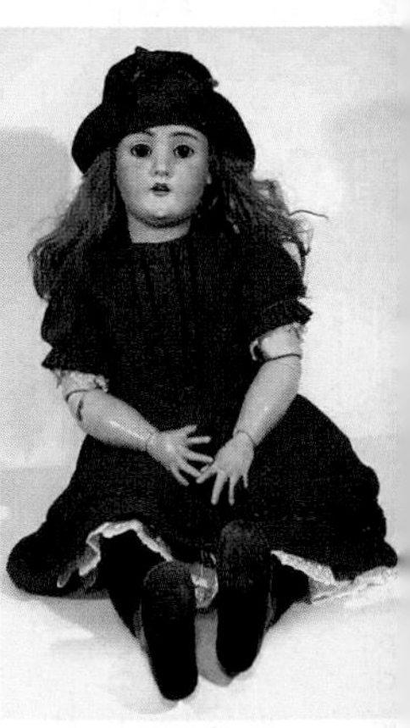

A Schönau & Hoffmeister bisque-headed doll, with sleeping eyes, open mouth, wig and jointed body, 1915–20, 39in (99cm) high.
£2,050–2,450
€2,950–3,500
$3,450–4,100 ⚒ AH

A Schützmeister & Quendt character doll, mould 201, with crying mechanism, German, c1910, 17in (43cm) high.
£290–330 / €410–470 $490–550 ⊞ BaN

A Schultz celluloid doll, in national costume, German, c1925, 25in (63.5cm) high.
£250–280 / €360–400 $420–470 ⊞ DOL

A S. F. B. J. character doll, mould 236, with toddler body, French, c1910, 27in (68.5cm) high.
£850–950 / €1,200–1,350 $1,450–1,600 ⊞ DOL

A S. F. B. J. Jumeau-style character doll, with weighted glass eyes, open mouth, upper teeth, pierced ears, mohair wig and fully jointed composition body, incised marks, French, c1910, 33in (84cm) high.
£1,050–1,250 €1,500–1,800 $1,750–2,100 ⚒ B(Kn)

A Simon & Halbig doll, mould 950, with closed mouth and original clothes, German, c1880, 14in (35.5cm) high.
£580–650 / €830–950 $970–1,100 ⊞ DOL

A Simon & Halbig/ Kämmer & Reinhardt bisque-headed doll, with weighted glass eyes, open mouth, upper teeth, mohair wig and fully jointed composition body, wearing original clothes, German, c1910, 13in (33cm) high.
£410–490 / €590–700 $690–820 ⚒ B(Kn)

A Simon & Halbig bisque-headed doll, with original clothes and wig, German, c1920, 15in (38cm) high.
£330–370 / €470–530 $550–620 ⊞ POLL

A Steiff policeman doll, with velvet face and hands, button eyes, the felt uniform with stitched and printed detail, German, c1910, 18in (45.5cm) high.
£1,200–1,400 €1,750–2,000 $2,000–2,350 ⚒ FHF

A Steiner bisque-headed *bébé* doll, with fixed paper-weight glass eyes, closed mouth, feather brows, pierced ears, mohair wig and fully-jointed composition body with fixed wrists, wearing original clothes, French, c1880, 22in (56cm) high.
£1,400–1,650 €2,000–2,350 $2,350–2,750 ⚒ B(Kn)

A Wagner & Zetzsche bisque-headed doll, the head by Gebrüder Heubach, marked, German, c1910, 18in (45.5cm) high.
£400–450 / €570–650 $670–760 ⊞ DOL

An Izannah Walker doll, with hand-painted hair and face, applied ears, on a muslin body, wearing original suit, hat and leather boots, damage and losses, American, c1873, 19in (48.5cm) high.
£4,900–5,800 €7,000–8,400 $8,200–9,800 ⚒ Bert

A C. & H. White leather-headed pedlar doll, with bead eyes, wearing traditional clothes and carrying a basket of wares, in a glass dome, c1840, 10¼in (26cm) high.
£430–510 / €620–730 $720–860 ⚒ S(O)

Unknown Makers

A composition doll, with painted features, mohair wig, fixed eyes and jointed leather body, early/mid-19thC, 15¾in (40cm) high.
£610–730 / €880–1,050
$1,000–1,200 ⚒ Bea

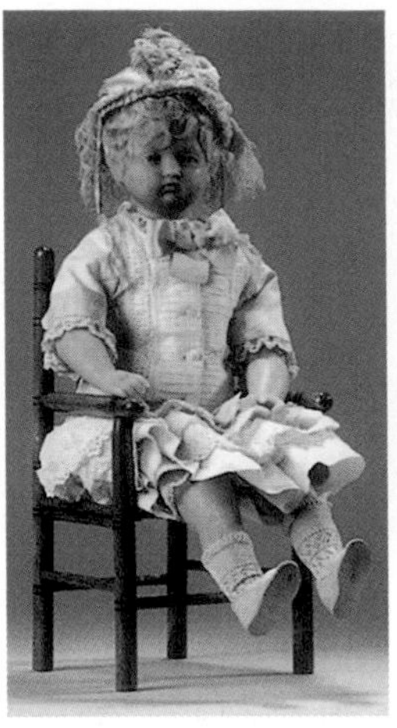

A poured wax portrait doll of Princess Louise, with glass eyes and painted mouth, cloth body with wax lower arms and legs, c1845, 21½in (51cm) high, seated on a turned wooden chair.
£2,700–3,250
€3,900–4,700
$4,550–5,500 ⚒ B(Kn)

A Victorian peg doll, with painted head, shoulders and lower limbs, wearing a contemporary dress, 10¾in (27.5cm) high.
£2,000–2,400
€2,900–3,450
$3,350–4,000 ⚒ CHTR

An early Victorian composition doll, with carved pine arms and legs, the bodice decorated with beads, 7¾in (19.5cm) high.
£440–530 / €630–760
$740–890 ⚒ SWO

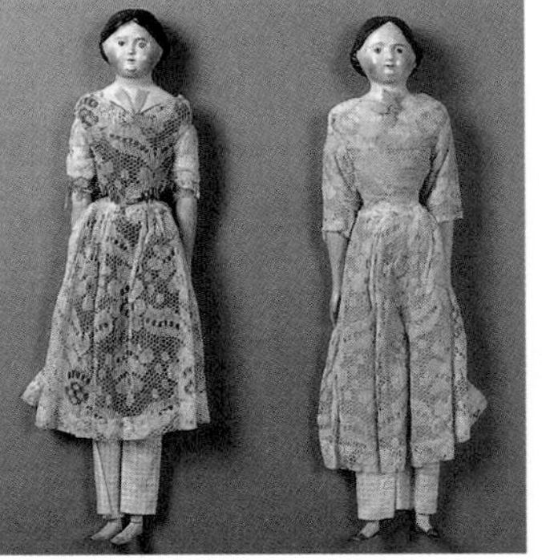

◄ A pair of papier-mâché and fabric dolls, with carved and painted arms and legs, wearing original clothes, probably German, c1850, 14½in (37cm) high.
£1,050–1,250
€1,500–1,800
$1,750–2,100
⚒ S(NY)

A wax-over-composition lady doll, with glass eyes, open mouth, upper teeth, wig and moulded boots, the cloth body with wax over composition, German, c1850, 12in (61cm) high.
£540–650 / €780–930
$910–1,100 ⚒ B(Kn)

◄ A papier-mâché doll, with painted features, moulded hair and jointed carved peg body, wearing original Welsh costume, German, c1850, 7in (18cm) high, in a papered and glazed case.
£370–440 / €530–630
$620–740 ⚒ B(Kn)

A wax doll, with cloth body, late 19thC, 8in (20.5cm) high.
£145–160 / €210–230
$240–270 ⊞ BaN

A china shoulder-headed fortune teller doll, the skirt made of paper fortunes, German, c1870, 5½in (14cm) high.
£240–280 / €340–400
$400–470 ⚒ G(L)

A bisque baby doll, German, c1900, 4in (10cm) high, in original presentation box.
£270–300 / €390–430
$450–500 ⊞ Beb

► A bisque-headed doll, with sleeping eyes, open mouth and real hair, leather body and bisque hands, impressed '28 Germany', early 20thC, 15in (38cm) high.
£410–490 / €590–700
$690–820 ⚒ TMA

DOLLS

Dolls' Houses & Accessories

A doll's house, the exterior with brickwork façade and balcony, the front opening into sections to reveal each floor with two rooms, some original wallpaper and fitted for electricity, with a later upper floor, c1890, 34in (86.5cm) wide, with a collection of furniture.
£4,250–5,100 / €6,100–7,300
$7,200–8,600 G(L)
This is known as The Henderson Doll's House and is described and illustrated in *English Dolls' Houses* by Vivien Greene, Bell & Hyman, 1979.

A painted doll's house, the hinged exterior with balustrade and porticoed front door, the interior with four rooms, two fireplaces and staircase, 19thC, 25¼in (64cm) wide.
£445–530 / €640–770
$750–900 Oli

A Moritz Göttschalk doll's house, in the form of a suburban villa, German, c1900, 17¼in (44cm) wide, with various contents.
£360–430 / €520–620
$600–720 HOK

A painted wooden doll's house, applied with copper relief panels and painted decoration, dated 1929, 32in (81.5cm) high.
£175–210 / €250–300
$290–350 G(L)

A Tri-ang wooden doll's house, with opening metal windows and garage, the front opening in two sections to reveal two rooms, garden attached, some wear, 1930s, 27in (68.5cm) wide.
£190–220 / €270–310
$320–370 WAL

A bisque doll's house doll, with glass eyes and jointed body, German, c1900, 4in (10cm) high.
£220–250 / €320–360
$370–420 YC

◄ A wooden doll's house bedroom suite, comprising bed, three-drawer chest, washstand and wardrobe, covered in wood effect paper, German, c1860, wardrobe 6in (15cm) high.
£520–620 / €750–890
$870–1,050 B(Kn)

A wooden doll's house dining suite, comprising table, six chairs, settee and footstool, covered in wood effect paper and velvet upholstery, German, c1860, table 2½in (6cm) high.
£220–260 / €320–370
$370–440 B(Kn)

A set of birds'-feather doll's house furniture, comprising six chairs and a settee, 19thC, largest 3in (7.5cm) high.
£165–195 / €240–280
$280–330 SWO

A set of Waltershausen wooden doll's house furniture, comprising a secretaire with fall-front, sewing table with two drawers containing buttons, ribbons and sewing utensils, cradle with silk blanket, slight damage, German, late 19thC, secretaire 5½in (14cm) high.
£490–580 / €710–840
$820–970 B(Kn)

Teddy Bears

A Bing teddy bear, with boot-button eyes, German, c1910, 24in (61cm) high.
£1,950–2,200
€2,800–3,150
$3,300–3,700 ⊞ BaN

A Chad Valley mohair teddy bear, with glass eyes, stitched nose and mouth, the fully jointed body with felt paw pads, labelled, c1935, 27in (69cm) high.
£590–700 / €850–1,000
$990–1,150 ⚒ B(Kn)

A Bing mohair teddy bear, with glass eyes, German, 1920s, 13in (33cm) high.
£1,400–1,550
€2,000–2,250
$2,350–2,600 ⊞ BBe

A Chad Valley plush teddy bear, with glass eyes, jointed limbs and velvet paw pads, labelled, 1950s, 23in (58.5cm) high.
£260–310 / €370–450
$440–520 ⚒ G(L)

Miller's Compares

I. A Chiltern pink and blue mohair Hugmee bear, with glass eyes and cotton pads, c1940, 15in (38cm) high.
£720–800
€1,050–1,200
$1,200–1,350 ⊞ BBe

II. A Chiltern mohair Hugmee bear, with glass eyes and cotton pads, 1930s, 22in (56cm) high.
£300–330 / €430–480
$500–550 ⊞ BBe

Item I is larger and probably slightly later in date than Item II and not in as good condition. However, it is made in a rare colour combination of pink and blue mohair and for this reason is worth more than double the amount of Item II.

A Chad Valley mohair teddy bear, with boot-button eyes, stitched nose, mouth and claws and jointed limbs, labelled, straw-filled, some wear, c1918, 16in (41cm) high.
£700–840 / €1,000–1,200
$1,200–1,400 ⚒ B(Kn)

A Chad Valley silk plush 'Patriotic' bear, labelled, 1950s, 26in (66cm) high.
£135–150 / €195–210
$220–250 ⊞ BBe

A Dean's mohair plush teddy bear, with cotton pads, 1950s, 16in (40.5cm) high.
£180–200 / €260–290
$300–330 ⊞ BBe

A Farnell mohair teddy bear, with glass eyes, 1930s, 19in (48.5cm) high.
£540–600 / €780–860
$900–1,000 ⊞ BBe

A Chad Valley mohair teddy bear, with glass eyes, 1920s–30s, 21in (53.5cm) high.
£670–750 / €960–1,100
$1,100–1,250 ⊞ BBe

A Chiltern pink mohair teddy bear, with glass eyes, stitched nose, mouth and claws, the fully jointed body with cloth paw pads, substantial wear, c1935, 19in (48cm) high.
£370–440 / €530–630
$620–740 ⚒ B(Kn)

A Merrythought Mr Woppit teddy bear, with glass eyes, stitched nose and mouth and felt ears and feet, labelled, c1956, 9in (23cm) high.
£610–730 / €880–1,050
$1,000–1,200 ⚒ B(Kn)

◄ **A Schuco plush mohair bear,** German, 1950s, 26in (66cm) high.
£310–350 / €440–500
$520–590 ⊞ BaN

A Steiff mohair teddy bear, with boot-button eyes, German, c1908, 19in (48.5cm) high.
£3,600–4,000
€5,200–5,800
$6,000–6,700 ⊞ BBe

A Steiff mohair teddy bear, button to ear, damaged, German, 1910–15, 12in (30.5cm) high.
£1,200–1,350
€1,750–1,950
$2,000–2,250 ⊞ BBe

A Steiff mohair teddy bear, button to ear missing, German, c1950, 11in (28cm) high.
£360–400 / €520–570
$600–670 ⊞ Beb

Identification buttons were often removed from the ears of soft toys because of the danger they presented to children. It is advisable to check the ear for a hole.

A Steiff mohair Tumbling teddy bear, with boot-button eyes, jointed limbs, felt paw pads, with mechanism enabling the arms to move forward in tumbling position, some wear, paw pads restored, German, c1909, 11¾in (30cm) high.
£1,150–1,400
€1,650–2,000
$1,950–2,350 ⚒ B(Kn)

► **A Tara Toys musical bear,** Irish, late 1950s, 19in (48.5cm) high.
£145–160 / €200–230
$240–270 ⊞ BaN

A William Terry mohair teddy bear, 1918–20, 13in (33cm) high.
£630–700 / €900–1,000
$1,050–1,200 ⊞ BBe

TEDDY BEARS

A mohair teddy bear, with boot-button eyes, pre-1920, 21in (53.5cm) high.
£630–700 / €900–1,000
$1,050–1,200 ⊞ BBe

A plush teddy bear, the jointed, straw-filled body with cotton pads, early 20thC, 26in (66cm) high.
£280–330 / €400–480
$470–550 ⚒ DA

A bristle mohair teddy bear, with boot-button eyes, German, c1920, 24in (61cm) high.
£360–400 / €520–580
$600–670 ⊞ BBe

◄ A plush teddy bear, with boot-button eyes and felt pads, straw-filled, growler inoperative, probably German, early 20thC, 17in (43cm) high.
£190–230 / €270–320
$320–370 ⚒ CDC

► A plush teddy bear, with button ears, damaged, Continental, early 20thC, 24in (61cm) high.
£3,650–4,400
€5,300–6,400
$6,400–7,400 ⚒ AH

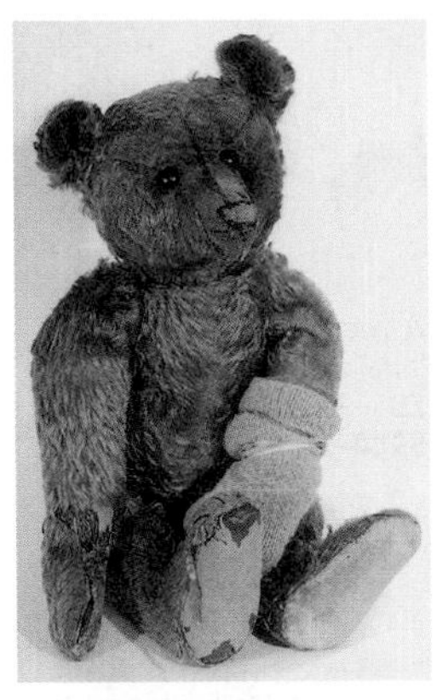

A plush teddy bear, with felt pads, straw-filled, some wear and restoration, later glass eyes, probably German, early 20thC, 13½in (34.5cm) high.
£120–145 / €170–200
$200–240 ⚒ CDC

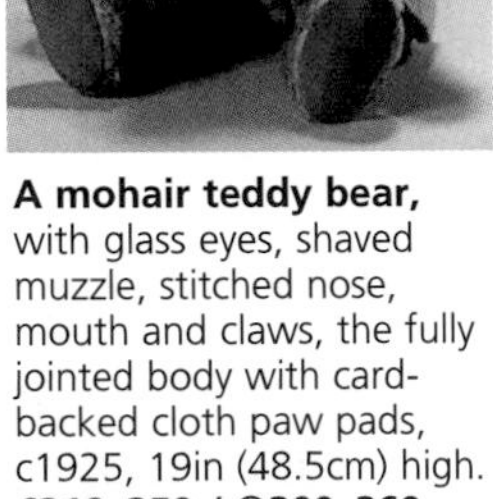

A mohair teddy bear, with glass eyes, shaved muzzle, stitched nose, mouth and claws, the fully jointed body with card-backed cloth paw pads, c1925, 19in (48.5cm) high.
£210–250 / €300–360
$350–420 ⚒ B(Kn)

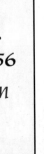

A plush teddy bear, with glass eyes and jointed limbs, excelsior filling, pre-1939, 18in (45.5cm) high.
£165–195 / €240–280
$280–330 ⚒ G(L)

◄ A plush teddy bear, with glass eyes and felt pads, straw-filled, probably German, pre-1939, 15in (38cm) high.
£190–230 / €270–320
$320–370 ⚒ CDC

Soft Toys

A Chad Valley golly, wearing original clothes, 1930s, 12in (30.5cm) high.
£270–300 / €390–430
$450–500 ⊞ BaN

◄ **A Farnell Alpha Toys monkey,** with fixed glass eyes, felt-covered face, hands and feet, jointed, labelled, c1930, 15in (38cm) high.
£2,250–2,700
€3,250–3,900
$3,750–4,500
CDC

A Kunsa Puss-in-Boots, marked, Austrian, 1940s, 21in (53.5cm) high.
£250–280 / €360–400
$420–470 ⊞ BaN

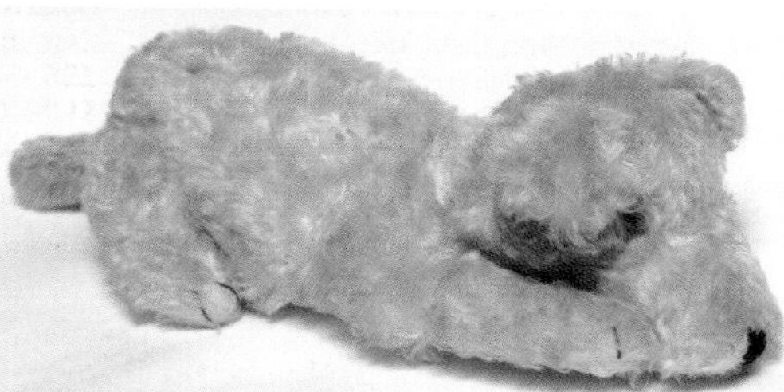

A Merrythought Terrier nightdress case, labelled, 1930s, 20in (51cm) long.
£85–95 / €120–135
$140–160 ⊞ DOL

A Roullet & Decamps mechanical cat, with rabbit-fur body, French, c1940, 15in (38cm) long.
£1,050–1,200
€1,500–1,700
$1,750–2,000 ⊞ AUTO
This cat walks, miaows and its tail moves.

A Steiff mohair dog, with boot-button eyes, jointed limbs, button to ear, some wear, German, c1904, 14½in (37cm) long.
£4,450–5,300 / €6,400–7,600
$7,500–8,900 G(L)

A Steiff rattle, in the form of a cat, with bead eyes, German, c1905, 5in (12.5cm) high.
£360–400 / €520–570
$600–670 ⊞ BaN

A Steiff felt pig, with button to ear, German, c1905, 5½in (14cm) long.
£270–300 / €390–430
$450–500 ⊞ BaN

◄ **A plush dog automaton,** with glass eyes, a weighted nodding head and clockwork mechanism, early 20thC, 15in (38cm) high.
£320–380 / €460–550
$540 640 Mit

A Scottie nightdress case, with collar and disc, 1930s, 22in (56cm) long.
£85–95 / €120–135
$140–160 ⊞ DOL

A wool poodle nightdress case, c1930, 18in (45.5cm) long.
£30–35 / €45–50
$50–60 ⊞ DOL

◄ **A Highland Terrier,** c1930, 13in (33cm) high.
£85–95 / €120–135
$140–160 ⊞ DOL

Toys

Aeroplanes & Airships

A Dinky Toys box of Hawker Hurricane single-seater fighters, No. 62, three camouflaged aircraft with wheels down, one camouflaged aircraft with wheels up and four damaged part models, one propeller missing, box dated 1940.
£350–420 / €500–600
$590–700 ⚒ VEC

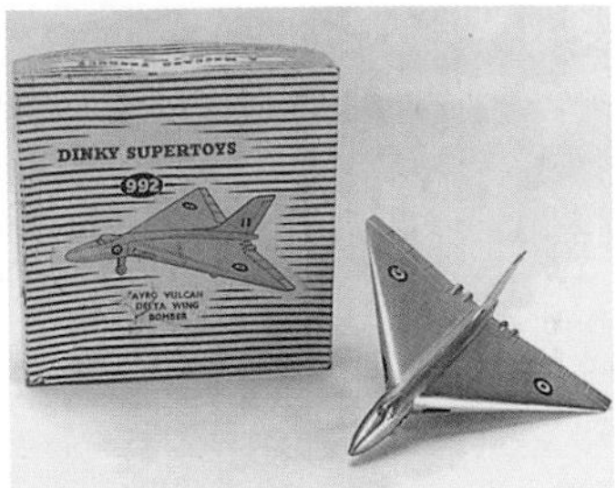

A Dinky Supertoys Avro Vulcan Delta Wing bomber, one roundel damaged, c1955, boxed.
£2,700–3,250 / €3,900–4,650
$4,550–5,400 ⚒ WAL

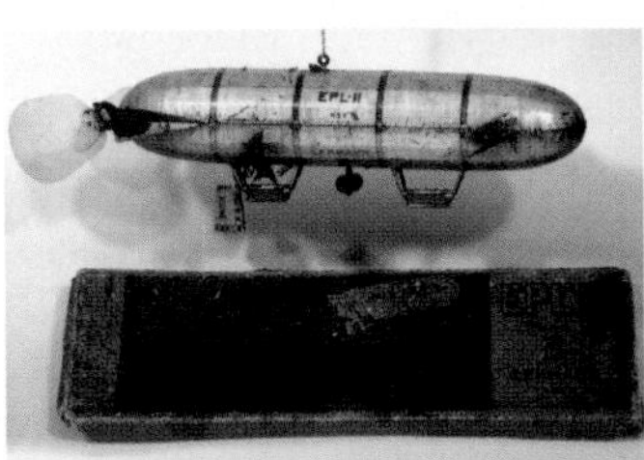

A Lehmann lithographed tinplate clockwork EPL 11 airship, worn, German, c1912, 9½in (24cm) long, boxed.
£1,100–1,300 / €1,600–1,900
$1,850–2,200 ⚒ CDC

Boats & Submarines

A Bing tinplate clockwork submarine, propeller and fore-and-aft flags missing, German, c1905, 13in (33cm) long, in original box.
£350–420 / €500–600
$590–710 ⚒ B(Kn)

► **A Bing tinplate clockwork liner,** motor, masts and lifeboats missing, some repainting, German, 1920s, 16½in (42cm) long.
£560–670 / €810–960
$930–1,100 ⚒ WAL

A Buffalo Toy Co tinplate Betsy Green side-wheeler steamboat, with pull-spring operation, American, early 1900s, 26in (66cm) long.
£540–600 / €780–860
$910–1,000 ⊞ TNS

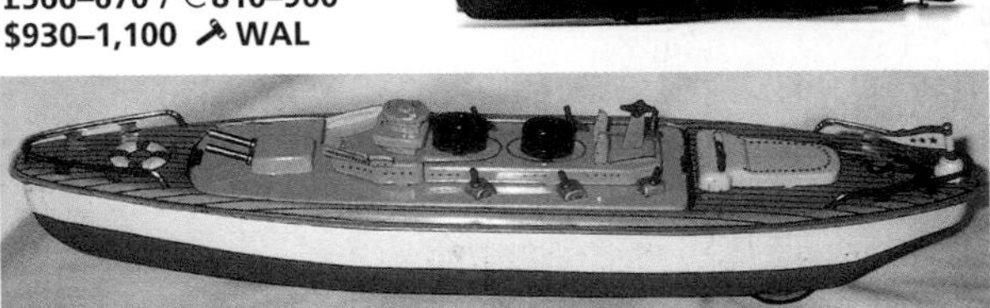

A tinplate friction motor 'flip-top' ship, Japanese, c1950, 12in (30.5cm) long.
£155–170 / €220–250
$260–290 ⊞ TNS
A lever on the back of this model flips the top and converts it from a cruise liner into a battleship.

Mechanical Toys

◄ **A Jumeau automaton,** with a key-wind mechanism enabling the head to move side-to-side and up-and-down to smell the flowers, arms replaced, French, c1890, 19in (48.5cm) high.
£1,450–1,750
€2,100–2,500
$2,450–2,950
⚒ B(Kn)

A Manivelle automaton, German, c1910, 10in (25.5cm) high.
£850–950 / €1,200–1,350
$1,450–1,600 ⊞ AUTO

◄ **A Lambert automaton Pierrot,** with a musical movement, French, c1890, 23in (58.5cm) high.
£3,550–3,950 / €5,100–5,700
$5,900–6,500 ⊞ KHW

A Moranghie dancing doll automaton, with a bisque head and original clothes, French, c1890, 11in (28cm) high.
£1,250–1,400
€1,800–2,000
$2,100–2,300 ⊞ AUTO

A Phalibois musical automaton, depicting two monkey figures in 18thC costume, the male playing a street organ, the female singing from a song sheet, under a glass dome, French, c1880, 23¾in (60.5cm) high.
£2,900–3,500
€4,200–5,000
$4,900–5,900 ⚒ B(WM)

A Renov 'The Magician' musical automaton, the doll with a bisque head and papier-mâché body, the musical box with five airs, c1890, 17in (43cm) high.
£7,600–8,500
€10,900–12,200
$12,800–14,300 ⊞ AUTO

A Roullet & Decamps electric monkey, covered in rabbit fur, with moving head, mouth and cello, French, c1920, 13in (33cm) high.
£680–750 / €980–1,100
$1,150–1,300 ⊞ AUTO

A Gustave Vichy clockwork musical automaton of a clown playing a banjo, some fading and wear, French, c1870, 22in (56cm) high.
£2,750–3,300
€4,000–4,750
$4,600–5,500 ⚒ B(Kn)

A Vichy musical girl mandolin-player, with moving head and strumming arm, French, c1880, 15¾in (40cm) high.
£4,000–4,400
€5,800–6,400
$6,700–7,400 ⊞ YC

An 'Antiques and Curios' pedlar doll, standing by a market stall, under a glass dome, 19thC, 17in (43cm) high.
£240–290 / €350–420
$400–480 ⚒ JM

A Victorian automaton, with a rocking ship flanked by a windmill and water wheel, with a train crossing a bridge, 24in (61cm) high.
£640–770 / €920–1,100
$1,100–1,300 ⚒ HYD

A clown automaton, the mechanism playing two airs, in need of restoration, French, late 19thC, 23¾in (60.5cm) high.
£1,200–1,450
€1,750–2,100
$2,000–2,400 ⚒ AMB

► **A clockwork clown advertising automaton,** with later clothes, German, c1880, 23in (58.5cm) high.
£1,600–1,750
€2,300–2,550
$2,650–2,950 ⊞ AUTO

A 'Rubber Neck' celluloid tramp, his neck extends as he walks, Japanese, c1930, 10in (25.5cm) high, boxed.
£140–170 / €200–240
$240–285 ⚒ BWL

A girl automaton, with moving head, eyes, arms and wrist, early 20thC, 21in (53.5cm) high.
£2,700–3,250
€3,900–4,650
$4,600–5,500 ⚒ FHF

◄ **A microphone dancer,** American, c1935, 12in (30.5cm) high.
£315–350 / €450–500
$530–590 ⊞ AUTO

Money Boxes

A painted copper money box, in the form of a cottage, c1830, 4in (10cm) high.
£270–300 / €390–430
$450–500 ⊞ F&F

A cast-iron Bulldog Bank money box, late 19thC, 8in (20.5cm) high.
£530–640 / €760–910
$1,000–1,100 ⚒ TMA

◄ **A cast-iron pillar-box money bank,** registered date for 1892, 6in (15cm) high.
£150–165 / €220–250
$250–280 ⊞ MFB

A cast-iron Transvaal money box, in the form of President Kruger, c1900, 6in (15cm) high.
£55–65 / €80–95
$90–105 ⚒ RTo

A spelter money box, in the form of a dog with a pipe, German, c1905, 4in (10cm) high.
£270–300 / €390–450
$430–500 ⊞ HAL

A spelter money box, in the form of a dog kennel with a dog and cat, c1910, 3in (7.5cm) high.
£310–350 / €450–500
$520–590 ⊞ HAL

◄ **A cast-iron money box,** in the form of a dovecote, c1910, 3½in (9cm) high.
£180–200 / €260–290
$300–340 ⊞ MFB

► **A cast-iron money box,** modelled as a house, c1910, 5½in (14cm) high.
£200–220 / €290–320
$330–370 ⊞ MFB

Noah's Arks

A wooden Noah's Ark, with carved and painted wooden animals, 19thC, 18in (45.5cm) wide.
£800–960 / €1,200–1,400
$1,350–1,600 ⚒ MAR

A painted wooden Noah's Ark, with 120 carved and painted wooden animals and seven figures, German, late 19thC, 19in (48.5cm) wide.
£940–1,150 / €1,350–1,600
$1,600–1,900 ⚒ B(Kn)

A painted wooden Noah's Ark, on wheels, with 20 carved and painted wooden animals and two figures, c1900, 31in (78.5cm) wide.
£390–470 / €560–670
$660–790 ⚒ SWO

Rocking Horses

A carved and painted wooden rocking horse, on a bow rocker, some losses, early 19thC, 76in (193cm) long.
£820–980 / €1,200–1,400
$1,400–1,650 WW

A Victorian painted wooden rocking horse, with glass eyes, on a pine safety rocker, later harness, some damage, 56in (142cm) long.
£1,400–1,700 / €2,000–2,450
$2,350–2,800 NSal

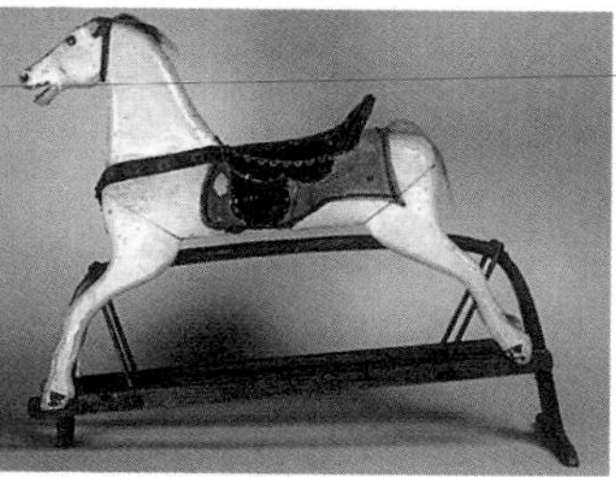

A painted wooden rocking horse, with horsehair mane and tail, glass eyes and studded saddle and bridle, on a wooden trestle base, one eye missing, German, late 19thC, 42in (106.5cm) long.
£350–420 / €500–600
$590–700 LHA

A painted pine rocking horse, with some original grey paint, leather harness, mane and tail detached, on a safety rocker, early 20thC, 51½in (131cm) high.
£1,000–1,200 / €1,500–1,750
$1,700–2,000 PFK

A G. & J. Lines wooden rocking horse, early 20thC, 32in (81.5cm) long.
£500–550 / €720–790
$840–920 GREE

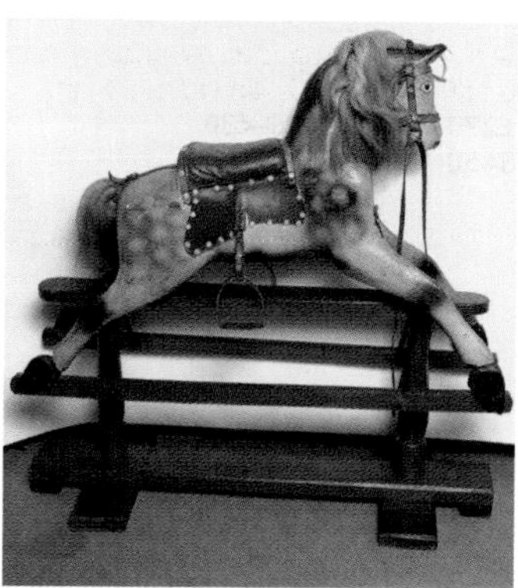

A wooden rocking horse, in original condition, 1920s, 36in (91.5cm) long.
£540–600 / €780–860
$910–1,000 BaN

TOYS

Soldiers

A Britains Royal Horse Artillery set, No. 39, first version, comprising a six-horse gun team, four seated men and a mounted officer, 1899.
£820–980 / €1,200–1,400
$1,400–1,650 B(Kn)

A Britains Kings African Rifles set, No. 225, comprising eight soldiers, in original box with tie-in card, minor wear to box, 1920s.
£190–230 / €270–320
$320–380 WAL

A Belgian Infantry set, No. 1389, minor wear, some chips, c1935, in original box.
£145–175 / €210–250
$240–280 WAL

◄ **A Britains Arabs of the Desert set,** No. 224, comprising two mounted camels, two warriors on horseback, three natives, a coconut palm and two palm trees, one native missing, c1946.
£120–145 / €170–200
$200–240 ⚒ CGC

A Britains Foreign Legion set, No. 1711, c1948, boxed.
£150–180 / €220–260
$250–300 ⚒ BR

A Britains Home Guard set, No. 1918, comprising eight soldiers, one figure retouched, late 1940s, in original box with packing card.
£165–200 / €240–280
$280–330 ⚒ WAL

A Britains Danish Guard Hussar regiment set, No. 2018, comprising six men with swords and an officer, all mounted, some paint chips and retouching, c1950, in original box.
£360–430 / €520–620
$600–720 ⚒ WAL

A Royal Corps of Signals dispatch riders set, No. 1791, comprising four riders on motorcycles, minor marking, 1950s, tied to original card in box.
£175–210 / €250–300
$290–340 ⚒ WAL

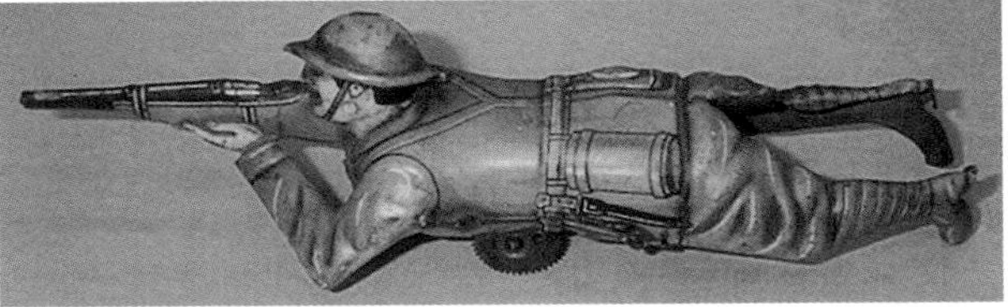

A lithographed tinplate automaton horizontal sniper, patent marks, German, c1900, 7½in (19cm) long.
£165–200 / €240–280
$280–330 ⚒ SPF

A CBG Mignot French Mountain Artillery set, comprising a mule towing a gun, three further pack mules, three mule handlers, four artillerymen and an officer, French, 1897, in original box.
£350–420 / €500–600
$590–710 ⚒ B(Kn)

Trains

◄ **A Bassett-Lowke gauge 0 live steam express 2–6–0 Mogul locomotive and tender,** 42980, with handbook, c1953, in original box.
£440–530 / €630–750
$740–890 ⚒ G(L)

A Bing gauge 1 clockwork 4–4–0 locomotive, No. 2631, with six-wheeled tender, German, c1906, 21in (53.5cm) long.
£590–710 / €850–1,000
$1,000–1,200 ⚒ G(L)

A Bing gauge 0 electric three-car LNER suburban train, with fitted interior and front and tail lights, two coaches RN2568 and a passenger brake end RN1234N, minor paint loss, some repainting, German, c1927.
£120–145 / €180–210
$200–240 ⚒ WAL

A Hornby Dublo tank goods set, with three wagons, track and controller, pre-WWII, boxed
£320–380 / €460–550
$540–640 ⚒ LAY

► **A Hornby gauge 0 saloon car,** early 1920s.
£115–130
€165–185
$200–220 ⊞ HAL

TOYS

◀ **A Hornby gauge 0 electric locomotive,** EPM16, c1934.
£1,350–1,500
€1,950–2,150
$2,250–2,500 ⊞ MDe
Green boxes denoted electrical items such as this locomotive. These were only made in small quantities and are rarely found in the condition pictured.

A Hornby Dublo 0–6–2 EDL 7 tank locomotive, 2594, pre-WWII, boxed.
£630–760 / €920–1,100
$1,050–1,250 ⚒ LAY

◀ **A Hornby Dublo D2 two-coach articulated unit,** pre-WWII.
£230–280 / €340–400
$390–460 ⚒ LAY

A Hornby Dublo painted wooden D402 goods depot, pre-WWII, boxed.
£320–380 / €460–550
$540–640 ⚒ LAY

A Märklin gauge 1 4–4–2 20v electric C-type Atlantic locomotive and tender, slight damage, German, c1930.
£1,750–2,100 / €2,500–3,000
$2,950–3,500 ⚒ AH

▶ **A Märklin gauge 1 4–4–2 electric locomotive,** No. HS 64/13021, with four opening cab doors, damaged, German, c1930.
£3,200–3,850 / €4,600–5,500
$5,400–6,500 ⚒ AH

A Schönner gauge 3 live steam Black Prince 4–4–0 locomotive and tender, No. 1502, slight paint loss, German, c1905.
£1,100–1,300 / €1,600–1,900
$1,850–2,200 ⚒ B(Kn)

A Tenshodo hand-built brass American locomotive, Japanese, c1958, 9in (23cm) long.
£90–100 / €130–145
$150–170 ⊞ WOS

A 2½in gauge steam-fired 2–6–0 locomotive and tender, c1950, on display track.
£550–660 / €790–950
$920–1,100 ⚒ DA

Vehicles

◄ **An Auto Dux Veritas racing car kit,** comprising pre-painted body, chassis, rear wheels, clockwork motor, front wheels, four tyres and two spanners, minor wear, German, 1950s, in original box.
£210–250 / €300–360
$350–420 ⚒ WAL

A Bandai tinplate battery-powered Saab 95 saloon car, Japanese, c1965, 7in (18cm) long.
£140–155 / €200–220
$230–260 ⊞ CBB

A Bing clockwork tinplate Model T Ford, German, c1923, 6½in (16.5cm) long.
£320–360 / €470–520
$540–600 ⊞ TNS
Bing's Fords are probably the most accurate wind-up tinplate models ever produced.

◄ **A Britains four-wheel farm lorry,** No. 59F, with a uniformed driver, 1939, in original box for army lorry.
£470–560 / €680–810
$790–940 ⚒ B(Kn)

► **A Burnett tinplate clockwork bus,** c1912, 9in (23cm) long.
£720–800 / €1,050–1,150
$1,200–1,350 ⊞ HAL

A Buddy L Coupé, American, early 20thC, 11in (28cm) long.
£1,050–1,250 / €1,500–1,800
$1,750–2,100 ⚒ JDJ
Buddy L toys were named after the son of Fred Lundahl, the owner of the company.

◄ **A Buddy L pressed-steel Railway Express vehicle,** with original Buddy L lock and pull cord, American, c1925, 24in (61cm) long.
£2,450–2,900
€3,500–4,200
$4,100–4,900
⚒ Bert

► **A Corgi Toys Bedford AFS fire service tender,** No. 405, late 1950s, 4in (10cm) long.
£100–110
€145–160
$170–190
⊞ HAL

A Dinky Toys Oldsmobile, American, late 1940s, 4in (10cm) long.
£90–100 / €130–145
$150–165 ⊞ CBB

TOYS

A Dinky Racing Cars gift set, No. 4, comprising a Cooper Bristol, Alfa Romeo, Ferrari, HWM and Maserati, paint chips to cars, c1956, in original box.
£470–560 / €680–810
$790–940 WAL

A Dinky Toys 25-pounder field gun set, No. 697, 1950s, 10in (25.5cm) long, boxed.
£90–100 / €130–145
$150–170 ⊞ HAL

A Dinky Toys Bentley Coupé, No. 194, 1950s, 4in (10cm) long, boxed.
£150–170 / €220–250
$250–280 ⊞ HAL
This car is scarcer in bronze than in the more usual silver-grey colourway.

A Hubley Manufacturing Co cast-iron Harley-Davidson Highway Patrol motorcycle and sidecar pull toy, with removable driver and passengers, American, c1928, 9in (23cm) long.
£900–1,000 / €1,300–1,450
$1,500–1,650 ⊞ TNS

A Dinky Supertoys Mighty Antar low loader with propeller, minor wear and chips, c1958, with original box and packaging.
£210–250 / €300–360
$350–420 WAL

A JNF tinplate clockwork Porsche, with lights and opening bonnet, German, c1954, 8in (20.5cm) long.
£490–540 / €700–780
$820–910 ⊞ TNS
The German company JNF was founded by Joseph Neuhierl in 1920.

A Lehmann Oho clockwork toy, German, c1903, 4in (10cm) long.
£140–170 / €200–240
$250–290 JDJ

◄ **A Lehmann Naughty Boy clockwork toy,** German, c1903, 5in (12.5cm) long.
£510–610 / €730–880
$860–1,000 JDJ

A Günthermann tinplate and clockwork double-decker bus, some rubbing and wear, German, c1920, 13¾in (35cm) long.
£610–730 / €880–1,050
$1,000–1,200 SWO

A Keystone pressed-steel circus truck, enclosing six animal cages, includes one animal, decorated with paper lithograph graphics to the side and interior of body, minor damage, American, c1932, 24¼in (61.5cm) long.
£12,500–15,000 / €18,000–21,600
$21,000–25,200 Bert

A Lesney Models of Yesteryear Gift Set, No. G7, comprising five vehicles, c1960, box 10in (25.5cm) wide.
£200–230 / €300–330
$340–380 ⊞ GTM

A Lines Bros tinplate pedal car, with rubber wheels, restored, 1930–40, 48in (122cm) long.
£530–640 / €760–910
$950–1,100 AH

► **A Märklin tinplate clockwork two-seat open tourer car,** repainted, some damage, three tyres missing, German, c1920, 4½in (11cm) wide.
£2,700–3,250
€4,000–4,700
$4,600–5,500
SWO

A Louis Marx tinplate Milton Berle Car, with figure of Milton Berle, clockwork mechanism, American, 1950s, 5½in (14cm) long, with original box.
£260–310 / €370–440
$440–520 Bert

A Mattel plastic Dream Car, with chrome-effect finish and trim, removable hardtop, American, c1953, 12in (30.5cm) long, with original box.
£160–190 / €230–270
$270–320 Bert

A Steelcraft pressed-steel Inter-City Bus, with electric lights, rubber tyres, window cut-outs and bench seats, paint chipped, American, c1927, 24in (61cm) long.
£390–460 / €560–670
$650–780 Bert

A Tri-ang Spot-On ERF lorry, 1960s, 8in (20.5cm) long, boxed.
£200–220 / €290–320
$330–370 HAL

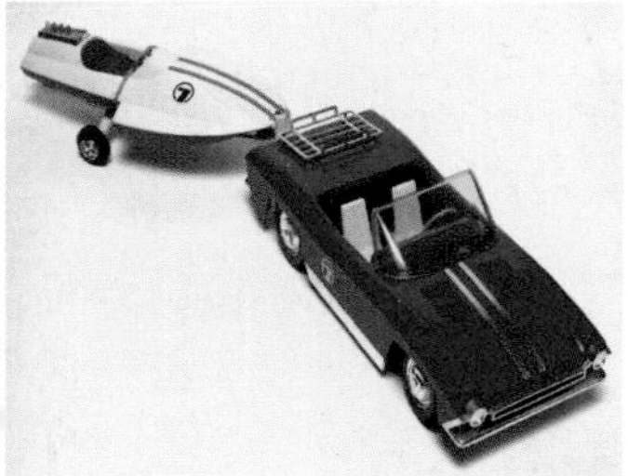

◄ **A Topper Toys battery-operated plastic Johnny 7 car and speedboat,** American, 1960s, 14in (35.5cm) long.
£110–120
€160–180
$185–210 HAL

A Whitanco tinplate clockwork bus, c1920, 14in (35.5cm) long.
£720–800 / €1,050–1,150
$1,200–1,350 HAL

► **A cast-iron tractor,** American, late 19thC, 5½in (14cm) long.
£75–90
€110–130
$125–150
DuM

► **A Wilkins metal tractor,** American, c1930, 8½in (21.5cm) long.
£120–145
€180–210
$200–240
DuM

◄ **A painted metal delivery wagon,** c1900, 11in (28cm) long.
£90–110
€135–160
$150–180
DuM

► **A Hessmobil tinplate touring car,** damaged, German, 1920s, 8in (20.5cm) long.
£210–250
€300–360
$350–420
MAR

◄ **A tinplate clockwork fire engine,** 1930s, 15in (38cm) long.
£150–180
€220–260
$250–300
AMB

Miscellaneous

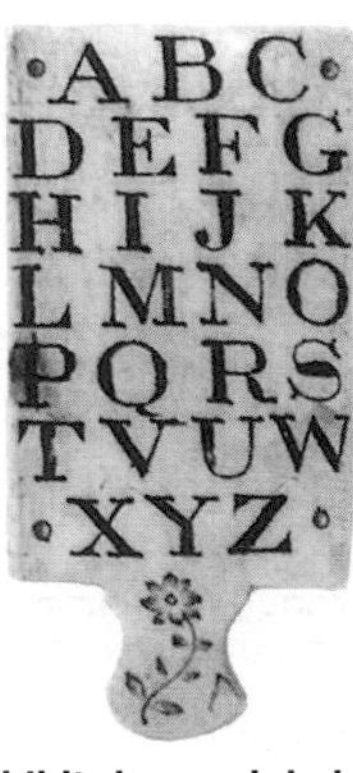

A child's bone alphabet tablet, engraved and coloured with the alphabet and a flower spray, early 19thC, 4¼in (11cm) high.
£500–600 / €720–860
$840–1,000 ⚒ Bri

A Bingoscope projector, with a boxed roll of Pathéscope 9.5mm Mickey Mouse safety film, 1930s, in original box with Mickey Mouse images.
£105–125 / €150–180
$175–210 ⚒ DW

A wood and metal doll's double pram, with a leatherette interior, late 19thC, 26in (66cm) wide.
£290–350 / €420–500
$490–590 ⚒ B(WM)

A boxed collection of bone alphabet letters and numbers, 19thC, each ½in (1cm) wide.
£370–440 / €530–630
$620–740 ⚒ G(B)

A Houghton & Gunn mahogany card board, the four hinged baize-lined sections locked by a brass slide bolt, with bezique markers and ivory maker's label, late 19th/early 20thC, 30 x 21¾in (76 x 55.5cm).
£315–350 / €450–500
$530–590 ⊞ ChC

An In Statu Quo patented travelling chess board, with red and white stained chessmen, in a mahogany folding case, 19thC, 9 x 5in (23 x 12.5cm), with a book-shaped outer case.
£350–420 / €500–600
$590–700 ⚒ BWL

A layered-paper doll on card, with 11 costumes, c1805, each card 5 x 5½in (12.5 x 14cm).
£1,100–1,300 / €1,600–1,900
$1,850–2,200 ⚒ BWL

A leather-bound folding backgammon and draughts board, the spine entitled 'Parlour Games', c1910, 15in (38cm) wide.
£450–500 / €650–720
$760–840 ⊞ MSh

A white-metal and enamel chess set, in the form of 16thC courtiers, Continental, early 19thC, with leather case for chess pieces.
£2,750–3,300 / €3,950–4,750
$4,600–5,500 ⚒ JAd

A set of boxwood chess pieces, 1930s, tallest 3in (7.5cm) high.
£110–120 / €160–180
$190–210 ⊞ MSh

A Schoenhut Humpty Dumpty Circus, comprising two clowns, three elephants, six horses, a giraffe and a rhinoceros, American, 1920–30, boxed.
£1,750–2,100 / €2,500–3,000
$2,950–3,500 ⚒ AH

A table football game, French, c1930, 21 x 36in (53.5 x 91.5cm).
£270–300 / €390–430
$450–500 ⊞ MSh

A wooden Frog game, the playing surface with a cast frog, rotating wheel flaps and hoops, above tiered scoring shelves, early 20thC, 22in (56cm) wide.
£550–660 / €790–950
$920–1,100 HYD

A Jeu de Course friction-powered horse race betting game, the six cast-metal horses with jockeys, in a lidded wooden case, late 19thC, 14¾in (37.5cm) square.
£105–125 / €150–180
$175–210 CDC

Myriorama, designed by Mr Clark, a collection of 16 hand-coloured aquatint cards forming an interchangeable landscape view, 1824, cards 8 x 2¾in (20 x 7cm), in original box.
£1,550–1,850 / €2,250–2,650
$2,600–3,100 BBA

A brass-mounted coromandel games compendium, with hinged top and front, the fitted interior with two lift-out trays containing bone chess pieces, draughts, dominoes and dice, a cribbage board, bezique markers and instruction book, late 19thC, box 12½in (32cm) wide.
£1,400–1,700 / €2,000–2,400
$2,350–2,800 SWO

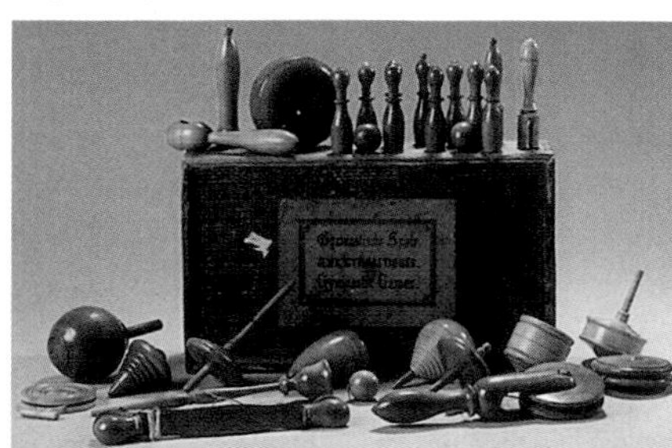

A Gymnastic Games collection of turned whitewood toys, including nine-pins, cup-and-ball, yo-yo and a selection of spinning tops, German, late 19thC.
£840–1,000 / €1,200–1,400
$1,400–1,650 B(Kn)

A set of seven painted wood skittles, carved as soldiers, c1890, 10½in (26.5cm) high.
£380–460 / €550–660
$640–770 G(B)

◄ **A turned mahogany solitaire board,** c1830, 12in (30.5cm) diam.
£90–100 / €130–145
$150–165 F&F

A mahogany games scorer, crossbanded with flame veneers, the cornice with a gilt-metal mount above two classical female figures, the two short drawers with turned handles, French, c1840, 37in (94cm) wide.
£330–400 / €480–570
$560–670 DN

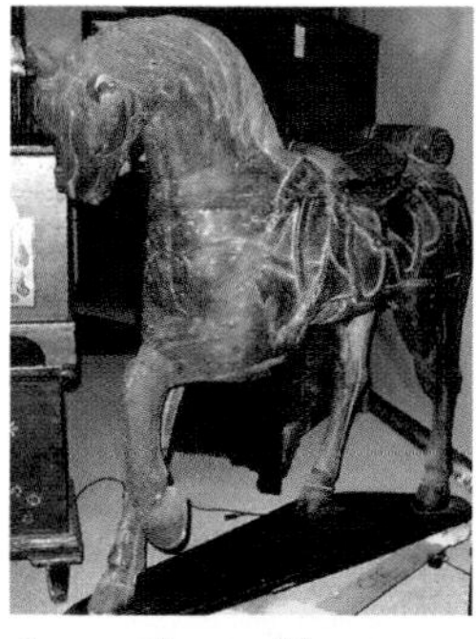

A carved wood horse, on a wooden base, 19thC, 54in (137cm) high.
£1,500–1,700
€2,200–2,500
$2,600–2,800 CHES

◄ **A Victorian painted wood and cast-iron horse tricycle,** some losses, 39in (99cm) long.
£440–530 / €630–750
$740–890 BR

A toy theatre, with printed decoration, late 19th/early 20thC, 12in (30.5cm) wide.
£165–200 / €250–290
$280–330 G(L)

Further reading

Miller's Toys & Games Buyer's Guide, Miller's Publications, 2004

Ephemera

Annuals, Books & Comics

◄ ***Charlie Chaplin's Funny Stunts,*** published by J. Keeley, 1917, 12 x 16in (30.5 x 40.5cm).
£20–25
€30–35
$35–40 JAA

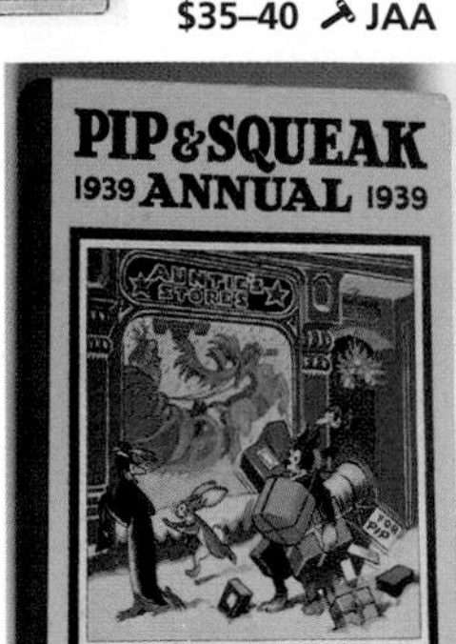

The Rupert Story Book, published by Sampson Low, colour-in pages neatly coloured, cut-out Rupert and Friends all uncoloured, 1938.
£270–320 / €390–460
$450–540 CBP

Pip & Squeak Annual, 17th year, 1939, 10 x 8in (25.5 x 20.5cm).
£25–30 / €35–40
$45–50 HTE

More Adventures of Mickey Mouse, published by Dean & Son, 1932, 8°.
£105–125 / €150–180
$175–210 CBP

Wonder, issue No. 13, with Schomburg bondage cover, 1947.
£120–145 / €175–200
$200–240 CBP

The Adventures of Mickey Mouse, Book 1, first edition, with colour illustrations, rebacked with cloth, slight wear, 1931, 8°.
£470–560 / €870–800
$790–940 BBA
This copy is inscribed by a member of Walt Disney's studio.

All Top, issue No. 13, 1948.
£90–105 / €130–150
$150–175 CBP

◄ ***Dennis the Menace,*** Book 1, some wear, 1956.
£145–175 / €210–250
$240–290 CBP

The Incredible Hulk, issue No. 1, some wear, minor damage, 1962.
£480–570 / €690–820
$810–960 CBP

◄ ***X-Men,*** issue No. 1, 196
£300–360 / €430–510
$500–600 CBP

EPHEMERA

Autographs

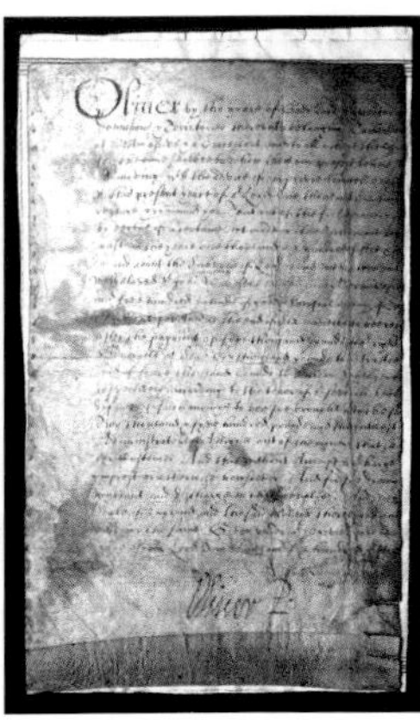

Oliver Cromwell, a signed part document on vellum, missing seal and right-hand half of each line, 1656, 9 x 5in (23 x 12.5cm), with a 19thC woodcut of Cromwell.
£3,400–3,800
€4,900–5,500
$5,700–6,400 ⊞ CFSD
This document details the payment of money collected under an act 'preventing the Multiplicity of Buildings in and about the suburbs of London'. The act was a barely concealed device to raise money. A Commission was to collect one year's rent of the full improved value of all properties of less than four acres built since 1620. There were exceptions such as hospitals and the developments in Covent Garden and Lincoln's Inn Fields. It also provided that all new building should be brick or stone, without 'butting or jettying out into the street'.

Queen Victoria, a signed cabinet photograph, 1887, 5¾ x 4¼n (14.5 x 11cm), mounted, framed and glazed.
£4,500–5,000
€6,500–7,200
$7,600–8,400 ⊞ FRa

BOSTON, April, 1767.
Faneuil-Hall LOTTERY, Number EIGHT.
This Ticket [No. 034] entitles the Possessor to any Prize drawn against said Number, in a LOTTERY granted by an Act of the General Court of the Province of the Massachusetts-Bay, for Re-building FANEUIL-Hall; subject to no Deduction.
John Hancock

► **John Hancock,** a signed lottery ticket for a draw to be held at Boston's Faneuil Hall in April 1767, American, 1¾ x 3½in (4.5 x 9cm).
£2,350–2,800
€3,400–4,000
$3,950–4,700 ⚒ JDJ

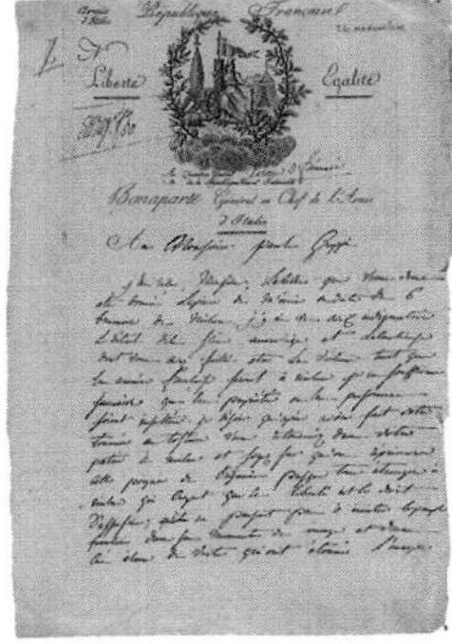

Napoleon Bonaparte, a letter to Paul Greppi, with 11 lines written by Bonaparte as General-in-Chief of the Italian Army, on the agitators: 'object of the eternal hatred of the French people', 1796, 2°.
£2,350–2,800
€3,400–4,000
$3,950–4,700 ⚒ S(P)

Charlotte Brontë, a signed pencil portrait of the Marquis of Douro, 1833, 3¾ x 3in (9.5 x 7.5cm).
£10,000–12,000
€14,400–17,300
$16,800–20,100 ⚒ BBA
Charlotte Brontë was 17 when she drew this portrait of one of the characters from her *Tales from Angria*, which is probably based on a likeness of the Duke of Wellington as a young man. The Brontë children were given lessons by John Bradley, an architect in Keighley, and both Charlotte and her brother Branwell hoped for artistic careers.

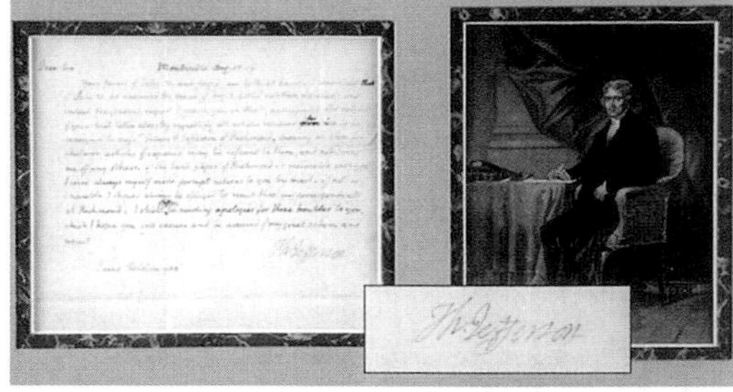

Thomas Jefferson, a signed one-page letter to David Gelston Esq, Collector of Port of New York, American, 1816, letter 6¼ x 7½in (16 x 19cm), in a painted wood frame with an engraving of Jefferson.
£12,300–14,800 / €17,700–21,000
$21,000–25,000 ⚒ JDJ

◄ **Queen Victoria,** a hand-written letter to Lady Mary Hood from Windsor Castle, 1860, 7 x 4½in (18 x 11.5cm).
£500–550 / €720–790
$830–920 ⊞ AEL

Johannes Brahms, a signed four-page letter to his friend Antonia Speyer, written in reply to her letter describing her father's last days during which he struggled to complete a piano arrangement of Brahms' clarinet quintet, 1896, 8°, with a signed envelope dated by Speyer.
£2,000–2,400
€2,900–3,450
$3,350–4,000 ⚒ B

Alexandra Feodorovna, a signed photograph of the Tsarina of Nicholas II of Russia, 1896, 6 x 4in (15 x 10cm), in a gilt mount and French-style glass box frame.
£5,200–5,800
€7,500–8,400
$8,700–9,700 ⊞ CFSD

► **George Gershwin,** a signed black and white photograph, 1935, 8 x 6in (20.5 x 15cm).
£1,800–2,150 / €2,600–3,100
$3,000–3,600 ⚒ DW
It is unusual to find a signed photograph of Gershwin.

Cigarette Cards

Barratt & Co, Famous Footballers, set of 60, 1956.
£130–150 / €185–210
$220–250 ⊞ SOR

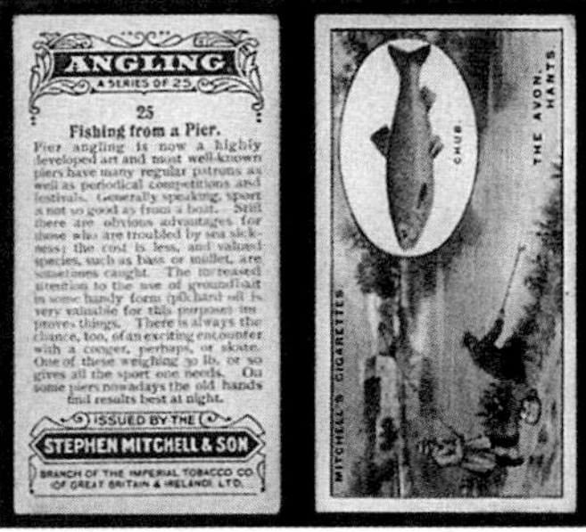

Stephen Mitchell & Son, Angling, set of 25, c1928.
£55–65 / €80–90
$90–105 ⚒ RTo

John Player & sons, Life on Board a Man of War in 1805 and 1905, set of 50, 1905.
£100–110 / €145–160
$170–190 ⊞ LCC

W. D. & H. O. Wills, Signalling, set of 50, 1911.
£70–80 / €100–115
$120–135 ⊞ SOR

Churchman, In Town Tonight, set of 50, 1938.
£45–50 / €65–75
$75–85 ⊞ LCC

Lambert & Butler, Aeroplane Markings, set of 50, 1937.
£80–90 / €115–130
$135–150 ⊞ MUR

Smiths, Cricketers, 1st Series, set of 50, 1912.
£240–290 / €340–410
$400–480 ⚒ AH

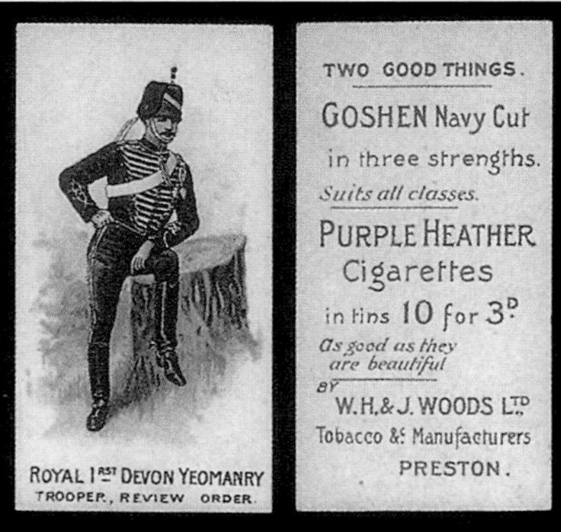

W. H. & J. Woods, Types of Volunteers and Yeomanry, set of 25, c1902.
£490–590 / €710–850
$820–990 ⚒ WAL

Hignett Bros & Co, International Caps & Badges, set of 25, 1924.
£80–90 / €115–130
$135–150 ⊞ SOR

◀ **Lambert & Butler,** Motor Cars, set of 25, 1922.
£55–65 / €80–90
$90–105 ⊞ LCC

Ogden's, Soldiers of the King, set of 50, 1909.
£190–220 / €270–320
$320–370 ⚒ WAL

Taddy & Co, Autographs, set of 25, 1912.
£165–195 / €240–280
$280–330 ⚒ AH

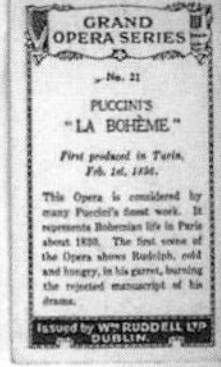

Wm Ruddell, Grand Opera Series, set of 25, c1924.
£90–105 / €130–150
$150–175 ⚒ RTo

Postcards

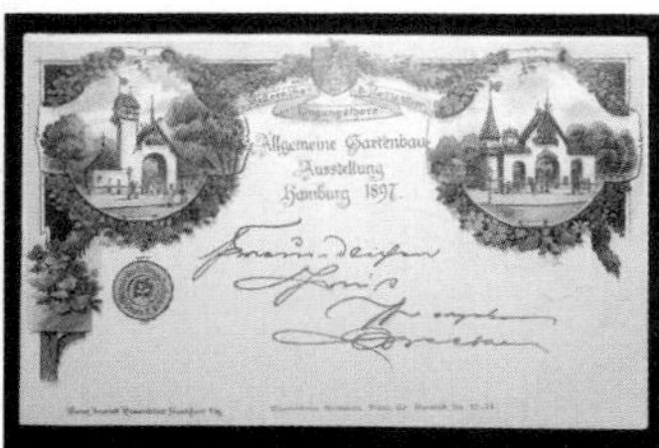

A horticultural exhibition postcard, German, Hamburg, 1897.
£25–30 / €35–40
$45–50 ⊞ S&D

A postcard, depicting the Prisoner of War Camp at Deadwood, St Helena, damaged, 1901.
£30–35 / €45–50
$50–60 ⚒ VS

A postcard, depicting the arrest of a militant suffragette, early 20thC.
£175–210 / €250–300
$290–350 ⚒ VS

▶ **A postcard,** depicting a suffragette campaigning for votes for women, early 20thC.
£175–210 / €250–300
$290–350 ⚒ VS

An Official Postal Union postcard, Russo-Japanese War, 1904–05.
£22–26 / €32–38
$38–44 ⊞ S&D

A set of six postcards, depicting glamour girls wearing gemstones, German, 1904.
£145–160 / €210–230
$240–270 ⊞ S&D

A postcard, depicting the Cement Works fire at Northfleet, Kent, 1909.
£35–40 / €50–60
$60–70 ⚒ VS

A postcard, depicting a barber supply automobile, American, 1911.
£120–145 / €170–200
$200–240 ⚒ JAA

A postcard, depicting a ladies' meeting in Patterson, American, 1913.
£750–900 / €1,100–1,300
$1,250–1,500 ⚒ JAA

A souvenir postcard, of the Adria Exhibition, by Kalmsteiner, Austrian, Vienna, 1913.
£25–30 / €40–45
$45–50 ⊞ S&D

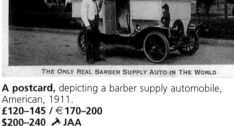

Posters

A lithographic poster, by Jules Chéret, 'Olympia', minor losses and staining, signed in print, French, 1892, 15¾in (40cm) high.
£120–145 / €170–200
$200–240 WW

A poster, by Paul Berthon, 'Les Boulles de Neige', from an edition of 200, on paper, printed by Chaix, slight creases, French, Paris, 1900, 15½ x 21¼in (39.5 x 54cm), framed.
£520–620 / €750–890
$870–1,050 BB(L)

◄ **A poster,** by Jules Chéret, 'Le Punch Grassot', printed by Chaix, minor repair, French, Paris, 1895, 49 x 34½in (124.5 x 87.5cm), framed.
£1,750–2,100 / €2,500–3,000
$2,950–3,550 BB(L)

A poster, by Alphonse Mucha, 'L'Habitation Pratique', slight damage, French, 1906, 15½ x 13in (39.5 x 33cm), framed.
£380–450 / €550–650
$640–760 BB(L)

A Northern Eastern Railway poster, by Frank Mason, advertising the Yorkshire coast, 'Alice in Holidayland', c1910, 40 x 50in (101.5 x 127cm).
£6,700–7,500 / €9,600–10,800
$11,200–12,600 ⊞ REN

A poster, by Franc-Malzac, after Laumont, 'A La Grosse Contrebasse, Espagnet', printed by Verneau, French, Paris, c1910, 54¾ x 39¼in (139 x 99.5cm).
£360–430 / €520–620
$600–720 BBA

◄ **An Isle of Man Steam Packet Co poster,** after Norman Wilkinson, advertising turbine steamers, printed by David Allen & Sons, early 20thC, 40¼ x 25¼in (102 x 64cm).
£350–420 / €500–600
$590–700 RTo

An Anchor Line poster, after Boydell, advertising 'Glasgow and New York via Londonderry', printed by Publicity Arts, early 20thC, 43¼ x 23½in (110 x 59.5cm).
£150–180 / €220–260
$250–300 RTo

An Anchor Line poster, after Kenneth D. Shoesmith, advertising 'Glasgow and New York via Londonderry', printed by Thos Foreman & Sons, early 20thC, 38¾ x 23¾in (98.5 x 60.5cm).
£220–260 / €320–370
$370–440 RTo

► **A poster,** by Werner, advertising *Vendetta*, with Pola Negri and Emil Jannings, printed by Hollerbaum & Schmidt, slight damage, German, Berlin, c1920, 48¼ x 35½in (122.5 x 90.5cm).
£260–310 / €370–440
$440–520 BBA

A poster, by Camille Bouche advertising Cognac Jacquet, printed by Vercasson, one repair, French, Paris, c1920, 46¼ x 62¼in (117.5 x 158cm).
£700–860 / €1,050–1,250
$1,200–1,400 BBA

A poster, after Roger Broders, advertising 'Paris-Lyon-Mediterranée, Calvi Beach, Corsica', printed by Lucien Serre et Cie, French, Paris, early 20thC, 40¼ x 13½in (102 x 34.5cm).
£560–670 / €810–960
$940–1,100 ⚒ RTo

A poster, advertising a summer exhibition, c1930, 30 x 20in (76 x 51cm).
£200–240 / €290–350
$340–400 ⚒ DW

► **An Imperial Airways poster,** 'Round the World on Airey's Projection', printed by Curwen Press, 1939, 40¼ x 25¼in (102 x 64cm).
£350–420 / €500–600
$590–700 ⚒ ONS

A Travel Association poster, by Terence Cuneo, advertising 'Britain in Winter', printed by W. S. Cowell, minor damage, 1948, 30 x 19¾in (76 x 50cm).
£300–360 / €430–510
$500–600 ⚒ BBA

A poster, by Kennedy North, advertising the British Empire Exhibition, with a stylized map of the London Underground, the reverse with monochrome images and information on the pavilions, minor damage, 1924, 19¼ x 29in (49 x 73.5cm), framed.
£100–120 / €145–170
$170–200 ⚒ BBA

A film poster, advertising *Frankenstein*, with Boris Karloff, 1931, 39¾ x 30in (101 x 76cm).
£890–1,050 / €1,300–1,500
$1,500–1,750 ⚒ BR

Further reading

Miller's Movie Collectibles, Miller's Publications, 2002

A poster, by Eric Vilhelm Rohman, 'Gläd Dig I Din Ungdom', printed by Ljunglöfs, creased, Swedish, Stockholm, 1939, 39¼ x 27¼in (99.5 x 69cm).
£120–145 / €170–200
$200–240 ⚒ BUK

◄ **A Royal Mail Lines poster,** by Jarvis, advertising voyages to Argentina, c1950s, 40¼ x 21in (102 x 53.5cm).
£240–290 / €340–410
$400–480 ⚒ DW

A Southern Railway poster, by Walter E. Spradbury, advertising Guildford, printed by Waterlow & Sons, with later stamp 'By Courtesy of Cunard Line, Boston, Massachusetts', c1930, 39½ x 24¾in (100.5 x 63cm).
£220–260 / €320–370
$370–440 ⚒ DW

An RKO Radio Pictures film poster, by Ronald Coudon, advertising *King Kong*, with Fay Wray, Robert Armstrong and Bruce Cabot, linen-backed, restored, French, 1933, 63 x 47in (160 x 119.5cm).
£4,100–4,900
€5,900–7,000
$6,900–8,200 ⚒ B(Kn)

A British Railways poster, by Lance Cattermole, advertising Portrush in Northern Ireland, printed by Jordinson & Co, 1950s, 39¾ x 25in (101 x 63.5cm).
£260–310 / €370–440
$440–520 ⚒ DW

◄ **An Iberia Airlines poster,** advertising Majorca, printed by Rasgo-Jerez Industrial, minor damage, Spanish, 1950s, 37 x 24½in (94 x 62cm).
£120–145 / €170–200
$200–240 DW

A poster, advertising skiing, 1950s, 30 x 24in (76 x 61cm).
£220–250 / €320–360
$370–420 Do

A P&O poster, by Clive Uptton, advertising cruises, printed by Brown, Knight & Truscott, minor damage, 1950s, 39¼ x 24½in (99.5 x 62cm).
£150–180 / €220–260
$250–300 DW

A BRSR poster, by Albert Brenet, advertising southern England, printed by Waterlow, mounted on linen, 1960, 40¼ x 24¾in (102 x 63cm).
£330–390 / €470–560
$550–650 ONS

GUINNESS
-HIM STRONG
See what Big Chief Toucan do

A poster, advertising Guinness, printed by Mills & Rockleys, folded, 1960, 59¾ x 40¼in (152 x 102cm).
£150–180 / €220–260
$250–300 ONS

A film poster, advertising Alfred Hitchcock's *The Birds*, folded, at fault, 1963, 30 x 39¾in (76 x 101cm).
£165–195 / €240–280
$280–330 BR

A United Airlines poster, advertising San Francisco, mounted on linen, minor staining, 1967, 39½ x 25¾in (100.5 x 65.5cm).
£90–105 / €130–150
$150–175 NSal

VEZELAY
COLLINE ÉTERNELLE
PAR
MAURICE DRUON
MUSIQUE DE DARIUS MILHAUD
RÉALISATION DE GEORGES VITALY
SON ET LUMIÈRE
TOUS LES SOIRS DE MAI A OCTOBRE

A poster, by Bernard Buffet, 'Vezelay', printed by Mourlot, pinholes, French, c1968, 39½ x 25½in (100.5 x 65cm).
£190–220 / €270–320
$320–370 DW

A film poster, advertising Gerry Anderson's *Thunderbirds are Go*, 1960s, 27½ x 37in (70 x 94cm), framed and glazed.
£370–440 / €530–630
$620–740 WAL

◄ **A poster,** by Arnold Skolnick, advertising 'Woodstock Music & Art Fair', American, 1969, 30 x 22in (76 x 56cm), framed, with original ticket for Friday August 15.
£490–590 / €710–850
$820–990 NSal

► **A poster,** by Salvidor Dali, 'Auvergne, Chemin De Fer Francais', some creasing, French, 1970, 39 x 24½in (99 x 62cm).
£140–165 / €200–230
$230–270 NSal

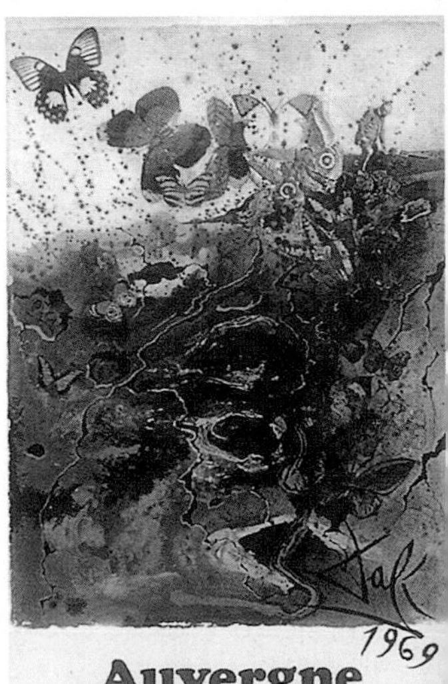

EPHEMERA

Rock & Pop

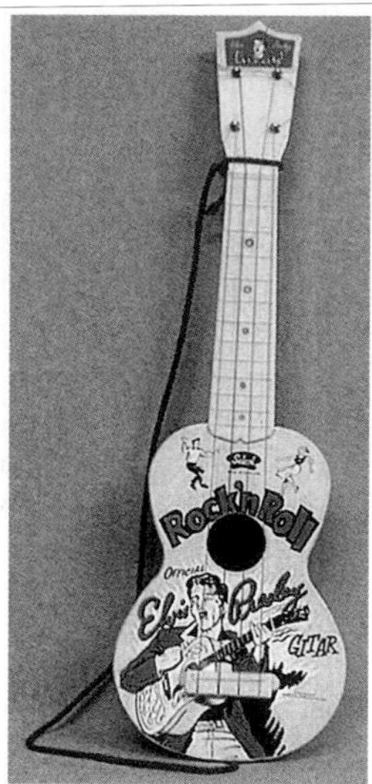

A Setcol Elvis Presley 'Rock 'n Roll' guitar, 1957, with box, bill of sale and instruction leaflet.
£370–440 / €530–630
$620–740 PF

Bravo, signed by Elvis Presley, German, 1958, 11 x 8½in (28 x 21.5cm), mounted, framed and glazed.
£1,750–1,950
€2,500–2,800
$2,950–3,250 FRa

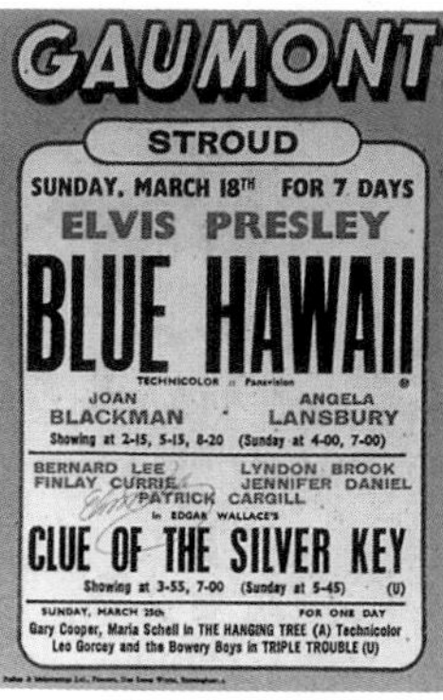

A cinema advertising card, *Blue Hawaii*, signed by Elvis Presley, from the Gaumont, Stroud, 1962, 11¾ x 8in (30 x 20.5cm).
£660–790 / €950–1,150
$1,100–1,300 S(O)

A Beatles single record, 'Love Me Do', signed by all four members of the group, 1962.
£4,600–5,500
€6,600–7,900
$7,700–9,200 B(Kn)

► ***Elvis Express,*** a full set of 19, published by Albert Hands Productions, dated 1962–64, 8 x 5in (20.5 x 12.5cm).
£105–120 / €150–170
$175–200 CTO

Mersey Beat, Vol. 1, No. 13, with headline 'Beatles Top Poll', 1962.
£1,100–1,300
€1,600–1,900
$1,850–2,200 S(O)

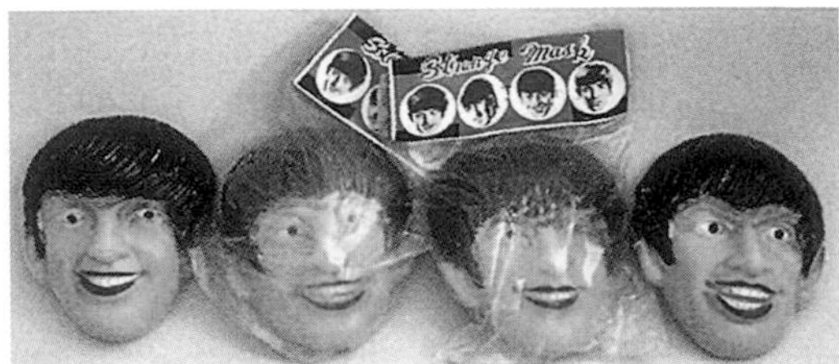

A set of four plastic Beatles face masks, Hong Kong, c1964, in original cellophane bags.
£175–210 / €250–300
$290–350 ⚒ CO

A set of four Beatles dolls, by Remco, with real hair, 1964, 6½in (16.5cm) high, in original boxes.
£480–570 / €690–820
$800–960 ⚒ S(O)

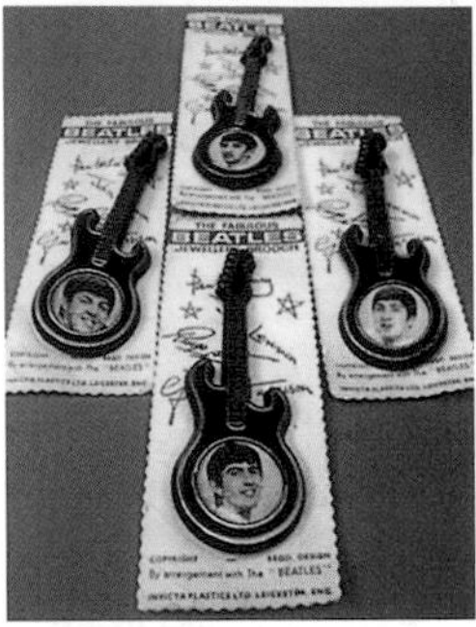

A set of four plastic Beatles brooches, by Invicta, in the form of guitars, set with pictures of John, Paul, George and Ringo, early 1960s, 3in (7.5cm) long.
£85–100 / €120–140
$145–170 ⚒ AMB

A concert programme, the front cover signed by the Rolling Stones, the inside signed by the Hollies, the Checkmates, Goldie and the Gingerbreads and compere Johnny Ball, 1965.
£1,000–1,200
€1,450–1,700
$1,700–2,000 ⚒ S(O)

A New Beat Beatles guitar, with facsimile signatures, 1960s, in original box.
£1,050–1,250 / €1,500–1,800
$1,750–2,100 ⚒ CHTR

◄ An Apple Corps Beatles single record acetate, 'Revolution', titled in ballpoint, 1968.
£1,050–1,250
€1,500–1,800
$1,750–2,100 ⚒ CO

A Fresh Cream LP sleeve, signed by Eric Clapton, Jack Bruce and Ginger Baker, mid-1960s.
£260–310 / €370–440
$440–520 ⚒ CO

A silkscreen poster, by Mike McInnerney, announcing the '14 Hour Technicolour Dream', 1967, 30 x 19¾in (76 x 50cm).
£450–500 / €650–720
$760–840 ⊞ ASC
The '14 Hour Technicolour Dream' benefit was held for *International Times* at Alexandra Palace in north London on 29th April 1967.

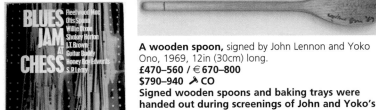

A wooden spoon, signed by John Lennon and Yoko Ono, 1969, 12in (30cm) long.
£470–560 / €670–800
$790–940 ⚒ CO
Signed wooden spoons and baking trays were handed out during screenings of John and Yoko's films at the London's New Cinema Club. The intention was for the audience to make a noise during the showing of *Two Virgins*.

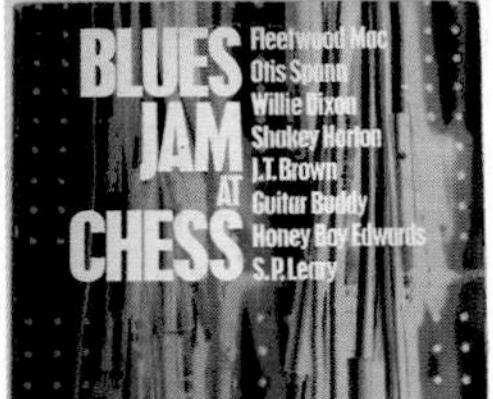

A Stereo UK double LP, 'Blues Jam at Chess', 1969.
£65–75 / €95–110
$110–125 ⊞ BNO

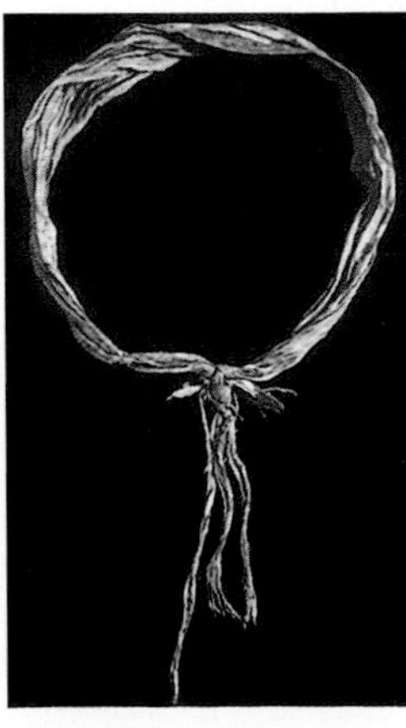

► A Jimi Hendrix bandana, c1970.
£600–720
€860–1,050
$1,000–1,200
⚒ S(O)

◄ A silkscreen poster, advertising Colosseum at the Guildhall, Portsmouth, c1970, 30 x 20in (76 x 51cm).
£120–140
€170–200
$200–230 ⚒ CO

An invitation/flyer, to a promotional evening for the release of the album *David Bowie* at the Purcell Room, London, tape markings, 1969, 9½ x 19in (24 x 48.5cm).
£230–270 / €330–390
$390–450 ⚒ CO

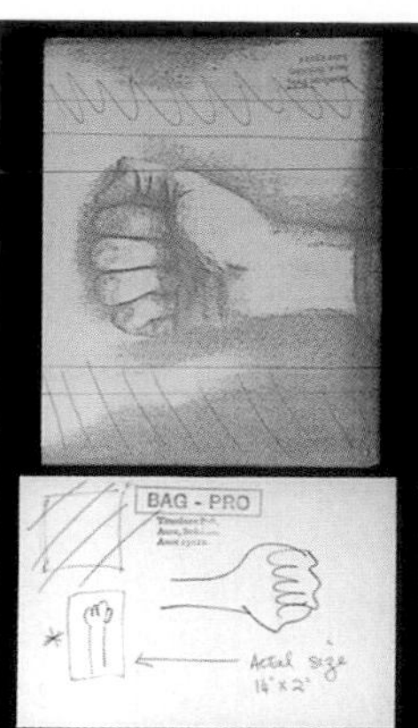

◄ **A design for a postage stamp,** by John Lennon, comprising an envelope, several sketches and a photocopy of John Lennon's right fist, 1971, envelope 6 x 9in (15 x 23cm).
£1,250–1,500 / €1,800–2,150
$2,100–2,500 ⚒ S(O)
In the 1971 UK postal service strike the GPO developed a scheme to license parties who applied to run alternate services. A group of artists and poets, including Richard Hamilton, David Hockney and Allen Jones, who were sympathetic to the postal workers' cause, set up a service entitled 'Culture Carriers', the funds going to support the strikers. A series of stamps and postcards were designed by the artists/poets and Lennon was one of those asked to contribute. However, the strike was over before his design could be turned into an editioned stamp.

A gold sales award, for the Simon & Garfunkel album 'Bridge Over Troubled Water', RIAA certified, early 1970s.
£2,600–3,100
€3,700–4,450
$4,350–5,200 ⚒ S(O)
'Bridge Over Troubled Water' was a number one album and single on both sides of the Atlantic and the LP spent 303 weeks in the UK chart.

An Elton John stage costume, embroidered with beach motifs and lettering, labelled 'Annie Reavey London', c1972.
£9,000–10,800
€13,000–15,600
$15,100–18,100 ⚒ S(O)

A Sex Pistols press book, by Glitterbest, 16pp, printed by the Suburban Press, slight damage, 1976, 12 x 8½in (30.5 x 21.5cm).
£135–150 / €195–210
$220–250 ⊞ ASC
This was the original booklet issued to the press before the Sex Pistols signed to EMI. It was assembled by Jamie Reid and consisted of numerous clippings relating to the Sex Pistols from the music and daily press.

LOCATE THE SOURCE

The source of each illustration in Miller's can be found by checking the code letters below each caption with the Key to Illustrations, pages 794–800.

► **A film poster,** *The Great Rock 'n' Roll Swindle*, with the Sex Pistols, 1979, 30 x 40in (76 x 101.5cm).
£500–550
€710–790
$830–920 ⊞ PLB

A U2 LP sleeve, 'Under a Blood Red Sky', signed by all four members of the band, c1983.
£165–195 / €240–280
$280–330 ⚒ CO

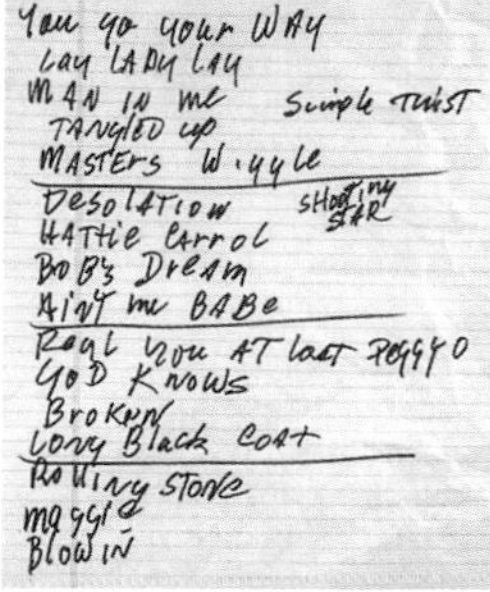
You go your WAY
Lay LAdy Lay
MAN in me Simple Twist
Tangled up
MASTERS Wiggle
Desolation Shooting Star
Hattie Carrol
Bob's Dream
Ain't me BABE
Real You At last Peggy O
God Knows
Broken
Long Black Coat
Rolling Stone
Maggie
Blowin

Bob Dylan, a hand-written set list, 1980s, 10½ x 8½in (26.5 x 21.5cm).
£660–790 / €950–1,100
$1,100–1,300 ⚒ S(O)

► **Paul McCartney,** a signed Concorde menu, 'To Julia, with love from Paul McCartney', c1985.
£210–250
€300–360
$350–420
⚒ LAY

Scientific Instruments

Calculating Instruments

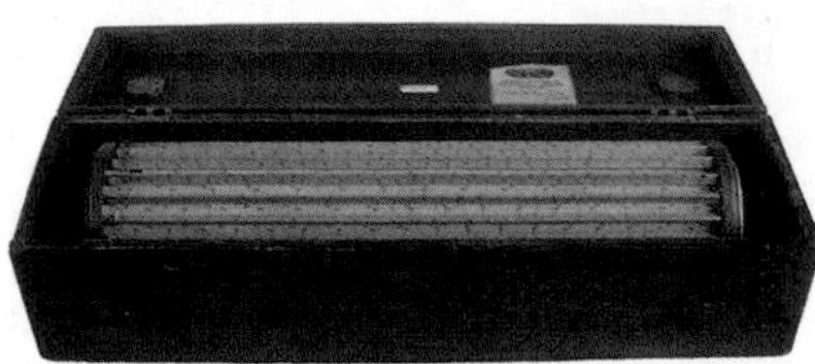

A Thatcher's calculator, by Keuffel & Esser, model 4012, with a sliding inner and revolving outer cylinder, No. 2963, marked, American, New York, c1910, 22½in (57cm) wide, in a mahogany case.
£1,100–1,300 / €1,600–1,850
$1,850–2,200 JDJ

Thatcher's calculators

The Thatcher's calculator is probably the most complex calculator ever made. Invented in 1881 by Edwin Thacher, (the spelling in usage is due to a typographical error on the label of the original piece), the 4in (10cm) diameter cylinder has one scale on it and 20 angled scales above, allowing the owner to quickly calculate figures to an accuracy of four or five decimal places. A slide rule containing this amount of information would need to be 10m (30ft) long; the instruction book extends to 71 pages. Thatcher's calculators were made by Stanley in Britain and by Keuffel & Esser in the United States and were produced well into the 1930s.

A white and yellow metal perpetual calender, engraved with a sunrise and a sunset, 19thC, ¾in (2cm) diam.
£140–165 / €200–230
$230–270 PFK

A Fuller calculator, by W. F. Stanley & Co, c1925, 18in (45.5cm) wide, in a mahogany case.
£430–480 / €620–690
$720–810 ETO

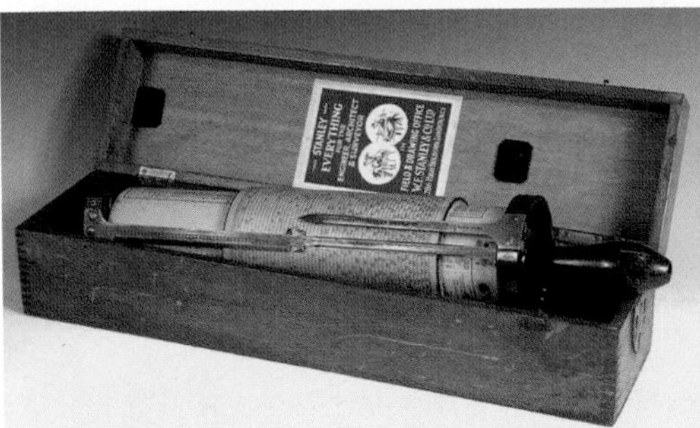

A Fuller calculator, by W. F. Stanley & Co, on a Bakelite mount, c1947, 18in (45.5cm) wide, in a fitted case.
£300–360 / €430–510
$500–600 SWO

Compasses & Dials

An ivory diptych dial, engraved with a sun and floral and geometric decoration, with pin gnomon, German, probably mid-18thC, 3in (7.5cm) long.
£840–1,000
€1,200–1,400
$1,400–1,650 S(O)

A brass pocket equinoctial dial, with engraved plate and inset compass, hinged hour ring, pin gnomon and adjustable latitude, the reverse engraved with European cities and their latitudes, German, 18thC, 2in (5cm) diam.
£420–500 / €600–720
$700–840 S(O)

A brass universal equinoctial dial, with engraved decoration, the underside engraved with five European cities, signed 'L Grafl', German, late 18thC, 2½in (6.5cm) diam.
£820–980 / €1,200–1,500
$1,400–1,650 TEN

An ivory travelling sundial, with folding metal dial and a turned wood finial, the shaft engraved with a gentleman holding a similar sundial, the base engraved with the signs of the zodiac, inscribed, dated 1629, 4¾in (12cm) high.
£3,300–3,950
€4,750–5,700
$5,500–6,600 S(Am)

◄ **A bronze plate sundial,** by Bate, signed, mid-18thC, 13¾in (35cm) diam.
£310–370
€440–530
$520–620
S(O)

◄ **A carved slate sundial,** by James Smith, dated 1864, 9in (23cm) wide.
£200–260 / €320–370
$370–440 EH

Globes & Armillary Spheres

A pocket globe, in a paper-covered case, marked 'A Correct Globe with New Corrections of Dr. Halley & Co', early 19thC, 2¾in (7cm) diam.
£2,900–3,500 / €4,200–5,000
$4,900–5,900 LHA

Globes

- Celestial globes show the map of the heavens often incorporated with the signs of the zodiac
- Terrestrial globes display the map of the earth. They were often made as pairs and as such are more valuable if found as originally designed
- Library globes are larger floor-standing globes that can measure up to 24in (61cm) in diameter and appeal to furniture as well as globe collectors
- Table globes are smaller in size, and even smaller are pocket globes, about 3in (7.5cm) in diameter and made with fishskin cases

A Navisphere celestial globe, by Commander M. H. DeMagnac, illustrating constellations, with fitted brass measuring gauge, on a lacquered brass stand, French, late 19thC, 13¼in (33.5cm) high, with instruction pamphlet, in a mahogany case.
£1,500–1,800 / €2,200–2,600
$2,500–3,000 G(L)

A 3in travelling globe, by C. Abel Klinger, entitled 'The Earth', the continents outlined in colours, with papered box, the cover depicting a lesson, German, Nuremberg, late 19thC.
£1,300–1,550 / €1,900–2,250
$2,200–2,600 BR

A pair of 12in terrestrial and celestial globes, by J. & W. Cary, the terrestrial globe showing the journey of Captain Cook and other circumnavigators, celestial globe missing meridian ring and stand and dated 1800, early 19thC.
£4,950–5,900 / €7,100–8,500
$8,300–9,900 L&T

A terrestrial globe, by Cruchley, with brass scale, on a turned wooden base, 19thC, 10in (25.5cm) high.
£440–520 / €630–750
$740–870 HYD

A Victorian terrestrial globe, damaged, 2¾in (7cm) diam.
£175–210 / €250–300
$290–350 RTo

► **A celestial globe,** by G. Philip & Son, on a vase-turned stem, c1910, 10½in (26.5cm) high.
£260–310 / €370–440
$440–520 WW

An armillary sphere, in the manner of Delamarche, the wooden sun surrounded by a series of paper-on-board concentric circles representing the signs of the zodiac, with meridian ring, card moon, calender ring and ecliptic ring, on an ebonized stand, French, c1820, 17in (43cm) high.
£3,100–3,700
€4,450–5,300
$5,200–6,200 S(O)

A terrestrial globe, by William Bardin, with brass engraved meridian circle and paper horizon, on a mahogany part-ebonized stand, 19thC, 45¼in (115cm) high.
£880–1,050
€1,250–1,500
$1,500–1,750 TEN

Medical & Dental

A mahogany apothecary box, the fitted interior with a shelf of bottles and fitted drawers, the rear door enclosing two fitted shelves, early 19thC, 10½in (26.5cm) wide.
£570–680 / €820–980
$960–1,150 AH

A mahogany apothecary box, comprising bottles, scales and weights and mortar and pestle, c1830, 7in (18cm) wide.
£1,450–1,650
€2,150–2,400
$2,500–2,750 ⊞ JTS

An ebony-strung mahogany travelling apothecary box, the two doors enclosing a fitted interior comprising bottle compartments with bottles and five drawers, with a single drawer, 19thC, 18in (45.5cm) high.
£760–910 / €1,100–1,300
$1,300–1,550 DMC

Apothecary boxes

The British National Health Service did not come into existence until after WWII and prior to that all medical care had to be paid for. Most middle-class homes would therefore have a well-stocked apothecary box, which usually included substances such as mercury, arsenic and opium which would be illegal to buy today. When purchasing an apothecary box, check that the contents are as original as possible and that replacement bottles fit properly into the apertures. Such bottles are acceptable as they would have been replaced as the contents were used up, but they should ideally be as close as possible in appearance to the originals.

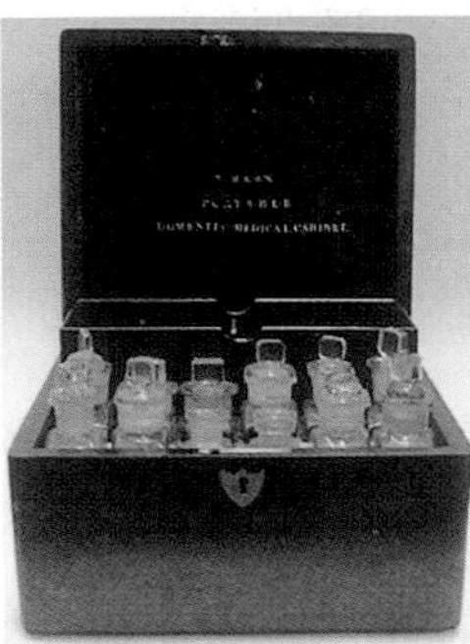

A mahogany St Maw's apothecary chest, opening to reveal a tray with glass bottles and stoppers, 19thC, 8¼in (21cm) wide.
£125–150 / €180–210
$210–250 HOLL

A Victorian mahogany apothecary box, the two doors opening to reveal glass bottles, five drawers and a concealed panel enclosing further bottles, some bottles missing, 11¾in (30cm) wide.
£500–600 / €720–860
$840–1,000 BR

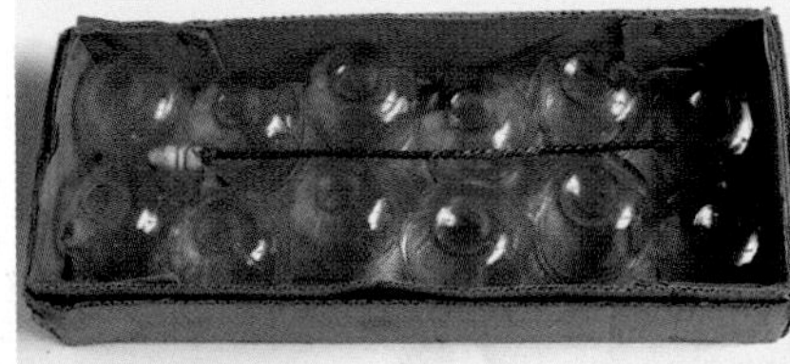

A set of 12 closed mould blood cupping glasses, 1880–1900, glasses 2¼in (5.5cm) high, in original box with taper.
£270–300 / €390–430
$450–500 ⊞ FOF

The doctor would make a cut on the patient's back and then place a lighted taper inside the cup to heat the air inside, which created a vacuum as it cooled. The cup was then placed quickly over the cut, allowing the vacuum to draw a good flow of blood from the wound. Closed mould glasses such as these were first produced towards the end of the 19th century, the slightly thicker rims preventing damage to the surface of the skin.

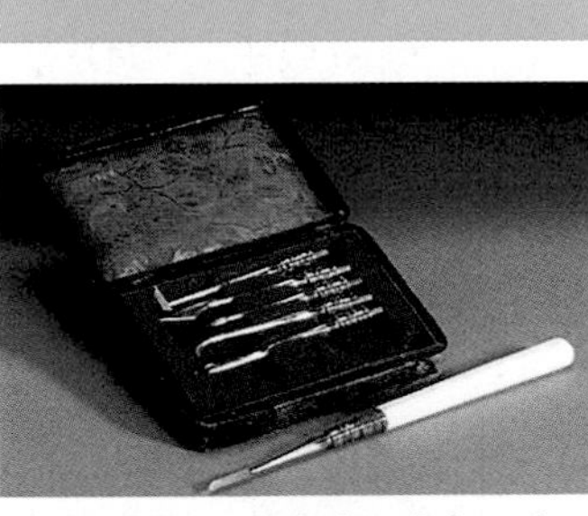

A set of six metal-plated dental scalers, in a velvet-lined leather case, c1820, 3½in (9cm) wide.
£175–195 / €210–280
$290–330 B(Kn)

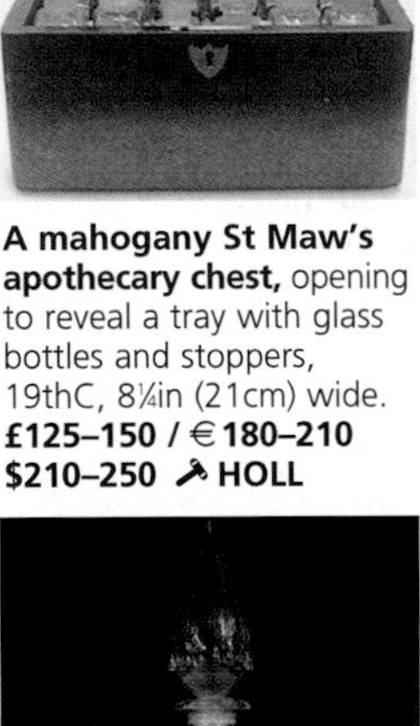

A chemist's glass carboy, with a faceted spire stopper, 19thC, 26in (66cm) high.
£105–125 / €150–180
$175–210 SWO

A brass extending ear trumpet, by R. J. Dowling, London, c1890, 18in (45.5cm) long.
£90–100 / €130–145
$150–170 ⊞ TOM

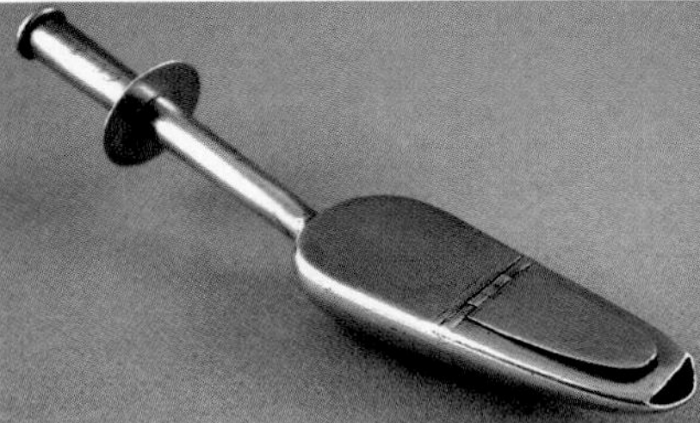

A silver medicine spoon, the covered bowl with hinged cover, inscribed 'C. Gibson', London 1828, 5½in (14cm) long, 1½oz.
£610–730 / €880–1,050
$1,000–1,200 WW

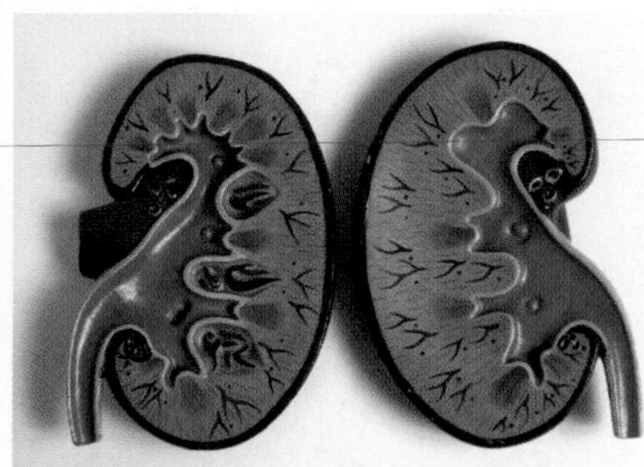

A two-piece plaster model of a kidney, with hand-painted decoration, c1900, 7½in (19cm) long.
£130–145 / €190–210
$220–250 ⊞ FOF

An apothecary's brass pestle and mortar, c1750, 4in (10cm) high.
£55–65 / €80–95
$95–110 ⊞ F&F

A creamware phrenology bust, by Fowler, with annotations of the mental faculties, c1850, 11in (28cm) high.
£660–790 / €950–1,100
$1,100–1,300 ⚒ S(O)

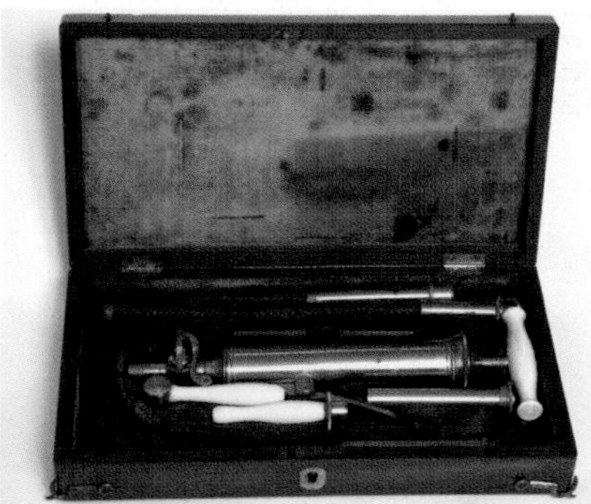

An ivory and lacquered-brass enema set, by Laundy, London, with cotton-covered vulcanized tubes, the velvet-lined mahogany case with brass cartouche, lock plate and swing hinges, c1810, 10½ x 6in (26.5 x 15cm).
£540–600 / €780–860
$900–1,000 ⊞ FOF

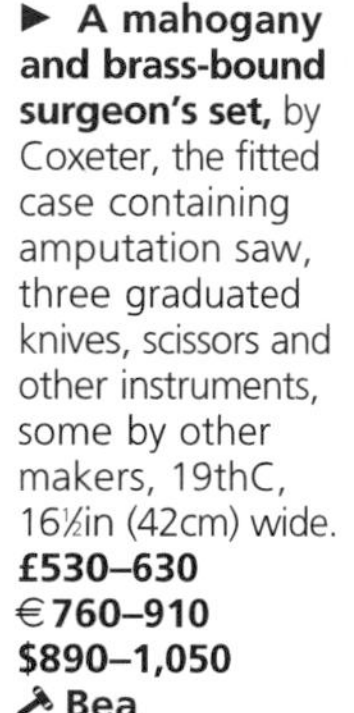

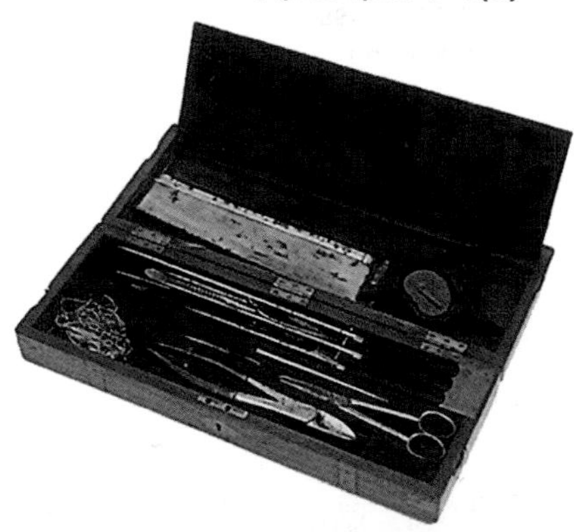

► A mahogany and brass-bound surgeon's set, by Coxeter, the fitted case containing amputation saw, three graduated knives, scissors and other instruments, some by other makers, 19thC, 16½in (42cm) wide.
£530–630
€760–910
$890–1,050
⚒ Bea

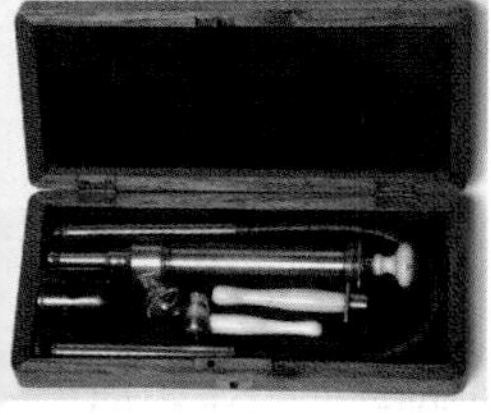

A brass and ivory enema set, by Coxeter, in a mahogany case, c1860, 9in (23cm) wide.
£260–290 / €380–420
$440–490 ⊞ ETO

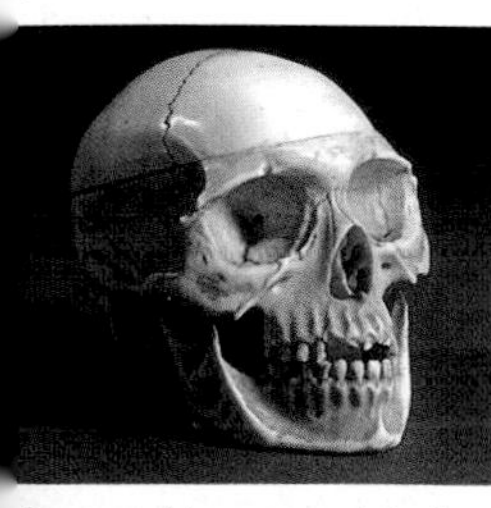

A carved ivory model of a human skull, the removable top enclosing a detailed interior, front teeth missing, 19thC, 3¼in (8cm) long.
£1,200–1,400
€1,750–2,000
$2,000–2,350 ⚒ B(Kn)

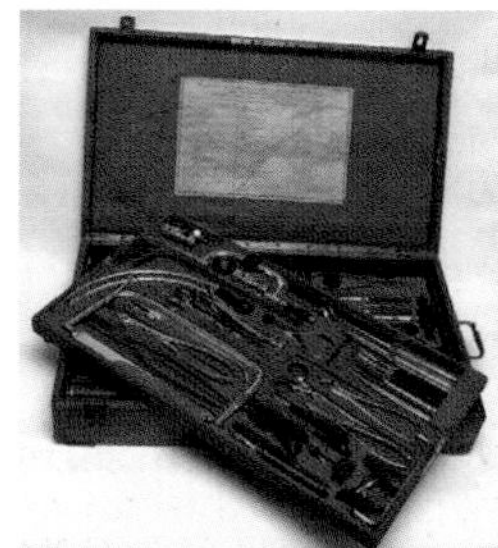

A marine surgeon's set, in a mahogany case, French, c1870, 13 x 22½in (33 x 57cm).
£5,000–5,500
€7,200–7,900
$8,400–9,300 ⊞ CuS

A wooden monaural stethoscope, c1900, 6¾in (17cm) long.
£85–95 / €120–135
$140–160 ⊞ CuS

Meteorological Instruments

A Robinson's copper cup anemometer, by L. Casella, with recording dial, c1880, 16in (40.5cm) diam.
£380–420 / €540–600
$640–710 ⊞ RTW

Further reading

Miller's Collecting Science & Technology, Miller's Publications, 2001

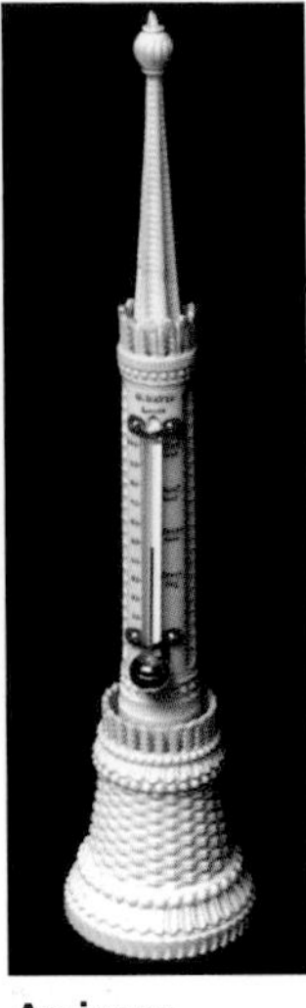

An ivory thermometer, by Gabriel Davis, 1822–47, 9in (23cm) high.
£340–380
€490–550
$570–740
⊞ ETO

A presentation weather station, by Chadburn & Son, comprising a timepiece with eight-day movement, thermometer and aneroid barometer, in a glazed walnut case, brass plaque engraved '*Thermopylae* in commemoration of a fine passage 1882', 26in (66cm) wide.
£4,100–4,900 / €5,900–7,000
$6,900–8,200 ⚒ B(Kn)

***Thermopylae* was designed for the China tea trade and rigged as a three-masted ship. Built in 1868, for George Thompson's White Star Line, she was the fastest of all the clipper ships and was involved in the famous race against her rival *Cutty Sark* from Shanghai to London in 1872 which she won due to *Cutty Sark* losing her rudder after having passed the Sunda Straits.**

According to family records, this weather station was presented to Captain Henderson who captained *Thermopylae* on her last tea voyage. He set out from Kowloon in November 1881 and arrived in Liverpool a record 81 days later.

Microscopes

A brass pocket microscope, by George Lindsay, with a brass stage, signed, tripod base missing, c1743, 3½in (9cm) long, in a fishskin case, with brass specimen holders.
£11,400–13,700
€16,400–19,700
$19,100–23,000 ⚒ S(O)

◄ A brass Culpeper monocular microscope, c1820, 13in (33cm) high, in original mahogany box.
£540–600 / €780–860
$900–1,000 ⊞ TOM

► A brass compound drum microscope, with six lenses, live box and a set of bone specimen holders, c1820, in a rosewood case, 11in (28cm) high.
£350–420 / €500–600
$590–700 ⚒ B(Kn)

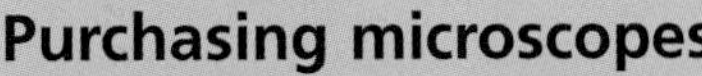

Purchasing microscopes

Microscopes are a popular collecting field as they are readily available from simple 20th-century examples at prices from £100 / €145 / $170 up to 18th-century examples at five-figure sums.

When buying a microscope make sure that it comes with its original carrying case which should be fitted with all its accessories including the all-important eyepieces and objective lenses. To ensure that the optics are all in place, set up the instrument and see if it works.

◄ A brass compound microscope, by Charles Baker, with mechanical stage and sub-stage, in a mahogany case with six drawers of accessories including four oculars and two objectives, signed, c1868, case 22in (56cm) high.
£1,150–1,350 / €1,650–1,950
$1,950–2,250 ⚒ B(Kn)

A brass compound microscope, by Smith & Beck, with racked body tube and removable Wenham binocular, the limb supported on twin columns and rotatable disk to tripod base, stamped mid-19thC, 18in (45.5cm) high, with two mahogany cases containing lenses, plates, slides and loose draw tube all contained in a large mahogany case.
£2,100–2,500 / €3,000–3,600
$3,550–4,200 ⚒ G(L)

A Victorian lacquered-brass monocular microscope, by Andrew Ross, with rack-and-pinion focus, directional table and folding triform base, engraved mark, 21½in (54.5cm) high, in original fitted mahogany case with spare lenses and slides.
£1,900–2,250 / €2,750–3,250
$3,200–3,800 EH

A lacquered-brass compound monocular microscope, by M. Pillischer, c1870, 11in (28cm) high, in original fitted mahogany case.
£180–200 / €260–290
$300–330 ⊞ TOM

◄ **A brass and lacquered binocular microscope,** by Henry Crouch, No. 3561, late 19thC, 15in (38cm) high, with fitted mahogany carrying case.
£590–700
€850–1,000
$990–1,150
DN

A botanical microscope, the turned bone lens mounted on a gilt-brass column, in a fitted mahogany case, c1800, 4¾in (12cm) long, with paper instructions, spare lenses and steel tweezers.
£350–420 / €500–600
$590–700 G(L)

A lacquered and japanned compound monocular microscope, by E. Leitz, in a mahogany case, German, c1900, 17in (43cm) high, with accessories.
£310–350 / €440–500
$520–590 ⊞ TOM

A monocular microscope, by Carl Zeiss, with two eyepieces and lenses, marked, German, early 20thC, 16in (40.5cm) extended, in a mahogany case.
£120–145 / €170–200
$200–240 SWO

Surveying & Drawing Instruments

A prismatic vernier mining/surveying compass, by Stanley, with jewelled bearing, original filters, c1890, 5½in (14cm) diam, with steel and leather cases.
£330–370 / €470–530
$550–620 ⊞ FOF

A mahogany and brass military surveyor's compass and clinometer, by J. H. Steward, c1910, 3in (7.5cm) diam.
£330–370 / €470–530
$550–620 ⊞ ETO

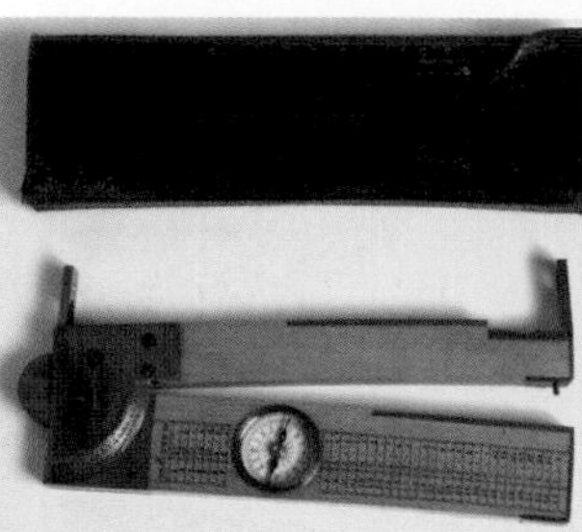

A Victorian boxwood and brass surveyor's compendium, by J. H. Steward, with twin alidade sights, scales, clinometer, inset compass and spirit level, 6¼in (16cm) long, with a leather carrying case.
£220–250 / €320–360
$370–420 ⊞ FOF

A set of draughtsman's instruments, in a shagreen case with hinged cover, case repaired, early 19thC, 7in (18cm) high.
£260–310 / €370–440
$440–520 ⚒ NSal

An anodized-brass pocket Abney inclinometer/level, by F. Barker & Son, with a silvered scale and water-filled level, c1890, in a lined leather-covered wooden case, 2¾ x 5¼in (7 x 13.5cm).
£500–560 / €720–800
$840–940 ⊞ FOF

A brass surveyor's level, on a wooden base, with a later lens cap, Italian, c1812, 13¼in (33.5cm) long.
£200–240 / €290–340
$340–400 ⚒ GK

A boxwood collapsible plane-table rule, with brass hinges, mid-19thC, 19½in (49.5cm) square.
£480–570 / €690–820
$810–960 ⚒ S(O)

An anodized-brass surveyor's level and tripod, by Patrick Adie, with four levelling screws and water-filled level, labelled, c1855, in a mahogany case with leather exterior case, 5¼ x 11in (13.5 x 28cm).
£500–560 / €720–800
$840–940 ⊞ FOF

A brass odometer, by E. Nairne, the silvered 4in calibrated dial with subsidiary dial and convex glass cover, on two brass and iron wheels, late 18thC, 9in (23cm) high, with a mahogany case.
£1,400–1,650 / €2,000–2,350
$2,350–2,750 ⚒ G(L)
This is a particularly rare instrument for measuring distances. Edward Nairne (working 1749–1806) made instruments for George III.

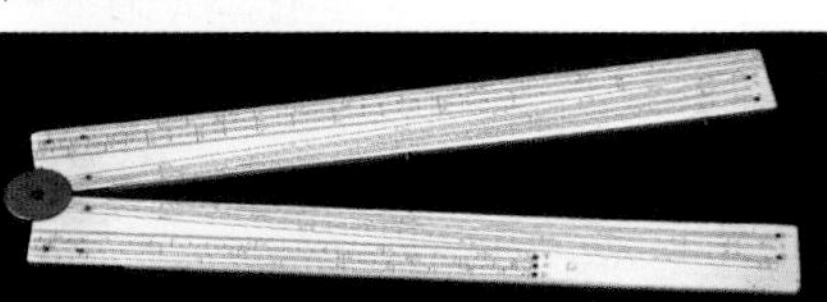

► **A brass and ivory sector,** c1830, 6in (15cm) long.
£75–85 / €110–125
$125–140 ⊞ ETO

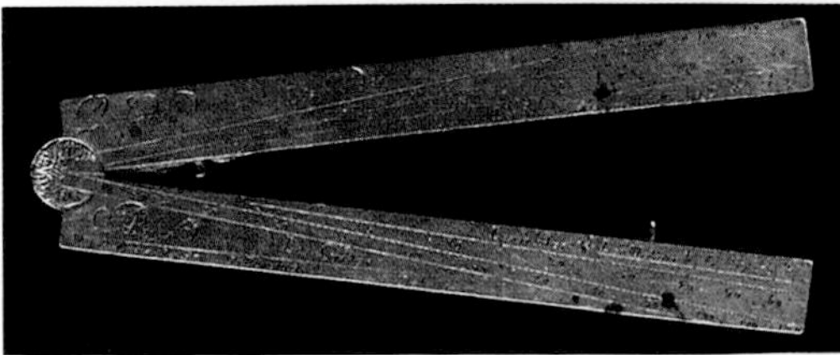

◄ **A brass sector,** inscribed with scales for equal parts, planes and polygons, on the reverse for chords and metal solids, signed 'Pierre Sevin à Paris', French, c1690, 4½in (11.5cm) long.
£1,200–1,400 / €1,750–2,000
$2,000–2,350 ⚒ S(O)
Pierre Sevin, *Ingénieur du Roi* and a leading maker of the late 17th century, supplied instruments to the Académie des Sciences and to the crown.

Telescopes

A 2½in brass refracting telescope, by Ramsden, with two rack-and-pinion and screw focusing, opens to reveal storage for the brass tripod and stand, signed, c1760, 15¾in (40cm) long, with velvet-lined mahogany case.
£3,600–4,300
€5,200–6,200
$6,000–7,200 S(O)

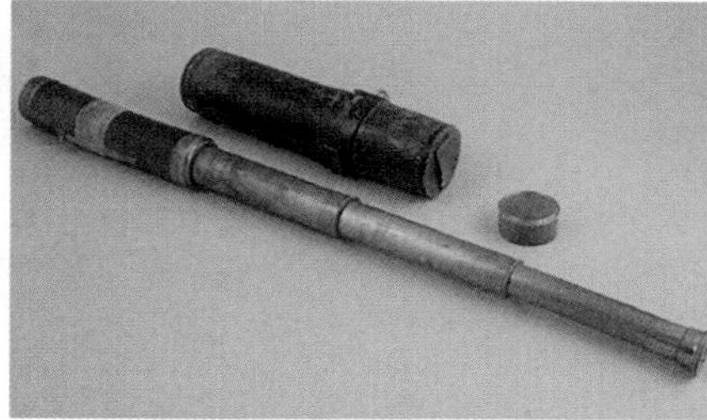

◄ **A George III brass three-draw telescope,** by Ramsden, with a mahogany grip, in a leather case, 22½in (57cm) extended.
£120–145
€170–200
$200–240 WW

► **A gilt-metal eye glass,** decorated with mother-of-pearl panels and a band of trailing flowers set with turquoise beads, French, 19thC, 3¾in (9.5cm) extended.
£120–145
€170–200
$200–240 FHF

A 1½in brass eight-draw refracting telescope, by George Adams, with japanned tube, signed, c1800, 28in (71cm) extended.
£570–680
€820–980
$960–1,150
B(Kn)

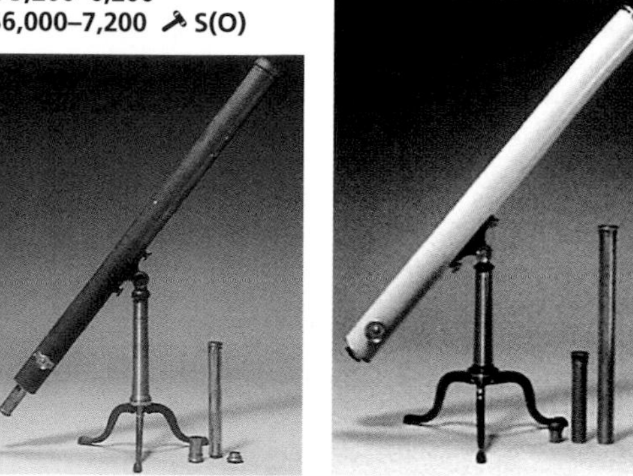

A 3in refracting telescope, by Dollond, the brass tube with later coating, with rack-and-pinion focusing, mounted on a column above a folding iron base, mid-19thC, 43in (109cm) long, with a mahogany case.
£560–670 / €810–960
$940–1,100 B(Kn)

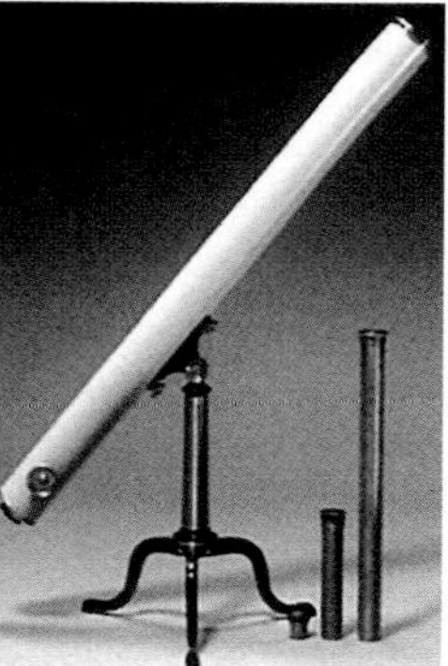

A 3in refracting telescope on stand, by Negretti & Zambra, the repainted brass tube with rack-and-pinion focusing, on a brass column and painted folding tripod, late 19thC, 37in (94cm) long, in a fitted case.
£490–590 / €710–850
$820–990 B(Kn)

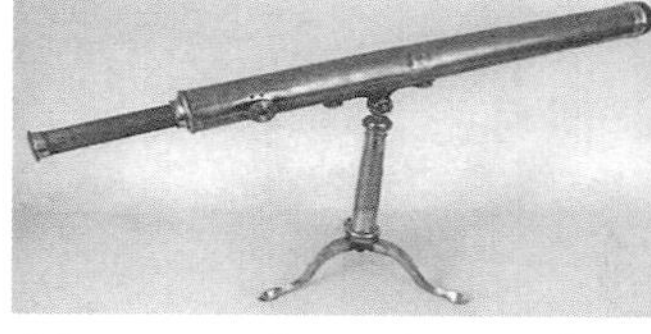

A brass two-draw telescope, by J. B. Dancer, on a column with folding cabriole legs, mid-19thC, 26in (66cm) long, with a mahogany case.
£470–560 / €680–810
$790–940 EH

► **A Signals and General Service three-drawer telescope,** by T. T. & H., with leather mounts, shoulder strap and spare objective lens, c1915, 36in (91.5cm) long.
£120–145
€170–200
$200–240 G(B)

Weights & Measures

A brass and steel pocket chondrometer, by Isaac Bradford, with removable brass pan and bone roller, in a mahogany case, c1808, 3 x 9in (7.5 x 23cm).
£430–480 / €620–690
$720–860 ⊞ FOF
This device was used to weigh samples of grain to determine quality and dryness. The bone roller was used to level the pan.

An ebonized and polished-brass spectroscope, late 19thC, 18in (45.5cm) long, with a fitted case.
£160–190 / €230–270
$270–320 G(B)

A set of gilt-metal chemical scales, in an oak-veneered and glazed case, upper glass broken, c1900, 18¼in (46.5cm) wide, with seven weights.
£260–310 / €370–440
$440–520 LCM

Marine

The national celebrations organized for the forthcoming 200th anniversary of the Battle of Trafalgar in October 2005 have stimulated great interest in works of art relating to ships and the sea. Consequently, although commemorative ceramics, silver and bronzes relating to Admiral Lord Nelson, Emma Hamilton and the Napoleonic Wars have always been avidly collected, they are currently the focus of even more attention.

As with many other areas of the art market, the prices realized for fine and rare pieces continue to accelerate far beyond run-of-the-mill collectables. A good example of this is a model of a fifth-rate ship-of-the-line which was made between 1710 and 1724 as a scale model of the full-size ship, which sold at Christie's for £667,000 / €960,000 / $1,121,000. More affordable are the bone models of ships made by French prisoners incarcerated in English hulks and jails during the Napoleonic Wars. Examples can be bought for £5,000–20,000 / €7,200–29,000 / $8,400–33,600 depending on size, quality and condition.

Navigational instruments including chronometers continue to be good buys with prices having remained stable for several years. Nineteenth-century sextants by known makers, in their original cases with a full set of accessories can still be found for £500–800 / €720–1,150 / $840–1,340. Two-day marine chronometers, used in conjunction with the sextant to determine longitude, in working order and contained in attractive double hinged cases, generally sell for around £1,800 / €2,600 / $3,000 if not by a prestigious maker.

American collectors of folk art are beginning to buy the 19th-century naïve works made by British sailors. Woolwork ship portraits have risen rapidly in price over the last year, those with strong colours and in good condition fetching over £5,000 / €7,200 / $8,400. Scrimshaw, the art of decorating whale bone and ivory, continues to appreciate in value, especially for examples that can be attributed to known artists. British-decorated whales' teeth can be bought for between £500–2,000 / €720–2,900 / $840–3,350 in the UK depending on the condition and subject matter.

Ever popular with the owners of yachts and seaside residences or those just passionate about ships and the sea, marine works of art continue to be a major part of the antiques and collectables market and, with the increased affluence in the West, are likely to remain so. **Jon Baddeley**

Chronometers & Timekeepers

A one-day marine chronometer, by Thomas Earnshaw, No. 1024, with a silvered dial, the freesprung fusee movement with maintaining power and diamond endstone, in a two-tier mahogany case with applied ivory plaque and sliding cover, c1818, 3in (7.5cm) diam.
£12,000–14,400
€17,500–21,000
$20,000–24,000 B
This chronometer was the personal property of the Arctic explorer Captain John Ross (1777–1856).

A two-day marine chronometer, by Litherland Davies & Co, the enamel dial with gold hands, the four-pillar movement with Earnshaw's spring detent escapement, maintaining power, signed, c1830, in a three-tier rosewood case, 3¾in (9.5cm) diam.
£4,400–5,300
€6,300–7,600
$7,400–8,900 TEN

A two-day marine chronometer, by John Fletcher, No. 1164, with silvered dial, the movement with fusee and chain, maintaining power and spotted plates, Earnshaw's detent escapement with free-sprung helical spring, cover missing, signed, c1847, in a three-tier brass-bound mahogany case, 3¾in (9.5cm) diam.
£900–1,050 / €1,300–1,500
$1,500–1,750 S(O)

A two-day marine chronometer, by Charles Shepherd, the silvered dial with gold hands, the movement with fusee and chain and Earnshaw's detent escapement, spotted plates and maintaining power, dial signed, c1850, with a later gimbal and three-tier brass-bound oak case, 3¾in (9.5cm) diam.
£1,100–1,300
€1,600–1,850
$1,850–2,200 S(O)

Chronometers

Chronometers are essential navigational instruments for mariners and used in conjunction with the sextant they can determine an accurate calculation of the latitude and longitude of a vessel. Prices are determined by the maker, whether of eight or two-day duration, the quality of the casing and, most importantly, by the condition of the movement and whether it has been altered or not.

◄ **A two-day marine chronometer,** by Russells, the silvered dial with gilt hands, the freesprung movement with Poole's auxiliary compensation, Earnshaw-type detent escapement, maintaining power, c1875, in a three-tier brass-bound mahogany case with later cover, 3¾in (9.5cm) diam.
£1,700–2,000 / €2,450–2,900
$2,900–3,350 ⚒ B

A Victorian two-day marine chronometer, by Charles Shepherd, with a brass-bound rosewood travelling case, hands missing, gimbal detached, signed, box with plaque inscribed 'James Gardner Greenock', 3¾in (9.5cm) diam.
£1,400–1,650 / €2,000–2,350
$2,350–2,750 ⚒ CHTR

A two-day marine chronometer, by Clerke, the silvered dial with gold hands, the fusee and chain movement with spotted plates, Earnshaw's detent escapement, maintaining power, c1890, in a three-tier brass-inlaid mahogany case, 4¼in (11cm) diam.
£2,900–3,500
€4,200–5,000
$4,900–5,900 ⚒ S(O)

A clock, from the *Discovery*, the barrel movement with four pillars, lever platform escapement, inscribed '"The Discovery" leads to Discovery', initialled 'FAH', 1901–04, 11in (28cm) diam.
£7,300–8,700 / €10,500–12,500
$12,300–14,600 ⚒ B
According to the vendor this clock was supplied to the National Antarctic Expedition by an anonymous donor and won by his father in a raffle at the end of the voyage. This would explain other items from the ship that have been offered at auction in recent years, particularly tableware, although fittings seem much more rare.

A brass bulkhead timepiece, with painted dial, signed 'Smith, Astral', c1930, 8in (20.5cm) diam.
£720–860 / €1,050–1,250
$1,200–1,450 ⚒ S(O)

MARINE

Model Ships

A bone model of a 100-gun prisoner of war first-rate ship-of-the-line, with galleried stern, warrior figurehead and deck details including capstan and stairways, French, c1800, 7¼in (18.5cm) long, mounted on original straw-work base and within a glazed case.
£7,200–8,600 / €10,400–12,400
$12,100–14,500 ⚒ S(O)

A bone model of a man-o'-war, with three masts, two gun decks presenting 44 guns, on a wooden stand, with later parts and repairs, 19thC, 24¼in (61.5cm) high.
£2,100–2,500 / €3,000–3,600
$3,500–4,200 ⚒ CDC

A painted wood model of the first America's Cup race, in a glazed case, mid-19thC, 28¼in (72cm) wide.
£11,200–12,500 / €16,200–18,000
$18,900–21,000 ⊞ RYA
The famous challenge for the America's Cup was conceived in 1851, when the first Commodore of the New York Yacht Club, John C. Stevens and his syndicate commissioned the 170 ton schooner *America* to be built in New York to compete in the Royal Yacht Squadron regatta around the Isle of Wight. A crew of 13 sailed *America* across the Atlantic to the Solent and subsequently challenged and beat a fleet of 14 vessels around the island, to win by eight minutes.

◄ **A builder's gold-mounted half-model of a merchantman,** with two masts and a bowsprit, mounted on a board, 19thC, 48¾in (124cm) long.
£610–730 / €880–1,050
$1,000–1,200 ⚒ SWO

A wooden model of HMS *Sapphire*, with paper-covered decks and a gilded figurehead, with anchors, galley chimney, windlass, wheel, drum skylight and ship's boats on davits, in a glazed case, 19thC, 21½in (54.5cm) wide.
£590–700 / €850–1,000
$990–1,150 ⚒ B(Kn)

A model of a man-o'-war, with two masts, rigging and brass cannon, in a glazed mahogany case, late 19thC, 27in (68.5cm) long.
£300–360 / €430–520
$500–600 ⚒ G(L)

A set of 16 Board of Enquiry model boats, by Droosten Allan & Co, cased, c1890.
£320–380 / €460–550
$540–640 ⚒ IM
These were used to show how accidents at sea occurred. Such items are seldom seen.

A shipping diorama, depicting a paddle steamer with painted figures, a yacht and a small steamer, against a background of houses and gardens, on simulated sea, in a burr-maple glazed frame, 19thC, 28in (71cm) wide.
£780–930 / €1,100–1,300
$1,300–1,550 ⚒ S(O)

A wooden model of a rowing boat, the pinned and plank hull with brass pins and ribbed inner frame, with rudder and interior thwarts, late 19thC, 24in (61cm) long.
£720–860 / €1,050–1,250
$1,200–1,400 ⚒ S(O)

A wooden pond yacht, the pinned and plank hull with gaff-rigged main mast, jib and fore sails, lead-weighted keel and linen sails, mounted on a wooden frame, early 20thC, 67½in (172cm) high.
£1,000–1,200 / €1,450–1,650
$1,700–2,000 ⚒ S(O)

A pine gaff-rigged pond yacht, on stand, c1900, 64in (162.5cm) wide.
£1,050–1,200 / €1,500–1,700
$1,750–2,000 ⊞ MINN

A carved and painted wood model of a steamship, with four masts, together with three small boats and a lighthouse, in a glass bottle with stopper, late 19thC, 15in (38cm) long.
£120–140 / €170–200
$200–230 ⚒ TMA

A wooden pond yacht, with a lead-weighted keel, operating rudder, mast, mainsail and jib, 1930s, 58in (147.5cm) long.
£610–730 / €880–1,050
$1,000–1,200 ⚒ G(L)

Nautical Handicrafts

A woolwork picture of a ship, c1830, 13 x 18in (33 x 45.5cm).
£1,050–1,200
€1,500–1,750
$1,750–2,000 ⊞ HIS

A woolwork picture of a three-masted sailing vessel, in a maple frame, 19thC, 10½ x 10in (26.5 x 25.5cm).
£2,000–2,400
€2,900–3,450
$3,350–4,000 ⚒ BWL

A woolwork picture of a merchantman, 19thC, 14¼ x 17¾in (36 x 45cm).
£590–700 / €850–1,000
$990–1,150 ⚒ SWO

For further information on
Textiles see pages 519–532

A woolwork picture of a frigate, in a bird's-eye maple frame, 19thC, 8¼ x 15in (21 x 38cm).
£880–1,050 / €1,250–1,500
$1,500–1,750 ⚒ RTo

A sailor's woolwork picture of *Ariel* and another sailing vessel, by D. Ames, framed and glazed, mid-19thC, 13½ x 20½in (34.5 x 52cm).
£820–980 / €1,200–1,400
$1,400–1,650 ⚒ F&C

An early Victorian woolwork picture of a royal ship, with three masts and 86 guns, 23¼ x 31in (59 x 78.5cm).
£6,800–8,100 / €9,800–11,600
$11,400–13,600 ⚒ CGC

An oil painting of a clipper, on sailcloth stretched on board, c1850, 18 x 34in (45.5 x 86.5cm).
£2,500–2,800 / €3,600–4,000
$4,200–4,700 ⊞ DeG

A Victorian woolwork picture of two ships and a yacht, 6¼ x 13in (16 x 33cm), in a glazed maple frame.
£1,000–1,200 / €1,450–1,750
$1,700–2,000 ⚒ G(L)

Handicrafts made by sailors are growing in popularity and often include woolwork pictures depicting ship portraits and other nautical themes such as 'The Sailor's Return'. The whaling industry, which rapidly grew during the 19th century to supply the very valuable oils used for lighting and heating, produced a wide range of decorative arts. Whale material such as ivory teeth and bone from sperm whales and baleen from blue whales was often engraved with domestic or whaling scenes. This type of material is called scrimshaw and collectors should be aware that many modern resin replicas have been reproduced. When buying a piece a full descriptive invoice should be obtained, including a date of production. Carved coconut shells, shell valentines, and tools used in sail-making such as seam rubbers and fids used in splicing rope were also produced by sailors.

► **A woolwork picture of a Japanese warship,** c1900, 12½ x 13¼in (32 x 35.5cm).
£240–290
€340–410
$400–480
⚒ SWO

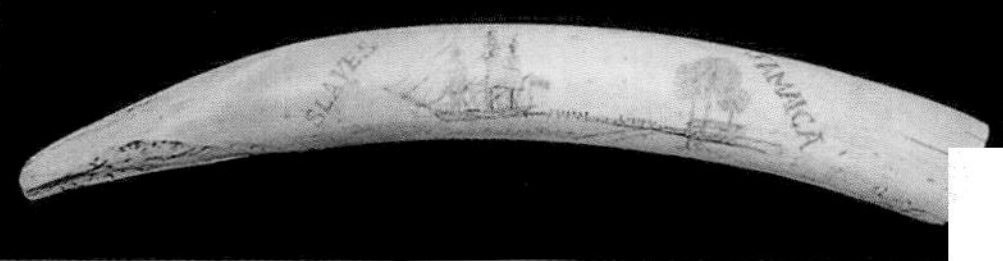

A scrimshaw walrus tusk, 'Slaves to America', engraved with a three-masted ship-of-the-line anchored off the island of Jamaica with a group of chained slaves, mid-19thC, 17¼in (44cm) long.
£3,000–3,600 / €4,400–5,200
$5,000–6,000 ⚒ S(O)

A nautilus shell, by C. Wood, engraved with SS *Great Britain*, SS *Great Eastern*, the Royal coat-of-arms and Prince of Wales feathers, with inscription, 19thC, 8in (20.5cm) wide.
£700–840 / €1,000–1,200
$1,200–1,400 ⚒ B(Kn)

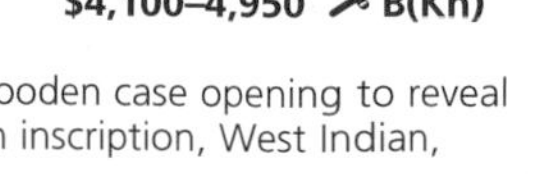

A double shell valentine, in a wooden case, 19thC, 10in (25.5cm) diam.
£2,450–2,950
€3,500–4,200
$4,100–4,950 ⚒ B(Kn)

A double shell valentine, in a wooden case, Caribbean, c1850, 10in (25.5cm) diam.
£2,700–3,000 / €3,900–4,300
$4,500–5,000 ⊞ RdeR

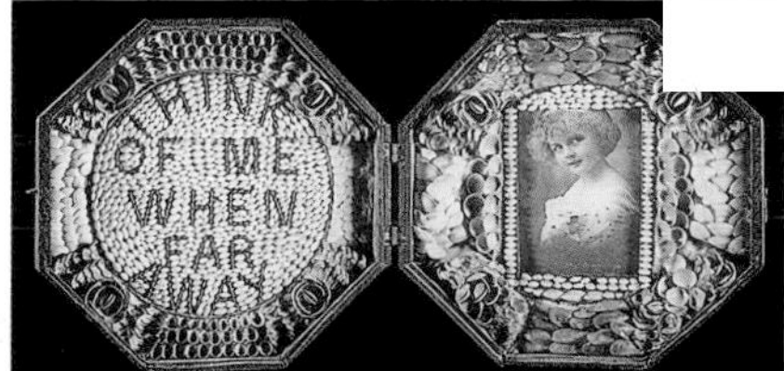

► **A double shell valentine,** the wooden case opening to reveal a black and white photograph and an inscription, West Indian, late 19thC, 9¾in (24.5cm) diam.
£2,250–2,700 / €3,250–3,900
$3,800–4,550 ⚒ S(O)

MARINE

Navigational Instruments

A bronze binnacle compass, the brass shaped cover with window to the front housing the gimbal-mounted compass, mounted on a tripod base in the form of three hippocampi, on a mahogany base, late 19thC, 43¾in (111cm) high.
£4,300–5,100
€6,200–7,300
$7,200–8,600 S(O)

The binnacle took its name from the place near the helm where the compass was kept. The term came to mean the receptacle, usually a box or cupboard with a glass top, in which it was housed.

A brass octant, with plate index arm, one set of filters, sighting mirror, horizon mirror and sight, applied with a cherub, signed 'Jan Cornelisen', Dutch, late 18thC, 13in (33cm) radius.
£5,400–6,500
€7,800–9,400
$9,100–10,900 S(O)

Jan Cornelisen, although his name seems to imply that he was of Dutch origin, lived and worked on the island of Fohr situated in the North Sea, just off the German coast immediately to the south of the frontier with Denmark, in the latter half of the 18th century. Five instruments, apart from the present one, are known by him. Although none are dated by him, one carries an ownership date of 1777.

A brass and oak binnacle compass, by W. Boosmann, Dutch, Amsterdam, late 19thC, 48in (122cm) high.
£1,300–1,500
€1,850–2,250
$2,200–2,600 Herm

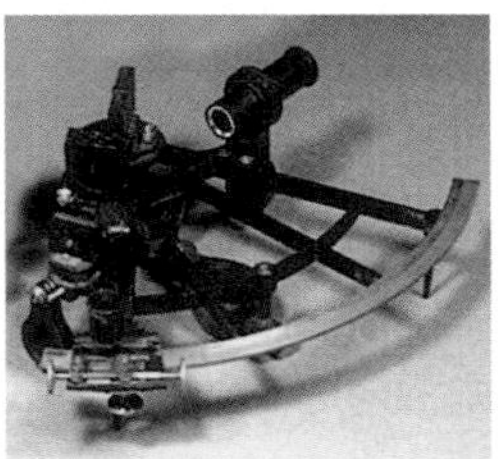

A radius ladder frame quintant, by Lorieux, with a silvered scale, the index arm with swivel magnifying glass and ground glass screen, fitted with a vernier reading to 10 seconds, nameplate for Captain Oudet, French, Paris, 19thC, 10¼in (26cm) wide, with a mahogany carrying case, together with two telescopes, a star scope, two lenses, magnifying glass, adjusting key and screwdriver.
£490–590 / €710–850
$820–990 B(Kn)

An Edwardian brass sextant, by Henry Hughes & Son, No. 5917, with a silvered vernier scale, 6in (15cm) radius, in a fitted mahogany case, together with shades, mirrors and telescopic lenses.
£500–600 / €720–860
$840–1,000 BR

A steel-mounted instrument panel, comprising clock, two statute fathoms and an hours/miles dial, with silvered dials, inscribed 'Henley, London', late 19thC, 35in (89cm) wide.
£340–400 / €490–580
$570–670 SWO

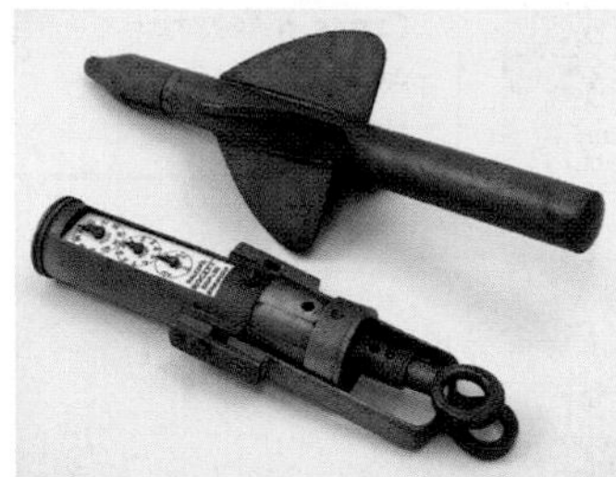

◄ **A Walker's patent Rocket ship log,** the brass measuring gauge with three dials, late 19thC, 14½in (36cm) extended.
£280–330
€400–480
$470–550 G(L)

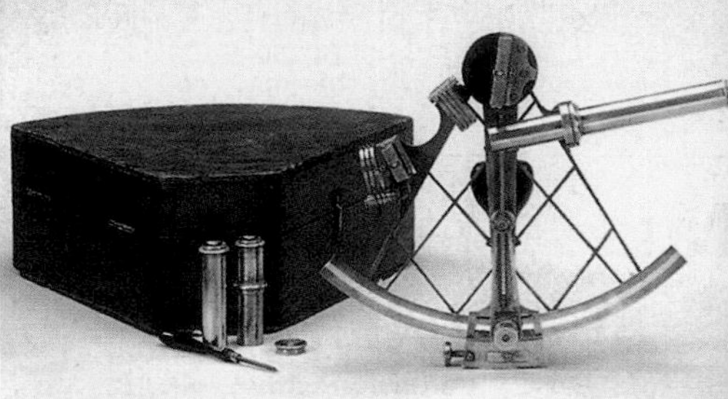

A brass lattice frame sextant, by H. Hughes, the index arm with vernier, two sets of interchangeable filters, mirror, split level mirror and telescope holder, signed, 1850–75, 9½in (24cm) radius, with three telescopes and one eyepiece.
£600–720 / €860–1,050
$1,000–1,200 S(O)

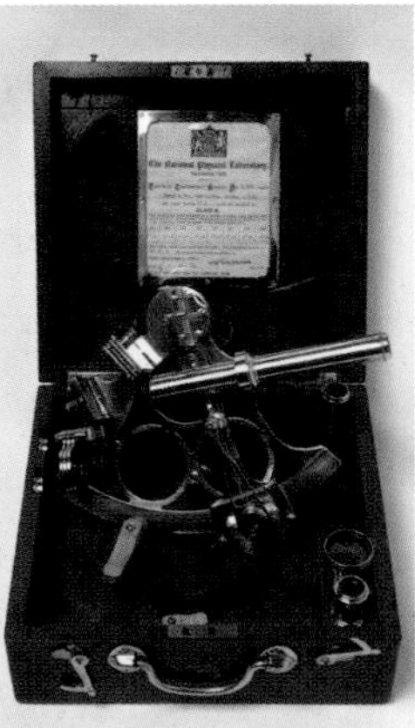

A sextant, by Heath & Co, c1938, in original mahogany case, 11in (28cm) wide, with accessories.
£580–650 / €830–940
$970–1,100 ⊞ PHo

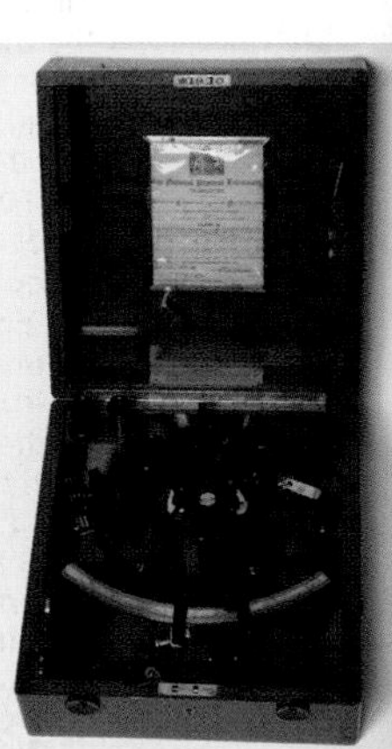

A sextant, by Henry Hughes & Son, c1939, in a mahogany case, 12in (30.5cm) wide, with accessories.
£1,350–1,500
€1,950–2,150
$2,250–2,500 ⊞ ETO

MARINE

Ship's Fittings

A brass ship's bell, inscribed 'Hing Chong', late 19thC, 11½in (29cm) high.
£150–180 / €220–260
$250–300 ⚒ SWO

A carved, gilded and painted pine sternboard eagle, holding a United States shield and a banner inscribed 'Active Padanaram', mounted on a wooden backboard, damaged, American, c1880, 71in (180.5cm) wide.
£17,800–21,400 / €25,000–30,000
$30,000–36,000 ⚒ S(NY)
Padanaram, Massachusetts, is home to the famous Concordia yacht-building company.

A carved wood ship's figurehead, 1800–25, 13in (33cm) high.
£4,000–4,800
€5,700–6,900
$6,700–8,000 ⚒ B(Kn)
The small size of this figurehead suggests two possible options; either that it is a model of a larger figurehead and used in a workshop or as a travelling piece to represent to potential clients the quality of the workshop's craftmanship, or that she was carved for a small coastal vessel and would have been removed from the bow once the vessel was out at sea, and only returned in port.

Cross reference
American Folk Art
see page 743

◄ **A carved wood merchant ship's figurehead,** in the form of a young woman, losses and damage, mid-19thC, 54in (137cm) high.
£4,250–5,100
€6,100–7,300
$7,200–8,600 ⚒ B(Kn)

A mahogany ship's wheel, with ten spokes, central brass hub and brass band to rim, late 19thC, 67¾in (172cm) diam.
£720–860
€1,050–1,250
$1,200–1,400 ⚒ S(O)

MARINE

Miscellaneous

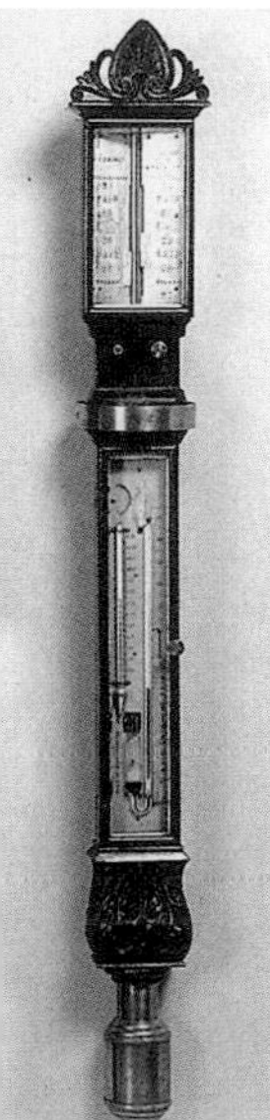

◄ **A rosewood marine barometer with sympiesometer,** by J. Hughes, with anthemion carved cresting and brass collar, the signed ivory dial with twin scales, the sympiesometer with moveable scale, mercury thermometer and recording dial, c1850, 40¼in (102cm) high.
£3,000–3,600
€4,300–5,200
$5,000–6,000 ⚒ B
Joseph Hughes was a London manufacturer of all manner of scientific instruments for much of the first half of the 19th century. He is first listed as working in 1818 and his son, Joseph II, continued the family firm into the 1870s.

A tin of dehydrated onions, by Andrew Lusk & Co, from Robert Scott's Antarctic expedition on the *Terra Nova*, 1910–12, 7in (18cm) high, with a letter and a photographic picture postcard.
£340–400 / €490–570
$570–670 ⚒ PFK

A journal/log book, with coloured maps and drawings of people and plants with mythical and religious sentiments in Latin, Greek and French, c1770, 8°.
£1,300–1,550 / €2,200–2,600
$2,500–3,000 ⚒ G(L)
This journal/log book relates to a naval expedition to the Antipodes and Galapagos islands to undertake research.

A set of four silver menu holders, Chester 1909, 1½in (4cm) high.
£420–500 / €600–720
$700–840 ⚒ G(L)

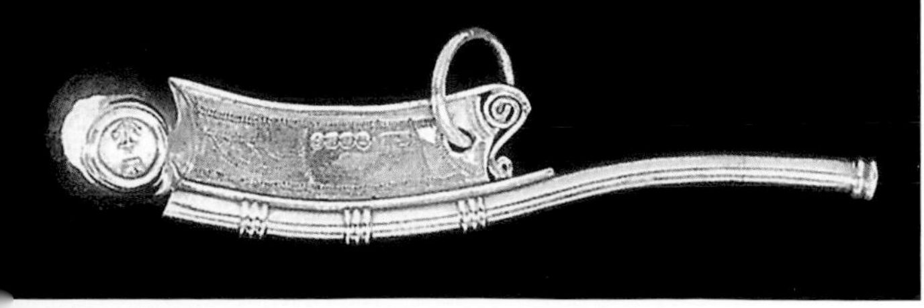

◄ **A silver boatswain's whistle,** by George Unite, Birmingham 1886, 4¼in (11cm) long.
£320–380 / €460–540
$540–640 ⚒ S(O)

The Death of Nelson, 21st October 1805

An enamel patch box, painted with a portrait of Admiral Lord Nelson at the Battle of Trafalgar, with the motto 'Nelson & Victory', the lid lined with a mirror, c1805, 2in (5cm) diam.
£1,550–1,850 / €2,250–2,650
$2,600–3,100 S

An oak snuff box, by Phipps & Robinson, the cover set with a silver plaque inscribed 'The oak of this box is part of a plank from the starboard gunnel of the *Victory* severed by a 36th shot in the Glorious Battle of Trafalgar 21 Octr 1805', the front of box inscribed 'Admiral Lord Nelson', 1808, 3in (7.5cm) wide.
£6,100–7,300 / €8,800–10,500
$10,200–12,200 B

A creamware jug, commemorating Admiral Lord Nelson, printed with a portrait above the dates of his birth and death, the reverse printed with a map and description of the Battle of Trafalgar, c1805, 6¾in (17cm) high.
£2,350–2,800
€3,400–4,000
$3,950–4,700 CGC

Nelson commemorative wares

As 2005 is the 200th anniversary of the Battle of Trafalgar and the focus of a major exhibition at the National Maritime Museum, prices are likely to take a leap forward. At the lower price range, ceramics made in the early 20th century in the image of Nelson, including Toby jugs, can still be found for under £1,000 / €1,450 / $1,700. Ceramics, prints, jewellery, medals and glass paintings made at the time of Trafalgar are substantially more expensive and items used by or owned by Nelson himself are extraordinarily rare, commanding very high prices. As with all material associated with celebrities, the provenance or proof of association is of paramount importance and buyers should be wary of items described as being 'purported to be' or 'associated with' the person concerned.

A Sunderland lustre documentary jug, printed with Admiral Lord Nelson, the Battle of Trafalgar and the Iron Bridge over the Wear, inscribed 'Peter and Harriet Palmer, married Jan 2nd 1825', minor damage, early 19thC, 8½in (21.5cm) high.
£840–1,000
€1,200–1,400
$1,400–1,650 SWO

A Royal Doulton stoneware loving cup, moulded with a quarter-length portrait of Admiral Lord Nelson within a rope-twist cartouche, flanked by the dates of his birth and death, impressed mark and inscribed 'HW', c1905, 5¾in (14.5cm) high.
£660–790 / €950–1,100
$1,100–1,300 S(O)

A Castleford-type feldspathic stoneware teapot, commemorating Admiral Lord Nelson, c1805, 7in (18cm) high.
£770–850 / €1,100–1,250
$1,300–1,450 AUC

A reverse painting on glass, depicting Admiral Lord Nelson, framed, c1905, 12in (30.5cm) high
£420–500 / €600–720
$700–840 S

◄ **A glass goblet,** decorated with a bust profile of Admiral Lord Nelson within laurel wreaths and inscriptions, on a waisted stem and stepped foot, c1905, 8¾in (22cm) high.
£410–490
€590–700
$690–820 DN

◄ **A pair of painted print on glass,** commemorating Admiral Lord Nelson, framed, c1805, 12¾ x 17ir (32.5 x 43cm).
£1,900–2,250
€2,750–3,250
$3,200–3,800 S

MARINE

Titanic Memorabilia

◄ **A maid's apron from RMS *Titanic*,** worn by Laura Mabel Francatelli, decorated with broderie anglaise and waist tie, with Red Cross label, minor repairs, c1912.
£1,000–1,200 / €1,450–1,700
$1,700–2,000 ⚒ B(Kn)
Laura Mabel Francatelli accompanied her employer, Lady Lucy Duff, on a business trip to Paris in April 1912 and thence to Cherbourg, boarding RMS *Titanic* for passage to New York. When disaster struck, Miss Francatelli and her employers were placed in a lifeboat and were rescued. On board *Carpathia*, it was Miss Francatelli who was responsible for writing out the £5 cheques, signed by Sir Cosmo Duff Gordon, as a token of thanks for the seamen in the lifeboat.

A letter, hand-written on RMS *Titanic* stationery, postmarked 'Queenstown 3.45am 11th April 1912', with original envelope.
£27,600–33,000 / €40,000–48,000
$46,000–55,000 ⚒ HAld
This letter was sent by second-class passenger, Clear Cameron, who was travelling to the USA with her companion, Nellie Walcroft.

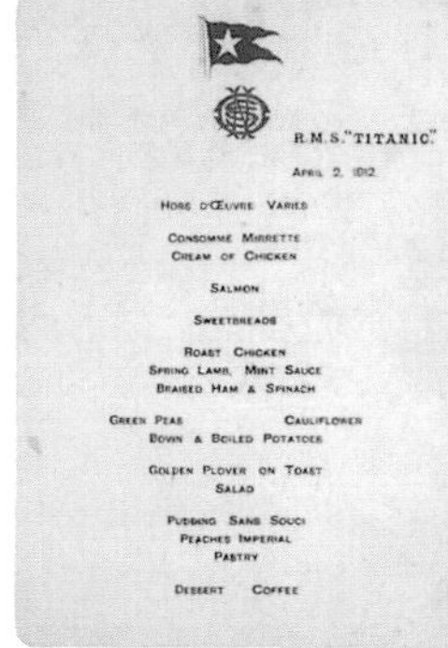

R.M.S. "TITANIC."
April 2, 1912

Hors d'Œuvre Varies

Consomme Mirrette
Cream of Chicken

Salmon

Sweetbreads

Roast Chicken
Spring Lamb, Mint Sauce
Braised Ham & Spinach

Green Peas Cauliflower
Down & Boiled Potatoes

Golden Plover on Toast
Salad

Pudding Sans Souci
Peaches Imperial
Pastry

Dessert Coffee

An RMS *Titanic* lunch menu, embossed with White Star Line flag, Oceanic Steam Navigation Company and RMS *Titanic* logos, 1912, 6¼ x 4in (16 x 10cm).
£28,000–33,000
€40,000–48,000
$47,000–56,000 ⚒ S
This menu was formerly the property of the family of the *Titanic*'s most senior surviving officer, Second Officer Herbert Charles Lightoller. The menu was for the first meal taken on board ship by the crew and officers on the occasion of *Titanic*'s sea trials from Belfast to Southampton.

A picture of RMS *Titanic*, hand-painted on tin, in a painted wood lifebelt frame, signed 'W. H. Duff, Belfast', c1911, 9in (23cm) diam.
£2,250–2,700 / €3,250–3,900
$3,800–4,550 ⚒ S(O)
The original owners of this lifebelt lived in Holywood, along the coast from Belfast where the *Titanic* was first launched. It is the belief of their descendants, the vendors of this piece, that it was purchased in Belfast at the time of the launch.

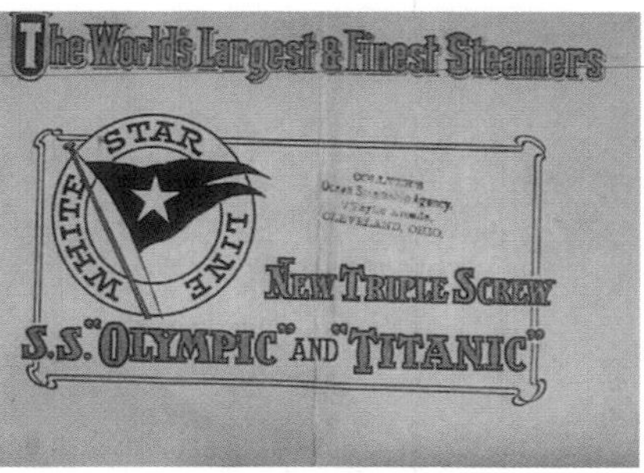

An SS *Olympic* and *Titanic* publicity brochure, with black and white illustrations, c1912.
£900–1,050 / €1,300–1,500
$1,500–1,750 ⚒ HAld

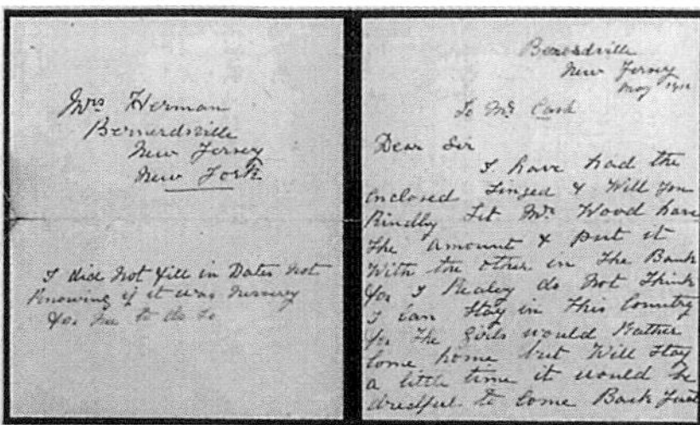

A four-page letter, written by second-class passenger Mrs Jane Herman describing her state of mind, dated May 1912.
£2,100–2,500 / €3,300–3,600
$3,500–4,200 ⚒ HAld
Mr Herman died in the disaster.

***The Shipbuilder*,** souvenir number, 'The White Star Triple-Screw Atlantic Liners *Olympic* and *Titanic*', with plates and illustrations of the exterior and interior of the liners, the builders and the owners, together with pull-outs of the deck plans and elevations of the engine rooms, 1911, 9¾ x 7¾in (25 x 19.5cm).
£1,400–1,650 / €2,000–2,350
$2,350–2,750 ⚒ S

A postcard of the *Titanic*, some wear, posted April 1912.
£45–50 / €65–75
$75–85 ⚒ JAA

◄ **A portrait photograph of RMS *Titanic* 5th Officer Harold Lowe,** by Vanderbilt, wearing White Star Line uniform, with dedication 'Yours sincerely, H. G. Lowe', c1912.
£2,300–2,750 / €3,300–3,950
$3,850–4,600 ⚒ HAld

Cameras

An Adams Idento folding camera, c1905.
£220–250 / €310–360
$370–420 ⊞ APC

A George Hare mahogany full-plate field camera, c1885.
£360–400 / €520–570
$600–670 ⊞ APC

A Multiscope Al-Vista 5B panoramic camera, c1905.
£180–210 / €260–300
$300–350 ⚒ JAA

A Teddy Camera Co camera, tank missing, c1924.
£450–500 / €650–720
$760–840 ⊞ APC

A Beck Frena 0 magazine camera, c1901.
£90–100 / €130–145
$150–170 ⊞ ARP

A Kodak B Boy Scout camera, with instructions, in original leather case, c1932.
£105–125 / €150–180
$175–210 ⚒ DD

A late Victorian Perken Son & Rayment mahogany and brass full-plate bellows camera, No. 5028, with a Primms Rapid rectilinear brass lens by Philips & Co, with three mahogany and brass plate-holders and leather case.
£210–250 / €300–360
$350–420 ⚒ BR

An Eastman Kodak 2-D camera, c1900.
£65–75 / €95–110
$110–125 ⚒ JAA

A Meagher mahogany full-plate tailboard camera, c1885.
£270–300 / €390–430
$450–500 ⊞ APC

A Ricoh Steky 111b camera, with telescopic lens, boxed, c1950.
£180–200 / €260–290
$300–340 ⊞ APC

A mahogany and brass studio plate camera, with a Voigtlander & John No. 6 Portrait Euroscop lens, Fresnel screen, plate back with masks, 1880–1900.
£2,100–2,350 / €3,000–3,400
$3,500–3,950 ⊞ CaH

◄ **A Williamson Kinematograf mahogany 35mm movie camera,** hand-cranked, with original leather case, c1910.
£90–100 / €130–145
$150–170 ⊞ TOM

Optical Devices & Viewers

◄ **A Victorian burr-walnut stereo graphoscope,** with ebonized eyepieces and rack-and-pinion focusing, the interior with wire holders for over 100 views on a continuous belt wound by a wooden hand-wheel, 52in (132cm) high.
£3,900–4,700 / €5,600–6,700
$6,600–7,900 ⚒ B(WM)

► **A kaleidoscope,** with rotating end, late 19thC, 9in (23cm) long.
£310–350 / €440–500
$520–590 ⊞ APC

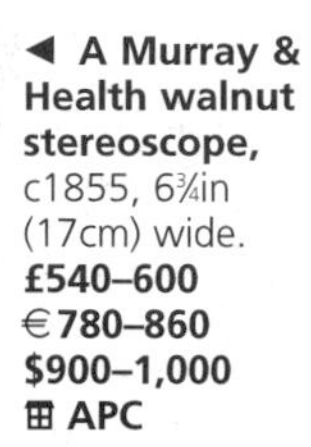

◄ **A Murray & Health walnut stereoscope,** c1855, 6¾in (17cm) wide.
£540–600
€780–860
$900–1,000
⊞ APC

A Victorian burr-walnut London Stereoscopic Exhibition achromatic revolving stereoscope, 10¼in (26cm) high.
£760–910 / €1,100–1,300
$1,300–1,550 ⚒ WilP

A painted-metal Mutoscope, by International Mutoscope Reel Company NY, with one reel depicting a scantily-clad woman, mounted with a framed photograph, American, late 19thC, 74in (188cm) high.
£1,200–1,400
€1,750–2,000
$2,000–2,350 ⚒ B

A J. J. Mathewson opaline glass viewer, with four colour lithographic views of the Thames Tunnel, c1860, 5in (12.5cm) high.
£610–730 / €880–1,050
$1,000–1,200 ⚒ TEN

A burr-walnut stereo viewer, with 50 cards, c1865, 11in (30cm) wide.
£900–1,000
€1,300–1,450
$1,500–1,700 ⊞ APC

A London Stereoscopic Photographic Co figured walnut cabinet stereo viewer, with internal wooden frames for 50 views on a rotating belt, sliding box focusing, 19thC, 23¾in (55.5cm) high, with four glass views.
£750–900 / €1,100–1,300
$1,250–1,500 ⚒ B(WM)

A London Stereoscopic & Photographic Co painted metal zoetrope, on a turned fruitwood and boxwood-strung pillar, early 20thC, 14in (35.5cm) high, with 13 coloured picture strips depicting acrobats, a whale, spider and various comical images.
£660–790 / €950–1,150
$1,100–1,300 ⚒ S(O)

A mahogany Holmes-style stereo viewer on stand, c1880, 11¾in (30cm) high.
£180–200 / €260–290
$300–330 ⊞ APC

► **A mahogany zograscope,** 18thC, 31in (78.5cm) high.
£490–590 / €710–850
$820–990 ⚒ AH

Photographs

Berenice Abbott, 'James Joyce', stamped, American, 1920s–30s, 14 x 11in (35.5 x 28cm).
£920–1,100 / €1,350–1,600
$1,550–1,850 ⚒ JDJ

Ansel Adams, 'Cloud, Hill, Philmont', matted, signed and titled by the photographer in ink, with San Francisco letterpress label, mounted, American, c1960, 9½ x 13½in (24 x 34.5cm).
£2,650–3,150 / €3,800–4,550
$4,450–5,300 ⚒ S(NY)

Edouard Baldus, 'Arles Amphithéâtre', albumen print, mounted on album page, facsimile signature, titled, French, c1859, 13¼ x 17in (33.5 x 43cm).
£480–570 / €690–820
$810–960 ⚒ S(O)

► **Cecil Beaton,** 'Princess Marina (Duchess of Kent)', signed, 1950, 13¼ x 10in (33.5 x 25.5cm)
£200–240 / €290–350
$340–400 ⚒ MUL
Beaton's photographic portraits of the senior members of the Royal Family, particularly the Queen Mother, are legendary. This is a particularly fine example.

Ansel Adams, 'Snow Scene in Yosemite', signed by the photographer in pencil, on mount, American, 1948–49, 6¼ x 9in (16 x 23cm).
£3,900–4,600 / €5,600–6,600
$6,600–7,700 ⚒ S(NY)

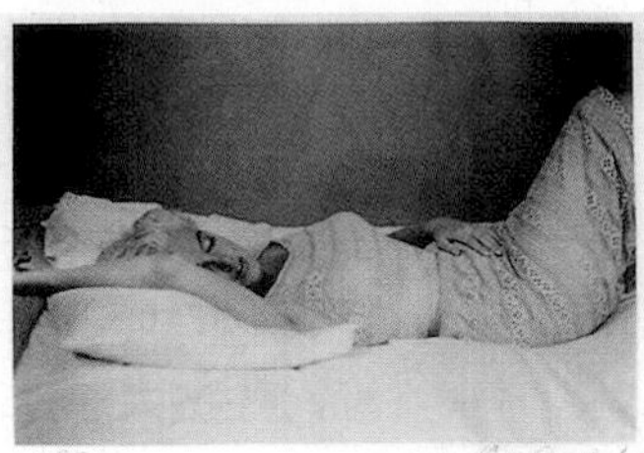

Eve Arnold, 'Marilyn Monroe resting before giving her speech, Bement, Illinois', pigment transfer print, signed and inscribed 'AP 1', American, 1955, printed later, 7¼ x 10½in (18.5 x 26.5cm), framed and glazed.
£2,750–3,300 / €3,950–4,750
$4,600–5,500 ⚒ S(O)
This is an artist's proof from an edition of 15.

Ansel Adams, 'Young Oaks', silver print, signed by the photographer in ink, edition wetstamp on reverse, mounted, American, c1938, printed 1960s, 6½ x 9½in (19 x 24cm), framed.
£1,050–1,250 / €1,500–1,800
$1,750–2,100 ⚒ S(O)

Eugène Atget, 'Grand Trianon', albumen print, numbered '1223' by the photographer in the negative, inscribed 'This is an original/vintage print by Atget mounted by me in 1930 – London June 4 1979', signed by Berenice Abbott, copyright stamp and title to reverse, mounted, French, c1920, 6¾ x 8¼in (17 x 21cm).
£4,250–5,100 / €6,100–7,300
$7,100–8,500 ⚒ S(NY)

◄ **Felice Beato,** 'Nautch Girls, India', albumen print, c1858, 8 x 6in (20.5 x 15cm).
£540–600 / €780–860
$900–1,000 ⊞ RMe

Cecil Beaton, 'Monroe by Beaton: The Eternal Marilyn a little bird told her...', with mounted paper label with note 'Please acknowledge: photograph by Cecil Beaton Camera Press London', wear, two ink stamps to reverse, c1956, possibly printed later, 8¾ x 8in (22 x 20.5cm).
£350–420 / €500–600
$590–700 ⚒ RTo

Bourne and Shepherd, 'Shipping on the Hooghly', albumen print, c1865, 9¼ x 11¼in (23.5 x 28.5cm).
£160–180 / €230–260
$270–300 ⊞ RMe

Wynn Bullock, 'Let There Be Light', matted, signed and titled, mounted, American, 1954, probably printed later, 7½ x 9½in (19 x 24cm).
£5,000–6,000 / €7,200–8,600
$8,400–10,100 ⚒ S(NY)

► **Julia Margaret Cameron,** 'Queen Henrietta telling her children of the coming fate of their father King Charles I', albumen print, mounted on card, inscribed 'Photograph by Mrs Cameron', 19thC, 13¾ x 8¾in (35 x 22cm), framed and glazed.
£540–650 / €780–940
$910–1,100 ⚒ SWO

LOCATE THE SOURCE

The source of each illustration in Miller's can be found by checking the code letters below each caption with the Key to Illustrations, pages 794–800.

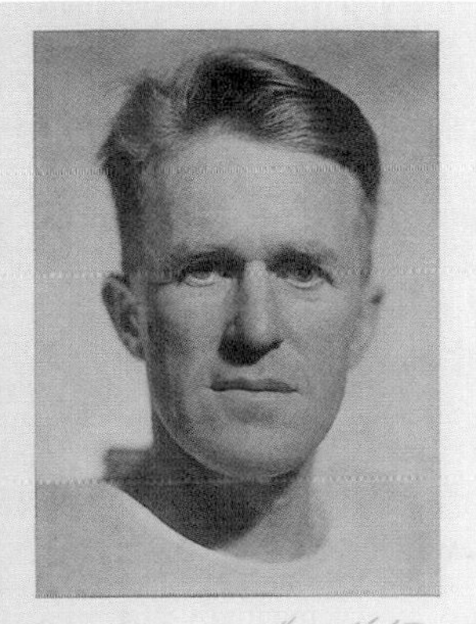

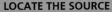

Howard Coster, 'T. E. Lawrence', printed on canvas wove, mounted, signed, photographer's label, slight damage, 1931, 17 x 12¼in (43 x 31cm).
£540–650 / €780–940
$910–1,100 ⚒ B

Matthew Brady, 'Chauncey Allen Goodrich', half-plate daguerreotype, in a velvet-lined leather case, slight damage, 6¼ x 4¾in (16 x 12cm).
£340–400 / €490–580
$570–670 ⚒ JDJ

Goodrich was a professor at Yale from 1817. Son-in-law of Noah Webster, he became Editor-in-Chief of Webster's Dictionaries from 1829 until his death in 1860. This fine daguerreotype is most likely from the series of Yale professors taken in the mid-1850s.

Ernest L. Crandall, 'The US Senate, Washington DC', silver print, photographer's copyright stamp, American, probably 1930s, 13¼ x 9½in (33.5 x 24cm).
£450–540 / €650–780
$750–900 ⚒ S(O)

Bill Brandt, 'East Sussex Coast', silver print, mounted on board, signed, 1958, printed later, 13¼ x 11½in (33.5 x 29cm), framed and glazed.
£4,300–5,100 / €6,200–7,300
$7,200–8,600 ⚒ S(O)

Julia Margaret Cameron, 'A study of the Beatrice Censi', albumen print, mounted on card with gilt-ruled border, titled, signed and inscribed by the photographer, with Royal Photographic Society labels on the reverse, 1870, 13¼ x 10in (33.5 x 25.5cm), framed and glazed.
£1,650–1,950 / €2,350–2,800
$2,750–3,250 ⚒ S(O)

André Disdéri, 'The Prince Imperial', albumen print on *carte de visite*, French, c1865.
£90–100 / €130–145
$150–170 ⊞ RMe

◄ **F. E. Evans,** 'A Chief of Geronimo's Band', cabinet card photograph, American, c1880, 7 x 4in (18 x 10cm).
£240–290 / €350–420 $400–480 ⚒ JDJ

Roger Fenton, 'Arab Study', albumen print, c1858, printed in the 1860s by Francis Frith, 8 x 6½in (120.5 x 16.5cm).
£580–650 / €830–930 $970–1,100 ⊞ RMe

Frederick H. Evans, 'Chateau Amboise', platinum print, mounted on paper with pencil and watercolour borders, signed and titled, early 1900s, 9½ x 6in (24 x 15cm).
£2,150–2,550 €3,100–3,650 $3,600–4,300 ⚒ S(NY)

Roger Fenton, 'Captain Adolphus Burton, 5th Dragoon Guards', salt print, 1855, 7 x 6in (18 x 15cm).
£900–1,000 €1,300–1,450 $1,500–1,700 ⊞ RMe

Foy Bros, 'Study of a Maori Woman', albumen print, with an arrangement of pressed leaves on the reverse, 1870, 3¼ x 2in (8.5 x 5cm).
£140–165 / €200–230 $230–270 ⚒ S(O)

Robert Frank, 'Cowboy and Girl', signed and matted by the photographer, annotated on the reverse, American, c1955, printed c1960, 8½ x 13in (21.5 x 33cm).
£2,500–3,000 / €3,600–4,300 $4,200–5,000 ⚒ S(NY)

Alexander Gardner, 'American Horse, Oglala Sioux', framed and matted, with pencil annotation on reverse, mid-19thC, 7½ x 5½in (19 x 14cm).
£820–980 / €1,200–1,400 $1,400–1,650 ⚒ JDJ

American Horse was one of the more reasoned and conciliatory of the Sioux chiefs, and encouraged his followers to cooperate with the demands of the whites in order to prevent the annihilation of their tribes. He was an eloquent speaker and was influential in keeping the peace, especially during the uprisings surrounding the Ghost Dance movement. Photographer Alexander Gardner was Matthew Brady's assistant, and was appointed to the staff of General George McClellan as a Captain. His photographs of the battles of Antietam, Fredericksburg, Gettysburg and Petersburg, among others, are classics and he published a two-volume set of them after the war. He later became the official photographer of the Union Pacific Railroad and took many photographs of Western scenes and people, including notable Native Americans.

Francis Frith, 'The Lake District', comprising 29 albumen prints, mounted on 13 card leaves, c1886, prints 7½ x 11½in (19 x 29cm).
£200–240 / €290–340 $340–400 ⚒ RTo

Christopher S. German, 'Portrait of Lincoln', varnished salt print, mounted, in a giltwood frame, American, 1858, 8 x 6in (20.5 x 15cm).
£4,250–5,100 €6,100–7,300 $7,200–8,600 ⚒ S(NY)

◄ **Bert Hardy,** 'The Gorbals. Europe's Worst Slum. Two Boys on a Shopping Errand', silver print, signed in ink, the reverse with photographer's Limpsfield Chart wetstamp, 1948, printed later, 12 x 16in (30.5 x 40.5cm).
£1,900–2,250 €2,750–3,250 $3,200–3,800 ⚒ S(O)

Alexander Hesler, 'Abraham Lincoln', in a painted frame, slight damage, American, 1860, 26½ x 19½in (67.5 x 49.5cm).
£390–460 / €560–660
$650–770 JDJ

Lewis W. Hine, 'Glass Works Boy, Night Shift, Indiana', matted, titled and numbered '90' by the photographer in pencil on the reverse, 1908, 6¾ x 4¾in (17 x 12cm).
£1,950–2,350
€2,800–3,350
$3,300–3,950 S(NY)

André Kertész, 'Nat. Museum Garden Budapest Oct 30 – 1919', silver print, titled and dated in pencil on the reverse, with photographer's wetstamp, Hungarian, 1919, printed later, 9¾ x 7¾in (25 x 19.5cm).
£480–570 / €690–820
$800–960 S(O)

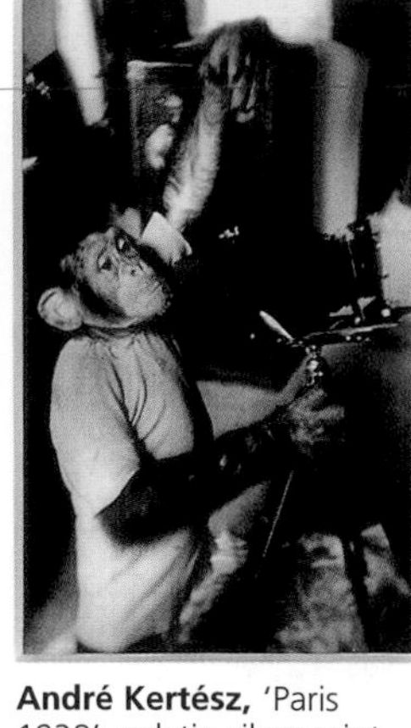

André Kertész, 'Paris 1928', gelatin silver print, printed c1980, French, 9½ x 6in (24 x 15cm).
£810–900 / €1,150–1,300
$1,350–1,500 RMe
André Kertész was born in Budapest in 1894 and served as a photographer with the Hungarian army in WWI. He then moved to Paris and was a great influence on Brassaï and Cartier-Bresson. He emigrated to the United States in 1936 and became an American citizen in 1944.

Heinrich Kühn, 'The Reaper', matted, bromoll print on tissue, signed and dated by the photographer in pencil, Austrian, c1930, 11¼ x 8½in (28.5 x 21.5cm).
£2,650–3,200
€3,800–4,600
$4,500–5,400 S(NY)

Jacques-Henri Lartigue, 'Simone', silver print, signed in ink, French, 1913, printed later, 12 x 16in (30.5 x 40.5cm), framed and glazed.
£960–1,150 / €1,400–1,650
$1,600–1,950 S(O)

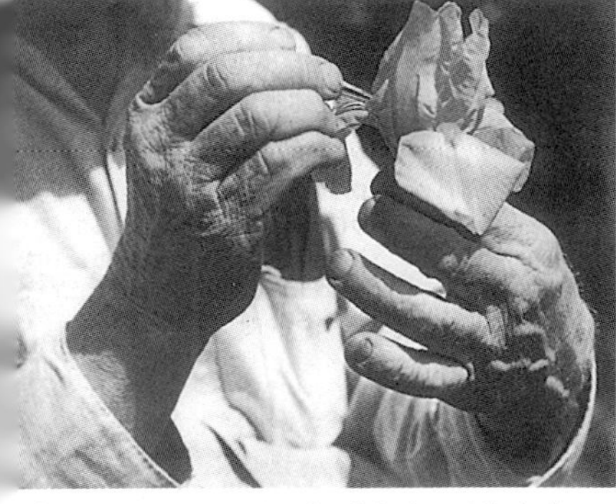

Alma Lavenson, 'Hands of Sydney Mitchell, iris breeder', matted, signed twice, titled and dated by the photographer in pencil on the reverse, framed, American, 1932, 8 x 10in (20.5 x 25.5cm).
£1,750–2,100 / €2,500–3,000
$2,950–3,500 S(NY)

► **Gaspard-Félix Tournachon (Nadar),** 'Sarah Bernhardt', Woodburytype, mounted on paper, French, 1880s, 5¾ x 4in (14.5 x 10cm), framed and glazed.
£330–390 / €470–560
$550–650 S(O)

William Notman, 'The Montreal Snow-Shoe Club', composite albumen print, impressed mark of the photographer, Canadian, 19thC, 6 x 8¾in (15 x 22cm), in an ebonized and gilt frame.
£140–165 / €200–240
$240–280 PFK

◄ **Timothy H. O'Sullivan,** 'Snake River Canyon, Idaho – View From Above Shoshone Falls', No. 25, US Army Corp of Engineers Expedition, mounted, American, 1874, 8 x 10¾in (20.5 x 27.5cm).
£470–560 / €670–800
$790–940 JDJ

Paul Outerbridge Jnr, 'Scrubbing The Hull', colour carbro print, with photographer's estate stamp, numbered '810' in an unidentified hand in pencil on the reverse, American, c1937, 16½ x 12¾in (42 x 32.5cm).
£4,250–5,100
€6,100–7,300
$7,100–8,500 S(NY)

Norman Parkinson, 'Lady Melissa and Lady Caroline Wyndham-Quin posing in Sybil Connolly dresses, the little dining room, Petworth', silver print, mounted on board, signed in ink, 1954, printed later, 20 x 16in (51 x 40.5cm), framed and glazed.
£1,000–1,200 / €1,450–1,700
$1,700–2,000 S(O)

Pascal Sebah, 'Grande Pyramide de Cheops a Gyzeh', albumen print, mounted on album page, Turkish, c1877, 10¼ x 13¼in (26 x 33.5cm), framed and glazed.
£330–390 / €470–560
$550–650 S(O)

Plate, 'Singhalese Beauty', platinum print, French, c1880, 9 x 11in (23 x 28cm).
£220–250 / €320–360
$370–420 ⊞ RMe

Robertson & Beato, 'Mount Katam & La Mosquee D'Omar', albumen print, signed in the negative, c1858, 10 x 11½in (25.5 x 29cm).
£840–1,000 / €1,200–1,400
$1,400–1,650 S(O)

Man Ray, Study of 'Danger/Dancer' and Other Works, inscribed 'To André Breton' by the photographer in pencil on the reverse, American, c1920, 4¾ x 3in (12 x 7.5cm).
£6,700–8,000
€9,600–11,500
$11,200–13,400 S(NY)

August Sander, 'Young Farmers', silver print, titled, dated, inscribed 'Antlitz der Zeit' and printed in 1978 by Günther Sander, German, 1914, 12 x 9½in (30.5 x 24cm), framed and glazed.
£960–1,150
€1,400–1,650
$1,600–1,950 S(O)

Count Vittorio Sella, 'K2', silver print, with climbers' signatures, stamped 'Istituto di Fotografia Alpina' on the reverse, Italian, 1909, printed 1954, 15½ x 11¾in (39.5 x 30cm).
£1,100–1,300
€1,600–1,850
$1,850–2,200 S(O)
This is one of a limited number of prints issued in 1954 to celebrate the conquest of K2 by the Italian climbers whose signatures appear on it.

► **Anon,** 'Man with Skull', a quarter-plate daguerreotype, later seal, in a leather case with gilt detail, inscribed 'Feb 1852', 4¼ x 3¼in (11 x 8.5cm).
£3,000–3,600
€4,300–5,100
$5,000–6,000 S(NY)

Carleton E. Watkins, 'Yosemite Woods and River', albumen print, with later inscription, American, 19thC, 21 x 15½in (53.5 x 39.5cm), framed.
£240–290 / €340–410
$400–480 JDJ

Anon, 'The Keyboard Musician', a sixth-plate daguerreotype, with an old seal, cased, 1840s, 3¼ x 2¾in (8.5 x 7cm).
£1,750–2,100
€2,500–3,000
$2,950–3,550 S(NY)

Anon, 'Girl in Paisley Shawl', a sixth-plate daguerreotype, in a signed leather case, c1850, 3¼ x 2¾in (8.5 x 7cm).
£200–240 / €290–340
$340–400 JDJ

◄ **Anon,** 'Two Girls Standing in Matching Dresses', a quarter-plate daguerreotype, gilt matt, in a velvet-lined tooled leather case, 1850s, 4¼ x 3¼in (11 x 8.5cm).
£420–500 / €600–720
$710–840 S(O)

Anon, 'The Military Trombonist', a quarter-plate daguerreotype, hand-tinted, with gilt detail, later seal, in a thermoplastic case, American, 1850s, 4¼ x 3¼in (11 x 8.5cm).
£1,750–2,100 / €2,500–3,000
$2,950–3,500 S(NY)

Anon, 'J. S. Boyd and Mr Strandley with flute and sheet music', sixth-plate daguerreotype, with inscription, later seal, cased, American, dated 1857, 3¼ x 2¾in (8.5 x 7cm).
£1,600–1,900 / €2,300–2,750
$2,700–3,200 S(NY)

Anon, 'New York, End of Wall, Central Park', albumen print, mounted on paper with later overmount, probably 1870s, 6 x 7¾in (15 x 19.5cm).
£380–450 / €550–650
$640–760 S(O)

► **Anon,** an albumen photograph of Stonehenge, mounted, slight damage, with Miell's label on reverse, c1870, 7 x 11¾in (18 x 30cm).
£190–220 / €270–320
$320–370 DW

Anon, a photograph of David Livingstone's coffin on board the SS *Calcutta* accompanied by Jacob Wainwright, an African member of his expedition, albumen print, mounted on paper, slight damage, 1874, 6¾ x 8¼in (17 x 21cm).
£840–1,000 / €1,200–1,400
$1,400–1,650 S

Anon, 'Chinese woman with bound feet', albumen print, c1875, 10 x 8in (25.5 x 20.5cm).
£400–450 / €580–650
$670–760 RMe

Anon, 'View in China', albumen print, probably 1870s, 8¼ x 10½in (21 x 26.5cm).
£310–370 / €440–530
$520–620 S(O)

Anon, 'Mode of dressing hair', albumen print, Kashmir, 1875–80, 8 x 6in (20.5 x 15cm).
£180–200 / €260–290
$300–330 RMe

Anon, a cabinet photograph of Geronimo posing with a cut-down musket, back-stamped 'A. Mancel, Pensacola', slight damage, American, c1887, 6½ x 4¼in (16.5 x 11cm).
£1,050–1,250
€1,500–1,800
$1,750–2,100 JDJ

◄ **Anon,** a portrait of Queen Alexandra's family, Danish, dated 1902, 7 x 9in (18 x 23cm).
£670–750 / €960–1,100
$1,100–1,250 AEL

Anon, a panoramic photograph of Cape Town, in four sections, slight wear, c1905, 8¼ x 43in (21 x 109cm), mounted, framed and glazed.
£1,000–1,200 / €1,450–1,750
$1,700–2,000 S

Arms & Armour

Armour

◄ **A three-quarter armour,** Nuremberg stamp to breastplate, German, c1560.
£13,400–14,900
€19,300–21,500
$22,000–25,000 ⊞ WSA

► **A horseman's composite armour,** c1575.
£17,000–19,000
€25,000–28,000
$29,000–32,000 ⊞ TLA
This armour was originally made in the Elizabethan era but used in the English Civil War with an adapted 'death's head' helmet.

A pikeman's armour, damaged, German, Nuremberg, c1600.
£4,250–5,100
€6,100–7,300
$7,200–8,600 ⚒ Herm

A gorget, south German/Italian, c1560, 13¼in (33.5cm) wide.
£1,250–1,500 / €1,800–2,150
$2,100–2,500 ⚒ Herm

A burgonet, Flemish, c1580.
£5,200–5,800 / €7,500–8,400
$8,700–9,700 ⊞ FAC
This helmet demonstrates many characteristics of Flemish construction including knurled main edges, and may have been made in Antwerp.

A cabasset, with brass rosettes, acid cleaned, slight damage, struck with armourer's mark, c1600.
£590–700 / €850–1,000
$990–1,150 ⚒ WAL

A cabasset, with brass rivet heads, acid cleaned, struck with crowned armourer's mark, c1600.
£600–720 / €860–1,000
$1,000–1,200 ⚒ WAL

A lobster-tailed pot, with two-piece skull and three-bar face-guard, later ear pieces, with domed steel lining rivets, struck with the letter 'N', mid-17thC, 14¾in (37.5cm) high.
£1,500–1,800 / €2,200–2,600
$2,500–3,000 ⚒ B(Kn)

A painted funerary helmet, the two-piece skull with tall comb and rivetted spike, the visor fixed with four bars and rivet heads, slight damage, covered with paint, 17thC.
£1,500–1,800
€2,200–2,600
$2,500–3,000 ⚒ WAL
These helmets were made to hang as 'funerary achievements' over tombs inside churches; the spikes were for securing it to a timber beam.

◄ **A harquebusier's helmet,** with 13 overlapping plates, eastern European, c1680.
£3,900–4,300 / €5,600–6,200
$6,500–7,200 ⊞ FAC
Helmets of this form were used in both Poland and Hungary.

Edged Weapons

A ballock dagger, with a tapered wood grip, the brass pommel decorated with a radial line and punch work, north European, 1450–1500, blade 10in (25.5cm) long.
£2,900–3,250 / €4,200–4,700
$4,900–5,500 ⊞ FAC

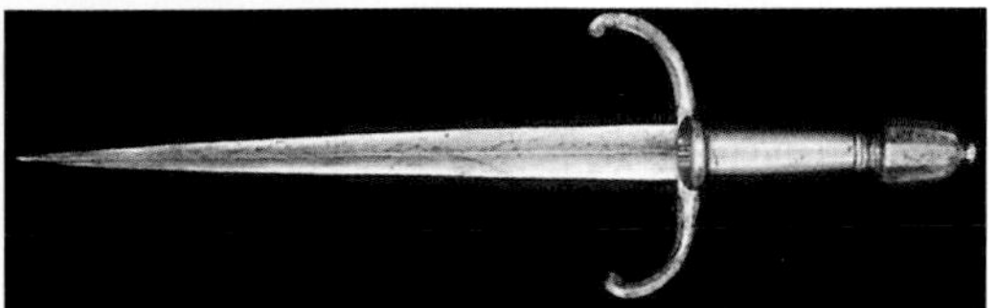

A left-hand dagger, the hilt with arched faceted quillons and side ring, the grip bound with silver wire, Italian, early 17thC, blade 12in (30.5cm) long
£1,500–1,800 / €2,150–2,600
$2,500–3,000 ⚒ B(Kn)

A sword/rapier, the iron hilt with double shell guard, with wooden grip, rust-patinated, American, 1650–1700, blade 35in (89cm) long.
£880–980 / €1,250–1,400
$1,500–1,650 ⊞ FAC
The guard and probably the blade of this sword are European but it was assembled or re-manufactured in Colonial America and the pommel and grip added, probably c1700. It was necessary for the Colonials to take up arms against the British on a regular basis throughout the period, although most occurrences were settled peacefully.

A matross cutlass, 17thC, 32in (81.5cm) long.
£810–900 / €1,150–1,300
$1,350–1,500 ⊞ TLA
Matrosses were the swords used by the guards of the Royal Navy gunner's mates.

A plug bayonet, with scabbard, late 17thC, 23in (58.5cm) long.
£1,800–2,000 / €2,600–2,900
$3,000–3,350 ⊞ WSA

A left-hand dagger, Spanish, 1570–85, 11in (28cm) long.
£5,700–6,300 / €8,200–9,100
$9,600–10,600 ⊞ FAC
This dagger was made *en suite* with a rapier and was used for duelling.

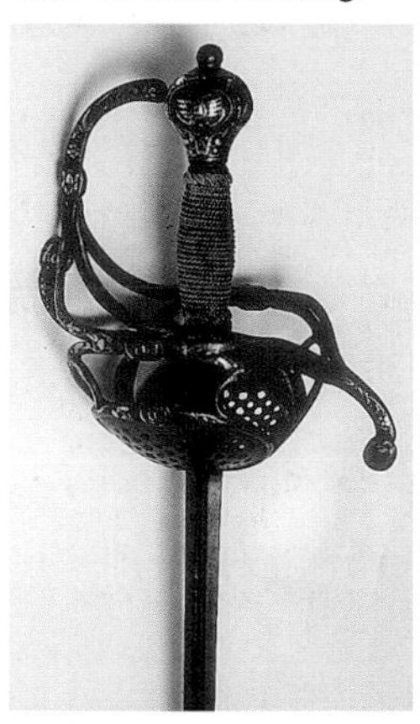

A rapier, c1620, 48in (122cm) long.
£3,600–4,000
€5,200–5,800
$6,000–6,700 ⊞ ARB

A mortuary backsword, the blade with double fullers, c1640, 32in (81.5cm) long.
£3,600–4,000
€5,200–5,800
$6,000–6,700 ⊞ WSA

◄ **A cup-hilt rapier,** Spanish, c1650, 48in (122cm) long.
£3,650–4,400 / €5,300–6,400
$6,100–7,300 ⚒ Herm

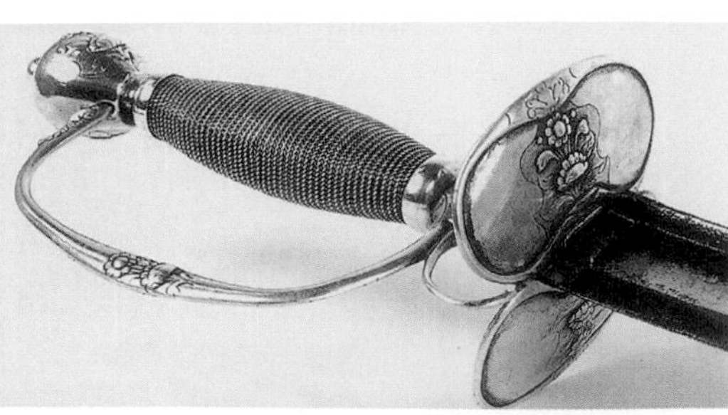

A curving sword, the silver handle embossed with flowers, marked 'GW', possibly George Weir, London 1723, 36in (91.5cm) long.
£940–1,100 / €1,350–1,600
$1,600–1,850 JNic

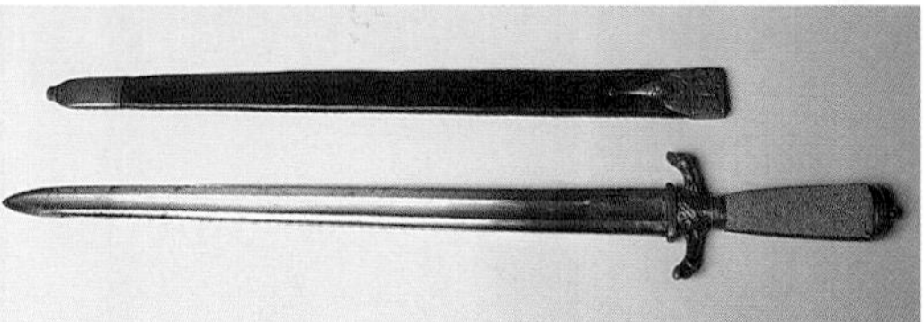

A silver-hilted hunting hanger, with shagreen grip, the locket chased with hunting scenes, north European, c1740, 23in (58.5cm) long.
£1,350–1,500 / €1,950–2,150
$2,250–2,500 WSA

A rapier shortsword, with silver hilt, 18thC, 38in (96.5cm) long.
£1,050–1,200 / €1,500–1,700
$1,750–2,000 TLA
General George Washington used an almost identical sword.

A rococo sword, with a silver swept hilt, Italian, Turin, c1780, 36½in (92.5cm) long.
£1,350–1,600 / €1,950–2,300
$2,250–2,700 DORO

▶ **A smallsword,** the brass hilt with traces of original gilding, with a wire-bound grip, the blade etched with flowers, c1725, blade 29¼in (74.5cm) long.
£350–420 / €500–600
$590–700 WAL

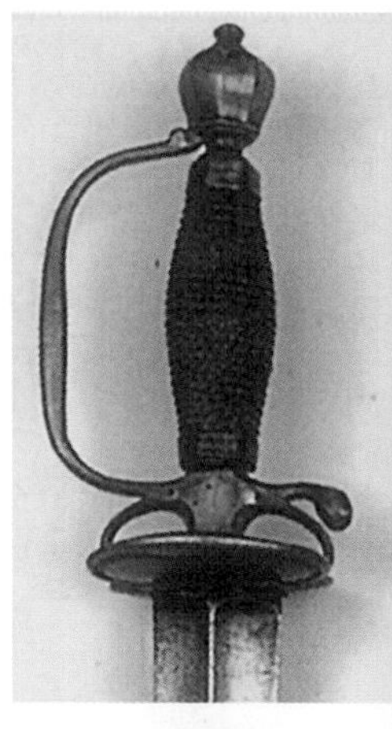

A hanger, with silver hilt, the expanded pommel cap with high-relief horseman motif, with a gnarled antler grip, king's head mark, German, c1760, 18½in (47cm) long.
£510–570 / €730–820
$860–960 FAC

A naval artillery sword, the brass hilt with lion's head pommel and bone-form guard, American, c1780, 28½in (72.5cm) long.
£1,100–1,250
€1,600–1,800
$1,850–2,100 FAC

A rapier shortsword, embellished with over 600 gold stars, 18thC, 38in (96.5cm) long.
£1,050–1,200
€1,500–1,700
$1,750–2,000 TLA

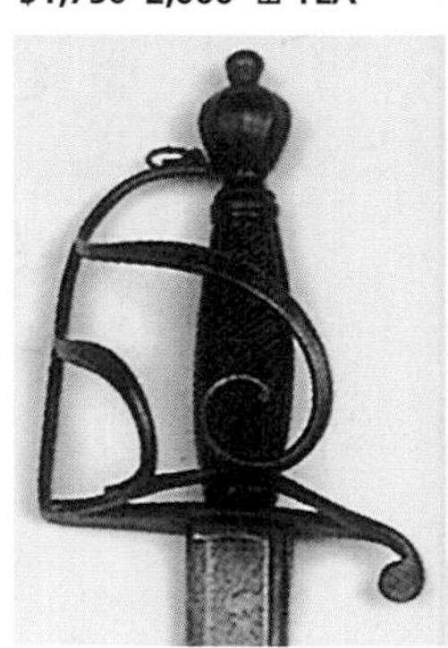

A cavalry officer's sword, the single-edged blade etched with martial trophies and foliate ornaments, the steel hilt with an ebony grip, tip slightly shortened and one scrolling side bar incomplete, late 18thC, blade 32¼in (82cm) long.
£470–560 / €680–810
$790–940 WAL

▶ **A midshipman's dirk,** with an ivory handle, the stiletto blade in a gilt-metal sheath cast in relief with the bust of a classical warrior, c1800, 7¼in (18.5cm) long.
£330–390 / €470–560
$550–650 G(L)

A naval dirk, c1800, 13in (33cm) long.
£420–470 / €600–670
$710–790 MDL

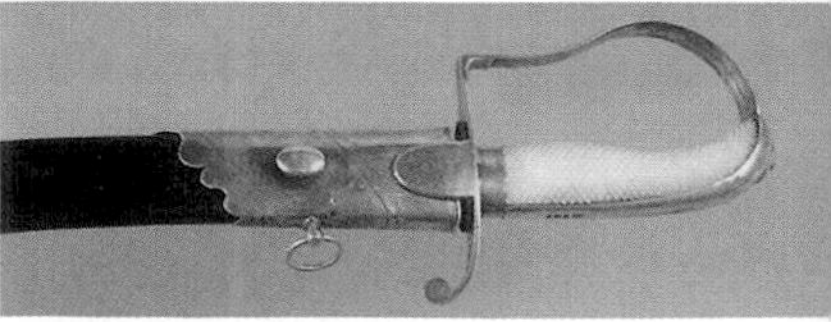

A cavalry sword, by Johnstons Sword Cutlers, with single-edged curved blade, the silver-mounted scabbard with later leather, initialled 'JJ', London 1803, blade 30½in (77.5cm) long.
£640–770 / €920–1,100
$1,100–1,300 L

An NCO's sword, with a brass hilt and leather-covered grips, worn, American, c1812, 27½in (70cm) long.
£460–520 / €660–750
$770–870 ⊞ FAC

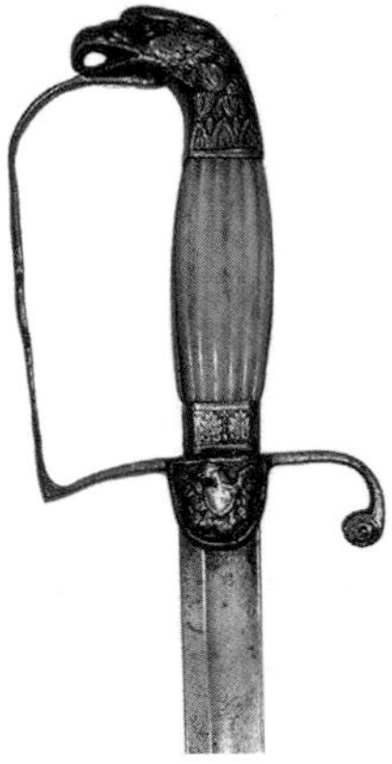

An officer's sword, the spadroon blade etched with sprigs of foliage, the brass hilt with eagle-head pommel and bone grip, American, 1815–30, blade 29in (73.5cm) long.
£580–650 / €830–930
$970–1,100 ⊞ FAC

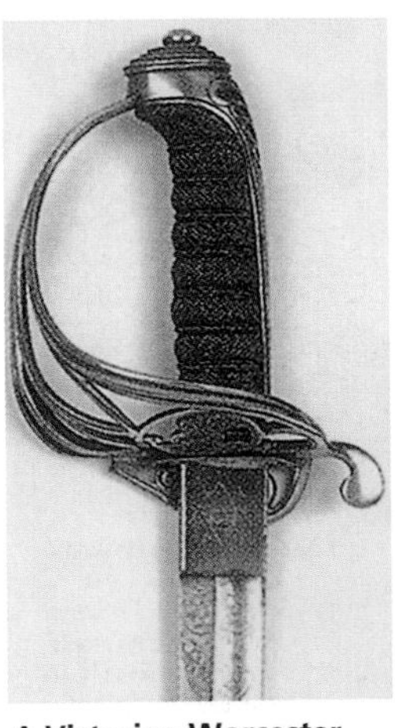

A Victorian Worcester Rifles officer's 1827 pattern sword, by Dolan & Co, etched with a crown and 'VR', 'Worcester Rifles' and foliage, with wirebound fishskin grip, the leather scabbard with nickel mounts, blade 32½in (82.5cm) long.
£350–420 / €500–600
$590–700 ⚒ WAL

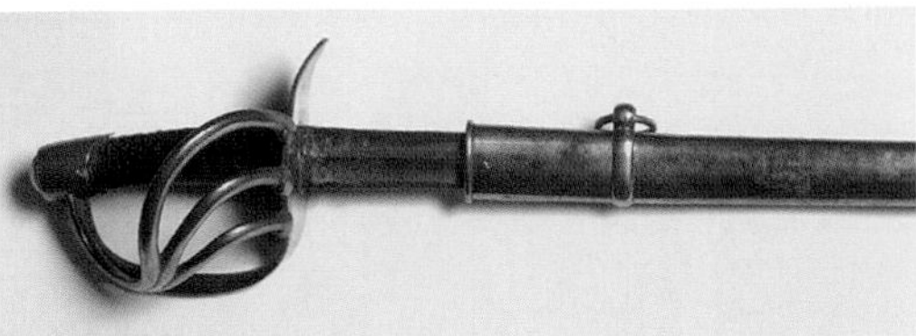

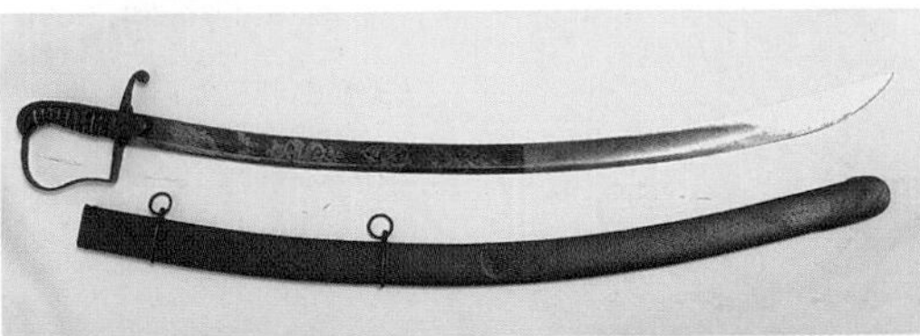

A 1796 patent cavalry sword, c1815, 39in (99cm) long.
£720–800 / €1,050–1,150
$1,200–1,350 ⊞ ChM

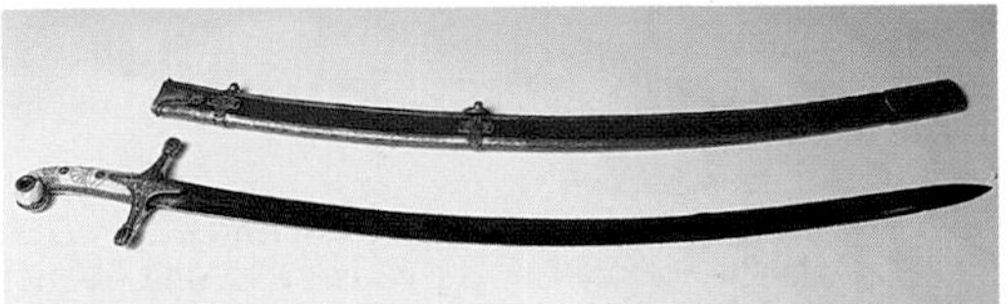

An officer's mameluke-hilted sword, the blade etched to the King's Hussars, c1830, 37in (94cm) long.
£1,800–2,000 / €2,600–2,900
$3,000–3,350 ⊞ WSA

A naval officer's dirk, the double-edged blade with gilt-brass hilt, with a turned bone grip, the gilt-brass sheath engraved with flowerheads, gilding worn, Continental, c1830, blade 8in (20.5cm) long.
£360–430 / €520–620
$600–720 ⚒ WAL

A sword, the silver-plated hilt with an eagle-head pommel and bone grip, the blade decorated with patriotic motifs, the leather scabbard with silver-plated mounts inscribed 'Capt. A. Gallatin Blanchard/USA', c1847, American, blade 32½in (82.5cm) long.
£3,100–3,700 / €4,450–5,300
$5,200–6,200 ⚒ JDJ
Blanchard was born in Massachusetts. He attended West Point where his classmates were Robert E. Lee and Joseph E. Johnston. He later moved to Louisiana, joined the militia and during the Mexican War served with distinction at the Battle of Monterey and Vera Cruz. At the outbreak of the Civil War he joined the Confederate Infantry and later was promoted to Brigadier General.

A naval cutlass, standard pattern, the brass hilt with scales, the pommel with eagle motif, blade marked 'U. S. N.', guard stamped '74' and stipple marked '297 3 Div', some staining, American, c1841, 21in (53.5cm) long.
£520–580 / €750–830
$870–970 ⊞ FAC

◀ **A Napoleonic cuirassier's sword,** French, c1814, 45in (114.5cm) long.
£860–950 / €1,200–1,350
$1,450–1,600 ⊞ TLA

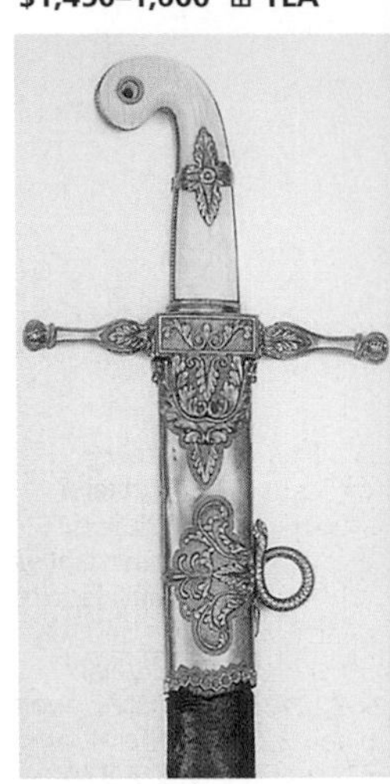

An officer's mameluke-hilted sword, with curved, fullered single-edged blade and gilt-copper-mounted shagreen-covered wooden scabbard, early 19thC, blade 31in (78.5cm) long.
£830–980 / €1,200–1,400
$1,400–1,650 ⚒ B(Kn)

A military sword and sheath, by Vernon & Cameron, with a scale and copper wire handle, the blade decorated with a crown above 'VR' and foliage, 19thC, 38in (96.5cm) long.
£135–150 / €195–230
$230–270 ⚒ SJH

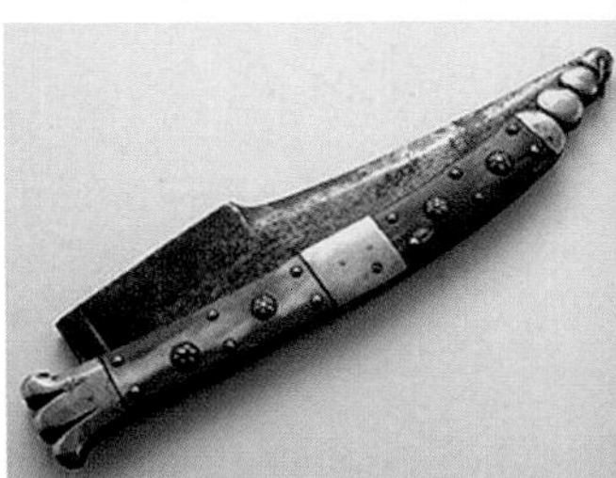

A Narafa folding knife, Spanish, 1850–80, 8in (20.5cm) closed.
£210–240 / €300–340
$350–400 ⊞ SPA

A Victorian infantry officer's 1845 pattern sword, by Lyon & Son, etched with a crown above 'VR' within scrolling frosted panels, with wire-bound fishskin grip and steel scabbard, slight rusting, worn, blade 32½in (82.5cm) long.
£220–260 / €320–370
$370–440 WAL

A Bowie knife, by Alexander Sheffield, the white metal hilt with shell pommel, the chequered horn grips with silver escutcheon engraved 'Capt. A. D. Robinson', the leather scabbard with white metal mounts engraved with the Southern Hemisphere and the button in the form of a whale, signed, mid-19thC, 15¼in (38.5cm) long.
£880–1,050 €1,250–1,500
$1,450–1,750 WD

◄ A Victorian officer's sword, with an infantry hilt and cavalry single-edged blade, with a fishskin grip and steel scabbard, slight rusting, stamped 'Mole Birmn', blade 32¾in (83cm) long.
£350–420 / €500–600
$590–700 WAL

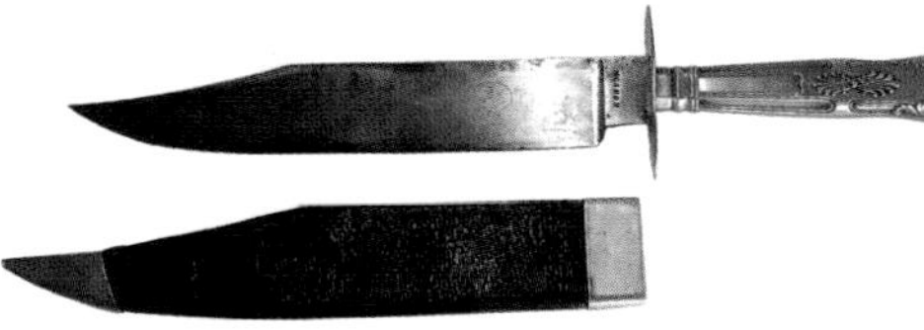

A Bowie knife, the blade by Hobson and etched 'Ask for nothing save what is right and submit to nothing that is wrong, draw me not in haste' and with an eagle, with King's pattern nickel hilt, the leather sheath with gilt mounts, 19thC, 13½in (34.5cm) long.
£1,050–1,250 / €1,500–1,800
$1,750–2,100 F&C

A sabre, German, 1914–18, 39in (99cm) long.
£440–500 / €630–720
$740–840 TLA

An infantry officer's 1897 pattern sword, by Mole, with 'GV' monogram, 1910–36, 38in (96.5cm) long.
£270–300 / €390–430
$450–500 SPA

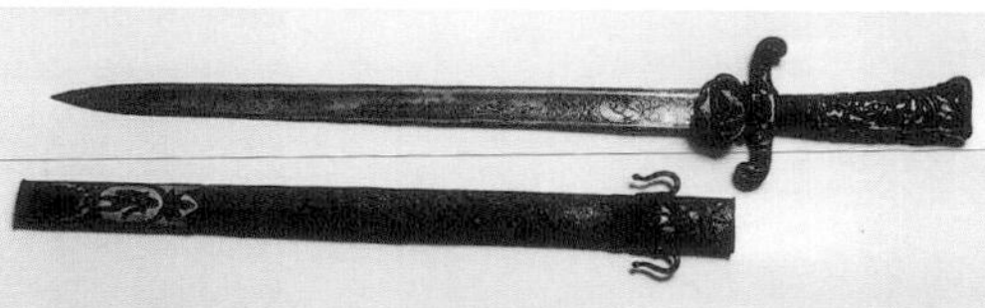

A hunting sword, the sharkskin scabbard with cut-steel handle and gilding, signed 'W. Clauberg à Solingen', German, c1870, 21in (53.5cm) long.
£3,150–3,500 / €4,500–5,000
$5,300–5,900 ARB
This German sword may have been made for a French client but it was also common to engrave blades with inscriptions in French, Italian or Latin in the 18th and 19th centuries.

A Bowie knife, by Joseph Rogers & Sons, with horn grip and German silver mounts, stamped, c1870, 12in (30.5cm) long.
£770–850 / €1,100–1,250
$1,300–1,450 MDL

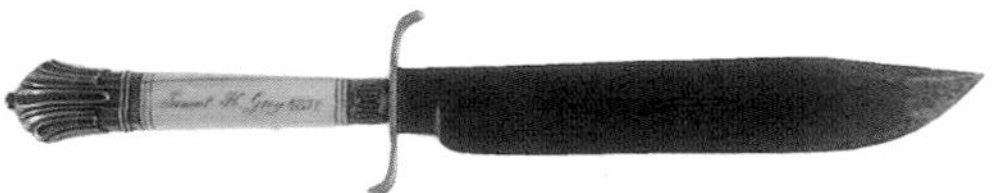

A Bowie knife, the ivory hilt engraved 'Samuel H. Grey 1877', with a silver pommel, marked 'Herbert / Robinson / Sheffield / Handforged', c1881, blade 8¾in (22cm) long.
£540–650 / €780–940
$910–1,100 JDJ

Firearms

A flintlock blunderbuss, with brass barrel and trigger guard, the lock marked 'Dublin Castle' and crowned 'GR', 18thC, 31in (78.5cm) long.
£350–420 / €500–600
$590–700 ⚒ LAY

A flintlock blunderbuss, by George Turner, with figured full stock, brass mounts and horn-tipped ramrod, signed in full and struck with an Irish registration mark beyond, later ramrod, Irish, Dublin, early 19thC, barrel 15¼in (38.5cm) long.
£700–840 / €1,000–1,200
$1,200–1,400 ⚒ B(Kn)

A flintlock blunderbuss, with brass barrel, c1820, 30in (76cm) long.
£1,150–1,300 / €1,650–1,850
$1,950–2,200 ⊞ MDL

A flintlock blunderbuss, with walnut stock, engraved brass butt plate and trigger guard, original steel lockplate and ramrod, the brass flaring barrel with London proof marks, stock with clean break, 18thC, 28¾in (73cm) long.
£1,250–1,500 / €1,800–2,150
$2,100–2,500 ⚒ F&C

A blunderbuss, by Archer, with spring-loaded bayonet, c1790, 30in (76cm) long.
£2,150–2,400 / €3,100–3,450
$3,600–4,000 ⊞ TLA

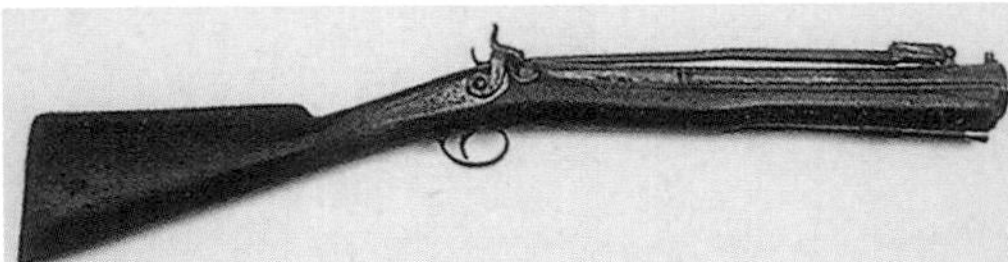

A percussion blunderbuss, with steel barrel, hinged bayonet, fully stocked with ramrod below, steel furniture and butt cap, signed 'Waterford', Irish, 19thC, barrel 16in (40.5cm) long.
£520–620 / €750–890
$870–1,050 ⚒ Bea

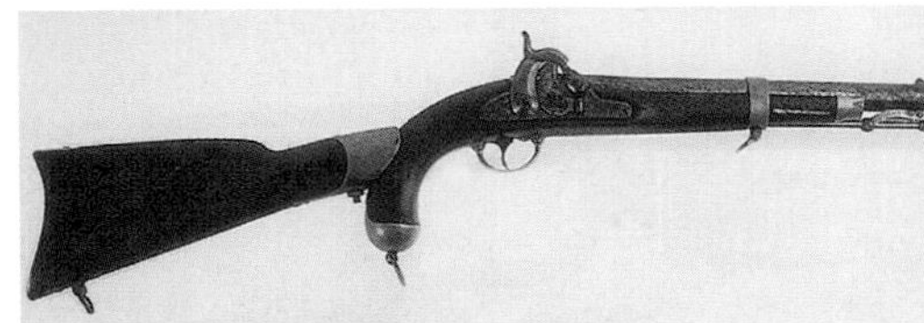

A .54 Springfield 1855 model pistol carbine, slight damage, American, 1855–56, barrel 12in (30.5cm) long.
£2,200–2,650 / €3,150–3,800
$3,700–4,450 ⚒ JDJ

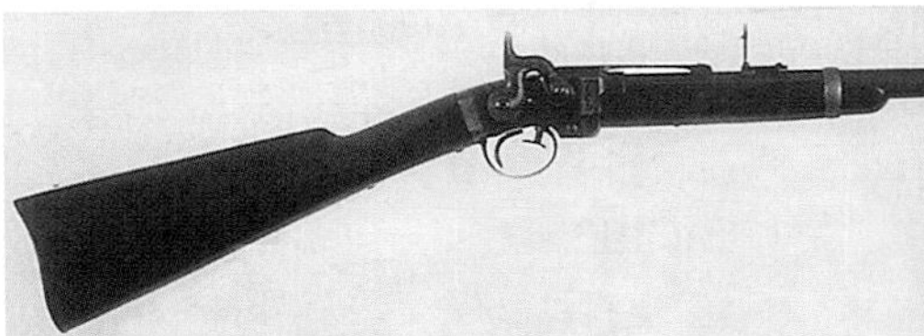

A .50 Smith carbine, by Mass Arms Co, inscribed 'JM', American, c1860, barrel 21½in (54.5cm) long.
£950–1,100 / €1,350–1,600
$1,600–1,850 ⚒ JDJ

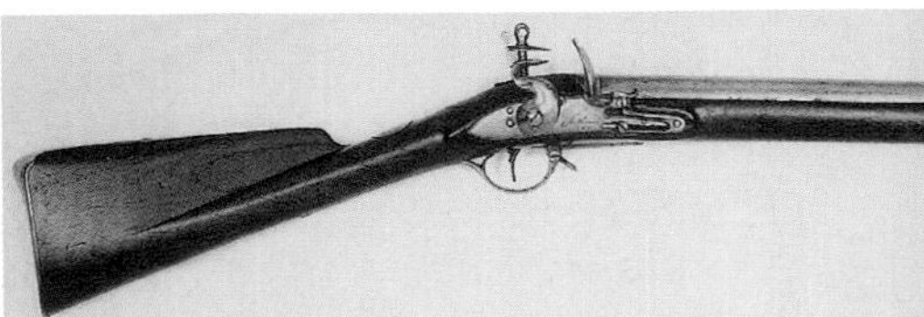

A 10 bore Short Land pattern flintlock service musket, by Ketland & Co, for a volunteer regiment, with figured full stock, brass mounts, steel ramrod, c1800, barrel 41¾in (106cm) long, with a socket bayonet stamped 'Woolley'
£1,400–1,650 / €2,000–2,350
$2,350–2,750 ⚒ B(Kn)

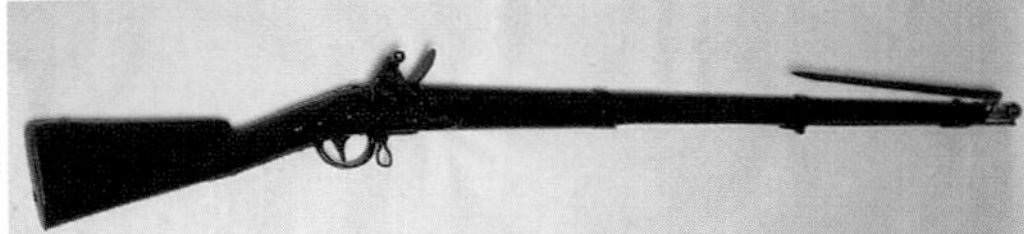

A Harpers Ferry flintlock musket, American, c1812, 57in (145cm) long.
£1,700–1,900 / €2,450–2,750
$2,850–3,200 ⊞ TLA
This musket dates from the war of 1812 between Great Britain and America, which was fought mainly on the Canadian border.

► **A flintlock coaching blunderbuss pistol,** by Barwick, Norwich, with brass barrel, 1798–1805, 13½in (34.5cm) long.
£990–1,100 / €1,400–1,600
$1,650–1,850 ⊞ SPA

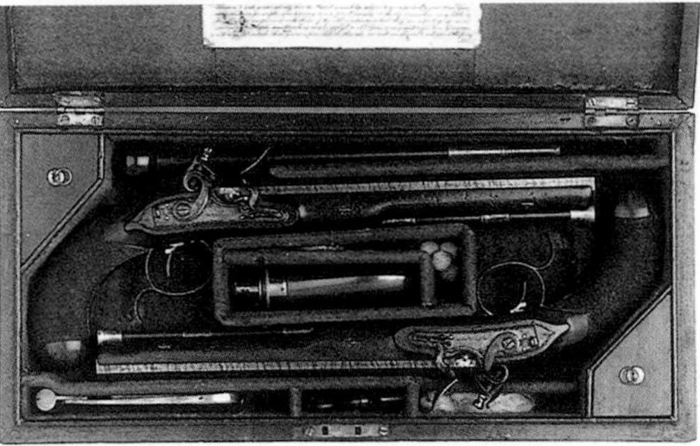

A pair of 28 bore flintlock duelling pistols, by Jas Wilkinson, London, the walnut full stocks with chequered butts and steel mounts, the brass ramrods with exposed steel worms, small repairs, c1815, 15in (38cm) long, in original mahogany case, with a later copper flask, pincer mould, screwdriver and cleaning rod.
£6,800–8,100 / €9,800–11,600
$11,400–13,600 ⚒ WAL

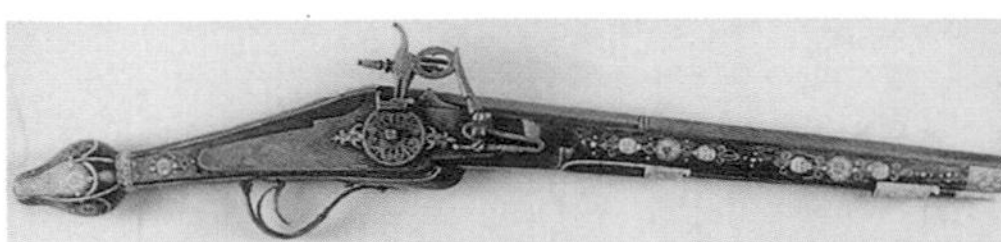

A wheel lock pistol, the walnut stock inlaid with bone, German, dated 1617, 26in (66cm) long.
£4,100–4,900 / €5,900–7,000
$6,900–8,200 ⚒ DORO

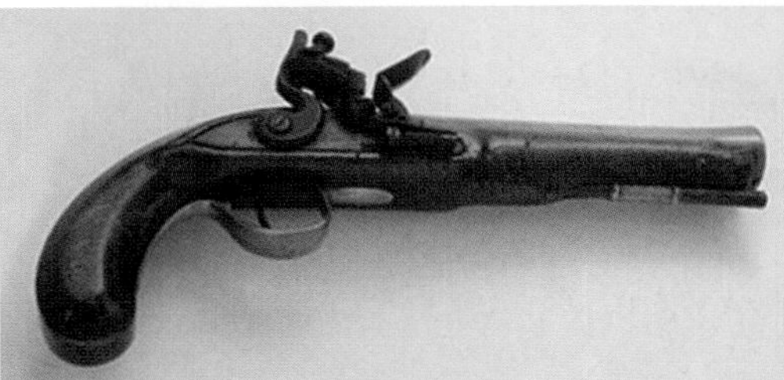

A sea service pistol, with walnut full stock and brass mounts, c1805, 19in (48.5cm) long.
£1,800–2,000 / €2,600–2,900
$3,000–3,350 ⊞ ARB

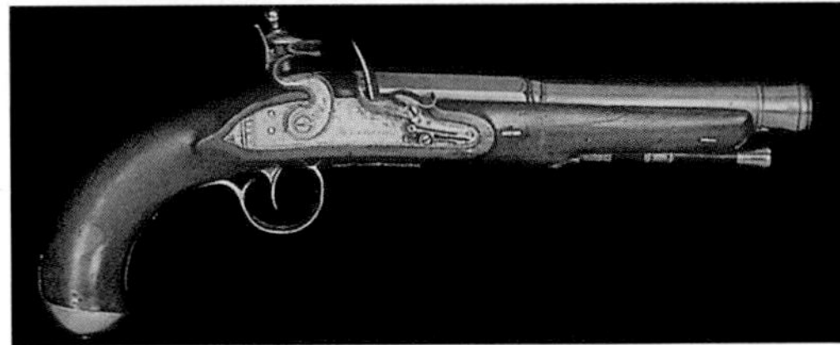

A flintlock blunderbuss pistol, by Meredith, London, with two-stage brass barrel, figured full stock, engraved brass mounts with pineapple finials, brass ramrod pipes, Birmingham proof marks, early 19thC, barrel 8in (20.5cm) long.
£1,000–1,200 / €1,450–1,700
$1,700–2,000 ⚒ B(Kn)

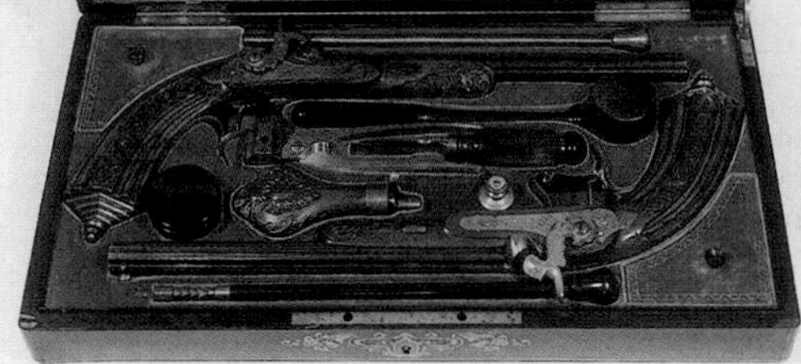

A pair of target or duelling pistols, the walnut stocks with ribbed grips and carved with leaves, the ornately chased percussion action inscribed 'Lissoride Arqr. A Pau', French, c1830, 16½in (42cm) long, in a brass-inlaid rosewood case with accessories.
£3,950–4,700 / €5,700–6,800
$6,600–7,900 ⚒ AH

A pair of Wender flintlock turnover pistols, probably by Samuel Brummett, Worksop, c1830, 13in (33cm) long.
£4,500–5,000 / €6,500–7,200
$7,600–8,400 ⊞ WSA

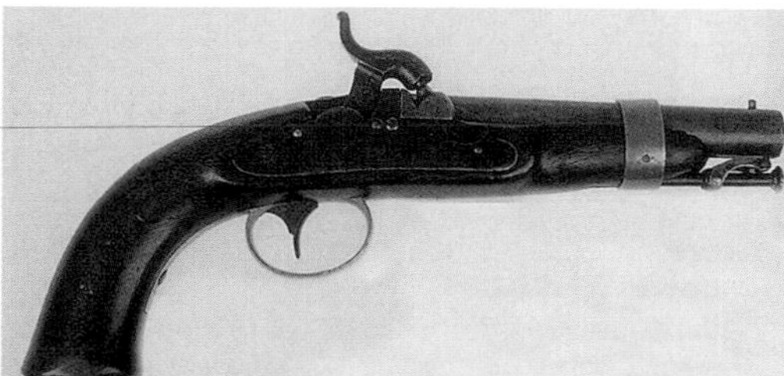

A .52 Ames 1842 model boxlock naval pistol, with later sight and band, repairs, American, dated 1844, barrel 6in (15cm) long.
£470–560 / €680–810
$790–940 JDJ

A British cavalry volunteer percussion pistol, with swivel ramrod, rifle barrel and walnut stock, marked 'V PEI 30', Canadian, Prince Edward Island, dated 1855, 13in (33cm) long.
£1,150–1,300 / €1,650–1,850
$1,950–2,200 ⊞ ARB

◄ A .41 Colt No. 3 Derringer pistol, American, c1875, 5in (12.5cm) long.
£630–700 / €900–1,000
$1,050–1,200 ⊞ WSA

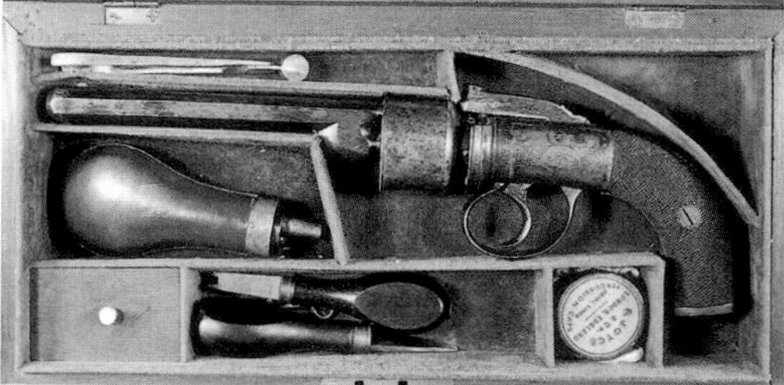

An 80 bore Laird patent transitional percussion revolver, engraved with foliage, chequered walnut grips and colour-hardened butt cap with engraved trap cover, marked, c1830, barrel 6in (15cm) long, in original mahogany case with accessories.
£1,800–2,150 / €2,600–3,100
$3,000–3,600 WD

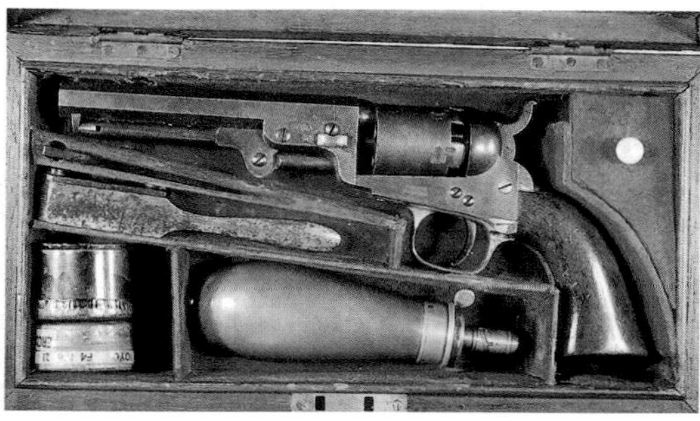

A .31 Colt 1849 model London pocket percussion revolver, with an iron silver-plated trigger-guard and back strap, walnut grip, in original mahogany case with accessories, c1849, barrel 5in (12.5cm) long.
£1,500–1,800 / €2,150–2,600
$2,500–3,000 WD

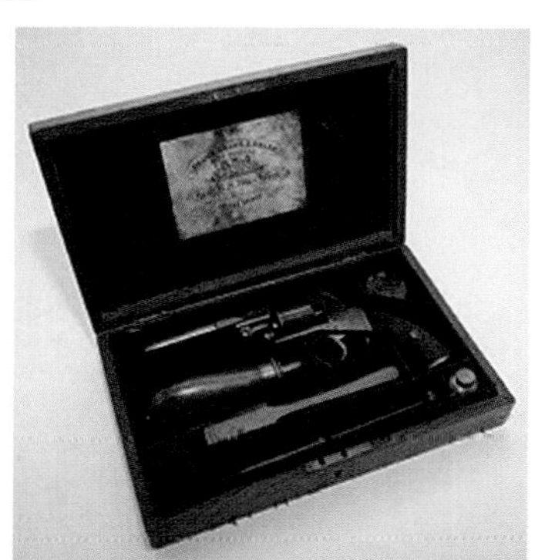

► An 80 bore five-shot percussion revolver, by Bentley, cased, with tools, c1850, box 7 x 11½in (18 x 29cm).
£1,350–1,500
€1,950–2,150
$2,250–2,500
⊞ SPA

A Victorian .45 Baker 1852 patent six-shot percussion revolver, 11in (28cm) long.
£700–790 / €1,000–1,150
$1,200–1,350 ⊞ ABCM

ARMS & ARMOUR

A .31 Colt 1849 pocket revolver, barrel address 'Sam Colt-New York U.S. America', 1864, barrel 5in (12.5cm) long.
£270–320 / €390–470
$450–540 COBB

A .22 Ponds patent front-loading seven-shot revolver, the brass frame with sheath trigger and varnished walnut grips, marked, American, c1870, barrel 3½in (9cm) long.
£370–440 / €530–630
$620–740 WD

A .35 Colt-type Brevette naval revolver, with bone handle and brass mounts, the steel barrel with foliate decoration and stamp, Belgian, late 19thC, 13in (33cm) long.
£140–165 / €200–240
$240–280 G(L)

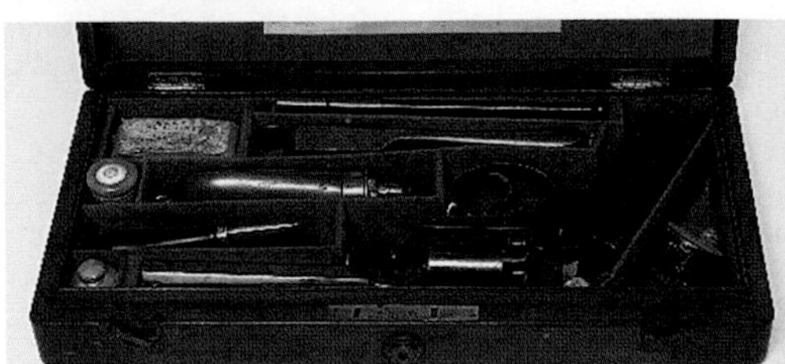

A 54 bore Adams patent revolver, by John Blissett, London, engraved maker's mark, the trigger strap engraved 'J. B.', c1885, box 7 x 14in (18 x 35.5cm).
£3,150–3,500 / €4,500–5,000
$5,300–5,900 MDL
This revolver possibly belonged to John Blissett himself.

Polearms & Axes

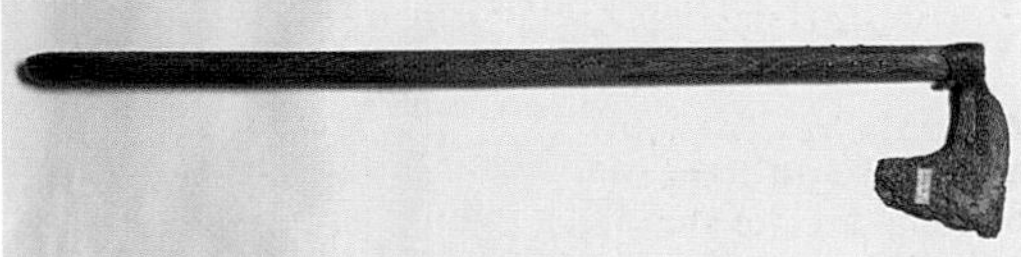

A battle-axe, with armourer's anchor marks, rehafted with antique oak, 12thC, 37in (94cm) long.
£810–900 / €1,150–1,300
$1,350–1,500 TLA

A partisan, the forged head on conical socket, chisel mark 'AN', French, 1350–1450, 102in (259cm) long.
£790–880 / €1,100–1,250
$1,350–1,500 FAC
'AN' is the mark of the Arsenal National repository of weapons which supported Napoleon's troops.

A halberd, on a later wooden staff, probably German, late 15thC, head 16in (40.5cm) long.
£2,250–2,700 / €3,250–3,900
$3,800–4,550 B(Kn)

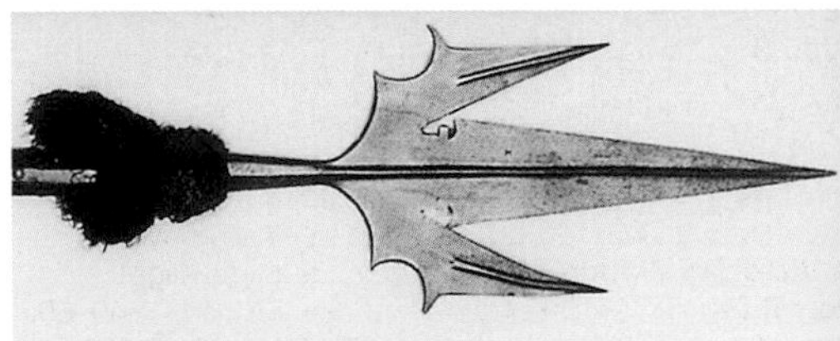

A corseca, on a wooden staff with traces of punched scrollwork, Italian, c1500, head 24in (61cm) long.
£2,100–2,500 / €3,000–3,600
$3,550–4,200 B(Kn)

A captain's leading staff, with pierced side wings, on a wooden haft, with small metal spike at base for steadying in the ground, 17thC, 52in (132cm) long.
£970–1,150 / €1,400–1,650
$1,600–1,900 WAL

A halberd, pierced with key motifs, the oak haft with beaded edge, Austrian, 1570–80, 104in (264cm) long.
£1,200–1,350 / €1,750–1,950
$2,000–2,250 FAC

► **An officer's gilt spontoon,** with original wooden haft, German, 18thC, 92½in (235cm) long.
£930–1,100 / €1,350–1,600
$1,550–1,850 Herm

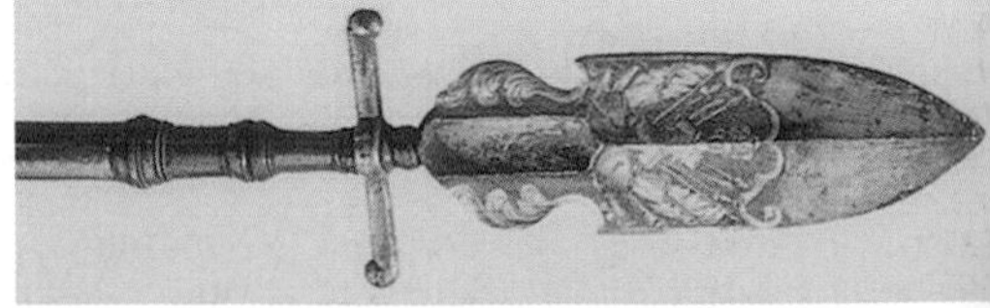

Militaria

Badges & Plates

An officer's gilt-brass shako plate, depicting a shield bearing the Imperial eagle, French, early 19thC.
£610–730 / €880–1,050
$1,050–1,250 DNW

A Marine Guards copper shako plate, depicting an eagle on a crowned anchor, French, early 19thC.
£300–360 / €430–520
$500–600 WAL

◄ **A 1st Madras Native Infantry officer's gilt shoulder belt plate,** with silver and gilt overlays, 1830–55.
£1,000–1,200
€1,450–1,750
$1,700–2,000 B(O)

An artillery officer's silver-plated helmet plate, depicting a double-headed eagle above a fused grenade, slight damage, Russian, 1840–60.
£270–320 / €390–460
$450–540 DNW

A Victorian Cinque Port Rifles other ranks' bi-metal shako badge.
£440–530 / €630–760
$740–890 WAL

A Worcestershire Rifle Volunteers silver-plated 1855 pattern shako plate, depicting the pear tree from the county arms, 1859–61.
£270–320 / €390–460
$450–540 DNW

A Victorian 6th West Suffolk RV Corps white metal helmet plate, slight damage.
£120–140 / €170–200
$200–240 WAL

A 30th Line Regiment officer's gilt-brass shako plate, with a shield bearing three fleur-de-lys, French, 1816–30.
£175–210 / €250–300
$290–350 DNW

A 1st Madras Native Infantry (Light Company) officer's bronze shoulder belt plate, with leather trim, 1830–55.
£640–770 / €920–1,100
$1,100–1,300 B(O)

An Irish Militia Westmeath Rifles other ranks' brass glengarry badge, pre-1881.
£120–140 / €170–200
$200–240 WAL

A 69th South Lincolnshire Regiment officer's gilt shoulder belt plate, overlaid with a silver beaded star, inscribed 'Waterloo Ava Bourbon India', with leather backing, 1826–55.
£1,650–1,950
€2,350–2,800
$2,700–3,250 DNW

A Victorian Marines Light Infantry other ranks' helmet plate, slight damage.
£165–195 / €240–280
$280–330 WAL

◄ **A Cardiff Rifle Volunteers, 10th Glamorgan, officer's silver-plated pouch belt plate,** bearing the city arms and inscribed 'Ich Dien' above the Prince of Wales's crest, 1860–83.
£640–770 / €920–1,100
$1,100–1,300 DNW

A Victorian 2nd Volunteer Battalion The Royal Sussex Regiment officer's silver-plated helmet plate, with enamel decoration.
£420–500 / €600–720
$700–840 WAL

Costume

An officer's patent leather snake belt, with embroidered gilt decoration, American, 19thC.
£340–400 / €490–580
$570–670 ⚒ JDJ

A drummer's coatee, repair and restoration, Russian, c1812.
£2,000–2,400
€2,900–3,450
$3,350–4,000 ⚒ WAL

A United States Cavalry short uniform jacket, lined with woven wool, with an interior pocket, marked on right sleeve 'H. Shafer/U.S./Inspector, slight damage, American, c1865.
£1,700–2,000
€2,450–2,900
$2,850–3,350 ⚒ JDJ

A Victorian Royal Engineers Lieutenant-Colonel's full dress uniform, comprising cocked hat, tunic, shoulder belt, waist belt and sling, with a leather suitcase marked 'Maj T. T. Oakes'.
£760–910 / €1,100–1,300
$1,250–1,500 ⚒ WAL

A Royal Engineers ceremonial jacket, the interior with label dated '1914'.
£70–80 / €100–115
$115–135 ⚒ AMB

An 8th Punjab Regiment 2nd Battalion three-piece mess kit, the jacket with four plated buttons and one silver collar badge, with waistcoat and overalls, c1935.
£300–360 / €430–510
$500–600 ⚒ DNW

◄ A WWII Air Transport Auxiliary pilot's tunic and sidecap, with gilt embroidered wings and two rank bars, integral belt with buckle, slight wear.
£440–520 / €630–750
$740–870 ⚒ WAL

A pair of military leather boots, by Moore Bros, Salisbury, c1910.
£105–120 / €150–170
$175–200 ⊞ MINN

Drums

A snare drum, painted with foliate decoration and an eagle on a patriotic shield, with an ivory peephole, maker's label 'Henry Eisele, successor to William Sempf manufacturer of base and snare drums, 209 & 211 Grand Street New York', American, c1865, 16in (40.5cm) diam.
£1,100–1,300 / €1,600–1,850
$1,850–2,200 ⚒ JDJ

A copper kettle drum, by V. A. Chaine, London, dated 1892, 26in (66cm) diam.
£540–600 / €780–860
$900–1,000 ⊞ Q&C

A 1st Battalion The Royal Munste Fusiliers half shallow drum, c1918 14in (35.5cm) wide.
£220–250 / €320–360
$370–420 ⊞ Q&C

► A 1st Battalion The Queen's Royal Regiment painted wood side drum, with regimental badges and 41 honour scrolls, with chords and tensioners, signed 'M. O. Donnell', c1950, 15in (38cm) diam.
£430–510 / €620–730
$720–860 ⚒ WAL

MILITARIA

Helmets & Headdresses

A National Field Batallion subaltern's shako, German, Bavarian, 1813–15.
£2,500–3,000
€3,600–4,300
$4,200–5,000 Herm

A Prince Albert's Somersetshire Light Infantry 1878 pattern officer's Home Service helmet, by Hawkes & Co, label inscribed 'Wardlaw 2 Som LI'.
£480–570 / €690–820
$810–960 DNW

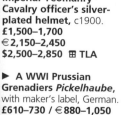

A Montgomeryshire Imperial Yeomanry Cavalry officer's silver-plated helmet, c1900.
£1,500–1,700
€2,150–2,450
$2,500–2,850 TLA

► A WWI Prussian Grenadiers *Pickelhaube*, with maker's label, German.
£610–730 / €880–1,050
$1,000–1,200 TRM

A cuirassier's white metal helmet, with shaving brush front plume and later feather side plume, leather lining restored, minor damage, Belgian, c1843.
£760–910 / €1,100–1,300
$1,300–1,550 WAL

A Victorian 1st Royal Dragoons other ranks' brass Albert pattern helmet, with hair plume and rebacked chin chain.
£880–1,050
€1,300–1,500
$1,500–1,750 WAL

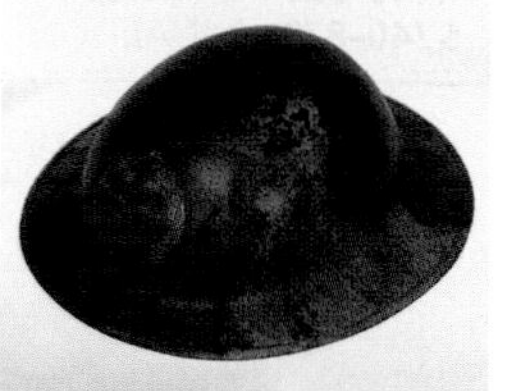

A Brodie helmet, decorated with camouflage, with advance sector division badge, 1917–18.
£260–290 / €370–420
$440–490 TLA
This British helmet was supplied to the American forces.

A naval helmet, the later front plate with double-headed eagle holding sceptre, orb and St George shield above anchors, with lobster tail chin strap, Russian, 19thC.
£300–360 / €430–510
$500–600 JAA

► A Victorian Royal Berkshire Yeomanry Cavalry helmet, with acanthus leaf finial and chain link chin strap, plume missing.
£1,000–1,200
€1,450–1,700
$1,700–2,000 CHTR

A Depot Light Cavalry 1857 pattern dragoon shako, with horsehair plume and velvet-backed gilt chin chain, some lining missing, mid-19thC.
£1,550–1,850
€2,250–2,650
$2,600–3,100 DNW

Orders & Medals

A Military General Service medal, awarded to Pte John Coombs, 61st Foot, with four bars, Egypt, Maida, Talavera and Salamanca, 1793–1814.
£1,800–2,150
€2,600–3,100
$3,000–3,600 JM

◄ **A 22nd Light Dragoons regimental silver medal,** depicting a Light Dragoon holding a shield, inscribed on reverse 'Valour Rewarded. Given to Wm Taylor, 1801'.
£280–330
€400–470
$470–550
WAL

An Order of St Patrick breast star, by Rundell, Bridge & Rundell, with silver, gold and enamels, the motto set with diamonds, maker's mark, 1810–15.
£7,000–8,400 / €10,100–12,100
$11,800–14,100 DNW

An Army of India medal, awarded to Lieutenant Jas Smith, with three bars, Assye, Argaum and Gawilghur, with a portrait miniature of the recipient.
£8,000–9,600 / €11,500–13,800
$13,400–16,100 DNW

A group of three, awarded to Sergeant Robert Cripps 1st Madras Fusiliers: Army of India, with one bar, Ava; India General Service 1854–95, with one bar, Pegu; Honourable East India Company, MSM, VR.
£2,350–2,800 / €3,400–4,000
$3,950–4,700 DNW

A 3rd Dragoon Guards regimental silver medal, with Prince of Wales's plume and motto, engraved on reverse 'A Reward of Merit to John Martin From his brethren in arms 1817'.
£140–165 / €200–230
$230–270 WAL

◄ **An India group of four,** awarded to Private George Merrick, 16th Lancers: Ghuznee 1839; Punniar Star 1843; Sutlej 1845, with one bar, Sobraon; Army Long Service & Good Conduct, damaged.
£1,450–1,750 / €2,100–2,500
$2,450–2,950 DN

A group of three, awarded to Thomas Patrick Matthew: Crimea 1854, with two bars, Sebastopol and Inkermann; France Legion of Honour Knights badge; Turkish Crimea, Sardinian issue, some damage.
£470–560 / €670–810
$790–940 WAL

A Crimea medal, awarded to David Robertson 50th Regiment, with two bars, Inkermann and Alma.
£490–590 / €710–850
$820–990 G(L)

A South Africa medal, awarded to Carpenter P. Hayes, HMS *Boadicea*, with one bar, 1879.
£360–400 / €520–580
$600–670 JBM

A pair, awarded to Carpenter and Leading Shipwright V. Urell, RN: Queen's South Africa 1899; Royal Navy, Long Service & Good Conduct.
£320–380 / €460–550
$540–640 HOLL

MILITARIA

A Queen's South Africa medal, awarded to Private A. Hennessy, 9th Lancers, with five bars, Paardeberg, Relief of Kimberley, Modder River, Belmont and Natal.
£210–250 / €300–360
$350–420 CDC

A group of twelve, awarded to Lieutenant-Colonel William A. Davenport, West Yorkshire Regiment: Distinguished Service Order GVR; OBE (Military), 2nd type; Military Cross GVR; 1914–15 Star; British War and Victory medals with MID oak leaf; Defence medal; Egypt Order of the Nile 4th class breast badge; France Legion of Honour 5th class breast badge; Khedive's Sudan 1910–21, with one bar; Hedjaz Order of El Nahda 3rd class neck badge; Boy Scout's Association Medal of Merit, cased.
£13,500–15,000
€19,400–22,000
$22,000–25,000 GBM
Lieutenant Davenport was a prominent participant in the 'Desert Revolt' with Lawrence of Arabia, particularly in the South Hedjaz where he carried out many important raids on the railway.

A group of six, awarded to Major General Sir H. B. B. Watkins, 31st Punjab Infantry: KCB; KCB neck badge; India medal, with one bar; 1914–15 Star; British War & Victory medals, MID oak leaf, in a glazed mahogany Spink case with miniatures, a photograph, a pencil sketch dated 1914 and a silver two-handled vase.
£3,500–4,200
€5,000–6,000
$5,900–7,000 CHTR

A group of four, awarded to Lieutenant Norman James Macdonald, R. Can Dragoons: comprising WWI trio and M.C. with inscription, with original newspaper cutting of the citation, dog tag, cap badges and regimental enamel cuff links.
£1,500–1,800
€2,200–2,600
$2,500–3,000 G(L)

The Order of St Michael and St George, Knight Commander Insignia, awarded to Rear Admiral John Frederick Ernest Green R.N.: comprising star on ribbon and badge, by Garrard & Co, London, 1919, with signed and sealed letter of appointment.
£640–770 / €920–1,100
$1,100–1,300 AH

A pair, awarded to Major General Edward Tanner 8th Liverpool Regiment: a gold Order of the Bath (CB); Afghan medal, with one bar, Peiwar Kotal, in a fitted case.
£2,600–2,900
€3,750–4,150
$4,350–4,850 JBM

A pair, awarded to Thomas Kenner: Royal Geographic Society Polar medal, with one bar, Antarctic 1901–04; Royal Geographic Society Scott medal 1904 inscribed 'Discovery'.
£8,000–9,600
€11,500–13,800
$13,400–16,100 B

A group of eight, awarded to Boatswain R. MacDonald R.N.: Distinguished Service medal; British Empire medal; Queen's South Africa medal; 1914–15 Star; British War medal; Victory medal; Long Service medal; Belgian Order of Leopold.
£1,800–2,000 / €2,600–2,900
$3,000–3,350 JBM

A group of four, awarded to Rear Admiral Sears: Distinguished Service Order; 1914 Star; British War & Victory medals, with MID oak leaf.
£1,400–1,600 / €2,000–2,300
$2,350–2,700 GBM

A group of eight, awarded to Lieutenant-Colonel Donough Carroll: Order of the British Empire (Military), 2nd type; India General Service medal 1908–36, with one bar; India General Service medal 1936–39, with one bar; 1939–45 Star; Africa Star; Burma Star; Defence medal; War medal, accompanied by printed research matter.
£700–840 / €1,000–1,200
$1,200–1,400 WW

Powder Flasks & Horns

◄ **A powder horn,** with owner's name and date, Scandinavian, 1599, 17¼in (44cm) long.
£2,100–2,500
€3,000–3,600
$3,550–4,200 Herm

A musketeer's powder flask, the velvet-covered iron frame with belt hook, c1600, 10in (25.5cm) high.
£810–900 / €1,150–1,300
$1,350–1,500 WSA

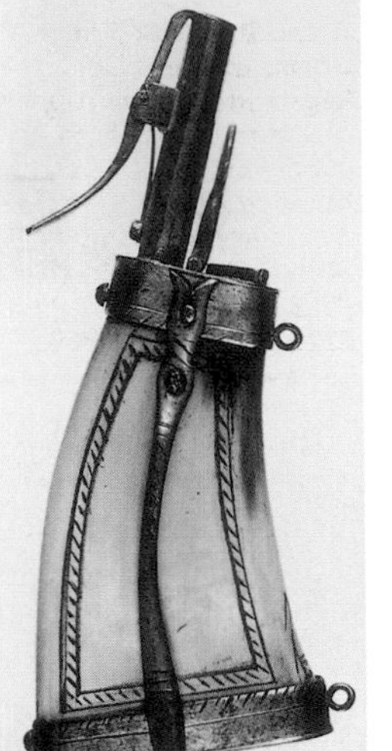

► **A brass-mounted cowhorn powder flask,** probably for Rifle Volunteers, with sprung lever and adjustable nozzle, leather cover and suspension cords, late 18thC, 11in (28cm) long.
£240–290 / €350–420
$400–480 WAL

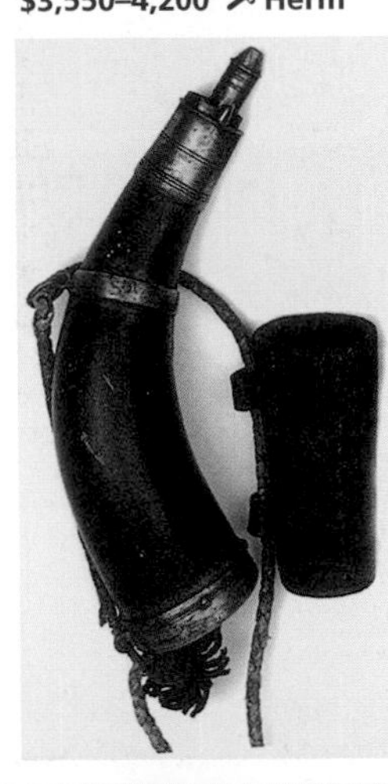

◄ **A powder flask,** with brass base, suspension rings and top with adjustable charger, c1750, 6½in (16.5cm) long.
£55–65 / €80–95
$90–105 WD

► **A powder monkey,** painted canvas on coopered oak, with royal coat-of-arms, c1850, 16in (40.5cm) long.
£100–115 / €145–165
$175–195 WSA

A brass-mounted horn powder flask, with folding top, c1850, 9in (23cm) long.
£160–180 / €230–260
$270–300 MDL

Miscellaneous

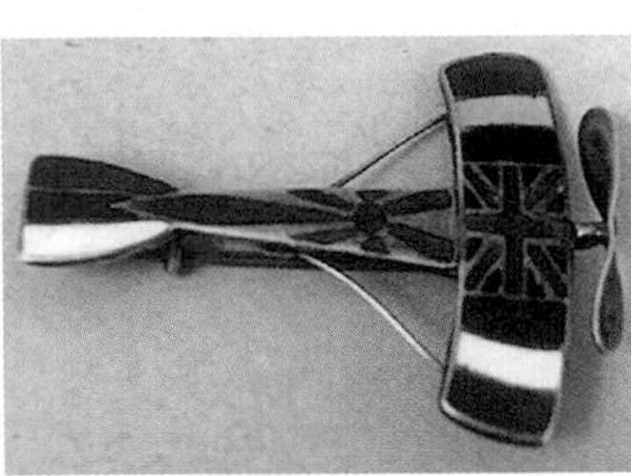

◄ **A silver and enamel brooch,** in the form of a WWI aeroplane, decorated with allied flags, stamped 'The Allies Aeroplane', early 20thC, 1½in (4cm) long.
£175–210 / €250–300
$290–350 BR

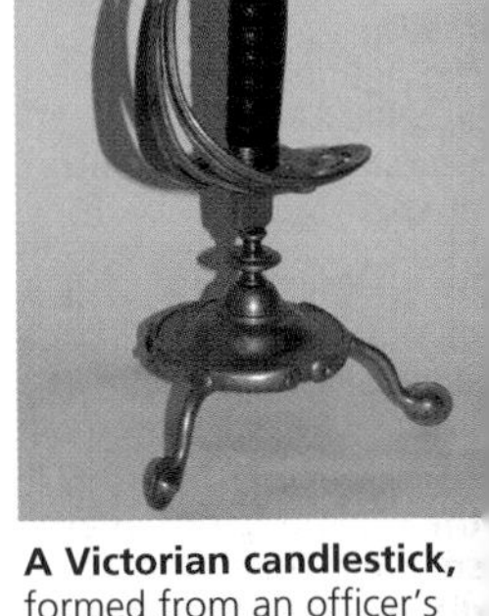

A Victorian candlestick, formed from an officer's sword, spurs, grip and cross belt, 12in (30.5cm) high.
£90–100 / €130–145
$150–165 GBM

A .36 Colt navy bullet mould, marked 'Colt's/Patent', '36' and a 'USC' monogram, American, c1860.
£480–570 / €690–820
$810–960 JDJ

A cartridge pouch, in a leather box, the reverse marked 'H. White/U.S./Ord.Dept/Sub Inspector', the front marked 'S. W. Young/Co./Newark/N. J.', American, c1865.
£240–290 / €350–420
$400–480 JDJ

◄ **A prison diary,** by Lance Bombadier Gladwyn Cecil John Winfield, Anti Tank R. A., written on airmail forms tied together with string, with four pencil sketches of Changi Hospital, Singapore and notations, 1943–45, 8°.
£270–320 / €390–460
$450–540 L

MILITARIA

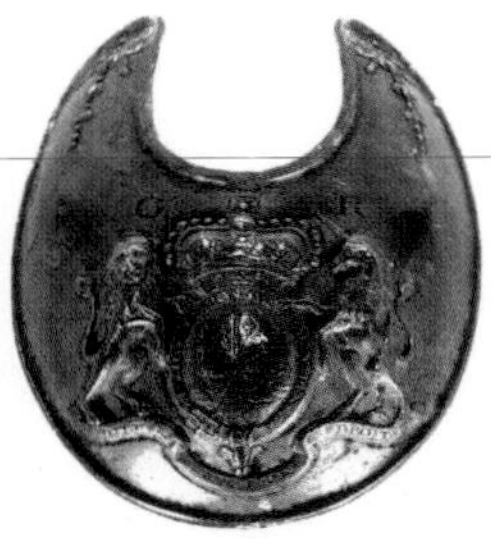

A George III officer's silver gorget, with embossed and engraved royal coat-of-arms, 4½in (11cm) high.
£880–1,050
€1,250–1,500
$1,500–1,750 F&C

A wooden model in a bottle, made by a prisoner of war, depicting a Masonic ceremony at a table, possibly French, late 18thC, 8¼in (21cm) high.
£1,300–1,550
€1,850–2,200
$2,200–2,600 B(L)

A Victorian silver-plated and wood military mace, surmounted with an eagle, 58¾in (149cm) long, with newspaper cutting.
£440–520 / €630–750
$740–870 L&E

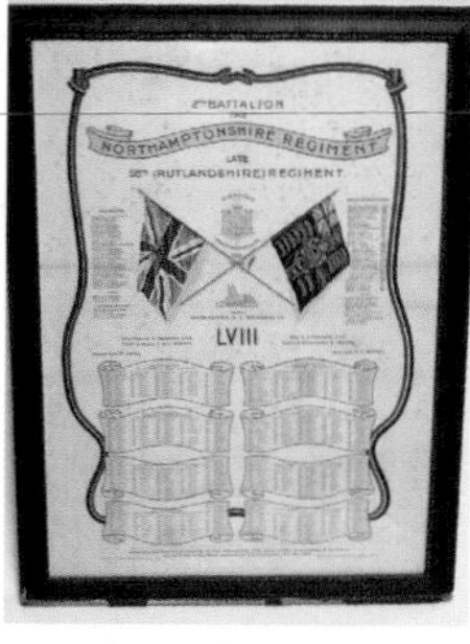

A 2nd Battalion The Northamptonshire Regiment muster roll, on the trooping of the colours and celebration of the 50th anniversary of their presentation 10th May 1860, 1910, 31 x 22in (78.5 x 56cm).
£220–250 / €320–360
$370–420 Q&C

A wool patchwork, made by a Crimean War soldier, with pieced and appliquéd uniform fragments, with a velvet back, 1853–56, 65in (165cm) square.
£1,800–2,150
€2,600–3,100
$3,000–3,600 S(O)

The Crimean War was fought betweem 1853 and 1856 with huge loss of life. A coalition of the United Kingdom, France, Sardinia and the Ottoman Empire were ranged against the Russian bid under Tsar Nicholas I to control the Straits between the Black Sea and the Mediterranean. One of the most memorable and wasteful events (in terms of human life and casualties) was the Charge of the Light Brigade at Sevastopol. Florence Nightingale first came to public notice there for her services ministering to the wounded but even so, more men died of disease than in battle.

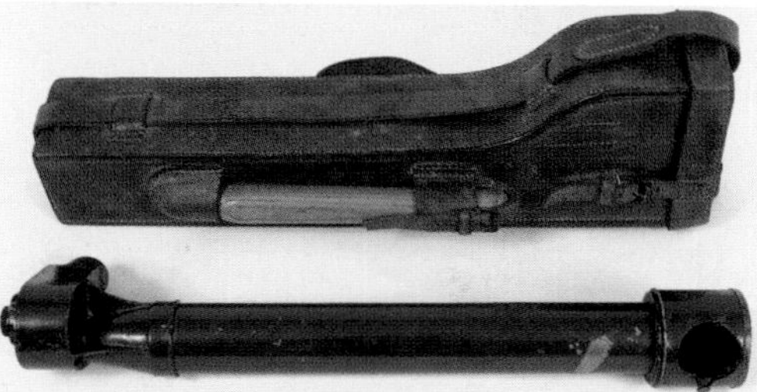

► A WWI Beck No. 14 painted trench periscope, No. 3642, 19¾in (50cm) long, with a leather carrying case with a wooden grip.
£175–210 / €250–300
$290–350 CHTR

Lord Roberts of Khandahar, two signed letters and a photograph by Lafayette, early 20thC.
£90–105 / €130–150
$150–175 SWO

Frederick Sleigh Roberts commanded the British forces in Afghanistan during Baden-Powell's service from 1881 to 1882 and was awarded the Victoria Cross during the Indian Mutiny.

A Parliamentary Recruiting Committee poster, 'Boys, Come Over Here, You're Wanted', published by David Allen & Sons, slight damage, 1915, 40¼ x 50in (102 x 127cm).
£155–185 / €220–260
$260–310 BBA

A military drum sextant, by T. A. Reynolds, Son & Wardale, with lacquered brass fittings and silvered scale, reference table inside cover, c1900, 2¾in (7cm) diam, with original leather case.
£590–650 / €850–940
$990–1,100 FOF

◄ A poster, 'Line Up, Boys!, Enlist – Today', 1915, 30 x 20in (76 x 51cm).
£190–220 / €270–310
$320–370 ONS

A trunk, marked 'Air Service U. S. Army', containing a pair of aviator goggles belonging to Lt H. C. Davis RMA, a group photograph and a copy of the magazine *The Call Field Stabilizer* depicting Davis, American, 1914–18, trunk 30½in (77.5cm) wide.
£180–210 / €260–300
$300–350 JDJ

Sport

Archery

◄ **A set of arrows,** with a leather quiver, in a fitted case, c1930, 38in (96.5cm) wide.
£125–140 / €180–200
$210–240 ⊞ MSh

A Robin Hood Society silver prize medal, by Phipps & Robinson, depicting an archer in sporting attire, 1789, 2¼in (5.5cm) high.
£670–750 / €960–1,100
$1,100–1,250 ⊞ TML
The Robin Hood Society was founded in Lower Holloway in 1787 and was active at Blackheath General Meetings between 1789 and 1793 when they appear to have disbanded. The writer Edward Lear was born in 1812 at Bowman's Lodge, the headquarters of the society.

A child's yew wood bow, c1900, 56in (142cm) long.
£95–110 / €135–150
$160–185 ⊞ MSh

◄ **A child's mug,** entitled 'Archery', c1860, 3in (7.5cm) high.
£105–120 / €150–170
$175–200 ⊞ RdV

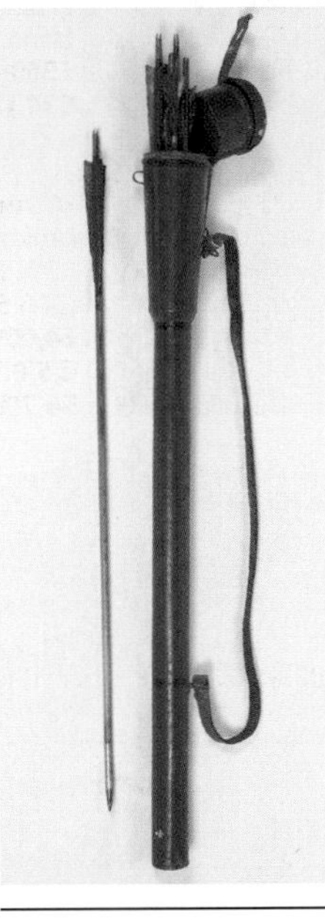

► **A tin quiver,** with arrows, c1900, 35in (89cm) long.
£125–140 / €180–200
$210–240 ⊞ MSh

Billiards

A pair of mahogany billiard room benches, with removable folding footrests, stamped 'Jacob', French, early 19thC, 40¼in (102cm) wide.
£13,200–15,800 / €20,000–23,000
$22,000–26,000 ⚒ S

Items in the Sport section have been arranged in alphabetical order within each sub-section.

◄ **A Thurston & Co snooker, billiard and life pool scoreboard,** c1890, 75in (190.5cm) high.
£1,500–1,800
€2,200–2,600
$2,500–3,000 ⊞ MSh

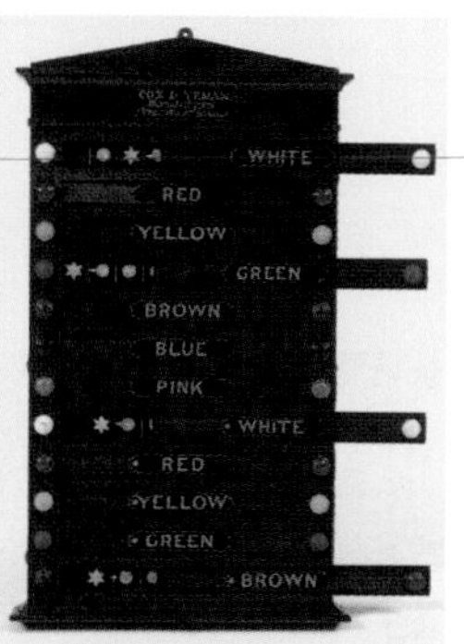

◄ **A mahogany snooker scoreboard,** by Cox & Yeman, London, with ivory-mounted sliders and mother-of-pearl markings, late 19thC, 16in (40.5cm) wide.
£1,050–1,250
€1,500–1,800
$1,750–2,100 ⚒ GAK

A mahogany snooker scoreboard, the revolving score panels above a glazed ball box flanked by drawer fronts, c1900, 44½in (113cm) wide.
£560–670 / €810–960
$940–1,100 ⚒ AH

A hand-held billiard score marker, c1910, 12in (30.5cm) long.
£240–270 / €340–390
$400–450 ⊞ MSh

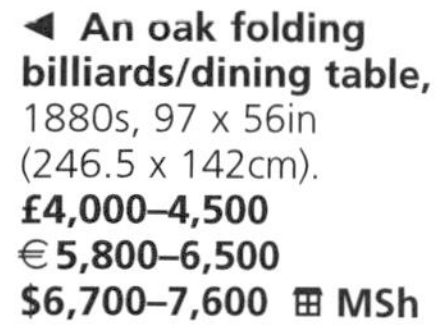

◄ **An oak folding billiards/dining table,** 1880s, 97 x 56in (246.5 x 142cm).
£4,000–4,500
€5,800–6,500
$6,700–7,600 ⊞ MSh

► **A Stevens & Son mahogany billiards/dining table,** with an elevating mechanism and two leaves, early 20thC, 84 x 48in (213.5 x 122cm), with two rests, three cues, balls and scoreboard.
£2,400–2,900
€3,450–4,150
$4,000–4,800 ⚒ BWL

A Riley's oak billiards/dining table, with removable top and adjustable height, c1900, 77 x 41in (195.5 x 104cm).
£2,400–2,700 / €3,450–3,900
$4,000–4,550 ⊞ MSh

Cricket

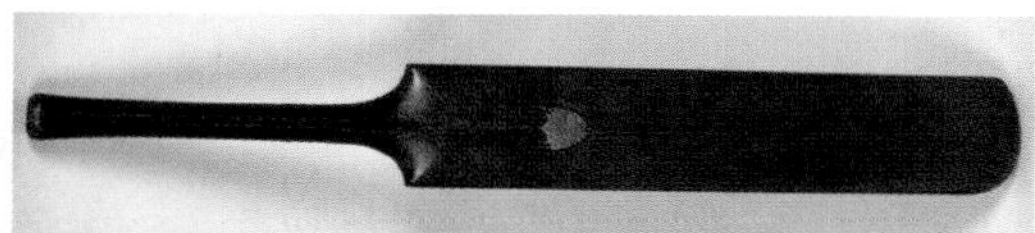

A cricket bat, with silver presentation plaque, dated 1889, 34in (86.5cm) long.
£220–250 / €320–360
$370–420 ⊞ MSh

A Gray & Nicholls Crusader cricket bat, signed by the West Indies and Warwickshire cricket team, 1963.
£120–145 / €170–200
$200–240 ⚒ FHF

◄ **Nicholas Wanostrocht,** *Felix on the Bat; Being A Scientific Inquiry into the Use of the Cricket Bat,* Third Edition, published by Baily Brothers, with seven hand-coloured lithographic plates, diagrams and illustrations, 1855, small 4°.
£630–750 / €910–1,050
$1,050–1,250 ⚒ L

SPORT

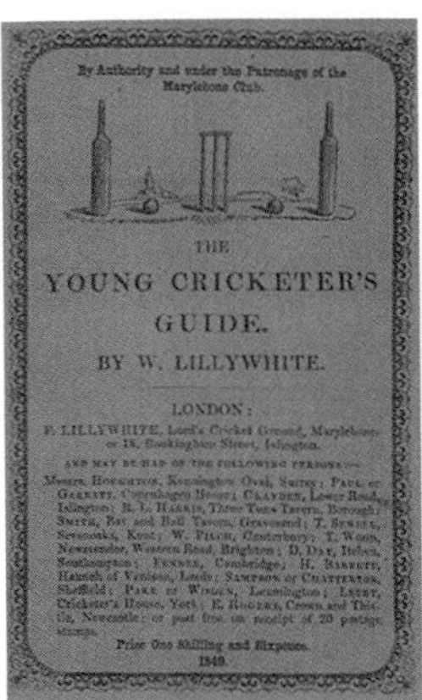

◄ **Frederick William Lillywhite,** *The Young Cricketer's Guide*, near-complete set of 19 issues, 1848–66.
£82,000–98,000 / €118,000–141,000
$138,000–165,000 L

This set, and the book pictured on page 731, are from the collection of a man considered by many to be the doyen of cricket book collecting, the late Leslie Gutteridge. He amassed a collection that comprised pamphlets, letters, books and memorabilia ranging across nearly 250 years. With what was generally thought to be a realistic estimate of £8,000–10,000 / €11,500–14,400 / $13,400–16,800, this rare, near-complete set of F. W. Lillywhite's *Young Cricketer's Guide* was battled out by two enthusiasts to a sum vastly in excess of any price previously paid for similar guides.

A silver goblet, by Duncan Urquhart & Naphtali Hart, chased with a band of vine and fruit, engraved 'Given by J. Brown to the best bowler, AD1831', London 1811, 6½in (16.5cm) high, 12oz.
£540–650 / €780–940
$910–1,100 BR

► **A photograph of the MCC Australian Touring side,** framed, 1928, 11 x 15in (28 x 38cm).
£1,000–1,100
€1,450–1,600
$1,650–1,850
MSh

A plated tin belt buckle, depicting a cricketer, 1880s, 3in (7.5cm) high.
£115–130 / €165–185
$195–220 MSh

◄ **A photograph of the Australian Cricket team,** signed in ink, including Don Bradman, 1930s, 12¼ x 13in (31 x 33cm).
£470–560
€670–800
$790–940
GTH

A cricket pitch tape measure, 1890s, 4½in (11.5cm) diam.
£95–110 / €135–160
$160–185 MSh

Equestrian

A horn beaker, etched with a hunting scene, c1780, 3½in (9cm) high.
£440–490 / €630–700
$740–820 SEA

A silver snuff box, by Joseph Ash I, decorated in high relief with a hunting scene, London 1809, 3in (7.5cm) wide.
£1,250–1,400 / €1,800–2,000
$2,100–2,350 BEX

A composite box, impressed with the Derby winner of 1863, 4 x 5in (10 x 12.5cm).
£700–780 / €1,000–1,100
$1,150–1,300 RGa

An enamelled cigarette box, by George Heath, depicting a group of jockeys and their trainers, with a gilt interior and lined with cedarwood, raised on ball feet, 1888, 3¾ x 5½in (9.5 x 14cm).
£4,700–5,600 / €6,800–8,100
$7,900–9,400 B

► **A silver-plated cigarette case,** the enamel cover decorated with a horse race, Continental, 1920–30, 3½in (9cm) wide.
£190–220 / €280–320
$320–370 WW

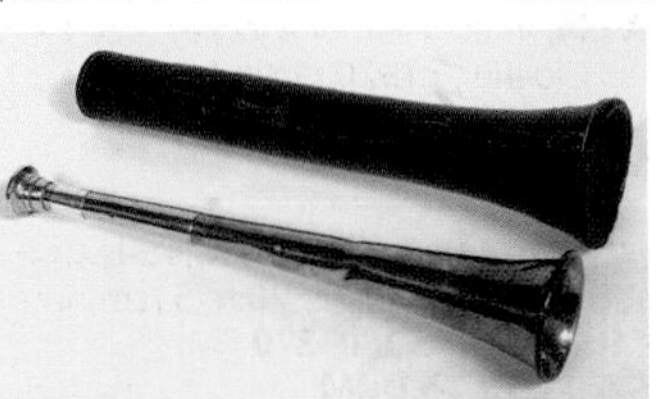

◄ **A hunting horn,** by Köhler & Son, in original leather sleeve, c1880, 10in (25.5cm) long.
£160–180 / €230–260
$270–300 MSh

A mounted horse's hoof inkwell, by Messrs Betjeman, with a glass liner, inscribed 'Winner of Viceroy's Cup Calcutta 1887–88 Died on Calcutta Race Course November 1893', London 1894, 3¼in (8.5cm) high.
£520–620 / €750–890
$870–1,050 ⚒ WW

A Spode stoneware jug, moulded in relief with a hunting scene, c1810, 7½in (19cm) high.
£210–240 / €300–340
$350–400 ⊞ AUC

A mug, by Lloyd & Co, Middlesbro-on-Tees, commemorating the centenary of the St Leger, 1776–1876, late 19thC, 7in (18cm) high.
£280–330 / €400–470
$470–550 ⚒ MAR

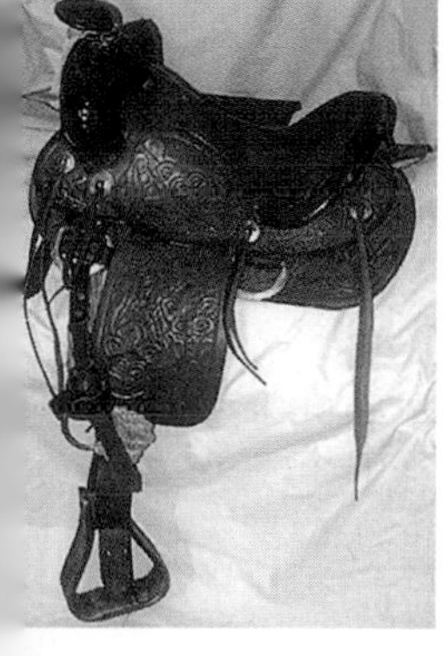

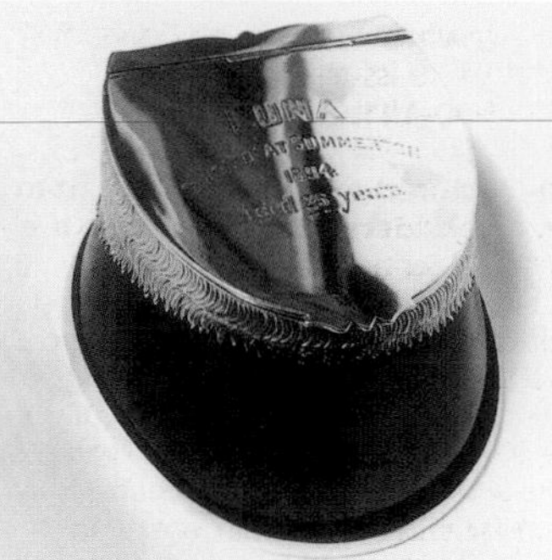

A silver-mounted horse's hoof match holder, by C. Lambe, Irish, Dublin 1894, 5in (12.5cm) diam.
£990–1,100 / €1,400–1,600
$1,650–1,850 ⊞ SIL

A pearlware jug, moulded in relief with a hunting scene, decorated with Pratt colours, c1820, 6in (15cm) high.
£810–900 / €1,150–1,300
$1,350–1,500 ⊞ HOW

A gilt-bronze image of a jockey and a racehorse, mounted and framed, c1820, 10 x 11in (25.5 x 28cm).
£380–420 / €540–600
$640–710 ⊞ RGa

A pin, in the form of a jockey, inscribed 'La Cloche', c1920, 1½in (4cm) high.
£590–650 / €850–940
$990–1,100 ⊞ SGr

◄ **A US Army cavalry tooled-leather saddle,** dated 1942, 20in (51cm) long.
£160–190 / €230–270
$270–320 ⚒ DuM

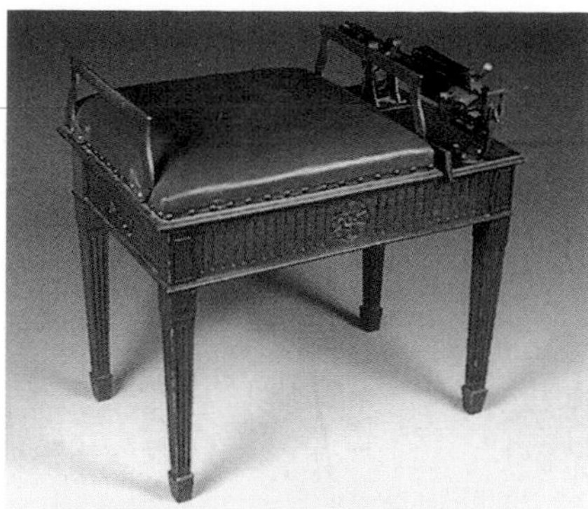

A set of oak jockey scales, early 20thC, 25¼in (64cm) wide.
£790–950 / €1,150–1,350
$1,350–1,600 ⚒ B(Kn)

A set of four lampshades, painted with polo scenes, signed 'N. Willows', c1930, 4in (10cm) high.
£320–360 / €460–520
$540–600 ⊞ MSh

A bronze model of a jockey and a racehorse, by Ludovico-Marazhani Auter, reins detached, signed, inscribed 'Fondria Artistica, Sperati Emilio, Torino', Italian, early 20thC, 13¼in (33.5cm) high.
£1,100–1,300 / €1,600–1,900
$1,850–2,200 ⚒ B(Kn)

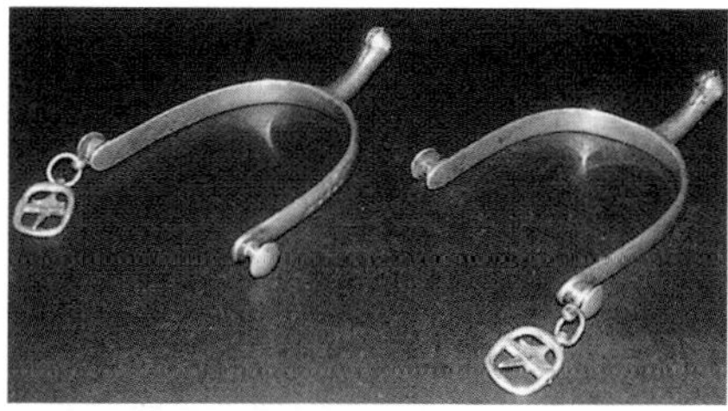

A pair of silver spurs, by B. & P., with buckles and steel rowels, Birmingham 1864, 7oz.
£300–360 / €430–520
$500–600 ⚒ PFK

◄ **A carved and painted pine horse's head trade sign,** c1870, 14in (35.5cm) high.
£1,350–1,500
€1,950–2,150
$2,250–2,500
⊞ RYA

Fishing

A late Victorian Royal Lifeboat Institution fisherman's cast-metal aneroid barometer, by Dollond, with a brass bezel, London, 6in (15cm) diam.
£200–220 / €290–320
$330–370 ⊞ RTW

A silver fly box, inscribed 'Forsinard, Aug 10th 1910', London 1893, 11in (28cm) long.
£2,900–3,250 / €4,200–4,700
$4,850–5,500 ⊞ SHa

A japanned fishing bait box, with lures, bait and minnows, c1920, 11in (28cm) wide.
£210–240 / €300–340
$350–400 ⊞ MSh

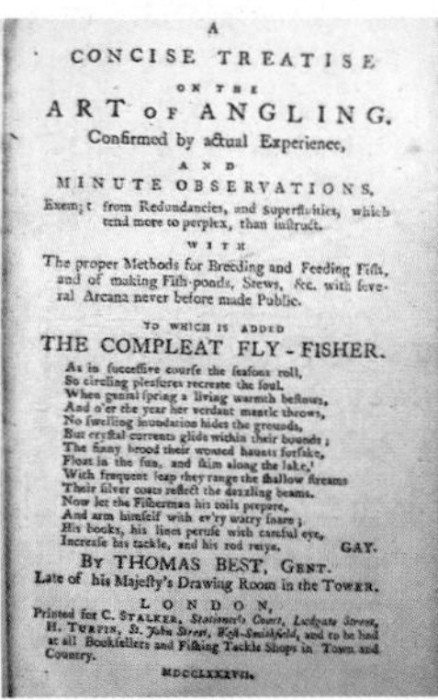

A
CONCISE TREATISE
ON THE
ART OF ANGLING.
Confirmed by actual Experience,
AND
MINUTE OBSERVATIONS,
Exempt from Redundancies, and Superfluities, which tend more to perplex, than instruct.
WITH
The proper Methods for Breeding and Feeding Fish, and of making Fish-ponds, Stews, &c. with several Arcana never before made Public.
TO WHICH IS ADDED
THE COMPLEAT FLY-FISHER.

As in successive course the seasons roll,
So circling pleasures recreate the soul.
When genial spring a living warmth bestows,
And o'er the year her verdant mantle throws,
No swelling inundation hides the grounds,
But crystal currents glide within their bounds;
The finny brood their wonted haunts forsake,
Float in the sun, and skim along the lake,
With frequent leap they range the shallow streams
Their silver coats reflect the dazzling beams.
Now let the Fisherman his toils prepare,
And arm himself with ev'ry watry snare;
His books, his lines peruse with careful eye,
Increase his tackle, and his rod retye. GAY.

BY THOMAS BEST, GENT.
Late of his Majesty's Drawing Room in the TOWER.
LONDON,
Printed for C. STALKER, Stationer's Court, Ludgate Street, H. TURPIN, St. John Street, West-Smithfield, and to be had at all Booksellers and Fishing Tackle Shops in Town and Country.
MDCCLXXXVII.

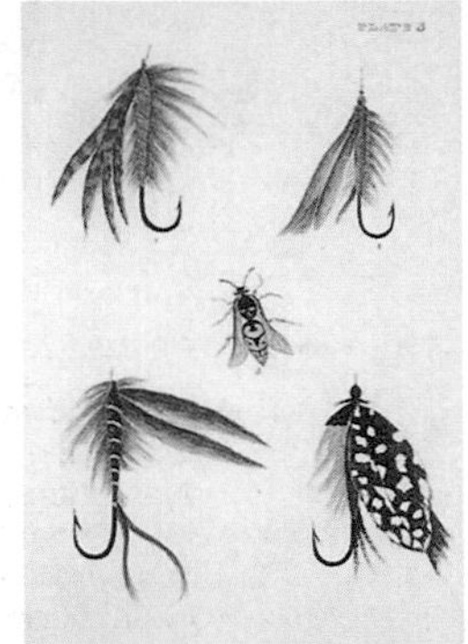

▶ **Thomas Best,** *The Art of Angling,* first edition, with half leather spine, 1787.
£360–430 / €520–620
$600–720 ⚒ MUL

◀ **George Cole Bainbridge,** *The Fly Fisher's Guide,* first edition, 1816, 4°, with eight hand-coloured engraved plates, minor damage.
£13,000–15,600
€19,000–22,000
$22,000–26,000 ⚒ BBA
This is one of only 12 large paper copies and was published at two guineas.

▶ **Sir Herbert Maxwell (Ed),** *Fishing at Home & Abroad,* published by the London & Counties Press Association, 1913, large 4°, No. 566 of 750, with two chromolithographed plates, five colour plates and 53 black and white plates, illustrations.
£190–220 / €270–320
$320–370 ⚒ RTo

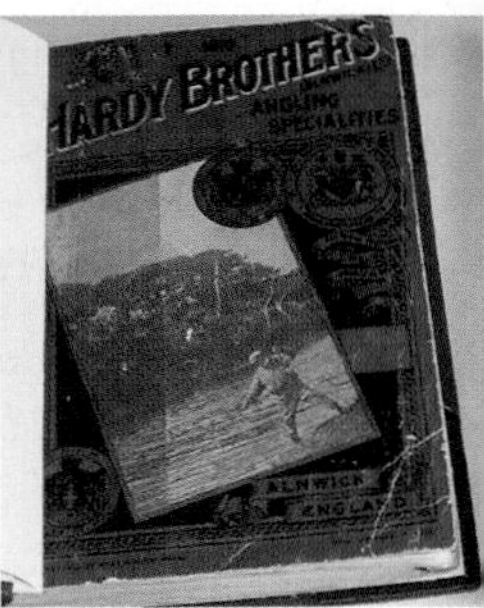

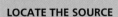

Hardy's Angler's Guide and Catalogue, 1910, 9 x 6in (23 x 15cm), with soft card cover and later leather binding.
£200–220 / €290–320
$330–370 ⊞ OTB

LOCATE THE SOURCE
The source of each illustration in Miller's can be found by checking the code letters below each caption with the Key to Illustrations, pages 794–800.

A stuffed and mounted golden roach, in a bowfronted case, with label 'Taken by Capt. J. B. Brander Sept 15th 1882 weight 2lb 1oz', with later label 'Exhibited by St Ives Angling Society', c1882, case 19¼in (49cm) wide.
£530–630 / €760–910
$890–1,050 ⚒ SWO

A stuffed and mounted salmon, by J. Cooper & Sons, in a bowfronted glazed case, the paper label inscribed 'Hertford Angling Preservation Society, Taken by Mr A. Berger in Hertford, September 1893, weight 5lbs 2oz', case 27in (68.5cm) wide.
£700–840 / €1,000–1,200
$1,200–1,400 ⚒ LFA

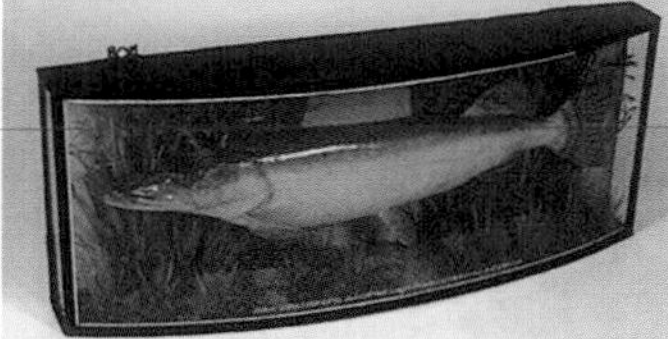

A stuffed and mounted pike, in a bowfronted glazed case, inscribed 'Taken by Walter King, January 31st 1896 length 39in, weight 17lbs 2oz', case 45in (114.5cm) wide.
£1,200–1,400 / €1,750–2,000
$2,000–2,350 ⚒ HYD

A stuffed and mounted tench, by J. Cooper & Sons, in a gilt-lined bowfronted case, with label inscribed 'Tench caught by G. C. Brewer Feby 10th 1901 Weight 3lb 4oz', case 23in (58.5cm) wide.
£820–980 / €1,200–1,400
$1,400–1,650 ⚒ B(W)

A stuffed and mounted carp, in a glazed bowfronted case, with label inscribed 'Carp Weight 6lbs 4oz Caught by R. C. Davies at Romney Marshes, October 26th 1930', case 26¾in (68cm) wide.
£320–380 / €460–550
$550–640 ⚒ WW

A stuffed and mounted perch, in a bowfronted case, with label for J. Cooper & Sons, entitled 'Caught by Henry Pratt at Widdicombe Ley, Devon Feb 3rd, 1932, Wght 2lbs', case 19¾in (50cm) wide.
£490–590 / €710–850
$820–990 ⚒ Bea

A stuffed and mounted chub, in a glazed case, label inscribed 'Chub Weight 4lbs. Caught by D. G. A. Newman, River Wye, Ross, March 26th 1951', case 26in (66cm) wide.
£400–480 / €580–690
$670–800 ⚒ GTH

► **A salesman's trout fly folio,** with 76 flies, c1920, 9in (23cm) wide.
£670–750 / €960–1,100
$1,100–1,250 ⊞ MSh

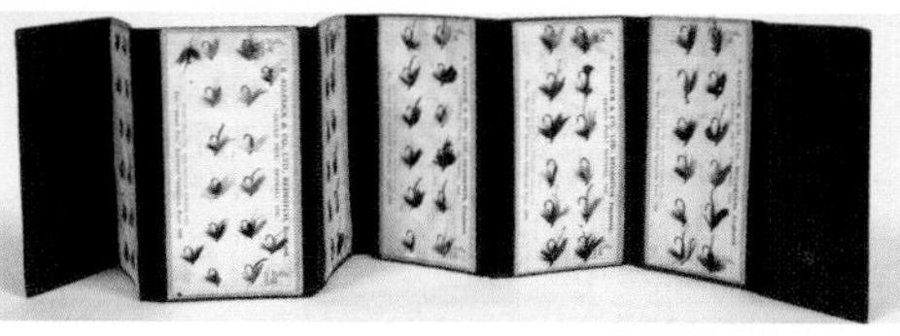

A leather fly wallet, with enamelled fly compartment, late 19thC, pouch 4 x 5½in (10 x 14cm), with original greetings cards.
£105–120 / €150–170
$175–200 ⊞ OTB
This wallet was presented to the original owner by his two sons on his 50th birthday in 1889.

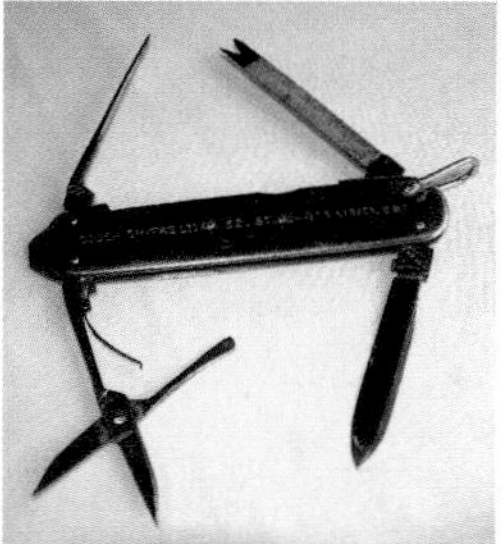

A Test angler's knife, by Ogden Smith, with tools and engraved hook size scale, c1935, 4in (10cm) long.
£160–180 / €230–260
$270–300 ⊞ OTB

Creel – A Fishing Magazine, edited by Bernard Venables, the first 12 volumes in a publisher's binding, 1963–67.
£230–270 / €330–390
$390–450 ⚒ MUL

A set of four silver-mounted and glazed menu holders, each set with a fly, Chester 1910, 2in (5cm) high.
£490–590 / €710–850
$820–990 ⚒ RTo

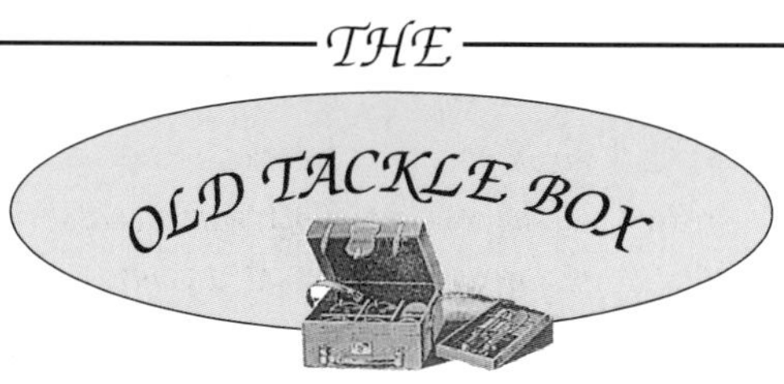

SPORT

◄ **A Hardy Zephyr alloy oil bottle,** c1920, 2¾in (7cm) high.
£140–160 / €200–230
$230–270 ⊞ OTB
This bottle was catalogued as alloy with a glass liner but is seen in various forms including brass and nickel silver.

A **group of six prints of fish,** by Denton, hand-coloured and engraved, American, late 19thC, 8 x 10¾in (20.5 x 27.5cm).
£520–620 / €750–890
$870–1,050 ⚒ LHA

A Royal Doulton Isaac Walton ceramic plate, decorated with a proverb and a fisherman, signed 'Noke', c1906, 10in (25.5cm) diam.
£160–180 / €230–260
$270–300 ⊞ MSh

An Allcock Ariel 3in reel, with optional check, brass foot and nickel-plated guard, c1910.
£220–250 / €320–360
$370–420 ⊞ MSh

A Hardy Perfect 4in salmon fly reel, with brass face, c1910.
£420–470 / €600–670
$700–790 ⊞ MSh

A Hardy Farne Ebona 5in ebonite sea fishing reel, with nickel-silver fittings, engraved 'Silex' and heat-stamped 'Hardy's Patent Ebona Reel', c1910.
£630–700 / €900–1,000
$1,050–1,200 ⊞ OTB

A Hardy Davey 3½in reel, the contract drum model with handles, telephone latch, rim tension regulator, brass foot with twin screw fixing, the interior stamped 'JS', 1930–39.
£1,900–2,250
€2,750–3,250
$3,200–3,800 ⚒ MUL
The Davey reel was produced between 1930 and 1939 – Hardy records show only 187 reels were made during this period.

A Hardy Super Silex Multiplier 3½in alloy casting drum reel, the external gear housing with handle, ivorine dial indicator operated by rim tension regulator, ribbed brass foot, ivorine casting brake knob and lacquered faceplate, 1930–39.
£610–730 / €880–1,050
$1,000–1,200 ⚒ MUL

A Hardy Super Silex multiplier 3½in alloy reel, with extra wide drum, ridged brass foot and ivorine tension indicator, c1935.
£630–700 / €900–1,000
$1,050–1,200 ⊞ OTB
Hardy records indicate that only 85 examples of this extra wide drum model were made.

◄ **A Hardy Perfect 2⅞in trout fly reel,** 1950s.
£220–250 / €320–360
$370–420 ⊞ OTB

SPORT

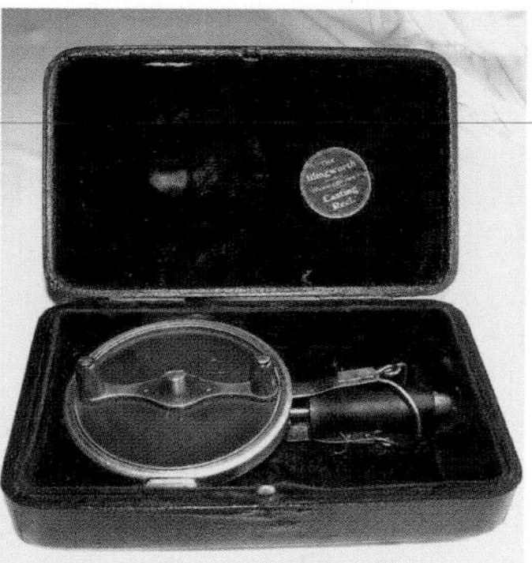

An Illingworth thread line casting reel, first model, c1910, in original Rexine case, 4½ x 7in (11.5 x 18cm).
£630–700 / €910–1,000
$1,050–1,350 ⊞ OTB

A David Slater 4in walnut combination fly and casting reel, with line guide on raised pillars and cruciform brass back engraved 'D. Slater's Patent 1447', c1890.
£180–200 / €260–290
$300–330 ⊞ OTB

A 2in brass multiplier fishing reel, with bone handle, c1860.
£140–160 / €200–230
$230–270 ⊞ MSh

For further information on
Scrimshaw see Marine pages 696–703

► **A Starback 5in walnut and brass reel,** with optional check tension screw and horn handles, c1910.
£105–120 / €150–170
$175–200 ⊞ MSh

A scrimshaw bone fishing rod case, engraved with 14 fish, with a cane fishing rod, signed 'Burgess 1879', case 22in (60cm) long.
£700–840 / €1,000–1,200
$1,200–1,400 ⚒ B(Kn)

A wrought-iron fish spear, c1840, 15in (38cm) long.
£125–140 / €180–200
$210–240 ⊞ MSh

A carved wood salmon trophy, inscribed 'Caught by Major E. A. Pope – caught in the rock pool, Symonds Yat on the River Wye, weight 30lbs 2oz, length 43in, March 14th 1913', 48in (122cm) wide.
£3,500–4,200 / €5,000–6,000
$5,900–7,000 ⚒ HYD

A carved and painted wood pike trophy, in a glazed case, inscribed and dated 1924, 43½in (110.5cm) wide.
£2,500–2,800 / €3,600–4,000
$4,200–4,700 ⊞ RYA

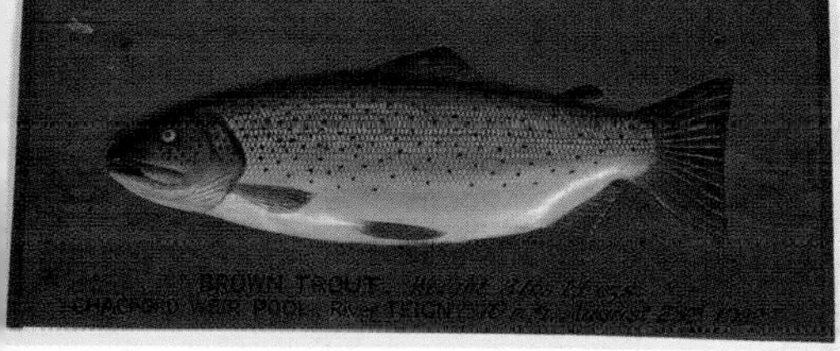

A carved wood model of a trout, by W. B. Griggs, London, mounted on an oak board, with inscription, dated 1932, 25in (63.5cm) wide.
£990–1,100 / €1,400–1,600
$1,650–1,850 ⊞ MSh

Football

A photograph of the England World Cup Team, with 11 signatures, 1966, 23 x 30in (58.5 x 76cm).
£2,700–3,000 / €3,900–4,300
$4,500–5,000 ⊞ SSL

Signatures of the 1966 England World cup winning team, on a 1985 newspaper clipping, 7 x 11in (18 x 28cm).
£1,350–1,500 / €1,950–2,150
$2,250–2,500 ⊞ FRa

A spelter figure of a footballer, by Ruffony, c1920, 25in (63.5cm) high.
£1,400–1,600
€2,000–2,300
$2,350–2,700 ⊞ MSh

◄ **An England v Italy International cap,** worn by Wilf Mannion, inscribed 'Italy', 1947–48,
£1,100–1,300 / €1,600–1,850
$1,850–2,200 ⚒ S(O)
Wilf Mannion, dubbed by journalists 'The Golden Boy of Soccer', won a total of 26 England International caps between 1947 and 1956. He also played in four wartime Internationals. The Middlesbrough inside-forward was famed for his exceptional ball control and passing ability.

A painted spelter figure of a footballer, by Rigual, c1900, 11¾in (30cm) high.
£770–850 / €1,050–1,200
$1,300–1,450 ⊞ MSh

► **An England International goalkeeping jersey,** worn by Reg Allen, with an embroidered three-lions cloth badge, 1940.
£720–860 / €1,050–1,250
$1,200–1,450 ⚒ S(O)

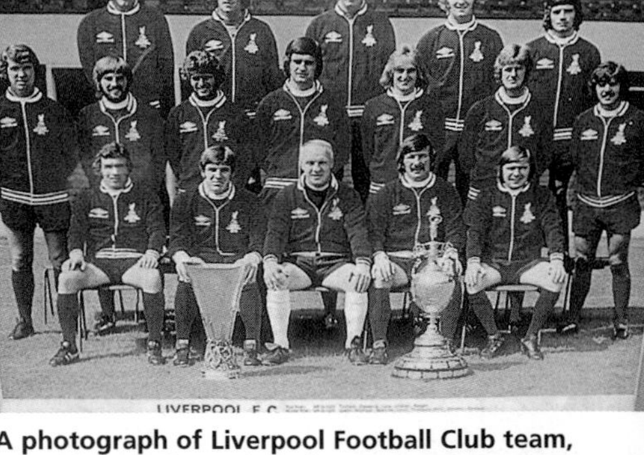

A photograph of Liverpool Football Club team, signed by the players, including Kevin Keegan, 1974, 17¼ x 23¼in (44 x 59cm).
£110–130 / €160–185
$185–220 ⚒ TRM

► **A West Germany International shirt,** No. 10, worn by Alfred Pfaff, with embroidered DFB cloth badge, c1955, with a signed photocard of Alfred Pfaff.
£450–540 / €650–780
$760–910 ⚒ S(O)

Golf

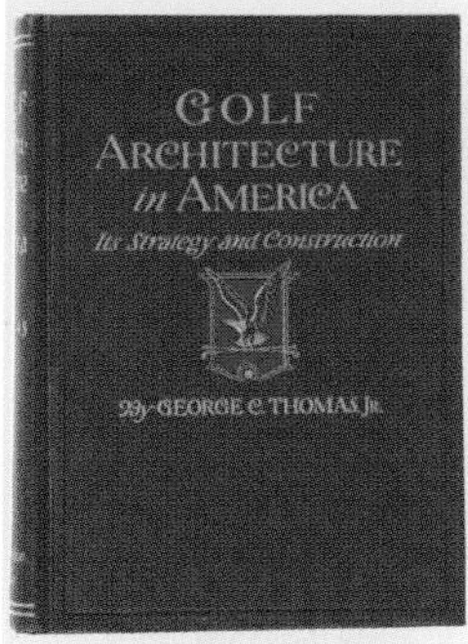

George C. Thomas Jr, *Golf Architecture in America, Its Strategy and Construction*, first edition, published by The Times – Mirror Press, America, Los Angeles, 1927, 9in (23cm) high.
£240–270 / €340–390
$400–450 ⊞ MSh

◄ **A pair of spelter bookends,** modelled as a golfer and a caddy, on marble bases, c1930, 10in (25.5cm) high.
£720–800
€1,000–1,150
$1,200–1,350
⊞ MSh

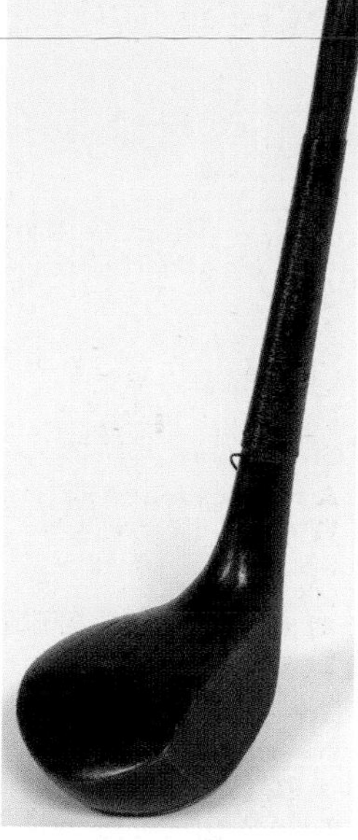

An Adams scared head driver, 1890s.
£90–100 / €130–145
$150–170 ⊞ MSh

A Hunt A. & C. P. Co niblick golf club, c1900.
£180–200 / €260–290
$300–330 ⊞ MSh

A Sunday golf club, with a marble head and a silver plaque, dated 1910.
£105–125 / €150–180
$175–210 ⚒ B(NW)

A Copeland Spode earthenware jug, decorated with golfers and young caddies, impressed with geometric motifs, printed and impressed marks, c1892, 6¼in (16cm) high.
£570–680 / €820–980
$960–1,150 ⚒ S(O)

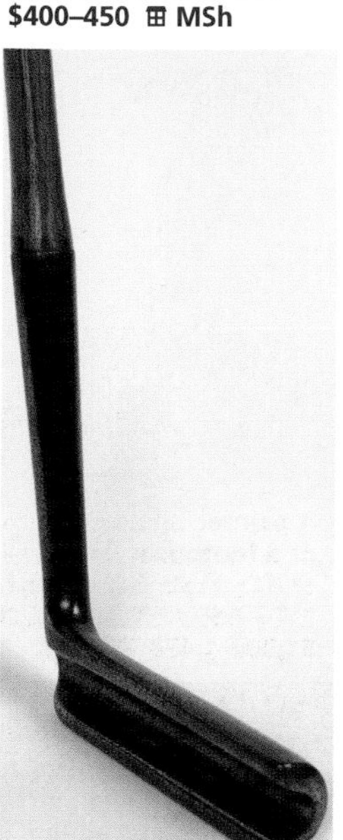

A Hendry & Bishop Perwhitt putter, c1910.
£380–420 / €550–600
$640–710 ⊞ MSh

A Foley cup and saucer, transfer-printed and hand-coloured with a golfing scene, c1900.
£160–180 / €230–260
$270–300 ⊞ MSh

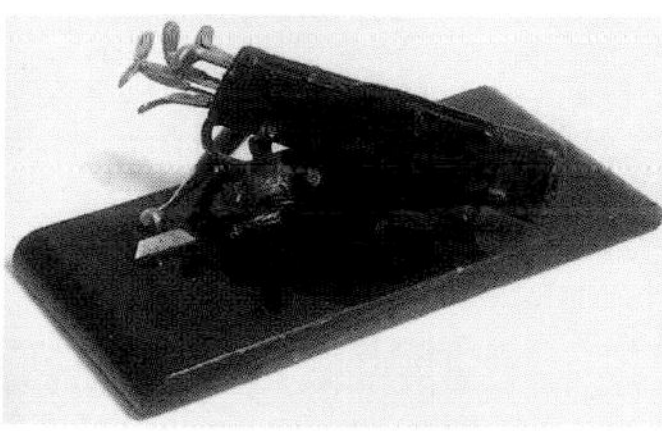

◄ **A desk stand,** in the form of a golf bag and clubs, on an onyx base, 1920s, 11¾in (30cm) wide.
£70–80
€100–120
$120–140 ⚒ TRM

► **A pair of silver napkin rings,** mounted with golf clubs, c1920, 3in (7.5cm) diam.
£270–300
€390–430
$450–500
⊞ MSh

A postcard, depicting two caddies from Pinehurst, North Carolina, American, 1910.
£200–240 / €290–340
$340–400 ⚒ JAA

A golfing poster, 'Evian Les Bains', c1920, 39 x 24in (99 x 61cm).
£1,700–1,900
€2,450–2,750
$2,850–3,200 ⊞ MSh

An oak putting practice cage, 19thC, 7¼in (18.5cm) long, with a photograph of a print by Frank Moss Bennett depicting golfers using similar devices.
£530–630 / €760–910
$890–1,050 PFK

► **A pair of silver salts,** modelled as golf balls, with gilt interiors, maker's mark BHJ for B. H. Joseph, Chester 1890, 1¼in (3cm) high.
£300–360 / €430–520
$500–600 BR

◄ **A Ronson table lighter,** mounted with a figure of a golfer, c1930, 7¼in (18.5cm) wide.
£600–720
€860–1,000
$1,000–1,200
S(O)

A walking stick, in the form of a golf club, with horn insert and silver mount, 1890s, 37in (94cm) long.
£290–320 / €410–460
$490–540 MSh

A Carlton Ware tobacco jar, printed and painted with golfing characters, printed marks and painted number 2633, c1930, 5½in (14cm) high.
£270–320 / €390–460
$450–540 PFK

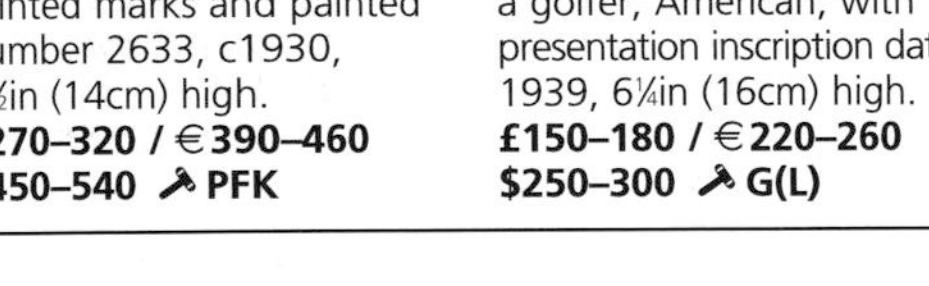

A silver-plated trophy, mounted with a figure of a golfer, American, with presentation inscription dated 1939, 6¼in (16cm) high.
£150–180 / €220–260
$250–300 G(L)

◄ **A silver trophy,** the ebonized base decorated with winners' shields, 1914, 28in (71cm) high.
£900–1,000
€1,300–1,450
$1,500–1,650 MSh

Rugby

A Mitre leather rugby ball, c1930, 13in (33cm) long.
£70–80 / €100–115
$115–135 MSh

► **A Copeland jug,** entitled 'Scrum Down', c1890, 5½in (14cm) high.
£680–760 / €980–1,100
$1,150–1,300 RdV

◄ **A spelter figure of a rugby player,** French, c1900, 7in (43cm) high.
£470–530
€670–760
$790–890
MSh

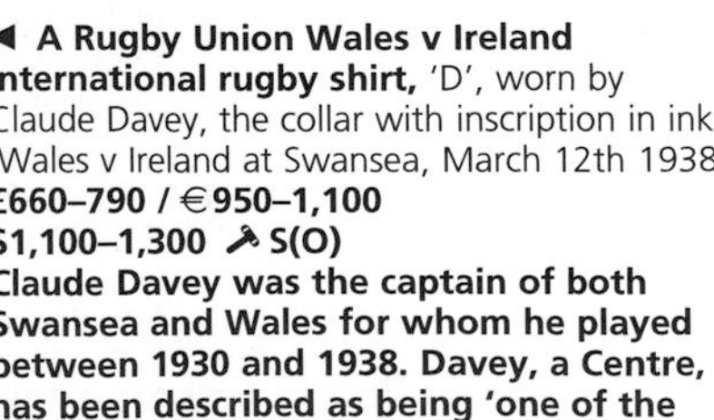

◄ **A Rugby Union Wales v Ireland International rugby shirt,** 'D', worn by Claude Davey, the collar with inscription in ink 'Wales v Ireland at Swansea, March 12th 1938'.
£660–790 / €950–1,100
$1,100–1,300 S(O)
Claude Davey was the captain of both Swansea and Wales for whom he played between 1930 and 1938. Davey, a Centre, has been described as being 'one of the finest tacklers of his or any other era.'

A glass tumbler, etched 'A Noble Fight, Wales v All Blacks, Cardiff, Dec 16 1905', 5in (12.5cm) high.
£220–245 / €320–350
$370–410 PEZ

Shooting

A silver butt marker, with eight ivory peg markers, damaged, Birmingham 1889, 3¼in (8.5cm) long.
£1,750–2,100 / €2,500–3,000
$2,950–3,500 RTo

► **An Edwardian oak gun cabinet,** by Army & Navy C. S. L, the glazed baize-lined interior with adjustable shelves, above a pair of panelled doors enclosing one long and two short drawers, with maker's ivory plaque, 32¾in (83cm) wide.
£560–670 / €800–960
$940–1,100 WW

A 30 bore air gun, by W. Parker, London, with walnut half stock and cheekpiece, steel mounts, with engraved decoration, copper reservoir, maker's mark, 19thC, barrel 34in (86.5cm) long, with brass-mounted pump with wooden handles.
£1,750–2,100 / €2,500–3,000
$2,950–3,500 WAL

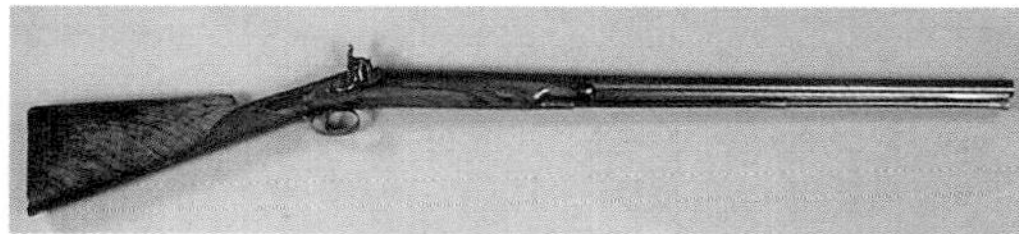

A single-barrelled percussion shotgun, by H. Bowman, with walnut half stock, engraved with floral scrollwork and 'Penrith', 19thC, 47in (119cm) long.
£440–520 / €630–750
$740–870 PFK

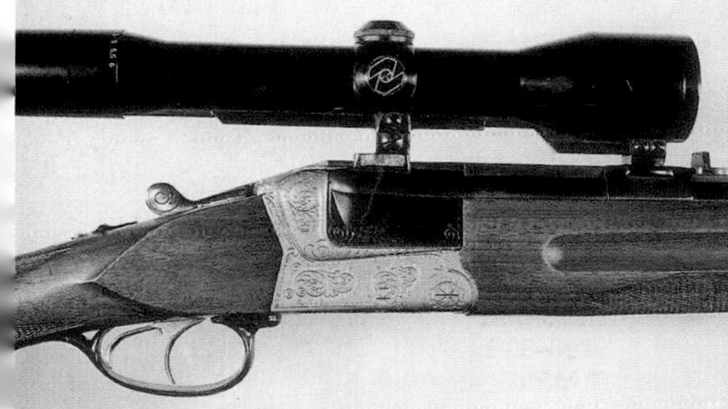

A .375 Mag double-barrelled over-and-under ejector sporting rifle, with fitted Zeiss variable telescopic sight on detachable scope mounts, German, c1960, barrel 25in (63.5cm) long.
£2,450–2,950 / €3,500–4,200
$4,100–4,900 WD

A leather cartridge magazine case, with brass corners, c1900, 13 x 18in (33 x 45.5cm).
£580–650 / €830–940
$970–1,100 ⊞ MSh

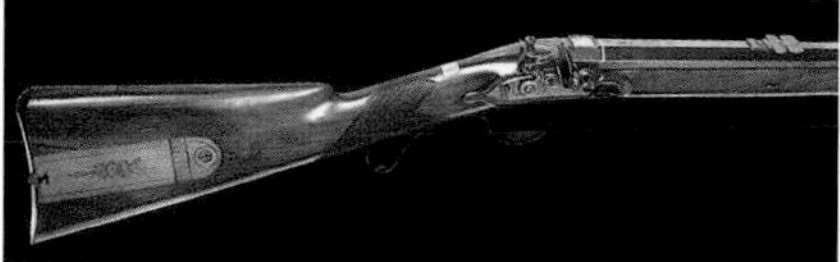

A 26 bore flintlock sporting rifle, by Henry Tatham, made for presentation to Canadian Indian Chiefs, with figured full stock, the butt with horn toe, cheekpiece and stamped War Department marks, the steel mounts engraved with martial trophies and foliage, the barrel forge by William Fullered, c1816, barrel 31in (78.5cm) long.
£10,600–12,700 / €15,200–18,300
$17,800–21,000 B(Kn)

Henry Tatham Sr was appointed Sword Cutler and Beltmaker-in-Ordinary to King George III in 1798 and Gunmaker to the Prince of Wales in 1799.

This rifle is one of a series commissioned by the British Government in 1816 for presentation to Canadian Indian Chiefs in order to foster their loyalty to the Crown. The largest surviving group is in the Royal Armouries in Leeds.

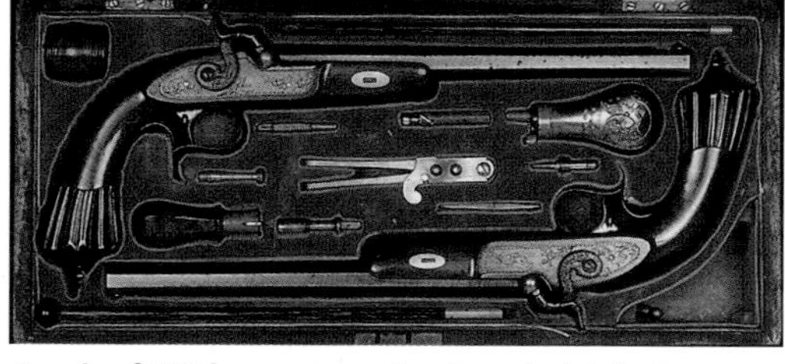

A pair of 120 bore percussion target pistols, by H. Berg, Davenport, No. 370, the figured half stocks carved with flowerheads, with steel mounts, signed, American, c1865, barrels 11in (28cm) long, in a mahogany case with accessories, lid missing.
£3,650–4,400 / €5,300–6,300
$6,200–7,400 B(Kn)

Henry Berg of Davenport, Iowa, America, is recorded 1860–75. He emigrated from Schleswig-Holstein in 1850.

A leather and brass shot pouch, c1850, 7½in (19cm) long.
£50–55 / €70–80
$85–95 ⊞ SPA

◄ **A shooting stick,** with a carved walnut seat, c1890, 32in (81.5cm) long.
£190–210 / €270–300
$320–360 ⊞ MSh

Tennis

A carved ivory and bronze figure of a tennis player, by Ferdinand Preiss, on an onyx and marble base, signed, c1925, 10¾in (27.5cm) high.
£13,800–16,600
€19,900–24,000
$24,000–28,000 S(O)

► **A silver pin cushion,** mounted with crossed tennis rackets, 1908, 2in (5cm) high.
£230–260 / €330–370
$390–440 ⊞ MSh

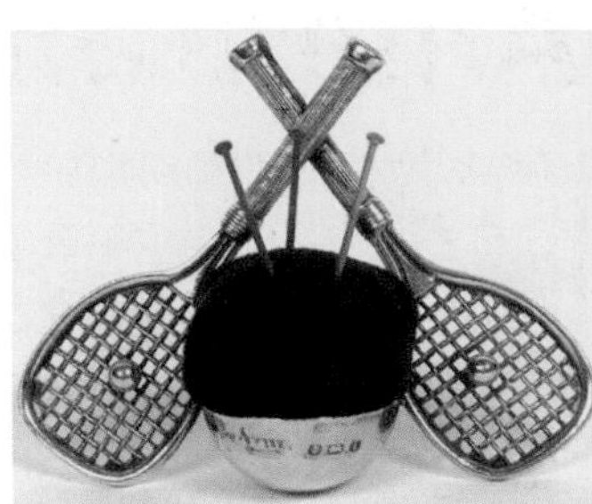

A lop-sided lawn tennis racket, 1870s, 27in (68.5cm) long.
£810–900 / €1,150–1,300
$1,350–1,500 ⊞ MSh

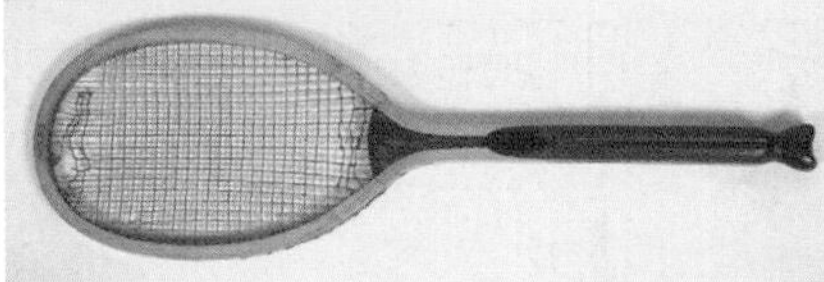

A Slazenger Demon lawn tennis racket, c1905, 27in (68.5cm) long.
£170–190 / €240–270
$290–320 ⊞ MSh

A leather lawn tennis tape measure, 1890s, 5in (12.5cm) diam.
£190–210 / €270–300
$320–360 ⊞ MSh

Miscellaneous

Items in the Miscellaneous section have been arranged in alphabetical order.

A croquet set, by F. H. Ayres, 'The Usborne', with boxwood balls and mallets, on original mahogany stand, c1880, 39in (99cm) high.
£1,200–1,350
€1,700–1,950
$2,000–2,250 ⊞ MSh

► **A Royal Worcester porcelain trophy cup,** painted by Harry Davis with a view of Worcester Bowling Club pavilion, printed mark, year mark for 1912, 6in (15cm) high.
£1,650–1,950 / €2,350–2,800
$2,750–3,250 TEN

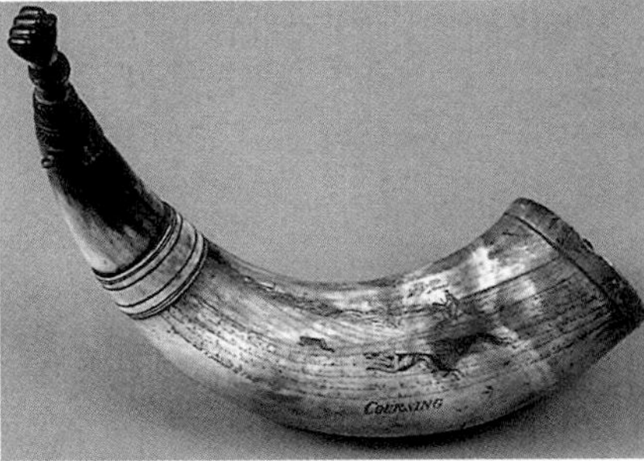

A carved and engraved drinking horn, engraved with a coursing scene, inscribed 'An Australian Bottle for W. J. Jones Esq.r. Coursing', signed by C. Wood, 19thC, 19in (48cm) long.
£750–900 / €1,100–1,300
$1,250–1,500 B(NW)

A spelter figure of a skier, on a marble base, 1930s, 5½in (14cm) high.
£170–190 / €250–280
$290–320 ⊞ MSh

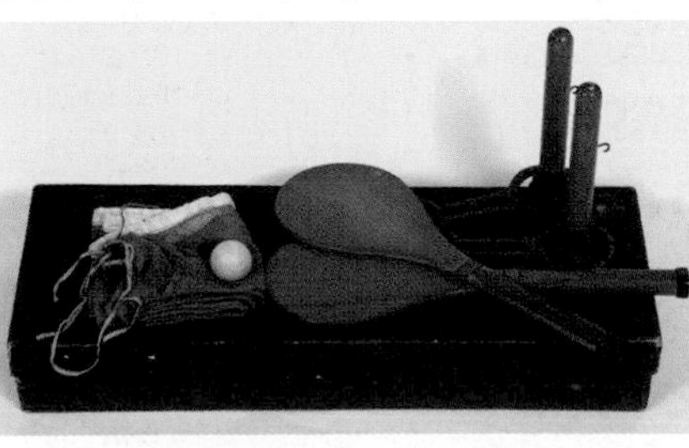

A Cavendish table tennis set, boxed, c1920, 22in (56cm) wide.
£170–190 / €250–280
$290–320 ⊞ MSh

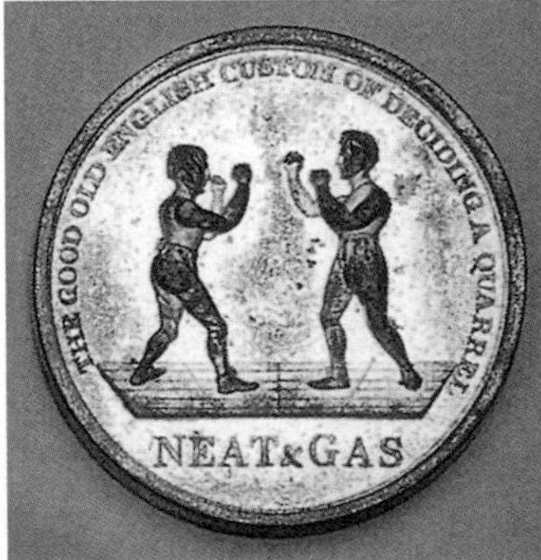

A white metal medal, depicting two prize fighters, inscribed 'Neat and Gas The Good Old English Custom of Deciding a Quarrel', the reverse with scenes of various sports, 1821, 1½in (4cm) diam.
£200–230 / €290–330
$340–390 ⊞ TML
It is recorded that Bill Neat fought Tom Hickman at Hungerford on 11 December 1921. Hickman's nickname was Gaslight Man.

American Folk Art

◄ **A burr-maple chopping bowl,** c1800, 18in (45.5cm) diam.
£2,250–2,700
€3,250–3,900
$3,800–4,550
JDJ

Folk Art is a very broad term, encompassing many collecting areas. For other examples refer to the sections on Kitchenware, Marine, Metalware, Treen, Boxes, Textiles and Toys.

A carved wood wall-mounted stick rack, modelled as Caesar holding a snake, c1900, 24in (61cm) wide.
£590–710 / €850–1,000
$1,000–1,200 SWO
Caesar was a freed boy slave.

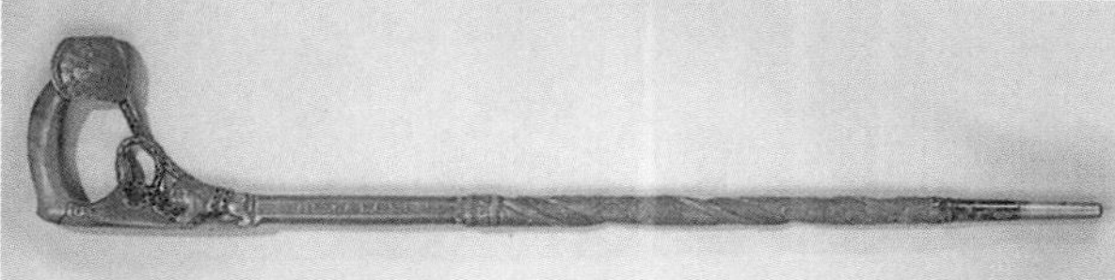

An applewood walking stick, carved with quotations and figures from the prophecy of Isaiah, signed 'Isaac S. Beecher', New York, dated 1878, 33½in (85cm) long.
£7,800–9,300 / €11,200–13,400
$13,100–15,600 S(NY)

► **A weathervane,** in the form of a trotting horse, attributed to Harris & Co, 19thC, 36in (91.5cm) wide.
£2,550–3,000
€3,700–4,300
$4,300–5,000
JDJ

A carved and painted wood cigar store, attributed to Samuel Anderson Robb, in the form of a Native American Chief, on a framed wooden base, c1900, 73in (185.5cm) high.
£11,300–13,600
€16,300–19,600
$20,000–23,000 JDJ
A letter sold with this Native American states it was part of a collection owned by the Schulte Cigar Store, a small chain of stores that operated in New York City up until the early 1940s.

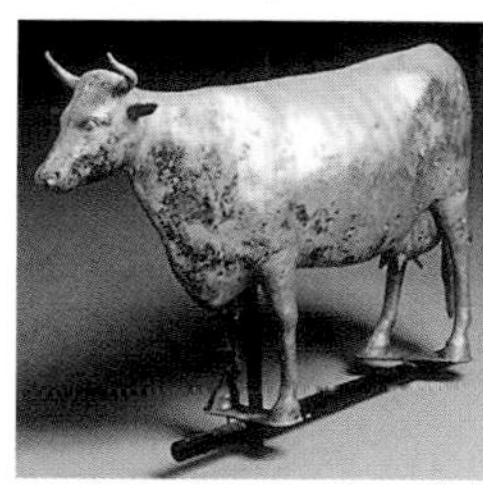

A moulded sheet copper and zinc weathervane, in the form of a cow, with later gilding and painted rod, early 20thC, 23¼in (59cm) high.
£2,350–2,800
€3,400–4,000
$3,950–4,700 B(Kn)

◄ **A sheet metal weathervane,** in the form of a locomotive and caboose, on a later metal base, c1900, 63in (160cm) wide.
£11,400–13,700
€16,400–19,800
$19,100–23,000 S(NY)

A carved and painted maple busk, inscribed 'Henry Tolman made with a Jack Knife', 18thC.
£100–120
€145–170
$170–200
COBB

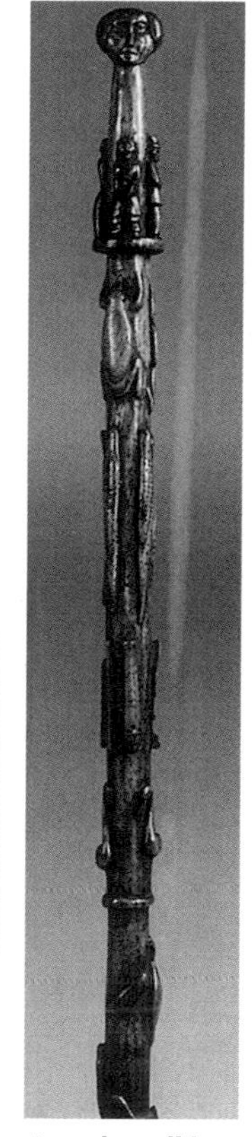

An ash walking stick, carved with a head finial, figures, frogs, snake, anchor, heart, hand, mug and fowl, with an iron tip, 19thC, 35¾in (91cm) long.
£910–1,100
€1,300–1,550
$1,550–1,850
SK

Focus on Scotland

The market for Scottish antiques is buoyant. The strength of the economy, distinctive nature of many of the items and limited supply of good material ensure that quality pieces sell easily.

Antique Scottish furniture is still a growth area. Georgian examples often follow generic British patterns, with restrained decoration and an emphasis on fine quality timbers. Many Scottish pieces are often only distinguishable by the presence of special features (see various footnotes on pages 744–45) and can therefore go unrecognized by dealers and auction houses. Prices for vernacular chairs continue to rise: those from Orkney regularly fetch four-figure sums.

Scottish pottery figures and commemorative wares from the 1820s and '30s do appear but are scarce in comparison with the huge amount of transfer-printed earthenware produced from c1850, much of which is still inexpensive. Dunmore art pottery also represents excellent value for money whereas Wemyss ware, popular for over 30 years with afficionados including the late Queen Mother, can fetch high prices.

Scottish silver is one of the strongest areas but buyers are highly selective and the market is driven by two factors: early date and manufacture outside Edinburgh or Glasgow. The most prolific centres of provincial silver production are Aberdeen, Perth and Dundee, while wares from Inverness, Greenock and Dumfries are less common and those from Tain, Peterhead and Wick represent the pinnacle of achievement for collectors. A single spoon from one of these last three towns will usually fetch over £1,000 / €1,450 / $1,700 and any piece of hollowware on offer causes great excitement.

Many small towns in Scotland had their own clockmakers from the late 1700s to the early 1800s, and the large number of surviving long-case clocks suggests that they enjoyed a steady trade. Consequently Scottish longcase clocks are remarkably good value but bracket and mantel clocks are scarcer and more expensive.

As prices for Charles Rennie Macintosh's furniture level out, the demand for items from the Arts and Crafts, Art Nouveau and Glasgow-style movements strengthens. The designs of Robert Lorimer, Scotland's foremost Arts and Crafts designer, came to prominence recently with the sale of the contents of Glencruitten House, near Oban. Glasgow-style metalwork also continues to appreciate in value. Pieces by Margaret Gilmour and Marion Henderson Wilson, formerly regarded as minor figures, regularly fetch four-figure sums and the Celtic revival metalwork of Alexander Ritchie is also increasingly sought after. **Gordon McFarlan**

Furniture

A mahogany breakfront bookcase, with astragal-glazed doors enclosing adjustable shelves, the lower section with a shallow drawer with hinged writing slope above panelled doors, early 19thC, 88½in (255cm) wide.
£10,300–12,400 / €14,800–17,800 $17,300–20,800 L&T

A Regency mahogany cellaret, with bead and reel moulding and paw feet, on a panelled base with casters, 31in (78.5cm) wide.
£3,750–4,500 / €5,400–6,500 $6,300–7,600 L&T
The sunken beaded panels seen on this cellaret are a common feature on Scottish Regency furniture. The lion-paw feet on Scottish pieces are also more likely to be carved than cast in brass.

A mahogany display cabinet, by T. Justice & Sons, Dundee, with astragal-glazed doors, early 20thC, 48½in (123cm) wide.
£1,050–1,250 €1,500–1,800 $1,750–2,100 B(Ed)

Further reading

Miller's Late Georgian to Edwardian Furniture Buyer's Guide, Miller's Publications, 2003

► **A elm and beech Darvel chair,** by Hugh Shields, with bobbin-turned supports, legs and stretchers, 19thC.
£960–1,150 / €1,400–1,650 $1,600–1,900 B(Ed)
From the 18th century the Ayrshire textile towns of Darvel and Newmilns were the centres of production for this distinctive type of Scottish stick-back chair. The bobbin-turned supports are characteristic of the work of Hugh Shields.

A child's oak Orkney chair, with rushwork back and seat, early 20thC.
£750–900 / €1,050–1,300
$1,250–1,500 B(Ed)
The Orkney chair is one of the most distinctive of British chair designs. The design is largely credited to a native Orcadian, David Munro Kirkness, who opened a workshop in Kirkwall in 1876 to produce frames, which were then shipped to outworkers on neighbouring islands who fitted the coiled straw backs. Due to the fact that the design remained largely unchanged, these chairs are difficult to date with accuracy, but earlier examples tend to be made of dark stained pine, while later examples use oak which has been fumed to darken the wood. Kirkness's Orkney chair was immensely popular, particularly with aficionados of the Arts and Crafts movement. They were retailed through shops in Glasgow, Manchester and London and also exported to Canada, South Africa and Australia. Kirkness died in 1936 but his workshop was revived after WWII by another Orcadian, Reynold Eunson.

► **A mahogany bowfronted sideboard,** with boxwood stringing, the three frieze drawers flanked by cupboards, altered, early 19thC, 83½in (212cm) wide.
£1,050–1,250
€1,500–1,800
$1,750–2,100 Bea

A mahogany Friendly Society money chest, the hinged cover with ebonized frieze and painted inscription 'Instituted July 15th 1768', the interior with cash and till box and six short drawers, the front painted with city crest shields and the verse 'We of the Lothians did unite, The Lawdable scheme to prosecute, With open hearts we sink our cash, To help our breatheren in distress', c1770, 25¼in (64cm) wide.
£11,500–13,800 / €16,600–19,900
$19,300–23,100 WL
There was an enormous gap between the rich and the poor in 18th-century Scotland. The lower classes had practically no say in the great social and economic changes that were being thrust upon them. The Friendly Societies that began to be formed at this time were set up specifically to protect lower-paid workers in times of trouble. Funds contributed were held in coffers such as this and paid to families of the members should they fall ill or die.

A Regency mahogany sideboard, with ebony stringing, the sliding doors above a bowfronted section with drawers, 91¼in (232cm) wide.
£2,800–3,350 / €4,000–4,800
$4,700–5,600 L&T
This sideboard has a 'stage' around three sides, indicating that it was made in Glasgow.

◄ **A Regency mahogany fold-over tea table,** with beaded edges, on scroll supports terminating in paterae, Edinburgh, 36¼in (92cm) wide.
£2,800–3,350 / €4,000–4,800
$4,700–5,600 B(Ed)
The table support composed of four scrolls terminating in paterae above four hipped claws was a typical product of Edinburgh workshops from c1815. Good examples by William Trotter can be seen at Paxton House, Berwickshire.

A Victorian mahogany chest, with four small, one deep and three long drawers, 48¾in (124cm) wide.
£650–780 / €940–1,100
$1,100–1,300 B(Kn)
This type of chest is currently unfashionable and is therefore inexpensive. The example pictured here has beautifully matched flame mahogany veneers.

A flame mahogany chest, with ogee upper drawers, c1860, 50in (127cm) high.
£880–980 / €1,250–1,400
$1,450–1,650 GEO

A George III mahogany and crossbanded Pembroke table, the hinged top above a frieze drawer, 43¼in (110cm) wide.
£820–980 / €1,200–1,400
$1,350–1,650 B(Ed)
This straightforward but distinctive Edinburgh pattern can be found in the *Edinburgh Book of Prices for Manufacturing Cabinet Work*, 1805, a publication that described all the regional preferences for fashionable furniture in the city. The price paid for the journeyman maker for a basic square-topped Pembroke table was 11 shillings but this table has various extras such as 'making the top octagon cornered cost 8d, working an astragal moulding along the edge was 9d, and the addition of socket casters was 6d.'

Ceramics

A Seaton Pottery agate ware money box, modelled as a hen, 1860–80, 4in (10cm) high.
£110–125 / €160–180
$185–210 ⊞ GAU

A pair of pottery pug dogs, with glass eyes, c1890, 12in (30.5cm) high.
£450–500 / €650–720
$750–840 ⊞ HOW
This type of 'wally dug' is traditionally ascribed to the Bo'ness Pottery.

A Wemyss model of a tabby cat, with glass eyes, repaired, possible impressed mark, c1900, 13in (33cm) high.
£4,700–5,600
€6,800–8,100
$7,900–9,400 ⚒ B(Ed)
Based on a French original by Gallé, these Wemyss cats are found with a variety of different markings.

◄ **A Wemyss model of a pig,** with painted patches, restored, impressed marks, c1900, 17¼in (44cm) long.
£820–980 / €1,200–1,400
$1,300–1,650 ⚒ DN
Wemyss pigs came in two sizes and the large ones were made as doorstops. Consequently, they are frequently damaged at the extremities. Provided the damage is minor, the value is not severely affected.

A Wemyss basket, painted with carnations, c1900, 8in (20.5cm) wide.
£720–800 / €1,050–1,200
$1,200–1,350 ⊞ RdeR

A Wemyss biscuit jar and cover, painted with strawberries, impressed mark, c1900, 6in (15cm) high.
£330–390 / €470–560
$550–660 ⚒ G(L)

A Wemyss honeycomb dish and cover, impressed mark, 1920, dish 7½in (19cm) square.
£720–800 / €1,050–1,150
$1,200–1,350 ⊞ RdeR

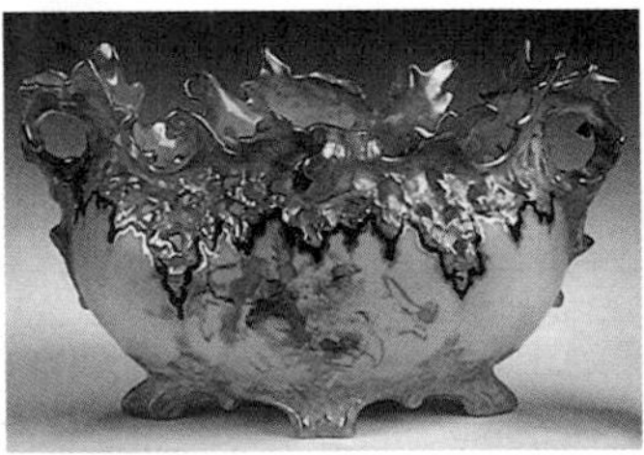

A Nautilus porcelain jardinière, decorated with sprays of poppies and other flowers, printed marks, c1900, 10¼in (26cm) long.
£530–630 / €760–910
$890–1,050 ⚒ B(Ed)
Nautilus porcelain was made in the Possil or Saracen Pottery in Glasgow from 1896 to 1911. It is hard-paste Parian porcelain and is usually hand-painted in colours and gilded. Inspired by contemporary Limoges and, to a lesser extent, Belleek porcelain, it has little in common with the types of ware traditionally made in Scotland. The tea wares in particular are so close to their French prototypes that it has been suggested, but never proved, that French potters might have been employed. The most characteristic wares are a very varied range of vases, centrepieces and baskets decorated in flamboyant late Victorian or Art Nouveau style.

A Wemyss hot milk jug, decorated with a cockerel, inscribed 'Bon Jour', c1900, 4in (10cm) high.
£360–400 / €520–580
$610–680 ⊞ GLB

Wemyss ware

Wemyss ware was first produced in 1882 when Robert Heron, the owner of the Fife Pottery, brought a group of Bohemian craftsmen to the factory, one of whom, Karol Nekola, became Heron's master painter. Nekola died in 1915 and was succeeded by Edwin Sandland who, in turn, was succeeded in 1928 by Nekola's son Joseph. Wares were initially sold through Thomas Goode's china shop in Mayfair, London. A victim of the economic depression, the factory closed in 1930, and Joseph Nekola was taken on by the Bovey Tracey Pottery Company in Devon, which had been producing unmarked Wemyss-style wares since c1916. They also acquired many of the Fife Pottery moulds and the remaining undecorated biscuit pottery, as well as the rights to the goodwill in the Wemyss name. Nekola died in 1952 but Wemyss ware continued to be produced at Bovey Tracey until the factory closed in 1957.

Wemyss was fired at a low temperature in order to preserve the brilliance of the underglaze colours. The body is soft and therefore prone to damage.

A Wemyss Plichta mustard pot, c1930, 3in (7.5cm) high.
£110–125 / €160–180 $185–210 ⊞ RdeR

Confusion is sometimes caused by wares marked 'Plichta' or 'Plichta London England'. Jan Plichta was an importer and wholesaler of pottery and glass, who acquired the rights to Wemyss ware in the 1930s. Although this is a Wemyss piece, Plichta also put his mark on Wemyss-style wares from other factories.

◄ **A pottery plate,** moulded and painted with a bust of George IV and a border of crowns, Prince of Wales feathers and foliage, minor chip, impressed mark, c1821, 8½in (21.5cm) diam.
£400–480 / €580–690 $670–800 ⚒ SAS

A Wemyss plate, painted with blackcurrants, c1930, 5½in (14cm) diam.
£220–250 / €320–360 $370–420 ⊞ RdeR

A Wemyss powder box, painted with roses, c1915, 4in (10cm) diam.
£450–500 / €650–720 $750–840 ⊞ GLB

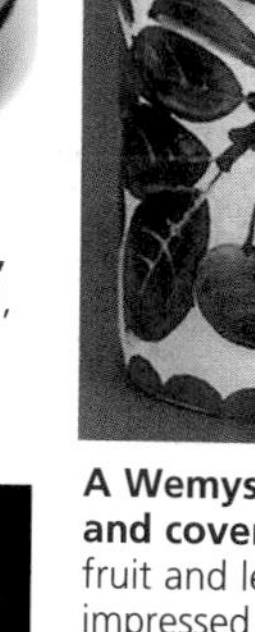

A Wemyss preserve jar and cover, painted with fruit and leaves, faults, impressed mark and Goode & Co retailer's stamp, early 20thC, 4¾in (12.5cm) high.
£90–105 / €130–150 $150–175 ⚒ DMC

► **A Wemyss tyg,** painted with raspberries, impressed mark, c1900, 5½in (14cm) high.
£700–780 / €1,000–1,100 $1,150–1,300 ⊞ RdeR

A Wemyss Toby jug, modelled as a sailor, minor damage, impressed mark, c1900, 11in (28cm) high.
£600–720 / €860–1,000 $1,000–1,200 ⚒ S(O)

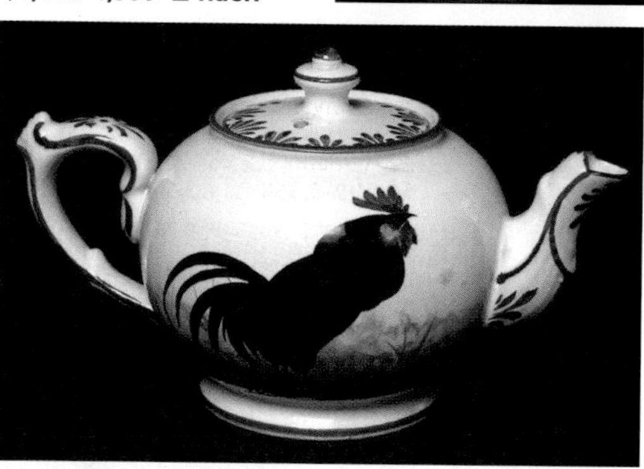

◄ **A Wemyss teapot,** painted with cockerels, c1900, 4in (10cm) high.
£430–480 / €620–690 $720–810 ⊞ RdeR

► **A Britannia Pottery agate ware vase,** by Cochran & Fleming, Glasgow, 1900–20, 5½in (14cm) high.
£110–125 / €160–180 $185–210 ⊞ GAU

FOCUS ON SCOTLAND

Silver

A pair of silver owl peppers, by Marshall & Sons, Edinburgh 1887, 3in (7.5cm) high, with a fitted case.
£1,800–2,150 / €2,600–3,100
$3,000–3,600 ⚒ S
Novelty peppers of this type are rare in Scottish silver.

A silver brandy saucepan, by William Jamieson, engraved with a crest and a motto, Aberdeen, c1810, 4¼in (11cm) wide, 9¼oz.
£2,350–2,800 / €3,400–4,000
$3,950–4,700 ⚒ L

A silver dish cross, by Milne & Campbell, cast with shell motifs, marked, Glasgow, c1760, 13½in (34.5cm) wide.
£1,200–1,400 / €1,750–2,000
$2,000–2,350 ⚒ L&T
As is usual with a dish cross, the feet are adjustable to accommodate bowls of varying diameter. Unlike English examples, it is unusual to find a Scottish dish cross with a burner.

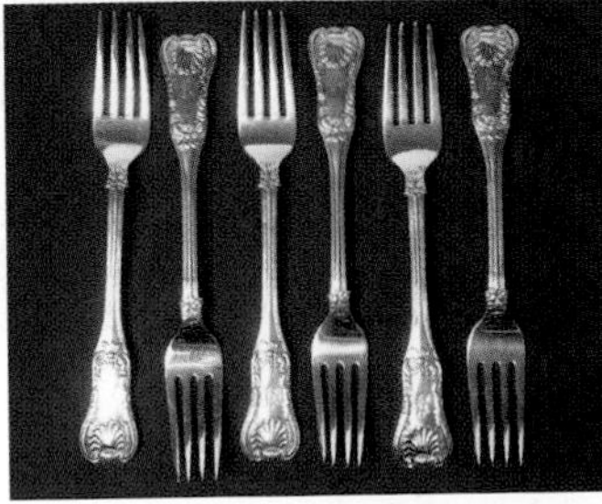

A set of six silver forks, by Alexander Mitchell, Glasgow 1831, 8½in (21.5cm) long.
£270–300 / €390–430
$450–500 ⊞ WAC

A silver snuff box, the base with presentation inscription for 1824, the cover depicting a coat-of-arms, the gilt interior with further presentation inscription for 1850, maker's mark AW, Edinburgh 1823, 4¾in (12cm) wide.
£1,250–1,500 / €1,800–2,150
$2,100–2,500 ⚒ B(Ed)
The three-towered castle seen on the coat-of-arms, which is that of Edinburgh, is also the mark for Edinburgh in the silver hallmarking system.

A silver chamberstick, by Hamilton & Inches, Edinburgh 1901, 3½in (9cm) high.
£120–140 / €170–200
$200–230 ⚒ GAK

A sugar bowl, by James Mitchellson, assay master Edward Penman, Edinburgh 1728, 2½in (6.5cm) high, 6½oz.
£2,900–3,500 / €4,200–5,000
$4,900–5,900 ⚒ B(Ed)
This form of wavy edge, which was cast and applied as a separate piece, is often seen on Scottish sugar bowls, waiters and teapot stands of the 1720s and 1730s.

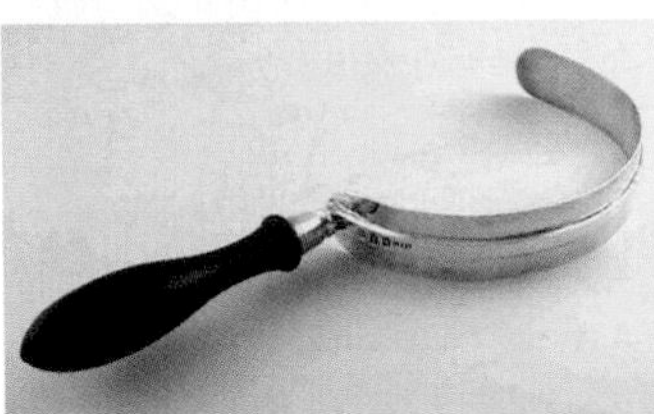

A silver crumb scoop, by Thomas Smith & Sons, with a turned hardwood handle, Glasgow 1897, 11½in (29cm) long.
£280–330 / €400–470
$470–550 ⚒ WW
This is a typically Scottish implement. They are found from the late 18th century onwards and were almost certainly used for scraping the crumbs from a tablecloth.

Miller's Compares

I. A silver dram cup, by Hugh Ross, Tain, of thistle form, with applied central band and calyx to the base, engraved with betrothal initials 'AS' over 'MF', with strap handle, maker's mark, early 18thC, 1¾in (4.5cm) high.
£26,000–31,000
€38,000–45,000
$44,000–52,000 ⚒ L&T
Hugh Ross is the earliest and best-known Tain silversmith.

II. A silver dram cup, of thistle form, with applied lobing beneath a moulded band, strap handle, engraved with initial 'M', 1710–20, 1½in (4cm) high.
£2,800–3,350 / €4,000–4,800
$4,700–5,600 ⚒ L&T

Dram cups are exclusively Scottish and were produced in the late 17th and early 18th centuries. Item I is engraved with typically Scottish betrothal initials (in Scotland the bride retained her maiden name, hence the need for four rather than three initials). The quality of the design and the workmanship of Item II is in fact superior to that of Item I. The huge price differential, however, is due to the enormous appeal of a piece of hollowware from one of Scotland's smallest and remotest centres of provincial silver production. Item I has now returned home, having been acquired by Tain Museum.

◄ **A pair of silver toddy ladles,** Edinburgh 1845, 6in (15cm) long.
£160–185 / €230–270
$270–310 ⊞ GRe
Toddy is a spirit-based drink stronger than punch. The ladles were made in sets and were used by guests to serve themselves from a bowl.

A silver mug, by William Jamieson, Aberdeen, engraved with Elder of Scotland crest and motto, marked, c1851, 3¼in (8.5cm) high.
£2,000–2,400 / €2,900–3,450
$3,350–4,000 ⚒ L&T

A silver gravy spoon, Dundee, c1795, 13in (33cm) long.
£470–520 / €680–750
$790–870 ⊞ WELD

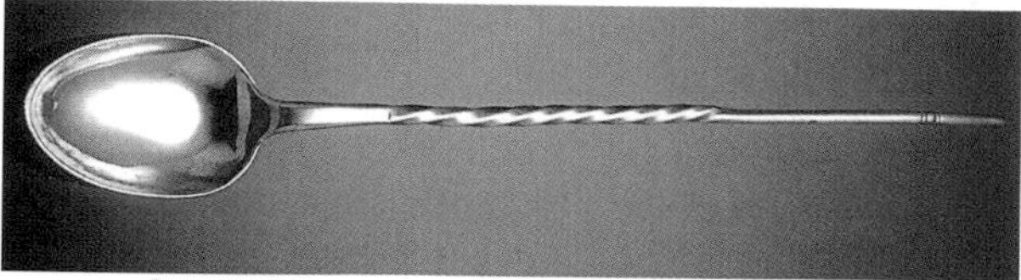

A masking spoon, by John Argo, Banff, with a twist stem, engraved 'W I.D', c1800, 6¼in (16cm) long.
£640–770 / €920–1,100
$1,100–1,300 ⚒ B(Ed)
The masking spoon, a typical Scottish utensil, was used for stirring a teapot. Often the form is exactly that of a teaspoon but half an inch (1.25cm) longer and it is not uncommon to find a set of six teaspoons and a masking spoon. The spike at the end of this example was presumably for unblocking the spout.

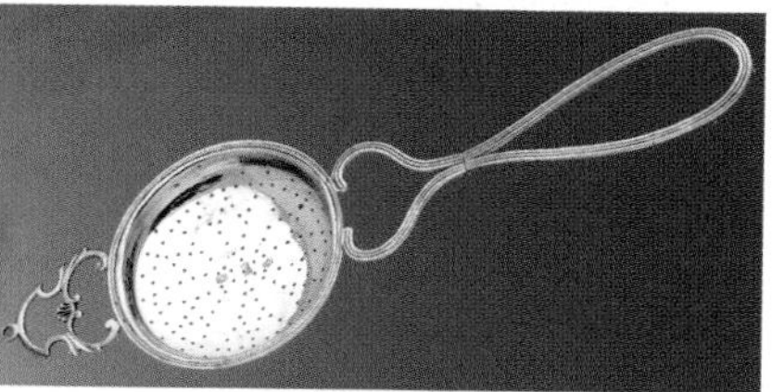

A silver punch strainer, with a folding handle, with marks for Dundee and JS, probably John Steven, c1760, 11¾in (30cm) long.
£2,600–3,100 / €3,700–4,500
$4,400–5,200 ⚒ L&T

A silver nutmeg grater, by Robert Gray & Sons, Glasgow, engraved with Stirling of Keir crest, Edinburgh 1814, 2½in (6.5cm) high.
£1,300–1,550
€1,900–2,250
$2,200–2,600 ⚒ L&T
It was not until 1819 that Glasgow got its own assay office. Prior to that date, the Glasgow goldsmiths had to go to the trouble and expense of sending their wares to Edinburgh to be assayed. This practice has resulted in a large amount of Glasgow-made silver bearing Edinburgh hallmarks.

A silver teapot-on-stand, by Francis Howden, engraved with chased swags and beaded borders, Edinburgh 1785, 9in (23cm) high, 30oz.
£1,000–1,200 / €1,450–1,700
$1,700–2,000 ⚒ S(O)

A pair of silver tea caddies, by Alexander Spence, engraved with stylized bands and a crest, with lockable lids, Edinburgh 1789, 4¾in (12cm) high, 19½oz.
£14,500–17,400 / €21,000–25,000
$24,000–29,000 ⚒ B(Ed)
Scottish silver tea caddies are extremely rare and this pair is a remarkable survival.

A silver salver, by Leonard Urquart, the border embossed with shells and flowerheads, the centre engraved with C-scrolls and fruiting vines, with triple feet, Edinburgh 1835, 13¼in (33.5cm) diam, 30oz.
£340–400 / €490–580
$570–670 ⚒ GH

A set of three wine labels, by Edward Livingstone, Dundee, marked with EL and vase of lilies, c1780.
£1,300–1,550 / €1,900–2,250
$2,200–2,600 ⚒ L&T

For further information on
Wine Antiques see pages 378–379

Clocks

A brass-mounted ebonized bracket clock, by Laurence Dalgleish, Edinburgh, the engraved silvered dial with subsidiaries for rise/fall and strike/silent, the five-pillar twin-train fusee and chain movement with anchor escapement and striking on a bell, mounted with female busts and trailing flowers, c1780, 20in (51cm) high.
£3,700–4,450
€5,400–6,400
$6,200–7,400 S(Am)
Laurence Dalgleish was a member of the Clockmakers Company and is recorded as working in Edinburgh between 1771 and 1821.

An oak longcase clock, by T. Reid, Edinburgh, the eight-day movement striking the hours on a bell, c1800, 79in (200.5cm) high.
£4,500–5,000
€6,500–7,200
$7,600–8,400 ⊞ PAO

Miller's Compares

I. A George III mahogany longcase clock, by M. Dickman, Perth, the painted dial with subsidiary seconds and date dials, the trunk door inlaid with a Masonic plaque, 88¼in (224cm) high.
£2,700–3,200
€3,900–4,600
$4,550–5,400 B(Ed)

II. A mahogany crossbanded and line-inlaid longcase clock, by Jas Allan, Kilmarnock, the painted dial with subsidiary seconds and date dials, the four-pillar movement with anchor escapement striking on a bell, base missing, early 19thC, 87in (221cm) high.
£880–1,050
€1,250–1,500
$1,500–1,750 B(Kn)
James Allan is listed as working in Kilmarnock from 1820 to 1837.

Item I has a slimmer, more elegant profile than the rather pedestrian example by Allan of Kilmarnock, even allowing for the fact that the latter has lost its base. The case of Item I also has several refined details that are absent on Item II, namely, the fluted quarter columns flanking the door and fully modelled columns flanking the hood, as well as a very unusual inlaid Masonic panel on the door. The swan-neck pediment on the hood of Item II looks like an afterthought and the painted swans in the arch of the dial appear crude rather than naive.

A George III mahogany longcase clock, by C. Merrilees, Edinburgh, the enamelled dial painted with a country house, with seconds and date dials, the eight-day twin-train movement with anchor escapement striking on a bell, 84¼in (214cm) high.
£2,800–3,350
€4,000–4,800
$4,700–5,600 L&T
Any Scottish longcase clock of this type is a collaborative effort. The case was made by a local cabinet maker, the face painted by a local painter on a sheet of steel possibly imported from England and the 'maker' produced the movement and retailed the clock.

A mahogany longcase clock, by David Straiton, Montrose, the dial painted with depictions of architectural ruins, subsidiary seconds and date dials, the eight-day movement striking on a bell, early 19thC, 82¼in (209cm) high.
£1,750–2,100
€2,500–3,000
$2,950–3,550 B(Ed)

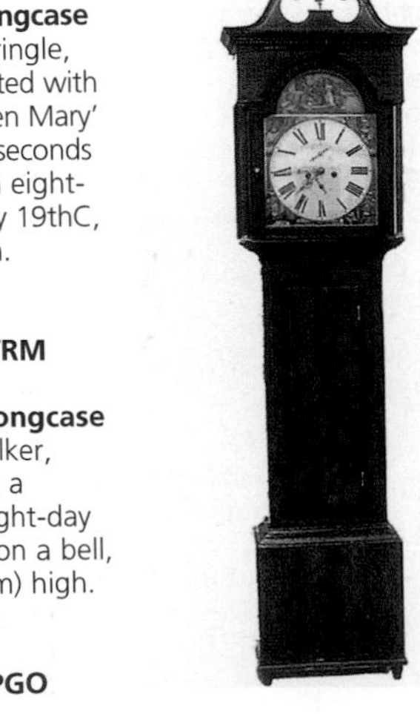

► A mahogany longcase clock, by George Pringle, Denny, the dial painted with 'The Escape of Queen Mary' and with subsidiary seconds and date dials, with eight-day movement, early 19thC, 88½in (225cm) high.
£1,100–1,300
€1,600–1,900
$1,850–2,200 TRM

◄ A mahogany longcase clock, by Frans Walker, Kirkcudbright, with a painted dial, the eight-day movement striking on a bell, c1800, 89in (226cm) high.
£3,300–3,700
€4,750–5,300
$5,500–6,200 ⊞ PGO

A mahogany longcase clock, by Halbert, Glasgow, the dial painted with representations of the four continents, the arch painted with a seated lady and a sailing ship, with a rack and bell striking movement, the case inlaid with stringing, apron missing, c1830, 82½in (209.5cm) high.
£1,200–1,400
€1,750–2,000
$2,000–2,350 ⚒ S(O)

A carved mahogany longcase clock, by Robertson, Edinburgh, the painted dial with subsidiary dials, the movement with anchor escapement and rack striking on a bell, c1840, 85in (216cm) high.
£1,650–1,950
€2,350–2,800
$2,750–3,250 ⚒ S(Am)

► An ebony and glass mantel clock, by Alexander Mitchell, Glasgow, with silvered and engraved dial, c1850, 13in (33cm) high.
£6,300–7,000
€9,100–10,100
$10,600–11,800 ⊞ JeF

A mahogany and brass-inlaid mantel clock, by Brotherston & Thomson, Dalkeith, with silvered dial, the twin fusee movement striking on a coiled gong, the case with drop handles and grille panels, 1825–50, 20in (51cm) high.
£1,850–2,200
€2,650–3,150
$3,100–3,700 ⚒ B(Ed)

A mahogany longcase clock, the dial painted with Scottish figures, the eight-day twin-train movement with anchor escapement and rack-strike on a bell, 19thC, 80¾in (205cm) high.
£820–980 / €1,200–1,400
$1,400–1,650 ⚒ DN

A mahogany regulator, by J. Bainbridge, Portobello, the silvered minute dial with second and hour dials, the movement with pillars and plates, with deadbeat escapement and mercury jar pendulum, 19thC, 79in (200.5cm) high.
£4,700–5,600
€6,800–8,100
$7,900–9,400 ⚒ B

A mahogany longcase clock, by A. Stoddart, Leith, with subsidiary seconds and date dials, steel hands, the eight-day movement striking the hours on a bell, c1840, 79in (200.5cm) high.
£5,400–6,000
€7,800–8,600
$9,100–10,100 ⊞ PAO

► A Victorian mahogany longcase clock, the gilt dial with subsidiary seconds and date dial, the twin-train movement with strike mechanism and anchor escapement missing, 76¾in (195cm) high.
£1,700–2,000
€2,450–2,900
$2,850–3,350 ⚒ BR

A mahogany longcase clock, by P. Wood, Montrose, the enamelled dial painted with the seasons and a moonlight scene of Rob Roy fighting, inscribed 'Vide Rob Roy', with subsidiary seconds and date dials, the eight-day twin-train movement with deadbeat escapement and twelve-hour alarm striking on a bell, 19thC, 82¾in (210cm) high.
£940–1,100
€1,350–1,600
$1,550–1,850 ⚒ L&T

Barometers & Barographs

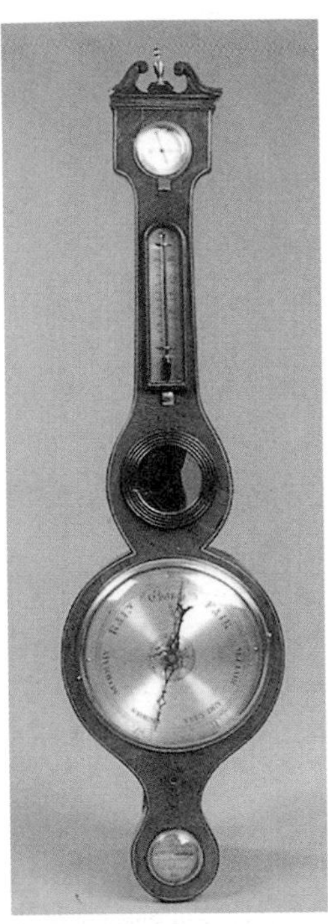

A late Georgian ebony and boxwood-strung mahogany wheel barometer, by D. Rivolta, Edinburgh, with hygrometer, later alcohol thermometer, mirror, silvered dial and spirit-level dial inscribed with maker's name, 37½in (95.5cm) high.
£330–390 / €480–560
$550–660 PFK

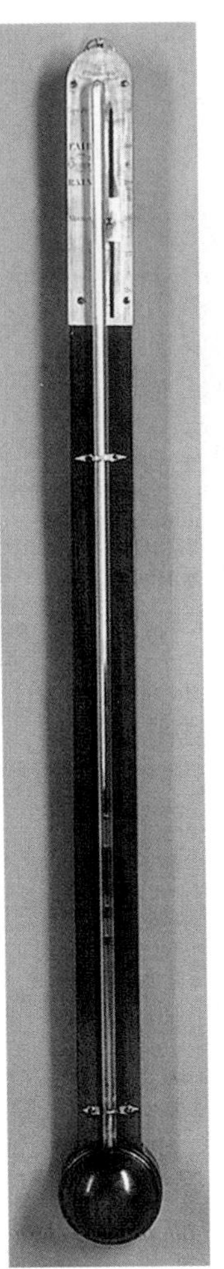

◄ **A mahogany stick barometer,** by Alexander Adie, Edinburgh, the silvered plate with vernier and signed 'Adie', c1830, 34½in (87.5cm) high.
£2,400–2,850 / €3,450–4,100
$4,000–4,800 S(O)
Alexander Adie was born in 1775 and apprenticed to his uncle, John Miller, one of the leading 18th-century Scottish barometer makers. He was taken into partnership with his uncle in 1804 under the name Miller & Adie. Miller died in 1815 but Adie continued to trade under the joint name until 1822. Adie invented and patented the sympiesometer in 1818 and for this, and other research, he was elected a Fellow of the Royal Society of Edinburgh in 1819. He was also optician to King William IV and Queen Victoria. In 1835 he took his son John into partnership. He died in 1858, his son having pre-deceased him the previous year.

A brass-mounted oak barograph, by Turnbull & Co, Edinburgh, c1900, 14in (35.5cm) wide.
£490–590 / €710–850
$820–990 GAK

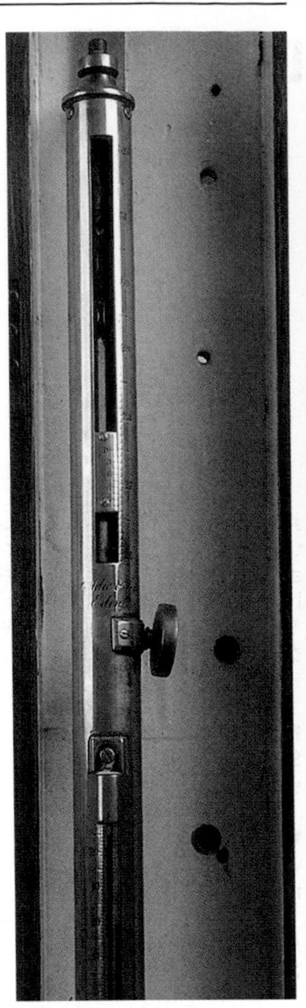

A Victorian brass lighthouse barometer, by Adie & Son, Edinburgh, with thermometer and adjustable vernier, 40¼in (102cm) long, with a later case.
£420–500 / €600–720
$710–840 B(Ed)

Architectural Antiques

A marble fire surround, c1820, 71in (180.5cm) wide.
£15,800–17,600 / €22,800–25,300
$26,600–30,000 ⊞ W&C
This surround comes from a Scottish country house.

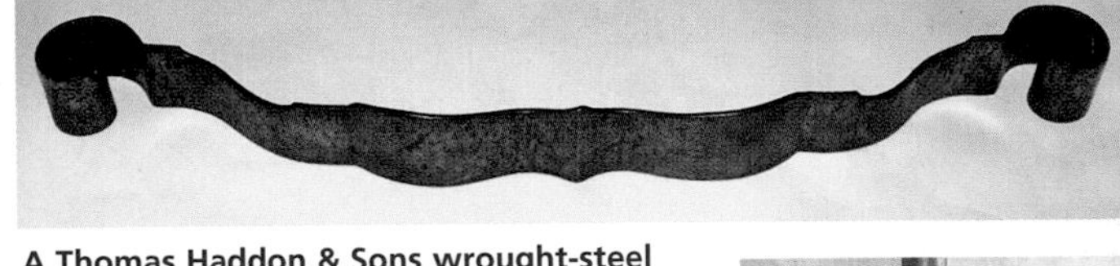

A Thomas Haddon & Sons wrought-steel fender, designed by Sir Robert Lorimer, c1910, 49in (124.5cm) wide.
£2,250–2,500 / €3,250–3,600
$3,800–4,200 ⊞ JSG

A pair of fireclay lions, c1870, 29½in (75cm) long.
£2,250–2,700 / €3,300–3,900
$3,800–4,500 S(S)
A number of Scottish potteries, including the Prestongrange Pottery and R. Brown of Paisley, produced models such as these.

A cast-iron and wrought-iron fire grate, c1880, 56¾in (144cm) wide.
£930–1,100 / €1,350–1,600
$1,550–1,850 S(O)

A laundry stove, by Balmain, c1900, 28in (71cm) high.
£630–700 / €900–1,000
$1,000–1,150 ⊞ B&R
This laundry stove was used for heating irons.

Decorative Arts

A walnut writing desk, by Sir Robert Lorimer, the stage-back flanked by veneered drawers above a frieze drawer with brass dolphin mask handles, stamped 'Whytock & Reid, Edinburgh', 1927–28, 59½in (151cm) wide.
£15,000–18,000 / €22,000–26,000
$35,000–30,000 ⚒ SH
This desk was designed by Sir Robert Lorimer for Glencruitten House in Oban. Lorimer was Scotland's premier architect and designer, working in the Arts and Crafts style.

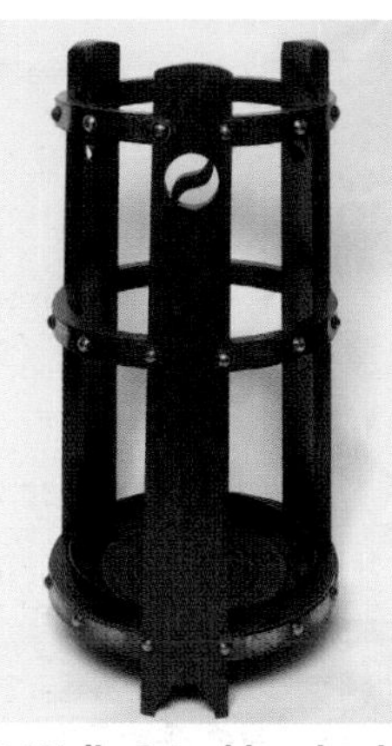

A Wylie & Lochhead oak stick stand, with copper and brass strapping and pierced decoration, c1900, 27in (68.5cm) high.
£500–550 / €720–800
$840–930 ⊞ TDG

A Dunmore Pottery model of a dragon, c1890, 8¼in (21cm) high.
£590–660 / €850–950
$990–1,100 ⊞ GLB
The Dunmore Pottery (1834–1902) near Airth in Stirlingshire, had its most productive period under Peter Gardner, who was the third generation of Gardners to pot at Dunmore. When he took over in 1866 output was changed from utility wares to decorative wares that were famed worldwide and attracted Queen Victoria as a patron. The Art Pottery produced in the late 19th century was influenced by the Aesthetic and Arts and Crafts movements. Wares were often inspired by natural form or mythical creatures and were decorated with rich, deeply-coloured lead glazes. The most common of these, derived from Chinese originals, were three-legged toads. Most Dunmore examples bear an impressed mark, though strangely this can appear on the body rather than the base of the piece.

► **A Monart glass bowl,** with aventurine inclusions, minor scratches, c1930, 12in (30.5cm) diam.
£175–210 / €250–300
$290–350 ⚒ BR

A Monart vase, shape 'N', c1924, 9½in (24cm) high.
£610–730 / €900–1,050
$1,000–1,200 ⚒ B(Ed)
This piece is characteristic of Monart's earliest production in that the colour decoration occurs on the surface of the piece. It was quickly realized that casing the pieces with a thin skin of clear glass increased the brilliance of the colours.

A Monart glass vase, 1930s, 9in (23cm) high.
£540–600 / €780–860
$900–1,000 ⊞ SAAC

Monart Glass

Monart Glass is French art glass made in Scotland by Spaniards. It was produced in Perth at the North British Glassworks of Moncreiff Ltd from 1924 to 1939, with production resuming after the war until 1961. All Monart was made by members of the Ysart family who originated from Barcelona, but who had worked at Cristallerie Schneider, near Paris. The earliest examples are surface-decorated, but the practice of casing in clear glass was soon adopted. The only means of marking was with a paper label stuck to the pontil mark, which usually does not survive. Prices, however, can be attributed on the basis of shape, size and colour combination.

A brass jardinière, by Margaret Gilmour, embossed with stylized foliage, stamped 'MG' monogram, early 20thC, 8¼in (21cm) square.
£540–650 / €780–940
$910–1,100 S(O)

◄ A copper wall sconce, by Alexander Ritchie, Iona, embossed with galleons and entwined lotus leaves, with Celtic knotwork borders, c1910, 16in (40.5cm) high.
£1,100–1,250 / €1,600–1,800
$1,850–2,100 ⊞ DAD
Alexander Ritchie produced substantial amounts of Celtic-revival silver jewellery and novelty items which he sold to visitors to the island of Iona. His silver is always marked but his larger beaten brass and copper pieces seldom are. These can be identified from contemporary photographs of his shop interior.

The Gilmour sisters

Margaret and Mary Gilmour studied at the Glasgow School of Art, one of whose functions was to provide educational opportunities for young ladies, who were directed towards suitable pursuits such as needlework, china decorating and, perhaps more surprisingly, metalwork. In 1893, the sisters established a studio in Glasgow where they worked for nearly 50 years, making a large range of domestic metalwork. Margaret undertook most of the design work while Mary concerned herself with the preparation and a third sister, Agnes, looked after the accounts. Much of their work is in the Celtic revival style, their designs being traced onto industrially manufactured sheet brass and then worked with a hammer and chisel in a repoussé technique. Pieces are marked with a stamped 'MG'.

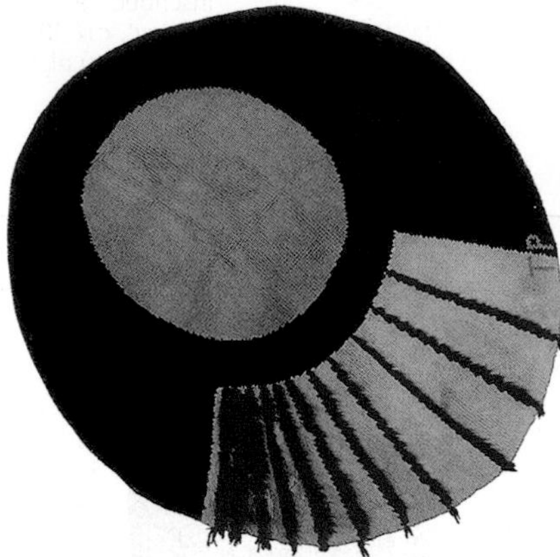

A hand-tufted wool rug, by Terence Prentice, woven by the Edinburgh Weavers, woven 'T.P.', 1936–37, 69¾in (177cm) wide.
£6,000–7,200 / €8,700–10,400
$10,100–12,100 S(O)

Jewellery

◄ A silver-gilt and paste-set pendant, by John Hay, Leith, with a glazed locket, maker's mark, c1820.
£300–360 / €440–520
$500–600 B(Ed)

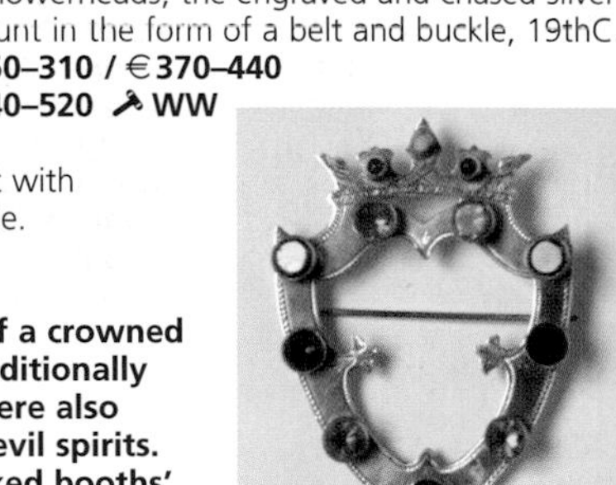

A hardstone bracelet, with five plaques carved as flowerheads, the engraved and chased silver mount in the form of a belt and buckle, 19thC.
£260–310 / €370–440
$440–520 WW

► A silver Luckenbooth-style brooch, set with foil-backed crystals, c1860, 2½in (6.5cm) wide.
£220–250 / €320–360
$370–420 ⊞ GAU
Luckenbooth brooches are in the form of a crowned heart or conjoined hearts. They were traditionally exchanged between sweethearts, but were also pinned to a child's clothing to ward off evil spirits. The name is said to derive from the 'locked booths' by St Giles Cathedral in Edinburgh from which they were first sold in the 17th century.

Treen

A sycamore and penwork snuff box, c1820, 3in (7.5cm) diam.
£180–200 / €260–290
$300–340 ⊞ MB

A yew wood and walnut three-handled quaich, bound with pewter bands, c1700, 7in (18cm) diam.
£420–500 / €600–720
$700–840 S(O)
The word quaich derives from the Gaelic 'cuach' meaning 'cup'.

A staved luggie, late 19thC, 2½in (6.5cm) wide.
£200–230 / €290–330
$340–390 ⊞ GAU
The individual staves are joined by feathering the edges – these slivers fit together and form a watertight seal.

Horn

◄ **A horn stirrup cup,** inscribed 'Ian McKay', c1800, 3in (7.5cm) high.
£430–480
€620–690
$720–800
⊞ SEA

A carved horn snuff mull, c1800, 4in (10cm) long.
£450–500 / €650–720
$760–840 ⊞ AEF

◄ **A carved horn snuff mull,** in the form of a cat, c1810, 2½in (6.5cm) high.
£800–890 / €1,150–1,300
$1,350–1,500 ⊞ GAU

Mauchline Ware

A Mauchline ware snuff box, decorated with penwork thistles and a painted scene of two lovers, c1810, 3½in (9cm) wide.
£1,100–1,250 / €1,600–1,800
$1,850–2,100 ⊞ GAU

A Mauchline ware snuff box, depicting Dunorlie Castle, Oban and Ballachullish Ferry and Hotel, 19thC, 5in (12.5cm) wide.
£55–65 / €80–95
$95–110 ⚒ BR

A Mauchline ware penwork workbox, depicting Scottish country houses including Barskinning in Ayrshire, the hinged lid enclosing a mirror and six compartments, feet missing, early 19thC, 9in (23cm) wide.
£1,400–1,650 / €2,000–2,350
$2,350–2,750 ⚒ B(Ed)

A Mauchline ware compass, depicting the White House in Washington, America, c1870, 2in (5cm) diam.
£120–135 / €170–195
$200–220 ⊞ GAU

Production of wooden boxes with their characteristic all-wooden hinge was begun in Laurenskirk in the east of Scotland in the late 18th century. By the early 19th century the industry was concentrated in Ayrshire around the town of Mauchline. The Smith company was the most prominent, and several hundred people were employed making high-quality sycamore snuff boxes, many of which were exported. They were hand-painted and then protected with up to 30 coats of copal resin varnish. Early 19th-century production was dominated by the snuff box, although larger items such as tea caddies were also made. Good examples will now fetch four-figure sums. By the 1840s, as snuff taking began to decline in popularity, the manufacturers had diversified into the production of a wide range of small domestic wares. Most late 19th- and early 20th-century Mauchline ware is decorated with transfer prints, often of popular resorts. This type is both more plentiful and much less expensive than the earlier hand-painted examples.

A Mauchline ware inkwell, decorated with a view of Tarbert, 1860–80, 2½in (6.5cm) high.
£210–240 / €300–340
$350–400 ⊞ GAU

A Mauchline ware money box, commemorating Queen Victoria's Golden Jubilee, the cover printed with a bust portrait and the body printed with an entitled view of 'Glasgow from the Clyde', 1887, 4in (10cm) high.
£90–105 / €130–150
$150–175 ⚒ PFK

A Mauchline ware tea caddy, transfer-printed with views of Taymouth Castle and Aberfeldy, signed 'Smith – Maker to His Majesty', c1900, 6¼in (16cm) wide.
£450–500 / €650–720
$760–840 ⊞ JTS

Tartan Ware

A Tartan ware box, decorated with the McLean tartan, c1870, 2½in (6.5cm) diam.
£100–110 / €145–160
$165–185 ⊞ RdeR

A Tartan ware notecase, decorated with the McFarlane tartan, with metal clasp, c1870, 3in (7.5cm) wide.
£250–280 / €360–400
$420–470 ⊞ RdeR

As the popularity of snuff-taking, and therefore snuff boxes, began to decline in the 1830s, the manufacturers of Mauchline ware were forced to find other ways of keeping their businesses afloat. One solution was devised by Smith of Mauchline who, in 1853, developed a machine that could automatically paint any one of several tartans using up to 16 pens. The tartan paper was stuck to the object, which was usually made of sycamore, and the joins concealed with black paint and sometimes a painted gold line. Finally, the piece was coated with many layers of shellac. Victorian inventiveness had been applied to what was essentially a craft process and a new type of souvenir ware had entered the market, taking advantage of the fashion for all things Scottish.

A Tartan ware pen tray, decorated with the Stuart tartan, damaged, 19thC, 9in (23cm) long.
£130–155 / €185–220
$220–260 ⚒ BR

A Tartan ware egg spool-holder, containing a silver thimble, c1870, 1½in (4cm) wide.
£250–280 / €360–400
$420–470 ⊞ RdeR

A Tartan ware egg timer, decorated with the McGregor tartan, slight damage, 19thC, 3in (7.5cm) high.
£95–110 / €135–160
$160–185 ⚒ BR

A Tartan ware photograph album, containing 200 *carte-de-visite* portrait photographs, decorated with the Stuart tartan, with gilt-metal clasps and inset silver presentation plaque, slight damage, c1867, 12¼ x 9¼in (31 x 23.5cm).
£260–310 / €380–450
$440–520 ⚒ RTo

A Victorian Tartan ware thimble container, 3in (7.5cm) high.
£220–250 / €320–360
$370–420 ⊞ HTE

◀ **A Tartan ware thread box,** decorated with the McIntosh tartan, with a picture of Adolphe Thiens, c1870, 4in (10cm) diam.
£220–250 / €320–360
$370–420 ⊞ GAU
Adolphe Thiens was the first president of France after the fall of Napoleon.

Metalware

A pewter laver, with cusped thumbpiece, c1780, 8½in (21.5cm) high.
£500–600 / €720–860
$840–1,000 S(O)

A pewter measure, engraved 'Wine Company of Scotland', Edinburgh, c1800, 8¾in (22cm) high.
£2,700–3,000
€3,900–4,300
$4,500–5,000 ⊞ DML

► **A pewter tappit hen measure,** 18thC, 7½in (19cm) high.
£610–680 / €880–980
$1,000–1,100 ⊞ KEY
A tappit hen or Scot's pint is equal to three imperial pints. The shape resembles pewter measures from Normandy and the name may be derived from the French quart measure *Topynett*. Tappit hens are seldom found with maker's marks.

LOCATE THE SOURCE
The source of each illustration in Miller's can be found by checking the code letters below each caption with the Key to Illustrations, pages 794–800.

A set of three pewter measures, marked 'D. B. & B. R.', early 19thC, largest 11in (28cm) high.
£3,800–4,250 / €5,500–6,100
$6,400–7,100 ⊞ HWK
The largest measure (tappit hen) holds three pints, the middle (chopin) holds one and a half pints and the smallest sized (mutchkin) holds three-quarters of a pint.

A pewter baluster measure, with ball thumbpiece, c1840, 4in (10cm) high.
£500–600 / €720–790
$830–920 ⊞ SEA
Scottish baluster measures of ball type were produced from c1750 to 1830.

A pair of Victorian tin tea canisters and covers, painted with a cartouche of exotic birds and flowers, with painted labels for Lowe of Glasgow, 19in (48.5cm) high.
£1,700–2,000 / €2,450–2,900
$2,850–3,350 G(L)

Weapons

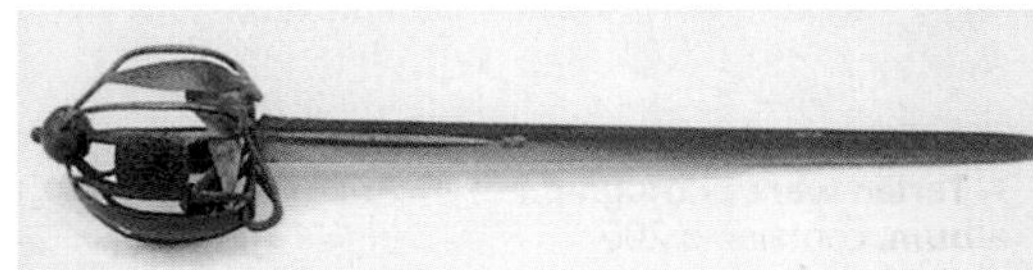

A basket-hilted sword, with steel pommel, armourer's mark, grip and half leather liner missing, blade shortened, 18thC, 27in (68.5cm) long.
£440–520 / €630–750
$740–870 WL

A basket-hilted broadsword, the blade by Andrea Ferrera, with Running Wolf mark, c1760, 40in (101.5cm) long.
£2,200–2,500 / €3,150–3,600
$3,700–4,200 ⊞ WSA

► **A basket-hilted broadsword,** by Walter Allen, Stirling, the iron hilt with baize-faced leather liner, with a later wire-bound leather grip, engraved 'W. A.' and stamped with various marks, 1725–50, blade 33¼in (84.5cm) long.
£20,000–24,000 / €29,000–35,000
$34,000–41,000 B(Kn)
Walter Allen was admitted Freeman of the Incorporation of Hammermen at Stirling in 1732 and is considered to be one of the most talented makers of Scottish basket hilts. The basket-hilted broadsword is the best known of all Scottish weapons. In 1797, a specific pattern of broadsword was introduced for officers in Scottish regiments.

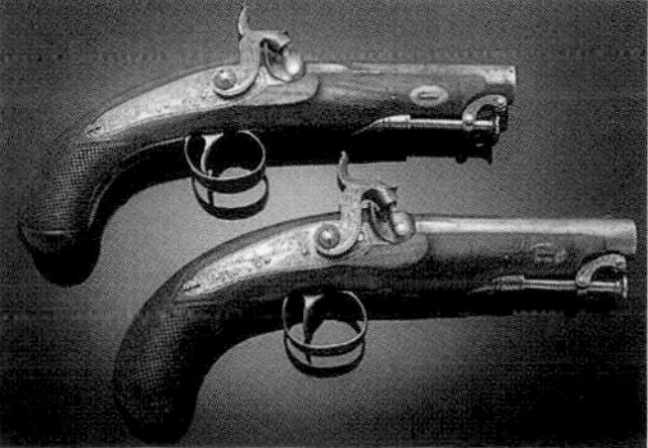

A pair of percussion travelling pistols, with walnut full stocks, silver bolt escutcheons, engraved trigger guards and chequered grips, signed 'MacLauchlan' and engraved 'Edinburgh', 19thC, 8in (20.5cm) long.
£1,400–1,650 / €2,000–2,350
$2,350–2,750 L&T

Scientific Instruments

A stained beech celestial globe, by Kirkwoods, Edinburgh, c1820, 15in (38cm) diam.
£5,000–5,500
€7,200–7,900
$8,400–9,300 ⊞ GEO

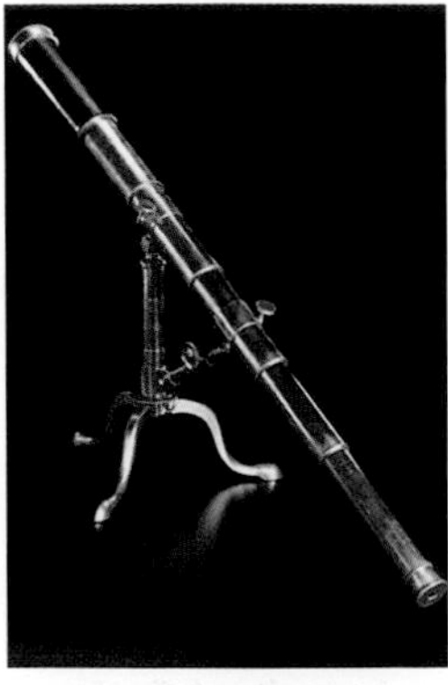

◄ A 2¾in nickel-plated refracting telescope, by Smith & Ramage, Aberdeen, with five draws and leather-bound body tube, two eyepieces, tripod stand and attachments, in a velvet-lined mahogany case, mid-19thC, 18in (46cm) long.
£3,100–3,700
€4,450–5,300
$5,200–6,200 ⚒ S(O)
This firm have specialized in the manufacture of large telescopes.

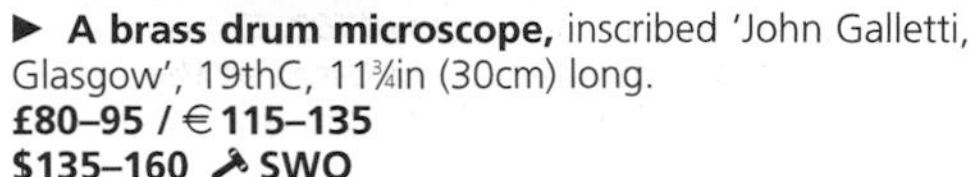

► A brass drum microscope, inscribed 'John Galletti, Glasgow', 19thC, 11¾in (30cm) long.
£80–95 / €115–135
$135–160 ⚒ SWO

Sport

For further information on
Sport see pages 730–742

A Scottish Football Association player's cap, 1963–64.
£1,800–2,000 / €2,600–2,900
$3,000–3,350 ⊞ EE

► A Scottish International football jersey, No. 8, worn by John White, with embroidered cloth badge, c1960.
£1,200–1,450 / €1,750–2,100
$2,000–2,400 ⚒ S(O)

◄ A gold and enamel Scottish Football League Cup winner's medal, awarded to Jim Baxter, with inscription, in original case, 1963–64.
£1,350–1,600 / €1,950–2,300
$2,250–2,700 ⚒ S(O)
In the 1964 Scottish League Cup Final, Rangers demolished Greenock Morton 5–0. Rangers won the Scottish domestic treble in this season. Jim Baxter was the Ranger's left-half between 1960 and 1965 and during this highly successful period won three Championship, three Scottish Cup and four Scottish League Cup medals.

A Brown's patent Major niblick golf rake iron, by Winton of Montrose, c1905.
£3,400–4,000
€4,900–5,900
$5,700–6,800 ⚒ SWO

A driver golf club, by Auchterlouie of St Andrews, c1915.
£40–45 / €55–65
$70–80 ⊞ MSh

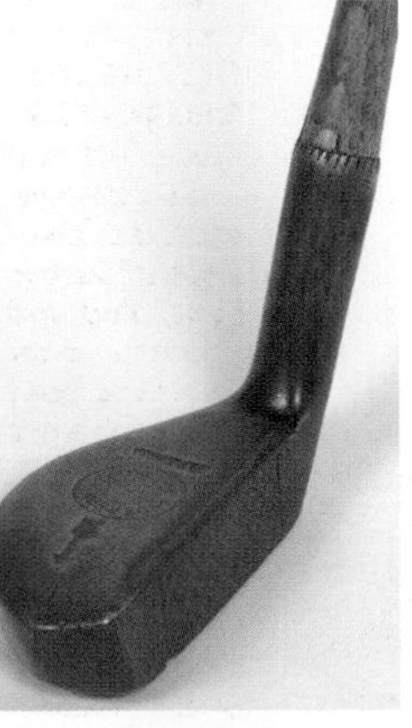

A brass head golf putter, by Anderson of Anstruther, c1910.
£105–120 / €150–170
$175–200 ⊞ MSh

A Mammoth niblick golf club, by Cochranes of Edinburgh, c1920.
£590–650 / €850–940
$990–1,100 ⊞ MSh

A smooth face lofting iron, by W. Park of Musselburgh, c1895.
£125–140 / €180–200
$210–230 ⊞ MSh

Miscellaneous

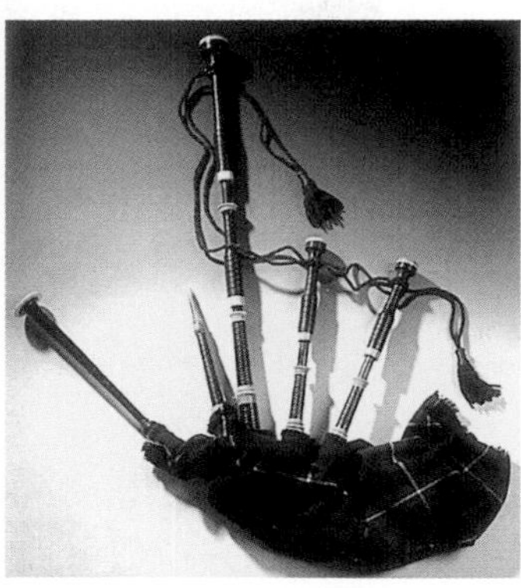

A set of tropical hardwood bagpipes, by Donald MacDonald, with ivory fittings, the chanter stamped 'MacDonald', early 19thC.
£1,550–1,850 / €2,250–2,650
$2,600–3,100 B(Ed)
Donald MacDonald holds a special place in the history of bagpipe manufacture. Not only was he one of the first makers in Scotland to mark his pipes but he was the first to publish Highland bagpipe music with his *Collection of the Ancient Martial Music of Caledonia called Piobaireachd*, issued 1819–20. MacDonald produced bagpipes from 1806 to 1839 in his workshop in the Lawnmarket in Edinburgh, succeeding the celebrated Hugh Robertson. MacDonald was in turn replaced by Thomas Glen.

A Paul Ysart paperweight, 1930s, 3½in (9cm) diam.
£860–950 / €1,200–1,350
$1,450–1,600 SWB
Paul Ysart was born in Barcelona of Bohemian parents. The family emigrated to Scotland in 1915 when Paul's father Salvador, also a glass-maker, obtained employment at the Edinburgh and Leith Flint Glassworks as a senior glass-blower, with Paul as an apprentice. The pair joined the Moncrieff Glassworks in 1922 and Paul began making weights in the 1930s. He remained with the company until 1963 when he moved to Caithness Glass, where he made many beautiful weights in his spare time. Those with canes inscribed 'PY' were sold to America. In 1970, he set up on his own and used an H cane to identify his weights. Examples that are scratch-signed are particularly interesting because they are the ones he gave to family and friends.

► **A pair of crewelwork bedhangings,** the embroidered flowering branches dotted with baskets, insects, birds and beasts, early 18thC, 104¼ x 43¼in (265 x 110cm).
£25,000–30,000 / €36,000–43,000
$42,000–50,000 S(O)
This pair of crewelwork bedhangings were worked by a Scottish noblewoman, probably a member of the Baird family 1690–1700. They originally would have formed part of a set of curtains and pelmets to hang on a four-poster bed to keep out the draughts. They originally came from Lennoxlove, an imposing house near Edinburgh – so called after Frances Stuart, Duchess of Richmond and Lennox, a renowned beauty and favourite of Charles II who bought the house c1702. These hangings have been exhibited at the National Museum of Edinburgh.

► **A pine model of a fishing boat,** entitled 'Glenbarry', c1880, 20in (51cm) wide.
£400–450 / €580–650
$670–760 GAU

An Argyll & Sutherland Highlanders officer's khaki serge doublet, worn by Col A. Douglas-Dick, with brass buttons and bronze lapel badges, with ribbons of C.B., Q.S.A. and 1911 Coronation, c1914.
£1,000–1,200
€1,450–1,700
$1,700–2,000 WAL

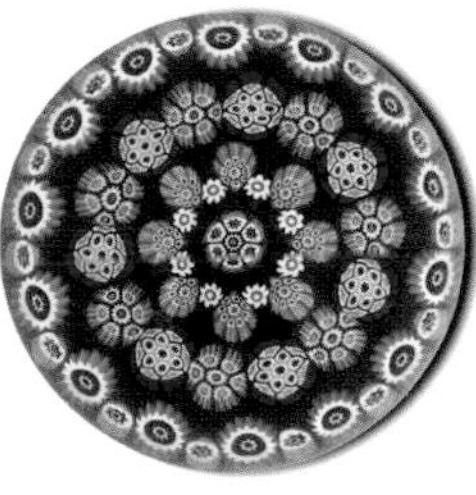

A Paul Ysart paperweight, scratch-signed 'P. Ysart' on base, 1930s, 3in (7.5cm) diam.
£590–650 / €850–940
$990–1,100 SWB

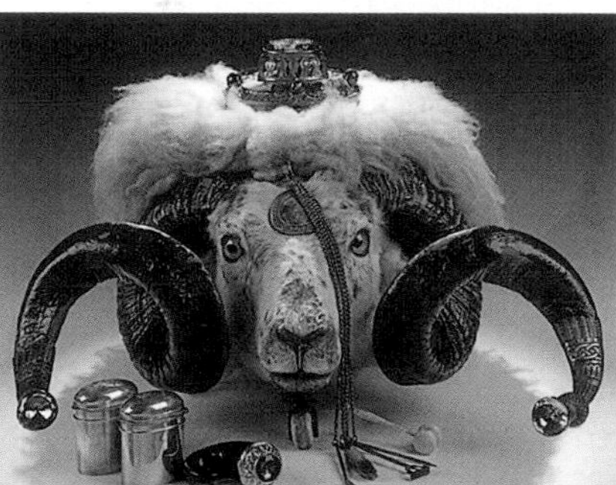

A ram's head table snuff mull, by Mackay & Chisholm, the silver lid chased with Celtic zoomorphic strapwork and centred by a faceted quartz, the forehead applied with a plaque below a ring from which five snuff tools are suspended from chains, on three ceramic casters, Edinburgh, 1880, 13¼in (33.5cm) high.
£7,700–9,200 / €11,100–13,300
$13,000–15,500 B(Ed)
This snuff mull incorporates a range of tools deemed useful for the preparation of snuff, attached by chains to the head. A more unusual feature is the three separate canisters concealed under the lid, which is set with agates and modelled on a plaid brooch. The engraved coat-of-arms indicate that it was made for a grand house – fitted with casters, it would have been wheeled up and down the dining table after the meal.

The fascination with all things Scottish began in the early 19th century with the visit of George IV to Edinburgh in 1822 being a milestone in its development, and Queen Victoria's purchase of Balmoral Castle in 1852 and her widely publicized love of the Highlands its apotheosis. A sentimental view of Scotland evolved in which thistles, tartan and broadswords feature prominently.

Glossary

Below are explanations of some of the terms that you will come across in this book.

agate ware: 18thC pottery, veined or marbled to resemble the mineral agate.

***aikuchi*:** Japanese dagger without a guard.

***albarello*:** Drug jar, usually of waisted cylindrical form, used in most major European countries from the 15thC.

anchor escapement: Said to have been invented c1670 by Robert Hooke or William Clement. A type of escape mechanism shaped like an anchor, which engages at precise intervals with the toothed escape wheel. The anchor permits the use of a pendulum (either long or short), and gives greater accuracy than was possible with the verge escapement.

***anhua*:** Hidden decoration on Chinese porcelain.

associated: Term used in antiques, in which one part of an item is of the same design but not originally made for it. See *marriage* and *made up*.

automaton: Any moving toy or decorative object, usually powered by a clockwork mechanism.

***basma*:** Silk threads couched at right angles giving the appearance of surface ribbing.

bezel: Ring, usually brass, surrounding the dial of a clock, and securing the glass dial cover.

***bianco-sopra-bianco*:** Literally white-on-white. Used in ceramics to describe an opaque white pattern painted on an off-white background.

Biedermeier: Style of furniture made principally in the 1820s and '30s in Austria, Germany and parts of Scandinavia and characterized by simple, heavy Classical forms. It is named after a fictional character who symbolized the German bourgeoisie of the early 19thC.

biggin: Form of coffee percolator invented c1799 by George Biggin.

***bijin*:** Japanese term for a beautiful woman.

bisque: French term for biscuit ware, or unglazed porcelain.

***blanc-de-Chine*:** Translucent white Chinese porcelain, unpainted and with a thick glaze, made in kilns in Dehua in the Fujian province from the Song Dynasty and copied in Europe.

Bodhisattva: Attendant of Buddha.

***bombé*:** Bulbous, curving form, a feature often seen on wares produced during the rococo period.

***bonbonnière*:** Sweet jar or box.

bordalou: Lady's portable commode.

***boteh*:** Stylized design of a floral bush found on rugs, similar to a Paisley design.

Britannia Standard: Higher standard of silver required between 1697 and 1720. Denoted by Britannia and a lion's head in profile on the hallmark.

***bureau de dame*:** Writing desk of delicate appearance and designed for use by ladies. Usually raised above slender cabriole legs and with one or two external drawers.

***bureau plat*:** French writing table with a flat top and drawers in the frieze.

cabaret set: Tea set on a tray for three or more people.

calamander: Hardwood, imported from Sri Lanka (of the same family as ebony), used in the Regency period for making small articles of furniture, as a veneer and for crossbanding.

cameo glass: Two or more layers of coloured glass in which the top layer/s are then cut or etched away to create a multi-coloured design in relief. An ancient technique popular with Art Nouveau glassmakers in the early 20thC.

cannetille: Extremely thin gold wirework decoration.

cartouche: Ornate tablet or shield surrounded by scrollwork and foliage, often bearing an inscription, monogram or coat-of-arms.

celadon: Chinese stoneware with an opaque grey-green glaze, first made in the Song Dynasty and still made today, principally in Korea.

cellaret: Lidded container on legs designed to hold wine. The interior is often divided into sections for individual bottles.

***champlevé*:** Enamelling on copper or bronze, similar to cloisonné, in which a glass paste is applied to the hollowed-out design, fired and ground smooth.

character doll: One with a naturalistic face, especially laughing, crying, pouting, etc.

***chilong*:** Small lizard, often portrayed on Chinese ceramics.

Chinese Imari: Chinese imitations of Japanese blue, red and gold painted Imari wares, made from the early 18thC.

chinoiserie: The fashion, prevailing in the late 18thC, for Chinese-style ornamentation on porcelain, wall-papers, fabrics, furniture and garden architecture.

***chuval*:** Turkic word meaning bag.

cistern tube: Mercury tube fitted into stick barometers, the lower end of which is sealed into a boxwood cistern.

clock garniture: Matching group of clock and vases or candelabra made for the mantel shelf. Often highly ornate.

cloisonné: Enamelling on metal with divisions in the design separated by lines of fine metal wire. A speciality of the Limoges region of France in the Middle Ages, and of Chinese craftsmen to the present day.

close-concentric paperweight: One which consists of concentric circles of canes arranged tightly together so that the clear glass cannot be seen between the rings of canes.

close-pack paperweight: One which is characterized by canes closely packed together without a pattern.

***coiffeuse*:** French dressing table.

coin silver: Silver of the standard used for coinage, ie .925 or sterling.

***coffor bach*:** Small Welsh coffer.

coromandel: Imported wood from the Coromandel coast of India, of similar blackish appearance to calamander and used from c1780 for banding, and for small pieces of furniture.

countwheel: Wheel with segments cut out of the edge or with pins fitted to one face, which controls the striking of a clock. Also known as a locking plate.

***crespina*:** Shallow Italian dish with a fluted border.

***cuerda seca*:** Technique of tile-making, developed in Iran in the 15thC, whereby the colours of the design were separated by an oily substance which leaves a brownish outline.

culet: Bottom facet or point of a faceted gemstone.

***cwpwrdd deuddarn*:** Welsh variety of the press cupboard with two tiers.

***cwpwrdd tridarn*:** Welsh variety of the press cupboard with three tiers.

cyma: Double-carved moulding. Cyma recta is concave above and convex below; cyma reversa the other way round. Also known as ogee and reverse ogee moulding. Popular with 18thC cabinet makers.

Cymric: Trade-name used by Liberty & Co for a mass-produced range of silverware inspired by Celtic art, introduced in 1899 and often incorporating enamelled pictorial plaques.

deadbeat escapement: Type of anchor escapement, possibly invented by George Graham and used in precision pendulum clocks.

Delft: Dutch tin-glazed earthenwares named after the town of Delft, the principal production centre, from the 16thC onwards. Similar pottery made in England from the late 16thC is also termed 'delft' or 'delftware'.

dentils: Small rectangular blocks applied at regular intervals as a decorative feature.

DEP: Abbreviation of the French *déposé* or German *deponiert*, indicating a registered patent. Used on French and German bisque dolls and often appearing as an incised mark on the head.

***dhurrie*:** Cotton flatweave rug or carpet from India.

diaper: Surface decoration composed of repeated diamonds or squares, often carved in low relief.

dog of *Fo*: Buddhist guardian lion.

***doucai*:** Decoration on Chinese porcelain using five colours.

drabware: Pottery or stoneware distinguished by its greenish-brown or pale coffee-coloured glaze, mainly produced from the late 18thC to c1860, by Staffordshire potters including Minton, Wedgwood and Spode.

***duchesse brisée*:** a type of chaise longue of French origin, consisting of one or two tub-shaped chairs and a stool to extend the length. Popular in Britain during the late 18thC.

***encre de chine*:** Indian ink.

***en grisaille*:** Monochrome decoration, usually grey, used on ceramics and furniture during the 18th and 19thC.

***ensi*:** Rug used as a tent door by Turkoman tribes.

escapement: Means or device which regulates the release of the power of a timepiece to its pendulum or balance.

***façon de Venise*:** Literally 'in the Venetian style', used to describe high quality, Venetian-influenced glassware made in Europe during the 16th to 17thC.

faïence: Tin-glazed earthenware named after the town of Faenza in Italy, but actually used to describe products made anywhere but Italy, where they are called maiolica.

***famille jaune/noire/rose/verte*:** Chinese porcelain in which yellow, black, pink or green respectively are the predominant ground colours.

***fauteuil*:** French open-armed drawing room chair.

feldspar: Rock-forming mineral used to make hard-paste porcelain.

fielded panel: Panel with bevelled or chamfered edges.

firing glass: Low drinking glass with a short, thick stem and a thick foot, used on ceremonial occasions when, after toasting, the glass would be hammered on the table to make a sound like gunfire.

flambé: Glaze made from copper, usually deep crimson, flecked with blue or purple, and often faintly crackled.

flatware (1): Collective name for flat pottery and porcelain, such as plates, dishes and saucers.

flatware (2): Cutlery.

fluted: Border that resembles a scalloped edge, used as a decoration on furniture, glass, silver and porcelain items.

fusee: 18thC clockwork invention; a cone-shaped drum, linked to the spring barrel by a length of gut or chain. The shape compensates for the declining strength of the mainspring thus ensuring constant timekeeping.

gadroon: Border or ornament comprising radiating lobes of either curbed or straight form. Used from the late Elizabethan period.

girandole: Carved and gilt candle sconce incorporating a mirror.

***guéridon*:** Small circular table designed to carry some form of lighting.

guglet: Type of water bottle, often accompanied by a small basin and used for minor ablutions.

***guilloche*:** Decorative motif of interlacing circles forming a continuous figure-of-eight pattern.

***gul*:** From the Persian word for flower – usually used to describe a geometric flowerhead on a rug.

***guri*:** Chinese layered lacquer or metalwork, carved to reveal the separate layers.

halberd: Spear fitted with a double axe.

hard paste: True porcelain made of china stone (petuntse) and kaolin; the formula was long known to, and kept secret by, Chinese potters but only discovered in the 1720s at Meissen, Germany, from where it spread to the rest of Europe and the Americas. Recognized by its hard, glossy feel.

***herati*:** Overall repeating design of a flowerhead within a lozenge issuing small leaves.

***hiramakie*:** Japanese term for sponged gold applied level with the surface.

***ho-o*:** Mythical Chinese bird, similar to a phoenix, symbolizing wisdom and energy.

hydria: Ancient Greek water vessel characterized by a vertical handle at the back for dipping and two horizontal handles for lifting.

Imari: Export Japanese porcelain of predominantly red, blue and gold decoration which, although made in Arita, is called Imari after the port from which it was shipped.

***indianische Blumen*:** German for 'indian flowers'; painting on porcelain in the Oriental style, especially on mid-18thC Meissen.

***inro*:** Japanese multi-compartmental medicine or seal container, carried suspended from the sash of a kimono.

***iroe hiramakie*:** Japanese term for lacquer decorated with gold and silver leaf.

ironstone: Stoneware, patented 1813 by Charles James Mason, containing ground glassy slag, a by-product of iron smelting, for extra strength.

***jambiya*:** Arabic dagger.

Kakiemon: Family of 17thC Japanese porcelain decorators who produced wares decorated with flowers and figures on a white ground in distinctive colours: azure, yellow, turquoise and soft red. Widely imitated in Europe.

kantharos: Ancient Greek stemmed deep drinking cup with high flung, ear-like handles.

***karakusa*:** 'Chinese grasses' – a common decoration on Chinese ceramics.

***katana*:** Long Japanese sword.

***kelleh*:** Long narrow carpets which are wider than runners.

***kendi*:** Chinese or Japanese globular drinking vessel which is filled through the neck, the liquid being drunk through the spout.

***khula khud*:** Indo-Persian term for helmet.

knop: Knob, protuberance or swelling in the stem of a wine glass, of various forms which can be used as an aid to dating and provenance.

***koro*:** Japanese incense burner.

***kotile*:** Ancient Greek vessel in the form of a bowl.

***kovsh*:** Russian vessel used for measuring drink, often highly decorated for ornamental purposes.

***kozuka*:** Small Japanese utility knife.

krater: Ancient Greek vessel for mixing water and wine in which the mouth is always the widest part.

***kris*:** Indonesian or Malaysian dagger with a scalloped edge.

***kylix*:** Ancient Greek shallow two-handled drinking vessel.

***laque burgauté*:** Asian lacquer wares, inlaid with mother-of-pearl, gold or precious stones.

latticinio: Fine threads of white or clear glass forming a filigree mesh effect enclosed in clear glass.

***lingzhi*:** Type of fungus or mushroom, used as a motif on Chinese works of art.

loaded: Term used for a silver candlestick with a hollow stem filled with pitch or sand for weight and stability.

***lohan*:** Saintly or worthy Chinese man.

Longquan: Chinese ceramics with a pale grey body covered by a thick, opaque, bluish-green, slightly bubbly glaze.

made up: Piece of furniture that has been put together from parts of other pieces of furniture. See *associated* and *marriage*.

maiolica: Tin-glazed earthenware produced in Italy from the 15thC to the present day.

majolica: Heavily-potted, moulded ware covered in transparent glazes in distinctive, often sombre colours, developed by the Minton factory in the mid-19thC.

***mandau*:** Bornean short sword.

marriage: Joining together of two unrelated parts to form one piece of furniture. See *associated* and *made up*.

***martelé*:** Term for silverware with a fine, hammered surface, first produced in France and later revived by the American silversmiths Gorham Manufacturing Co during the Art Nouveau period.

***meiping*:** Chinese for cherry blossom, used to describe a tall vase with high shoulders, small neck and narrow mouth, used to display flowering branches.

***menuki*:** Hilt ornaments for Japanese sword mountings.

merese: Flat disc of glass which links the bowl and stem, and sometimes the stem and foot, of a drinking glass.

***mihrab*:** Prayer niche with a pointed arch; the motif which distinguishes a prayer rug from other types.

milk glass: Term for glass made with tin oxide, which turns it an opaque white. Developed in Venice in the late 15thC.

millefiori: Italian term meaning 'thousand flowers'. A glassmaking technique whereby canes of coloured glass are arranged in bundles so that the cross-section creates a pattern. Commonly used in paperweights.

***mon*:** Japanese crest or coat-of-arms.

muntins: Uprights between the corner posts of a cabinet or the stiles of a door, to support and enclose panels.

near pair: Two items that are very similar in appearance and give the appearance of being a pair. Also known as a matched pair.

***netsuke*:** Japanese carved toggles made to secure *sagemono* (hanging things) to the *obi* (waist belt) from a cord; usually of ivory, lacquer, silver or wood, from the 16thC.

Newcastle light baluster glass: Type of drinking glass made in the north east of England from 1730 to 1755, distinguished by the lightness of the glass of which they are made. The stems often had knops with tears in them to create the impression of light within the stem.

niello: Black metal alloy or enamel used for filling in engraved designs on silverware.

ogee: Double curve of slender S shape.

oinochoe: Small ancient Greek jug with handles.

***ojime*:** Japanese word meaning bead.

***okimono*:** Small, finely carved Japanese ornament.

oklad: Silver or gold icon cover, applied as a tribute or in gratitude for a prayer answered. Also known as a riza or basma.

***oni*:** Chinese devil.

ormolu: Strictly, gilded bronze but used loosely for any yellow metal. Originally used for furniture handles and mounts but, from the 18thC, for inkstands, candlesticks etc.

overlay: In cased glass, the top layer, usually engraved to reveal a different coloured layer beneath.

palmette: Stylized palm-leaf motif.

***pâte-de-cristal*:** Glass that is crushed into fine crystals and then bound together so that it can be moulded rather than having to be worked in its molten state.

***pâte-de-verre*:** 'glass paste' – translucent glass created by melting and applying powdered glass in layers or by casting it in a mould.

***pâte-sur-pâte*:** 19thC Sèvres porcelain technique, much copied, of applying coloured clay decoration to the body before firing.

pavé: Setting that has been paved with snugly fitting gemstones, so that little or no metal shows through.

penwork: Type of decoration applied to japanned furniture, principally in England in the late 18th/early 19thC. Patterns in white japan were applied to a piece which had already been japanned black, and then the details and shading were added using black Indian ink with a fine quill pen.

pier glass: Mirror designed to be fixed to the pier, or wall, between two tall window openings, often partnered by a matching pier table. Made from the mid-17thC.

***pietra dura*:** Italian term for hardstone, applied to a mosaic pattern of semi-precious stones and marble.

pinchbeck: Alloy of copper and tin, used as imitation gold.

***piqué*:** Technique in which a material such as tortoiseshell is inlaid with metal decoration.

plum pudding: Type of figuring in some veneers, produced by dark oval spots in the wood. Found particularly in mahogany.

***polos*:** Tall, generally ornamental headdress, often worn by ancient Greek goddesses.

pole screen: Small adjustable screen mounted on a pole and designed to stand in front of an open fire to shield a lady's face from the heat.

***poudreuse*:** French dressing table.

powder flask: Device for measuring out a precise quantity of priming powder, suspended from a musketeer's belt or bandolier and often ornately decorated. Sporting flasks are often made of antler and carved with hunting scenes.

powder horn: Cow horn hollowed out, blocked at the wide end with a wooden plug and fitted with a measuring device at the narrow end, used by musketeers for dispensing a precise quantity of priming powder.

prie-dieu: Chair with a low seat and a tall back designed for prayer. Usually dating from the 19thC.

printie: Circular or oval hollow cut into glass for decorative effect, sometimes called a lens.

prunt: Blob of glass applied to the stem of a drinking vessel both as decoration and to stop the glass from slipping in the hand.

***qilin*:** Chinese mythical beast. Also spelt *kilin*.

Qingbai: White ware produced by potters in the Jingdezhen area of China throughout the Song Dynasty.

quarter-veneered: Four consecutively cut, and therefore identical, pieces of veneer laid at opposite ends to each other to give a mirrored effect.

register plate: Scale of a barometer against which the mercury level is read.
regulator: Clock of great accuracy, thus sometimes used for controlling or checking other timepieces.
repoussé: Relief decoration on metal made by hammering on the reverse so that the decoration projects.
***rhyton*:** Ancient Greek ritual pouring vessel.
rocaille: Shell and rock motifs found in rococo work.
***rouge de fer*:** Iron-red colour produced with iron-oxide, used on Chinese ceramics.
rummer: 19thC English low drinking goblet.
***ruyi*:** Chinese presentation sceptre.
***sancai*:** Three-colour decoration on Chinese porcelain.
***schwarzlot*:** German term for black lead enamel painting on porcelain and glass used from c1650.
scratch stock: Very fine incised groove running around the edge of a piece of furniture.
S. F. B. J.: *Société de Fabrication de Bébés et Jouets*; association of doll makers founded 1899 by the merger of Jumeau, Bru and others.
sgraffito: Form of ceramic decoration incised through a coloured slip, revealing the ground beneath.
***shakudo*:** Japanese term for an alloy of copper and gold.
***Shibayama*:** Japanese term for lacquer applied with semi-precious stones and ivory.
***shishi*:** Japanese mythical beast, a lion-dog.
shoulder-head: Term for a doll's head and shoulders below the neck.
shoulderplate: Area of a doll's shoulder-head below the neck.
siphon tube: U-shaped tube fitted into wheel barometers where the level of mercury in the short arm is used to record air pressure.
skyphos: Ancient Greek vessel.
***soffreh*:** Persian bread cloth.
soft paste: Artificial porcelain made with the addition of ground glass, bone-ash or soap-stone. Used by most European porcelain manufacturers during the 18thC. Recognized by its soft, soapy feel.
spadroon: Cut-and-thrust sword.
spandrel: Element of design, closing off a corner.
spelter: Zinc treated to look like bronze and much used as an inexpensive substitute in Art Nouveau appliqué ornament and Art Deco figures.
strapwork: Repeated carved decoration suggesting plaited straps.
stuff-over: Descriptive of upholstered furniture where the covering extends over the frame of the seat.
stumpwork: Embroidery which incorporates distinctive areas of raised decoration, formed by padding certain areas of the design.
***sugán*:** Twisted lengths of straw: referring to a type of Irish country chair which has a seat of this type.
***susani*:** Central Asian hand-embroidered bridal bed-cover.
sympiesometer: Instrument that uses a gas and coloured oil to record air pressure.
***takamakie*:** Technique used in Japanese lacquerware in which the design is built up and modelled in a mixture of lacquer and charcoal or clay dust, and then often gilded.
***tanto*:** Japanese dagger.
***Taotie*:** Chinese mythical animal which devours wrong-doers.
tassets: Overlapping plates in armour for the groin and thighs.
tazza: Wide but shallow bowl on a stem with a foot; ceramic and metal tazzas were made in antiquity and the form was revived by Venetian glassmakers in the 15thC. Also made in silver from the 16thC.
teapoy: Piece of furniture in the form of a tea caddy on legs, with a hinged lid opening to reveal caddies, mixing bowl and other tea drinking accessories.
tear: Tear-drop-shaped air bubble in the stem of an early 18thC wine glass, from which the air-twist evolved.
tête-à-tête: Tea set for two people.
thuyawood: Reddish-brown wood with distinctive small 'bird's-eye' markings, imported from Africa and used as a veneer.
***tiki*:** Symbol of the procreative power of the Maori god Tane.
timepiece: Clock that does not strike or chime.
tin glaze: Glassy opaque white glaze of tin oxide; re-introduced to Europe in the 14thC by Moorish potters; the characteristic glaze of delftware, faïence and maiolica.
toleware: Items made from tinplated sheet iron which is varnished and then decorated with brightly coloured paints.
touch: Maker's mark stamped on much, but not all, early English pewter. Their use was strictly controlled by the Pewterer's Company of London: early examples consist of initials, later ones are more elaborate and pictorial, sometimes including the maker's address.
trumeau: Section of wall between two openings; a pier mirror.
***tsuba*:** Guard of a Japanese sword, usually consisting of an ornamented plate.
***tsuboya*:** Japanese kiln.
Tudric: Range of Celtic-inspired Art Nouveau pewter of high quality, designed for mass-production by Archibald Knox and others, and retailed through Liberty & Co.
***tughra*:** Official mark of the Ottoman sultans.
tulipwood: Yellow-brown wood with reddish stripe, imported from Central and South America and used as a veneer and for inlay and crossbanding.
tyg: Mug with three or more handles.
***uraeus*:** Symbol of kingship in ancient Egypt, in the form of a cobra.
***vargueño*:** Spanish cabinet with a fall-front enclosing drawers.
verge escapement: Oldest form of escapement, found on clocks as early as 1300 and still in use in 1900. Consisting of a bar (the verge) with two flag-shaped pallets that rock in and out of the teeth of the crown or escape wheel to regulate the movement.
vernier scale: Short scale added to the traditional 3in (7.5cm) scale on stick barometers to give more precise readings than had previously been possible.
***verre églomisé*:** Painting on glass. Often the reverse side of the glass is covered in gold or silver leaf through which a pattern is engraved and then painted black.
vesta case: Ornate flat case of silver or other metal for carrying vestas, an early form of match. Used from the mid-19thC.
***vide-poche*:** Table or receptacle for holding the contents of one's pockets.
vitrine: French display cabinet which is often of *bombé* or serpentine outline and ornately decorated with marquetry and ormolu.
***wakizashi*:** Japanese sword shorter than a *katana*.
WMF: Short for Württembergische Metallwarenfabrik, a German foundry that was one of the principal producers of Art Nouveau metalware.
***wucai*:** Type of five-colour Chinese porcelain decoration, executed in vigorous style.
***wufu*:** Chinese term meaning 'the five happinesses' (long life, riches, tranquility, love of virtue and a good end to one's life).
***yaki*:** Japanese term for ware.
***zhadou*:** A particular shape of Chinese vessel.

Directory of Specialists

If you wish to be included in next year's directory, or if you have a change of address or telephone number, please contact Miller's Advertising Department on 01580 766411 by April 2005. We advise readers to make contact by telephone before visiting a dealer, therefore avoiding a wasted journey.

20TH CENTURY DESIGN
Kent
20th Century Marks, 12 Market Square, Westerham TN16 1AW Tel: 01959 562221 Mobile: 07831 778992 info@20thcenturymarks.co.uk www.20thcenturymarks.co.uk *20th century furniture and design.*

AMERICANA
USA
American West Indies Trading Co Antiques & Art awindies@worldnet.att.net www.goantiques.com/members/awindiestrading *Ethnographic, Folk, Tribal, Spanish Colonial, Santos & Retablos, American Indian, Indonesian Keris, southeast Asian antiquities, orientalia, Art Deco and Floridiana.*

ANTIQUE DEALERS ASSOCIATION
London
Portobello Antiques Dealers Association, 223a Portobello Road, W11 1LU Tel: 020 7229 8354 info@portobelloroad.co.uk www.portobelloroad.co.uk

Oxfordshire
T.V.A.D.A., The Old College, Queen Street, Dorchester-on-Thames OX10 7HL Tel: 01865 341639 antiques@tvada.co.uk www.tvada.co.uk

ANTIQUITIES
Dorset
Ancient & Gothic, PO Box 5390, Bournemouth BH7 6XR Tel: 01202 431721 *Antiquities from before 300,000 BC to about 1500 AD.*

USA
Hurst Gallery, 53 Mt Auburn Street, Cambridge MA 02138 Tel: 617 491 6888 www.hurstgallery.com manager@hurstgallery.com www.hurstgallery.com *Art of the Pacific, Africa, Asia, The Americas and the ancient world.*

ARCHITECTURAL ANTIQUES
Cheshire
Nostalgia, Hollands Mill, 61 Shaw Heath, Stockport SK3 8BH Tel: 0161 477 7706 www.nostalgia-uk.com

Gloucestershire
Minchinhampton Architectural Salvage Company, Cirencester Road, Chalford, Stroud GL6 8PE Tel: 01285 760886 masco@catbrain.com www.catbrain.com *Architectural antiques, garden statuary, bespoke chimney pieces and traditional flooring. MASCo specializes in large architectural features and garden ornaments. The company also carries extensive stocks of hard and soft wood flooring as well as reclaimed building materials. Call or email for further details. Subscribers to the SALVO code. We also offer a Garden Design service.*

Kent
Catchpole & Rye, Saracens Dairy, Jobbs Lane, Pluckley, Ashford TN27 0SA Tel: 01233 840840 info@crye.co.uk www.crye.co.uk

Lancashire
John Cowell Ltd, Antique Exports info@john-cowell.com www.john-cowell.com

Surrey
Drummonds Architectural Antiques Ltd, The Kirkpatrick Buildings, 25 London Road (A3), Hindhead GU26 6AB Tel: 01428 609444 www.drummonds-arch.co.uk

ARMS & MILITARIA
Cheshire
Armourer – The Militaria Magazine, Published by Beaumont Publishing Ltd, 1st floor Adelphi Mill, Bollington SK10 5JB Tel: 01625 575700 editor@armourer.co.uk www.armourer.co.uk *A bi-monthly magazine for military antique collectors and military history enthusiasts offering hundreds of contacts for buying and selling, articles on all aspects of militaria collecting plus the dates of UK militaria fairs and auctions. Available on subscription.*

Gloucestershire
Q & C Militaria, 22 Suffolk Road, Cheltenham GL50 2AQ Tel: 01242 519815 Mobile: 07778 613977 qcmilitaria@btconnect.com www.qcmilitaria.com

Kent
Sporting Antiques, 10 Union Square, The Pantiles, Tunbridge Wells TN4 8HE Tel: 01892 522661 *Specialist dealers in antique arms, armour, pistols – sporting and military inclusive of all accessories and tools. Books and prints. We buy and sell.*

Lincolnshire
Garth Vincent, The Old Manor House, Allington, Nr Grantham NG32 2DH Tel: 01400 281358 garthvincent@aol.com www.guns.uk.com

Surrey
Alan Cook Tel: 01932 228328 Mobile: 07785 252120 antiquearms@btinternet.com www.antiquearms.co.uk

West Street Antiques, 63 West Street, Dorking RH4 1BS Tel: 01306 883487 weststant@aol.com www.antiquearmsandarmour.com

East Sussex
The Lanes Armoury, 26 Meeting House Lane, The Lanes, Brighton BN1 1HB Tel: 01273 321357 enquiries@thelanesarmoury.co.uk www.thelanesarmoury.co.uk

Wallis & Wallis, West Street Auction Galleries, Lewes BN7 2NJ Tel: 01273 480208 auctions@wallisandwallis.co.uk www.wallisandwallis.co.uk *Auctioneers of militaria, arms and armour and medals.*

USA
Faganarms, Box 425, Fraser MI 48026 Tel: 586 465 4637 info@faganarms.com www.faganarms.com

Warwickshire
London Antique Arms Fairs Ltd, 35 Rosefield Street, Leamington Spa CV32 4HE Tel: 01432 355416 & 01926 883665 info@antiquearmsfairsltd.co.uk www.antiquearmsfairsltd.co.uk

BAROGRAPHS
Somerset
Richard Twort Tel: 01934 641900 Mobile: 07711 939789

BAROMETERS
Berkshire
Alan Walker, Halfway Manor, Halfway, Nr Newbury RG20 8NR Tel: 01488 657670 Mobile: 07770 728397 www.alanwalker-barometers.com

Cheshire
Derek & Tina Rayment Antiques, Orchard House, Barton Road, Barton, Nr Farndon SY14 7HT Tel: 01829 270429/07860 666629 & 07702 922410 raymentantiques@aol.com www.antique-barometers.com *Also repair and restoration.*

Somerset
Knole Barometers, Bingham House, West Street, Somerton TA11 7PS Tel: 01458 241015 Mobile: 07785 364567 dccops@btconnect.com

Wiltshire
P. A. Oxley Antique Clocks & Barometers, The Old Rectory, Cherhill, Calne SN11 8UX Tel: 01249 816227 info@paoxley.com www.british-antiqueclocks.com

Yorkshire
Weather House Antiques, Kym S. Walker, Foster Clough, Hebden Bridge HX7 5QZ Tel: 01422 882808/886961 Mobile: 07889 750711 kymwalker@btinternet.com

BEDS
Wales
Seventh Heaven, Chirk Mill, Chirk, Wrexham, County Borough LL14 5BU Tel: 01691 777622/773563 requests@seventh-heaven.co.uk www.seventh-heaven.co.uk

Worcestershire
S. W. Antiques, Newlands (road), Pershore WR10 1BP Tel: 01386 555580 sw-antiques@talk21.com www.sw-antiques.co.uk

BILLIARD TABLES
Surrey
Academy Billiard Co, 5 Camp Hill Industrial Estate, Camphill Road, West Byfleet KT14 6EW Tel: 01932 352067

BOOKS
Surrey
David Aldous-Cook, PO Box 413, Sutton SM3 8SZ Tel: 020 8642 4842 office@davidaldous-cook.co.uk www.davidaldous-cook.co.uk *Reference books on antiques and collectables.*

Wiltshire
Dominic Winter Book Auctions, The Old School, Maxwell Street, Swindon SN1 5DR Tel: 01793 611340 info@dominicwinter.co.uk www.dominicwinter.co.uk

BOTTLES
Staffordshire
Gordon Litherland, 25 Stapenhill Road, Burton-on-Trent DE15 9AE Tel: 01283 567213 Mobile: 07952 118987 *Bottles, breweriana and pub jugs, advertising ephemera and commemoratives.*

BOXES & TREEN
London
Gerald Mathias, Antiquarius, 135–142 Kings Road, Chelsea, SW3 4PW Tel: 020 7351 0484

fineantiqueboxes@geraldmathias.com
www.geraldmathias.com

BRITISH ANTIQUE FURNITURE RESTORERS' ASSOCIATION
BAFRA Head Office, The Old Rectory, Warmwell, Dorchester, Dorset DT2 8HQ
Tel: 01305 854822
headoffice@bafra.org.uk
www.bafra.org.uk

Berkshire
Ben Norris & Co, Knowl Hill Farm, Knowl Hill, Kingsclere, Newbury RG20 4NY
Tel: 01635 297950
Gilding, carving and architectural woodwork. Antique furniture restorer.

Cambridgeshire
Ludovic Potts, Unit 1 & 1A, Haddenham Business Park, Station Road, Ely CB6 3XD
Tel: 01353 741537
mail@restorers.co.uk
www.restorers.co.uk
Traditional repairs, boulle, walnut, oak, veneering, upholstery, cane, rush and gilding.

Derbyshire
A. Allen Conservation & Restoration Ltd, The Old Wharf Workshop, Redmoor Lane, New Mills, High Peak SK22 3JL
Tel: 01663 745274
Conservation and restoration of furniture, clocks and artifacts.

Devon
Tony Vernon, 15 Follett Road, Topsham, Exeter EX3 0JP
Tel: 01392 874635
tonyvernon@antiquewood.co.uk
www.antiquewood.co.uk
All aspects of conservation and restoration including gilding, carving, upholstery, veneering and polishing. Accredited member of BAFRA; the British Antique Furniture Restorers' Association.

Essex
Clive Beardall Restorations Ltd, 104B High Street, Maldon CM9 5ET
Tel: 01621 857890
www.clivebeardall.co.uk

Gloucestershire
Alan Hessel, The Old Town Workshop, St George's Close, Moreton-in-Marsh GL56 0LP
Tel: 01608 650026
Our skilled craftsmen have restored fine furniture since 1976. We accept commissions from galleries and private collections. Our specialism is from the late 17thC to early 19thC furniture.

Hampshire
David C. E. Lewry, Wychelms, 66 Gorran Avenue, Rowner, Gosport PO13 0NF
Tel: 01329 286901
Consultancy only.

Hertfordshire
John B. Carr, Charles Perry Restorations Ltd, Praewood Farm, Hemel Hempstead Road, St Albans AL3 6AA
Tel: 01727 853487
cperry@praewood.freeserve.co.uk
Specialists in restoration and conservation of all types of antique furniture.

Kent
Timothy Akers, The Forge, 39 Chancery Lane, Beckenham BR3 6NR
Tel: 020 8650 9179
enquiries@akersofantiques.co.uk
www.akersofantiques.co.uk
Longcase and bracket clocks, cabinet-making and French polishing. Dealers of selected fine English furniture.

Benedict Clegg, Rear of 20 Camden Road, Tunbridge Wells TN1 2PT
Tel: 01892 548095
All aspects of 17th–19thC furniture.

Bruce Luckhurst, Little Surrenden Workshops, Ashford Road, Bethersden, Ashford TN26 3BG
Tel: 01233 820589
woodwise@tiscali.co.uk
www.bruceluckhurst.co.uk
Weekend and 5 day courses available.

Lancashire
Eric Smith Antique Restorations, The Old Church, Park Road, Darwen BB3 2LD Tel: 01254 776222
eric.smith@restorations.ndo.co.uk
www.ericsmithrestorations.co.uk
Accredited member of the British Antique Furniture Restorers' Association. Consultant to Galway Claire Castle Galway Ireland. Workshop is included on the Conservation register maintained by the United Kingdom Institute for Conservation in London.

Lincolnshire
Michael E. Czajkowski BSc, Czajkowski & Son, 96 Tor O Moor Road, Woodhall Spa LN10 6SB
Tel: 01526 352895
michael.czajkowski@ntlworld.com
Conservation and restoration of antique furniture, clocks (dials, movements and cases) and barometers. Skills include: marquetry Buhle and inlay work; carving and gilding; lacquer work, re-upholstery and upholstery conservation; clockwork and associated metal work. Regular collection service to the East Midlands and London. Member of BAFRA and Accredited Member United Kingdom Institute of Conservation.

London
Rodrigo Titian, Titian Studio, 32 Warple Way, Acton W3 0DJ Tel: 020 8222 6600
enquiries@titianstudios.co.uk
www.titianstudios.co.uk
Carving, gilding, lacquer, painted furniture and French polishing. Caning and rushing.

Norfolk
Michael Dolling, Church Farm Barns, Glandford, Holt NR25 7JR
Tel: 01263 741115
Also at: 44 White Hart Street, East Harling NR16 2NE. Tel: 01953 718658.
Restoration of Antique and fine furniture including marquetry, carving, gilding, upholstery and caning.

Roderick Nigel Larwood, The Oaks, Station Road, Larling, Norwich NR16 2QS
Tel: 01953 717937
rodlar@tinyworld.co.uk
Restorers of fine antiques and traditional finishers.

Somerset
Stuart Bradbury, M. & S. Bradbury, The Barn, Hanham Lane, Paulton, Bristol BS39 7PF
Tel: 01761 418910
enquiries@mandsbradbury.co.uk
www.mandsbradbury.co.uk
Antique furniture conservation and restoration.

North Somerset
Robert P. Tandy, Lake House Barn, Lake Farm, Colehouse Lane, Kenn, Clevedon BS21 6TQ Tel: 01275 875014
robertptandy@hotmail.com
Traditional antique furniture restoration and repairs.

Staffordshire
Stefan Herberholz, Middleton Hall, Middleton B78 2AE Tel: 01827 282858

Surrey
Hedgecoe & Freeland Antique Furniture Restoration and Upholstery, 21 Burrow Hill Green, Chobham, Woking GU24 8QP Tel: 01276 858206/07771 953870
hedgecoefreeland@aol.com

Timothy Naylor, 24 Bridge Road, Chertsey KT16 8JN
Tel: 01932 567129
timothy.naylor@talk21.com

West Sussex
Albert Plumb, Albert Plumb Furniture Co, Briarfield, Itchenor Green, Chichester PO20 7DA
Tel: 01243 513700
Cabinet making and upholstery.

West Midlands
Phillip Slater, 93 Hewell Road, Barnt Green, Birmingham B45 8NL
Tel: 0121 445 4942
Inlay work and marquetry.

Wiltshire
William Cook, High Trees House, Savernake Forest, Nr Marlborough SN8 4NE
Tel: 01672 512561
wcook_uk@yahoo.com

CAMERAS
Lincolnshire
Antique Photographic Company Ltd Tel: 01949 842192 alpaco47@aol.com

CLOCKS
Cheshire
Coppelia Antiques, Holford Lodge, Plumley Moor Road, Plumley WA16 9RS
Tel: 01565 722197
www.coppeliaantiques.co.uk

Devon
Carnegie Paintings & Clocks, 15 Fore Street, Yealmpton, Plymouth Pl8 2JN
Tel: 01752 881170
info@paintingsandclocks.com
www.paintingsandclocks.com

Musgrave Bickford Antiques, 15 East Street, Crediton EX17 3AT
Tel: 01363 775042
Antique clocks and barometers.

Essex
Bellhouse Antiques
Tel: 01268 710415
Bellhouse.Antiques@virgin.net

It's About Time, 863 London Road, Westcliff-on-Sea SS0 9SZ Tel: 01702 472574
sales@antiqueclock.co.uk
www.antiqueclock.co.uk

Gloucestershire
The Grandfather Clock Shop, Styles of Stow, The Little House, Sheep Street, Stow-on-the-Wold GL54 1JS
Tel: 01451 830455
info@stylesofstow.co.uk
www.stylesofstow.co.uk

Gloucestershire
Woodward Antique Clocks, 21 Suffolk Parade, Cheltenham
Tel: 01242 245667
woodwardclocks@onetel.net.uk
www.woodwardclocks.com

Greater Manchester
Northern Clocks, Boothsbank Farm, Worsley, Manchester M28 1LL
Tel: 0161 790 8414
Mobile: 07970 820258
info@northernclocks.co.uk
www.northernclocks.co.uk

Hampshire
Bryan Clisby Antique Clocks, at Cedar Antiques Centre Ltd, High Street, Hartley Wintney RG27 8NY
Tel: 01252 843222
www.bryanclisby-antiqueclocks.co.uk

The Clock-Work-Shop (Winchester), 6A Parchment Street, Winchester SO23 8AT Tel: 01962 842331
Mobile: 07885 954302
www.clock-work-shop.co.uk

Kent
Gaby Gunst, 140 High Street, Tenterden TN30 6HT
Tel: 01580 765818

The Old Clock Shop, 63 High Street, West Malling ME19 6NA
Tel: 01732 843246
theoldclockshop@tesco.net
www.theoldclockshop.co.uk

Derek Roberts Antiques, 25 Shipbourne Road, Tonbridge TN10 3DN
Tel: 01732 358986
drclocks@clara.net
www.qualityantiqueclocks.com

London
The Clock Clinic Ltd, 85 Lower Richmond Road, Putney, SW15 1EU
Tel: 020 8788 1407
clockclinic@btconnect.com
www.clockclinic.co.uk

Pendulum, King House, 51 Maddox Street, W1R 9LA Tel: 020 7629 6606 www.pendulumofmayfair.co.uk

Roderick Antique Clocks, 23 Vicarage Gate, W8 4AA Tel: 020 7937 8517 rick@roderickantiqueclocks.com www.roderickantiqueclocks.com

W. F. Turk, 355 Kingston Road, Wimbledon Chase, SW20 8JX Tel: 020 8543 3231 www.wfturk.com

Scotland
John Mann Antique Clocks, The Clock Showroom, Canonbie, Near Carlisle, Galloway DG14 0SY Tel: 013873 71337/71827 Mobile: 07850 606 147 jmannclock@aol.com www.johnmannantiqueclocks.co.uk

Somerset
Kembery Antique Clocks Ltd, George Street Antique Centre, 8 Edgar Buildings, George Street, Bath BA1 2EH Tel: 0117 9565 281 Mobile: 07850 623 237 kembery@kdclocks.co.uk www.kdclocks.co.uk

Surrey
Antique Clocks by Patrick Thomas, 62a West Street, Dorking RH4 1BS Tel: 01306 743661 patrickthomas@btconnect.com www.antiqueclockshop.co.uk

The Clock House, 75 Pound Street, Carshalton SM5 3PG Tel: 020 8773 4844 Mobile: 07850 363 317 markcocklin@theclockhouse.co.uk www.theclockhouse.co.uk

The Clock Shop, 64 Church Street, Weybridge KT13 8DL Tel: 01932 840407/855503 www.theclockshopweybridge.co.uk

East Sussex
Sam Orr Antique Clocks, 34–36 High Street, Hurstpierpoint, Nr Brighton BN6 9RG Tel: 01273 832081 Mobile: 07860 230888 clocks@samorr.co.uk www.samorr.co.uk

USA
R. O. Schmitt Fine Art, Box 1941, Salem, New Hampshire 03079 Tel: 603 893 5915 bob@roschmittfinearts.com www.antiqueclockauction.com *Specialist antique clock auctions.*

Setniks In Time Again, 815 Sutter Street, Suite 2, Folsom, California 95630 Tel: 916 985 2390 Toll Free 888 333 1715 setniks@pacbell.net setniksintimeagain.com

Warwickshire
Summersons, 172 Emscote Road, Warwick CV34 5QN Tel: 01926 400630 clocks@summersons.com www.summersons.com *We offer a complete restoration service for antique clocks and barometers. We also undertake the following: Dial restoration, cabinetwork and French polishing, wheel cutting, one-off parts made, clock hands cut, fretwork, silvering/gilding, polishing/lacquering, restoration parts and materials, insurance valuations, free estimates and advice. WANTED: Clocks & barometers purchased in any condition.*

Wiltshire
P. A. Oxley Antique Clocks & Barometers, The Old Rectory, Cherhill, Calne SN11 8UX Tel: 01249 816227 info@paoxley.com www.british-antiqueclocks.com

Allan Smith Clocks, Amity Cottage, 162 Beechcroft Road, Upper Stratton, Swindon SN2 7QE Tel: 01793 822977 Mobile: 07778 834342 allansmithclocks@lineone.net www.allansmithantiqueclocks.co.uk

Yorkshire
Time & Motion, 1 Beckside, Beverley HU17 0PB Tel: 01482 881574

North Yorkshire
Brian Loomes, Calf Haugh Farm, Pateley Bridge HG3 5HW Tel: 01423 711163 clocks@brianloomes.com www.brianloomes.com

COMICS
London
Comic Book Postal Auctions Ltd, 40–42 Osnaburgh Street, NW1 3ND Tel: 020 7424 0007 comicbook@compuserve.com www.compalcomics.com

DECORATIVE ARTS
Dorset
Delf Stream Gallery Tel: 07974 926137 nic19422000@yahoo.co.uk www.delfstreamgallery.com

Greater Manchester
A. S. Antique Galleries, 26 Broad Street, Pendleton, Salford M6 5BY Tel: 0161 737 5938 Mobile: 07836 368230 as@sternshine.demon.co.uk

Kent
The Design Gallery 1850–1950, 5 The Green, Westerham TN16 1AS Tel; 01959 561234 Mobile: 07974 322858 sales@thedesigngalleryuk.com www.thedesigngalleryuk.com

London
Artemis Decorative Arts Ltd, 36 Kensington Church Street, W8 4BX Tel: 020 7376 0377 Artemis.w8@btinternet.com www.artemisdecorativearts.com

Crafts Nouveau, 112 Alexander Park Road, Muswell Hill, N10 2AE Tel: 0208 444 3300 Mobile: 07958 448 380 craftsnouveau@btconnect.com www.craftsnouveau.co.uk

Shapiro & Co, Stand 380, Gray's Antique Market, 58 Davies Street, W1K 5LP Tel: 020 7491 2710 *Fabergé.*

Republic of Ireland
Mitofsky Antiques, 8 Rathfarnham Road, Terenure, Dublin 6 Tel: 00 353 1492 0033 info@mitofskyartdeco.com www.mitofskyartdeco.com

Scotland
decorative arts@doune, Scottish Antique & Arts Centre, By Doune, Stirling FK16 6HD Tel: 01786 834401 or 07778 475974 decorativearts.doune@btinternet.com www.decorativearts-doune.com

Worcestershire
Art Nouveau Originals, The Bindery Gallery, 69 High Street, Broadway WR12 7DP Tel: 01386 854645 Mobile: 07774 718 096 cathy@artnouveauoriginals.com www.artnouveauoriginals.com

Yorkshire
Muir Hewitt Art Deco Originals, Halifax Antiques Centre, Queens Road Mills, Queens Road/Gibbet Street, Halifax HX1 4LR Tel: 01422 347377 muir.hewitt@virgin.net www.muirhewitt.com *Clarice Cliff.*

EPHEMERA
Nottinghamshire
T. Vennett-Smith, 11 Nottingham Road, Gotham NG11 0HE Tel: 0115 983 0541 info@vennett-smith.com www.vennett-smith.com *Ephemera auctions.*

EXHIBITION & FAIR ORGANISERS
Devon
Trident Exhibitions, West Devon Business Park, Tavistock PL19 9DP Tel: 01822 614671 info@trident-exhibitions.co.uk www.tridentexhibitions.co.uk www.interfine.co.uk www.surreyantiquesfair.co.uk www.buxtonantiquesfair.co.uk

Nottinghamshire
DMG Fairs, PO Box 100, Newark NG24 1DJ Tel: 01636 702326 www.dmgantiquefairs.com

Warwickshire
London Antique Arms Fairs Ltd, 15 Burbury Court, Emscote Road, Warwick CV34 5LD Tel: 01432 355416 & 01926 883665 Mobile: 07801 943983 info@antiquearmsfairsltd.co.uk www.antiquearmsfairsltd.co.uk

West Midlands
Antiques for Everyone Fair, NEC House, National Exhibition Centre, Birmingham B40 1NT Tel: 0121 780 4141 antiques@necgroup.co.uk

EXPORTERS
Devon
McBains of Exeter, Exeter Airport, Clyst, Honiton, Exeter EX5 2BA Tel: 01392 366261 mcbains@netcom.co.uk

Pugh's Antiques, Pugh's Farm, Monkton, Nr Honiton EX14 9QH Tel: 01404 42860 sales@pughsantiques.com www.pughsantiques.com

Gloucestershire
Piano-Export, Bridge Road, Kingswood, Bristol BS15 4FW Tel: 0117 956 8300

Lancashire
John Cowell Ltd, Antique Exports info@john-cowell.com www.john-cowell.com

Staffordshire
Acorn G.D.S. Ltd, 183 Queens Road, Penkhull, Stoke-on-Trent ST4 7LF Tel: 01782 817700 or 01782 845051 acorn@acorn-freight.co.uk www.acorn-freight.co.uk *Export shipping.*

East Sussex
International Furniture Exporters Ltd, Old Cement Works, South Heighton, Newhaven BN9 0HS Tel: 01273 611251 ife55@aol.com www.int-furniture-exporters.co.uk

The Old Mint House, High Street, Pevensey BN24 5LF Tel: 01323 762337 antiques@minthouse.co.uk www.minthouse.co.uk

Wiltshire
North Wilts. Exporters, Farm Hill House, Brinkworth SN15 5AJ Tel: 01666 510876 mike@northwilts.demon.co.uk www.northwiltsantiqueexporters.com

FISHING
Hampshire
Evans & Partridge, Agriculture House, High Street, Stockbridge SO20 6HF Tel: 01264 810702 *Sporting auctions.*

Kent
Old Tackle Box, PO Box 55, Cranbrook TN17 3ZU Tel: 01580 713979 Mobile: 07729 278 293 tackle.box@virgin.net

London
Angling Auctions, PO Box 2095, W12 8RU Tel: 020 8749 4175 Mobile: 07785 281349 neil@anglingauctions.demon.co.uk

Yorkshire
James M. Fielding Tel: 0114 235 0185 m.fielding@btinternet.com

FURNITURE
Berkshire
Hill Farm Antiques, Hill Farm, Shop Lane, Leckhampstead, Nr Newbury RG20 8QG Tel: 01488 638541/638361 Mobile: 07836 503561 beesley@hillfarmantiques.demon.co.uk *Specialists in antique dining tables.*

The Old Malthouse, Hungerford RG17 0EG Tel: 01488 682209 hunwick@oldmalthouse30.freeserve.co.uk

Cumbria
Anthemion, Cartmel, Grange Over Sands LA11 6QD Tel; 015395 36295 Mobile: 07768 443757

Derbyshire
Spurrier-Smith Antiques, 28, 39 Church Street, Ashbourne DE6 1AJ Tel: 01335 342198/343669 ivan@spurrier-smith.fsnet.co.uk

Devon
Pugh's Antiques, Pugh's Farm, Monkton, Nr Honiton EX14 9QH Tel: 01404 42860 sales@pughsantiques.com www.pughsantiques.com

Jane Strickland & Daughters, 71 High Street, Honiton EX14 1PW Tel: 01404 44221 JSandDaughtersUk@aol.com www.janestricklanddaughters.co.uk

Essex
F. G. Bruschweiler (Antiques) Ltd, 41–67 Lower Lambricks, Rayleigh SS6 8DA Tel: 01268 773 761/773 932 info@fgbantiques.com www.fgbantiques.com

Hertfordshire
Collins Antiques, Corner House, Wheathampstead AL4 8AP Tel: 01582 833111

Kent
Flower House Antiques, 90 High Street, Tenterden TN30 6JB Tel: 01580 763764

Pamela Goodwin, 11 The Pantiles, Royal Tunbridge Wells TN2 5TD Tel: 01892 618200 mail@goodwinantiques.co.uk www.goodwinantiques.co.uk *Antique furniture, clocks, oil lamps, mirrors and decorative items.*

Lincolnshire
Seaview Antiques, Stanhope Road, Horncastle LN9 5DG Tel: 01507 524524 tracey.collins@virgin.net www.seaviewantiques.co.uk

London
Oola Boola Antiques London, 139–147 Kirkdale, SE26 4QJ Tel: 020 8291 9999 Mobile: 07956 261252 oola.boola@telco4u.net

Oxfordshire
Blender Antiques Limited, Cotefield Farm, Oxford Road, Bodicote, Nr Banbury OX15 4AQ Tel: 01295 254754 blenderantiques@btopenworld.com www.blenderantiques.co.uk

The Chair Set, 18 Market Place, Woodstock OX20 1TA Tel: 01428 707301 Mobile: 07711 625 477 allanjames@thechairset.com www.thechairset.com *Specialists in sets of chairs, furniture and accessories for the dining room.*

Georg S. Wissinger Antiques, Georgian House Antiques, 2, 21 & 44 West Street, Chipping Norton OX7 5EU Tel: 01608 641369

Surrey
Dorking Desk Shop, J. G. Elias Antiques Limited, 41 West Street, Dorking RH4 1BU Tel: 01306 883327/880535 info@dorkingdeskshop.co.uk www.desk.uk.com

J. Hartley Antiques Ltd, 186 High Street, Ripley GU23 6BB Tel: 01483 224318

East Sussex
M. D. Johnson Antiques, 14–16 High Street, Seaford BN25 1PG Tel: 01323 897777 Mobile: 07860 899774

The Old Mint House, High Street, Pevensey BN24 5LF Tel: 01323 762337 antiques@minthouse.co.uk www.minthouse.co.uk

Pastorale Antiques, 15 Malling Street, Lewes BN7 2RA Tel: 01273 473259 or 01435 863044 pastorale@btinternet.com *Large showrooms. Genuine Georgian and Victorian furniture as seen in Miller's Antiques Price Guide. Also French provincial and old pine.*

Seahaven Antiques, 87 Railway Road, Newhaven Tel: 01273 611899

West Sussex
British Antique Replicas, 22 School Close, Queen Elizabeth Avenue, Burgess Hill RH15 9RX Tel: 01444 245577 www.1760.com

Stable Antiques, Adrian Hoyle, 98a High Street, Lindfield RH16 2HP Tel: 01444 483662 Mobile: 07768 900331 herbon@btopenworld.com

USA
Antiquebug, Frank & Cathy Sykes, 85 Center Street, Wolfeboro, New Hampshire 03894 Tel: 603 569 0000 www.antiquebug.com *Also Folk Art, mahogany speed boat models, maps and antiquarian books.*

Warwickshire
Coleshill Antiques & Interiors, 12–14 High Street, Coleshill B46 1AZ Tel: 01675 467416 enquiries@coleshillantiques.com www.coleshillantiques.com *Dealers in fine antiques and exclusive interiors.*

West Midlands
Martin Taylor Antiques, 323 Tettenhall Road, Wolverhampton WV6 0JZ Tel: 01902 751166 enquiries@mtaylor-antiques.co.uk www.mtaylor-antiques.co.uk

Yoxall Antiques, 68 Yoxall Road, Solihull B90 3RP Tel: 0121 744 1744 Mobile: 07860 168078 sales@yoxallantiques.co.uk www.yoxall-antiques.co.uk

Wiltshire
Cross Hayes Antiques, Units 6–8 Westbrook Farm, Draycot Cerne, Chippenham SN15 5LH Tel: 01249 720033 david@crosshayes.co.uk www.crosshayes.co.uk *Shipping furniture.*

ICONS
London
The Temple Gallery, 6 Clarendon Cross, Holland Park, W11 4AP Tel: 020 7727 3809 info@templegallery.com www.templegallery.com

JEWELLERY
Canada
Fiona Kenny Antiques Tel: 905 682 0090 merday@cogeco.ca www.trocadero.com/merday www.fionakennyantiques.com *18th–20thC jewellery and antiques, sterling and silver plate, china and pottery, 20thC modern, collectibles and advertising.*

KITCHENWARE
East Sussex
Ann Lingard, Ropewalk Antiques, Rye TN31 7NA Tel: 01797 223486 ann-lingard@ropewalkantiques.freeserve.co.uk

LIGHTING
Devon
The Exeter Antique Lighting Co, Cellar 15, The Quay, Exeter EX2 4AP Tel: 01392 490848 Mobile: 07702 969438 www.antiquelightingcompany.com *Antique lighting and stained glass specialists.*

Somerset
Joanna Proops Antique Textiles & Lighting, 34 Belvedere, Lansdown Hill, Bath BA1 5HR Tel: 01225 310795 antiquetextiles@aol.co.uk www.antiquetextiles.co.uk

USA
Lamps: By The Book, Inc, 514 14th West Palm Beach, Florida 33401 Tel: 561 659 1723 booklamps@msn.com www.lampsbythebook.com *Gift lamps. Also buy leather bound books.*

MARKETS & CENTRES
Bedfordshire
Woburn Abbey Antiques Centre, Woburn MK17 9WA Tel: 01525 290350 antiques@woburnabbey.co.uk www.woburnabbey.co.uk/antiques *The centre has 40 quality dealer shops, 2 art galleries and a fine selection of porcelain, silver and jewellery in 30 showcases. Just 10 minutes from Junction 13 of the M1 (junction 12, 15 minutes) in the wonderful surroundings of Woburn Abbey. Open every day except Christmas Eve, Christmas Day and Boxing Day from 10am–5pm. For further information about the centre and its' events please contact us by phone or email.*

Derbyshire
Chappells Antiques Centre – Bakewell, King Street, Bakewell DE45 1DZ Tel: 01629 812496 ask@chappellsantiquescentre.com www.chappellsantiquescentre.com *30 established dealers inc LAPADA members. Quality period furniture, ceramics, silver, plate, metals, treen, clocks, barometers, books, pictures, maps, prints, textiles, kitchenalia, lighting and furnishing accessories from the 17th–20thC. Open Mon–Sat 10–5pm Sun 12–5pm. Closed Christmas Day, Boxing Day and New Year's Day. Please ring for brochure, giving location and parking information.*

Matlock Antiques, Collectables & Riverside Café, 7 Dale Road, Matlock DE4 3LT Tel: 01629 760808 bmatlockantiques@aol.com www.matlock-antiques-collectables.cwc.net *Proprietor W. Shirley. Over 70 dealers. Open 7 days 10am–5pm including Bank Holidays. Parking available.*

Devon
Colyton Antiques Centre, Dolphin Street, Colyton EX24 6LU Tel: 01297 552339 colytonantiques@modelgarage.co.uk www.modelgarage.co.uk

Essex
Debden Antiques, Elder Street, Debden, Saffron Walden CB11 3JY Tel: 01799 543007 info@debden-antiques.co.uk www.debden-antiques.co.uk *Mon–Sat 10am–5.30pm Sundays and Bank Holidays 11am–4pm. 30 quality dealers in a stunning 17thC Essex barn. Large selection of 16th–20thC oak, mahogany and pine furniture, watercolours and oil paintings, rugs, ceramics, silver and jewellery. Plus garden furniture and ornaments in our lovely courtyard.*

Gloucestershire
Antiques Centre Gloucester, 1 Severn Road, The Historic Docks, Gloucester GL1 2LE Tel: 01452 529716 www.antiques.center.com *The Gloucester Antiques Centre makes a fine day out, with antiques and collectibles of every description. There is something for everyone, even those that are not antiques collectors will find items to decorate any home. Collectors of modern items are catered for. Open Mon–Sat 10am–5pm Sunday 1pm–5pm.*

Durham House Antiques, Sheep Street, Stow-on-the-Wold GL54 1AA Tel: 01451 870404 *30+ dealers. Town and country furniture, metalware, books, ceramics, kitchenalia, sewing ephemera, silver, jewellery and samplers. Mon–Sat 10am–5pm, Sun 11am–5pm. Stow-on-the-Wold, Cotswold home to over 40 antique shops, galleries and bookshops.*

Jubilee Hall Antiques Centre, Oak Street, Lechlade-on-Thames GL7 3AY Tel: 01367 253777 mail@jubileehall.co.uk www.jubileehall.co.uk

The Top Banana Antiques Mall, 1 New Church Street, Tetbury GL8 8DS Tel: 0871 288 1102 info@topbananaantiques.com www.topbananaantiques.com

Kent
Malthouse Arcade, High Street, Hythe CT21 5BW Tel: 01303 260103 *Open Fri, Sat and Bank Holiday Mon 9.30am–5.30pm. 37 Stalls and cafe. Furniture, china and glass, jewellery, plated brass, picture postcards, framing etc.*

Lancashire
The Antique Centre, 56 Garstang Road, Preston PR1 1NA Tel: 01772 882078 info@paulallisonantiques.co.uk www.paulallisonantiques.co.uk *Open 7 days a week. Free admission and free parking.*

GB Antiques Centre, Lancaster Leisure Park, (the former Hornsea Pottery), Wyresdale Road, Lancaster LA1 3LA Tel: 01524 844734 *Over 140 dealers in 40,000 sq ft of space. Showing porcelain, pottery, Art Deco, glass, books and linen. Also a large selection of mahogany, oak and pine furniture. Open 7 days a week 10am–5pm.*

Kingsmill Antique Centre, Queen Street, Harle Syke, Burnley BB10 2HX Tel: 01282 431953 antiques@kingsmill.demon.co.uk www.kingsmill.demon.co.uk *Open 7 days 10am–5pm, 8pm Thurs. 8,500 sq ft. Trade welcome.*

Leicestershire
Oxford Street Antique Centre, 16–26 Oxford Street, Leicester LE1 5XU Tel: 0116 255 3006 *Vast selection of clean English furniture ideal for home and overseas buyers, displayed in 14 large showrooms on 4 floors, covering 30,000 sq ft. Reproduction furniture and accessories also stocked.*

Lincolnshire
Hemswell Antique Centres, Caenby Corner Estate, Hemswell Cliff, Gainsborough DN21 5TJ Tel: 01427 668389 info@hemswell-antiques.com www.hemswell-antiques.com

London
Antiquarius Antiques Centre, 131/141 King's Road, Chelsea, SW3 5ST Tel: 020 7351 5353 antique@dial.pipex.com

Atlantic Antiques Centres, Chenil House, 181–183 Kings Road, SW3 5EB Tel: 020 7351 5353 antique@dial.pipex.com

Bond Street Antiques Centre, 124 New Bond Street, W1Y 9AE Tel: 020 7351 5353 antique@dial.pipex.com

Nottinghamshire
Antiques Trade Space, Brunel Drive, Newark NG24 2DE Tel: 01636 651444 info@antiquestradespace.com

Newark Antiques Warehouse Ltd, Old Kelham Road, Newark NG24 1BX Tel: 01636 674869 enquiries@newarkantiques.co.uk www.newarkantiques.co.uk

Oxfordshire
Swan at Tetsworth, The High Street, Tetsworth, Nr Thame OX9 7AB Tel: 01844 281777 antiques@theswan.co.uk www.theswan.co.uk *'Best Antiques Centre in Great Britain'. 2003/4 BACA Award. 80 dealers displaying good quality antiques in 40 showrooms. Large selection of furniture, Georgian through to Art Deco. Wonderful selection including silver, mirrors, rugs, glass, ceramics, jewellery, boxes and lots more all housed in a Grade II listed Elizabethan Coaching Inn. Garden Statuary Area. Open every day 10am–6pm. Large Car Park 5 mins Junctions 6/8 M40 Motorway. Award winning restaurant. Tel 01844 281777 for brochure or visit website www.theswan.co.uk*

Scotland
Scottish Antique and Arts Centre, Carse of Cambus, Doune, Perthshire FK16 6HD Tel: 01786 841203 sales@scottish-antiques.com www.scottish-antiques.com *Over 100 dealers. Huge gift and collectors sections. Victorian and Edwardian furniture. Open 7 days 10am–5pm.*

Scottish Antique Centre, Abernyte PH14 9SJ Tel: 01828 686401 sales@scottish-antiques.com www.scottish-antiques.com *Over 100 dealers. Huge gift and collectors sections. Victorian and Edwardian furniture. Open 7 days 10am–5pm.*

East Sussex
Church Hill Antiques Centre, 6 Station Street, Lewes BN7 2DA Tel: 01273 474 842 churchhilllewes@aol.com www.church-hill-antiques.co.uk

Hastings Antique Centre, 59–61 Norman Road, St Leonards-on-Sea TN38 0EG Tel: 01424 428561 www.hastingsantiquecentre.co.uk *Open Mon–Sat 9am–5.30pm. Over 20 dealers. Good trade call. 3 floors of antiques, Continental and English furniture.*

USA
Chesapeake Antique Center, Inc, Rt 301, PO Box 280 Queenstown MD 21658 Tel: 410 827 6640 antiques@chesapeakeantiques.com www.chesapeakantiques.com

Wales
Afonwen Craft & Antique Centre, Afonwen, Nr Caerwys, Nr Mold, Flintshire CH7 5UB Tel: 01352 720965 *Open all year Tue–Sun 9.30am–5.30pm, closed Mon, open Bank Holidays. The largest centre in North Wales and the borders. 14,000 sq ft, 40 dealers. Fabulous selection of antiques, china, silver, crystal, quality collectables, fine furniture, oak, walnut, mahogany and pine from around the world. Excellent restaurant, free entrance and free large car park.*

Offa's Dyke Antique Centre, 4 High Street, Knighton, Powys LD7 1AT Tel: 01547 528635/520145 *Open Mon–Sat 10am–5pm. Wide ranging stock. Specialists in ceramics and glass, fine art of the 19th & 20thC. Country antiques and collectables.*

Warwickshire
Barn Antiques Centre, Station Road, Long Marston, Nr Stratford-upon-Avon CV37 8RB Tel: 01789 721399 www.barnantique.co.uk *Huge old barn crammed full of affordable antiques. Over 13,000 sq ft and 50 established dealers. Open daily 10am–5pm, Sun 12pm–6pm. Large free car park. Licensed bistro.*

Yorkshire
Cavendish Antique & Collectors Centre, 44 Stonegate, York YO1 8AS Tel: 01904 621666 sales@yorkantiquescentre.co.uk www.cavendishantiques.co.uk *Open 7 days 9am–6pm. Browse at leisure. Over 70 dealers on 3 floors. Jewellery, silver, porcelain, glass engravings and prints, furniture, oils and watercolours, watches, collectables.*

The Court House, 2–6 Town End Road, Ecclesfield, Sheffield S35 9YY Tel: 0114 257 0641 thecourthouse@email.com www.courthouseantiques.co.uk

MONEY BOXES

Yorkshire
John & Simon Haley, 89 Northgate, Halifax HX1 1XF Tel: 01422 822148/360434 toysandbanks@aol.com

MUSICAL INSTRUMENTS

Gloucestershire
Keith Harding's World of Mechanical Music, The Oak House, High Street, Northleach GL54 3ET Tel: 01451 860181 keith@mechanicalmusic.co.uk www.mechanicalmusic.co.uk *Mechanical music and automata, antique and modern. Also antique musical boxes and clocks.*

Kent
Stephen T. P. Kember, Pamela Goodwin, 11 The Pantiles, Royal Tunbridge Wells TN2 5TD
Tel: 01959 574067
Mobile: 07850 358067
steve.kember@btinternet.com
www.antique-musicboxes.co.uk
Antique cylinder and disc musical boxes.

London
Piano Auctions Ltd, Conway Hall, 25 Red Lion Square, Holborn, WC1 R4RL
Tel: 01234 831742
www.pianoauctions.co.uk
Specialist valuers and auctioneers of pianos and keyboard instruments.

Nottinghamshire
Turner Violins, 1–5 Lily Grove, Beeston NG9 1QL
Tel: 0115 943 0333
info@turnerviolins.co.uk

Somerset
Piano-Export, Bridge Road, Kingswood, Bristol BS15 4FW Tel: 0117 956 8300

West Midlands
Turner Violins, 1 Gibb Street, Digbeth High Street, Birmingham B9 4AA
Tel: 0121 772 7708
info@turnerviolins.co.uk

OAK & COUNTRY
Surrey
The Refectory, 38 West Street, Dorking RH4 1BU
Tel: 01306 742111
www.therefectory.co.uk
Oak & country – Refectory table specialist.

Kent
Douglas Bryan Antiques, The Old Bakery, St David's Bridge, Cranbrook TN17 3HN Tel: 01580 713103
Mobile: 07774 737303
By appointment only.

London
Robert Young Antiques, 68 Battersea Bridge Road, SW11 3AG
Tel: 020 7228 7847
office@robertyoungantiques.com
Country furniture and Folk Art.

Northamptonshire
Paul Hopwell, 30 High Street, West Haddon NN6 7AP Tel: 01788 510636
Mobile: 07836 505950
paulhopwell@antiqueoak.co.uk
www.antiqueoak.co.uk

Oxfordshire
Key Antiques of Chipping Norton, 11 Horsefair, Chipping Norton OX7 5AL
Tel: 01608 644992/643777
info@keyantiques.com
www.keyantiques.com

Surrey
Anthony Welling, Broadway Barn, High Street, Ripley GU23 6AQ
Tel: 01483 225384
ant@awelling.freeserve.co.uk

ORIENTAL
USA
Mimi's Antiques Tel: 410 381 6862/443 250 0930
mimisantiques@comcast.net
www.mimisantiques.com
www.trocadero.com/mimis antiques
18th and 19thC Chinese export porcelain, American and English furniture, continental porcelain, paintings, sterling and oriental rugs.

PACKERS & SHIPPERS
Dorset
Alan Franklin Transport, 26 Blackmoor Road, Ebblake Industrial Estate, Verwood BH31 6BB
Tel: 01202 826539

Gloucestershire
The Shipping Company, Bourton Industrial Park, Bourton on the Water, Cheltenham GL54 2HQ
Tel: 01451 822451
enquiries@theshippingcompanyltd.com
www.theshippingcompanyltd.com

PAPERWEIGHTS
Cheshire
Sweetbriar Gallery Paperweights Ltd, 3 Collinson Court, off Church Street, Frodsham WA6 6PN
Tel: 01928 730064
sales@sweetbriar.co.uk
www.sweetbriar.co.uk

USA
The Dunlop Collection, PO Box 6269, Statesville NC 28687 Tel: (704) 871 2626 or Toll Free Telephone (800) 227 1996

PEWTER
Warwickshire
David Moulson, The Gorralls, Cold Comfort Lane, Alcester B49 5PU
Tel: 01789 764092
dmoulson@hotmail.com
Specialist dealer and consultant in antique pewter.

PHOTOGRAPHS
London
Jubilee Photographica, 10 Pierrepoint Row, Camden Passage, N1 8EE
Tel: 07860 793707
Specialist shop and gallery dealing in rare and collectable photographs from the 19th & 20thC. We sell and hold a large and constantly changing stock of cartes de visite, stereocards, daguerreotypes and ambrotypes, albums of travel, topographical and ethic photographs, art photographs and a range of books on the art and history of photography. We also have magic lanterns and lantern slides, and stereoscopic viewers. The shop is open on Wed and Sat 10am–4pm.

PINE
Cornwall
Julie Strachey, Trevaskis Barn, Gwinear Road, Nr Hayle TR27 5JQ
Tel: 01209 613750
Antique farm and country furniture in pine, oak, etc. Ironwork and interesting pieces for the garden (no repro).

Gloucestershire
Cottage Farm Antiques, Stratford Road, Aston Subedge, Chipping Campden GL55 6PZ
Tel: 01386 438263
info@cottagefarmantiques.co.uk
www.cottagefarmantiques.co.uk

Hampshire
Pine Cellars, 39 Jewry Street, Winchester SO23 8RY
Tel: 01962 777546/867014

Republic of Ireland
Ireland's Own Antiques, Alpine House, Carlow Road, Abbeyleix, Co Laois
Tel: 353 502 31348
Ireland's Own Antiques have a fine stock of original country furniture, which for years has been collected from country cottages and mansions all over Ireland by Peter and Daniel Meaney. Years of experience in the art of packing and shipping, and have many customers. This is a well worthwhile call for overseas buyers.

Somerset
Gilbert & Dale Antiques, The Old Chapel, Church Street, Ilchester, Nr Yeovil BA22 8ZA Tel: 01935 840464
roy@roygilbert.com

Westville House Antiques, Westville House, Littleton, Nr Somerton TA11 6NP
Tel: 01458 273376
Mobile: 07941 510823
antique@westville.co.uk
www.westville.co.uk

East Sussex
Ann Lingard, Ropewalk Antiques, Rye TN31 7NA Tel: 01797 223486
ann-lingard@ropewalkantiques.freeserve.co.uk

Wiltshire
North Wilts. Exporters, Farm Hill House, Brinkworth SN15 5AJ Tel: 01666 510876
Mobile: 07836 260730
mike@northwilts.demon.co.uk
www.northwiltsantiqueexporters.com

PORCELAIN
Essex
Barling Porcelain
Tel: 01621 890058
stuart@barling.uk.com
www.barling.uk.com

Bellhouse Antiques
Tel: 01268 710415
Bellhouse.Antiques@virgin.net

Hampshire
The Goss & Crested China Club & Museum, incorporating Milestone Publications, 62 Murray Road, Horndean PO8 9JL
Tel: (023) 9259 7440
info@gosschinaclub.demon.co.uk
www.gosscrestedchina.co.uk

Shropshire
Harvey Antiques
Tel: 01584 876375
christopher-harvey@tesco.net
By appointment only.

East Sussex
Tony Horsley, PO Box 3127, Brighton BN1 5SS
Tel: 01273 550770
Candle extinguishers, Royal Worcester and other fine porcelain.

Warwickshire
Coleshill Antiques & Interiors, 12–14 High Street, Coleshill B46 1AZ
Tel: 01675 467416
enquiries@coleshillantiques.com
www.coleshillantiques.com

Wiltshire
Andrew Dando, 34 Market Street, Bradford-on-Avon BA15 1LL
Tel: 01225 865444
andrew@andrewdando.co.uk
www.andrewdando.co.uk
English, oriental and continental porcelain.

Yorkshire
The Crested China Co, Highfield, Windmill Hill, Driffield YO25 5YP
Tel: 0870 300 1 300
dt@thecrestedchinacompany.com
www.thecrestedchinacompany.com

PORTRAIT MINIATURES
Gloucestershire
Judy & Brian Harden, PO Box 14, Bourton-on-the Water, Cheltenham GL54 2YR Tel: 01451 810684
Mobile: 07831 692252
harden@portraitminiatures.co.uk
www.portraitminiatures.co.uk

POTTERY
Berkshire
Special Auction Services, Kennetholme, Midgham, Reading RG7 5UX
Tel: 0118 971 2949
www.invaluable.com/sas/
Specialist auctions of commemoratives, pot lids and Prattware, Fairings, Goss & Crested, Baxter & Le Blond prints.

Buckinghamshire
Gillian Neale Antiques, PO Box 247, Aylesbury HP20 1JZ Tel: 01296 423754/07860 638700
gillianneale@aol.com
www.gilliannealeantiques.co.uk
Blue and white transfer-printed pottery 1780–1860.

Dorset
Greystoke Antiques, 4 Swan Yard, (off Cheap Street), Sherborne DT9 3AX
Tel: 01935 812833
Established 28 years. Adjacent to town centre car park. 10am–4.30pm daily, closed Wed. Also blue transfer-printed pottery 1800–50. Always some 200–300 pieces in stock.

Kent
Serendipity, 125 High Street, Deal CT14 6BB Tel: 01304 369165/01304 366536
dipityantiques@aol.com
Staffordshire pottery.

London
Jonathan Horne, 66 Kensington Church Street, W8 4BY Tel: 020 7221 5658
JH@jonathanhorne.co.uk
www.jonathanhorne.co.uk
Early English pottery.

Rogers de Rin, 76 Royal Hospital Road, SW3 4HN
Tel: 020 7352 9007
Wemyss ware.

Scotland
Becca Gaudie Antiques, The Old School, Glendoick, Perthshire PH2 7NR

Tel: 01738 860 870
Mobile: 07770 741 636
becca@scottishantiques.freeserve.co.uk
Scottish country antiques and Folk Art circa 1750–1900, snuff boxes, sewing tools and Mauchline ware.

Glebe Antiques, Scottish Antique Centre, Doune FK16 6HG
Tel: 01259 214559
Mobile: 07050 234577
rrglebe@aol.com
Wemyss ware.

Surrey
Judi Bland Antiques
Tel: 01536 724145 or 01276 857576
18th and 19thC English Toby jugs and Bargeware.

Julian Eade
Tel: 01865 300349
Mobile: 07973 542971
Doulton Lambeth stoneware and Burslem wares. Royal Worcester, Minton and Derby.

Tyne & Wear
Ian Sharp Antiques, 23 Front Street, Tynemouth NE30 4DX
Tel: 0191 296 0656
sharp@sharpantiques.com
www.sharpantiques.com
Tyneside and Wearside ceramics.

Warwickshire
Janice Paull, PO Box 100, Kenilworth CV8 1JX
Tel: 07876 284647
janicepaull@yahoo.com
www.janicepaull.com
Masons Ironstone.

Wiltshire
Andrew Dando, 34 Market Street, Bradford-on-Avon BA15 1LL
Tel: 01225 865444
andrew@andrewdando.co.uk
www.andrewdando.co.uk
English, oriental and continental pottery.

PUBLICATIONS

West Midlands
Antiques Magazine, H.P. Publishing, 2 Hampton Court Road, Harborne, Birmingham B17 9AE
Tel: 0121 681 8000
Subs 01562 701001
subscriptions@antiquesmagazine.com

RESTORATION (See also BRITISH ANTIQUE FURNITURE RESTORERS' ASSOCIATION)

Northamptonshire
Leather Conservation Centre, University College Campus, Boughton Green Road, Moulton Park, Northampton NN2 7AN
Tel: 01604 719766
lcc@northampton.ac.uk
Conservation and restoration of leather screens, wall hangings, car, carriage and furniture upholstery, saddlery, luggage, firemens' helmets and much, much more. The Centre is included on the Register maintained by the United Kingdom Institute for Conservation.

ROCK & POP

Cheshire
Collector's Corner, PO Box 8, Congleton CW12 4GD
Tel: 01260 270429
dave.popcorner@ukonline.co.uk

Lancashire
Tracks, PO Box 117, Chorley PR6 0UU Tel: 01257 269726
sales@tracks.co.uk

RUGS & CARPETS

West Sussex
Wadsworth's, Marehill, Pulborough RH20 2DY
Tel: 01798 873555
info@wadsworthsrugs.com
www.wadsworthsrugs.com

SCIENTIFIC INSTRUMENTS

Cambridgeshire
Fossack & Furkle, PO Box 733, Abington CB1 6BF
Tel: 01223 894296
Mobile: 07939078719
fossack@btopenworld.com
www.fossackandfurkle.freeservers.com

Cheshire
Charles Tomlinson, Chester
Tel: 01244 318395
charlestomlinson@tiscali.co.uk

Kent
Sporting Antiques, 10 Union Square, The Pantiles, Tunbridge Wells TN4 8HE
Tel: 01892 522661
Theodolites, sextants, levels, marine and military compasses, microscopes, telescopes and drawing instruments. We buy and sell.

Scotland
Early Technology, Monkton House, Old Craighall, Musselburgh, Midlothian EH21 8SF Tel: 0131 665 5753
Mobile: 07831 106768
michael.bennett-levy@virgin.net
www.earlytech.com
www.rare78s.com
www.tvhistory.tv

SCULPTURE

East Sussex
Garret & Hazlehurst, PO Box 138, Hailsham BN27 1WX
Tel: 01580 241993
Mobile: 07976 247942
garhaz.com@btopenworld.com
www.garretandhazlehurst.co.uk

SERVICES

Hampshire
Securikey Ltd, PO Box 18, Aldershot GU12 4SL
Tel: 01252 311888
enquiries@securikey.co.uk
www.securikey.co.uk
Underfloor safes.

Surrey
The Internet Fine Art Bureau, The Elms, Alma Way, Farnham GU9 0QN
Tel: 01252 640 666
enquiries@interfine.com
www.interfine.com
Specialist designers of websites for the antiques and fine art trade.

USA
Go Antiques, 1350 W.5th Ave, Suite 230, Columbus, Ohio 43212 Tel: 614 481 5750 www.goantiques.com
Antiques online.

Trocadero.com
admin@trocadero.com
www.trocadero.com
Antiques and art online.

SILVER

Dorset
Greystoke Antiques, 4 Swan Yard, (off Cheap Street), Sherborne DT9 3AX
Tel: 01935 812833
Adjacent to town centre car park. 10am–4.30pm daily, closed wed. Georgian, Victorian and later silver.

London
Daniel Bexfield, 26 Burlington Arcade, W1J 0PU Tel: 020 7491 1720
antiques@bexfield.co.uk
www.bexfield.co.uk

Lyn Bloom & Jeffrey Neal, Vault 27, The London Silver Vaults, Chancery Lane, WC2A 1QS Tel: 0207 242 6189
Mobile: 07768 533055
bloomvault@aol.com
www.bloomvault.com
We stock fine quality silver items ranging from £70 to £20,000 which includes anything from silver napkin rings and flatware to large centrepieces. Our speciality is a range of over 200 antique miniature silver toys.

Shropshire
Harvey Antiques
Tel: 01584 876375
christopher-harvey@tesco.net
By appointment only.

SPORTS & GAMES

Kent
Sporting Antiques, 10 Union Square, The Pantiles, Tunbridge Wells TN4 8HE
Tel: 01892 522661
Fishing rods, reels, trophies, books and prints. Golf and general antique sporting goods.

Nottinghamshire
T. Vennett-Smith, 11 Nottingham Road, Gotham NG11 0HE
Tel: 0115 983 0541
info@vennett-smith.com
www.vennett-smith.com
Sporting auctions.

TEDDY BEARS

Gloucestershire
Bourton Bears
Tel: 01993 824756
help@bourtonbears.co.uk
www.bourtonbears.com

Oxfordshire
Teddy Bears of Witney, 99 High Street, Witney OX28 6HY
Tel: 01993 702616/706616

TEXTILES

London
Erna Hiscock & John Shepherd, Chelsea Galleries, 69 Portobello Road, W11 Tel: 01233 661407
Mobile: 0771 562 7273
erna@ernahiscockantiques.com
www.ernahiscockantiques.com
Antique samplers.

Somerset
Joanna Proops Antique Textiles & Lighting, 34 Belvedere, Lansdown Hill, Bath BA1 5HR
Tel: 01225 310795
antiquetextiles@aol.co.uk
www.antiquetextiles.co.uk

USA
Antique European Linens, PO Box 789, Gulf Breeze, Florida 32562-0789
Tel: 850 432 4777
staff@antiqueeuropeanlinens.com
www.antiqueeuropeanlinens.com

TOYS

Berkshire
Special Auction Services, Kennetholme, Midgham, Reading RG7 5UX
Tel: 0118 971 2949
www.invaluable.com/sas/
Specialist auctions of toys for the collector including Dinky, Corgi, Matchbox, lead soldiers and figures, tinplate and model railways, etc.

Kent
The Collector's Toy & Model Shop, 49 Canterbury Road, Margate CT9 5AS
Tel: 01843 232301
Mobile: 07973 232778

East Sussex
Wallis & Wallis, West Street Auction Galleries, Lewes BN7 2NJ Tel: 01273 480208
auctions@wallisandwallis.co.uk
grb@wallisandwallis.co.uk
www.wallisandwallis.co.uk
Auctioneers of diecast toys, model railways, tinplate toys and models.

Yorkshire
John & Simon Haley, 89 Northgate, Halifax HX1 1XF
Tel: 01422 822148/360434
toysandbanks@aol.com

TRIBAL ART

USA
Hurst Gallery, 53 Mt Auburn Street, Cambridge MA 02138 Tel: 617 491 6888
manager@hurstgallery.com
www.hurstgallery.com
Art of the Pacific, Africa, Asia, The Americas and the ancient world.

TUNBRIDGE WARE

Kent
Dreweatt Neate formerly Bracketts Fine Art Auctioneers, The Auction Hall, The Pantiles, Tunbridge Wells TN2 5QL
Tel: 01892 544500
tunbridgewells@dnfa.com
www.dnfa.com/tunbridgewells
Tunbridge ware auctioneers.

WATCHES

Kent
Tempus Tel: 01344 874007
www.tempus-watches.co.uk

Lancashire
Brittons Jewellers, 4 King Street, Clitheroe BB7 2EP
Tel: 01200 425555
Mobile: 0789 008 1849
sales@brittonswatches.com
www.internetwatches.co.uk

London
Pieces of Time, (1–7 Davies Mews), 26 South Molton Lane, W1Y 2LP
Tel: 020 7629 2422
info@antique-watch.com
www.antique-watch.com
www.cufflinksworld.com

Yorkshire
Harpers Jewellers Ltd, 2/6 Minster Gates, York YO1 7HL Tel: 01904 632634
york@harpersjewellers.co.uk
www.vintage-watches.co.uk
Vintage and modern wrist and pocket watches.

Directory of Auctioneers

Auctioneers who hold frequent sales should contact us on +44 (0) 1580 766411 by April 2005 for inclusion in the next edition.

UNITED KINGDOM

Bedfordshire

W. & H. Peacock, 26 Newnham Street, Bedford MK40 3JR Tel: 01234 266366

Berkshire

Cameo Auctions, Kennet Holme Farm, Bath road, Midgham, Reading RG7 5UX Tel: 01189 713772 cameo-auctioneers@lineone.net

Dreweatt Neate, Donnington Priory, Donnington, Newbury RG14 2JE Tel: 01635 553553 donnington@dnfa.com www.dnfa.com/donnington

Law Fine Art Tel: 01635 860033 info@lawfineart.co.uk www.lawfineart.co.uk

Padworth Auctions, 30 The Broadway, Thatcham RG19 3HX Tel: 01734 713772

Shiplake Fine Art, 31 Great Knollys Street, Reading RG1 7HU Tel: 01734 594748

Special Auction Services, Kennetholme, Midgham, Reading RG7 5UX Tel: 0118 971 2949 www.invaluable.com/sas/

Buckinghamshire

Amersham Auction Rooms, Station Road, Amersham HP7 0AH Tel: 01494 729292 info@amershamauctionrooms.co.uk

Bosley's, 42 West Street, Marlow SL7 2NB Tel: 01628 488188

Bourne End Auction Rooms, Station Approach, Bourne End SL8 5QH Tel: 01628 531500

Dickins Auctioneers Ltd, The Claydon Saleroom, Middle Claydon MK18 2EZ Tel: 01296 714434 info@dickins-auctioneers.com www.dickins-auctioneers.com

Cambridgeshire

Cheffins, Clifton House, Clifton Road, Cambridge CB1 7EA Tel: 01223 213343 www.cheffins.co.uk

Rowley Fine Art, The Old Bishop's Palace, Little Downham, Ely CB6 2TD Tel: 01353 699177 mail@rowleyfineart.com www.rowleyfineart.com

Willingham Auctions, 25 High Street, Willingham CB4 5ES Tel: 01954 261252 info@willinghamauctions.com www.willinghamauctions.com

Channel Islands

Bonhams and Langlois, Westaway Chambers, 39 Don Street, St Helier, Jersey JE2 4TR Tel: 01534 722441 www.bonhams.com

Cheshire

Bonhams, New House, 150 Christleton Road, Chester CH3 5TD Tel: 01244 313936 www.bonhams.com

Halls Fine Art Auctions, Booth Mansion, 30 Watergate Street, Chester CH1 2LA Tel: 01244 312300/312112

Frank R. Marshall & Co, Marshall House, Church Hill, Knutsford WA16 6DH Tel: 01565 653284

Maxwells of Wilmslow inc Dockree's, 133A Woodford Road, Woodford SK7 1QD Tel: 0161 439 5182 www.maxwells-auctioneers.co.uk

Wright Manley, Beeston Castle Salerooms, Tarporley CW6 9NZ Tel: 01829 262150 www.wrightmanley.co.uk

Cleveland

Vectis Auctions Ltd, Fleck Way, Thornaby, Stockton-on-Tees TS17 9JZ Tel: 01642 750616 admin@vectis.co.uk www.vectis.co.uk

Co Durham

Addisons Auctions, The Auction Rooms, Staindrop Road, Barnard Castle DL12 8TD Tel: 01833 690545 enquiries@addisons-auctions.co.uk www.addisons-auctioneers.co.uk

Cornwall

Bonhams, Cornubia Hall, Eastcliffe Road, Par PL24 2AQ Tel: 01726 814047 www.bonhams.com

Lambrays, Polmorla Walk Galleries, The Platt, Wadebridge PL27 7AE Tel: 01208 813593

W. H. Lane & Son, Jubilee House, Queen Street, Penzance TR18 2DF Tel: 01736 361447 graham.bazlet@excite.com

David Lay ASVA, Auction House, Alverton, Penzance TR18 4RE Tel: 01736 361414 david.lays@btopenworld.com

Martyn Rowe, The Truro Auction Centre, Triplets Business Park, Poldice Valley, Nr Chacewater, Truro TR16 5PZ Tel: 01209 822266 www.invaluable.com/martynrowe

Cumbria

Bonhams, 48 Cecil Street, Carlisle CA1 1NT Tel: 01228 542422 www.bonhams.com

Kendal Auction Rooms, Sandylands Road, Kendal LA9 6EU Tel: 01539 720603 www.kendalauction.co.uk/furniture

Mitchells Auction Company, The Furniture Hall, 47 Station Road, Cockermouth CA13 9PZ Tel: 01900 827800

Penrith Farmers' & Kidd's plc, Skirsgill Salerooms, Penrith CA11 0DN Tel: 01768 890781 info@pfkauctions.co.uk www.pfkauctions.co.uk

Thomson, Roddick & Medcalf Ltd, Coleridge House, Shaddongate, Carlisle CA2 5TU Tel: 01228 528939 www.thomsonroddick.com

Devon

Bearnes, St Edmund's Court, Okehampton Street, Exeter EX4 1DU Tel: 01392 207000 enquiries@bearnes.co.uk www.bearnes.co.uk

Bonhams, Dowell Street, Honiton EX14 1LX Tel: 01404 41872 www.bonhams.com

Bonhams, 38/39 Southernhay East, Exeter EX1 1PE Tel: 01392 455 955 www.bonhams.com

Michael J. Bowman, 6 Haccombe House, Nr Netherton, Newton Abbott TQ12 4SJ Tel: 01626 872890

Dreweatt Neate formerly Honiton Galleries, inc Robin A. Fenner, 205 High Street, Honiton EX14 1LQ Tel: 01404 42404 honiton@dnfa.com www.dnfa.com/honiton

Eldreds Auctioneers & Valuers, 13–15 Ridge Park Road, Plympton, Plymouth PL7 2BS Tel: 01752 340066

S. J. Hales, 87 Fore Street, Bovey Tracey TQ13 9AB Tel: 01626 836684

The Plymouth Auction Rooms, Edwin House, St John's Road, Cattedown, Plymouth PL4 0NZ Tel: 01752 254740

Rendells, Stonepark, Ashburton TQ13 7RH Tel: 01364 653017 stonepark@rendells.co.uk www.rendells.co.uk

G. S. Shobrook & Co, 20 Western Approach, Plymouth PL1 1TG Tel: 01752 663341

John Smale & Co, 11 High Street, Barnstaple EX31 1BG Tel: 01271 42000/42916

Martin Spencer-Thomas, Bicton Street, Exmouth EX8 2SN Tel: 01395 267403

Dorset

Chapman, Moore & Mugford, 9 High Street, Shaftesbury SP7 8JB Tel: 01747 852400

Charterhouse, The Long Street Salerooms, Sherborne DT9 3BS Tel: 01935 812277 enquiry@charterhouse-auctions.co.uk www.charterhouse-auctions.co.uk

Cottees of Wareham, The Market, East Street, Wareham BH20 4NR Tel: 01929 552826 www.auctionsatcottees.co.uk

Hy Duke & Son, The Dorchester Fine Art Salerooms, Weymouth Avenue, Dorchester DT1 1QS Tel: 01305 265080 www.dukes-auctions.com

Onslow's Auctions Ltd, The Coach House, Manor Road, Stourpaine DT8 8TQ Tel: 01258 488838

Riddetts of Bournemouth, 1 Wellington Road, Bournemouth BH8 8JQ Tel: 01202 555686 auctions@riddetts.co.uk www.riddetts.co.uk

Semley Auctioneers, Station Road, Semley, Shaftesbury SP7 9AN Tel: 01747 855122/855222

Essex

Ambrose, Ambrose House, Old Station Road, Loughton IG10 4PE Tel: 020 8502 3951

Cooper Hirst Auctions, The Granary Saleroom, Victoria Road, Chelmsford CM2 6LH Tel: 01245 260535

Leigh Auction Rooms, John Stacey & Sons, 88–90 Pall Mall, Leigh-on-Sea SS9 1RG Tel: 01702 477051

Saffron Walden Auctions, 1 Market Street, Saffron Walden CB10 1JB Tel: 01799 513281 www.saffronwaldenauctions.com

Sworders, 14 Cambridge Road, Stansted Mountfitchet CM24 8BZ Tel: 01279 817778 auctions@sworder.co.uk www.sworder.co.uk

Flintshire

Dodds Property World, Victoria Auction Galleries, 9 Chester Street, Mold CH7 1EB Tel: 01352 752552

Gloucestershire

Bruton, Knowles & Co, 111 Eastgate Street, Gloucester GL1 1PZ Tel: 01452 521267

The Cotswold Auction Company Ltd, inc Short Graham & Co and Hobbs and Chambers Fine Arts, The Coach House, Swan Yard, 9–13 West Market Place, Cirencester GL7 2NH Tel: 01285 642420 info@cotswoldauction.co.uk www.cotswoldauction.co.uk

The Cotswold Auction Company Ltd, inc Short Graham & Co and Hobbs and Chambers Fine Arts, Chapel Walk Saleroom, Cheltenham GL50 3DS Tel: 01242 256363 info@cotswoldauction.co.uk www.cotswoldauction.co.uk

The Cotswold Auction Company Ltd, inc Short Graham & Co and Hobbs and Chambers Fine Arts, 4–6 Clarence Street, Gloucester GL1 1DX Tel: 01452 521177 info@cotswoldauction.co.uk www.cotswoldauction.co.uk

Dreweatt Neate formerly Bristol Auction Rooms, St John's Place, Apsley Road, Clifton, Bristol BS8 2ST Tel: 0117 973 7201 bristol@dnfa.com www.dnfa.com/bristol

Dreweatt Neate formerly Bristol Auction Rooms, Bristol Saleroom Two, Baynton Road, Ashton, Bristol BS3 2EB Tel: 0117 953 1603 bristol@dnfa.com www.dnfa.com/bristol

Mallams, 26 Grosvenor Street, Cheltenham GL52 2SG Tel: 01242 235712

Moore, Allen & Innocent, The Salerooms, Norcote, Cirencester GL7 5RH Tel: 01285 646050 fineart@mooreallen.co.uk www.mooreallen.co.uk

Specialised Postcard Auctions, 25 Gloucester Street, Cirencester GL7 2DJ Tel: 01285 659057

Tayler & Fletcher, London House, High Street, Bourton-on-the-Water, Cheltenham GL54 2AP Tel: 01451 821666 bourton@taylerfletcher.com www.taylerfletcher.com

Wotton Auction Rooms, Tabernacle Road, Wotton-under-Edge GL12 7EB Tel: 01453 844733 info@wottonauctionrooms.co.uk www.wottonauctionrooms.co.uk

Greater Manchester

Bonhams, The Stables, 213 Ashley Road, Hale WA15 9TB Tel: 0161 927 3822 www.bonhams.com

Capes Dunn & Co, The Auction Galleries, 38 Charles Street, Off Princess Street M1 7DB Tel: 0161 273 6060/1911 capesdunn@yahoo.co.uk

Hampshire

Bonhams, 54 Southampton Road, Ringwood BH24 1JD Tel: 01425 473333 www.bonhams.com

Evans & Partridge, Agriculture House, High Street, Stockbridge SO20 6HF Tel: 01264 810702

Jacobs & Hunt, 26 Lavant Street, Petersfield GU32 3EF Tel: 01730 233933 www.jacobsandhunt.co.uk

George Kidner, The Old School, The Square, Pennington, Lymington SO41 8GN Tel: 01590 670070 info@georgekidner.co.uk www.georgekidner.co.uk

May & Son, The Old Stables, 9A Winchester Road, Andover SP10 2EG Tel: 01264 323417 office@mayandson.com www.mayandson.com

D. M. Nesbit & Co, Fine Art and Auction Department, Southsea Salerooms, 7 Clarendon Road, Southsea PO5 2ED Tel: 023 9286 4321 auctions@nesbits.co.uk www.nesbits.co.uk

Odiham Auction Sales, Unit 4, Priors Farm, West Green Road, Mattingley RG27 8JU Tel: 01189 326824 auction@dircon.co.uk

Herefordshire

Brightwells Fine Art, The Fine Art Saleroom, Easters Court, Leominster HR6 0DE Tel: 01568 611122 fineart@brightwells.com www.brightwells.com

Morris Bricknell, Stroud House, 30 Gloucester Road, Ross-on-Wye HR9 5LE Tel: 01989 768320 morrisbricknell@lineone.net www.morrisbricknell.com

Nigel Ward & Co, The Border Property Centre, Pontrilas HR2 0EH Tel: 01981 240140 www.nigel-ward.co.uk

Williams & Watkins, Ross Auction Rooms, Ross-on-Wye HR9 7QF Tel: 01989 762225

Hertfordshire

Sworders, The Hertford Saleroom, 42 St Andrew Street, Hertford SG14 1JA Tel: 01992 583508 auctions@sworder.co.uk www.sworder.co.uk

Tring Market Auctions, The Market Premises, Brook Street, Tring HP23 5EF Tel: 01442 826446 sales@tringmarketauctions.co.uk www.tringmarketauctions.co.uk

Kent

Bonhams, 49 London Road, Sevenoaks TN13 1AR Tel: 01732 740310 www.bonhams.com

Calcutt Maclean Standen, The Estate Office, Stone Street, Cranbrook TN17 3HD Tel: 01580 713828

The Canterbury Auction Galleries, 40 Station Road West, Canterbury CT2 8AN Tel: 01227 763337 auctions@thecanterburyauctiongalleries.com www.thecanterburyauctiongalleries.com

Mervyn Carey, Twysden Cottage, Scullsgate, Benenden, Cranbrook TN17 4LD Tel: 01580 240283

Dreweatt Neate formerly Bracketts Fine Art Auctioneers, The Auction Hall, The Pantiles, Tunbridge Wells TN2 5QL Tel: 01892 544500 tunbridgewells@dnfa.com www.dnfa.com/tunbridgewells

Gorringes, 15 The Pantiles, Tunbridge Wells TN2 5TD Tel: 01892 619670 www.gorringes.co.uk

Ibbett Mosely, 125 High Street, Sevenoaks TN13 1UT Tel: 01732 456731 auctions@ibbettmosely.co.uk www.ibbettmosely.co.uk

Lambert & Foster, 102 High Street, Tenterden TN30 6HT Tel: 01580 762083 saleroom@lambertandfoster.co.uk www.lambertandfoster.co.uk

B. J. Norris, The Quest, West Street, Harrietsham, Maidstone ME17 1JD Tel: 01622 859515

Wealden Auction Galleries, Desmond Judd, 23 Hendly Drive, Cranbrook TN17 3DY Tel: 01580 714522

Lancashire

Smythes Fine Art, Chattel & Property Auctioneers & Valuers, 174 Victoria Road West, Cleveleys FY5 3NE Tel: 01253 852184 smythes@btinternet.com www.smythes.net

Tony & Sons, 4–8 Lynwood Road, Blackburn BB2 6HP Tel: 01254 691748

Leicestershire

Gilding's Auctioneers and Valuers, 64 Roman Way, Market Harborough LE16 7PQ Tel: 01858 410414 sales@gildings.co.uk www.gildings.co.uk

Lincolnshire

Batemans Auctioneers, The Exchange Hall, Broad Street, Stamford PE9 1PX Tel: 01780 766466 www.batemans-auctions.co.uk

DDM Auction Rooms, Old Courts Road, Brigg DN20 8JD Tel: 01652 650172 www.ddmauctionrooms.co.uk

Thomas Mawer & Son, Dunston House, Portland Street, Lincoln LN5 7NN Tel: 01522 524984 mawer.thos@lineone.net

Marilyn Swain Auctions, The Old Barracks, Sandon Road, Grantham NG31 9AS Tel: 01476 568861

Walter's, No. 1 Mint Lane, Lincoln LN1 1UD Tel: 01522 525454

London

Angling Auctions, PO Box 2095, W12 8RU Tel: 020 8749 4175 Mobile: 07785 281349 neil@anglingauctions.demon.co.uk

Bloomsbury Auctions Ltd, Bloomsbury House, 24 Maddox Street, W1S 1PP Tel: 020 7495 9494 info@bloomsburyauctions.com www.bloomsburyauctions.com

Bonhams, 65–69 Lots Road, Chelsea, SW10 0RN Tel: 020 7393 3900 www.bonhams.com

Bonhams, 101 New Bond Street, W1S 1SR Tel: 020 7629 6602 www.bonhams.com

Bonhams, 10 Salem Road, Bayswater, W2 4DL Tel: 020 7313 2700 www.bonhams.com

Bonhams, Montpelier Street, Knightsbridge, SW7 1HH Tel: 020 7393 3900 www.bonhams.com

Bonhams, 101 New Bond Street, W1S 1SR Tel: 020 7629 6602 www.bonhams.com

Christie's, 8 King Street, St James's, SW1Y 6QT Tel: 020 7839 9060 www.christies.com

Christie's, 85 Old Brompton Road, SW7 3LD Tel: 020 7930 6074 www.christies.com

Comic Book Postal Auctions Ltd, 40–42 Osnaburgh Street, NW1 3ND Tel: 020 7424 0007 comicbook@compuserve.com www.compalcomics.com

Cooper Owen, 10 Denmark Street, WC2H 8LS Tel: 020 7240 4132 www.CooperOwen.com

Criterion Salerooms, 53 Essex Road, Islington, N1 2BN Tel: 020 7359 5707

Dix-Noonan-Webb, 16 Bolton Street, W1J 8BQ Tel: 020 7016 1700 auctions@dnw.co.uk www.dnw.co.uk

Glendining's (A division of Bonhams specialising in coins & medals), 101 New Bond Street, W1S 1SR Tel: 020 7493 2445

Harmers of London, 111 Power Road, Chiswick, W4 5PY Tel: 020 8747 6100 auctions@harmers.demon.co.uk www.harmers.com

Lloyds International Auction Galleries, Lloyds House, 9 Lydden Road, SW18 4LT Tel: 020 8788 7777 www.lloyds-auction.co.uk

Lots Road Auctions, 71–73 Lots Road, Chelsea, SW10 0RN Tel: 020 7351 7771 www.lotsroad.com

Morton & Eden Ltd, In association with Sotheby's, 45 Maddox Street, W1S 2PE Tel: 020 7493 5344 info@mortonandeden.com

Piano Auctions Limited, Conway Hall, 25 Red Lion Square, Holborn, WC1R 4RL Tel: 01234 831742

Proud Oriental Auctions, Proud Galleries, 5 Buckingham Street, WC2N 6BP Tel: 020 7839 4942

Rosebery's Fine Art Ltd, 74/76 Knights Hill, SE27 0JD Tel: 020 8761 2522 auctions@roseberys.co.uk

Sotheby's, 34–35 New Bond Street, W1A 2AA Tel: 020 7293 5000 www.sothebys.com

Sotheby's Olympia, Hammersmith Road, W14 8UX Tel: 020 7293 5555 www.sothebys.com

Spink & Son Ltd, 69 Southampton Road, Bloomsbury, WC1B 4ET Tel: 020 7563 4000

Merseyside

Cato Crane & Company Antiques & Fine Art Auctioneers, 6 Stanhope Street, Liverpool L8 5RF Tel: 0151 709 5559 johncrane@cato-crane.co.uk www.cato-crane.co.uk

Outhwaite & Litherland, Kingsway Galleries, Fontenoy Street, Liverpool L3 2BE Tel: 0151 236 6561

Middlesex

West Middlesex Auction Rooms, 113–114 High Street, Brentford TW8 8AT Tel: 020 8568 9080

Norfolk

Garry M. Emms & Co Ltd Auctioneers, Valuers & Agents, Great Yarmouth Salerooms, Beevor Road (off South Beach Parade), Great Yarmouth NR30 3PS Tel: 01493 332668 g_emms@gt-yarmouth-auctions.com www.gt-yarmouth-auctions.com

Thomas Wm Gaze & Son, Diss Auction Rooms, Roydon Road, Diss IP22 4LN Tel: 01379 650306 sales@dissauctionrooms.co.uk www.twgaze.com

Horners Professional Valuers & Auctioneers, inc Howlett & Edrich and Jonathan Howlett, North Walsham Salerooms, Midland Road, North Walsham NR28 9JR Tel: 01692 500603

Keys, Off Palmers Lane, Aylsham NR11 6JA Tel: 01263 733195 www.aylshamsalerooms.co.uk

Knight's, Cuckoo Cottage, Town Green, Alby, Norwich NR11 7HE Tel: 01263 768488

Northamptonshire

Denise E. Cowling FGA Tel: 01604 686219 Mobile: 0781 800 3786 northants@peacockauction.co.uk

J. P. Humbert Auctioneers Ltd, The Salerooms, Unit 2A, Burcote Road Estate, Towcester NN12 6TF Tel: 01327 359595 www.invaluable.com/jphumbert www.jphumbertauctioneers.co.uk

Merry's Auctioneers Tel: 01604 769990

Northern Ireland

Anderson's Auction Rooms Ltd, Unit 7, Prince Regent Business Park, Prince Regent Road, Castereagh, Belfast BT5 6QR Tel: 028 9040 1888

Northumberland

Jack Dudgeon, The New Saleroom, 76 Ravensdowne, Berwick-upon-Tweed TD15 1DQ Tel: 01289 332700 Mobile: 07968 207575 jack@jackdudgeon.co.uk www.jackdudgeon.co.uk

Nottinghamshire

Bonhams, 57 Mansfield Road, Nottingham NG1 3PL Tel: 0115 947 4414 www.bonhams.com

Arthur Johnson & Sons Ltd, The Nottingham Auction Centre, Meadow Lane, Nottingham NG2 3GY Tel: 0115 986 9128 arthurjohnson@btconnect.com

Mellors & Kirk, The Auction House, Gregory Street, Lenton Lane, Nottingham NG7 2NL Tel: 0115 979 0000

Neales, 192 Mansfield Road, Nottingham NG1 3HU Tel: 0115 962 4141 fineart@neales-auctions.com www.neales-auctions.com

C. B. Sheppard & Son, The Auction Galleries, Chatsworth Street, Sutton-in-Ashfield NG17 4GG Tel: 01773 872419

T. Vennett-Smith, 11 Nottingham Road, Gotham NG11 0HE Tel: 0115 983 0541 info@vennett-smith.com www.vennett-smith.com

Oxfordshire

Bonhams, 39 Park End Street, Oxford OX1 1JD Tel: 01865 723524 www.bonhams.com

Holloway's, 49 Parsons Street, Banbury OX16 5PF Tel: 01295 817777 enquiries@hollowaysauctioneers.co.uk www.hollowaysauctioneers.co.uk

Mallams, Bocardo House, 24 St Michael's Street, Oxford 0X1 2EB Tel: 01865 241358 oxford@mallams.co.uk

Simmons & Sons, 32 Bell Street, Henley-on-Thames RG9 2BH Tel: 01491 612810 www.simmonsandsons.com

Soames County Auctioneers, Pinnocks Farm Estates, Northmoor OX8 1AY Tel: 01865 300626

Scotland

Bonhams, 65 George Street, Edinburgh EH2 2JL Tel: 0131 225 2266 www.bonhams.com

Bonhams, 176 St Vincent Street, Glasgow G2 5SG Tel: 0141 223 8866 www.bonhams.com

William Hardie Ltd, 15a Blythswood Square, Glasgow G2 4EW Tel: 0141 221 6780

Loves Auction Rooms, 52 Canal Street, Perth PH2 8LF Tel: 01738 633337

Lyon & Turnbull, 33 Broughton Place, Edinburgh EH1 3RR Tel: 0131 557 8844 info@lyonandturnbull.com

Macgregor Auctions, 56 Largo Road, St Andrews, Fife KY16 8RP Tel: 01334 472431

Shapes Fine Art Auctioneers & Valuers, Bankhead Avenue, Sighthill, Edinburgh EH11 4BY Tel: 0131 453 3222 auctionsadmin@shapesauctioneers.co.uk www.shapesauctioneers.co.uk

L. S. Smellie & Sons Ltd, Within the Furniture Market, Lower Auchingramont Road, Hamilton ML10 6BE Tel: 01698 282007 or 01357 520211

Sotheby's, 112 George Street, Edinburgh EH2 4LH Tel: 0131 226 7201 www.sothebys.com

Thomson, Roddick & Medcalf Ltd, 60 Whitesands, Dumfries DG1 2RS Tel: 01387 279879 trmdumfries@btconnect.com www.thomsonroddick.com

Thomson, Roddick & Medcalf Ltd, 20 Murray Street, Annan DG12 6EG Tel: 01461 202575 www.thomsonroddick.com

Thomson, Roddick & Medcalf Ltd, 43/4 Hardengreen Business Park, Eskbank, Edinburgh EH22 3NX Tel: 0131 454 9090 www.thomsonroddick.com

Shropshire

Halls Fine Art Auctions, Welsh Bridge, Shrewsbury SY3 8LA Tel: 01743 231212

McCartneys, Ox Pasture, Overture Road, Ludlow SY8 4AA Tel: 01584 872251

Mullock & Madeley, The Old Shippon, Wall-under-Heywood, Nr Church Stretton SY6 7DS Tel: 01694 771771 auctions@mullockmadeley.co.uk www.mullockmadeley.co.uk

Nock Deighton, Livestock & Auction Centre, Tasley, Bridgnorth WV16 4QR Tel: 01746 762666

Walker, Barnett & Hill, Cosford Auction Rooms, Long Lane, Cosford TF11 8PJ Tel: 01902 375555 wbhauctions@lineone.net www.walker-barnett-hill.co.uk

Welsh Bridge Salerooms, Welsh Bridge, Shrewsbury SY3 8LH Tel: 01743 231212

Somerset

Aldridges, Newark House, 26–45 Cheltenham Street, Bath BA2 3EX Tel: 01225 462830

Bonhams, 1 Old King Street, Bath BA1 2JT Tel: 01225 788 988 www.bonhams.com

Clevedon Salerooms, The Auction Centre, Kenn Road, Kenn, Clevedon, Bristol BS21 6TT Tel: 01934 830111 clevedon.salerooms@blueyonder.co.uk www.clevedon-salerooms.com

Gardiner Houlgate, The Bath Auction Rooms, 9 Leafield Way, Corsham, Nr Bath SN13 9SW Tel: 01225 812912 auctions@gardiner-houlgate.co.uk www.invaluable.com/gardiner-houlgate

Greenslade Taylor Hunt Fine Art, Magdelene House, Church Square, Taunton TA1 1SB Tel: 01823 332525

Lawrence Fine Art Auctioneers, South Street, Crewkerne TA18 8AB Tel: 01460 73041 www.lawrences.co.uk

Tamlyn & Son, 56 High Street, Bridgwater TA6 3BN Tel: 01278 458241

Staffordshire

Louis Taylor Auctioneers & Valuers, Britannia House, 10 Town Road, Hanley, Stoke-on-Trent ST1 2QG Tel: 01782 214111

Potteries Specialist Auctions, 271 Waterloo Road, Cobridge, Stoke-on-Trent ST6 3HR Tel: 01782 286622

Wintertons Ltd, Lichfield Auction Centre, Fradley Park, Lichfield WS13 8NF Tel: 01543 263256 enquiries@wintertons.co.uk www.wintertons.co.uk

Suffolk

Abbotts Auction Rooms, Campsea Ashe, Woodbridge IP13 0PS Tel: 01728 746323

Boardman Fine Art Auctioneers, Station Road Corner, Haverhill CB9 0EY Tel: 01440 730414

Bonhams, 32 Boss Hall Road, Ipswich IP1 5DJ Tel: 01473 740494 www.bonhams.com

Diamond Mills & Co, 117 Hamilton Road, Felixstowe IP11 7BL Tel: 01394 282281

Dyson & Son, The Auction Room, Church Street, Clare CO10 8PD Tel: 01787 277993 info@dyson-auctioneers.co.uk www.dyson-auctioneers.co.uk

Lacy Scott and Knight, Fine Art Department, The Auction Centre, 10 Risbygate Street, Bury St Edmunds IP33 3AA Tel: 01284 763531

Neal Sons & Fletcher, 26 Church Street, Woodbridge IP12 1DP Tel: 01394 382263

Olivers, Olivers Rooms, Burkitts Lane, Sudbury CO10 1HB Tel: 01787 880305 oliversauctions@btconnect.com

Vost's, Newmarket CB8 9AU Tel: 01638 561313

Surrey

Bonhams, Millmead, Guildford GU2 4BE Tel: 01483 504030 www.bonhams.com

Clarke Gammon, The Guildford Auction Rooms, Bedford Road, Guildford GU1 4SJ Tel: 01483 880915

Ewbank Auctioneers, Burnt Common Auction Rooms, London Road, Send, Woking GU23 7LN Tel: 01483 223101 antiques@ewbankauctions.co.uk www.ewbankauctions.co.uk

Hamptons International, Baverstock House, 93 High Street, Godalming GU7 1AL Tel: 01483 423567 fineartauctions@hamptons-int.com www.hamptons.co.uk

Lawrences Auctioneers Limited, Norfolk House, 80 High Street, Bletchingley RH1 4PA Tel: 01883 743323 www.lawrencesbletchingley.co.uk

John Nicholson, The Auction Rooms, Longfield, Midhurst Road, Fernhurst GU27 3HA Tel: 01428 653727

Richmond & Surrey Auctions Ltd, Richmond Station, Kew Road, Old Railway Parcels Depot, Richmond TW9 2NA Tel: 020 8948 6677 rsatrading.richmond@virgin.net

P. F. Windibank, The Dorking Halls, Reigate Road, Dorking RH4 1SG Tel: 01306 884556/876280 sjw@windibank.co.uk www.windibank.co.uk

East Sussex

Burstow & Hewett, Abbey Auction Galleries, Lower Lake, Battle TN33 0AT Tel: 01424 772374 www.burstowandhewett.co.uk

Dreweatt Neate formerly Edgar Horns, 46–50 South Street, Eastbourne BN21 4XB Tel: 01323 410419 eastbourne@dnfa.com www.dnfa.com/eastbourne

Gorringes Auction Galleries, Terminus Road, Bexhill-on-Sea TN39 3LR Tel: 01424 212994 bexhill@gorringes.co.uk www.gorringes.co.uk

Gorringes Inc Julian Dawson, 15 North Street, Lewes BN7 2PD Tel: 01273 478221 auctions@gorringes.co.uk www.gorringes.co.uk

Raymond P. Inman, 98a Coleridge Street, Hove BN3 5AA Tel: 01273 774777 www.invaluable.com/raymondinman

Rye Auction Galleries, Rock Channel, Rye TN31 7HL Tel: 01797 222124 sales@ryeauction.fsnet.co.uk

Scarborough Perry Fine Art, Hove Auction Rooms, Hove Street, Hove BN3 2GL Tel: 01273 735266

Wallis & Wallis, West Street Auction Galleries, Lewes BN7 2NJ Tel: 01273 480208 auctions@wallisandwallis.co.uk www.wallisandwallis.co.uk

West Sussex

Henry Adams Fine Art Auctioneers, Baffins Hall, Baffins Lane, Chichester PO19 1UA Tel: 01243 532223 enquiries@henryadamsfineart.co.uk

John Bellman Auctioneers, New Pound Business Park, Wisborough Green, Billingshurst RH14 0AZ Tel: 01403 700858 jbellman@compuserve.com

Peter Cheney, Western Road Auction Rooms, Western Road, Littlehampton BN17 5NP Tel: 01903 722264 & 713418

Denham's, The Auction Galleries, Warnham, Nr Horsham RH12 3RZ Tel: 01403 255699 Tel/Fax: 01403 253837 enquiries@denhams.com www.denhams.com

R. H. Ellis & Sons, 44–46 High Street, Worthing BN11 1LL Tel: 01903 238999

Sotheby's Sussex, Summers Place, Billingshurst RH14 9AD Tel: 01403 833500 www.sothebys.com

Stride & Son, Southdown House, St John's Street, Chichester PO19 1XQ Tel: 01243 780207

Rupert Toovey & Co Ltd, Spring Gardens, Washington RH20 3BS Tel: 01903 891955 auctions@rupert-toovey.com www.rupert-toovey.com

Worthing Auction Galleries Ltd, Fleet House, Teville Gate, Worthing BN11 1UA Tel: 01903 205565 info@worthing-auctions.co.uk www.worthing-auctions.co.uk

Tyne & Wear

Anderson & Garland (Auctioneers), Marlborough House, Marlborough Crescent, Newcastle-Upon-Tyne NE1 4EE Tel: 0191 232 6278

Boldon Auction Galleries, 24a Front Street, East Boldon NE36 0SJ Tel: 0191 537 2630

Bonhams, 30–32 Grey Street, Newcastle-Upon-Tyne NE1 6AE Tel: 0191 233 9930 www.bonhams.com

Sneddons, Sunderland Auction Rooms, 30 Villiers Street, Sunderland SR1 1EJ Tel: 0191 514 5931

Wales

Anthemion Auctions, 2 Llandough Trading Park, Penarth Road, Cardiff CF11 8RR Tel: 029 2071 2608

Bonhams, 7–8 Park Place, Cardiff CF10 3DP Tel: 029 2072 7980 cardiff@bonhams.com www.bonhams.com

Peter Francis, Curiosity Sale Room, 19 King Street, Carmarthen SA31 1BH Tel: 01267 233456 Peterfrancis@valuers.fsnet.co.uk www.peterfrancis.co.uk

Morgan Evans & Co Ltd, 30 Church Street, Llangefni, Anglesey LL77 7DU Tel: 01248 723303/421582 gaerwen.auction@morganevans.i12.com www.morganevans.com

Rogers Jones & Co, The Saleroom, 33 Abergele Road, Colwyn Bay LL29 7RU Tel: 01492 532176 www.rogersjones.co.uk

J. Straker, Chadwick & Sons, Market Street Chambers, Abergavenny, Monmouthshire NP7 5SD Tel: 01873 852624

Wingetts Auction Gallery, 29 Holt Street, Wrexham, Clwyd LL13 8DH Tel: 01978 353553 auctions@wingetts.co.uk www.wingetts.co.uk

Warwickshire

Bigwood Auctioneers Ltd, The Old School, Tiddington, Stratford-upon-Avon CV37 7AW Tel: 01789 269415

Locke & England, 18 Guy Street, Leamington Spa CV32 4RT Tel: 01926 889100 www.auctions-online.com/locke

West Midlands

Biddle and Webb Ltd, Ladywood, Middleway, Birmingham B16 0PP Tel: 0121 455 8042 antiques@biddleandwebb.freeserve.co.uk www.biddleandwebb.co.uk

Bonhams, The Old House, Station Road, Knowle, Solihull B93 0HT Tel: 01564 776151 www.bonhams.com

West Midlands

Fellows & Sons, Augusta House, 19 Augusta Street, Hockley, Birmingham B18 6JA Tel: 0121 212 2131 info@fellows.co.uk www.fellows.co.uk

Weller & Dufty Ltd, 141 Bromsgrove Street, Birmingham B5 6RQ Tel: 0121 692 1414 sales@welleranddufty.co.uk www.welleranddufty.co.uk

Wiltshire

Henry Aldridge & Son Auctions, Unit 1, Bath Road Business Centre, Devizes SN10 1XA Tel: 01380 729199 www.henry-aldridge.co.uk

Finan & Co, The Square, Mere BA12 6DJ Tel: 01747 861411 post@finanandco.co.uk www.finanandco.co.uk

Kidson Trigg, Estate Office, Friars Farm, Sevenhampton, Highworth, Swindon SN6 7PZ Tel: 01793 861000

Netherhampton Salerooms, Salisbury Auction Centre, Netherhampton, Salisbury SP2 8RH Tel: 01722 340 041

Dominic Winter Book Auctions, The Old School, Maxwell Street, Swindon SN1 5DR Tel: 01793 611340 info@dominicwinter.co.uk www.dominicwinter.co.uk

Woolley & Wallis, Salisbury Salerooms, 51–61 Castle Street, Salisbury SP1 3SU Tel: 01722 424500/411854 junebarrett@woolleyandwallis.co.uk www.woolleyandwallis.co.uk

Worcestershire

Andrew Grant, St Mark's House, St Mark's Close, Cherry Orchard, Worcester WR5 3DL Tel: 01905 357547 www.andrew-grant.co.uk

Philip Laney, The Malvern Auction Centre, Portland Road, off Victoria Road, Malvern WR14 2TA Tel: 01684 893933 philiplaney@aol.com

Philip Serrell, The Malvern Saleroom, Barnards Green Road, Malvern WR14 3LW Tel: 01684 892314 serrell.auctions@virgin.net www.serrell.com

Yorkshire

BBR, Elsecar Heritage Centre, Elsecar, Barnsley S74 8HJ Tel: 01226 745156 sales@onlinebbr.com www.onlinebbr.com

Paul Beighton Auctioneers Ltd, Woodhouse Green, Thurcroft, Rotherham S66 9AQ Tel: 01709 700005 www.paulbeightonauctioneers.co.uk

Bonhams, 17a East Parade, Leeds LS1 2BH Tel: 0113 2448011 www.bonhams.com

Boulton & Cooper, St Michael's House, Market Place, Malton YO17 0LR Tel: 01653 696151

H. C. Chapman & Son, The Auction Mart, North Street, Scarborough YO11 1DL Tel: 01723 372424

Cundalls, 15 Market Place, Malton YO17 7LP Tel: 01653 697820

Dee, Atkinson & Harrison, The Exchange Saleroom, Driffield YO25 6LD Tel: 01377 253151 info@dahauctions.com www.dahauctions.com

David Duggleby, The Vine St Salerooms, Scarborough YO11 1XN Tel: 01723 507111 auctions@davidduggleby.com www.davidduggleby.com

ELR Auctions Ltd, The Nichols Building, Shalesmoor, Sheffield S3 8UJ Tel: 0114 281 6161

Andrew Hartley, Victoria Hall Salerooms, Little Lane, Ilkley LS29 8EA Tel: 01943 816363 info@andrewhartleyfinearts.co.uk www.andrewhartleyfinearts.co.uk

Lithgow Sons & Partners, The Auction Houses, Station Road, Stokesley, Middlesbrough TS9 7AB Tel: 01642 710158 info@lithgowsauctions.com www.lithgowsauctions.com

Malcolm's No. 1 Auctioneers & Valuers Tel: 01977 684971 info@malcolmsno1auctions.co.uk www.malcolmsno1auctions.co.uk

Christopher Matthews, 23 Mount Street, Harrogate HG2 8DQ Tel: 01423 871756

Morphets of Harrogate, 6 Albert Street, Harrogate HG1 1JL Tel: 01423 530030

Sheffield Railwayana Auctions, 43 Little Norton Lane, Sheffield S8 8GA Tel: 0114 274 5085 ian@sheffrail.freeserve.co.uk www.sheffieldrailwayana.co.uk

Tennants, The Auction Centre, Harmby Road, Leyburn DL8 5SG Tel: 01969 623780 enquiry@tennants-ltd.co.uk www.tennants.co.uk

Tennants, 34 Montpellier Parade, Harrogate HG1 2TG Tel: 01423 531661 enquiry@tennants-ltd.co.uk www.tennants.co.uk

Wilkinson & Beighton Auctioneers, Woodhouse Green, Thurcroft, Rotherham SY3 8LA Tel: 01709 700005

Wombell's Antiques & General Auction, The Auction Gallery, Northminster Business Park, Northfield Lane, Upper Poppleton, York YO26 6QU Tel: 01904 790777 www.invaluable.com/wombell

AUSTRALIA

Leonard Joel Auctioneers, 333 Malvern Road, South Yarra, Victoria 3141 Tel: 03 9826 4333 decarts@ljoel.com.au or jewellery@ljoel.com.au www.ljoel.com.au

Shapiro Auctioneers, 162 Queen Street, Woollahra, Sydney NSW 2025 Tel: 612 9326 1588

AUSTRIA

Dorotheum, Palais Dorotheum, A–1010 Wien, Dorotheergasse 17, 1010 Vienna Tel: 515 60 229 client.services@dorotheum.at

BELGIUM

Bernaerts, Verlatstraat 18–22, 2000 Antwerpen/Anvers Tel: +32 (0)3 248 19 21 edmond.bernaerts@ping.be www.auction-bernaerts.com

BRUSSELS

Horta, Hotel de Ventes, 16 Avenue Ducpetiaux 1060 Tel: 02 533 11 11

CANADA

Bailey's Auctioneers & Appraisers Tel: 001 519 823 1107 www.BaileyAuctions.com

Ritchies Inc, Auctioneers & Appraisers of Antiques & Fine Art, 288 King Street East, Toronto, Ontario M5A 1K4 Tel: (416) 364 1864 auction@ritchies.com www.ritchies.com

Sotheby's, 9 Hazelton Avenue, Toronto, Ontario M5R 2EI Tel: (416) 926 1774 www.sothebys.com

A Touch of Class Auction & Appraisal Service Tel: 705 726 2120 info@atouchofclassauctions.com www.atouchofclassauctions.com

Waddington's Auctions, 111 Bathurst Street, Toronto M5V 2R1 Tel: 001 416 504 9100 www.waddingtons.ca

When the Hammer Goes Down, 440 Douglas Avenue, Toronto, Ontario M5M 1H4 Tel: 416 787 1700 TOLL FREE 1 (866) BIDCALR (243 2257) BIDCALR@rogers.com www.bidcalr.com

CHINA

Sotheby's, 5/F Standard Chartered Bank Building, 4–4A Des Voeux Road, Central Hong Kong Tel: 852 2524 8121 www.sothebys.com

DENMARK

Bruun Rasmussen-Havnen, Pakhusvej 12, DK–2100, Copenhagen Tel: +45 70 27 60 80 havnen@bruun-rasmussen.dk www.bruun-rasmussen.dk

FINLAND

Bukowskis, Horhammer, Iso Roobertink, 12 Stora Robertsg, 00120 Helsinki Helsingfors Tel: 00 358 9 668 9110 www.bukowskis.fi

Hagelstam, Bulevardi 9 A, II kerros, 00120 Helsinki Tel: 358 (0)9 680 2300 www.hagelstam.fi

FRANCE

Sotheby's France SA, 76 rue du Faubourg, Saint Honore, Paris 75008 Tel: 33 1 53 05 53 05 www.sothebys.com

GERMANY

Auction Team Koln, Postfach 50 11 19, 50971 Koln Tel: 00 49 0221 38 70 49 auction@breker.com

Hermann Historica OHG, Postfach 201009, 80010 Munchen Tel: 00 49 89 5237296

Sotheby's Berlin, Palais anmFestungsgraben, Unter den Linden, Neue Wache D–10117 Tel: 49 (30) 201 0521 www.sothebys.com

Sotheby's Munich, Odeonsplatz 16, D–80539 Munchen Tel: 49 (89) 291 31 51 www.sothebys.com

HONG KONG

Christie's Hong Kong, 2203–8 Alexandra House, 16–20 Chater Road Tel: 852 2521 5396 www.christies.com

ISRAEL

Sotheby's Israel, 46 Rothschild Boulevard, Tel Aviv 66883 Tel: 972 3 560 1666 www.sothebys.com

ITALY

Christie's, Palazzo Massimo, Lancellotti, Piazza Navona 114, 00186 Rome Tel: 39 06 686 3333 www.christies.com

Sotheby's, Palazzo Broggi, Via Broggi 19, Milan 20129 Tel: 39 02 295 001 www.sothebys.com

Sotheby's Rome, Piazza d'Espana 90, Rome 00186 Tel: 39(6) 69941791/6781798 www.sothebys.com

MEXICO

Galeria Louis C. Morton, GLC A7073L IYS, Monte Athos 179, Col Lomas de Chapultepec CP11000 Tel: 52 5520 5005 glmorton@prodigy.net.mx www.lmorton.com

MONACO

Sotheby's Monaco, B. P. 45 Le Sporting d'Hiver, Place du Casino, Monte Carlo, Cedex MC 98001 Tel: 377 93 30 88 80 www.sothebys.com

NETHERLANDS

Christie's, Cornelis Schuystraat 57, 1071 JG Amsterdam Tel: 020 575 5255 www.christies.com

Sotheby's Amsterdam, De Boelelaan 30, Amsterdam 1083 HJ Tel: 31 20 550 2200 www.sothebys.com

Van Sabben Poster Auctions, PO Box 2065, 1620 EB Hoorn Tel: 31 229 268203 uboersma@sabbenposterauctions.nl www.vsabbenposterauctions.nl

REPUBLIC OF IRELAND

James Adam & Sons, 26 St Stephen's Green, Dublin 2 Tel: 00 3531 676 0261 www.jamesadam.ie/

Hamilton Osborne King, 4 Main Street, Blackrock, Co Dublin Tel: 353 1 288 5011 blackrock@hok.ie www.hok.ie

Mealy's, Chatsworth Street, Castle Comer, Co Kilkenny Tel: 00 353 564 441 229 info@mealys.com www.mealys.com

Whyte's Auctioneers, 38 Molesworth Street, Dublin 2 Tel: 00 353 1 676 2888 info@whytes.ie www.whytes.ie

SINGAPORE

Sotheby's (Singapore) Pte Ltd, 1 Cuscaden Road, 01–01 The Regent 249715 Tel: 65 6732 8239 www.sothebys.com

SWEDEN

Bukowskis, Arsenalsgatan 4, Stockholm Tel: +46 (8) 614 08 00 info@bukowskis.se www.bukowskis.se

SWITZERLAND

Bonhams, 7 Av Pictet-de-Rochemont, 1207 Geneva Tel: (0) 22 300 3160

Christie's, 8 Place de la Taconnerie, 1204 Geneva Tel: 022 319 1766 www.christies.com

Phillips, Kreuzstrasse 54, 8008 Zurich Tel: 00 41 1 254 2400

Phillips Geneva, 9 rue Ami-Levrier, CH–1201 Geneva Tel: 00 41 22 738 0707

Sotheby's, 13 Quai du Mont Blanc, Geneva CH–1201 Tel: 41 22 908 4800 www.sothebys.com

Sotheby's Zurich, Gessneralee 1, CH–8021 Zurich www.sothebys.com

TAIWAN R.O.C.

Sotheby's Taipei, 1st Floor, No. 79 Secl, An Ho Road, Taipei Tel: 886 2 755 2906 www.sothebys.com

USA

Bertoia Auctions, 2141 DeMarco Drive, Vineland, New Jersey 08360 Tel: 856 692 1881 bill@bertoiaauctions.com www.bertoiaauctions.com

Bloomington Auction Gallery, 300 East Grove St, Bloomington, Illinois 61701 Tel: 309 828 5533 joyluke@aol.com www.joyluke.com

Bonhams & Butterfields, 220 San Bruno Avenue, San Francisco CA 94103 Tel: 415 861 7500

Bonhams & Butterfields, 7601 Sunset Boulevard, Los Angeles CA 90046 Tel: 323 850 7500

Bonhams & Butterfields, 441 W. Huron Street, Chicago IL 60610 Tel: 312 377 7500

Frank H. Boos Gallery, 420 Enterprise Court, Bloomfield Hills, Michigan 48302 Tel: 248 332 1500 www.boosgallery.com

Braswell Galleries, 125 West Ave, Norwalk CT06854 Tel: 001 203 899 7420

Chesapeake Antique Center, Inc, Rt 301, PO Box 280, Queenstown MD 21658 Tel: 410 827 6640 antiques@chesapeakeantiques.com www.chesapeakantiques.com

Christie's, 20 Rockefeller Plaza, New York NY 10020 Tel: 212 636 2000 www.christies.com

The Cobbs Auctioneers LLC, Noone Falls Mill, Peterborough NH 03458 Tel: 603 924 6361 info@thecobbs.com www.thecobbs.com

Copake Auction, Inc, 266 Rt 7A, Copake NY 12516 Tel: 518 329 1142 info@copakeauction.com www.copakeauction.com

Doyle New York, 175 East 87th Street, New York NY 10128 Tel: 212 427 2730 info@doylenewyork.com www.doylenewyork.com

Du Mouchelles, 409 East Jefferson, Detroit, Michigan 48226 Tel: 313 963 6255

Eldred's, Robert C. Eldred Co Inc, 1475 Route 6A, East Dennis, Massachusetts 0796 Tel: 508 385 3116 www.eldreds.com

Freeman Fine Art Of Philadelphia Inc, 1808 Chestnut Street, Philadelphia PA 19103 Tel: 215 563 9275

The Great Atlantic Auction Company, 2 Harris & Main Street, Putnam CT 06260 Tel: 860 963 2234 www.thegreatatlanticauction.com

Green Valley Auctions, Inc, 2259 Green Valley Lane, Mt. Crawford VA 22841 Tel: (540) 434 4260 gvai@shentel.net www.greenvalleyauctions.com

Gene Harris Antique Auction Center, 203 S. 18th Avenue, PO Box 476, Marshalltown, Iowa 50158 Tel: 641 752 0600 geneharris@geneharrisauctions.com geneharrisauctions.com

Leslie Hindman Inc, 122 North Aberdeen Street, Chicago, Illinois 60607 Tel: 312 280 1212 www.lesliehindman.com

Hunt Auctions, 75 E. Uwchlan Avenue, Suite 130, Exton, Pennsylvania 19341 Tel: 610 524 0822 info@huntauctions.com www.huntauctions.com

Randy Inman Auctions Inc, PO Box 726, Waterville, Maine 04903–0726 Tel: 207 872 6900 inman@inmanauctions.com www.inmanauctions.com

Jackson's International Auctioneers & Appraisers of Fine Art & Antiques, 2229 Lincoln Street, Cedar Falls IA 50613 Tel: 319 277 2256/800 665 6743 www.jacksonsauction.com

James D. Julia, Inc, PO Box 830, Rt 201 Skowhegan Road, Fairfield ME 04937 Tel: 207 453 7125 www.juliaauctions.com

Mastronet, 660 Kingery HWY, Willowbrook, Illinois 60527 Tel: 630 472 1200 www.mastronet.com

Paul McInnis Inc Auction Gallery, 21, Rockrimmon Road, Northampton, New Hampshire Tel: 603 964 1301

New Orleans Auction Galleries, Inc, 801 Magazine Street, AT 510 Julia, New Orleans, Louisiana 70130 Tel: 504 566 1849

Northeast Auctions, 93 Pleasant St, Portsmouth NH 03810–4504 Tel: 603 433 8400 neacat@ttlc.net

Phillips, de Pury & Co, 3 West 57 Street, New York NY 10019 Tel: 212 570 4830 phillips-auctions.com

Phillips New York, 406 East 79th Street, New York NY10021 Tel: 212 570 4830

R. O. Schmitt Fine Art, Box 1941, Salem, New Hampshire 03079 Tel: 603 893 5915 bob@roschmittfinearts.com www.antiqueclockauction.com

Skinner Inc, 357 Main Street, Bolton MA 01740 Tel: 978 779 6241

Skinner Inc, The Heritage On The Garden, 63 Park Plaza, Boston MA 02116 Tel: 617 350 5400

Sloan's & Kenyon, 4605 Bradley Boulevard, Bethesda, Maryland 20815 Tel: 301 634 2330 info@sloansandkenyon.com www.sloansandkenyon.com

Sotheby's, 1334 York Avenue at 72nd St, New York NY 10021 Tel: 212 606 7000 www.sothebys.com

Sotheby's, 9665 Wilshire Boulevard, Beverly Hills, California 90212 Tel: (310) 274 0340 www.sothebys.com

Sotheby's, 215 West Ohio Street, Chicago, Illinois 60610 Tel: 312 670 0010 www.sothebys.com

Sprague Auctions, Inc, Rt 5, Dummerston VT 05301 Tel: 802 254 8969 bob@spragueauctions.com www.spragueauctions.com

Stair Galleries, PO Box 418, Claverack, New York 12513 Tel: 518 851 2544 www.stairgalleries.com

Strawser Auctions, Michael G. Strawser, 200 North Main Street, Wolcottville, Indiana 46795 Tel: 260 854 2859 info@strawserauctions.com www.strawserauctions.com www.majolicaauctions.com

Theriault's, PO Box 151, Annapolis MD 21404 Tel: 410 224 3655 info@theriaults.com www.theriaults.com

Treadway Gallery, Inc, 2029 Madison Road, Cincinnati, Ohio 45208 Tel: 513 321 6742 www.treadwaygallery.com

TreasureQuest Auction Galleries, Inc Tel: 772 781 8600 TQAG@TQAG.com www.TQAG.com

Weschler's Auctioneers & Appraisers, 909 E Street NW, Washington DC2004 Tel: 202 628 1281/800 331 1430 www.weschlers.com

Wolfs Gallery, 1239 W 6th Street, Cleveland OH 44113 Tel: 216 575 9653

Swann, 104 East 25th Street, New York 10010 Tel: 212 254 4710 swann@swanngalleries.com

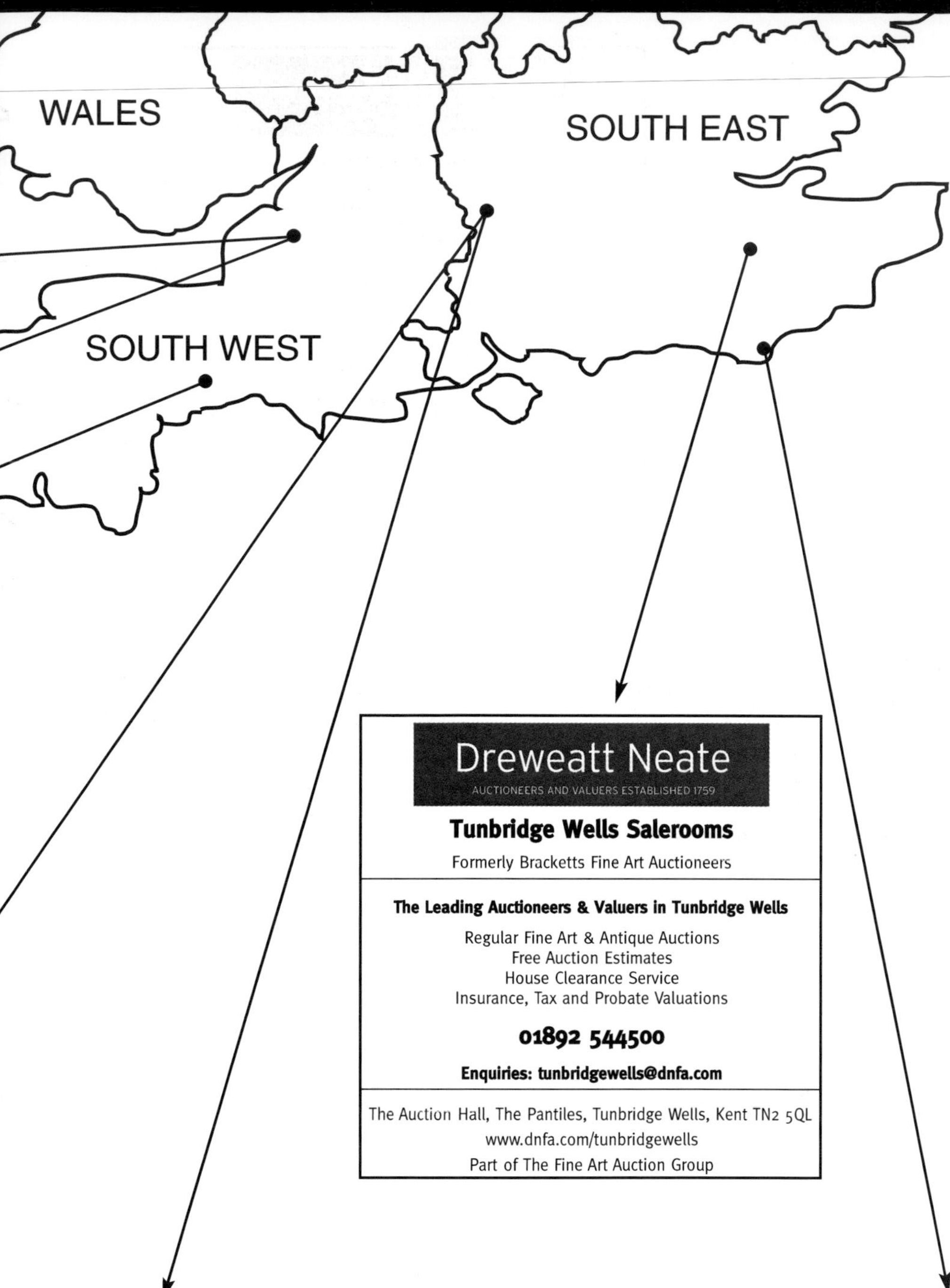
WALES
SOUTH EAST
SOUTH WEST

SIMMONS & SONS

CHARTERED SURVEYORS · INDEPENDENT SINCE 1802

32 Bell Street, Henley-on-Thames, Oxfordshire
Telephone: 01491 571111
Fax: 01491 579833
www.simmonsandsons.com

AUCTIONEERS & VALUERS OF
ANTIQUES, FINE ART & CHATTELS

MAY & SON

(Established 1925)
Auctioneers in Andover, Hampshire
Monthly catalogued auctions of Antiques & Collectables
Periodical Specialist Sales
Invaluable Auction Contributor – House Clearances & Removals
No Trade items entered

Good friendly Auctions with fascinating and interesting items

For information on viewing & catalogues
Tel: 01264 323417 Fax: 01264 338841
Email: office@mayandson.com Website: www.mayandson.com

1964

LAWRENCES

AUCTIONEERS LIMITED

Regular Sales of Fine Art & Chattels
Single Items or Complete House Contents
Free Auction Estimates
Valuation for Probate & Insurance
Collection & Delivery Available
30 years experience in Auctions

Norfolk House, 80 High Street
Bletchingley, Surrey RH1 4PA

Telephone: 01883 743323

www.lawrencesbletchingley.co.uk

Ibbett Mosely

AUCTIONEERS & VALUERS

A Regular Programme of Sales

of Antique, Victorian and Edwardian Furniture, Works of Art, Silver, Glass, Watches, China, Musical Instruments, Jewellery, etc. etc.

Held in our Saleroom at Otford, Nr. Sevenoaks, Kent

Also valuations carried out for Probate, Insurance and Family Division

Complete house clearances undertaken with personal supervision

Storage facilities available for short periods pending sale

125 High Street, Sevenoaks, Kent TN13 1UT

Telephone: 01732 456731 Fax: 01732 740910
Email: auctions@ibbettmosely.co.uk Website: www.ibbettmosely.co.uk

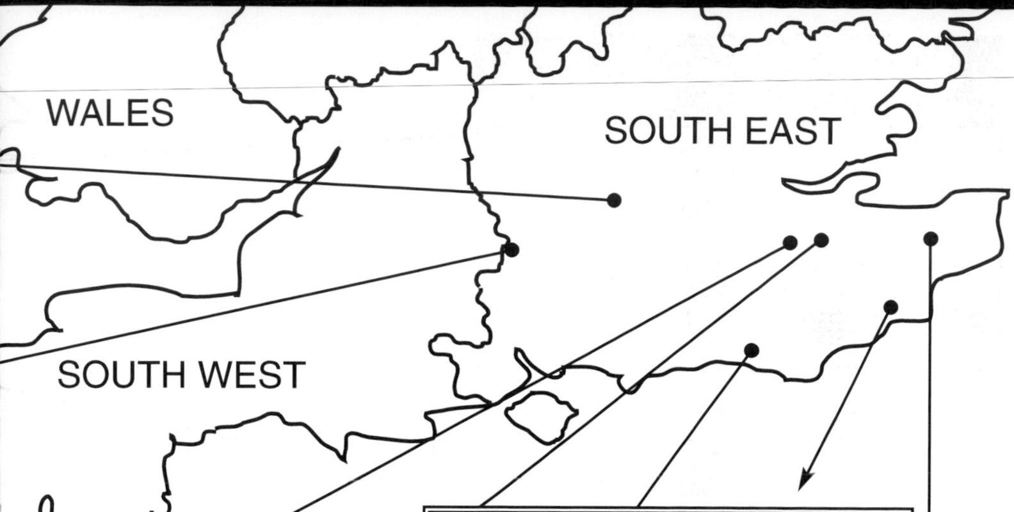

WALES
SOUTH EAST
SOUTH WEST

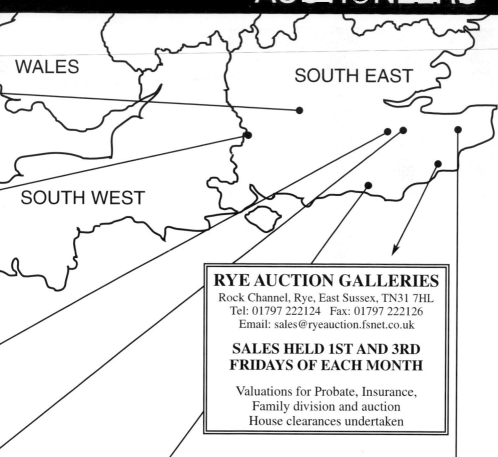

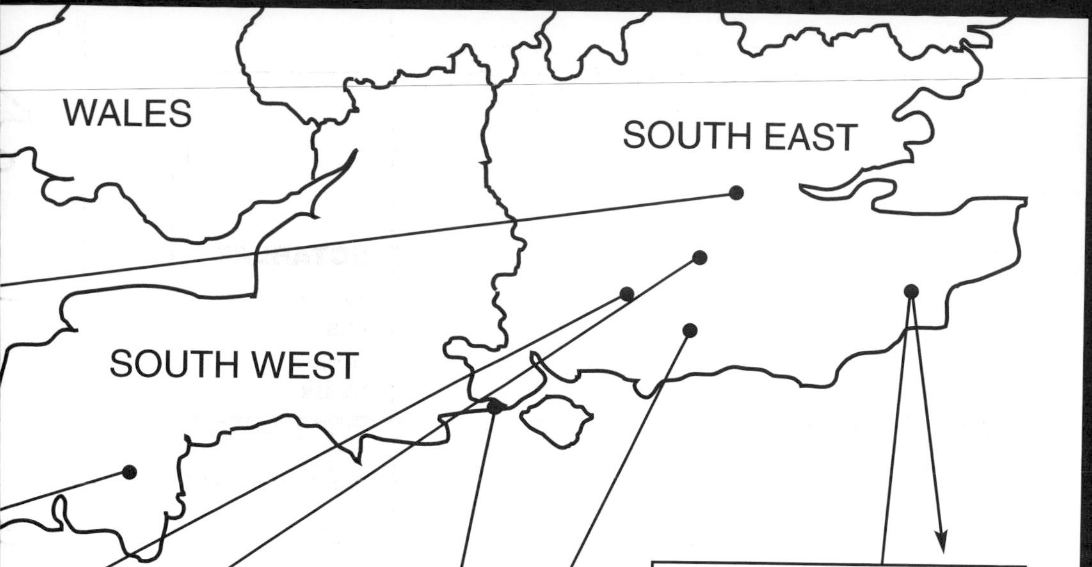

WALES
SOUTH EAST
SOUTH WEST

CAMEO

D.M. NESBIT & Company

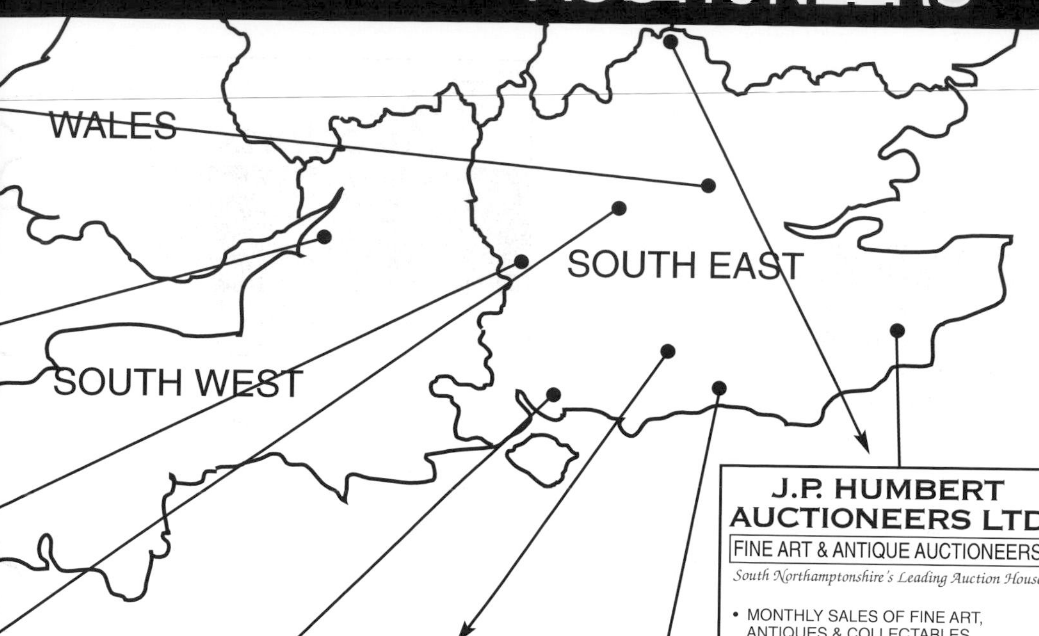

DENHAM'S

THE SUSSEX AUCTIONEERS – FOUNDED 1884

Monthly Fine Art Auctions & Collectors Auctions
Also monthly Secondary Antiques and General Effects sales

☆ FREE PRE-SALE VALUATIONS ALSO VALUATIONS FOR INSURANCE, PROBATE & FAMILY DIVISION PURPOSES

EXCELLENT FACILITIES INCLUDING

Easy access and substantial free parking. Refreshments

THE AUCTION GALLERIES (On the A24 two miles north of Horsham)
Warnham, Nr. Horsham, Sussex Tel: 01403 255699 Tel & Fax: 253837

www.denhams.com Email: enquiries@denhams.com

J.P. HUMBERT AUCTIONEERS LTD

FINE ART & ANTIQUE AUCTIONEERS

South Northamptonshire's Leading Auction House

- MONTHLY SALES OF FINE ART, ANTIQUES & COLLECTABLES
- REGULAR GENERAL & HOUSEHOLD SALES
- REGULAR SPECIALIST SALES
- VALUATIONS & HOUSE CLEARANCE
- EASY ACCESS, EXCELLENT PARKING & FACILITIES
- 5000 SQUARE FOOT OF SALES AREA

FURNITURE, PICTURES, CERAMICS, GLASSWARE, SILVERWARE, PEWTER, CLOCKS, BOOKS, TOYS, MUSICAL INSTRUMENTS, JEWELLERY, COLLECTABLES, ARCHITECTURAL & AGRICULTURAL BYGONES

The Sale Rooms, Unit 2A, Burcote Road
Trading Estate, Towcester NN12 6TF
Tel: 01327 359595 Fax: 01327 352038
(Only an hour from London, 8 miles from J15A, M1)

Also at:
www.invaluable.com/jphumbert
www.jphumbertauctioneers.co.uk

Est. 1929

Auctioneers and valuers of furniture and fine art

RAYMOND P. INMAN

FREE AUCTION ADVICE THROUGHOUT SUSSEX

Regular Sales of Antique and Reproduction Furniture, Pictures, Silver, Jewellery, Ceramics, Glassware, Collectors Items, etc.

RICS

PROBATE VALUATIONS AND EXECUTORS SERVICES
WRITTEN VALUATIONS FOR INSURANCE

98a COLERIDGE STREET, HOVE BN3 5AA

TEL: 01273 774777 www.invaluable.com/raymondinman

ESTABLISHED 1790
MARK ELLIN FNAVA

ABBEY AUCTION GALLERIES

Lower Lake, Battle, E. Sussex
Tel: 01424 772374
Fax: 01424 772302

Illustrated website:
www.burstowandhewett.co.uk

Monthly Sales of Antique and Fine Furniture, Silver, Jewellery, etc.
Specialist monthly Art sales
Valuations for all purposes

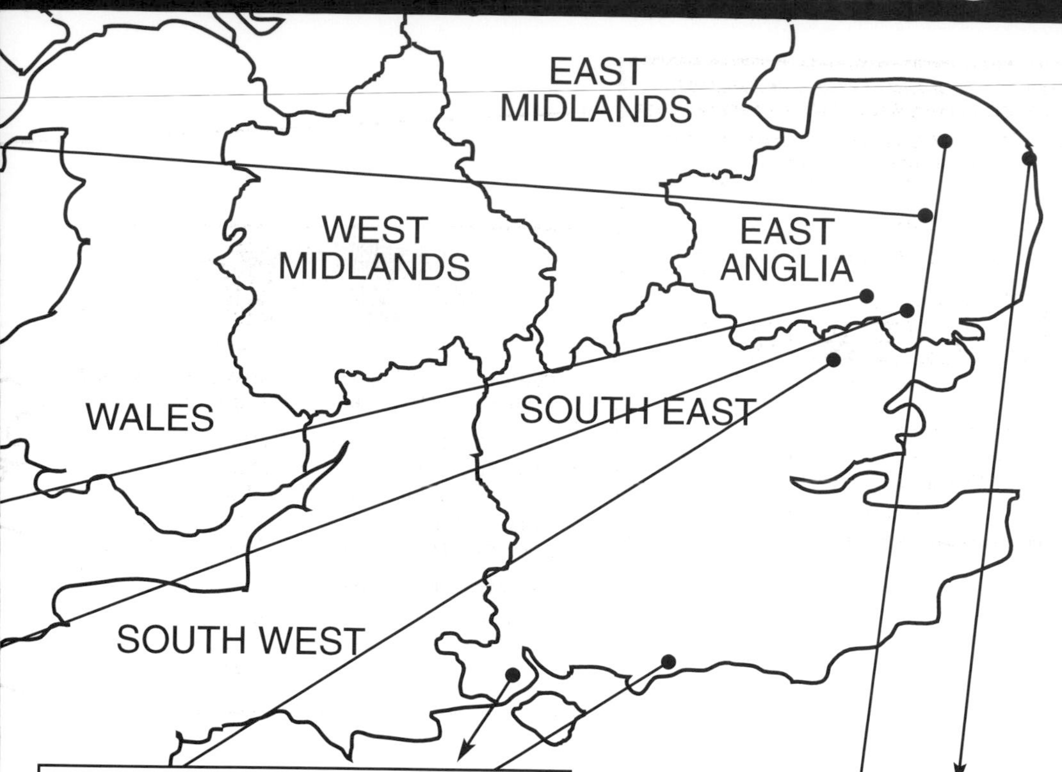
EAST
MIDLANDS
WEST
MIDLANDS
EAST
ANGLIA
WALES
SOUTH EAST
SOUTH WEST

GEORGE KIDNER

AUCTIONEERS AND VALUERS

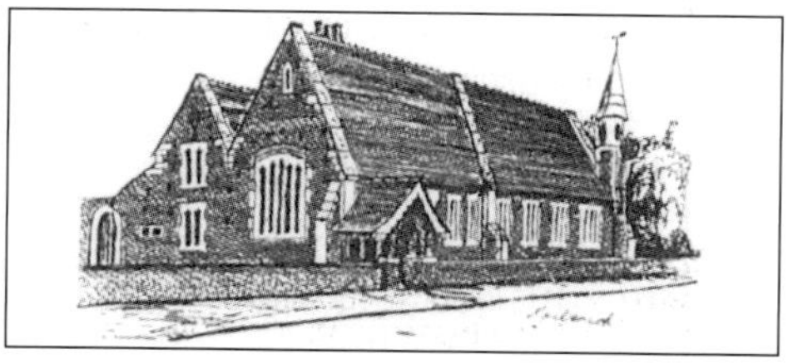

The Old School, The Square,
Pennington, Lymington
Hampshire SO41 8GN
Tel: 01590 670070 Fax: 01590 675167
www.georgekidner.co.uk
info@georgekidner.co.uk

Garry M. Emms & Co. Ltd

AUCTIONEERS, VALUERS & AGENTS

GREAT YARMOUTH SALEROOMS

Auctions of Antique, Reproduction, Furniture and Effects held most Wednesdays at Great Yarmouth Salerooms, Beevor Road (off South Beach Parade), Great Yarmouth, Norfolk NR30 3PS.

Bi-monthly Picture Sales that now include Great Yarmouth pottery tankards plus items of Beswick & Doulton.
Plus Special Sales and On-Site Auctions etc.
Appointed Auctioneer for the County Court.
We offer Free Valuations and of course a full and comprehensive House Clearance Service.
Valuations also for Probate and Family Division.
Shipping arranged, Small Removals and Carriage undertaken.
For further help and advice please contact:

Saleroom: 01493 332668 Fax: 01493 728290
Email: g_emms@gt-yarmouth-auctions.com
www.gt-yarmouth-auctions.com

keys

AYLSHAM SALEROOMS
East Anglia's leading Auction House
Antique, Fine Art and General Auctioneers
Freephone valuation line on 0800 163894
for auction estimates

AYLSHAM AUCTION MARKET
Every week throughout the year
A miscellany of Furniture and Effects,
Motor Vehicles, Cycles etc.

Antique Sales
(every 3 weeks)

Book Sales
(every 2 months)

Picture Sales
(every 2 months)

Collectors' Sales
(every 2 months)

ALL TYPES OF VALUATIONS UNDERTAKEN

One name, one company with 50 years of service and expertise

off Palmers Lane, Aylsham, Norfolk NR11 6JA
Tel 01263 733195 Fax 01263 732140
www.aylshamsalerooms.co.uk

AUCTIONEERS

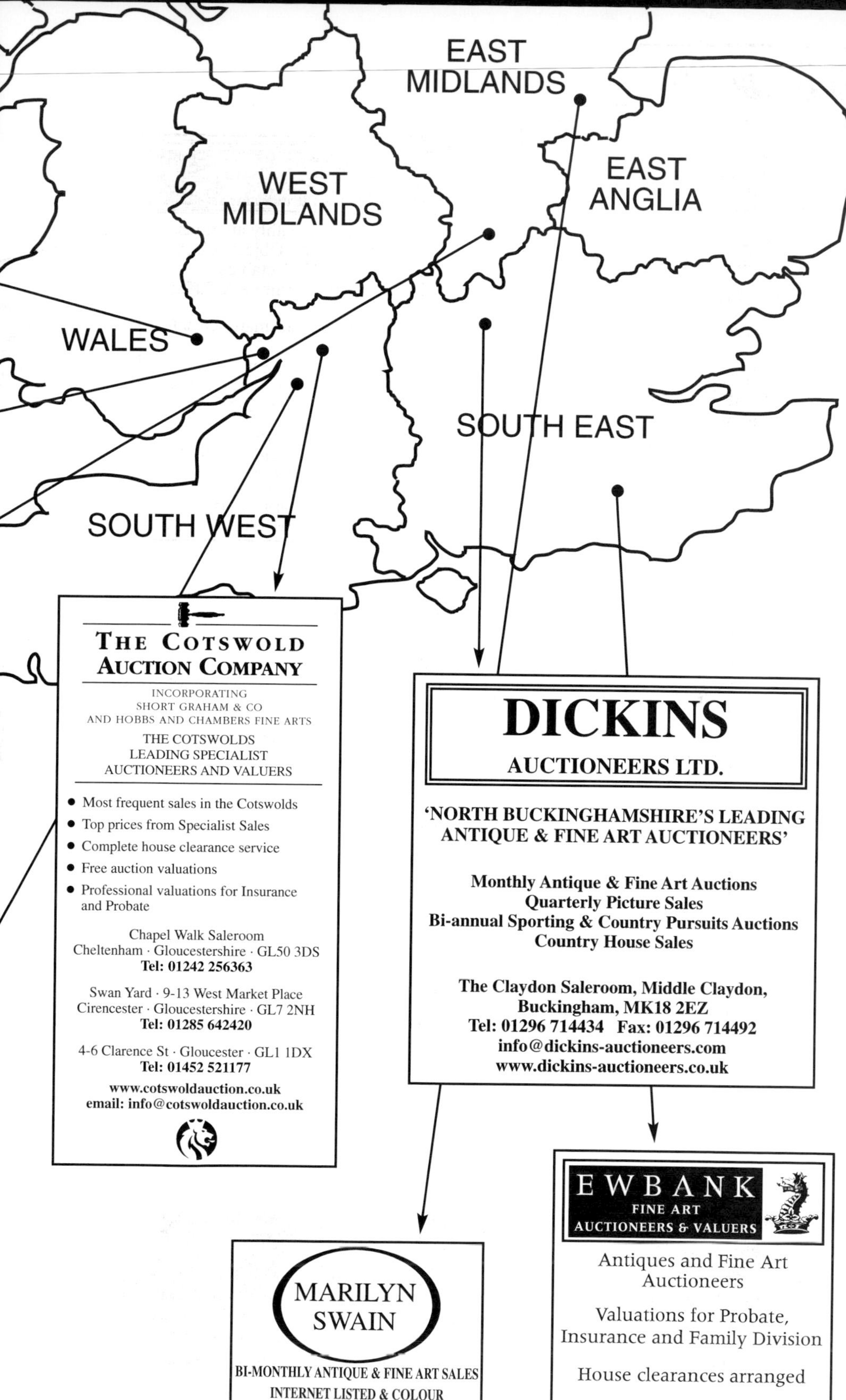
EAST MIDLANDS
WEST MIDLANDS
EAST ANGLIA
WALES
SOUTH EAST
SOUTH WEST

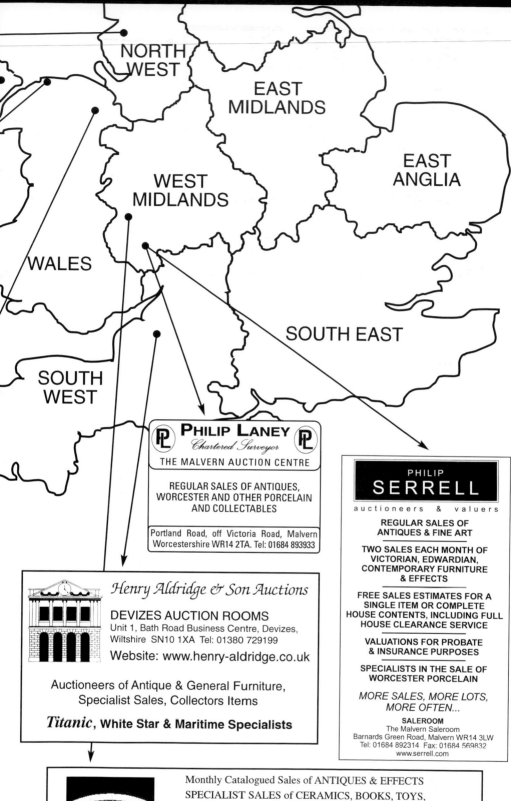

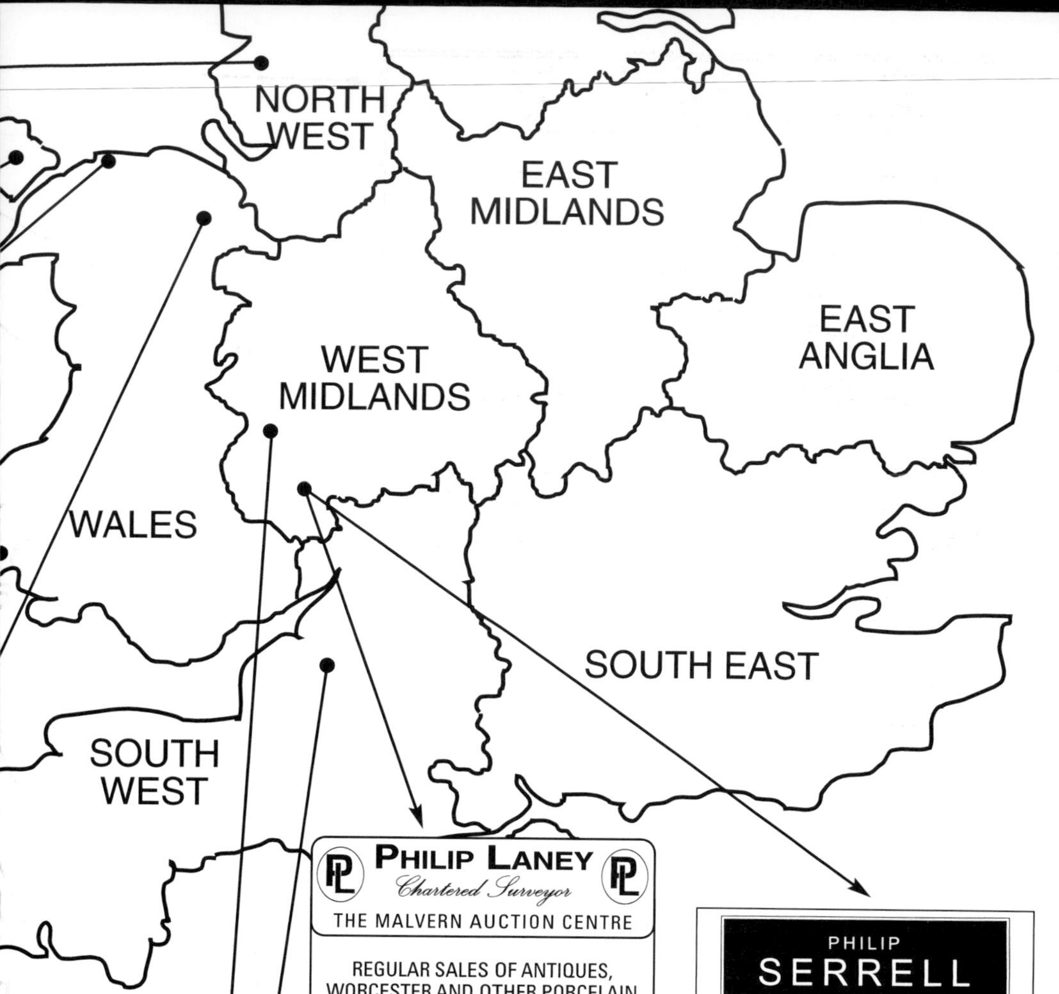

NORTH WEST
EAST MIDLANDS
EAST ANGLIA
WEST MIDLANDS
WALES
SOUTH EAST
SOUTH WEST

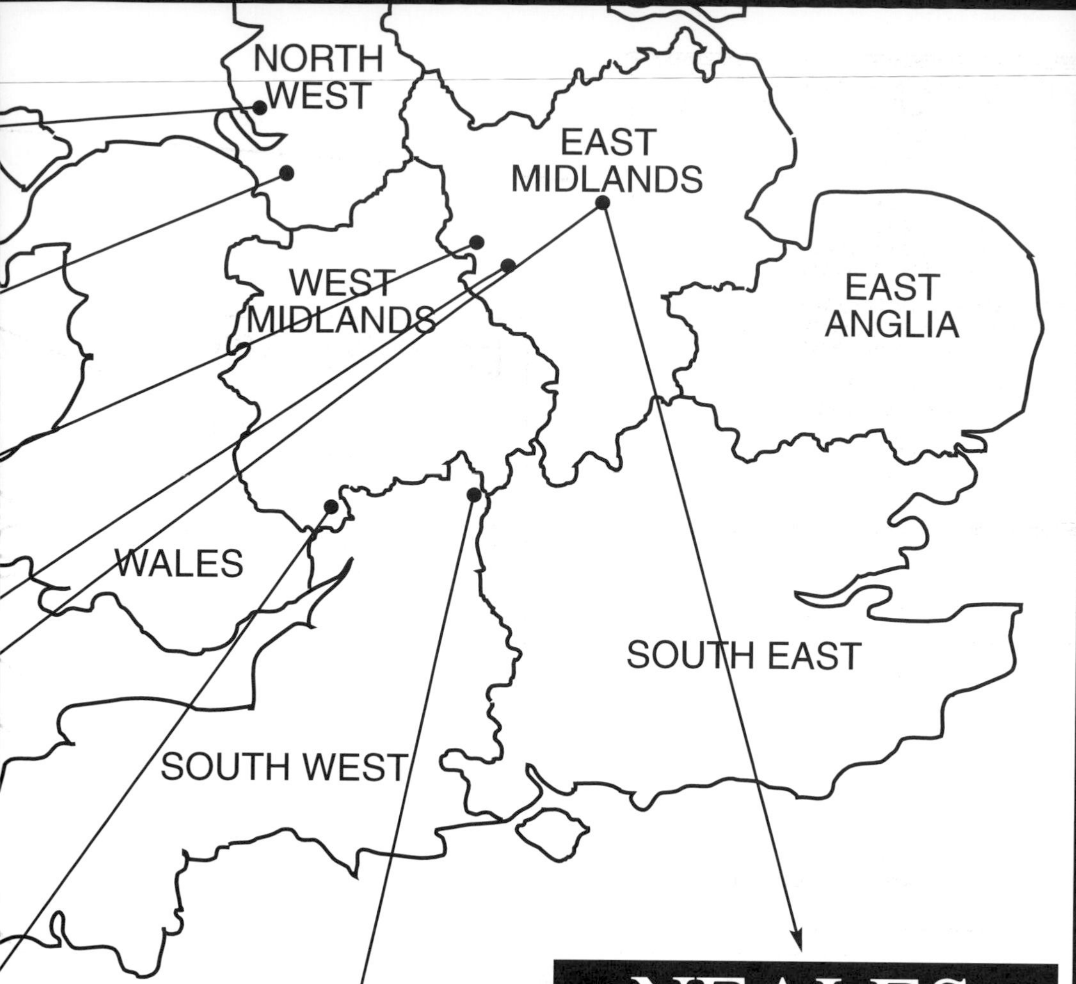

NORTH WEST
EAST MIDLANDS
WEST MIDLANDS
EAST ANGLIA
WALES
SOUTH EAST
SOUTH WEST

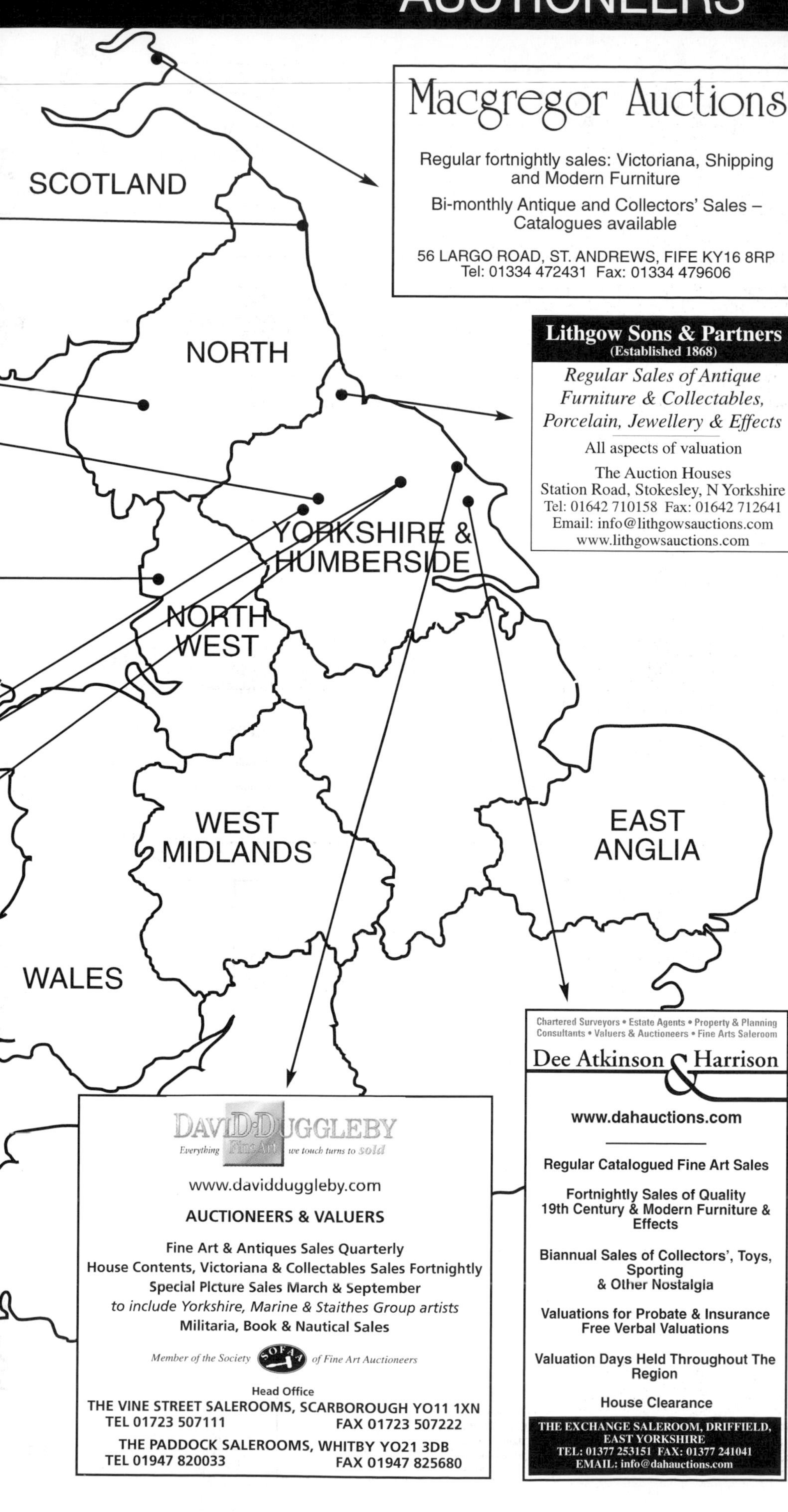
SCOTLAND
NORTH
YORKSHIRE & HUMBERSIDE
NORTH WEST
WEST MIDLANDS
EAST ANGLIA
WALES

Key to Illustrations

Each illustration and descriptive caption is accompanied by a letter code. By referring to the following list of auctioneers (denoted by ⚒) and dealers (⊞) the source of any item may be immediately determined. Inclusion in this edition in no way constitutes or implies a contract or binding offer on the part of any of our contributors to supply or sell the goods illustrated, or similar articles, at the prices stated. Advertisers in this year's directory are denoted by †.

If you require a valuation for an item, it is advisable to check whether the dealer or specialist will carry out this service and if there is a charge. Please mention Miller's when making an enquiry. Having found a specialist who will carry out your valuation it is best to send a photograph and description of the item to the specialist together with a stamped addressed envelope for the reply. A valuation by telephone is not possible.

Most dealers are only too happy to help you with your enquiry; however, they are very busy people and consideration of the above points would be welcomed.

A&O ⊞ Ancient & Oriental Ltd Tel: 01664 812044 alex@antiquities.co.uk

ABCM ⊞ A. B. Coins & Medals, 23–25 'Old' Northam Road, Southampton, Hampshire SO14 Tel: 02380 233393 Mobile: 07759 655739 or 07770 671832

ACAN ⊞ Acanthus, Chipping Norton, Oxfordshire OX7 7WB Tel: 01869 340009 www.acanthusonline.co.uk

ADD ⊞ Addyman Books, 39 Lion Street, Hay-on-Wye, Herefordshire HR3 5AD Tel: 01497 821136

AEF ⊞ A. & E. Foster Tel: 01494 562024

AEL ⊞ Argyll Etkin Ltd, 1–9 Hills Place, Oxford Circus, London W1F 7SA Tel: 020 7437 7800 philatelists@argyll-etkin.com www.argyll-etkin.com

AFD ⊞ Afford Decorative Arts Tel: 01827 330042 Mobile: 07831 114909 afforddecarts@fsmail.net

AG ⚒ Anderson & Garland (Auctioneers), Marlborough House, Marlborough Crescent, Newcastle-upon-Tyne, Tyne & Wear NE1 4EE Tel: 0191 232 6278

AGO ⊞ Ashton Gower Antiques, 9 Talbot Court, Market Square, Stow-on-the-Wold, Gloucestershire GL54 1BQ Tel: 01451 870699 ashtongower@aol.com

AH ⚒† Andrew Hartley, Victoria Hall Salerooms, Little Lane, Ilkley, Yorkshire LS29 8EA Tel: 01943 816363 info@andrewhartleyfinearts.co.uk www.andrewhartleyfinearts.co.uk

AL ⊞† Ann Lingard, Ropewalk Antiques, Rye, East Sussex TN31 7NA Tel: 01797 223486 ann-lingard@ropewalkantiques.freeserve.co.uk

AM ⊞ Alison Massey, MBO 32/33 Grays Antiques, 1–7 Davies Mews, London W1K 5AB Tel: 020 7629 7034

AMB ⚒ Ambrose, Ambrose House, Old Station Road, Loughton, Essex IG10 4PE Tel: 020 8502 3951

AMC ⊞ Amelie Caswell Tel: 0117 9077960

AMG ⊞ Amphora Galleries, 16–20 Buchanan Street, Balfron, Glasgow, Scotland G63 0TT Tel: 01360 440329

AMH ⊞ Amherst Antiques, Monomark House, 27 Old Gloucester Street, London WC1N 3XX Tel: 01892 725552 Mobile: 07850 350212 amherstantiques@monomark.co.uk

ANAn ⊞ Angel Antiques, Church Street, Petworth, West Sussex GU28 0AD Tel: 01798 343306 Mobile: 07980 617591 swansonantiques@aol.com www.angel-antiques.com

ANG ⊞† Ancient & Gothic, PO Box 5390, Bournemouth, Dorset BH7 6XR Tel: 01202 431721

ANO ⊞† Art Nouveau Originals, The Bindery Gallery, 69 High Street, Broadway, Worcestershire WR12 7DP Tel: 01386 854645 Mobile: 07774 718 096 cathy@artnouveauoriginals.com www.artnouveauoriginals.com

APC ⊞ Antique Photographic Company Ltd Tel: 01949 842192 alpaco47@aol.com

APO ⊞ Apollo Antiques Ltd, The Saltisford, Birmingham Road, Warwick CV34 4TD Tel: 01926 494746/494666 mynott@apolloantiques.com

APS ⊞ The Antique Print Shop, 11 Middle Row, East Grinstead, West Sussex RH19 3AX Tel: 01342 410501 printsandmaps@www.theantiqueprintshop.com

ARB ⊞ Arbour Antiques Ltd, Poet's Arbour, Sheep Street, Stratford-on-Avon, Warwickshire CV37 6EF Tel: 01789 293453

ARP ⊞ Arundel Photographica, The Arundel Antiques Centre, 51 High Street, Arundel, West Sussex BN18 9AJ Tel: 01903 882749

ARTi ⊞ Artifactory, 641 Indiana Ave. NW, Washington DC 20004, USA Tel: 202 393 2727 artifactorydc@msn.com www.artifactorydc.com

ASA ⊞† A. S. Antique Galleries, 26 Broad Street, Pendleton, Salford, Greater Manchester M6 5BY Tel: 0161 737 5938 Mobile: 07836 368230 as@sternshine.demon.co.uk

ASC ⊞ Andrew Sclanders, 32 St Paul's View, 15 Amwell Street, London EC1R 1UP Tel: 020 7278 5034 sclanders@beatbooks.com www.beatbooks.com

ASH ⊞ Adrian Ager Ltd, Great Hall, North Street, Ashburton, Devon TQ13 7QD Tel: 01364 653189 afager@tinyworld.co.uk www.adrianager.co.uk

ASP ⊞ Aspidistra Antiques, 51 High Street, Finedon, Wellingborough, Northamptonshire NN9 5JN Tel: 01933 680196 Mobile: 07768 071948 info@aspidistra-antiques.com www.aspidistra.antiques.com

AU ⊞ Auto Suggestion Tel: 01428 751397

AUA ⊞ Austin's Antiques, PO Box 4723, Ringwood, Hampshire BH24 2DN Tel: 07880 663823 austinsantiques@ukonline.co.uk austinsantiques@btclick.com www.austins-antiques.co.uk

AUC ⊞ Aurea Carter, PO Box 44134, London SW6 3YX Tel: 020 7731 3486 aureacarter@englishceramics.com www.englishceramics.com

AUTO ⊞ Automatomania, Stands 23 & 24, 284 Westbourne Grove (corner of Portobello road), London W11 2QA Tel: 07790 719097 magic@automatomania.com www.automatomania.com

AWI ⊞† American West Indies Trading Co Antiques & Art awindies@worldnet.att.net www.goantiques.com/members/awindiestrading

B ⚒ Bonhams, 101 New Bond Street, London W1S 1SR Tel: 020 7629 6602 www.bonhams.com

B(B) ⚒ Bonhams, 1 Old King Street, Bath, Somerset BA1 2JT Tel: 01225 788 988 www.bonhams.com

B(EA) ⚒ Bonhams, 32 Boss Hall Road, Ipswich, Suffolk IP1 5DJ Tel: 01473 740494 www.bonhams.com

B(Ed) ⚒ Bonhams, 65 George Street, Edinburgh, Scotland EH2 2JL Tel: 0131 225 2266 www.bonhams.com

B(Kn) ⚒ Bonhams, Montpelier Street, Knightsbridge, London SW7 1HH Tel: 020 7393 3900 www.bonhams.com

B(L) ⚒ Bonhams, 17a East Parade, Leeds, Yorkshire LS1 2BH Tel: 0113 2448011 www.bonhams.com

B(NW) ⚒ Bonhams, New House, 150 Christleton Road, Chester CH3 5TD Tel: 01244 313936 www.bonhams.com

B(O) ⚒ Bonhams, 39 Park End Street, Oxford OX1 1JD Tel: 01865 723524 www.bonhams.com

B(Pr) ⚒ Bonhams, Cornubia Hall, Eastcliffe Road, Par, Cornwall PL24 2AQ Tel: 01726 814047 www.bonhams.com

B(W) ⚒ Bonhams, Dowell Street, Honiton, Devon EX14 1LX Tel: 01404 41872 www.bonhams.com

B(WM) ⚒ Bonhams, The Old House, Station Road, Knowle, Solihull, West Midlands B93 0HT Tel: 01564 776151 www.bonhams.com

B&L ⚒ Bonhams and Langlois, Westaway Chambers, 39 Don Street, St Helier, Jersey, Channel Islands JE2 4TR Tel: 01534 722441 www.bonhams.com

B&R ⊞ Bread & Roses Tel: 01926 817342

BAC ⊞ The Brackley Antique Cellar, Drayman's Walk, Brackley, Northamptonshire NN13 6BE Tel: 01280 841841 antiquecellar@tesco.net

BaN ⊞ Barbara Ann Newman Tel: 07850 016729

BAY ⊞ George Bayntun, Manvers Street, Bath, Somerset BA1 1JW Tel: 01225 466000 EBayntun@aol.com

BB(L) ⚒ Bonhams & Butterfields, 7601 Sunset Boulevard, Los Angeles CA 90046, USA Tel: 323 850 7500

BBA ⚒ Bloomsbury Auctions Ltd, Bloomsbury House, 24 Maddox Street, London W1S 1PP Tel: 020 7495 9494 info@bloomsburyauctions.com www.bloomsburyauctions.com

BBe ⊞† Bourton Bears Tel: 01993 824756 help@bourtonbears.co.uk www.bourtonbears.com

BBo ⊞ Bazaar Boxes Tel: 01992 504 454 Mobile: 07970 909 206 bazaarboxes@hotmail.com commerce.icollector.com/BazaarBoxes/

BD ⊞ Banana Dance Ltd, 155A Northcote Road, Battersea, London SW11 6QT Tel: 01634 364539 Mobile: 07976 296987 jonathan@bananadance.com www.bananadance.com

Bea ⚒ Bearnes, St Edmund's Court, Okehampton Street, Exeter, Devon EX4 1DU Tel: 01392 207000 enquiries@bearnes.co.uk www.bearnes.co.uk

Beb ⊞ Bebes et Jouets, c/o Post Office, Edinburgh, Scotland EH7 6HW Tel: 0131 332 5650 Mobile: 0771 4374995 bebesetjouets@u.genie.co.uk www.you.genie.co.uk/bebesetjouets

BeF ⊞ Bevan Fine Art, PO Box 60, Uckfield, East Sussex TN22 1ZD Tel: 01825 766649 Mobile: 07711 262022 bevanfineart@quista.net

BELL ⊞† Bellhouse Antiques, Chelmsford, Essex Tel: 01268 710415 Bellhouse.Antiques@virgin.net

BERN ⚒ Bernaerts, Verlatstraat 18–22, 2000 Antwerpen/Anvers, Belgium Tel: +32 (0)3 248 19 21 edmond.bernaerts@ping.be www.auction-bernaerts.com

BEV ⊞ Beverley, 30 Church Street, Marylebone, London NW8 8EP Tel: 020 7262 1576 Mobile: 07776136003

BEX † Daniel Bexfield, 26 Burlington Arcade, London W1J 0PU Tel: 020 7491 1720 antiques@bexfield.co.uk www.bexfield.co.uk

BHa † Judy & Brian Harden, PO Box 14, Bourton-on-the Water, Cheltenham, Gloucestershire GL54 2YR Tel: 01451 810684 Mobile: 07831 692252 harden@portraitminiatures.co.uk www.portraitminiatures.co.uk

BHA Bourbon-Hanby Antiques Centre, 151 Sydney Street, Chelsea, London SW3 6NT Tel: 020 7352 2106

BIB Biblion, Grays Antique Market, 1–7 Davies Mews, London W1K 5AB Tel: 020 7629 1374 info@biblion.com www.biblion.com www.biblionmayfair.com

BLm Lyn Bloom & Jeffrey Neal, Vault 27, The London Silver Vaults, Chancery Lane, London WC2A 1QS Tel: 0207 242 6189 Mobile: 07768 533055 bloomvault@aol.com www.bloomvault.com

BMi Bobbie Middleton, 58 Long Street, Tetbury, Gloucestershire GL8 8AQ Tel: 01666 502761 Mobile: 07774 192660 bobbiemiddleton@lineone.net

BNO Beanos, Middle Street, Croydon, London CR0 1RE Tel: 020 8680 1202 enquiries@beanos.co.uk www.beanos.co.uk

Bns † Brittons Jewellers, 4 King Street, Clitheroe, Lancashire BB7 2EP Tel: 01200 425555 Mobile: 0789 008 1849 sales@brittonswatches.com www.internetwatches.co.uk

BP † Barling Porcelain Tel: 01621 890058 stuart@barling.uk.com www.barling.uk.com

BrL The Brighton Lanes Antique Centre, 12 Meeting House Lane, Brighton, East Sussex BN1 1HB Tel: 01273 823121 Mobile: 07785 564337 peter@brightonlanes-antiquecentre.co.uk www.brightonlanes-antiquecentre.co.uk

BROW David Brower, 113 Kensington Church Street, London W8 7LN Tel: 0207 221 4155 David@davidbrower-antiques.com www.davidbrower-antiques.com

BrW Brian Watson Antique Glass, Foxwarren Cottage, High Street, Marsham, Norwich, Norfolk NR10 5QA Tel: 01263 732519 brian.h.watson@talk21.com By appointment only

BSA Bartlett Street Antiques Centre, 5–10 Bartlett Street, Bath, Somerset BA1 2QZ Tel: 01225 466689/469998 info@antiques-centre.co.uk www.antiques-centre.co.uk

BUK Bukowskis, Arsenalsgatan 4, Stockholm, Sweden Tel: +46 (8) 614 08 00 info@bukowskis.se www.bukowskis.se

BWL † Brightwells Fine Art, The Fine Art Saleroom, Easters Court, Leominster, Herefordshire HR6 0DE Tel: 01568 611122 fineart@brightwells.com www.brightwells.com

ByI Bygones of Ireland Ltd, Lodge Road, Westport, County Mayo, Republic of Ireland Tel: 00 353 98 26132/25701 bygones@anu.ie www.bygones-of-ireland.com

C&A Campbell & Archard Ltd, Lychgate House, Church Street, Seal, Kent TN15 0AR Tel: 01732 761153 campbellarchard@btclick.com www.campbellandarchard.co.uk

C&R † Catchpole & Rye, Saracens Dairy, Jobbs Lane, Pluckley, Ashford, Kent TN27 0SA Tel: 01233 840840 info@crye.co.uk www.crye.co.uk

C&W Carroll & Walker Tel: 01877 385618

CaF Caren Fine, U.S.A Tel: 301 854 6262 jdcicca@bellatlantic.net

CaH The Camera House, Oakworth Hall, Colne Road, Oakworth, Keighley, Yorkshire BD22 7HZ Tel: 01535 642333 colin@the-camera-house.co.uk www.the-camera-house.co.uk

CANI Caniche Decorative Arts, PO Box 350, Watford, Hertfordshire WD19 4ZX Tel: 01923 251 206 Mobile: 07860 833 170

Cas Castle Antiques www.castle-antiques.com

CAT Lennox Cato, 1 The Square, Church Street, Edenbridge, Kent TN8 5BD Tel: 01732 865988 Mobile: 07836 233473 cato@lennoxcato.com www.lennoxcato.com

CAV Rupert Cavendish Antiques, 610 King's Road, London SW6 2DX Tel: 020 7731 7041 www.rupertcavendish.co.uk

CB Christine Bridge Antiques, 78 Castelnau, London SW13 9EX Tel: 07000 445277 christine@bridge-antiques.com www.bridge-antiques.com www.antiqueglass.co.uk

CBB Colin Baddiel, Gray's Mews, 1–7 Davies Mews, London W1Y 1AR Tel: 020 7408 1239/ 020 8452 7243

CBP † Comic Book Postal Auctions Ltd, 40–42 Osnaburgh Street, London NW1 3ND Tel: 020 7424 0007 comicbook@compuserve.com www.compalcomics.com

CDC Capes Dunn & Co, The Auction Galleries, 38 Charles Street, Off Princess Street, Greater Manchester M1 7DB Tel: 0161 273 6060/1911 capesdunn@yahoo.co.uk

CFSD Clive Farahar & Sophie Dupre, Horsebrook House, XV The Green, Calne, Wiltshire SN11 8DQ Tel: 01249 821121 post@farahardupre.co.uk www.farahardupre.co.uk

CGA Castlegate Antiques Centre, 55 Castlegate, Newark, Nottinghamshire NG24 1BE Tel: 01636 700076 Mobile: 07860 843739

CGC Cheffins, Clifton House, Clifton Road, Cambridge CB1 7EA Tel: 01223 213343 www.cheffins.co.uk

CHA Chislehurst Antiques, 7 Royal Parade, Chislehurst, Kent BR7 6NR Tel: 020 8467 1530

CHAC † Church Hill Antiques Centre, 6 Station Street, Lewes, East Sussex BN7 2DA Tel: 01273 474 842 churchhilllewes@aol.com www.church-hill-antiques.co.uk

ChC Christopher Clarke (Antiques) Ltd, The Fosseway, Stow-on-the-Wold, Gloucestershire GL54 1JS Tel: 01451 830476 cclarkeantiques@aol.com www.campaignfurniture.com

Che Chevertons of Edenbridge Ltd, 71–73 High Street, Edenbridge, Kent TN8 5AL Tel: 01732 863196 chevertons@msn.com www.chevertons.com

CHES † Chesapeake Antique Center, Inc, Rt 301, PO Box 280, Queenstown, MD 21658, USA Tel: 410 827 6640 antiques@chesapeakeantiques.com www.chesapeakantiques.com

CHI Chinasearch Ltd, 4 Princes Drive, Kenilworth, Warwickshire CV8 2FD Tel: 01926 512402 helen@chinasearch.uk.com jackie@chinasearch.uk.com www.chinasearch.uk.com

ChM Chelsea Military Antiques, F4 Antiquarius, 131/141 Kings Road, Chelsea, London SW3 4PW Tel: 020 7352 0308 richard@chelseamilitaria.com

CHTR Charterhouse, The Long Street Salerooms, Sherborne, Dorset DT9 3BS Tel: 01935 812277 enquiry@charterhouse-auctions.co.uk www.charterhouse-auctions.co.uk

CO Cooper Owen, 10 Denmark Street, London WC2H 8LS Tel: 020 7240 4132 www.CooperOwen.com

COBB † The Cobbs Auctioneers LLC, Noone Falls Mill, Peterborough, NH 03458, USA Tel: 603 924 6361 info@thecobbs.com www.thecobbs.com

COF Cottage Farm Antiques, Stratford Road, Aston Subedge, Chipping Campden, Gloucestershire GL55 6PZ Tel: 01386 438263 info@cottagefarmantiques.co.uk www.cottagefarmantiques.co.uk

CoHA Corner House Antiques and Ffoxe Antiques, Gardners Cottage, Broughton Poggs, Filkins, Lechlade-on-Thames, Gloucestershire GL7 3JH Tel: 01367 860078 jdhis007@btopenworld.com www.corner-house-antiques.co.uk

CoS Corrine Soffe Tel: 01295 730317 soffe@btinternet.co.uk

CPC † Carnegie Paintings and Clocks, 15 Fore Street, Yealmpton, Plymouth, Devon Pl8 2JN Tel: 01752 881170 info@paintingsandclocks.com www.paintingsandclocks.com

CS Christopher Sykes, The Old Parsonage, Woburn, Milton Keynes, Buckinghamshire MK17 9QM Tel: 01525 290259 www.sykes-corkscrews.co.uk

CTO † Collector's Corner, PO Box 8, Congleton, Cheshire CW12 4GD Tel: 01260 270429 dave.popcorner@ukonline.co.uk

CUN † Cundalls, 15 Market Place, Malton, North Yorkshire YO17 7LP Tel: 01653 697820

CuS Curious Science, 319 Lillie Road, Fulham, London SW6 7LL Tel: 020 7610 1175 Mobile: 07956 834094 curiousscience@medical-antiques.com

CVA Courtville Antiques, Powerscourt Townhouse Centre, South William Street, Dublin 2, Republic of Ireland Tel: 01 679 4042

DA † Dee, Atkinson & Harrison, The Exchange Saleroom, Driffield, East Yorkshire YO25 6LD Tel: 01377 253151 info@dahauctions.com www.dahauctions.com

DAC No longer Trading

DAD † decorative arts@doune, Scottish Antique & Arts Centre, By Doune, Stirling, Scotland FK16 6HD Tel: 01786 834401 Mobile: 07778 475974 decorativearts.doune@btinternet.com www.decorativearts-doune.com

DAN Andrew Dando, 34 Market Street, Bradford-on-Avon, Wiltshire BA15 1LL Tel: 01225 865444 andrew@andrewdando.co.uk www.andrewdando.co.uk

DAV Hugh Davies, The Packing Shop, 6–12 Ponton Road, London SW8 5BA Tel: 020 7498 3255

DD † David Duggleby, The Vine St Salerooms, Scarborough, Yorkshire YO11 1XN Tel: 01723 507111 auctions@davidduggleby.com www.davidduggleby.com

DeA Delphi Antiques, Powerscourt Townhouse Centre, South William Street, Dublin 2, Republic of Ireland Tel: 01 679 0331 declancorrigan@netscape.net

DeG Denzil Grant, Suffolk Fine Arts, Drinkstone House, Drinkstone, Bury St Edmunds, Suffolk IP30 9TG Tel: 01449 736576

Del Delomosne & Son Ltd, Court Close, North Wraxall, Chippenham, Wiltshire SN14 7AD Tel: 01225 891505

DeP De Parma, Core One, The Gasworks, 2 Michael Road, London SW6 2AN Tel: 0207 736 3384 Mobile: 07976 280 275 info@deparma.com www.deparma.com

DFA Delvin Farm Antiques, Gormonston, Co Meath, Republic of Ireland Tel: 353 1 841 2285 info@delvinfarmpine.com john@delvinfarmpine.com www.delvinfarmpine.com

DIA Mark Diamond London Tel: 020 8508 4479 mark.diamond@dial.pipex.com

DJH David J Hansord & Son, 6 & 7 Castle Hill, Lincoln LN1 3AA Tel: 01522 530044 Mobile: 07831 183511

DLP † The Dunlop Collection, P.O. Box 6269, Statesville, NC 28687, USA Tel: (704) 871 2626 or Toll Free Tel: (800) 227 1996

DMa David March, Abbots Leigh, Bristol, Gloucestershire BS8 Tel: 0117 937 2422

DMC Diamond Mills & Co, 117 Hamilton Road, Felixstowe, Suffolk IP11 7BL Tel: 01394 282281

DMe Ireland's Own Antiques, Alpine House, Carlow Road, Abbeyleix, Co Laois, Republic of Ireland Tel: 353 502 31348

DML David Moulson, The Gorralls, Cold Comfort Lane, Alcester, Warwickshire B49 5PU Tel: 01789 764092 dmoulson@hotmail.com

DN † Dreweatt Neate, Donnington Priory, Donnington, Newbury, Berkshire RG14 2JE Tel: 01635 553553 donnington@dnfa.com www.dnfa.com/donnington

DN(BR) † Dreweatt Neate formerly Bracketts Fine Art Auctioneers, The Auction Hall, The Pantiles, Tunbridge Wells, Kent TN2 5QL Tel: 01892 544500 tunbridgewells@dnfa.com www.dnfa.com/tunbridgewells

DN(Bri) † Dreweatt Neate formerly Bristol Auction Rooms, St John's Place, Apsley Road, Clifton, Bristol, Gloucestershire BS8 2ST Tel: 0117 973 7201 bristol@dnfa.com www.dnfa.com/bristol

DN(EH) † Dreweatt Neate formerly Edgar Horns, 46–50 South Street, Eastbourne, East Sussex BN21 4XB Tel: 01323 410419 eastbourne@dnfa.com www.dnfa.com/eastbourne

DNo Desmond & Amanda North, The Orchard, 186 Hale Street, East Peckham, Kent TN12 5JB Tel: 01622 871353

DNW Dix-Noonan-Webb, 16 Bolton Street, London W1J 8BQ Tel: 020 7016 1700 auctions@dnw.co.uk www.dnw.co.uk

Do Liz Farrow T/A Dodo, Stand F071/73, Alfie's Antique Market, 13–25 Church Street, London NW8 8DT Tel: 020 7706 1545

DOL Dollectable, 53 Lower Bridge Street, Chester CH1 1RS Tel: 01244 344888/679195

DOR Dorset Reclamation, Cow Drove, Bere Regis, Wareham, Dorset BH20 7JZ Tel: 01929 472200 info@dorsetrec.u-net.com www.dorset-reclamation.co.uk

DORO Dorotheum, Palais Dorotheum, A–1010 Wien, Dorotheergasse 17, 1010 Vienna, Austria Tel: 515 60 229 client.services@dorotheum.at

DRU † Drummonds Architectural Antiques Ltd, The Kirkpatrick Buildings, 25 London Road (A3), Hindhead, Surrey GU26 6AB Tel: 01428 609444 www.drummonds-arch.co.uk

DSA David Scriven Antiques, PO Box 1962, Leigh-on-Sea, Essex SS9 2YZ Mobile: 07887 716677 david@david-scriven-antiques.fsnet.co.uk

DSG † Delf Stream Gallery, Bournemouth, Dorset Tel: 07974 926137 nic19422000@yahoo.co.uk www.delfstreamgallery.com

DUK Dukeries Antiques Centre, Thoresby Park, Budby, Newark, Nottinghamshire NG22 9EX Tel: 01623 822252

DuM Du Mouchelles, 409 East Jefferson, Detroit, Michigan 48226, USA Tel: 313 963 6255

DW † Dominic Winter Book Auctions, The Old School, Maxwell Street, Swindon, Wiltshire SN1 5DR Tel: 01793 611340 info@dominicwinter.co.uk www.dominicwinter.co.uk

DY Dycheling Antiques, 34 High Street, Ditchling, Hassocks, West Sussex BN6 8TA Tel: 01273 842929 Mobile: 07785 456341 www.antiquechairmatching.com

E † Ewbank Auctioneers, Burnt Common Auction Rooms, London Road, Send, Woking, Surrey GU23 7LN Tel: 01483 223101 antiques@ewbankauctions.co.uk www.ewbankauctions.co.uk

EAL † The Exeter Antique Lighting Co., Cellar 15, The Quay, Exeter, Devon EX2 4AP Tel: 01392 490848 Mobile: 07702 969438 www.antiquelightingcompany.com

Ech Echoes, 650a Halifax Road, Eastwood, Todmorden, Yorkshire OL14 6DW Tel: 01706 817505

EE Empire Exchange, 1 Newton Street, Piccadilly, Manchester Tel: 0161 2364445

ETO Eric Tombs, 62a West Street, Dorking, Surrey RH4 1BS Tel: 01306 743661 ertombs@aol.com www.dorkingantiques.com

EXC Excalibur Antiques, Taunton Antique Centre, 27–29 Silver Street, Taunton, Somerset TA13DH Tel: 01823 289327/07774 627409 pwright777@btopenworld.com www.excaliburantiques.com

F&C Finan & Co, The Square, Mere, Wiltshire BA12 6DJ Tel: 01747 861411 post@finanandco.co.uk www.finanandco.co.uk

F&F Fenwick & Fenwick, 88–90 High Street, Broadway, Worcestershire WR12 7AJ Tel: 01386 853227/841724

FAC † Faganarms, Box 425, Fraser, MI 48026, USA Tel: 586 465 4637 info@faganarms.com www.faganarms.com

FHA † Flower House Antiques, 90 High Street, Tenterden, Kent TN30 6JB Tel: 01580 763764

FHF Fellows & Sons, Augusta House, 19 Augusta Street, Hockley, Birmingham, West Midlands B18 6JA Tel: 0121 212 2131 info@fellows.co.uk www.fellows.co.uk

FOF † Fossack & Furkle, PO Box 733, Abington, Cambridgeshire CB1 6BF Tel: 01223 894296 Mobile: 07939078719 fossack@btopenworld.com www.fossackandfurkle.freeservers.com

FOX Fox Cottage Antiques, Digbeth Street, Stow-on-the-Wold, Gloucestershire GL54 1BN Tel: 01451 870307

FRa Fraser's, 399 Strand, London WC2R OLX Tel: 020 7836 9325 sales@frasersautographs.co.uk www.frasersautographs.com

G(B) Gorringes Auction Galleries, Terminus Road, Bexhill-on-Sea, East Sussex TN39 3LR Tel: 01424 212994 bexhill@gorringes.co.uk www.gorringes.co.uk

G(L) Gorringes Inc Julian Dawson, 15 North Street, Lewes, East Sussex BN7 2PD Tel: 01273 478221 auctions@gorringes.co.uk www.gorringes.co.uk

G&G Guest & Gray, 1–7 Davies Mews, London W1K5 AB Tel: 020 7408 1252 info@chinese-porcelain-art.com www.chinese-porcelain-art.com

G&H † Garret & Hazlehurst, PO Box 138, Hailsham, East Sussex BN27 1WX Tel: 01580 241993 Mobile: 07976 247942 garhaz.com@btopenworld.com www.garretandhazlehurst.co.uk

GAK † Keys, Off Palmers Lane, Aylsham, Norfolk NR11 6JA Tel: 01263 733195 www.aylshamsalerooms.co.uk

Gam Clarke Gammon, The Guildford Auction Rooms, Bedford Road, Guildford, Surrey GU1 4SJ Tel: 01483 880915

GAU † Becca Gauldie Antiques, The Old School, Glendoick, Perthshire, Scotland PH2 7NR Tel: 01738 860 870 Mobile: 07770 741 636 becca@scottishantiques.freeserve.co.uk

GBM GB Military Antiques, Antiquarius Antiques Centre, 131/141 Kings Road, Chelsea, London SW3 4PW Tel: 020 7351 5357 info@gbmilitaria.com www.gbmilitaria.com

GBr Geoffrey Breeze Antiques, Top Banana Antiques Mall, 1 New Street, Tetbury, Gloucestershire GL8 8OS Tel: 01225 466499 Mobile: 077 404 35844 antiques @geoffreybreeze.co.uk www.antiquecanes.co.uk

GD † Gilbert & Dale Antiques, The Old Chapel, Church Street, Ilchester, Nr Yeovil, Somerset BA22 8ZA Tel: 01935 840464 roy@roygilbert.com

GDB G D Blay Antiques, 56 West Street, Dorking, Surrey RH4 1BS Tel: 07785 767718 gdblay@gdblayantiques.com www.gdblayantiques.com

GDO Gavin Douglas Fine Antiques Ltd, 75 Portobello Road, London W11 2QB Tel: 01444 414040 Mobile: 07860 680521 gavin@antique-clocks.co.uk www.antique-clocks.co.uk

GEO Georgian Antiques, 10 Pattinson Street, Leith Links, Edinburgh, Scotland EH6 7HF Tel: 0131 553 7286 info@georgianantiques.net JDixon7098@aol.com www.georgianantiques.net

GFA Goodfaith Antiques and Fine Art, USA Tel: 518 854 7844 ntk@goodfaithantiques.com www.goodfaithantiques.com By appointment only

GGD Great Grooms of Dorking, 50/52 West Street, Dorking, Surrey RH4 1BU Tel: 01306 887076 laurence@greatgrooms.co.uk www.great-grooms.co.uk

GH Gardiner Houlgate, The Bath Auction Rooms, 9 Leafield Way, Corsham, Nr Bath, Somerset SN13 9SW Tel: 01225 812912 auctions@gardiner-houlgate.co.uk www.invaluable.com/gardiner-houlgate

GLB † Glebe Antiques, Scottish Antique Centre, Doune, Scotland FK16 6HG Tel: 01259 214559 Mobile: 07050 234577 rrglebe@aol.com

GLD Glade Antiques, PO Box 873, High Wycombe, Buckinghamshire HP14 3ZQ Tel: 01494 882818 Mobile: 07771 552 328 sonia@gladeantiques.com www.gladeantiques.com

GN † Gillian Neale Antiques, PO Box 247, Aylesbury, Buckinghamshire HP20 1JZ Tel: 01296 423754 Mobile: 07860 638700 gillianneale@aol.com www.gillianneale antiques.co.uk

GoW Gordon Watson Ltd, 50 Fulham Road, London SW3 6HH Tel: 020 7589 3108

GRe Greystoke Antiques, 4 Swan Yard, (off Cheap Street), Sherborne, Dorset DT9 3AX Tel: 01935 812833

GREE Greenway Antiques, 90 Corn Street, Witney, Oxfordshire OX28 6BU Tel: 01993 705026 Mobile: 07831 585014 jean_greenway@hotmail.com

GRG Gordon Reece Galleries, Finkle Street, Knaresborough, Yorkshire HG5 8AA Tel: 01423 866219 www.gordonreecegalleries.com

GRI Grimes House Antiques, High Street, Moreton-in-Marsh, Gloucestershire GL56 0AT Tel: 01608 651029 grimes_house@cix.co.uk www.grimeshouse.co.uk www.cranberryglass.co.uk

GS Ged Selby Antique Glass, Yorkshire Tel: 01756 799673 By appointment only

GTH Greenslade Taylor Hunt Fine Art, Magdelene House, Church Square, Taunton, Somerset TA1 1SB Tel: 01823 332525

GTM Gloucester Toy Mart, Ground Floor, Antique Centre, Severn Road, Old Docks, Gloucester GL1 2LE Tel: 07973 768452

HA Hallidays, The Old College, Dorchester-on-Thames, Oxfordshire OX10 7HL Tel: 01865 340028/68 Mobile: 07860 625917 antiques@hallidays.com www.hallidays.com

HAA Hampton Antiques, The Crown Arcade, 119 Portobello Road, London W11 2DY Tel: 01604 863979 Mobile: 07779 654879 info@hamptonantiques.co.uk www.hamptonantiques.co.uk

HAL John & Simon Haley, 89 Northgate, Halifax, Yorkshire HX1 1XF Tel: 01422 822148/360434 toysandbanks@aol.com

HAld Henry Aldridge & Son Auctions, Unit 1, Bath Road Business Centre, Devizes, Wiltshire SN10 1XA Tel: 01380 729199 www.henry-aldridge.co.uk

HAM Hamptons International, Baverstock House, 93 High Street, Godalming, Surrey GU7 1AL Tel: 01483 423567 fineartauctions@hamptons-int.com www.hamptons.co.uk

HCFA Henry T. Callan, 162 Quaker Meeting House Road, East Sandwich, MA 02537–1312, USA Tel: 508-888-5372

HEL Helios Gallery, 292 Westbourne Grove, London W11 2PS Tel: 077 11 955 997 info@heliosgallery.com www.heliosgallery.com

Herm Hermann Historica OHG, Postfach 201009, 80010 Munchen, Germany Tel: 00 49 89 5237296

HiA Rupert Hitchcox Antiques, Warpsgrove, Nr Chalgrove, Oxford OX44 7RW Tel: 01865 890241 www.ruperthitchcoxantiques.co.uk

HIS Erna Hiscock & John Shepherd, Chelsea Galleries, 69 Portobello Road, London W11 Tel: 01233 661407 Mobile: 0771 562 7273 erna@ernahiscockantiques.com www.ernahiscockantiques.com

HL Honiton Lace Shop, 44 High Street, Honiton, Devon EX14 1PJ Tel: 01404 42416 shop@honitonlace.com www.honitonlace.com

HOK Hamilton Osborne King, 4 Main Street, Blackrock, Co Dublin, Republic of Ireland Tel: 353 1 288 5011 blackrock@hok.ie www.hok.ie

HOLL Holloway's, 49 Parsons Street, Banbury, Oxfordshire OX16 5PF Tel: 01295 817777 enquiries@hollowaysauctioneers.co.uk www.hollowaysauctioneers.co.uk

HON Honan's Antiques, Crowe Street, Gort, County Galway, Republic of Ireland Tel: 00 353 91 631407 www.honansantiques.com

HOW John Howard at Heritage, 6 Market Place, Woodstock, Oxfordshire OX20 1TA Tel: 01993 811332/0870 4440678 Mobile 07831 850544 john@johnhoward.co.uk www.antiquepottery.co.uk www.atheritage.co.uk

HRQ Harlequin Antiques, 79–81 Mansfield Road, Daybrook, Nottingham NG5 6BH Tel: 0115 967 4590 sales@antiquepine.net www.antiquepine.net

HTE Heritage, 6 Market Place, Woodstock, Oxfordshire OX20 1TA Tel: 01993 811332/0870 4440678 Mobile: 07831 850544 dealers@atheritage.co.uk www.atheritage.co.uk

HUM Humbleyard Fine Art, Unit 32 Admiral Vernon Arcade, Portobello Road, London W11 2DY Tel: 01362 637793 Mobile: 07836 349416

HUN The Country Seat, Huntercombe Manor Barn, Henley-on-Thames, Oxfordshire RG9 5RY Tel: 01491 641349 wclegg@thecountryseat.com www.thecountryseat.com

HUR Hurst Gallery, 53 Mt. Auburn Street, Cambridge, MA 02138, USA Tel: 617 491 6888 manager@hurstgallery.com www.hurstgallery.com

HWK H W Keil Ltd, Tudor House, Broadway, Worcestershire WR12 7DP Tel: 01386 852408 hans@hwkeil.co.uk

HYD Hy Duke & Son, The Dorchester Fine Art Salerooms, Weymouth Avenue, Dorchester, Dorset DT1 1QS Tel: 01305 265080 www.dukes-auctions.com

ICO Iconastas, 5 Piccadilly Arcade, London SW1 Tel: 020 7629 1433 info@iconastas.com www.iconastas.com

IM Ibbett Mosely, 125 High Street, Sevenoaks, Kent TN13 1UT Tel: 01732 456731 auctions@ibbettmosely.co.uk www.ibbettmosely.co.uk

IS Ian Sharp Antiques, 23 Front Street, Tynemouth, Tyne & Wear NE30 4DX Tel: 0191 296 0656 sharp@sharpantiques.com www.sharpantiques.com

JAA Jackson's International Auctioneers & Appraisers of Fine Art & Antiques, 2229 Lincoln Street, Cedar Falls, IA 50613, USA Tel: 319 277 2256/800 665 6743 www.jacksonsauction.com

JAd James Adam & Sons, 26 St Stephen's Green, Dublin 2, Republic of Ireland Tel: 00 3531 676 0261 www.jamesadam.ie/

JAS Jasmin Cameron, Antiquarius, 131–141 King's Road, London SW3 4PW Tel: 020 7351 4154 Mobile: 077 74 871257 jasmin.cameron@mail.com

JBL Judi Bland Antiques, Surrey Tel: 01536 724145 or 01276 857576

JBM Jim Bullock Militaria, PO Box 217, Romsey, Hampshire SO51 5XL Tel: 01794 516455 jim@jimbullockmilitaria.com www.jimbullockmilitaria.com

JC J. Collins & Son, The Studio, 28 High Street, Bideford, Devon EX39 2AN Tel: 01237 473103

JCH Jocelyn Chatterton, 126 Grays, 58 Davies St, London W1Y 2LP Tel: 020 7629 1971 Mobile: 07798 804 853 jocelyn@cixi.demon.co.uk www.cixi.demon.co.uk

JDJ James D Julia, Inc, P O Box 830, Rte.201 Skowhegan Road, Fairfield, ME 04937, USA Tel: 207 453 7125 www.juliaauctions.com

JE Julian Eade, Surrey Tel: 01865 300349 Mobile: 07973 542971

JeA Jess Applin, 8 Lensfield Road, Cambridge CB2 1EG Tel: 01223 315168

JeF Jeffrey Formby, The Gallery, Orchard Cottage, East Street, Moreton-in-Marsh, Gloucestershire GL56 0LQ Tel: 01608 650558 www.formby-clocks.co.uk

JHo Jonathan Horne, 66 Kensington Church Street, London W8 4BY Tel: 020 7221 5658 JH@jonathanhorne.co.uk www.jonathanhorne.co.uk

JM Maxwells of Wilmslow Inc Dockree's, 133A Woodford Road, Woodford, Cheshire SK7 1QD Tel: 0161 439 5182 www.maxwells-auctioneers.co.uk

JNic John Nicholson, The Auction Rooms, Longfield, Midhurst Road, Fernhurst, Surrey GU27 3HA Tel: 01428 653727

JON Jonkers, 24 Hart Street, Henley on Thames, Oxfordshire RG9 2AU Tel: 01491 576427 bromlea.jonkers@bjbooks.co.uk www.bjbooks.co.uk

JOP Jonathan Potter Ltd, Antique Maps, 125 New Bond Street, London W1S 1DY Tel: 020 7491 3520 jpmaps@attglobal.net www.jpmaps.co.uk

JP Janice Paull, PO Box 100, Kenilworth, Warwickshire CV8 1JX Tel: 07876 284647 janicepaull@yahoo.com www.janicepaull.com

JPr Joanna Proops Antique Textiles & Lighting, 34 Belvedere, Lansdown Hill, Bath, Somerset BA1 5HR Tel: 01225 310795 antiquetextiles@aol.co.uk www.antiquetextiles.co.uk

JRe John Read, 29 Lark Rise, Martlesham Heath, Ipswich, Suffolk IP5 7SA Tel: 01473 624897

JSG James Strang Tel: 01334 472 566 Mobile: 07950 490088 jameslstrang@hotmail.com www.mod-i.com

JSt Jane Strickland & Daughters, 71 High Street, Honiton, Devon EX14 1PW Tel: 01404 44221 JSandDaughtersUk@aol.com www.janestricklanddaughters.co.uk

JTS June & Tony Stone Fine Antique Boxes, PO Box 106, Peacehaven, Sussex BN10 8AU Tel: 01273 579333 rachel@boxes.co.uk www.boxes.co.uk

JUP Jupiter Antiques, PO Box 609, Rottingdean, East Sussex BN2 7FW Tel: 01273 302865

K&D Kembery Antique Clocks Ltd, George Street Antique Centre, 8 Edgar Buildings, George Street, Bath, Somerset BA1 2EH Tel: 0117 9565 281 Mobile: 07850 623 237 kembery@kdclocks.co.uk www.kdclocks.co.uk

KEY Key Antiques of Chipping Norton, 11 Horsefair, Chipping Norton, Oxfordshire OX7 5AL Tel: 01608 644992/643777 info@keyantiques.com www.keyantiques.com

KHW Keith Harding's World of Mechanical Music, The Oak House, High Street, Northleach, Gloucestershire GL54 3ET Tel: 01451 860181 keith@mechanicalmusic.co.uk www.mechanicalmusic.co.uk

KK Karl Kemp & Assoc, Ltd Antiques, 36 East 10th Street, New York, NY 10003, USA Tel: (212) 254 1877 info@karlkemp.com www.karlkemp.com

KMG Karen Michelle Guido, Karen Michelle Antique Tiles, PMB 243, 1835 US 1 South #119, St Augustine, FL 32084, USA Tel: (904) 471 3226 karen@antiquetiles.com www.antiquetiles.com

L Lawrence Fine Art Auctioneers, South Street, Crewkerne, Somerset TA18 8AB Tel: 01460 73041 www.lawrences.co.uk

L(r) LASSCO, 41 Maltby Street, London SE1 3PA Tel: 020 7394 7494 marketing@lassco.co.uk www.lassco.co.uk

L(sm) LASSCO St Michael's, Mark Street, London EC2A 4ER Tel: 020 7749 9944 www.lassco.co.uk

L&E Locke & England, 18 Guy Street, Leamington Spa, Warwickshire CV32 4RT Tel: 01926 889100 www.auctions-online.com/locke

L&L Linen & Lace, Shirley Tomlinson, Halifax Antiques Centre, Queens Road/Gibbet Street, Halifax, Yorkshire HX1 4LR Tel: 01422 366657 Mobile: 07711 763454

L&T Lyon & Turnbull, 33 Broughton Place, Edinburgh, Scotland EH1 3RR Tel: 0131 557 8844 Mobile:07714699802 info@lyonandturnbull.com

LaF La Femme Tel: 07971 844279 jewels@joancorder.freeserve.co.uk

LAY David Lay ASVA, Auction House, Alverton, Penzance, Cornwall TR18 4RE Tel: 01736 361414 david.lays@btopenworld.com

LBe Linda Bee, Art Deco Stand L18–21, Grays Antique Market, 1–7 Davies Mews, London W1Y 1AR Tel: 020 7629 5921

LBO Laura Bordignon Antiques, PO Box 6247, Finchingfield, Essex CM7 4ER Tel: 01371 811 791 Mobile: 07778 787929 laurabordignon@hotmail.com

LBr Lynda Brine lyndabrine@yahoo.co.uk www.scentbottlesandsmalls.co.uk By Appointment only

LCC The London Cigarette Card Co Ltd, Sutton Road, Somerton, Somerset TA11 6QP Tel: 01458 273452 cards@londoncigcard.co.uk www.londoncigcard.co.uk

LCM Galeria Louis C. Morton, GLC A7073L IYS, Monte Athos 179, Col. Lomas de Chapultepec CP11000, Mexico Tel: 52 5520 5005 glmorton@prodigy.net.mx www.lmorton.com

LDC L. & D. Collins, London Tel: 020 7584 0712

LF Lambert & Foster, 77 Commercial Road, Paddock Wood, Kent TN12 6DR Tel: 01892 832325

LFA † Law Fine Art, Berkshire Tel: 01635 860033 info@lawfineart.co.uk www.lawfineart.co.uk

LHA † Leslie Hindman, Inc, 122 North Aberdeen Street, Chicago, Illinois 60607, USA Tel: 312 280 1212 www.lesliehindman.com

LJ Leonard Joel Auctioneers, 333 Malvern Road, South Yarra, Victoria 3141, Australia Tel: 03 9826 4333 decarts@ljoel.com.au jewellery@ljoel.com.au www.ljoel.com.au

LOP Lopburi Art & Antiques, 5 Saville Row, Bath, Somerset BA1 2QP Tel: 01225 322947 mail@lopburi.co.uk www.lopburi.co.uk

LUA Linda's Unique Antiques, PO Box 143, Ardsley, NY 10502, USA Tel: 914 693 4245 Unique@arsh.com www.lc-tiffany.com

LUNA Luna, 23 George Street, Nottingham NG1 3BH Tel: 0115 924 3267 info@luna-online.co.uk www.luna-online.co.uk

M Morphets of Harrogate, 6 Albert Street, Harrogate, Yorkshire HG1 1JL Tel: 01423 530030

MAA Mario's Antiques, 288 Westbourne Grove, London W11 2PS Tel: 020 8902 1600 Mobile: 07956 580772 marwan@barazi.screaming.net www.marios_antiques.com

Man Mansers, 31 Wyle Cop, Shrewsbury, Shropshire SY1 1XF Tel: 01743 240328 info@fineartdealers.co.uk www.fineartdealers.co.uk

MAR Frank R. Marshall & Co, Marshall House, Church Hill, Knutsford, Cheshire WA16 6DH Tel: 01565 653284

MARG Margaret Williamson, Vintage Modes, Grays Antique Market, 1–7 Davies Mews, Mayfair, London W1K 5AB Tel: 0207 40 90 400 chelsealace@aol.com www.vintagemodes.co.uk

MARK † 20th Century Marks, 12 Market Square, Westerham, Kent TN16 1AW Tel: 01959 562221 Mobile: 07831 778992 info@20thcenturymarks.co.uk www.20thcenturymarks.co.uk

MB Mostly Boxes, 93 High Street, Eton, Windsor, Berkshire SL4 6AF Tel: 01753 858470

MCA † Mervyn Carey, Twysden Cottage, Scullsgate, Benenden, Cranbrook, Kent TN17 4LD Tel: 01580 240283

MCO Mary Cooke Antiques Ltd, 12 The Old Power Station, 121 Mortlake High Street, London SW14 8SN Tel: 020 8876 5777

McP R. & G. McPherson Antiques, 40 Kensington Church Street, London W8 4BX Tel: 020 7937 0812 Mobile: 07768 432 630 rmcpherson@orientalceramics.com www.orientalceramics.com

MDe Mike Delaney, Oxfordshire Tel: 01993 840064 Mobile: 07979 919760 mike@vintagehornby.co.uk www.vintagehornby.co.uk

MDL Michael D Long Ltd, 96–98 Derby Road, Nottingham NG1 5FB Tel: 0115 941 3307 sales@michaeldlong.com www.michaeldlong.com

MEA Mealy's, Chatsworth Street, Castle Comer, Co Kilkenny, Republic of Ireland Tel: 00 353 564 441 229 info@mealys.com www.mealys.com

MFB Manor Farm Barn Antiques Tel: 01296 658941 Mobile: 07720 286607 mfbn@btinternet.com btwebworld.com/mfbantiques

MHA Merchant House Antiques, 19 High Street, Honiton, Devon EX14 1PR Tel: 01404 42694/44406 antiquesmerchant@ndirect.co.uk

MI † Mitofsky Antiques, 8 Rathfarnham Road, Terenure, Dublin 6, Republic of Ireland Tel: 00 353 1492 0033 info@mitofskyartdeco.com www.mitofskyartdeco.com

MIL Millennia Antiquities, Lancashire Tel: 091204 690175 Mobile: 07930 273998 millenniaant@aol.com www.AncientAntiquities.co.uk

MIN Ministry of Pine, Timsbury Village Workshop, Unit 2, Timsbury Industrial Estate, Hayeswood Road, Timsbury, Bath, Somerset BA2 0HQ Tel: 01761 472297 Mobile: 07770 588536 ministryofpine.uk@virgin.net www.ministryofpine.com

MINN Geoffrey T. Minnis, Hastings Antique Centre, 59–61 Norman Road, St Leonards-on-Sea, East Sussex TN38 0EG Tel: 01424 428561

MIR Mir Russki, Scotland Tel: 01506 843973 Mobile: 07979 227779 info@russiansilver.co.uk www.russiansilver.co.uk

Mit Mitchells Auction Company, The Furniture Hall, 47 Station Road, Cockermouth, Cumbria CA13 9PZ Tel: 01900 827800

MLa Marion Langham Limited, Claranagh, Tempo, Co Fermanagh, Northern Ireland BT94 3FJ Tel: 028 895 41247 marion@ladymarion.co.uk www.ladymarion.co.uk

MLL Millers Antiques Ltd, Netherbrook House, 86 Christchurch Road, Ringwood, Hampshire BH24 1DR Tel: 01425 472062 mail@millers-antiques.co.uk www.millers-antiques.co.uk

MPC M C, Cheshire Tel: 01244 301800 Sales@Moorcroftchester.co.uk www.Moorcroftchester.co.uk

MSh Manfred Schotten, 109 High Street, Burford, Oxfordshire OX18 4RG Tel: 01993 822302 www.antiques@schotten.com

MTay † Martin Taylor Antiques, 323 Tettenhall Road, Wolverhampton, West Midlands WV6 0JZ Tel: 01902 751166 Mobile: 07836 636524 enquiries@mtaylor-antiques.co.uk www.mtaylor-antiques.co.uk

MUL Mullock & Madeley, The Old Shippon, Wall-under-Heywood, Nr Church Stretton, Shropshire SY6 7DS Tel: 01694 771771/ 07803 276394 auctions@mullockmadeley.co.uk www.mullockmadeley.co.uk

MUR Murray Cards (International) Ltd, 51 Watford Way, Hendon Central, London NW4 3JH Tel: 020 8202 5688 murraycards@ukbusiness.com www.murraycard.com/

NART Newel Art Galleries, Inc, 425 East 53rd Street, New York 10022, USA Tel: 212 758 1970 info@newel.com www.Newel.com

NAW † Newark Antiques Warehouse Ltd, Old Kelham Road, Newark, Nottinghamshire NG24 1BX Tel: 01636 674869 Mobile: 07974 429185 enquiries@newarkantiques.co.uk www.newarkantiques.co.uk

NBL N. Bloom & Son (1912) Ltd, 12 Piccadilly Arcade, London SW1Y 6NH Tel: 020 7629 5060 nbloom@nbloom.com www.nbloom.com

NMA Noel Mercer Antiques, Aurora House, Hall Street, Long Melford, Sudbury, Suffolk CO10 9RJ Tel: 01787 311882/01206 323558

NOA New Orleans Auction Galleries, Inc, 801 Magazine Street, AT 510 Julia, New Orleans, Louisiana 70130, USA Tel: 504 566 1849

NoC No.1 Castlegate Antiques, 1–3 Castlegate, Newark, Nottinghamshire NG24 1AZ Tel: 01636 701877 Mobile: 07850 463173

NOST † Nostalgia, Hollands Mill, 61 Shaw Heath, Stockport, Cheshire SK3 8BH Tel: 0161 477 7706 www.nostalgia-uk.com

NS Nicholas Shaw Antiques, Virginia Cottage, Lombard Street, Petworth, West Sussex GU28 0AG Tel: 01798 345146/01798 345147 Mobile: 07885 643000/07817 572746 silver@nicholas-shaw.com www.nicholas-shaw.com

NSal Netherhampton Salerooms, Salisbury Auction Centre, Netherhampton, Salisbury, Wiltshire SP2 8RH Tel: 01722 340 041

OE Orient Expressions, Bath

OH Old Hat, 66 Fulham High Road, London SW6 3LQ Tel: 020 7610 6558

OLA Olliff's Architectural Antiques, 19–21 Lower Redland Road, Redland, Bristol, Gloucestershire BS6 6TB Tel: 0117 923 9232 marcus@olliffs.com www.olliffs.com

Oli † Olivers, Olivers Rooms, Burkitts Lane, Sudbury, Suffolk CO10 1HB Tel: 01787 880305 oliversauctions@btconnect.com

OND Ondines Tel: 01865 882465

ONS Onslow's Auctions Ltd, The Coach House, Manor Road, Stourpaine, Dorset DT8 8TQ Tel: 01258 488838

OTB † Old Tackle Box, PO Box 55, Cranbrook, Kent TN17 3ZU Tel: 01580 713979 Mobile: 07729 278 293 tackle.box@virgin.net

P&T Pine & Things, Portobello Farm, Campden Road, Nr Shipston-on-Stour, Warwickshire CV36 4PY Tel: 01608 663849 www.pinethings.co.uk

PaA Pastorale Antiques, 15 Malling Street, Lewes, East Sussex BN7 2RA Tel: 01273 473259 or 01435 863044 pastorale@btinternet.com

PAO † P. A. Oxley Antique Clocks & Barometers, The Old Rectory, Cherhill, Calne, Wiltshire SN11 8UX Tel: 01249 816227 info@paoxley.com www.british-antiqueclocks.com

PAS Tina Pasco, Waterlock House, Wingham, Nr Canterbury, Kent CT3 1BH Tel: 01227 722151 tinapasco@tinapasco.com www.tinapasco.com

PAY Payne & Son, 131 High Street, Oxford OX1 4DH Tel: 01865 243787 silver@payneandson.co.uk www.payneandson.co.uk

PBA Paul Beighton Auctioneers Ltd, Woodhouse Green, Thurcroft, Rotherham, Yorkshire S66 9AQ Tel: 01709 700005 www.paulbeightonauctioneers.co.uk

PCA Patricia Cater Oriental Art, Gloucestershire Tel: 01451 830944 Patriciacaterorg@aol.com www.PatriciaCater-OrientalArt.com

Penn Penny Fair Antiques Tel: 07860 825456

PEx † Piano-Export, Bridge Road, Kingswood, Bristol, Somerset BS15 4FW Tel: 0117 956 8300

PEZ Alan Pezaro, 62a West Street, Dorking, Surrey RH4 1BS Tel: 01306 743661

PF † Peter Francis, Curiosity Sale Room, 19 King Street, Carmarthen, Wales SA31 1BH Tel: 01267 233456 Peterfrancis@valuers.fsnet.co.uk www.peterfrancis.co.uk

PFK † Penrith Farmers' & Kidd's plc, Skirsgill Salerooms, Penrith, Cumbria CA11 0DN Tel: 01768 890781 info@pfkauctions.co.uk www.pfkauctions.co.uk

PGO † Pamela Goodwin, 11 The Pantiles, Royal Tunbridge Wells, Kent TN2 5TD Tel: 01892 618200 mail@goodwinantiques.co.uk www.goodwinantiques.co.uk

PHo Paul Howard Mobile: 07881 862 375 scientificantiques@hotmail.com

PIC David & Susan Pickles Tel: 01282 707673 Mobile: 07976 236983

PICA Piccadilly Antiques, 280 High Street, Batheaston, Bath BA1 7RA Tel: 01225 851494 Mobile: 07785 966132 piccadillyantiques@ukonline.co.uk

PLB Planet Bazaar, 149 Drummond Street, London NW1 2PB Tel: 020 7387 8326 Mobile: 07956 326301 info@planetbazaar.co.uk www.planetbazaar.co.uk

POLL Pollyanna, 34 High Street, Arundel, West Sussex BN18 9AB Tel: 01903 885198 Mobile: 07949903457

POT Pot Board Tel: 01834 842699 Gill@potboard.co.uk www.potboard.co.uk

POW Sylvia Powell Decorative Arts, Suite 400, Ceramic House, 571 Finchley Road, London NW3 7BN Tel: 020 8458 4543 Mobile: 07802 714998 dpowell909@aol.com

PSC Peter & Sonia Cashman, The Emporium, Tetbury, Gloucestershire GL8 8AA Tel: 01225 469497 Mobile: 0780 8609860 www.cashman-antiques.co.uk

PT † Pieces of Time, (1–7 Davies Mews), 26 South Molton Lane, London W1Y 2LP Tel: 020 7629 2422 info@antique-watch.com www.antique-watch.com www.cufflinksworld.com

PTh Antique Clocks by Patrick Thomas, 62a West Street, Dorking, Surrey RH4 1BS Tel: 01306 743661 patrickthomas@btconnect.com www.antiqueclockshop.co.uk

PUGH † Pugh's Antiques, Pugh's Farm, Monkton, Nr Honiton, Devon EX14 9QH Tel: 01404 42860 sales@pughsantiques.com www.pughsantiques.com

PVD Puritan Values at the Dome, St Edmunds Business Park, St Edmunds Road, Southwold, Suffolk IP18 6BZ Tel: 01502 722211 Mobile: 07966 371676 sales@puritanvalues.com www.puritanvalues.com

Q&C † Q & C Militaria, 22 Suffolk Road, Cheltenham, Gloucestershire GL50 2AQ Tel: 01242 519815 Mobile: 07778 613977 qcmilitaria@btconnect.com www.qcmilitaria.com

QM The Wyndham Gallery, Lafayette Antiques Center, 401E 110th Street, New York, USA Tel: 212 722 8400 john_cullis@hotmail.com

RAN Ranby Hall-Antiques, Barnby Moor, Retford, Nottinghamshire DN22 8JQ Tel: 01777 860696 Mobile: 07860 463477 paul.wyatt@virgin.net www.ranbyhall.antiques-gb.com

RAP Rapparee Antiques at Louisa Frances Fine Antiques, High Street, Brasted, Westerham, Kent TN16 1JB Tel: 01959 561222 or 020 8777 4016

RAY † Derek & Tina Rayment Antiques, Orchard House, Barton Road, Barton, Nr Farndon, Cheshire SY14 7HT Tel: 01829 270429/07860 666629 and 07702 922410 raymentantiques@aol.com www.antique-barometers.com

RBA Roger Bradbury Antiques, Church Street, Coltishall, Norfolk NR12 7DJ Tel: 01603 737444

RBM Robert Morley & Co Ltd, 34 Engate Street, London SE13 7HA Tel: 020 8318 5838 jvm@morley-r.u-net.com www.morleypianos.com

RdeR † Rogers de Rin, 76 Royal Hospital Road, London SW3 4HN Tel: 020 7352 9007

RdV Roger de Ville Antiques Tel: 01629 812496 Mobile: 07798 793857 www.rogerdeville.co.uk

REI Reindeer Antiques Ltd, 43 Watling Street, Potterspury, Northamptonshire NN12 7QD Tel: 01908 542200 nicholasfuller@btconnect.com www.reindeerantiques.co.uk

REN Paul & Karen Rennie, 13 Rugby Street, London WC1N 3QT Tel: 020 7405 0220 info@rennart.co.uk www.rennart.co.uk

RGa Richard Gardner Antiques, Swanhouse, Market Square, Petworth, West Sussex GU28 0AN Tel: 01798 343411

RGC Ronald G. Chambers Fine Antiques, Market Square, Petworth, West Sussex GU28 0AH Tel: 01798 342305 jackie@ronaldchambers.com www.ronaldchambers.com

RGe Rupert Gentle Antiques, The Manor House, Milton Lilbourne, Nr Pewsey, Wiltshire SN9 5LQ Tel: 01672 563344

RH Rick Hubbard Art Deco, 3 Tee Court, Bell Street, Romsey, Hampshire SO51 8GY Tel: 01794 513133 Mobile: 07767 267607 rick@rickhubbard-artdeco.co.uk www.rickhubbard-artdeco.co.uk

RHa Robert Hall, 15c Clifford Street, London W1X 1RF Tel: 020 7734 4008

RICC Riccardo Sansoni

RKa Richardson & Kailas, London Tel: 020 7371 0491 By appointment only

RMe Jubilee Photographica, 10 Pierrepoint Row, Camden Passage, London N1 8EE Tel: 07860 793707

ROH Roy C. Harris Tel: 01283 520355 Mobile: 0771 8500961 rchclocks@aol.com rch-antique-clocks.com

ROSc † R. O. Schmitt Fine Art, Box 1941, Salem, New Hampshire 03079, USA Tel: 603 893 5915 bob@roschmittfinearts.com www.antiqueclockauction.com

RPA Richard Price & Associates Tel: 01784 452990 www.antiqueclocks.tv

RPh No Longer trading

RTo † Rupert Toovey & Co Ltd, Spring Gardens, Washington, West Sussex RH20 3BS Tel: 01903 891955 auctions@rupert-toovey.com www.rupert-toovey.com

RTW † Richard Twort, Somerset Tel: 01934 641900 Mobile: 07711 939789

RUSK Ruskin Decorative Arts, 5 Talbot Court, Stow-on-the-Wold, Cheltenham, Gloucestershire GL54 1DP Tel: 01451 832254 william.anne@ruskindecarts.co.uk

RYA † Robert Young Antiques, 68 Battersea Bridge Road, London SW11 3AG Tel: 020 7228 7847 office@robertyoungantiques.com

S Sotheby's, 34–35 New Bond Street, London W1A 2AA Tel: 020 7293 5000 www.sothebys.com

S(Am) Sotheby's Amsterdam, De Boelelaan 30, Amsterdam 1083 HJ, Netherlands Tel: 31 20 550 2200 www.sothebys.com

S(HK) Sotheby's, 5/F Standard Chartered Bank Building, 4–4A Des Voeux Road, Central Hong Kong, China Tel: 852 2524 8121 www.sothebys.com

S(Mi) Sotheby's, Palazzo Broggi, Via Broggi, 19, Milan 20129, Italy 39 02 295 001 www.sothebys.com

S(NY) Sotheby's, 1334 York Avenue at 72nd St, New York, NY 10021, USA Tel: 212 606 7000 www.sothebys.com

S(O) Sotheby's Olympia, Hammersmith Road, London W14 8UX Tel: 020 7293 5555 www.sothebys.com

S(P) Sotheby's France SA, 76 rue du Faubourg, Saint Honore, Paris 75008, France Tel: 33 1 53 05 53 05 www.sothebys.com

S(S) Sotheby's Sussex, Summers Place, Billingshurst, West Sussex RH14 9AD Tel: 01403 833500 www.sothebys.com

S&D S. & D. Postcards, Bartlett Street Antique Centre, 5–10 Bartlett Street, Bath, Somerset BA1 2QZ Tel: 07979 506415 wndvd@aol.com

SAAC Scottish Antique Centre, Abernyte, Scotland PH14 9SJ Tel: 01828 686401 sales@scottish-antiques.com www.scottish-antiques.com

SAM Samarkand Galleries, 7–8 Brewery Yard, Sheep Street, Stow-on-the-Wold, Gloucestershire GL54 1AA Tel: 01451 832322 mac@samarkand.co.uk www.samarkand.co.uk

SAS † Special Auction Services, Kennetholme, Midgham, Reading, Berkshire RG7 5UX Tel: 0118 971 2949 www.invaluable.com/sas/

SAT The Swan at Tetsworth, High Street, Tetsworth, Nr Thame, Oxfordshire OX9 7AB Tel: 01844 281777 antiques@theswan.co.uk www.theswan.co.uk

SAW Salisbury Antiques Warehouse Ltd, 94 Wilton Road, Salisbury, Wiltshire SP2 7JJ Tel: 01722 410634 Mobile: 07703 211151 kevin@salisbury-antiques.co.uk

SAY Charlotte Sayers, 360 Grays Antique Market, 58 Davies St, London W1K 5LP Tel: 020 7499 5478

SCO Peter Scott Tel: 0117 986 8468 Mobile: 07850 639770

SDA Stephanie Davison Antiques, Bakewell Antiques Centre, King Street, Bakewell, Derbyshire DE45 1DZ Tel: 01629 812496 Mobile: 07771 564 993 bacc@chappells-antiques.co.uk www.chappells-antiques.co.uk

SEA Mark Seabrook Antiques, PO Box 396, Huntingdon, Cambridgeshire PE28 0ZA Tel: 01480 861935 Mobile: 07770 721931 enquiries@markseabrook.com www.markseabrook.com

SeH † Seventh Heaven, Chirk Mill, Chirk, Wrexham, County Borough, Wales LL14 5BU Tel: 01691 777622/773563 requests@seventh-heaven.co.uk www.seventh-heaven.co.uk

SER † Serendipity, 125 High Street, Deal, Kent CT14 6BB Tel: 01304 369165/01304 366536 dipityantiques@aol.com

SERR † Philip Serrell, The Malvern Saleroom, Barnards Green Road, Malvern, Worcestershire WR14 3LW Tel: 01684 892314 serrell.auctions@virgin.net www.serrell.com

SET † Setniks In Time Again, 815 Sutter Street, Suite 2, Folsom, California 95630, USA Tel: 916 985 2390 Toll Free 888 333 1715 setniks@pacbell.net setniksintimeagain.com

SGA † Stair Galleries, P O Box 418, Claverack, New York 12513, USA Tel: 518 851 2544 www.stairgalleries.com

SGr Sarah Groombridge, Stand 335, Grays Market, 58 Davies Street, London W1K 5LP Tel: 020 7629 0225 Mobile: 07770 920277 sarah.groombridge@totalise.co.uk

SH Shapes Fine Art Auctioneers & Valuers, Bankhead Avenue, Sighthill, Edinburgh, Scotland EH11 4BY Tel: 0131 453 3222 auctionsadmin@shapesauctioneers.co.uk www.shapesauctioneers.co.uk

SHa † Shapiro & Co, Stand 380, Gray's Antique Market, 58 Davies Street, London W1K 5LP Tel: 020 7491 2710

SHSY Shapiro Auctioneers, 162 Queen Street, Woollahra, Sydney NSW 2025, Australia Tel: 612 9326 1588

SIE Sieff, 49 Long Street, Tetbury, Gloucestershire GL8 8AA Tel: 01666 504477 sieff@sieff.co.uk www.sieff.co.uk

SIL The Silver Shop, Powerscourt Townhouse Centre, St Williams Street, Dublin 2, Republic of Ireland Tel: 01 679 4147 ianhaslam@eircom.net

SJH S.J. Hales, 87 Fore Street, Bovey Tracey, Devon TQ13 9AB Tel: 01626 836684

SK Skinner Inc, The Heritage On The Garden, 63 Park Plaza, Boston, MA 02116, USA Tel: 617 350 5400

SMI Skip & Janie Smithson Antiques, Lincolnshire Tel: 01754 810265 Mobile: 07831 399180 smithsonantiques@hotmail.com

Som Somervale Antiques, 6 Radstock Road, Midsomer Norton, Bath, Somerset BA3 2AJ Tel: 01761 412686 Mobile: 07885 088022 ronthomas@somervaleantiquesglass.co.uk www.somervaleantiquesglass.co.uk

SOR Soldiers of Rye, Mint Arcade, 71 The Mint, Rye, East Sussex TN31 7EW Tel: 01797 225952 rameses@supanet.com chris@johnbartholomewcards.co.uk www.rameses.supanet.com

SPA Sporting Antiques, 10 Union Square, The Pantiles, Tunbridge Wells, Kent TN4 8HE Tel: 01892 522661

SPE Sylvie Spectrum, Stand 372, Grays Market, 58 Davies Street, London W1Y 2LB Tel: 020 7629 3501

SPF Scarborough Perry Fine Art, Hove Auction Rooms, Hove Street, Hove, East Sussex BN3 2GL Tel: 01273 735266

SSL Star Signings Ltd, The Burbeque Gallery, 16A New Quebec Street, London W1H 7DG Tel: 020 7723 8498 starsignings@btconnect.com

SSW Spencer Swaffer, 30 High Street, Arundel, West Sussex BN18 9AB Tel: 01903 882132

STA George Stacpoole, Main Street, Adare, Co Limerick, Republic of Ireland Tel: 6139 6409 stacpoole@iol.ie www.georgestacpooleantiques.com

SV Sutton Valence Antiques, North Street, Sutton Valence, Nr Maidstone, Kent ME17 3AP Tel: 01622 843333/01622 675332 svantiques@aol.com www.svantiques.co.uk

SWA † S. W. Antiques, Newlands (road), Pershore, Worcestershire WR10 1BP Tel: 01386 555580 sw-antiques@talk21.com www.sw-antiques.co.uk

SWB † Sweetbriar Gallery Paperweights Ltd, 3 Collinson Court, off Church Street, Frodsham, Cheshire WA6 6PN Tel: 01928 730064 sales@sweetbriar.co.uk www.sweetbriar.co.uk

SWN Swan Antiques

SWO † Sworders, 14 Cambridge Road, Stansted Mountfitchet, Essex CM24 8BZ Tel: 01279 817778 auctions@sworder.co.uk www.sworder.co.uk

TASV Tenterden Antiques & Silver Vaults, 66 High Street, Tenterden, Kent TN30 6AU Tel: 01580 765885

TDG The Design Gallery 1850–1950, 5 The Green, Westerham, Kent TN16 1AS Tel: 01959 561234 Mobile: 07974 322858 sales@thedesigngalleryuk.com www.thedesigngalleryuk.com

TDS The Decorator Source, 39a Long Street, Tetbury, Gloucestershire GL8 8AA Tel: 01666 505358

TeG The Temple Gallery, 6 Clarendon Cross, Holland Park, London W11 4AP Tel: 020 7727 3809 info@templegallery.com www.templegallery.com

TEM † Tempus, Kent Tel: 01344 874007 www.tempus-watches.co.uk

TEN † Tennants, The Auction Centre, Harmby Road, Leyburn, Yorkshire DL8 5SG Tel: 01969 623780 enquiry@tennants-ltd.co.uk www.tennants.co.uk

TH † Tony Horsley, PO Box 3127, Brighton, East Sussex BN1 5SS Tel: 01273 550770

TIC Tickers, 37 Northam Road, Southampton, Hampshire SO14 0PD Tel: 02380 234431 kmonckton@btopenworld.com

TIM S. & S. Timms, 2–4 High Street, Shefford, Bedfordshire SG17 5DG Tel: 01462 851051 info@timmsantiques.com www.timmsantiques.com

TIN Tin Tin Collectables, G38–42 Alfies's Antique Market, 13–25 Church Street, Marylebone, London NW8 8DT Tel: 020 7258 1305 leslie@tintincollectables.com www.tintincollectables.com

TLA † The Lanes Armoury, 26 Meeting House Lane, The Lanes, Brighton, East Sussex BN1 1HB Tel: 01273 321357 enquiries@thelanesarmoury.co.uk www.thelanesarmoury.co.uk

TMA † Tring Market Auctions, The Market Premises, Brook Street, Tring, Hertfordshire HP23 5EF Tel: 01442 826446 sales@tringmarketauctions.co.uk www.tringmarketauctions.co.uk

TML Timothy Millett Ltd, Historic Medals and Works of Art, PO Box 20851, London SE22 0YN Tel: 020 8693 1111 Mobile: 07778 637 898 tim@timothymillett.demon.co.uk

TNS Toy's N Such Toy's – Antiques & Collectables, 437 Dawson Street, Sault Sainte Marie, MI 49783–2119, USA Tel: 906 635 0356

TOM † Charles Tomlinson, Chester Tel: 01244 318395 charlestomlinson@tiscali.co.uk

TOP † The Top Banana Antiques Mall, 1 New Church Street, Tetbury, Gloucestershire GL8 8DS Tel: 0871 288 1102 info@topbananaantiques.com www.topbananaantiques.com

TPC † Pine Cellars, 39 Jewry Street, Winchester, Hampshire SO23 8RY Tel: 01962 777546/867014

TREA Treadway Gallery, Inc, 2029 Madison Road, Cincinnati, Ohio 45208, USA Tel: 513 321 6742 www.treadwaygallery.com

TRI Trident Antiques, 2 Foundry House, Hall Street, Long Melford, Suffolk CO10 9JR Tel: 01787 883388 Mobile: 07860 221402 tridentoak@aol.com

Trib Tribal Gathering, No 1 Westbourne Grove Mews, Notting Hill, London W11 2RU Tel: 020 7221 6650 Mobile: 07720 642539 bryan@tribalgathering.com www.tribalgatheringlondon.com

TRM Thomson, Roddick & Medcalf Ltd, 60 Whitesands, Dumfries, Scotland DG1 2RS Tel: 01387 279879 trmdumfries@btconnect.com www.thomsonroddick.com

TRM Thomson, Roddick & Medcalf Ltd, Coleridge House, Shaddongate, Carlisle, Cumbria CA2 5TU Tel: 01228 528939 www.thomsonroddick.com

TRM Thomson, Roddick & Medcalf Ltd, 20 Murray Street, Annan, Scotland DG12 6EG Tel: 01461 202575 www.thomsonroddick.com

TRM Thomson, Roddick & Medcalf Ltd, 43/4 Hardengreen Business Park, Eskbank, Edinburgh, Scotland EH22 3NX Tel: 0131 454 9090 www.thomsonroddick.com

TSC The Silver Collection Ltd Tel: 01442 890954 Mobile: 07802 447813

UD Upstairs Downstairs, 40 Market Place, Devizes, Wiltshire SN10 1JG Tel: 01380 730266 or 07974 074220 devizesantiques@amserve.com

US Ulla Stafford Tel: 0118 934 3208 Mobile: 07944 815104

VB Variety Box Tel: 01892 531868

VEC Vectis Auctions Ltd, Fleck Way, Thornaby, Stockton-on-Tees, Cleveland TS17 9JZ Tel: 01642 750616 admin@vectis.co.uk www.vectis.co.uk

VICT June Victor, Vintage Modes, S041–43, Alfies Antique Market, 13–25 Church Street, London NW8 8DT Tel: 020 7723 6066 Mobile: 07740704723

VS † T. Vennett-Smith, 11 Nottingham Road, Gotham, Nottinghamshire NG11 0HE Tel: 0115 983 0541 info@vennett-smith.com www.vennett-smith.com

VSP Van Sabben Poster Auctions, PO Box 2065, 1620 EB Hoorn, The Netherlands Tel: 31 229 268203 uboersma@sabbenposterauctions.nl www.vsabbenposterauctions.nl

W&C Westland & Co, St Michael's Church, Leonard Street (off Great Eastern Street), London EC2A 4ER Tel: 0207 7398094 westland@westland.co.uk www.westland.co.uk

WAA † Woburn Abbey Antiques Centre, Woburn, Bedfordshire MK17 9WA Tel: 01525 290350 antiques@woburnabbey.co.uk

WAC Worcester Antiques Centre, Reindeer Court, Mealcheapen Street, Worcester WR1 4DF Tel: 01905 610680 WorcsAntiques@aol.com

WADS Wadsworth's, Marehill, Pulborough, West Sussex RH20 2DY Tel: 01798 873555 info@wadsworthsrugs.com www.wadsworthsrugs.com

WAL † Wallis & Wallis, West Street Auction Galleries, Lewes, East Sussex BN7 2NJ Tel: 01273 480208 auctions@wallisandwallis.co.uk www.wallisandwallis.co.uk

WD Weller & Dufty Ltd, 141 Bromsgrove Street, Birmingham, West Midlands B5 6RQ Tel: 0121 692 1414 sales@wellerandduftv.co.uk www.wellerandduftv.co.uk

WeA Wenderton Antique Tel: 01227 720295 By appointment only

WELD J. W. Weldon, 55 Clarendon Street, Dublin 2, Republic of Ireland Tel: 00 353 1 677 1638

WiB Wish Barn Antiques, Wish Street, Rye, East Sussex TN31 7DA Tel: 01797 226797

WilP W&H Peacock, 26 Newnham Street, Bedford MK40 3JR Tel: 01234 266366

WIM Wimpole Antiques, Stand 349, Grays Antique Market, 58 Davies Street, London W1K 5LP Tel: 020 7499 2889 WimpoleAntiques@compuserve.com

WL † Wintertons Ltd, Lichfield Auction Centre, Fradley Park, Lichfield, Staffordshire WS13 8NF Tel: 01543 263256 enquiries@wintertons.co.uk www.wintertons.co.uk

WOS Wheels of Steel, Grays Antique Market, Stand A12–13, Unit B10 Basement, 1–7 Davies Mews, London W1Y 2LP Tel: 0207 629 2813

WRe Walcot Reclamations, 108 Walcot Street, Bath, Somerset BA1 5BG Tel: 01225 444404 rick@walcot.com www.walcot.com

WRi Linda Wrigglesworth, 34 Brook Street, London W1K 5DN Tel: 020 7408 0177 linda@wrigglesworth.demon.co.uk www.artnet.com/chinesetextileswrigglesworth.html

WSA † West Street Antiques, 63 West Street, Dorking, Surrey RH4 1BS Tel: 01306 883487 weststant@aol.com www.antiquearmsandarmour.com

WW Woolley & Wallis, Salisbury Salerooms, 51–61 Castle Street, Salisbury, Wiltshire SP1 3SU Tel: 01722 424500/411854 junebarrett@woolleyandwallis.co.uk www.woolleyandwallis.co.uk

YC Yesterday Child Tel: 020 7354 1601 or 01908 583403

YOX † Yoxall Antiques, 68 Yoxall Road, Solihull, West Midlands B90 3RP Tel: 0121 744 1744 Mobile: 07860 168078 sales@yoxallantiques.co.uk www.yoxall-antiques.co.uk

Index to Advertisers

Index

Bold page numbers refer to information and pointer boxes

C

D

INDEX

INDEX

INDEX

INDEX

T

INDEX